Contracts: Law in Action

STEWART MACAULAY
Malcolm Pitman Sharp Professor &
Theodore W. Brazeau Professor
University of Wisconsin Law School

JOHN KIDWELL
Kathleen M. & George I. Haight Professor
University of Wisconsin Law School

WILLIAM WHITFORD
George H. Young-Bascom Professor
University of Wisconsin Law School

MARC GALANTER
Evjue-Bascom Professor
University of Wisconsin Law School

THE MICHIE COMPANY
Law Publishers
CHARLOTTESVILLE, VIRGINIA

1246910

CONTRACTS:
LAW IN ACTION

CONTEMPORARY
LEGAL EDUCATION SERIES

PREFACE

The Wisconsin Contracts Group produced these materials. While those listed as authors played major roles in writing them, others taught from them and argued over what worked in the classroom. Arlen Christenson, Kenneth Davis, Robert Gordon, Jo Pasqualucci, Joseph Thome, Pat Williams, Jennifer Moore, and Cliff Thompson all put their stamp on what finally emerged. Jay Feinman, William Woodward and Jean Braucher used excerpts from an earlier version of *Contracts: Law in Action*, and gave us detailed and valuable comments.

Most course materials rest on earlier casebooks. The influence of Lon Fuller's articles and casebook will be obvious to contracts scholars. *Contracts: Law in Action* began as a supplement to Kessler and Sharp and then re-emerged as a supplement to Macneil's[1] first edition. Most of us used Richard Danzig's course materials, part of which became his supplementary book, *The Capability Problem in Contract Law*, which we use as a supplement to *Contracts: Law in Action*. Contracts has provoked some very good legal writing, and we have tried to excerpt or cite much of it. Of course, we have read these articles from the law in action perspective of the University of Wisconsin Law School. As a result, we may have interpreted these articles in ways which might surprise their authors.

We wish to acknowledge support from the National Institute for Dispute Resolution and the William and Flora Hewlett Foundation. We are grateful to the Institute for Legal Studies here at the University of Wisconsin Law School for publishing these materials during their transition to book form. We must thank Deans Orrin Helstad, Cliff Thompson, and Dan Bernstine for support for this project. The University of Wisconsin Law Library staff contributed to our efforts. Cynthia May, in particular, served as detective and skilled advocate as she found briefs and records and persuaded other law libraries to lend them to us. Michael Morgalla continually called our attention to relevant material in obscure sources. Theresa Dougherty and Linda Hicks produced skilled typing and desktop publishing. We too often pressed Ruth Saaf and David Ward to photocopy and publish the materials for our classes under tight, if not impossible, deadlines. They always got materials to our students on time.

We owe a large debt to Wisconsin law students who have taught us so much, as they coped with our efforts to offer an unusual contracts course. Wisconsin law students often come to us with relevant experience, and we took advantage of this. Many of them obtained information for us from contacts made in their

---

[1]MacNeil, Cases and Materials on Contracts — Exchange Transactions and Relationships (1971).

earlier careers. Some wrote detailed memos about business practices related to problems raised in class. We learned to be careful about jokes at the expense of the parties and lawyers in the cases we considered. Far too often a son, daughter or close friend of a party or a lawyer was sitting in our class. We learned to put these students to work as researchers.

We originally wrote most of the text on a word-processing program that would have required our repeating many formatting commands to generate one set of footnote numbers for our own text, and a different set for opinions and articles. We have chosen to number *all* the footnotes sequentially in each chapter. This means that the footnote numbers in articles are not as they appear in the originals. Readers should have no difficulty distinguishing our footnotes from those of courts and other authors. Where we thought there might be some confusion, we introduced our footnotes as "Eds. note." We have also eliminated some citations and footnotes from judicial opinions, often without noting the omission.

Summary Table of Contents

Table of Contents

Chapter 1

INTRODUCTION

Most of those who take a contracts course are beginning law students, unfamiliar with both the study of law and the subject of contracts. In this chapter we first offer a summary written by Professor Stewart Macaulay to introduce law study and contracts to those starting their legal career. Even though oversimplified, it is unlikely that beginners will understand everything in this chapter completely on first reading. Read it at the outset of the course and then again later when you have sampled law school classes and can put the material presented here into the context of your experience.

A. STUDYING LAW

Beginning law students often have difficulty understanding what their professors want them to learn. These students may bring expectations with them to law school that cause part of the problem. Some assume that being a law student is a larger version of learning the rules of the road in order to get a motor vehicle driver's license. Law is rules, and the best student is the one who knows the most rules. Some expect to be offered a cookbook approach to such things as how to write and probate a will, how to draft a contract and how to transfer real estate. Others expect basic training in how to try a lawsuit, including how to trip up a lying witness by vigorous cross-examination. These students' model is learning golf or tennis from a pro — law, as life, is a game, and they want to know how to win. Most law schools — certainly those with the highest prestige — will disappoint all of these expectations. Legal education directs primary attention elsewhere. Memorizing rules alone will not get a student very far. Moreover, while in the last decade there have been some changes, those teaching in the classical manner assume that things such as legal drafting, cross-examination techniques, and questions of tactics and strategy will be learned in practice once formal legal education is over.

The traditional style of law school teaching causes many law students to misunderstand the game they are called upon to play. In this grand style, a professor assigns a collection of legal raw materials — appellate opinions and occasionally statutes — for preparation before class. Then the professor questions students about them, pointing out flaws in their answers. If a student takes the plaintiff's side in discussing a case, the professor attacks with challenges supporting the defendant. But if another student offers support for the defendant's arguments, the professor neatly leaps to the other side and attacks the defendant's case. The professor never answers his or her questions and never summarizes.

Student questions are answered with other questions. A Yale law student said that one of that school's most famous professors would respond to "what time is it?" by a series of questions about the functions of time in modern society. Students complain that their notes are nothing but a list of questions, but the professor refuses to see this as a criticism of the class. Such professors observe "*I* don't teach; *you* learn!"

At the very least, students in such a class are supposed to learn to impose structure on what seem to be a jumble of case summaries, questions, their fellow students' attempts at answers, jokes and professorial war stories. They are supposed to recognize that plausible arguments can be made by a lawyer for just about any proposition but that some arguments are easier to sell than others. Professors and judicial opinions offer examples of formal legal argument and conventional assumptions of legal culture. Needless to say, students who assume that studying involves only memorizing what a professor or textbook author certifies to be the truth are misguided. Students who have firm but simple ideas of right and wrong often are disturbed by what they see as the chaos and relativism of many law school classes.

Law professors often speak of class discussion, but this phrase suggests more equality between professor and student than usually exists. Students cannot remain passive note takers. Students can be forced to participate and risk making fools of themselves. Moreover, the professor controls the agenda, grants and withholds permission to speak, and is armed with rhetorical ploys that few in the class will have mastered. Students learn to make qualified statements and recognize that the other side always has a good argument. Beginning law students often find themselves at the end of a limb arguing that a particular result is "just" or "fair." After having the limb sawed off a few times, students learn to say something such as "one might argue that a particular result promotes efficiency but one must remember that many would object to the distributional consequences." Moreover, even a beginning law teacher will have spent more time preparing for class than the most conscientious law student, and the professor will be far better able to see any particular discussion in the total context of the course.

As students progress through law school they learn how to cope with this teaching style. Some master the game. Many tend to become more and more cautious about participating in class and more tentative in their answers. This style of teaching in its pure form may be passing into history, but enough remains to cause problems for many students who have to learn the game.

Some of the difficulty experienced by many students flows from the three-ring-circus nature of law teaching. The topic, in the center ring, may be the definition of a part of a rule of law. But at the same time, in a side ring, may be a procedural point essential to the case. Students may have to explore points of legal philosophy or legal ethics. The rule in the case may operate together with another rule that the class has yet to study. Lawyers may have to choose between, say, contracts or torts theories, and thus the contracts professor may find herself trespassing on another course. New students often raise concerns not directly relevant to the materials under discussion but important in their own right. Many professors think that it is a good idea to follow what seems to interest the class rather than hold the discussion in narrow channels. However, this means that a transcript of a class rarely takes the form of a neatly organized outline. Organizing one's notes is a distinct step that must take place after class or a series of classes. Sometimes it is hard to see whether a discussion was related directly to a major theme, a subtheme, or was but a pure digression.

1. LAW SCHOOL CLASSES AND CONTRACT THEORIES

What goes on in law school classes? Probably no two professors' classes are alike, and all of them pursue multiple and often conflicting goals. However, we can sketch a number of models of what it is "they want me to learn." Classes reflect professors' theoretical assumptions about their fields as well as their assumptions about legal education and law practice. We will take an historical approach. The current fashion in legal education is a reaction to what went before, but one cannot just turn to the latest fad and ignore earlier styles. Professors usually want you to master the older approaches and something else as well. Almost all modern law professors at least touch on most of the models we will describe. They differ largely in emphasis. With few exceptions, professors do not follow a party line. Some champion an approach that their colleagues reject with contempt. We will discuss, in turn, what we can label the (a) classic, (b) realist, (c) neutral principles and procedures, (d) law and economics, (e) critical legal studies, and (f) law and society approaches. We will describe these approaches and sketch some of the objections to each.

2. LAW SCHOOL CLASSES

a. The Classic Approach

In classic legal education, one learns the law and its application to particular situations. For example, suppose the tort of X allows a plaintiff to recover damages from a defendant if the plaintiff can prove (1) defendant hit plaintiff, (2) defendant intended to hit plaintiff, and (3) plaintiff did not consent to being hit. A professor expects students to discover "the elements" (that is, factors (1), (2), and (3)) of the tort of X from reading one or more cases, but this is only the start of the game.

A classic law professor would push students to unearth many difficult problems of definition lurking within this seemingly simple example. At the outset, what does "hit" mean? Suppose Defendant (hereafter D) tried to hit Plaintiff (hereafter P) but missed. However, as D's fist swung past P's chin, the sleeve of D's jacket brushed the sleeve of P's shirt. Did D "hit" P? And what does "intend" mean? Suppose D tried to hit Mr. A, but hit P instead when P jumped in the way trying to defend Mr. A. Suppose, alternatively, D intended to swing his fist at P but only to scare P, not to hit him. However, P moved into the path of D's punch and took it on the chin. Suppose, to change the case again, D swung his fist at P but was indifferent whether he hit P or came close enough to scare him. Suppose, finally, D testifies at trial that he actually intended only to make a broad gesture while arguing with P, but D's fist came in contact with P's chin by accident. X, Y, and Z, three reasonable people who watched the encounter, testify that D seemed to them to have intended to hit P. Does the definition of "intend" in the tort refer to some subjective inner state? Must actors in the legal system judge it objectively by outward appearances?

The classic law professor would not be through yet. What does "consent" mean?[1] Few people who are not masochists would want others to hit them. Nevertheless, many do put themselves into situations where it is likely they will be hit. Does this constitute "consent" and thus a defense to the tort of X? Suppose that both P and D are professional football players for rival teams. In the course of a game, D hits P to block him so that a runner can advance the ball. Does P "consent" to D's hitting him just by participating in the game of football? Or does consent require a formal act such as signing a written contract whereby P gives up his protection from being hit by D in exchange for the privilege of playing the game? Suppose that D's block was illegal under the rules of football.[2] Would P's consent to being blocked in the game extend to being blocked illegally under the league rule? Would it matter if the rule were frequently broken or almost never broken? Suppose during a time out, P took off his helmet, and D then punched P in the face. Does P's consent to being hit during the course of a game extend to this kind of behavior that is not part of the contest?

Suppose, to shift the situation again, P and D are baseball players. P, a pitcher, threw a ball at D, a batter, that just missed him. D ran to the mound and hit P in the face. P knew that while this is not an everyday occurrence, it is not unheard of. Did P consent to D's retaliatory blow just by playing the game? Suppose that P is a spectator at a baseball game and a foul ball off D's bat went into the stands hitting P. Did P consent to being hit in this way just by attending

---

[1]The meaning of consent has become the focus of political controversy in the crime of rape. A man has not raped a woman who consented to sexual intercourse. However, how free must her choice be? Whatever the formal definition of consent, what is the folk definition of the term imposed by juries? One study suggests that American jurors often rule that if the woman knew the man, if sexual intercourse took place in a social situation, and if no weapon were used, the woman will be deemed to have consented. Many feminists see the social definition of rape as a reflection of the sexism in the society. Apart from the merits of their argument, the example suggests that consent is not a simple concept, and its definition often involves controversial normative choices.

[2]Notice the interesting use of the term illegal. Can we say that the National Football League has its own "LAW?" If so, should lawyers, and law students, concern themselves with this kind of "private government"? Is this footnote an example of a digression from the main theme of the discussion? If so, is it unimportant? Can you just ignore these questions without fear of sanction?

the game? Suppose P is French, and this is the first time he has ever seen a baseball game. On the back of P's ticket of admission to the game a number of sentences appear printed in tiny type. They say that anyone attending the game shall be deemed to have consented to being hit by foul balls coming into the stands. Is P bound by a contract whereby he gave up his rights as a result of accepting such a ticket and entering the stadium?

Of course, law professors and law students who have learned to play the game can dream up hypothetical situations endlessly that test what seems to be a straightforward rule of law. This illustrates something about the nature of the words so often used to state legal rules such as "hit," "intend," and "consent." Is hypothetical construction just a game or is there an important lawyer's skill involved? Could we avoid all of these problems by drafting rules of law more carefully and using more precise terms? Those drafting legal rules pay a price when they try to anticipate most situations. Think of the Internal Revenue Code and the regulations drafted under it. They are exceedingly complex, and complexity creates work for accountants and tax lawyers.

How do we answer these endless questions? The classic law professor, by question and body language, would push students toward several possible sources of answers. First, we could search for *authority* — cases, statutes, administrative regulations, and other sources of law dealing with some aspect of the problems we have posed. Suppose we add to one of our hypothetical cases that P played football for the Chicago Bears, and D played for the Green Bay Packers. D hit P in a game played in Milwaukee. Thus, we can assume that the case is governed by the law of Wisconsin. Suppose, further, that the Supreme Court of Wisconsin decided in 1960 that professional football players consent, within the meaning of that term in the tort of X, to the common and ordinary hitting involved in the game by their participation in the sport. If we assume that the Wisconsin court would not reverse its 1960 decision (and this might be a large assumption), then we could answer some of the questions about the meaning of consent with a degree of assurance.

We could consider the implications of this decision by using the techniques of common law case analysis. This is the art of generating both broad holdings for cases, so that they may be applied beyond their intuitive scope, and narrow holdings, so that they will not apply where it seems they should. Most narrowly, a court could limit the 1960 decision to professional football and the particular facts of the case. More broadly, a court could read the decision as establishing that a player takes the risk of common and ordinary physical contact in *any* sport. Of course, we still would have to determine whether the particular hitting involved in our case would be deemed to be common and ordinary within the sport. We might expect that some hitting would clearly be part of football while other hitting clearly would outside the ordinary risks assumed by anyone who played the game. Having established this, however, we might expect to find a large range of cases in the middle where reasonable people might differ about how common and ordinary the type of hitting involved was. These would be the close and difficult cases where both P and D would have good arguments — the type of case likely to be posed on a law school examination. Even skilled and experienced lawyers would not be able to be certain of the outcome of these cases; at best, they could make informed judgments about the probabilities that P or D would win.

Law students are expected to learn "to spot the issues" — that is, to identify ambiguities in rules, conflicts among rules, and gaps where particular situations fail to fit rules. Clearly, this 1960 decision does not answer all the questions we raised. For example, does it apply to baseball players as well as football players? The classic law professor would push his or her students to reason by *analogy*. One could say, for example, that the key idea in the 1960 decision was that professional athletes — whatever the sport — can be assumed to understand the ordinary risks of the game. As a result, they can be deemed to choose to take those risks when they choose to play. In this sense, baseball is like (analogous to) football, although the precise risks assumed by baseball and football players would differ as the two sports differ. Of course, this judgment based on an analogy would be strengthened if we were to discover that the highest courts in ten other states had decided just this way on these very grounds. Then we could combine an argument by analogy with an appeal to authority. While the decisions of the courts in other states would not bind the Supreme Court of Wisconsin in interpreting its 1960 decision, it is likely that its members would find these other cases *persuasive* since, absent good reason to the contrary, uniformity among the states itself is an important value.

Classic law professors often refer to the ordinary meaning of language as a second major source of answers to the questions we raised earlier. They might ask whether most people (they often mean most educated people, or most members of the same socio-economic class as the legal elite) understand "hit," "intend," or "consent" to include or exclude the cases presented. On occasion, judges, lawyers, and law professors look to dictionary definitions. The problem, of course, is justifying the assumption that words have clear fixed meanings apart from context and that dictionaries capture those meanings accurately. Sometimes the argument is put less elegantly. A professor asserts "it is just common sense that P did not consent to being hit in the face by D during a time out from play." Without a great deal of analysis, he just knows that this is true.

b. Legal Realism

Beginning just before the First World War, a group of American law professors attacked the kinds of approaches we have just described. Their movement was called "legal realism," but it is far easier to describe what they were against than what they were for. One idea common to the group was that judges do not "find" the law in the clouds or by manipulating techniques of distinguishing cases. Rather judges "make" the law by normative choices. And if this is true, the realists told us that we would get better decisions if judges openly recognized their role and explained how they arrived at their choices. Many realists relied on the teachings that came to be known as general semantics to attack definitional approaches. Words such as "hit," "intend," and "consent" have many meanings in ordinary speech, and definitions serve better to rule out extreme cases than to decide close ones. Since past decisions almost never involve the identical situation now brought before the court, cases almost always can be distinguished if a judge wants to do so. Thus, appeals to authority may affect judgment but they do not compel one result rather than another.

Analogies, too, are suspect. For example, baseball and football are both professional sports, and those who play them are likely to be aware of certain risks of being hit by another player that are just part of the game. But football is supposed to be a contact sport while baseball is not. We could say that a football player has less need of the deterrent of the law of torts than a baseball player because of the nature of his athletic equipment and the opportunity to retaliate. Or one could argue that football needs the support of tort law more than baseball because it is necessary to control the violence inherent in the sport. Whatever the merit of these arguments, they illustrate that the very nature of an analogy is that the things being viewed are *both* like one another in some respects and not like one another in others. The problem is to decide if the common factors are more important than the uncommon ones. However, this is a judgment that rests on values, facts, and predictions about the consequences of decisions each way. Analogy may be a step in the process of decision, but it does not end the discussion.

A law professor who embraced realism would ask a student to argue in terms of the goals to be served by one decision or another. For example, a student might argue for a consent rule in professional sports that turned on the likely reaction of fans viewing the event. A player should be deemed to consent to the normal risks of the game even including blows that violate its rules, but those blows that would likely incite fans to violence should be deterred by all means available including tort liability. This, the student might argue, would aid in crowd control — a worldwide problem at sporting events — and, in the long run, in the continuation of professional sports. Another student might disagree, arguing that the private government of professional sports has enough internal sanctions to control the behavior of competitors so that we need not incur the costs of trying lawsuits between athletes. She might remind us that players in any sport, from golf to boxing, who hit others outside the rules of the game can be suspended or thrown out of the game for good. Those who violate the working norms of competitors are subject to a variety of sanctions ranging from attacks on their reputation in the form of gossip, to ostracism, and to physical retaliation. We need evidence that more is needed before we waste the time of overcrowded judicial machinery on such cases.

Whatever the merit of these arguments, they accept that the term "consent" could be interpreted to include or exclude the behavior in question, and they attempt to influence the choice of a meaning in a particular situation on the basis of some impact on behavior that the advocate thinks good or bad. Definitions and analogies only offer a number of possibilities. Choices must be made on the basis of normative evaluation of statements of the rule or predictions about its consequences. This being the case, one must argue policy just as if one were trying to convince a legislator to vote for passage or defeat of a statute.

Realism, of course, relies on wise judges to make policy choices. How, then, does law differ from politics? Republican governors appoint one group of judges while Democratic governors appoint another. Then each judge has a roving commission to do good as he or she sees fit. Many find this unsatisfactory, an abandonment of the rule of law. Indeed, some even recall the Nazi judges in Germany who applied their policy approach to legal problems with disastrous consequences.

c. Neutral Principles and Procedures

By the 1950s, most law professors accepted many of the teachings of realism. And, as we might have predicted, there was a reaction. Many legal scholars were critical of the approach taken in *Brown v. Board of Education* (the school desegregation case of 1954). Mr. Justice Warren's opinion for the unanimous court was widely criticized as not measuring up to the high standards of legal craft. Members of the legal elite saw it as a prime example of illegitimate judicial law making. The Supreme Court decided that the constitution prohibited states from offering separate but equal public schools to whites and blacks.[3] The court overruled *Plessy v. Ferguson*, an 1895 decision upholding separate but equal railway carriages "for the white and colored races." The court in *Brown* could not rest its decision on the inconclusive evidence of the intention of the framers of the Fourteenth Amendment concerning equal protection. The Supreme Court said that segregated education, even if such tangible things as buildings and books were equal, harmed children of both races. It cited modern "psychological knowledge" not available at the time of the *Plessy* decision. Thus, in many ways the decision reflected a legal realist approach to the role of appellate judging.

Many law professors argued, and taught, that *courts* should not attempt to desegregate public schools, supervise prisons, regulate abortion or contraception and the like. We may favor reforms, but it is not a judge's role to bring them about. These are political decisions, and in a representative democracy it is not the business of judges to make them. The courts lack the capacity to make such decisions well and to implement them. The adversary system offers judges an incomplete picture of the impact of their decisions. Courts lack independent investigators and experts; they are dependent on what the parties bring before

---

[3]Of course, black segregated schools seldom, if ever, were physically equal to white schools, but neither the NAACP nor the court wanted to decide the case on that narrow basis.

them. Judges themselves may be expert in law but not in school administration, penology, or changing views about sexuality.

Moreover, these scholars stress that there is an important question of legitimacy. To a very large degree, in a democracy the majority has a right to be wrong as judged by elite values. The judiciary has limited power to coerce people to abide by its decisions; it has no army at its command. The power of courts rests largely on the perception of the public that judges are applying the law and not their own views of the good, the true, and the beautiful. The solution these professors advocate is legal craft and procedure that would restrain judicial innovation to an incremental step-by-step approach. Judges and lawyers can claim no special understanding of what to do, but can demand that whatever society wants be done using proper procedures.

Of course, not every legal scholar accepts this craft and procedural fairness position. Some doubt "if you do it the right way, you will get the right result." Some insist that the major role of courts in the American legal system is the interpretation of fundamental political and social values found in federal and state constitutions. Some wonder about the continued legitimacy of the Supreme Court had it decided *Brown v. Board of Education* the other way. Some point out that a Bill of Rights necessarily limits the power of majorities to implement their will. Some insist that representative democracy in the United States had broken down so that needed and acceptable change through legislative action had been blocked by unrepresentative minorities. At the time of *Brown*, Blacks could not register to vote in many states, in many parts of the country voting districts were gerrymandered so that certain groups would retain control of the political process, and the committee system in the Congress plus the filibuster gave power to established minorities such as white Southerners. These critics challenged the advocates of neutral principles and procedures to move from formal neutrality to a view of the actual operation of the United States political system. Formal neutrality would only insure that things stayed as they were. The privileged would keep their advantages while those at the bottom would stay there. Given the system's flawed nature, they saw a role for an activist judiciary to set things right.

d. Economics-and-Law

The economics-and-law approach has become popular in many American law schools. The founding fathers of the movement are identified with the University of Chicago and its tradition in economics. Realism tells judges and other decision-makers to make normative choices openly, but offers little advice about how to choose among possible normative positions. Legal proceduralism imposes a requirement of due process on almost every important decision but accepts whatever substantive choices emerge from formally fair procedures. Economics-and-law says that a decision-maker should consider the impact of his or her decision on efficiency; if one wants to seek some other goal, at least one should be aware of the costs of such a policy.

For example, we must pay a price if we insist that all decisions be taken only after procedures that comply with due process. Sometimes the cost will be outweighed by the benefits, but often it will not. The position teaches a powerful lesson overlooked in much of legal realism, 1930s liberalism or legal proceduralism — sometimes the lesson is summarized as "there's no such thing as a free lunch." In the 1960s and 1970s, Congress decided to regulate the safety of automobile design, environmental pollution caused by automotive exhaust, and the fuel consumption of cars. The economics-and-law approach emphasizes that such regulation is not free, and the cost of these changes in the design of vehicles will raise prices for cars. This, in turn, is likely to have many consequences, some of which may be hard to see at first. Less transportation, for example, may be available to the poor if higher prices cause middle class owners to drive their cars longer so there is less usable life left when they trade in the cars. The total market for automobiles may contract as prices increase, and this will limit the number of available jobs connected with automobile manufacture, servicing, tourism and so on. People may be willing to accept these costs of regulation as the price for what they see as real benefits. Nonetheless, we cannot pretend that there are no costs or that they just will come out of the pocket of wealthy corporations in some magical fashion. Most simply, the approach reminds us that law is not free.

The economics-and-law approach also suggests that, absent transaction costs, it makes no difference where legislatures and courts place liability for accidental injuries and deaths. Suppose we have a rule that says car buyers must pay for repairs to their vehicles whatever the cause of damage. A court or legislature changes the rule to place the burden of certain repairs on car sellers. We then can expect sellers to raise prices or to make contracts shifting the burden of repairs back to buyers. In either event buyers will still pay for repairs.

Many of those who advocate the economics-and-law approach see it as value neutral. Insofar as we care about efficiency, we must try to predict the economic consequences of a proposed change in legal rules. Moreover, we can explain much of what courts have done since the Industrial Revolution in terms of seeking efficiency. Most of the proponents of this economics-and-law approach tell us that it does not deal with the justice or fairness of the present distribution of wealth, status, privilege, or power in the society. Economics-and-law, however, has a great deal to say about the costs of measures designed to change such distributions.

Critics of the approach see it as a highly successful effort to legitimate the position of the well-off in society. Economics-and-law just ignores law's role in symbolizing values and morals.[4] Often the message of the approach is that reform

---

[4]See Friedman, Two Faces of Law, 1984 Wisconsin Law Review 13.

is impossible or unwise, and if only government would go away, all would be as good as it can be. These scholars hold as an article of faith that competition and free markets solve all problems, and they deny that there can be any private power unchecked by the market apart from advantages granted by government.

Critics point out that its approach is highly abstract and based on logical deduction from doubtful assumptions. A great deal of economics-and-law assumes a world without transaction costs, but that is not the world in which we live. Too little attention is given to implementation of rules — writers sometimes treat people as if they were puppets tied by strings to legal rules that control their behavior. That the formal statement of a legal rule can be rationalized in efficiency terms does not necessarily indicate that the rule promotes efficiency in practice. Of course one could take an economics-and-law approach to the law in action. It just hasn't been done often.

e. Critical Legal Studies

Occasionally, some professors will ask students to make radical or "critical" appraisals of legal problems. From this perspective, the existing distribution of wealth, status, privilege, and power is central. Those who adopt a critical approach see legal doctrine as mystification. For example, in the 19th Century lawyers and judges came to see the business corporation as a legal person with all the rights of real individuals. The law treats General Motors and an individual consumer *as if* they were equal before the law. If General Motors were to infringe the rights of an individual, in theory, he could sue and recover damages as compensation. But all of this is ideology that ignores the advantages General Motors has over any individual who attempts to assert legal rights against it.[5] Lawyers are both necessary and expensive. Wealth has impact on the outcome of litigation. People and organizations with wealth can better afford the long delays that so characterize our legal system. Moreover, organizations that engage in repeated standardized transactions can plan these relationships to their advantage. Individuals who deal with them sign standard form contracts that serve to ward off most unwanted liability from the large organization. Most individuals are not aware of what they are giving away when they sign. If they were, they would have what one taking a radical position would call little *real* choice but to sign away their rights.

Scholars associated with the Conference on Critical Legal Studies (CLS) examine the assumptions hidden within legal doctrine concerning what is necessary, tolerable, and just. What do those who make and work with our law take as "common sense"? Do these assumptions add up to a coherent and defensible political philosophy? Which groups in society benefit from these tacit

---

[5]See Galanter, Why the "Haves" Come Out Ahead: Speculations on the Limits of Legal Change, 9 Law & Society Review 95 (1974).

assumptions in our law; which are disadvantaged by them? Critical scholars see American legal consciousness as favoring wealth and privilege and harming working class and poor people. Some of these scholars find American law characterized by contradictory principles. They hope that by showing underdeveloped but long established counterthemes in our law, they can open the way to a new conception of rights more consistent with a less competitive and more cooperative society. For example, contract law celebrates both individual selfishness and altruism although since the last century, the individualist strand has been dominant. Lawyers, judges, and scholars could develop altruistic notions such as fiduciary duties and expand them to cover any long-term continuing relationship. To some degree, this might offset disparities in power between contracting parties.

Critical Feminists and Critical Race Theorists have challenged the white male law professors who make up most of CLS. They have charged them with insensitivity to the benefits of a rule of law. While rights may be flawed weapons, women and people of color can use them both as symbols, and as instruments to better their position. Moreover, when we look at any body of law, including contracts, from the perspective of gender or race we recognize easily overlooked and debatable assumptions. For example, the alleged neutrality of contract ideas served well the institution of slavery in the United States until the Civil War — humans bought and sold other people under a law that claims to be one of the foundations of liberty.[6] People of color are almost entirely absent from contracts casebooks, suggesting that this body of law deals with power as much as it deals with questions of free choice. Many of the defenses to contracts law suits involve a claim of weakness, and it is women willing to play this stereotypical feminine role who claim these defenses successfully. A leading Critical Feminist wrote an analysis of how a popular contracts casebook treated women either as sex objects or as the subject of paternal care.[7]

Radical lawyers sometimes see all varieties of critical legal thinkers as trying to bring about a revolution from within the academy rather than taking risks fighting the battle in the front lines. Critical scholars respond that it is better to change ideas about what must and what could be, than to win victories seeking rights: lawyers championing the "have nots" can implement rights only marginally in legal institutions controlled by the powerful. Whenever workers, people of color, women, or other less powerful groups threaten to win significant victories through the assertion of rights, the system adjusts to support the status quo. Statutes are construed narrowly, procedural rules are put in place to minimize the chances of success, the costs of asserting rights are raised to limit their use, and jurors reject valid claims as something they do not wish to believe.

---

[6]Williams, The Alchemy of Rights, 17-21, 216, 224 (1991).

[7]Frug, Re-reading Contracts: A Feminist Analysis of a Contracts Casebook, 34 American University Law Review 1065 (1985).

We could debate most of these assertions. Nonetheless, all varieties of critical legal thought invite students to consider how the legal system works in practice and what kinds of people benefit. Seemingly neutral legal rules may privilege certain positions.[8] Whatever the statement of legal ideals, the law on the books may differ from the law in action. The impact of these differences may not be random or neutral.

f. Law and Society

All of the approaches we have considered so far call for a student to appraise and work with legal doctrine. Students learn to predict what a court will do. But those who think about law in these ways assume that rules are the most important part of the legal system. The final approach — the law-and-society or the empirical view — questions overemphasis of legal rules. Here one asks how people solve problems that in some way are deemed legal ones and what role, if any, law and lawyers play.

Those few law professors who stress this approach emphasize that very few cases ever get to litigation, let alone to an appeal that produces the appellate opinions typically studied in law schools. In most situations, legal rights serve as but a vague bargaining entitlement in a negotiation process. People settle differences in the shadow of the law; they reach negotiated solutions where the chance that each party could win before the courts is discounted. For example, the victim and an insurance adjuster who is not a lawyer settle most auto accident claims in a fairly routine way. Even in the small percentage of cases where the victim hires a lawyer, they are likely to negotiate a settlement without filing a complaint. In those few cases where complaints are filed in court, lawyers settle most before the trial begins. Of course, legal rules play a part in the outcome, but often a minor one. As a result, the liability rules discussed in law school classes often will not have the impact on behavior assumed in approaches such as legal realism or economics-and-law.

Moreover, we may err if we assume that these appellate decisions are final resolutions of matters. The loser may battle on through administrative agencies or state and national legislatures to change the rules. And sometimes people win victories in these other law-making institutions so slighted in traditional legal education. Even where a plaintiff wins an appellate decision affirming a judgment for a large sum of damages one must execute the judgment and turn it into money. However, the defendant may have no assets subject to execution in the jurisdiction. The defendant may file for bankruptcy or delay matters through a state creditor-debtor proceeding. One of the lessons of a law and society

---

[8]Anatole France once wryly noted that "The law in its majestic egalitarianism, forbids the rich as well as the poor to sleep under bridges, to beg in the streets, and to steal bread." Le lys rouge, 1894, Ch. 7.

approach is that while rules and upper level decisions are important, one has to look at the real options open to the parties. This approach insists that we look at the legal system from the bottom up as well as from the top down. Criminal law, for example, is both a matter of the statutory definitions of crimes as interpreted by appellate courts and behavior as seen from the front seat of a police squad car.

As we might expect, this approach too has its critics. Law and society research undervalues the impact of legal doctrine as that research debunks and stresses other-than-legal factors. In American culture, law matters. Also, behavioral studies of law often stray far from ideal social science methods because of the difficulties in studying the functioning legal system. Radicals attack the approach for emphasizing details that can be studied empirically rather than broader questions such as the functions of liberal views of law in continuing the existing distributions of wealth and power.

3. LAW SCHOOL EXAMINATIONS

Once a student masters the blend of these approaches demanded by his or her professor, the student still must pass a law school examination. Typically, a student will be confronted with a story and asked to play the role of judge or that of a lawyer for plaintiff or defendant. To take a very simple example, suppose the question set out the story of P and D, two professional baseball players employed by rival teams. P, a pitcher, threw a ball that just missed hitting D who was batting. D ran to the mound and threw a punch at P. However, D hit U, the first base umpire. U had come to the mound to try to prevent a fight. You are U's lawyer. Make the best case you can to justify recovery of a judgment against D.

Your first task would be to try to fit these facts into some legal category. You recognize that it is worth considering the tort of X. There is no question that D hit U, and so the first element of the tort seems to be present. However, unless you can persuade a judge and jury to interpret the word "intent" very broadly, you face trouble establishing the second element of the tort. Moreover, you should at least recognize the possibility that D's lawyer is going to argue that just by being an umpire U "consented" to the risks of getting hit in a fight between players. (Law students call the process of fitting facts into legal categories we have just gone through "spotting the issues." Most of those who get low grades do so because they fail to see that they should discuss the tort of X or that there would be a problem in establishing that D "intended" to hit U.)

How would you argue that it was enough that D intended to hit someone and that the tort of X does not, or should not, require that he have intended to hit his actual victim, your client U? You could turn to whatever authority had been discussed in your course. You probably would not have a case directly deciding the question. You would have to draw analogies to those decisions that adopted a broader definition of "intent" in other contexts. You would do what you could with the ordinary understanding of the word "intent." Perhaps you could argue that in common speech we assume that one "intends" the ordinary consequences of one's actions, and one consequence of throwing a punch is missing the intended target and hitting something else. You would make policy arguments that would justify an expanded definition of the term so that the rule would include third parties such as U. You would deal with D's likely arguments that changes in liability rules are properly the task of a legislature and that such broader liability is economically inefficient. You might consider whether all a new rule would do is prompt disclaimer clauses in umpires' contracts. You might consider a distributional argument concerning highly paid players striking lesser paid employees of organized baseball such as umpires.

Then after all of this analysis concerning "intent," you would turn to the consent issue. Do umpires assume the risk of injury in fights between players just by being umpires? Again you would make all the types of arguments we've catalogued. You would anticipate those your opponent is likely to make and deal with them as best as you could.

Once you had dealt with the tort of X, you would then consider whether D's conduct came within the tort of Y. It applies to unintentional but "negligent" hitting of others. Why not start with tort Y and avoid all the difficult problems with the idea of "intent" in tort X? Because, as you would have stated in your answer, U might be able to get punitive damages in addition to compensation for his actual injuries if the hitting were deemed intentional. He could recover only actual compensatory damages for negligence. Indeed, this possibility might affect arguments about how a court should define intent for purposes of tort — in essence, you would assert that D's conduct warranted strong punishment so both he and others would be deterred in the future and therefore the word "intent" should be defined broadly to achieve this goal. D's lawyer, of course, would argue that D's conduct did not warrant such punishment. This may seem to be arguing backwards. Logically, one might expect a determination of whether D has committed tort X and then the remedies would just follow if he had. Here, we begin by asking what remedy makes sense in light of D's conduct. You will find that many of your courses reflect this concern with the bottom line. This is another example of the realists' point that deciding cases involves policy choices and not just definitions and deductions.

4. ENDS AND MEANS: WHAT AM I HERE FOR?

Yet, you might ask, what am I here for? What does all this have to do with becoming a lawyer? You did not come to law school to become an examination answering expert. Examinations are supposed to be a means to the end of becoming a lawyer. The faculty believes and hopes that those who can write good answers will be able to evaluate and make persuasive arguments to legal decision-makers. Lawyers who are good at evaluating arguments will know what cases to accept from potential clients and what to do with those they do take.

Where one has a strong legal argument — assuming all other things are equal — he or she can demand far more as the price of a settlement than when he or she has a weaker but possible legal position.

Notice that here we arrive at an explanation for the law professor's emphasis on arguments rather than answers. One who can fashion a plausible argument, even one involving creative new theories, usually is in a better bargaining position in settlement negotiations than a lawyer who can do little more than blunder through a cookbook approach to practice. All lawyers are equal only in the yellow pages of the telephone directory; smart lawyers do better than stupid ones. Of course, creative theories must fall within the range of arguments acceptable within legal culture. Whatever the merit of Marxist theories about American law, one would be a fool to offer them so labelled to most American judges. There are fashions in ideas acceptable to the courts. Certain views are "in the air" at one time but not another. A wise lawyer would not make the same arguments in the same way before the present Supreme Court of the United States as she made when Earl Warren was Chief Justice. Consumer protection was far more popular in the early 1970s than in the early 1980s. Also, some judges delight in technical lawyering while others are annoyed by nice distinctions among cases and clever readings of statutes.

Indeed, the law of nearly every state as applied in its cities, towns, and villages will reflect the state's diversity and is likely to differ substantially around a common core found in the state's statutes, administrative regulations, and appellate cases. Knowing what is likely to sell before the judges who would decide a case also is part of a lawyer's skill. Of course, a sociologist of law would remind us that bargaining power flows from far more than legal arguments and so settlements may turn on other factors. For example, one party may need money immediately while the other is able to await a final decision after several appeals, and this fact is likely to affect how they settle a case. This, too, is part of our subject matter.

In a sense, good lawyers never cease being law students. As this essay emphasizes, the practice of law is far more than knowing a body of formal statements of rules. Of course, learning certain rules and a vocabulary is an essential step in the process of becoming a lawyer. However, it is but one step. Moreover, many of the rules one must learn to practice are not what one normally thinks of as laws. Both lawyers who represent those injured in auto accidents and lawyers who represent insurance companies know the going rate for various kinds of accidents. They know about what it will take to settle a rear-end collision where the police gave neither driver a traffic ticket and where the plaintiff has suffered damage to his car and personal injuries. While all this is true, a great deal of law practice also involves judgments about probabilities in light of specialized knowledge. One must cope with the knowledge that one cannot be certain: a court or legislature may change the rule, there are good arguments for alternative interpretations of the rule as applied in the present situation, and what one knows and what one can prove in court are very different things. A major goal of legal education is to provide part of the basis for making such informed judgments in the practice of law.

While legal education always could do a better job in preparing students for practice, it would be impossible to mint finished lawyers in but three years at a university. "Lawyer" is a label applied to many distinct professions, and faculty and students cannot predict whether certain students will go to Wall Street or Main Street, whether they will work in governmental agencies, or whether they will enter politics.

After reading this essay, ·tudents should consider the professors they encounter in all the classes they are taking. What blend of the styles identified here does each reflect? What does this essay omit? One might question such an approach: ideally, the goal of education would be knowledge rather than how to play each professor. Yet all people, even professors trying to be objective and neutral, are products of their experiences, values, and biases. To understand what is being communicated, one must understand the communicator. Moreover, by learning to read professors a law student should gain skill in learning to read judges and other decision makers he or she will seek to influence in practice. Far too often all of us, particularly law professors, think only of what we mean to say rather than what others are likely to understand from what we communicate. This is an expensive conceit for a lawyer. Perhaps by watching the faculty struggle to communicate, you can learn to do better.

It is not easy to be a law student. There is too much to learn and too little time in which to master it. Nonetheless, there is no reason to make it harder by forgetting what you are trying to do. A few moments thought devoted to "what am I here for?" now and then is likely to pay off.

B. CONTRACTS COURSES

Almost all law students in what was once the British Empire begin their study with a course called "contracts." Students naturally assume that the course deals with an important part of law practice. However, in recent years many law professors and others have questioned this. They point out that there is a large gap between the law school law of contract, what happens in courts, and what practicing lawyers do. *Contracts: Law in Action* reflects our doubts about the traditional course. In this introductory essay we, the authors and editors, describe what we think contract study should be in light of the social functions played by this area of law in modern society.

1. THE GOALS OF THE COURSE: LAWYERS AND CONTRACTS

Professors and students long assumed that contract rules were fundamental to the practice of law. While this may or may not be the case, contract doctrine clearly is only part of what lawyers need to understand to serve their clients. Lawyers are involved in the planning and structuring of business relationships.

Producing a successful contract involves, first, an assessment of the goals and positions of the parties. What a lawyer proposes must be acceptable so that the parties can make a deal. Second, success involves planning a relationship so that both sides will be satisfied with the performance of the contract. Thus, the lawyer must understand business and social relationships, the techniques of planning and writing, and many bodies of law so that the arrangement will have desired legal consequences. Clearly, a good deal more is involved than a knowledge of contract doctrine.

Lawyers also perform an important advisory role in managing ongoing contractual relationships. For example, the parties may disagree about their obligations under a contract. One party may come close to performing but not quite make it. Is a miss as good as a mile or must a client accept substantial but not complete performance? Or the seller may fall far short of full performance, but the buyer may need the defective performance so badly that she takes it. Once the need has passed, can the buyer assert the original obligation or has she modified the contract by accepting the defective performance? Or the seller's failure to live up to the letter of the contract may have been caused by an unexpected event such as a fire, strike, or a flood. To what extent, if at all, do such contingencies constitute excuses from contractual duties? Finally, once relationships are wrecked, lawyers may face questions of salvage. Can one turn to the legal system to force the other to assume some or all of the losses caused by the breach of the contract? Again, contract doctrine speaks to all these questions, but lawyers and clients often must make difficult business judgments that are more important than legal arguments.

Lawyers do play a part in planning contracts, carrying them out, and clearing away the wreckage of those that fail, but business people are often able to handle these problems themselves without legal advice and real estate brokers, land developers, investment bankers, sales people, engineers, and accountants all compete with lawyers to offer this kind of advice. Nevertheless, complicated contracts problems do arise in many contexts — not just in business — and their solution may require the services of someone who understands the law of contract. However, lawyers are more likely to face some questions than others. All lawyers must recognize the important contracts issues, but exposing every law student to all the classic contracts puzzles is an inefficient use of law school time and resources.

Contract ideas are indirectly relevant to most lawyers' practices. Contract ideas form part of the ideology[9] of capitalism, and this ideology affects many branches of the law and many lawyers' tasks. The ideology is familiar to us all. Many writers see contract as the solution to the conflict between individualism and community. In a society based on command, rulers order people to perform

---

[9]We use the term "ideology" rather than political philosophy because ideology connotes a system accepted and assumed rather than a thought-out view.

tasks. In a free society, individuals make choices about what they will and will not do. There are, however, ends that cannot be achieved without social interaction that is only possible by coordinating individual choices. By exchanging some measure of our freedom or property for what we value, our choices serve to allocate resources to desired uses. Contract, thus, enables people to unlock the value of their labor and the tangible and intangible things they control. I want your money more than I want my Chevrolet. You want a car more than you want your money. By making an exchange we are both better off. Neither of us can take advantage of the other in a market society. Others will offer you automobiles and others will offer me money for my car. These alternative potential contracts serve to limit our bargain so that we exchange the automobile at close to what some are willing to call a just price — that is, a price within the range of many similar choices by willing sellers and buyers. Self interest, in this way, is channeled into a tool for cooperation in collective action.

Many theorists see contract law in capitalist societies as providing needed security of transactions. Any bargain where people exchange goods and money at the same time is almost self-policing. This is not true, however, when the exchange involves complex performances that take place over time. Suppose I am to paint your house and you are to pay me when I finish. Until I complete the job, you risk losing opportunities to hire someone else who might do the job more quickly and better. I risk your willingness and ability to pay me when I finish. Of course, many nonlegal sanctions give both of us incentives to perform. For example, we both may not want to be known as people who fail to carry out commitments. We may want to deal again, and I must worry that what I do under this contract will affect your willingness to enter new ones in the future. Members of my family may work for members of yours and depend on their good will for their economic success. Nonetheless, those who write about law see a need for official sanctions to reinforce nonlegal ones that support the making and performance of contracts. Contracts are too important to leave to other-than-legal sanctions.

Contract law tells those who would plan and take risks how to make legally binding commitments. One who follows the accepted formula can know that she has made a contract. Contract law provides standardized interpretations of forms of language — it is a kind of authoritative dictionary. Contract law fills in gaps in agreements so that it is unnecessary to plan everything in each contract. Contract law also offers remedies for breach. While these remedies may provide some salvage of wrecked bargains, perhaps their most important function is to deter breach in the first place. One who would default must consider the threat that contract law will cause trouble. It costs money to defend oneself, even if one is successful. Moreover, contract law symbolizes the importance of commitments. Society spends resources supporting performance of bargains, and this itself is a statement of what is right.

There is a vast literature debating the assumptions we have sketched. If one truly believes in freedom, why say that a person loses it by making a promise?

To reject freedom to change one's mind, one must look to policies other than choice. Suppose, for example, University makes a five year contract with Coach to guide its football team. Two years later, State University offers Coach twice the salary to coach its team. Why should he not be free to change his mind and take the offer? Suppose Manufacturer Corporation orders parts from Supplier Corporation but then finds that the sales of the product in which it used these parts are very disappointing. Why should it not be free to cancel the order? If we look at customs in the football and manufacturing industries, we find that coaches and industrial buyers do feel free to cancel their commitments, whatever contract law says. Both universities and suppliers often accept cancellations without too much objection. And we should note that the law of contracts seldom, if ever, would tell judges to order either Coach or Manufacturer Corporation to perform or send them to jail for breach. Both could buy their way out by paying damages if either University or Supplier Corporation did not release them. Thus, the law itself suggests there may be reasons to allow people to break promises at not too great a price. Capitalist law does not seem to find absolute security of transactions an overriding value.

Some writers argue that free choice never really exists anyway, except in theorists' ivory towers. Suppose a robber with a gun sticks it in the back of a man walking past and says, "your money or your life!" The victim cannot say "none of the above"; he is being given a choice between unpleasant alternatives. In the example about buying a car, your real preference might have been a better car for a lower price. Realistically, people are always constrained by their circumstances. The line between a choice we deem free and one we call coerced usually is difficult to draw. It is a normative evaluation rather than a description of a situation. The distribution of advantages in society affects freedom of choice in important ways. Perhaps seeing all but a few choices as free and not the product of coercion is a useful working assumption, but it cannot be confused with an empirical description.

Furthermore, the theorists' model is that of a negotiated deal. The parties give and take. They are aware of the terms or accept the risks of incomplete knowledge. While this may describe some transactions involving expert buyers and sellers, it is a poor representation of many bargains. It is hard for most consumers to appraise products before they buy them. Few consumers understand that the form contracts they sign drastically limit their ability to do anything about unsatisfactory purchases. Of course, other-than-legal sanctions operate in this area, and many consumers' complaints will prompt real efforts to produce a remedy. However, the power of these sanctions is not equally distributed across society. Despite efforts to do better in recent years, Mercedes Benz buyers are likely to have more attention paid to their complaints than Chevrolet buyers, and buyers of new Chevrolets will do better than buyers of used ones.

When you examine contract law closely, you will discover that it reflects competing tendencies. Scholars have fashioned an abstract system of rules that appear relatively clear and suitable for use for about any purpose by anyone.

Courts have used some parts of this system at various times and places. Nonetheless, if we look carefully in area after area within the body of contract doctrine, we find counterrules and approaches that seek substantive justice at the expense of predictable abstraction. While skilled lawyers can predict the results of cases with some degree of accuracy, they must draw on information outside of the rules of law to do this.

It is a mistake, then, to assume that your professors are going to hand you a beautifully worked out, consistent and coherent system called "contract law." We doubt that such a system could exist without great changes in American society. Instead we hope to show you the contradictions within contract law, and how to use this imperfect language to accomplish your clients' goals. This is what the good contracts lawyer must take from a law school class rather than details of doctrinal refinements.[10] First, you should understand the rhetoric of contract with all of its ambiguities and inconsistencies. Whatever the doctrinal area, you will find that certain basic but inconsistent themes appear again and again. Lawyers have to learn to speak contract rhetoric because it will be the accepted vocabulary in negotiation as well as before trial and appellate courts.

Second, you must understand that contract law is a tool that you can use trying to solve your client's problems rather than a set of answers to all your questions. Rather than offering certainty and predictability, often it offers good arguments for all concerned. Lawyers are people who know how things work and how to get things done. They spend a good deal of their time coping with uncertainty and risk. For example, they may turn to drafting contract provisions that define what the law has left unclear. They may use uncertainty about the meaning of rules or about proving facts as bargaining tools and not as legal arguments before decision makers — for example, a client's uncertain chance of winning at trial is something you can sell to the other side for a price.

Lawyers often turn out to be policy makers. The actual jobs of lawyers often surprise law students. Rather than spending all their time in trial or appellate courtrooms, many lawyers act politically, both directly and indirectly. They are in the business of making deals with both public officials and representatives of private organizations. Contract often provides a vocabulary for negotiations in all kinds of settings. Furthermore, large numbers of lawyers are elected to legislatures at all levels of government and even more serve on legislative staffs. Much legislation of the past century has involved withdrawing areas from the domain of contract and creating specialized bodies of law. However, when we

---

[10]Details of doctrinal refinements might prove important sometime in your practice. However, there is not time to teach everything in three years of law school. Furthermore, contracts doctrine, as all law, has a short shelf life; details learned today may be out of date tomorrow. Fortunately, there is an impressive literature in contract law to help you exhaust the refinements of any nice point of doctrine. This course certainly should acquaint you with enough of the conventional wisdom in the field so that you will recognize a problem and understand what you read in treatises and journal articles.

shift to these new areas, we do not leave contract assumptions behind. They continue to color thought, particularly in labor law, real estate transactions, business organizations, commercial law, family law, trusts and estates, and regulation of specific areas. For example, during the past two or three decades, consumer advocates have made effective use of phrases, such as inequality of bargaining power and unconscionability, that have long been a countertheme in contract. In the 1980s, ideas about consumers' needs for protection began to change. Once again there was talk of self-reliance, efficiency, and the power of the market to impose all the discipline needed. Both in the 1970s and 1980s, the debate was about where we should draw the boundaries of free contract and social control, and much of it was carried on in contract rhetoric. Of course, we must be sensitive to the possibility that the terms of that debate get in the way of seeing what really is at stake, but that, too, is on our agenda.

2. CONTRACTS: LAW IN ACTION

These materials, *Contracts: Law in Action*, try to put contract law into its full context. We stress such things as the costs of using courts and bringing appeals. We see lawyers playing active roles reflecting both their clients' and their own interests. We see litigation and appeals as only part of a much larger social process. The chance that one might sue plays an important part in negotiation. Processes such as mediation and arbitration are supported by tacit threats of what might happen if one party declined to participate. Lawyers themselves often judge the merits of both sides' claims and attempt to work out problems in acceptable ways. We also try to keep students well aware that modern law involves legislation and administrative regulation. We see our course as helping beginning law students learn to be lawyers rather than just masters of the fine points of legal doctrine. At the same time, legal craft demands that lawyers recognize the conflicting goals of the field. Good lawyers understand the ways things work whether or not they work as they should.

Students have mixed reactions to the course. Some find to their surprise that our contracts course is not as dull as they feared the subject would be. It is, after all, about very real problems. Other students, however, sometimes find it hard to understand what we are driving at. "First, teach us the rules," they say, "and then we can learn how to apply them in new situations and to see exceptions." Or, as Betty Mensch[11] notes,

> Viewed in retrospect, Williston's majestic doctrinal structure may have been silly, but ... appeals to reasonableness and justice appear sloppy and formless by comparison. Williston's structure was, at least, a real structure, however misguided. Perhaps much Willistonian dogma survives simply

---

[11]Mensch, Freedom of Contract as Ideology, 33 Stanford Law Review 753, 769 (1981).

because it provides a challenging intellectual game to learn and teach in law school — more fun than the close attention to commercial detail required by thorough-going realism.

This demand for structure reminds us of a statement printed on a bookbag carried by one of our former students. It said, "I have given up the search for truth. Now all I want is a good fantasy." We understand our students' desire for simple answers and structure. Students, particularly beginners, assume there are clear rules and seek to master them. Commercial publishers play to that demand and offer outlines and books aimed at students. Generally, professors hope to encourage students to go beyond the comforting half-truths of doctrinal knowledge. However, they are relatively simple and reassuring if one does not read them too carefully, and may assist some students in their struggle with the basic issues of a topic.

Some students fight *Contracts: Law in Action* because of the pressure to get what they see as acceptable grades. Law students are people who have done well in academic competition. However, most recognize that not everyone can be in the top ten percent of his or her law school class, as unfair as that may seem. All those others sitting in a first year class room are also accustomed to high grades. Those who gathered the low Bs and Cs in undergraduate days no longer are in the race. One's own self-definition of acceptable grades creates tension when the material seems disorganized, class involves unanswered questions and no single clear theme, and examinations get closer and closer. Law students with better grades find it easier to get jobs they want when they graduate — there are real rewards for doing well in law school. This, too, fans the student demand for a clear structure and rules they can grasp. If the teacher would stop "suppressing the truth" and teach "law," then students could use the techniques that won the grades that got them into law school.

Moreover, the approach taken in these materials questions many things some students want to hold dear. Macaulay[12] suggests:

The classical model of contract ... appeals to many legal professionals [and law students] because it seems to offer those without political or economic power the possibility of overturning the structures of the powerful in the society. Judges are supposed to respond to reasoned argument, and if their decisions importantly affect behavior, then a single skilled advocate or author of a law review article, armed only with reason, could right wrongs by persuading judges. Not only would the powerless win, but the legal professional who championed their cause would need to do only honorable and enjoyable things in order to help them. The champion works through

---

[12]Macaulay, Elegant Models, Empirical Pictures, and the Complexities of Contract, 11 Law & Society Review 507, 521-522 (1977).

appeals to reason and intelligence, and talks of economic and social norms, the "findings of science," efficiency, or some other highly valued body of thought. Problems of politics, interest, power, and dominance need not be faced because they do not appear to be relevant in the world of doctrine, where it is assumed that right ideas will be crystallized into rules that are self-enforcing.... But many of those who examine the legal process in operation today find it difficult to retain their faith that the key to the good society resides in appellate judges, administrative agencies exercising discretion, pluralism, the morality of adjudication, or economic theory. Instead of justice, the empiricists describe a system of bargaining where "the haves come out ahead."[13]

One major theme of the course is that things are not as they seem. But debunking can be upsetting. It can lead to a resigned cynicism that undercuts any effort toward bettering the world. It is true that naive idealism may seriously mislead those whose goal is to effect change. However, legal rules do often matter. Lawyers for various causes have won remarkable victories, and reform efforts have affected life in the United States over the past thirty years or so. We think good lawyers are skeptical idealists, aware of how the system works but unwilling to retreat into an easy cynicism.

The authors of these materials organized them to emphasize what they see as important problems. In many places this calls for something other than a doctrinal arrangement. Indeed, often a doctrinal arrangement would distort our thinking. For example, David Trubek argues that the behavioral system related to processing particular types of disputes — including the relevant doctrine — "not only transforms the various individual conflicts: in so doing it 'transforms,' so to speak, a raw conflict of interest into a social process with limited possibilities. The disputes that do emerge are those in which basic economic relationships are not challenged: all other possibilities are filtered out."[14] We want to avoid these limitations on what we can see. Nonetheless, we make a major effort to explain the ins and outs of the doctrines and traditional approaches. We accept the point that as silly as some may be, they exist and influence the vocabulary and expectations of lawyers. We have struggled to explain the logical structure of, say, the consideration doctrine without allowing that structure to set boundaries around our thought.

Some students will find the materials difficult, but they only reflect the difficulty in both the claims of contract law and its actual role in social life in this country. Those who find the materials disorganized are looking for something

---

[13]See Galanter, Why the "Haves" Come Out Ahead: Speculations on the Limits of Legal Change, 9 Law & Society Review 95 (1974).

[14]Trubek, The Construction and Deconstruction of a Disputes Focused Approach, 15 Law & Society Review 727, 743 (1980-81).

other than the organization that is there. We have made great efforts to signal where we are going and why. Attempting to transform this course into the one oversimplified by a commercial publisher's canned outline seems a strange way to cope with the material, somewhat like shuffling the deck midway through a game of solitaire when you find the cards arranged the wrong way. You may feel better, but you do not really win.

Our experience is that few students will find these materials boring. They do not teach the artificial rules of a board game but accept that messy reality provokes messy answers to difficult questions. The discussion in class flowing from the materials may push you to the boundaries of your Republican, Democratic, reactionary or radical beliefs. You should expect this, for most of the fights about the good, the true and the beautiful lurk just beneath the surface of the law of contracts. It mirrors the conflicting visions that many of us accept as just common sense. Whether or not you find satisfying answers will depend in large part on your vision of the society in which you live, and your definition of social justice. In good liberal fashion, we have not written the materials to indoctrinate students with any political point of view. During the late 1960s and early 1970s, those teaching from the earliest versions questioned students from somewhat to the right of the accepted wisdom of the vocal members of the class. In the 1990s, many students seem to have moved toward the right, and our challenges seem to come from the left. Whatever challenges can be made to American liberalism, we think its ideal of testing ideas and assumptions valuable for those learning to be lawyers.

After many years of exploring the area, those who have contributed to these materials still find the subject fascinating and find something new each trip through them. The process of learning anything worth learning probably must involve a degree of frustration. Everything is related to everything else, and it seems impossible to understand anything without understanding everything. Moreover, most Americans expect law to be clear and consistent with simple ideas of right and wrong. Whatever the merit of that idea, students find that concepts of right and wrong prove to be anything but simple, and law reflects this complexity. We have tried to keep inevitable frustration within bounds. We hope that you will share our interest in contracts as a way of learning about life in this country and considering possibilities for stability and change.

Chapter 2
REMEDIES FOR BREACH OF CONTRACT

We begin with contract remedies, the "so what?" of the subject. Suppose Williston makes a contract to supply goods to Corbin at an agreed price. Williston fails to deliver the goods and has no excuse that the law recognizes. What can Corbin do? He is likely to talk with Williston to try to persuade him to perform. If that fails, Corbin can buy from someone else and resolve never to deal with Williston again. Corbin can gossip at a trade show, telling atrocity stories about Williston which will make it harder for Williston to make contracts with other potential customers. Corbin might decide to consult a lawyer to see whether it made sense to seek legal relief against Williston.

What would the lawyer tell Corbin? He would state facts and opinions about what the law might offer, what it might cost to get it, and the chances of winning. Law school courses too seldom stress the costs and risks involved in delivering law to its consumers, but lawyers and clients must confront these factors. We will continually remind you that law is not free. Keeping this in mind, what has the legal system to offer someone when another has breached their contract? In a famous article, Fuller and Perdue[1] tell us that the law could protect the *expectation, the reliance, or the restitution interests*, or some combination of them. While there are problems with Fuller and Perdue's classification since the categories overlap, one must master it because these terms have become part of the vocabulary of the contracts field. This first chapter of the Wisconsin Contracts Materials will take up the expectation, reliance and restitution interests and then turn to some difficult problems drawing on aspects of all of them.

A. PROTECTING THE EXPECTATION INTEREST

From the middle of the 19th century to today, judges and legal writers have told us that the goal of contracts remedies primarily is to protect what Fuller and Perdue call the "expectation interest." The Uniform Commercial Code announces in § 1-106:

> [t]he remedies provided by this Act shall be liberally administered to the end that the aggrieved party may be put in as good a position as if the other

---

[1]Fuller and Perdue, The Reliance Interest in Contracts Damages (pts. 1-2), 46 Yale Law Journal 52, 373 (1936 & 1937).

party had fully performed but ... penal damages may [not] be had except as specifically provided in this Act or by other rule of law.

While the Code does not apply to all contracts cases, it shares this statement of goals with all the other bodies of contract law. Thus, the law says that it will attempt to put aggrieved parties where they expected to be as the result of performance. The ordinary objective is to approximate a hypothetical state — where the aggrieved would have been had the contract been performed — and not to punish breach or put the aggrieved party in a better position than would have resulted from performance.

The goal is easy enough to state, but it ought to provoke questions. Why seek this objective? What function does it serve? And what about the means to the end? We have no contract police to watch those who enter into contracts. One who threatens breach or does not perform is not arrested or subject to large penalties. Such an approach might encourage performance but few of us would be willing to pay to have contract police to ensure performance. We have balanced the ends and costs of alternative ways to respond to breach and collectively chosen to protect the "expectation interest" — hoping this will achieve an optimal level of performance at an acceptable cost.

But what do we mean by the phrase, "the expectation interest?" What are the likely actual consequences of the compromises embodied in our contracts damages norms when they are filtered through the legal system in operation? How far is the law of contract remedies actually an instrument designed to produce changes in behavior, and how far is it an exercise in political and cultural symbolism and ideology? This is the agenda for our first body of material.

1. A LONG, BUT NECESSARY, DIGRESSION: OF TWO CODES, READING STATUTES, AND THE APPLICATION OF ARTICLE II OF THE U.C.C.

We want to begin with some simple examples of how the Uniform Commercial Code attempts to put aggrieved buyers and sellers of goods in as good a position as they would have been had the contract been performed and why the law dealing with sales of goods adopts this as a goal. Also we will examine assumptions and compromises involved in the techniques which the U.C.C. uses to protect the expectation interest. Then we can turn to examples of the expectation interest in areas not covered by the Code.

However, before beginning students can embark on this enterprise, they have to learn a little about what the Uniform Commercial Code is, techniques of reading statutes, and, since Article II of the Code does not apply to all contracts, when they can use its provisions. We will also (very briefly) mention another important codification of commercial law — the United Nations Convention on Contracts for the International Sale of Goods (CISG). The Convention will be of increasing significance, and it is important that you know just a bit about it. We will advert to its provisions from time to time in these materials.

The Uniform Commercial Code: A great deal of this course will involve learning about the Uniform Commercial Code. It is a lengthy statute which has been the law in all but one state since the late 1960s. However, it is not all of commercial law. It does not cover taxation, bankruptcy, government contracts, patents and copyrights, consumer protection, environmental protection, cooperatives, antitrust and the protection of competitive markets, the regulation of banks and securities markets and a lot more.

What does the Code deal with? It has nine articles or major sections: Article I covers the purposes of the Code, definitions, and a few provisions that apply to all the other articles. Article II deals with transactions in goods — roughly, buying and selling cars, computers, cows, crowbars and other tangible things. Article III covers the law of commercial paper — checks and promissory notes, for example. Article IV concerns bank deposits and collections. Article V governs letters of credit. Article VI regulates bulk transfers. Article VII covers warehouse receipts, bills of lading and other documents of title. Article VIII deals with some aspects of investment securities, and Article IX has provisions relating to secured transactions (buying a car "on time," for example), sales of accounts and chattel paper. We will be concerned in Contracts almost entirely with Articles I and II. The rest of the Code is the turf of courses in Commercial Law.

Uniform laws attempt to deal with some of the costs of federalism. The United States has fifty states, as well as districts and territories, all with power to make laws affecting transactions within their borders. However, the economy of this country does not respect national or state lines. It would be difficult for Ford to sell cars under fifty different state laws, and it would be even harder for smaller companies which could not afford to hire a staff of lawyers to keep things straight. The Congress of the United States could pass national legislation. However, it is questionable under the Constitution whether it would have power to regulate entirely intrastate business transactions.

The U.C.C. is the product of a collaboration between The National Conference of Commissioners on Uniform State Laws and the American Law Institute. Both are examples of the odd mixture of public and private functions so often found in this country. The National Conference promotes uniform laws. It is largely funded by state governments which appoint its members, but it has no official powers. It supervises experts who draft proposed uniform laws to submit to the state legislatures. Sometimes legislatures pass these model laws as written; sometimes they tinker with them; sometimes they ignore them. Between 1896 and 1933, the Commissioners proposed seven different uniform laws dealing with negotiable instruments, sales, warehouse receipts, stock transfers, bills of lading, conditional sales, and trust receipts. They had mixed success. By 1955, forty eight states had passed the negotiable instruments, warehouse receipts and stock transfer uniform laws; only ten had passed the Uniform Conditional Sales Act.

Many groups were dissatisfied with provisions of these various uniform acts, and they proposed many amendments.

The American Law Institute is a private group performing what we might see as public functions. It has attempted to distill, organize and state precisely the judge-made common law developed by state appellate courts. Its most famous project has been the publication of "restatements of the law", including the Restatement of the Law of Contracts.[2] Restatements are essentially proposals to judges who may or may not choose to follow the version of a common law rule put forward. However, these restatements are influential for many reasons. They are the product of drafting by experts and careful review by committees of elite judges, lawyers, and law professors.

The Uniform Commercial Code did not appear by magic on the pages of statute books. People with thought-out positions, biases, and human failings drafted proposed versions which committees reviewed. These groups insisted on revisions. Then their final product had to be sold to fifty legislatures. While the proponents of the Code tried to claim that it was the work of neutral experts and expressed a consensus of those who understood the area, opposition developed. In the late 1950s, many thought the whole project was dead and would never become law. The Code you will study reflects the process of drafting, editing, fighting and compromising that produced it.

In the late 1930s, many commercial lawyers thought that the Uniform Sales Act was out of date. Professor Karl Llewellyn, who then taught at the Columbia Law School, sought radical reform of commercial law. Llewellyn was a member of the National Conference of Commissioners on Uniform State Laws. He maneuvered to take the leading role in a reform effort. Zipporah Wiseman tells us:

> In "five weeks' work by the clock, and uninterrupted," Llewellyn wrote an eighty-eight page draft of a "Uniform Sales Act 1940."...
>
> Llewellyn's vision of sales law, reflected in that 1940 draft and in his earlier writings and subsequent revisions of the draft, was no mere update of Williston's approach.... Obsolescence in general was an important starting point, but modernization was not Llewellyn's only end. Llewellyn's objective was to reformulate sales law in light of his normative vision of both merchant practice and judicial decision making.[3]

Llewellyn's work on the revised sales act led to a proposal to reform a broader area of commercial law. The Conference of Commissioners on Uniform State

---

[2] We discuss the Restatement of Contracts in note 1 following Lake River Corp. v. Carborundum Co., *infra* p. 77.

[3] Wiseman, The Limits of Vision: Karl Llewellyn and the Merchant Rules, 100 Harvard Law Review 465, 490-493 (1987).

Laws approved in principle the idea of a comprehensive "Uniform Commercial Code," and in 1942 the American Law Institute agreed to be a co-sponsor. Llewellyn's 1940 Sales Act revision was to become Article 2 of the new Code. Committees of academics and leading practitioners were established to draft other articles on other topics. All the Committees worked under the general supervision of Professor Llewellyn. By 1949 there was an integrated draft of nine articles, with notes and comments.[4]

As the Code neared completion, it began attracting a great deal of attention. Opposition to many of its innovations developed. Several state legislatures set up study committees to advise on enactment. The most extensive study occurred in New York. In 1956 the New York Committee issued its report. The Committee endorsed the idea of a Uniform Commercial Code, but it concluded that the then current draft was unsatisfactory and needed extensive revision. As a result, a Permanent Editorial Board that had been established by the two sponsoring organizations undertook a substantial revision, attempting to take account of many of the criticisms that had been made. A revised Uniform Commercial Code was published in 1958. It is basically this edition of the Code that was enacted by the states, though there have been some amendments since.

Prior to 1958 only two states, Pennsylvania and Massachusetts, had adopted the proposed Uniform Commercial Code. After publication of the revised Code, however, a major effort was made to secure enactment. Many academics who taught commercial law participated in a lobbying movement, reassuring legislators that the Code was a progressive reform.

It is unlikely that many state legislators read and understood the Code. In most states, scholars prepared lengthy section-by-section commentaries discussing the impact of the Code's provisions on the law of the state. A few legislators may have looked at these efforts, but their length and complexity suggest that most legislators had to take the Code on faith or rely on opinions of those they trusted.

By 1962, fourteen states had passed the U.C.C., including important commercial ones such as Illinois and New Jersey. By 1967 it was the law in 49 states, the District of Columbia, and the Virgin Islands. Louisiana, with its French Civil Code tradition, was the lone exception. Finally, in 1974, Louisiana passed all of the Code's articles but II and VI. Guam also adopted the entire U.C.C. in 1977. Many of the states passed the statute with their own amendments here and there so that the result is not complete uniformity.

The Uniform Commercial Code has a style that many lawyers dislike. Professor Karl Llewellyn, its Chief Reporter, was a famous jurisprudential

---

[4]For greater detail of this drafting process and the subsequent efforts, as described in the text, to get the code enacted, see Braucher, Legislative History of the Uniform Commercial Code, 58 Columbia Law Review 798 (1958).

scholar.[5] He thought that the common law tradition was one of the important inventions of English-speaking people. Llewellyn argued that American courts had engaged in three styles of reasoning since 1800. The "Grand Style" typified 1800 to 1850. This was a creative and flexible approach. Judges looked back to precedent but also forward to prospective consequences and prospective future problems. "[P]recedent is carefully regarded, but if it does not make sense it is ordinarily re-explored; 'policy' is explicitly inquired into; alleged 'principle' must make for wisdom as well as for order if it is to qualify as such...."[6] He contrasted this Grand Tradition with a "Formal Style" that predominated from 1850 to 1920. This approach was formal, logical but remote from life. Formal style opinions ignored or concealed change and growth in the law. Llewellyn said that since the mid-1920s, courts had attempted to recapture the Grand Style of an earlier time. Judges, he wrote, had a situation-sense that helped them find sensible results in particular cases, whatever the quality of the reasoning in opinions explaining what they had done. Rather than attempting to spell out precise rules in detail, lawmakers should attempt to help judges by giving guidance as to factors to consider. Thus, the Code often speaks qualitatively, using terms such as "good faith," "unconscionable," "commercial reasonableness," and the like. The Code does not purport to offer a solution for all possible problems.

Article II of the U.C.C. is not pure Llewellyn. While he wrote the first draft in 1940, by 1958 many cooks had had a hand in making the broth. Wiseman[7] has studied Llewellyn's original papers, and she details how much of Llewellyn's original vision was lost in the process of building coalitions and making compromises. Llewellyn, himself, said:

> I am ashamed of [the U.C.C.] in some ways; there are so many pieces that I could make a little better; there are so many beautiful ideas I tried to get in that would have been good for the law, but I was voted down. A wide body of opinion has worked the law into some sort of compromise after debate and after exhaustive work. However, when you compare it with anything that there is, it is an infinite improvement.[8]

---

[5]See, *e.g.*, Wm. Twining, Karl Llewellyn and the Realist Movement (1973); Casebeer, Escape from Liberalism: Fact and Value in Karl Llewellyn, 1977 Duke Law Journal 671; Note, How Appellate Opinions Should Justify Decisions Made Under the U.C.C., 29 Stanford Law Review 1245 (1977).

[6]Llewellyn, On the Current Recapture of the Grand Tradition, 9 University of Chicago Law Review 6 (1960).

[7]Wiseman, The Limits of Vision: Karl Llewellyn and the Merchant Rules, 100 Harvard Law Review 465 (1987).

[8]Llewellyn, Why a Commercial Code?, 22 Tennessee Law Review 779, 784 (1953).

While all states have passed a major part of the Code, there is a real gap between its text and the living law. Many lawyers and judges went to law school before courses taught its provisions. The Code is not easy to understand. At the most elementary level, it lacks an index compiled by its authors, and the cross references in the Official Comments often are incomplete. Some lawyers fight its underlying philosophy; they would be happier with a statute that provided more answers. Some lawyers and judges do not understand the U.C.C. They sometimes offer legal advice and write briefs based on pre-U.C.C. cases and general ideas about contracts and sales. Many appellate opinions display a deep misunderstanding of the logic and vocabulary of the Code.

Whatever your ultimate judgment about the U.C.C., it is the law. Command of its logic and vocabulary is an important skill for lawyers who encounter the subjects it deals with in their practice. One may have to do a good job educating judges, and it is hard to teach others what you do not understand.

United Nations Convention on Contracts for the International Sale of Goods: The development of trade across state boundaries led to the need for a code of commercial law which was more or less uniform from one state to another — hence the U.C.C. Similarly, growth of international trade led to a felt need for a code which would govern international sales of goods — hence the Convention on Contracts for the International Sale of Goods (CISG). The Convention was approved by a Diplomatic Conference in Vienna in 1980, and the process of adoption by individual countries began immediately. Though the pace of change of private international law proceeds slowly, some believe that forty to fifty nations may be parties to the Convention by 1995. By 1990 more than twenty countries, including the United States, Australia, China, France, Mexico, and Sweden had already subscribed to the Convention. Contracts for the international sale of goods which are entered into by parties in countries which have ratified the convention are subject to CISG unless the contract for sale explicitly designates another law (such as the U.C.C.) as the governing law. Many of the rules of the Convention are the same as those of the U.S. common law, or the U.C.C., but there are important differences. We will, on occasion, call your attention to the Convention when we think it would be useful or interesting to do so; we do not intend, however, to provide an exhaustive summary of the Convention's rules. It is important that you know that the Convention provides the presumptive standards for international sales of goods involving participating nations, and that the rules may be different from those you might otherwise expect to apply.

Reading Statutes: While in many ways the Uniform Commercial Code is an unusual statute, still it is a statute. Lawyers have techniques for reading and applying words passed by legislatures. Law students, professors, judges, and lawyers often forget an obvious and simple one: *you must read the statute.*, When section ten refers to section seven, and both use terms defined in section one, you must read all three sections and put them together in some plausible way. English may be a terribly imprecise language, far better suited to poetry than lawmaking, but this does not justify neglect of what precision it does have.

We cannot forget that the reader of anything written must create its meaning. Judges often write of seeking the "plain meaning" of legislation. Many legal scholars, borrowing the teaching of those who study language, have attacked the idea that documents can have a plain meaning. Words take on meaning *for me* as I interpret them in light of context and my experiences. However, the meaning I create by this active process may not be the one you create because we are different people. At the extreme, the plays of Pirandello assert that people cannot understand each other. Undoubtedly, the scholars' attack on the conceit that interpretation is a mechanical translation of a code available to everyone was a valuable corrective to the earlier position.

However, lawyers have a professional interest in asserting there is some possibility of communication among people. One who decides to interpret "yes" to mean "no," "stop" to mean "go," "up" to mean "down," "right" to mean "left," and "I promise" to mean "I will if I feel like it" is likely to experience a good deal of difficulty in interaction with others. Most lawyers share a culture, and they have some success in predicting how others might react if they translate words one way or another. The more you understand that culture, the better you will be able to predict how lawyers are likely to interpret language. To restate the first rule of statutory construction: read the statute, but read it intelligently.

Judges also say that when the language of a statute is "ambiguous," then they may use various extrinsic aids to give it meaning. Again, those who study language insist that all words, phrases, sentences and paragraphs are ambiguous. You and I each must give meaning to symbols on paper, and since we are different people, we bring different experiences and skills to the task. As a result, we should be surprised when our interpretations are precisely the same. Most lawyers would take the "ambiguity" rule to have a more complicated but acceptable meaning. When the words in a statute seem to draw on the meanings common to lawyers, probably it is not worth wasting a judge's time by asking him or her to consider other plausible meanings. It is a good idea to hold legislators to use words with something like the meaning expected in legal culture. Lawyers read laws so they can advise clients, and judges should help them in this translation process.

Ambiguity is a matter of degree. Two conductors will interpret Beethoven's Fifth Symphony differently, but all listeners will recognize it as the Fifth. Lawyers, as symphony conductors, will usually produce reasonably similar interpretations of familiar phrases. But at some point, even words taken in context may leave most lawyers uncertain. Then materials other than the text of a statute should be consulted.

Often judges say that the goal of statutory construction is the "intention" of the legislature. At first glance, you might find this a strange idea. A legislature, after all, is not a person but a collective body. Representative A votes for the Good Works Act because the Director of a Political Action Committee which contributes to A's reelection campaign tells him to do so. Representative B has studied the matter and reached a reasoned conclusion that the Good Works Act best balances the competing interests of all the affected public. Representative C relies on Representative B's judgments on such matters while she specializes in other legislative issues. And so on. Furthermore, a great deal of the work of modern legislatures is done by members of the legislative staff who, in turn, may draw on suggestions from lobbyists, the governor's staff, people in administrative agencies, and professors. Given the work load and the complexity of the issues coming before a legislature, there must be a great division of labor, and representatives must rely on others often.

To be sure, there are cases where we can assume that all those voting for a bill had more or less the same intention. However, those do not seem to be the situations that trouble us.

Judges seek to carry out the metaphor of legislative intent by interpreting provisions in light of "the purpose" of the legislation. For example, judges should not read a statute designed to benefit the poor so as to hurt them and benefit the rich. But how do we know the goals and purposes of legislation? Sometimes statutes have a preamble declaring all kinds of goals and purposes. (See, for example, Uniform Commercial Code, §§ 1-102(1) and (2).) Sometimes legislative committee reports contain express statements of purpose or language. The transcript of a legislative committee hearing may show that the Chair of the Committee that considered the bill said something relevant, and so on. Often, however, an imaginative lawyer can find indications of conflicting purposes in all this legislative material.

Returning to the Uniform Commercial Code, we can expect lawyers to read it technically — that is carefully and in light of its logical structure and definitions of terms, but also in light of the legal culture. Though the drafters of the Code were free to innovate, nevertheless if a provision looks like something well known to commercial lawyers, we can expect that lawyers and judges are likely to read it in the comfortable traditional way. Lawyers would also rely on arguments based on legislative intent. But what is legislative "intent" with respect to the U.C.C.? Most commercial publishers' editions of the U.C.C. contain "Official Comments" following most provisions. By the 1980s, courts routinely used the Official Comments in interpreting the Code. However, it was the text of the Code that was enacted as law by legislatures; the comments were not. While the comments may be highly influential, a reading of a comment that does violence to the text of a Code section may be hard to sell to a court.

Applicability of Article II of the U.C.C.: Article II of the Uniform Commercial Code governs many but not all contracts. It is important that you use Article II when it is clearly applicable. Before you turn to particular sections in Article II, you always must give some thought to whether you have an Article II transaction. Obviously, in many situations it will not matter whether a case fits into Article II because its rules and those of general contract law are the same. The problem comes when Article II has provisions which favor your client but which are not found in other bodies of law. We will explore some of these differences in due course. Appellate courts have had to wrestle with the scope of Article II in a surprising number of cases.

At this point you should read §§ 2-102, 2-105(1), 2-107(1) and (2), and 2-501(1) of the Uniform Commercial Code and related Comments. Then consider the following questions: Some of these questions are quite difficult and complicated.

(1) Owner buys a wooded hillside lot located at 123 N. Main Street for $20,000 from the Subdivision Development Corporation. Would Article II of the U.C.C. apply to this transaction? See §§ 2, 102, 2-105(1) and 2-107. If not, does this mean that their contract is not legally enforceable? See §§ 1-201(3), 1-103.

(2) Owner hires Architect to draw plans for a house to be built on Owner's lot. Under their contract Architect will own the drawings and plans he produces. Owner receives a right to build one house following them but may not sell the design to anyone else. Is this transaction within Article II of the U.C.C.? See § 2-105(1).

(3) Businessperson leases an automobile for one day from Rent-A-Car. Is this transaction within Article II of the Code? See §§ 2-101, 2-106(1).

(4) Owner buys components for a hi-fi system from StereoLand. Owner receives cartons containing components at the store, and she assembles the system at her house. Is this transaction within Article II of the U.C.C.? On the other hand, suppose the contract called for a StereoLand employee to go to Owner's house and install the system; would this affect your answer?

(5) Owner makes a contract with Engineer to produce a specially designed automobile. Engineer is to supply the design, labor and parts, and deliver a completed automobile to Owner. Is this transaction within Article II of the U.C.C.? See § 2-105(1) and compare § 2-704(2). What about a case in which Client consults Lawyer, and Lawyer prepares a will reflecting Client's wishes for the disposition of his property after his death. Lawyer produces a ten-page typewritten document on expensive paper with a fancy cover. This is handed to Client who pays Lawyer's fee. Does this transaction fall within the boundaries of Article II? If you have any question about the application of Article II here, how does the transaction differ from the production of a specially designed automobile?

In *Bonebrake v. Cox*[9], the court said:

> The test for inclusion or exclusion [in Article II of the U.C.C.] is not whether they [goods and services] are mixed, but, granting that they are mixed, whether their predominant factor, their thrust, their purpose, reasonably stated, is the rendition of service, with goods incidentally involved (*e.g.*, contract with artist for painting) or is a transaction of sale,

---

[9] 499 F.2d 951, 960 (8th Cir. 1974).

with labor incidentally involved (installation of a water heater in a bath-room).

Do you find that this test helps you solve these problems?

(6) Owner makes a contract with General Contractor to build a house as designed by Architect on Owner's lot. General Contractor is to supply labor and materials. Is this transaction within Article II of the U.C.C.? See § 2-501(1)(a) and (b).

(7) After the house is built, Owner sells it to Buyer. Is this transaction within Article II of the U.C.C.? Does it matter whether Owner sells only the house or sells the house and the lot on which it is built? See § 2-107(1).

(8) Oil Company enters a dealer franchise agreement with Charlie Grease. Under this agreement, Grease leases from Oil Company the land and building constituting the service station; agrees to provide various services such as keeping the station open certain hours, keeping records in certain forms, and running a clean station; and agrees to buy Oil Company gasoline, oil, tires, batteries and accessories. The franchise agreement provides that Oil Company can cancel the arrangement upon giving sixty days notice, and it exercises this right. Grease's lawyer wants to argue that Oil Company's action violated the obligation of "good faith" imposed by the Code under §§ 1-203 and 2-103(1)(b). Oil Company's lawyer argues that the U.C.C. is not applicable to this transaction, and general contract law imposes no such obligations. The courts have had a great deal of trouble with this problem. Do you see why?[10]

Can or should courts apply particular provisions found in Article II to transactions involving something other or more than a transaction in goods? Suppose a lawyer argued persuasively to a court that the reasons Article II adopted a particular rule make sense in the context of contracts for services as well as transactions in goods. Should a court extend the rule found in Article II to contracts for services? Those involved in drafting the Uniform Commercial Code were well aware of this problem and scholars have argued vigorously on both sides of the question.[11] The Code's Comments acknowledge the possibility of application by analogy.[12]

Article II of the U.C.C. applies to "transactions in goods." One may enter the labyrinths of this Article only if one has a "transaction in goods" in hand or,

---

[10]As we will see later, Charlie Grease may have rights under federal and state franchise protection statutes passed in the 1960s and 1970s, but those statutes do not cover all situations involving franchisees.

[11]Collins, Contracts, Annual Survey of American Law 243 (1961).

[12]See Uniform Commercial Code, § 1-102, Official Comment 1: "[Courts] have recognized the policies embodied in an act as applicable in reason to subject-matter which was not expressly included in the language of the act .... They have done the same where reason and policy so required, even where the subject-matter had been intentionally excluded from the act in general. ... Nothing in this Act stands in the way of the continuance of such action by the courts."

perhaps, if one can persuade a court to draw an analogy to goods cases and expand the Code's boundaries. How would you explain to someone what a transaction in goods is? Could you point to something all such transactions have in common? All transactions in goods somehow involve "goods." But what do all "goods" have in common? The Code suggests that they are "movable." What do all movable things have in common? And, if you can say what all goods have in common, can you also say how those goods must enter into a transaction for that transaction to be "a transaction in goods?"

If you are unable to say what all goods have in common, or are otherwise perplexed about this matter, you might find solace in suggestions by Ludwig Wittgenstein (1889-1951) in his Philosophical Investigations, an enigmatic landmark in twentieth century philosophy. Wittgenstein suggests a radical defect in a long tradition in philosophy that says one knows what a thing is (say a "game," or a "transaction in goods") only if one knows some property or set of proprieties which *all* things, and *only* things, of that type have.

Philosophical Investigations
Ludwig Wittgenstein[13]

66. Consider for example the proceedings that we call "games." I mean board-games, card-games, ball-games, Olympic games, and so on. What is common to them all? — Don't say: "There *must* be something in common, or they would not be called 'games'" — but *look and see* whether there is anything common to all. — For if you look at them you will not see something that is common to *all*, but similarities, relationships, and a whole series of them at that. To repeat: don't think, but look! — Look for example at board-games, with their multifarious relationships. Now pass to card-games; here you find many correspondences with the first group, but many common features drop out, and others appear. When we pass next to ball-games, much that is common is retained, but much is lost. — Are they all 'amusing'? Compare chess with noughts and crosses. Or is there always winning and losing, or competition between players? Think of patience. In ball games there is winning and losing; but when a child throws his ball at the wall and catches it again, this feature has disappeared. Look at the parts played by skill and luck; and at the difference between skill in chess and skill in tennis. Think now of games like ring-a-ring-a-roses; here is the element of amusement, but how many other characteristic features have disappeared! And we can go through the many, many other groups of games in the same way; can see how similarities crop up and disappear.

---

[13](3d ed.) Translated by G.E.M. Anscombe. Reprinted by permission of Macmillan Publishing Company. Copyright 1972 by Macmillan Publishing Company.

And the result of this examination is: we see a complicated network of similarities overlapping and criss-crossing: sometimes overall similarities, sometimes similarities of detail.

67. I can think of no better expression to characterize these similarities than "family resemblances"; for the various resemblances between members of a family: build, features, colour of eyes, gait, temperament, etc., etc. overlap and criss-cross in the same way. — And I shall say: 'games' form a family....

....

69. How shall we explain to someone what a game is? I imagine that we should describe *games* to him, and we might add: "This *and similar things* are called 'games.'" And do we know any more about it ourselves? Is it only other people whom we cannot tell exactly what a game is? — But this is not ignorance. We do not know the boundaries because none have been drawn. To repeat, we can draw a boundary — for a special purpose. Does it take that to make the concept usable? Not at all! (Except for that special purpose.) No more than it took the definition: 1 pace = 75 cm. to make the measure of length 'one pace' usable. And if you want to say "But still, before that it wasn't an exact measure", then I reply: very well, it was an inexact one. — Though you still owe me a definition of exactness.

70. "But if the concept 'game' is uncircumscribed like that, you don't really know what you mean by a 'game.'" — When I give the description: "The ground was quite covered with plants" — do you want to say I don't know what I am talking about until I can give a definition of a plant? ....

71. One might say that the concept 'game' is a concept with blurred edges. — "But is a blurred concept a concept at all?" — Is an indistinct photograph a picture of a person at all? Is it even always an advantage to replace an indistinct picture by a sharp one? Isn't the indistinct one often exactly what we need?

Wittgenstein's notion of "family resemblances" may be an incomplete solution to the problem he raises, but it does provide a provocative backdrop against which to think about the problem under discussion. For our purposes, it is especially useful to reflect upon the questions raised in § 71 of Wittgenstein's text. Why would it be an advantage for the U.C.C. to employ an indistinct or blurred concept of "transaction in goods?" What disadvantages can you see?

Our long march through this digression ends at last. Now you are ready to begin by reading some Uniform Commercial Code sections and applying them to problems dealing with the expectation interest.

2. THE EXPECTATION INTEREST: THE SUBSTITUTE CONTRACT AS THE PREFERRED MEANS TO THE END

Contract remedies generally are based on encouraging the aggrieved party to enter a substitute contract and then awarding damages to make up any loss remaining. Suppose Seller promises to sell 100 shares of Hot Property Software Corporation stock to Buyer for $10 a share. Seller breaches the contract. Buyer then immediately purchases 100 shares of this stock from someone else for $12 a share. Had the Seller - Buyer contract been performed, Buyer would have paid $1,000 for 100 shares of stock. Because of the breach, Buyer had to pay $1,200. A court would award Buyer damages of $200. Assuming no transaction costs, Buyer then will have paid $1,000 ($1,200 - 200 = $1,000) for the 100 shares — that is, Buyer will be where he or she would have been had the contract been performed. The expectation interest is protected.

We will illustrate this principle in more detail by a series of examples of how the Uniform Commercial Code has codified this simple approach. As so often is the case, complexity lurks at the margins of a seemingly simple idea. In each instance ask yourself not only what is the proper answer under the applicable statutes, but whether it is a sensible answer. First, read §§ 2-703, 2-706, and 2-708 of the Uniform Commercial Code as well as the relevant Official Comments. Then answer the following questions:

(1) On June 1st, Seller contracted to sell 100 crates of apples to Natural Foods at $8 per crate. The crates of apples were to be delivered to Natural Foods on July 1st. On July 1st, Seller arrived at Natural Foods with 100 crates of apples that met the quality the contract required. However, Natural Foods Produce Manager breached the contract by refusing to accept or pay for the apples. Seller returned to his farm and kept the apples. The market price for this quality and type of apples on July 1st was $7.10/crate. How much, if anything, should Seller recover under the U.C.C.?

(2) Suppose we learned that the market value of apples of this type and quality on both June 1st and July 1st was $7.10/crate. Would this charge the result? Why or why not?

(3) Suppose the facts are as stated in question (1), except that Seller had resold the apples on July 1st at $7/crate to a supermarket located near Natural Foods' place of business. The owner of the supermarket was Seller's neighbor and close personal friend. How much, if anything, would Seller recover from Buyer?

(4) Suppose the facts are as stated in question (1), except that Seller upon leaving Natural Foods' place of business parked his truck by the side of the road and resold all the apples to people who stopped at $7.50/crate. How much, if anything, would Seller recover from Buyer?

You will find later that the Uniform Commercial Code offers much the same pattern of remedies when sellers breach and buyers are the aggrieved parties. Generally, the Code treats buyers *as if* they had covered their needs from another seller and awards as damages the increased cost of obtaining such a substitute contract. See U.C.C. §§ 2-711, 2-712, and 2-713. White and Summers, *Uniform Commercial Code* (3d ed. 1988), is often quoted and cited by courts faced with difficult problems of construing the U.C.C. You may find it helpful.

B. THE EXPECTATION INTEREST: OF INFERIOR SUBSTITUTES, OTHER ENDS AND OTHER MEANS

The contract-price market-price approach offers a simple solution to many cases. However, it won't always work. For example, go back once again to our apple case. Suppose the Produce Manager at Natural Foods refuses to take the apples because there is a glut, and apples are so plentiful that one can buy them at every roadside for a penny an apple. Commercial buyers are not purchasing apples from anyone, and one cannot sell them to consumers at roadsides at prices adequate to pay for the gasoline burned to drive the truck there. Section 2-709 makes it clear that "if the seller is unable after reasonable effort to resell [the goods] at a reasonable price or the circumstances reasonably indicate that such effort will be unavailing," then the seller may recover the contract price from the buyer. The seller must hold the goods for the buyer unless resale becomes possible.

The next three cases illustrate some of the difficulties in the application of the expectation principle.

SHIRLEY MACLAINE PARKER v. TWENTIETH CENTURY-FOX FILM CORPORATION

3 Cal.3d 176, 474 P.2d 689 (1970)

BURKE, J. — Defendant Twentieth Century-Fox Film Corporation appeals from a summary judgment granting to plaintiff the recovery of agreed compensation under a written contract for her services as an actress in a motion picture. As will appear, we have concluded that the trial court correctly ruled in plaintiff's favor and that the judgment should be affirmed.

Plaintiff is well known as an actress, and in the contract between plaintiff and defendant is sometimes referred to as the "Artist." Under the contract, dated August 6, 1965, plaintiff was to play the female lead in defendant's contemplated production of a motion picture entitled "Bloomer Girl." The contract provided that defendant would pay plaintiff a minimum "guaranteed compensation" of $53,571.42 per week for 14 weeks commencing May 23, 1966, for a total of $750,000. Prior to May 1966 defendant decided not to produce the picture and by a letter dated April 4, 1966, it notified plaintiff of that decision and that it would not "comply with our obligations to you under" the written contract. By the same letter and with the professed purpose "to avoid any damage to you," defendant instead offered to employ plaintiff as the leading actress in another film tentatively entitled "Big Country, Big Man" (hereinafter, "Big Country"). The compensation offer was identical, as were 31 of the 34 numbered provisions or articles of the original contract. Unlike "Bloomer Girl," however, which was to have been a musical production, "Big Country" was a dramatic "western type" movie. "Bloomer Girl" was to have been filmed in California; "Big Country" was to be produced in Australia. Also, certain terms in the proferred contract varied from those of the original.

Plaintiff was given one week within which to accept; she did not and the offer lapsed. Plaintiff then commenced this action seeking recovery of the agreed guaranteed compensation.

... Defendant in its answer admits the existence and validity of the contract, that plaintiff complied with all the conditions, covenants and promises and stood ready to complete the performance, and that defendant breached and "anticipatorily repudiated" the contract. It denies, however, that any money is due to plaintiff either under the contract or as a result of its breach, and pleads as an affirmative defense to both causes of action plaintiff's allegedly deliberate failure to mitigate damages, asserting that she unreasonably refused to accept its offer of the leading role in "Big Country."

Plaintiff moved for summary judgment under Code of Civil Procedure § 437c, the motion was granted, and summary judgment for $750,000 plus interest was entered in plaintiff's favor. This appeal by defendant followed.

The familiar rules are that the matter to be determined by the trial court on a motion for summary judgment is whether facts have been presented which give rise to a triable factual issue. The court may not pass upon the issue itself. Summary judgment is proper only if the affidavits or declarations in support of the moving party would be sufficient to sustain a judgment in his favor and his opponent does not by affidavit show facts sufficient to present a triable issue of fact. The affidavits of the moving party are strictly construed, and doubts as to the propriety of summary judgment should be resolved against granting the motion. Such does not become a substitute for the open trial method of determining facts.

The moving party cannot depend upon allegations in his own pleadings to cure deficient affidavits, nor can his adversary rely upon his own pleadings in lieu or in support of affidavits in opposition to a motion; however, a party can rely on his adversary's pleadings to establish facts not contained in his own affidavits. Also, the court may consider facts stipulated to by the parties and facts which are properly the subject of judicial notice.

As stated, defendant's sole defense to this action which resulted from its deliberate breach of contract is that in rejecting defendant's substitute offer of employment plaintiff unreasonably refused to mitigate damages.

The general rule is that the measure of recovery by a wrongfully discharged employee is the amount of salary agreed upon for the period of service, less the amount which the employer affirmatively proves the employee has earned or with reasonable effort might have earned from other employment. However, before projected earnings from the employment opportunities not sought or accepted by the discharged employee can be applied in mitigation, the employer must show that the other employment was comparable, or substantially similar, to that of which the employee has been deprived; the employee's rejection of or failure to seek other available employment of a different or inferior kind may not be resorted to in order to mitigate damages.

In the present case defendant has raised no issue of *reasonableness of efforts* by plaintiffs to obtain other employment; the sole issue is whether plaintiff's refusal of defendant's substitute offer of "Big Country" may be used in mitigation. Nor, if the "Big Country" offer was of employment different or inferior when compared with the original "Bloomer Girl" employment, is there an issue as to whether or not plaintiff acted reasonably in refusing the substitute offer. Despite defendant's arguments to the contrary, no case cited or which our research has discovered holds or suggests that reasonableness is an element of a wrongfully discharged employee's option to reject, or fail to seek, different or inferior employment lest the possible earnings therefrom be charged against him in mitigation of damages.

Applying the foregoing rules to the record in the present case, with all intendments in favor of the party opposing the summary judgment motion — here, defendant — it is clear that the trial court correctly ruled that plaintiff's failure to accept defendant's tendered substitute employment could not be applied in mitigation of damages because the offer of the "Big Country" lead was of employment both different and inferior, and that no factual dispute was presented on that issue. The mere circumstance that "Bloomer Girl" was to be a musical review calling upon plaintiff's talents as a dancer as well as an actress, and was to be produced in the City of Los Angeles, whereas "Big Country" was a straight dramatic role in a "Western Type" story taking place in an opal mine in Australia, demonstrates the difference in kind between the two employments; the female lead as a dramatic actress in a western style motion picture can by no stretch of imagination be considered the equivalent of or substantially similar to the lead in a song-and-dance production.

Additionally, the substitute "Big Country" offer proposed to eliminate or impair the director and screenplay approvals accorded to plaintiff under the original "Bloomer Girl" contract (see fn. *ante*), and thus constituted an offer of inferior employment. No expertise or judicial notice is required in order to hold that the deprivation or infringement of an employee's rights held under an original employment contract converts the available "other employment" relied upon by the employer to mitigate damages, into inferior employment which the employee need not seek or accept. Statements found in affidavits submitted by defendant in opposition to plaintiff's summary judgment motion, to the effect that the "Big Country" offer was not of employment different from or inferior to that under the "Bloomer Girl" contract, merely repeat the allegations of defendant's answer to the complaint in this action, constitute only conclusionary assertions with respect to undisputed facts, and do not give rise to a triable factual issue so as to defeat the motion for summary judgment....

The judgment is affirmed.

(Opinion by Burke, J., with McComb, Peters and Tobriner, JJ., and Kraus and Roth, JJ., concurring. Separate dissenting opinion by Sullivan, Acting C.J.)

SULLIVAN, Acting C.J. — The basic question in this case is whether or not plaintiff acted reasonably in rejecting defendant's offer of alternate employment. The answer depends upon whether that offer (starring in "Big Country, Big Man") was an offer of work that was substantially similar to her former employment (starring in "Bloomer Girl") or of work that was of a different or inferior kind. To my mind this is a factual issue which the trial court should not have determined on a motion for summary judgment. The majority have not only repeated this error but have compounded it by applying the rules governing mitigation of damages in the employer-employee context in a misleading fashion. Accordingly, I respectfully dissent.

The familiar rule requiring a plaintiff in a tort or contract action to mitigate damages embodies notions of fairness and socially responsible behavior which are fundamental to our jurisprudence. Most broadly stated, it precludes the recovery of damages which, through the exercise of due diligence, could have been avoided. Thus, in essence, it is a rule requiring reasonable conduct in commercial affairs. This general principle governs the obligations of an employee after his employer has wrongfully repudiated or terminated the employment contract. Rather than permitting the employee simply to remain idle during the balance of the contract period, the law requires him to make a reasonable effort to secure other employment. He is not obliged, however to seek or accept any and all types of work which may be available. Only work which is in the same field and which is of the same quality need be accepted.

The relevant language excuses acceptance only of employment which is of a *different kind*. It has never been the law that the mere existence of *differences between two jobs in the same field* is sufficient, as a matter of law, to excuse an employee wrongfully discharged from one from accepting the other in order to mitigate damages. Such an approach would effectively eliminate any obligation of an employee to attempt to minimize damage arising from a wrongful discharge. The only alternative job offer an employee would be required to accept would be an offer of his former job by his former employer.

Although the majority appear to hold that there was a difference "in kind" between the employment offered plaintiff in "Bloomer Girl" and that offered in "Big Country," an examination of the opinion makes crystal clear that the majority merely point out differences between the two *films* (an obvious circumstance) and then apodictically assert that these constitute a difference in the *kind* of *employment*. The entire rationale of the majority boils down to this: that the "*mere circumstances*" that "Bloomer Girl" was to be a musical review while "Big Country" was a straight drama "demonstrates the difference in kind" since a female lead in a western is not "the equivalent of or substantially similar to" a lead in a musical. This is merely attempting to prove the proposition by repeating it. It shows that the vehicles for the display of the star's talents are different but it does not prove that her employment as a star in such vehicles is of necessity different *in kind* and either inferior or superior.

I believe that the approach taken by the majority (a superficial listing of differences with no attempt to assess their significance) may subvert a valuable legal doctrine. The inquiry in cases such as this should not be whether differences between the two jobs exist (there will always be differences) but whether the differences which are present are substantial enough to constitute differences in the *kind* of employment or, alternatively, whether they render the substitute work employment of an *inferior kind*.

It seems to me that *this* inquiry involves, in the instant case at least, factual determinations which are improper on a motion for summary judgment. Resolving whether or not one job is substantially similar to another or whether, on the other hand, it is of a different or inferior kind, will often (as here) require a critical appraisal of the similarities and differences between them in light of the importance of these differences to the employee. This necessitates a weighing of the evidence, and it is precisely this undertaking which is forbidden on summary judgment.

This is not to say that summary judgment would never be available in an action by an employee in which the employer raises the defense of failure to mitigate damages. No case has come to my attention, however, in which summary judgment has been granted on the issue of whether an employee was obliged to accept available alternate employment. Nevertheless, there may well be cases in which the substitute employment is so manifestly of a dissimilar or inferior sort, the declarations of the plaintiff so complete and those of the defendant so conclusionary and inadequate that no factual issues exist for which a trial is required. This, however, is not such a case.

It is not intuitively obvious, to me at least, that the leading female role in a dramatic motion picture is a radically different endeavor from the leading female role in a musical comedy film. Nor is it plain to me that the rather qualified rights of director and screenplay approval contained in the first contract are highly significant matters either in the entertainment industry in general or to this plaintiff in particular. Certainly, none of the declarations introduced by plaintiff in support of her motion shed any light on these issues. Nor do they attempt to explain why she declined the offer of starring in "Big Country, Big Man." Nevertheless, the trial court granted the motion, declaring that these approval rights were "critical" and that their elimination altered "the essential nature of the employment."

The plaintiff's declarations were of no assistance to the trial court in its effort to justify reaching this conclusion on summary judgment. Instead, it was forced to rely on judicial notice of the definitions of "motion picture," "screenplay" and "director" and then on judicial notice of practices in the film industry which were purportedly of "common knowledge."

Use of judicial notice was never intended to authorize resort to the dictionary to solve essentially factual questions which do not turn upon conventional linguistic usage.

The majority do not confront the trial court's misuse of judicial notice. They avoid this issue through the expedient of declaring that neither judicial notice nor expert opinion (such as that contained in the declarations in opposition to the motion) is necessary to reach the trial court's conclusion. *Something*, however, clearly *is* needed to support this conclusion. Nevertheless, the majority make no effort to justify the judgment through an examination of the plaintiff's declarations. Ignoring the obvious insufficiency of these declarations, the majority announce that "the deprivation or infringement of an employee's rights held under an original employment contract" changes the alternate employment offered or available into employment of an inferior kind.

I cannot accept the proposition that an offer which eliminates *any* contract right, regardless of its significance, is, as a matter of law, an offer of employment of an inferior kind. Such an absolute rule seems no more sensible than the majority's earlier suggestion that the mere existence of differences between two jobs is sufficient to render them employment of different kinds. Application of such per se rules will severely undermine the principle of mitigation of damages in the employer-employee context.

I remain convinced that the relevant question in such cases is whether or not a particular contract provision is so significant that its omission creates employment of an inferior kind. This question is, of course, intimately bound up in what I consider the ultimate issue: whether or not the employee acted reasonably. This will generally involve a factual inquiry to ascertain the importance of the particular contract term and a process of weighing the absence of that term against the countervailing advantages of the alternate employment. In the typical case, this will mean that summary judgment must be withheld.

In the instant case, there was nothing properly before the trial court by which the importance of the approval rights could be ascertained, much less evaluated. Thus, in order to grant the motion for summary judgment, the trial court misused judicial notice. In upholding the summary judgment, the majority here rely upon per se rules which distort the process of determining whether or not an employee is obliged to accept particular employment in mitigation of damages.

I believe that the judgment should be reversed so that the issue of whether or not the offer of the lead role in "Big Country, Big Man" was of employment comparable to that of the lead role in "Bloomer Girl" may be determined at trial.

Appellant's petition for a rehearing was denied October 28, 1970. Mosk, J., did not participate therein. Sullivan, J., was of the opinion that the petition should be granted.

NOTES AND QUESTIONS

1. *Case analysis*: *Parker v. Twentieth Century Fox* is the first case you have read in this course. It is appropriate to introduce some techniques of case analysis at this point. You have read a majority and dissenting opinion of the Supreme Court of California. That court reviewed decisions in this case by the trial court and the District Court of Appeal. California, as many states, has a system whereby appeals go to one of many intermediate appellate courts. Only cases presenting issues of general importance then go to the highest court in the state. There is no right to take civil cases to the Supreme Court; that court has discretion as to what civil cases to hear.

One District Court of Appeal does not have to follow the decisions of another. The Supreme Court of the state is not bound by decisions of an intermediate court. If decisions of two or more intermediate appellate courts conflict, the Supreme Court decides what the law should be. However, decisions of intermediate courts of appeal are *persuasive authority*. Absent good reason to the contrary, other courts of appeal and the highest court will follow them or interpret them so they are consistent with the pattern of decisions adopted in the state.

Under common theories of precedent, courts are bound only by holdings in past cases. Most narrowly, a case only "holds" what was absolutely necessary to decide to reach its result. Anything beyond that necessary minimum is dictum and does not become precedent.

Can lawyers ignore mere dicta? Not necessarily. Suppose a Justice of the Supreme Court of California writes an opinion for the court in which she comments far beyond what was necessary to decide the case. The opinion is published this week, and you are scheduled to argue before the same judges next week. You would be foolish to dismiss anything in such an opinion as "mere dicta." Moreover, even if all lawyers would agree that a particular discussion was not needed to decide the precise case before an appellate court, the members of another court might read the passage and decide that it was a powerful argument for what the law ought to be. Whatever the formal precedential standing of a passage in a judicial opinion, lawyers are more comfortable when they are able to indicate that some judge, somewhere and sometime, bought an argument they are trying to make.

When the lawyers argued the *Parker* case before the trial and intermediate appellate courts, both sides devoted attention to *de la Falaise v. Gaumont-British Picture Corp.*[14] In that case, Constance Bennett de la Falaise, a famous actress in the 1930s, contracted with Gaumont-British Picture Corporation [GBP]. She was to make two motion pictures, "Everything is Thunder" and "The Hawk." GBP was to pay her 10% of the United States gross distribution receipts or $35,000 per picture, whichever was more. Both pictures were to be made in

---

[14]39 Cal. App. 461, 103 P.2d 447 (1940).

London, England. She was to work no more than eight weeks on each. "Everything is Thunder" was filmed, and GBP paid her $35,000.

The contract called for production of "The Hawk" to begin between September 1, 1936 and November 14, 1936. Constance Bennett was to receive notice of the precise date no later than August 1, 1936. She did not receive timely notice of the starting date, and the picture was never made. The trial court found that GBP had breached the contract. This decision was affirmed by the District Court of Appeal.

Mitigation of damages was an issue on appeal. The appellate court reported that de la Falaise's agent

> ... made diligent attempts to secure employment for her as a motion picture actress but ... received no offers of employment and no compensation for her services in motion pictures between September 1, 1936, and January 1, 1937. However, she did receive the sum of $4,000 for two radio engagements on September 5 and 17, 1936, which took place in the evening at half past five and nine o'clock, respectively.

The court's opinion says nothing about the point, but if we assume that Constance Bennett de la Falaise performed in two American radio dramas, almost all such broadcasts at the time originated either in New York City or Los Angeles. She could not have been making a picture in London and simultaneously act in the radio dramas in New York or Los Angeles on September 5 and 17th. (Remember that passenger jet aircraft did not cross the Atlantic then.) The trial court awarded de la Falaise damages of $35,000 less the $4,000 she earned for the two radio broadcasts. On appeal she argued "the sum of $4,000 received by her in radio engagements was not earned during any period when [GBP] was entitled to her services and, therefore, cannot be offset in mitigation of damages." The appellate court's opinion does not explain this argument. However, we can assume that her lawyer was arguing that since GBP had not given notice on time, she was relieved from any duty to make the second picture when she appeared on the two radio broadcasts.

The District Court of Appeal affirmed the trial court's decision that the $4,000 was to be deducted from Constance Bennett de la Falaise's recovery. It quoted an earlier California decision as establishing that measure of damages for breach of an employment contract is the salary "less the amount which the servant has earned or with reasonable effort might have earned from other employment." The court said that the "'other employment' which the discharged employee is bound to seek is employment of a character substantially similar to that of which he has been deprived; he need not enter upon service of a different or inferior kind." The appellate court then said that while radio engagements "might be denominated different in character from [the work] required of a moving picture actress, it cannot be said to be inferior thereto." The court did not answer de la Falaise's argument that the radio broadcasts took place when GBP was not entitled to her services because of its failure to give timely notice when production of the second picture was to begin.

(A) Suppose you represented Twentieth Century Fox in the *Parker* case. How would you argue that *de la Falaise v. Gaumont-British Picture Corp.* establishes California law in a way that would help your client's position?

(B) Suppose you represented Parker. How would you distinguish the *de la Falaise* case?

2. *Summary judgment*: To understand many contracts cases, you have to understand something of procedure and evidence too. Though you will explore these subjects at great length elsewhere in law school, we offer a simplified introduction.

There are several procedural devices designed to avoid unnecessary trials. Suppose I sue you but I have a very weak case. Even the simplest trial takes valuable judicial time. Lawmakers have fashioned rules to limit the burdens imposed by groundless litigation. In the older common law procedure, one was a "demurrer." In essence, a defendant who demurs says that for purposes of this procedural argument only, I admit all the facts the plaintiff alleges. Even treating all these facts as true, I should win because they do not add up to a cause of action. Plaintiffs also could use demurrers against defendants' answers. Here, the motion would say, in substance, even if defendant proves all that he or she alleges, that is not a defense to my cause of action. Under modern procedure we no longer speak of demurrers but motions to dismiss for failure to state a cause of action or a defense. Nonetheless, you will often encounter the term demurrer.

While a complaint or answer may allege enough to escape being thrown out on a motion to dismiss for failure to state a cause of action or a defense, there may be no real legally relevant controversy between the parties. In such cases lawyers use motions for "summary judgment." Suppose that Shirley MacLaine Parker's case were as follows: she signed a contract with the studio to star in "Bloomer Girl," a story that features the female lead. When Twentieth Century Fox decided it did not want to make "Bloomer Girl," it offered her the part of, say, "Daisy" in "Big Country, Big Man." Daisy was on the screen less than two minutes out of a two hour picture, and she was but a minor character among many. Furthermore, the actual contract tendered MacLaine for "Big Country, Big Man" called for Fox to pay her only one tenth of the salary it promised her for appearing in "Bloomer Girl." Finally, in the movie business when a star takes a minor role, except in unusual circumstances, it shows that he or she has lost popularity, and, as a result, it is harder to get starring roles in the future.

Shirley MacLaine Parker's lawyer could move for "summary judgment," and attach sworn affidavits from those who would testify to all of these facts plus copies of the written contracts, the scripts and any other relevant documents. Twentieth Century Fox would have to respond to this motion to avoid losing the case on summary judgment. On the one hand, if its affidavits did not deny the sworn statements supporting her motion, the judge would grant summary judgment and Parker would win.

On the other hand, suppose Fox offered an affidavit that MacLaine had been offered the role of "Jane" in "Big Country, Big Man," and Jane was the featured part in the whole story. It offered another affidavit in which an official of the studio swore that she had been offered a contract calling for an increase in salary and had expressed interest in taking the part. A third affidavit indicated the studio was willing to shoot her scenes in California, and include a dance-hall scene in which she would be featured. In the face of such affidavits, the court would likely deny the motion for summary judgment since there would seem to be several real issues of fact between the parties. Summary judgment, then, forces parties to take a stand on what evidence they are going to offer. Judges hesitate to throw people out of court and so use summary judgment sparingly. Nonetheless, if the sworn affidavits show that there really is no argument about the facts, and if those facts establish the existence or absence of a cause of action or a defense, then a costly trial can be avoided.

In ruling on a motion for summary judgment, as well as making many other decisions, courts can take "judicial notice" of generally accepted facts. There is no question that they can take judicial notice that June 25, 1984 was a Monday, that in the usual system found in the United States there are 24 hours in a day and 60 minutes in an hour, that the sun sets in the West, that the Japanese bombed Pearl Harbor on December 7, 1941 and the like. Obviously, forcing people to prove such facts would be a waste of time.

However, judges are concerned about how far they should go in adding to what a party has proved or offered by way of affidavit on a preliminary motion. Suppose, for example, a party asked a court to take judicial notice that President Roosevelt knew that the Japanese were going to bomb Pearl Harbor but did not notify the military leaders in command there because he wanted to bring America into World War II in the face of a strong anti-war movement. One could cite several books making this assertion on the basis of historical records. One could cite a number of others, as well as many book reviews, contesting this argument. Clearly, this is no place for judicial notice. Yet it is far easier to offer examples of extreme situations than to state a test that will decide most or all cases. How much is the majority of the Supreme Court of California filling in on the basis of generally accepted facts in *Parker v. Twentieth Century Fox*? Is the majority taking judicial notice that the role in "Big Country, Big Man" is not comparable to the lead in "Bloomer Girl"? If so, is that more like the date on which Pearl Harbor was bombed or President Roosevelt's knowledge and motive concerning the Japanese attack?

Finally, judges bring their own experience with them to the bench. When they encounter a case from an area in which they specialized in practice, they are likely to make judgments based on their experience, adding to and interpreting the evidence. Even a judge who tried to avoid any bias produced by her experience would have difficulty putting such an interpretive framework aside. If the bias is too great, for example, where the judge is the defendant's parent, we expect the judge to decline to hear the case, but this solution only works in extreme situations. While we have no reason to think that this was the case, suppose Justice Burke, the author of the majority opinion in the *Parker* case, had been a specialist in entertainment law when he was a practicing lawyer. Would he have been justified in looking at the role and contract for "Big Country, Big Man," seeing that anyone in the industry would know it was inferior, and then writing the opinion he did?

3. *MacLaine's goals and constraints*: One of our former students interviewed two of Shirley MacLaine Parker's agents and one of her lawyers in 1979, about nine years after the Supreme Court of California's opinion. All answered questions on the basis of what they remembered without checking files. One agent said that Ms. MacLaine had been willing to settle throughout the trial and the appeal. He pointed out that in the motion picture industry there were only five major employers, not counting independent studios, and it is in a performer's best interest to maintain good relations with all of the major producers of motion pictures. Another agent said that he had worked out a tentative settlement with the head of the Fox studio, but the corporate board rejected it because Fox's legal department wanted to go to court since they felt their case was so strong. MacLaine's lawyer did not think that Fox's lawyers were so anxious to go to court. He remembered MacLaine asking about $600,000 and Fox offering $400,000 to settle, but neither was willing to move closer to the other's figure. MacLaine had turned down a $1 million contract to make *Casino Royale* for Columbia Pictures because she was under contract to do Bloomer Girl. The lawyer thought this affected MacLaine's advisors' judgment about what would be a fair settlement.

4. *Objective versus subjective interests*: Suppose the case had gone to trial. Would evidence of the following facts have been relevant to the issue of the comparability of roles in the two movies? MacLaine was married to a film producer in Japan; she often traveled to various parts of the world to meet him, and to make films on location. MacLaine has long been active in liberal causes. She participated in the civil rights movement of the 1960s. She was a delegate for Robert Kennedy at the 1968 Democratic Party Convention. She was active in the McGovern campaign four years later. She took stands against the war in Vietnam, and feminist issues interest her. *Bloomer Girl* was a popular musical produced in 1944 which had a theme likely to appeal to MacLaine. The story takes place in 1861. Dolly Bloomer advocates that women wear loose trousers fastened at the ankles instead of the fashionable hoopskirts which symbolize the subjugation of women. She also is an abolitionist who participates in the underground railway that helps slaves move to free states to escape their masters. Dolly's brother (the wicked capitalist) is a wealthy hoopskirt manufacturer. Her niece, Evelina, rebels against her father, and she accepts her aunt's progressive ideas. However, Evelina falls in love with Jeff Calhoun, a Southerner who has come North to find his runaway slave, Pompey. Pompey is the slave that Aunt Dolly has been hiding. At the end of the story, Jeff has a change of heart. He frees Pompey and marries Evelina to provide the happy ending.

Shirley MacLaine was to play Evelina. It was a good part in a well crafted musical. Harold Arlen composed the music for *Bloomer Girl*, and E. Y. (Yip) Harburg wrote the lyrics. Both were exceptionally talented; "Over the Rainbow" from the *Wizard of Oz*, is just one of their many famous songs. The critics praised the score, lyrics and choreography.

We know nothing about *Big Country, Big Man*. As far as we can tell, Fox never produced it. Nevertheless, the title suggests it was a common Western. Men do things. Women only talk or react. They try to keep men from getting killed by advocating cowardly retreat or they admire male heroism. Sometimes they are just objects. They serve as fair princesses rescued by heroes. They are the reward as the hero gets the girl in the last act.

Moreover, liberals would view the politics of many Westerns as decidedly right-wing. The good man is self-reliant. Men with guns defend honor and property. Organized society is weak or corrupt. Moral questions have simple answers. These films accept or justify violence as the solution to important problems. Heroes are white; villains are often Mexicans or Indians (they are not called Native Americans). Killing them is often treated as killing threatening wild animals. Of course, Westerns do not have to be written this way, but assume that *Big Country, Big Man* was the kind of a film that would offend Shirley MacLaine's political beliefs.

Suppose MacLaine's lawyer established in this fashion that Shirley MacLaine did not view the female lead in *Big Country, Big Man* as comparable to the part of Evelina in *Bloomer Girl* nor would any reasonable person holding MacLaine's political views see the parts as equivalent. Should this be relevant to her duty to mitigate damages flowing from Fox's breach of contract? Remember that she would earn about $800,000 for performing in either film. Furthermore, she was entitled to a percentage of the profits as part of her pay. Assume that *Big Country, Big Man* was likely to earn more profit than *Bloomer Girl*.

In considering this question, you might ask why Fox breached the contract. Darryl F. Zanuck, was one of the last of the great movie kings. He and his son, Richard, ran Twentieth Century Fox. Richard's strategy was to make blockbuster films such as *The Sound of Music*, *Patton*, and *M*A*S*H*. These pictures cost four to five times more than ordinary films, but the return could be much greater. In the mid-1960s, he was very successful. The 1966 gross income was the highest in the company's history. In 1967 seven blockbuster films were in production or planned. However, many Fox executives and bankers worried about the risks involved in Richard Zanuck's strategy. They pressed for restraint. Fox notified Shirley MacLaine in April of 1966 that it would not film *Bloomer Girl*. Fox pointed to script problems and high cost estimates.

Richard Zanuck resigned in January of 1971. The studio had produced too many costly failures such as *Tora! Tora! Tora!*, *Dr. Dolittle*, *Hello Dolly*, and *Beyond the Valley of the Dolls*. It lost $25 million in 1969, and $21 million in the first nine months of 1970, and its bankers demanded changes. Thus, from the standpoint of Twentieth Century Fox's stockholders and creditors, we can ask what Fox had to pay to end its mistaken *Bloomer Girl* venture and move its resources to films more likely to be profitable. Recall that the court awarded Shirley MacLaine about $750,000 plus interest. However, she did not have to perform to earn this money. She may have spent at least some of the time freed by Fox's cancellation of *Bloomer Girl* campaigning for Robert Kennedy in the Democratic Party's presidential primary elections in 1968.

Does any of this affect your judgment about the proper result in our hypothetical case about the comparability of the female lead in *Big Country, Big Man* and in *Bloomer Girl*? Finally, can courts make informed judgments about the comparability of two jobs in light of subjective preferences of employees? We have drawn a sharp contrast between *Bloomer Girl* and *Big Country, Big Man*. However, *Bloomer Girl* is not clearly a feminist musical. It treats women's claims for equality as the subject of humor. Evelina's political and moral principles are overcome by the sexual attraction of a handsome man. Some of the songs sung by Evelina suggest she is prepared to subordinate her pursuit of social causes to pursuit of a man.

Also *Big Country, Big Man* may not have been so clearly a right-wing script with a limited role for the female lead. The studio's letter offering the substitute part says that MacLaine had "already expressed an interest in performing the role in 'BIG COUNTRY, BIG MAN.'" (See the last paragraph in the court's second footnote.) Is the difficulty of deciding such issues of comparability reason enough for courts to limit the question to the economic or financial aspects of a substitute job which an employer asserts the employee should have accepted? If you accept this argument, have you necessarily rejected the idea that the law of contract rests on freedom and choice?

5. *Interpretation of the Parker case in later decisions*: As of 1994, the Supreme Court of California had not considered the problem raised by the *Parker* case again. However, one way a case takes on meaning is by the way lower courts interpret it over time. Of course, the Supreme Court of a state always could reject the accepted interpretation by intermediate appellate courts, but after time passes it is less likely to do this. The justices who decided a particular case are unlikely still to be on the court ten or fifteen years later. The new members of the highest court will be influenced by plausible interpretations written by their colleagues at the intermediate level. Unless there is a good reason to reject what has become accepted, predictability of the law is served by following the cases which have developed.

What have the intermediate appellate courts in California made of *Parker v. Twentieth Century Fox*? Two cases cite the *Parker* decision. In *California School Employees Assn. v. Personnel Com'n*[15] a school bus driver had been fired without cause. The driver did not take other jobs driving school buses. The jobs were in the same locale and the employee would not have had to move. There was only

---

[15]30 Cal.Ap.3d 241, 106 Cal.Rptr. 283 (1st Dist. 1973).

a few cents per hour difference in the pay and there was little variation in vacation and sick leave time among school districts. Unlike the school system that had terminated the employee without cause, the other school districts did not have a "merit system for classified employees." Probably, in the alternative school bus driving jobs, all employees within a particular classification received the same pay. In a merit system, supervisors could single out some employees and reward them for their better performance. Without discussing the issue, the District Court of Appeal said that lack of such a system was not enough to make the available jobs inferior, and the employee had failed to mitigate damages.

Currieri v. City of Roseville[16] ruled that a police officer who was reinstated with back pay after wrongful discharge had failed to mitigate damages, and so what he could have made was deducted from the amount of back pay due. When the officer was fired, he did not look for another police job but became a full time college student. Another officer fired at the same time found a job as a police officer in another city, and the court said there was sufficient evidence that police forces were hiring.

The United States Court of Appeals for the Fifth Circuit cited the *Parker* case as persuasive authority in a decision applying Florida law. In *Ballard v. El Dorado Tire Company*,[17] Ballard had been hired for a five-year term as Executive Vice President and General Manager of El Dorado's Florida subsidiary. One of El Dorado's stockholders wanted to take over management of the Florida subsidiary, and Ballard was fired without cause. Citing the *Parker* case, the court said "an employees' damages are reduced only if the employer proves with reasonable certainty that employment was available in the *specific line of work* in which the employee was engaged." An expert witness testified that employment statistics showed an extremely low rate of unemployment for "professional technicians and managers" in Orlando. The court found this insufficient to carry the employer's burden that the employee had failed to mitigate. It said:

> El Dorado could meet its burden of proof only by showing the availability of a managerial type position in the tire industry. Were the contrary true, the rule requiring the employer to prove the availability of similar employment would be meaningless. The employer could always meet the so-called "burden" simply by introduction of the help-wanted ads of a local newspaper. The law does not allow contract breachers to escape consequences of their wrongful acts in such a perfunctory fashion.

What do you conclude from these cases? Can we say that the law benefits upper-middle and middle class employees more than working class employees? Why do the courts seem to assume that one school bus driving job is like another

---

[16]50 Cal.Ap.3d 502, 123 Cal.Rptr. 314 (3d Dist. 1975).
[17]512 F.2d 901 (5th Cir. 1975).

but "Big Country, Big Man" is not like "Bloomer Girl" or any managerial, professional, technical job is not comparable to a managerial type position in the tire industry? Isn't the result that Shirley MacLaine could have devoted her time to peace and environmental activism during the time "Bloomer Girl" was to have been made, but that the police officer could not attend college? Is this an unfair reading of these cases?

ANTHONY NERI v. RETAIL MARINE CORPORATION

30 N.Y.2d 393, 334 N.Y.S.2d 165, 285 N.E.2d 311 (1972)

GIBSON, J. The appeal concerns the right of a retail dealer to recover loss of profits and incidental damages upon the buyer's repudiation of a contract governed by the Uniform Commercial Code. This is, indeed, the correct measure of damage in an appropriate case and to this extent the code (§ 2-708, subsection [2]) effected a substantial change from prior law, whereby damages were ordinarily limited to "the difference between the contract price and the market or current price." Upon the record before us, the courts below erred in declining to give effect to the new statute and so the order appealed from must be reversed.

The plaintiffs contracted to purchase from defendant a new boat of a specified model for the price of $12,587.40, against which they made a deposit of $40. They shortly increased the deposit to $4,250 in consideration of the defendant dealer's agreement to arrange with the manufacturer for immediate delivery on the basis of "a firm sale," instead of the delivery within approximately four to six weeks originally specified. Some six days after the date of the contract plaintiffs' lawyer sent to defendant a letter rescinding the sales contract for the reason that plaintiff Neri was about to undergo hospitalization and surgery, in consequence of which, according to the letter, it would be "impossible for Mr. Neri to make any payments." The boat had already been ordered from the manufacturer and was delivered to defendant at or before the time the attorney's letter was received. Defendant declined to refund plaintiffs' deposit and this action to recover it was commenced. Defendant counterclaimed, alleging plaintiffs' breach of the contract and defendant's resultant damage in the amount of $4,250, for which sum defendant demanded judgment. Upon motion, defendant had summary judgment on the issue of liability tendered by its counterclaim; and Special Term directed an assessment of damages, upon which it would be determined whether plaintiffs were entitled to the return of any portion of their down payment.

Upon the trial so directed, it was shown that the boat ordered and received by defendant in accordance with plaintiffs' contract of purchase was sold some four months later to another buyer for the same price as that negotiated with plaintiffs. From this proof the plaintiffs argue that defendant's loss on its contract was recouped, while defendant argues that but for plaintiffs' default, it would have sold two boats and have earned two profits instead of one. Defendant proved, without contradiction, that its profit on the sale under the contract in suit would have been $2,579 and that during the period the boat remained unsold incidental expenses aggregating $674 for storage, upkeep, finance charges and insurance were incurred. Additionally, defendant proved and sought to recover attorneys' fees of $1,250.

The trial court found "untenable" defendant's claim for loss of profit, inasmuch as the boat was later sold for the same price that plaintiffs had contracted to pay; found, too, that defendant had failed to prove any incidental damages ... and ... awarded ... defendant $500 upon its counterclaim and directed that plaintiffs recover the balance of their deposit, amounting to $3,750. The ensuing judgment was affirmed, without opinion, at the Appellate Division and defendant's appeal to this court was taken by our leave.

The issue is governed in the first instance by § 2-718 of the Uniform Commercial Code which provides, among other things, that the buyer, despite his breach, may have restitution ... Section 2-718, however, establishes ... [t]he buyer's right to restitution is subject to offset to the extent that the seller establishes (a) a right to recover damages under the provisions of this Article. ...

Among "the provisions of this Article ... are those to be found in § 2-708, which the courts below did not apply. Subsection (1) of that section provides that "the measure of damages for non-acceptance or repudiation by the buyer is the difference between the market price at the time and place for tender and the unpaid contract price together with any incidental damages provided in this Article (Section 2-710), but less expenses saved in consequence of the buyer's breach." However, this provision is made expressly subject to subsection (2), providing: "(2) If the measure of damages provided in subsection (1) is inadequate to put the seller in as good a position as performance would have done then the measure of damages is the profit (including reasonable overhead) which the seller would have made from full performance by the buyer, together with any incidental damages provided in this Article (Section 2-710), due allowance for costs reasonably incurred and due credit for payments or proceeds of resale."

Prior to the code, the New York cases "applied the 'profit' test, contract price less cost of manufacture, only in cases where the seller [was] a manufacturer or an agent for a manufacturer" (1955 Report of New York Law Review Commission, vol. 1, p. 693). Its extension to retail sales was "designed to eliminate the unfair and economically wasteful results arising under the older law when fixed price articles were involved. This section permits the recovery of lost profits in all appropriate cases, which would include all standard priced goods." (Official Comment 2, McKinney's Cons. Laws of N.Y., Book 62 1/2, Part 1, p. 605, under Uniform Commercial Code, § 2-708.) Additionally, and "[i]n all cases the seller may recover incidental damages" (id., Comment 3). The buyer's right to restitution was established at Special Term upon the motion for summary judgment, as was the seller's right to proper offsets ...; and, as the parties concede, the only question before us, following the assessment of damages at Special Term, is that as to the proper measure of damage to be applied. The conclusion is clear from the record — indeed with mathematical certainty — that "the measure of damages provided in subsection (1) is inadequate to put the seller in as good a position as performance would have done" (Uniform Commercial Code, § 2-708, subsection [2]) and hence — again under subsection (2) — that the seller is entitled to its "profit (including reasonable overhead) ... together with any incidental damages ..., due allowance for costs reasonably incurred and due credit for payments or proceeds of resale."

It is evident, first, that this retail seller is entitled to its profit and, second, that the last sentence of subsection (2), as hereinbefore quoted, referring to "due credit for payments or proceeds of resale" is inapplicable to this retail sales contract. Closely parallel to the factual situation now before us is that hypothesized by Dean Hawkland as illustrative of the operation of the rules: "Thus, if a private party agrees to sell his automobile to a buyer for $2,000, a breach by the buyer would cause the seller no loss (except incidental damages, i.e., expense of a new sale) if the seller was able to sell the automobile to another buyer for $2000. But the situation is different with dealers having an unlimited supply of standard-priced goods. Thus, if an automobile dealer agrees to sell a car to a buyer at the standard price of $2000, a breach by the buyer injures the dealer, even though he is able to sell the automobile to another for $2000. If the dealer has an inexhaustible supply of cars, the resale to replace the breaching buyer costs the dealer a sale, because, had the breaching buyer performed, the dealer would have made two sales instead of one. The buyer's breach, in such a case, depletes the dealer's sales to the extent of one, and the measure of damages should be the dealer's profit on one sale. Section 2-708 recognizes this, and it rejects the rule developed under the Uniform Sales Act by many courts that the profit cannot be recovered in this case." (Hawkland, Sales and Bulk Sales [1958 ed.], pp. 153-154; and see Comment, 31 Fordham Law Review 749, 755-756.)

The record which in this case establishes defendant's entitlement to damages in the amount of its prospective profit, at the same time confirms defendant's cognate right to "any incidental damages provided in this Article (Section 2-710)" (Uniform Commercial Code, § 2-708, subsection [2]). From the language employed it is too clear to require discussion that the seller's right to recover loss of profits is not exclusive and that he may recoup his "incidental" expenses as well (*Procter & Gamble Distr. Co. v. Lawrence Amer. Field Warehousing Corp.*, 16 N.Y.2d 344, 354)....

[T]here was an explicit finding "that defendant completely failed to show that it suffered any incidental damages." We find no basis for the court's conclusion with respect to a deficiency of proof inasmuch as the proper items of the $674 expenses (being for storage, upkeep, finance charges and insurance for the period between the date performance was due and the time of the resale) were proven without objection and were in no way controverted, impeached or otherwise challenged, at the trial or on appeal. Thus the court's finding of a failure of proof cannot be supported upon the record and, therefore, and contrary to plaintiffs' contention, the affirmance at the Appellate Division was ineffective to save it.

The trial court correctly denied defendant's claim for recovery of attorney's fees incurred by it in this action. Attorney's fees incurred in an action such as this are not in the nature of the protective expenses contemplated by the statute (Uniform Commercial Code, § 1-106, subd. [1]; § 2-710; § 2-708, subsection [2]) and by our reference to "legal expense" in *Procter & Gamble Distr. Co. v. Lawrence Amer. Field Warehousing Corp.* (16 N.Y.2d 344; 354-355, *supra*), upon which defendant's reliance is in this respect misplaced.

It follows that plaintiffs are entitled to restitution of the sum of $4,250 paid by them on account of the contract price less an offset to defendant in the amount of $3,253 on account of its lost profit of $2,579 and its incidental damages of $674.

The order of the Appellate Division should be modified, with costs in all courts, in accordance with this opinion, and, as so modified, affirmed....

NOTES AND QUESTIONS

1. *When would § 2-708(2) apply as written?* Apply §§ 2-708(2) and 2-704(2) to the following problem:

> Seller contracts with Buyer to build a custom made car for $22,000. When the car is about half completed, Buyer tells Seller that he will neither accept delivery of the car nor pay for it. This breaches their contract. At this point, Seller has spent $12,000 in labor and materials building the partially completed car. Seller estimates that it would cost $6,000 to complete the car, and the current salvage value of the car as it stands is $2,000. It would be very difficult to sell the completed car to anyone other than Buyer because Buyer had many peculiar features designed into the car.

What remedies under the Uniform Commercial Code might the seller seek with a chance of success? Does § 2-708(2) as written reach the right result in this kind of case?

2. *Questions of technique*: Does the Court's opinion in the *Neri* case suggest that we should ignore the last two phrases of § 2-708(2)? If so, is that consistent with the appropriate functions of courts and legislatures? Assume we accept some version of the idea that elected representatives make the law while judges play a more limited role. Didn't the Court of Appeal make new law to correct what it viewed as a legislative mistake in the *Neri* case? Hasn't it then usurped the New York Legislature's functions? Of course, a state legislature usually can overturn a decision of the state's supreme court by passing a statute. Is it enough that legislatures have this ultimate power?

Is there another way the court might have interpreted § 2-708(2) to reach the same result while keeping closer to traditional notions of a legislative role in creating law and a judicial role in interpreting and applying it? Look at U.C.C. § 2-708(2) again. Suppose, for example, the Court of Appeals had said that there had been no "resale" in the *Neri* situation, and thus there was nothing to deduct. Could this be argued to be the case? How? Would the argument be plausible?

3. *History of § 2-708(2)*: Richard Danzig, the author of *The Capability Problem in Contract Law*, which some of you will study in your Contracts course, studied the drafting history of § 2-708(2). He wanted to find out why a provision that apparently was designed to provide a remedy for a lost volume seller (Comment 2 so states) included the last two phrases concerning costs reasonably incurred and proceeds of resale. He discovered that the original drafts of the Section did not include these phrases. They were added in 1954, at the time the Code was going through extensive revision to respond to the many criticisms it had received. A drafter's note accompanying the addition of the last two phrases explained:

> The main purpose of the change is to clarify the privilege of the seller to realize junk value when it is manifestly useless to complete the operation of manufacture.

Relying on this note, Danzig speculates that an unspecified person working on the Code (not Llewellyn) got confused and thought that the purpose of § 2-708(2) was to replicate § 64(4) of the Uniform Sales Act (the predecessor uniform statute to Article II). Section 64(4) to deal with the situation where a seller had not completed manufacture of goods ordered by the buyer, which is the fact situation stated in note 1, *supra*. Without the last two phrases concerning costs reasonably incurred and proceeds of resale, of course, § 2-708(2) would not provide a sensible formula for measuring damages for the seller with unfinished goods.

At this time we cannot know for sure whether Danzig's speculations are correct. If they are, the draftsman's error passed undetected. Later legislative history on the U.C.C. makes no mention of this problem. As finally approved by the sponsoring agencies, the American Law Institute and the National Conference of Commissioners on Uniform State Laws, the Code continued to include Comment 2 suggesting that the purpose of § 2-708(2) was to deal with the lost volume seller.

Suppose we assume that Danzig's account correctly explains how the last two phrases of § 2-708(2) came to appear in the statute. Does this account have any bearing on the appropriateness of the New York Court of Appeals' interpretation of that section?

4. *Debate about Neri*: The position of the "lost volume" seller under the Uniform Commercial Code has been the subject of considerable academic controversy. Most commentators agree with the result reached by the New York Court of Appeals in *Neri v. Retail Marine*. See, *e.g.*, J. White and R. Summers, *Uniform Commercial Code* 225-32 (1972). For a contrary view, see Goetz and Scott, Measuring Sellers' Damages: The Lost-Profits Puzzle, 31 Stanford Law Review 323 (1979); Shanker, The Case for a Literal Reading of U.C.C. § 2-

708(2), 24 Case Western Law Review 697 (1974). Among other things, Goetz and Scott and Shanker argue since there are so few true lost volume sellers in the world, it is not worth a court's time to listen to evidence attempting to establish that a particular seller is one.

Are there many true lost volume sellers? How often can we be sure that if buyer #1 hadn't breached, seller would have earned two full profits by selling to buyer #2 as well as buyer #1? For example, how can we be sure that had buyer #1 bought the goods, he wouldn't have sold them to buyer #2? If he did this, seller wouldn't have made a sale to buyer #2. Furthermore, how can we be sure what seller's costs of making the second sale would have been? Can we assume that in some situations a seller will not make more items because the costs of producing additional ones will exceed the profit to be made on them? If there are but a very few clear situations where we are sure there are lost volume sellers, is this an argument for denying protection of their expectation interest?

Whether the *Neri* interpretation of § 2-708(2) was proper has not been a major issue before the courts. Typically, the decisions just cite *Neri* and turn to a more difficult problem. How does one establish that he or she is a "lost volume seller" when a buyer breaches? The *Neri* opinion quotes Dean Hawkland's discussion of "dealers having an unlimited supply of standard-priced goods." As of 1994, the cases are not entirely clear, but we have found no decision calling for proof of "an unlimited supply of standard-priced goods." Some courts seem willing to presume that if one is a retailer, one is a lost-volume seller. Others seem more demanding, insisting that one offer some proof that but for the breach there would have been two sales. For example, in *Famous Knitwear Corp. v. Drug Fair, Inc.,*[18] the court held that a buyer was entitled to prevail if it could show that the seller/broker could not have filled additional orders and that the sales which followed the buyer's breach were "substitute sales." The seller contended that it could have filled buyer's order as well as made the subsequent sales. The case was remanded to the trial court for findings of fact on the issue.[19]

5. *Briefs and record*: Professor Robert Gordon of the Stanford Law School examined the record in the *Neri* case and his observations raise a number of questions about the decision. We can summarize them by asking whether *Neri v. Retail Marine* was a good example of a *Neri* case.

Tony Neri took the purchase price of the boat, a 1970, 31-foot Broadwater "Bay Breeze," out of his pension. However, the day after he signed the contract, he learned that he had to be hospitalized. The Bay Breeze was delivered to Retail

---

[18]493 F.2d 251 (4th Cir. 1974).

[19]A more recent decision that upholds the availability of lost profits recovery for the lost volume seller but imposes a substantial burden on the seller to show that it lost a sale as a result of the breach is Davis Chemical Corp. v. Diasonics, 826 F.2d 678 (7th Cir., 1987). The contract was for the purchase of medical diagnostic equipment costing several hundred thousand dollars. Should courts require the seller to prove more to establish lost volume seller status when selling very expensive items than when selling boats as in the *Neri* case?

Marine's showroom in early May, 1970, a few days after Neri tried to back out of the contract. Retail Marine nonetheless installed all the accessories he had ordered. The Bay Breeze finally was sold in September to a Mr. Olsen, at the same price of $11,988 (plus 5% New York sales tax of $599.40) for a total of $12,587.40. Mr. Olsen did, however, receive a trade-in allowance of $2,988 for his 1969 Super Craft.

It is apparent from pre-trial documents that Retail Marine went into the case with a different legal theory than that which the New York Court of Appeals used to explain its decision. An affidavit of Mr. Meere, Retail Marine's Vice President, contended that,

> [a]s a result of the discount that was given to the new purchasers [Olsen] by way of an inflated trade allowance, and taking into consideration the additional expenses which accrued, such as interest on the financing of the boat, the second commission to the salesman, extra insurance, storage and upkeep, the defendant sustained damages in excess of $2,000, which does not contemplate any attorney's fees, which the defendant is going to be required to pay to defend this action.

By the time the case got to trial, Mr. Miller, Retail Marine's counsel, looked at it differently. He did not ask about the trade-in allowance on the sale to Olsen. He argued that the sale to Olsen was irrelevant, and when he asked Mr. Meere to compute Marine's incidental damages, there was no mention of a second salesman's commission. He did bring out that Retail Marine was the largest Broadwater boat dealer in the United States. Miller computed incidental damages as follows: storage and upkeep for the boat, $200; finance charges before resale, $375; and insurance, $99.

Mr. Razis, Neri's attorney, asked Meere about the Olsen sale:

> Q. When did you sell this boat, September? Isn't it rather unusual that it took you from May, June, July, August, and September to sell a boat?
> A. No, sir....
> Q. When is the best time to sell this boat?
> A. It is a very slow mover. There is no good time for it. [After Neri's repudiation] every sales person at our location was offered an additional commission to sell that boat.
> Q. Did you advertise it?
> A. Yes, we did. In the New York Times, Newsday.

Meere also testified that the 1971 models of the Broadwater boats came out in June, 1970.

Retail Marine's records of the Olsen sale, to which neither party referred at trial, tend to support the contention in Meere's affidavit that Marine took a lower profit on this sale of the boat originally ordered by Neri. Their "Dealer Advice Trade-In" form lists a "Trade Overallowance" of $988.

The briefs on appeal are short and unilluminating on the lost volume seller issue. Neither brief attempted to interpret the clause in § 2-708 about "due credit for payments or proceeds of resale." The judges on the Court of Appeals and their law clerks must have done most of the research for its opinion, rather than ordering the lawyers for both sides to rebrief the case in light of the lost volume seller theory. This meant Neri's lawyer had no chance to challenge adopting the lost volume seller rule or its application to this case. We can say that Neri's lawyer had a chance when he briefed the case originally to consider this question. However, the theory certainly wasn't obvious from the text of the statute, and Retail marine hadn't raised it at trial.

In view of what we learn from the briefs and record on appeal, does it seem likely that Olsen would have purchased a different boat from Retail Marine if he had not bought the Bay Breeze originally ordered for Neri? If he would not have bought a different boat, what recovery would have been proper? If he would have bought another Bay Breeze from Retail Marine as the Court of Appeals assumes, should recovery for lost profits have been limited to the profit Retail Marine would have made on the sale to Neri? And why was there no recovery for the advertising expenses incurred by Retail Marine?

All in all, it appears that Retail Marine set out to offset Tony Neri's attempt to recover his down payment by seeking its actual losses ($988 on the "over-allowance" on Mr. Olsen's trade-in, $250 on the second salesman's commission it had to pay when the Bay Breeze was sold to Olsen, and $647 in interest, storage, and insurance charges between the sales, or a total of $1,885) incurred from having to sell a slow-moving boat three months after the next year's models were out, plus its attorney's fees. Mr. Miller, Retail Marine's counsel, was asked at trial to estimate what his fees would be. He guessed $1,250, but of course this was before the case went through two appeals. Retail Marine was awarded $2,579 in lost profits on the lost volume seller theory adopted by the Court of Appeals as well as $674 for incidental damages or a total of $3,253. Nonetheless, if you add the likely additional legal expenses in taking the appeals to the costs we know about ($1,885 + $1,250 = $3,135), Retail Marine almost certainly ended with a net loss. However, it did keep Neri from recovering much of his down payment, and it did establish a rule of law helpful to automobile and boat dealers.

6. *Downpayments and cancellations*: Tony Neri bought a boat, but then he discovered that he could not use it. He tried to back out before the boat was delivered. Why can't Neri cancel his order without legal liability?

We must distinguish the legal situation from everyday practice. Once consumer and retailer make a legally enforceable contract, neither can back out free of liability without the consent of the other absent a legally recognized excuse. As we know, many stores will let customers cancel orders or return goods and refund what the customers have paid. Does this practice suggest that the law should not hold consumers to contracts unless the seller has relied in some unusual way? Or should retailers have the option to release some customers who have cancelled while holding others (like Neri) to their contracts?

John Miller and William Ross, students of Professor Wallace Loh at the University of Washington Law School, surveyed 16 new car dealers in Seattle, Bellevue, and Renton. Most dealers were unaware that they might be able to sue buyers who canceled orders for lost profits. "All the dealers we talked to thought that the idea of recovering lost profits was, from a practical standpoint, 'ludicrous.' As one dealer put it: 'Realistically, how long could a dealer who sues customers for lost profits last in a competitive market? Once the word got out, such a reputation would drive customers away.'"

Almost all dealers required a customer to make a deposit before they would order a car with particular features for the customer. "The refundability of the 'deposit' varied among dealers. Ten of the dealers said they would refund the deposit if the buyer canceled the order. Four of the dealers said they would not refund the deposit; two dealers said they would not refund only on special factory ordered cars or on slow selling cars." Miller and Ross commented that they "got the sense ... that if the customer is adamant in demanding a refund, and the customer has legitimate reasons for backing out, ... these nonrefunding dealers will grudgingly refund [the money]."

Miller and Ross did not interview a representative sample of dealers in the Puget Sound area, and we cannot be sure that practices there match practices elsewhere. Nonetheless, their work should prompt us to ask who is likely to use the rights created by the *Neri* case and when. Is Retail Marine more likely to use these rights than a Chevrolet dealer that sold Tony Neri a new car? Suppose an industrial purchaser cancels an order for steel or machine tools. Will the supplier or manufacturer always be free to use the rights created by the *Neri* case?

7. *Lawyer's fees for the winner*: The Court of Appeals follows the usual American rule when it refuses to allow the winning party to recover attorney's fees in a breach of contract action. The American rule stands in sharp contrast to the so-called "English rule" in which the loser must pay the winner's costs of litigation, including attorney's fees. In practice, English winners recover not their actual fees, but "reasonable legal costs" as assessed by a court official. Similar "loser pays" rules are prevalent throughout much of the world. Such "fee-shifting" rules can have profound effects on the incentives to pursue, avoid, or settle litigation. To encourage claimants to come forward, many American statutes in such areas as consumer protection and civil rights authorize courts to award attorneys fees to successful plaintiffs. Such "one way fee-shifting" is regarded as an exception to the American tradition of each side bearing its own costs. Critics concerned with excessive litigation propose the general introduction of "loser pays" to inhibit "frivolous litigation." Opponents are concerned about the chilling effect on claims that are not cut-and-dried. What effect, if any, might a "loser pays" rule have had on Neri's decision to sue? On Retail Marine's strategy in defending? For an overview of these issues, see Herbert M. Kritzer,

"The English Rule," 78 American Bar Association Journal (November, 1992) 54.

8. *Questions of overhead*: When a retailer (like Retail Marine) sells a product (like a boat) they receive an amount of money (revenue) which can be seen as consisting of three parts. First, part of the revenue can be allocated to cover the direct costs associated with the sale — such as the wholesale cost of the product and any commission paid the salesperson. Second, in order for the business to be profitable in the long run, some portion of the revenue must be allocated to cover the indirect costs of selling this and other products — such as rent, utilities, interest on loans, and so forth. This is often called overhead. Overhead expenses are expenses associated with running the business and are not clearly related to any particular transaction. Finally, any amount left after recovering *all* costs, both direct and indirect, represents the *net profit* on the transaction.

It is, unfortunately, common for retailers and others to refer to the difference between revenue from the sale and wholesale cost as profit. It is unfortunate because the use of the unmodified word "profit" creates the risk of confusing net and gross profit. Gross profit is the difference between revenue and direct costs or, to look at it another way, gross profit is the sum of net profit plus overhead. To say it again, in yet another form, the difference between net and gross profit is overhead.

The question for us is this: when a legal rule awards "profits" does it provide for an award of net or gross profit? Or, in other words, if a plaintiff is entitled to recover profits does this recovery include overhead? The U.C.C., in 2-708(2) provides (at one level) an easy answer to the question since it provides that the seller is entitled to "the profit (including reasonable overhead) which the seller would have made." But how easy is it to *apply* the § 2-708(2) rule?

How does this apply in the *Neri* case? Is Retail Marine entitled to recover overhead? What might that include? *Vitex Manufacturing Corp. v. Caribtex Corp.*[20] involved a seller that had closed its plant. Then it negotiated a contract with buyer to process woolen material. Seller reopened its plant, ordered the necessary chemicals, and recalled its work force. Buyer then breached. The trial court found that seller's gross revenues would have been $31,250, its costs $10,136, and so its damages were $21,114. Buyer argued that the trial court had erred by not subtracting seller's overhead expenses from the contract price in determining lost profits. The Third Circuit upheld the trial court:

> Although there is authority to the contrary, we feel that the better view is that normally, in a claim for lost profits, overhead should be treated as a part of gross profits and recoverable as damages, and should not be considered as a part of the seller's costs. A number of cases hold that since overhead expenses are not affected by the performance of the particular

---

[20]377 F.2d 795 (3d Cir. 1967).

contract, there should be no need to deduct them in computing lost profits....

[Buyer] may argue that this view ignores modern accounting principles, and that overhead is as much a cost of production as other expenses. It is true that successful businessmen must set their prices at sufficient levels to recoup all their expenses, including overhead, and to gain profits. Thus, the price the businessman should charge on each transaction could be thought of as that price necessary to yield a pro rata portion of the company's fixed overhead, the direct costs associated with production, and a "clear profit." Doubtless this type of calculation is used by businessmen and their accountants.... However, because it is useful for planning purposes to allocate a portion of overhead to each transaction, it does not follow that this allocate share of fixed overhead should be considered a cost factor in the computation of lost profits on individual transactions....

....

By the very nature of this allocation process, as the number of transactions over which overhead can be spread becomes smaller, each transaction must bear a greater portion or allocate share of the fixed overhead cost. Suppose a company has fixed overhead of $10,000 and engages in five similar transactions; then the receipts of each transaction would bear $2000 of overhead expense. If the company is now forced to spread this $10,000 over only four transactions, then the overhead expense per transaction will rise to $2500, significantly reducing the profitability of the four remaining transactions. Thus, where the contract is between businessmen familiar with commercial practices, as here, the breaching party should reasonably foresee that his breach will not only cause a loss of "clear" profit, but also a loss in that the profitability of other transactions will be reduced.... Therefore, this loss is within the contemplation of "losses caused and gains prevented," and overhead should be considered to be a compensable item of damage.

Other courts have demanded more precision in allocating costs to particular contracts. How precise must our calculations be? On one hand, we want to reach substantive justice. On the other hand, we must remember that law is not free. Proving damages with some precision requires experts and records. It also opens the door to longer trials and confused juries.

In addition to the difficulties just discussed, we need to be alert to calculating a plaintiff's claim in a way that yields overcompensation or "double recovery." Sometimes lawyers and courts become confused when calculating damages and award, for example, gross profits plus overhead. This is clearly improper since gross profit already includes overhead.

C. THE EXPECTATION INTEREST: PERFORMANCE RATHER THAN DAMAGES

COPYLEASE CORPORATION OF AMERICA v. MEMOREX CORPORATION

408 F. Supp. 758 (S.D.N.Y. 1976).

[Memorex manufactures supplies for copying machines. Copylease, a distributor of these supplies, made a contract with Memorex for three types of toner, a chemical used in copying machines. Copylease promised to buy specified minimum quantities of these products. Memorex, in return, granted Copylease 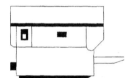 a favorable price and an exclusive dealership for Memorex toners in the Midwest. Soon after they signed a contract, Memorex's officials expressed dissatisfaction with various terms, which they considered unduly favorable to Copylease. For example, Copylease was free to devote its efforts to promoting a private label toner rather than Memorex toner. Although Memorex supplied both the private label and Memorex toner, sales of the Memorex product were more advantageous to it. Negotiations for modification of the contract followed. Though happy with the contract, Copylease was willing to consider changes if Memorex offered an attractive incentive. The negotiations, however, became quite heated, and officials of both firms exhibited great ill feeling. Memorex then notified Copylease that it was unilaterally altering the terms of their relationship. Memorex would no longer recognize Copylease as its exclusive dealer in any area. Copylease sued for breach of contract. It sought specific performance of the exclusive dealership as well as damages for losses suffered between the time Memorex took action and when a court entered an order.]

LASKER, J. By Memorandum Opinion dated November 12, 1975, 403 F. Supp. 625, we determined that Memorex Corporation (Memorex) breached its contract with Copylease Corporation of America (Copylease) for the sale of toner and developer and directed the parties to submit proposed judgments with supporting documentation relating to the availability of injunctive relief, or, more precisely, specific performance. We have studied the submissions and conclude that further testimony is necessary to determine the propriety of such relief. Memorex takes the position that under California law Copylease is not entitled to specific performance of this contract.... [The court agrees with Memorex' contention that California law applies. The court's reasoning is summarized in note 1 following the case.]

We ... agree with Memorex that the provision in the contract granting Copylease an exclusive territory, on which Copylease places primary reliance in its request for specific performance, is not in itself an adequate basis under

California law for an award of such relief. *Long Beach Drug Co. v. United Drug Co.*, 13 Cal.2d 158, 88 P.2d 698, 89 P.2d 386 (1939). California law does not consider a remedy at law inadequate merely because difficulties may exist as to precise calculation of damages. *Hunt Foods, Inc. v. Phillips*, 248 F.2d 23, 33 (N.D. Cal. 1957) (applying California law); *Thayer Plymouth Center, Inc. v. Chrysler Motors Corp.*, 255 Cal. App. 2d 300, 63 Cal. Rptr. 148, 152 (4th Dist. Ct. App. 1967) and cases cited there. *Long Beach Drug* and *Thayer Plymouth* also demonstrate the more fundamental refusal of California courts to order specific performance of contracts which are not capable of immediate enforcement, but which require a "continuing series of acts" and "cooperation between the parties for the successful performance of those acts." *Thayer Plymouth Center, Inc. v. Chrysler Motors Corp., supra*, 255 Cal. App. 2d at 303, 63 Cal. Rptr. at 150; *Long Beach Drug Co. v. United Drug Co., supra*, 13 Cal. 2d 158, 88 P.2d 698, 703-05, 89 P.2d 386. Absent some exception to this general rule, therefore, Copylease will be limited to recovery of damages for the contract breach.

An exception which may prove applicable to this case is found in Cal. U.C.C. § 2716(1). That statute provides that in an action for breach of contract a buyer may be entitled to specific performance "where the goods are unique or in other proper circumstances." Cal. U.C.C. § 2716(1) (West 1964). In connection with its claim for interim damages for lost profits from the time of the breach Copylease argues strongly that it could not reasonably have covered by obtaining an alternative source of toner because the other brands of toner are distinctly inferior to the Memorex product. If the evidence at the hearing supports this claim, it may well be that Copylease faces the same difficulty in finding a permanent alternative supplier. If so, the Official Comment to § 2716 suggests that a grant of specific performance may be in order:

> Specific performance is no longer limited to goods which are already specific or ascertained at the time of contracting. The test of uniqueness under this section must be made in terms of the total situation which characterizes the contract. Output and requirements contracts involving a particular or peculiarly available source or market present today the typical commercial specific performance situation ... However, uniqueness is not the sole basis of the remedy under this section for the relief may also be granted "in other proper circumstances" and *inability to cover is strong evidence of "other proper circumstances"*. Cal. U.C.C. § 2716, Comment 2 (West 1964). (emphasis added)

If Copylease has no adequate alternative source of toner the Memorex product might be considered "unique" for purposes of § 2716, or the situation might present an example of "other proper circumstances" in which specific performance would be appropriate.

If such a showing is made it will be necessary to reconcile California's policy against ordering specific performance of contracts which provide for continuing acts or an ongoing relationship with § 2716 of the Code. Although we recognize that the statute does not require specific performance, the quoted portion of the Official Comment seems clearly to suggest that where a contract calls for continuing sale of unique or "noncoverable" goods this provision should be considered an exception to the general proscription. Output and requirements contracts, explicitly cited as examples of situations in which specific performance may be appropriate, by their nature call for a series of continuing acts and an ongoing relationship. Thus, the drafters seem to have contemplated that at least in some circumstances specific performance will issue contrary to the historical reluctance to grant such relief in these situations. If, at the hearing, Copylease makes a showing that it meets the requirements of § 2716, the sensible approach would be to measure, with the particulars of this contract in mind, the uniqueness or degree of difficulty in covering against the difficulties of enforcement which have caused courts to refrain from granting specific performance. It would be premature to speculate on the outcome of such analysis in this case.

NOTES AND QUESTIONS

1. *Diversity of citizenship jurisdiction*: The United States is a federal system, and there are both federal and state courts. For the most part, problems involving contracts, torts, and property are matters of state law, while federal courts deal with statutes enacted by Congress. However, when the thirteen colonies became the United States, some worried that state courts might be unfair when one party was not a resident of the state where a trial was to be held. As a result, Congress gave federal courts jurisdiction over cases which parties otherwise would try in state courts where there was "diversity of citizenship." Large corporations today are often incorporated in states such as Delaware to take advantage of their favorable laws. Under a legal fiction, they are citizens of those states. Thus, diversity is very common when one of the parties is a corporation doing business nationally.

In a diversity case tried in a federal court what law does the court apply? Federal courts apply their own rules of procedure. However, they are supposed to apply the substantive law which would be applied in the courts of the state in which they sit. Often state law is unclear, and a federal court must do its best to determine what a state court would have done had the case been tried before it.

In the *Copylease* case, the United States District Court first had to decide whether awarding an injunction or decree of specific performance was a matter of substance or procedure. If it were but a matter of procedure, then a federal law would apply. However, the court decided that it had to follow state practice in this matter. But which state law should apply in a case being tried before a federal court sitting in New York to a contract action between what were in substance two Midwestern corporations? The written contract itself said that the law of California would apply, and the court decided to follow the choice of the parties since the "transaction bears a reasonable relation to" California.[21]

2. *California law, specific performance, and the long-term relationship*: The federal court considering the *Copylease* case had to consider California law concerning specific performance of a contract involving a long-term continuing relationship. California courts had decided two important cases before the Uniform Commercial Code went into effect in that state, and both decisions showed a great reluctance to award specific performance of a continuing contract of any complexity.

The first was *Long Beach Drug Co. v. United Drug Co.*[22] There, the parties entered a contract in 1909, appointing the plaintiff the exclusive sales agent in Long Beach, California for "Rexall" drug products. The contract was to last as long as plaintiff performed according to its terms, and one of the most important was that it sell only at prices established by defendant for Rexall products. In 1909, Long Beach had a population of 18,000, and plaintiff's store was centrally located. Sales of Rexall products increased from only a few thousand dollars in the early days to a high point in 1923 when plaintiff's sales were about $20,000.

From that high point sales fell until in 1934, during the depression, plaintiff sold only $2,800 worth of Rexall products. By 1930, Long Beach had grown to a population of 142,000, and plaintiff's store was no longer centrally located. In the early 1930s, the chain store, a new form of retailing, became popular. A firm operating many stores could buy in larger quantities at lower prices from manufacturers. Thus, it was able to offer more variety at lower prices than the older, smaller stores that stressed service and personal relationships.

In 1936, United Drug signed a contract with the Owl Drug Company which ran stores throughout Los Angeles County, including four in Long Beach. In about 14 months, the four Owl stores in Long Beach sold about $10,600 worth of Rexall products. At that point, United Drug stopped doing business with plaintiff.

---

[21]See U.C.C. § 1-105(1); a provision typically considered in courses on Conflict of Laws. The "reasonable relation" standard is not easy to apply in close cases. Suppose a Wisconsin manufacturer sells its product to an Illinois corporation. The one drafting the contract can specify that either Wisconsin or Illinois law governs, but not the law of Argentina. Suppose, however, the Illinois buyer is a subsidiary of a large multinational corporation. The multinational is incorporated in Delaware, has home offices in New York, and has told its Illinois subsidiary to buy the machine and ship it to Argentina. Now what law might a contract drafter specify validly under the Code's test? While we will give this problem no further attention in this course, you should be aware that those who draft contracts often do specify the applicable law, and there is some limitation on their freedom to shop for a law favorable to their interests. See Gruson, Governing Law Clauses in Commercial Agreements — New York's Approach, 18 Columbia Journal of Transnational Law, 323 (1979); Covey and Morris, The Enforceability of Agreements Providing for Forum and Choice of Law Selection, 61 Denver Law Journal 837 (1984).

[22]13 Cal.2d 158, 88 P.2d 698 (1939).

Long Beach Drug Co. sued for an injunction ordering United Drug to stop supplying other drug stores in Long Beach. The trial court granted the injunction. The Supreme Court of California reversed this order. First, Justice Shenk's opinion pointed out that the California Civil Code provided "an injunction cannot be granted to prevent the breach of a contract, the performance of which would not be specifically enforced." Second, specific performance of this contract would not be proper. "Equity will not decree specific performance of contracts which by their terms stipulate for a succession of acts whose performance cannot be consummated by one transaction, but will be continuous and require protracted supervision and direction." Justice Shenk explained that to "undertake to compel defendant to sell to plaintiff, and plaintiff to purchase from defendant and to uphold all products to the full list retail price set by defendant, over an indefinite term, would impose upon the court a duty well nigh impossible of performance." The court left plaintiff to seek whatever damages it could prove.

The *Long Beach Drug* case was followed in *Thayer Plymouth Center, Inc. v. Chrysler Motors Corp.*[23] Chrysler terminated a Plymouth dealer's franchise. The parties disputed whether Chrysler's action was justified. The trial court granted the dealer a preliminary injunction pending trial to keep the business alive until it could hear the case. The District Court of Appeal reversed. The decree "would impose upon the court the impossible task of supervising continuous performance by the parties." The dealer's difficulty in proving the amount of damages did not make the legal remedy inadequate.

3. *"Law" and "Equity"*: Specific performance is one of a number of "equitable" remedies a court has at its disposal. An "equitable remedy" requires a person to do, or refrain from doing, something. For example, one can be told to perform a contract or told not to compete against her former employer. A "legal" remedy awards a judgment calling for payment of damages. Typically, a person bringing a law suit can request damages. Equitable remedies, on the other hand, are available only in special situations at the discretion of the court.

When will courts award specific performance? (1) Almost always, a court will order a defaulting party to carry out a contract to convey land. (2) Also, a court will order it when a contract calls for a seller to deliver a rare item such as a painting by a famous artist. (3) Almost never will an employer be able to compel an employee to carry out a contract. An employer may be able to convince a court to order the employee not to compete with the employer.

Why do English and American courts award damages rather than order performance in ordinary situations? Part of the explanation is historical, but, as always, history is a better explanation of why something started than why it continued and was not changed. Law and equity arose as two separate branches of the English legal system long before there was a United States. Each system had its own sphere of authority, rules, and remedies. The English common law

---

[23] 255 Cal.App. 300, 63 Cal.Rptr. 148 (4th Dist. 1967).

system developed first from *writs* issued directly by the King and later by the King's courts. A person who felt that he had been wronged would petition for relief. A writ could be issued ordering the alleged wrongdoer to appear before one of the King's judges and explain why the wrongdoer should not give a remedy to the person injured. The court might issue a writ ordering an alleged wrongdoer to appear and show cause why a sheriff or other legal official should not carry out some action.

As this procedure became more common, the King's officials developed certain standard writs. They were used for particular types of actions. The system was frozen in the Thirteenth Century, and thereafter, for a long time, no new writs were developed, and courts did not allow parties to modify the standard language of the writs to fit their particular situations. If a wrong did not fit neatly into one of the writs, the victim had no remedy "at law." English law was narrow and technical; the King's judges could not be accused of usurping his powers.

Many people who thought they had been wronged were left without remedy by the common law courts. Those with access began to petition the King directly for the relief which the law courts would not give them. The King then referred these petitions to his Chancellor. The Chancellor could order the parties to appear before him, and if he found that a wrong had been done, he would fashion a remedy to meet the situation. A system of courts, called Chancery or Equity Courts, grew up to handle these exceptional cases. This system functioned alongside the common law court system, but equity was wholly separate, with its own personnel, rules of procedure, and substantive policies.

Equity courts claimed that their function was to see that justice was done where a legal remedy would be inadequate. At the outset their concern was for substantive justice rather than technical legal reasoning. However, equitable remedies were extraordinary and reserved for cases where some defect was perceived in what was available from the law courts. One had no right to demand equitable relief. It was given only by the grace of the King. The Chancellor exercised discretion in using the King's powers, on the King's behalf.

By the Seventeenth Century, the English legal system had institutionalized courts of equity. Written reports of decisions of the equity courts were published, and the equity judges came to rely on precedents and a formalized body of law rather than exercise discretion case by case. Equity and common law courts were rivals. Each sought to expand its jurisdiction at the expense of the other. Both systems changed by using legal fictions and tricky reasoning. They began to fall into a common pattern with a rough division of labor. Finally, the two systems were merged in England by the Common Law Procedure Act of 1854 and the Judicature Act of 1873. In the United States, merger of the courts of law and equity first came when New York adopted the Field Code of 1848. Today, all but a very few states have one court system. Judges have all the old powers of the courts of law as well as those of the courts of equity.

We can still find evidence of the old dual court system in modern American law even after merger. For instance, a court will not grant an equitable remedy unless it finds there is no adequate legal remedy. This principle is reflected in the law concerning the availability of specific performance as a remedy for breach of contract. Section 2-711 of the Uniform Commercial Code gives an aggrieved buyer many kinds of damages remedies, but subsection (2)(b) says that specific performance can be obtained only in "a proper case" as defined by § 2-716. Section 2-716(1) begins by saying "[s]pecific performance may be decreed where the goods are unique...." Suppose I own a painting by Degas, and I make a contract to sell it to you. I refuse to deliver it, breaching our contract. You recover a judgment against me for the difference between the contract price and the market price. I pay the judgment. Can you take this money, plus what you would have had to pay me had I performed, and buy the Degas painting? Not unless I change my mind and sell the painting to you or to another who is willing then to sell it to you. Thus, the legal remedy is inadequate to put you where you would have been had the contract been performed. This will be true whenever the goods are truly unique. Of course, the unique goods case is not the only one where the legal remedy will be inadequate as § 2-716(1) recognizes.

Even after law and equity systems merged, important differences remain. First, one has a right to a jury trial in an action that, before merger, would have been brought in the law courts. One has no such right in what would have been an equitable action.

Second, the remedies may be different. A judgment for damages gives the successful plaintiff the right to ask a sheriff to seize the defendant's non-exempt property. The sheriff then sells it at a foreclosure sale, and pays the judgment out of the proceeds of the sale. If the defendant has little non-exempt property, then he is "judgment proof." The victory before the court is worthless.

However, an equitable decree is another matter. In the extreme case one refusing to obey an order may be found in contempt, and imprisoned, either as punishment or until she performs as ordered. In some situations a judge exercising equitable powers can carry out the order directly. For example, if defendant breaches a contract by failing to convey real property, the court's decree, in most states, can be recorded with the same effect as a conveyance. The court may "reform" a legal document because of fraud or mistake, and the court's decree can be recorded as a substitute for the original one. Of course, in most instances the threat is enough; most of those subject to equitable decrees comply and obey them.

4. *Why damages rather than specific performance today?* As we said, history may explain how things began, but many legal procedures of the past (trial by battle, for example) have not survived. Why is specific performance not the basic remedy for breach of contract with damages serving only as an auxiliary remedy? There are three major possibilities: (1) no one cares enough to bother to make any changes; (2) the practice has continued because it serves the interest of someone or some group that counts; or (3) the practice serves some larger social interest. Consider the following elaborations of these positions. Do they overstate the arguments?

(1) The distinctions between law and equity began for some reason. Once lawyers accepted these distinctions, the distinctions became the "common sense" of this elite. The rule doesn't matter enough to provoke change. Most contracts are performed because it is in everyone's long term advantage to perform. Most breaches take place when a defendant no longer can perform or pay damages. Even when this is not true, neither a suit for damages nor specific performance is attractive. Lawsuits are expensive and time consuming. One can seldom prove enough damages as the result of a breach of contract so that litigation would pay. One who gains a decree of specific performance often would have an order for a "shotgun marriage," lacking all the cooperation needed to make a social relationship work. There are many ways to avoid the threat of a contempt penalty. In short, there isn't much of a market for either damages or specific performance, and so it doesn't matter much what the formal law says about the matter. Compared to abortion, women's rights, issues of war and peace, economic recovery, jobs and the like, the issue is trivial and we cannot expect action.

(2) The damages and specific performance pattern found in United States law serves the interests of the powerful with a covering gloss of legitimacy. This is why it has not been changed. Consider *Long Beach Drug Co. v. United Drug Co.*,[24] discussed above. Long Beach had grown, but Long Beach Drug Co. had remained a small business making an acceptable profit and had not changed to move with the times. Chain stores, such as the Owl Drug Co. with stores all over Los Angeles County, were able to use their size and skill in buying and marketing to offer greater variety at lower prices. They were able to open new stores to serve population shifts so products would be available. United Drug Co. needed to move Rexall products to Owl Drug for the well-being of United's management, its stockholders, and for the benefit of consumers in Long Beach as well. Long Beach Drug's actual damages would have been extremely difficult to prove. Jurors would have had to speculate about how long the contract would last. They would have had to determine what future sales and costs would be. These questions might have turned on innovations in products and marketing techniques such as competing chain stores. The net result of the case was to leave United Drug free to move Rexall products to the Owl Drug chain. United Drug risked a damages claim by Long Beach Drug's owners. Given the cost barriers to litigation, after the Supreme Court of California's decision, Long Beach Drug Co.'s owners probably were willing to accept a token settlement to dismiss the case.

(3) The present pattern of awarding damages as the primary remedy and reserving specific performance for exceptional situations promotes the best use of resources. At the same time, it protects the legitimate interests of the parties. Suppose a town contracts with a construction company to repair and widen a

---

[24] 13 Cal.2d 158, 88 P.2d 698 (1939).

bridge over a river that flows between the northern boundary of the town and the main highway. The town is to pay the builder $1,000,000 for its work on the project. Had the project been completed, it would have cost the builder $750,000 to do the work on the bridge; the builder would have made a profit of $250,000 ($1,000,000 - $750,000 = $250,000). However, after the contract is made, the town is notified that a new interstate highway will be built to the south of the town. The old main highway to the north will be closed and blocked off. If the builder had a right to specific performance, the town might find itself paying $1,000,000 for a bridge to nowhere. This would be a foolish waste of resources. Rather, the builder is given a right to damages. They would include its $250,000 profit plus any costs of doing the work incurred before the town notified it to stop performing. The town can avoid building a useless bridge, and the builder is put where it would have been had the contract been performed. Its legitimate interests and the town's are both protected.

Whatever the merit of the three explanations of the existing law, a number of writers have advocated that courts order specific performance more often.[25] These writers point out that the reality of the American legal system in action is bargaining in the shadow of the law. Judicial visions of courts supervising performance between angry and unwilling parties are unrealistic. A court's order for specific performance often only changes the bargaining position of the parties and seldom forces an unwilling party to perform or to accept an unwanted performance. The parties will negotiate a settlement to solve the problem in light of the court's action.

For example, we learn from an earlier opinion in the *Copylease* case[26] that the dispute between the parties was caused by Memorex' officials' dissatisfaction with the terms of the underlying contract. Copylease's officials thought that Memorex was doing everything to make life miserable for Copylease so that it would abandon the contract. Officers and lawyers for both sides argued heatedly at a meeting. Each side saw the other as behaving unreasonably.

Copylease sought a preliminary injunction pending trial to establish the contract and the breach and to make Memorex perform. Memorex made a cross motion for summary judgment, challenging the validity of the contract. This prompted an early trial on the merits that took only one day. Judge Lasker wrote an opinion finding the contract to be valid and Memorex to have breached. He wrote a second opinion which you read, suggesting that Copylease might be able to win a decree of specific performance after a further hearing.

What happened then? There was no hearing. A Copylease lawyer said that shortly after Judge Lasker issued his opinion, Memorex' executives suggested

---

[25]See, *e.g.*, Kronman, Specific Performance, 45 University of Chicago Law Review 351 (1978); Schwartz, The Case for Specific Performance, 89 Yale Law Journal 271 (1979); Laycock, The Death of the Irreparable Injury Rule, 103 Harvard Law Review 687 (1990)

[26]403 F.Supp. 625 (S.D.N.Y. 1975).

negotiations. They blamed the lawyers on both sides for having caused the trouble. The executives on both sides handled the negotiations without the presence of the lawyers who had excited so much bad feeling at their earlier meeting and reached a settlement under which Memorex made a substantial monetary payment to Copylease, and they rewrote the contract more to Memorex' liking. The parties then continued to do business amicably under the revised contract, until Copylease decided to go out of the toner business in 1978. Is it likely that a settlement on similar terms would have been reached if Judge Lasker had ruled that damages was Copylease's only remedy?

The authors we cited and others argue that bargained settlements typically follow orders for specific performance. The functions of the decree are, largely, to increase the cost that the one dissatisfied with a contract must pay to get out. This far better protects the other's expectations arising from the contract than the likely negotiations when the only remedy is the damages that can be proved. This suggests that if Long Beach Drug Co. had won their order for specific performance, the result would have been to increase the price it could charge to settle the case and give up its exclusive distributorship.

A negotiated settlement, it is argued, is likely to be the best possible conclusion to the end of a long-term continuing relationship. Courts will seldom face a supervision burden, and battles about whether a decree is being carried out will be rare and won't burden the courts. What do you think of this argument when you match it against the others we set out above? On what assumptions does it rest? Are those assumptions likely accurate in some, many or most situations?

5. *The buyer's damages remedies under the U.C.C.*: To discuss specific performance, we usually must contrast that remedy with money damages. A general map of a *buyer's* remedies where it has not accepted goods, appears in Uniform Commercial Code § 2-711. This section approach is roughly the mirror image of the provisions on *seller's* remedies in § 2-703. The law seeks to influence both aggrieved sellers and aggrieved buyers to find substitute contracts; this minimizes losses. Difference measures are used to compensate for having to sell at a loss or buy above the contract price. Other remedies apply only when the substitute contract approach will not work. More particularly, buyer may cover its needs (that is, buy them from someone else) and get the difference between the contract price and cover price under § 2-712. Buyer also may recover the difference between the market price and the contract price under § 2-713. Section 2-714 deals with the buyer's remedies where it has accepted goods but something is wrong with the seller's performance. Sections 2-712, 2-713, and 2-714, in turn, all say that a buyer can recover consequential damages in a proper case as defined by § 2-715(2). One requirement is that the consequential loss "could not reasonably be prevented by cover or otherwise." The other requirement is the Code's version of *Hadley v. Baxendale*. We will study the *Hadley* case after we deal with stipulated damage clauses.

6. *Does the U.C.C. make important changes in the law of specific performance?* Consider the following problems in light of §§ 2-709, 2-716, and 1-106. Assume for purposes of this exercise that the Wisconsin courts have decided no cases relevant to the problems.

Seller, located in Milwaukee, supplies meat to restaurants. It makes a contract with a large resort in Northern Wisconsin to supply 100 restaurant prime- grade aged sirloin steaks each day for the entire tourist season at a specified price. A truck takes about two hours to travel from Milwaukee to the resort. Seller buys meat for its entire business and does not identify specific steaks as those intended for the resort until they are wrapped the night before deliveries are to be made.

Other businesses able to supply this quantity and quality of meat are located in Milwaukee and in the Minneapolis-St. Paul area but nowhere else nearer the resort. These other suppliers are unwilling to make the four- to six-hour round-trip to supply only one customer.

(A) On June 1st, Seller's President announces that she will no longer perform the contract with the resort. Make an argument that a court should grant specific performance? Cite specific language in the Code and Comments. Would, or should, it matter whether Seller repudiates in order to use its truck to deliver the meat to a new customer who has agreed to a higher price or merely wishes to withdraw from long distance deliveries?

(B) Suppose the Resort is the one that refuses to proceed with the contract. Can Seller's lawyer make a strong argument that a court should award it the contract price? Cite Code and Comments. Would, or should, it matter whether Resort repudiates because it has found a more attractive contract with a meat supplier in Minneapolis or it has lost the chef whose specialty was making sauces that made these steaks so popular with resort customers? Assume that these factors don't excuse performance of the contract.

7. *The Convention on the International Sale of Goods and Specific Performance:* Generally the Convention on International Sale of Goods provides an even more liberal specific performance remedy for both buyers and sellers than does the U.C.C. This is consistent with the practice in much of the rest of the world, where specific performance is the preferred remedy. CISG Article 46(1) provides that, "The buyer may require performance by the seller of his obligations unless the buyer has resorted to a remedy which is inconsistent with such requirements." CISG Article 62, a parallel provision for sellers, provides "The seller may require the buyer to pay the price, take delivery or perform his other obligations, unless the seller has resorted to a remedy which is inconsistent with this requirement". It is also important to note, however, that in order to "ease the position of those States whose courts regarded specific performance as

an exceptional rather than a usual remedy"[27] CISG Article 28 *permits* (but does not require) a court to refuse specific performance if it would refuse specific performance for a contract governed under its own law. Whether United States courts will choose to refuse is something only experience will tell.

D. THE EXPECTATION INTEREST: BREACH DETERRENCE VERSUS LIQUIDATED DAMAGES

LAKE RIVER CORPORATION v. CARBORUNDUM COMPANY

769 F.2d 1284 (7th Cir. 1985)

POSNER, J. This diversity suit between Lake River Corporation and Carborundum Company requires us to consider questions of Illinois commercial law, and in particular to explore the fuzzy line between penalty clauses and liquidated-damages clauses.

Carborundum manufactures "Ferro Carbo," an abrasive powder used in making steel. To serve its midwestern customers better, Carborundum made a contract with Lake River by which the latter agreed to provide distribution services in its warehouse in Illinois. Lake River would receive Ferro Carbo in bulk from Carborundum, "bag" it, and ship the bagged product to Carborundum's customers. The Ferro Carbo would remain Carborundum's property until delivered to the customers.

Carborundum insisted that Lake River install a new bagging system to handle the contract. In order to be sure of being able to recover the cost of the new system ($89,000) and make a profit of 20 percent of the contract price, Lake River insisted on the following minimum-quantity guarantee:

> In consideration of the special equipment [i.e., the new bagging system] to be acquired and furnished by LAKE-RIVER for handling the product, CARBORUNDUM shall, during the initial three-year term of this Agreement, ship to LAKE-RIVER for bagging a minimum quantity of [22,500 tons]. If, at the end of the three- year term, this minimum quantity shall not have been shipped, LAKE-RIVER shall invoice CARBORUNDUM at the then prevailing rates for the difference between the quantity bagged and the minimum guaranteed.

If Carborundum had shipped the full minimum quantity that it guaranteed, it would have owed Lake River roughly $533,000 under the contract.

---

[27]Summary Records of Committee Meetings of the Vienna Conference, quoted in Kritzer, Guide to the Practical Applications of the United Nations Convention on Contracts for the International Sale of Goods, p. 213.

After the contract was signed in 1979, the demand for domestic steel, and with it the demand for Ferro Carbo, plummeted, and Carborundum failed to ship the guaranteed amount. When the contract expired late in 1982, Carborundum had shipped only 12,000 of the 22,500 tons it had guaranteed. Lake River had bagged the 12,000 tons and had billed Carborundum for this bagging, and Carborundum had paid, but by virtue of the formula in the minimum-guarantee clause Carborundum still owed Lake River $241,000 — the contract price of $533,000 if the full amount of Ferro Carbo had been shipped, minus what Carborundum had paid for the bagging of the quantity it had shipped.

When Lake River demanded payment of this amount, Carborundum refused, on the ground that the formula imposed a penalty. At the time, Lake River had in its warehouse 500 tons of bagged Ferro Carbo, having a market value of $269,000, which it refused to release unless Carborundum paid the $241,000 due under the formula. Lake River did offer to sell the bagged product and place the proceeds in escrow until its dispute with Carborundum over the enforceability of the formula was resolved, but Carborundum rejected the offer and trucked in bagged Ferro Carbo from the East to serve its customers in Illinois, at an additional cost of $31,000.

Lake River brought this suit for $241,000, which it claims as liquidated damages. Carborundum counterclaimed for the value of the bagged Ferro Carbo when Lake River impounded it and the additional cost of serving the customers affected by the impounding. The theory of the counterclaim is that the impounding was a conversion, and not as Lake River contends the assertion of a lien.[28] The district judge, after a bench trial, gave judgment for both parties. Carborundum ended up roughly $42,000 to the good: $269,000 + $31,000 - $241,000 - $17,000, the last figure representing prejudgment interest on Lake River's damages. (We have rounded off all dollar figures to the nearest thousand.) Both parties have appealed.

The only issue that is not one of damages is whether Lake River had a valid lien on the bagged Ferro Carbo that it refused to ship to Carborundum's customers — that, indeed, it holds in its warehouse to this day. Although Ferro Carbo does not deteriorate with age, the domestic steel industry remains in the doldrums and the product is worth less than it was in 1982 when Lake River first withheld it. If Lake River did not have a valid lien on the product, then it

---

[28][Eds. Note: A "conversion" is the legal term for the civil wrong of taking possession without the right to do so. The crime of theft may involve the tort, or civil wrong, of conversion. (Not all conversions, of course, are crimes.) Sometimes one has a privilege to take possession against the wishes of the owner. One such case arises when a creditor is granted a *lien* against the property; the holder of a lien has a right to demand that the property subject to the lien be sold and the proceeds used to pay the debt to the creditor. You may have heard of a "mechanic's lien"; statutes often grant garages, for example, a right to retain possession of a repaired car until the bill is paid. Lake River, in this case, is claiming it has a right analogous to a mechanic's lien.]

converted it, and must pay Carborundum the $269,000 that the Ferro Carbo was worth back then.

It might seem that if the minimum-guarantee clause was a penalty clause and hence unenforceable, the lien could not be valid, and therefore that we should discuss the penalty issue first. But this is not correct. If the contractual specification of damages is invalid, Lake River still is entitled to any actual damages caused by Carborundum's breach of contract in failing to deliver the minimum amount of Ferro Carbo called for by the contract. The issue is whether an entitlement to damages, large or small, entitles the victim of the breach to assert a lien on goods that are in its possession though they belong to the other party.

[The court rejected Lake River's claim that it was entitled to assert a lien on the Ferro Carbo in its possession, noting that

> When as a practical matter the legal remedy may be inadequate because it operates too slowly, self-help is allowed. But we can find no case recognizing a lien on facts like these, no ground for thinking that the Illinois Supreme Court would be the first court to recognize such a lien if this case were presented to it, and no reason to believe that the recognition of such a lien would be a good thing. It would impede the marketability of goods without responding to any urgent need of creditors.

The court then turned to the question of the validity of the liquidated damages clause.]

The hardest issue in the case is whether the formula in the minimum-guarantee clause imposes a penalty for breach of contract or is merely an effort to liquidate damages. Deep as the hostility to penalty clauses runs in the common law, see Loyd, Penalties and Forfeitures, 29 Harvard Law Review 117 (1915), we still might be inclined to question, if we thought ourselves free to do so, whether a modern court should refuse to enforce a penalty clause where the signator is a substantial corporation, well able to avoid improvident commitments. Penalty clauses provide an earnest of performance. The clause here enhanced Carborundum's credibility in promising to ship the minimum amount guaranteed by showing that it was willing to pay the full contract price even if it failed to ship anything. On the other side it can be pointed out that by raising the cost of a breach of contract to the contract breaker, a penalty clause increases the risk to his other creditors; increases (what is the same thing and more, because bankruptcy imposes "deadweight" social costs) the risk of bankruptcy; and could amplify the business cycle by increasing the number of bankruptcies in bad times, which is when contracts are most likely to be broken. But since little effort is made to prevent businessmen from assuming risks, these reasons are no better than makeweights.

A better argument is that a penalty clause may discourage efficient as well as inefficient breaches of contract. Suppose a breach would cost the promisee $12,000 in actual damages but would yield the promisor $20,000 in additional profits. Then there would be a net social gain from breach. After being fully compensated for his loss the promisee would be no worse off than if the contract had been performed, while the promisor would be better off by $8,000. But now suppose the contract contains a penalty clause under which the promisor if he breaks his promise must pay the promisee $25,000. The promisor will be discouraged from breaking the contract, since $25,000, the penalty, is greater than $20,000, the profits of the breach; and a transaction that would have increased value will be foregone.

On this view, since compensatory damages should be sufficient to deter inefficient breaches (that is, breaches that cost the victim more than the gain to the contract breaker), penal damages could have no effect other than to deter some efficient breaches. But this overlooks the earlier point that the willingness to agree to a penalty clause is a way of making the promisor and his promise credible and may therefore be essential to inducing some value- maximizing contracts to be made. It also overlooks the more important point that the parties (always assuming they are fully competent) will, in deciding whether to include a penalty clause in their contract, weigh the gains against the costs — costs that include the possibility of discouraging an efficient breach somewhere down the road — and will include the clause only if the benefits exceed those costs as well as all other costs.

On this view the refusal to enforce penalty clauses is (at best) paternalistic — and it seems odd that courts should display parental solicitude for large corporations. But however this may be, we must be on guard to avoid importing our own ideas of sound public policy into an area where our proper judicial role is more than usually deferential. The responsibility for making innovations in the common law of Illinois rests with the courts of Illinois, and not with the federal courts in Illinois. And like every other state, Illinois, untroubled by academic skepticism of the wisdom of refusing to enforce penalty clauses against sophisticated promisors, see, *e.g.*, Goetz & Scott, Liquidated Damages, Penalties and the Just Compensation Principle, 77 Columbia Law Review 554 (1977), continues steadfastly to insist on the distinction between penalties and liquidated damages. [Numerous citations omitted] To be valid under Illinois law a liquidation of damages must be a reasonable estimate at the time of contracting of the likely damages from breach, and the need for estimation at that time must be shown by reference to the likely difficulty of measuring the actual damages from a breach of contract after the breach occurs. If damages would be easy to determine then, or if the estimate greatly exceeds a reasonable upper estimate of what the damages are likely to be, it is a penalty. [citation omitted]

The distinction between a penalty and liquidated damages is not an easy one to draw in practice but we are required to draw it and can give only limited weight to the district court's determination. Whether a provision for damages is a penalty clause or a liquidated-damages clause is a question of law rather than fact, [citations omitted] and unlike some courts of appeals we do not treat a determination by a federal district judge of an issue of state law as if it were a finding of fact, and reverse only if persuaded that clear error has occurred, though we give his determination respectful consideration. [citations omitted]

Mindful that Illinois courts resolve doubtful cases in favor of classification as a penalty, [citations omitted] we conclude that the damage formula in this case is a penalty and not a liquidation of damages, because it is designed always to assure Lake River more than its actual damages. The formula — full contract price minus the amount already invoiced to Carborundum — is invariant to the gravity of the breach. When a contract specifies a single sum in damages for any and all breaches even though it is apparent that all are not of the same gravity, the specification is not a reasonable effort to estimate damages; and when in addition the fixed sum greatly exceeds the actual damages likely to be inflicted by a minor breach, its character as a penalty becomes unmistakable. [citations omitted] This case is within the gravitational field of these principles even though the minimum-guarantee clause does not fix a single sum as damages.

Suppose to begin with that the breach occurs the day after Lake River buys its new bagging system for $89,000 and before Carborundum ships any Ferro Carbo. Carborundum would owe Lake River $533,000. Since Lake River would have incurred at that point a total cost of only $89,000, its net gain from the breach would be $444,000. This is more than four times the profit of $107,000 (20 percent of the contract price of $533,000) that Lake River expected to make from the contract if it had been performed: a huge windfall.

Next suppose (as actually happened here) that breach occurs when 55 percent of the Ferro Carbo has been shipped. Lake River would already have received $293,000 from Carborundum. To see what its costs then would have been (as estimated at the time of contracting), first subtract Lake River's anticipated profit on the contract of $107,000 from the total contract price of $533,000. The difference — Lake River's total cost of performance — is $426,000. Of this, $89,000 is the cost of the new bagging system, a fixed cost. The rest ($426,000-$89,000 = $337,000) presumably consists of variable costs that are roughly proportional to the amount of Ferro Carbo bagged; there is no indication of any other fixed costs. Assume, therefore, that if Lake River bagged 55 percent of the contractually agreed quantity, it incurred in doing so 55 percent of its variable costs, or $185,000. When this is added to the cost of the new bagging system, assumed for the moment to be worthless except in connection with the contract, the total cost of performance to Lake River is $274,000. Hence a breach that occurred after 55 percent of contractual performance was complete would be expected to yield Lake River a modest profit of $19,000 ($293,000-$274,000). But now add the "liquidated damages" of $241,000 that Lake River claims, and the result is a total gain from the breach of $260,000, which is almost two and a half times the profit that Lake River expected to gain if there was no breach. And this ignores any use value or salvage value of the new bagging system, which is the property of Lake River — though admittedly it also ignores the time value of money; Lake River paid $89,000 for that system before receiving any revenue from the contract.

To complete the picture, assume that the breach had not occurred till performance was 90 percent complete. Then the "liquidated damages" clause would not be so one-sided, but it would be one-sided. Carborundum would have paid $480,000 for bagging. Against this, Lake River would have incurred its fixed cost of $89,000 plus 90 percent of its variable costs of $337,000, or $303,000. Its total costs would thus be $392,000, and its net profit $88,000. But on top of this it would be entitled to "liquidated damages" of $53,000, for a total profit of $141,000 — more than 30 percent more than its expected profit of $107,000 if there was no breach.

The reason for these results is that most of the costs to Lake River of performing the contract are saved if the contract is broken, and this saving is not reflected in the damage formula. As a result, at whatever point in the life of the contract a breach occurs, the damage formula gives Lake River more than its lost profits from the breach — dramatically more if the breach occurs at the beginning of the contract; tapering off at the end, it is true. Still, over the interval between the beginning of Lake River's performance and nearly the end, the clause could be expected to generate profits ranging from 400 percent of the expected contract profits to 130 percent of those profits. And this is on the assumption that the bagging system has no value apart from the contract. If it were worth only $20,000 to Lake River, the range would be 434 percent to 150 percent.... .

With the penalty clause in this case compare the liquidated-damages clause in *Arduini v. Board of Education, supra*, which is representative of such clauses upheld in Illinois. The plaintiff was a public school teacher whose contract provided that if he resigned before the end of the school year he would be docked 4 percent of his salary. This was a modest fraction of the contract price. And the cost to the school of an untimely resignation would be difficult to measure. Since that cost would be greater the more senior and experienced the teacher was, the fact that the liquidated damages would be greater the higher the teacher's salary did not make the clause arbitrary. Even the fact that the liquidated damages were the same whether the teacher resigned at the beginning, the middle, or the end of the school year was not arbitrary, for it was unclear how the amount of actual damages would vary with the time of resignation. Although one might think that the earlier the teacher resigned the greater the damage to the school would be, the school might find it easier to hire a replacement for the whole year or a great part of it than to bring in a replacement at the last minute to grade the exams left behind by the resigning teacher. Here, in contrast, it is apparent from the face of the contract that the damages provided for by the "liquidated damages" clause are grossly disproportionate to any probable loss and penalize some breaches much more heavily than others regardless of relative cost....

The fact that the damage formula is invalid does not deprive Lake River of a remedy. The parties did not contract explicitly with reference to the measure of damages if the agreed-on damage formula was invalidated, but all this means is that the victim of the breach is entitled to his common law damages. See, *e.g.*, Restatement, Second, Contracts § 356, Comment a (1981). In this case that would be the unpaid contract price of $241,000 minus the costs that Lake River saved by not having to complete the contract (the variable costs on the other 45 percent of the Ferro Carbo that it never had to bag). The case must be remanded to the district judge to fix these damages.

Two damage issues remain. The first concerns Carborundum's expenses of delivering bagged Ferro Carbo to its customers to replace that impounded by Lake River. The district judge gave Carborundum the full market value of the bagged Ferro Carbo. Lake River argues that it should not have to pay for Carborundum's expense of selling additional Ferro Carbo — additional in the sense that Carborundum is being given credit for the full retail value of the product that Lake River withheld. To explain, suppose that Carborundum had an order for $1,000 worth of bagged Ferro Carbo, which Lake River was supposed to deliver; and because it refused, Carborundum incurred a transportation cost of $100 to make a substitute shipment of bagged Ferro Carbo to the customer. Carborundum would still get $1,000 from the customer, and if that price covered the transportation cost it would still make a profit. In what sense, therefore, is that cost a separate item of damage, of loss? On all Ferro Carbo (related to this case) sold by Carborundum in the Midwest, Carborundum received the full market price, either from its customers in the case of Ferro Carbo actually delivered to them, or from Lake River in the case of the Ferro Carbo that Lake River refused to deliver. Having received a price designed to cover all expenses of sale, a seller cannot also get an additional damage award for any of those expenses.

If, however, the additional Ferro Carbo that Carborundum delivered to its midwestern customers in substitution for Ferro Carbo previously delivered to, and impounded by, Lake River would have been sold in the East at the same price but lower cost, Carborundum would have had an additional loss, in the form of reduced profits, for which it could recover additional damages. But it made no effort to prove such a loss. Maybe it had no unsatisfied eastern customers, and expanded rather than shifted output to fulfill its midwestern customers' demand. The damages on the counterclaim must be refigured also.

Finally, Lake River argues that Carborundum failed to mitigate its damages by accepting Lake River's offer to deliver the bagged product and place the proceeds in escrow. But a converter is not entitled to retain the proceeds of the conversion even temporarily. Lake River had an opportunity to limit its exposure by selling the bagged product on Carborundum's account and deducting what it claimed was due it on its "lien." Its failure to follow this course reinforces our conclusion that the assertion of the lien was a naked attempt to hold Carborundum hostage to Lake River's view — an erroneous view, as it has turned out — of the enforceability of the damage formula in the contract.

The judgment of the district court is affirmed in part and reversed in part, and the case is returned to that court to redetermine both parties' damages in accordance with the principles in this opinion. The parties may present additional evidence on remand, and shall bear their own costs in this court.

Affirmed in part, reversed in part, and remanded.

NOTES AND QUESTIONS

1. *The American Law Institute on stipulated damages*: Towards the end of his opinion Judge Posner cites Restatement (Second) of Contracts § 356(1), which provides:[29]

> Damages for breach by either party may be liquidated in the agreement but only at an amount that is reasonable in the light of the anticipated or actual loss caused by the breach and the difficulties of proof of loss. A term fixing unreasonably large liquidated damages is unenforceable on grounds of public policy as a penalty.

Compare the Restatement with U.C.C. § 2-718(1). How, if at all, does the Restatement differ from the Code? Is the difference likely to matter practically?

Students sometimes have difficulty understanding what the American Law Institute's Restatements are. It is tempting to take them as an accurate statement of "the law," but lawyers can never safely assume that this is the case. Restatements have been prepared for many areas of law including contracts. They represent an effort by a committee of legal scholars, judges and lawyers, acting under the auspices of the American Law Institute, to summarize and refine basic principles of common law developed by courts. These principles are set forth in numbered sections followed by explanatory notes. While at first glance, they may look like the Uniform Commercial Code in form, they differ in fundamental purpose. The U.C.C. is a statute passed by legislators; its text is the law. The Restatements are descriptions and refinements of court decisions. They are not law but suggestions of common law rules that courts could use in future cases. Only when courts accept the suggestion and follow a Restatement provision does it become a governing precedent for the court that adopted it.

The Restatement of Contracts was published in 1932. It reflected a compromise of the views of the leading scholars of its day. It has been very successful in prompting citations to itself by judges. Notice, however, that we cannot be sure whether a judge cites a Restatement to indicate that it caused her decision or only as part of the process of rationalizing a decision based on other grounds. A revised Restatement (Second) of Contracts was begun in 1962 and finally appeared in 1981. It, too, represents a compromise of the views of leading

---

[29]Although we quote the Restatement section here, henceforth in these materials we will just cite to the Restatement and expect the student to gain access to the text of the section cited from some other source.

scholars of the 1950s, 60s and 70s filtered through the elaborate committee process of the American Law Institute.

One tension in the Restatement process involves the conflict between the prescriptive and the descriptive. The ALI's presentation of its efforts stresses describing the law as fashioned by the courts. Nonetheless, the drafters face conflicting lines of authority and must make choices. And occasionally, the Restaters just innovate.

Another tension involves the ALI's image of apolitical neutrality when its work involves significant choices between competing norms. Left-wing radicals, right-wing religious fundamentalists, personal injury plaintiffs' lawyers, faculty members of smaller and lesser known law schools, and people of color are likely to be underrepresented on the American Law Institute committees. Perhaps this makes no difference. Nonetheless, students should always remember that individuals write and revise Restatements. They must be influenced by what passes for common sense in their time. Students would waste their time challenging the good faith and intelligence of those involved, but should feel free to challenge the assumptions and value judgments implicit in these documents.

2. *Stipulated damages and economic efficiency*: Judge Posner often casts his arguments in terms of advancing "economic efficiency." He raises questions in his opinion as to whether the law of stipulated damages is consistent with the operation of an efficient market. Students of welfare economics would recognize some of Posner's argument as pointing toward a *Pareto optimal* situation. Many writers tell us that the law should promote *Pareto optimal* transactions. When a particular activity makes at least some people better off while making no one worse off, the activity is in the general social interest. It enhances total social wealth. As a result, so-called efficient breaches of contract should be encouraged. This is the usual contemporary justification for refusing to enforce penalty clauses. They get in the way of efficient breach.

We can question this efficiency analysis in several ways. We might ask whether it takes account of the interests of all those potentially affected by a breach. What, for example, of the interests of persons other than the parties to the contract. What of the interests of employees? People who are not parties to the agreement itself may have relied on it, by taking jobs with the victim of the breach, for example. Furthermore, the analysis is most powerful when we assume that the victim's damages are easy to determine. When the amount of the damages is uncertain, we cannot be sure that a settlement will put the victim where it would have been had the contract been performed. There is a chance that the victim will be worse off, and then the situation will not be *Pareto optimal*.

Moreover, in recent years a number of writers have argued that it is not necessary to hold some stipulated remedy clauses unenforceable to prompt efficient breaches. They contend that a party who would make an efficient breach if there were no stipulated remedy clause would approach the other party and seek to negotiate an agreed cancellation of the clause. The party seeking release from the stipulated remedy clause would offer to share the benefits of an efficient breach in return for the release. The stipulated remedy provision in the contract would serve only as a bargaining entitlement.

Writers who offer this hypothetical negotiation which produces an efficient breach urge courts to enforce stipulated remedy clauses in most circumstances where such clauses are the product of free agreement. This will still produce *Pareto optimal* solutions in the kinds of cases we have described. Furthermore, this position avoids the difficulties that courts have long faced in distinguishing valid liquidated damages provisions from unenforceable penalty clauses.[30]

This analysis can be illustrated using the facts of *Lake River*. Judge Posner reasons that Lake River would have made a profit of $260,000 if the stipulated remedy clause had been enforced, whereas it anticipated a profit of only $107,000 if there had been no breach. If Carborundum anticipated that the stipulated remedy clause would have been enforced, it would have made sense to offer Lake River, before any breach, a lump sum considerably less than the stipulated remedy clause to induce them to tear up the contract. Suppose, for example, Carborundum offered Lake River $100,000 to terminate the contract. On Judge Posner's analysis, Lake River would still have made an overall profit of $119,000, which is more than it anticipated profit from complete performance of $107,000. Even if Lake River believed that Carborundum would continue with performance if its offer were declined, it would be in Lake River's self-interest to accept the $100,000 offer. Then the efficient breach would have occurred even if the law enforced all stipulated remedy clauses — even ones now considered penalties.

Do you agree with Judge Posner's position? Consider the next note and question before you reach a final conclusion.

3. *"A pound of flesh," popular culture, and the law*: Shakespeare's *The Merchant of Venice*, first produced in 1600, is the source of a vivid and influential image that to this day colors our culture's responses to forfeitures and penalty clauses — the pound of flesh.[31] In the play the law's reluctance to allow

---

[30]See Clarkson, Miller & Muris, Liquidated Damages v. Penalties: Sense or Nonsense, 1978 Wisconsin Law Review 351; Goetz and Scott, Liquidated Damages, Penalties and the Just Compensation Principle: Some Notes on an Enforcement Model and a Theory of Efficient Breach, 77 Columbia Law Review 554 (1977).

[31]Lawrence W. Levine notes that "Like the Elizabethans, a substantial portion of nineteenth-century American audiences knew their Shakespeare well." "Although nineteenth century Americans stressed the importance of literacy . . . , theirs remained an oral world in which the spoken word was central. In such a world Shakespeare had no difficulty finding a place. Nor was Shakespearean oratory confined to the professional stage; it often was a part of life. . . . In the 1850s Mark Twain worked as an apprentice to the pilot-master George Ealer on the steamboat Pennsylvania: 'He would read Shakespeare to me; not just casually, but by the hour, when it was his watch, and I was steering . . . He did not use the book, and did not need to; he knew his Shakespeare as well as Euclid ever knew his multiplication table.' Shakespeare became elite culture only toward the end of the 19th century and the beginning of the 20th." Levine, William

parties to deter breach by making the consequences for the breacher highly undesirable resonates with profound themes of hostility to outsiders. In *The Merchant of Venice* it is amplifed by the long established demonization of Jews,[32] but such hostility may be aroused by any outsider with whom one has economic relations but not shared communal fellowship. Does the play also suggest other reasons for the law's refusal to enforce what we call "penalty clauses" today?

Shakespeare's play begins with Bassanio in need of money so he might seek the hand of Portia, an heiress from Belmont. Bassanio is something of a spendthrift, constantly in debt. Most is owed to his friend Antonio, a merchant of Venice. Antonio, however, gives freely of his wealth and is willing to finance Bassanio, but there is a problem. All Antonio's money is tied up at present, his ships still at sea. Antonio sends Bassanio out into Venice to seek a loan using Antonio's credit rating for collateral. Bassanio goes to Shylock, a rich Jewish merchant of Venice, to seek three thousand ducats. Shylock agrees. Antonio, who has reviled Shylock, comes to close the deal. There being no love lost between the two merchants, an unusual contract is finally struck.

> *Shylock.* This kindness will I show.
> Go with me to a notary, seal me there
> Your single bond; and, in a merry sport,
> If you repay me not on such a day,
> In such a place, such sum or sums as are
> Express'd in the condition, let the forfeit
> Be nominated for an equal pound
> Of your fair flesh, to be cut off and taken
> In what part of your body pleaseth me.
> *Antonio.* Content, in faith; I'll seal to such a bond,
> And say there is much kindness in a Jew.

Shortly thereafter Shylock's reason for demanding the penalty clause becomes evident. He is asked why he wants a pound of flesh, "what's that good for?" He rages:

> *Shylock.* To bait fish withal: If it will feed nothing
> else, it will feed my revenge. He hath disgraced me, and
> hindered me half a million, laughed at my losses, mocked at
> my gains, scorned my nation, thwarted my bargains, cooled my

---

Shakespeare and the American People: A Study in Cultural Transformation, 89 American History Review 34 (1984).

[32] In a recent and comprehensive review of the Shylock legend, English critic John Gross observes that "behind the usurer enforcing his bond there looms that ultimate bogeyman, the Jew intent on shedding Christian blood for its own sake." John Gross, Shylock: A Legend and Its Legacy (New York: Touchstone Books, 1994) 29.

friends, heated mine enemies; and what's his reason? I am a
Jew. Hath not a Jew eyes? Hath not a Jew hands, organs,
dimensions, senses, affections, passions? -fed with the same
food, hurt with the same weapons, subject to the same
diseases, healed by the same means, warmed and cooled by the
same winter and summer, as a Christian is? If you prick us,
do we not bleed? If you tickle us, do we not laugh? if you
poison us, do we not die? And if you wrong us, shall we not
revenge? If we are like you in the rest, we will resemble
you in that. If a Jew wrong a Christian, what is his
humility? Revenge. If a Christian wrong a Jew, what should
his sufferance be by Christian example? Why, revenge. The
villainy you teach me I will execute, and it shall go hard
but I will better the instruction.

The inevitable occurs. Antonio's ships do not come in. Bassanio has better
fortune as he has succeeded in courting the heiress. The trial nears, and Antonio
and a friend discuss the legalities involved.

Solanio. I am sure the duke [the judge]
Will never grant this forfeiture to hold.
(Antonio) The duke cannot deny the course of law:
For the commodity that strangers have
With us in Venice, if it be denied,
Will much impeach the justice of the state;
Since that the trade and profit of the city
Consisteth of all nations. Therefore, go:
These griefs and losses have so bated me,
That I shall hardly spare a pound of flesh
To-morrow to my bloody creditor.

Antonio's friends offer Shylock more than 3,000 ducats if he agrees to waive the
bond. However, settlement attempts fail. The matter is now in the hands of the
Court. The duke calls Shylock to open court. The duke seeks to persuade
Shylock to have pity and not take his pound of flesh.
Shylock, undeterred, responds,

I have possess'd your Grace of what I purpose;
And by our Holy Sabbath have I sworn
To have the due and forfeit of my bond:
If you deny it, let the danger light
Upon your charter and your city's freedom.
You'll ask me, why I rather choose to have
A weight of carrion flesh than to receive

Three thousand ducats: I'll not answer that:
But say it is my humour: is it answer'd?
What if my house be troubled with a rat,
And I be pleas'd to give ten thousand ducats
To have it ban'd? What, are you answer'd yet?
Some men there are love not a gaping pig:
Some, that are mad if they behold a cat;
And others, when the bagpipe sings i' the nose,
Cannot contain their urine: for affection,
Master of passion, sways it to the mood
Of what it likes, or loathes. Now, for your answer:
As there is no firm reason to be render'd,
Why he cannot abide a gaping pig;
Why he a harmless necessary cat;
Why he, a woolen bagpipe; — but of force
Must yield to such inevitable shame
As to offend, himself being offended;
So can I give no reason, nor will I not,
More than a lodg'd hate and a certain loathing
I bear Antonio, that I follow thus
A losing suit against him. Are you answer'd?

[Stay tuned. What happens next will be reported in Chapter 4 of these materials.]

4. *Termination clauses in employee contracts*: Business practice usually moves ahead of legal form. People respond to a recurrent problem, and then later lawyers struggle to fit the response into existing legal categories. In the early 1970's the Wall Street Journal reported[33] that it was becoming increasingly common for companies, particularly troubled companies seeking to reverse their fortunes by bringing in outside managers, to give those executives contracts containing generous termination provisions. Sometimes those contracts provided that if the company terminated an employee for any reason that employee was entitled to one or more years of salary, or even to an amount greater than the annual salary.

(A) Suppose that an executive had a termination agreement of the type described above. The agreement provided for payment of a larger sum upon dismissal than the executive would be able to collect in a suit for breach of contract. For example, the employee was able to mitigate by finding another job shortly after termination. Are there any legal or policy objections to enforcing a termination agreement? For example, if courts would enforce the agreement, a company might be reluctant to fire an inefficient but minimally competent executive.

---

[33]Wall Street Journal, Dec. 11, 1972, p. 1, col. 6.

(B) Suppose it were established law that termination agreements of the type discussed in the Wall Street Journal article were legally unenforceable to the extent they provided for greater payments than could be collected in a suit for breach of contract. The authors of these materials would still expect most companies to honor the agreements. Why?

(C) What are the functions of employment contracts and termination agreements, and are they a good idea? Executives expressed a number of views in a 1984 Forbes magazine article.[34] One suggested that contracts were especially useful in high-risk, high-reward, intensively competitive industries in which companies were worried about talented employees being hired away by competitors. Another suggested that the contracts were useful in the recruitment of middle-managers who traditionally had little job security. But a consultant expressed skepticism. He found such contracts "neurotic" and suggested that they implied reciprocal doubts about the relationship.

5. *A stipulated damages clause is upheld*: The Supreme Court of Wisconsin considered termination clauses in *Wassenaar v. Panos*.[35] An employer hired plaintiff to manage a hotel for three years. The employer drafted a written contract which both signed. It provided that in case of termination without cause the employer would be "responsible for fulfilling the entire financial obligation as set forth within this agreement for the full period of three years." The employer fired plaintiff without cause about twenty-one months before the contract expired. He was out of work for about two-and-one-half months, and then another hotel hired him.

The Supreme Court of Wisconsin affirmed the trial court's finding that this was a liquidated damages clause and not a penalty. Justice Abrahamson discussed the legal standards at length in light of many law review articles on the subject. She considered both the Restatement and the Uniform Commercial Code. She said that two factors are important: First, whether the injury caused by the breach was difficult or incapable of accurate estimation when the parties made the contract. Second, whether the stipulated damages were a reasonable forecast of the harm caused by the breach. However, "reasonableness of the stipulated damages clause cannot be determined by a mechanical application of" these factors. She noted that these factors are intertwined, and both use a combined prospective-retrospective approach. While courts often say that the amount of actual loss at the time of trial is irrelevant, the cases show that "facts available at trial significantly affect the court's determination of the reasonableness of the stipulated damages clause. If the damages provided for in the contract are grossly disproportionate to the actual harm sustained, the courts usually conclude that the parties' original expectations were unreasonable."

---

[34]Forbes, February 13, 1984, pp. 150, 154

[35]111 Wis.2d 518, 331 N.W.2d 357 (1983).

The employer argued that the stipulated damages clause in the case was void as a penalty because the harm to the employee was capable of estimation when the contract was made and was relatively easy to prove at trial. Justice Abraham-son noted:

> [t]he standard calculation of damages after breach, however, may not reflect the actual harm suffered because of the breach. In addition to the damages reflected in the black-letter formulation, an employee may suffer consequential damages, including permanent injury to professional reputation, loss of career development opportunities, and emotional distress.... The usual arguments against allowing recovery for consequential damages — that they are not foreseeable and that no dollar value can be set by a court — fail when the parties foresee the possibility of such harm and agree on an estimated amount.

The clause passed the difficulty of estimation test. The employer also argued that since the employee obtained another job within a short time, this showed that the clause was unreasonable. Justice Abrahamson responded there was no evidence in the record showing that the stipulated amount was grossly disproportionate to the actual harm suffered. The employer had the burden of establishing this to overturn the clause once there was evidence that the employee had suffered some loss.

Are the *Lake River* and *Wassenaar* cases consistent?

5. *The Convention on the International Sale of Goods and Stipulated Damages*: CISG does not address the question of penalty clauses. This means that the parties will be able to enforce penalty clauses if the gap-filling law is the law of a jurisdiction that permits enforcement — which civil law countries generally do. On the other hand, if the gap-filling law is the law of the United States, for example, the U.S. law of liquidated damages would be applied.

E. THE EXPECTATION INTEREST: LOST ANTICIPATED PROFITS AND CONSEQUENTIAL DAMAGES

The announced goal of contracts damages is to protect the expectation interest — we say that we want to put the aggrieved parties where they would have been had the contract been performed. Typically, however, the law offers a measure of damages that treats aggrieved parties as if they had sold the goods or services to another or satisfied their needs by buying substitute goods elsewhere. The victim is entitled, under this measure, to the difference between the contract price and the cost of the available substitute. This measure is said to provide "difference money damages." It is hard to get specific performance, and one cannot structure a contract to deter breach by including a provision calling for a pound of flesh in the event of nonperformance. We already have asked whether the law has adopted means well suited to the announced end. However, conflicting policies and questions of means to achieve ends are highlighted when we turn to "consequential damages."

What are consequential damages? To take a very simple example, suppose Steak Restaurant makes a contract to buy its steaks from a wholesale butcher (Supplier) at a low price. The supplier makes a mistake in calculating its need for steaks, and has too little to fill the orders of all its customers. Supplier decides, a day before it is supposed to deliver steaks to Steak Restaurant to deliver the inventory it has to a different restaurant (its oldest customer). The failure to deliver the steaks in a timely fashion forces Restaurant to close for two days while substitute steaks are obtained. Restaurant loses not only the benefit of the low price for steaks specified by the contract, but the profit it would have made selling the steaks to restaurant patrons. In addition, some of the food it might have bought to serve with the steaks (fresh vegetables and salads) might be spoiled, or re-sold at a loss. In addition it might have to pay cooks and other employees while the restaurant was closed, and might also lose some of its "goodwill" in the community. In order to put Restaurant in the position it would have been in if the contract had been performed, substantial damages might be required in addition to any difference between the contract price of the steaks and its market price. As we shall learn, Restaurant may face real difficulty in winning such damages. We will be interested in when such damages can and cannot be won, and why.

At this point, we are ready to turn to *Hadley v. Baxendale*, a truly classic case. Many of you will read this case in Richard Danzig, *The Capability Problem in Contract Law* (Foundation Press 1978). We include the case subsequently in the text for classes that are not using the Danzig text as a supplement to the materials. For those readers using the Danzig text, we ask you to consider the utility of reading lengthy stories about several cases which we take up in this course. To this end, we offer, first, excerpts from a letter which was written by Professor Robert Gordon[36] at the request of the publisher of Danzig's book. Second, we offer excerpts from a review of the Danzig book by Professor Kevin Tierney which cautions against the dangers of too much realism.

---

[36]Professor Gordon is now a member of the Stanford Law School faculty. At the time he wrote this letter he was a member of the Wisconsin Law School faculty and a user of an earlier edition of these materials in his Contracts class.

1. CASES IN CONTEXT: LESSONS AND DANGERS

R. Danzig's The Capability Problem in Contract Law
Comment by Robert Gordon

... Yet I want to emphasize that I'm not pushing this book because I think it will show something of the "human side of practice" to law students, though in fact it will do that, but for the fundamental intellectual problems that it raises. Danzig's own introductory text (in contrast to some of the wicked questions he sticks after the stories) seems unduly selective in saying what these problems are. By calling them problems of "capability" he implies that what are being exposed are merely slippages or inefficiencies in the legal system, such as the difficulties in the way of using law to control primary behavior, or to vindicate grievances, or the unreliability of litigation process as a way of finding facts. These points are true and important, but by focusing scowlingly on inefficiencies he tends to reinforce the Mugwump Ideal that the stories themselves radically subvert. The stories subvert it because they reveal the great gulfs between the experiential worlds of appellate and trial courts, and of the legal and law participants. The "facts" recited in the appellate opinions bear a relation to the "facts" of Danzig's accounts similar to the *Odyssey's* relation to Mycenaean history (much less attenuated, to be sure). The facts receive a mythic rendering intended to satisfy the exacting literary form of the legal opinion (which requires, for example, that a "Contracts" case be a tale about two parties, given personal attributes despite their commonly corporate character, who at one time arrived at a mutual agreement about a future undertaking, which one of them has now broken, to the other's damage, etc.) and, of course, serving the institutional and ideological purposes of the reciters; and they tell you more about the social world of the story-teller than that of those whom the story concerns, and more about both worlds' aspirations than their practices....

[Danzig] has a potentially corrosive effect upon the neo-Realist assumptions on which I would guess most Contracts teachers now operate. We all learned that the judicial practice earlier in this century of characterizing the questions to be resolved in such ways as "Did offeror intend his offer as one for a unilateral or bilateral contract" was comically formalistic; and that it only thinly (and illegitimately) disguised the reality of exercise of judicial power by pretending to do no more than carry out the will of the parties. Candid, open-textured, policy-oriented decision-making, on the other hand, would reach behind this abstraction to find the concrete "offeror" in her particular trade and situation, and the "offeree" in his, would ask whether they had acted in accordance with reasonable good faith commercial standards, and would strive to find the remedies that would be fairest in the circumstances for everyone. (This is of course a parody of the prevailing orthodoxy, but not a grotesque one.) Danzig's stories help to reveal that the neo-Realist aspiration of substantively rational decision-making is scarcely more approachable than the late 19th century classical ideal of formal rationality, and that our present judicial ways of ordering experience are in their own fashion quite as abstract and mythic.

Students — the stories being well and simply told — have no difficulty seizing this point, which, once taken, allows the class to go farther and to try to discover the precise forms of these judicial story-structures and to ask how they came to look that way. Some are extremely threatened by these materials and seek to avoid the questions they raise by pushing them to the periphery of the "real" business of practical training and burying themselves in black-letter; but it's much harder to treat these very "real" stories that way than equally valuable but less obviously relevant theoretical, comparative, or historical materials. Other students find the stories simply reinforce their indwelling tendencies toward cynicism about the legal system. But I think that almost without exception they find the materials hypnotically fascinating, and their implications for the ways in which we all think about law fundamental. A teacher can't very well ask for more than that.

Professor Tierney was far more critical of Danzig's book. He warns:[37]

[The] trouble with Professor Danzig's book is that it is an oblique attack on the legal concept of relevance without any offer of a substitute. In general, first year law students need to be taught a sense of relevance, and to be weaned off the habit of crass generalization with which many of them have grown up. The free ranging approach of Professor Danzig is therefore a dangerous drug, not to be taken while still in the legal cradle, and even later in the legal life only to be ingested under careful professional supervision and with an antidote immediately to hand.

How would you expect Professor Gordon to respond to Professors Oldham and Tierney?

---

[37]Tierney, Book Review, 32 Hastings Law Journal 1071, 1091 (1981). Copyright 1981 Hastings School of Law, reprinted with permission.

2. HADLEY v. BAXENDALE: PUTTING AGGRIEVED PARTIES NOT QUITE WHERE THEY WOULD HAVE BEEN HAD THE CONTRACT BEEN PERFORMED

HADLEY AND ANOTHER v. BAXENDALE AND OTHERS

9 Ex. 341, 156 Eng. Rep. 145, 1854

[As with most old English appellate cases the account begins with a "headnote" by the Court Report describing the "facts" as they are revealed by the pleadings, and summarizing the proceedings below.]

… At the trial before Crompton, J., at the last Gloucester Assizes, it appeared that the plaintiffs carried on an extensive business as millers at Gloucester; and that, on the 11th of May, their mill was stopped by a breakage of the crank shaft by which Messrs. Joyce & Co., the engineers, at Greenwich, and it became necessary to send the shaft as a pattern for a new one to Greenwich. The fracture was discovered on the 12th, and on the 13th the plaintiffs sent one of their servants to the office of the defendants, who are the well-known carriers trading under the name of Pickford & Co., for the purpose of having the shaft carried to Greenwich. The plaintiff's servant told the clerk that the mill was stopped, and that the shaft must be sent immediately; and in answer to the inquiry when the shaft would be taken, the answer was, that if it was sent by twelve o'clock any day, it would be delivered at Greenwich on the following day. On the following day the shaft was taken by the defendants, before noon, for the purpose of being conveyed to Greenwich, and the sum of 2£. 4s. was paid for its carriage for the whole distance; at the same time the defendants' clerk was told that a special entry, if required, should be made to hasten its delivery. The delivery of the shaft at Greenwich was delayed by some neglect; and the consequence was, that the plaintiffs did not receive the new shaft for several days after they would otherwise have done, and the working of their mill was thereby delayed, and they thereby lost the profits they would otherwise have received.

On the part of the defendants, it was objected that these damages were too remote, and that the defendants were not liable with respect to them. The learned Judge left the case generally to the jury, who found a verdict with 25£. damages beyond the amount paid into Court.

Whateley, in last Michaelmas Term, obtained a rule nisi for a new trial, on the ground of misdirection.…

The judgement of the Court was now delivered by

ALDERSON, B. We think that there ought to be a new trial in this case; but, in so doing, we deem it to be expedient and necessary to state explicitly the rule which the Judge, at the next trial, ought, in our opinion, to direct the jury to be governed by when they estimate the damages.

It is, indeed, of the last importance that we should do this; for, if the jury are left without any definite rule to guide them, it will in such cases as these, manifestly lead to the greatest injustice....

Now we think the proper rule in such a case as the present is this:—Where two parties have made a contract which one of them has broken, the damages which the other party ought to receive in respect of such breach of contract should be such as may fairly and reasonably be considered either arising naturally, i.e., according to the usual course of things, from such breach of contract itself, or such as may reasonably be supposed to have been in the contemplation of both parties, at the time they made the contract, as the probable result of the breach of it. Now, if the special circumstances under which the contract was actually made were communicated by the plaintiffs to the defendants, and thus known to both parties, the damages resulting from the breach of such a contract, which they would reasonably contemplate, would be the amount of injury which would ordinarily follow from a breach of contract under these special circumstances so known and communicated. But, on the other hand, if these special circumstances were wholly unknown to the party breaking the contract, he, at the most, could only be supposed to have had in his contemplation the amount of injury which would arise generally, and in the great multitude of cases not affected by any special circumstances from such a breach of contract. For, had the special circumstances been know the parties might have specially provided for the breach of contract by special terms as to the damages in the case; and of this advantage it would be very unjust to deprive them. Now the above principles are those by which we think the jury ought to be guided in estimating the damages arising out of any breach of contract.... Now, in the present case, if we are to apply the principles above laid down, we find that the only circumstances here communicated by the plaintiffs to the defendants at the time the contract was made, were, that the article to be carried was the broken shaft of a mill, and that the plaintiffs were the millers of that mill. But how do these circumstances shew reasonably that the profits of the mill must be stopped by an unreasonable delay in the delivery of the broken shaft by the carrier to the third person? Suppose the plaintiffs had another shaft in their possession put up or putting up at the time, and that thy only wished to send back the broken shaft to the engineer who made it; it is clear that this would be quite consistent with the above circumstances, and yet the unreasonable delay in the delivery would have no effect upon the intermediate profits of the mill. Or, again, suppose that, at the time of the delivery to the carrier, the machinery of the mill had been in other respects defective, then, also, the same results would follow. Here it is true that the shaft was actually sent back to serve as a model for a new one, and that the want of a new one was the only cause of the stoppage of the mill, and that the loss of profits really arose from not sending down the new shaft in proper time, and that this arose from the delay in delivering the broken one to serve as a model. But it is obvious that, in the great multitude of cases of millers sending off broken shafts to third persons by a carrier under ordinary circumstances, such con-

probability, have occurred; and these special circumstances were here never communicated by the plaintiffs to the defendants. It follows, therefore, that the loss of the profits here cannot reasonably be considered such a consequence of the breach of contract as could have been fairly and reasonably contemplated by both the parties when they made this contract. For such loss would neither have flowed naturally from the breach of this contract in the great multitude of such cases occurring under ordinary circumstances, nor were the special circumstances, which, perhaps, would have made it a reasonable and natural consequence of such breach of contract, communicated to or known by the defendants. The Judge ought, therefore, to have told the jury, that, upon the facts before them, they ought not to take the loss of profits into consideration at all in estimating the damages. There must therefore be a new trial in this case.

Rule absolute.

NOTES AND QUESTIONS

1. *The buyer's remedies under the U.C.C.*: Sections 2-712, 2-713, and 2-714 all say that a buyer can recover consequential damages in a proper case as defined by § 2-715(2). One requirement is that the consequential loss "could not reasonably be prevented by cover or otherwise." The other is the Code's version of *Hadley v. Baxendale*. See Official Comments 2 and 3. The form of the test differs from that found in the *Hadley* opinion, but is the Code rule different in substance? How are we to determine when a seller "had reason to know" "at the time of contracting" of "general or particular requirements and needs" of the buyer?

2. *The seller's consequential damages under the U.C.C.*: There is no provision in the U.C.C. giving *sellers* a right to consequential damages. Normally, when a buyer breaches a contract the seller loses the gains it would have made from receiving money. Had the drafters of the Code written a consequential damages section for sellers, sellers seldom would recover under any provision that incorporated the ideas of *Hadley v. Baxendale*. Sellers might do many things with money. It would be hard to foresee what a seller might be planning to do with the proceeds from any particular contract. The typical common law approach was to award an aggrieved seller the difference between the contract price and the resale or market price. In addition, sellers can recover interest at the legal rate set by statute for interest on judgments. Often this rate is far less than the current price of borrowing money.

However, can a seller recover the actual cost of financing its performance of the contract with buyer? You may recall that in *Neri v. Retail Marine* the court awarded Retail Marine "finance charges" on the boat from the time of Neri's breach to the time Mr. Olsen bought it. These were "incidental damages" under § 2-710. The New York Court of Appeals read this section broadly. It followed the language of the Comment which says "[t]he section sets forth the principal normal and necessary additional elements of damage flowing from the breach but intends to allow all commercially reasonable expenditures made by the seller." In *Intermeat, Inc. v. American Poultry, Inc.*,[38] the court applied the *Neri* decision to allow an award of finance charges directly attributable to a shipment of meat.

The court in *Nobs Chemical, U.S.A., Inc. v. Koppers Co.*,[39] seems to reach a contrary result. Nobs agreed to sell Koppers cumene, an additive for high-octane motor fuel. Nobs then ordered a large quantity of cumene from a Brazilian supplier, including some which it planned to supply to Koppers under their contract. When Koppers canceled, Nobs had to pay the Brazilian supplier an extra $25 per ton on its order since it no longer qualified for a quantity discount. The court said that the lost quantity discount was consequential rather than incidental damage, and it did not allow any recovery for these reduced profits on other sales.[40]

3. *The "tacit agreement rule"*: Before passage of the Uniform Commercial Code many states interpreted *Hadley v. Baxendale* to require that sellers of goods or services make a "tacit agreement" to pay consequential damages if they did not perform. Courts and writers often quoted Judge Learned Hand's statement of the doctrine: "we know of no test other than the loose one that the loss must be such that, had the promisor been originally faced with its possibility, he would have assented to its inclusion in what he must make good."[41] Courts following the tacit agreement rule often balanced the benefits of the contract against the burdens of the damages sought. For example, in *Hooks Smelting Co. v. Planters' Compress Co.*,[42] the court said:

> ... the profits which the plaintiff might reasonably have expected to make on this contract did not probably exceed one or two hundred dollars.... And yet for the failure to properly perform this contract plaintiff is subjected to damages nearly ten times greater than the gross amount to be paid it for all the materials it furnished.

Official Comment 2 to U.C.C. § 2-715 states "[t]he 'tacit agreement' test for the recovery of consequential damages is rejected."[43] Can we conclude that the balance between the benefits of the contract and the burdens of consequential

---

[38]575 F.2d 1017 (2d Cir. 1978).

[39]616 F.2d 212 (5th Cir. 1980).

[40]For a case following the reasoning in Nobs Chemical, see Bulk Oil (U.S.A.), Inc. v. Sun Oil Trading Co., 697 F.2d 481 (2d Cir. 1983).

[41]Stamford Extract Mfg. Co. v. Oakes Mfg. Co., 9 F.2d 301, 303 (2d Cir. 1925).

[42]72 Ark. 275, 283, 79 S.W. 1052 (1904).

[43]In Troxler Electronics Laboratories, Inc. v. Solitron Devices, Inc., 722 F.2d 81 (4th Cir. 1983), the District Court denied recovery of lost profits because the defendant did not specifically agree to be liable for them when the parties made the contract. The Court of Appeals reversed. The U.C.C. requires only that damages be reasonably foreseeable.

damages is now irrelevant to whether a loss is one "resulting from general or particular requirements and needs of which the seller at the time of contracting had reason to know" under U.C.C. § 2-715(2)(a)?

4. *Disclaimers of consequential damages*: One of the most common provisions on the business forms used by sellers reads something as follows: "In no event shall seller be liable for any consequential damages." Does this limit the modern significance of *Hadley v. Baxendale* to cases where there has been a failure of planning caused by sloppy business practices? In other words, is the *Hadley v. Baxendale* case irrelevant in most cases, given the fact that the modern Baxendale would have tried to protect itself from consequential damages by inserting a provision in its form contracts excluding liability for all consequential damages? In chapter 4 of these materials we will study judicial regulation of terms hidden in fine print in standard form contracts. You should wait until after studying those materials before coming to a final conclusion about these questions.

3. PROOF OF DAMAGES WITH REASONABLE CERTAINTY: OF NEW BUSINESSES AND EXPERTS

In this section we will study the rule that requires damages to be proved "with reasonable certainty." We will see a common legal problem — do we spend the time and effort attempting to establish something hard to prove or do we adopt a *per se* rule? On one hand, Comment 1 to U.C.C. § 1-106 says "[c]ompensatory damages often are at best approximate: they have to be proved with whatever definiteness and accuracy the facts permit, but no more." See also Comment 4 to § 2-715.

On the other hand, some states follow a "new business" rule. As the court said in *Keener v. Sizzler Family Steak Houses*, "[u]nder Texas law prospective profits are not recoverable for a newly established business or for a business which has operated at a loss."[44]

EVERGREEN AMUSEMENT CORPORATION v. MILSTEAD

112 A.2d 901 (Md.1955)

HAMMOND, J. The Evergreen Amusement Corporation, the appellant, operator of a drive-in movie theater, was held liable by the court, sitting without a jury, to Harold D. Milstead, the appellee, a contractor, for the balance due on a written contract for the clearing and grading of the site of the theater and certain extras, less the cost of completing a part of the work and damages for delay in completion, based on rental value of the theater property during the period of delay and out-of-pocket costs for that time.

---

[44]597 F.2d 453, 458 (5th Cir. 1979).

The appellant, by counterclaim, sought recovery of lost profits for the period of delay. The court held the amount claimed to have been so lost to be too uncertain and speculative, and refused evidence proffered to support appellant's theory. [The appellant raised several issues on appeal — one of which was that the trial court had erred in refusing to consider evidence of lost profits due to plaintiff's unexcused delay in completing the work. After disposing of the other issues before it, the court turned to this issue.]

The real reliance of the Evergreen Amusement Corporation is on the slowness of the contractor in completing the work. It says that the resulting delay in the opening of the theater from June first to the middle of August cost it twelve thousand five hundred dollars in profits. It proffered a witness to testify that he had built and operated a majority of the drive-in theaters in the area, that he is in the theater equipment business and familiar with the profits that drive-in theaters make in the area, that a market survey was made in the area before the site of the theater was selected, and that it had shown the need for such a theater in the neighborhood. It was said he would testify as to the reasonably anticipated profits during the months in question by comparing the months in its second year of operation with those in which it could not operate the year before, and would say that the profits would have been the same. His further testimony would be, it was claimed, that weather conditions, the population, and competition were all approximately the same in the year the theater opened and the following year.

We think the court did not err in refusing the proffered evidence. Under the great weight of authority, the general rule clearly is that loss of profit is a definite element of damages in an action for breach of contract or in an action for harming an established business which has been operating for a sufficient length of time to afford a basis of estimation with some degree of certainty as to the probable loss of profits, but that, on the other hand, loss of profits from a business which has not gone into operation may not be recovered because they are merely speculative and incapable of being ascertained with the requisite degree of certainty. Restatement, Contracts, § 331, states the law to be that damages are recoverable for profits prevented by breach of contract "only to the extent that the evidence affords a sufficient basis for estimating their amount in money with reasonable certainty," and that where the evidence does not afford a sufficient basis, "damages may be measured by the rental value of the property." Comment "d" says this: "If the defendant's breach has prevented the plaintiff from carrying on *a well-established business*, the amount of profits thereby prevented is often capable of proof with reasonable certainty. On the basis of its past history, a reasonable prediction can be made as to its future." (Italics supplied.) That damages for profits anticipated from a business which has not started may not be recovered, is laid down in 25 C.J.S., Damages, § 42, and 15 Am.Jur., Damages, § 157; 5 Corbin, Contracts, §§ 1022, 1023; *Cramer v. Grand Rapids Show Case Co.,* 223 N.Y. 63, 119 N.E. 227, 1 A.L.R. 156; *Sinclair Ref. Co. v. Hamilton & Dotson,* 164 Va. 203, 178 S.E. 777, 99 A.L.R. 938. See also The Requirement of Certainty for Proof of Lost Profits, 64

Harvard Law Review 317. The article discusses the difficulties of proving with sufficient certainty the profits which were lost, and then says: "These difficulties have given rise to a rule in some states that no new business can recover for its lost profits." While this Court has not laid down a flat rule (and does not hereby do so), nevertheless, no case has permitted recovery of lost profits under comparable circumstances. In *Abbott v. Gatch,* 13 Md. 314, the claim for loss of profits arose because of delay in completion of a flour mill. The Court held that the mill owner's loss was to be established by fair rental value for the time of the delay resulting from failure to complete it according to contract, that he could not recover estimated profits, because it was dependent, as they were, upon the quality of flour available, the fluctuation of prices of flour, continuance of the mill in running order and other variants. The Court labelled the damages claimed speculative and refused to follow a Vermont case which had allowed them to be shown. The rule laid down in this case has been followed in a number of others. In *Winslow Elevator & Machine Co. v. Hoffman,* 107 Md. 621, 69 A. 394, 17 L.R.A.,N.S., 1130, an elevator was not installed within the specified time and was defective. The owner sought to recover loss of rents because of the refusal of prospective tenants to lease offices and the moving out of others. The Court followed *Abbott v. Gatch, supra,* and held that the claim for loss of rentals must be denied as too uncertain and remote. See also [citations omitted].

The appellant relies on cases in the Supreme Court of the United States and lower Federal Courts, ... [citations omitted]. With one exception they involved existing businesses or theaters. Each claim for lost profits was based on conspiracies in restraint of trade in violation of the anti-trust statutes. While the opinions do not articulate that the damages were allowed to make effective the civil sanctions of the anti-trust statutes and, indeed, in one case, perhaps self-consciously, suggest that there is no distinction in the rules as to damages between anti-trust cases and others, nevertheless, it seems clear that the courts, in order to lay a basis for punitive triple damages, have relaxed the standards of proof in anti-trust suits to permit the establishment of lost profits as basic damages. The author of the Harvard Law Review article cited above observes: "As the courts have become more favorably impressed by the desirability of civil anti-trust remedies there has been a steady relaxation of the standard of certainty required, and recovery has even been permitted in cases where the plaintiff's business has never before made a profit, and where the business has only been in operation for a matter of months". On the other hand, the uncertain nature of the business of the theater is noted in cases which have denied damages. In *Todd v. Keene, 167* Mass. 157, 45 N.E. 81, suit was brought by a theater owner against an actor who breached his agreement to appear. It was shown that the actor was of high repute, had played the same theater in previous years in the same type of play to large audiences and that a college nearby always insured a crowded house. It was held that the court properly excluded evidence based on past experience of the management of the theater as to the amount of cash receipts to be expected from the some type of play at the same place under the same auspices. In *Broadway Photoplay Co. v. World Film Corp.*, 225 N.Y. 104, 121 N.E. 756, the Court, speaking through Judge Cardozo, refused to allow loss of profits for failure to supply one feature film a week to a movie theater as agreed, although the proffer made and the evidence introduced would seem to have been as reliable a foundation as that in the case before us for their estimation. It would seem that a new theater would not for some time be well enough known to attract the same number of patrons it would draw after a period of operation. We think the court was right in basing the damages for delay in the completion of the site on fair rental value and the actual monetary losses incurred....

We think that the case below was tried and decided without reversible error. *Judgment affirmed, with costs.* Brune, C. J., dissents in part.

NOTES AND QUESTIONS

1. *What is the rule of the case?* The court says in its opinion that it has not laid down a "flat rule" prohibiting new businesses from recovering for lost profits. What do you think? Can you imagine circumstances in which an operator of a drive-in theatre in Maryland could recover lost profits if she had not yet opened for business?

What objective, or objectives, seem to have animated the court to choose a rule which makes it extremely difficult, if not impossible, for a plaintiff to seek lost profits if the plaintiff is a new business? Is it fairness to plaintiff? defendant? Suspicion of triers of fact? Judicial efficiency?

2. *A Secret Recovery of Lost Profits?* The court allows the plaintiff to recover the "fair rental value" of the theater property. We do not know what that fair rental value represents. Perhaps plaintiff rented the land on which the theater was located, in which case this recovery represents what we will come to know as a reliance recovery. Perhaps, however, the court allowed the plaintiff to recover the estimated fair rental value of the property, as a completed drive-in theater, for the months of the delay in completion of the construction. If the recovery was of the latter amount, has the court effectively allowed the plaintiff at least some recovery for lost profits?

3. *Briefs of the parties — a study in contrasts:* The briefs submitted provide an interesting contrast. Appellant's brief is 18 pages long, with a 39-page appendix. It cites 26 cases, in addition to Corbin, Williston, the Restatements of Contracts and Torts, and an article from the Harvard Law Review. Ten pages of the brief are addressed to the lost profits issue.

The appellee's brief is barely seven pages long, of which only a bit more than three comprise the argument. Only two short paragraphs address the legal issue of lost profits. The first such paragraph seeks to distinguish the Federal decisions allowing lost profits in antitrust cases. The second paragraph says simply:

No authority in Maryland would justify the Court in considering the testimony as profferred. Many cases justify its exclusion. [The brief then provides bare cites to three Maryland cases.]

One other case, and a citation to a Practice and Procedure manual constitute the balance of legal authority. Another paragraph from the brief seems worth quoting, because of its confident air, and slightly contemptuous dismissal of some of the arguments advanced by the appellant.

As a practical matter (and the law is sometimes practical), if the Judge who heard this case, without a jury, felt that the evidence tendered was too speculative to be a proper basis of an award of damages, and that other evidence in the case was more reliable for that purpose, then it makes no difference whether the evidence was in or out. Even if, as a Judge, he had admitted the evidence, then as the trier of facts, it is obvious that he would have given it no weight.

4. *Rejection of the new business rule*: The new business doctrine was rejected in *Chung v. Kaonohi Center Co,*[45] a case which may be emblematic of an emerging skepticism of the value of a flat prohibition of recovery of profits for new businesses. Though the case may reflect a growing trend, and relief for some potential plaintiffs, it also clearly suggests some of the difficulties in trying to prove the lost profits of a new venture.

In *Chung*, a stock broker and the operator of a Chinese restaurant made a contract to lease for ten years concession space for a fast-food Chinese kitchen as part of an international restaurant in a shopping mall. They arranged for financing, ordered equipment and furnishings, hired chefs and workers, and advertised in the Yellow Pages of the telephone directory. While they were preparing to begin operations, the promoters of the mall were negotiating secretly with others. The promoters leased the entire international kitchen restaurant concession to Battistetti, and they attempted to cancel their contract with plaintiffs by returning their deposit. The jury found a breach of contract and awarded damages of $50,000 for emotional distress[46] and $175,000 loss of future profits. The Supreme Court of Hawaii affirmed the judgment.

The Supreme Court first rejected the rule barring proof of the lost profits of a new business. It cited cases supporting this view from California, Kansas, Rhode Island, and Wyoming. It said "it would be grossly unfair to deny a plaintiff meaningful recovery for lack of a sufficient 'track record' where the

---

[45]62 Hawaii 594, 618 P.2d 283 (1980).

[46]Chung's wife had a miscarriage which the Chungs and the jury attributed to their difficulties with the promoters of the mall. The court recognized that emotional distress damages are not given ordinarily in breach of contract actions. However, it found the promoters' conduct so outrageous as to justify a recovery in this case.

plaintiff has been prevented from establishing such a record by defendant's actions."

It then said that the trier of fact "must be guided by some rational standard in making an award for loss of future profits." It found enough evidence to support the jury's verdict.

Plaintiffs' key witness was Don Voronaeff, a real estate and business appraiser. Voronaeff valued the proposed Chinese kitchen using three different valuation approaches — a reproduction costs analysis [the cost of reproducing the assets of the business], a comparative market analysis [plaintiffs' business was compared to recently sold businesses of a similar nature], and an income stream analysis. In reaching a final valuation figure, Voronaeff relied primarily on his income stream analysis, but included both the reproduction cost analysis and comparative market analysis as a check on that figure....

In his analysis, Voranaeff used $420,000 as the gross income for the first year of operation and projected that that figure would increase by ten percent each year. Voronaeff testified that he arrived at this figure by looking at the actual gross income of the Chinese kitchen in the Pearlridge International Kitchen run by Mr. Battistetti. The first year gross income of that operation was $417,000. A person employed by Voronaeff also conducted a one-day count of customers and gross receipts of the existing Chinese kitchen which, when projected over a year, indicated a gross income of $666,041. That survey figure, Voronaeff stated, supported the gross income figure from the Battistetti operation and, based on Battistetti's gross income and gross income figures from other Chinese restaurants, a $420,000 gross income was reasonable.

Appellants object to the gross income figure utilized by plaintiffs' expert since it was based on an existing operation *not* run by plaintiffs. We reject this argument for obvious reasons. Appellants' contract breach prevented appellees from establishing a profit and loss record on which to base a gross income figure. The restaurant most nearly approximating plaintiffs' proposed kitchen was Battistetti's Chinese kitchen....

The next stage in Voronaeff's analysis was estimating the cost of goods and expenses and subtracting them from the gross income to reach a net income figure.... [H]e subtracted estimates which he testified were based on industry standards. Voronaeff extensively detailed the cost of goods and other expenses in his testimony and on cross-examination stated that the expenses he had subtracted "covered everything that you should cover in operating a business." ... After subtracting each expense, Voronaeff derived a net income figure of $67,608 for the first year of operation. He then capitalized that net income figure at a rate of 20% over the ten-year life of the lease to reach a final value of approximately $225,000. [He testified that "What we're saying is that someone would pay $225,000 to obtain an annual net income of $67,000 and they'd be getting a 20 percent return on their investment."]

Appellants argue that Voronaeff's testimony as to cost of goods and expenses was speculative and lacked a factual basis.... Weaknesses in reaching the valuation go to the weight of such testimony. It is incumbent on the opposing party to bring out any such weaknesses on cross-examination or through presentation of counter evidence.... It [the jury] also knew that plaintiff Lum [a partner of Chung's and a co-plaintiff in the case] owned and operated two Chinese restaurants ... The profit and expense sheets from at least one of these restaurants was introduced into evidence, so the jury could reasonably have estimated the effectiveness of plaintiff Lum's management.

Is it likely that the *Chung* decision is a breakthrough for new small businesses? Will many be able to produce the kind of expert testimony the plaintiffs were able to offer? How many are likely to be able to afford the research and calculations that Don Voronaeff offered the jury?

3. *The expert witness — how expert?* The new business rule prevents some plaintiffs from even attempting to prove their lost profits. But even if the court decides that the new business rule is inapplicable (for instance because the business is established, or because the enterprise is a new venture for an established business) the plaintiff must offer satisfactory proof of lost profits. This almost always is done through the testimony of experts. But one soon discovers that the mere presence of experts, testifying for both sides, does little to eliminate the uncertainty. The case of *Eastern Airlines, Inc. v. McDonnell Douglas Corp.*[47] provides a vivid example. This case involved the late delivery by Douglas of ninety passenger jets to Eastern Airlines. Eastern's expert testified that the delay caused the airline to lose $23,400,000 in profits. McDonnell's expert, on the other hand, testified that the delay actually *saved* Eastern $1,294,000 because the tardy delivery reduced financing costs. In its decision remanding the case to the District Court for further proceedings the 5th Circuit suggested that the trial court consider calling its own expert witness, as it can do, in order to provide a more independent source of testimony on the damages question.

---

[47]532 F.2d 957 (5th Cir. 1976).

F. THE EXPECTATION INTEREST: FORESEEABILITY AND PROOF WITH REASONABLE CERTAINTY AS BARRIERS TO RELIEF

1. APPELLATE CASES AS A BIASED SAMPLE OF EVENTS IN THE WORLD

Beginning law students often assume that legal training involves little more than memorizing a series of rules hidden in appellate cases. Even in those areas where rules of law have great importance, it is not enough to know only the words which express the rules.

Hadley v. Baxendale is a good example. You know that damages are limited to those

> ... as may fairly and reasonably be considered either [1] arising naturally, i.e., according to the usual course of things, from such breach of contract itself, or [2] such as may reasonably be supposed to have been in the contemplation of both parties, at the time they made the contract as the probable result of the breach of it.

But what do those words mean? The application of the rule to the facts of that case itself ought to give us some clues about the meaning of the doctrine. However, what were the facts of *Hadley v. Baxendale* — what did the shipper say to the carrier's agent and what authority did that agent have to receive notices that would impose liability on the company? Furthermore, the *Evergreen, Lakota, Chung,* and *Eastern* decisions all tell us that lost anticipated profits must be proved with reasonable certainty. But what does this mean? Again the facts of the four cases do give us some idea, but it is not a very precise one.

Moreover, even after we read and think about all these decisions, we must confront one of the real problems of the case method of teaching. You cannot tell what the cases given you represent. You have an 1854 case from England, a forty-year old case from Maryland, a relatively recent decision from a United States Courts of Appeals purporting to apply the laws of Iowa, and a decision of the Supreme Court of Hawaii. Are the cases typical of current practice in these jurisdictions? Would courts follow them in, say, New York, California, Wisconsin, Virginia or South Dakota? And if so, what does "followed" mean? It was once fashionable to assume there was a single "thing" called the common law and any decision was but an example of it. Once we abandon that idea or reinterpret it to scale back its claims, we face the problem of sampling and bias. What does any casebook represent? Obviously, difficult questions of judgment are involved.

2. CONTENT ANALYSIS AND THE INTERACTION OF DOCTRINES

One way to give meaning to phrases such as "may reasonably be supposed," "may fairly and reasonably be considered," or "speculative or conjectural estimates" is to look at many decisions applying these rules to see if we find any patterns. A Comment in 65 Yale Law Journal 992 (1956), looked at the cases applying the *Hadley* and "proof with reasonable certainty" rules and found a pattern which might help us predict the outcome of cases involving claims for lost profits — if we can assume that the pattern still holds true today. The article reports the outcome of different types of cases under the *Hadley* and reasonable certainty rules:

> (1) The seller's claim for direct profits on the sale to the buyer.
> Here the seller is a manufacturer, builder, farmer or middleman who has a contract to sell goods to the buyer. His case is that if he could have performed the contract, he would have delivered goods at a cost less than the contract price. This difference is the profit he would have made on the sale. (He also may have to show that his supply of goods or capacity to produce them exceeded the demand after the breach. Unless he can qualify as a lost volume seller, he must make a substitute contract rather than seeking lost profits.) The judicial treatment of this kind of case is so favorable that the certainty and *Hadley v. Baxendale* rules rarely function as obstacles — in fact courts seem to presume forseeability and certainty rules have been met. One dealing with businessmen must foresee that they are trying to sell at a price above their costs, and most businessmen can supply enough data to prove their costs with "reasonable," if not exact, certainty.
> (2) Buyers' claims against sellers for collateral profits.
> (a) The Middleman's claim for resale profits.
> The buyer's theory here is that his supplier's breach of contract has prevented the buyer from realizing a profit on reselling the goods to his customers at a price greater than his costs. (To seek these lost profits, the buyer must also show that substitute goods were not available; otherwise, the buyer is expected to obtain the substitute and hold the original supplier who defaulted for any increased cost.) The middleman's theory involves proof of three things which are not always easy to establish:
> (i) the demand — the number of sales which would have been made if the supplier had not failed to deliver;
> (ii) the price at which the sales would have been made, and;
> (iii) the costs of the resales.

Today courts generally are favorable to this type of claim, although not as favorable as they are toward the seller's direct profits on a sale. Estimates and probabilities have sufficed; opinion evidence has been allowed. The foreseeability rule has been applied more favorably toward the middleman more recently. The older decisions required the defendant supplier to have notice of the particular resale or resales on which the middleman claimed a lost profit. The newer cases have been satisfied with the supplier's know ledge that the buyer was a merchant or that the buyer was ordering quantities too large for its own use.

(b) The manufacturer's claim for collateral profits.

The plaintiff is a buyer who expected to use the goods promised by the defaulting seller in order to process or manufacture other goods which he then would sell at a profit. For example, General Motors Corporation buys both machines and steel in order to make Chevrolets which G.M. then will sell to the public. (Again, in order to seek lost profits, the buyer must establish substitutes were not available.) Here the buyer must prove both demand and costs, and frequently this is very difficult. This is particularly true in the case of new businesses or new products. The judicial treatment is generally very unfavorable to the plaintiff. Foreseeability of profits is generally required. The certainty rule is applied strictly.

One can add another category to those of the Yale Comment:

(3) The claim for collateral profits of a purchaser of services from a common carrier or public utility.

A telegram or goods are not delivered. The purchaser of services seeks to recover its lost profits caused by this default. Judicial treatment is generally unfavorable. For example, it is not enough that the clerk accepting a message can see that it is a business telegram. Often the question is covered by statute or administrative regulation limiting the liability of the utility.

As we said, this is a 1956 article, written before the Uniform Commercial Code was adopted in all but a few states. Diane Thornberry, a University of Wisconsin Law Student, recently sought to replicate and extend the study. Her work generally supports its hypothesis.

Thornberry considered the *Hadley* rule in common carrier or telegraph company cases. She found the treatment totally inconsistent and unpredictable. She also found many cases that did not fit into the Yale Comment's categories. The *Hadley* and reasonable certainty tests were often applied in cases involving financial and securities transactions, breach of warranties in sales of goods, patents, collective bargaining agreements, and contracts governed by the law of admiralty.

Can you explain these categories and the results? Why is the foreseeability rule applied loosely in one situation and strictly in another? To what extent, if at all, is deterring breach of contract a goal of contract damages as far as you can tell from the way the foreseeability and reasonable certainty rules have been applied? To what extent, if at all, is the apparent goal to minimize the consequences of a breach of contract in order to make it easy to back out from what turns out to be a bad deal? To what extent, if at all, does the pattern of application found by the Yale Comment and confirmed by Thornberry indicate that the courts are unwilling to challenge the allocation of power within the society and are serving the interests of the "haves?" Suppose the foreseeability rule were repealed and one who breached a contract were responsible for all lost profits that plaintiff could prove by reasonable estimates. What effect, if any, would this have on what members of the society?

What, then, is the function of contract remedies? Contract law declares that it will attempt to put the aggrieved party in as good a position as had the contract been performed. Measures of damages based on the difference between the contract price and cover, resale or the market would seem to carry out this goal, until one discovers that an aggrieved party cannot recover lawyer's fees and remembers that the breaching party may be judgment-proof. The lost-volume-seller idea benefits some aggrieved sellers under some interpretations, but it might be extremely difficult to prove that a business was a lost volume seller under a strict reading of the uncertain tests of the *Neri* case. It is difficult to get specific performance, and it is not easy to have a stipulated damages clause enforced. The limitations on consequential damages defeat the expectation interest in many situations. The function of contract remedies, then, is not directly instrumental in many situations. Is it all a trick or might legal declarations of values serve some purpose?

Consider these questions in light of the following excerpts from articles by Llewellyn and Macaulay:

What Price Contract? — An Essay In Perspective
Karl N. Llewellyn[48]

Is the Law of Contract Necessary?

All of which, however, begs the question of why there need be any *legal* machinery at all for the purposes mentioned, other than mere protection of the factual results of accomplished bargains, work, deliveries, and payments. The peace, and more dubiously the law of alienability and of ownership, at least as against persons entrusted with possession — what more is needed? As one puts such a question, one recalls first how seldom law touches *directly* any case in which a promise has been performed, or in which an inadequate performance has been received in satisfaction. Promise, performance and adjustment are in this sense primarily extra-legal. It needs no argument that if they did not normally occur without law's intervention, no regime of future dealings would be possible. The lawyer's idea of "contract," applied to these normal cases, where performance and informal business adjustments proceed to occur, is thus a conceptual projection of trouble and the legal spawn of trouble upon the untroubled in fact.

---

[48]40 Yale Law Journal 704, 718-22 (1931). Copyright Yale Law Journal. Reprinted with permission.

Applied to such cases, the lawyer's idea of "contract" is unreal in genesis and misleading in implication — unless, which is the matter of inquiry, what the courts may do in the possible case of trouble is a needed factor, or at least a factor, in promise, or in performance, or in adjustment.

Neither will it do to treat the mere presence of legal machinery in any particular field as of itself demonstrating a *need* for it there. For such presence may merely be an instance of unneeded or even parasitic expansion of a going institution. Law early serves a prime function as offering means of dealing with some types of dispute not otherwise adjusted; I should indeed be tempted to argue that the differentiation of anything we can perceive as law begins with this. And even apart from the attribution of the results or their foundation to super-natural powers, even apart from the presence of felt Oughtness as to the content of decision, the last resort character of emerging law would seem to me enough to call forth the recurrent tendency we find in legal machinery to set itself up, *if* it be appealed to, as the *exclusive* means for dealing with any dispute. Law regularly purports, too, to speak for the group as a whole, and this of necessity bespeaks a constant pressure to draw into law's orbit any other important institution; it is the stuff of other institutions which offers the subject matter of disputes. Finally, rarely until modern times has expansion of jurisdiction or business been unprofitable to the law-men concerned. The chief counter-tendency to this expansiveness is found in law's own formalism (compare the impediments to assignability of choses in action) and in the tradition-set character of the molds within which law-men must move if their action is to have standing as official. Given, then, promises present, relied on, and broken, law will sooner or later wrestle with their breach; but it will do so whether or not society peculiarly requires the wrestling.

Yet as the specialization and credit, and particularly the industrial, aspects of an economy gain ground, it becomes hard to escape the positive case for utility of legal enforcement of promises. Credit or reliance on a purely customary or self-interest basis presupposes for effectiveness either permanence of dealings involving long-run mutual dependence, or an ingrained traditional morality covering the point, or dealings within a face-to-face community (or its equivalent, a close-knit though wandering guild-like interest-group such as the early medieval merchants seem to have made up) in which severe group pressure on delinquent promisors is available. These types of sanction fail in a society mobile as to institutions, mobile as to residence, mobile as to occupation; they fail increasing-ly as the market expands spatially and in complexity. They fail, in a word, as to long-run, long-range, impersonal bargains, as also in cases where death, or transfer of rights, removes from the relation what may at the outset have been a personal aspect.

Frequently enough no other sanction than the legal exists at all. Where other sanctions do exist (*e.g.,* desire for continued dealings, or for a business reputation) they show an unfortunate tendency to fail precisely where most needed, *i.e.,* when stress of loss (or gain: management manipulation of the market or merger of the debtor) is strong. Max Weber cogently remarks that expediency-founded ethics are less reliable factors in performance than are those founded in tradition. It results that even to some extent in short-run face-to-face dealings, and *a fortiori* and importantly in long-run ones, legal enforceability figures as an element of added security in credit matters; a partial insurance against the very case of need: when credit-judgment was misguided, or in case of death or assignment, or where supervening troubles disrupt either willingness or power to perform.

The Use and Non-Use of Contract in the Manufacturing Industry
Stewart Macaulay[49]

Most businessmen I have talked to have an attitude toward contracts that can best be described as indifferent or even hostile to the whole idea. They remark, "Contracts are a waste of time. We've never had any trouble, because we know our customers and our suppliers. If we needed a contract with a man, we wouldn't deal with him." "Lawyers are overprotective and just get in the way of buying or selling. If business had to be done by lawyers as buyers and sellers, the economy would stop. No one would buy or sell anything; they'd just negotiate forever."

Yet, some businessmen look at things differently: "We've been sued (or our competitor has been sued), and one ought to be careful. There is no need to skate on thin ice legally. We've learned the hard way." "If you get the intent spelled out, you won't have any trouble. People perform commitments they understand. It's worth a little extra time to make sure everyone is talking about the same thing."

The last statement indicates that people may be thinking of different things when they talk about a "contract." They may be talking about planning a transaction. Whether or not an arrangement is legally enforceable, people may want an understanding about who is to do what and the effect of certain events, such as, what happens if one or the other fails to perform in some respect, or what happens if there is a strike or fire.

On the other hand, people may use the word "contract" to refer to the effect of law, and they may be thinking of several different effects of law:

> — They may think of an understanding or a plan for a business exchange that will not run afoul of any of the many regulatory statutes: the Robinson-Patman, Sherman, or Clayton Acts, for example.
> — They may think of an understanding that will award off statutory or common law liability for their conduct: disclaimers or indemnity provisions for patent infringement, products liability, or negligence.

---

[49] 9 The Practical Lawyer 14 (Nov. 1963).

— They may think of a legal sanction that will induce one of the parties to perform his side of the agreement.

All of these ideas about contract are related, but they are sufficiently different to demand separate consideration.

I shall make one final comment about attitudes before reporting on practices. One's job influences his attitudes toward both planning a business exchange and the effect of law in this area:

— The salesman finds contract the work of the devil; it is just one more thing to get in the way of closing a sale. Moreover, suing or threatening to sue a customer who could place orders in the future is insanity.

— The purchasing agent tends to be indifferent. He may carefully plan transactions so that what he is buying and the price are defined, but he feels that provisions on strikes, late deliveries, warranties, etc., are a waste of time. Changed circumstances and disputes can be handled informally. Planning for such things and using, or threatening to use, legal sanctions is simply unnecessary. (Of course, if pressed, he may concede that he deals differently with building contractors on major construction jobs.)

— Financial people tend to be the strongest contract boosters. They want to "get the commitments spelled out."

— Outside counsel also tend to favor planning and the use of legal sanctions to settle disputes.

— The house counsel may have to temper his views favoring contract, because he is part of the organization.

Business Practices

Some businessmen say their firms carefully plan everything and arrange their agreements so they are legally enforceable contracts. But even these firms seldom use their legal rights openly. They are not going to sue anyone or threaten to do so, except in extraordinary situations. The contract remains in the background as a handy club to hold in reserve, in case it is necessary.

However, most firms I've seen do not plan this carefully, except in rare situations, and most are not concerned with legal sanctions. Important agreements often are worked out by the businessmen representing the buyer and the seller. Then an attorney is called in and told to draft something. He is given an hour or an afternoon for what should be several days' careful work. He is told, or he understands without being told, that he is not to "make it complicated." He is not going to be popular if he tries to make the businessmen "work out all the details." Too often the attorney discovers that the businessmen really have not reached agreement on the difficult issues, but have ignored them to avoid argument. If he wakes these sleeping dogs, he may cause his client to lose a bargain that his client thinks is a good one. If he drafts an ambiguous document avoiding hard issues, he exposes his client to serious risks, and his client will hold him responsible if any of the risks should materialize.

Alternatively, an attorney is not consulted at all at the planning stage. One businessman may write a letter with a proposal that is accepted by the other businessman. The letter will cover anything directly and immediately related to money, but little else. Or the businessmen may agree orally, and one may write a confirming letter stating his interpretation of their agreement. Often the one receiving such a letter remains silent, thus manifesting either acceptance of the interpretation in the confirmation, or complete disagreement and a refusal even to continue negotiations. Even when it is clear that the confirmation has been accepted, such letters are often terse and ambiguous.

When we turn to business practices concerning legal sanctions, we note many practices that make the enforceability of many business agreements very doubtful:
...

    — Firms often deal on the basis of "blanket orders subject to releases." Yet, the blanket order, if and when accepted by the seller, is no more than a continuing offer by the seller that the buyer accepts each time he sends the seller a release form. Moreover, these blanket orders frequently contain "agreements to agree in the future," termination-for-convenience clauses calling for cancellation charges to be "equitably adjusted," and change provisions that let the buyer make a completely different offer out of the order.

    — Then we have the case contracts teachers like to talk about: the purchase order and acknowledgment forms that have different and inconsistent terms and conditions printed on the back. A great deal of business is done on an offer and counteroffer.

When disputes occur, there is a hesitancy to use legal sanctions or even to refer to the contract. Businessmen try to "work things out without bringing lawyers into it." Contract lawsuits and appellate cases concerning contract problems are relatively rare.

Why Business Can and Does Ignore Contract

Businessmen can deal without contract for obvious reasons. They have little, if any, trouble, even if they run risks of trouble. It is in the interest of everyone to perform agreements. There are personal relationships between buyers and sellers on all levels of the two corporations. Purchasing agents know salesmen, corporate presidents know corporate presidents, and so forth. This creates an incentive to get along in a continuing relationship. Most importantly, the two businesses want to do business in the future. You don't get repeat orders from unsatisfied customers, and one's reputation can influence future business if word gets around. And word does get around.

Using contract, of course, can have a number of disadvantages. If, in planning a business transaction, one is going to mention all the horrible things that can happen, he may scare off the other side so that the deal is lost. If one does set up a contractual relationship, there is some risk that one will get only performance to the letter of the contract most narrowly construed. Conversely, there is also a risk that one will be held to the letter of the contract and lose "flexibility." Using legal sanctions for breach of contract to settle disputes is costly. Usually it ends the business relationship between the parties. Furthermore, I need not tell you that lawsuits and lawyers cost money.

Of course, there is some use of legal sanctions. Typically, this occurs when someone with power thinks the gains from proceeding this way outweigh the costs. Often this is the lawyer's view, but lawyers do not always get to run their clients' affairs in the way lawyers might wish to run them.

3. THE RELIANCE INTEREST

Contract remedies could, and sometimes do, seek to protect the *reliance interest*. Rather than trying to put aggrieved parties where they would have been had their contracts been performed, judges applying contract law might seek to compensate victims of breach for out-of-pocket losses. That is, rather than trying to approximate the situation had there been no breach, a court could instead seek to compensate for losses caused by reliance on the contract.

Suppose, for example, Buyer, thinking he has a contract with Seller, makes expenditures in order to *unlock the value* of Seller's performance. Seller is to supply a machine tool that will produce a product. Buyer orders a special type of steel which the machine will process. When Seller defaults, Buyer has to pay for the steel. However, Buyer now has no machine with which to turn it into something that can be sold (and cannot readily obtain a substitute machine). If Buyer must pay to cancel the contract with the steel supplier or if Buyer must resell steel that has been delivered at a loss, Buyer has suffered financial injury. This injury would considered a reliance loss.

Finally, there is another kind of reliance loss that is a necessary consequence of most contracts. Buyer, thinking he has a contract with Seller, does not continue to seek contracts to supply his need from other sellers. (Recall that Shirley MacLaine gave up the chance to make a million-dollar deal to star in *Casino Royale* for Columbia because she had a contract with Twentieth Century Fox to play Evelina in *Bloomer Girl*). This costs the buyer the chance to find out whether other suppliers would produce the machine or, indeed, supply a better one cheaper. This kind of reliance loss is called the reliance of lost opportunities. In most cases whether there is such a reliance loss, as well as its extent, is not susceptible to exact proof.

To what extent, if at all, does American law protect the reliance interest? If one asked the question in the early 1930s, she would discover that American law had no theory that directly protected the reliance interest as such. Of course, a remedy protecting the expectation interest often compensates for some kinds of reliance loss. Suppose a court awards a builder, for example, damages which consist of his lost net profit plus what he has spent trying to perform before the owner's breach. This remedy covers at least some of the builder's reliance loss as part of protecting his expectation interest.[50] However, many American lawyers before the mid-1930s would have seen compensation for reliance losses as applying a *tort* measure of damages to a *contracts* action, something illogical and foreign to the common law.

In 1936, Fuller and Perdue published "The Reliance Interest in Contracts Damages."[51] To simplify only a little, they looked at continental European legal systems and found that they often protected losses in reliance on contracts. They then looked at the common law and asked to what extent it offered such protection directly or indirectly. They were able to find some cases where our courts protected the reliance interest, although many seemed to involve instances where courts had just acted without analyzing what they were doing very carefully. Fuller and Perdue also argued that the law ought to protect the reliance interest in many situations, but it should do so openly by creating a new theory of contracts damages.

Fuller and Perdue's article has been very influential. Many contracts scholars accept their classification. The Restatement (Second) of Contracts states the argument of the article in code-like form. Law students have been taught the vocabulary of the article. Courts have begun to accept this part of the legal culture. However, you should distinguish an analytic concept — the reliance interest — that has proved useful for thinking about contracts remedies from a rule of law.

In the next few pages we will examine the idea of the reliance interest so we can understand the concept, considering what we can say for and against offering legal protection for some or all of the reliance interest. Why does protecting the reliance interest matter, and to whom? Are the courts likely to limit reliance recovery?

---

[50]We can illustrate this by assuming a contract to construct a building for $100,000. After the builder has spent $40,000 performing, the owner breaches the contract by stopping construction. Had the builder completed the structure, he would have spent an additional $35,000 for a total of $75,000 to complete the job. A court protects the expectation interest by awarding the builder the contract price less the cost of completion ($100,000 - $35,000 = $65,000). This award gives the builder the equivalent of the net profit he would have made ($100,000 - [$40,000 + $35,000 = $75,000] = $25,000) plus what he has lost relying on the contract and trying to perform it ($40,000). The $40,000 is a reliance loss included within the expectation recovery.

[51]46 Yale Law Journal 52 (1936)

SECURITY STOVE & MANUFACTURING CO. v. AMERICAN RAILWAYS EXPRESS CO.

51 S.W.(2d) 572. (Kansas City Court of Appeals, 1932)

BLAND, J. — This is an action for damages for the failure of defendant to transport, from Kansas City to Atlantic City, New Jersey, within a reasonable time, a furnace equipped with a combination oil and gas burner. The cause was tried before the court without the aid of a jury, resulting in a judgment in favor of plaintiff in the sum of $801.50 and interest, or in a total sum of $1000. Defendant has appealed.

The facts show that plaintiff manufactured a furnace equipped with a special combination oil and gas burner it desired to exhibit at the American Gas Association Convention held in Atlantic City in October, 1926. The president of plaintiff testified that plaintiff engaged space for the exhibit for the reason "that the Henry L. Dougherty Company was very much interested in putting out a combination oil and gas burner; we had just developed one, after we got through, better than anything on the market and we thought this show would be the psychological time to get in contact with the Dougherty Company;" that "the thing wasn't sent there for sale but primarily to show;" that at the time the space was engaged it was too late to ship the furnace by freight so plaintiff decided to ship it by express, and, on September 18, 1926, wrote the office of the defendant in Kansas City, stating that it had engaged a booth for exhibition purposes at Atlantic City, New Jersey, from the American Gas Association, for the week beginning October 11th; that its exhibition consisted of an oil burning furnace, together with two oil burners which weighed at least 1500 pounds; that, "In order to get this exhibit in place on time it should be in Atlantic City not later than October the 8th. What we want you to do is to tell us how much time you will require to assure the delivery of the exhibit on time."

Mr. Banks, chief clerk in charge of the local office of the defendant, upon receipt of the letter, sent Mr. Johnson, a commercial representative of the defendant, to see plaintiff. Johnson called upon plaintiff taking its letter with him. Johnson made a notation at the bottom of the letter giving October 4th, as the day that defendant was required to have the exhibit in order for it to reach Atlantic City on October 8th.

On October 1st, plaintiff wrote the defendant at Kansas City, referring to its letter of September 18th, concerning the fact that the furnace must be in Atlantic City not later than October 8th, and stating what Johnson had told it, saying: "Now, Mr. Banks, we want to make doubly sure that this shipment is in Atlantic City not later than October 8th and the purpose of this letter is to tell you that you can *have your truck call for the shipment between 12 and 1 o'clock on Saturday, October 2nd for this.*" (Italics plaintiff's.) On October 2nd, plaintiff called the office of the express company in Kansas City and told it that the shipment was ready. Defendant came for the shipment on the last mentioned day, received it and delivered the express receipt to plaintiff. The shipment contained twenty-one packages. Each package was marked with stickers backed with glue and covered with silica of soda, to prevent the stickers being torn off in shipping. Each package was given a number. They ran from one to twenty-one.

Plaintiff's president made arrangements to go to Atlantic City to attend the convention and install the exhibit, arriving there about October 11th. When he reached Atlantic City he found the shipment had been placed in the booth that had been assigned to plaintiff. The exhibit was set up, but it was found that one of the packages shipped was not there. This missing package contained the gas manifold, or that part of the oil and gas burner that controlled the flow of gas in the burner. This was the most important part of the exhibit and a like burner could not be obtained in Atlantic City.

Wires were sent and it was found that the stray package was at the "over and short bureau" of defendant in St. Louis. Defendant reported that the package would be forwarded to Atlantic City and would be there by Wednesday, the 13th. Plaintiff's president waited until Thursday, the day the convention closed, but the package had not arrived at the time, so he closed up the exhibit and left. About a week after he arrived in Kansas City, the package was returned by the defendant.

Banks testified that the reasonable time for a shipment of this kind to reach Atlantic City from Kansas City would be four days; that if the shipment was received on October 4th, it would reach Atlantic City by October 8th; that plaintiff did not ask defendant for any special rate; that the rate charged was the regular one; that plaintiff asked no special advantage in the shipment; that all defendant, under its agreement with plaintiff was required to do was to deliver the shipment at Atlantic City in the ordinary course of events; that the shipment was found in St. Louis about Monday afternoon or Tuesday morning; that it was delivered at Atlantic City at the Ritz Carlton Hotel, on the 16th of the month. There was evidence on plaintiff's part that the reasonable time for a shipment of this character to reach Atlantic City from Kansas City was not more than three or four days.

While the petition alleges that defendant agreed to deliver the shipment at Atlantic City on or before October 8, 1926, it also alleges that this was the reasonable and proper time necessary to transport said shipment to Atlantic City. Therefore, giving the petition a liberal construction, it would appear that all that plaintiff was contending therein was that defendant had agreed to transport the shipment within a reasonable time, and that delivery on or before October 8th was necessary to comply with the agreement.

There is nothing in the evidence tending to show any unjust discrimination between shippers in the agreement had between plaintiff and defendant. Boiled down to its last analysis, the agreement was nothing more than that the shipment would be transported within the ordinary time. Plaintiff sought no special advantage, was asking nothing that would be denied any other shipper, was asking no particular route, no particular train, nor for any expedited service. It was simply seeking the same rights any other shipper could have enjoyed on the same terms. No special instructions were given or involved in the case. It is well established that a shipper cannot recover on a special contract to move a shipment within a specified time, for such would work an unjust discrimination among shippers. The only duty that the carrier is under is to carry the shipment safely and to deliver it at its destination within a reasonable time.

Plaintiff asked damages, which the court in its judgment allowed as follows: $147 express charges (on the exhibit); $45.12 freight on the exhibit from Atlantic City to Kansas City; $101.39 railroad and pullman fares to and from Atlantic City, expended by plaintiff's president and a workman taken by him to Atlantic City; $48 hotel room for the two; $150 for the time of the president; $40 for wages of the plaintiff's other employee and $270 for rental of the booth, making a total of $801.51.

Defendant contends that its instructions in the nature of demurrers to the evidence should have been given for the reason that the petition and plaintiff's evidence show that plaintiff has based its cause of action on defendant's breach of a promise to deliver the shipment at a specified time and that promise is non-enforceable and void under the Interstate Commerce Act; that the court erred in allowing plaintiff's expenses as damages; that the only damages, if any, that can be recovered in cases of this kind, are for loss of profits and that plaintiff's evidence is not sufficient to base any recovery on this ground.

We think, under the circumstances in this case, that it was proper to allow plaintiff's expenses as its damages. Ordinarily the measure of damages where the carrier fails to deliver a shipment at destination within a reasonable time is the difference between the market value of the goods at the time of the delivery and the time when they should have been delivered. But where the carrier has notice of peculiar circumstances under which the shipment is made, which will result in an unusual loss by the shipper in case of delay in delivery, the carrier is responsible for the real damage sustained from such delay if the notice given is of such character, and goes to such extent, in informing the carrier of the shipper's situation, that the carrier will be presumed to have contracted with reference thereto.

In the case at bar defendant was advised of the necessity of prompt delivery of the shipment. Plaintiff explained to Johnson the "importance of getting the exhibit there on time." Defendant knew the purpose of the exhibit and ought to respond for its negligence in failing to get it there. As we view the record this negligence is practically conceded. The undisputed testimony shows that the shipment was sent to the over and short department of the defendant in St. Louis. As the packages were plainly numbered this, prima facie, shows mistake or negligence on the part of the defendant. No effort was made by it to show that it was not negligent in sending it there, or not negligent in not forwarding it within a reasonable time after it was found.

There is no evidence or claim in this case that plaintiff suffered any loss of profits by reason of the delay in the shipment. In fact defendant states in its brief:

The plaintiff introduced not one whit of evidence showing or tending to show that he would have made any sales as a result of his exhibit but for the negligence of the defendant. On the contrary Blakesley testified that the main purpose of the exhibit was to try to interest the Henry L. Dougherty Company in plaintiff's combination oil and gas burner, yet that was all the evidence that there was as to the benefit plaintiff expected to get from the exhibit.

As a matter of evidence, it is clear that the plaintiff would not have derived a great deal of benefit from the exhibit by any stretch of the imagination.... .

Nowhere does plaintiff introduce evidence showing that the Henry L. Doherty Company in all probability would have become interested in the combination oil and gas burner and made a profitable contract with the plaintiff.

There is evidence that the exhibit was not sent to make a sale.

In support of its contention that plaintiff can sue only for loss of profit, if anything, in a case of this kind, defendant, among other cases cites that of *Adams Exp. Co. v. Egbert,* 36 Pa. 360. That case involved the shipment of a box containing architectural drawings or plans for a building, to a building committee of the Touro Aimshouse, in New Orleans. This committee had offered a premium of $500 to the successful competitor. These plans arrived after the various plans had been passed upon and the award made to another person. It was sought in that case to recover the value of the plans. The evidence, however, showed that the plans would not have won the prize had they arrived on time. The court held that the plans, under the circumstances, had no appreciable value and recovery could not be had for them and there was no basis for recovery for loss of the opportunity to compete for the prize....

Defendant contends that plaintiff "is endeavoring to achieve a return of the *status quo* in a suit based on a breach of contract. Instead of seeking to recover what he would have had, had the contract not been broken, plaintiff is trying to recover what he would have had, had there never been any contract of shipment;" that the expenses sued for would have been incurred in any event. It is no doubt, the general rule that where there is a breach of contract the party suffering the loss can recover only that which he would have had, had the contract not been broken, and this is all the cases decided upon which defendant relies.... But this is merely a general statement of the rule and is not inconsistent with the holdings that, in some instances, the injured party may recover expenses incurred in relying upon the contract, although such expenses would have been incurred had the contract not been breached.

The case at bar was not to recover damages for loss of profits by reason of the failure of the defendant to transport the shipment within a reasonable time, so that it would arrive in Atlantic City for the exhibit. There were no profits contemplated. The furnace was to be shown and shipped back to Kansas City.

There was no money loss, except the expenses, that was of such a nature as any court would allow as being sufficiently definite or lacking in pure speculation. Therefore, unless plaintiff is permitted to recover the expenses that it went to, which were a total loss to it by reason of its inability to exhibit the furnace and equipment, it will be deprived of any substantial compensation for its loss. The law does not contemplate any such injustice. It ought to allow plaintiff, as damages, the loss in the way of expenses that it sustained, and which it would not have been put to if it had not been for its reliance upon the defendant to perform its contract. There is no contention that the exhibit would have been entirely valueless and whatever it might have accomplished defendant knew of the circumstances and ought to respond for whatever damages plaintiff suffered. In cases of this kind the method of estimating the damages should be adopted which is the most definite and certain and which best achieves the fundamental purpose of compensation.

In *Sperry et al. v. O'Neill-Adams Co.,* 185 Fed. 231, the court held that the advantages resulting from the use of trading stamps as a means of increasing trade are so contingent that they cannot form a basis on which to rest a recovery for a breach of contract to supply them. In lieu of compensation based thereon the court directed a recovery in the sum expended in preparation for carrying on business in connection with the use of the stamps. The court said, l. c. 239:

> Plaintiff in its complaint had made a claim for lost profits, but, finding it impossible to marshal any evidence which would support a finding of exact figures, abandoned that claim. Any attempt to reach a precise sum would be mere blind guesswork. Nevertheless a contract, which both sides conceded would prove a valuable one, had been broken and the party who broke it was responsible for resultant damage. In order to carry out this contract, the plaintiff made expenditures which otherwise it would not have made.... The trial judge held, as we think rightly, that plaintiff was entitled at least to recover these expenses to which it had been put in order to secure the benefits of a contract of which defendant's conduct deprived it.

Had the exhibit been shipped in order to realize a profit on sales and such profits could have been realized, or to be entered in competition for a prize, and plaintiff failed to show loss of profits with sufficient definiteness, or that he would have won the prize, defendant's cases might be in point. But as before stated, no such situation exists here.

While, it is true that plaintiff already had incurred some of these expenses, in that it had rented space at the exhibit before entering into the contract with defendant for the shipment of the exhibit and this part of plaintiff's damages, in a sense, arose out of a circumstance which transpired before the contract was even entered into, yet, plaintiff arranged for the exhibit knowing that it could call upon defendant to perform its common-law duty to accept and transport the shipment with reasonable dispatch. The whole damage, therefore, was suffered in contemplation of defendant performing its contract, which it failed to do, and would not have been sustained except for the reliance by plaintiff upon defendant to perform it. It can, therefore, be fairly said that the damages or loss suffered by plaintiff grew out of the breach of the contract, for had the shipment arrived on time, plaintiff would have had the benefit of the contract, which was contemplated by all parties, defendant being advised of the purpose of the shipment.

The judgment is affirmed. All concur.

NOTES AND QUESTIONS

1. *The briefs and record in the Security Stove case*: Both sides spent a great deal of time on research and argued their positions in the *Security Stove* case very well. This is, perhaps, surprising in view of the small stakes involved. The court awarded $800 damages plus interest bringing the judgment to $1,000. American Railway Express filed a brief and summary of the record of 104 pages; Security Stove responded with a 44-page brief; and American Railway Express' reply brief was 12 pages.

Security Stove was organized in 1926, the year the express company delayed the essential part of the shipment. Thus, Security Stove was a classic new business. In many states it could not have recovered lost profits since it could not have proved them with reasonable certainty. However, by the time of the trial in 1931, Security Stove had managed to remain in business for five years. It ceased making the particular furnace burner with the part that American Railway Express lost, but it continued to manufacture an improved version. The novel idea in Security Stove's furnace was that "it was so designed that by pulling a switch you could change from oil to gas or back from gas to oil." The gas manifold was the part that controlled the flow of natural gas in the burner. It was the key piece that did not arrive in Atlantic City for the trade show.

American Railway Express argued that Security Stove was suing on a special contract to deliver on time, and the Interstate Commerce Commission's rules specifically barred such contracts. These rules prevented a "common carrier," such as Railway Express, from offering services to one customer that were not available at similar prices to the general public. Security Stove responded by denying it was seeking to enforce a special contract. "Plaintiff asked for no service not open to all...." Rather, it sued on the common law duty of a carrier to carry all goods with reasonable dispatch and without delay, a rule not changed by the Interstate Commerce Act. There was no agreement to rush its shipment, no special instruction.

On the issue of damages, the American Railway Express lawyers argued "Blakesley [Security Stove's President] himself admitted that he would have had to pay these expenses [which Security Stove recovered as damages] anyway if there had been no breach of contract.... Instead of seeking to recover what he would have had, had the contract not been broken, plaintiff is trying to recover what he would have had, had there never been any contract of shipment...."

Then the American Railway Express lawyers turned to many cases involving the loss of a chance to win a prize, most of which denied recovery. They discussed *Adams Express Company v. Egbert*[52] at length. A committee offered a prize of $500 for the best design of the Touro Almshouse in New Orleans. Plaintiff, an architect, gave Adams Express a box containing plans and specifications to be sent to the Committee. The express company delivered the box after the day all entries were due. The court in the *Adams Express* case held that the chance of winning the prize was too remote and contingent to allow a jury to consider it in assessing damages.

Finally, the American Railway Express lawyers sought to apply the *Adams Express* case to the facts in *Security Stove v. American Railway Express*, saying:

> Nowhere does plaintiff introduce evidence showing that the Henry L. Doherty Company in all probability would have become interested in the combination oil and gas burner and made a profitable contract with the plaintiff.... What the plaintiff actually lost as a result of defendant's breach of contract to deliver on or before October 8 was the benefit of the exhibit, but the plaintiff introduces no evidence whatsoever to determine as a matter of law just what that benefit was. There is absolutely no evidence beyond a mere possibility tending to show that the plaintiff would have made $800 out of the exhibit but for the defendant's breach of contract.

Security Stove pointed out that in *Adams Express Co. v. Egbert* the jury found that had the box shipped arrived on time, plaintiff's plans would not have been selected to win the prize. An expert testified that the plans were "totally unsuited for the purpose for which the building was intended, and not at all adapted, in its ventilation, to the climate in which it was to be erected." The court said that "[i]f his plans were entirely defective, if they were suited better for a bridge than for an almshouse, it cannot be claimed that he was damaged." It was not established that Security Stove's exhibit would have been valueless. Security Stove's lawyer said:

> Clearly, had Mr. Blakesley known that he could not have made his exhibit, he would not have gone to Atlantic City. Neither would he have sent Mr. Lundgren to Atlantic City. The chance to make the exhibit was ruined by the failure of the defendant to perform the duty imposed upon it by law, to-wit: To deliver the shipment within a reasonable time. They had ample notice that special damages would result from their failure to deliver within a reasonable time.

---

[52]36 Pa. 360, 78 Am.Dec. 382 (1860).

In its reply brief, the American Railway Express lawyers responded that the "items of damage which plaintiff seeks to recover are not proper items of damage because the plaintiff did not incur its expenses by reason of the breach of contract.... [T]he only thing the plaintiff can recover in an action like this one is the loss of profits. There is no other possible, logical solution of the problem."

2. *Contract as contrasted with tort damages*: Cases such as *Security Stove* sometimes are litigated under a tort theory. Under this theory, a carrier such as American Railway Express assumes a duty of exercising reasonable care in handling the goods. The firm shipping the goods argues that the carrier negligently failed to perform thereby causing the loss. If the negligence is the proximate cause of a loss, shipper may recover the amount of this loss as damages. Tort damages seek to restore a victim to the position he was in before the wrong was committed. Such a recovery is very similar to Fuller and Perdue's concept of reliance damages. Often lawyers struggle over the classification of a case as contract or tort in order to gain an advantageous measure of damages, statute of limitations, or substantive rule. Judges could classify many situations involving contracts either as contract or tort. Judicial opinions deciding that particular cases are either tort or contract but not both, often are statements of conclusions. The reasons offered seldom are persuasive.

3. *Reliance damages and disclaimers*: Had the events in the *Security Stove* case taken place in the 1990s, Security Stove might have shipped its exhibit by a small package air freight service such as Federal Express. Federal Express' 1990 airbill contains a remedy limitation very similar to that used by American Railway Express in the late 1920's. Federal Express provides in tiny type above the shipper's place for signature:

> In the event of untimely delivery, Federal Express will at your request and with some limitations, refund all transportation charges paid. See Service Guide for further information.

The Service Guide is a 582-page book which lists the countries, states and cities served by Federal Express. Buried in the book is the following statement:

> WE WILL NOT BE LIABLE, IN ANY EVENT, FOR ANY DAMAGES, WHETHER DIRECT, INCIDENTAL, SPECIAL OR CONSEQUENTIAL, IN EXCESS OF THE DECLARED VALUE OF A SHIPMENT, WHETHER OR NOT WE KNEW OR SHOULD HAVE KNOWN THAT SUCH DAMAGES MIGHT BE INCURRED, INCLUDING, BUT NOT LIMITED TO, LOSS OF INCOME OR PROFITS.[53]

---

[53]Federal Express Worldwide Service Guide 46 (1990).

Another similar remedy limitation and disclaimer is printed on the back of the sender's copy of the airbill. This copy is on pink paper, and the clause is printed in light gray ink. It is almost impossible to read. Finally, the same remedy limitation as in the Service Guide appears in the lower right hand corner on the back side of the FedEx Pac envelope in which documents are placed by the sender.

We will consider, in Chapter IV, arguments that Federal Express' disclaimer would not become part of the contracts between it and shippers. Assuming that a court would hold the provisions to be part of their contracts, do these provisions wipe out any general impact of *Security Stove v. American Railway Express*? For example, are the damages in these cases "special, incidental or consequential" or are they other kinds of damages? Can you fashion an argument that we are all better off if companies such as Security Stove cannot recover reliance damages from express companies? If you can fashion such an argument, might you want to regulate Federal Express' advertising campaign that speaks of "when it absolutely, positively has to get there overnight?" Again, much of this note is a preview of coming attractions for Chapter IV, but, practically, it is difficult to separate reliance damages and disclaimers.

4. *Is Security Stove the law? Where?* The *Security Stove* case's history is odd. It is a decision by a relatively obscure court. Judges and lawyers might give some extra weight to a commercial law decision by the United States Court of Appeals for the Second Circuit, the Court of Appeals of New York, or, perhaps, the Supreme Court of California. However, few who practice outside of Missouri (and perhaps even few who practice in Missouri but not in Kansas City) pay much attention to the Kansas City Court of Appeals. According to Shepard's Citator, the *Security Stove* decision has been cited in only nine other cases as of July, 1989. When we read these nine decisions, we discover that few involve the issue of reliance recovery as contract damages.

On the other hand, when we turn to the law of the law schools, the picture changes. Of fourteen contracts casebooks available in 1993, the case is a principal case in four, a note case in four more. Indeed, it even appears in Macneil, *Contracts: Instruments for Social Cooperation — East Africa* (1968), a case book written for use in East Africa. The case appears to have been the discovery of Fuller and Perdue in their influential article, "The Reliance Interest in Contracts Damages: 1," 46 Yale Law Journal 52, 88 n.57, 91 n.63 (1936). What, if anything is the significance of academic contract law? Does it matter to anyone who is not a law professor or a law student? In what ways and to what extent?

L. ALBERT & SON v. ARMSTRONG RUBBER CO.

178 F.2d 182 (2d Cir. 1949)

L. HAND, C.J. Both sides appeal from the judgment in an action brought by the Albert Company, which we shall speak of as the Seller, against the Armstrong Company, which we shall call the Buyer. The action was to recover the agreed price of four "Refiners," machines designed to recondition old rubber; the contract of sale was by an exchange of letters in December, 1942, and the Seller delivered two of the four "Refiners" in August, 1943, and the other two on either August 31st or September 8th, 1945. Because of the delay in delivery of the second two, the Buyer refused to accept all four in October, 1945 — the exact day not being fixed — and it counterclaimed for the Seller's breach. The judge dismissed both the complaint and the counterclaim; but he gave judgment to the Seller for the value without interest of a part of the equipment delivered — a 300 horse-power motor and accessories — which the Buyer put into use on February 20th, 1946. On the appeal the Seller's position is that its delay was not too long; that in any event the Buyer accepted delivery of the four "Refiners"; and that they were in accordance with the specifications. As an alternative it insists that the Buyer is liable, not only for the value of the motor, but for interest upon it; and, as to the counterclaim, that the Buyer proved no damages, assuming that there was a breach. The judge found that all four "Refiners" conformed to the specifications, or could have been made to do so with slight trouble and expense; that the contract was inseparable and called for four not two and two; that the delivery of the second two was too late; and that, as the Buyer rejected all four, it was not liable on the contract at all. On the other hand, as we have said, he found that the Buyer's use for its own purposes of the motor, although not an acceptance of the "Refiners," made it liable for the value of the motor in quasi contract, but without interest. He dismissed the Buyer's counterclaim because it had failed to prove any damages.

The first issue is whether the Seller's delivery of the second two "Refiners" was too late, and justified the Buyer's rejection of all four in October of that year. [We have omitted discussion of this issue. The Court upheld the trial court's determination.]

Upon the Seller's appeal there remains only the question whether it was entitled to interest upon the value of the motor and its accessories, which the judge denied. The Buyer's use of his property was indeed a conversion, for which the Seller might sue in quasi-contract, as it did; and the judge found that the motor, although it was secondhand machinery originally, had a "fair market value of $4,590." We follow the law of Connecticut upon the point, and we read *Regan v. New York & New England R. Co.*[54] and *Healy v. Fallon*[55] as establish-

---

[54] 60 Conn. 124, 22 A. 503, 25 Am. St. Rep. 306.

[55] 69 Conn. 228, 37 A. 495.

ing the principle that, when the value of goods can be "ascertained with reasonable certainty as of a definite time," interest should be recovered. Hence we hold that the Seller should have been awarded interest on the value of the motor and its accessories from the date of the Buyer's appropriation — February 20th, 1946.

Coming next to the Buyer's appeal, it does not claim any loss of profit, but it does claim that expenses which it incurred in reliance upon the Seller's promise. These were of three kinds: its whole investment in its "reclaim department," $118,478; the cost of its "rubber scrap," $27,555.63; the cost of the foundation which it laid for the "Refiners," $3,000. The judge in his opinion held that the Buyer had not proved that "the lack of production" of the reclaim department "was caused by the delay in delivery of plaintiff's refiners"; but that that was "only one of several possible causes. Such a possibility is not sufficient proof of causation to impose liability on the plaintiffs for the cost of all machinery and supplies for the reclaim department." The record certainly would not warrant our holding that this holding was "clearly erroneous"; indeed, the evidence preponderates in its favor. The Buyer disposed of all its "scrap rubber" in April and May, 1945; and, so far as appears, until it filed its counterclaim in May, 1947, it never suggested that the failure to deliver two of the four "Refiners" was the cause of the collapse of its "reclaim department." The counterclaim for these items has every appearance of being an afterthought, which can scarcely have been put forward with any hope of success.

The claim for the cost of the foundation which the Buyer built for the "Refiners," stands upon a different footing. Normally a promisee's damages for breach of contract are the value of the promised performance, less his outlay, which includes, not only what he must pay to the promisor, but any expenses necessary to prepare for the performance; and in the case at bar the cost of the foundation was such an expense. The sum which would restore the Buyer to the position it would have been in, had the Seller performed, would therefore be the prospective net earnings of the "Refiners" while they were used (together with any value they might have as scrap after they were discarded) less their price — $25,500 — together with $3,000, the cost of installing them. The Buyer did not indeed prove the net earnings of the "Refiners" or their scrap value; but it asserts that it is nonetheless entitled to recover the cost of the foundation upon the theory that what it expended in reliance upon the Seller's performance was a recoverable loss. In cases where the venture would have proved profitable to the promisee, there is no reason why he should not recover his expenses. On the other hand, on those occasions in which the performance would not have covered the promisee's outlay, such a result imposes the risk of the promisee's contract upon the promisor. We cannot agree that the promisor's default in performance should under this guise make him an insurer of the promisee's venture; yet it does not follow that the breach should not throw upon him the duty of showing that the value of the performance would in fact have been less than the promisee's outlay. It is often very hard to learn what the value of the performance would have been;

and it is a common expedient, and a just one, in such situations to put the peril of the answer upon that party who by his wrong had made the issue relevant to the rights of the other.(footnote omitted) On principle therefore the proper solution would seem to be that the promisee may recover his outlay in preparation for the performance, subject to the privilege of the promisor to reduce it by as much as he can show that the promisee would have lost, if the contract had been performed.

The decisions leave much to be desired. There is language in *United States v. Behan*[56] which, read literally, would allow the promisee to recover his outlay in all cases: the promisor is said to be "estopped" to deny that the value of the performance would not equal it. We doubt whether the Supreme Court would today accept the explanation, although the result was right under the rule which we propose. Moreover, in spite of the authority properly accorded to any decision of that court, we are here concerned only with Connecticut law; and the decisions in that state do not seem to be in entire accord. In the early case of *Bush v. Canfield*[57] the buyer sued to recover a payment of $5,000 made in advance for the purchase of 2,000 barrels of flour at $7.00 a barrel. Although at the time set for delivery the value of the flour had fallen to $5.50, the seller for some undisclosed reason failed to perform. The action was [for breach of contract, and not for restitution] and the court, Hosmer, J., dissenting, allowed the buyer to recover the full amount of his payment over the seller's objection that recovery should be reduced by the buyer's loss. The chief justice gave the following reason for his decision which we take to be that of the court, 2 Conn. page 488: "The defendant has violated his contract; and it is not for him to say that if he had fulfilled it, the plaintiffs would have sustained a great loss, and that this ought to be deducted from the money advanced." If there is no difference between the recovery of money received by a promisor who later defaults, and a promisee's outlay preparatory to performance, this decision is in the Buyer's favor. However, when the promisor has received any benefit, the promisee's recovery always depends upon whether the promisor has been "unjustly enriched"; and, judged by that nebulous standard, there may be a distinction between imposing the promisee's loss on the promisor by compelling him to disgorge what he has received and compelling him to pay what he never has received. It is quite true that the only difference is between allowing the promisee to recover what he has paid to the promisor and what he has paid to others; but many persons would probably think that difference vital.

In any event, unless this be a valid distinction, it appears to us that *Santoro v. Mack*[58] must be read as taking the opposite view. The plaintiff, the vendee under a contract for the sale of land, had paid an electrician and an architect whom he

---

[56]110 U.S. 338, 345, 346, 4 S. Ct. 81, 28 L.Ed. 168 [1884].

[57]2 Conn. 485 [1818].

[58]108 Conn. 683, 145 A. 273 [1929].

had employed in reliance upon the promised conveyance. These payments he sought to recover, and was unsuccessful on the ground that they had not benefited the vendor, and that they had been incurred without the vendor's knowledge or consent. Yet it would seem that such expenses were as much in reasonable preparation for the use of the land, as the cost of the foundation was for the use of the "Refiners." The point now before us was apparently not raised, but the decision, as it stands, seems to deny any recovery whatever....

The result is equally inconclusive if we consider the few decisions in other jurisdictions. The New Jersey Court of Errors and Appeals in *Hold v. United Security Life Insurance & Trust Co.*[59] recognized as the proper rule that, although the promisor had the burden of proving that the value of the performance was less than the promisee's outlay, if he succeeded in doing so, the recovery would be correspondingly limited. In *Bernstein v. Meech*[60] the promisee recovered his full outlay, and no limitation upon it appears to have been recognized, as may be inferred from the following sentence: "it cannot be assumed that any part of this loss would have been sustained by the plaintiff if he had been permitted to perform his contract." In Reynolds v. Levi[61] the promisee was a well digger, who had made three unsuccessful efforts to reach water, and the promisor — a farmer — stopped him before he had completed his fourth. The court limited the recovery to the amount earned on the fourth attempt, but for reasons that are not apparent. It appears to us therefore that the reported decisions leave it open to us to adopt the rule we have stated. Moreover, there is support for this result in the writings of scholars. The Restatement of Contracts[62] allows recovery of the promisee's outlay "in necessary preparation" for the performance, subject to several limitations, of which one is that the promisor may deduct whatever he can prove the promisee would have lost, if the contract had been fully performed. Professor McCormick thinks[63] that "the jury should be instructed not to go beyond the probable yield" of the performance to the promisee, but he does not consider the burden of proof. Much the fullest discussion of the whole subject is Professor Fuller's in the Yale Law Journal.[64] The situation at bar was among those which he calls cases of "essential reliance," and for which he favors the rule we are adopting. It is one instance of his "very simple formula: We will not in a suit for reimbursement of losses incurred in reliance on a contract knowingly put the plaintiff in a better position than he would have occupied, had the contract been fully performed."

---

[59]76 N.J.L. 585, 72 A. 301, 21 L.R.A., N.S., 691.

[60]130 N.Y. 354, 360, 29 N.E. 255, 257.

[61]122 Mich. 115, 80 N.W. 999.

[62]§ 333(d).

[63]McCormick on Damages, § 142, p. 584.

[64]46 Yale Law Journal, 752, pp. 75-80.

The judgment will therefore be affirmed with the following modifications. To the allowance for the motor and accessories will be added interest from February 20th, 1946. The Buyer will be allowed to set off $3,000 against the Seller's recovery with interest from October, 1945, subject to the Seller's privilege to deduct from that amount any sum which upon a further hearing it can prove would have been the buyer's loss upon the contract, had the "Refiners" been delivered on or before May 1st, 1945.

Judgment modified as above, and affirmed as so modified.

NOTES AND QUESTIONS

1. *Judge Hand and the law of Connecticut*: Once again we read an opinion of a federal court deciding a case brought to it under diversity of citizenship jurisdiction. Under *Erie v. Thompkins*, the federal court should apply state law. In his *L. Albert & Sons* opinion, Judge Hand discusses *Bush v. Canfield* and *Santoro v. Mack* in some detail. He concludes "[i]t appears to us ... that the reported decisions leave it open to us to adopt the rule we have stated." Has Judge Hand successfully distinguished *Bush v. Canfield* and *Santoro v. Mack* from the case he was deciding? Can you think of distinctions he might have suggested but did not? Consider *Hadley v. Baxendale, supra*.

2. *Judge Hand and causation*: Judge Hand says that there was no merit in buyer's claim for its investment in the "reclaim department" and for the rubber scrap. What is his reasoning? Is Judge Hand consistent in his denial of recovery of these items while allowing recovery for buyer's investment in the foundation, subject to seller's right to show that the investment would have been a loss if there had been no breach? Does Judge Hand seem to impose *on the buyer* the burden of proof of showing that the investment in the "reclaim department" and the rubber scrap would not have been lost if there had been no breach, whereas with respect to the foundation he imposes that burden on the seller?

In thinking about these questions, it might be helpful to ask whether if there had been no contract at all buyer would have made the investment in (1) the reclaim department, (2) the rubber scrap, or (3) the foundations. Suppose the investment in (1) and (2) would have been made even if seller had refused to enter into any contract at all with buyer, whereas the investment in (3) was made only because of the contract. Would that have any bearing on the decision in this case?

Some World War II history may provide some context for answering these questions. When the Japanese won their early victories in Southeast Asia, they cut off most American supplies of natural rubber. While German technology had developed synthetic rubber, the United States was far behind in developing it. Reclaimed rubber was a costly way to produce an inferior substitute. As the war went on, American technology developed synthetic rubber. As allied victories pushed the Japanese back from Southeast Asia, America regained supplies of natural rubber. Thus, had the seller delivered the machines on time, what would have been the likely position of the buyer toward the end of the war? There was a market for reclaimed rubber both before and after World War II, but the demand was nothing like that in the early wartime period.

The seller's brief tells us more about this issue:

> From the evidence, largely out of the mouths of the defendant's own officers, it appeared that the defendant did not try very hard to put its reclaiming department in operation. It had just a few men working on one shift, while the rest of its factory was working 24 hours a day. After a small experimental output, the department was disbanded. While the defendant originally relied upon getting the refiners from the plaintiff to start production in this department, it duplicated its order by securing the four so-called Stuart-Bolling refiners from another party. If it really wanted to reclaim rubber, it had all the equipment it needed.... No witness ever intimated that the Stuart-Bolling refiners were not suitable for the purpose.

3. *Reliance damages and the U.C.C.:* The Restatement (Second) of Contracts, § 349, embodies the Learned Hand limitation on recovery of reliance expenses set out in the *L. Albert* case. If a court decided *L. Albert & Son v. Armstrong Rubber* today, Article 2 of the Uniform Commercial Code would apply. What result would it reach?

Perhaps the first question that should be asked is whether reliance expenditures that buyer sought to recover could be considered "consequential damages" under § 2-715(2)? There is no explicit definition of "consequential damages" in Article 2. Comment 3 to § 1-106 provides that " 'consequential' ... damages ... are used in the sense given them by leading cases on the subject." The treatises suggest that the term "consequential" damage is used in the same sense as the term "special" damage is used in *Hadley v. Baxendale* (i.e., as distinguished from damages arising "naturally").[65] Under that test, would the expenditures for the foundation in *L. Albert & Son* be considered "consequential" damages? If they were consequential damages, would the result in the case be the same as the result reached by Judge Hand? In particular, under the Code would the seller have the option of showing that the foundation expenditures would have been losses even if there had been no breach?

If not consequential damages, the reliance damages might be considered "incidental damage" under § 2-715(1). There are few cases distinguishing between incidental damages under § 2-715(1) and consequential damages under § 2-715(2). Could it matter whether we consider reliance damages one or the other?

---

[65]Farnsworth, Contracts 913 (2d ed., Little, Brown & Co., 1990); Dobbs, Remedies 138 (West Publishing Co., 1973).

If reliance damages are not either incidental or consequential damage, could the buyer in *L. Albert & Sons* recover under § 1-103?

4. *Consequential Damages and the Seller in the U.C.C.:* There is no section of the U.C.C. that provides for consequential damages for the seller. Normally the seller does not have consequential damages, but it is possible. The Code does have a section providing for incidental damages for the seller — § 2-710. Perhaps because there is no section providing for consequential damages for the seller, some courts have interpreted § 2-710 in a very expansive way. It is an unsettled question whether these expansive decisions would be applied to § 2-715(1) — the buyer's incidental damages section. Of course, such application would matter only if it made any difference whether buyer damages were labeled "incidental" or "consequential" damages, a question posed in the previous note.

G. RESTITUTION AND EXIT AS ALTERNATIVES TO CONTRACT REMEDIES FOR BREACH OF CONTRACT

1. INTRODUCTION

When the other party breaches your contract, you may want nothing more than to forget the whole thing. You may decide that the deal was not that good or another is better. You may think the costs of litigation will be too great. However, are you free to forget the whole thing? Sometimes yes, sometimes no. Much complicated law governs the right to exit. Here we introduce the problem and show some of the main approaches; in chapter 9 we return to this topic and cover it in much greater depth.

There is another closely related problem. You may want to forget the contract. However, you, as buyer, may have made a down payment or, as seller, delivered some or all of the goods. You want your money or your property back. Not surprisingly, there are legal remedies designed to get them back. Occasionally, these remedies may be more valuable than contract damages. For example, suppose you have sold what you thought was just an old book to someone for $5. However, the buyer fails to pay the $5. Then you discover that the book is a rare first edition of a classic. You may want to get the book back rather than be put where you would have been had the contract been performed. Can you do this?

Here we encounter the third and last of Fuller and Perdue's interests protected by contracts remedies — "the restitution interest." Restitution means, roughly, giving back. Fuller and Perdue note that we can see the restitution interest as a special case of the reliance interest. However, lawyers think the restitution situation often presents a stronger argument for relief. You, the breacher, are "unjustly enriched." I have relied on the contract and money or other assets have left my pocket. Moreover, they have ended up in your pocket. You have a gain while I have a loss. Restitutionary remedies are available in many situations other than contract breaches. For example, I have a remedy to recover property from a thief, one who has defrauded me, or from a trustee who has misused property which the trustee was to hold for my benefit. While all restitution situations are similar in some ways, they also differ. Restitution is a potential alternative remedy in many situations: breach of contract, mutual mistake, fraud, breach of fiduciary duty, and so on. But in each of these situations, the rules governing restitution may differ importantly.

We can illustrate some of the interplay between the expectation, reliance and restitution interests with a simplified example. Suppose Seller contracts to deliver 3,000 bushels of apples to Buyer for $8,000. Buyer pays $1,000 as a down payment. In anticipation of delivery Buyer hires two laborers to unload the apples, paying them $100 each in advance for their time. At the time for delivery, Buyer is ready and willing to pay the remaining $7,000 to Seller, but Seller breaches the contract by refusing to deliver. The market price when Buyer learned of the breach is $9,000. Buyer has no other work for the laborers to do, and sends them home. Buyer then arranges for purchase of more apples (at $9000), to replace those he did not obtain from Seller, and makes new arrangements to have them unloaded, but this time must pay 2 laborers $125 each. Buyer sues Seller.

(A) What recovery would protect Buyer's expectation interest? Her reliance interest? Her restitution interest? Are the interests mutually exclusive? Cumulative?

(B) What would Buyer recover under the Uniform Commercial Code? See §§ 2-711(1); 2-713.

(C) What would Buyer recover under the Uniform Commercial Code if the market price of apples had been $6,000 at the time the Buyer learned of the breach, and the Buyer had purchased replacement apples for $6,000? Recall Judge Hand's discussion of *Bush v. Canfield* in his *L. Albert & Son v. Armstrong Rubber Co.* opinion. Does this recovery protect the expectation, the reliance or the restitution interest or some combination of them? Compare U.C.C. § 2-706(6) governing cases where the seller resells goods for more than the contract price. What if the buyer had chosen not to buy any replacement apples?

(D) Would it matter if the replacement laborers were paid $100 each? $200 each?

2. WALKING AWAY FROM A DEAL: EXIT AND RESTITUTION

a. Sales of Goods

Exit and restitution are important remedies. Buyers often find exit and restitution important when they question a seller's performance. Even if the buyer finds that it would not pay to sue for the difference between the contract and cover price as damages, the right to exit allows him to avoid or minimize loss and go on about his business. Sellers, too, may value the right to walk away from a buyer who fails to make payments. Furthermore, parties may be able to threaten to cancel a contract as a tactic in negotiating settlements.

However, the law limits the use of these remedies. If a failure to perform is not important, then calling off a deal is a drastic therapy. Normally we expect, for example, a buyer to accept goods and deal with a minor defect in any of a number of ways. He can ask the seller to fix the defect. He can deduct a sum representing the cost of fixing the defect from his payment. He can accept all the good items and reject only the few bad ones. Indeed, if a buyer tries to exit when a seller's default is only trivial, we can suspect that defective performance is only a pretext. A book by Bertell Ollman, *Class Struggle Is the Name of the Game*, illustrates the tactical advantages of exit and restitutionary remedies as well as suggesting why courts have not granted these remedies freely.

Ollman is a professor of political science. He devised "Class Struggle," a board game designed to teach a Marxist perspective about capitalism. However, he and his friends who backed the game found that it had to be marketed through the capitalist system. In order to teach revolution, they had to play the role of entrepreneur. Initially the game was a success. They sold over twenty-five thousand games in the first six months. Ollman and his friends then ordered fifty thousand games from Bill Finn's company which manufactured the board, the game pieces and the boxes. They agreed to pay $160,000, and made a $65,000 down payment. This was a mistake. A lender decided that their accounts receivable did not warrant a loan, stores were slow in paying for games they had bought, Bloomingdales in New York decided not to feature the game, and a customer in Holland who had asked for five thousand games changed his mind. Finn demanded payment of the $95,000 balance due, but they did not have enough to pay him. "The whole business was about to come crashing down on our heads. Class Struggle was on the verge of bankruptcy."

Ollman, in the extract presented below, has just finished preparing the board of directors for the news that they will have to declare bankruptcy.

Class Struggle Is the Name of the Game
Bertell Ollman[66]

But before I could continue, Paul interrupted. "Not yet. First, take a look at this." With that, he opened up a Class Struggle game box he was carrying, and took out two game boards. He pointed to the low ridge that followed the fold in the middle of the board. "These are the new boards. I picked them up in the factory today. The ridge in the middle is so high it disfigures the board. I also think these boards are a little lighter than the ones we got last time. Wasn't Finn supposed to give us the same board?" ...

---

[66]172-81, 201. Copyright 1983 by William Morrow and Company, Inc. Reprinted with the permission of William Morrow and Company, Inc.Publishers, New York.

"Are they really that bad?" I asked. I could see what Paul was talking about, but the difference between the boards seemed to be very slight.

"I think so." Howard said angrily. "If I was a customer, I wouldn't buy a board like this."

"No, the real problem is not with customers," Paul corrected him, "but with store buyers. Some of them look the game over very carefully. They may be indifferent to its politics, but they want it to be well made. This sloppy manufacturing is going to turn them off." Paul spoke with great certainty, and then more tentatively. "A few of them, anyway."

"But they're already made, all fifty thousand of them." Ed shook his head in disgust.

"And we haven't paid for them." Howard finally spoke the words that we had all begun to think. "Izzy, what does our agreement with Finn say, I mean about this new edition?"

"That he produce the same game he did the last time. Yes," Izzy specified, noting the question in our eyes, "that means exactly the same."

"And if he doesn't?" Milt broke in before Izzy had a chance to finish.

"If he doesn't," Izzy continued, "I guess that means he is in breach of contract."

"Finn's about to sue us for the ninety-five thousand dollars we still owe him," I interjected. "That's the good news I was saving for tonight's meeting."

"Sue us? Sue us?" Howard shouted. "That bastard has just about destroyed our business by giving us a shoddy game. We should sue him for ... for a million dollars."...

It was as if a great natural force, a hurricane or a river of lava, that was about to engulf us all had been stopped dead by Howard's words, and had now begun to recede. My tiredness, the tiredness of months, had given way to an energy, indeed an exhilaration. I thought I'd lost. This was, as they say, a new ball game. Finn had outsmarted himself.... He had given us something other than what we had contracted for. Whether customers were actually pressing us for games at this time was irrelevant. He had our sixty-five thousand dollars, and we had received nothing....

The next day, Howard and I went to see Finn.... [They showed him the defect.]

"Look ...," Finn shot back. "I've been making game boards for twenty years. I'm telling you there is nothing wrong with this board."

"The feel of a game, how heavy it is — and that includes how heavy the board is — all enter into the consciousness of a buyer." I said. "It's related to quality. The buyer for Toys-R-Us made a big point of this."

Finn's original defensiveness was now turning into annoyance. "This board is no lighter than the boards I make for Scrabble."

"Maybe so," Howard replied. "But as you can see, it is lighter than the board you made for the last edition of Class Struggle, and therefore it is lighter than the board you contracted to make this time."

With the mention of our contract, Finn flushed, stopped all movement, and looked at us long and hard.

Howard was the first to break the silence, but Finn had already understood. "As it stands, we don't think we can use these games. So...."

"You guys are really something. You can't pay for what you ordered, so you decide after they're made that you don't want them. It isn't my fault that you're having a lousy Christmas. Where did you professors learn how to do business?" His face had turned deep red.

Finn's barbs contained enough half-truths to hurt. "Look, Bill, it's nobody's fault," I intoned without much conviction. "And business isn't bad — we really could use the games. But if we feel we can't sell them or that selling them will damage our reputation, then we have to take some action to protect ourselves. We want new game boards, just like the ones we had last time, just like the ones we ordered this time."

"There is also the matter of the damage done to our business," Howard added gravely, "due to the delay this will cause in getting games with acceptable boards. We will probably lose a lot of orders."

Finn had heard enough. The lines were now drawn. He would sue us for the money we owed him "and collect to the last penny," he promised, hissing the words out between his teeth. Straining to keep our cool, we replied that we would be suing him for breach of contract, asking for our sixty-five thousand dollars back and damages.

On leaving his office, something in me rebelled against the strictures of my new role. Finn wasn't a bad sort. We had shared some hopes and laughs together about his business as well as mine. On my last visit, he had talked about a daughter who was having a serious operation. "I hope your daughter recovers quickly, Bill," I said, turning toward him. I don't know why but I held out my hand. No, I do know why, but it made no difference. Finn put his hands behind his back and just glared at me.

Business. Wasn't I just being a good businessman? We had to protect our investment. Finn, too, was just trying to be a good businessman. I mustn't let any human feelings interfere with what business required. That is being a bad businessman. Unless those human feelings clear the way for more and better business, and that was not the case here....

We received court papers announcing Finn's suit, and sent him court papers announcing ours. But Finn knew that suing us would take years, during which he would be stuck with a lot of games he couldn't use or sell, and that even if he won his suit, all that would happen was that he would force us into bankruptcy. Only a quick settlement offered him any hope of recuperating part of his investment. A few weeks went by when his lawyer, Herbert Jason, Jr., called our lawyer, Izzy, and asked whether something couldn't be worked out. "Like what?" Izzy asked. After several more calls, an appointment was made for Izzy and me to meet with Finn and Jason at the latter's office.

The evening before, the board met to hammer out a bargaining position. We had practically run out of games. If we were to stay in business, we needed more and we needed them quickly. We also reached an uneasy consensus that we could sell the new games despite the inferior board. Paul was unhappy with this decision, but eventually he, too, agreed. We would conduct business as usual, but if a customer complained, we would refund his or her money. Before he halted production, Finn had finished twenty-two thousand games, and he had the parts on hand to produce another twenty-eight thousand. The key question was how much was all this worth above the sixty-five thousand dollars we had already paid.

Izzy met me at Jason's plush Park Avenue office wearing the kind of three-piece tailored suit he puts aside for occasions such as this....[67] Jason began by announcing rather formally that Mr. Finn wanted ninety-five thousand dollars that was owed him for producing fifty thousand games for Class Struggle, Inc. Whereupon, Izzy responded just as formally that Class Struggle, Inc., wanted its sixty-five thousand dollars back, as well as a half-million dollars for damages to our business firm. He could keep the damaged games. Then, less formally, Jason said, "But there does seem to be some room for a compromise." When Izzy asked what he suggested, Jason responded that Mr. Finn would kindly extend the length of time for paying the money which we owed. Jason then asked Izzy what we had in mind, to which Izzy responded that we might consider dropping our suit for damages to the business if Mr. Finn returned our sixty-five thousand dollars and gave us all the finished games. This was one of the occasions on which Finn shot me a particularly hostile glance.

From these two extreme positions, both lawyers began to edge toward a common center. Each lawyer would introduce his "last best offer" by turning to his client to make sure he had not gone too far. Every now and then Finn would put on a show of total opposition, and once he even stalked from the room. Each time Jason would soothe him, saying that such an act of generosity and statesmanship on his part would surely bring Class Struggle to settle the matter right here. After witnessing this imaginative charade a couple of times, I decided to include it in my own act. Feigning outrage at their offer, I blew up. Izzy caught on, and gave me a chance to appear as the generous statesman. Business has provided me with the occasion for many kinds of acting — comedy, farce, adventure — but this was my first essay into Shakespearean tragedy.

After an hour and a half, we had crawled to offering them fifteen thousand dollars on top of the sixty-five thousand dollars they had for the games already produced and all the raw materials (estimating it would take another fifteen thousand to twenty thousand dollars to produce twenty-eight thousand more games from these materials); and Finn had reduced his demand to thirty thousand

---

[67]Why did the meeting take place at a "plush Park Avenue office"? Why did Izzy, Class Struggle, Inc.'s lawyer, wear a costume to the performance?

dollars for everything. But I had already gone higher than I had been authorized by the board to go, and Finn had been more conciliatory than he had expected to be. Finn's temper was flaring more frequently now. No further progress could be made today. I had received his very last offer, and he took note of mine. The lawyers agreed to keep in touch....

NOTES AND QUESTIONS

1. *The end of the story*: Class Struggle, Inc., and Finn finally settled their dispute. Class Struggle agreed to pay Finn $20,000 more. Finn agreed to hand over twenty-two thousand finished games and the parts for twenty-eight thousand others.[68]

2. *The human side of playing "hardball"*: The chance that Class Struggle, Inc. might have been able to exit from the transaction without any legal obligation to Finn had great tactical value in the negotiations. Finn, however, was angry. Why? Ollman reports his own doubts about his part in dealing with Finn. Why did he have doubts? Isn't it the American norm that "all's fair in love, war and business?"

3. *A legislative proposal*: Professor Karl Llewellyn's original draft of what became Article II of the Uniform Commercial Code proposed a substantial performance rule for merchant buyers. This meant that buyers could not refuse to accept a tender of goods unless there were important defects in them. (They would, however, have been able to sue for damages to cover defects which were not substantial.) Llewellyn tried to avoid giving a buyer a right to get out of a contract when his real motive was to take advantage of a falling market. (Professor Ollman and his colleagues might not have been able to use the defects in the game boards to ward off bankruptcy either.) Consumer buyers, however, could insist on exact performance.

The New York Merchants' Association objected.[69] The merchants worried about a substantial performance rule in the hands of judges and juries. The Merchants' Association representative said,

> Now, one merchant I was speaking [to,] an officer of R.H. Macy & Company and a lawyer, said, "My Lord, what a chance for sellers to unload all their shopworn and defective goods and then let a jury decide whether they can't do it. It's wonderful."

---

[68]For a critical review of Ollman's book, see Zukin, Book Review, 14 Theory and Society 247 (1985)("As a board game, 'Class Struggle' was neither well designed nor well crafted, and people who played it reported that the rules were complex, it took too long to play, and playing it wasn't very much fun.")

[69]Wiseman, The Limits of Vision: Karl Llewellyn and the Merchant Rules, 100 Harvard Law Review 465, 526 (1987).

Merchants thought they could solve the problem that concerned Llewellyn by "relational sanctions;" that is, by threatening or using the informal sanctions that accompany any long term relationship, such as declining to enter into future transactions, or withholding cooperation in situations in which cooperation is not legally required, but is necessary, as a practical matter.

The provisions of the U.C.C. as enacted are a compromise. No distinctions here are made between merchant and consumer buyers. Under § 2-601, a buyer may reject goods that "fail in any respect to conform to the contract." However, after a rejection, § 2-508 gives sellers a right to cure defective tenders of goods, subject to a number of qualifications. Once a buyer accepts goods, then § 2-608 says that the buyer may revoke his acceptance only in certain limited situations. One important limitation is that the non-conformity [of the goods] must substantially impair [their] value to him." Different rules apply to installment contracts. Under § 2-612, a buyer may reject an installment "if the non-conformity substantially impairs the value of that installment...." A buyer may call off the entire installment contract when a default "substantially impairs the value of the whole contract."

As so often is the case, compromises yield complexity. Complexity gives lawyers on both sides good arguments. It seldom gives them answers.

COLONIAL DODGE, INC. v. MILLER

116 Mich.App. 78, 322 N.W.2d 549 (1982)

DEMING, J. On May 28, 1976, Clarence R. Miller went to the plaintiff's dealership to pick up his new Dodge station wagon. He signed one form and drove the vehicle a short distance, exchanging cars with his wife. Mr. Miller drove an older car to work while Mrs. Miller returned home with the new car at about 3:00 p.m. When Mr. Miller returned home his wife informed him that the new car had no spare tire. Because Miller worked the night shift and the dealership was not open when he received word that his new car had no spare tire, Miller waited until the next morning to phone the salesman who had sold him the car. When Mr. Miller expressed dissatisfaction, the salesman informed him that he knew that the car had no spare tire because of a tire strike but that he (the salesman) had other things on his mind.

When Mr. Miller reiterated that he drove long distances to and from work on Detroit area expressways, up to 170 miles per day, and that he had paid extra money for high quality steel-belted radial tires, he received no satisfactory answer. Miller then told the salesman to come and get the car and that he didn't want it and that he was going to stop payment on two checks given in payment for the automobile.[70]

After Miller stopped payment on the checks, he parked the automobile in front of his house, later refusing receipt of license plates for the car. When the temporary vehicle registration expired, 10 days after the car was purchased, police officers towed the new car and impounded it.

The plaintiff concedes that the automobile did not have a spare tire but argues that one finally did arrive after the tire strike ended. Plaintiff also concedes that it is reasonable to expect, and that defendant in fact paid for, five tires with the car that he purchased.

Plaintiff sued defendant Miller for the purchase price of the car. Miller defended on the basis that he had either never accepted the car or had properly revoked acceptance under provisions of the Uniform Commercial Code. The trial court found that plaintiff was entitled to the contract price of the vehicle, less what it would have received from resale of the car within a reasonable period after the defendant breached the sales contract. Judgment was entered for $1,342.31. The plaintiff appeals.

At issue is whether Mr. Miller ever accepted the automobile within the meaning of M.C.L. § 440.2606; M.S.A. § 19.2606, and, if so, whether that acceptance was properly revoked pursuant to M.C.L. § 440.2608; M.S.A. § 19.2608....

It is clear that, under the Code, delivery does not in and of itself constitute acceptance. In White & Summers, Handbook of the Law Under the Uniform Commercial Code (2d ed.), § 8-2, p. 296, the concept of acceptance as within the meaning of § 2-606 is discussed. The authors point out that, because acceptance is a term of art which must be sharply distinguished from a variety of other acts which a buyer might commit, the Code first distinguishes and separates title problems from the problem of acceptance. Secondly, acceptance is only tangentially related to a buyer's possession of the goods, and in the usual case the buyer will have had possession of the goods for some time before he has accepted them within the meaning of the Code.

The mere taking of possession of goods by a delivery of goods to a buyer does not equal automatic acceptance, for the U.C.C. makes an important and just allowance of a "reasonable opportunity" to inspect goods. M.C.L. § 440.2606(1)(a), (b); M.S.A. § 19.2606(1)(a), (b)...

In *Zabriske Chevrolet, Inc. v. Smith*, 99 N.J. Super. 441, 240 A.2d 195 (1968), the court viewed a similar circumstance. Plaintiff sold defendant a new Chevrolet automobile. After driving it a short distance, the automobile became inoperable. Defendant phoned the dealership, "canceled" the sale, and stopped

---

[70] We take judicial notice of the fact that Detroit area freeways and expressways have been the scene of violent crime and that many citizens justifiably fear automobile breakdowns while travelling on the expressways and the danger attendant thereto.

payment on the check written in purchase of the automobile. The dealer thereafter sued for the purchase price of the car. Plaintiff repaired the vehicle and notified defendant that the automobile was now operable. The car that the Smiths purchased remained in storage for a lengthy period of time.

In *Zabriske*, as here, plaintiff argued strongly that § 2-607(1), M.C.L. § 440.2607(1); M.S.A. § 19.2607(1), applied and that, having accepted the vehicle, defendant was bound to pay for it according to the terms of the contract. In specifically rejecting plaintiff's argument, the *Zabriske* court said:

> It is clear that a buyer does not accept goods until he has had a "reasonable opportunity to inspect." Defendant sought to purchase a new car. He assumed that every new car buyer has a right to assume and, indeed, has been led to assume by the high powered advertising techniques of the auto industry — that his new car, with the exception of very minor adjustments, would be mechanically new and factory-furnished, operate perfectly, and be free of substantial defects. The vehicle delivered to defendant did not measure up to these representations. Plaintiff contends that defendant had "reasonable opportunity to inspect" by the privilege to take the car for a typical "spin around the block" before signing the purchase order. If by this contention plaintiff equates a spin around the block with "reasonable opportunity to inspect," the contention is illusory and unrealistic. To the layman, the complicated mechanisms of today's automobiles are a complete mystery. To have the automobile inspected by someone with sufficient expertise to disassemble the vehicle in order to discover latent defects before the contract is signed, is assuredly impossible and highly impractical..... Consequently, the first few miles of driving become even more significant to the excited new car buyer. This is the buyer's first reasonable opportunity to enjoy his new vehicle to see if it conforms to what it was represented to be and whether he is getting what he bargained for. How long the buyer may drive the new car under the guise of inspection of new goods is not an issue in the present case. It is clear that defendant discovered the nonconformity within 7/10 of a mile and minutes after leaving plaintiff's showroom. Certainly this was well within the ambit of "reasonable opportunity to inspect". *Id*. 452-453, 240 A.2d 195.

Moreover, the court specifically recognized the perfect tender rule of § 2-601 specifically rejecting pre-code cases which held that substantial compliance with contract terms entitled the seller to force a buyer to accept nonconforming goods and pay for them.

We conclude that the trial court's finding that defendant Miller had accepted the automobile is clearly erroneous. Acceptance, as that term is used in the Uniform Commercial Code, is much more than taking delivery. Acceptance cannot occur, as a matter of law, unless and until the buyer has had a "reasonable" opportunity to inspect the purchased goods. M.C.L. § 440.2606(1); M.S.A. § 19.2606(1)....

Since Mr. Miller did not have a reasonable opportunity to inspect the automobile and did not act inconsistently with the seller's ownership after the hidden defect was in fact found, we hold that he had an absolute right to reject the automobile because it failed to conform to the contract, *i.e.*, it did not have five tires....

Having concluded that Mr. Miller never accepted the vehicle, we turn to the facts surrounding his rejection. M.C.L. § 440.2602; M.S.A. § 19.2602. It is undisputed that on the morning after taking delivery of the station wagon, Mr. Miller phoned the dealership, discussed the absence of the spare tire, and, after receiving no satisfactory explanation orally rejected the automobile as not conforming to the purchase contract. He told the dealer's agent to come and pick up the car because he refused to drive it at all without a spare tire.

At issue is the propriety of defendant's rejection. M.C.L. § 440.2602; M.S.A. § 19.2602 requires a nonmerchant buyer who has rightfully rejected goods to seasonably inform the seller of the fact of rejection. Thereafter, the buyer has no further obligations with regard to goods rightfully rejected. M.C.L. § 440.2602(2)(c); M.S.A. § 19.2602(2)(c). The duty of the seller to remove or repossess the nonconforming goods is universally recognized....

Nor do we find that defendant's method of notice, the telephone, was inappropriate under these circumstances. There is no dispute concerning the unequivocal nature of Mr. Miller's rejection of the automobile or the reason for the rejection....

Having properly rejected nonconforming goods, defendant Miller had no other obligation and properly parked the vehicle in front of his house. M.C.L. § 440.2602(2)(c); M.S.A. § 19.2602(2)(c). However, we direct that, on remand, Mr. Miller execute whatever documents are required to vest legal title in the plaintiff, forthwith.

Reversed and remanded. Costs to appellee. [Brennan, J., concurred.]

CYNAR, J. (dissenting). Defendant Miller entered into a special purchase order with plaintiff for the purchase of a station wagon specified as a "Heavy Duty Trailer Package" which included "heavy duty oversized tires". The specially ordered station wagon was delivered to plaintiff and Miller picked up the vehicle after Miller executed an application for Michigan Title and made payment for the vehicle with checks. The invoice indicated that the spare tire was not included in the delivery and would be shipped later, the delay being attributed to a nationwide tire strike. The following day Miller called plaintiff and complained about the missing tire, stopped payment on the checks, and advised plaintiff to pick up the station wagon, which was parked in front of his home. Plaintiff advised Miller when the replacement tire became available.

In *Zabriske Chevrolet, Inc. v. Smith*, 99 N.J. Super. 441, 240 A.2d 195 (1968), an automobile became inoperable 7/10 of a mile and minutes after leaving the dealer's showroom. The court decided that the buyer had a right to assume that his new car, with the exception of very minor adjustments, would be mechanically new, factory-furnished, operate perfectly, and be free of substantial defects. While I am in total agreement with the *Zabriske* decision, it must be pointed out that the facts in the matter submitted for our decision are not similar.

A buyer may properly revoke acceptance where the nonconformity substantially impairs its value. The existence of such nonconformity depends on the facts and circumstances of each case....

The trial judge's determination that the temporarily missing spare tire did not constitute a substantial impairment in value under either the subjective or objective test was not clearly erroneous. I therefore disagree with the majority finding that defendant Miller properly rejected the vehicle, and I would affirm the trial court's finding in that regard.

Having determined that defendant Miller wrongfully revoked acceptance in this case, the trial court found that the vehicle would have been resold for $1,000 less, on or about September 1, 1976, than the sales price to defendant Miller and therefore this was the amount of damages the plaintiff was entitled to recover. With this determination, I must disagree.... [T]he trial court should have awarded the full contract price to plaintiff.

NOTES AND QUESTIONS

1. *Rejection and revocation*: The court tells us that the buyer in this case argued that "he had either never accepted the car or had properly revoked acceptance under provisions of the Uniform Commercial Code." There are a number of very important questions which must be asked in order to understand the arguments implicit in the preceding statement. See if you can unpack the statement.

a. First, what are the relevant code sections?

b. Under what circumstances may a buyer refuse to accept tendered goods? Sometimes the argument will be about whether or not the goods meet the standard required by the contract, and by the law. Was the argument in *Colonial Dodge* about whether the buyer had a right to reject?

c. What acts constitute an acceptance? Sometimes the argument will assume some defect in the goods, but argue that buyer failed to reject them. Was that the argument here?

d. When may a buyer revoke an acceptance? Sometimes a buyer who has accepted may undo the acceptance? Is that a possibility here?

e. How do the standards for rejection, and revocation of acceptance, differ?

2. *The beat goes on*: The Michigan intermediate appellate court subsequently granted a rehearing. (The opinion issued after the rehearing is reprinted in Chapter 8. You may, if overcome by curiosity, read it now.) If you were a law clerk asked to draft an opinion in which you reached a different conclusion in this case, what arguments would you make? Where would you attack the majority opinion?

3. *Remedies for buyers who have accepted goods*: What if one concluded that Mr. Miller had accepted the car, and had no right to revoke his acceptance. Would that mean he would be entitled to no remedy for the dealer's failure to include the spare tire? Section 2-714(2) would grant Mr. Miller "the difference at the time and place of acceptance between the value of the goods accepted and the value they would have had if they had been as warranted, unless special circumstances show proximate damages of a different amount." See, also, § 2-714(3). How much would that be? Would Mr. Miller be content with such a remedy?

4. *Flowchart for buyer's options*: The following diagram shows the buyer's options on the seller's tender of goods which fail to conform to the contract.

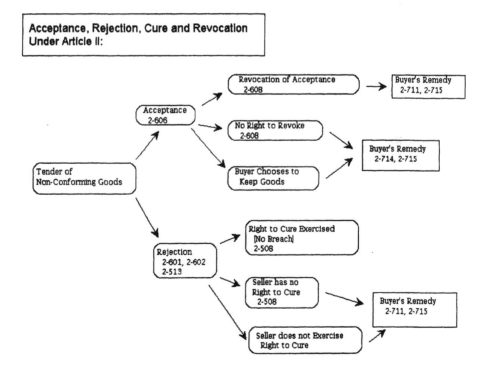

b. Substantial Performance in Building Contracts

Courts have long struggled with the conflict between personal taste and objective material defects in the area of residential building construction. Houses and apartment buildings are not precision products built to exact specifications. Nonetheless, the owner or buyer may be very unhappy with defects which only he or she can see. In *Plante v. Jacobs*,[71] for example, Frank and Carol Jacobs contracted with Plante in 1956. Plante was to build a house upon their lot in Brookfield according to plans and specifications. They were to pay him $26,765 as construction progressed. They paid him a total of $20,000 in several installments.

The Jacobs were unhappy about Plante's work. They failed to make their last payment, Plante sued, and then they, or their attorney, gathered everything they could call a defect in an attempt to offset Plante's claim. There were twenty-four entries in their "schedule of items not performed or not properly performed." They estimated that the most expensive to remedy was a misplaced wall between the living room and the kitchen. It narrowed the living room and expanded the kitchen by about one foot. The Jacobs offered evidence that it would cost $4,000 to tear down this wall and rebuild it according to the plans and specifications.

The trial court said "[b]ased on the testimony of the defendants' witness Harrigan and the plaintiff's witness Ruby, the Court will find that the misplacing of this wall caused no damage to the defendants." Since the wall and the other defects were not a material failure to perform, Plante had substantially performed his side of the deal. This meant he was entitled to the contract price minus any damages that the Jacobs could prove. They had no right to withhold the last payment because of Plante's failure to follow plans and specifications.

Harrigan, a real estate broker, appraised the Jacobs' house as having a market value of $35,000. He testified that his opinion about the fair market value "was not greatly influenced by this difference in dimensions. The kitchen being a foot wider was not a great factor." Roland Ruby, another real estate broker and a Vice-President of the Elm Grove Savings and Loan Association, testified for Plante:

> Q. And having that living room — what effect would it have on the market value of that house to have that living room one foot wider?
> A. I don't think it would be a factor.
> Q. You don't think it would make any difference to anybody who bought it?
> A. No, I don't.

---

[71] 10 Wis.2d 567, 103 N.W.2d 300 (1960).

Frank M. Jacobs, the buyer of the house, testified:

> The living room is now 15x32 ft. instead of 16x32 ft. Such narrowness of the living room of course has changed our plans so far as what we could do in decorating the room and the access to the west end of the room through the kitchen door. We had a custom built davenport and you can't cut a foot off to give proper walking space. If another chair is at the end as it should be that is a group. The kitchen is a foot wider than the plans called for. That makes a larger kitchen so far as walking back and forth in it is concerned.

Don E. Knoblauch, an architect, testified:

> [a]s an architect it is my opinion that it was a serious error in narrowing the living room and widening the kitchen. I would say it would make the house less desirable to live in and to own.... It is standard practice in construction where an error of this magnitude occurs that the wall would be ordered to be removed and placed in the position indicated on the plans.

Why did the trial court, as trier of fact, accept the views of the two real estate appraisers rather than those of the buyer of the home and an architect? What kinds of values does each group see as important?

Justice Hallows wrote the opinion for the Supreme Court of Wisconsin affirming the trial court's decision. There was substantial performance. The Jacobs could not walk away from the deal. They could recover appropriate damages. The measure of damages was the cost of repair for items that did not involve "an unreasonable economic waste." However, this measure is inappropriate when repair would involve such waste. Then all a plaintiff can recover is the "difference in value of the house as it stands with faulty and incomplete construction and the value of the house if it had been constructed in strict accordance with the plans and specifications." The court said:

> To tear down the wall now and rebuild it in its proper place would involve a substantial destruction of the work, if not all of it, which was put into the wall and would cause additional damage to other parts of the house and require replastering and redecorating the walls and ceilings of at least two rooms. Such economic waste is unreasonable and unjustified.

Justice Hallows explained: "[t]here may be situations in which features or details of construction of special or of great personal importance, which if not performed, would prevent a finding of substantial performance." Nevertheless, in the *Plante* case, "the plan was a stock floor plan." "There were no blueprints." "Many of the problems that arose during the construc-

tion had to be solved on the basis of practical experience." Do you infer that a court would require a builder to come closer to the plans to perform substantially a contract to build an architect designed house with artistic features? If so, is the court's decision an example of the law favoring the wealthy over the middle and working class? Or is it an example of the law favoring small businesses and stopping home buyers from searching for minor defects to escape paying all they agreed to pay?

3. RESTITUTION AS AN ALTERNATIVE REMEDY FOR BREACH OF CONTRACT

a. The Remedy and Its Impact

In addition to contract remedies that protect the expectation and reliance interests, aggrieved parties may seek a recovery based on a quasi-contract[72] or restitutionary theory. The traditional logical dance goes this way: Plaintiff performed and handed over goods and services to Defendant. Defendant, however, failed to pay. As a result of this breach, Plaintiff may "rescind" the contract. Once the contract is out of the way, then Defendant has Plaintiff's property to which he is not entitled. In order to prevent Defendant's "unjust enrichment," the law will offer many of the restitutionary remedies fashioned for wrongful takings of property. While Plaintiff may wish to recover specific goods he has delivered to Defendant, more commonly Plaintiff seeks the fair market value of what he has handed over to Defendant.

Why do we have alternative remedies? As you will see, at times restitution will be inconsistent with the goal of putting an aggrieved party where she would have been had the contract been performed. Indeed, restitution sometimes can be used to put her in a much better position. Are there any limitations on using restitution to avoid facing the requirements of contracts damages rules?

OLIVER v. CAMPBELL

43 Cal.2d 298, 273 P.2d 15 (1954)

CARTER, J. — Plaintiff appeals from a judgment for defendant, administratrix of the estate of Roy Campbell, deceased, in an action for attorney's fees.

---

[72]Quasi-contracts are situations where the law treats people *as if* they had made a contract. For example, suppose I am a popular singer. I ask you to be my personal manager, but we never sign a written contract nor specify how much you are to be paid. You work for me for six months, but I fail to pay you. Then I fire you without cause. You have a quasi-contract action against me for the fair market value of your services. Sometimes you will see judicial opinions call this a quantum meruit action. This phrase refers to one of the common law writs used to plead this kind of action. Modern writers prefer to use the term restitution to cover all legal theories designed to give back unjust enrichment.

Plaintiff's cause of action was stated in a common count alleging that Roy Campbell became indebted to him in the sum of $10,000, the reasonable value of services rendered as attorney for Campbell; that no part had been paid except $450. Campbell died after the services were rendered by plaintiff. Plaintiff filed a claim against his estate for the fees which defendant rejected. Defendant in her answer denied the allegations made and as a "further" defense alleged that plaintiff and Campbell entered into an "express written contract" employing plaintiff as attorney for a stated fee of $750, and all work alleged to have been performed by plaintiff was performed under that contract.

According to the findings of the trial court the claim against the estate was founded on the alleged reasonable value of legal services rendered by plaintiff for Campbell in an action for separate maintenance by defendant, Campbell's wife, against Campbell and in which the latter cross-complained for a divorce. Plaintiff was not counsel when the pleadings in that action were filed. He came into the case on December 16, 1949, before trial of the action. He and Campbell entered into a written contract on that date for plaintiff's representation of Campbell in the action, the contract stating that plaintiff agrees to represent Campbell in the separate maintenance and divorce action which has been set for trial in the superior court for a "total fee" of $750 plus court costs and other incidentals in the sum of $100 making a total of $850. The fees were to be paid after trial. Plaintiff represented Campbell at the trial consuming 29 days and lasting until May, 1950. (Defendant's complaint for separate maintenance was changed to one for divorce.) After the trial ended the court indicated its intention to give Mrs. Campbell a divorce. But while her proposed findings were under consideration by plaintiff and the court, defendant Campbell substituted himself instead of plaintiff and thereby the representation by plaintiff of Campbell was "terminated." The findings in the divorce action were filed in May, 1951. Plaintiff's services were furnished pursuant to the contract. The reasonable value of the services was $5,000. Campbell paid $450 to plaintiff and the $100 costs.

The court concluded that plaintiff should take nothing because neither his claim against the estate nor his action was on the contract but were in *quantum meruit* and no recovery could be made for the reasonable value of the services because the compensation for those services was covered by the express contract.

According to plaintiff's undisputed testimony Campbell told him after defendant had offered proposed findings in the divorce action that he was dissatisfied with plaintiff as his counsel and would discharge him and asked him if he would sign a substitution of attorneys under which Campbell would represent himself. Plaintiff replied that he recognized Campbell had a right to discharge him but that he was prepared to carry the case to conclusion; that he expected to be paid the reasonable value of his services which would be as much as defendant's counsel in the divorce action received, $9,000, to which Campbell replied he was not going to pay "a cent more." (At that time Campbell had paid $450.) Thereupon the substitution (dated January 25, 1951) was signed and Campbell took plaintiff's file in the divorce case with him.

It seems that the contract of employment contemplated that plaintiff was to continue his services and representation at least until and including final judgment in the divorce action. (See *Neblett v. Getty*, 20 Cal.App.2d 65 [66 P.2d 473].) It might thus appear that plaintiff was discharged before he had fully completed his services under the contract and the discharge prevented him from completing his performance. (That question is later discussed.)

One alleged rule of law applied by the trial court and that urged by defendant is that where there is a contract of employment for a definite term which fixes the compensation, there cannot be any recovery for the reasonable value of the services even though the employer discharges the employee — repudiates the contract before the end of the term; that the only remedy of the employee is an action on the contract for the fixed compensation or damages for the breach of the contract. The trial court accepted that theory and rendered judgment for defendant because plaintiff did not state a cause of action on the contract nor for damages for its breach; it was for the reasonable value of the services performed before plaintiff's discharge. Accordingly there is no express finding on whether the discharge was wrongful or whether there was a rescission of the contract by plaintiff because of Campbell's breach of it, or whether plaintiff had substantially performed at the time of this discharge.

The rule applied is not in accord with the general contract law, the law applicable to employment contracts or employment of an attorney by a client. The general rule is stated:

> ... that one who has been injured by a breach of contract has an election to pursue any of three remedies, to wit: "He may treat the contract as rescinded and may recover upon a quantum meruit so far as he has performed; or he may keep the contract alive, for the benefit of both parties, being at all times ready and able to perform; or, third, he may treat the repudiation as putting an end to the contract for all purposes of performance, and sue for the profits he would have realized if he had not been prevented from performing." *Alder v. Drudis*, 30 Cal.2d 372, 381 [182 P.2d 195].

See 12 Cal.Jur.2d, Contracts, § 253; Restatement of Contracts, § 347. It is the same in agency or contract for services cases.

> If the principal, in violation of the contract of employment, terminates or repudiates the employment, or the agent properly terminates it because of breach of contract by the principal, the agent is entitled at his election to receive either:
>
> (a) the amount of the net losses caused and gains prevented by the principal's breach, or, if there are no such losses or gains, a small sum as nominal damages; or

(b) the reasonable value of the services previously rendered the principal, not limited by the contract price, except that for services for which a price is apportioned by the terms of the contract he is entitled to receive the contract price and no more.

Comment:

a. In no event is the agent entitled to compensation for services unperformed. If, however, the principal terminates the relationship in breach of contract, or if the agent chooses to terminate it because of a total breach by the principal, the agent is entitled, at his option, to affirm or disaffirm the contract. If he affirms the contract, he can maintain an action for its breach and recover damages in accordance with the rule stated in Clause (a). For a complete statement as to the amount of damages recoverable, if he choose this alternative, see the Restatement of Contracts, §§ 326-346. The rule stated in Clause (b) is based upon the disaffirmance of the contract by the agent, and damages are given him by way of restitution. The Restatement of Contracts, § 347, states the consequences of disaffirmance and the non-availability of restitution as a remedy where part performance has been completed, for which compensation has been apportioned. Restatement of Agency, § 455.

[The court then quoted from Williston's famous treatise.]

If the performance rendered consists of services, there cannot ordinarily, from the nature of legal remedies, be actual restitution, but it is possible to give the equivalent in value under a common count. Since money paid may be thus recovered and similarly in the United States in many instances, land, logic would require such a remedy; and it is allowed in part, but only in part. If the plaintiff has fully performed the contract, or a severable part thereof, and "if the only part of the agreed exchange for such performance that has not been rendered by the defendant is a sum of money constituting a liquidated sum," the only redress he has for breach of contract by the other side is damages for the breach. It is true that if the performance to which he is entitled in return is a liquidated sum of money, he may sue in *indebitatus assumpsit* and not on the special contract, but the measure of damages is what he ought to have received — not the value of what he has given. If, however, the plaintiff has only partly performed and has been excused from further performance by prevention or by the repudiation or abandonment of the contract by the defendant, he may recover, either in England or America, the value of the services rendered, though such a remedy is no more necessary than where he has fully performed, since in both cases alike the plaintiff has an effectual remedy in an action on the contract for damages. In some jurisdictions, if a price or rate of compensation is fixed by the contract, that is made the conclusive test of the value of the services rendered. More frequently, however, the plaintiff is allowed to recover the real value of the services though in excess of the contract price. The latter rule seems more in accordance with the theory on which the right of action must be based — that the contract is treated as rescinded, and the plaintiff restored to his original position as nearly as possible. (Williston on Contracts (rev. ed.), § 1459.)

... And in entire contracts employing an attorney for a fixed fee it has been said that when the client wrongfully discharges the attorney before he has completed the contract, the attorney may recover the reasonable value of the services performed to the time of discharge.... Inasmuch as the contract has been repudiated by the employer before its term is up and after the employee has partly performed and the employee may treat the contract as "rescinded," there is no longer any contract upon which the employer can rely as fixing conclusively the limit of the compensation — the reasonable value of services recoverable by the employee for his part performance. Hence it is stated in *Lessing v. Gibbons, supra,* 6 Cal.App.2d 598, 607, that:

> It is well settled that one who is wrongfully discharged and prevented from further performance of his contract may elect as a general rule to treat the contract as rescinded, may sue upon a *quantum meruit* as if the special contract of employment had never been made and may recover the reasonable value of the services performed even though such reasonable value exceeds the contract price.

That statement is quoted with approval in *Neblett v. Getty, supra,* 20 Cal.App.2d 65, 70 (dictum).... Of course the contract price is competent evidence bearing on the reasonable value of the services....

The question remains, however, of the application of the foregoing rules to the instant case. Plaintiff had performed practically all of the services he was employed to perform when he was discharged. The trial was at an end. The court had indicated its intention to give judgment against Campbell and all that remained was the signing of findings and judgment. The full sum called for in the contract was payable because the trial had ended. Under these circumstances it would appear that in effect, plaintiff had completed the performance of his services and the rule would apply that:

> The remedy of restitution in money is not available to one who has fully performed his part of a contract, if the only part of the agreed exchange for such performance that has not been rendered by the defendant is a sum of money constituting a liquidated debt; but full performance does not make restitution unavailable if any part of the consideration due from the defendant in return is something other than a liquidated debt. Rest. Contracts, § 350.

... The judgment is therefore reversed and the trial court is directed to render judgment in favor of plaintiff for the sum of $300.

Shenk, Acting C. J., Traynor, J., and Spence, J., concurred. Edmonds, J., concurred in the judgment.

SCHAUER, J. — I dissent. I agree with a great deal of the discussion in the majority opinion, and even to a larger extent with the authorities therein cited, relative to the rules of law which should govern this case but I think this court misapplies the very rules it cites.

Specifically, I think this court errs when it says "there being no dispute as to the amount called for in the contract, the services having been in effect fully performed, the court should have rendered judgment for the balance due on the contract which is conceded to be $300." The foregoing statement is neither supported factually by the record nor legally by the authorities cited.

Upon the record and the authorities the judgment should be reversed and the cause remanded either (a) with directions to the trial court to enter judgment for the plaintiff for $5,000 or (b) for a retrial upon all issues. I would prefer to end the litigation by adopting alternative (a) and in my view the record fully justifies that disposition of the cause. Directed to that conclusion is the succinctly stated opinion prepared by Justice Vallee when the cause was before the District Court of Appeals (reported by (Cal.App.) pp. 932-933, 265 P.2d) and I adopt it as a most worthy presentation of the views which I think should prevail:

> I am of the opinion that the judgment should be reversed with directions to the superior court to render judgment for plaintiff for $5,000. The court found that the reasonable value of the services performed by plaintiff is $5,000. Plaintiff was the only witness who testified concerning his discharge by Dr. Campbell. The opinion of this court fails to state all of the testimony of plaintiff with respect to his discharge. I set it forth *in toto* in the margin.[73]

---

[73]   Q. Mr. Oliver, did you have any discussion with Dr. Campbell about that contract or as to the writing of that contract sometime after Judge Clark had announced his decision, and about the time that you had received the proposed findings of fact drawn by Mr. Shoemaker for Mrs. Campbell....
The Witness: I did not.
By Mr. Neblett: [Attorney for plaintiff].
Q. Did you have a discussion with Dr. Campbell about that time in your office? A. I did.
Q. What was said? ... A. Dr. Campbell came into my office and stated that he was dissatisfied with the announced judgment of the court. In his opinion, Mrs. Campbell should have been allowed nothing in way of alimony. I told Dr. Campbell that after 28 years of married life and with his property and his earning capacity that I thought the least the court would have allowed would have been possibly $250.00 a month.
He also stated to me at that time that he was dissatisfied with the proposed amendments that I had prepared on the findings of fact and conclusions of law because he thought the

I think no reasonable conclusion can be drawn from the evidence other than that the discharge amounts to a clear repudiation and abrogation of the contract in its entirety, in which case plaintiff is entitled to recover the reasonable value of the service performed. *The contract plaintiff made with Dr. Campbell did not limit his services to the trial of the case.*[74] [Italics

---

findings should state in there that Mr. Shoemaker had suborned and bribed certain witnesses for the plaintiff.

I told Dr. Campbell that there was no evidence of any such action on the part of Mr. Shoemaker and that I was not going to submit to the court any proposed findings in that regard.

He stated at that time that if I wouldn't run this case the way he wanted it that he would discharge me, and asked me if I would sign a substitution of attorneys. I told him that I recognized that he had the power to discharge me as his attorney, that I was prepared to carry the case through to a conclusion, *and I thought the case would be reversed on appeal.* [Italics added.]

He said "no," he wanted to act as his own attorney, so he could argue the proposed findings himself; and with that I prepared the substitution of attorneys which is in the file, and Dr. Campbell signed it and I signed it.

He left the office carrying the files of this case, the divorce case, and also the file of the Municipal Court case with him, and that is the substance of the conversation.

Q. You turned over to Dr. Campbell at that time all of the files in Campbell against Campbell? A. The two cases.

Q. And the other case that is, the case in the Municipal Court? A. The entire file.

Q. You have had nothing to do with the case from that time until now? A. I have not.

Q. Mr. Oliver, will you look in the file of Campbell against Campbell, Number D370,670, and find the substitution to which you have just referred? A. Here it is.

Q. This substitution which you have presented to me appears to have been signed by Dr. Campbell, January 25, 1951, and by John Oliver on account of Ralph D. Paonessa and John Oliver on the same day? A. That is correct.

Q. That is Dr. Campbell's signature? A. That is Dr. Campbell's signature; he signed that in my presence; and that is my signature.

Q. That reads: "Defendant and cross-complainant hereby substitutes himself Roy Campbell in *pro. per.* as his attorney of record in place of Ralph D. Paonessa and John Oliver." and under that: "We consent to the above substitution, dated: January 25, 1951."

Then on the other page there is another signature of Dr. Campbell above "substitution accepted." A. That is correct.

Q. Did you have any conversation at that time with Dr. Campbell about compensation? A. Yes, I told him that I expected to be paid the reasonable value...

(Continuing) That I expected to be paid a reasonable value for my services. He says: "What do you think the reasonable value of your services are?" I said, "I expect to be paid as much as Mr. Shoemaker."...

Q. When you told Dr. Campbell that you expected to be paid and you expected to be paid approximately, or the same amount that was allowed Mr. Shoemaker what did Dr. Campbell say? A. He said, "I am not going to pay you a cent more."

[74]The contract reads:
December 16th, 1949

We, the undersigned do hereby agree to represent Roy Campbell in an action for separate maintenance instituted by his wife, Iva Lee Campbell and on cross-complaint for divorce filed

added.] Under the contract he agreed to represent the doctor until final judgment, and he told the doctor that he *"thought the case would be reversed on appeal."* [Italics added.] Manifestly, the evidence will be no different on a retrial. Dr. Campbell is dead. Plaintiff is the only witness who can testify to the conversation. There is nothing in plaintiff's testimony to impugn his integrity. He did all any lawyer of the highest professional standards could have done under the conditions. ... Defendant will be unable to make any showing to the contrary of the testimony of plaintiff. Under these circumstances, the judgment should be reversed with directions as I have indicated. ...

DOOLING, J. pro tem., concurred.

NOTES AND QUESTIONS

1. *Briefs and record*: The briefs and record in the case tell us little about why Oliver agreed to represent Dr. Campbell for only $750 when the fair market value of Oliver's work was $5,000. Oliver had some warning that Dr. Campbell might not be an easy client to satisfy. Iva Lee Campbell sued for divorce on November 5, 1948, alleging extreme cruelty. Roy Campbell answered and cross-complained for divorce on November 23d, represented by Carl S. Kegley. On December 20th, Ross, Goldstone & Saunders were substituted as Dr. Campbell's lawyers, and they filed an amended cross-complaint. On September 7, 1949, Iva Lee Campbell filed a supplement to her complaint, charging new acts of cruelty after the commencement of the action. Oliver became Dr. Campbell's lawyer on December 16, 1949. Why might Oliver have agreed to represent Dr. Campbell for such a low fee, knowing that he faced a long and difficult legal battle and suspecting that Dr. Campbell might be a difficult client?

Those who enjoy mild irony should note that Oliver was fired by Dr. Campbell because he would not make allegations of unprofessional behavior against Mr. Shoemaker, Iva Lee Campbell's lawyer. When Dr. Campbell died, Iva Lee Campbell inherited his estate. Thus, the lawyer who successfully defended Oliver's claim against the estate was the same Mr. Shoemaker.

---

by Roy Campbell against his wife, and which has been set for trial for February 20th, 1950 in Department 1 of the Superior Court of the County of Los Angeles State of California for a total fee of $750.00 plus Court Costs and other incidentals in the sum of $100.00 making a total sum of $850.00. Said fees of $750.00 to be paid after trial.

    (signed) Ralph D. Paonessa
    John Oliver

I accept the services of Ralph D. Paonessa and John Oliver as per above agreement.
    (signed) RC

2. *New limitations on damages in lawyer's suits against clients*: You should realize that contracts between lawyers and their clients raise special concerns. The Supreme Court of California, in *Fracasse v. Brent*,[75] decided that a client could discharge an attorney at any time with or without cause. In either case, the attorney was entitled to recover only the reasonable value of his or her services. A basic term of the contract between attorney and client will be implied by law making it terminable by the client at will. Thus, the attorney may not sue for damages for breach of contract measured by the expectation interest even when discharged without cause. The court explained the new rule by saying

> [t]he relation of attorney and client is one of special confidence and trust and the dignity and integrity of the legal profession demand that the interests of the client be fully protected.... The right to discharge is of little value if the client must risk paying the full contract price for services not rendered upon a determination by a court that the discharge was without legal cause.

If we were to extend the logic of this policy concern, we would expect a court to refuse to award restitution damages when they exceed the contract price. To rule otherwise would encourage a client to stay in a relationship with an attorney in whom they had lost confidence.

3. *Restitution and "benefit"*: Suppose a client hires a lawyer to do a certain task for $5,000. After the lawyer has worked but has not completed the job, the client discharges him without cause. The client then hires a second lawyer who agrees to do the task for $6,000. The second lawyer is unable to make use of any of the first lawyer's work. She completes the task and is paid $6,000. The first lawyer then sues the client for the reasonable value of his work. Many courts have allowed him to recover. However, how can we say that it is based on restitution? The lawyer may have relied and expended time and money trying to perform, but in what way did all this effort produce a "benefit" to the client? Suppose the fair market value of the first lawyer's work was $4,000. If the client has to pay this amount, he will have to pay $10,000 ($6,000 + 4,000) to get the task performed. We can be fairly sure that the task is not worth this amount. What does the client "have" which he ought to give back to avoid "unjust enrichment?" Isn't this just another example of what Fuller and Perdue would call "the reliance interest?" If so, why clutter up matters with all the talk of rescission and quantum meruit?

4. *What's a benefit*? Traditionally, one recovers "benefits conferred" in a restitution action. We could say that you benefit me when you do what I want you to do. We then could value my benefit by what it would cost to get someone else to do what I asked you to do. On the other hand, we could insist on finding an actual increase in my assets before concluding there is a benefit. Do we focus

---

[75]100 Cal.Rptr. 385, 494 P.2d 9 (1972).

on what it cost you or what I got from your efforts? Put another way, how far are we interested in compensating your reliance loss and how far are we interested in making sure that I am not unjustly enriched? While in many cases this will amount to the same thing, in others there will be a difference. Section 371 of the Restatement (Second) offers important clarifications and innovations concerning the definition of benefit when restitution is used as an alternative remedy for breach of contract. If, at the time the court decided *Oliver v. Campbell*, California had followed the rules stated in § 371, would the court have decided the case the same way?

The Restatement (Second) of Contracts originally proposed another major change but then dropped it. Section 373 states the traditional rule that a plaintiff may choose restitution as a remedy instead of expectation or reliance recoveries. However, where the benefits conferred on the breaching party are goods or services, § 373(2) provided that plaintiffs could recover no more than the amount they would have received had the parties performed their contract. In *Oliver v. Campbell*, this approach would limit recovery to the contract price or rate regardless of whether plaintiff had completed performance. The reform was deleted when the American Law Institute published the final version of the Restatement. The Comment states now:

> In the case of a contract on which he [an injured party] would have sustained a loss instead of having made a profit, however, his restitution interest may give him a larger recovery than would damages on either basis. The right of the injured party under a losing contract to a greater amount in restitution than he could have recovered in damages has engendered much controversy. The rules stated in this Section give him that right.

The Reporter's Note does not explain why the ALI dropped the reform from the Restatement (Second).

b. Difficulties with Restitution as a Remedy for Breach of Contract

The law offers restitution as an alternative remedy for breach of contract. However, as *Oliver v. Campbell* suggests, but does not hold, this alternative remedy may serve to put an aggrieved party in a much better position than had the contract been performed. Those who write about law say that contract remedies protect the expectation interest. Restitution can serve, in some situations, as a kind of offsetting counterrule that undercuts a number of other contracts policies. At least in some instances, the chance that the other party might be able to win a large restitutionary award may serve as a deterrent to breaching contracts, paying damages, and turning to more efficient uses of one's resources. While some may see rules matched by counterrules serving to free courts to do justice as they see fit, many are offended by such a messy, contradictory system. Here we will examine some of the debate about this alternative remedy.

NOTES AND QUESTIONS

1. *When can one get restitution as an alternative remedy for breach of contract*? In what kinds of cases are lawyers likely to use the doctrine? The court cited Restatement of Contracts [1st] § 347 in the *Oliver* decision. It summarizes the requirements for the remedy. First, there must be a "total breach of contract." Restitution is a drastic remedy. It is not available for minor or partial failures to perform. It is not available if the defaulting party has substantially performed as in *Plante v. Jacobs*. The aggrieved party cannot have performed fully. An injured party entitled to restitution gets a judgment for "the reasonable value of a performance rendered by him, measured as of the time it was rendered, less the amount of benefits received as part performance of the contract and retained by him." However, the "performance" must have been "rendered," and it must have been "(a) part or all of a performance for which the defendant bargained."

2. *The vanishing contract in construction contracts*: The doctrine of the "vanishing contract" can be useful to plaintiffs in building contracts. Suppose, for example, Builder agrees to construct a structure for $90,000. When Owner breaches this contract, Builder has spent $90,000 performing, but it would have cost him $30,000 to complete the job. Had Builder finished performance, Builder would have spent $120,000 but only received $90,000. It was a losing deal. Owner did Builder a favor by breaching their contract. Builder's expectation recovery here, in a strict sense, should be $60,000. Do you see why? If Builder sought his reliance losses (the $90,000 he spent performing the contract), Judge Hand, in *L. Albert & Son v. Armstrong Rubber Co.*, said that the defendant Owner can reduce the recovery "by as much as he can show that the promisee would have lost, if the contract had been performed."

Things improve if Builder forgets contract damages and turns to restitution. Once Owner defaults, Builder may elect to rescind the contract. *Oliver v. Campbell* says that once the contract is rescinded, it "vanishes." Then the defendant Owner cannot refer to it to limit his obligations to restore to Builder all benefits conferred. An earlier California case, *Boomer v. Muir*,[76] applied just this theory in a losing bargain situation. Thus, applying the rescission rule to the facts we've assumed, Builder would recover $90,000. We ignore that had the contract been performed, Builder would have lost $30,000. Instead of putting plaintiff where he would have been had the contract been performed, restitution puts him where he would have been had he not made such a lousy deal (ignoring the attorney's fees he pays to bring this about).

---

[76] 24 P.2d 570 (D.C.A. Calif. 1933).

In both the *Boomer* and *Oliver* cases, the California courts wrote as if the logic of rescission and restitution theory compelled the result. Once a plaintiff exercises his right to rescind the contract, it "ceases to exist." Then nothing exists to limit recovery. The situation is exactly as if Owner had asked Builder to build, but the parties said nothing about the price. In that case, Builder could recover the fair market value of his work.

However, this argument proves too much. Suppose Builder is out of work. He decides the Owner needs a nice building on his property and can afford to pay for it. Without making a contract or saying a word to Owner who is away on an extended trip, Builder starts work and invests $90,000 in materials, subcontracts, wages and his own overhead. Owner returns and stops everything. Builder could not sue Owner successfully for $90,000 as a benefit conferred. Owner never asked for this benefit. Builder would be an "officious intermeddler," and Owner would not be "unjustly enriched." Would it matter if the Owner used the building, thus "accepting" the benefit? It might; there is substantial authority (though not necessarily in cases of officiously constructed buildings) that one who retains and uses the unrequested benefit may forfeit the defense that the party conferring the benefit was an intermeddler.

How does our hypothetical case where Builder "rescinds" the contract differ from one involving an officious intermeddler? Of course, there was a contract by which Owner asked for the benefit. Yet if rescission causes the contract to cease to exist, then how can we look to the contract to avoid the officious intermeddler rule if we cannot look to it to limit recovery to the contract price or rate? A contract is not a tangible thing but an idea. If we say that plaintiff has a right to rescind, this does not mean that the contract never existed. Rather, the courts are saying that they will treat the contract *as if* its limitations were not controlling because this serves some purpose.

One older New Jersey case, *Kehoe v. Rutherford*,[77] took a compromise view that seems to appeal to many students. It made the builder take some but not all of the loss he would have incurred had the owner not defaulted. Recall our hypothetical figures:

Contract price:	$90,000
Cost of work done:	$90,000
Cost of work to be done:	$30,000

The total cost of performance would have been $120,000, and the builder would have lost $30,000 but for the breach by the Owner. The court in the *Kehoe* case said that the builder's recovery should be the cost of the work done divided by the total cost of the work times the contract price. On our facts, then:

---

[77] 56 N.J.L. 23, 27 A. 912 (1893).

$$\frac{90,000}{120,000} \times 90,000 \ or \ \sfrac{3}{4} \times 90,000 = \$67,500$$

This would mean that the builder would take a loss of $22,500, or 3/4 of the loss he would have taken had the contract been performed (3/4 x $30,000 = $22,500). In terms of the costs of doing the job, the builder had done 3/4 the work, and so he should take 3/4 the loss. Does this follow? How can we be sure, for example, that the builder might not have been able to reduce the loss during the last quarter of the job?

3. *Restitution to wipe out reliance*? At this point, some might be tempted to downgrade the importance of the *L. Albert & Son* case. Judge Hand said that a defendant could reduce the recovery by showing plaintiff had made a losing bargain. However, a plaintiff can sometimes avoid being held to the contract's allocation of gains and losses by taking the restitution route. *Oliver v. Campbell* shows one important limitation on restitution: plaintiff has no such right if he has completed his performance and is entitled to the contract sum.

There are other problems as well. *L. Albert & Son* involved a reliance loss which did not benefit the defaulting seller. The very idea of restitution is giving back benefits conferred. Rescission and restitution will only work to avoid the burdens of a losing bargain if there is something that a court is willing to call a benefit. Comment c. to Restatement of Contracts § 348, stressed that if,

> the performance that the contract required of the plaintiff has been wholly prevented, and if the result of his labor and expenditure still belongs to him, he has no remedy by way of restitution. If the performance required was the production and delivery of a finished article, and the defendant wrongfully prevents completion and delivery of the article, the plaintiff cannot get judgment for the reasonable value of his work and labor in preparation to perform, except insofar as it may be included in a claim for damages.

Restatement (Second) of Contracts § 373(1) seems to change this rule. It provides "the injured party is entitled to restitution for any benefit that he has conferred on the other party by way of *part performance or reliance.* [Emphasis added]." Many cases support Comment c. to Restatement of Contracts § 348. We will see whether courts accept Restatement (Second) of Contracts § 373(1)'s invitation to overturn those cases. Should they accept it?

4. *What's the right rule*? Should restitution be available to plaintiffs in some instances to aid them in escaping losing bargains when defendants have breached? Professor John Kidwell suggests that, despite their wooden reasoning, cases such as *Boomer v. Muir* may reach the right result.

The principle that allows the parties to allocate risk does facilitate planning and serves to support the market, and *is* deeply imbedded in the law of contracts. The principle that exchanges should be *fair*, I argue, is also an indispensable part of contract law. The fairness principle is, however, not normally stated so boldly; but it lurks beneath the surface in the rules of duress, capacity, unconscionability, mistake, impossibility, frustration, and even in the law of consideration.[78] If the contracting parties have expressly allocated a risk, the freedom of contract/expectation principle will be honored even though it results in recognizing the expectations of a contracting party that involved an unequal exchange. In the preceding sentence I referred to an *unequal* exchange. The idealized, archetypical aspiration that lies behind contract law is a *fair exchange* and that is thought, in the absence of special circumstances, to mean an exchange of equal values. This does not mean *precisely* equal, but generally equal, in light of the incomparability of individual preferences *and* in light of the risks contemplated by the parties....

And in a case like *Boomer v. Muir* the court may simply be signalling that one who wishes to have the benefit of the expectation principle in the case of a dramatically unequal exchange must have scrupulously complied with the formal requirements of contract law. The court may have believed that the owner was trying to take unfair advantage of the contractor; and it may have simply employed a convenient escape hatch to reach what it found the preferable result. Note that *Boomer* comes perilously near a mistake or impossibility case. *How* express — that is, how knowing — was the allocation of the risks of unexpected conditions which caused the work to be so expensive?

The principle of fair exchange presumes a certain equality of value. It is very nearly as central to the law of contracts as the expectation principle. The cases in which unjust enrichment principles are applied in contract cases are *not* inconsistent with contract law; they are merely cases in which the expectation principle has appropriately been subordinated to fair exchange.[79]

4. RESTITUTION FOR THE PLAINTIFF IN DEFAULT

To this point, we considered the aggrieved party who suffers a breach by the other. Now we look at matters from the other side. Particularly in a long-term contract, one may invest much trying to perform, produce clear benefits to the other party, but then be unable to complete the job. Clearly, a party in default

---

[78]Most of these rules will be considered later in these materials.

[79]Kidwell, Association of American Law Schools, Section on Remedies Newsletter (1981).

must pay damages to the other party. However, may she recover any balance of benefits conferred over damages suffered in her favor?

Some 19th century cases denied recovery. Several involved a farm laborer who contracted to work for a year. The farmer agreed to supply room and board and then to pay the laborer a sum of money at the end of the term. The laborer worked ten or eleven months and then quit. Could he recover compensation for his work? In *Hansell v. Erickson*,[80] the Supreme Court of Illinois denied recovery, saying that the "special contract must govern." The court thought the "principles involved in this case have been so long settled that it seems a waste of time to argue upon them." Its reaction to the claim speaks loudly of the assumptions of those likely to rise to the appellate bench at that time about farming, work, and immigration:

> The pretext that appellee was a Swede, and did not understand our language, is too flimsy to deserve notice. He made the contract — it is abundantly proved, and he must abide by it. He left his employer in the midst of his harvest, probably under the promise, from some meddlesome person, to give him higher wages. This is contrary to justice and good morals, and cannot be tolerated.

Britton v. Turner[81] is a famous decision reaching the opposite result on similar facts. The New Hampshire court said "we have abundant reason to believe, that the general understanding of the community is, that the hired laborer shall be entitled to compensation for the service actually performed, though he does not continue the entire term contracted for." The opinion concluded,

> This rule, by binding the employer to pay the value of the service he actually receives, and the laborer to answer in damages where he does not complete the entire contract, will leave no temptation to the former to drive the laborer from his service, near the close of his term, by ill treatment, in order to escape from payment; nor to the latter to desert his service before the stipulated time, without a sufficient reason....

The problem of the farm laborer has vanished from our appellate courts. However, the treatment of the plaintiff in default remains alive and troublesome in other areas. When a party to a contract risks forfeiting what he has done trying to perform, this is an incentive to complete performance. However, breaches of contracts are not always the result of morally bad conduct. Particularly in long-term contracts, one may encounter unexpected trouble only remotely related to one's own actions. Moreover, some writers see no reason to

---

[80]28 Ill. Rep. 257 (1862).
[81]6 N.H. 481 (1834).

perform contracts if there is a better use for resources elsewhere. These writers want to minimize the costs of breach. Those costs include benefits already conferred on the other party. These writers, therefore, believe that these benefits should be forfeited only where the amount of forfeiture roughly equals the other party's damages resulting from breach. In other words, these writers would bar a restitution claim by a plaintiff-in-default only when a liquidated damages clause to the same effect would be enforced under the standards discussed in *Lake River Corp. v. Carborundum Co.*, *supra*.

Despite these arguments favoring restitution recovery for the plaintiff-in-default, the law remains somewhat unclear. What is called the "forfeiture" rule was once the majority rule in the United States. That has changed now, and a majority of the states will uphold a restitution claim by the plaintiff-in-default, at least in many circumstances. But many vestiges of the older forfeiture rule remain.

NOTES AND QUESTIONS

1. *Land contracts*: Some states distinguish the rights of a defaulting party in contracts to buy land and those who have entered land contracts. The two phrases can be confusing, but they refer to distinct parts of a real estate sales transaction. All real estates sales begin with a contract to sell (or buy) land, formed in the conventional way after an offer and an acceptance. Later an event called "closing" occurs. Normally at "closing" the seller transfers the deed to the real estate and the buyer pays whatever part of the agreed price had not been earlier paid as a downpayment or escrow payment. Sometimes, however, the seller agrees to allow the buyer some additional number of years after "closing" to pay the balance of the purchase price. In that circumstance, at "closing" the parties enter into a second contract, called a "land contract," in which the buyer agrees to pay the unpaid purchase price within an agreed time period and the seller receives the right to reacquire title to the land upon default.

Wisconsin and some other states follow the "forfeiture" rule in land contract cases. If the buyer fails to make timely payments, the seller has the option to sue in "strict foreclosure." The seller establishes the contract and the buyer's failure to pay. Then the seller reacquires title to the real estate and all interests of the buyer in return of any amounts already paid are forfeited. The seller is free to deal with the property in any way. The seller may use it herself rather than resell it. If she does resell it to a third party for more than the unpaid portion of the defaulting buyer's contract price, the "profit" inures solely to the seller's benefit. Of course, sellers have practical reasons in some situations to wait for a defaulting buyer to perform rather than asserting their rights.[82]

---

[82] The foregoing rule applies only to strict foreclosures of land contracts. Schwartz v. Syver, 264 Wis. 526, 59 N.W.2d 489 (1953), says that a vendee in a contract to purchase land can recover that amount of his down payment or earnest money that he can prove is over and above the vendor's damages. There is no indication that the Supreme Court of Wisconsin has considered

In a strict foreclosure action, a Wisconsin court may delay foreclosure for a reasonable time to permit the buyer to pay the entire remaining contract balance. However, only payment of the entire balance will forestall forfeiture of the buyer's rights under the land contract. Payment of only past due amounts will not prevent foreclosure. In setting a time by which buyer may prevent foreclosure by paying the contract balance, the court "must bear in mind that in fairness the vendor should not be deprived of his land for any considerable length of time, unless there appears to be a reasonable possibility for the vendee to redeem."[83]

2. *The right to appreciation in the value of land*: The rights of the purchaser of real estate who is in default and liquidated damages come together in *Vines v. Orchard Hills, Inc.*[84] Husband and wife gave seller $7,880 as a down payment on the purchase of a condominium in New Canaan for $78,800. The contract provided that seller "shall retain all sums of money paid under this Contract, as liquidated damages." The husband's employer transferred him to New Jersey about six months after the contract was made, and the buyers decided not to take the condominium. Husband and wife sued to recover their down payment. They claimed that the liquidated damages clause was invalid, and that seller suffered no damages as a result of their breach. The condominium they had agreed to buy for $78,800 in 1973 had, by the time of the trial in 1979, a fair market value of $160,000. The trial court relied on this figure and concluded that seller had gained a windfall of about $80,000. Purchasers were entitled to recover their down payment.

The Supreme Court of Connecticut decided first that a defaulting vendee on a land contract was entitled to restitution of any balance in its favor when payments and the vendor's damages were matched. Justice Peters noted "there are those who argue that repudiation of contractual obligations is socially desirable, and should be encouraged, whenever gain to the party in breach exceeds loss to the party injured by breach." She responded "[t]o assign such primacy to inferences drawn from economic models requires great confidence that the person injured by breach will encounter no substantial difficulties in establishing the losses for which he is entitled to be compensated." She concluded, "a purchaser whose breach is not willful has a restitutionary claim to recover moneys paid that unjustly enrich his seller." However, the purchaser must establish that the seller has been unjustly enriched.

The trial court thought that the liquidated damages clause was invalid because the purchasers had shown that seller had suffered no damages at all. However, the case was reversed and remanded. "The relevant time at which to measure the seller's damages is the time of breach.... Benefits to the seller that are attribut-

---

why one rule should apply to formal land contracts and another to contracts to buy real estate where earnest money is paid to close the deal.

[83]Kallenback v. Lake Publication, Inc., 30 Wis.2d 647, 658, 142 N.W.2d 212 (1966).

[84]181 Conn. 501, 435 A.2d 1022 (1980).

able to a rising market subsequent to breach rightfully accrue to the seller." There was no evidence that seller was not injured at the time of purchasers' breach. The court remanded the case to give purchasers a chance to offer evidence that seller could have sold the condominium at the time of their breach at a price which would have covered its damages.

Justice Peters was once Professor Peters of the Yale Law School. Writing about her colleague, friend and mentor after his death, she reported that she had sent Professor Grant Gilmore a copy of her opinion in the *Vines* case. He responded: "I appreciate the logic of your position. And yet I wonder whether the trial judge may not have blundered into a sort of truth (judicial ignorance is the greatest of law reformers). No doubt the economists would have an answer ready-made." Justice Peters notes "I shall always treasure the comment as quintessentially Grant's, and I still wonder which answer is right."[85]

3. *Plaintiff in default under the U.C.C.*: Mr. Neri, as you will recall, began his famous case with a claim for a return of his $4,250 downpayment. See Neri v. Retain Marine Corp., *supra*. What is his entitlement to that downpayment under U.C.C. §§ 2-718(2) and (3)?[86] How, if at all, would answer be different if instead of a cash downpayment Neri had received a trade allowance of $4250 on his old boat? See U.C.C. § 2-708 (4).

H. FULLER AND PERDUE'S CATEGORIES AS SURRO-GATES FOR DIFFICULT NORMATIVE CHOICES

Fuller and Perdue's categories — the expectation, the reliance and the restitution interests — have advanced thinking about contract law. As is true of all analytic categories, they cannot explain everything. We have already seen some of the difficulties with the expectation, reliance and restitution interest scheme. However, our emphasis to this point has been on understanding Fuller and Perdue and the extent to which the law attempts to further the three interests. In this section, we bring the difficulties front and center. We will emphasize such things as normative conflict. How do judges manipulate contract remedies when they recognize that a problem involves two or more valued but inconsistent objectives? We will talk about the symbolic functions of law. Contract rules may declare something to be good, true and beautiful but may do little directly to bring about that something. We will stress a bottom-up or consumer perspective on contract remedies. Whatever appellate opinions and law professors say, does

---

[85]Peters, Grant Gilmore and the Illusion of Certainty, 92 Yale Law Journal 8, 11 (1982).

[86]What justification, if any, is there for the limitation on the buyer's restitution rights contained in U.C.C. § 2-718(2)(b)? In the *Neri* case, in a part of the opinion we omitted, the New York Court of Appeals held that the limitations on a buyer's restitution rights contained in 2-718(2)(b) and 2-718(3)(a) are in the alternative and not cumulative. That interpretation is now generally accepted.

contract law as delivered through the American legal system come close to protecting the expectation, reliance, and restitution interests of all or some citizens? Our goal is not to undercut or destroy Fuller and Perdue, but to teach both the values and limitations of their analysis.

We will look at three cases which should serve to review what you have studied as well as to raise a number of these problems. Some students object that these are three freak cases, atypical of American business transactions in the second half of the 20th century. However, before you dismiss this section on that ground, you must ask whether a primary function of contract law is to deal with what are in some sense freak cases. Ordinary business deals are performed or defaults are written off as parties go on to the next transaction. Disputes worth litigating come in unusual situations. However, our contract law may be fashioned to cope with certain kinds of transactions and may not fit others very well. It may be impossible to fashion a general contract law that applies the same principles to sales of machines, to business and to consumer products, to employment contracts involving famous actresses and to ordinary employees, to sales of condominiums and houses and to complex real estate development schemes or the exploitation of mineral rights and so on. Each situation has its own particular nature, and we generalize only by denying particularity.

PEEVYHOUSE v. GARLAND COAL & MINING COMPANY

392 P.2d 109 (Okla. 1962), *cert. denied*, 375 U.S. 906 (1963).

JACKSON, J. In the trial court, plaintiffs Willie and Lucille Peevyhouse sued the defendant, Garland Coal and Mining Company, for damages for breach of contract. Judgment was for plaintiffs in an amount considerably less than was sued for. Plaintiffs appeal and defendant cross-appeals.

In the briefs on appeal, the parties present their argument and contentions under several propositions; however, they all stem from the basic question of whether the trial court properly instructed the jury on the measure of damages.

Briefly stated, the facts are as follows: plaintiffs owned a farm containing coal deposits, and in November, 1954, leased the premises to defendant for a period of five years for coal mining purposes. A "strip-mining" operation was contemplated in which the coal would be taken from pits on the surface of the ground, instead of from underground mine shafts. In addition to the usual covenants found in a coal mining lease, defendant specifically agreed to perform certain restorative and remedial work at the end of the lease period. It is unnecessary to set out the details of the work to be done, other than to say that it would involve the moving of many thousands of cubic yards of dirt, at a cost estimated by expert witnesses at about $29,000.00. However, plaintiffs sued for only $25,000.00.

During the trial, it was stipulated that all covenants and agreements in the lease contract had been fully carried out by both parties, except the remedial work mentioned above; defendant conceded that this work had not been done.

Plaintiffs introduced expert testimony as to the amount and nature of the work to be done, and its estimated cost. Over plaintiffs' objections, defendant thereafter introduced expert testimony as to the "diminution in value" of plaintiffs' farm resulting from the failure of defendant to render performance as agreed in the contract — that is, the difference between the present value of the farm, and what its value would have been if defendant had done what it agreed to do.

At the conclusion of the trial, the court instructed the jury that it must return a verdict for plaintiffs, and left the amount of damages for jury determination. On the measure of damages, the court instructed the jury that it might consider the cost of performance of the work defendant agreed to do, "together with all of the evidence offered on behalf of either party."

It thus appears that the jury was at liberty to consider the "diminution in value" of plaintiffs' farm as well as the cost of "repair work" in determining the amount of damages.

It returned a verdict for plaintiffs for $5000.00 — only a fraction of the "cost of performance," *but more than the total value of the farm even after the remedial work is done.*

On appeal, the issue is sharply drawn. Plaintiffs contend that the true measure of damages in this case is what it will cost plaintiffs to obtain performance of the work that was not done because of defendant's default. Defendant argues that the measure of damages is the cost of performance "limited, however, to the total difference in the market value before and after the work was performed."

It appears that this precise question has not heretofore been presented to this court. In *Ardizonne v. Archer*, 72 Okl. 70, 178 P. 263, this court held that the measure of damages for breach of a contract to drill an oil well was the reasonable cost of drilling the well, but here a slightly different factual situation exists. The drilling of an oil well will yield valuable geological information, even if no oil or gas is found, and of course if the well is a producer, the value of the premises increases. In the case before us, it is argued by defendant with some force that the performance of the remedial work defendant agreed to do will add at the most only a few hundred dollars to the value of plaintiffs' farm, and that the damages should be limited to that amount because that is all plaintiffs have lost.

Plaintiffs rely on *Groves v. John Wunder Co.*, 205 Minn. 163, 286 N.W. 235, 123 A.L.R. 502. In that case, the Minnesota court, in a substantially similar situation, adopted the "cost of performance" rule — as opposed to the "value" rule. The result was to authorize a jury to give plaintiff damages in the amount of $60,000, where the real estate concerned would have been worth only situation$12,160, even if the work contracted for had been done.

It may be observed that *Groves v. John Wunder Co.*, *supra*, is the only case which has come to our attention in which the cost of performance rule has been followed under circumstances where the cost of performance greatly exceeded the diminution in value resulting from the breach of contract. Incidentally, it appears that this case was decided by a plurality rather than a majority of the members of the court.

Defendant relies principally upon *Sandy Valley & E. R. Co., v. Hughes*, 175 Ky. 320, 194 S.W. 344; *Bigham v. Wabash-Pittsburg Terminal Ry. Co.*, 223 Pa. 106, 72 A. 318; and *Sweeney v. Lewis Const. Co.*, 66 Wash. 490, 119 P. 1108. These were all cases in which, under similar circumstances, the appellate courts followed the "value" rule instead of the "cost of performance" rule. Plaintiff points out that in the earliest of these cases (*Bigham*) the court cites as authority on the measure of damages an earlier Pennsylvania *tort* case, and that the other two cases follow the first, with no explanation as to why a measure of damages ordinarily followed in cases sounding in tort should be used in contract cases. Nevertheless, it is of some significance that three out of four appellate courts have followed the diminution in value rule under circumstances where, as here, the cost of performance greatly exceeds the diminution in value.

The explanation may be found in the fact that the situations presented are artificial ones. It is highly unlikely that the ordinary property owner would agree to pay $29,000 (or its equivalent) for the construction of "improvements" upon his property that would increase its value only about $300). The result is that we are called upon to apply principles of law theoretically based upon reason and reality to a situation which is basically unreasonable and unrealistic.

In *Groves v. John Wunder Co.*, *supra*, in arriving at its conclusions, the Minnesota court apparently considered the contract involved to be analogous to a building and construction contract, and cited authority for the proposition that the cost of performance or completion of the building as contracted is ordinarily the measure of damages in actions for damages for the breach of such a contract.

In an annotation following the Minnesota case beginning at 123 A.L.R. 515, the annotator places the three cases relied on by defendant (*Sandy Valley*, *Bigham*, and *Sweeney*) under the classification of cases involving "grading and excavation contracts."

We do not think either analogy is strictly applicable to the case now before us. The primary purpose of the lease contract between plaintiffs and defendant was neither "building and construction" nor "grading and excavation." It was merely to accomplish the economical recovery and marketing of coal from the premises, to the profit of all parties. The special provisions of the lease contract pertaining to remedial work were incidental to the main object involved.

Even in the case of contracts that are unquestionably building and construction contracts, the authorities are not in agreement as to the factors to be considered in determining whether the cost of performance rule or the value rule should be applied. The American Law Institute's Restatement of the Law, Contracts, Volume 1, §§ 346(1)(a)(i) and (ii) submits the proposition that the cost of performance is the proper measure of damages "if this is possible and does not involve *unreasonable economic waste*"; and that the diminution in value caused by the breach is the proper measure "if construction and completion in accordance with the contract would involve *unreasonable economic waste*." (Emphasis supplied.) In an explanatory comment immediately following the text, the Restatement makes it clear that the "economic waste" referred to consists of the destruction of a substantially completed building or other structure. Of course no such destruction is involved in the case now before us.

On the other hand, in McCormick, Damages, § 168, it is said with regard to building and construction contracts that "... in cases where the defect is one that can be repaired or cured without *undue expense*" the cost of performance is the proper measure of damages, but where "... the defect in material or construction is one that cannot be remedied without *an expenditure for reconstruction disproportionate to the end to be attained*" (emphasis supplied) the value rule should be followed. The same idea was expressed in *Jacob & Youngs, Inc. v. Kent*, 230 N.Y. 239, 129 N.E. 889, 23 A.L.R. 1429, as follows:

> The owner is entitled to the money which will permit him to complete, unless the cost of completion is grossly and unfairly out of proportion to the good to be attained. When that is true, the measure is the difference in value.

It thus appears that the prime consideration in the Restatement was "economic waste"; and that the prime consideration in McCormick, Damages, and in *Jacob & Youngs, Inc. v. Kent, supra*, was the relationship between the expense involved and the "end to be attained" — in other words, the "relative economic benefit."

In view of the unrealistic fact situation in the instant case, and certain Oklahoma statutes to be hereinafter noted, we are of the opinion that the "relative economic benefit" is a proper consideration here. This is in accord with the recent case of *Mann v. Clowser*, 190 Va. 887, 59 S.E.2d 78, where, in applying the cost rule, the Virginia court specifically noted that "... the defects are remediable from a practical standpoint and the costs *are not grossly disproportionate to the results to be obtained*" (Emphasis supplied).

23 O.S. 1961 §§ 96 and 97 provide as follows:

> § 96. ... Notwithstanding the provisions of this chapter, no person can recover a greater amount in damages for the breach of an obligation, than he would have gained by the full performance thereof on both sides ....

§ 97. ... Damages must, in all cases, be reasonable, and where an obligation of any kind appears to create a right to unconscionable and grossly oppressive damages, contrary to substantial justice no more than reasonable damages can be recovered.

Although it is true that the above sections of the statute are applied most often in tort cases, they are by their own terms, and the decisions of this court, also applicable in actions for damages for breach of contract. It would seem that they are peculiarly applicable here where, under the "cost of performance" rule, plaintiffs might recover an amount about nine times the total value of their farm. Such would seem to be "unconscionable and grossly oppressive damages, contrary to substantial justice" within the meaning of the statute. Also, it can hardly be denied that if plaintiffs here are permitted to recover under the "cost of performance" rule, they will receive a greater benefit from the breach than could be gained from full performance, contrary to the provisions of § 96.

An analogy may be drawn between the cited sections, and the provisions of 15 O.S.1961 §§ 214 and 215. These sections tend to render void any provisions of a contract which attempt to fix the amount of stipulated damages to be paid in case of a breach, except where it is impracticable or extremely difficult to determine the actual damages. This results in spite of the agreement of the parties, and the obvious and well known rationale is that insofar as they exceed the actual damages suffered, the stipulated damages amount to a penalty or forfeiture which the law does not favor.

23 O.S.1961 §§ 96 and 97 have the same effect in the case now before us. *In spite of the agreement of the parties*, these sections limit the damages recoverable to a reasonable amount not "contrary to substantial justice"; they prevent plaintiffs from recovering a "greater amount in damages for the breach of an obligation" than they would have "gained by the full performance thereof."

We therefore hold that where, in a coal mining lease, lessee agrees to perform certain remedial work on the premises concerned at the end of the lease period, and thereafter the contract is fully performed by both parties except that the remedial work is not done, the measure of damages in an action by lessor against lessee for damages for breach of contract is ordinarily the reasonable cost of performance of the work; however, where the contract provision breached was merely incidental to the main purpose in view, and where the economic benefit which would result to lessor by full performance of the work is grossly disproportionate to the cost of performance, the damages which lessor may recover are limited to the diminution in value resulting to the premises because of the non-performance.

We believe the above holding is in conformity with the intention of the Legislature as expressed in the statutes mentioned, and in harmony with the better-reasoned cases from the other jurisdictions where analogous fact situations have been considered. It should be noted that the rule as stated does not interfere with the property owner's right to "do what he will with his own" (*Chamberlain v. Parker*, 45 N.Y. 569), or his right, if he chooses, to contract for "improvements" which will actually have the effect of reducing his property's value. Where such result is in fact contemplated by the parties, and is a main or principal purpose of those contracting, it would seem that the measure of damages for breach would ordinarily be the cost of performance.

The above holding disposes of all of the arguments raised by the parties on appeal.

Under the most liberal view of the evidence herein, the diminution in value resulting to the premises because of non-performance of the remedial work was $300.00. After a careful search of the record, we have found no evidence of a higher figure, and plaintiffs do not argue in their briefs that a greater diminution in value was sustained. It thus appears that the judgment was clearly excessive, and that the amount for which judgment should have been rendered is definitely and satisfactorily shown by the record.

We are asked by each party to modify the judgment in accordance with the respective theories advanced, and it is conceded that we have authority to do so. 12 O.S.1961 § 952; *Busboom v. Smith*, 199 Okl. 688, 191 P.2d 198; *Stumpf v. Stumpf*, 173 Okl. 1, 46 P.2d 315.

We are of the opinion that the judgment of the trial court for plaintiffs should be, and it is hereby, modified and reduced to the sum of $300.00, and as so modified it is affirmed.

Welch, Davison, Halley, and Johnson, JJ., concur. Williams, C. J., Blackbird, V. C. J., and Irwin and Berry, JJ., dissent.

IRWIN, J. (dissenting). By the specific provisions in the coal mining lease under consideration, the defendant agreed as follows:

> ... 7b Lessee agrees to make fills in the pits dug on said premises on the property line in such manner that fences can be placed thereon and access had to opposite sides of the pits.
>
> 7c Lessee agrees to smooth off the top of the spoil banks on the above premises.
>
> 7d Lessee agrees to leave the creek crossing the above premises in such a condition that it will not interfere with the crossings to be made in pits as set out in 7b.
>
> ....
>
> 7f Lessee further agrees to leave no shale or dirt on the high wall of said pits....

Following the expiration of the lease, plaintiffs made demand upon defendant that it carry out the provisions of the contract and to perform those covenants contained therein.

Defendant admits that it failed to perform its obligations that it agreed and contracted to perform under the lease contract and there is nothing in the record which indicates that defendant could not perform its obligations. Therefore, in my opinion defendant's breach of the contract was wilful and not in good faith.

Although the contract speaks for itself, there were several negotiations between the plaintiffs and defendant before the contract was executed. Defendant admitted in the trial of the action, that plaintiffs insisted that the above provisions be included in the contract and that they would not agree to the coal mining lease unless the above provisions were included.

In consideration for the lease contract, plaintiffs were to receive a certain amount as royalty for the coal produced and marketed and in addition thereto their land was to be restored as provided in the contract.

Defendant received as consideration for the contract, its proportionate share of the coal produced and marketed and in addition thereto, the *right to use* plaintiffs' land in the furtherance of its mining operations.

The cost for performing the contract in question could have been reasonably approximated when the contract was negotiated and executed and there are no conditions now existing which could not have been reasonably anticipated by the parties. Therefore, defendant had knowledge, when it prevailed upon the plaintiffs to execute the lease, that the cost of performance might be disproportionate to the value or benefits received by plaintiff for the performance.

Defendant has received its benefits under the contract and now urges, in substance, that plaintiffs' measure of damages for its failure to perform should be the economic value of performance to the plaintiffs and not the cost of performance.

If a peculiar set of facts should exist where the above rule should be applied as the proper measure of damages, (and in my judgment those facts do not exist in the instant case) before such rule should be applied, consideration should be given to the benefits received or contracted for by the party who asserts the application of the rule.

Defendant did not have the right to mine plaintiffs' coal or to use plaintiffs' property for its mining operations without the consent of plaintiffs. Defendant had knowledge of the benefits that it would receive under the contract and the approximate cost of performing the contract. With this knowledge, it must be presumed that defendant thought that it would be to its economic advantage to enter into the contract with plaintiffs and that it would reap benefits from the contract, or it would have not entered into the contract.

Therefore, if the value of the performance of a contract should be considered in determining the measure of damages for breach of a contract, the value of the benefits received under the contract by a party who breaches a contract should also be considered. However, in my judgment, to give consideration to either in the instant action, completely rescinds and holds for naught the solemnity of the contract before us and makes an entirely new contract for the parties.

In *Goble v. Bell Oil & Gas Co.*, 97 Okl. 261, 223 P. 371, we held:

Even though the contract contains harsh and burdensome terms which the court does not in all respects approve, it is the province of the parties in relation to lawful subject matter to fix their rights and obligations, and the court will give the contract effect according to its expressed provisions, unless it be shown by competent evidence that the written agreement as executed is the result of fraud, mistake, or accident.

In *Cities Service Oil Co. v. Geolograph Co. Inc.*, 208 Okl. 179, 254 P.2d 775, we said:

While we do not agree that the contract as presently written is an onerous one, we think the short answer is that the folly or wisdom of a contract is not for the court to pass on.

In *Great Western Oil & Gas Company v. Mitchell*, Okl., 326 P.2d 794, we held:

The law will not make a better contract for parties than they themselves have seen fit to enter into, or alter it for the benefit of one party and to the detriment of the others; the judicial function of a court of law is to enforce a contract as it is written.

I am mindful of Title 23 O.S.1961 § 96, which provides that no person can recover a greater amount in damages for the breach of an obligation than he could have gained by the full performance thereof on both sides, except in cases not applicable herein. However, in my judgment, the above statutory provision is not applicable here.

In my judgment, we should follow the case of *Groves v. John Wunder Company*, 205 Minn. 163, 286 N.W. 235, 123 A.L.R. 502, which defendant agrees "that the fact situation is apparently similar to the one in the case at bar," and where the Supreme Court of Minnesota held:

The owner's or employer's damages for such a breach (i.e. breach hypothesized in 2d syllabus) are to be measured, not in respect to the value of the land to be improved, but by the reasonable cost of doing that which the contractor promised to do and which he left undone.

The hypothesized breach referred to states that where the contractor's breach of a contract is wilful, that is, in bad faith, he is not entitled to any benefit of the equitable doctrine of substantial performance.

In the instant action defendant has made no attempt to even substantially perform. The contract in question is not immoral, is not tainted with fraud, and was not entered into through mistake or accident and is not contrary to public policy. It is clear and unambiguous and the parties understood the terms thereof, and the approximate cost of fulfilling the obligations could have been approximately ascertained. There are no conditions existing now which could not have been reasonably anticipated when the contract was negotiated and executed. The defendant could have performed the contract if it desired. It has accepted and reaped the benefits of its contract and now urges that plaintiffs' benefits under the contract be denied. If plaintiffs' benefits are denied, such benefits would inure to the direct benefit of the defendant.

Therefore, in my opinion, the plaintiffs were entitled to specific performance of the contract and since defendant has failed to perform, the proper measure of damages should be the cost of performance. Any other measure of damage would be holding for naught the express provisions of the contract; would be taking from the plaintiffs the benefits of the contract and placing those benefits in defendant which has failed to perform its obligations; would be granting benefits to defendant without a resulting obligation; and would be completely rescinding the solemn obligation of the contract for the benefit of the defendant to the detriment of the plaintiffs by making an entirely new contract for the parties.

I therefore respectfully dissent to the opinion promulgated by a majority of my associates.

NOTES AND QUESTIONS

1. *Rehearing and vote switching:* Following the Supreme Court of Oklahoma's decision, the Peevyhouses' lawyer petitioned for a rehearing. Ten highly regarded lawyers and academics from Oklahoma City filed an amicus curiae brief in support of the Peevyhouses, arguing for the sanctity of contracts:

> [T]he express and unambiguous terms of contracts entered into by private individuals... cannot ... be abrogated.... [W]hen contractual promises are broken, this Court should lend its aid to promisees relying on the promises of competent promisors and lend its most vigorous sanction, to insure to future promisees that the aid of this Court is certain and unwavering, particularly being mindful of the interests sought to be safeguarded by the promisee in stipulating for terms, and not alone the objective of the promisor.

The Supreme Court denied the petition for rehearing, but there was a vote switch. The vote on the original decision was 5 to 3, with Justice Welch not participating. On rehearing Justice Williams switched his vote, resulting in a 4-4 split among the participating justices. However, Justice Welch then decided to vote on the side of Garland and the rehearing petition was denied 5-4. Later the official report was amended to reflect the votes of Justices Williams and Welch after rehearing.

2. *Stripmining*: Stripmining has been defined as follows:

> Stripmining entails digging a long, open trench through the overburden to expose a part of the seam for removal. After the exposed coal is removed, the operator makes a second, parallel cut with the overburden placed as spoil material into the first cut. The operator continues with successive cuts until the remaining coal lies too deep below the overburden to be mined economically. The last cut leaves a pit, or open trench bounded on one side by the last spoil bank, and on the other side by the highwall.... If the bottom of the last cut is beneath the water table, the pit eventually fills with water, and is then euphemistically called the "pond."[87]

At the time of this case, environmental regulations did not require restoration of the Peevyhouse land after the stripmining. Hence, the Peevyhouse's only legal claim was for breach of contract. Should the decision of the Oklahoma Supreme Court nonetheless have been influenced by environmental concerns? Try to construct an argument that a judge should *not* have looked to such things as his or her own views about the environment in deciding the case.

Since the *Peevyhouse* decision, there has been a great deal of environmental legislation regulating stripmining. In 1967, the Oklahoma Legislature passed the Open Cut Land Reclamation Act (now 45 Okla.Stat.Ann. §§ 721-792). It declares the policy of the State to be preservation of natural resources. It imposes a duty on mine operators to restore the land, and before operations begin they must post a bond covering the estimated cost of reclamation. The state is authorized to have the work done if the operator fails to carry out the duty. There is no exception where the cost of reclamation is disproportionate to the increased value of the land. In 1977, Congress enacted the Surface Mining Control and Reclamation Act (30 U.S.C.A. ch. 25.). It also is designed to assure that mined areas are reclaimed. However, during the tenure of James Watt as Secretary of the Interior in the first Reagan Administration, the Office of Surface Mining's penalty assessments department was abolished without congressional approval; members of Congress were very critical of the refusal to enforce the law and subsequently, portions of accumulated penalties were paid by the stripminers.

3. *Background of the case*: The briefs in the *Peevyhouse* case throw some light on the facts. The following excerpt from the transcript, taken from plaintiffs' brief, reveals some of the circumstances surrounding the negotiation of the contract. The testimony is by Burl Cumpton, who admitted negotiating and executing the contract on behalf of Garland Coal and Mining Co.

---

[87] Maute, *supra*.

Q. Isn't it true Mr. Peevyhouse insisted upon those provisions being included in that lease?

A. That's true.

Q. Before he agreed to sign it?

A. That's right.

Q. Mr. Cumpton when you negotiated and obtained that lease from the Peevyhouses did you intend to comply with the terms of that contract, those specific terms of that lease that are included in there?

A. Yes, we did.

Q. Your company hasn't complied with them?

A. No, that's right....

Q. Could you, with the equipment you have, could you have complied with those terms of that lease?

A. Yes, we could, but I want to qualify that statement....

The Court: You can bring it [the qualification] out on cross examination.

The following excerpt, taken from plaintiffs' reply brief, may explain why plaintiffs wanted the remedial work done:

> From the terms of the mining lease it is clearly apparent that plaintiffs insisted upon the insertion of the terms ... for the reason they wanted to assure their continued right to the use of their land in connection with their stock farming operations. I am sure that this Court is cognizant of what effect the bisecting of a tract of land by deep, east-west, 45-foot water-filled pit, rendering inaccessible the northern portion of plaintiffs' lands (ed. note: about 7 acres) along with 80 acres of leased land, would have on a stockman. It is quite obvious from the facts of this case that when the contract was executed between the parties that the plaintiffs had in mind only the assurance of the continued future use of their land as a stock farm and that the defendant was thoroughly cognizant of these desires and agreed to them.

Professor Judith Maute has done an extensive study of the *Peevyhouse* case, including extensive interviews of Peevyhouses themselves. She describes Garland's failure to perform the remedial work in the following terms:

> Actual mining on Peevyhouse land was short-lived. Garland began coal removal on their land in February, 1957 and ended sometime that spring. Exceptionally heavy spring rains broke a six year drought.... The flood conditions must have resolved any doubts Garland had about continuing to mine at this location. Garland pulled the dragline from the worksite and resumed mining at a higher and drier site....
>
> Garland had no contractual duty to remove a specific quantity of coal from Peevyhouse land.... Nonperformance of the remedial work was the

only breach.... As Garland prepared to leave the site, Burl Cumpton and Willie discussed the remedial work.... A bulldozer spent one day smoothing off the sharp peaks on the spoil banks and building a dirt levee across the pit. More heavy rains interrupted these makeshift efforts. When saturated ground caused unstable conditions that endangered workers, Garland ceased all remedial efforts.Willie then offered to accept $500 so he could hire a bulldozer and level the ground himself. Garland refused. Willie then told Cumpton that the price of the settlement would increase $500 each time he returned to Garland's Stigler office about the matter. Six fruitless visits later brought the settlement demand to $3,000. Finally, Garland presented a check for $3,000 conditioned on signing a release.

Peevyhouses knew of Woodrow McConnell because he was from Stigler and had represented their neighbor, Clifton Few, in a pending tort claim against Garland. That week-end the Peevyhouses went to Oklahoma City to discuss the proposed settlement with McConnell. He advised them against signing the release unless one paragraph was deleted. They recall his explanation: "If you sign this, you take full responsibility to your neighbors for damage being done to their land from the creek, and your neighbors will look to you." Settlement discussions ended when Garland refused to delete the objectionable paragraph.

Professor Maute describes the condition of the Peevyhouse farm today. Apparently the dirt levee constructed by Garland quickly washed out. There have been no crossings across the pit since then, and the pit is filled with water. Professor Maute continues:

Willie and Lucille still live on the land located just outside Stigler. The land they leased to Garland has changed little from when mining stopped over thirty-five years ago. The rough, rocky surface on the high wall and spoil banks is sparsely vegetated. About half of the leased acreage remains unusable....

Lucille is bitter and distrustful of the legal system. She wants to move into the town of Stigler, leaving behind the scarred land and her memories of the legal dispute. Willie still wants the land fixed: "It's just not right to do something with land that makes it useless for the future."... [A]pproximately thirty acres are practically worthless to the Peevyhouses.

4. *Specific performance*: Some have argued that the ideal solution in cases such as *Peevyhouse v. Garland Coal & Mining Co.* would be an order of specific performance requiring Garland to fill in the hole. If a court issued such an order, what do you think would have been the likely consequence? Would the pits on the Peevyhouse's land have been filled in?

5. *Other possible outcomes:* The Oklahoma Supreme Court analyzed the case as if the only possible outcomes were either to award the cost of performance or

the diminution in value of the land. Both of these damages formulas reflect the expectation principle: they constitute different methods of estimating the position of the plaintiff if the contract had not been breached. There have many cases in other states discussing which approach to measuring expectation damages is most appropriate. Some of these cases are discussed in the *Peevyhouse* opinion. Another is *Plante v. Jacobs, supra,* p. 146. If you are using the Danzig book entitled *The Capability Problem in Contract Law,* the very famous Cardozo opinion in *Jacob & Youngs v. Kent,* 230 N.Y. 239, 129 N.E. 889 (1921), is contained therein. Subsequent Oklahoma decisions on this question are summarized in note 7, *infra.*

In *Peevyhouse* the Oklahoma Supreme Court did not discuss possible damages calculations reflecting reliance or restitution principles. What possibilities can you construct? Consider the following additional information about the case. Much of this information comes from Professor Maute's study of the case and was not included in the trial record because the lawyer for the Peevyhouses did not introduce it at trial.

(a) It is unclear how much Garland expected the remedial work to cost at the time it signed the contract. Normally Garland paid landowners a surface damage payment in addition to royalties. In the Peevyhouses' situation, that payment would have been $3,000 but it was not included in the contract because Garland agreed to the remedial work. On the other hand the Peevyhouses negotiated a 20 cents per ton royalty for mined coal instead the normal 15 cents per ton in Garland contracts. Undoubtedly the cheapest way to do the remedial work would have been for Garland to do it when its earth moving equipment was on site, but as indicated above the soil was so water-logged at the time Garland decided to quit the site that the work could not practically be done. The $29,000 estimate of the cost of doing the remedial work at a later time, which is mentioned in the Court's opinion, comes from testimony at trial by an expert witness for Peevyhouse. At trial Garland's lawyer challenged the basis of this estimate. An expert for Garland testified that the cost of the doing the work at the time of trial would have been only $8500. Writing in 1994, Professor Maute concluded that the best guess she could make about the cost of doing the remedial work at the time of the trial in this case was $17,000.

(b) Garland was especially anxious to sign a contract with the Peevyhouses because it needed to divert the creek. Diversion of the creek was necessary so that the water from the creek would not run into the various "cuts" Garland would make, not only on Peevyhouse's land but also the land of neighbors with whom Garland signed contracts. Because of the topography of the land, the most practical place to divert the creek was through Peevyhouse's land.

(c) The Peevyhouses received $2500 in royalties under the Garland contract. Professor Maute's estimate of Garland's profits from the coal mined from Peevyhouse's land is between $25,000 and $34,000.

(d) If the fills had been made in the pits as promised in the contract, Peevyhouse would have had access to approximately 4.5 acres of unspoiled land that he owned and which was separated from the rest of the land. The fills would also have provided access to leased land. If in addition the spoil banks had been leveled, Peevyhouse would have regained nearly 7 acres of pasture land. At the time undisturbed land in the area had a market value of about $50 per acre.

6. *The authority of Peevyhouse*: Professor John H. Jackson, of the University of Michigan Law School, in his *Contract Law in Modern Society* 44 (West Publishing Co. 1973) points out that a year after the *Peevyhouse* decision, there was a scandal involving the Supreme Court of Oklahoma. Several of its members were accused of taking bribes to decide cases, but they were *not* accused of taking a bribe in *Peevyhouse v. Garland Coal & Mining Co.* Two of the justices who concurred in the majority opinion in that case were implicated. One resigned and one was impeached. An Oklahoma Bar Association Committee investigated, and said that the other seven justices "were proved to be honest men and have not been paid, nor have they received any bribe in any case."[88] Could a lawyer in Oklahoma use this scandal as a basis for attacking the *Peevyhouse* decision? Could a lawyer in another state use it to argue that her highest court should not follow the decision? Does the fact that a judge was bribed in one case indicate necessarily there is something wrong with his or her decision in another one?

Peevyhouse's lawyer was a solo practitioner, based in Oklahoma City. Peevyhouse learned of him because he was originally from Stigler and had represented some neighbors in lawsuits against Garland. Garland was represented by one of Oklahoma City's largest law firms. Many persons question some of the decisions made by Peevyhouse's lawyer. He chose not to introduce much potentially relevant evidence, including Peevyhouse's waiver of a surface damage payment in exchange for the remedial clauses. He chose to appeal the jury verdict of $5,000 even though Garland probably would have settled for that amount, with the result that Garland cross appealed and obtained a significant reduction in the size of the judgment. Is the authority of the *Peevyhouse* decision lessened because Peevyhouse's lawyer made decisions that with the advantage of hindsight seem clearly unfortunate?

A cynic might say that it did not matter whether Peevyhouse was well represented or whether someone bribed members of the Supreme Court of Oklahoma. Any lawyer in Oklahoma who would come within the charmed circle from which appellate judges are picked in that state would be sympathetic to extractive industries. These people usually hold positive views of oil, gas and coal companies, and they favor exploitation of resources over the interests of individuals such as the Peevyhouses or environmental concerns. Their "common sense" views of what was necessary, tolerable or just would prompt them to define the situation as wasting a lot of money to truck in fill to suit the Peevyhouses' whims or to manufacture a lawsuit where the Peevyhouses and their lawyer could reap a windfall. Is this cynicism or realism?

---

[88] 36 Oklahoma Bar Association Journal 1507 (1965).

7. *Subsequent Oklahoma decisions.* There have been a number of subsequent decisions in Oklahoma discussing the current status of the *Peevyhouse* holding.

(a) A 1983 10th Circuit decision in the case of *Rock Island Improvement Co. v. Helmerich & Payne, Inc.*[89] raised the same issue as that posed in the *Peevyhouse* case. A mining company leased the right to mine coal on two tracts of land in Oklahoma. The lease required that the surface be restored to its condition prior to the mining operations. The tracts of land were strip mined but not reclaimed. The parties stipulated that the value of the land was $6,797 less after the mining than it would have been had the reclamation been carried out. Expert testimony established that restoring the land as called for by the lease would cost $375,000. The jury awarded the land owner $375,000. The 10th Circuit noted that there was a strong dissent in *Peevyhouse* and that since the *Peevyhouse* decision, the public policy of the state had changed as expressed by the adoption of a law regulating reclamation of open cut mines. The court felt that it was unlikely that the Oklahoma Supreme Court would follow its decision in *Peevyhouse* and thus the court indicated that it need not adhere to the decision. The court found that the parties expressly included the reclamation clause which required the lessee to bear the cost of reclamation and the court felt that the agreement should be given force. The court said nothing about the likelihood that the $375,000 less attorney's fees would be spent on reclamation or the wisdom of spending that much to produce an economic benefit of $6,797.

(b) A year later the Oklahoma Court of Appeals decided *Thompson v. Andover Oil Co.*[90] In this case, plaintiffs brought a nuisance action against holders of an oil and gas lease for damages to the land surface resulting from oil and gas operations. The plaintiff testified that the diminution in the value of the land was $50,000. Expert testimony indicated that the cost of restoring the land was $70,000. The jury awarded $50,000. The Oklahoma Court of Appeals upheld the jury's award. The court reasoned that damages must be limited to the cost of restoring the land but twice noted that they cannot exceed the depreciated value of the land itself; the court cited *Peevyhouse* for this proposition and made no mention of the 10th Circuit's decision in *Rock Island*.

(c) *Davis v. Shell Oil Co.*, 795 F.Supp. 381 (W.D. Okl. 1992) was decided by the Federal District court for the Western District of Oklahoma in 1992. In discussing the amount of damages that the plaintiff could claim, the court rejected defendant's claim that damages must be limited to diminution in value. The court cited *Rock Island* as if it held that courts in Oklahoma do not follow *Peevyhouse*. The court also noted that the citation of *Peevyhouse* in *Thompson* was in dicta and characterized *Thompson* as unpersuasive authority.

(d) In *Schneberger v. Apache Corp.*, 1994 WL 580878 (Okla.S.Ct., Oct. 25, 1994), the Oklahoma Supreme Court addressed the continuing vitality of the

---

[89]698 F.2d 1075 (10th Cir. 1983).

[90]691 P.2d 77 (Okl. App. 1984).

Peevyhouse rule. Apache agreed to clean up ground water contaminated by drilling for oil and gas wells. They abandoned their clean up efforts. Plaintiff's estimate of the cost of completing the clean up was $1.3 million. Apache's experts estimated the diminution in market value of the land because of ground water contamination was $5,175. The Court held that damages would be limited to the diminution in value. The Court held that the *Peevyhouse* rule was not limited to cases where the remedial work was "incidental to the main purpose of the contract."

ALICE SULLIVAN v. JAMES H. O'CONNER

363 Mass. 579, 296 N.E.2d 183 (1973)

[If you are using Danzig, *The Capability Problem in Contract Law,* as a supplement to this text, you should read the case and accompanying notes at pages 5-43. For other students, the edited opinion is reproduced below.]

KAPLAN, J.

The plaintiff patient secured a jury verdict of $13,500 against the defendant surgeon for breach of contract in respect to an operation upon the plaintiff's nose. The substituted consolidated bill of exceptions presents questions about the correctness of the judge's instructions on the issue of damages.

The declaration was in two counts. In the first count, the plaintiff alleged that she, as patient, entered into a contract with the defendant, a surgeon, wherein the defendant promised to perform plastic surgery on her nose and thereby to enhance her beauty and improve her appearance; that he performed the surgery but failed to achieve the promised result; rather the result of the surgery was to disfigure and deform her nose, to cause her pain in body and mind, and to subject her to other damage and expense. The second count, based on the same transaction, was in the conventional form for malpractice, charging that the defendant had been guilty of negligence in performing the surgery. Answering, the defendant entered a general denial.

On the plaintiff's demand, the case was tried by jury. At the close of the evidence, the judge put to the jury, as special questions, the issues of liability under the two counts, and instructed them accordingly. The jury returned a verdict for the plaintiff on the contract count, and for the defendant on the negligence count. The judge then instructed the jury on the issue of damages.

As background to the instructions and the parties' exceptions, we mention certain facts as the jury could find them. The plaintiff was a professional entertainer, and this was known to the defendant. The agreement was as alleged in the declaration. More particularly, judging from exhibits, the plaintiff's nose had been straight, but long and prominent; the defendant undertook by two operations to reduce its prominence and somewhat to shorten it, thus making it more pleasing in relation to the plaintiff's other features. Actually the plaintiff was obliged to undergo three operations, and her appearance was worsened. Her nose now had a concave line to about the midpoint, at which it became bulbous; viewed frontally, the nose from bridge to midpoint was flattened and broadened, and the two sides of the tip had lost symmetry. This configuration evidently could not be improved by further surgery. The plaintiff did not demonstrate, however, that her change of appearance had resulted in loss of employment. Payments by the plaintiff covering the defendant's fee and hospital expenses were stipulated at $622.65.

The judge instructed the jury, first, that the plaintiff was entitled to recover her out-of-pocket expenses incident to the operations. Second, she could recover the damages flowing directly, naturally, proximately, and foreseeably from the defendant's breach of promise. These would comprehend damages for any disfigurement of the plaintiff's nose — that is, any change of appearance for the worse — including the effects of the consciousness of such disfigurement on the plaintiff's mind, and in this connection the jury should consider the nature of the plaintiff's profession. Also consequent upon the defendant's breach, and compensable, were the pain and suffering involved in the third operation, but not in the first two. As there was no proof that any loss of earnings by the plaintiff resulted from the breach, that element should not enter into the calculation of damages.

By his exceptions the defendant contends that the judge erred in allowing the jury to take into account anything but the plaintiff's out-of-pocket expenses (presumably at the stipulated amount). The defendant excepted to the judge's refusal of his request for a general charge to that effect, and, more specifically, to the judge's refusal of a charge that the plaintiff could not recover for pain and suffering connected with the third operation or for impairment of the plaintiff's appearance and associated mental distress.

The plaintiff on her part excepted to the judge's refusal of a request to charge that the plaintiff could recover the difference in value between the nose as promised and the nose as it appeared after the operations. However, the plaintiff in her brief expressly waives this exception and others made by her in case this court overrules the defendant's exceptions; thus she would be content to hold the jury's verdict in her favor.

We conclude that the defendant's exceptions should be overruled.

It has been suggested on occasion that agreements between patients and physicians by which the physician undertakes to effect a cure or to bring about a given result should be declared unenforceable on grounds of public policy.... But there are many decisions recognizing and enforcing such contracts, see annotation, 43 A.L.R.3d 1221, 1225, 1229-1233, and the law of Massachusetts has treated them as valid.... (citations omitted) These causes of action are, however, considered a little suspect, and thus we find courts straining sometimes to read the pleadings as sounding only in tort for negligence, and not in contract for breach of promise, despite sedulous efforts by the pleaders to pursue the latter theory. See ... annotation, *supra*, at 1225, 1238-1244.

It is not hard to see why the courts should be unenthusiastic or skeptical about the contract theory. Considering the uncertainties of medical science and the variations in the physical and psychological conditions of individual patients, doctors can seldom in good faith promise specific results. Therefore it is unlikely that physicians of even average integrity will in fact make such promises. Statements of opinion by the physician with some optimistic coloring are a different thing, and may indeed have therapeutic value. But patients may transform such statements into firm promises in their own minds, especially when they have been disappointed in the event, and testify in that sense to sympathetic juries.[91] If actions for breach of promise can be readily maintained, doctors, so it is said, will be frightened into practicing "defensive medicine." On the other hand, if these actions were outlawed, leaving only the possibility of suits for malpractice, there is fear that the public might be exposed to the enticements of charlatans, and confidence in the profession might ultimately be shaken. See Miller, The Contractual Liability of Physicians and Surgeons, 1953 Wash.L.Q. 413, 416-423. The law has taken the middle of the road position of allowing actions based on alleged contract, but insisting on clear proof. Instructions to the jury may well stress this requirement and point to tests of truth, such as the complexity or difficulty of an operation as bearing on the probability that a given result was promised. See annotation, 43 A.L.R.3d 1225, 1225-1227.

If an action on the basis of contract is allowed, we have next the question of the measure of damages to be applied where liability is found. Some cases have taken the simple view that the promise by the physician is to be treated like an ordinary commercial promise, and accordingly that the successful plaintiff is entitled to a standard measure of recovery for breach of contract — "compensatory" ("expectancy") damages, an amount intended to put the plaintiff in the position he would be in if the contract had been performed, or, presumably, at the plaintiff's election, "restitution" damages, an amount corresponding to any benefit conferred by the plaintiff upon the defendant in the performance of the contract disrupted by the defendant's breach. See Restatement: Contracts § 329 and Comment a, §§ 347, 384(1). Thus in *Hawkins v. McGee*, 84 N.H. 114, 146 A. 641, the defendant doctor was taken to have promised the plaintiff to convert his damaged hand by means of an operation into a good or perfect hand, but the doctor so operated as to damage the hand still further. The court, following the usual expectancy formula, would have asked the jury to estimate and award to the plaintiff the difference between the value of a good or perfect hand, as promised, and the value of the hand after the operation. (The same formula would apply, although the dollar result would be less, if the operation had neither

---

[91]Judicial skepticism about whether a promise was in fact made derives also from the possibility that the truth has been tortured to give the plaintiff the advantage of the longer period of limitations sometimes available for actions on contract as distinguished from those in tort or for malpractice. See Lillich, The Malpractice Statute of Limitations in New York and Other Jurisdictions, 47 Cornell Law Quarterly 339; annotation, 80 A.L.R.2d 368.

worsened nor improved the condition of the hand.) If the plaintiff had not yet paid the doctor his fee, that amount would be deducted from the recovery. There could be no recovery for the pain and suffering of the operation, since that detriment would have been incurred even if the operation had been successful; one can say that this detriment was not "caused" by the breach. But where the plaintiff by reason of the operation was put to more pain ... [than] he would have had to endure, had the doctor performed as promised, he should be compensated for that difference as a proper part of his expectancy recovery. It may be noted that on an alternative count for malpractice the plaintiff in the *Hawkins* case had been nonsuited; but on ordinary principles this could not affect the contract claim, for it is hardly a defence to a breach of contract that the promisor acted innocently and without negligence....

Other cases, including a number in New York, without distinctly repudiating the *Hawkins* type of analysis, have indicated that a different and generally more lenient measure of damages is to be applied in patient-physician actions based on breach of alleged special agreements to effect a cure, attain a stated result, or employ a given medical method. This measure is expressed in somewhat variant ways, but the substance is that the plaintiff is to recover any expenditures made by him and for other detriment (usually not specifically described in the opinions) following proximately and foreseeably upon the defendant's failure to carry out his promise.... (citations omitted) This, be it noted, is not a "restitution" measure, for it is not limited to restoration of the benefit conferred on the defendant (the fee paid) but includes other expenditures, for example, amounts paid for medicine and nurses; so also it would seem according to its logic to take in damages for any worsening of the plaintiff's condition due to the breach. Nor is it an "expectancy" measure, for it does not appear to contemplate recovery of the whole difference in value between the condition as promised and the condition actually resulting from the treatment. Rather the tendency of the formulation is to put the plaintiff back in the position he occupied just before the parties entered upon the agreement, to compensate him for the detriments he suffered in reliance upon the agreement. This kind of intermediate pattern of recovery for breach of contract is discussed in the suggestive article by Fuller and Perdue, The Reliance Interest in Contract Damages,[92] where the authors show that, although not attaining the currency of the standard measures, a "reliance" measure has for special reasons been applied by the courts in a variety of settings, including noncommercial settings.

For breach of the patient-physician agreements under consideration, a recovery limited to restitution seems plainly too meager, if the agreements are to be enforced at all. On the other hand, an expectancy recovery may well be excessive. The factors, already mentioned, which have made the cause of action somewhat suspect, also suggest moderation as to the breadth of the recovery that

---

[92]Eds. Note: This article is cited and discussed on p. 124 *supra*.

should be permitted. Where, as in the case at bar and in a number of the reported cases, the doctor has been absolved of negligence by the trier, an expectancy measure may be thought harsh. We should recall here that the fee paid by the patient to the doctor for the alleged promise would usually be quite disproportionate to the putative expectancy recovery. To attempt, moreover, to put a value on the condition that would or might have resulted, had the treatment succeeded as promised, may sometimes put an exceptional strain on the imagination of the fact finder. As a general consideration, Fuller and Perdue argue that the reasons for granting damages for broken promises to the extent of the expectancy are at their strongest when the promises are made in a business context, when they have to do with the production or distribution of goods or the allocation of functions in the market place; they become weaker as the context shifts from a commercial to a noncommercial field. 46 Yale Law Journal at 60-63.

There is much to be said, then, for applying a reliance measure to the present facts, and we have only to add that our cases are not unreceptive to the use of that formula in special situations. We have, however, had no previous occasion to apply it to patient-physician cases.[93]

The question of recovery on a reliance basis for pain and suffering or mental distress requires further attention. We find expressions in the decisions that pain and suffering (or the like) are simply not compensable in actions for breach of contract. The defendant seemingly espouses this proposition in the present case. True, if the buyer under a contract for the purchase of a lot of merchandise, in suing for the seller's breach, should claim damages for mental anguish caused by his disappointment in the transaction, he would not succeed; he would be told, perhaps, that the asserted psychological injury was not fairly foreseeable by the

---

[93]In Mt. Pleasant Stable Co. v. Steinberg, 238 Mass. 567, 131 N.E. 295, the plaintiff company agreed to supply teams of horses at agreed rates as required from day to day by the defendant for his business. To prepare itself to fulfill the contract and in reliance on it, the plaintiff bought two "Cliest" horses at a certain price. When the defendant repudiated the contract, the plaintiff sold the horses at a loss and in its action for breach claimed the loss as an element of damages. The court properly held that the plaintiff was not entitled to this item as it was also claiming (and recovering) its lost profits (expectancy) on the contract as a whole.... (The loss on sale of the horses is analogous to the pain and suffering for which the patient would be disallowed a recovery in Hawkins v. McGee ... because he was claiming and recovering expectancy damages.) The court in the *Mt. Pleasant* case referred, however, to Pond v. Harris, 113 Mass. 114, as a contrasting situation where the expectancy could not be fairly determined. There the defendant had wrongfully revoked an agreement to arbitrate a dispute with the plaintiff (this was before such agreements were made specifically enforceable). In an action for the breach, the plaintiff was held entitled to recover for his preparations for the arbitration which had been rendered useless and a waste, including the plaintiff's time and trouble and his expenditures for counsel and witnesses. The context apparently was commercial but reliance elements were held compensable when there was no fair way of estimating an expectancy. See, generally, annotation, 17 A.L.R.2d 1300. A noncommercial example is Smith v. Sherman, 4 Cush. 408, 413–414, suggesting that a conventional recovery for breach of promise of marriage included a recompense for various efforts and expenditures by the plaintiff preparatory to the promised wedding....

defendant as a probable consequence of the breach of such a business contract. See Restatement of Contracts, § 341, and Comment a. But there is no general rule barring such items of damage in actions for breach of contract. It is all a question of the subject matter and background of the contract, and when the contract calls for an operation on the person of the plaintiff, psychological as well as physical injury may be expected to figure somewhere in the recovery, depending on the particular circumstances.... Suffering or distress resulting from the breach going beyond that which was envisaged by the treatment as agreed, should be compensable on the same ground as the worsening of the patient's condition because of the breach. Indeed it can be argued that the very suffering or distress "contracted for" — that which would have been incurred if the treatment achieved the promised result — should also be compensable on the theory underlying the New York cases. For that suffering is "wasted" if the treatment fails. Otherwise stated, compensation for this waste is arguably required in order to complete the restoration of the status quo ante.[94]

In the light of the foregoing discussion, all the defendant's exceptions fail: the plaintiff was not confined to the recovery of her out-of-pocket expenditures; she was entitled to recover also for the worsening of her condition, and for the pain and suffering and mental distress involved in the third operation. These items were compensable on either an expectancy or a reliance view. We might have been required to elect between the two views if the pain and suffering connected with the first two operations contemplated by the agreement, or the whole difference in value between the present and the promised conditions, were being claimed as elements of damage. But the plaintiff waives her possible claim to the former element, and to so much of the latter as represents the difference in value between the promised condition and the condition before the operations.

What is a promise? Justice Kaplan indicates that courts require plaintiffs to present clear proof to juries that a doctor has made a contractual promise about

---

[94]Recovery on a reliance basis for breach of the physician's promise tends to equate with the usual recovery for malpractice, since the latter also looks in general to restoration of the condition before the injury. But this is not paradoxical, especially when it is noted that the origins of contract lie in tort. See Farnsworth, The Past of Promise: An Historical Introduction to Contract, 69 Columbia Law Review 576, 594--596; Breitel, J. in Stella Flour & Feed Corp. v. National City Bank, 285 App.Div. 182, 189, 136 N.Y.S.2d 139 (dissenting opinion). A few cases have considered possible recovery for breach by a physician of a promise to sterilize a patient, resulting in birth of a child to the patient and spouse. If such an action is held maintainable, the reliance and expectancy measures would, we think, tend to equate, because the promised condition was preservation of the family status quo. See Custodio v. Bauer, 251 Cal.App.2d 303, 59 Cal.Rptr. 463; Jackson v. Anderson, 230 So.2d 503 (Fla.App.).... See also annotation, 27 A.L.R.3d 906. It would, however, be a mistake to think in terms of strict "formulas." For example, a jurisdiction which would apply a reliance measure to the present facts might impose a more severe damage sanction for the wilful use by the physician of a method of operation that he undertook not to employ.

the outcome of the operation. But clear proof about what? Suppose that Dr. O'Conner had presented incontrovertible proof that he did not want or intend to make any contractual obligations respecting the nature of Ms. Sullivan's nose at the conclusion of the surgery. Should the trial court then have directed a verdict for the defendant on the contract count in the complaint?

Chapter 3

CONTRACT AND CONTINUING RELATIONS

A. INTRODUCTION

Writers discussing contracts often assume that people usually engage in discrete transactions. Strangers meet, they bargain cautiously, and they close a contract that covers their complete agreement. Scholars sometimes call this the horse-trade model of contract. The traveling horse trader comes to the farm for the first, and probably the last, time. Both trader and farmer know they must take care of themselves. Horse trades involve sharp bargaining, and the parties have few obligations to each other.[1]

While there are one-shot contractual deals, long-term continuing business relations are common. We must change many of our assumptions when we consider relational bargaining. For example, a year-round resident in a resort community, who needs car repairs, may get different treatment than a tourist would get — especially from a merchant who values relationships with regular customers. The impact of contract law may differ as the underlying situation resembles one or the other of these examples.

The organization of this chapter sometimes may be hard to follow because we are trying to teach several things at once. Chapter 2 was an overview of the legal and practical protection given by the private law remedy system for breach of voluntarily assumed obligations. Most, but not all, of the materials in that chapter dealt with relatively simple kinds of agreements — one-shot deals or transactions in which the relationship of the parties began when they entered their agreement and ended when they performed or breached it. (*Copylease v. Memorex*, of course, was an exception.) Chapter 3 develops many of the ideas found in Chapter 2 in complex social and economic contexts. Here we consider what, if anything, the law has to offer to support complex contractual relationships. We ask whether the legal system can offer more than salvage when they are wrecked.

We can arrange contracts on a spectrum from discrete transactions to long-term continuing relations. Agreements become more relational as contacts between the parties become more frequent, and as their demands upon one another become less standardized and more idiosyncratic.[2] Consider the following situations:

---

[1]Compare Issacs, The Industrial Purchaser and the Sales Act, 34 Columbia Law Review 262, 263 (1934); Llewellyn, Across Sales on Horseback, 52 Harvard Law Review 725 (1939); Llewellyn, The First Struggle to Unhorse Sales, 52 Harvard Law Review 873 (1939).

[2]The idea of idiosyncrasy as the identifying characteristic of relational contracts comes from Williamson, Transaction-Cost Economics: The Governance of Contractual Relations, 22 Journal of Law & Economics 233 (1979).

(1) Company Executive rents a car from a local firm for a business trip, in a place she has never been before and never expects to be again.

(2) Company regularly calls on Rent-a-Car, a national organization, whenever Company's officials need a car. Company has seasonal needs, requests for different car types for different jobs, and so on. Rent-a-Car makes a special effoi. to fill Company's orders to keep its good will. Rent-a-Car assigns particular employees to service the Company account, and they form personal relationships with Company executives and employees who deal with rental automobiles and trucks.

(3) Company leases a whole fleet of cars from Rent-a-Car, and Rent-a-Car agrees to service them and replace them after they have travelled a certain number of miles. Rent-a-Car employees now regularly work at Company's headquarters and divisional offices in connection with maintaining this fleet.

(4) Company decides to integrate a fleet of cars into its own organization. It ends the agreement with Rent-a-Car and takes on the former Rent-a-Car employees who serviced its account as its own employees.

These arrangements illustrate points along the spectrum from discrete transaction to relation. The first three will use what we can call a "contract," a more or less formal statement of the terms of the agreement. However, as the arrangements become more relational, the formal contract will be a less adequate description of the parties' actual expectations, which develop through experience and personal contact. Rent-a-Car's employees assigned to the Company account will develop special working relationships with Company's people, a specialized knowledge about Company's problems, and an interest in solving them. Rent-a-Car employees and Company employees are likely to become involved in a network of exchanging favors and information.[3] Indeed, some employees of both concerns may find their loyalties unclear. A particular Company employee may become Rent-a-Car's informal advocate within Company. The reputation and status of the employee who selected Rent-a-Car and recommends continuing doing business with it may turn on Rent-a-Car's performance. The employee and Rent-a-Car's representatives may work closely to keep everyone satisfied with its performance and repair, or even cover up, any failures to perform.

We also can see the final stage where Company absorbs the car fleet as a contract. The elaborate transaction may be affected by one or more labor union's

---

[3]See Haas and Deseran, Trust and Symbolic Exchange, 44 Social Psychology Quarterly 3 (1981). Trust is a belief that another will fulfill his or her obligations and pull his or her weight in their relationship. Symbolic gestures and experience create and maintain trust. One invests in a relationship by offering food and drink, gifts and favors. Moore, Law and Social Change: the Semi-Autonomous Social Field as an Appropriate Object of Study, 7 Law & Society Review 719 (1973), points out that American business is characterized by what she calls "fictive friendships." The parties to a business deal often use first names, ask about family events, give gifts, and engage in business entertaining. A lawyer who deals with contracts and fails to understand the power and the limits of trust and the social sanctions flowing from "fictive friendships" is incompetent.

collective bargaining agreements with Company and Rent-a-Car. If Company is big enough, it may decide to treat its own divisions as independent units and make arrangements resembling contracts with them to supply its needs. It may even make them compete with real outside contractors for its business.

The materials in this chapter deal mostly with agreements falling toward the relational side of the spectrum. We start with family relationships, a seemingly eccentric choice in a contracts course where students expect to focus on business. However, the choice is justifiable. All our readers have some experience in this area but only a few know much about business relations. Also, regulation of family relations is not very different from regulation of business relations in the problems it poses for the legal system. In fact, business people sometimes describe partnerships as a kind of "marriage," and those working face to face over time take on aspects of family relations. After working through contract and the family, we will turn to employment and other business relationships.

One purpose of this chapter is simply to take another look at the whole battery of contract remedies from Chapter 2 — expectation damages, reliance, restitution, specific performance, and all the rest — in this new context of complex ongoing relations. As we saw in Chapter 2, especially in *Sullivan v. O'Connor*, seeking vindication through civil litigation processes is far from costless in money, time, and emotional energy. Even winners often wonder whether their victory was worth the price. The costs usually increase when people involved in a long term continuing relationship take disputes to courts. You will have an opportunity here to compare the effectiveness and fairness of the contract remedies system to some alternatives — including such non-judicial means of dispute processing as arbitration, mediation, and private sanctions devised and imposed by the parties themselves.

A second purpose of Chapter 3 is to consider legal enforcement and regulation of contract relations as a form of official intervention into the lives and dealings of parties. To simplify considerably, someone asks an agency — court, regulatory body, or arbitration board — to intervene in a set of contract relations. The agency has three choices: (i) It can intervene primarily to *facilitate* the relationship according to the wishes of the parties. (ii) It can *regulate* it, imposing on it notions of policy not derived from the interests of the immediate parties. (iii) It can *abstain* because the parties' problems are beyond the agency's competence or concern or because the parties' freedom to do as they please is itself an important value.

We will be considering from two different perspectives how legal agencies make these choices:

(a) We will look at *contract doctrine*. Contract law has a number of standards to help legal officials decide when and how to intervene. We have encountered some of them already. For example, many writers claim that the expectation principle of contract damages facilitates planning and risk assumption. The courts' refusal to enforce penalty clauses is regulatory. The refusal to award speculative damages is a doctrine of abstention.

In this chapter we consider a collection of doctrines that common law judges and treatise-writers developed in the "classical" period of contract law in the late 19th century. Judges and scholars said that these rules drew lines between situations in which courts would enforce contracts and those in which they had to abstain — doctrines marking off "enforceable" from "unenforceable" transactions. The doctrinal devices that marked boundaries were: (1) formation rules (those dealing with "offers" and "acceptances") that specified the types of signs and forms that parties had to use toward one another to persuade a court that they had agreed to a deal. (2) Rules derived from the Statute of Frauds, a phrase used by lawyers covering rules requiring that certain kinds of contracts be in writing (see, *e.g.*, U.C.C. § 2-201). (3) The doctrine of "consideration" — one of the strangest of all legal concepts. In the classical period, for example, consideration doctrine made promises to make gifts unenforceable.

This "classical" doctrine is still with us in some form, but it now co-exists with a whole new set of 20th century rules that add to, qualify, and frequently contradict the traditional learning. Among these new ideas is § 90 of the Restatement of Contracts, which appears to authorize enforcement of non-bargained-for promises and much else besides. Indeed, § 90 may contradict much of the Statute of Fraud's demand for a writing. Courts also have read it to impose a kind of promissory liability for negotiating behavior where the parties failed to conclude a bargain. Part of our task, of course, is to get a sense of when the old-fashioned contracts religion will hold sway and when judges and lawyers will use these newer ideas.

(b) We view legal doctrine as primarily *a set of tools used in the service of substantive social policies*. Conflict in the rules reflects conflict in larger social values. The major focus of this chapter will be on these social policies, and we will look at doctrine as a means to an end.

Doctrine may serve another function. The way we state legal rules may limit the way we see problems and solutions. We can become so accustomed to certain rules that they just seem to reflect common sense. Yet that common sense may reflect a distinct way of looking at the world which is questionable. We will try to look behind and within legal rules to make these assumptions explicit so we can ask whether we want to accept them. Professor Feinman asserts "[t]he ideological function of contract law is to conceal ... choices, to make results seem determinate when they are not."[4] He continues: "As contract law is one realm of elite ideology, the concealment it produces typically legitimates the status quo."[5] We will test his assertions in the materials which follow.

---

[4]Feinman, The Significance of Contracts Theory 41, University of Cincinnati Law Review 1283 (1990).

[5]*Ibid.*

1. THE VOCABULARY OF CONTRACT FORMATION

At the beginning of Chapter Two we offered a relatively extended "digression" on the history of the development of the U.C.C. We felt that this was necessary background for a discussion of the expectation principle, its role in contract doctrine, and its codification in the Uniform Commercial Code. We offer, at this point,[6] another digression from our main objective. This "digression" is more controversial, however. At least to label it as a digression is controversial.

Many contracts books begin with a long series of cases designed to introduce the doctrines of contract formation. These doctrines are commonly known as the rules of "offer and acceptance" and "consideration." We believe that such presentations both exaggerate the practical significance of those particular legal rules and obscure the ways in which the formation rules are used as tools by lawyers and courts in pursuit of particular ends. In addition, by giving excessive attention to some questions that are, frankly, largely of academic interest less time remains for more practical concerns. We have chosen, therefore, to present the formation rules differently. First, we offer a brief summary of some of the formation rules in a textual note. We then turn to principles governing what kinds of promises courts will enforce, reading some appellate opinions and exploring some rather simple examples. After studying the *Marvin v. Marvin* case in some detail, we offer another textual note, addressing another formation doctrine — the doctrine of consideration. We are convinced that we can familiarize you with most of the formation rules in just a few pages, with little loss to your capacity to solve the puzzles these rules are designed to solve. We then introduce you to the ins and outs of the rules which govern whether or not agreements need to be in writing in much the same way, with an emphasis on a descriptive textual note rather than on appellate opinions. Finally, we return to many of the formation rules in a context in which the organizing structure is more oriented to exposing policy conflicts, and less oriented to doctrinal explication. In the long run we believe you will have a richer understanding of both doctrine and policy.

You should regard the summary of doctrine which follows as you would the vocabulary list at the beginning of a lesson in the grammar of a foreign language. In the foreign language course your principal objective is to learn the grammar of the language, though you need a vocabulary to do so and must inevitably learn both grammar and vocabulary simultaneously. Read the note which follows as you would that vocabulary list — as an essential, but subordinate, part of the lesson of Chapter 3.

---

[6]You should not be surprised if your teacher asks you to read this on your own, or later in the course, or even skips it entirely.

a. An Introduction to the Rules of Offer and Acceptance

A Doctrinal Note — Contract Formation
Stewart Macaulay
John Kidwell

Offer-and-acceptance law is a late development in the common law of contract. It did not become a separate topic in the law until the classical period of the mid to late 19th century. Before then, lawyers were only trained to ask whether defendant had made, and broken, a *promise* of some type that was "actionable," — that is, one they could make the basis of a lawsuit under the writs available. The classical lawyers changed the question from, "Was there an actionable promise?" to "Was there a *contract*?" They said that a contract required (1) an offer, (2) an acceptance of the terms of that offer, and (3) consideration.

Once the problem was put this way, academic writers and judges put an enormous amount of energy into elaborating the new topic. Almost half of the first American treatise on contract law, Langdell's *Cases and Summary of the Law of Contracts* (1871), deals with offer-and-acceptance (the rest deals with consideration and the Statute of Frauds). The writers and judges wanted to develop rules that would fix the *exact moment* that parties created a contract. Before this instant, the parties were completely free, after, completely bound.

Contracts scholars said that offer-and-acceptance law served to (1) enable the court to mark off a dividing line between "preliminary negotiations" toward a deal and the closing of a bargain; (2) ensure that the parties had agreed on some minimum quantity of sufficiently defined terms so that a court could find that they actually *had* made a deal; and (3) give the court a reliable method to determine the content of their deal.

We can imagine these scholars' ideal world. The offeror says during the negotiations: "I offer you the following terms, and if you accept, there is a deal." Then the offeror states all the essential terms unambiguously. The offeree responds: "I accept your offer." At this moment (assuming consideration) their actions would form a contract, and a court could easily determine its existence and content.

Real life, unfortunately, is messy. It frequently produces situations that do not look anything like a neat offer followed by a clear acceptance. For example, parties may be negotiating even after they start performance. We cannot be sure whether they are in or out of the contract. They may leave the content of the deal to be worked out as the relationship develops. Instead of a one-shot, comprehensive offer, they will make a long strung-out series of proposals and adaptations. They cannot determine the content of their contract until they have fully performed. This is likely to be the case with the highly relational contracts dealt with in Chapter 3 of these materials. Furthermore, real life communication must rely on language and silence. It is riddled with ambiguities and potentials for misunderstanding. When I hear the words of your "offer," and say, "I accept," what is our deal? Am I consenting to the deal you thought you were proposing or the one I thought I heard, or something else? Notice also there may be a big difference between what we said and what we can prove at trial.

In the face of all this indeterminacy, classical courts and commentators nonetheless went sturdily ahead. They tried to find a magic moment at which the parties had manifested their intention to be bound contractually. To cover the bewildering variety of human contracting behavior, this effort rapidly produced a complex body of rules. It would have been a miracle had they been consistent. The miracle did not occur.

One result was, as with any technically intricate body of law, offer and acceptance became something of a Law of Loopholes. Much of this law today serves as a collection of ploys used by lawyers to get their clients out of perfectly good contracts — in the sense that the parties intended a deal — that have gone sour. If a client wants to get out of a deal, one promising avenue for its lawyer to investigate is the body of rules dealing with formation of contract.[7] It may be enough for a lawyer to assert a barely plausible offer-and-acceptance theory which would let his or her client escape contractual liability. Often the other party will not think it worth debating fine points of arcane law. Faced with the threat of litigation, a person may decide to drop the whole matter or offer or accept a token settlement.

Courts have frequently exploited the technicality of these rules for regulatory purposes — they use them to punish bad faith conduct and protect good faith reliance. (Advertisements, for example, usually are not offers. However, courts sometimes find *misleading* ads designed to lure customers into a store where a salesperson will sell them something else that is more expensive — bait and switch tactics — to be offers. It serves the store right to have its lies taken literally).

The other result of the complexity of these rules is that, to a large extent, they have collapsed of their own weight. Many courts and writers saw the technicality of these rules as leading either to contradictory results or results that were bothersome to common sense. As elsewhere in the law, writers exposed the failure of the roles to work, and they built a climate of opinion supporting reform. Some courts have been willing to use doctrines such as Restatement of Contracts, § 90, to protect reliance even where the formation rules have not been satisfied. Article 2 of the Uniform Commercial Code swept away nearly all of the fine points of classic offer-and-acceptance and much of consideration. For

---

[7] A major reason for using formation rules to bail out of a deal is to avoid the law governing performance of contracts. Performance law is highly qualitative and uncertain. For example, I need not continue to perform if you have failed "to substantially perform." I need not continue to perform if something has happened "the non-occurrence of which was a basic assumption on which the contract was made." We cannot blame lawyers for trying to avoid wading in these dismal swamps.

example, § 2-204 repeals rules that require courts to find a precise instant when parties made a contract. It says:

> (1) A contract for sale of goods may be made in any manner sufficient to show agreement, including conduct by both parties which recognizes the existence of such a contract.
> (2) An agreement sufficient to constitute a contract for sale may be found even though the moment of its making is undetermined.
> (3) Even though one or more terms are left open a contract for sale does not fail for indefiniteness if the parties have intended to make a contract and there is a reasonably certain basis for giving an appropriate remedy.

Furthermore, the Restatement (Second) of Contracts invites courts to abandon the old religion and follow the Code's approach in areas other than sales of goods where Article 2 applies.

Having said all this, you need to learn something about formation of contracts. While this law may be ill, it is not dead. In a particular case before a particular judge, you could find it necessary to be a master of its rhetoric and the tricks used by the profession to work with it. Classic contracts courses began with "offer and acceptance." This body of law constitutes a vocabulary and common culture of the bar. Offer-and-acceptance law is like a field of land mines left over from a past war. It still strews the landscape with traps for the unwary lawyer and opportunities for the canny one. The following outline is a sketch of the minefield. It will not get you through it, but it will tell you as much of what you need to know now about what it looks like. Treatises and law review articles treat these issues in exhaustive detail. Thus, help is at hand in walking through the minefield if you recognize in time that you are about to enter it. We address some contemporary, and more lively, formation problems in Contracts II.

The standard of interpretation — a meeting of minds versus objective signs of agreement: Throughout most of the 19th century, judges said contract rested on the "intention of the parties," and there had to be "meeting of the minds." The requirement that there be a subjective union of the wills of the parties became, not just a metaphor representing an idealized vision of agreement, but a legal standard. The rhetoric links theories of individual autonomy and liability based on choice. At the extreme, it suggests that I am not bound to a contract that I did not *intend* (subjectively) to make. While intellectual developments of the late 19th and early 20th century attacked the requirement that the parties must simultaneously share an intention to make legally binding promises, the residue of the idea still remains as a tool occasionally called on by courts to rationalize, if not motivate, decision. Lawyers and judges still speak lovingly of "a meeting of the minds" as a term of art in the technical vocabulary of the bar.

Writers such as Holmes and Williston campaigned for an "objective theory of contract." They argued that actual intention and real choice is irrelevant; liability rests on outward objective manifestations. If I look *as if* I am making a promise, I have made one. I can commit a contract whether or not I really (subjectively) intend to make one. Does this mean that two actors in a stage play who exchange promises have made a contract because they appear to be doing so? Of course not — because the context of their behavior includes the fact that they are actors in a play and, once one broadens the context they no longer objectively can be said to manifest agreement.

Professor Malcolm Sharp rationalized the imposition of liability a bit differently. Drawing on some ideas usually associated with tort law he suggested that parties are held liable for intentional or negligent communication that causes loss. I am responsible for your reasonable interpretations of my behavior. Instead of concepts of individual *choice*, contract turns on either fault-based, or strict, liability. This position promotes easy reliance on promises and protects plans and risk taking. It avoids problems that would arise if contract were really based on subjective choice. For example, I can fail to read or misunderstand a printed form contract which I sign, and still be bound by it. I may be bound to a contract which I would not have accepted if I had understood the terms. I am not bound because I choose to make a promise, but because I behaved in a way that could reasonably lead another to rely on my apparent promise to perform, to that other's injury.

Applying the principle of objectivity, courts hold people to offers made as a joke if the offeree has no reason to see the humor of the situation. Similarly, one who has reason to know that raising his or her hand is a symbol meaning "I raise the bid" or "I accept" has symbolized just that, and is bound, although she forgot the code or did not intend the gesture to have that meaning. The principle of objective interpretation may explain why advertisements are usually not offers; a reasonable person cannot read them as commitments to supply an indefinite number of people with an unlimited quantity of the thing publicized. On the other hand, if you made an inquiry about a product and I responded by sending you a clipped advertisement, the circumstances might lead a court to say that the clipped newspaper ad *was* an offer, even though the same ad would *not* constitute an offer to those who read it in The Daily News. Normal ads are not offers because there is no reason to think a merchant takes either the risk of a large demand or the risk that a printed ad might contain a mistake. This means that a merchant is not legally bound, by contract law, to provide advertised merchandise at the advertised price, let alone at a price that is the result of a typographical error.[8] Advertisements of rewards may be construed as offers, which ripen into contracts by doing the requested action. This may be because reward offers

---

[8]There are rules, of course, prohibiting deliberately false statements in advertisements, "bait and switch" techniques, and so forth — but these, to the classical lawyer, are not generally seen as rules of contract doctrine. They are rules governing unfair trade practices.

don't generally create the risk of excessive acceptances.[9] Courts interpret contracts in context in terms of what a reasonable person should understand from the communication. Secret reservations and private meanings of words do not control; I can't avoid being bound by my promise even though I cross my fingers behind my back, and have a witness. *Shared* special meanings and usages and customs of a shared trade may color or alter the meaning of the words, however. If a court believes that you and I have agreed that "I am not interested," means "I accept your offer" (to confuse competitors, for example) then the court will respect our private meaning, and create a contract.

Silence in the face of an offer: Silence in response to an offer is not acceptance, except when it is. Suppose S writes to B, "unless I hear from you in two days, you will be deemed to have accepted my offer." Generally B is free to ignore S's statement. Doing nothing does not create contractual liability. This rule protects free choice, and avoids what could be a burdensome commercial practice — responding to ward off liability. *However*, in a continuing relationship, the parties can agree that renewals of their arrangement will take place automatically unless one gives notice of a desire to cancel it. This agreement can be implied from custom and past practice. (Examples are book and record clubs where customers agree to accept the monthly selection unless they send notice before a specified time.) This means that if S and B had often done business in the past, and B had agreed that it was reasonable for S to treat his (B's) silence as an acceptance, then B could be bound to a contract.

   There are difficult cases involving B's reliance on S's statements about silence as acceptance. Most of these involve purchases of insurance where an agent represents that the customer is covered, unless notified by the company. The courts usually found a way in which to protect the customer who had relied in such cases, sometimes by using the theory of estoppel — which is a trick used to preserve doctrine while not applying it. The court might say that the conduct of the agent "raised an estoppel" and that the company was forbidden to assert that no contract arose, even though *theoretically* there was no contract. The modern practice of agent's binders has arisen to deal with the problem of coverage while awaiting a decision by the home office, and so the problem is not a common one any longer. A few cases involve reliance by a retailer on a "silence as acceptance" practice of a wholesaler. A retailer orders "subject to acceptance at the home office," the time to order elsewhere for the season passes, and the wholesaler refuses to fill the order. Some courts have strained to find any communication from the seller to be an acceptance to protect the reliance.

---

[9]Reward offers also pose special conceptual problems insofar as revocation is concerned. The problem isn't important enough to go into here, but you might ask yourself why a conceptual problem might arise, and how you think the courts have responded.

The duration of offers: People must accept offers to create conventional contracts, but they cannot accept the offers after they have expired. How long does an offer last? An offer lasts only to any limit specified in its terms; if it says "this offer will lapse next Wednesday," one cannot accept it on Thursday. Offers which specify no expiration time, but are on their face unlimited are, nevertheless, open only for a reasonable time. How long is reasonable depends on the circumstances. In a rapidly fluctuating market this might be as short as the time it takes to place a long-distance telephone call. On the other hand, an offer to sell a business, or a vacant lot, might remain open for weeks.

Sometimes, the question is not whether the offer has expired, but whether it has been revoked. Generally, an offeror can revoke an offer until it has been accepted. Can an offeror revoke an offer before the time set for it to expire? Suppose S offers to sell a house to B and promises to hold the offer open until next Wednesday. On Tuesday, S gets a much better proposal from T. Can S revoke the offer to B and sell to T without liability to B? The answer provided in classical doctrine might surprise you. Traditionally, an offeror could revoke at any time before acceptance *despite* a promise not to do this. The explanation lies in another formation doctrine. As we will see shortly, a promise not to revoke lacks consideration since the buyer gave nothing for it, and so that promise was not enforceable. There *is* a way for B to secure an irrevocable offer under classical doctrine; B could buy an option by giving S consideration (something valuable) for the promise not to revoke, making the promise enforceable.

Some courts have applied Restatement of Contracts, § 90 to irrevocable, or "firm," offers. Once there is reliance on the promise not to revoke, the offeror loses his or her power to revoke. Many of these cases involve subcontractors' bids on work (that is, offers) to general contractors who use the sub's bid in making their own bid. Most modern cases hold that the sub's bid cannot be revoked. In many instances, the sub's bid is not accompanied by an express promise not to revoke, but courts imply such a promise. Then the courts protect reliance on the just-fashioned promise. U.C.C. § 2-205 says that a merchant can make an irrevocable offer in writing which will stay open despite the absence of consideration or any proof of actual reliance. The statute limits the duration of such an offer.

The manner of acceptance: One must use a reasonable means to communicate his/her acceptance. For example, it usually is safer to accept by FAX an offer made by FAX, since the use of a FAX suggests the need for quick action. In some circumstances one might not need to respond by a rapid means of communication. Suppose, for example, it is clear from the circumstances that an offeror used a FAX only to attract attention and the market is not a fluctuating one. Probably a letter would still be a reasonable means of acceptance.

Under classical doctrine, one must accept the precise offer made in order to create a contract. "The offeror is master of the offer," as the saying goes. For example, one cannot accept an offer to sell a 1980 Ford for $1,000 by saying "I accept your offer to sell a 1981 Chevrolet for $500." Could you accept the offer to sell the 1980 Ford by saying, "I accept your offer to sell the 1980 Ford for $1000 and I will give you a personal check next Monday?" That would depend on whether the court would interpret the offer as requiring payment in cash; some courts might do so, and see the statement proposing payment by check as an imperfect acceptance or counteroffer.

It is useful to distinguish between the revocation of an offer, which is what an offeror does to terminate it, and a rejection. The offeree rejects an offer by expressly or impliedly communicating disinterest. And, importantly, a counteroffer is treated as a rejection. This means that in our hypothetical in the preceding paragraph involving the 1980 Ford, IF the proposal to pay by check was treated as a counteroffer, the buyer could no longer accept the offer even if agreeing to pay cash. In other words, if you offer to sell your car to me for $1000 and I respond, "Would you take $950?" I have rejected your offer by making a counteroffer and have terminated my power to accept it even on the original terms.

Modern business practice appears inconsistent with the rule requiring the acceptance to mirror the offer — which creates a problem called "the battle of the forms." The parties exchange business documents with different or conflicting terms, but both think they have a deal. For example, buyer uses a *purchase order* with terms on the back, one of which grants a right to cancel for any delay. Seller accepts on *an acknowledgment of order* form with terms on *its* back, one of which says that delivery dates are only approximate, and seller will satisfy the contract if it delivers goods within a reasonable time. At common law, there was *no contract* at this point because of the failure of the acceptance to mirror the offer; insofar as the effect of delay was concerned the acceptance was not identical to the offer. However, if seller shipped goods and buyer accepted them, courts might say that seller's "Acknowledgment of Order" (which looked like an acceptance) was in law a counteroffer — which was accepted by Buyer's action of accepting the goods. That is, Buyer's original purchase order would be treated as an offer which had been rejected by counteroffer. What looked at first like an acceptance would be treated as an offer, and that offer was accepted when the Buyer took control of the goods and paid for them. Buyer could not return the goods on the ground that its form said it could cancel for any delay, because *its* form is altogether irrelevant.

The Uniform Commercial Code has done a major remodeling job on the classical laws governing inconsistent forms. Under U.C.C. § 2-207, if there is a "definite and seasonable expression of acceptance," there is a contract. There are elaborate provisions on how courts will fashion the terms, which will be taken up in Contracts II. If there is no such expression of acceptance, the parties conduct may create a contract, the terms of which will be all those upon which their writings agree plus the provisions of the U.C.C. where they disagree. The section is complex and has prompted a great deal of litigation.

The acceptance-when-mailed rule: Generations of law students have cut their legal teeth on "the mail box rule." Suppose the following sequence:

> (1) An offer is mailed on Nov. 10th at 1:00 p.m., and it arrives on Nov. 12th at 2:00 p.m.
> (2) A letter of acceptance, properly addressed, is deposited in a mail box on Nov. 12th at 3:00 p.m. It arrives on Nov.14th at 1:00 p.m. (or there is an airplane crash and the letter never arrives at all.)
> (3A) The offeror telephones the offeree on Nov. 12th at 3:05 p.m., and says "I revoke my offer." OR
> (3B) The offeree telephones the offeror at that time and says "Disregard the letter you will get. I do not want to buy the goods, and I call off my acceptance."

Although there are very few cases, writers said that a contract was formed when a letter of acceptance was placed in the mail. Neither telephone call (3A or 3B) is effective to prevent the formation of a contract. That is, neither attempt to back out (3A or 3B) is effective. (Of course, the other party always could consent to calling off the deal, but does not have to do this.)

Writers have attacked the rule as an overgeneralization, and have suggested that it may be appropriate to find a contract in one case (3A) but not in the other (3B). We can defend the general rule binding the offeror once the offeree deposits a letter of acceptance — 3A — since the offeree may rely from that point. At the least, the offeree won't look for other deals from then on. It may be that an efficient economy results when offerees can begin to rely at once, without needing to wait for a confirmation that their acceptance has been received by the offeror. On the other hand, it is harder to build a case for binding the offeree when the first thing the offeror hears from the offeree is the message that the offeree doesn't want a deal. There would be, of course, no reliance from the offeree (who has changed her mind). And the letter of acceptance, though posted by the offeree, cannot prompt reliance by the offeror because the offeror doesn't see it before knowing that the offeree wants it disregarded. Nonetheless, most courts have opted for a flat, symmetrical rule; both are bound, at least insofar as the rules of offer and acceptance are concerned, when the letter is posted.

The requirement of certainty: Finally, contracts must be reasonably certain to be enforceable. How certain is certain enough is hard to say. A contract to sell a named product, "quantity and price to be agreed" would not be definite enough at common law. Even an open price term was probably enough to prevent a contract from forming under classical rules. Once again, the Uniform Commercial Code has liberalized the standard, seeking to ratify common commercial practices. U.C.C. § 2-204(3) expresses the standard as "a contract does not fail for indefiniteness if the parties have intended to make a contract and there is a reasonably certain basis for giving an appropriate remedy." Section 2-305 governs "open price terms," and provides that a contract may legitimately leave the price unspecified; in such a case the price is taken to be a reasonable price at the time and place of delivery. Of course, the parties may have intended to be bound only after settling on the price term, and in such a case there would be no contract until the issue of the price was settled.

A great deal more could be said about offer and acceptance rules. We will explore some of the finer points of formation doctrine in the pages that follow. But the summary you have just read embodies much of the content of the doctrine that occupies some law students for several weeks. We might add at this point that there is nothing wrong with using formation rules as the subject of study in a basic contracts course. Usually we suspect that the real agenda in extensive study of the mailbox rule, and the other chestnuts of offer and acceptance law, is not the content of the rules themselves, but rather legal analysis. We simply believe the analysis of different rules is, in the long run, just as effective in teaching the general skill of analysis, and more meaningful insofar as substantive knowledge is concerned.

2. A POLICY APPROACH TO JUDICIAL INTERVENTION

Finally, we return to explore the main theme of this Chapter. What factors should a legal agency such as a court or administrative office consider in deciding how to respond to a request to intervene in a relationship? Should the agency help or regulate the relationship? Or should it stand aside and leave parties where it finds them when one asks for help? We often will repeat this question in specific contexts. However, for now, you may find it useful to consider some general observations that Professor Zechariah Chafee made over 50 years ago in a famous article.[10] Chafee identified four policies that he thought should govern the decision to intervene — the first favors intervention; the last three oppose it.

(1) The "Strangle-Hold" Policy. Sometimes a relationship is so important to the parties that changing or leaving it would have unusually serious consequences for their lives. It is not easy for them to "exit" if the relationship goes wrong. They can't pack up and go elsewhere. (Chafee gives as examples workers expelled from unions, doctors from medical societies, or brokers from the stock exchange). In such cases, only outside intervention may prevent or compensate what we see as serious harm. The fact that one or both of the parties is in a strangle-hold is a reason for intervention.

(2) The "Dismal Swamp" Policy. The agency may be getting in over its head. It may not be able to sort out conflicting claims of right and wrong in a complex relationship. The relationship has its own unique history, specialized vocabulary, power hierarchies, personal animosities, and implicit understandings. (An

---

[10]Chafee, The Internal Affairs of Associations not for Profit, 43 Harvard Law Review 993, 1021-29 (1930).

obvious example is the difficulty faced by courts asked to decide contending claims to church property among schismatic factions. Each asserts it, and it alone, represents the true religion of the church. It is easy to see why courts are reluctant to intervene.)

(3) The "Hot Potato" Policy. If most of the parties think that outside intervention is undesirable and would be an uncalled-for interference in their affairs, the agency's attempt to intervene may simply cause resentment and resistance. This is particularly true if the legal agency operates as a court and uses an adversarial procedure. Such procedures invite parties to show their opponents in the worst possible light. When a plaintiff charges a defendant with wrongful conduct, it may aggravate an already difficult relationship. As a result, parties may not cooperate in fact-finding, settlement or enforcement processes.[11]

(4) The "Living Tree" Policy. The autonomy of the relationship itself may be independently valuable. Chafee says that the "health of society will usually be prompted if the groups within it which serve the industrial, mental, and spiritual needs of citizens are genuinely alive.... Legal supervision must often be withheld for fear that it may do more harm than good." [p. 1027] If parties "legalize" their relationship, and structure it with a view toward invoking outside legal regulation to enforce their demands, they may sacrifice cooperation.

Chafee's list of policies obviously is not exhaustive. Moreover, they seem to emphasize passive virtues rather than legal action to carry out valued goals. Chafee's legal agencies would be cautious. Perhaps he is right, but you do not have to accept this view. You may want to see the right judges given a roving commission to do good. You may see Chafee's statement of the policies as a useful way to hide legal support for power as it exists in the society. Chafee's article does not justify active intervention in relationships to carry out fundamental values.

Nonetheless, Chafee is descriptively accurate. Legal agencies recognize the four policies he identifies, although they seldom offer such colorful names. You should keep the four policies in mind, along with further policies thought important by the judges you read, as you consider the *Balfour*, *Miller*, and *Marvin* cases that follow. You should also remember them when we move from contract in the family setting to employment and other business contexts.

---

[11]One of the authors remains puzzled at why "Hot Potato" is the name for this policy, and would prefer "Poison Ivy" — but "Hot Potato" is the name Chafee chose.

B. CONTRACT IN THE FAMILY SETTING

1. WHICH PROMISES SHOULD THE LAW ENFORCE? — ILLUSTRATIONS AND ISSUES

Should the courts, as the arm of the state, enforce every statement in the form of a promise? The courts have never thought so. But as soon as we accept the need to divide the enforceable from the nonenforceable we encounter the difficult issue of articulating the criteria for making the division.

a. Courts and Contracts Between Husband and Wife

Can husbands and wives make contracts with each other? Yes. For example, the wealthy often come to marriages, particularly second or third marriages, agreeing to keep their property separate. Yet one spouse may wish to buy the land, or artwork, or automobile of the other spouse. One agrees to buy, the other to sell. If we assume that the transaction meets the general rules of contract, this contract would be as enforceable as if they were strangers. But husbands and wives make many promises to each other of a different character. Some are trivial; some are serious. They can range from agreements about who will pick up the wine and who will shop for what is needed to make the meal at a dinner party, to whether his elderly father will be invited to live with them in the family home. We can think of almost all human interaction as contractual, but this does not mean that all human interaction will be transformed into contracts legally enforceable by courts.

We will begin with a traditional view. Ask yourself if it is a view that would be especially appealing to male judges, most of whom are white, middle-aged and from the middle-class.

BALFOUR v. BALFOUR

In the Court of Appeal, 2 K.B. 571 [1919]

[Mrs. Balfour sued her husband for breach of contract. Mr. and Mrs. Balfour lived together in Ceylon for 15 years. He was given leave from his position with the Government of Ceylon, and the Balfours returned to England for an eight month vacation. They were to return to Ceylon in August of 1916, but Mrs. Balfour was suffering from rheumatic arthritis and her doctor advised her to remain in England for another three months. Before Mr. Balfour sailed on August 8, 1916, he gave his wife a check for 24 pounds, and he promised to give her 30 pounds a month until she returned to Ceylon. Afterward, Mr. Balfour wrote his wife suggesting that they remain apart. He did not send the 30 pounds each month, and Mrs. Balfour sued for the balance due. The trial judge held that Mr. Balfour was under an obligation to support his wife, and her consent to define that obligation as 30 pounds monthly was consideration to support a contract. He awarded Mrs. Balfour judgment. The Court of Appeal reversed.]

WARRINGTON, L.J. ... The matter really reduces itself to an absurdity when one considers it, because if we were to hold that with regard to all the more or less trivial concerns of life where a wife, at the request of her husband, makes a promise to him, that is a promise which can be enforced in law.... All I can say is that there is no ... contract here. These two people never intended to make a bargain which could be enforced in law. The husband expressed his intention to make this payment, and he promised to make it, and was bound in honour to continue it so long as he was in a position to do so. The wife, on the other hand, so far as I can see, made no bargain at all....

DUKE, L.J. ... The proposition that the mutual promises made in the ordinary domestic relationship of husband and wife of necessity give cause for action on a contract seems to me to go to the very root of the relationship, and to be a possible fruitful source of dissension and quarreling. I cannot see that any benefit would result from it to either of the parties, but on the other hand it would lead to unlimited litigation in a relationship which should be obviously as far as possible protected from possibilities of that kind....

ATKIN, L.J. ... The defence to this action on the alleged contract is that the defendant, the husband, entered into no contract with his wife, and for the determination of that it is necessary to remember that there are agreements between parties which do not result in contracts within the meaning of that term in our law. The ordinary example is where two parties agree to take a walk together, or where there is an offer and acceptance of hospitality. Nobody would suggest in ordinary circumstances that those agreements result in what we know as a contract, and one of the most usual forms of agreement which does not constitute a contract appears to me to be the arrangements which are made between husband and wife. It is quite common, and it is the natural and inevitable result of the relationship of husband and wife, that the two spouses should make arrangements between themselves — agreements such as are in dispute in this action — agreements for allowances, by which the husband agrees that he will pay to his wife a certain sum of money, per week, or per month, or per year, to cover either her own expenses or the necessary expenses of the household and of the children of the marriage, and in which the wife promises either expressly or impliedly to apply the allowance for the purpose for which it is given.

To my mind those agreements, or many of them, do not result in contracts at all, and they do not result in contracts even though there may be what as between other parties would constitute consideration for the agreement. The consideration, as we know, may consist either in some right, interest, profit or benefit accruing to one party, or some forbearance, detriment, loss or responsibility given, suffered or undertaken by the other. That is a well-known definition, and it constantly happens, I think, that such arrangements made between husband and wife are arrangements in which there are mutual promises, or in which there is consideration in form within the definition that I have mentioned. Nevertheless they are not contracts, and they are not contracts because the parties did not intend that they should be attended by legal consequences.

To my mind it would be of the worst possible example to hold that agreements such as this resulted in legal obligations which could be enforced in the Courts. It would mean this, that when the husband makes his wife a promise to give her an allowance of 30 shillings or 2 pounds a week, whatever he can afford to give her, for the maintenance of the household and children, and she promises so to apply it, not only could she sue him for his failure in any week to supply the allowance, but he could sue her for non-performance of the obligation, express or implied, which she had undertaken upon her part. All I can say is that the small Courts of this country would have to be multiplied one hundredfold if these arrangements were held to result in legal obligations. They are not sued upon, not because the parties are reluctant to enforce their legal rights when the agreement is broken, but because the parties, in the inception of the arrangement, never intended that they should be sued upon. Agreements such as these are outside the realm of contracts altogether. The common law does not regulate the form of agreements between spouses. Their promises are not sealed with seals and sealing wax. The consideration that really obtains for them is that natural love and affection which counts for so little in these cold Courts. The terms may be repudiated, varied or renewed as performance proceeds or as disagreements develop, and the principles of the common law as to exoneration and discharge and accord and satisfaction are such as find no place in the domestic code. The parties themselves are advocates, judges, Courts, sheriff's officer and reporter. In respect of these promises each house is a domain into which the King's writ does not seek to run, and to which his officers do not seek to be admitted. The only question in this case is whether or not this promise was of such a class or not. For the reasons given by my brethren it appears to me to be plainly established that the promise here was not intended by either party to be attended by legal consequences. I think the onus was upon the plaintiff, and the plaintiff has not established any contract. The parties were living together, the wife intending to return. The suggestion is that the husband bound himself to pay 30 pounds a month under all circumstances, and, although she was in ill-health and alone in this country, that out of that sum she undertook to defray the whole of the medical expenses that might fall upon her, whatever might be the development of her illness, and in whatever expenses it might involve her. To my mind neither party contemplated such a result....

NOTES AND QUESTIONS

1. *Mrs. Balfour's tactics*: Sometime in 1918, Mrs. Balfour obtained a legal separation and an order for alimony. Hedley tells us, "[i]t is unclear what

advantage Mrs Balfour was seeking by exercising both contractual and matrimonial rights. The only plausible explanation seems to be that she wanted alimony *plus* 30 pounds per month; I am informed that maintenance awards at that date were not generous."[12]

2. *Intent to create legal relations*: Consider critically the following hypothetical statement that might be made by a law professor:

> Sometimes courts say that social promises and promises between family members are unenforceable because the parties did not intend them to have legal consequences. This explanation, as has been repeatedly recognized, is artificial. In most instances, including business transactions, the parties have no intention one way or the other about legal enforceability. They have made promises which they assume will be performed. If they were concerned about breach and legal consequences, they wouldn't enter the arrangement or they would structure the transaction to provide security.

> Suppose two law professors agree to have lunch tomorrow, and they state in the presence of another faculty member that they intend their promises to be legally enforceable. How should the common law treat this "contract?" Apart from any appropriate sanction a court might impose because lawyers fabricated the transaction, it should throw them out as quickly as possible. Whatever their intention, courts are not free and have more important things to do than deal with trivial promises. Social promises and those among family members, in most instances, just are not important enough to justify wasting scarce resources on their resolution. The question of social importance, rather than a fictional intention to have legal consequences, is a key to solving what is really a question of priorities in allocating resources.

· Hedley comments on the *Balfour* case and the requirement that parties intend to create legal relationships. He says "[a] marriage run on the common law principles designed for businesses would indeed be a sorry affair, but so would a business run on those same principles. Willing co-operation without reference to legal entitlements is normal (and indeed, essential) in both spheres." He continues "since there are such obvious differences between the two, there must be something very wrong with a theoretical approach that claims to distinguish them *only* by reference to a presumed, unquantifiable and highly questionable difference in willingness to sue." Hedley concludes "the modern law of 'intent to create legal relations' essentially reduces to this: that where the parties were dealing at arms' length, promises will generally be enforced; but in domestic contexts, contractual liability will be imposed only if the party seeking

---

[12]Hedley, Keeping Contract in its Place — *Balfour v. Balfour* and the Enforceability of Informal Agreements, 5 Oxford Journal of Legal Studies 391, 392 n.4 (1985).

enforcement has already performed one side of the bargain and is simply seeking reciprocity. The courts will not enforce an executory agreement [in a domestic context]. Beyond this, I argue, there is no requirement of an agreement of an 'intention to create legal relations.'"[13]

3. *The broken date*: In 1978 the New York Times[14] reported the story of accountant Tom Horsley who brought a suit in a San Francisco small claims court seeking damages from Alyn Chesslet. He asked for $38 in damages because Ms. Chesslet had failed to notify him she was canceling a dinner date, with the result that he had fruitlessly driven 50 miles to pick her up. He asked to be reimbursed for 17 cents per mile for the 100 mile trip plus $8.50 per hour for 2 hours of his time; $8.50 was his minimum professional billing rate. Ms. Chesslet testified she had tried to reach Mr. Horsley to notify him that she had to work, but that he was not in his office. Ms. Chesslet also testified that "Mr. Horsley had been abusive on the night of the broken date and had harassed her later." Judge Figone dismissed the suit, observing that "... the promise to attend a social engagement is always conditioned on the promisor's ability or disposition to attend the event ... particularly ... within the context of a 'dating' situation."

(a) Suppose Ms. Chesslet had broken her promise to go to dinner and the theater with Mr. Horsley because another person, whose company she preferred, had asked her out for the same evening after she had accepted Mr. Horsley's invitation, *and* she had made no effort at all to contact Mr. Horsley but had just failed to appear at a place they were to meet. Would this affect your view about the merits of the case? When, if ever, may one break a promise for a social engagement? How hard must we try to notify another of the change in plans? Are there other-than-legal sanctions for violating these expectations? Do you think rules of law could answer these questions? Would such rules be difficult to state with any precision in a judicial opinion?[15]

(b) Assuming that a court would enforce Ms. Chesslet's promise, do you see any problem with charging her for two hours of Mr. Horsley's time at his rate for providing accounting services? Can you think of a better measure of contract damages? If Mr. Horsley could get to court in time, would or should it award him specific performance?

(c) We might guess that a good part of Mr. Horsley's injury was his sense of rejection and disappointment prompted by losing a dinner and evening at the theater with Ms. Chesslet. If this were true, what remedies does the legal system have to offer Mr. Horsley?

---

[13]*Id.* at 396.

[14]New York Times, July 28, 1978.

[15]Lempert, Norm-Making in Social Exchange: A Contract Law Model, 7 Law & Society Review 1 (1972), suggests that dating and other social behavior are permeated by contract ideas.

MILLER v. MILLER

78 Iowa 177, 35 N.W. 464, 42 N.W. 641 (1887).[16]

[Nancy Miller sued Robert Miller, her husband, for breach of a written contract. The trial court sustained the husband's demurrer. The Supreme Court of Iowa affirmed the judgment.

The contract stated:

> *This agreement, made this fifth day of August, 1885, between the under-signed, husband and wife, in the interests of peace and for the best interests of each other and of their family, is signed in good faith by each party, with the promise, each to the other, and to their children, that they will each honestly promise to help each other to observe and keep the same, which is as follows, to wit: All past causes and subjects of dispute, disagreement and complaint of whatever character or kind shall be absolutely ignored and buried, and no allusion thereto by word or talk to each other or any one else shall ever be made. Each party agrees to refrain from scolding, fault-finding and anger in so far as relates to the future, and to use every means within their power to promote peace and harmony, and that each shall behave respectfully, and fairly treat each other; that Mrs. Miller shall keep her home and family in a comfortable and reasonably good condition, and Mr. Miller shall provide for the necessary expenses of the family, and shall, in addition thereto, pay Mrs. Miller for her individual use two hundred dollars per year, payable, sixteen and two-thirds dollars per month in advance, so long as Mrs. Miller shall faithfully observe the terms and conditions of their contract. They agree to live together as husband and wife and observe faithfully the marriage relation, and each to live virtuously with the other.*

Mrs. Miller's petition alleged, and for purposes of the demurrer it was taken as true, that Mr. Miller "while improperly spending money upon other women, refused to furnish the plaintiff with necessary clothing, and she had been compelled to furnish it herself by her personal earnings."

One of Mr. Miller's arguments in support of his demurrer was there was no consideration for his promises under the contract. He said that his wife only was promising to do what the law already required of her as a wife. Thus he gained and she gave up nothing to which he was not already entitled. There was no real bargain. The Supreme Court of Iowa found it unnecessary to reach this question

---

[16]Oddly, there are two opinions in this case, published two years apart. The first was prepared by a member of the court who did not agree with the decision; most of that opinion (at 35 N.W. 464) is an argument against the dismissal of the complaint. A rehearing was granted, apparently so that the majority of the court could publish an opinion which contained the prevailing arguments!

because it accepted Mr. Miller's alternative argument — that the contract was void as against public policy. The court explained its decision as follows:]

Whatever may have induced the making of the contract, one thing is certain, — the ground of recovery from time to time is a faithful observance of the contract. If payment of the amounts is enforced, this observance must be pleaded, and, if denied, it must become a matter of judicial inquiry. Now, looking to the contract, we find that the plaintiff has agreed to do just what is demanded by her marital relations and is essential to domestic felicity. If she does this, under the letter of her contract, she may recover; if she does not, she cannot recover.... Now, if a husband and wife, without any domestic discord to serve as an inducement to such a contract, should make an agreement that the husband should pay to the wife, monthly, a stated sum, merely because of her observance of an agreement not to scold, find fault, or get angry, and to use every means in her power to promote peace and harmony, and behave respectfully towards her husband, would the court, upon a refusal by the husband, compel a payment? We think not, nor do we think counsel would seriously contend, in such a case, that it should; for the reason that judicial inquiry into matters of that character, between husband and wife, would be fraught with irreparable mischief, and forbidden by sound considerations of public policy.

It is of the genius of our laws, as well as of our civilization, that matters pertaining so directly and exclusively to the home, and its value as such, and which are so generally susceptible of regulation and control by those influences which surround it, are not to become matters of public concern or inquiry.... It is said in argument that in this case the husband had been guilty of such conduct as to justify the wife in leaving him, and would have been entitled to a separate support, and it was because of this contract that she consented to live with defendant, and that the amount was settled upon the wife in pursuance of the agreement. Stripped of the conditions upon which payment is to be made, such a contract might not be questioned. The enforcement of this contract as to payments involves an inquiry into just the facts which we have been urging as against public policy.... Was she not at some time angry? Has she kept the family in a comfortable condition? ... It needs no argument to show that such inquiries in public would strike at the very foundations of domestic life and happiness.... What element could be introduced into a family that would tend more directly to breed discord than this contract? ... An effort at compulsory payment would almost certainly bring before the courts allegations of misconduct, based upon incidents of little moment, to be magnified or belittled in the interest of success in court.

NOTES AND QUESTIONS

1. *Intention to create legal relations*: Did the parties in *Miller v. Miller* actually intend their agreement to be legally enforceable? Who do you think wrote their contract?

2. *Judicial Capacity*: Are the factual determinations suggested by the Court more difficult than those involved in a long-term complex commercial contract? Than those involved in a contested divorce action in a state where one must prove grounds for a divorce? In *Bohanan v. Maxwell*[17], the Supreme Court of Iowa suggested that the rule of the Miller case rests, at least in part, on the possibility of fraud on creditors. What did it mean by this? How might husbands and wives use contracts to defraud creditors? What priorities are implied by this suggestion?

3. *Consideration*: Both the *Balfour* and *Miller* cases referred to the doctrine of "consideration." You might already have read the note on consideration that appears later in this chapter[18]; if so, you will have a good understanding of the consideration problem of *Balfour*. If you haven't already read the note, Lord Atkin's statement in his *Balfour* opinion — that consideration may consist "either in some right, interest, profit or benefit accruing to one party, or some forbearance, detriment, loss or responsibility given, suffered or undertaken by the other" — will suffice as a working introduction to the concept. The argument in *Miller v. Miller* was that because the law of marital relations already imposed upon Mrs. Miller the duties she promised to perform, her promise conferred no new benefits upon her husband. Thus, her promise could not serve as consideration for his.

How can we determine what legal duties were imposed on Mrs. Miller as part of her status as Mr. Miller's wife? Was she promising nothing beyond her legal obligations?

(a) Brown, Emerson, Falk and Freedman, The Equal Rights Amendment: A Constitutional Basis for Equal Rights for Women, 80 Yale Law Journal 871, 943, 944 (1971), tells us:

> One of the law's most comprehensive efforts to define the rights and obligations of the partners to a marriage relationship occurs in personal injury actions, after one or the other spouse has been seriously incapacitated. In order to instruct the jury as to the proper standards for awarding damages, the judge must define what benefits the plaintiff should have expected from his or her now incapacitated spouse. At common law these standards were rigidly defined and totally male-oriented. A man had a right to recover damages for loss of his wife's services when she was injured by intentional or negligent action. In time, a husband's rights of consortium were defined to include love, affection, companionship, society, and sexual relations. A woman, by contrast, had no right to sue for loss of her husband's services, since in theory, he provided none.... Courts in many states have ... extended to women the right to sue for loss of consortium....

---

[17]190 Iowa 1308, 181 N.W. 683 (1921).

[18]The note is after the case of Hamer v. Sidway, *infra*.

(b) *In re Callister's Estate*,[19] an attorney's wife worked for him as his secretary and clerk, and the Iowa Supreme Court used this as an example of duties which would be outside of the marriage relationship and thus could constitute the consideration needed to make a contract enforceable. However, *In re Straka's Estate*,[20] the Supreme Court of Iowa found that there was no consideration for a note given to a wife by her husband. She was the second wife who raised his children by his first marriage and who did the work of a hired man on the farm. Relying on an earlier case[21] the Iowa court remarked, "[s]he may have done more than her share. But it is no more than the wives of most farmers have done. They usually do more than their share."

4. *Wives benefiting from the Miller rule*: The *Balfour, Miller, Bohanan*, and *Straka* cases all involve a wife's unsuccessful attempt to enforce a promise made to her by her husband. However, wives who want to avoid contracts which they made with husbands may assert a lack of consideration. Two decisions in the 1960s involved situations which were similar to that in the *Miller* case. After a marital dispute, the husbands and wives had entered reconciliation agreements. The wives agreed to a certain division of property, alimony and child support if the reconciliation failed. In both cases the reconciliations failed, and the wives sought to get a more favorable property division, alimony and child support than the contract called for. Both wives asserted that the contract was invalid, relying in part on the dicta in the *Miller* case.

In *Hoyt v. Hoyt*,[22] the court upheld the contract. It found the wife estopped to assert lack of consideration because the husband had paid her $45,000 under the contract. However, in *Clark v. Clark*,[23] the court found that the husband had made the contract to "facilitate the obtention of a divorce" and, hence, the contract was against the public policy of the state. The court went on to say that even if the contract did not offend the public policy of the state, it was of "such a nature as to require careful scrutiny in a court of equity." "Equity will not countenance overreaching by either party." It then found "[i]t is apparent the husband was seeking to arrange in advance the terms of a divorce decree with respect to alimony and maintenance, and the terms were greatly to his advantage." Interestingly, there was consideration because "[n]ot only had she fulfilled her duties and responsibilities as a housewife for many years but she had also contributed a great deal to the husband's accumulation of his wealth" by doing manual labor and doing all of the bookkeeping.

5. *Cultural norms:* Could we defend the courts by arguing persuasively that cases such as *Balfour* and *Miller* protect women as a group? Any contract reflects

---

[19]153 N.Y. 294, 47 N.W. 268 (1897).

[20]224 Iowa 109, 275 N.W. 490 (1937).

[21]Sinift v. Sinift, 229 Iowa 56, 293 N.W. 841 (1940).

[22]213 Tenn. 117, 372 S.W.2d 300 (1963).

[23]425 S.W. 2d 745 (Ky. 1968),

the power positions of the parties. In most instances men are more powerful than women because men control economic wealth. Thus, most contracts between husbands and wives will be unfavorable to the wife. While courts could supervise all contracts between husbands and wives for fairness, cost barriers to litigation block access to the courts in most cases. The best the courts can do is refuse to enforce all of these contracts affecting ongoing relationships. In most instances, this will avoid adding judicial power to that which husbands have as a result of their economic position. Courts leave the parties to the legal regulation of the status of marriage. Mrs. Balfour and Mrs. Miller must use the divorce courts to protect their interests. Usually, wives do better under this regulation than do husbands. Would you accept the assumptions on which this argument rests?

We suggest that Chafee's "living tree" and "stranglehold" policies are not value neutral in their impact. They reflect assumptions of judges and lawyers arguing to them about particular relationships and transactions. Professor Kathryn Powers points out that American law has offered ideals of equality and justice, but women have a subordinate status. [24]To rationalize this contradiction,

> a legal tradition evolved which recognized a world split into public and private spheres and segregated women into the private sphere where such legal ideals did not apply.... The public sphere is the official world of the workplace, the marketplace, and the government, and is predominantly male. The private sphere is the domestic world of family, child rearing, and household maintenance, and is almost exclusively female."

Law left most aspects of private life unregulated. "By refusing to substantially regulate the private sphere, the legal order left the resolution of ... disputes to the parties and thereby permitted custom to dictate the appropriate conduct for marital parties.... As Professor Unger has observed, business relations in the public sphere were likely to be governed by what amounted to the 'law of communal solidarity' reflected in standards of good faith and fairness while, by contrast, familial relationships were likely to be governed by what amounted to the 'law of the jungle,' reflected in the legal order's noninterference with the 'exploitation of power advantages within the family.' "

b. Marriage and Cohabitation Contracts

In the 1970s many feminist books and magazines attacked traditional marriage. While some writers argued "freedom for women cannot be won without the abolition of marriage,"[25] others thought that marriage contracts, negotiated

---

[24]Powers, Sex, Segregation and the Ambivalent Directions of the Sex Discrimination Law, 1979 Wisconsin Law Review 1. Copyright 1979 by the University of Wisconsin.

[25]Cronan, Marriage, Notes from the Third Year, at 62.

between spouses, could reform the institution. During the 1980s, there were reports that many engaged couples were entering these contracts. Marriage contracts can deal with very different things, and thinking about marriage contracts can illuminate issues arising in commercial relationships. It is important to draw some distinctions in order to think about them:

(1) One highly publicized agreement was between Alix Cates Shulman and her husband, drafted after two children had been born. The contract seems to focus primarily on the allocation of domestic duties. A part entitled "Children" consists of many paragraphs assigning tasks connected with mornings, transportation, helping with homework, personal questions and explaining things, nighttime, baby-sitters, sick care and weekends. "Housework" deals with cooking, shopping, cleaning and laundry. The allocations are detailed and specific. For example, he is to deal with the children at night (baths, stories, bed routine and waking up in the middle of the night) three nights a week; she does it three other nights, and they use Friday to compensate the one who has done extra work during the week.[26]

(2) Other proposed marriage contracts focus on the economic side of marriage, and require men to pay women for housework, child care and lost opportunities or provide for earned income to be community property.

(3) Some marriage contracts deal with another range of problems in conventional marriage which are of concern to some women. For example, these contracts have clauses relating to a woman's interest in her family name, the right to sexual access, and the domicile of the couple. These contracts clauses also purport to change many of the laws dealing with these matters. Again, whether courts would enforce them is open to question.

(4) Other proposals are even more far reaching. For example, some call for new forms of marriage such as marriages among three or more people or people of the same sex. Some propose a termination fee for the dissolution of marriage. Some deal with whether the right to sexuality will be exclusive. Most of these provisions purport to change the laws dealing with these matters.

Necessarily, this is not a complete catalog of all proposals for marriage contracts. There seem to be few dealing directly with alimony and child support upon separation or divorce. However, under some contracts the wife would have less need for support since she would have her half interest in the community property or have received payments for her household and child care services.

"Marriage contracts" are more than a feminist concern. Consider the following extract from an advertisement which appeared in the New York Times Book Review, Sept. 8, 1974, at 21:

---

[26]The contract appears in Ms., 66, 72 (Spring 1972), and Up from Under 5-8 (Aug.-Sept. 1970).

I am fifty years old, and a chemist. I worry about my weight, but not about my bifocal glasses, graying hair, or the fact that after a lifetime of marriage, I am now living with a woman I hired through a newspaper ad....

Contract Cohabitation
An Alternative to Marriage

... **Now** — at last — here's a revolutionary lifestyle that'll be cheered by both feminists and male chauvinists, by all men and women who seek their true identities, desire emotional and financial independence and the *freedom* to mold their lives. *Contract Cohabitation* will give you a new alternative to marriage, and inspire you to start life afresh — regardless of your age, sex or occupation!

[The book is described as a combination of a "candid memoir" and "practical how-to handbook about a person who, after 26 years of marriage and 5 children, frustrated by the pattern of family life dictated by society, learned how to opt for his own life and identity."]

Divorce alone was not the answer

Edmund L. Van Deusen is a real person. He is a chemist, writer, and former associate editor of *Fortune* magazine. He is also an inventor, sculptor, ...d the father of five children. Simply, eloquently, and without bitterness, he confesses the dissatisfactions within his marriage. We follow him through the "nether world of one-night stands" that first exhilarated and then exhausted him.... We watch as he evolves the new concept of a lifestyle that demands *both* partners be strong, independent, even selfish adults able to stand alone — without being lonely. This, then, is the crux of Contract Cohabitation: *a relationship based on that of the employer and the employee, complete with the unique benefits of our working life: vacations, salaries, regular hours and set responsibilities!* ...

What Is Contract Cohabitation?

— An eating, and living arrangement, based on a written or unwritten employment contract....
— An employer/employee relationship that can be man-woman or woman-man, depending only on the financial strength and personal goals of the individuals involved....
— All contract terms are defined by the employer and accepted by the employee *in advance* ... including salary, free hours, annual vacations, social and work activities outside the CC relationship....

— Sex is not an object of the arrangement, or a subject of the contract: both parties are free to be together, apart or with someone else....

— The employment contract can be cancelled at any time within 30 days by *either* party — without reason or explanation.

[The advertisement closes with a suggestion that existing social norms lead to a "stultifying togetherness" that leads to a loss of individuality "for the sake of an ideal, illusory partnership." The suggestion is that the philosophical basis for the "CC relationship" is the use of money as emotional currency, and the substitution of the employer-employee model for the partnership model.]

NOTES AND QUESTIONS

1. *Latent functions of marriage contracts*: Sometimes engaged couples find they cannot negotiate marriage contracts successfully because their disagreements are fundamental. As a result, they break the engagement and call off the wedding. (Is this good? or bad?) Contrast cultures in which parents arrange marriages. The husband and wife must work out most matters on a day by day basis within their cultural context. What can we say for one system as contrasted with the other? To what extent, if at all, does contractual cohabitation avoid these problems?

2. *Law is not free*: While a couple can draft a marriage contract aided by books and magazine articles, many see lawyers for help. A prenuptial agreement could cost from as little as $500 to as much as $10,000 (or more) for a complex agreement where both prospective spouses have a great deal of property. Should people draft their own contracts, following advice in a book? Should they see lawyers? How many lawyers would be experts in contract cohabitation?

c. Contracts Between "Husband" and "Wife" Who Are Not Married: Courts Swim in the Dismal Swamp

Changes in the law often mirror changes in the larger society. Views about sexuality and marriage have changed in the past three decades or so. Of course, not everyone accepts the challenges to traditional marriage and the new lifestyles. The following materials report two distinct judicial reactions to social change. As you read them, remember writers such as Chafee, Powers and Olsen. Notice too that common law ideas provide rationalizations and rhetoric for all sides in the debate.

MARVIN v. MARVIN

134 Cal. Rptr. 815, 557 P.2d 106 (Cal. 1976)

TOBRINER, J. — During the past 15 years, there has been a substantial increase in the number of couples living together without marrying. Such nonmarital relationships lead to legal controversy when one partner dies or the couple separates. Courts of Appeal, faced with the task of determining property rights in such cases, have arrived at conflicting positions: two cases (*In re Marriage of Cary* (1973) 34 Cal. App. 3d 345 [109 Cal. Rptr. 862]; *Estate of Atherley* (1975) 44 Cal. App. 3d 758 [119 Cal. Rptr. 41]) have held that the Family Law Act (Civ. Code, § 4000 et seq.) requires division of the property according to community property principles, and one decision (*Beckman v. Mayhew* (1975) 49 Cal. App. 3d 529 [122 Cal. Rptr. 604]) has rejected that holding. We take this opportunity to resolve that controversy and to declare the principles which should govern distribution of property acquired in a nonmarital relationship.

We conclude: (1) The provisions of the Family Law Act do not govern the distribution of property acquired during a nonmarital relationship; such a relationship remains subject solely to judicial decision. (2) The courts should enforce express contracts between nonmarital partners except to the extent that the contract is explicitly founded on the consideration of meretricious sexual services. (3) In the absence of an express contract, the courts should inquire into the conduct of the parties to determine whether that conduct demonstrates an implied contract, agreement of partnership or joint venture, or some other tacit understanding between the parties. The courts may also employ the doctrine of quantum meruit, or equitable remedies such as constructive or resulting trusts, when warranted by the facts of the case.

In the instant case plaintiff and defendant lived together for seven years without marrying; all property acquired during this period was taken in defendant's name. When plaintiff sued to enforce a contract under which she was entitled to half the property and to support payments, the trial court granted judgment on the pleadings for defendant, thus leaving him with all property accumulated by the couple during their relationship. Since the trial court denied plaintiff a trial on the merits of her claim, its decision conflicts with the principles stated above, and must be reversed.

1. *The factual setting of this appeal.*

Since the trial court rendered judgment for defendant on the pleadings, we must accept the allegations of plaintiff's complaint as true, determining whether such allegations state, or can be amended to state, a cause of action. We turn therefore to the specific allegations of the complaint.

Plaintiff avers that in October of 1964 she and defendant "entered into an oral agreement" that while "the parties lived together they would combine their efforts and earnings and would share equally any and all property accumulated as a result of their efforts whether individual or combined." Furthermore, they agreed to "hold themselves out to the general public as husband and wife" and that "plaintiff would further render her services as a companion, homemaker, housekeeper and cook to ... defendant."

Shortly thereafter plaintiff agreed to "give up her lucrative career as an entertainer [and] singer" in order to "devote her full time to defendant ... as a companion, homemaker, housekeeper and cook"; in return defendant agreed to "provide for all of plaintiff's financial support and needs for the rest of her life."

Plaintiff alleges that she lived with defendant from October of 1964 through May of 1970 and fulfilled her obligations under the agreement. During this period the parties as a result of their efforts and earnings acquired in defendant's name substantial real and personal property, including motion picture rights worth over $1 million. In May of 1970, however, defendant compelled plaintiff to leave his household. He continued to support plaintiff until November of 1971, but thereafter refused to provide further support.

On the basis of these allegations plaintiff asserts two causes of action. The first, for declaratory relief, asks the court to determine her contract and property rights; the second seeks to impose a constructive trust[27] upon one half of the property acquired during the course of the relationship.

Defendant demurred unsuccessfully, and then answered the complaint. Following extensive discovery and pretrial proceedings, the case came to trial. Defendant renewed his attack on the complaint by a motion to dismiss. Since the parties had stipulated that defendant's marriage to Betty Marvin did not terminate until the filing of a final decree of divorce in January 1967, the trial court treated defendant's motion as one for judgment on the pleadings augmented by the stipulation.

After hearing argument the court granted defendant's motion and entered judgment for defendant. Plaintiff moved to set aside the judgment and asked leave to amend her complaint to allege that she and defendant reaffirmed their agreement after defendant's divorce was final. The trial court denied plaintiff's motion, and she appealed from the judgment.

---

[27]Eds. Note: A constructive trust is a remedy which is imposed to avoid unjust enrichment. One person, who holds legal title to property, is ruled to hold that property for the benefit of another. Many kinds of circumstances might cause a court to use the remedy of the imposition of a constructive trust. Constructive trusts are part of the substantive law of restitution. Constructive trusts are not real trusts, any more than quasi-contracts are real contracts. Some would argue that the constructive trust is the equitable equivalent to the quasi-contract.

2. *Plaintiff's complaint states a cause of action for breach of an express contract.*

In *Trutalli v. Meraviglia* (1932) 215 Cal. 698 [12 P.2d 430] we established the principle that nonmarital partners may lawfully contract concerning the ownership of property acquired during the relationship. We reaffirmed this principle in *Vallera v. Vallera* (1943) 21 Cal.2d 681, 685 [134 P.2d 761], stating that "If a man and woman [who are not married] live together as husband and wife under an agreement to pool their earnings and share equally in their joint accumulations, equity will protect the interests of each in such property."

In the case before us plaintiff, basing her cause of action in contract upon these precedents, maintains that the trial court erred in denying her a trial on the merits of her contention. Although that court did not specify the ground for its conclusion that plaintiff's contractual allegations stated no cause of action, defendant offers some four theories to sustain the ruling; we proceed to examine them.

Defendant first and principally relies on the contention that the alleged contract is so closely related to the supposed "immoral" character of the relationship between plaintiff and himself that the enforcement of the contract would violate public policy.

A review of the numerous California decisions concerning contracts between nonmarital partners, however, reveals that the courts have not employed such broad and uncertain standards to strike down contracts. The decisions instead disclose a narrower and more precise standard: a contract between nonmarital partners is unenforceable only *to the extent* that it *explicitly* rests upon the immoral and illicit consideration of meretricious sexual services.

Numerous cases have upheld enforcement of agreements between nonmarital partners in factual settings essentially indistinguishable from the present case.

Although the past decisions hover over the issue in the somewhat wispy form of the figures of a Chagall painting, we can abstract from those decisions a clear and simple rule. The fact that a man and woman live together without marriage, and engage in a sexual relationship, does not in itself invalidate agreements between them relating to their earnings, property, or expenses. Neither is such an agreement invalid merely because the parties may have contemplated the creation or continuation of a nonmarital relationship when they entered into it. Agreements between nonmarital partners fail only to the extent that they rest upon a consideration of meretricious sexual services. Thus the rule asserted by defendant, that a contract fails if it is "involved in" or made "in contemplation" of a nonmarital relationship, cannot be reconciled with the decisions.

The three cases cited by defendant which have *declined* to enforce contracts between nonmarital partners involved consideration that *was* expressly founded upon an illicit sexual service. In *Hill v. Estate of Westbrook*, 95 Cal.App.2d 599, the woman promised to keep house for the man, to live with him as man and wife, and to bear his children; the man promised to provide for her in his will, but died without doing so. Reversing a judgment for the woman based on the reasonable value of her services, the Court of Appeal stated that "the action is predicated upon a claim which seeks, among other things, the reasonable value of living with decedent in meretricious relationship and bearing him two children.... The new law does not award compensation for living with a man as a concubine and bearing him children.... As the judgment is at least in part, for the value of the claimed services for which recovery cannot be had, it must be reversed." (95 Cal.App.2d at p. 603.) Upon retrial, the trial court found that it could not sever the contract and place an independent value upon the legitimate services performed by claimant. We therefore affirmed a judgment for the estate. (*Hill v. Estate of Westbrook* (1952) 39 Cal.2d 458 [247 P.2d 19].)

In the only other cited decision refusing to enforce a contract, *Updeck v. Samuel* (1954) 123 Cal.App.2d 264 [266 P.2d 822], the contract "was based on the consideration that the parties live together as husband and wife." (123 Cal.App.2d at p. 267.) Viewing the contract as calling for adultery, the court held it illegal.

The decisions in the *Hill* and *Updeck* cases thus demonstrate that a contract between nonmarital partners, even if expressly made in contemplation of a common living arrangement, is invalid only if sexual acts form an inseparable part of the consideration for the agreement. In sum, a court will not enforce a contract for the pooling of property and earnings if it is explicitly and inseparably based upon services as a paramour. The Court of Appeal opinion in *Hill*, however, indicates that even if sexual services are part of the contractual consideration, any *severable* portion of the contract supported by independent consideration will still be enforced.

The principle that a contract between nonmarital partners will be enforced unless expressly and inseparably based upon an illicit consideration of sexual services not only represents the distillation of the decisional law, but also offers a far more precise and workable standard than that advocated by defendant. Our recent decision in *In re Marriage of Dawley* (1976) 17 Cal.3d 342 [131 Cal.Rptr. 3, 551 P.2d 323] offers a close analogy. Rejecting the contention that an antenuptial agreement is invalid if the parties contemplated a marriage of short duration, we pointed out in *Dawley* that a standard based upon the subjective contemplation of the parties is uncertain and unworkable; such a test, we stated, "might invalidate virtually all antenuptial agreements on the ground that the parties contemplated dissolution ... but it provides no principled basis for determining which antenuptial agreements offend public policy and which do not." (17 Cal.3d 342, 352.)

Similarly, in the present case a standard which inquires whether an agreement is "involved" in or "contemplates" a nonmarital relationship is vague and unworkable. Virtually all agreements between nonmarital partners can be said to be "involved" in some sense in the fact of their mutual sexual relationship, or to "contemplate" the existence of that relationship. Thus defendant's proposed standards, if taken literally, might invalidate all agreements between nonmarital partners, a result no one favors. Moreover, those standards offer no basis to distinguish between valid and invalid agreements. By looking not to such uncertain tests, but only to the consideration underlying the agreement, we provide the parties and the courts with a practical guide to determine when an agreement between nonmarital partners should be enforced.

[The court rejected a second contention by defendant that enforcement of the 1964 contract would impair the community property rights of Betty Marvin, defendant's lawful wife, and so violate public policy.]

Defendant's third contention is noteworthy for the lack of authority advanced in its support. He contends that enforcement of the oral agreement between plaintiff and himself is barred by Civil Code § 5134, which provides that "All contracts for marriage settlements must be in writing...." A marriage settlement, however, is an agreement in contemplation of marriage in which each party agrees to release or modify the property rights which would otherwise arise from the marriage. . . . The contract at issue here does not conceivably fall within that definition, and thus is beyond the compass of § 5134.

[The court rejected defendant's fourth argument which was that enforcement of the contract would violate a California statute barring suits for breach of promise to marry, finding that the statute did not address agreements between nonmarital partners to pool property.]

In summary, we base our opinion on the principle that adults who voluntarily live together and engage in sexual relations are nonetheless as competent as any other persons to contract respecting their earnings and property rights. Of course, they cannot lawfully contract to pay for the performance of sexual services, for such a contract is, in essence, an agreement for prostitution and unlawful for that reason. But they may agree to pool their earnings and to hold all property acquired during the relationship in accord with the law governing community property; conversely they may agree that each partner's earnings and the property acquired from those earnings remains the separate property of the earning partner. So long as the agreement does not rest upon illicit meretricious consideration, the parties may order their economic affairs as they choose, and no policy precludes the courts from enforcing such agreements.

In the present instance, plaintiff alleges that the parties agreed to pool their earnings, that they contracted to share equally in all property acquired, and that defendant agreed to support plaintiff. The terms of the contract as alleged do not rest upon any unlawful consideration. We therefore conclude that the complaint furnishes a suitable basis upon which the trial court can render declaratory relief.

The trial court consequently erred in granting defendant's motion for judgment on the pleadings.

3. *Plaintiff's complaint can be amended to state a cause of action founded upon theories of implied contract or equitable relief.*

As we have noted, both causes of action in plaintiff's complaint allege an express contract; neither assert any basis for relief independent from the contract. In *In re Marriage of Cary, supra*, 34 Cal.App.3d 345, however, the Court of Appeal held that, in view of the policy of the Family Law Act, property accumulated by nonmarital partners in an actual family relationship should be divided equally. Upon examining the *Cary* opinion, the parties to the present case realized that plaintiff's alleged relationship with defendant might arguably support a cause of action independent of any express contract between the parties. The parties have therefore briefed and discussed the issue of the property rights of a nonmarital partner in the absence of an express contract. Although our conclusion that plaintiff's complaint states a cause of action based on an express contract alone compels us to reverse the judgment for defendant, resolution of the *Cary* issue will serve both to guide the parties upon retrial and to resolve a conflict presently manifest in published Court of Appeal decisions.

Both plaintiff and defendant stand in broad agreement that the law should be fashioned to carry out the reasonable expectations of the parties. Plaintiff, however, presents the following contentions: that the decisions prior to *Cary* rest upon implicit and erroneous notions of punishing a party for his or her guilt in entering into a nonmarital relationship, that such decisions result in an inequitable distribution of property accumulated during the relationship, and that *Cary* correctly held that the enactment of the Family Law Act in 1970 overturned those prior decisions. Defendant in response maintains that the prior decisions merely applied common law principles of contract and property to persons who have deliberately elected to remain outside the bounds of the community property system. *Cary*, defendant contends, erred in holding that the Family Law Act vitiated the force of the prior precedents.

As we shall see from examination of the pre-*Cary* decisions, the truth lies somewhere between the positions of plaintiff and defendant. The classic opinion on this subject is *Vallera v. Vallera, supra*, 21 Cal.2d 681. Speaking for a four-member majority, Justice Traynor posed the question: "whether a woman living with a man as his wife but with no genuine belief that she is legally married to him acquires by reason of cohabitation alone the rights of a co-tenant in his earnings and accumulations during the period of their relationship." (21 Cal.2d at p. 684.)....

Vallera explains that "Equitable considerations arising from the reasonable expectation of the continuation of benefits attending the status of marriage entered into in good faith are not present in such a case." (p. 685.) In the absence of express contract, *Vallera* concluded, the woman is entitled to share in property jointly accumulated only "in the proportion that her funds contributed toward its acquisition." (p. 685.) Justice Curtis, dissenting, argued that the evidence showed an implied contract under which each party owned an equal interest in property acquired during the relationship.

The majority opinion in *Vallera* did not expressly bar recovery based upon an implied contract, nor preclude resort to equitable remedies. But *Vallera's* broad assertion that equitable considerations "are not present" in the case of a nonmarital relationship (21 Cal.2d at p. 685) led the Courts of Appeal to interpret the language to preclude recovery based on such theories....

This failure of the courts to recognize an action by a nonmarital partner based upon implied contract, or to grant an equitable remedy, contrasts with the judicial treatment of the putative spouse. Prior to the enactment of the Family Law Act, no statute granted rights to a putative spouse. The courts accordingly fashioned a variety of remedies by judicial decision. Some cases permitted the putative spouse to recover half the property on a theory that the conduct of the parties implied an agreement of partnership or joint venture.... Others permitted the spouse to recover the reasonable value of rendered services, less the value of support received. Finally, decisions affirmed the power of a court to employ equitable principles to achieve a fair division of property acquired during putative marriage.

Thus in summary, the cases prior to *Cary* exhibited a schizophrenic inconsistency. By enforcing an express contract between nonmarital partners unless it rested upon an unlawful consideration, the courts applied a common law principle as to contracts. Yet the courts disregarded the common law principle that holds that implied contracts can arise from the conduct of the parties. Refusing to enforce such contracts, the courts spoke of leaving the parties "in the position in which they had placed themselves" (*Oakley v. Oakley*, 82 Cal.App.2d 188, 192), just as if they were guilty parties *in pari delicto*.

Justice Curtis noted this inconsistency in his dissenting opinion in *Vallera*, pointing out that "if an express agreement will be enforced, there is no legal or just reason why an implied agreement to share the property cannot be enforced."...

Still another inconsistency in the prior cases arises from their treatment of property accumulated through joint effort. To the extent that a partner had contributed *funds* or *property*, the cases held that the partner obtains a proportionate share in the acquisition, despite the lack of legal standing of the relationship. (citations omitted) Yet courts have refused to recognize just such an interest based upon the contribution of *services*. As Justice Curtis points out [in the *Vallera* case] "Unless it can be argued that a woman's services as cook, housekeeper, and homemaker are valueless, it would seem logical that if, when she contributes money to the purchase of property, her interest will be protected, then when she contributes her services in the home, her interest in property accumulated should be protected." ...

Thus as of 1973, the time of the filing of *In re Marriage of Cary, supra,* 34 Cal.App.3d 345, the cases apparently held that a nonmarital partner who rendered services in the absence of express contract could assert no right to property acquired during the relationship. The facts of *Cary* demonstrated the unfairness of that rule.

Janet and Paul Cary had lived together, unmarried, for more than eight years. They held themselves out to friends and family as husband and wife, reared four children, purchased a home and other property, obtained credit, filed joint income tax returns, and otherwise conducted themselves as though they were married. Paul worked outside the home, and Janet generally cared for the house and children.

In 1971, Paul petitioned for "nullity of the marriage." Following a hearing on that petition, the trial court awarded Janet half the property acquired during the relationship, although all such property was traceable to Paul's earnings. The Court of Appeals affirmed the award.

Reviewing the prior decisions which had denied relief to the homemaking partner, the Court of Appeals reasoned that those decisions rested upon a policy of punishing persons guilty of cohabitation without marriage. The Family Law Act, the court observed, aimed to eliminate fault or guilt as a basis for dividing marital property. But once fault or guilt is excluded, the court reasoned, nothing distinguishes the property rights of a nonmarital "spouse" from those of a putative spouse. Since the latter is entitled to half the " 'quasi marital property'" (Civ. Code, § 4452), the Court of Appeal concluded that, giving effect to the policy of the Family Law Act, a nonmarital cohabitator should also be entitled to half the property accumulated during an "actual family relationship." (34 Cal.App.3d at p. 353.)

If *Cary* is interpreted as holding that the Family Law Act requires an equal division of property accumulated in nonmarital "actual family relationships," then … *Cary* distends the act. No language in the Family Law Act addresses the property rights of nonmarital partners, and nothing in the legislative history of the act suggests that the Legislature considered that subject. The delineation of the rights of nonmarital partners before 1970 had been fixed entirely by judicial decision; we see no reason to believe that the Legislature, by enacting the Family Law Act, intended to change that state of affairs.

But although we reject the reasoning of *Cary*, we share the perception of the *Cary* courts that the application of former precedent in the factual setting of those cases would work an unfair distribution of the property accumulated by the couple. We should not, therefore, reject the authority of *Cary* without also examining the deficiencies in the former law which led to those decisions.

The principal reason why the pre-*Cary* decisions result in an unfair distribution of property inheres in the court's refusal to permit a nonmarital partner to assert rights based upon accepted principles of implied contract or equity. We have examined the reasons advanced to justify this denial of relief, and find that none have merit.

First, we note that the cases denying relief do not rest their refusal upon any theory of "punishing" a "guilty" partner. Indeed, to the extent that denial of relief "punishes" one partner, it necessarily rewards the other by permitting him to retain a disproportionate amount of the property. Concepts of "guilt" thus cannot justify an unequal division of property between two equally "guilty" persons.

Other reasons advanced in the decisions fare no better. The principal argument seems to be that "[e]quitable considerations arising from the reasonable expectation of ... benefits attending the status of marriage ... are not present [in a nonmarital relationship]." (*Vallera v. Vallera, supra,* 21 Cal.2d at p. 685.) But, although parties to a nonmarital relationship obviously cannot have based any expectations upon the belief that they were married, other expectations and equitable considerations remain. The parties may well expect that property will be divided in accord with the parties' own tacit understanding and that in the absence of such understanding the courts will fairly apportion property accumulated through mutual effort. We need not treat nonmarital partners as putatively married persons in order to apply principles of implied contract, or extend equitable remedies; we need to treat them only as we do any other unmarried persons.

The remaining arguments advanced from time to time to deny remedies to the nonmarital partners are of less moment. There is no more reason to presume that services are contributed as a gift than to presume that funds are contributed as a gift; in any event the better approach is to presume, as Justice Peters suggested, "that the parties intend to deal fairly with each other."

The argument that granting remedies to the nonmarital partners would discourage marriage must fail.... Although we recognize the well-established public policy to foster and promote the institution of marriage ... perpetuation of judicial rules which result in an inequitable distribution of property accumulated during a nonmarital relationship is neither a just nor an effective way of carrying out that policy.

In summary, we believe that the prevalence of nonmarital relationships in modern society and the social acceptance of them, marks this as a time when our courts should by no means apply the doctrine of the unlawfulness of the so-called meretricious relationship to the instant case. As we have explained, the nonenforceability of agreements expressly providing for meretricious conduct rested upon the fact that such conduct, as the word suggests, pertained to and encompassed prostitution. To equate the nonmarital relationship of today to such a subject matter is to do violence to an accepted and wholly different practice.

We are aware that many young couples live together without the solemnization of marriage, in order to make sure that they can successfully later undertake marriage. This trial period, preliminary to marriage, serves as some assurance that the marriage will not subsequently end in dissolution to the harm of both parties. We are aware, as we have stated, of the pervasiveness of nonmarital relationships in other situations.

The mores of the society have indeed changed so radically in regard to cohabitation that we cannot impose a standard based on alleged moral considerations that have apparently been so widely abandoned by so many. Lest we be misunderstood, however, we take this occasion to point out that the structure of society itself largely depends upon the institution of marriage, and nothing we have said in this opinion should be taken to derogate from that institution. The joining of the man and woman in marriage is at once the most socially productive and individually fulfilling relationship that one can enjoy in the course of a lifetime.

We conclude that the judicial barriers that may stand in the way of a policy based upon the fulfillment of the reasonable expectations of the parties to a nonmarital relationship should be removed. As we have explained, the courts now hold that express agreements will be enforced unless they rest on an unlawful meretricious consideration. We add that in the absence of an express agreement, the courts may look to a variety of other remedies in order to protect the parties' lawful expectations.

The courts may inquire into the conduct of the parties to determine whether that conduct demonstrates an implied contract or implied agreement of partnership or joint venture ... or some other tacit understanding between the parties. The courts may, when appropriate, employ principles of constructive trust ... or resulting trust. Finally, a nonmarital partner may recover in quantum meruit for the reasonable value of household services rendered less the reasonable value of support received if he can show that he rendered services with the expectation of monetary reward.

Since we have determined that plaintiff's complaint states a cause of action for breach of an express contract, and, as we have explained, can be amended to state a cause of action independent of allegations of express contract, we must conclude that the trial court erred in granting defendant a judgment on the pleadings.

The judgment is reversed and the cause remanded for further proceedings consistent with the views expressed herein.

Wright, C.J., McComb, J., Most, J., Sullivan, J., and Richardson, J., concurred.

CLARK, J., Concurring and Dissenting. — The majority opinion properly permit recovery on the basis of either express or implied in fact agreement between the parties. These being the issues presented, their resolution requires reversal of the judgment. Here, the opinion should stop.

This court should not attempt to determine all anticipated rights, duties and remedies within every meretricious relationship — particularly in vague terms. Rather, these complex issues should be determined as each arises in a concrete case.

The majority broadly indicate that a party to a meretricious relationship may recover on the basis of equitable principles and in quantum meruit. However, the majority fail to advise us of the circumstances permitting recovery, limitations on recovery, or whether their numerous remedies are cumulative or exclusive. Conceivably, under the majority opinion a party may recover half of the property acquired during the relationship on the basis of general equitable principles, recover a bonus based on specific equitable considerations, and recover a second bonus in quantum meruit.

The general sweep of the majority opinion raises but fails to answer several questions. First, because the Legislature specifically excluded some parties to a meretricious relationship from the equal division rule of Civil Code § 4452, is this court now free to create an equal division rule? Second, upon termination of the relationship, is it equitable to impose the economic obligations of lawful spouses on meretricious parties when the latter may have rejected matrimony to avoid such obligations? Third, does not application of equitable principles — necessitating examination of the conduct of the parties — violate the spirit of the Family Law Act of 1969, designed to eliminate the bitterness and acrimony resulting from the former fault system in divorce? Fourth, will not application of equitable principles reimpose upon trial courts the unmanageable burden of arbitrating domestic disputes? Fifth, will not a quantum meruit system of compensation for services — discounted by benefits received — place meretricious spouses in a better position than lawful spouses? Sixth, if a quantum meruit system is to be allowed, does fairness not require inclusion of all services and all benefits regardless of how difficult the evaluation?

When the parties to a meretricious relationship show by express or implied in fact agreement they intend to create mutual obligations, the courts should enforce the agreement. However, in the absence of agreement, we should stop and consider the ramifications before creating economic obligations which may violate legislative intent, contravene the intention of the parties, and surely generate undue burdens on our trial courts.

By judicial overreach, the majority perform a nunc pro tunc marriage, dissolve it, and distribute its property on terms never contemplated by the parties, case law or the Legislature.

NOTES AND QUESTIONS

1. *The background of the case*: According to newspaper accounts, Michelle Triola started singing professionally in nightclubs in Hollywood after she graduated from high school. She then went on the Playboy Club circuit. When she was 20, she was a dancer featured in Las Vegas and Reno. In 1963, she went to Europe and sang in nightclubs for $300 to $1,000 a week. She returned the next year and joined the cast of the film, "Ship of Fools." She met Lee Marvin, one of the stars of the picture. After a few weeks of dating, Lee moved into Michelle's Hollywood Hills apartment. They spent the next six years together. She spent most of her time decorating the couple's $250,000 Malibu beach house and entertaining show business friends. In 1970, she changed her last name legally to Marvin. A few months later, Lee Marvin left to marry his high school sweetheart.

Michelle Marvin tried to resume her career, but no one was interested in a 37-year-old singer who had not performed regularly in years. Lee Marvin promised to give her $833 a month for five years. He stopped payments after 14 months because he thought she had told a Hollywood gossip columnist that his new marriage was failing. She supported herself by watering plants, typing scripts and doing odd jobs for friends. Finally, she found a $125-a-week secretarial position at the William Morris Agency in Beverly Hills.

Marvin Mitchelson, Michelle's lawyer, wrote a book called "Made in Heaven, Settled in Court." He said that Michelle came to him, broke, frightened, and miserable. She was seeking some way to make Lee Marvin resume making the promised payments of $833 a month for four more years. Mitchelson relates,

> She was entitled to a great deal more.... I felt that she had a right to half of the assets acquired during the time they lived together as "man and wife." Anything less would not only be an injustice but, I strongly felt, probably unconstitutional as well....
>
> I explained my beliefs on the subject to Michelle, and she agreed it was very important that some precedents be set in this particular area of the law. She remained willing to test it even after I told her we'd probably lose in the lower courts, and any hope of a voluntary financial settlement might be ruined by the very act of raising the issue at all.

2. *The impact of Marvin v. Marvin on those involved — a third Marvin case?*
The Supreme Court of California said that the facts alleged by Marvin Mitchelson for Michelle Marvin stated a cause of action. This clearly was a victory in terms of creating new law. However, Michelle Triola Marvin still had to prove her case. She had to establish an express or implied contract to share property. Or she had to prove facts establishing some other theory of relief found within the Supreme Court's opinion. The much publicized trial took eleven weeks and featured the testimony of many famous people from the film industry about the couple's relationship. Michelle was her own chief witness, and Lee's lawyer cross-examined her at length pointing to inconsistencies in her story. Lee Marvin's testimony told a very different story about their relationship.

The trial judge, sitting as trier of fact, found that Michelle Marvin had not proved a contract to share property existed. He wrote:

> ... the basic statement on which plaintiff relies is the one which she says (and defendant denies) was made by defendant at San Blas — "What I have is yours and what you have is mine." Considering the circumstances from which it allegedly sprung, the lack of intent to make a contract is immediately apparent. In 1964-1965 defendant was married; he had considerable unresolved financial problems; he had repeatedly informed plaintiff that he did not believe in marriage because of the property rights which a wife

thereby acquires. Plaintiff could not have understood that phrase to accord the same rights to one who was *not* defendant's wife.

The judge pointed out that it was not clear what they were to share over what period. During the time Lee and Michelle lived together, he deposited his salary into his separate bank account. He always bought and sold property in his name. Michelle had her own bank account. She deposited into it an allowance Lee gave her as well as the sums she earned as a singer. Lee created joint bank accounts when they were "on location" making a motion picture, but when the pictures were finished Lee withdrew the remaining balances and deposited them back into his separate account. She could not show that she had given up her career at his request. Indeed, he had done several things to further her career as a singer while they lived together. It was unclear whether she would have had a successful career as a singer had she never lived with Lee Marvin.

The National Law Journal reported that Marvin Mitchelson, Michelle's lawyer, said that she did not have a perfect *Marvin* case. "There are better witnesses than Michelle.... She is not as good an actor as Lee, but then he won an Academy Award. I think she told the truth about the relationship as she remembered it." He also said that if Ms. Marvin had had greater financial resources, he might have done more pre-trial investigation. The Los Angeles Times News Service reported "Mitchelson lost the almost $100,000 it cost to try the case."

In its *Marvin* opinion, the Supreme Court of California suggested the possibility of other theories of recovery which might be applicable when unwed couples lived together. For example, if a couple produced property through "mutual effort," it should be divided even though there was no contract. However, the trial court said:

> ... where both wanted to be free to come and go without obligation, the basis for any division of property surely cannot be her "giving up" her career for him. It then can only be her work as cook, homemaker and companion that can be considered as plaintiff's contribution to the requisite "mutual effort." Yet, where $72,000 has been disbursed by defendant on behalf of plaintiff in less than six years, where she has enjoyed a fine home and travel throughout the world for about 30 months, where she acquired whatever clothes, furs and cars she wished and engaged in a social life amongst screen and stage luminaries, such services as she has rendered would appear to have been compensated.

Finally, in the last two paragraphs of his opinion, the trial judge awarded Michelle Marvin $104,000 "for rehabilitation purposes so that she may have the economic means to re-educate herself and to learn new, employable skills or to refurbish those utilized, for example, during her most recent employment and so that she may return from her status as companion of a motion picture star to a separate, independent but perhaps more prosaic existence." The judge noted that it was unlikely that Michelle could resume her career as a singer, and she was supporting herself by unemployment insurance benefits. Lee Marvin owned property worth more than a million dollars. The judge explained that $104,000 would be about equivalent to the highest rate that she ever had earned as a singer, $1,000 per week, for the two years he estimated that she would need to rehabilitate herself.

In August of 1981, a three judge panel of the Court of Appeals of California reversed the trial court's award of $104,000 for rehabilitation.[28] The vote was two to one. The majority said that the award was without support in either equity or law. The rehabilitation remedy had to rest on some recognized cause of action, and the trial court's award did not. Michelle noted that two men on the court had voted against her while the one woman voted to remand for additional findings. Marvin Mitchelson promised to take the case to the Supreme Court of California, but less than a month later it refused to hear the case. The battle ended after eleven years.

Michelle Marvin received nothing from her suit but publicity. Many saw her as a feminist heroine. She said that she had gained real satisfaction in establishing the rights of women living in relationships with men other than marriage. Marvin Mitchelson, her lawyer, called her "the Joan of Arc of live-in women." However, in July of 1981, she was convicted of shoplifting from a Beverly Hills department store, fined $250, and placed on six months' probation. In 1986 The Los Angeles Times News Service reported, "Michelle Triola Marvin, 48, now works in public relations and lives in the Los Angeles area with comedian Dick Van Dyke."

Lee Marvin continued to earn large sums as an actor until his death in 1987. He saw the case as a cause, and he was determined not to pay Michelle anything. His lawyer said that his client was fighting the case because he was highly principled, and he wanted to erase from the public mind the "grand illusion that merely living together generates some rights." Ten years later Marvin said, "[i]t was a comedy." "I didn't have anything else to do that year. I enjoyed it. It probably disturbed my wife and family, but it didn't bother me. It was a learning experience. I learned how little truth there is in court."

Marvin Mitchelson, Michelle's lawyer, became famous and gained many clients in the divorce and family law areas. Newspaper accounts say that in 1982, he charged $200 an hour but preferred taking a $15,000 retainer for cases in California and $25,000 to $50,000 for cases elsewhere. Some large cases involve much more. He remarked that publicized cases are hard to handle, but "if you win one, you can make millions." Mitchelson is a workaholic, putting in long hours. He has a large caseload and often speaks to bar groups.

A lawyer who is one of his friends said, "Marvin would be the first to tell you he is not a research man. He's not going to go into the library and start pulling

---

[28]Marvin v. Marvin, 122 Cal.App.3d 871, 176 Cal.Rptr. 555 (Dist. Ct.Ap. 1981).

the books and look at detailed aspects of the law. He's not that kind of lawyer. But he always has an overall grasp of the strategy of the cases he's handling." The research is assigned to others who work with him. Family law experts have praised his effort in *Marvin v. Marvin*. Lee Marvin's lawyer credited Mitchelson with "tenacity and persistence" in pushing a case no other lawyer would have taken.

Recall Mitchelson's comments about the *Marvin* case in his book. Michelle came to him in a dependent situation; she was hardly an arm's length bargainer. She regarded Mitchelson as a professional expert. He told her that he thought "she was entitled to a great deal more" than the $833 a month payments. He felt that she "had a *right*" to half the assets. Was he defining the expectation in their lawyer-client undertaking? Was he promising her the equivalent of a "perfect hand" or a "Hedy LaMarr nose?" If so, is there a contract remedy for failure to deliver on such a promise? Mitchelson apparently induced Michelle to forego pursuit of the $38,318 ($833 x 46 months remaining of the 60 months Marvin had promised to pay) in remaining promised monthly support payments. Could she recover this sum from Mitchelson under a reliance theory of contract damages if it were recognized in California?

Was it responsible lawyering for an attorney to advise a destitute and desperate client to pursue a protracted campaign to reform the law? In Mitchelson's words, "any hope of a voluntary financial settlement might be ruined" Would this depend on what he knew when he gave the advice, what he told her, and whether she was able to make an informed choice? Remember that the lawyer-client relationship is a fiduciary one. Lawyers are responsible for their client's welfare. They should not maximize their own gains from the service they give. Might Michelle Marvin have been better off to have consulted a legal aid office or some kind of group legal practice that would not have had the time to pursue legal change to establish novel theories? As far as we know, Mitchelson's representation pleased Michelle. If she is happy, does that answer all questions about the attorney-client relationship involved in this case?

The major beneficiary of *Marvin v. Marvin* seems to be Marvin Mitchelson. Were Michelle and Mitchelson, unmarried parties, engaged in a "mutual effort" or partnership? Could another lawyer turn some of the theories in Justice Tobriner's opinion against Marvin Mitchelson? Does Michelle deserve a share of the benefits — fame, new business, ability to charge higher fees, speaker's fees and so on — that Mitchelson has derived from his association with the *Marvin* case?

3. *The impact of Marvin v. Marvin on the law*: The courts in about half of the states have considered the *Marvin* case and most of them have followed the California rule. A few have gone further and enforced agreements even where sexual relations were part of the agreement. Many bills were introduced in state legislatures which would require that legally enforceable agreements between unmarried cohabitants be in writing.

Although it was ultimately reversed, the trial court in the *Marvin* case fashioned the unique rehabilitation remedy. Some courts have used conventional family law remedies in enforcing agreements between unmarried couples. For example, in *McCullon v. McCullon*,[29] a New York court ordered Mr. McCullon to pay Ms. McCullon alimony of $50 per week and child support of $50 per week. They had lived together for 28 years without marriage. He had promised to support her for life in exchange for her implied promise to perform household services for him. In a similar case, *Kozlowski v. Kozlowski*,[30] the New Jersey Superior Court awarded Ms. Kozlowski a lump sum equal to the present value of an annuity to support her for the rest of her life. The court refused to compensate her for past services and lost opportunities. Mr. Kozlowski had fulfilled his obligation by supporting Ms. Kozlowski for the previous 15 years.

Other courts have been unwilling to require people to provide future support to others with whom they have cohabited. However, they have ordered that property accumulated during the term of the relationship be partitioned between the two parties. In deciding these cases, courts usually begin by solemnly declaring that the intentions of the parties are the key to the matter. However, in most cases there is perilously little evidence of any actual intention about the rights to property if the unimaginable — the breakup of a wonderful relationship — happened. Courts often presume that parties intended to divide property accumulated during the course of the relationship equally. See *Carlson v. Olsen*;[31] *Beal v. Beal*.[32]

While couples who live together without marriage often talk about a free and easy arrangement, breaking up any relationship is difficult. Many troubled cohabiting couples seek counselling when they find they have a marriage in substance if not in form. Lawyers find they face real difficulties in working out terminations. Joseph Summers, a St. Paul, Minnesota Family Court Judge, says a typical situation involves a young man who moves out of his female friend's apartment in anger. He returns to claim his water bed. She refuses to return it, presenting him with a bill for her money spent for payments on his car. Also, the judge says "what was a gift when it was given often turns into a loan after a couple breaks up." There has been a great growth in mediation, attempting to lead parties to agree about ending relationships and paying past debts and dividing property. Litigation is seen as a bad, but sometimes necessary, technique for dealing with such questions. While there are folk norms about washing dirty linen in public, people do seem willing today to take family cases before judges. The threat that one might go to court may play a role in persuading the other to negotiate or accept mediation.

---

[29] 419 N.Y.S.2d 226 (1979).

[30] 395 A.2d 913 (1978).

[31] 256 N.W.2d 249 (Minn. 1977).

[32] 577 P.2d 507 (Ore. 1978).

4. *Not all states follow Marvin v. Marvin*: Throughout the 1960s and 1970s, there was a great change in the laws of many states related to sexuality, marriage and cohabitation by unwed couples. Many state supreme courts seemed eager to recognize *Marvin v. Marvin* or go beyond it. However, not everyone in the United States welcomed these changes. Defense of traditional marriage, the family, and sex roles were adopted as symbols by a number of groups. For example, this was an important issue for those groups opposed to the Equal Rights Amendment, and religious fundamentalists used it as part of their attack on reforms which liberals and feminists had pushed over the previous two decades.

Some of this thinking, perhaps, can be found in *Hewitt v. Hewitt*.[33] It is a major victory of those opposed to *Marvin v. Marvin* and the cluster of ideas for which it stands. Victoria Hewitt alleged she lived with Robert Hewitt "from 1960 to 1975 in an unmarried, family-like relationship to which three children have been born." She sued to recover "an equal share of the profits and properties accumulated by the parties" during that period. The trial court dismissed her complaint, but the Appellate Court reversed. It adopted the rule of *Marvin v. Marvin*, at least for situations where the parties had lived "a most conventional, respectable and ordinary family life." The court noted that fornication was an offense in Illinois only when it is "open and notorious."

Victoria Hewitt had an appealing case. In June of 1960, when Victoria and Robert were students at Grinnell College, she became pregnant. Robert told her that they were husband and wife, and no formal ceremony was necessary. He would "share his life, his future, his earnings and his property" with her. Victoria and Robert told their parents they were married, and they lived as if they were. She devoted efforts to Robert's professional education and establishing his practice of pedodontia. She obtained financial assistance from her parents to support the practice in its early days, and she worked to create and maintain the business records of the practice. The practice paid her for services in the office, but she deposited her checks into their joint account. Robert owned nothing when they began living together. He now earned over $80,000 a year and owned much property. She alleged she had given him every assistance a wife and mother could. She organized and participated in social and community activities designed to enhance his professional reputation.

The Supreme Court of Illinois unanimously reversed the Appellate Court, affirming the trial court's decision dismissing Victoria Hewitt's complaint. One should compare the kinds of arguments made in the *Hewitt* opinion with those offered by Justice Tobriner in the *Marvin* case in light of the introductory essay — "What Am I Here For?" — to these materials.

---

[33]77 Ill.2d 49, 394 N.E.2d 1204 (1979).

What follows is taken from the Illinois Supreme Court's opinion:

The increasing incidence of nonmarital cohabitation referred to in *Marvin* and the variety of legal remedies therein sanctioned seem certain to result in substantial amounts of litigation, in which, whatever the allegations regarding an oral contract, the proof will necessarily involve details of the parties' living arrangements.

Apart, however, from the appellate court's reliance upon *Marvin* to reach what appears to us to be a significantly different result, we believe there is a more fundamental problem. We are aware, of course, of the increasing judicial attention given the individual claims of unmarried cohabitants to jointly accumulated property, and the fact that the majority of courts considering the question have recognized an equitable or contractual basis for implementing the reasonable expectations of the parties unless sexual services were the explicit consideration.

The issue of unmarried cohabitants' mutual property rights, however, as we earlier noted, cannot appropriately be characterized solely in terms of contract law, nor is it limited to considerations of equity or fairness as between the parties to such relationships. There are major public policy questions involved in determining whether, under what circumstances, and to what extent it is desirable to accord some type of legal status to claims arising from such relationships. Of substantially greater importance than the rights of the immediate parties is the impact of such recognition upon our society and the institution of marriage. Will the fact that legal rights closely resembling those arising from conventional marriages can be acquired by those who deliberately choose to enter into what have heretofore been commonly referred to as "illicit" or "meretricious" relationships encourage formation of such relationships and weaken marriage as the foundation of our family-based society? In the event of death shall the survivor have the status of a surviving spouse for purposes of inheritance, wrongful death actions, workmen's compensation, etc.? And still more importantly: what of the children born of such relationships? What are their support and inheritance rights and by what standards are custody questions resolved? What of the sociological and psychological effects upon them of that type of environment? Does not the recognition of legally enforceable property and custody rights emanating from non-marital cohabitation in practical effect equate with the legalization of common law marriage — at least in the circumstances of this case? And, in summary, have the increasing numbers of unmarried cohabitants and changing mores of our society reached the point at which the general welfare of the citizens of this State is best served by a return to something resembling the judicially created common law marriage our legislature outlawed in 1905?

The real thrust of plaintiff's argument here is that we should abandon the rule of illegality because of certain changes in societal norms and attitudes.

It is urged that social mores have changed radically in recent years, rendering this principle of law archaic. It is said that because there are so many unmarried cohabitants today the courts must confer a legal status on such relationships. This, of course, is the rationale underlying some of the decisions and commentaries. (See, *e.g.*, Marvin v. Marvin (1976), 18 Cal.3d 660, 683, 134 Cal.Rptr. 815, 831, 557 P.2d 106, 122; *Beal v. Beal* (1978), 282 Or. 115, 577 P.2d 507; Kay & Amyx, *Marvin v. Marvin: Preserving the Options*, 65 California Law Review 937 (1977).) If this is to be the result, however, it would seem more candid to acknowledge the return of varying forms of common-law marriage than to continue displaying the naivete we believe involved in the assertion that there are involved in these relationships contracts separate and independent from the sexual activity, and the assumption that those contracts would have been entered into or would continue without that activity.

Even if we were to assume some modification of the rule of illegality is appropriate, we return to the fundamental question earlier alluded to: If resolution of this issue rests ultimately on grounds of public policy, by what body should that policy be determined? *Marvin*, viewing the issue as governed solely by contract law, found judicial policy-making appropriate. Its decision was facilitated by California precedent and that state's no-fault divorce law. In our view, however, the situation alleged here was not the kind of arm's length bargain envisioned by traditional contract principles, but an intimate arrangement of a fundamentally different kind. The issue, realistically, is whether it is appropriate for this court to grant a legal status to a private arrangement substituting for the institution of marriage sanctioned by the state. The question whether change is needed in the law governing the rights of parties in this delicate area of marriage-like relationships involves evaluations of sociological data and alternatives we believe best suited to the superior investigative and fact-finding facilities of the legislative branch in the exercise of its traditional authority to declare public policy in the domestic relations field.

That belief is reinforced by the fact that judicial recognition of mutual property rights between unmarried cohabitants would, in our opinion, clearly violate the policy of our recently enacted Illinois Marriage and Dissolution Marriage Act. Although the Act does not specifically address the subject of nonmarital cohabitation, we think the legislative policy quite evident from the statutory scheme is .... "to ... strengthen and preserve the integrity of marriage and safeguard family relationships."

We cannot confidently say that judicial recognition of property rights between unmarried cohabitants will not make that alternative to marriage more attractive by allowing the parties to engage in such relationships with greater security. As one commentator has noted, it may make this alternative especially attractive to persons who seek a property arrangement that the law does not permit to marital partners. (Comment, 90 Harvard Law Review 1708, 1713 (1977).) ...

The Act also provides: "Common law marriages contracted in this State after June 30, 1905 are invalid."...

While the appellate court denied that its decision here served to rehabilitate the doctrine of common law marriage, we are not persuaded. Plaintiff's allegations disclose a relationship that clearly would have constituted a valid common law marriage in this State prior to 1905. The parties expressly manifested their present intent to be husband and wife; immediately thereafter they assumed the marital status; and for many years they consistently held themselves out to their relatives and the public at large as husband and wife. Revealingly, the appellate court relied on the fact that the parties were, to the public, husband and wife in determining that the parties' living arrangement did not flout Illinois public policy. It is of course true, as plaintiff argues, that unlike a common law spouse she would not have full marital rights in that she could not, for example, claim her statutory one-third share of defendant's property on his death. The distinction appears unimpressive, however, if she can claim one-half of his property on a theory of express or implied contract....

These circumstances in our opinion constitute a recent and unmistakeable legislative judgment disfavoring the grant of mutual property rights to knowingly unmarried cohabitants. We have found no case in which recovery has been allowed in the face of a legislative declaration as recently and clearly enacted as ours. Even if we disagreed with the wisdom of that judgment, it is not for us to overturn or erode it.

Actually, however, the legislative judgment is in accord with the history of common law marriage in this country. "Despite its judicial acceptance in many states, the doctrine of common-law marriage is generally frowned on in this country, even in some of the states that have accepted it." Its origins, early history and problems are detailed in *In re Estate of Soeder*, where that court noted that some 30 states did not authorize common law marriage. "It tends to weaken the public estimate of the sanctity of the marriage relation. It puts in doubt the certainty of the rights of inheritance. It opens the door to false pretenses of marriage and the imposition on estates of suppositious heirs." 7 Ohio App.2d 271, 290, 220 N.E.2d 547, 561 (1966).

We do not intend to suggest that plaintiff's claims are totally devoid of merit. Rather, we believe that our statement in *Mogged v. Mogged* (1973), 55 Ill.2d 221, 225, 302 N.E.2d 293, 295, made in deciding whether to abolish a judicially created defense to divorce, is appropriate here:

Whether or not the defense of recrimination should be abolished or modified in Illinois is a question involving complex public-policy considerations as to which compelling arguments may be made on both sides. For the reasons stated hereafter, we believe that these questions are appropriately within the province of the legislature, and that, if there is to be a change in the law of this State on this matter, it is for the legislature and not the courts to bring about that change.

We accordingly hold that plaintiff's claims are unenforceable for the reason that they contravene the public policy, implicit in the statutory scheme of the Illinois Marriage and Dissolution of Marriage Act, disfavoring the grant of mutually enforceable property rights to knowingly unmarried cohabitants. The judgment of the appellate court is reversed and the judgment of the circuit court of Champaign County is affirmed.

5. *The direct impact of Marvin*: The Los Angeles Times News Service surveyed the situation ten years after the *Marvin* decision. It reported that the flood of cases anticipated in 1976 never materialized. "[O]bservers say palimony has largely fallen into disuse, although specific numbers are hard to come by." The number of couples cohabiting has not increased in the 1980s. The publicity given to the *Marvin* case has prompted more written agreements, and those without them know or learn that their chances of winning a judgment are slim. Palimony suits are expensive to litigate, and since they seldom result in a large award, few lawyers will take them on contingent fees. Nonetheless, "Marvin may be moribund, but nobody considers it dead." If lawyers are likely to bring very few cases under the *Marvin* theory, why then do professors teach it in one or more courses in most law schools?

2. WHICH PROMISES SHOULD THE LAW ENFORCE? RESPONSE OF CONTRACTS DOCTRINE AND ROLE OF FORM

a. "Bait": Promises by a Family Member with Money to Influence the Lives of Those Without It

In this section we seek to develop several ideas related to contracts doctrine. For the most part, we look at promises made to family members to induce them to do things desired by the one with money. These are not commercial situations, but courts often use contract law as a tool to resolve problems that do not fit into family or property law.

Although, as we shall see, there is no "typical" bait situation, there are a great many cases in which aging farmers, or other small businessmen, promise to turn their property over to one or more children in exchange for a promise by the children to support their parents for their remaining lifetimes. Later, or sometimes sooner, conflicts arise and one or the other of the parties seeks either to enforce or repudiate the bargain. A disproportionate number of well known contract cases follow this pattern, and so it is a useful paradigm for the study of contract doctrine, the limits of judicial capability, and the advantages and disadvantages of thinking of agreements as creating relationships rather than transactions.

Before narrowing our focus to contract, we should briefly consider some of the other legal devices that may apply to the "bait" situation. As you will see, lawyers often press contract into service when they find these other theories don't quite work. Suppose a father is unhappy about the purposeless life of his son who has graduated from college but has refused to follow a conventional career. The father wants the son to go to law school. However, the father also wants evidence that the son will work to the full level of his ability. Thus he writes his son:

> I will give you tuition and a reasonable allowance for books, room and board, clothes and recreation. I will do this only if you go to the University of Wisconsin Law School and if you pass the examinations at the end of the first semester with at least the average grade needed for graduation.

The son is admitted to law school, pays his expenses from his own money and what he can earn from a part time job, and goes to classes. Before final examinations at the end of the first semester, his father dies. There is no provision in the father's will calling for payment of his son's law school expenses. The will leaves all the father's money to the son's stepmother who dislikes him. The son takes examinations and receives the highest grade average in the class. The executor of the father's estate refuses to pay any money to the son without an order of a court to do so. What theories might the son assert against the estate, and what chances for success would each have?

Conventional ways to transfer property in families: There are a number of traditional legal categories into which our facts almost but do not quite fit. The letter to the son would not itself serve as a *will*, or as an amendment to the original one. The letter does not purport to be a will, and the father did not sign it in the presence of two witnesses. Under some circumstances, a few states will accept a little less formality. However, the legal system demands relatively precise compliance with the formal requirements of creating wills. The transaction between father and son was not a legally effective *gift* either. To make a gift, the law insists on donative intent plus a delivery of property. Whatever the father's intention, here he delivered nothing to complete a gift.

Could we call the arrangement a *trust*? Restatement (Second) of Trusts, § 2, defines a trust as "a fiduciary relationship with respect to property, subjecting the person by whom the title to the property is held to equitable duties to deal with the property for the benefit of another person." People may create trusts in several ways, including a declaration by the owner of property that he or she holds property as trustee for another. Thus, suppose *X* stated that he was the owner of 100 shares of AT&T stock and was holding it in trust for the benefit of his granddaughter until her twenty-first birthday. This declaration would create a trust. *X* would have a legal obligation to deal with the 100 shares of stock only for the benefit of his granddaughter. It is questionable whether the father's letter to this son in our case reasonably could be construed as such a declaration. The father did not state he was holding *specific property* as a trustee, ready to devote it to paying law school bills. Instead, the father stated that he would pay in the future without segregating assets for this purpose.

Contract to the rescue? Finally, can we call the transaction between father and son a *contract*? This raises the question of whether there was "consideration" for the father's promise. Was this "a bargained-for exchange between the parties," or, rather, was it no more than "a statement of intention or a promise to make a gift to the son on a certain condition?" A completed gift requires no consideration to be enforced. However, a promise to make a gift in the future — or for that matter, a promise to make a will or create a trust — typically will be unenforceable without it. There are some exceptions, but we will come to them later. Often it is difficult to distinguish a conditional gift from a bargain.

Legal formality: We can view the requirements for making a legally enforceable will, gift, trust or contract as *forms*. That is, there is a necessary pattern of conduct or ceremony which people must follow to trigger a particular legal relationship. For example, wills require a writing witnessed by two people. Gifts require intent plus delivery. Trusts require a declaration to hold specific assets for another, and contracts require an exchange (and often, but not always, a writing as well). We can ask about the costs and benefits of formal requirements. This will help us understand whether the law is likely to insist firmly there is one and only one way to make, for example, a will. Assume that our son cannot establish a will, gift, trust or conventional contract. We will ask whether he could turn to some less formal way of having his father's promise enforced.

The *costs of form* are obvious. One person may clearly intend to transfer property, and the other may expect to get it and even rely on the transaction. However, if they have not met a formal requisite, the attempted transfer of rights fails. Justice is defeated by a mere technicality. One who has purported to transfer or promise can, in bad faith and without any excuse, refuse to carry out the transaction and hide behind the legal rule. Moreover, knowledge of legal forms is not widespread, and people must hire lawyers to be sure that they achieve their purposes.

The *functions or benefits of form* may not be obvious to everyone. The persistence of formal requirements in many legal systems suggests, but does not prove, there may be some utility in them. Professor Lon Fuller says that legal formalities have three functions — cautionary, evidentiary and channeling. Let's examine what he means.

Cautionary: If people must go through a formal ceremony to create legal relationships, it may warn them that they are doing something serious and important. Such a warning should serve to prompt thought about the commitment being made. "Do I really want to give away Grandfather's watch?" "Do I want to do it unconditionally or should I attach some strings to be sure that my son is worthy?" Many people avoid thinking about their own death. The will ceremony with witnesses (and even the usual presence of a lawyer who asks questions) may shock them into recognizing what they are doing. Handing over a valued possession in order to make a delivery for a gift should be more than just talk. Insofar as people view exchange-based bargains as serious and as slightly dangerous, a contract also serves as a form. Bargaining warns people not to be careless in the promises they make. In this view, people who make benevolent promises from which they receive only intangible satisfactions such as gratitude need protection against their own generous impulses.

Obviously, legal formalities can provide greater or lesser degrees of caution. An oral exchange of promises between business bargainers may involve more caution than an oral promise to make a gift. A signed written promise may have more shock value. There are customs in our society about the magical impact of signing documents. All sales people know that it is a long step from orally closing a deal to getting the papers signed. Requiring parties to put contracts in writing and then appear before a government official who cross-examines them about their understanding of what they have done seems to offer even more caution. Some legal systems require just this kind of procedure to make certain transactions legally enforceable.

Evidentiary: Some forms give us evidence that a transaction took place while others also tell us what the terms of the transaction are. A will signed before two witnesses, apart from a risk of forgery, tells us that the testator made a will and who gets what. Contrast the situation that would exist under oral wills if the law were to recognize them. Courts would have to rely on testimony about what the deceased said and intended. Those most likely to have heard the deceased also are the likely beneficiaries, or their relatives, who would have reason to shade their stories. Written contracts serve the evidentiary function nicely, provided the parties understand what they have signed. Oral contracts are less useful. Perhaps it is easier to believe that a person made a promise when the other party gave something in exchange for it. It is, for example, easier to believe that a person made an oral promise when the other party has performed and seeks payment.

Channeling: A legal form is important to people who want to do something with legal consequences. The law says that you have no gift if there is no intent or delivery. It also says that you can make a gift successfully if you do intend to make one and hand over property or a token representing it. If you want to be sure that you have a legally enforceable contract, it is useful to find a blueprint telling you how to build one.

Courts need channels too. The more objective the formal requirements, the easier it is for judges. Contrast two types of legal rules. One rule says that a manufacturer may sell an item without responsibility for its defects if the seller uses a certain form of words. The other rule allows disclaimers only if a buyer "should reasonably have known" that seller intended an "as is" sale. In the first case, the question is little more than did the seller use the magic words? In the second, one must weigh and balance norms and facts to determine what the buyer should have known. Moreover, the channel serves more than the judge's convenience. It is easier for others who care to predict what any judge might do if the law says that certain words and only those words are effective. This last point concerns the legitimacy of the judicial role in a society where legislatures are supposed to have primary rulemaking power. Some think that the more clearly judges are in the rule-applying rather than rulemaking business, the easier it is to defend what they do.

Consideration, Fuller says, may serve some of this channeling function. In planning a contract, a lawyer knows that she is taking far fewer risks if she casts the arrangement as an exchange. The courts can quickly sort clear-cut exchanges from all other promissory transactions, and they may refuse to act or demand strong reasons for enforcement of non-exchanges. Nonetheless, we can ask to what extent consideration is an effective form compared to the requirement that a certain type of contract be in writing. To say that a doctrine serves some formal functions does not mean that other doctrines might not serve the same functions better.

We now turn to some cases dealing with consideration, and reliance as a substitute for consideration, in the family bait situation. Remember that in all of the situations we will consider, there were other ways that the person making the promise could have structured things to make it easier to enforce the promise in question. Should we hold to form or seek substantive justice on the facts of each particular case?

HAMER v. SIDWAY

124 N.Y. 538, 27 N.E. 256 (1891)

The plaintiff presented a claim to the executor of William E. Story, Sr., for $5,000 and interest from the 6th day of February, 1875. She acquired it through several ... assignments from William E. Story, 2d. The claim being rejected by the executor, this action was brought. It appears that William E. Story, Sr., was the uncle of William E. Story, 2d; that at the celebration of the golden wedding of Samuel Story and wife, father and mother of William E. Story, Sr., on the 20th day of March, 1869, in the presence of the family and invited guests, he promised his nephew that if he would refrain from drinking, using tobacco, swearing, and playing cards or billiards for money until he became 21 years of age, he would pay him the sum of $5,000. The nephew assented thereto, and fully performed the conditions inducing the promise. When the nephew arrived at the age of 21 years, and on the 31st day of January, 1875, he wrote to his uncle, informing him that he had performed his part of the agreement, and had thereby become entitled to the sum of $5,000. The uncle received the letter, and a few days later, on the 6th day of February, he wrote and mailed to his nephew the following letter:

Buffalo, Feb. 6, 1875. W.E. Story, Jr. — Dear Nephew: Your letter of the 31st ult. came to hand all right, saying that you had lived up to the promise made to me several years ago. I have no doubt but you have, for which you shall have five thousand dollars, as I promised you. I had the money in the bank the day you was twenty-one years old that I intend for you, and you shall have the money certain. Now, Willie, I do not intend to interfere with this money in any way till I think you are capable of taking care of it, and the sooner that time comes the better it will please me. I would hate very much to have you start out in some adventure that you thought all right and lose this money in one year. The first five thousand dollars that I got together cost me a heap of hard work. You would hardly believe me when I tell you that to obtain this I shoved a jack-plane many of day, butchered three or four years, then came to this city, and, after three months' perseverance, I obtained a situation in a grocery store. I opened this store early, closed late, slept in the fourth story of the building in a room 30 by 40 feet, and not a human being in the building but myself. All this I done to live as cheap as I could to save something. I don't want you to take up with this kind of fare. I was here in the cholera season of '49 and '52 and the deaths averaged 80 to 125 daily, and plenty of smallpox. I wanted to go home, but Mr. Fisk, the gentleman I was working for, told me, if I left them, after it got healthy he probably would not want me. I stayed. All the money I have saved I know just how I got it. It did not come to me in any mysterious way, and the reason I speak of this is that money got in this way stops longer with a fellow that gets it with hard knocks than it does when he finds it. Willie, you are twenty-one, and you have many a thing to learn yet. This money you have earned much easier than I did, besides acquiring good habits at the same time, and you are quite welcome to the money. Hope you will make good use of it. I was ten long years getting it together after I was your age. Now, hoping this will be satisfactory, I stop. One thing more. Twenty-one years ago I bought you 15 sheep. These sheep were put out to double every four years. I kept track of them the first eight years. I have not heard of them since. You father and grandfather promised me that they would look after them till you were of age. Have they done so? I hope they have. By this time you have between five and six hundred sheep, worth a nice little income this spring. Willie, I have said much more than I expected to. Hope you can make out what I have written. To-day is the seventeenth day that I have not been out of my room, and have had the doctor as many days. Am a little better to day. Think I will get out next week. You need not mention this to your father, as he always worries about small matters. Truly yours, W.E. STORY. P.S. You can consider this money on interest.

The nephew ... consented that the money should remain with his uncle in accordance with the terms and conditions of the letter. The uncle died on the 29th day of January 1887, without having paid over to his nephew any portion of the said $5,000 and interest....

PARKER, J., ... The question which ... lies at the foundation of plaintiff's asserted right of recovery, is whether by virtue of a contract defendant's testator, William E. Story, became indebted to his nephew, William E. Story, 2d, on his twenty-first birthday in the sum of $5,000. The trial court found as a fact that "on the 20th day of March, 1869, ... William E. Story agreed to and with William E. Story, 2d, that if he would refrain from drinking liquor, using tobacco, swearing, and playing cards or billiards for money until he should become twenty-one years of age, then he, the said William E. Story, would at that time pay him, the said William E. Story, 2d, the sum of $5,000 for such refraining, to which the said William E. Story, 2d, agreed," and that he "in all things fully performed his part of said agreement." The defendant contends that the contract was without consideration to support it, and therefore invalid. He asserts that the promisee, by refraining from the use of liquor and tobacco, was not harmed, but benefited; that that which he did was best for him to do, independently of his uncle's promise, — and insists that it follows that, unless the promisor was benefited, the contract was without consideration, — a contention which, if well founded, would seem to leave open for controversy in many cases whether that which the promisee did or omitted to do was in fact of such benefit to him as to leave no consideration to support the enforcement of the promisor's agreement. Such a rule could not be tolerated, and is without foundation in the law. The exchequer chamber in 1875 defined "consideration" as follows: "A valuable consideration, in the sense of the law, may consist either in some right, interest, profit, or benefit accruing to the one party, or some forbearance, detriment, loss, or responsibility given, suffered, or undertaken by the other." Courts "will not ask whether the thing which forms the consideration does in fact benefit the promisee or a third party, or is of any substantial value to any one. It is enough that something is promised, done, forborne, or suffered by the party to whom the promise is made as consideration for the promise made to him." Anson, Cont. 63.... Pollock in his work on Contracts, (page 166) after citing the definition given by the exchequer chamber, already quoted, says: "The second branch of this judicial description is really the most important one. 'Consideration' means not so much that one party is profiting as that the other abandons some legal right in the present, or limits his legal freedom of action in the future, as an inducement for the promise of the first." Now, applying this rule to the facts before us, the promisee used tobacco, occasionally drank liquor, and he had a legal right to do so. That right he abandoned for a period of years upon the strength of the promise of the testator that for such forbearance he would give him $5,000. We need not speculate on the effort which may have been required to give up the use of those stimulants. It is sufficient that he restricted his lawful freedom of action within certain prescribed limits upon the faith of his uncle's agreement, and now, having fully performed the conditions imposed, it is of no moment whether such performance actually proved a benefit to the promisor, and the court will not inquire into it; but, were it a proper subject of inquiry, we see nothing in this record that would permit a determination that the uncle was not benefited in a legal sense....

[T]he agreement which we have been considering was within the condemnation of the statute of frauds, because not to be performed within a year, and not in writing. But this defense the promisor could waive, and his letter and oral statements subsequent to the date of final performance on the part of the promisee must be held to amount to a waiver....

[I]t must be deemed established for the purposes of this appeal that on the 31st day of January, 1875, defendant's testator was indebted to William E. Story, 2d, in the sum of $5,000; and, if this action were founded on that contract, it would be barred by the statute of limitations, which has been pleaded, but on that date the nephew wrote to his uncle.... [O]n February 6th, the uncle replied ... as follows: "Dear Nephew: Your letter of the 31st ult. came to hand all right, saying that you had lived up to the promise made to me several years ago. I have no doubt but you have, for which you shall have $5,000, as I promised you. I had the money in the bank the day you was 21 years old that I intend for you, and you shall have the money certain. Now, Willie, I do not intend to interfere with this money in any way till I think you are capable of taking care of it, and the sooner that time comes the better it will please me. I would hate very much to have you start out in some adventure that you thought all right and lose this money in one year.... W. E. STORY. P.S. You can consider this money on interest." The trial court found as a fact that "said letter was received by said William E. Story, 2d, who thereafter consented that said money should remain with the said William E. Story in accordance with the terms and conditions of said letter." And further, "that afterwards, on the 1st day of March 1877, with the knowledge and consent of his said uncle, he duly sold, transferred, and assigned all his right, title, and interest in and to said sum of $5,000 to his wife, Libbie H. Story, who thereafter duly sold, transferred, and assigned the same to the plaintiff in this action." We must now consider the effect of the letter and the nephew's assent thereto. Were the relations of the parties thereafter that of debtor and creditor simply, or that of trustee and *cestui que trust*? If the former, then this action is not maintainable, because barred by lapse of time. If the latter, the result must be otherwise. No particular expressions are necessary to create a trust. Any language clearly showing the settler's intention is sufficient if the property and disposition of it are definitely stated.... A person in the legal possession of money or property acknowledging a trust with the assent of the *cestui que trust* becomes from that time a trustee if the acknowledgment be founded on a valuable consideration. His antecedent relation to the subject, whatever it may have been, no longer controls.... If before a declaration of trust a party be a mere debtor, a subsequent agreement recognizing the fund as already in his hands, and stipulating for its investment on the creditor's account, will have the effect to create a trust.... It is essential that the letter, interpreted in the light of surrounding circumstances, must show an intention on the part of the uncle to become a trustee before he will be held to have become such; but in an effort to ascertain the construction which should be given to it we are also to observe the rule that the language of the promisor is to be interpreted in the sense in which he had reason to suppose it was understood by the promisee.... At the time the uncle wrote the letter he was indebted to his nephew in the sum of $5,000, and payment had been requested. The uncle, recognizing the indebtedness, wrote the nephew that he would keep the money until he deemed him capable of taking care of it. He did not say, "I will pay you at some other time," or use language that would indicate that the relation of debtor and creditor would continue. On the contrary, his language indicated that he had set apart the money the nephew had "earned," for him, so that when he should be capable of taking care of it he should received it with interest.... Certainly the uncle must have intended that his nephew should understand that the promise not "to interfere with the money" referred to the money in the bank, which he declared was not only there when the nephew became 21 years old, but was intended for him. True, he did not use the word "trust," or state that the money was deposited in the name of William E. Story, 2d, or in his own name in trust for him, but the language used must have been intended to assure the nephew that his money had been set apart for him, to be kept without interference until he should be capable of taking care of it.... In this declaration there is not lacking a single element necessary for the creation of a valid trust, and to that declaration the nephew assented.... *The order appealed from should be reversed, and the judgment of the special term affirmed, with costs payable out of the state. All concur.*

NOTES AND QUESTIONS

1. *Bargains and contingent gifts*: What is consideration and how does it differ from a contingent gift? Does the promisor's true subjective motive matter? Consider the following classic and influential statement from Oliver Wendell Holmes, and then compare his views with the current statement of the consideration doctrine in Restatement (Second) of Contracts, § 71.

It is said that consideration must not be confounded with motive. It is true that it must not be confounded with what may be the prevailing or chief motive in actual fact. A man may promise to paint a picture for five hundred dollars, while his chief motive may be a desire for fame. A consideration may be given and accepted, in fact, solely for the purpose of making a promise binding. But, nevertheless, it is the essence of a consideration, that, by the terms of the agreement, it is given and accepted as the motive or inducement of the promise. Conversely, the promise must be made and accepted as the conventional motive or inducement for furnishing the consideration. The root of the whole matter is the relation of reciprocal conventional inducement, each for the other, between consideration and promise.[34]

2. *Problems in application*: Do Holmes and the Restatement help sort out when courts will find bait situations to be enforceable contracts and when they will classify them as contingent gifts?

How do we know if someone is bargaining for action or making a gratuity in a family setting? Suppose you wish to help support your poor but proud aunt who will not accept charity. You agree to buy her five-year-old automobile for twice the fair market value of this kind of car. You know that the car is in excellent condition, and she has not driven it very much. The car will be useful, but you would not have purchased a second car had your aunt not needed money. Is this a bargain, a gift or some of both? How would Holmes classify this transaction?

3. *Williston's tramp case*: In *Maughs v. Porter*,[35] the defendant advertised in a newspaper that there would be an auction of residence lots. The advertisement's heading was "NEW MODEL FORD FREE." The text said that everyone "has an equal chance at the new Ford regardless of buying or bidding. Come to the auction...." Plaintiff went to the auction. She placed her name on a slip of paper in a box held by the auctioneer. Defendant drew her name as the winner of the Ford. Defendant placed an order for the car with a Ford dealer but refused to pay for it when it was ready for delivery. Defendant demurred to plaintiff's complaint. He alleged that his promise lacked consideration, and so it was unenforceable. He also argued that the drawing was an illegal lottery, and so any contract resulting from it was unenforceable.

The Supreme Court of Virginia first noted that a promise to make a gift is legally unenforceable. It remarked that it was often difficult to determine whether there was consideration. It then quoted 1 *Williston on Contracts* § 112 (1920) to illustrate the difficulty and a method for resolving it:

> If a benevolent man says to a tramp: "If you go around the corner to the clothing shop there, you may purchase an overcoat on my credit," no reasonable person would understand that the short walk was requested as the consideration for the promise, but that in the event of the tramp going to the shop the promisor would make him a gift. Yet the walk to the shop is in its nature capable of being consideration. It is a legal detriment to the tramp to make the walk, and the only reason why the walk is not consideration is because on a reasonable construction it must be held that the walk was not requested as the price of the promise, but was merely a condition of a gratuitous promise. It is often difficult to determine whether words of

---

[34]O.W. Holmes, Jr., The Common Law 230 (1881; M. Howe ed. 1963).

[35]157 Va. 415, 161 S.E. 242 (1931).

condition in a promise indicate a request for consideration or state a mere condition in a gratuitous promise. An aid, though not a conclusive test, in determining which construction of the promise is more reasonable is an inquiry whether the happening of the condition will be a benefit to the promisor. If so, it is a fair inference that the happening was requested as a consideration. On the other hand, if, as in the case of the tramp stated above, the happening of the condition will be not only of no benefit to the promisor but is obviously merely for the purpose of enabling the promisee to receive a gift, the happening of the event on which the promise is conditional, though brought about by the promisee in reliance on the promise, will not properly be construed as consideration. In case of doubt where the promisee has incurred a detriment on the faith of the promise, courts will naturally be loath to regard the promise as a mere gratuity and the detriment incurred as merely a condition. But in some cases it is so clear that a conditional gift was intended that even though the promisee has incurred detriment, the promise has been held unenforceable.

The court in the *Maughs* case found there was consideration for the promise of a car to the winner of the drawing. "The object of the defendant unquestionably was to attract persons to the auction sale with the hope of deriving benefit from the crowd so augmented. Even though persons attracted by the advertisement of the free automobile might attend only because hoping to draw the automobile, and with the determination not to bid for any of the lots, some of these even might nevertheless be induced to bid after reaching the place of sale." However, the court then affirmed sustaining the demurrer because the advertisement was for a lottery which "contravenes public policy and avoids the agreement."

Courts and writers have said that the law looks only for the existence and not the adequacy of consideration. However, as the *Maughs* case and the tramp illustration show, we cannot rely solely on the form of the transaction. Both situations fit neatly into the form of "if you do X, then I'll do Y." Are we interested in the subjective state of mind of the one making the promise? Williston tells us that the person talking to the tramp is "a benevolent man." Suppose that the giver of the coat is an ambitious politician who wishes to be seen, and photographed, walking with the tramp and giving him the overcoat, in order to project an image of concern and generosity to the voting public? Would this matter?

Professor Clare Dalton notes[36] that many judges and law professors assert that consideration is principally a formal requirement. She argues that they want us to think that courts do not intervene in private bargains and make substantive

---

[36]Dalton, An Essay in the Deconstruction of Contract Doctrine, 94 Yale Law Journal 997, 1094 95 (1985).

judgments about what agreements should and should not be enforced. These writers insist that the law is not concerned with the adequacy of the parties' exchange but only whether the parties intended to trade one item for something else. However, when exchanges are significantly unequal, judges inevitably look behind formal rules and consider the substance of objective value. To hide this state intervention in private transactions, judges and law professors often are tempted to talk about the intention of the parties to bargain rather than the fairness of their agreement.

How might Dalton apply her argument to *Hamer v. Sidway* and Williston's tramp case? Why do we need a neutral apolitical contract doctrine? Who is in the audience that applauds neutral apolitical judging in contracts cases? Suppose we find that the intentions of the parties at the time of the transaction are too unclear to answer the question of liability. On what other grounds can a court decide whether to enforce their transaction? Can we have a single rule resting on choice and bargain or must we have many rules dealing with different situations in light of different policy considerations?

4. ***Promises to make gifts distinguished from trusts***: In *Hamer v. Sidway*, the uncle sent a letter from Buffalo, telling the nephew about some sheep bought at the nephew's birth and put in the possession of the nephew's father and grandfather. The uncle's gift of the sheep created a trust. The uncle could not reclaim these sheep before the nephew reached the age of majority. If the father sold some of the sheep and invested the money in corporate securities, the courts would hold him to the fiduciary duties of a trustee. If this were an unreasonable investment or if the father were unwilling to hand over the stock or proceeds when the nephew/son reached the age of majority, the nephew/son could sue the father successfully for breach of trust. Courts protect trust beneficiaries with remedies more powerful than those used for breaches of contract. For example, the nephew/son could trace the money his father gained by selling the sheep into the corporate securities. The nephew/son could recover those securities. However, if they were now valueless, the nephew/son could recover the fair market value of the sheep misappropriated by his father, the trustee. Students consider these subjects at length in other courses. All you need know for purposes of a contracts course is that often lawyers for claimants will want to classify a transaction as a trust rather than as a contract. The remedies differ and, as *Hamer v. Sidway* indicates, often so does the applicable statute of limitations.

5. ***Bargains distinguished from statements of intention***: The uncle also mentioned a transaction between Mr. Fisk and himself. Suppose the uncle stayed with Fisk through the cholera epidemic but then Fisk fired him. Could the uncle sue Mr. Fisk for breach of contract successfully? How, if at all, does this transaction differ from that found to be a contract between the uncle and the nephew in *Hamer v. Sidway*? Why does the law intervene in a transaction such as *Hamer v. Sidway* but refuse to do so in those such as *Balfour v. Balfour*? Are the questions a court must answer less difficult in the *Hamer* case? Is the court less likely to fall into a "dismal swamp" while holding a "hot potato?" Are

transactions such as those between the uncle and the nephew more socially important in some way than those between husband and wife?

3. AN INTRODUCTION TO THE DOCTRINE OF CONSIDERATION

Although it has been our experience that a careful and thorough study of the *Hamer v. Sidway* case serves to reveal a great deal about the doctrine of consideration, we offer at this point another note. This one summarizes the doctrine of consideration, and we intend that you read it in the same spirit as the note summarizing the offer and acceptance doctrine. Some of this note repeats things you should already know, other parts of it introduce some special applications of the doctrine, as well as some exceptions. Just as with the note dealing with offer and acceptance, you should not be surprised if your teacher asks you to read it on your own, or at another point in the text.

A Doctrinal Note — Consideration
John Kidwell
Stewart Macaulay

Courts, as we have already said more than once, will enforce some promises but not others. The doctrine of consideration has been one of the tools used to distinguish one kind from the other. Professor John Murray speaks of consideration as the most significant of several "validation devices" found in the law. Murray also observes "the reason the doctrine of consideration is so well remembered by most lawyers, and a greater importance attributed to it than it deserves, is the difficulty which most students have in understanding it." One reason for the difficulty is that consideration really is a number of rules, and it is impossible to capture it in a single, concrete statement. Most attempts are so abstract and qualified as to communicate little to one not already well-versed in contracts lore. Another reason for confusion is that consideration is a legal construct without a counterpart in human perception. Any person might see a contract as "fair" or "unfair," but only a lawyer could characterize one as "supported by consideration."

Someone must make a promise to another to create a contract. Often both people involved make promises to each other. For example, seller promises to deliver a car if buyer will pay $1,000. Buyer in turn promises to pay $1,000 if seller will deliver the car. Law professors often speak of the *promisor* — the one who makes a promise — and the *promisee* — the one who receives the promise. In our car case, seller and buyer are both promisor and promisee; each promise (and each made a promise) has both a promisor and a promisee. That is only a complicated, but conventional, way of saying that each made a promise to the other.

Consideration — A promise for an act: Suppose that a seller refused to deliver the car although the buyer had paid seller the money. Could the buyer sue the seller for damages? To succeed, the buyer would have to establish there was a legally enforceable contract which was breached. Buyer would have to prove that seller made the promise, and then show that the promise was of the kind the law enforces. One way to validate the promise is to show that buyer gave *consideration* for it. The $1,000 buyer paid seller would be consideration to support enforcement of seller's promise to deliver the car. This is the easiest case. Buyer paid the money, and this was the price for the promise. Contracts writers call this a "half-completed exchange," and many see it as the paradigmatic case for enforcement of a promise. Not only has buyer failed to get what he expected, but seller has his money.

Consideration — A promise for a promise: Suppose buyer had never paid the $1,000 as promised. However, buyer was ready, willing and able to do so when seller refused to deliver the car. There would still be consideration for seller's promise. Buyer's promise to pay would serve as consideration for seller's promise to deliver. *Consideration can be either an action or a promise to act.*

A promise is consideration, however, only if performing it would be consideration. Suppose, in exchange for your promise to pay me $1,000, I promise not to smash the windows of your store. Since I have no legal right to smash your windows, my promise is not consideration for yours. Of course, this does not mean that my promise might not be valuable if I had the power to smash your windows and the police were unlikely to protect you. Consideration is not just something you want or value. It must be something I have a legal right to withhold from you if you do not pay.

Consideration — bargained for and given in exchange: Not just any act or promise will serve as consideration. This is true even if the action or the promise was or would be very valuable to the one getting it. Consideration must be *bargained for and given in exchange*. Suppose last year Bill gave his sister, June, $5,000. She needed money to pay living expenses and tuition at the university. June graduated and has a good job. June owns a 1978 MGB sports car in excellent condition which Bill has always admired. June, out of gratitude for all Bill's previous help, promises to give the car to Bill when she takes delivery of a new car she is buying. However, before June gets the new car, Bill and June have a serious fight over politics and religion and June refuses to carry out her promise. If Bill wishes to pursue the matter, is June's promise to transfer title to the MGB supported by consideration?

This question may give some students trouble. Both the $5,000 and the MGB are valuable. June wanted the $5,000, and Bill wants the MGB. However, the $5,000 given by Bill to June is *not consideration* for her promise to give him the MGB. It was not "bargained for and given in exchange." "Bargained for" does not mean "haggled over" but rather paying the $5000 would have to be the inducement for her promise to transfer title to the car.

Bill's kind act in the past prompted her promise, but he gave her the money as a gift with no strings attached. If at the outset of their dealings she had said, "I will transfer title to the MGB next year IF you now pay me $5,000," and he had agreed to this deal, then there would have been consideration. But as we have posed the case, while she may have felt morally bound to her brother, she did not bargain to get the needed money. Thus, her promise would lack consideration. That is, she could back out without being liable to pay her brother damages. He could not win a specific performance action even if a court might consider the MGB unique.

Consideration — transforming gifts into bargains to make them legally enforceable: Let's change the case. Suppose June wants to promise to give her MGB to Bill. However, her good friend Fred Firstyear, a law student, told her that promises to make gifts are not legally enforceable. Bill protests that it doesn't matter, but June wants to make a legally enforceable promise to hand over the car. She asks Bill to promise to give her a paperback book regularly sold for $3.25, in exchange for her promise to deliver the MGB. Bill said that the whole thing was silly, but he finally agreed to go through with the ceremony to please her. Now is June's promise enforceable as supported by consideration?

Some courts have said things such as, "We look for only the presence and not the adequacy of consideration." Some have refused to look behind the form of the transaction to the real transaction. However, the Restatement of Contracts follows the bargain theory of consideration. Since the promise to deliver the book in no way induced June's promise, it says there is no consideration.

Even here, the Restatement is not perfectly clear. It says there would be consideration if June's motives were mixed. If she acted both to get the book and to express her gratitude, then there would be consideration. Suppose, for example, June needed more money because she had to pay bills piled up while she was in school. She agrees to sell the MGB to Bill for $500, although the market value of the car is from $2,500 to $3,500. She would not sell the car to anyone else for $500. However, this way she can discharge her sense of obligation and get some cash too. There would be consideration for her promise since a material part of the inducement to hand over the MGB was the $500. In sum, courts and law book writers are not clear on how free people are to transform gifts into the form of bargains and still satisfy the consideration requirement.

Consideration — policing bargains for equality? A promise and the consideration for it need not be of equal value. Remember that consideration is a legal construct and not a free floating fairness doctrine. A prominent exception to this rule concerns an exchange of unequal sums of money. A promise to pay $100 in exchange for $5 is unenforceable for want of consideration. Courts often explain by reciting that while they will not *investigate* the adequacy of consideration, they will not enforce a bargain which on its face can be nothing but an unequal exchange. Despite the form of bargain, the transaction would be a gift of $95.

How far can we take this idea? Some have said that we cannot compare personal utility. Suppose Bob agrees to exchange a book for Ann's used automobile worth about $1,500. Anyone can buy another copy of the book for

$20. Nonetheless, how do we know how much the book was worth to Ann? The statements in the cases probably reflect a genuflection in the direction of the extravagant ideas of individual autonomy prevalent in the 19th century. Courts were reluctant to attempt to regulate contracts openly. Obviously, there are very few reported cases where someone has traded a $20 book for a $1,500 automobile. Thus, we have few tests of a court's willingness to follow past declarations about disinterest in the adequacy of consideration.

So long as the consideration is sufficient to make credible the idea that it was bargained for and given in exchange, courts do not ask whether one party made a good deal and the other a very bad one. Suppose Bob agreed to buy Ann's used car for $8,500. There is consideration for Bob's promise to pay $8,500. The solution to this problem is to teach people such as Bob to be better shoppers and bargainers. However, at some point a disparity in value suggests that we are not looking at a bargain at all. It would be far easier, for example, to argue that the disparity in values between the $20 book and Ann's car showed only a sham bargain, and thus no consideration, than to argue there was a true exchange.

Courts have hesitated to use the consideration doctrine openly to investigate the equality of exchanges. They will, however, refuse to enforce grossly dispropor-tionate exchanges on the ground that they were procured by fraud, are unconscionable, or were the product of duress. But each of these attacks on the contract opens questions very different from those posed by consideration. They force us to face directly many difficult issues. How much do I have to tell you when we are bargaining? To what extent may I take advantage of your difficult circumstances which I did not create? What kinds of leverage so interfere with what we want to call free choice that we should label use of such leverage duress, and refuse to enforce the promise?

Consideration — benefit or detriment: Let's change the facts again. Suppose June promises to transfer title to the MGB if Bill agrees to serve as the county chairperson for a Red Cross Blood Drive. June will not benefit financially, and Bill's action will aid the community rather than June alone. Bill's promise is consideration for June's. June, for her own reasons, has diverted Bill's activities, and this is enough. No tangible benefit need move to the promisor. Serving as chairperson is a legal detriment to Bill. He has agreed to do something he was free not to do. This is true although Bill finds the job rewarding and satisfying rather than personally detrimental.

Consideration — modifications of bargains and preexisting legal obligations: One of the standard consideration problems involves the modification of ongoing bargains. Suppose Dan Architect agrees to superintend a construction project for Bruce Builder for a $10,000 fee. During the project, Dan unjustifiably takes the plans and refuses to continue supervising the work or to make the plans available to Builder unless Builder pays Architect an additional $2,000. Builder promises to do so since it is cheaper to buy off Dan than do anything else. Is there consideration for Builder's promise to pay Dan an additional $2,000? No, because Dan demanded an additional amount to do no more than he originally promised. Consideration serves to protect reliance on bargains and blunt the leverage people in Dan's position get when their trading partner cannot replace them easily.

But there are good reasons to modify bargains where coercion is not a major factor. Consideration can get in the way of these modifications. Suppose Angela borrowed $500 from Julia and agreed to repay the money on December 1st. On December 1st, Angela had only $400. Julia needed money then, and so she promised to discharge the debt if Angela paid her the $400. Payment of $400 would not be consideration for Julia's promise. Angela had a pre-existing duty to pay the debt in full. She promised nothing she was not already bound to give.

Notice that as a practical matter this lack of consideration for the promise seldom presents problems. Why would Julia want to sue Angela for the balance after having made the promise to take $400 in full settlement? Most non-lawyers would not know about the consideration rule and think themselves bound to the settlement. However, suppose Julia discovered that Angela had tricked her. Angela easily could have paid the full $500 on December 1st, but she made up a sad story to cheat Julia and pay her only part of what she owed her. Or, suppose on December 2d, Angela learned that she had just inherited $1,000,000 from her long lost Uncle Harvey. Julia might think that Angela ought to share the wealth, at least to the extent of the $100 gift that Julia was forced to give her. In either of these situations, Julia might see a lawyer who could give her the good news about the consideration doctrine.

However, there must be a pre-existing legal obligation to trigger the rule. Suppose Angela owes Julia $500, payable on December 1st. However, Julia needs money because of unexpected obligations. She asks Angela if she could repay her on November 25th. Angela says she has only $400, but is willing to pay that then in full satisfaction of the debt. Julia promises to discharge the debt for $400. Since Angela's payment was early, she was under no pre-existing legal obligation to pay then. The payment is consideration for Julia's promise.

How far can we push this idea to beat the consideration doctrine? Suppose Angela comes to Julia on December 1st, and tells her that she has only $400. Julia agrees to release the debt for that amount. However, Fred Firstyear, the law student, accompanies Angela. He has told her about the consideration doctrine. Angela tells Julia to agree to release the debt in exchange for the payment of the $400 plus a copy of a $3.95 paperback book which Angela has brought with her. Julia laughs but goes along with Fred's structuring of the transaction. Angela did not owe Julia $400 plus a paperback book — there was no pre-existing duty to give this performance. The Restatement of Contracts, § 71, would insist that the different performance be "bargained for and given in exchange." However, many courts have accepted $1.00 thrown in to make a deal legal, and some have required only a trivial modification to find consideration.

Another question that sometimes arises in applying the pre-existing duty rule concerns the question of the nature of the pre-existing duty itself. Does there have to be a real, substantial duty? Is it enough there might be one? Suppose

Stuart thinks he has a claim against the Marx Publishing Company for infringement of copyright. Marx has published a book that Stuart thinks steals his ideas. Stuart makes a demand, and Marx offers $500 in full settlement of all claims. Stuart accepts this sum and releases his claim. Suppose we brought together a group of 1,000 copyright lawyers and asked whether Stuart had a claim against Marx. Assume 200 would say he did because of their interpretation of the law, 200 would say he did because of their interpretation of the application of the law to the facts, and 600 would say Stuart had no claim at all. Marx, of course, settled to avoid having to litigate and having a claim pending against it. There is consideration for the release. One can give up a chance to litigate a claim that is doubtful because of uncertainty about the facts or the law.

Furthermore, it is enough for some courts that the one in Stuart's position honestly believed that he had a claim even if he was wrong. The Restatement (Second) of Contracts § 74 says that it is enough that Stuart "honestly believes that his claim or defense is just and may be determined valid." Notice that this would include a situation where Stuart's lawyer told him that the cases were against him but thought there was some chance that they could get the courts to overturn their old decisions and make new law. Thus, in our previous examples, if Angela had any reason to think she had a defense against Julia's claim for the $500, there would be consideration for the promise to settle for $400.

We are not yet finished with qualifications to the pre-existing duty rule. Suppose the builder promises to construct an apartment building according to plans and specifications in exchange for $750,000. However, once the excavation for the foundation is underway, the builder discovers an underground stream flowing through the property. The builder must divert the stream and use a different foundation than the one specified. Owner promises to pay 3/4th of the increased costs so builder will go ahead. At first glance, this would seem to be an example of a pre-existing duty case and so owner's promised additional payment would lack consideration. However, if the unforeseen event causes a great additional expense, some courts have been willing to say that this is an exception to the consideration doctrine and enforce the promise.

Some courts have, in effect, almost abandoned the pre-existing duty rule. Some talk about the one performing the duty for an increased payment, giving up her right to breach and pay damages. In Wisconsin, as long as a sum certain has not become due, older cases say that the consideration from the original promise "relates forward" to support a second promise modifying the original obligation.

The pre-existing duty rule is shot through with exceptions and qualifications. It is difficult to state when it will and will not apply. Section 2-209 of the Uniform Commercial Code opens with the bold statement, "[a]n agreement modifying a contract within this article needs no consideration to be binding." The comments say that the parties must modify their contract in "good faith." The comments invite courts to deal with extortion of modifications by using the good faith requirement rather than the common law pre-existing duty rule. Of course, this leaves it to the courts to work out which are good modifications and which are bad ones. Few standards exist to tell us how hard one may twist the arm of the other before crossing the line into the zone of bad faith. The Restatement (Second) of Contracts § 89 says that a promise modifying a contract is binding without consideration:

> (a) if the modification is fair and equitable in view of circumstances not anticipated by the parties when the contract was made; or
> (b) to the extent provided by statute; or
> (c) to the extent that justice requires enforcement in view of material change of position in reliance on the promise.

Once again we have qualitative standards courts must work out in the future on a case-by-case basis. We shall have to see how far courts abandon older views and embrace the Restatement to deal with modifications.

Consideration — illusory and alternative promises: Illusory and alternative promises pose still further difficulties for the consideration doctrine. Suppose Joe makes raspberry, strawberry, and grape jam which he sells at a local farmers' market every weekend. He puts the jam into used jam/jelly containers and seals them with wax on top. He tells a local boys' club that he will pay five cents for every jar with a top they bring him. The 11 year old president of the club says "That's great. We know where there are a lot of them. We'll do it." Shortly afterward, Joe finds a better source of used jars and does not need anymore. He tells the president of the boys' club that the deal is off.

You are the parent of the disappointed 11 year old president, and you are also a lawyer. Your son asks whether Joe made a legally binding contract with the club to buy jars from it. The answer would depend on a court's interpretation of what your son said. If it interpreted his remarks as "we have access to a supply of jars, and we promise to deliver them to you," there would be consideration. Your son would have promised to deliver the jars. Suppose, on the other hand, his words conveyed the idea "we think we can find jars, and if we still feel like gathering them, we will bring them to you." Then your son has made "an illusory promise" which would not be consideration for Joe's promise to buy. This is a statement in the form of a promise that does not limit the options open to your son. In effect, he said "I'll perform, if I feel like it." Whether a promise is illusory often turns on how we translate it. If your son committed the club to deliver jars, or not to deliver them to anyone else, then his promise would not be illusory but would limit his freedom. In that event, it would be good consideration for Joe's promise.

It is often difficult to spot illusory promises because they seldom are as blatant as "I'll perform if I feel like it." Sometimes, for example, A may hire B to act as agent for three years. However, buried in the mass of clauses in their printed form contract is one that provides that either A or B can end the agreement at any time. As you can see, this gives either party the legal right to perform or not to perform the agency agreement. Without more, this would be an illusory promise.

Suppose you represented A, and it was important that the contract be legally binding. Many lawyers provide some period of notice before a party can end the agreement. If the contract requires notice, then both parties are bound at least until the period expires. This would be enough to make the promise real and not illusory. A court might imply such an obligation to give reasonable notice before exercising a right to cancel at will. If it were willing to do this, the implied promise would salvage the deal. Parties who overlook the illusory promise trap, however, cannot always rely on courts to bail them out.[37]

Consideration — requirements and output contracts: In the past, courts had problems with consideration and requirements and output contracts. Suppose Al Artisan, a skilled sandal maker, agrees to sell all the sandals he makes to Rolph Retailer, or Rolph agrees to buy all his requirements of sandals from Al. Reading the contract literally, Al could make no sandals at all, or Rolph could arrange things so he had no requirements. Courts have imposed obligations of good faith so neither Al nor Rolph could turn off the contract at will.[38]

Other courts argue that the promises properly interpreted restrain freedom enough to constitute consideration. Al has promised to sell his output of sandals to Rolph and not anyone else. Rolph has promised to sell Al's sandals or sell no sandals at all.

Promises enforceable without consideration: It would be nice if we could stop here, but we cannot. You must at least cast your eye over the cases that the Restatement of Contracts candidly refers to as promises enforceable *without* consideration. Some are cases where courts in the past strained to find consideration and seemed to stretch even this malleable doctrine beyond its limits. Others are pure "exceptions," fashioned to patch up unsatisfactory results yielded by a strict application of the consideration notion.

Promises to repay despite defenses to the debt: Suppose Bill owes Jane $1,000, and he did not repay the money when payment was due. Then Bill discovers he has one of several defenses to the debt:

(1) he was a minor when he contracted the debt, it was not for "necessaries," and he disaffirms the debt within a reasonable time after he reaches the age of majority; or

(2) the statute of limitations runs before Jane files an action to collect the debt.

Despite having one of these defenses, Bill promises Jane that she will be repaid. Jane gives no new consideration for the promise. Nonetheless, common law courts would enforce it. They made a great deal of noise trying to square this position with orthodox notions of consideration, but all attempts seemed to be fudging the rules. Some courts used the common law's all purpose wild card —

---

[37] U.C.C. § 2-309(3).

[38] See U.C.C. § 2-306(1), especially Comment 2 thereto.

"waiver." Others talked about "moral consideration" to support the second promise. This suggests the reason for the result. These defenses were seen as technical evasions of a real obligation to repay debts. In the society from which judges came, it was a true moral obligation.

Waiver: As we suggested, waiver is one of the wild cards in the common law. The term means that a person may lose a right when she voluntarily gives it up. Of course, she might be estopped if she misled the other party into relying on her statements so allowing her to assert the right would be unjust. However, a waiver does not require proof of reliance. Can one waive a right without receiving consideration for giving it up? This has been the subject of some dispute. Professor Williston insisted that, with a few exceptions, consideration was necessary. However, the common law cases did not support his position.

The Restatement (Second) of Contracts § 84, deals with promises to perform despite the nonoccurrence of a condition — the typical situation where we find waivers. For example, Bill promises to pay, but only if A, B, and C happen. A and B happen, but C does not. Bill then promises to pay anyway. The Restatement says that Bill's promise is enforceable unless the condition is material. While there are cases supporting the Restatement position, not all the decisions impose this limitation. Some just say or assume that waivers do not require consideration. There is a great deal more to this problem than we can present here. For now, it is enough to recognize that this is a complex and inconsistent body of law. Your legal research in this area is likely to produce more plausible arguments than real answers.

Consideration and anti-consideration — Restatement § 90: The major exception to the consideration offered by the Restatement of Contracts is § 90. As you will learn from the cases which follow this note, courts can enforce promises without consideration on the basis of reliance to the extent required to prevent injustice. While the comment and illustrations are suggestive, the boundaries of this idea remain open. A court could use it to cancel a great deal of the impact of the consideration rule. It is unclear when or how courts will use the reliance doctrine. It does seem clear that courts talk more about § 90 than actually find liability based on an application of the section. Those who assert it usually lose. However, many states have accepted the doctrine, and courts always could develop it much more.

Consideration — conclusions: This brief essay is only a quick introduction to the complexities of consideration. The rules in any particular state would require research and difficult analysis. In many states, there is enough contradiction so we cannot state any rule or rules of consideration. There are good treatments of the doctrine in Corbin and Williston, Farnsworth and Murray. The important thing is to recognize when you face a consideration problem so you will see that you need to research it.

No matter how many pages we devote to the subject, we must be modest about claiming to have captured the intricacy of the consideration doctrine. Arthur Corbin devoted a good part of his professional life to thinking about the doctrine.

However, at § 109 of the one volume edition taken from his magnificent treatise on Contracts, Professor Corbin begins,

> [We must] discover ... our doctrine of "consideration" from the reports and records of recent times, containing as they do the customs, the decisions, the doctrines, and the reasoning of the men who have been the ministers of justice.
>
> The reports and records of recent times! Courts and jurisdictions scattered over all the continents and the seven seas! Cases by the million! Libraries so labyrinthine as to require a guide! The leaves of the books like the leaves of the trees! Who can now read all the reports of cases dealing with the law of consideration for informal purposes, stating the reasons deemed sufficient for enforcing such promises, laying down the doctrines and constructing the definitions? Certainly not the writer of this volume. He has merely read enough of them to feel well assured that the reasons for enforcing informal promises are many, that the doctrine of consideration is many doctrines, that no definition can rightly be set up as the one and only correct definition, and that the law of contract is an evolutionary product that has changed with time and circumstance and that must ever continue so to change.

4. THE CONDITIONAL GIFT REVISITED

The next case revisits, for the third time, the problem of the conditional gift, but also provides a transition to our investigation of a doctrine in which post-promise reliance serves to justify enforcing a promise.

KIRKSEY v. KIRKSEY

8 Ala. 131 (S. Ct. of Ala. 1845)

Assumpsit by the defendant, against the plaintiff in error. The question is presented in this court, upon a case agreed, which shows the following facts:

The plaintiff was the wife of defendant's brother, but had for some time been a widow, and had several children. In 1840, the plaintiff resided on public land, under a contract of lease, she had held over, and was comfortably settled, and would have attempted to secure the land she lived on. The defendant resided in Talladega county, some sixty or seventy miles off. On the 10th October, 1840, he wrote to her the following letter:

> *Dear sister Antillico — Much to my mortification, I heard, that brother Henry was dead, and one of his children. I know that your situation is one*

of grief and difficulty. You had a bad chance before, but a great deal worse now. I should like to come and see you, but cannot with convenience at present.... I do not know whether you have a preference on the place you live on or not. If you had, I would advise you to obtain your preference, and sell the land and quit the country, as I understand it is very unhealthy, and I know society is very bad. If you will come down and see me, I will let you have a place to raise your family, and I have more open land than I can tend; and on account of your situation, and that of your family, I feel like I want you and the children to do well.

Within a month or two after the receipt of this letter, the plaintiff abandoned her possession, without disposing of it, and removed with her family, to the residence of the defendant, who put her in comfortable houses and gave her land to cultivate for two years, at the end of which time he notified her to remove, and put her in a house not comfortable, in the woods, which he afterwards required her to leave.

A verdict being found for the plaintiff, for two hundred dollars, the above facts were agreed, and if they will sustain the action, the judgment is to be affirmed, otherwise it is to be reversed.

ORMOND, J. The inclination of my mind, is, that the loss and inconvenience, which the plaintiff sustained in breaking up and moving to the defendant's, a distance of sixty miles, is a sufficient consideration to support the promise, to furnish her with a house, and land to cultivate, until she could raise her family. My brothers, however, think that the promise on the part of the defendant was a mere gratuity, and that an action will not lie for its breach.

The judgment of the Court below must therefore be reversed, pursuant to the agreement of the parties.

NOTES AND QUESTIONS

1. *Distinctions*: Does this case differ significantly from *Hamer v. Sidway*? In both, a relative with wealth wants to influence the behavior of a family member "for his (or her) own good." In both, the one receiving the promise had expectations and relied. Shouldn't courts decide the cases the same way?

2. *Modern approaches*: In the 1990s is it likely that courts would decide *Kirksey v. Kirksey* the same way for the same reasons? Could Sister Antillico rely on the estoppel doctrine enunciated in the next case?

ANDREW D. RICKETTS, EXECUTOR v. KATIE SCOTHORN

57 Neb. 51, 77 N.W. 365 (1898)

SULLIVAN, J. In the district court of Lancaster county the plaintiff Katie Scothorn recovered judgment against the defendant Andrew D. Ricketts, as executor of the last will and testament of John C. Ricketts, deceased. The action was based upon a promissory note, of which the following is a copy:

> *May the first, 1891. I promise to pay to Katie Scothorn on demand, $2,000, to be at 6 per cent per annum.*
>
> *J. C. Ricketts.*

In the petition the plaintiff alleges that the consideration for the execution of the note was that she should surrender her employment as bookkeeper for Mayer Bros. and cease to work for a living. She also alleges that the note was given to induce her to abandon her occupation, and that, relying on it, and on the annual interest, as a means of support, she gave up the employment in which she was then engaged. These allegations of the petition are denied by the executor. The material facts are undisputed. They are as follows: John C. Ricketts, the maker of the note, was the grandfather of the plaintiff. Early in May, — presumably on the day the note bears date, — he called on her at the store where she was working. What transpired between them is thus described by Mr. Flodene, one of the plaintiff's witnesses:

> A. Well the old gentleman came in there one morning about 9 o'clock, — probably a little before or a little after, but early in the morning, — and he unbuttoned his vest and took out a piece of paper in the shape of a note; that is the way it looked to me; and he says to Miss Scothorn, "I have fixed out something that you have not got to work any more." He says, "None of my grandchildren work and you don't have to."
>
> Q. Where was she?
>
> A. She took the piece of paper and kissed him; and kissed the old gentleman and commenced to cry.

It seems Miss Scothorn immediately notified her employer of her intention to quit work and that she did soon after abandon her occupation. The mother of the plaintiff was a witness and testified that she had a conversation with her father, Mr. Ricketts, shortly after the note was executed in which he informed her that he had given the note to the plaintiff to enable her to quit work; that none of his grandchildren worked and he did not think she ought to. For something more than a year the plaintiff was without an occupation; but in September, 1892, with the consent of her grandfather, and by his assistance, she secured a position as bookkeeper with Messrs. Funke & Ogden. On June 8, 1894, Mr. Ricketts died. He had paid one year's interest on the note, and a short time before his death expressed regret that he had not been able to pay the balance. In the summer or fall of 1892 he stated to his daughter, Mrs. Scothorn, that if he could sell his farm in Ohio he would pay the note out of the proceeds. He at no time repudiated the obligation. We quite agree with counsel for the defendant that upon this evidence there was nothing to submit to the jury, and that a verdict should have been directed peremptorily for one of the parties. The testimony of Flodene and Mrs. Scothorn, taken together, conclusively establishes the fact that the note was not given in consideration of the plaintiff pursuing, or agreeing to pursue, any particular line of conduct. There was no promise on the part of the plaintiff to do or refrain from doing anything. Her right to the money promised in the note was not made to depend upon an abandonment of her employment with Mayer Bros. and future abstention from like service. Mr. Ricketts made no condition, requirement, or request. He exacted no *quid pro quo*. He gave the note as a gratuity and looked for nothing in return. So far as the evidence discloses, it was his purpose to place the plaintiff in a position of independence where she could work or remain idle as she might choose. The abandonment by Miss Scothorn of her position as bookkeeper was altogether voluntary. It was not an act done in fulfillment of any contract obligation assumed when she accepted the note. The instrument in suit being given without any valuable consideration, was nothing more than a promise to make a gift in the future of the sum of money therein named. Ordinarily, such promises are not enforceable even when put in the form of a promissory note. But it has often been held that an action on a note given to a church, college, or other like institution, upon the faith of which money has been expended or obligations incurred, could not be successfully defended on the ground of a want of consideration.

In this class of cases the note in suit is nearly always spoken of as a gift or donation, but the decision is generally put on the ground that the expenditure of money or assumption of liability by the donee, on the faith of the promise, constitutes a valuable and sufficient consideration. It seems to us that the true reason is the preclusion of the defendant, under the doctrine of estoppel, to deny the consideration. Such seems to be the view of the matter taken by the supreme court of Iowa in the case of *Simpson Centenary College v. Tuttle*, 71 Ia. 596, where Rothrock, J., speaking for the court, said: "Where a note, however, is based on a promise to give for the support of the objects referred to, it may still be open to this defense [want of consideration], unless it shall appear that the donee has, prior to any revocation, entered into engagements or made expenditures based on such promise, so that he must suffer loss or injury if the note is not paid. This is based on the equitable principle that, after allowing the donee to incur obligations on the faith that the note would be paid, the donor would be estopped from pleading want of consideration."

Under the circumstances of this case, is there an equitable estoppel which ought to preclude the defendant from alleging that the note in controversy is lacking in one of the essential elements of a valid contract? We think there is. An estoppel *in pais* is defined to be "a right arising from acts, admissions, or conduct which have induced a change of position in accordance with the real or apparent intention of the party against whom they are alleged." Mr. Pomeroy has formulated the following definition: "Equitable estoppel is the effect of the voluntary conduct of a party whereby he is absolutely precluded, both at law and in equity, from asserting rights which might perhaps have otherwise existed, either of property, or contract, or of remedy, as against another person who in good faith relied upon such conduct, and has been led thereby to change his position for the worse, and who on his part acquires some corresponding right either of property, of contract, or of remedy." (2 Pomeroy, Equity Jurisprudence 804.)

According to the undisputed proof, as shown by the record before us, the plaintiff was a working girl, holding a position in which she earned a salary of $10 per week. Her grandfather, desiring to put her in a position of independence, gave her the note, accompanying it with the remark that his other grandchildren did not work, and that she would not be obliged to work any longer. In effect he suggested that she might abandon her employment and rely in the future upon the bounty which he promised. He, doubtless, desired that she should give up her occupation, but whether he did or not, it is entirely certain that he contemplated such action on her part as a reasonable and probable consequence of his gift. Having intentionally influenced the plaintiff to alter her position for the worse on the faith of the note being paid when due, it would be grossly inequitable to permit the maker, or his executor, to resist payment on the ground that the promise was given without consideration. The petition charges the elements of an equitable estoppel, and the evidence conclusively establishes them. If errors intervened at the trial they could not have been prejudicial. A verdict for the defendant would be unwarranted.

The judgment is right and is affirmed.

NOTES AND QUESTIONS

1. *Restatement § 90*: Section 90 is probably the most influential single section of the Restatement. The original version read,

> Section 90. Promise Reasonably Inducing Definite and Substantial Action.
> A promise which the promisor should reasonably expect to induce action or forbearance of a definite and substantial character on the part of the promisee and which does induce such action or forbearance is binding if injustice can be avoided only by enforcement of the promise.

Compare Restatement (Second) of Contracts, § 90. How, if at all, is the text modified? What would the result in *Ricketts v. Scothern* be under the new Restatement? How is that different from the result reached in the case?

2. *Of Restatements and political compromises*: Section 90 is widely attributed to Samual Williston's successful efforts, in the first Restatement, to adopt the Holmesian view as the definition of consideration. Holmes, however, had never claimed that his view was a correct restatement of all the holdings. Those holdings reflected several different and conflicting views of the nature of consideration. As a result, when Williston, as the reporter for Restatement (First) of Contracts imposed the Holmesian view as *the* definition of consideration, it

left unaccounted for several well known cases enforcing promises which lacked consideration under Holmes' test. Section 90 was his attempt to account for the results of these cases. Relatively few of the cases used the language of estoppel, with *Ricketts v. Scothern* being one of the few exceptions. Today promissory estoppel is thought of as being largely the invention of the Restatement (First). It could be seen as an example of the Restatement actually changing the law, though perhaps it just changes the rationale (from consideration to estoppel) for results that would have been reached in any event.

3. ***Statutory construction of § 90***: Is serious reliance enough or must we take the clause about "avoiding injustice" seriously? If we must apply all of the terms of the section, what does this last clause mean?

(a) Suppose that before his death, John C. Ricketts discovered that Katie had left her career as a bookkeeper for Mayer Bros. and become a mass murderer or a prostitute. Could John or his executor defend against enforcement of the promise in either or both of these cases? Suppose she had become an advocate of women's suffrage or gone to law school with the plan of becoming a lawyer? Assume that her grandfather thought these were outrageous things for a woman to do.

(b) In *Kirksey v. Kirksey*, why did the brother-in-law invite his brother's widow to live in a house on his land, give her a comfortable house, then give her a house in the woods, and finally notify her to remove? Suppose "Dear Sister Antillico" was an impossible person to live near. She complained constantly and she could not control her children. Can injustice then be avoided only by forcing the brother-in-law to pay damages based on his promise to let Antillico "have a place to raise" her family, at least until her children are grown?

The cynical reader might see another explanation for the situation. The brother-in-law may have been interested in Antillico sexually. She resisted his advances or he tired of her, and then he tried to get rid of her. Wouldn't such a story be relevant to avoiding injustice? However, suppose both stories were true — she proved to be impossible to live with or be near, and he had tried to exploit her sexually. What now should a judge do with the case? Recall Chafee's categories in our introduction. Do you get a whiff of the smell of a dismal swamp?

(c) Suppose the grandfather or the brother-in-law tried to perform their promises but then faced a financial crisis. Each had to pay for an exceedingly expensive operation to save the lives of young children who were related to Katie and Antillico. As a result, there was no money or property left to carry out the promise. Under any or all of the doctrines we have considered which bear on the bait problem, should a court consider the merits of those who would get the money or property if the promise were not enforced? Could it do this legitimately under any of the doctrines other than Restatement of Contracts, § 90?

4. ***The impact of § 90 in family cases***: We can get a very rough idea of the impact of § 90 if we look at reported cases which cite it. The American Law Institute has collected references in *The Restatement in the Courts* until 1976, and

since then in pocket parts to the Restatement of Contracts. Of course, reported cases do not necessarily reflect the impact of any rule of law. There may be many trial court decisions influenced by a doctrine which never prompt written opinions and never get appealed. Lawyers may give advice or negotiate based on their view of what a court would or might do if the case ever were litigated and appealed. Rules may influence a folk-view of what is right and wrong so people accept a situation and do not complain. Nonetheless, reported cases are fairly easy to count, and they are the best indication we have of the impact of § 90.

From 1932 to 1978, there were about 350 cases that cited Restatement of Contracts, § 90 reported in the ALI publications. Only six of these cases involve bait offered by one family member to another. By far, most of the cases involve commercial situations concerning long-term continuing relationships. Jay M. Feinman surveyed cases involving Restatement of Contracts, § 90, by looking at the cases reported from 1967 to 1983, in the West Digest system. He states "[a]lthough my survey of the recent case law revealed a few ... family promises, promissory estoppel cases now arise chiefly in commercial contracts." Farber and Matheson report "[d]espite its tentative origins and its initial restriction to donative promises, promissory estoppel is regularly applied to the gamut of commercial contexts." We will consider promissory estoppel in commercial contexts later in the course.

5. *Expectation or reliance remedies?* In *Hamer v. Sidway* and *Ricketts v. Scothorn* the courts found family promises created liability. In both cases courts gave remedies designed to protect the expectation interest. Have the courts been too generous? Why should a family member who has relied on a nonbusiness promise recover more than compensation for his reliance?

Much of the debate about reliance remedies in family cases was prompted by the two Restatements of Contracts. The first Restatement of Contracts seemed not to recognize the possibility of reliance remedies. The Restatement (Second) of Contracts, however, does recognize this possibility. An exchange between Samuel Williston and Mr. Coudert in the course of the American Law Institute's discussion of § 90 of the first Restatement of Contracts has achieved a certain notoriety in the world of contracts teachers. Williston offered an example. An uncle promised Johnny, his nephew, $1,000 so that he could buy a car. Johnny then contracted with an auto dealer to buy a car for $1,000. Several members of the ALI, in good law teacher fashion, changed the facts to test the principle. They asked for Williston's opinion about the result under § 90 if the nephew bought a car for only $500. Williston responded "If Johnny had done what he was expected to do, or is acting within the limits of his uncle's expectation, I think the uncle would be liable for $1,000; but not otherwise." He explained, "Either the promise is binding or it is not. If the promise is binding, it has to be enforced as it is made."

Fuller and Perdue argue that as a matter of policy Williston is wrong. They say that the reasons that courts measure damages for breach of contract by the expectation interest do not apply when promises are enforced only because people have relied on them.

> The suggestion that the expectation interest is adopted as a kind of surrogate for the reliance interest because of the difficulty of proving reliance can scarcely be applicable to a situation where we actually insist on proof of reliance, and indeed, reliance of a "definite and substantial character." The notion that the expectancy is granted as compensation for foregoing the opportunity to enter other similar contracts is also without application in this situation, if for no other reason than because no contract is here "entered" at all. Finally the policy in favor of facilitating reliance can scarcely be extended to all promises indiscriminately. Any such policy must presuppose that reliance in the particular situation will normally have some general utility. Where we are dealing with "exchanges" or "bargains" it is easy to discern this utility since such transactions form the very mechanism by which production is organized in a capitalistic society. There seems no basis for assuming any such general utility in the promises coming under § 90, since they are restricted only by a negative definition — they are not bargains.

Restatement (Second) of Contracts, § 90 largely accepts Fuller and Perdue and rejects Williston on the remedy appropriate when promises are enforced on the basis of reliance.

5. THE STATUTE OF FRAUDS AND FAMILY "BAIT" PROMISES

Once again we turn to the family bait problem to illustrate another issue. Perhaps the best example of a formal legal requirement is the rule that certain contracts must be in writing to be enforceable. Such a requirement runs counter to the way people often act. People make oral promises and rely on them. This often happens in situations where the parties are supposed to trust one another. Asking for a written contract might seem an attack on the integrity of the other party. In family transactions, particularly, people feel they should trust one another. It might seem greedy to press a relative to make a will, a conveyance or a written detailed contract. Legislators and judges can insist on written documents. On the other hand, they can offer aid to those who have been trusting. Sometimes it looks as if they are trying to do both at once.

Lawyers speak of requirements that certain contracts be in writing as "Statute of Frauds requirements." The English "Act for the Prevention of Frauds and Perjuries" was enacted in 1677. It contained twenty five sections designed to control perjury by requiring written evidence of conveyances, wills, trusts and contracts. Many of the patterns found in this early statute are still with us.

The 1677 Act provided that a person may not sue for breach of several categories of contracts "unless the agreement upon which such action shall be brought, or some memorandum or note thereof, shall be in writing, and signed by the party to be charged therewith." You should notice several things. The complete contract itself does not have to be in writing. It is enough that there is a memorandum or note. One might write a letter describing an earlier oral agreement. This probably would satisfy the requirement of the statute.

Both parties do not have to sign the writing. Only "the party to be charged" need sign it. This means that one who signed can be bound although the other is not — because he or she never signed. (You should be careful here, however, since some contemporary statutes require that both parties sign writings, at least with respect to some kinds of transactions.)

And, finally, the English statute, unlike those in some American states, does not say that an oral agreement within the statute is void. It says it is unenforceable in courts. This distinction has various legal consequences. For example, Rule 8(c) of the Federal Rules of Civil Procedure provides that a litigant must raise the statute of frauds by way of affirmative defense. If a defendant fails to raise it, a court will enforce an oral contract although it is within the statute.

What contracts must be in writing? Today in most American states those contracts listed by the original English statute still must be in writing. They are:

(1) a contract of an executor or administrator to answer for a duty of his decedent (the executor-administrator provision);

(2) a contract to answer for the duty of another (the suretyship provision);

(3) a contract made upon consideration of marriage (the marriage provision);

(4) a contract for the sale of an interest in land (the land contract provision);

(5) a contract that cannot be performed within one year from its making (the one-year provision); and

(6) a contract for the sale of goods in excess of a certain value. The English statute has been superseded by § 201 of the U.C.C., which generally requires a writing when the contract price is $500 or more.

The Statute of Frauds involves both the benefits and the costs of form. The statute announces that it has an *evidentiary* purpose — it is to prevent perjury. Required writings may serve to *caution* people and remind them they are making a commitment. Many people seem to believe in the magical significance of signing a writing. It is an important symbol of commitment. They may well think that if they do not sign, they are not bound. The writing requirement also may help *channel* behavior. Those who want to make a binding conveyance, will or contract of the type that must be within the statute can do so. As always, formal requirements also have costs. Not everyone knows that these contracts must be in writing. People can be fooled and rely on oral promises.

The Statute of Frauds is a statute. Virtually every American jurisdiction has legislation patterned on the 1677 English Act, and many legislatures have added writing requirements governing other contracts as well. Nonetheless, the courts have not given the usual deference to this legislation. To a great extent, they have treated the Statute of Frauds as if it were a common law principle and developed it incrementally. The courts have not been sympathetic to writing requirements, and they have worked hard to limit the impact of these provisions. However, at times the rule can block enforcement of an oral contract when the plaintiff has what seems a good case but for the statute.

Professor Corbin suggests the difficulty in generalizing about the Statute of Frauds:

> There is much conflict and lack of uniformity. Two conflicting tendencies have been evident for the whole two hundred and seventy years. One of these is to regard the statute as a great and noble preventive of fraud and to apply it against the plaintiff with a good conscience even in cases where no doubt exists that the defendant made the promise with which he is charged. The other and much more frequent one is to enforce promises that a jury would find to have been in fact made, and if necessary to this end to narrow the operation of the statute. This narrowing of application was sometimes accompanied by general words of encomium for the great statute; but in recent years the courts nearly always say nothing on the subject except what may be necessary to the business actually in hand, the enforcement of the promise. The narrowing process has been in part one of supposed interpretation of language and in part one of permitting the jury to determine the application of the statute by a general verdict under instructions that do not in fact hamper the jury in its effort to do "justice."

We cannot provide anything approaching a comprehensive analysis of the statute as interpreted by courts. Nonetheless, the following few pages depict some of the ironies and fine-line drawing that have resulted from the effort to offset the costs of imposing formal requirements.

Contracts not to be performed within one year: The statute calls for contracts performed over time to be in writing. How do we know if we have one? An employment contract calling for the employee to work 367 days would fall within the statute. There is no way the employee can perform it in less than a year. However, courts will not look into the transaction to determine the likelihood that performance will take more than a year. It is enough that there is no legal barrier to performance within that time. For example, suppose Willie's uncle promises to pay $5,000 per year to Willie for the remainder of Willie's life if Willie will run Uncle's store for the next six months. The contract is not within the Statute of Frauds. Courts have construed the statute to apply only to contracts which a party cannot possibly perform within a year. Although Willie is still young, it is possible that he might die within a year from the time they made the contract. If this happened, the uncle would complete his performance in less than a year.

Similarly, suppose an oral contract for the construction of a building which would be impossible for anyone to build in less than five years. This oral contract would not fall within the statute. It would be enforceable, even though oral, since legally the builder would not breach the contract if it found a way to complete it within 364 days, and the court would not consider the practical feasibility of such a pace of construction.

Contracts to answer for debts of another: The law has sought to protect sureties who agree to pay debts of others if they fail to do so. There is an important exception, however. Suppose Edward Entrepreneur's business has suffered losses. Bert Banker, to whom Edward owes $10,000, is threatening to foreclose his mortgage on Edward's factory and put him out of business. Sam Samaritan is one of Edward's major suppliers. He thinks that foreclosure will ruin Entrepreneur, cost Samaritan a good customer, and make certain that Entrepreneur will pay only a fraction of what he owes Samaritan for past deliveries. Samaritan and Banker orally agree that if Banker refrains from foreclosing, Samaritan will pay the debt if Entrepreneur fails to do so.

Courts have said that this oral contract is not within the statute. Samaritan would seem to have made an oral promise to answer for the debt of another. However, courts have developed an exception to this provision known as the "main purpose" or "leading object" rule. They reason that the policy of the provision is that often people promise to pay another's debt for sentimental or gratuitous purposes. Where a promisor's main purpose is his or her own economic well being, there is less need for protection. Courts then will enforce the promise. Bert Banker can sue Sam although his promise to pay Eddie's debt was oral. Had Sam been Eddie's old army buddy, with no financial stake in Eddie's business, Sam's oral promise would have been unenforceable.

What kind of a writing will be enough, and what is a signature?: Certainly, the statute is satisfied if parties prepare a document they call a "Contract," which contains all the terms of their agreement, and which they both sign at the bottom. However, how much less will do? Suppose Vera Vendor orally agrees to sell her farm, Plumacre, to Pete Purchaser for $150,000. They do not sign a written contract. One week after the agreement, Vera dictates a memorandum detailing her agreement with Pete. Her secretary transcribes it. Vera proofreads the transcribed memorandum, initials it, and places it in her files. One week later, she calls Pete to tell him that the deal is off. Pete sues Vera for specific performance and through pretrial discovery obtains a copy of the memorandum. Does it satisfy the Statute of Frauds?

This contract is one for the sale of an interest in land, and so the Statute of Frauds requires it to be in writing. Whether Vera's memorandum is enough depends on the language of the particular statute and its construction by the courts in the state. The memorandum initialed by Vera would appear to satisfy the English statute of 1677. It required either a written contract or "some note or memorandum thereof" signed by the party to be charged. Courts have held initials satisfy the requirement of a signature. However, the rule in some states would be different. For example, the Wisconsin statute governing conveyances of land requires a written instrument signed by all parties. Vera's memorandum would not be enough in Wisconsin and in other states with similar statutes.

What must be in the memorandum? Restatement (Second) of Contracts § 131 says that the writing must (a) reasonably identify the subject matter of the contract, (b) be sufficient to indicate that the parties have made a contract with respect to that subject, and (c) state with reasonable certainty the essential terms of the unperformed promises in the contract. Often these tests leave matters uncertain. Something less than the high point of drafting will do, but how much less is unclear. A series of memoranda, taken together, might satisfy the statute.

The effect of part performance and promises to convey land: Courts often depart from the requirements of form to relieve undue hardship, and the Statute of Frauds cases are no exception. The so-called part performance doctrine is a major example. This doctrine developed in cases involving land. Not surprisingly, one area where the Statute of Frauds requires a writing is transactions concerning interests in land. Land is economically important. In England, where the rule developed, land ownership played a key role in the culture as well, often determining social rank. Given the importance of the transaction and the fact that many third parties may have an interest in who owns real estate or who has mortgages or other interests, contracts involving land seem perfect candidates for a strong formal requirement. However, at least in some situations, courts have recognized the claims of those who have relied on oral promises to convey. In fact, the Court of Chancery began to fashion the doctrine of part performance only nine years after the passage of the Statute of Frauds. We will consider this way of getting around the writing requirement in this section. We will look first at some early Wisconsin cases, then at an attempt at statutory codification of the part-performance doctrine, and finally at the courts' treatment of the statute.

The Rodman case: The first Wisconsin case we will consider is *Rodman v. Rodman*.[39] In *Rodman*, a son sought specific performance of an oral contract which he had made with his father. The son alleged that his father had promised to make a will leaving real estate to him. The trial court entered a judgment for the estate and the son appealed. The Supreme Court of Wisconsin affirmed the trial court's decision.

The facts revealed that the elder Rodman (age 67) owned a 500 acre farm. He wanted to cease active operation of the farm. In 1873, he persuaded Winfield, his 22 year old son, to return to the farm. Winfield was to operate the farm on shares and they were to live in the homestead together. Winfield married soon after they made this arrangement. Winfield managed the farm for 22 years until his father's death in 1895. The father attempted to make a will in 1881 which would have left the farm to Winfield. The will, however, was invalid because the father did not sign it in the presence of two witnesses. Winfield testified that his

[39]112 Wis. 378, 88 N.W. 218 (1901).

father told him that if he stayed home and cared for his father, he would get the homestead. Winfield and his father had a dispute in 1886, and the father said that Winfield and his wife must leave the farm. Two older sons resolved the quarrel.

The trial court ruled that Winfield had not proved an oral contract to make a will. The Supreme Court found this finding was not against the weight of the evidence. The Supreme Court pointed out that when Winfield and his father had their dispute, Winfield did not make any claim of contractual rights. They made the alleged contract in 1873, but the father attempted to execute a will to carry out the contract eight years later. During that time, an earlier will existed with provisions inconsistent with the alleged contract.

The Supreme Court also affirmed the finding because, even if Winfield had proved an oral contract to make a will, it would have been invalid under the Statute of Frauds. The alleged contract concerned the transfer of an interest in real estate. Winfield's work on the farm for 22 years did not serve to take the case out of the provisions of the Statute of Frauds. The father had never given Winfield exclusive possession of the premises. Mere performance of services is not enough. The father remained in possession of the property until his death. The court pointed out:

> During all of this time the plaintiff and Robert L. Rodman [the father] lived upon the homestead, the plaintiff doing the work necessary to the operation of the farm and the gathering of the crops, but the father remaining the final director of farm operations, in that he dictated what kind of crops should be raised, rented parts of the farm to third persons at various times, and deeded two acres ... to a third person. The father also made and paid for all substantial repairs and improvements in the place, and paid all taxes, except the road tax, which was worked out by the plaintiff.... It is true that plaintiff also lived upon the premises, but such possession as he had was subordinate to his father's superior possession and was plainly due to the sharing agreement and not to the alleged contract to will.

The Powell case: The second Wisconsin case is *Estate of Powell.*[40] Lottie and George Wilcox sued for specific performance of an oral contract to transfer a farm to them by will or by deed. The executor and beneficiaries under the deceased's will appealed. The decree for Lottie and George was affirmed.

Lottie alleged that her uncle had promised to transfer a farm to her if she and her husband would work it on shares until the uncle's death. Lottie was the child of her uncle's sister who died when she was two years old. The uncle took her into his home and reared her as his own child. Lottie "performed services in the home as great as any daughter could." The uncle's son was "demented." Lottie cared for him, attending to his personal cleanliness. She married George Wilcox

---

[40] 206 Wis. 513, 240 N.W. 122 (1932).

who rented on shares a large highly improved, well-stocked farm. The uncle asked them to return to his farm, and they moved back and remained until the uncle's death nearly twenty years later.

The Court observed:

> The Powell farm was ill-kept and run down; the buildings were dilapidated, except the barn which was unfinished; it was not nearly so attractive or remunerative as a renting proposition as the farm the Wilcoxes left. Powell [the uncle] lived at a small hamlet a half mile from the farm, but a room was always kept ready for his use in the house on the farm. Mrs. Wilcox did his washing mostly and looked after him in a general way until his marriage eight or nine years before his death. From the time they went on the Powell farm the Wilcoxes worked and managed it as they would a farm of their own. Wilcox cleaned it and kept it clean of quack grass and Canada thistles; cleaned out fence rows; built new fences; repaired the house and kept it in repair; helped finish a barn in process of construction; built a hog pen, hen house, and other outbuildings; tore down and removed dilapidated outbuildings; did work on a silo; made a driveway; wired outbuildings for electric lights; grubbed out an old and set out a new orchard and small fruit; bred the scrub cattle into a fifteen-sixteenths and better blooded Guernsey herd; kept purebred China hogs, — all beyond the work and conduct of a tenant and without being paid for the extra work or reimbursed his expenditures. Powell paid for most of the material that went into the improvements and did some work upon them, but the evidence tends to show the aggregate value of Wilcox's work and material not paid for or reimbursed amounted to upwards of $4,000. The receipts of the farm were divided equally between Powell and Wilcox, without any strict or regular accounting. Powell's income from it was far beyond what would be realized from renting on shares to an ordinary tenant, as Wilcox was an excellent farmer.

Four disinterested people testified that Powell said "Lottie and George would have the farm some day...." "Lottie was to him a daughter, nearest and dearest to him of any one on earth...." "When Powell was through with the farm it went to Lottie." Others testified, however, about statements Powell made after his marriage that the Wilcoxes had no claim to the farm. These statements were made when the new wife was suspicious of the Wilcoxes and hostile to them.

Lottie and George testified that Powell had entered into an agreement with them before they moved back to his farm. They were to repair the place as if it were their own. They went back to the farm solely because of the agreement, and they expected Powell to will the farm to her.

The Supreme Court of Wisconsin said that a trial court should not decree specific performance of a contract unless the plaintiff establishes the promise by clear, satisfactory, and convincing proof. However, "[t]he trial judge might properly find the evidentiary facts as above stated, and we consider that their cumulative force warranted the inference of ultimate fact that a contract to transfer the farm was made." The statements made after Powell's marriage were self-serving.

Then the Supreme Court turned to the Statute of Frauds issue:

> It is urged that there was no such partial performance by the respondents [Lottie and George Wilcox] as to warrant specific enforcement of the contract because the proof does not show that the respondents entered upon the land as and solely as a result of the contract.... But there is testimony of the respondents themselves to the precise point that they did so enter, and the circumstances indicate that they would not have gone upon the farm as mere tenants and that they did not so enter. It is urged that possession alone and that services alone do not constitute sufficient performance. While it may be that no one act or no one class of acts of the respondents would alone have constituted sufficient partial performance to warrant specific enforcement, their acts in the aggregate throughout the twenty years that were beyond the requirements of ordinary tenancy and husbandry were such that to deny them specific enforcement would operate as a fraud upon them, and the prevention of fraud is the basis of and reason for the equitable relief of specific performance.
>
> ....
>
> [I]t is to be regretted that the wishes of the testator, which were entirely reasonable and which he endeavored to place in legal and binding form, failed to become effective by reason of a failure to properly witness the will, of which he knew nothing. These matters, however, are of little moment in the consideration of the issues of this case.

The 1969 statute: In 1969, Wisconsin enacted a statute drafted by a committee of the State Bar Association of Wisconsin, presumably to clarify the extent of the rule which had emerged from cases like *Rodman* and *Powell*. The legislation stated both the writing requirement and the exceptions to protect reliance on oral promises. Section 706.01(1) says that subject to a few exceptions, Chapter 706 of the statutes "shall govern every transaction by which any interest in land is created, aliened, mortgaged, assigned or may be otherwise affected in law or equity." The major exceptions are wills and leases for less than a year. Section 706.02(1) provides, in relevant part, as follows:

706.02 Formal requisites. (1) Transactions under § 706.01(1) shall not be valid unless evidenced by a conveyance which:
  (a) Identifies the parties; and
  (b) Identifies the land; and
  (c) Identifies the interest conveyed,...; and
  (d) Is signed by or on behalf of each of the grantors; and

(e) Is signed by or on behalf of all parties, if a lease or contract to convey; and

(f) ...

(g) ...

Section 706.04 states the counterrules. It provides,

> **706.04 Equitable relief**. A transaction which does not satisfy one or more of the requirements of § 706.02 may be enforceable in whole or in part under doctrines of equity, provided all of the elements of the transaction are clearly and satisfactorily proved and, in addition:
>
> **(1)** The deficiency of the conveyance may be supplied by reformation in equity; or
>
> **(2)** The party against whom enforcement is sought would be unjustly enriched if enforcement of the transaction were denied; or
>
> **(3)** The party against whom enforcement is sought is equitably estopped from asserting the deficiency. A party may be so estopped whenever, pursuant to the transaction and in good faith reliance thereon, the party claiming estoppel has changed his position to his substantial detriment under circumstances such that the detriment so incurred may not be effectively recovered otherwise than by enforcement of the transaction, and either:
>
>> (a) The grantee has been admitted into substantial possession or use of the premises or has been permitted to retain such possession or use after termination of a prior right thereto; or
>>
>> (b) The detriment so incurred was incurred with the prior knowing consent or approval of the party sought to be estopped.

In addition, § 706.01(6) provides "[t]his chapter shall be liberally construed, in cases of conflict or ambiguity, so as to effectuate the intentions of parties who have acted in good faith."

NOTES AND QUESTIONS

1. *Examples of the part performance exception*: Other states have grappled with the reach of the part-performance exception to the Statute of Frauds. Consider, for example, *Seavey v. Drake*[41] where, as had been alleged in *Rodman*, a father made an oral promise to convey to his son. The son took possession of part of his father's land, built a house, barn and stable and made other improvements. He did all of this with his father's help. The father died, and the son brought a bill in equity for specific performance of an oral promise to

---

[41]62 N.H. 393 (1882).

convey the land. The son held his father's note for $200, and he alleged that he returned the note to his father after he took possession. The executor moved to dismiss the bill because there was an oral promise to convey land not supported by consideration. The court denied the motion. Equity removes the bar of the Statute of Frauds when there has been part performance. "[I]t is a fraud for the vendor to insist upon the absence of a written instrument, when he has permitted the contract to be partly executed." The absence of consideration is not important "for equity protects a parol gift of land equally with a parol agreement to sell it, if accompanied by possession, and the donee has made valuable improvements upon the property induced by the promise to give it." How, if at all, does *Seavey v. Drake* differ from the situation in *Rodman v. Rodman*?

Perhaps the most extreme example of the hard line is *Boone v. Coe*. W. H. Boone and J. T. Coe, the plaintiffs, were farmers living with their families in Kentucky. In the fall of 1909, the defendant, J. F. Coe[42], orally promised that if Boone and Coe would move to Texas and manage defendant's farm there for a year, they would receive a portion of the crops raised. Plaintiffs moved from Kentucky to Texas with their families, wagons, horses and camping outfit. The trip took 55 days. When they arrived, the defendant would not allow them to begin performing the contract, and they returned to Kentucky. They alleged that they:

> ... spent in going to Texas, in cash, the sum of $150; that the loss of time to plaintiffs and their teams [of horses] in making the trip to Texas was reasonably worth $8 a day for a period of 55 days, or the sum of $440; that the loss of time to them and their teams during the period they remained in Texas was $8 a day for 22 days, or $176; that they paid out in actual cash for transportation for themselves, families and teams from Texas to Kentucky, the sum of $211.80; that the loss of time to them and their teams in making the last named trip was reasonably worth the sum of $100; that in abandoning and giving up their homes and businesses in Kentucky, they had been damaged in the sum of $150, making a total damage of $1,387.80, for which judgment was asked.

Defendant's demurrer to the petition was sustained, and the trial court's decision was affirmed on appeal. The court explained that allowing such damages would be an indirect enforcement of the oral contract which was barred by the Statute of Frauds. Plaintiffs could sue in quantum meruit, but for such a recovery it "must appear that the defendant has actually received or will receive some benefit from the acts of part performance. It is immaterial that the plaintiff may have suffered a loss because he is unable to enforce his contract." "In the case under

---

[42]The opinion does not state his relationship to the plaintiff, J. T. Coe., but we can suspect that this is another family bait situation.

consideration, the plaintiffs merely sustained a loss. Defendant received no benefit." Would *Boone v. Coe* be decided differently under Wis Stat. § 706.04-(3)?

2. *The Restatement:*   Study § 139 of the Restatement (Second) of Contracts. How is it different from Wis. Stat. § 706.04? From Restatement, § 90?

3. *Restitution of benefits conferred under contracts made unenforceable by the Statute of Frauds*:

In *Montanaro Brothers Builders, Inc. v. Snow*,[43] the court said that:

> It is hornbook law that a party whose agreement is unenforceable under the Statute of Frauds or because of indefiniteness is generally entitled to restitution.... When a landowner relies upon the Statute of Frauds as a basis for repudiating his agreement, it is unjust to permit him to retain payments or services that he has received and to transfer nothing in return.... The plaintiffs' claim in restitution is not a claim arising out of an express or an implied contract but invokes instead an obligation, independent of contract, "based on equitable principles to operate whenever justice requires compensation to be made."

Restatement (Second) of Contracts, § 375 provides that one is not barred from restitution "because of the Statute of Frauds unless the Statute provides otherwise or its purpose would be frustrated by allowing restitution." When might the purpose of the Statute of Frauds be frustrated by restitution of benefits conferred? Why is there such a requirement? Doesn't an award of reliance damages under § 139 of the second Restatement always frustrate the purposes of the Statute of Frauds? Professor Knapp says "the Statute of Frauds, given three hundred years of judicial whittling-down, capped by the recent tendency to hold that the Statute bends to substantial reliance on an oral bargain" is a "rule that can be understood only in light of its exceptions." He then asks whether one should now ask "whether the exceptions together do not now make up 'the rule' with the former rule being itself relegated to the status of an exception."[44]

4. *Professional responsibility.*   Suppose a vendor made an oral agreement to convey but did not sign a written contract. Can the vendor's lawyer ethically defend the vendor's refusal to convey by asserting the Statute of Frauds? Can the lawyer ethically *refuse* to assert the Statute of Frauds as a defense to a claim against her client? Would it depend on why the vendor wants to back out of the oral arrangement?

5. *Contracts for the sale of goods*: "Transactions in goods" are now covered by Article 2 of the Uniform Commercial Code. Those who drafted it had a chance to consider the older writing requirement, and the various exceptions and

---

[43]190 Conn. 481, 460 A.2d 1297 (1983).

[44]Knapp, Book Review, 82 Michigan Law Review 932, 944-945 (1984).

constructions courts had fashioned. How did the drafters respond to problems such as the tension between the virtues of form and reliance on oral contracts? In addition to reading § 2-201, you should read the Official Comments. We will return to the study of the Statute of Frauds as it applies to a sale of goods later in these materials.

6. *CISG and the Statute of Frauds*: The CISG in Article 11 explicitly provides that contracts of sale need not be in writing. This is in keeping with the fact that the majority of the world's countries have no statute of frauds requirements. But the repudiation of writing requirements is significantly undercut by the fact that Article 96 authorizes a country to make a declaration that Articles of CISG that eliminate writing requirements are inoperative when one party has a place of business in the country making the declaration. However, the United States has not made a declaration under Article 96.

7. *Should we repeal the Statute of Frauds?* Many jurisdictions have modified or repealed the Statute of Frauds, including the United Kingdom, New Zealand, and several Canadian provinces. G.H.L. Fridman[45] conducted a study for the Ontario Law Reform Commission. He attacked the Statute and advocated repeal. He charges that the courts have had to

> ... engage upon casuistry and legal sophistry of the most blatant kind in order to avoid the consequences that would flow from what would otherwise be the logical and correct application of the statute's provisions. The statute has been the cause of the invention of an equitable doctrine [part performance] that, frankly and plainly, contradicts the statute and contravenes the law.... If there is one thing that would suggest that the present law is absurd, outdated, inconvenient, and unduly complex it is this doctrine. If the repeal of ... the Statute of Frauds would have the result of eradicating the doctrine of part performance, that alone would justify such repeal.... In the end what has emerged is what might be called a 'make-do-and-mend' type of justice. Such an approach ... cannot but encourage reasonable people to think less favorably of the law, and of a system of justice that allows, even promotes, such judicial chicanery.

Fridman asserts that the writing requirement serves no important purpose in today's world. He looks at Professor Fuller's functions of form — evidence, caution and channeling. He concludes that the Statute and its exceptions fail to attain enough of the benefits of these functions to justify its costs. We often do not gain evidence there was a contract and the nature of its terms. The Statute fails to cover some important contracts which are enforceable although oral. The

---

[45]Fridman, The Necessity for Writing in Contracts Within the Statute of Frauds, 35 University of Toronto Law Journal 43 (1983). Copyright University of Toronto Law Journal. Reprinted with permission.

Statute seems to cover other important contracts, but they are enforceable because they fall into one of the many exceptions to the rule.

Fridman concedes there may be something to the cautionary function, but he says that writers carry the argument too far.

> It may be true that people who have to enter into a written document take more care and pay more attention to what they are doing, but not necessarily. Every lawyer is familiar with the contracting party who signs without reading, only to find the true nature of his obligation later, if and when litigation is threatened.... The contracting party may not have read it ... because he was too lazy or disinclined to attempt to understand its meaning, or because he was acting in reliance upon the word of the other party or his own recollections of what was said or what was intended. For whatever reason, there are many parties who do not take any more care about contracting because the contract is written or is contained more or less in some written form than they do or would if the contract were merely oral.

Fridman also questions the channeling function:

> Just as the fact that a contract is in writing, or is evidenced by writing, does not always lead to more careful consideration of what one is doing, so, too, the fact that there has to be some kind of writing may not necessarily bring home to a party that he is bound, or may not always and sufficiently distinguish a binding obligation from one that is not. The man in the street often has peculiar ideas about whether a contract has to be in writing. He may think that, unless there is a document, there is no contract, when — save for special situations ... — this is not the case. He may, on the other hand, regard "a man's word as his bond" and so think that he has a valid, enforceable contract when, because of the Statute of Frauds, or something else, he has not.

Moreover, the Statute opens the possibility of fraud when a buyer signs a writing but the seller does not. The buyer cannot hold the seller to the contract, but the seller can hold the buyer who signed. Thus, the seller may look for a better price while having the buyer's deal to fall back on if he does not find a better purchaser. Most buyers would not be aware of what they had done, and so a seller could trick a buyer into this kind of disadvantageous situation.

Fridman concludes, "[w]hether the ultimate answer is to allow all contracts to be oral or to make it mandatory for all contracts to be in writing, the conclusion that is ineluctable is that the provisions of the Statute of Frauds dealing with contracts will have to be repealed."

Does Professor Fridman convince you? Whether requiring a writing promotes evidence, caution and channeling is, in part, an empirical question. From where does Professor Fridman get his facts? Furthermore, what is wrong with a rule partially offset by a counterrule? We begin with a rule that contracts for the sale of land must be in a signed writing. Then we fashion a limited counterrule that says in exceptional cases where our writing rule would produce clearly unfair results, we might enforce an oral promise. Does this necessarily or usually lead to bad results?

6.   FAMILY BAIT: REACHING THE RIGHT RESULT BY MANIPULATING DOCTRINES OF CONTRACT FORMATION

Suppose a father makes a statement which might or might not be a promise to make a present gift, write a will, or create a trust. A member of his family relies on this statement. Then the father fails to act. If you represent the father in such a situation, a handy tool is the idea of a "unilateral contract." Most simply, I promise a reward if you will do something I want done. You do not commit yourself to do this something, and so you are free to back out at any time. However, suppose that you do not back out but perform. This, usually, is an easy case. I made a promise and you gave me what I had demanded. When this happened it created a binding contract. You have earned the reward, and courts will enforce my promise. We can exchange my promise for your act. When you perform the act I sought, you then create a binding contract.

However, suppose you are performing, and I back out before you complete the task. Classic law assumed that since you had made no commitment to complete the performance which I wanted, then either of us could back out of the deal for any reason. Equality seemed to demand that both or neither of us be bound to a contract. However, at times courts protected your reliance by fudging the rules. Scholars then rushed to provide rationalizations. A later generation of writers came to see the unilateral contract as both a silly play with words and an unimportant back water in the law of contracts.[46] The Restatement (Second) of Contracts tries to erase the term "unilateral contract" from legal vocabulary and speaks of promises calling for performances but not promises.

Courts, however, hate to throw away useful tools. Despite all the trashing by contracts professors, the unilateral contract apparently is alive and well. Thus, you must understand the idea, the scholarly objections, and how courts use the tool — even if using the doctrine resembles driving nails with a wrench.

1. *The doctrinal twists of Davis v. Jacoby*: Casebook authors often reprint Davis v. Jacoby,[47] a California case. We can illustrate some of the problems with a unilateral contract analysis by simplifying the facts of this case. Caro Davis was Rupert and Blanche Whitehead's daughter. Caro was married to Frank

---

[46]See Llewellyn, On Our Case-Law of Contract: Offer and Acceptance(pts. 1 & 2), 48 Yale Law Journal 1, 779 (1938-1939).

[47]1 Cal.2d 370, 34P.2d 1026 (1934).

Davis, and they lived in Windsor, Ontario, Canada. Rupert and Blanche lived in Oakland, California.

In 1930, Blanche became seriously ill. Early in 1931,Rupert had suffered severe financial reverses, and he was in ill health. Rupert wrote Frank and Caro asking them to come to California. Caro would care for her mother, and Frank would help Rupert with his business affairs. Rupert stated that under his will all his property was to go to Blanche. He said that under Blanche's will everything was to go to Caro. He also said, "The next attack will be my end, I am 65 and my health has been bad for years, so, the Drs. don't give me much longer to live. So if you can come, Caro will inherit everything and you will make our lives happier and see Blanche is provided for to the end... [Y]ou can help me and Blanche and gain in the end." On April 14, 1931, Frank wrote Rupert and said that they would come to California. They planned to leave Windsor on April 25th. Frank and Caro closed Frank's business and closed their home. Rupert committed suicide on April 22 before Frank and Caro had left Windsor. Frank and Caro came to Oakland and took care of Blanche for about a month until she died.

After Blanche's death, Frank and Caro discovered that Rupert's statement about the Whitehead's wills was false. Rupert left his estate to his nephews, and Blanche's will left nothing to Caro. Frank and Caro sued the estates of her parents for specific performance of a contract to make a will.

2. *The legatee's argument:* The court in Davis v. Jacoby deals with the unilateral contract argument made by the legatees under Rupert Whitehead's will. They attempt to defeat the Davis' claim to all of his property. The legatees conceded that Mr.Whitehead had made an offer to Caro and Frank Davis, but they argued that it had been an offer contemplating a unilateral contract. They said that Rupert's promise was offered for action and not for a return promise.

Their argument continued: One can accept an offer for a unilateral contract only by full performance; only then does it become a contract. Until the Davis' performed the requested action, the offeror (Mr. Whitehead) was free to revoke his offer and back out without liability to the offerees (the Davis'). Another rule of law says that death revokes all outstanding offers. Since the Davis' had not fully performed before Mr.Whitehead committed suicide, there was no contract to make a will. The will as written stands, the legatees win and the Davis' do not get any of the Whitehead's property as promised.

The court rejected this argument. It found that Mr.Whitehead's offer contemplated a bilateral contract. A contract was formed when Frank Davis sent his letter to Mr. Whitehead, promising to come to California and perform the services. Therefore, the legatees under the will take subject to this contract, and they get little or nothing. How can we tell whether Rupert was bargaining for the Davis' promise or only their act of coming to California and offering care? Did Frank and Caro's letter saying that they were coming to California contain a promise to come and provide the services or was it only an expression of their present intention which might change at any time?

3. *The unilateral contract paradigm*: A transaction such as that put forward by the legatees is conceivable. Suppose Rupert Whitehead had written to the Davis' exactly as reported in the case. However, he also explained that he was concerned about the quality of care which Caro might give his wife and about the quality of business services which Frank might provide because of Frank's drinking problem. Therefore, suppose Rupert continued:

> I promise to arrange our wills so that we will leave everything we own to Caro if Caro properly cares for Blanche and if Frank properly handles the business. However, I reserve the right to revoke this offer without any need to show cause at any time before you two complete your performances. I recognize that I am asking you to move here and try to perform. You run the risk that I might be unreasonably dissatisfied with what you do and the risk that I might die before you finish the job. Nonetheless, you'll just have to trust me and take your chances.

Rupert would gain maximum leverage over Caro and Frank, if they started to perform. The more they invested in trying to perform (leaving their home and business in Ontario and providing services in California), the more they would have to lose if they displeased Rupert.

There is just one difficulty with the offer we've imagined. Rupert Whitehead wants to induce Caro and Frank to tear up their lives in Windsor, Ontario, to make a commitment to him and to perform the services in a manner above and beyond the call of duty. How can he hope to persuade them to do this in the face of the distrust reflected in his letter and in the face of the risks he is forcing them to take?[48] The expression of distrust might cut against the emotional ties between Caro and her Aunt which Rupert Whitehead was counting on. Many would think it improper to force family members to wager their home and business on the whims of an old man facing the loss of his wife and his wealth at the same time. And we must recall economic conditions at the time of this transaction. If Frank Davis gave up his insurance business and failed to gain from managing Rupert's business, it would not be easy to start again.

There are not many true unilateral contracts in the world. Few people are willing to place significant reliance on a promise that an offeror can revoke at

---

[48]See Haas and Deseran, Trust and Symbolic Exchange, 44 Social Psychology Quarterly 3 (1981): Trust "is established in various ways, one of which is investment in expensive gestures of good faith. We have called the exchange of such tokens of good faith 'symbolic exchanges.' We have argued that the use of symbolic exchange requires the existence of a standardized vocabulary of symbolic exchange . . . [A] refusal to reciprocate. . . or indeed any violation of the canons of symbolic exchange may signify a refusal of the relationship indicated by the exchange.'"Indeed, if Caro and Frank come to California after the hypothetical letter in the text, wouldn't they seem to be greedy and not motivated by the proper family spirit? Compare Bilder, Managing the Risks of International Agreement (University of Wisconsin Press 1981), dealing with another situation in which trust must be created before risks will be accepted.

any time. Of course, some reward situations fit this legal category. Suppose I offer a reward of $10,000 to anyone who captures a criminal. Suppose I offer a commission to any real estate broker who finds a buyer to whom I sell my house. In each instance, the person seeking the reward runs the risk that someone will beat her to it. In each case, the person seeking the reward can invest as much effort in trying to perform as she thinks warranted in light of the risks.

Courts often call settlement agreements unilateral contracts. They read these contracts as "I give up my right to sue you in exchange for your act of paying me, say, $10,000." This means that I do not lose my right to sue until you pay the$10,000. I do not run the risk that you will promise to pay the money, fail to do it, but then limit my claim to the amount of the settlement.

4. *Unilateral contracts and reliance:* If the act to be performed in a unilateral contract is complex, you may need time to accomplish it. Moreover, you may invest much trying to perform. However, under the classic doctrine, I can revoke my offer until you complete your performance. This opens the door to reliance loss on your part. How might courts respond to the situation?

(1) In some instances they might allow the offeror to back out if he or she managed to reserve this right clearly. Suppose a couple is considering divorce. They contact a real estate broker and explain that they are thinking of selling their house, but they are not sure that they will divorce and move. They make a nonexclusive listing with the broker because, as they make clear, they plan to show it themselves. The broker shows the house to a number of people. The couple reconcile and want to keep their house. It is unlikely that the broker would have any rights because the couple managed to explain the situation. The broker had the choice in light of the situation to invest no time or only a little in trying to find a buyer. Moreover, the transaction is not unusual but rather common. The broker should not be surprised when the couple take the house off the market.

(2) The easiest solution when the facts lend themselves to it, is the one taken in *Davis v. Jacoby.* The court finds that the offeror was bargaining for a promise which the offeree made. Thus, we have a bilateral contract. The deal was closed when the promise to come to California and provide care was made, and the offeror no longer could back out at will. This solution often is slightly messy. Suppose, for example, Caro and Frank sent the letter promising to come to California and perform the services. They begin preparations to leave Canada, but they discover that the loss they would have to take would be fantastically large. They telephone Rupert and tell him they are not coming. Could Rupert, or his executor, sue Caro and Frank for breach of their promise to come? If you follow the logic of the court's opinion, the answer is yes. Somehow one wonders if a court would reach that result on the facts.

(3) The original Restatement of Contracts, § 45, became the most commonly accepted solution to the problem of the unilateral contract. It provided:

If an offer for a unilateral contract is made, and part of the consideration requested in the offer is given or tendered by the offeree in response thereto, the offeror is bound by a contract, the duty of immediate performance of which is conditional on the full consideration being given or tendered within the time stated in the offer, or, if no time is stated therein, within a reasonable time.

(4) At one time the doctrine offered a possible loophole for a clever lawyer who wanted to break a contract for his client. Suppose a buyer, the client, ordered goods from seller, saying, "Please send me one model number 1000 automated thing." The seller responded by sending buyer an acknowledgment of order form which is a promise to ship the goods. Before the goods arrive, buyer wants to backout because he has a better offer from another seller. The buyer's lawyer might send a notice revoking his client's "unaccepted offer." The lawyer would claim that the offer had been a unilateral one, calling for the act of shipping goods. A promise to ship would not close the deal. The argument was just good enough to make the seller's case difficult. Some sellers would drop the whole thing and let the buyer out of his order.

Professor Llewellyn, the drafter of Article 2 of the Uniform Commercial Code, plugged this loophole in § 2-206.

Unless otherwise unambiguously indicated by the language or circumstances ... (b) an order or other offer to buy goods for prompt or current shipment shall be construed as inviting acceptance either by a prompt promise to ship or by the prompt or current shipment of conforming or non-conforming goods....

Restatement (Second) of Contracts, § 29(2) says that essentially the same rule extends to all contracts.

5. *Failure to observe form versus expectation and reliance:* What was involved in *Davis v. Jacoby*? Given the formalities of the Statute of Wills, why do Caro and Frank Davis have any claim against the estate? Rupert did request services. It was clear that he did not think he could ask for what he wanted as a gift without offering compensation. Caro and Frank performed some services. Thus, Caro, and perhaps Frank, would have a claim to restitution for the fair market value of Caro's work in caring for Blanche and for any services which Frank offered while in California. However, they want much more than the fair market value of a few weeks of nursing care. They did close a business and a house in Windsor, Ontario and travel to California, but it is unclear what that cost them. Their reply brief said that they returned to Canada. They reopened their home, and Frank was reemployed by the insurance company.

Would the case have been better analyzed by using Restatement of Contracts, § 90 and focusing on the amount of foreseeable substantial reliance and whether injustice could be avoided only by enforcing, in whole or in part, the promise?

Suppose you thought that Frank and Caro could not prove that they relied very substantially. They were able to reclaim their home and Frank's insurance business in Canada.

Are there some promises that courts ought enforce apart from a return promise, performance or reliance? Professor Mark Pettit, Jr. argues that courts think this is the case, and they often use the idea of a unilateral contract to achieve the result they seek. Despite the academic attack on the idea following Llewellyn's great articles of the 1930's, Pettit says "in fact unilateral contract never died, but is alive and thriving as never before."[49] We will see the doctrine again when we look at employment contracts.

6. *Contracts subject to conditions of personal satisfaction:* After considering unilateral contracts, we must examine a distinct but similar legal category into which the facts such as those in Davis v. Jacoby might fit. Recall our hypothetical version of the facts in the Davis case where we created an express unilateral contract to give Rupert leverage over the performances of Caro and Frank. Suppose, instead, Rupert had promised to will all his property to Caro in exchange for Caro and Frank's promises to perform services "to the satisfaction of Rupert Whitehead." Assume that Caro and Frank accepted this offer. The appropriate legal classification now is that the parties made a bilateral contract, subject to the condition of Rupert's satisfaction. That is, Rupert promises to pay PROVIDED THAT he is satisfied with their work. Of course, this would still place a tremendous risk on to Caro and Frank, but it would be somewhat different from the risks involved in a unilateral contract or from a promise enforced because of reliance under Restatement § 90.

(a) Unlike the promise of Rupert subject to enforcement under Restatement § 90, Caro and Frank would have made a promise to come to California and give services. Rupert's estate could sue them if they never left Windsor, if they came to California and then abandoned the project, or if they performed poorly.

(b) Unlike the situation under the classic unilateral contract unencumbered by reforms such as Restatement § 45, Caro and Frank would not be taking the risk of Rupert revoking his offer either by choice or by death. Their promise would form a contract, and death only revokes offers and not contracts. Of course, Rupert would have tremendous leverage under a "personal satisfaction" condition. Caro and Frank would have to satisfy him before he would have perform his promise. Under this assumption, Rupert only promised to make the will IF HE WERE SATISFIED. Nonetheless, courts would be likely to insist that Rupert act in good faith in asserting that he was dissatisfied. They might even require that he be reasonable in his judgment, but this is not clear. He could not call the whole thing off on a whim as he could if we were dealing with a revocable offer.

---

[49] Pettit, Modern Unilateral Contracts, 63 Boston University Law Review 551 (1983).

(c) Obviously, the deal still is risky for Caro and Frank. They would prefer that their performance be measured by an objective standard. If anyone could think of one, it might serve the interests of all concerned better. Yet it would not be easy to spell out just what Caro and Frank were to do. Imagine trying to write the clause concerning Frank's drinking problem. It might be easy to write a provision prohibiting his drinking a drop of liquor. However, it might not be easy to prove that he didn't honor the requirement. If he were willing to discuss the subject at all, Frank probably would ask for a clause speaking of drinking so much that it impaired his ability to perform business services regularly. Yet this would pose difficult questions of proof and judgment. In light of the difficulties, some contract drafters would not raise the question expressly. They would try to include language requiring adequate business services, hoping it might offer some support for negotiations if Frank's drinking became a problem.

7. CONTRACTS TO PROVIDE FOR THE OLD: CONTRACT AND RESTITUTION AS A SUBSTITUTE FOR AN EXTENDED FAMILY

Arrangements to provide for old people offer another example of the tension between legal formality and protecting reliance on promises. As people get old, often they become unable to care for themselves alone. Some need nursing care. Almost all want companionship. Spouses usually take care of spouses. But what happens when both are incapacitated or one dies? The three-generation family is a solution common throughout the world, but one not customary in middle class American society.

Rich older people can hire a staff to provide care. Today upper middle class people can pay a great deal to segregate themselves from younger society. They move into the "Golden Years" retirement home, complete with golf course, bridge club, and staff nurse. Poorer older people who cannot take care of themselves while living on welfare, social security or a pension, are also segregated from the larger society. However, the surroundings are not likely to be so architecturally pleasing. Many counties in many states have the "old folks home" and the mental institution. After being stripped of friends, dignity and family, the old are sent to these institutions when they become senile or bothersome. In between these extremes of wealth, older people often use the assets they have (usually their homes or farms as well as their pensions) to make arrangements so that they can live in their own homes while receiving care. These arrangements bump into the law of wills, gifts, contracts, and restitution and produce a surprising number of disputes, litigation, and appellate opinions in every state.

These problems are less likely to develop if an older person has money. The present generation is generally better off than preceding generations. The Wall Street Journal reported that in 1984 one in seven over-65's was below the poverty line while in 1964, one in four was. However, we may see such problems increasingly in the future as people live longer and costs of care increase.

Even older people with assets may want care from a relative and not a hired nurse. An older person may own a house or a farm plus some savings but be uncertain that this will cover all expenses of care until death. In these cases, he or she may pursue a strategy of reward. This chapter contains several cases in which an older person promised to exchange their property for care from a relative, or a friend. At the other extreme, an older person may rely on family ties so that one of his or her children will stay home or return to provide care and companionship. Often this role falls to the unmarried daughter, who, tradition would have it, has nothing better to do with her life.[50]

Of course, there are many strategies to induce grown children to care for their aged parents. For example, suppose an unmarried daughter comes home to take care of Mom and Dad. She is likely to expect to be better treated in their wills than her brothers who send Christmas cards or gifts and visit whenever they find it convenient. The brothers and other sisters may make financial contributions to run the household. However, neither the brother who writes the check nor the sister who cares for their aged parents wants to label her actions as motivated by a desire for gain. Aged parents, too, may want to imagine the situation as one held together by love rather than work now for pay later when the will is probated. For many people, contracts and wills along with death are taboo subjects. The law reflects this ambivalence about the true nature of the situation.

Even the hired nurse or housekeeper may become "a member of the family." She may hear countless expressions of gratitude, including expressions or intimations of the idea "you deserve more than I am paying you and I will make it right in my will." Then, too, a neighbor who assumes the duty of "just running next door to see that everything is okay" may give important services. She may provide nursing care during serious illness because no one else is available. Such a generous neighbor may expect the older person to remember her in the will, but custom dictates that she not voice this expectation while the older person is alive.

Throughout this section, we must remember that the law has provisions about wills and what happens if a person fails to make one. People have great freedom

---

[50]Some students have objected to this sentence as sexist. We think it descriptively accurate. The sexism is in the assumption that the customary role of women is their correct or only role and that it should be the model for the future. A description of what that role has been is either accurate or not. Care of the old can be a demanding and thankless job. Often there is a tremendous loss of freedom for the one giving care since it is so difficult to leave for more than a short time. The burden most often falls on daughters who do not at the time have families or socially valued careers of their own. As so often is true, litigation of the sort described in the following sections probably is a surrogate for deeper problems in families and general social problems in dealing with the increasing life span. See Emily Abel, Adult Daughters and Care for the Elderly, 12 Feminist Studies 479 (1986).

to will property to anyone. However, wills are revocable until death. A writer of a newspaper column about problems of the elderly emphasizes that an older person should use the leverage created by the right to make and revoke wills in order to get adult children to behave decently. Wills, however, can be attacked by charges of duress, undue influence, and lack of a testator's mental capacity. Judges seek to protect one whom age has robbed of defenses from predators — actually, those protected usually are the spouse and children who do not get "enough" under the will.

Often people fail to make wills or they have invalid ones. Statutes then divide property among relatives based on family relationships. For example, children take equally, whether or not they shared the work of caring for elderly parents. Relatives take the entire estate although a nurse or neighbor was considered "one of the family" and did all of the dirty work. If the deceased did not leave you enough in the will, or if the deceased did not make a valid will, you must find a legal theory to justify any recovery. Contract and restitution are the most likely avenues open.

We will consider a number of common situations related to care for the elderly and the legal problems involved.

Contracts to make wills and the dead man's statute: First, suppose an older person promises to leave everything to the one giving care in exchange for services. The older person fails to execute such a will and then dies. The one who made a contract to give care can get the promise enforced. However, those who gave care must prove that there was a valid contract. They may run into trouble with the "dead man's statute." This doctrine prevents parties, in most instances, from testifying on their own behalf about conversations with people who are now dead. There are exceptions and qualifications to the dead man's statute in most states. Nonetheless, as a practical matter, one who gave care will have a much easier time proving his or her case if there is written evidence that a contract existed or if there is a disinterested witness who can testify to the making of an oral contract.

Payment for care when there is no express contract: Second, suppose that a person renders services with an expectation of compensation, through a will or otherwise. However, the recipient does not make a will or even an express contract to make one. For example, in *Estate of Voss*,[51] an elderly man advertised in the newspaper for a housekeeper. Plaintiff worked for him, but they never made a definite arrangement concerning wages. She lived in his house and ate food for which he paid. Plaintiff alleged that the elderly man promised to marry her, and that, as a result, she was lulled into continuing to work for him. No marriage took place, she testified, because the elderly man's son strongly opposed it. A fair wage would have been $35 per week, which was more than the value of her room and board. The plaintiff might have claimed that there was

---

[51]20 Wis.2d 238, 121 N.W.2d 744 (1963).

a contract implied in fact, or an obligation imposed by law to avoid unjust enrichment — which is sometimes called a contract implied in law.

The plaintiff's theory in the *Voss* case was restitution of benefits conferred. The old man accepted a benefit fully aware that it was not being offered as a gift. The court sustained plaintiff's claim. It awarded the housekeeper the going price for her services, less the value of her board and room, and not the value to the elderly man which might have been more or less. Under this theory, the award pays her for her work, but she does not get the entire estate. After she is paid, the balance of the estate goes to the legatees under the will or to the relatives if there is no will.

Courts thus need not venture into the dismal swamp of evaluating family members' actions in time of need. Courts can avoid assessing the quality of the caregiver's services as well. The one receiving care can value contributions above and beyond the call of duty in a will. If the deceased fails to execute a will recognizing a housekeeper's work, then the caregiver is limited to the fair market value of services rendered for which she has not been paid. Courts do not attempt to measure intangible subjective values often involved in these relationships. Of course, this result may not please a housekeeper who is not a relative. She was there in the hour of need while the relatives did little or nothing. But, the deceased may have thought the housekeeper was paid all she had coming.

Recovery by family members: A family member who cares for an elderly relative faces a major problem in recovering restitution of benefits conferred. Courts have long said there is a presumption that services given by one member of the family to another are gratuitous.[52] The one receiving the benefit may not

---

[52]In Estate of Steffes, 95 Wis.2d 490, 290 N.W.2d 697 (1980), the court considered compensation for services rendered by persons cohabiting but not related by marriage. Mary Lou Brooks and Virgil Steffes each were married to other persons. They met in a tavern where she worked, and then, at his request, she lived in his home on his farm from 1969 to 1976 when he died. She cleaned, cooked, washed, and ironed, and she picked corn, ran the combine, loaded silage, helped pour concrete walls, helped remodel the house, and paid the bills. Until 1974, Brooks and Steffes had sexual relations. In 1974, Steffes's wife died. In that same year, doctors found that Steffes had a brain tumor. Brooks gave nursing care and drove him to a hospital for 28 consecutive days for cobalt treatments. He said that he would leave her the proceeds of the sale of the farm, but he did not make such a will. She sued for the value of her services. The trial court found that she expected compensation, and that he had requested the services. The court awarded her $14,600 as compensation for the work during the last two years of Steffe's life (his gross estate was $733,644.65).

On appeal, the personal representative (Virgil Steffe's son) argued that because Virgil Steffes had treated Mary Lou Brooks as part of the family, the presumption of gratuitous services should apply. Justice Abrahamson wrote the majority opinion which affirmed the trial court's decision. It was necessary to decide whether the presumption was applicable because if "a promise can be implied from the facts, then the plaintiff is entitled to compensation regardless of the fact that she rendered services with a sense of affection, devotion and duty." Plaintiff expected payment, and deceased expressed his intention to provide for her.

know that the person offering services expects payment for them. Thus he has not had a chance to reject services he would do without if he knew that he had to pay for them.

A family member must overcome a strong presumption to recover for benefits conferred. For example, in *Miller v. Estate of Bell*,[53] there were four children, two sons and two daughters. At the time of the litigation, the daughters were age 50 and 56 and living with families of their own. The two daughters, who lived near their parents, had cleaned and shopped for them and given them some personal care for six years before their deaths. Both parents had stated that all of the property should go to the daughters because they had taken care of them. The father made a will. It gave all of his property to his wife if she survived him. If she did not, the property went to the daughters except $100 which he left to each of the sons. The mother made no will because she told their lawyer that she had no property. Actually, she owned a half interest in most of the property which the couple held jointly. The father died first. Since the mother survived her husband, she inherited a half interest in the property and had her own half interest as well. When she died without a will, all of this property went to the four children equally, and not according to the terms of her husband's will. The court rejected the daughters' restitution claim against their mother's estate since their services were presumed to have been gratuitous. However, the court noted that their bequests under their father's will were more than the fair value of all their services.

One can contrast *Estate of Grossman*.[54] A daughter lived in Milwaukee where she worked as a waitress, and her parents lived in Dale, Wisconsin. Dale is about 100 miles north of Milwaukee. When her mother became seriously ill, her father asked her to return home. She cared for her mother for about six weeks until her death. A doctor testified that the daughter's services had been necessary. The daughter sacrificed an average of $8.00 per day which she would have earned had she stayed at work in Milwaukee. The trial court allowed her claim against the estate for $4.00 per day for her services. The Supreme Court of Wisconsin affirmed, saying, "[w]hile the proof offered by claimant to overcome the presumption that the services were gratuitous is not too strong, it is considered sufficient to overcome the presumption and sustain the trial court in granting judgment...."

The daughter also made trips to Dale from Milwaukee between February 1st and July 1, 1942, on September 1, 1942, and on November 22, 1945. Her father

---

The personal representative also argued that she could not recover on an implied contract because she was living in an adulterous relationship. The trial court found that the illicit bargain was incidental to the plaintiff's performance of lawful services. It was not a condition of nor a consideration for decease's implied promise to compensate. The majority of the Supreme Court accepted this finding, citing Marvin v. Marvin.

[53]224 Wis. 593, 273 N.W. 67 (1937).

[54]250 Wis. 457, 27 N.W.2d 365 (1947).

was "an aged man" with a heart condition. During her visits she cared for him and did housework. The father died on December 13, 1945. The Supreme Court disallowed a claim for these trips and services. It said,

> While claimant is to be complimented on the interest shown in her father and her desire to be helpful to him, and without doubt the father was happy to see her and such services as she rendered were helpful to him, nevertheless these trips home were no different than the trips she made home prior to the time her mother was taken sick, even though they may have been a little more frequent and the services rendered were somewhat greater. There is nothing to indicate that the father requested her to come home at the times in question, and certainly no parent would expect to pay a child for services when she occasionally drops in to visit for a day or two at a time.

Another factor, perhaps relevant, in the *Grossman* case was the disposition of the father's estate. The claimant and her brother survived the father. The brother was in the army during the time the daughter performed the services. In 1942, the father deeded the family house to his daughter, reserving a life estate. This property was appraised at $2,750. In his will, the father gave the daughter $500, and then divided the balance of his estate equally between the daughter and the son.

Restitution for friendly neighbors: Family members are not the only ones to face the gratuitous services problem. Neighbors and friends also help old people. They may mow the lawn, do odd jobs, visit, bring in food, and offer some household service and nursing care. Then the older person dies. May the neighbor make a claim for the reasonable value of his or her services against the estate? There is no presumption as in the case of family. However, the neighbor will have difficulty establishing that the older person should have known that the neighbor expected payment. Sometimes the older person did not ask for the services and, as a practical matter, would have had difficulty rejecting them if he or she wanted to do so.

In re Goldricks Will[55] involved the helpful neighbor story. The Supreme Court reversed a judgment for $500. It noted that the services were "various things that a friendly neighbor might well perform for a widow next door, whose relations to her husband and to her had always been friendly and neighborly." Consider that statement in light of the record of the trial. The neighbor's evidence concerning the work done was as follows:

> George Goldrick was buried on the 13th day of June, 1918, and after his death I performed services for Mrs. Goldrick in looking after her mortgages, insurance, taxes, collected her interest, worked around her house, looked

---

[55]198 Wis. 500, 224 N.W. 741 (1929).

after the building of a porch, re-roofed the house, built a cistern, cleaned the house and put in ice for her, mowed the lawn, drove her around about five thousand miles, looked after selling land, sold lots and land; looked after some trespass, and went to see town boards with reference to her assessments, and whatever business she had to do I did for her.

Had quite a job looking after the interest. Don't think one out of twenty-five could pay the interest and pay the taxes, and had quite a lot of trouble with that. A lot of times they would come and pay twenty or thirty dollars to Mrs. Goldrick, and she would not keep track of it, and had quite a job trying to keep that straightened out. A lot of receipts were not dated, and it was pretty hard to read her writing. I made out her income reports, both state and federal, looked after the payment of all taxes at all times; attended to mortgage foreclosures and bid in the property. Went to Oshkosh for her. When the Goldrick estate was probated a forty was omitted and I had to see about going through all that again. Drove out to different farmers in regard to interest, looked after the Mattoon farm, and had to do quite a lot of chasing around. Went to Oshkosh to look over some lots which a man wanted to trade for some property in Aniwa. Went to the Town of Plover when the equalization board was in session to get her valuation down. Went to the Town of Harrison to see about getting taxes lower in that town.

I looked after a trespass for her. When she sold 200 acres of timber I went and looked over that for her. Sold eight, ten or twelve pieces of land for her and looked after her business in general whatever she had to do. She couldn't even sign anything, she wanted to know from me whether she should sign it or not.

After Goldrick's death Mr. Cady was the attorney for the estate and I sent in whatever papers I had, and perhaps once in every five or six weeks I would get a letter from him wanting to know about which or when this property was bought or that property was bought, and had a lot of trouble with the government over income tax.

Had to make good on some abstracts which Mr. Goldrick had gotten for people. Looked after the building of line fences and looked after her checking accounts. Such services were worth at least $25.00 per month.

They covered a period of eight and a half years up to the time of her death. She was seventy-four when she died. She had heart trouble and rheumatism and was not able to look after her own affairs. For the last two years she has not been just right mentally.

In addition to the work I mentioned I also helped build a cement sidewalk, helped clean the windows, cleaned the furnace, and helped set out some shrubs, filled in manure, shoveled the walks, put on screens, took off screens, attended to locks, put on the storm windows and storm doors, emptied out slop and put on and took off the screen doors and windows. Packed the ice in the ice house. Shoveled off the roads and moved the furniture, looked after moneys, mortgages and notes, made out deeds; nobody had anything to do with the property excepting myself.

The Supreme Court explained:

> There is undoubtedly a strong temptation to participate in the estates of deceased persons by magnifying trifling services into large claims, when the persons to whom the supposed services were rendered are dead and have no answer to make. Claimants silent in lifetime, become voluble when their pretended debtors no longer can speak. Such claims are not favored in law.

Mrs. Goldricks had remembered her neighbor in her will. The court characterized the situation as one where the neighbor expected a larger legacy than he received. The value of the estate was $88,000, and there were no children. A year before the widow died, she executed a will under which she left the friendly neighbor $9,000. Later she executed the will which was probated under which the friendly neighbor took only $1,000. There was no evidence as to why she changed her mind.

Promises recognizing past services: Finally, it is not uncommon for elderly people to recognize that they are receiving services above and beyond the call of duty. They then promise to pay a family member or a neighbor for them. For example, *In re Estate of Tulley*[56] involved a woman who was once a neighbor of the claimant. The woman was in ill-health, and the claimant helped her find and furnish an apartment. The claimant visited the woman daily and did the shopping and cleaning. The woman told her landlord that she did not know what she would do without claimant's help. On September 11, 1975, the woman gave claimant a check for $5,000 and a handwritten note. It said, "Jean I am leaving a check for you rather than putting you in the will. This way you won't have to pay tax on it. I only hope there is enough left to cover it by the time I die." The woman died on November 1, 1975. There was not enough in the bank account to cover the check, but she left an estate of about $40,000.

The Supreme Court of Wisconsin found that the $5,000 check was an invalid testamentary disposition because it failed to follow the formalities of execution prescribed by the Statute of Wills. The court said that people could make a contract and delay payment until after death. However, there was no proof that claimant ever expected compensation for her services or that they had bargained. The check and the note were not a promise to pay in exchange for the services. "[I]t was the intent of decedent to show appreciation for the kindnesses of the claimant and ... it was the intent of claimant to render assistance to the decedent without expectation of monetary compensation."

---

[56] 86 Wis.2d 593, 273 N.W.2d 329 (1979).

Suppose the woman had written a slightly different note. Suppose she had said, "Jean, you have been wonderful and done so much for me. And so I promise to pay you $5,000 when I die. You can collect it by cashing this check." In other words, the older woman's promise recognizes an obligation she felt because of all Jean's kindness to her. Such a transaction would not be a bargain, and there would be no consideration for it under an orthodox view.

The problem is that there was no swap but only a recognition that Jean had done so much. You cannot bargain for a performance you already have.[57]

Most states do recognize "past consideration" as enough to justify enforcing a promise in a narrowly limited class of cases involving commercial transactions and far from our kindly neighbor situation. Suppose you and I made a contract under which you conferred a benefit on me. However, I had or acquired a defense to your rights under that contract because:

(1) I was under the age of majority (usually 18 or 21) when I entered the agreement,

(2) the Statute of Limitations had run on your claim, or

(3) I received a discharge of all my debts in bankruptcy. Then, I, being over 18 and knowing of my defense, made a new promise to pay you for the benefit which you had conferred. Most courts would award you damages if I then failed to pay after this second promise.[58] Some courts explained the case as one where I waived my defense, and so you can sue on the original promise which was supported by consideration. The original Restatement of Contracts recognized these three situations as exceptions to the rule of § 75, in §§ 86, 87 and 89. These sections, together with § 90, were grouped under the heading "Contracts Without Consideration." However, many judges who decided the cases which established these rules did not concede that promises were being enforced without consideration. They looked hard and found some. They asserted there was a moral obligation to pay any debt despite the existence of "technical" defenses (and immoral ones?) such as bankruptcy, the Statute of Limitations or infancy.

---

[57]Reliance theories, such as Restatement (Second) of Contracts, § 90, may not work either. In these cases, the claimant conferred the benefit first and not in reliance on a promise which came later. Section 90 might help if Jean could show that she had continued providing services relying on the promise.

[58]Under changes in bankruptcy law which first became effective in October of 1979, and then were amended in both 1984 and 1994, significant limitations have been placed on the enforceability of promises to pay debts discharged in bankruptcy. To a great extent, promises to pay a debt discharged in bankruptcy have been removed from the general law of contracts and subjected to regulation. Compare the following: "The most dramatic changes touching the significance of contract law in modern life ... came about, not through internal developments in contract law, but through developments in public policy which systematically robbed contract of its subject-matter." Friedman, Lawrence, Contract Law in America: a Social and Economic Case Study © 1965 (Madison: The University of Wisconsin Press). This material protected by copyright: permission to copy must be obtained from The University of Wisconsin Press.

What they called a moral obligation served as consideration for the debtor's subsequent promise to pay.

Recognition of a moral obligation as consideration: The supreme courts of Wisconsin and a very few other states have expanded this idea of a moral consideration to pay for past benefits. Some of the Wisconsin cases deal with commercial situations, but many concern promises by older people to pay family members and neighbors for care and services. See, *e.g.*, *Estate of Hatten*,[59] *Estate of Schoenkerman*,[60] *Estate of Gerke*.[61] Yet there must be a moral obligation to pay for the services, and the court is the judge of whether or not such a moral obligation exists. For example, in *Estate of Briese*,[62] the court found there was no such moral obligation in a case involving family services. Husband promised dying First Wife to take care of her Mother who had lived with them for over 30 years. A year after First Wife's death, Husband remarried. Mother left in anger although Husband did not tell her to leave. Mother sued for breach of Husband's promise to First Wife to take care of Mother. She lost. There was no consideration for Husband's promise. Moral consideration does not apply. The benefits Husband had received from First Wife (the promisee) were benefits "which it was the legal and moral duty of the promisee to confer without compensation, else any promise made by a husband to his wife becomes legally enforceable." Mother also claimed that she had furnished moral consideration to support the husband's promise to First Wife (her daughter) because she had done housework with her daughter while living with them from 1905 to 1935 and then had continued to run the house for two years until the dispute after the remarriage. The Supreme Court of Wisconsin did not respond to this argument in its opinion.

The drafters of Restatement (Second) of Contracts accepted some part of the Wisconsin moral consideration cases and in § 86 codified their view of them. Do you see any difference between the Wisconsin cases and § 86? See especially § 86(2)(a), and suppose a promise by an aged father to give a daughter a new stereo after the daughter has cared for him for years out of a sense of familial duty. For a discussion of Restatement (Second) of Contracts, § 86, see Henderson, Promises Grounded in the Past: The Idea of Unjust Enrichment and the Law of Contracts, 57 Virginia Law Review 1115 (1971).

---

[59]233 Wis. 199, 288 N.W. 278 (1940).

[60]236 Wis. 311, 294 N.W. 810 (1940).

[61]271 Wis. 297, 73 N.W.2d 506 (1955).

[62]240 Wis. 426, 3 N.W.2d 691 (1942).

8. IF LAW IS TO INTERVENE, WHAT REMEDIES ARE APPROPRIATE?

a. Reliance and the Expectation Interest in the Family Context

Promises enforced because of reliance and the measure of recovery: We've considered several cases where courts protected reliance on promises where there was doubt whether the transaction should be called a bargain. When we looked at *Hamer v. Sidway* (the generous uncle case) and *Ricketts v. Scothorn*, (the generous grandfather case) we considered whether expectation or reliance damages should be awarded in such cases. We noted the Restatement (Second) of Contracts § 90's recognition of reliance recovery. We could raise similar questions about the appropriate remedy in *Davis v. Jacoby*. Assuming you conclude that Caro deserves something more than restitution, why should she recover the full estate? However, suppose you thought that the *Davis* case would be better decided under Restatement § 90. What award would she recover under this section? Could a court split the estate into equal amounts among Caro and the two nephews? Should it?

Recognition of past benefits and limited remedies: Suppose an older person makes a promise to pay for care and housekeeping services rendered in the past. Assume that the circumstances make this promise enforceable under the "moral consideration" doctrine in Wisconsin. How much can the one performing services recover? Will the court enforce the older person's promise or will it limit the remedy?

In *Estate of Hatten*,[63] plaintiff sued on a promissory note given by an older person to pay for past services. The note was for $25,000. The court stated,

> Were we required to determine whether the services, meals, etc., were reasonably worth the sum of $25,000, — in other words, if this action were one to recover quantum meruit, we should have no hesitation in holding that they were not reasonably worth that amount.

Yet the court found the note a valid claim against the estate because "whether or not the consideration was adequate is a matter exclusively for the decision of the parties."

On the other hand, in *Estate of Gerke*,[64] the older person had promised to leave "everything" to the plaintiff upon the older person's death as compensation for past services. The court enforced the promise because of moral consideration. However, it limited plaintiff's recovery to the reasonable value of "that which the claimant furnished, in return for which the promise was made." The court

---

[63] 233 Wis. 199, 288 N.W. 278 (1940).

[64] 271 Wis. 297, 73 N.W.2d 506 (1955).

explained that to "measure recovery by the value of the estate would circumvent the statute of wills ... and will not be countenanced."

Suppose Daughter has taken care of her elderly father. He promises to leave everything to her under circumstances where his promise would be enforceable in Wisconsin because of the doctrine of moral consideration. Why aren't her expectations important enough to deserve full protection?

b. Specific Performance and "Shotgun Marriages"

Up to this point our focus has been on contracts to care for the elderly and fights between relatives and caretakers after care was given. Usually the older person has died, and then the contracts litigation is part of the process of dividing the estate. In this section, however, we return to the problems of legal intervention in ongoing relationships. To what extent, if at all, can courts police the quality of care? To what extent, if at all, can they protect the interests of the caregiver in the face of the desires of the older person to break off the relationship? These relationships are subjective and involve human feeling. They are not primarily economic. It is difficult to care for the old, and it is difficult to be old and lose independence and control after a lifetime of running things. It is easy to dismiss these situations and say that people should not run to court to cope with such problems. If, however, courts are not the place for resolving such battles, where then is the place? First, we will look at the rights of the one entitled to receive care under a contract. Then we will consider the rights of the one giving it.

The rights of the one receiving care: The following excerpt is from Lawrence M. Friedman, Contract Law in America 36-39 (1965). He tells us that the "decisions of the Wisconsin Supreme Court on contract questions form the basic material of this study. These cases have been drawn from three periods." His first period is 1836-61, the "frontier" period in the state's history; the second is 1905-15, the "Progressive" era; and the third is the decade of the 1950s.

> The single most frequent fact-situation underlying the land cases of Period II was the "support contract" — a conveyance, usually of a farm, in exchange for a promise to support the former owner. Almost all of these transfers took place within the immediate family circle and from the older to the younger generation — *e.g.*, from father to son. In many cases, the family was of German descent. It seems pretty clear that immigrants from Central Europe brought the traditional form of the support contract with them to Wisconsin. This in itself is striking. Foreign legal practice rarely survived passage over the Atlantic. But the support contract was a legal institution only in a narrow sense; more accurately, it was a custom which contract law, basically permissive, recognized and enforced. (Other foreign customs, such as the *padrone* labor system among Italian immigrants of the 1890's, could not be readily assimilated into American law.) The support

contract survived in Wisconsin and reached its legal climax in the 1900's. Reported cases were at their peak in Period II; field studies of the actual use of these contracts confirm the fact that these contracts were never so popular before or after. Yet the Germans had been flocking into Wisconsin since at least 1848.

The support contract permitted the head of a family to retire from active farming, with enough income (in cash and kind) to live on, while he used the farm itself as security. The farm secured performance of the contract not through any formal institutional set of doctrines (such as clustered about the mortgage), but because the court would allow rescission for breach of contract. The contract also kept the family farm in the family; and it let the children stay on the farm as owners, without waiting for their parents to die. In theory, both sides benefited. The sons got independence and their own farm; the old folks enjoyed a dignified and comfortable retirement.

The use of the support contract implied a definite social and economic pattern: a stable family unit, rooted to a particular plot of land. In the pioneer days, the sons of the farmers — or even the farmers themselves — were apt to pull up stakes and follow the agricultural frontier. Probably most farms did not produce enough to support more than one adult family. And the population of the state was composed of relatively young men and young women. By the turn of the century, however, many Wisconsin farms had been "in the family" for two generations. Problems of continuity and succession had become more important. Sons were no longer so likely to leave home for the new west. The drift to the west was replaced, though not completely, by the drift to the cities. But an old farmer could not usually afford to retire to town or city. In later times, when the old folks were more likely to go to the city, the support contract lost much of its importance. Beyond a doubt, most such contracts were carried out without trouble. But the contracts and deeds were often home-made and artlessly written. Trouble lurked in traditional phrases. Some agreements set out far too much detail, inviting quarrels over trifles. For example, in one such contract (which ended in the courts), the grantee agreed to pay "yearly to plaintiff twenty bushels of wheat, three hundred pounds of dressed pork, fifty pounds of beef, fifteen bushels of potatoes, feed and pasture for one cow, twelve chickens and feed for same, twelve cords of four foot hardwood, $20 in cash"; the grantor could also "have the main room and bedroom in the stone house on the premises," "medical treatment" during illness, and in general, "good care." The excessive detail was bad enough, although the realities of farming made it easier to pay in chickens than in cash. "Good care" was, however, much harder to measure than chickens. Some contracts invited controversy by setting even vaguer standards of performance; in one example, the grantees promised to be "good and kind" to the grantor. Case after case in the tabulation showed the same pathology: bad blood, a little quarrel getting bigger, then accusations of bad faith and the collapse of the whole arrangement. As far as the evidence of the Supreme Court cases goes, the old folks were almost invariably the plaintiffs, bitterly complaining about their children and demanding rescission of the entire arrangement. In the language of Timlin, J., "unfortunate family controversies [are] almost inevitable when exacting and irritable old age contracts with selfish youth for those attentions which are ordinarily the gift of filial love rather than the obligations of contract." Another case the court called a "tale of insult, abuse, crimination, and personal violence upon both sides which is not pleasant to contemplate."

Timlin's characterization of these situations is worth stressing, since it points to a fact of the deepest significance for the law of contract. These were "contract" cases, but they had almost nothing to do with the market. By stretching a point, one might make a market case out of *Gall v. Gall*, where the plaintiff and her witnesses said that "some of the pork was too hard ... to eat.... The beef was not so very bad. The wheat was pretty bad, it was fit for chicken feed." Possibly these failures of quality of performance could be measured objectively. But what of *Mash v. Bloom*, where defendants failed to keep the plaintiff company and "entertain her in her loneliness"? And even in *Gall v. Gall*, Kerwin, J., had to scold the defendant for bad conduct: "though bound by contract, if by no other tie, to care for and minister to the wants of his aged mother, [he] did not speak to her when he met her on the road ... and spoke in the most cruel and inhuman manner of her in public...." Obviously, whatever technical language the court might speak in these cases, the abstraction of the market did not fit the relationships. The judges' comments show that they were aware what these cases were really about. Yet, most of these cases were brought *as* contract cases, and the results were embodied in decisions that talked this language."

Again, the land cases of Period III formed a quite distinctive group. The support contract cases had vanished. Investment land reappeared as a significant element in appellate litigation; this land was not, however, the cut-over lands of the north, but subdivision land on the outskirts of the cities.

NOTES AND QUESTIONS

1. *Social and legal change*: Why have support contract cases vanished from the Wisconsin courts? Suppose today an owner of a family farm is nearing retirement age, and he has a married son who wishes to take over the business. How might they handle the transaction?

2. *Of hot potatoes and dismal swamps*: To what extent do the policies that pressed against judicial intervention in promises between husband and wife also apply to the support contract? To the extent that they apply, why didn't the courts reach the same results in the older Wisconsin cases?

The rights of the one giving care: The following cases introduce problems in running ongoing relationships. On one hand, they force us to ask what courts could and should do when relationships of this kind are in trouble. On the other hand, they also should suggest questions related to preventing the trouble in the first place. Could lawyers have anticipated and prevented the problems that arose in these cases? One lawyer's task is to draft legal instruments such as contracts, wills and trusts so that they are legally enforceable. However, this is hardly enough. The more important task is to plan transactions so they will work without being enforced by the courts.

FITZPATRICK v. MICHAEL

9 A.2d 639 (Md. Ct. App. 1939)

OFFUTT, J. In the Summer of 1936, Marie Ellen Fitzpatrick, a native and resident of Harford County, who was then about fifty two years old, was employed by Orion C. Michael of Aberdeen in that county as a practical nurse for his wife who was an invalid, and she remained in that employment until the wife's death in February 1937. Upon Mrs. Michael's death, Miss Fitzpatrick informed her employer that she was about to leave his home, and Michael, who was then about seventy six years old, and apparently in uncertain health, asked her to wait a few days, that he wanted to talk over his plans for the future with her. She did remain and a few days later he spoke to her of his age, told her that he had no relatives or friends, and that "he wanted company and someone to look after and take charge of his home, his flowers, drive him around in the automobile, care for him, when he was sick or needed attention, and as she had been so kind and attentive to his sick wife, had rendered her such valuable services in nursing and caring for her for about five or six months in the last months of her life, that he wanted the Complainant to remain with him the balance of his life, and take full charge of his home, nurse him when it was necessary, look after his flowers, drive him around in the automobile and be company for him, that while he could not pay her much money, only eight ($8.00) per week, that his home on the said Bel Air Avenue would be her home with board as long as he lived, and that he would make a Will that upon his death his home property with all the furniture and furnishings should be hers for the balance of her life, and that his automobiles would be hers absolutely." Miss Fitzpatrick accepted the offer and continued to serve Michael under the contract until April 6th, 1939, when he terminated the employment. During that period Michael appears to have been entirely satisfied with her services and she took "full charge of his large home, looking after his flower garden, the furnace in his residence, driving him to his office and back daily, as well driving him on pleasure and business trips of many thousand miles on a trip, nursing him at times when he would be confined to his bed for as long as four or five weeks at a time, as well looking after him both daily and at night from causes such as arterial sclerosis that comes with age, a heart with a missing beat, as well on many nights requiring to keep hot water bottles to his back and feet all night to make him a little comfortable, all of these services the Defendant apparently appreciated and valued by telling the neighbors what a wonderful nurse and housekeeper the Complainant had been, and if it were not for her, he did not know what he would do, for he was not on very friendly terms with the distant relatives, who did not visit him, and several did not speak to him." In March 1939 she drove him to Miami, Florida, accompanied him to Cuba, and drove him back to his home in Aberdeen, and on their return he had the following personal item published in a local newspaper: — "Mr. O. C. Michael, prominent business man of Aberdeen, and Miss Mazie Fitzpatrick, also of Aberdeen, have returned to their home after a vacation of several weeks in Florida. The trip was made by automobile, Miss Fitzpatrick driving the entire distance of 4,400 miles without the least mishap either with motor or tires. Cuba was also visited."

To carry out his undertaking, Michael in the Summer of 1937 executed a will in which he left to Miss Fitzpatrick his home and its furnishings for life, and his automobiles absolutely. Then on or about December 21st 1938, he executed a second will with her consent in which he changed the term of her tenancy from life to fifteen years. Finally he executed in March 1939 a third will in which while making changes as to other bequests and devices he left the provisions affecting her unchanged.

After the trip to Florida Michael's attitude towards Miss Fitzpatrick underwent a complete and to her highly objectionable change. On April 4th of this year he left his home for his office and did not return, although so far as she knew their friendly relations were unchanged, and on April 6th he attempted to force her to leave the home by cutting off the light, water, heat and telephone, and also the food supplies, and when that blockade proved ineffective, he had her arrested for trespass and while she was under arrest he locked up the house so that she was unable to enter it although she had property of her own in it.

Miss Fitzpatrick attributes the change to the jealousy of relatives, for she alleges "the Defendant until he left his home as aforesaid had been carrying out his promises under his said agreement for valuable services rendered and to be rendered until his death, with the exception that he had not fully paid her the weekly wages due, and no doubt would have returned to his own home as he always did, but for the jealousies of some distant relatives, who succeeded in keeping him away from his home by making him believe the Courts would not allow him to return, until they had so poisoned his mind against your Complainant to take steps to force her out of his home, that the Respondent stated that the reason he did not return to his home, was because he was under the law and could not return, notwithstanding the Complainant was ready, willing and able to provide him with all the comforts, nursing and the necessary attention for properly looking after and caring for him, and would have been glad to have continued to perform her agreement with the Respondent for his comfort." Following her removal from Michael's home, Miss Fitzpatrick on May 9th of this year filed the bill of complaint in this case against Michael and in it after alleging the facts which have been stated she asked that the respondent be required to specifically perform his contract with her, and that a receiver be appointed to take charge of "all the estate, both real and personal of the Respondent, to collect all money, rents, etc., and to pay this Complainant the weekly sum of eight dollars ($8.00) per week as long as the Respondent lives, and to provide her in the Respondent's Aberdeen residence a home with board and lodging so long as the Respondent lives, upon the Complainant looking after the Respondent's home, flowers, driving his automobile, and nursing and caring for the Respondent in compliance with her said agreement, with the said Respondent."

The defendant demurred to the bill for a general want of equity, the demurrer was sustained and the bill dismissed, and from that decree the plaintiff appealed.

There can be no possible doubt that upon those facts the plaintiff should be entitled to some relief against the defendant, but the question in this case is, whether the remedy is in equity.

A contract to make a will is not invalid because of its subject matter, for since one may bargain and sell, give away or otherwise surrender every right and property interest which he has there can be no sound reason why he cannot also validly agree to dispose of it by will, nor, since Michael may not have lived for a year after it was made can it be said that apart from any question of part performance that the contract is invalid because it was not embodied in a writing signed by the party to be charged as required by clause 5 of the Fourth Section of the Statute of Frauds, Alexander's British Statutes, pp. 511, 534, because there was a possibility that it might be performed within a year. But as it relates to an interest in land it is within clause 4 of the Section and unenforceable unless the bar of the statute is removed. That may be done by sufficient proof that the plaintiff has performed it in part and is willing and able to continue to do those things which under it she undertook to do.... The doctrine of part performance, however, is peculiar to equity and may not be invoked in courts of law, so that unless the facts present a case of equitable jurisdiction the appellant has no remedy on the contract either at law or in equity.

But no ground of equitable jurisdiction can be found in the facts stated unless it be that she has no adequate remedy at law. But even though there is no adequate remedy at law equity will not ordinarily specifically enforce a contract for personal service, for these reasons, one, that the mischief likely to result from the enforced continuance of the relationship incident to the service when it has become personally obnoxious to one of the parties is so great that the best interests of society require that the remedy be refused, Fry on Spec. Perf. 50, for as stated by Fry "The relation established by the contract of hiring and service is of so personal and confidential a character that it is evident that such contracts cannot be specifically enforced by the Court against an unwilling party with any hope of ultimate and real success; and accordingly the Court now refuses to entertain jurisdiction in regard to them.... But the difficulty of enforcing such contracts in specie is now admitted by the Courts. It is not for the interest of society that persons who are not desirous of maintaining continuous personal relations with one another should be compelled so to do." The other reason is, that courts have not the means or the ability to enforce such decrees. Nevertheless there is a class of cases in which although the contract is not actionable under the Statute of Frauds it has been performed by the rendition of services the value of which cannot be estimated in terms of money, and in such cases when it appears that a monetary award will not place the parties in statu quo, or adequately compensate the complaining party, equity may grant relief in the nature of a specific performance of the contract....

Executory contracts are not, however, within the scope of that principle which can only be invoked where the employment has been terminated by the expiration of the term of employment, by the death of one of the parties, or in some other manner inconsistent with the possibility of future or continuing service under the contract. For during the term of employment, where it is for an indefinite period, when both parties are living and specific performance would mean compelling one party to accept and the other to render services, the reasons for the refusal of courts of equity to decree specific performance of such contracts apply and that relief will be refused even though there be no adequate remedy at law, for it would result in a species of peonage on the part of the servant, or, an enforced association with an obnoxious employee on the part of the master which would be intolerable. So it is said: "By reason of the doctrine of mutuality, a court of equity will refuse to decree the specific performance of an executory contract wherever it creates a duty from the plaintiff of such confidential or personal nature that the court could not have enforced it at the instance of the defendant. After the services have been rendered, however, the reason for the foregoing rule no longer applies, the contract having become mutual in both obligation and remedy, and specific performance of a contract will not be denied because the consideration consists of personal services, where all such services have been fully performed." 25 R.C.L. 305....

The limitation which the rule imposes upon equitable jurisdiction at times results in the denial of any adequate remedy to one who has been injured by the breach of such a contract and courts have striven to discover some alternate remedy which in cases of unusual and extreme hardship would afford to the promisee some measure of relief. So in England where such contracts contained negative covenants, while the courts at first in cases where specific performance of the affirmative covenants could not be enforced also refused to enforce the negative covenants, later, beginning with *Lumley v. Wagner*, 1 DeG. M. & G. 604, their power to enforce negative covenants was recognized although that might indirectly result in compelling the specific performance of the affirmative covenants. In *Lumley v. Wagner*, the negative stipulation was express, but later cases upon its reasoning extended the principle which it announced to cover implied covenants, but that extension appears to have been disapproved in *Whitwood Chemical Co. v. Hardman*, [1891] 2 Ch. pp. 427, 430, and Fry, criticizing the extension of the doctrine, says: "It is not easy to see the limits to which the doctrine of an implied negative might be carried; for as A and not-A. include the whole world, it follows that a contract to sell to A. or to sing at A. must imply a negation of a sale to not-A. or a singing at not-A.: and if injunction is to be granted where specific performance might be impossible, the logical conclusion of the doctrine would be a great and rather formidable enlargement of the jurisdiction of Equity." Fry Spec. Perf. § 857....

There is a distinction between cases in which the contract provides merely for employment and compensation in which a refusal to serve or to pay is the negation of a promise to pay or to serve, and cases where the services involve and imply some rare and unusual quality in the promisor which if given to a competitor of the promisee might cause him a loss by the diversion of custom in addition to what he might suffer from the loss of custom which the services of the promisor might attract, and that consideration apparently underlies the decisions in many of the cases enforcing negative covenants. There are, however, cases in which the doctrine of the enforcement of implied negative covenants has been carried far beyond the present state of the law in England, and beyond what seems to be the weight of the best considered authority here, but taking the law as we find it, it may safely be said that equity will not enforce a negative covenant, express or implied, in a contract which it can not specifically enforce, unless a breach of the negative covenant will cause loss to the promisee distinct from that resulting from the mere failure of the promisor to carry out his affirmative promise. Applying that principle to contracts for personal services the sounder rule is that equity will not enforce negatively a contract which it could not enforce affirmatively, nor will it enjoin the breach of a negative covenant, express or implied, unless the breach will cause a loss to the promisee independent of the loss caused by the mere failure of the promisor to keep and perform his affirmative covenants.

Applying those principles to the facts of this case the conclusion that the plaintiff is not entitled to any relief in equity seems inevitable. The contract was essentially one for the rendition of personal services. They were varied it is true, but they required no extraordinary or unusual skill, experience or capacity. Under the employment the appellant acted as nurse, chauffeur, companion, gardener and housekeeper and while it may be difficult to appraise in monetary terms the value of services so varied, nevertheless, they involved no more than doing such things as a housewife often does as a part of the ordinary routine of life. The reasons for the general rule that equity will not specifically enforce contracts for personal service apply with plenary force to the facts conceded here. Assuming that appellee broke the contract, that the breach was whimsical, arbitrary and unjust, and induced by the intrigue of greedy relatives, nevertheless its enforcement would compel him to accept the personal services of an employee against his wish and his will. The court can no more compel him to accept her services under such conditions, than it could compel her to render them if he demanded them and she were unwilling to give them. It follows that the decree must be affirmed.

Decree affirmed, with costs.

NOTES AND QUESTIONS

1. *Later developments in Maryland*: If Mr. Michael had died before Ms. Fitzpatrick had sued, would the result have been different? For a somewhat similar case suggesting that Ms. Fitzpatrick would then have received specific performance, see *Hanson v. Urner.*[65]

2. *Negative injunctions*: In *Fitzpatrick v. Michael*, the court considers the possibility of a "negative injunction." Ordinarily, courts will not order specific performance of contracts involving personal services. However, where an employee leaves an employer and competes directly with the employer some relief seemed warranted. The court would not order the employee to perform the employment contract and continue working, but it might negatively enjoin the employee from working for someone else. The employee could sit idle or, perhaps, work in jobs that were not in competition with the employer — subject to liability to pay any damages that could be proved. In *Warner Bros. Pictures, Inc. v. Nelson*,[66] for example, the court ordered the actress Bette Davis not to render "any services for or in any motion picture or stage production or productions of any person, firm or corporation other than the plaintiffs." She was not ordered to carry out her contract with Warner Bros. Pictures. She was told not to work as an actress for anyone else. The indirect coercion supporting the contract worked. Bette Davis resumed making pictures for Warner Bros. Soon thereafter Davis and Warner Bros. renegotiated her contract.

The court in the *Fitzpatrick* case said that such an injunction required that the services be of some rare and unusual quality so that if they were given to a competitor, they might cause a loss by the diversion of custom. The court said that in the *Fitzpatrick* case, the personal services required no unusual skill. They "involved no more than doing such things as a housewife often does as part of the ordinary routine of life." In the 1990s, a court probably would not devalue nursing or housewife services in these terms. Nonetheless, in the *Fitzpatrick* case, the nurse's services were not being diverted to a competitor thereby causing a loss of custom. It is important to realize that normally it is the employer who seeks to enjoin the employee from working for a competitor. If the "diversion of business" criteria is essential to obtaining a negative injunction, it is hard to imagine a case in which an employee could enjoin an employer from hiring a substitute. Moreover, Orien C. Michael, the employer, was not trying to avoid

---

[65] 111 A.2d 649 (Md. Ct. App., 1955).

[66] [1937] 1 KB 209.

competitive injury by an injunction. Thus, the nurse could not get an injunction, the equitable remedy which she needed to avoid the Statute of Frauds.

BRACKENBURY v. HODGKIN

102 A. 106. (Me. 1917)

CORNISH, C. J. The defendant Mrs. Sarah D. P. Hodgkin on the 8th day of February, 1915, was the owner of certain real estate — her home farm, situated in the outskirts of Lewiston. She was a widow and was living alone. She was the mother of six adult children, five sons, one of whom, Walter, is the codefendant, and one daughter, who is the coplaintiff. The plaintiffs were then residing in Independence, Mo. Many letters had passed between mother and daughter concerning the daughter and her husband returning to the old home and taking care of the mother, and finally on February 8, 1915, the mother sent a letter to the daughter and her husband which is the foundation of this bill in equity. In this letter she made a definite proposal, the substance of which was that if the Brackenburys would move to Lewiston, and maintain and care for Mrs. Hodgkin on the home place during her life, and pay the moving expenses, they were to have the use and income of the premises, together with the use of the household goods, with certain exceptions, Mrs. Hodgkin to have what rooms she might need. The letter closed, by way of postscript, with the words, "you to have the place when I have passed away."

Relying upon this offer, which was neither withdrawn nor modified, and in acceptance thereof, the plaintiffs moved from Missouri to Maine late in April, 1915, went upon the premises described and entered upon the performance of the contract. Trouble developed after a few weeks, and the relations between the parties grew most disagreeable. The mother brought two suits against her son-in-law on trifling matters, and finally ordered the plaintiffs from the place, but they refused to leave. Then on November 7, 1916, she executed and delivered to her son, Walter C. Hodgkin, a deed of the premises, reserving a life estate in herself. Walter, however, was not a bona fide purchaser for value without notice, but took the deed with full knowledge of the agreement between the parties and for the sole purpose of evicting the plaintiffs. On the very day the deed was executed he served a notice to quit upon Mr. Brackenbury, as preliminary to an action of forcible entry and detainer which was brought on November 13, 1916. This bill in equity was brought by the plaintiffs to secure a reconveyance of the farm from Walter to his mother, to restrain and enjoin Walter from further prosecuting his action of forcible entry and detainer, and to obtain an adjudication that the mother holds the legal title impressed with a trust in favor of the plaintiffs in accordance with their contract.

The sitting justice made an elaborate and carefully considered finding of facts and signed a decree, sustaining the bill with costs against Walter C. Hodgkin, and granting the relief prayed for. The case is before the law court on the defendants' appeal from this decree.

Four main issues are raised.

1. As to the completion and existence of a valid contract.

A legal and binding contract is clearly proven. The offer on the part of the mother was in writing, and its terms cannot successfully be disputed. There was no need that it be accepted in words, nor that a counter promise on the part of the plaintiffs be made. The offer was the basis, not of a bilateral contract, requiring a reciprocal promise, a promise for a promise, but of a unilateral contract requiring an act for a promise. "In the latter case the only acceptance of the offer that is necessary is the performance of the act. In other words, the promise becomes binding when the act is performed." 6 R. C. L. 607. This is elementary law.

The plaintiffs here accepted the offer by moving from Missouri to the mother's farm in Lewiston and entering upon the performance of the specified acts, and they have continued performance since that time so far as they have been permitted by the mother to do so. The existence of a completed and valid contract is clear.

2. The creation of an equitable interest.

This contract between the parties, the performance of which was entered upon by the plaintiffs, created an equitable interest in the land described in the bill in favor of the plaintiffs. The letter of February 8, 1915, signed by the mother, answered the statutory requirement that "there can be no trust concerning lands, except trusts arising or resulting by implication of law, unless created or declared by some writing signed by the party or his attorney." R. S. 1903, c. 75, § 14. No particular formality need be observed; a letter or other memorandum is sufficient to establish a trust provided its terms and the relations of the parties to it appear with reasonable certainty. Bates v. Hurd, 65 Me. 181; McClellan v. McClellan, 65 Me. 500. The equitable interest of the plaintiffs in these premises is obvious, and they are entitled to have that interest protected.

3. Alleged breach of duty on the part of the plaintiffs.

The defendants contend that, granting an equitable estate has been established, the plaintiffs have failed of performance because of their improper and unkind treatment of Mrs. Hodgkin, and therefore have forfeited the right to equitable relief which they might otherwise be entitled to. The sitting justice decided this question of fact in favor of the plaintiffs, and his finding is fully warranted by the evidence. Mrs. Hodgkin's temperament and disposition, not only as described in the testimony of others, but as revealed in her own attitude, conduct, and testimony as a witness, as they stand out on the printed record, mark her as the provoking cause in the various family difficulties. She was "the one primarily at fault."

4. Adequate relief at law.

The defendants finally invoke the familiar rule that the plaintiffs have a plain and adequate remedy at law, and therefore cannot ask relief in equity.

The answer to this proposition is that this rule does not apply when the court has been given full equity jurisdiction, or has been given special statutory jurisdiction covering the case.... The court in equity in this state is given special statutory jurisdiction to grant relief in cases of trusts (R. S. 1903, c. 79, § 6, par. 4), and therefore the exception and not the rule must govern here.

The plaintiffs are entitled to the remedy here sought, and the entry must be: *Appeal dismissed.* Decree of sitting justice affirmed, with costs against Walter C. Hodgkin.

NOTES AND QUESTIONS

1. *Background of the case*: Dawson and Harvey, in their case book on contracts, tell us "[o]ur informant learned from Mr. Brackenbury that the latter secured a transcript of the record in the equity case and 'would from time to time, read from it to the old lady.'" In their teacher's manual to the case book, Dawson and Harvey add more details. A younger brother of Mrs. Brackenbury sided with his mother, Mrs. Hodgkin. He said that,

> Conditions got to be unbearable for my mother chiefly from Brackenbury. I have been in when they were eating and food was not passed to her, but rather thrown to her by Brackenbury. I never did hear my sister in any argument with mother, but apparently approving what her husband did. The fork which she always had to use was an old iron one with two tines broken off, fit only for the waste cart. I went into the house once when he followed with a gun and threatened to shoot me. But I did not budge.

Douglas I. Hodgkin is Sarah Hodgkin's great grandson. He is a Professor of Political Science at Bates College in Lewiston, Maine. He compiled information about the family feud that continued from 1916 to 1922. The feud received extensive coverage in the local newspapers. He says "[t]he feud arose from the irascible personality of Sarah D. Purinton Hodgkin and the rivalries among her six living children over the family property." None of Mrs. Hodgkin's sons would live with her, and she attempted to recruit her daughter Bertha and her husband Joe Brackenbury. They knew what they might face, and they insisted on a letter that made detailed promises.

Trouble flared within the first month of the Brackenbury's arrival. Joe Brackenbury and Sarah Hodgkin argued about who would decide what work needed to be done. Sarah Hodgkin went to bed at 4:30 or 5:00 p.m. during the winter, and she demanded that the house be quiet. She did not like Bertha's cooking. Sarah Hodgkin tried to get the Brackenbury's to leave. Finally, she sold the property to her son Walter, and this prompted the case which you have read.

Battles continued after the decision. Joe Brackenbury cut wood on the property, and Sarah Hodgkin sued him for trespass. The jury found for Sarah Hodgkin but awarded her only one cent as damages. The brothers who sided with their mother came to the house and attempted to remove a bed at her request. Bertha stopped them. Walter Hodgkin called the police and asserted that Bertha had threatened to shoot him if he tried to move the bed. The jury found Bertha not guilty. She then sued Walter for $3,000 because of the embarrassment of the criminal complaint. She was awarded $212.14 damages. Irving and Russell Hodgkin had an argument that ended when Irving hit Russell in the face. Once again the family returned to the local courts. Russell was awarded $66.71.

Sarah Hodgkin died on January 4, 1921. She left Bertha and her brother Russell nothing in her will "because I have assisted them each to a great extent in the past with financial and other assistance." Bertha and Russell contested the will, alleging undue influence and lack of testamentary capacity. The court admitted the will to probate. Joe and Bertha Brackenbury then sold the property and moved back to Independence, Missouri. Bertha died in 1961 at the age of 97. She corresponded with her nieces and nephews, but she remained estranged from her brothers for the rest of their lives.

2. *Coerced performance and personal relationships*: Why didn't the court consider the "shotgun marriage" aspects of specific performance? The final decree provided "Sarah D.P. Hodgkin shall hold said land which shall be impressed with a trust in their [the Brackenburys] favor and in accordance with the terms of the contract so long as the plaintiffs hereafter perform their contract according to the language and spirit thereof." Could the court have done more to police the relationship? Was it necessary to leave Mrs. Hodgkin at the mercy of Brackenbury?

3. *Review of themes to this point*: Consider the following situation as a way of reviewing what you should have learned to this point in the course:

Husband and wife agree in writing[67] that wife will work while husband begins law school. After he finishes the second year, she will start the first year at the same law school. assuming she is admitted. After graduation, he will take a job in the area to support the two of them while she finishes law school.

They perform the agreement, and she gains admission to the law school he is attending. At graduation a law firm in San Diego, California offers him a job. He is to begin immediately. He wants to take it. He insists that his wife come with him to San Diego. He does not want to be separated from her and their children. He argues that they cannot afford to maintain two households. She does not want to change law schools. The only law

---

[67]This may be an agreement that they cannot perform within one year. Many professional schools require students to be enrolled for a specified time. As a result, the contract might come within the Statute of Frauds. Absent an exception to the Statute such as part performance, oral promises for performances that would take more than a year would not be legally enforceable. While we have made the promises in writing here, how likely are husband and wife to make this kind of arrangement in writing if they are living together?

schools in the San Diego area which will accept her as a transfer student are of much lesser status than her current law school. If she transferred she would probably have fewer job opportunities at graduation. She does not want a divorce.[68] She believes that if they can solve this problem, the marriage will survive. If there is nothing else that can be done, she will go to the San Diego area as he insists. However, she has not told him this.

You are a practicing lawyer. Wife is an old friend and you have offered her a summer job between her first and second year in law school. She asks for your advice, and suggests that she sue her husband for specific performance or for damages caused by his anticipatory breach of contract.[69] She will care for their children while she finishes law school. However, this will require both tuition and support, including money to replace the child care services which the husband would have given as well as to pay for the expenses of finishing law school. She believes that he can borrow any money he cannot save by living very frugally in San Diego. What advice would you give the wife? Should she sue? If so, for what? Is she likely to win a decree of specific performance or a judgment for a sum of money as damages? Would filing a complaint be a good or bad bargaining strategy? Are there ways other than litigation to handle a dispute of this kind?

C. ALTERNATIVES TO LITIGATION IN FAMILY MATTERS

We have looked at relationships between husbands and wives and between families and those who care for the old. Traditionally, courts said that litigation was an inappropriate way to deal with problems between spouses. Similarly, there might be better ways than litigation to compensate meritorious services to

---

[68]In Morgan v. Morgan, 366 N.Y.S.2d 977 (1975), a wife worked to put a husband through medical school. She was awarded enough alimony as part of their divorce action to "so that she can finish her premedical education of one and a half years and then go to medical school for four years, although she was capable of supporting herself working as a secretary." A number of other courts in divorce actions have found ways in which to compensate a spouse who has worked to put the other through school. For example, the Supreme Court of Wisconsin decided that a court could award a combination of property division and maintenance payments although the wife who had done the work was able to support herself. See In re Marriage of Lundberg, 107 Wis.2d 1, 318 N.W.2d 918 (1982); Roberto v. Brown, 107 Wis.2d 17, 318 N.W. 2d 358 (1982). Our interest is in contract and restitutionary theories, but you should be aware of the alimony possibility. While the wife now does not want a divorce, if this matter cannot be resolved in a satisfactory fashion, she may change her mind. Furthermore, she may be able to use the possibility of alimony in negotiations about the contract dispute.

[69]You may assume that the husband's statements about moving to San Diego would themselves breach their contract when he made them. Although the date for his performance — supporting her during her last two years of law school — may not have yet come, the law would allow her to sue now as a result of his clear repudiation of his obligations under the contract. Obviously, we are assuming away a difficult problem. In the usual situation, the husband's statements would not be so clear. You would face difficulty establishing that he had repudiated the contract at this point.

the elderly. During the 1970s and 1980s, there was much debate about "alternatives to litigation." Critics said that American courts were crowded. Litigation was costly and served to enrich lawyers. Public formal adversary procedures injured or destroyed long-term relationships. Radicals saw the American legal system as part of a system of repression. Elite lawyers saw the courts being overwhelmed by an outpouring of relatively minor disputes. Both drew on the work of anthropologists and the peoples' courts found in socialist societies in suggesting that there should be nonadversarial ways of resolving disputes involving long-term continuing relationships. We will consider sketches of the ways in which societies very different from our own resolve disputes, and then we will ask to what extent we find analogous procedures in this country.

1. STORIES FROM OTHER SOCIETIES

Comparative approaches to law often open our eyes to the nature of our own legal system and assumptions on which it rests. Clearly, we do not ask you to read about African tribal law or social control in socialist societies because we think you are likely to make direct use of this information in your law practice.

There are a number of classic problems in comparative work. It is misleading to compare a formal, idealized version of, say, French law with the day-to-day reality of courts in Milwaukee or Chicago. Furthermore, we always have trouble defining the boundaries of what we want to call the legal system. What is part of government in a Chinese setting may be within the jurisdiction of family therapists and parish priests or rabbis in the United States. Consider the following materials in light of a broad view of American social structure, asking whether we have analogous institutions and looking for similarities as well as differences. Then ask whether it makes any difference if a social function is assigned to the public or private sector, insofar as those labels have any connection with reality.

James Gibbs' description of the Kpelle[70] moot[71] proved a provocative example for those seeking to reform the American legal system's way of coping with interpersonal disputes in families and neighborhoods. The Kpelle were a group of about 175,000 people who lived in Central Liberia and adjoining regions of Guinea. They had a formal court system which was "particularly effective in settling cases such as assault, possession of illegal charms, or theft where the litigants are not linked in a relationship which must continue after trial."

---

[70]A Peace Corps worker with experience in the area tells us that the pronunciation is something like "Gah-Bell-ah."

[71]Gibbs, The Kpelle Moot, in Law and Warfare: Studies of the Anthropology of Conflict, at 277-289 (Bohanan ed. 1967). First published in Africa, Journal of the International African Institute, 33(1) 1963.

However, the court was "particularly inept at settling ... matrimonial disputes because its harsh tone tends to drive spouses farther apart rather than to reconcile them."

For cases involving such continuing relationships, the Kpelle used a moot which was more effective than a court in many cases. Gibbs says the "genius of the moot lies in the fact that it is based on a covert application of the principles of psychoanalytic theory which underlie psychotherapy." First, the moot took place before a group including the kin of the litigants and neighbors from the quarter in which the case was being heard. Second, it was held on Sunday, a day of rest, at the home of the complainant. Third, the complainant selected as mediator a kinsman who was a town chief or elder. Fourth, an introductory ceremony was held which focused attention on maintaining harmony and the well-being of the group. Fifth, the proceeding was informal but structured. The complainant spoke but might be interrupted by the mediator or anyone else who wished to challenge what was said or add to it. The mediator might fine those who spoke out of turn — for example, he might order them to bring rum for all to drink. Sixth, the mediator and the others present would point out the various faults of both parties, and at the end of the proceeding, the mediator would express the consensus of the group. Seventh, the one mainly at fault would formally apologize to the other by giving token gifts which must be accepted; the one found less at fault would return a smaller token to signify acceptance of the apology.

Gibbs points out that the process resulted in an airing of all grievances between the parties. The process took place in a familiar setting soon after the matter had come up and before positions had hardened. Both parties were required to consent to bring the matter to the moot although there was social pressure to consent. Fault usually was attributed to both sides. Those who participated in the moot knew the parties and their history, and so they could judge behavior in its full context. They could see how what an outsider might view as trivial had significance in light of past events. Behavior was judged against traditional customary norms of the Kpelle that defined the behavior of a good wife, a good son, a good cousin who was a neighbor and so on. Furthermore, the sanctions imposed were largely symbolic. They were not so burdensome as to prompt resentment. Both parties were re-educated by the reactions of relatives, friends and neighbors to their attitude and conduct. For example, Gibbs reports that a husband learned that the group viewed his customary mildly paranoid sarcasm as destructive of harmony in his marriage, and it did not accept his view of the situation. Presumably, he mended his ways. Disputants were coaxed to conformity by the granting of rewards. The major one was group approval which "goes to the wronged person who accepts an apology and to the person who is magnanimous enough to make one." Thus, successful moots involved changing attitudes and perceptions of situations as the foundation of behavior in the future. Finally, we can note that it would be difficult for a Kpelle to run away from his or her troubles — there was a strong sense of extended family obligation, and it was difficult to leave one's place in the social organization and find needed social and economic support.

Gibbs' conclusions include important qualifications often overlooked by Americans who advocate some version of Kpelle moots for the United States. First, Gibbs stresses:

> A moot is not always successful.... Both parties must have a genuine willingness to cooperate and a real concern about their discord. Each party must be willing to list his grievances, to admit his guilt, and to make an open apology. The moot, like psychotherapy, is impotent without well-motivated clients.

Second, Gibbs notes that courts have a complementary function to the moots. Courts declare rights. In the case of matrimonial disputes, they grant divorces which sometimes are the appropriate remedy. "The essential point is that both formal and informal dispute-settlement procedures serve significant functions in Kpelle society and neither can be fully understood if studied alone." Although Gibbs does not say so, Kpelle might have accepted the risks involved in going to the moot to avoid the greater risks involved in going to court.

Those who have lived under communitarian regimes may pay a price in loss of privacy. Are Kpelle moots and community courts consistent with American or British views of individual rights and privacy? What would the judges who decided *Balfour v. Balfour* say about such institutions? People from other parts of the world might have very different norms about privacy, families and communities. Can we say that European and American societies value privacy so greatly that people who live in them are not subject to social control by their friends and neighbors? Does the answer turn on your social class?

All of us who have attended high school or lived in group residences know that there is such a thing as social control apart from the public legal system in our society. Nauta[72] studied 196 women living in blocks of twelve adjoining houses in the eastern part of Amsterdam. The researcher asked for details of quarrels between neighbors, who quarreled with whom, why, and what happened exactly. We could interpret almost all the quarrels as sanctions against infringements of norms. The exerter of sanctions turned out time and again to be the controlling neighbor. Most of those controlled were younger, had lived for shorter times in the block, were more permissive, and worked more outside the home. Other women felt that they were being controlled by their neighbors although they avoided quarrels. Some withdrew from contact with neighbors, but many were dependent on their neighbors for assistance and sociability. It was easy to gossip about neighbors, and those with restrictive views about proper conduct felt under

---

[72]Nauta, Social Control and Norm Restrictiveness: Some Results of an Inquiry into Neighbour Relationships, 10 Sociologia Neerlandia 233 (1974).

pressure to conform. You can make your own judgment about the extent to which you would find similar forms of social control in American apartment and suburban living. Insofar as you found something of this sort, how does it differ from Kpelle moots?

2. "ALTERNATIVES" IN AMERICAN SOCIETY

To what extent do we find institutions similar to Kpelle moots and community courts in the United States? Is it true that we can solve personal disputes only by withdrawal, violence or litigation? Suppose a middle or an upper middle class family faces marital difficulties. Is it likely that either the husband's or the wife's parents will play a role in trying to resolve the problems? Will neighbors play a role? What professionals might they call on? How might they go about coping with the problems? Might contract in some form play a part? Remember *Miller v. Miller*, *supra*. Do courts and other state institutions have an informal side, in which officials behave more like a Kpelle moot than their formal job descriptions would suggest?

Suppose a working class or poor family has an ongoing dispute. What do police do with family disputes when the neighbors call them? Parnas,[73] in a description which predated mandatory arrest laws in domestic disturbance cases and at least some greater appreciation of the significance of such behavior, told us:

> If the victim and offender are both present when the police arrive and the victim has not sustained serious injury, the police, depending upon the circumstances of the incident and their own individual inclination, may use one or more of the following procedures: mediation; referral [to private or public agencies]; threats of arrest or other forms of indirect sanctions; voluntary, temporary separation of the disputants; the threat of filing cross-complaints; refusal to arrest except on a warrant.

Of course, police in a smaller city might act differently from police in a major metropolitan center. In addition, we note that expectations and procedures seem to be changing with a realization of the stakes in these cases. What differences are there in the approaches which we might expect from, on the one hand American police and, on the other hand, from Li Erh-ma?[74]

Some groups in American society run their own "private legal systems," and often they deal with family matters. For example:

---

[73]Parnas, "The Police Response to the Domestic Disturbance," 1967 Wisconsin Law Review 914, 932. Copyright c. by The University of Wisconsin.

[74]The role of police in family disputes is controversial. Many argue that battering husbands ought to be arrested and jailed rather than subjected to slaps on the wrist. Often, however, the battered wife needs the husband's income and faces difficult choices.

Jewish Conciliation Board (JCB): The JCB, established in New York City in the early 1920's, is an interdenominational Jewish court of arbitration. It currently handles close to one thousand widely varied cases yearly. The majority of the cases are family and marital problems: children refusing to support elderly relatives; financial responsibilities in second marriages; and typical husband-wife problems that seem to be leading the couple down the road to divorce.... The Board also deals with minor problems between Jewish businessmen and with miscellaneous problems between individuals.

From the close to one thousand cases that are brought to the JCB each year, only 8 1/2 per cent actually go to trial. A look at the Board's procedure explains why.

The first step in bringing a problem before the Board is an interview with the executive secretary in the Board's office. Many of the cases brought are not proper for adjudication; some are merely personal problems that require a helping hand and not a court. Nobody is ever turned away. If possible, the troubled person is sent to a government or private agency where assistance is available. If not, there is still an open and sympathetic ear at the JCB which often is very useful.

For those complaints that are fit for adjudication, the party coming to the Board fills out a complaint form after the interview. This is given a case number, put into the Board's file and a copy sent to the other party who is asked to come to the office to explain his side. If the party refuses to come, follow-up letters are sent. Although there is no way to force parties to appear, they usually do. When both parties appear at the Board's office together, mediation by the executive secretary is attempted. In many cases, face-to-face confrontation plus the prodding and logical and objective view of the mediator is all that is needed for agreement. If this is not successful, the case then goes on the docket. Before any case is officially taken up by the Board of judges, a signed submission agreement is required. This makes the JCB's decision legally binding.

The method used by the judges in deciding cases is *mishpat shalom*, a judgment of peace. It has been described as a combination of "a paragraph of (Jewish) law and human intuition." The three judges provide the human intuition as well as the law, so in theory the outcome is sensible, logical and equitable. The method has also been described as "an act of conciliation. We try not to say 'you are right, you are wrong.' Rather we try to convince the parties to do what is proper." The fact that these decisions are rarely, if ever, appealed is perhaps proof enough that the method is successful.

In a recent session, the practical effects of the Board's philosophy were clearly seen. Four marital cases were before the Board. Two of those cases were concluded with the complaint being withdrawn and the parties kissing and making up in the courtroom. In another case, the husband and wife were sent to a marriage counsellor with certain conditions, and in the fourth case, the wife was sent to a free treatment center for necessary psychiatric help.

The JCB has no machinery to enforce its decisions, and none is usually necessary. If one of the parties is reluctant to abide by the decision, a letter from the Board is usually enough to make the party comply. If, as very rarely happens, these letters fail, the winning party can sue in civil court for his award and the court will grant and enforce it.

Sitting on each case is a board of three judges, a rabbi, a businessman, and a lawyer, chosen by the executive secretary. Where necessary, a psychiatrist may sit on a case in order to give the judges the benefit of his professional knowledge. Since many people who come to the Board are disturbed and need professional guidance, this innovation is quite helpful.

There are court sessions about every two or three weeks with a few cases heard at each session. When the parties come to court, the hearings are quite informal. The parties present their own side in an informal manner, and the lawyer-judge handles any of the necessary legal issues. Witnesses appear and are questioned and cross-examined informally by the judges. When the parties finish their stories, they leave the room and the judges discuss the case. A decision is then reached and written up by the lawyer-judge. The decision is then read to the parties and put in the Board's files. A complete record of all cases is kept, including a transcript of the trial.[75]

What differences are therein in the approaches we might expect from, on the one hand a Kpelle moot, and on the other hand either the American police or a Jewish Conciliation Board?

3. CALLS FOR NEW APPROACHES AND THE PRACTICE OF LAW

Apart from the many "private governments" found in American society, people often consult lawyers when they face problems. One who knew about lawyers only from the articles in the popular press published in the 1970s and 1980s might assume that all clients who enter lawyers' offices engage in bitter protracted litigation. Clearly some lawyers representing some clients do appear before juries and carry appeals to the highest available court. However, frequently this is not what happens.

---

[75]Note, Rabbinical Courts: Modern Day Solomons, 6 Columbia Journal of Law and Social Problems 49, 66-68 (1970). Copyright Columbia Journal of Law and Social Problems. Reprinted with permission. See, also, James Yaffe, So Sue Me (Saturday Review Press 1972).

a. Calls for Mediation Rather than Adjudication

Even if we cannot help parties find a way to continue a long-term relationship, they may need help in finding a way out of one. Many now believe that when marriages end, mediated settlements are better than litigation for all concerned. Some seeking divorce have decided to try to attempt to avoid court battles, and the bitterness and antagonism they often cause, and have sought out divorce mediators. The mediators, most of them trained as lawyers, social workers, or psychologists, help the parties work out an agreement. Many who have used mediators have been very pleased with the results, commenting on the absence of bad feelings in the process.[76] But there are problems with trying to move away from power and legal coercion towards consent as a way of dealing with questions that arise when marriages end. Some critics suggest that mediators, in their focus on producing an agreement without confrontation, may sacrifice the interests of one of the parties. Just because something is a compromise doesn't mean that it is fair.

b. Alternative Dispute Resolution and the Practice of Law

The following material deals with areas other than family disputes. Nonetheless, it suggests that lawyers regularly play roles other than that of courtroom advocate. We can ask whether lawyers in family disputes also play the part of mediator. Macaulay studied lawyers and consumer protection laws.[77] He found that lawyers played the roles of gatekeeper who teaches clients about the costs of using the legal system, the knowledgeable friend or therapist, the broker of information or coach, the go between or informal mediator, the legal technician, and the adversary bargainer-litigator.[78] However, most lawyers would not do anything with a consumer matter beyond letting a client or potential client express anger, attempting to change the client's view of the situation, telling the client how to complain, or directing him or her to a state or local agency. Thus, lawyers played the role of gatekeeper to the legal system, filtering out potential claims.

Attorneys who became more involved in a dispute might find themselves playing the part of go-between or informal mediator. They might telephone or

---

[76]Mediating a Less Hostile End to a Marriage, New York Times, August 3, 1981 at p. 16, cols. 2-6.

[77]Macaulay, Lawyers and Consumer Protection Laws, 14 Law & Society Review 115 (1979).

[78]We can also distinguish styles in playing these roles. For example, Neustadter studied lawyers handling individuals seeking relief from debts in bankruptcy. Some lawyers sought to counsel clients and explain all options open to them. Others created a routine and mass processed clients through the legal system as quickly as possible. See Neustadter, When Lawyer and Client Meet: Observations of Interviewing and Counseling Behavior in the Consumer Bankruptcy Office, 35 Buffalo Law Review 177 (1986).

write the seller or creditor. The lawyer may be able to present the complaint so that it is more understandable, and transform the presentation so that it is more persuasive. The complaint, restated by a lawyer, may gain legitimacy. The lawyer is saying that he or she has reviewed the buyer's or debtor's story, the assertions of fact are at least plausible, and the buyer or debtor has reason to complain if these are the facts. The lawyer is more likely than the consumer to talk to someone who has authority to do something about a problem. And a tacit threat always lurks in the background; lawyers are people who can make trouble if a settlement isn't reached.

When they talk with the seller or creditor, lawyers often learn that their clients did not tell them the whole story — there usually is another side. However, lawyers may be able to reach a settlement if they do not ask for too much. Good lawyers know how much is too much. A skillful lawyer may be able to avoid confrontation and give the seller or creditor a graceful way to agree to a settlement. Ideally, the lawyer and the seller or creditor will fashion a solution that both looks good to the client and does not hurt the seller or creditor very much.[79]

Once a lawyer obtains such an offer, the next step is to sell it to the client. The client may want to fight to the Supreme Court, but the lawyer must persuade the client that the settlement is fair and litigation would not be profitable. Often enough, the client takes the settlement but remains unhappy with the lawyers' services. The client thought he or she had rights and expected vindication. Instead, all the lawyer produced was a deal.

Why don't lawyers accept all clients who come to their offices and immediately turn to litigation? Would we expect lawyers to treat family matters much as they treat consumer protection questions? Insofar as the practice of law often involves negotiating settlements, what role do legal rules and procedures play? Consider the following excerpts from Professor Galanter's article and ask why legal educators want to stress doctrine and adjudication rather than what he calls "litigotiation?"

Worlds of Deals: Using Negotiation to Teach about Legal Process
Marc Galanter[80]

[The phrase] ... alternative dispute resolution strikes me as revealing something about the tacit picture of the legal world which permeates American legal

---

[79]For example, a used car dealer might offer to take back a car with which the lawyer's client is dissatisfied. However, the dealer is unlikely to offer to refund the purchase price. Rather, the dealer might offer to take the car plus an additional amount of money in exchange for another car on the dealer's lot. The net price paid by the client will be far less than the asking price for the substitute car. Nonetheless, the dealer may still be able to profit on the entire transaction.

[80]34 Journal of Legal Education 268 (1984) Copyright Journal of Legal Education. Reprinted with permission.

education. It links negotiation with alternatives and implicitly juxtaposes them to something unspecified. Alternatives, we may ask, to what? To adjudication, to courts. Even while affirming that negotiation is important, the title reflects the view that negotiation (and mediation and so forth) occupies the outer edges of the legal realm — peripheral to the real thing, adjudication in courts; they are soft as opposed to the hard core of legal doctrine. Negotiation is something apart from the real law that occupies legal educators.

This picture is misleading in several ways. It implies that negotiation (and other so-called alternatives) are infrequent, new, unproven, marginal. But the gravitation to the mediative posture by judges and other decision makers armed with arbitral powers is surely one of the most typical patterns of disputing on the American scene — as an examination of our courts and administrative agencies will attest. The linking of negotiation to "alternatives" to litigation is misleading in another sense. On the contemporary American legal scene the negotiation of disputes is not an alternative to litigation. It is only a slight exaggeration to say that it *is* litigation. There are not two distinct processes, negotiation and litigation; there is a single process of disputing in the vicinity of official tribunals that we might call *litigotiation*, that is, the strategic pursuit of a settlement through mobilizing the court process. Full-blown adjudication of the dispute — running the whole course — might be thought of as an infrequently-pursued alternative to the ordinary course of litigotiation. I do not minimize its importance: adjudication remains a compelling presence even when it does not occur.

The courts are central to the litigotiation game because of the "bargaining endowments" they bestow on the parties. What might be done by (or in or near) a court, that is, gives the parties bargaining chips or counters. Bargaining chips derive from the substantive entitlements conferred by legal rules and from the procedural rules that enable these entitlements to be vindicated. But rules are only part of the endowment conferred by the law — the delay, cost, and uncertainty of eliciting a favorable determination also confer bargaining counters on the disputants. Everything that might affect outcome counts — all the outcome for the party, not just that encompassed by the rules. The ability to impose delay, costs, risk, embarrassment, publicity comes into play along with the rules. Rules are important but they interact with a host of other factors in ways that do not correspond to the nearly separated background and foreground of the law school classroom.

The settlement process is not some marginal, peripheral aspect of legal disputing in America; it is the central core. Something like 90 percent of civil cases are settled (and of course many more disputes are settled before reaching the stage of filing). Lawyers spend more time on settlement discussions than on research or on trials and appeals. Much of the other activity that lawyers engage in is articulated to the settlement process. Even in the case that departs from the standardized routines of settlement, negotiation and litigation are not separate processes, but are inseparably entwined. Negotiation, then, is not the law's soft penumbra, but the hard heart of the process. The so-called hard law turns out to be only one (often malleable) set of counters in the litigotiation game....

[T]he world of negotiation [is] made up of different bargaining arenas. By this I mean some more or less bounded constellation of lawyers (and in some cases other actors such as insurance adjusters or detectives or judges) who interact with one another in connection with the settlement (and occasional adjudication) of particular kinds of cases in a particular locality. They share (more or less) expectations and understandings about procedures, applicable norms, outcomes. In a particular locality there may be a personal injury bargaining arena, a medical malpractice bargaining arena, a family law arena, an antitrust arena and so forth. Individual lawyers may participate in one or several; lawyers may be comfortably familiar with a certain arena or find it strange and intimidating. Such arenas may be more or less differentiated and more or less bounded. A lawyer may spend his whole working life in a single arena in which everybody knows everybody, one's reputation in the arena is a prime concern, and everybody knows what every case is worth. (I gather that criminal law in some middle-sized cities approximates this.) Or an arena may be diffuse — one may constantly encounter antagonists who are strangers, with little concern about reputation and little shared knowledge about standards and benchmarks. An arena may deal with cases that are exhaustively researched and investigated, or with cases that are too small to support much investment in generating information.

So, preparing to negotiate involves not only acquiring generalized skills, but learning to read the landscape, to dope out the features of the bargaining arena. It is crucial to know whether you are dealing with people who are concerned to deal with you again, whether deals are standardized here or custom made, and what expectations are shared about the process and outcome.

c. Effectiveness of Mediation

Mediation is a process in which parties to a dispute use a third party who does not have power to dictate an outcome — as does an arbitrator. Mediators act in a number of ways: They can suggest new solutions to parties; they can help parties recharacterize events; they can separate parties and act as go-betweens, translating their concerns into less emotional language. Not all mediation is the same, however. Those who have studied mediation suggest that it ranges from a bargaining process conducted in the shadow of a court, to a communication process which resembles therapy in its focus upon exploring and enunciating feelings.[81] Mediation rarely can be found in its "ideal" form. Mediators, for example, often have some degree of power over one or both parties. When a judge acts as a mediator in order to help the parties to settle a case, the judge may have the power to retaliate against one who blocks a solution to the

---

[81]Silbey and Merry, Mediator Settlement Strategies, 8 Law & Policy 7 (1986).

problem. In addition, the parties may want to look good to the mediator, who may be a friend, or respected person who has agreed to play the role.

Mediation should not be romanticized. It doesn't always work. While mediators may help open lines of communication, and suggest solutions, mediation may also reveal that the disputant's objectives are genuinely incompatible. A mediator might pressure parties to reach an agreement that might not be long-lasting, or that ratifies existing patterns of domination.[82] How would one go about testing the hypothesis that mediation often fails to protect the weaker party?

When is mediation likely to work? When is it likely to fail? Felstiner, one of the leading scholars of the subject, notes that conflicts of values are less likely to produce mediated agreements than conflicts over interests.[83] For example, Lee Marvin probably could have saved money by agreeing to pay Michelle the amount awarded by the trial court for rehabilitation rather than paying his lawyer to take the case to the appellate court. However, Marvin reportedly saw the matter as a cause. He thought women should not have claims to money just because they lived with a man. This suggests mediation might not have worked between Lee and Michelle.

Felstiner also points out that the claim may be but a surrogate for a real dispute. If the underlying causes are rooted in patterns established by years of coping, mediation will not address them. What seems to be a reasonable solution to a relatively minor problem, will not touch the real difficulty if the minor problem is but part of a much larger balance sheet of interpersonal claims. The Balfours and the Millers are unlikely to become warm caring people concerned with each other as a result of two or three mediating sessions. In short, mediation is not deep psychotherapy.

Mediation is difficult when there are many parties. Lawyers often tell stories about clients who would have been willing to settle claims against others but who were pushed into litigating by their spouses. If many know about a dispute, considerations of pride and reputation may make it difficult for some people to back down. Felstiner says that success requires some rough status equality

---

[82]See, *e.g.*, Bedlin and Nejelski, Unsettling Issues About Settling Civil Litigation, 68 Judicature 9 (1984). In contrast, however, Janet Rifkin argues:

"Although critics of mediation charge that it may keep the less powerful party from achieving equality and equal bargaining power, it is not so clear ... how this operates in practice. These objections to mediation are inextricably tied to the view that the formal legal system offers both a better alternative and a greater possibility of achieving a fair and just resolution to the conflict. The general assumption that the lawyer can "help" the client more meaningfully than a mediator is part of the problem with this view. In many instances, although new substantive rights or legal protections are realized, patterns of domination are reinforced by the lawyer-client relationship, in which the client is a passive recipient of the lawyer's expertise. This is particularly true for women clients, for whom patterns of domination are at the heart of the problem." Rifkin, Mediation From a Feminist Perspective: Promise and Problems, 2 Law & Inequality 21, 30 (1984).

[83]Felstiner, The Logic of Mediation, in Toward a General Theory of Social Control (Donald Black ed. 1981).

between the parties. Mr. Balfour, for example, had no apparent reason to mediate his dispute with Mrs. Balfour. He had the money, he had left her, and the situation as it stood pleased him. He had already earned the disapproval of relatives and friends as a result of separating from his wife. He was unlikely to reap much goodwill by participating in mediation.

d. Compensating Care for the Old

We talked with officials familiar with the probate and administration of estates in Dane County, Wisconsin. They told us that care for the elderly poses common problems. While they process most estates in what is essentially an administrative procedure, enough flawed wills and family situations occur so they know the situation well. For example, a common case involves a farm estate. Suppose a farm family consists of husband and wife and five children. Four children leave the farm and go to cities to pursue careers. One brother stays and works the farm with his father. The father dies and leaves everything to the mother. She never makes a will. She lives until the child who stayed and worked the farm is in his fifties. Then she dies. Under intestate succession, all five children take equally. The four who left the farm want to sell and divide the proceeds. However, this would leave the one who worked the farm all his life with no future. Another common case involves the daughter who comes home to take care of aged parents. Trouble comes when their wills do not honor her or when they do not remember her special contribution.

Commissioners and clerks who handle probate say that they tell the lawyers that they do not want to see such cases as disputes. They hold pre-trial conferences as well as informal discussions so that the lawyers do not lose the forest by concentrating on the trees. Lawyers for the estate may forget that the estate is the client rather than the executor or particular heirs. It makes no sense to spend thousands of dollars to resolve claims that lawyers could settle for much less. 95% of these claims for caring for the old are settled for something less than the claimant asked for but for more than the law might require the estate to pay. Wisconsin law allows a lawyer to make a good case for those who cared for the old, and this is enough to justify a settlement. One always seeks to get all those with any claim to the estate to agree to these settlements so no one later can attack the final distribution of the estate.

Lawyers learn how to handle matters sensibly. In smaller counties the same group of lawyers handles most of the estates. Older lawyers appear most often. They have drafted the wills and outlived their clients. In Dane County, there are many lawyers and the group appearing to probate estates changes over time. Senior lawyers delegate all but the very difficult ones to junior lawyers. Lawyers just out of law school get small estates as some of the first matters they see. Younger lawyers sometimes see things as all or nothing. Those who handle probate explain that one has to consider the costs to the estate and the various claimants as contrasted with what they might gain by litigation. The probate commissioners in Dane County are lawyers, and so they can educate lawyers in the advantages of settling these claims.

Of course, the lawyers have to persuade their clients to settle. However, these matters involve family members who seldom are eager to battle each other if they can work out anything acceptable to everyone. Families do not want to wash their dirty linen in public. Family members may feel guilty about allowing a sister or brother to care for their elderly parent. If handled properly, lawyers can use this guilt in suggesting a settlement that pays for care. If the estate is large enough, payments for services will be a deduction against the gross estate when they calculate the estate tax. The parties can see the government paying part of what extra is given to the brother or sister who cared for the elderly parent. Lawyers, themselves, can push hard for settlements. They can explain both the law and the equities of the claim in such a way that most relatives will accept that a settlement may be best for all concerned. It would seldom pay for a lawyer to encourage taking a family fight through litigation. Few potential heirs can pay large fees, and a contingent fee would make economic sense only when there is a good chance of winning a large sum against a wealthy estate.

D. FRANCHISE AND EMPLOYMENT RELATIONS

Much of what we have seen in studying contract and family relationships returns when we look at franchises and employment. When we considered *Copylease v. Memorex* (the photocopy-toner case) we saw that the California courts were no more willing to attempt to regulate ongoing franchise relationships than other courts have been to deal with contracts between husband and wife. Furthermore, the reasons offered for hesitating to venture into what Chafee called "the dismal swamp" were much the same. However, the legal system sometimes intervenes in employment and franchise relationships. Over the past thirty years, those championing employees and franchisees have increasingly called for more intervention. While we can distinguish the situations at the extremes, in practice many franchises come close to employment relationships. Indeed, often the franchisor seeks both the control which an employer has over employees and the image of "running your own business" to provide incentives for hard work.

Automobile dealerships, fast food restaurants, motels, dry cleaners, gasoline service stations and nationwide real estate firms all are examples of the franchise. A firm granting a franchise usually provides a trade name, products, and procedures. The one receiving a franchise agrees to follow the procedures and invest both labor and capital. Absent legal regulation, franchisors retain great influence on the day-to-day operations of the business. They reserve almost absolute power to end the arrangement without any need to show cause. The threat of taking away the sign that says "Mobil," "Holiday Inn," "One-Hour Martinizing," "McDonalds," or "Chevrolet" turns requests into commands. Franchisees may be so productive that they command real independence. In some situations, however, a franchisee resembles an employee since the franchisor exercises almost complete control of the operation. This is particularly the case where the franchisee does not invest large sums of capital at the outset, but invests his or her labor in creating a going business. Even where this is the case, franchisees may have greater incentives than most employees to work hard, and many of the statutes regulating wages and hours of employment do not apply to their efforts.

Until the 1950s, franchisees had only the rights which franchisors gave them in franchise agreements. Franchisors seemed more concerned with protecting their interests than creating systems of due process for those who ran their local retailing outlets. Over the last thirty to forty years, franchisees often have appealed to the American legal system with mixed success.

1. THE FRANCHISE

a. Creating the Relationship

Many franchises are very valuable. A good manager, with only a little luck, can make a great deal of money being the local Chevrolet dealer or running a Holiday Inn. One probably never will get rich running a Mobil service station or a One-Hour Martinizing dry cleaning establishment; nonetheless, it is a chance at upward mobility for many. "The Commerce Department predicts that franchising will account for more than half of retail sales by the year 2000.... [It] estimates that franchising accounted for $456.7 billion in sales ... [in 1984], a jump of more than 270 percent from 1969, when only $112.8 billion came from franchising."[84]

However, franchisors do not hand out franchises just for the asking. Those seeking them will have to convince a franchisor's representatives that they have enough skill and capital to succeed in business. Furthermore, the person seeking a franchise will want to enter business as soon as possible after the franchisor awards it. If a local representative says that the home office will approve; the applicant may be tempted to invest in signs, inventory and the like. Once again, courts could draw sharp lines to serve as forms. They could say that a person who has a franchise agreement signed by the franchisor has whatever rights it grants. One who has yet to receive a signed document has nothing. Many courts have taken just this position. However, other courts have offered relief even to those who have yet to pass through the formality creating the status of franchisee.

HOFFMAN v. RED OWL STORES, INC.

26 Wis.2d 683, 133 N.W.2d 267 (1965)

Action by Joseph Hoffman (hereinafter "Hoffman") and wife, plaintiffs, against defendants Red Owl Stores, Inc. (hereinafter "Red Owl") and Edward Lukowitz.

---

[84]New York Times, Jan. 20, 1985, at F4, col. 3.

The complaint alleged that Lukowitz, as agent for Red Owl, represented to and agreed with plaintiffs that Red Owl would build a store building in Chilton and stock it with merchandise for Hoffman to operate in return for which plaintiffs were to put up and invest a total sum of $18,000; that in reliance upon the above-mentioned agreement and representations plaintiffs sold their bakery building and business and their grocery store and business; also in reliance on the agreement and representations Hoffman purchased the building site in Chilton and rented a residence for himself and his family in Chilton; plaintiffs' actions in reliance on the representations and agreement disrupted their personal and business life; plaintiffs lost substantial amounts of income and expended large sums of money as expenses. Plaintiffs demanded recovery of damages for the breach of defendants' representations and agreements....

Hoffman assisted by his wife operated a bakery at Wautoma from 1956 until sale of the building late in 1961. The building was owned in joint tenancy by him and his wife. Red Owl is a Minnesota corporation having its home office at Hopkins, Minnesota. It owns and operates a number of grocery supermarket stores and also extends franchises to agency stores which are owned by individuals, partnerships, and corporations. Lukowitz resides at Green Bay and since September, 1960, has been divisional manager for Red Owl in a territory comprising Upper Michigan and most of Wisconsin in charge of 84 stores. Prior to September, 1960, he was district manager having charge of approximately 20 stores.

In November, 1959, Hoffman was desirous of expanding his operations by establishing a grocery store and contacted a Red Owl representative by the name of Jansen, now deceased. Numerous conversations were made in 1960 with the idea of establishing a Red Owl franchise store in Wautoma. In September, 1960, Lukowitz succeeded Jansen as Red Owl's representative in the negotiations. Hoffman mentioned that $18,000 was all the capital he had available to invest and he was repeatedly assured that this would be sufficient to set him up in business as a Red Owl store. About Christmastime, 1960, Hoffman thought it would be a good idea if he bought a small grocery store in Wautoma and operated it in order that he gain experience in the grocery business prior to operating a Red Owl store in some larger community. On February 6, 1961, on the advice of Lukowitz and Sykes, who had succeeded Lukowitz as Red Owl's district manager, Hoffman bought the inventory and fixtures of a small grocery store in Wautoma and leased the building in which it was operated.

After three months of operating this Wautoma store, the Red Owl representatives came in and took inventory and checked the operations and found the store was operating at a profit. Lukowitz advised Hoffman to sell the store to his manager, and assured him that Red Owl would find a larger store for him elsewhere. Acting on this advice and assurance, Hoffman sold the fixtures and inventory to his manager on June 6, 1961. Hoffman was reluctant to sell at that time because it meant losing the summer tourist business, but he sold on the assurance that he would be operating in a new location by fall and that he must sell this store if he wanted a bigger one. Before selling, Hoffman told the Red Owl representatives that he had $18,000 for "getting set up in business" and they assured him that there would be no problems in establishing him in a bigger operation. The makeup of the $18,000 was not discussed; it was understood plaintiff's father-in-law would furnish part of it. By June, 1961, the towns for the new grocery store had been narrowed down to two, Kewaunee and Chilton. In Kewaunee, Red Owl had an option on a building site. In Chilton, Red Owl had nothing under option, but it did select a site to which plaintiff obtained an option at Red Owl's suggestion. The option stipulated a purchase price of $6,000 with $1,000 to be paid on election to purchase and the balance to be paid within thirty days. On Lukowitz's assurance that everything was all set plaintiff paid $1,000 down on the lot on September 15th.

On September 27, 1961, plaintiff met at Chilton with Lukowitz and Mr. Reymund and Mr. Carlson from the home office who prepared a projected financial statement. Part of the funds plaintiffs were to supply as their investment in the venture were to be obtained by sale of their Wautoma bakery building.

On the basis of this meeting Lukowitz assured Hoffman: "... [E]verything is ready to go. Get your money together and we are set." Shortly after this meeting Lukowitz told plaintiffs that they would have to sell their bakery business and bakery building, and that their retaining this property was the only "hitch" in the entire plan. On November 6, 1961, plaintiffs sold their bakery building for $10,000. Hoffman was to retain the bakery equipment as he contemplated using it to operate a bakery in connection with his Red Owl store. After sale of the bakery Hoffman obtained employment on the night shift at an Appleton bakery.

The record contains different exhibits which were prepared in September and October, some of which were projections of the fiscal operation of the business and others were proposed building and floor plans. Red Owl was to procure some third party to buy the Chilton lot from Hoffman, construct the building, and then lease it to Hoffman. No final plans were ever made, nor were bids let or a construction contract entered. Some time prior to November 20, 1961, certain of the terms of the lease under which the building was to be rented by Hoffman were understood between him and Lukowitz. The lease was to be for ten years with a rental approximating $550 a month.... At the end of the ten-year term he was to have an option to renew the lease for an additional ten-year period or to buy the property at cost on an installment basis. There was no discussion as to what the installments would be or with respect to repairs and maintenance.

On November 22 or 23, Lukowitz and plaintiffs met in Minneapolis with Red Owl's credit manager to confer on Hoffman's financial standing and on financing the agency. Another projected financial statement was there drawn up entitled, "Proposed Financing For An Agency Store." This showed Hoffman contributing

$24,100 of cash capital of which only $4,600 was to be cash possessed by plaintiffs. Eight thousand was to be procured as a loan from a Chilton bank secured by a mortgage on the bakery fixtures, $7,500 was to be obtained on a 5 percent loan from the father-in-law, and $4,000 was to be obtained by sale of the lot to the lessor at a profit.

A week or two after the Minneapolis meeting Lukowitz showed Hoffman a telegram from the home office to the effect that if plaintiff could get another $2,000 for promotional purposes the deal could go through for $26,000. Hoffman stated he would have to find out if he could get another $2,000. He met with his father-in-law, who agreed to put $13,000 into the business provided he could come into the business as a partner. Lukowitz told Hoffman the partnership arrangement "sounds fine" and that Hoffman should not go into the partnership arrangement with the "front office." On January 16, 1962, the Red Owl credit manager teletyped Lukowitz that the father-in-law would have to sign an agreement that the $13,000 was either a gift or a loan subordinate to all general creditors and that he would prepare the agreement. On January 31, 1962, Lukowitz teletyped the home office that the father-in-law would sign one or other of the agreements. However, Hoffman testified that it was not until the final meeting some time between January 26 and February 2, 1962, that he was told that his father-in-law was expected to sign an agreement that the $13,000 he was advancing was to be an outright gift. No mention was then made by the Red Owl representatives of the alternative of the father-in-law signing a subordination agreement. At this meeting the Red Owl agents presented Hoffman with the following projected financial statement:

Capital required in operation:

Cash	$ 5,000.00
Merchandise	$20,000.00
Bakery	$18,000.00
Fixtures	$17,500.00
Promotional Funds	$ 1,500.00
TOTAL	$62,000.00

Source of funds:

Red Owl 7-day terms	$ 5,000.00
Red Owl Fixture contract (Term 5 years)	14,000.00
Bank loans (Term 9 years)	
Union State Bank of Chilton	8,000.00
(Secured by Bakery Equipment)	
Other loans (Term No-pay)	
No interest	13,000.00
Father-in-law	
(Secured by None)	
(Secured by Mortgage on Wautoma Bakery Bldg.)	2,000.00

Resale of land   6,000.00
Equity Capital: $ 5,000.00 — Cash
                    17,500.00 — Bakery Equip.
      Amount owner has to invest: 22,500.00
                         TOTAL: $70,500.00

Hoffman interpreted the above statement to require of plaintiffs a total of $34,000 cash made up of $13,000 gift from his father-in-law, $2,000 on mortgage, $8,000 on Chilton bank loan, $5,000 in cash from plaintiff, and $6,000 on the resale of the Chilton lot. Red Owl claims $18,000 is the total of the unborrowed or unencumbered cash, that is, $13,000 from the father-in-law and $5,000 cash from Hoffman himself. Hoffman informed Red Owl he could not go along with this proposal, and particularly objected to the requirement that his father-in-law sign an agreement that his $13,000 advancement was an absolute gift. This terminated the negotiations between the parties.

The case was submitted to the jury on a special verdict with the first two questions answered by the court. This verdict, as returned by the jury, was as follows:

"*Question No. 1*: Did the Red Owl Stores, Inc., and Joseph Hoffmann on or about mid-May of 1961 initiate negotiations looking to the establishment of Joseph Hoffmann as a franchise operator of a Red Owl Store in Chilton? Answer: Yes. (Answered by the Court.)

"*Question No. 2*: Did the parties mutually agree on all of the details of the proposal so as to reach a final agreement thereon? Answer: No. (Answered by the Court.)

"*Question No. 3:* Did the Red Owl Stores, Inc., in the course of said negotiations, make representations to Joseph Hoffmann that if he fulfilled certain conditions that they would establish him as a franchise operator of a Red Owl Store in Chilton? Answer: Yes.

"*Question No. 4*: If you have answered Question No. 3 'Yes,' then answer this question: Did Joseph Hoffmann rely on said representations and was he induced to act thereon? Answer: Yes.

"*Question No. 5:* If you have answered Question No. 4 'Yes,' then answer this question: Ought Joseph Hoffmann, in the exercise of ordinary care, to have relied on said representations? Answer: Yes.

"*Question No. 6:* If you have answered Question No. 3 'Yes' then answer this question: Did Joseph Hoffmann fulfill all the conditions he was required to fulfill by the terms of the negotiations between the parties up to January 26, 1962? Answer: Yes.

"*Question No. 7:* What sum of money will reasonably compensate the plaintiffs for such damages as they sustained by reason of:

      "(a) The sale of the Wautoma store fixtures and inventory?
         "Answer: $16,735.
      "(b) The sale of the bakery building?

"Answer: $2,000.

"(c) Taking up the option on the Chilton lot?

"Answer: $1,000.

"(d) Expenses of moving his family to Neenah?

"Answer: $140.

"(e) House rental in Chilton?

"Answer: $125."

Plaintiffs moved for judgment on the verdict while defendants moved to change the answers to Questions 3, 4, 5, and 6 from "Yes" to "No," and in the alternative for relief from the answers to the subdivisions of Question 7 or a new trial. On March 31, 1964, the circuit court entered the following order:

It Is Ordered in accordance with said decision on motions after verdict hereby incorporated herein by reference:

1. That the answer of the jury to Question No. 7 (a) be and the same is hereby vacated and set aside and that a new trial be had on the sole issue of the damages for loss, if any, on the sale of the Wautoma store, fixtures and inventory.

2. That all other portions of the verdict of the jury be and hereby are approved and confirmed and all after-verdict motions of the parties inconsistent with this order are hereby denied.

Defendants have appealed from this order and plaintiffs have cross-appealed from paragraph 1, thereof.

CURRIE, C.J. The instant appeal and cross appeal present these questions:

(1) Whether this court should recognize causes of action grounded on promissory estoppel as exemplified by § 90 of Restatement, 1 Contracts?

(2) Do the facts in this case make out a cause of action for promissory estoppel?

(3) Are the jury's findings with respect to damages sustained by the evidence?

Recognition of a Cause of Action Grounded on Promissory Estoppel.

... The Wisconsin Annotations to Restatement, Contracts, prepared under the direction of the late Professor William H. Page and issued in 1933, stated (at p. 53, § 90):

> The Wisconsin cases do not seem to be in accord with this section [§ 90] of the Restatement. It is certain that no such proposition has ever been announced by the Wisconsin court and it is at least doubtful if it would be approved by the court.

... Because we deem the doctrine of promissory estoppel, as stated in § 90 of Restatement, 1 Contracts, is one which supplies a needed tool which courts may employ in a proper case to prevent injustice, we endorse and adopt it.

Applicability of Doctrine to Facts of this Case.

The record here discloses a number of promises and assurances given to Hoffman by Lukowitz in behalf of Red Owl upon which plaintiffs relied and acted upon to their detriment.

Foremost were the promises that for the sum of $18,000 Red Owl would establish Hoffman in a store. After Hoffman had sold his grocery store and paid the $1,000 on the Chilton lot, the $18,000 figure was changed to $24,100. Then in November, 1961, Hoffman was assured that if the $24,100 figure were increased by $2,000 the deal would go through. Hoffman was induced to sell his grocery store fixtures and inventory in June, 1961, on the promise that he would be in his new store by fall. In November, plaintiffs sold their bakery building on the urging of defendants and on the assurance that this was the last step necessary to have the deal with Red Owl go through.

We determine that there was ample evidence to sustain the answers of the jury to the questions of the verdict with respect to the promissory representations made by Red Owl, Hoffman's reliance thereon in the exercise of ordinary care, and his fulfillment of the conditions required of him by the terms of the negotiations had with Red Owl.

There remains for consideration the question of law raised by defendants that agreement was never reached on essential factors necessary to establish a contract between Hoffman and Red Owl. Among these were the size, cost, design, and layout of the store building; and the terms of the lease with respect to rent, maintenance, renewal, and purchase options. This poses the question of whether the promise necessary to sustain a cause of action for promissory estoppel must embrace all essential details of a proposed transaction between promisor and promisee so as to be the equivalent of an offer that would result in a binding contract between the parties if the promisee were to accept the same.

... If promissory estoppel were to be limited to only those situations where the promise giving rise to the cause of action must be so definite with respect to all details that a contract would result were the promise supported by consideration, then the defendants' instant promises to Hoffman would not meet this test. However, § 90 of Restatement, 1 Contracts, does not impose the requirement that the promise giving rise to the cause of action must be so comprehensive in scope as to meet the requirements of an offer that would ripen into a contract if accepted by the promisee. Rather the conditions imposed are:

(1) Was the promise one which the promisor should reasonably expect to induce action or forbearance of a definite and substantial character on the part of the promisee?

(2) Did the promise induce such action or forbearance?

(3) Can injustice be avoided only by enforcement of the promise?

We deem it would be a mistake to regard an action grounded on promissory estoppel as the equivalent of a breach-of-contract action.... While the first two of the above-listed three requirements of promissory estoppel present issues of fact which ordinarily will be resolved by a jury, the third requirement, that the remedy can only be invoked where necessary to avoid injustice, is one that involves a policy decision by the court. Such a policy decision necessarily embraces an element of discretion.

We conclude that injustice would result here if plaintiffs were not granted some relief because of the failure of defendants to keep their promises which induced plaintiffs to act to their detriment.

Damages.

Defendants attack all the items of damages awarded by the jury.

The bakery building at Wautoma was sold at defendants' instigation in order that Hoffman might have the net proceeds available as part of the cash capital he was to invest in the Chilton store venture. The evidence clearly establishes that it was sold at a loss of $2,000. Defendants contend that half of this loss was sustained by Mrs. Hoffman because title stood in joint tenancy. They point out that no dealings took place between her and defendants as all negotiations were had with her husband. Ordinarily only the promisee and not third persons are entitled to enforce the remedy of promissory estoppel against the promisor. However, if the promisor actually foresees, or has reason to foresee, action by a third person in reliance on the promise, it may be quite unjust to refuse to perform the promise.... Here not only did defendants foresee that it would be necessary for Mrs. Hoffman to sell her joint interest in the bakery building, but defendants actually requested that this be done. We approve the jury's award of $2,000 damages for the loss incurred by both plaintiffs in this sale.

Defendants attack on two grounds the $1,000 awarded because of Hoffman's payment of that amount on the purchase price of the Chilton lot. The first is that this $1,000 had already been lost at the time the final negotiations with Red Owl fell through in January, 1962, because the remaining $5,000 of purchase price had been due on October 15, 1961. The record does not disclose that the lot owner had foreclosed Hoffman's interest in the lot for failure to pay this $5,000. The $1,000 was not paid for the option, but had been paid as part of the purchase price at the time Hoffman elected to exercise the option. This gave him an equity in the lot which could not be legally foreclosed without affording Hoffman an opportunity to pay the balance. The second ground of attack is that the lot may have had a fair market value of $6,000, and Hoffman should have paid the remaining $5,000 of purchase price. We determine that it would be unreasonable to require Hoffman to have invested an additional $5,000 in order to protect the $1,000 he had paid. Therefore, we find no merit to defendants' attack upon this item of damages.

We also determine it was reasonable for Hoffman to have paid $125 for one month's rent of a home in Chilton after defendants assured him everything would be set when plaintiff sold the bakery building. This was a proper item of damage.

Plaintiffs never moved to Chilton because defendants suggested that Hoffman get some experience by working in a Red Owl store in the Fox River Valley. Plaintiffs, therefore, moved to Neenah instead of Chilton. After moving, Hoffman worked at night in an Appleton bakery but held himself available for work in a Red Owl store. The $140 moving expense would not have been incurred if plaintiffs had not sold their bakery building in Wautoma in reliance upon defendants' promises. We consider the $140 moving expense to be a proper item of damage.

We turn now to the damage item with respect to which the trial court granted a new trial, i.e., that arising from the sale of the Wautoma grocery-store fixtures and inventory for which the jury awarded $16,735. The trial court ruled that Hoffman could not recover for any loss of future profits for the summer months following the sale on June 6, 1961, but that damages would be limited to the difference between the sales price received and the fair market value of the assets sold, giving consideration to any goodwill attaching thereto by reason of the transfer of a going business. There was no direct evidence presented as to what this fair market value was on June 6, 1961. The evidence did disclose that Hoffman paid $9,000 for the inventory, added $1,500 to it and sold it for $10,000 or a loss of $500. His 1961 federal income-tax return showed that the grocery equipment had been purchased for $7,000 and sold for $7,955.96. Plaintiffs introduced evidence of the buyer that during the first eleven weeks of operation of the grocery store his gross sales were $44,000 and his profit was $6,000 or roughly 15 percent. On cross-examination he admitted that this was gross and not net profit. Plaintiffs contend that in a breach-of-contract action damages may include loss of profits. However, this is not a breach-of-contract action.

The only relevancy of evidence relating to profits would be with respect to proving the element of goodwill in establishing the fair market value of the grocery inventory and fixtures sold. Therefore, evidence of profits would be admissible to afford a foundation for expert opinion as to fair market value.

Where damages are awarded in promissory estoppel instead of specifically enforcing the promisor's promise, they should be only such as in the opinion of the court are necessary to prevent injustice. Mechanical or rule-of-thumb approaches to the damage problem should be avoided.

> ... Enforcement of a promise does not necessarily mean Specific Performance. It does not necessarily mean Damages for breach. Moreover the amount allowed as Damages may be determined by the plaintiff's expenditures or change of position in reliance as well as by the value to him of the promised performance. Restitution is also an 'enforcing' remedy, although it is often said to be based upon some kind of a rescission. In determining what justice requires, the court must remember all of its powers, derived from equity, law merchant, and other sources, as well as the common law. Its decree should be molded accordingly. 1A Corbin, Contracts, p. 221, § 200.

The wrong is not primarily in depriving the plaintiff of the promised reward but in causing the plaintiff to change position to his detriment. It would follow that the damages should not exceed the loss caused by the change of position, which would never be more in amount, but might be less, than the promised reward. Seavey, Reliance on Gratuitous Promises or Other Conduct, 64 Harvard Law Review (1951), 913, 926.

At the time Hoffman bought the equipment and inventory of the small grocery store at Wautoma he did so in order to gain experience in the grocery-store business. At that time discussion had already been had with Red Owl representatives that Wautoma might be too small for a Red Owl operation and that a larger city might be more desirable. Thus Hoffman made this purchase more or less as a temporary experiment. Justice does not require that the damages awarded him, because of selling these assets at the behest of defendants, should exceed any actual loss sustained measured by the difference between the sales price and the fair market value.

Since the evidence does not sustain the large award of damages arising from the sale of the Wautoma grocery business, the trial court properly ordered a new trial on this issue.

By the Court. — Order affirmed. Because of the cross appeal, plaintiffs shall be limited to taxing but two thirds of their costs.

NOTES AND QUESTIONS

1. *The promise on which Hoffman relied*: Restatement of Contracts § 90 speaks of relying on a promise. Did Red Owl make a promise to Joseph Hoffman? His expectations and reliance were based on the conduct and statements of Edward Lukowitz, District Manager of the Agency Division of Red Owl Stores. Hoffman knew that Lukowitz could not award franchises. He knew that power belonged to officials at Red Owl's home office in Hopkins, Minnesota, a suburb of Minneapolis. However, under the law of agency, Red Owl was responsible for Lukowitz' conduct in the usual course of his job. Joseph Hoffman testified:

> There was further discussion ... based on the results of the three-month operation.... I says, "Fellows, you know how much money I got — approximately eighteen thousand dollars. Will this put me in a bigger operation or won't it." I was assured at that time there would be no problems. With this assurance and advice I proceeded to sell the store I was operating.... The decision to sell the grocery business was made on May 6. As to who made that decision, Ed told me if I wanted this bigger store, I would have to sell this one. The actual decision to sell I made, with Red Owl's advice.
>
> I drove down to Chilton and met the fellows [Lukowitz and his assistant] there, and they had a map of the City of Chilton. We looked at the piece of

property together. We discussed the location of the lot in connection with the main intersection in the town and so forth. At that time they asked me for a list of my assets and liabilities which they filled out on a piece of paper. They felt this whole thing looked real good. I had been assured all the time this thing was going ahead with no hitches. They assured me that day there appeared to be no hitch in the setup and that we should be getting our building started and underway in the not too distant future.

At the time of this discussion I just related the dollars I had to have to have this building project proceed was $18,000 and then there was going to be a little profit from the lot, which they projected. That was their projection. Eighteen thousand dollars was the only figure we ever had. As to whether anyone ever told me that $18,000 would do it, I had been assured. I wouldn't have sold my store if I felt $18,000 wouldn't. Ed Lukowitz assured me it would be sufficient ...

I was told that Red Owl wanted me to sell the store business because they felt I was capable and I had enough money to go into a bigger operation. I was a little reluctant. I thought I should run my store possibly a little longer. They said, "Now is the time to sell; and we can get you going by fall." and so I went into it.... As to whether there were representations or statements by Mr. Lukowitz to the effect that he had contacted Minneapolis and gotten approval from them at this stage, I was assured that Minneapolis was in accord with what he was telling me. That is why I sold my grocery business....

On November 22 or 23, just prior to Thanksgiving week, Ed Lukowitz and myself went from Green Bay to Minneapolis to the home office up there. At the home office I met with Mr. Carlson [and] Mr. Hall.... Mr. Carlson is the developer. Mr. Hall is credit manager.... They had a sheet there and Mr. Carlson took down my financial standing.... Ed Lukowitz and Carlson and myself went into Mr. Hall's office, which is across the hallway and Mr. Hall looked it over. This is the first that I find out that they are pressing for more money.... By adjusting the land value a little bit we come up with $24,100.00, I believe, the form shows, and they had a discretion there and they said, "This is a little bit tight, but I think they will put this store up for this amount of money."...

Cross-examination of Joseph Hoffman:

As to whether I claim that by June of 1961 there was a definite complete agreement to set me up in a store in one of these towns at an investment on my part of not to exceed $18,000.00, it was an agreement that this would be done by fall if I would be able to meet certain requirements. The store had to be sold. Something had to be done with my bakery, which I still had. These things had to transpire. As of that time I hadn't yet sold my grocery store. I still owned the bakery. I hadn't decided yet whether to sell my bakery until I knew when we were going into our store and where. The matter of selling my bakery didn't come up at this inventory time. There wasn't a definite thing established on that.

Edward Lukowitz, called by plaintiffs adversely, testified as follows:

I was on friendly terms with Joe Hoffman and was trying to set him up in business in a Red Owl store. That was part of my duty.... I would say I got to know Joe fairly well.

In the course of these visits from place to place and looking over these different locations I had discussions with Mr. Hoffman.... As to when we got talking about Chilton we discussed specifically the figure $18,000.00, my answer is "never specifically." That had been an approximation. He said he could make $18,000.00 available. I could not feel that $18,000.00 was satisfactory because every town is different. $18,000.00 could set him up in certain towns but we would have to find a town we could do it in. We were not talking about Chilton at that time....

As to whether during this period of time I was assisting and counseling and aiding and abetting Mr. Hoffman in getting set up in this new store in Chilton, I was trying to be helpful. As to whether I had made different projections, not only on what it would cost, what type of building it would be, what the amount would be, what the terms of the lease would be, how long the terms would be, and what the option terms were, it was just in general discussion, nothing specific.....

Red Owl had not picked out this lot for the building as yet. It was still under discussion. That is the lot I had suggested, yes.... This is a map of a proposed site plan that was prepared by Red Owl stores for the particular location on a particular lot and showing the customer parking lot and was prepared on the Chilton store....

As to whether at this point I felt that $24,100.00 was all that was needed in the way of capital, the way I felt I thought we could possibly work something out on this basis. There was never an assurance of that to Mr. Hoffman.... My being satisfied ... would not be enough. It was my opinion that there was a possibility it could be done. As a matter of fact I recommended it be done. I knew that Mr. Hoffman knew that at that point, that I recommended it to Hoffman. I supposed he was satisfied with my judgment. I supposed he relied on me. I hope that he had confidence in me....

What do you think Edward Lukowitz intended to communicate to Joseph Hoffman about the $18,000 amount? Do you think that Lukowitz cared whether Hoffman became a Red Owl franchisee? What did Hoffman understand? Does the Red Owl decision impose liability on those negotiating? Is the decision a major interference with free choice and business convenience, and a reflection of a self-defeating anti-big business theme in American consciousness? European law generally recognizes a duty to negotiate in good faith once contractual negotiation reach a stage where good faith can reasonably be expected by both parties.[85] Some scholars have suggested that the Hoffman case shows that a duty to negotiate in good faith may be creeping into the law of the United States as well.[86] Do you agree?

2. *Interpreting Lukowitz' communications in light of Hoffman's background:* The record on appeal also shows that Joseph Hoffman was a high school graduate and had attended vocational school for one year, taking business courses. In November of 1956, he bought a bakery in Wautoma and ran it with his wife. He worked night and day and got so little sleep that his wife listened to all long-distance telephone conversations "to be sure he [Joe Hoffman] was wide awake and that he knew what he was doing...." At the time of the trial, Hoffman was 31, and he and his wife had seven children. Assuming that Lukowitz knew all this, does it help a court interpret his statements and conduct to decide if he made a promise? Does this information help establish Lukowitz' intentions or something else?

3. *Judicial practice under Restatement 90:* Professor Jay Feinman surveyed the reported cases discussing § 90. He reports a major difference in approach:

> In circumstances that depart from the promissory norm, courts are variously strict and flexible in determining whether a manifestation of intention may furnish a basis for actionable reliance. The strict view holds that a statement that is not specifically demonstrative of an intention respecting future conduct or that is indefinite or limited cannot be the basis for promissory estoppel. Under a more flexible view, courts have held such statements to suffice.
>
> The strict view carefully distinguishes promises, which are future oriented, from statements of belief, which concern only the present. For example, in cases involving franchisors who have made representations about the business potential that franchisees may expect or about their own policies of support for franchisees, some courts have held that such representations may not reasonably be relied upon as indications of future conduct. Courts usually view these representations, unlike promises to grant franchises, as statements of "belief" (that is, predictions or statements of current company policy) rather than intention. The statements are, therefore, not promises.

---

[85]See Kessler & Fine, Culpa in Contrahendo, Bargaining in Good Faith, and Freedom of Contract: A Comparative Study, 77 Harvard Law Review 401(1964).

[86] Temkin, When does the "Fat Lady" Sing: An analysis of "Agreements in Principal" in Corporate Acquisitions, 55 Fordham Law Review 125 (1987).

The strict view also requires that the promise be definite and unequivocal. The court may determine that the promisor's expression concerning its future conduct is insufficiently certain and specific to give rise to promissory estoppel. Similarly, if the expression is made in the course of preliminary negotiations when material terms of the agreement are lacking, the degree of certainty necessary in a promise is absent. Finally, when the intention manifested is conditional, the promissory ideal is not met unless the event constituting the condition occurs. This rule holds good even when the event is within the control of the promisor, as is a condition of approval by a home office or higher official or a condition of execution of a final written agreement....

The alternative, more flexible approach to promise allows reliance recovery in a wider variety of settings. Courts adopting this perspective hold that a promise need not be explicitly expressed but may be inferred from, for example, statements about future conduct or factual representations about a present state of affairs. The standard, consistent with the definition in § 90, is not whether the promisor clearly made a promise, but whether, given the context in which the statement at issue was made, the promisor should reasonably have expected that the promisee would infer a promise. This standard may be met not only by a particular promise or representation, but also by general statements of policy or practice, such as published plans for employee compensation or benefits. In appropriate cases of this type, the court may infer a promise even in the face of inconsistent expressions.[87]

Feinman is very critical of the "flexible" approach. He summarizes his objections:

First, the courts are so distant from the actual contexts of cases that judicial application of the method is properly characterized as interpretive rather than empirical. Second, the courts' interpretive activity is not and cannot be consistently executed. Third, judicial interpretation is necessarily based on a subjective application of policies more complex than any simple preference for facilitation of commercial exchange.[88]

Compare Farber and Matheson's argument:

Courts often resort to conclusory language in finding that a manifestation rises to the level of a promise. This is not surprising. Judges called upon to determine whether a promise has been made must look beyond the words

---

[87]Feinman, Promissory Estoppel and Judicial Method, 97 Harvard Law Review 678, 691-692 (1984). Copyright Harvard Law Review. Reprinted with permission.

[88]Feinman, *supra* at 703.

and acts which constitute the transaction to the nature of the relationship between the parties and the circumstances surrounding their actions. But relationships and surrounding circumstances do not speak for themselves. They must be interpreted by judges on the basis of the expectations likely to arise between similarly situated parties. The conclusory tone follows because we are being told what we ought to already understand as members of the community. It is inherent in the use of an objective standard — under both traditional contract and promissory estoppel theories of obligation — to determine whether a commitment was voluntarily made.[89]

Do Farber and Matheson answer Feinman's objections?

4. *Of promises and regulation:* Farber and Matheson surveyed 222 promissory estoppel cases decided between 1975 and 1985. Courts apply the doctrine regularly in commercial contexts. They use it as a primary basis of enforcement even where they could have applied traditional contract theory. Reliance plays little role in the determination of remedies. Expectation damages are the norm. Furthermore, reliance plays a diminished role in determining liability. The new rule that is emerging is quite simple: "any promise made in furtherance of an economic activity is enforceable."[90]

5. *Impact on Red Owl:* Suppose it is a few weeks after the *Red Owl* opinion became final. You represent Red Owl. You are asked to prepare a memorandum suggesting what the organization should do to avoid future Hoffman v. Red Owl situations. Remember that your legal advice must seem practical and realistic to Red Owl's executives, who are not lawyers, or they will ignore it.

6. *Impact on Hoffman and his lawyer:* Hoffman's attorney wrote the authors:

> After the Supreme Court remand, the case was re-tried to a jury in the Circuit Court of Outagamie County and was settled after approximately one and one-half days of trial for $10,600.
>
> This was certainly one of the most interesting cases I have handled even though not the most remunerative. Hoffman received $6,600. My fees were $4,000.00. Two thirds of costs were paid by Red Owl Stores, Inc. in accordance with the Supreme Court decision.
>
> Shortly after Joseph Hoffman's experience with Red Owl, he started to work for Metropolitan Life Insurance Company as a salesman. He immediately won honors for highest sales and was promoted to District Manager in Milwaukee. I am informed within the next couple of months he will be transferred to Indiana in a managerial capacity.

---

[89]Farber and Matheson, Beyond Promissory Estoppel: Contract Law and the "Invisible Handshake," 52 University of Chicago Law Review 903 (1985). Copyright c. University of Chicago.

[90]Farber and Matheson, *supra* at 905.

Hoffman's lawyer won a victory and created new law in Wisconsin. Did Hoffman win a victory? While $6,600 is not a lot of money, Hoffman did make Red Owl's officials defend themselves. Furthermore, the court labeled their actions as "wrong," at least in some sense. Was this enough? Would you expect that Hoffman's experience left him dissatisfied with the American legal system, one of its champions, or just indifferent? [91]

b. Ending the Relationship

Those who create franchises structure relationships to achieve several purposes. Franchisors seek to build and guard the reputation of their product or service. Franchisors want franchisees who are honest and efficient, and who represent the product and trade-name in their locality in a manner that enhances its reputation. Franchisees can benefit greatly from these relationships. A local dealer representing, for example, the Ford Motor Company gains the use of a valuable trade name, national advertising, and a great deal of training and systems of marketing. Or, to take another example, almost always it will be more profitable to run a McDonald's fast food franchise than "Joe's Eats."

Lawyers for franchisors usually draft elaborate standard form agreements to govern these relationships. In the past, these documents almost always reserved to the franchisors the right to end the relationships at will. Furthermore, franchises usually run for a specified term that is not too long. Thus, instead of termination, a franchisor could refuse to renew the arrangement when it expired. This structure aided franchisors to end relationships when franchisees didn't perform or when a franchisor found another person who might perform better at the same location. It also served to reinforce the power of the franchisor to gain compliance with its requests and demands. A franchisee might want to free ride and gain the benefits of the franchise's reputation without investing much to maintain it. The threat of cancellation or nonrenewal always was present, although when things went well the threat would be in the background and almost never mentioned.

Franchisees who had served long and hard often thought the arrangement poorly protected their interests. Franchisors and academics who champion their cause sometimes argue that franchisors have no reason to treat efficient franchisees poorly.

The franchisor is not likely to terminate franchisees merely to confiscate their sunk investments opportunistically because franchisors must be

---

[91]Those students who read Sullivan v. O'Conner, *supra* in the Danzig book should compare the response of Alice Sullivan to her experience with the legal system.

concerned about their reputations when attempting to sell additional franchise locations.[92]

However, sometimes a franchisor makes a business judgment that profits it but injures dealers. For example, automobile manufacturers have moved to sell and service cars in fewer but larger dealerships to gain some economies of scale. This may benefit the manufacturer and perhaps many consumers, but it came at the expense of many smaller dealerships that had been in operation for years. Petroleum refiners decided to convert many gasoline stations from places where cars were repaired to convenience stores where customers pumped gasoline into their cars. This maximized the refiners' profits and benefited those dealers who could make more from a convenience store than car repairs. However, the change was a devastating blow to those dealers who had built a reputation as experts in car service and who were poorly situated to compete in the convenience store market.

To complicate matters further, middle managers who deal with franchisees often act for their own interests. Sometimes dealers were required to give bribes or kickbacks in order to keep their franchises. In addition, middle management might sometimes be evaluated in terms of short-term rather than long-term performance, and this might cause them to encourage franchisees to resort to questionable, or illegal, business practices. In addition, the evaluation of the performance of franchisees is often largely a matter of judgment by middle-management, who may make mistakes.

Just before and just after the Second World War, automobile dealers in about a third of the states lobbied for statutes to defend their interests. A federal statute was passed in 1956. Retail gasoline dealers battled for legislation through the states and finally at the federal level from the 1950s to the middle 1970s. As a result of this lobbying by gasoline dealers, some states passed general franchise protection acts, not limited to those who sold particular products such as automobiles and gasoline.

We will look at the Wisconsin Fair Dealership Act as an example of similar statutes found in many states. Section 135.03 says that no franchisor may "terminate, cancel, fail to renew or substantially change the competitive circumstances of a dealership agreement ... without good cause." Section 135.02(4) defines good cause as:

> (a) Failure by a dealer to comply substantially with essential and reasonable requirements imposed upon him by the grantor, or sought to be imposed by the grantor, which requirements are not discriminatory as

---

[92]Klein and Saft, The Law and Economics of Franchise Tying Contracts, 28 Journal of Law & Economics 345, 356 (1985). For a similar argument, see Wiggins, Franchising — A Case of Long-Term Contracts, 144 Journal of Institutional and Theoretical Economics 149, 151 (1988).

compared with requirements imposed on other similarly situated dealers either by their terms or in the manner of their enforcement; or

(b) Bad faith by the dealer in carrying out the terms of the dealership.

The burden of proving good cause is on the franchisor. The provisions of the statute may not be varied by contract.

The following case raises many of the difficulties in legal regulation of long-term continuing relationships. Walgreen Drug Stores had long operated in many states through its agency division. Agency stores could purchase Walgreen's house brand drugs, and they could use Walgreen's trade name. Walgreen decided to close its entire agency division, and it terminated many stores in Wisconsin. However, it was not withdrawing from business in Wisconsin. It planned to remain in Wisconsin, running its own large stores in shopping centers in the best areas for high volume sales.

Thirteen pharmacies in southern Wisconsin brought a class action suit. The Wisconsin Pharmaceutical Association helped coordinate the suit although the WPA remained neutral. Walgreen is a member of WPA. Fighting a major corporation is never easy. Notice the number of difficult issues which the lawyers for the pharmacies had to brief and argue.

COLLINS DRUGS, INC. v. WALGREEN CO.[93]

539 F. Supp. 1357 (W.D.Wis. 1982)

CRABB, CHIEF JUDGE. These civil actions for injunctive and monetary relief under the Wisconsin Fair Dealership Law, Wis. Stats. § 135.01 *et seq.*, are before the court on defendant's motions for summary judgment. Both actions were begun in state court and removed here by defendant. Diversity jurisdiction is present. 28 U.S.C. § 1332. The issue in both cases is whether the Wisconsin Fair Dealership Law permits a grantor to cancel *all* of its dealership arrangements within the state for bona fide economic reasons such as a change in its manner of doing business. For the reasons that follow, I conclude that the Wisconsin Fair Dealership Law does not permit grantors to terminate dealerships for any reason other than "good cause," as that term is defined in the Act; that defendant Walgreen's termination of its dealership agreements was without good cause; and that those plaintiff-dealers whose agreements are covered under the Act are entitled to damages and to partial summary judgment in their favor, but that none of the plaintiffs is entitled to injunctive relief.

From the record, I find that there is no genuine issue with respect to the following material facts.

---

[93] On appeal, the caption for this case changed to Kealey pharmacy & Home Care Services, Inc. v. Walgreen. This case has had several captions, but for the sake of uniformity, we will try to refer to it as the "Walgreen case."

FACTS

Plaintiffs are pharmacies doing business in the State of Wisconsin. Defendant is a corporation organized under the laws of the State of Illinois....

Defendant manufactures and sells under its own private labels a wide variety of drugs, beauty aids, and household commodities. It also sells similar products manufactured by other companies. Prior to October 1, 1980, defendant sold these products to the consuming public through a nation-wide system of both company-owned and independently-owned stores.

Every independently-owned drug store which sold Walgreen brand products operated under a standard written agreement (the "Retailer's Agreement"). At the beginning of 1980, approximately 1,400 independently-owned drug stores operated throughout the United States under such agreements.

The Retailer's Agreement governed all aspects of the contractual relationship between defendant and its dealers including such matters as the right of the independently-owned store to use the Walgreen trade name and trademark, defendant's right to locate a company-owned store near the independently-owned store, and the minimum amount of Walgreen products that the retailer must purchase each year. Paragraph "Fourth. (c)" of the Retailer's Agreement expressly provided that "[i]n the event Walgreen determines at any time to discontinue all similar Agreements, it may, at its option, terminate this agreement upon thirty days' written notice" to the dealer. Under the terms of the Retailer's Agreement, the plaintiff dealers were permitted to, and did, purchase additional goods for resale from suppliers other than defendant.

On April 14, 1980, defendant's board of directors met and decided to discontinue the operations of its Agency Division, which administered the defendant's relationship with its dealers, and to terminate all of the Retailer's Agreements as of October 1, 1980, on the ground that these independently-owned drug stores were producing an inadequate rate of return.

By letter dated April 17, 1980, defendant informed plaintiffs and each of its other approximately 1,400 independent dealers that, pursuant to paragraph "Fourth. (c)" of its Retailer's Agreement, defendant had elected to terminate the agreements, effective October 1, 1980.

By letter dated April 28, 1980, defendant informed every dealer that defendant would furnish the dealer's name and address to manufacturers, wholesalers, suppliers, and vendors for the purpose of assisting the dealers in finding alternative sources of supply. Subsequently, defendant gave to other drug store companies the names and addresses of most of its dealers.

As a result of defendant's April, 1980 decision to terminate the Agency Division and all of its Retailer's Agreements, the division was disbanded. Division staff was reduced from 110 persons to 3; over half of the staff left defendant's employment and the remainder were transferred to other positions within the Walgreen organization. The division field personnel responsible for the dealers in the State of Wisconsin are no longer employed by defendant....

Defendant continues to operate company-owned stores in Wisconsin.

OPINION

A. *Dealership Agreements Covered by the Wisconsin Fair Dealership Law*

Defendant does not contend that plaintiffs are not dealers within the meaning of that term in Wis. Stats. § 135.02. It contends, however, that not all of the plaintiffs are parties to agreements subject to the provision of the Wisconsin Fair Dealership Law, either because they were operating under agreements executed prior to the effective date of the law or because they were operating under "renewal agreements" executed prior to the effective date of the amendment to the Fair Dealership Law which specified that the provisions of the law extended to renewal agreements. Therefore, the threshold inquiry is to determine which of the plaintiffs are parties to agreements subject to the provisions of the Wisconsin Fair Dealership Law....

[The Court concluded that the Wisconsin Fair Dealership Law applied to all original or renewal agreements signed after April 5, 1974. It dismissed the complaints of two plaintiffs whose agreements were signed before that date.]

B. *Scope and Constitutionality of the Wisconsin Fair Dealership Law*

Defendant musters two arguments against binding it to the provisions of law: the first is that the legislature never intended to make the Fair Dealership Law applicable to statewide terminations of dealerships effected for legitimate business reasons, and the second is that if the legislature did intend such a broad application of the law, it was acting unconstitutionally in violation of defendant's rights to due process and to freedom of contract.

1. *Applicability of Wisconsin Fair Dealership Law to Statewide Dealership Terminations*

Section 135.03 of the Wisconsin Fair Dealership Law proscribes the termination, cancellation, failure to renew, or substantial change in the competitive circumstances of a dealership agreement "without good cause."...

The statute says nothing about any circumstances in which a grantor may terminate an agreement for any reason other than the dealer's bad faith or failure to perform its obligations under the agreement. The fair inference is that any other terminations are violative of the statute. In this respect, the statute is clear and unequivocal. Ordinarily, when the language of a statute is unambiguous, judicial inquiry is at an end, ... Defendant counters, correctly, that the rules of statutory construction do not bind a court to a literal reading of a statute, where literalism would lead to a result wholly at odds with the legislature's intent, ... or where a clearly expressed legislative intention compels a construction contrary to the language of the statute itself....

However, a heavy burden of persuasion rests on the party urging that a statute should be read to mean something other than what it appears to mean on its face. Two arguments may be marshalled in support of defendant's position that, despite the clear language dictating coverage, the statute should be declared inapplicable to the terminations at issue here. The first is what I will call the "fair treatment" argument; the second, I will refer to as the "omission of non-judicial remedies" argument.

a. *Fair Treatment Argument*

Relying on the statutory statement that the Wisconsin Fair Dealership Law has as one of its purposes, "the continuation of dealerships on a *fair* basis," defendant suggests that the legislature's concern was directed solely at the discriminatory termination of one dealership or of a small number of dealerships without statutory good cause, and not about the nondiscriminatory, evenhanded, and impartial terminations at issue here. Defendant argues that the statutory references to fairness are evidence that the legislature never considered or addressed the possibility of wholesale dealership terminations and never intended to prohibit such terminations. This argument fails upon a reading of the statute, a review of the legislative history, and the application of logic.

First, nothing in the language of the statute compels the interpretation defendant suggests. It is true that "fair" can mean evenhanded and impartial; it can also mean "just" and "equitable." The American Heritage Dictionary of the English Language, p. 471 (1970). Given the legislature's expressed concern with the imbalance of power between dealers and grantors, it seems unlikely that the framers of the statute intended "fair" to refer only to evenhanded, nondiscriminatory treatment as between one dealer and another, and not to refer as well to the fairness, or equitableness, of the relationship between a grantor and its dealer. It seems even more unlikely that the legislature intended to permit a grantor to take any kind of action adverse to its dealers, provided only that it took the same action with respect to all of its dealers.

Second, the legislative history of the Fair Dealership Law refutes defendant's suggestion that the legislature might not have been thinking of the possibility of statewide dealership terminations when it enacted the law. In 1973, the entire United States began to feel the effects of the concerted actions of the Organization of Petroleum Exporting Countries. Many American oil companies began reducing the number of their retail gasoline outlets in Wisconsin and, in some instances, ceased supplying gasoline altogether to their independently-operated dealerships in Wisconsin. The Wisconsin legislature was aware of this phenomenon. Indeed, one proposed version of the Fair Dealership Law, Senate Substitute Amendment 3, would have limited its scope to gasoline dealership terminations only.

Moreover, in the course of enacting the Act, the Wisconsin legislature considered, but failed to adopt, Senate Amendment 4 to 1973 Assembly Bill 837.

Had it adopted the amendment, the legislature would have provided exceptions from the Fair Dealership Law for actions taken by grantors to

(a) vertically integrate;

(b) alter or adjust its marketing technique, scheme or plan;

(c) withdraw from a geographic marketing area; or

(d) dispose of, through sale or lease, any parcel of real estate occupied by a dealer upon the expiration of the dealer's lease for the parcel as long as the parcel of real estate ceases to be the site of a branded outlet of the grantor.

Although the legislature's failure to enact this amendment is not dispositive of the question of its intent, it is supportive of the view that the statute should not be read in the restrictive manner urged by defendant.

Finally, logic alone would compel the conclusion that the legislature did not intend to provide an exception from the Fair Dealership Law for large scale terminations of dealerships, any more than it intended to permit exceptions for the termination of a single dealership for a bona fide business reason. As several commentators have pointed out, the adverse impact upon a dealer of a unilateral termination of its dealership is not lessened because the grantor is acting in good faith for sound business reasons. Neither is the adverse impact lessened because all other similarly situated dealers are being terminated as well.

b. *The Absence of Non-Judicial Remedies Argument*

Under the Fair Dealership Law, *all* terminations, cancellations, or failures to renew dealership agreements are violative of the statute unless they are effected for "good cause." Any dealer whose dealership is terminated in violation of the statute has one remedy only: a suit for damages or injunctive relief or both. The statute makes no provision for negotiated terminations under any circumstances and it makes no provision for protecting dealers from the loss of their investment upon termination other than by legal action.

The absence of any non-judicial remedy for termination or of any provision under which a dealer can effect a valid termination of a dealership it no longer wants to continue suggests two possibilities. The first is that urged by defendant: the absence of these provisions demonstrates that the legislature was addressing only the discriminatory termination of individual dealerships, effected under circumstances in which the grantor remains a viable franchisor within the state, continuing to operate through independent dealerships. Surely, the argument continues, the legislature neither desired nor intended to lock every grantor into eternal dealership agreements with each of its Wisconsin dealers, despite the grantor's desire to withdraw from an entire geographic area, or to cease production of the kinds of products sold through the dealerships, or to change its entire system of marketing its products. Thus, the legislature must have intended an exception for such major changes in the grantor's method of doing business.

The flaw in this interpretation is that it is no more reasonable to assume that the legislature intended to prohibit forever the closing down of *one* of a grantor's dealerships than to assume that the legislature intended to prohibit forever the closing down of *all* of the grantor's dealerships. The defendant's interpretation ignores the fact that, just as there are instances in which a grantor has sound business reasons for closing all of its dealerships, there are instances in which a grantor has equally sound business reasons (but not the "good cause" required under the statute) for ending its relationship with a particular dealer.

The second and more plausible interpretation of the Fair Dealership Law's omission of non-judicial remedies is that the legislature was not trying to create a system of "perpetual care" dealerships, but rather that it believed that only the threat of a civil action for money damages or injunctive relief would give sufficient support to a dealer's bargaining position to allow the dealer to negotiate a fair termination agreement.

The legislature may well have concluded that when a grantor terminates a dealership for any reason other than good cause, the dealer should be reimbursed for any loss of investment caused by the termination. Having reached this conclusion, it may have decided that, rather than try to fashion a procedure that would permit terminations subject to some statutory damage formula, it would leave the task of determining a dealer's fair compensation to the courts to be determined on a case-by-case basis. Creating a cause of action for damages based on all terminations except those motivated by good cause was the most expeditious way to draft a statute which would achieve this legislative objective.

The legislature's concern was to protect dealers. It is consistent with this concern that the legislature would have provided that in any termination not undertaken for good cause, the dealer is entitled to a judicial determination of the damages it has incurred as a result of its termination and, in appropriate instances, to an injunction against the termination.

At first reading, the statutory provision of injunctive relief against invalid terminations supports the view that application of the Act to statewide dealership terminations would have the effect of prohibiting any business changes from ever occurring, an effect that the legislature could not have intended. However, a closer look at the statute reveals that the grant of injunctive relief is discretionary with the court. Section 135.06 provides that a dealer "also *may* be granted injunctive relief against unlawful termination, cancellation, nonrenewal, or substantial change of competitive circumstances." Wis. Stats. § 135.06 (Emphasis supplied). By making the granting of injunctive relief discretionary, the legislature gave implicit recognition to the fact that there would be instances of dealership terminations where permanent injunctive relief would be wholly inappropriate.

For the foregoing reasons, I conclude that a Wisconsin court considering this issue would hold that the Wisconsin Fair Dealership Law is not limited in its application to only those terminations or other adverse actions that discriminate against one dealer in relation to other dealers; rather, a Wisconsin court would conclude that the law was intended to, and does, cover nondiscriminatory, across-the-board terminations of dealerships even if those terminations are undertaken because the grantor decides to withdraw from an entire geographic area, or to cease production of the products sold by its dealers, or to change its marketing structure, or for any other business reason.

2. Constitutionality of the Wisconsin Fair Dealership Law as Applied to Across-the-Board Dealership Terminations

The remaining question is whether the application of the Fair Dealership Law to company-wide dealership terminations is constitutional or whether it violates defendant's rights to freedom of contract and to due process....

As an exercise of Wisconsin's power to regulate private business for the public welfare, the Fair Dealership Law is attended by a presumption of constitutionality. The courts have no power to review these determinations; they are not authorized to substitute their own views for those of the legislature about what is economically wise or necessary. The popularly-elected legislature is vested with the exclusive authority to determine the need for economic regulation and the appropriate response to such needs....

It is not for this court to say whether the Wisconsin legislature acted wisely in choosing to penalize, and in some instances prohibit, terminations of dealerships except for specified causes....

Under the Fair Dealership Law, grantors remain free to enter into dealership agreements with Wisconsin dealers, subject only to certain restrictions upon their ability to modify or cancel those agreements. The restrictions are set out in the statute, they are known in advance to the grantor, and they apply equally to all grantors. The strict prohibitions upon termination are a rational means of preventing grantors from subjecting economically-weaker dealers to severe financial hardship through termination or nonrenewal of dealership agreements; they serve to redress the imbalance of bargaining power between grantor and dealer....

Moreover, the legislature avoided the constitutional problem that would attend a statute that required a grantor to continue doing business forever with its Wisconsin dealers, whatever the economic consequences, when it committed the issuance of permanent injunctive relief to the court's discretion. As a consequence, a grantor is not prohibited entirely from terminating its dealers when it wishes to withdraw from the state, to cease production, or to change its marketing structure.

I conclude that the application of the Wisconsin Fair Dealership Law to the terminations at issue herein does not violate any constitutional right of the defendant.

C. *Remedy*

All of the plaintiffs are seeking damages and all plaintiffs except Collins are seeking permanent injunctions forbidding defendant from terminating their dealerships.

1. *Money Damages*

The plaintiffs have not moved for summary judgment on the issue of defendant's liability for money damages under the Fair Dealership Law. However, it is proper for a court to enter summary judgment for non-moving parties, if no factual dispute exists and if the non-movants are entitled to summary judgment as a matter of law.

There is no dispute of fact among the parties, only a dispute as to whether on the non-disputed facts defendant has any liability to those plaintiffs covered by the provisions of the Fair Dealership Law. On that issue, plaintiffs are entitled to partial summary judgment in their favor. Defendant is liable to all plaintiffs except Genoa City Pharmacy and Bernie's Walgreen Agency for money damages resulting from the terminations of plaintiffs' dealerships effected in violation of Chapter 135, the Wisconsin Fair Dealership Law. The appropriate damages remain to be determined in a subsequent proceeding.

2. *Injunctive Relief*

The basis for injunctive relief in the federal courts is irreparable harm and inadequacy of legal remedies....

In addition, the court must balance the probabilities of harm to the individual parties if an injunction is or is not issued, and determine whether the public interest will be disserved by its issuance. In the cases before the court, there is no showing that the harm to plaintiffs cannot be compensated adequately by an award of damages. Moreover, I am persuaded that it would be unduly burdensome to require defendant to maintain its distribution system in Wisconsin when it has abandoned that system in every other state. Finally, societal interests are not served by prohibiting businesses from ever changing their business structures or their methods of operation. I conclude, therefore, that a grant of permanent injunctive relief is not justified in these cases, and I will grant defendant's motion for summary judgment on plaintiffs' claims for permanent injunctive relief requiring the reinstatement of the dealerships....

Judge Crabb later awarded the eleven successful plaintiffs $431,182 in damages. Included in this amount were their attorneys' fees of $75,407 and costs of $15,428 which are reimbursable under § 135.06. Walgreen appealed the award of damages to the United States Court of Appeals for the Seventh Circuit. It affirmed her decisions except for an award of pre-judgment interest. The Seventh Circuit's discussion about computing damages follows:

Judge Crabb awarded plaintiffs $431,182 in damages. Her division of that amount among the plaintiffs is not contested....

The only significant argument defendant has made with respect to damages concerns the $294,705 the district court allowed plaintiffs for lost future profits. Plaintiffs' expert witness on this subject was Donald Nichols, Chairman of the Department of Economics of the University of Wisconsin in Madison. He was formerly Deputy Assistant Secretary of Labor of the United States and served as an expert witness as to lost future profits in two WFDL cases tried in the district court for the Eastern District of Wisconsin. His testimony was summarized in [Walgreen II] and produced a present value of lost sales for the eleven stores of $3,237,872. [The lost sales amount was calculated by projecting an estimated decline in the rate of increase of gross sales for plaintiffs' stores over the twenty-year estimated life of these stores, and then discounting the resulting estimate to a present value using a real interest rate of three percent.] He determined that their variable profit rate was 9.4% Multiplying those two figures produced the $295,000 lost future profits allowed by the district court.... This was the most conservative of three estimates Nichols provided for plaintiffs' loss of future profits and was the one selected by Judge Crabb as the proper amount of damages plaintiffs should recover in that category ....

Defendant argues that plaintiffs did not present adequate evidence to support the $295,000 lost profits figure accepted by the court. Walgreen sets forth numerous factors that bear upon the profitability of various plaintiff stores and Walgreen-owned stores which might explain the four percent decrease in growth rate observed by Nichols apart from the Walgreen termination decision. Defendant asserts that the court and plaintiffs' expert overlooked or ignored such factors as new competition, increased advertising and store improvements with regard to both individual Walgreen and former Walgreen Agency stores. Both Judge Crabb and Professor Nichols, however, were aware of these factors, presented in detail below by defendant, and agreed that they demonstrated all the more clearly that Walgreen's termination caused the 1981 four percent decline in gross sales:

... the only event common to all the stores is the plaintiffs' termination as agency stores in October, 1980. It is more probable than not that this event was the cause of the 1981 decline in the rate of annual sales growth for plaintiffs. The probability is enhanced by the evidence adduced by defendant to show that in 1981 some of the plaintiffs had increased competition, some had less; that some plaintiffs increased their advertising budgets, some decreased them; that some plaintiffs felt the effects of the economic recession in their towns; that some plaintiffs increased their business dramatically by emphasizing a special line of products ... or by negotiating exclusive prescription contracts with nursing homes ... In other words, defendant has helped show that there was no one event common to all the plaintiffs that would account for the change in behavior in their average rate of sales growth other than their termination as Walgreen agencies....

Future profits are difficult to prove and an estimate of lost future profits is inherently speculative to some degree, but these problems do not preclude recovery of damages under Wisconsin law.... The conservative estimates utilized by the plaintiffs' expert and adopted by the district court were computed with the reasonable certainty required and were not the result of mere guesswork.... It is not irrelevant to our holding that despite defendant's offer of numerous observations and criticisms, both here and below, regarding the damages figure adopted by the district court, Walgreen produced no expert witness on the issue of future profits.

NOTES AND QUESTIONS

1. *Later interpretations*:   In *St. Joseph Equipment Co. v. Massey-Ferguson, Inc.,*[94] Massey-Ferguson terminated a dealership as part of withdrawing from the entire North American construction equipment market. Judge Evans held that this did not violate the Wisconsin Fair Dealership Act. He said that the analysis, but not the result, in the *Walgreen* decision was wrong. The *Walgreen* opinion did not consider fairness from the grantor's perspective. The statute permits evenhanded, non-discriminatory actions. The Legislature did not intend WFDA to isolate dealers from economic reality.

In *Ziegler v. Rexnord,*[95] a majority of the Supreme Court of Wisconsin said:

The real issue is whether a grantor ... may alter its method of doing business with its dealers ... to accommodate its own economic problems, or whether it must subordinate those problems — regardless how real, how legitimate, or how serious — in all respects and permanently if the dealer wishes to continue the dealership. We find that the grantor's economic circumstances may constitute good cause to alter its method of doing business with its dealers, but such changes must be essential, reasonable and nondiscriminatory....

The WFDL meant to afford dealers substantial protections previously unavailable at common law; however, the Wisconsin legislature could not have intended to impose an eternal and unqualified duty of self-sacrifice upon every grantor that enters into a distributorship agreement....

Put another way, the grantor may terminate, cancel or fail to renew a dealership if the dealer refuses to accept proposed changes in the dealership

[94]546 F.Supp. 1245 (E.D.Wis. 1982).
[95]149 Wis.2d 308, 433 N.W.2d 8 (1988).

relationship provided that the changes are essential, reasonable and not discriminatory between similarly situated dealers. In determining whether the changes are essential and reasonable, a balancing must be done. Whether the changes are essential and reasonable must also be considered in regard to the effect on the grantee....

The court relied on the WFDL's statement of purpose: "To promote the compelling interest of the public in fair business relations between dealers and grantors, and in the continuation of dealerships on a fair basis." Justices Abrahamson and Heffernan dissented because "the majority's interpretation of the good cause requirement focuses on the grantor and therefore contravenes the plain language of § 135.02(4), [Wis.] Stats. which focuses entirely on the conduct of the dealer." What does the decision in the *Ziegler* case leave of Judge Crabb's opinion in the Walgreen case?

2. *Proof of damages with reasonable certainty*: The group claim helped the plaintiffs' lawyers and expert make a statistical case for damages. The lawyers for Walgreen's were critical of Judge Crabb's acceptance of the statistical argument of the plaintiffs; they believed that the statistical summary obscured some very important differences between stores in Milwaukee and all other stores, as well as failing to account for changing competitive conditions in the stores sampled by plaintiffs.

You should not underestimate the difficulties involved in proving lost profits of a franchisee. The requirement to prove those damages with reasonable certainty is likely to be one of the most difficult challenges for a plaintiff in a franchise termination case, if they seek damages. The court in *C.A. May Marine Supply Co. v. Brunswick Corp.*,[96] discussed measuring damages under the Wisconsin Fair Dealership Act:

> A showing of the profits lost by the dealer as a result of the breach of contract is the usual and most common procedure to prove the damage... Where the business is new and the dealer goes out of business before he is able to compile an earnings record, the amount of lost profits is gauged by a 'yardstick" study of the business profits of a closely comparable business.... Otherwise, the dealer's profit record prior to the violation is compared with his performance subsequent thereto. This method is often called the "before and after" theory....

Loss of business value is the second major measure of damages in dealership cases. This method focuses upon the change in worth of a going concern after total or almost total destruction caused by a breach of contract.... Both business goodwill and future profits are computed into the "going concern" value loss.

---

[96]649 F.2d 1049, 1053 (5th Cir. 1981).

Hence, damage awards which include recovery for lost future profits and "going concern" value are impermissibly duplicitous.

Another possibility would be to award reliance losses. The 8th Circuit in *Central Microfilm Service Corp. v. Basic/Four Corp.,*[97] suggested that where the "peculiar circumstances of the case involved" make use of an expectation measure impossible to apply accurately, an alternative measure of damages would be available.

3. *Consequences of the statute*: What can we say about the impact of the statute? Lawyers seem relatively well-informed about the statute's potential. This may be partly due to the fact that the statute does authorize awards of attorney's fees, making litigation under it somewhat more economical for plaintiffs. We found 227 cases reported from 1976 to 1995 where the statute was in issue.[98] any involve people in various kinds of relationships trying to claim that they have a dealership covered by the statute. These cases suggest plaintiffs' lawyers see the statute as offering real advantages to their clients which they do not find in other bodies of law. For example, courts have held manufacturers' representatives and freight forwarders did not have sufficient "community of interest" to fall within the statutory definition of "dealership."

Not everyone is enthusiastic about the statute's consequences. A prominent Wisconsin lawyer commented about the consequences of the statute:

> As an aside, it is interesting to note that the WFDL has had just the opposite effect than was anticipated. Before the enactment of the WFDL, usually only the very large grantors (*e.g.*, petroleum refiners, brewers, distillers, etc.) entered into detailed dealership agreements. Other grantors simply left the relationship with their dealers quite vague and usually did not have any written dealership agreement whatsoever. Now because the only way a relationship can normally be terminated or changed is when the grantor can *prove* that the dealer breached a dealership agreement term, it is essential that those terms be specified with excruciating detail. Today even the smallest grantors must resort to written and tight contracts in order to protect their own rights. Moreover, the WFDL has injured many good dealers as well as the general public because many grantors are now afraid to terminate marginal dealers for fear of being sued. Those marginal dealers are many times reducing the level of service normally provided by the grantor's dealers and are, in some instances, injuring the grantor's good will

---

[97] 688 F.2d 1206 (1982).

[98] You will notice that federal courts acting under diversity of citizenship jurisdiction have made most of the decisions under the Wisconsin Fair Dealership Law. Wisconsin courts have written opinions in only 53 of the 227 cases reported as of 1995. As always, it is difficult to judge how far the Supreme Court of Wisconsin will follow this body of case law created by federal courts "applying Wisconsin law" under diversity of citizenship jurisdiction.

which affects the ability of the better dealers to sell the same products and services.

William Nelson, the draftsman of the statute, noted that another reason for preferring WFDA actions if you are a plaintiff, (and disliking them if you are a defendant-franchisor) was the non-discrimination clause in the Act. This permits plaintiffs to go through all the franchisor's records, which makes them unhappy, but is essential. In addition, of course, attorney's fees are recoverable under the WFDA, which may advantage plaintiffs with strong claims but few resources.

4. *What is "good cause" for ending a dealership?* Section 135.02(4) defines "good cause" as the failure "to comply substantially with essential and reasonable requirements" which "are not discriminatory as compared with requirements imposed on other similarly situated dealers either by their terms or in the manner of their enforcement." Notice that "substantially," "essential," "reasonable," and "discriminatory" are all qualitative terms, calling for judgment in their application in a particular case. However, remember that the burden of proof to show good cause for terminating a dealership is on the *franchisor*.

In *Al Bishop Agency, Inc. v. Lithonia-Div. of National Service Industries, Inc.,*[99] the court applied the statutory definition of good cause. One of the issues in the case was whether Lithonia was justified in terminating the plaintiff for failure to meet certain sales volume requirements. The court held that the law required that such requirements be both essential and reasonable. In this case the requirements met both criteria, and so defendant was justified in terminating plaintiff. The court went on, however, to find that since Lithonia had not given proper notice, or allowed cure of plaintiff's default as required, the plaintiff was entitled to an injunction prohibiting the termination of the dealership.

5. *The continuing battle — amendment, repeal, or avoidance*: Throughout the early 1980's franchisors sought to amend or repeal the statute. They charged that the statute prohibited franchisors from effectively policing franchisees in situations involving franchisee dishonesty, laziness, uncleanliness, or other behavior which destroyed franchisor goodwill. Franchisors were particularly frustrated at the clause which required 90-day notice of changes in franchisee behavior, and an additional 60 days to comply.

Wisconsin's 4500 registered franchise holders fought back, characterizing the Wisconsin law as "the nation's finest franchise law" and "the Magna Carta of franchise protection laws." To some extent Wisconsin became a battleground between the International Franchise Association (IFA), an organization representing franchisors, and the National Franchisee Association (NFA), representing franchisees. The arguments in Wisconsin paralleled those made in other states, where changes in franchise laws were under consideration. The IFA claimed to have been successful in blocking developments in many states which

---

[99]474 F. Supp. 828 (E.D.Wis. 1979).

it claimed would unfairly restrict franchising practices. There is little doubt that the battle will be a continuing one in the 90s.

At the same time that efforts were being made to repeal or amend the statute, lawyers for franchisors were seeking ways to limit the statute's impact. Judge Crabb has ruled that the Wisconsin Fair Dealership Act is subject to the Federal Arbitration Act, because of the supremacy clause in the U.S. Constitution.[100] This means that if the franchise contract contains an arbitration clause, dealers seeking to assert claims must present those claims to arbitrators rather than courts and juries. Is there any reason for dealers to care whether their claims are heard by arbitrators or courts?

2. GRIEVANCE PROCESSES UNDER COLLECTIVE BARGAINING

Contracts relating to employment are the source of many disputes. One kind of employment related contract is the collective bargaining agreement which is negotiated by a union on behalf of its members. Courses in labor law teach a great deal about unions, managements and collective bargaining. Here we offer only the briefest introduction to a small part of the area.

The contracts which unions negotiate on behalf of their membership nearly always contain a procedure for processing grievances. This grievance procedure usually provides for binding arbitration if the parties cannot otherwise agree. Having a brief picture of grievance arbitration provides a useful contrast with how courts deal with relationships between employer and employee in the absence of a collective bargaining agreement. What kinds of rules and procedures govern disputes between employers and nonunionized employees? Do they work? For whom? How do formal systems actually work in practice? What are the costs of the various procedures?

a. Grievance Systems

Grievance systems vary. Nonetheless, most procedures involve a filtering system that handles disputes quickly and informally. An employee who claims to have been the victim of improper application of the collective bargain usually must present the complaint to a supervisor. A worker may appeal an adverse judgment to a superintendent who will meet with a union grievance committee. If this process does not solve the problem, then the dispute may go to the personnel department of the company. An official will deal with a representative of the regional or national office of the union. If the problem still is unsettled, most collective agreements then call for arbitration. Sometimes there is a panel with a representative of the union and management as well as a neutral. Sometimes there is a single arbitrator. There are procedures for choosing

---

[100]Good(e) Business Systems, Inc. v. Raytheon Co., 614 F.Supp. 428 (W.D. Wis. 1985)

arbitrators. Some aspects of the arbitration decision are subject to review in the courts. Most grievances relate to employee discipline. Others concern job assignments, overtime, or seniority.

The system does not always work as we might think it should. On one hand, union officials may stir up grievances for political purposes, to strengthen their chances for re-election, or to gain interpretations of the contract to trade in the collective bargaining process. On the other hand, workers do not always take their problems to the process, fearing the loss of the good will of their supervisor, or lacking faith in their local union officials. Those who support the local officials may get more effort expended in pressing their grievances than others despite the legal duty of fair representation. The international union may be pursuing policies that particular members dislike, and its officials may be seen as unlikely to press particular claims.

Others attack the grievance procedure because it places maximum value on avoiding interruption of production, even if that is at the expense of employee health and safety.[101]

b. Arbitration Versus Adjudication

To what extent, if at all, does arbitration of a grievance differ from adjudication before a court? Consider the following case. How might a court have decided it had TWA and the flight attendant been operating under a binding employment contract and taken the case to a judge and jury?

---

[101]   Capitalist class bias favors uninterrupted production, even at the probable expense of employee health and safety. The mistaken good faith belief that hazards exist will not support unilateral employee cessation of work; instead, the employee must be supported by objective evidence of abnormally dangerous conditions in fact. The same class bias also underlies the fact that the fundamental purpose of the grievance procedure is to ensure the continued subordination of labor to ownership interests. Employee grievances are relegated to the grievance arbitration provisions of the collective bargaining agreement.

In grievance arbitration, which operates within the contractual constraints actually set management, the employee bears adverse disciplinary action or is discharged, while the production process continues without interruption. Termination can thus be imposed on the employee, who must bear this draconian sanction without proper prior impartial corroboration of culpability. Meanwhile, arbitration, the primary means for employee vindication, remains at least several months in the future. Even if the employee is ultimately vindicated by the arbitrator, no punitive sanction is imposed upon the employer.

Professor David L. Gregory, reviewing James B. Atleson, Values and Assumptions in American Labor Law (1983) in 62 Texas Law Review 389, 396-97 (1983).

IN RE TRANS WORLD AIRLINES, INC.

System Board of Adjustment
46 Lab. Arb. Rep. 611 (1965)

Decision of Arbitrators

WIG DEMONSTRATION

WALLEN, ARBITRATOR: — The facts of the case are fairly clear. X — is a Stewardess in the International Division. She has been employed by TWA since 1956 and apparently has a clear record. The difficulties which led to her discharge grew out of a hostess grooming and appearance inspection scheduled beginning February 1, 1964. Pursuant to a posted notice, all Idlewild International-Based Hostesses were to appear for such an inspection after pre-flight briefing for their first trip in February. Particular emphasis was to be placed on personal appearance — "weight, length, color and styling of hair, complexion and make-up, as covered in the Flight Service Manual."

The Flight Service Manual, § 01.10.01 dated February 1, 1963 sets forth detailed regulations concerning their hair styles. One regulation provides: "The hair shall be worn close to the head, and when pulled straight from the hairline at the nape of the neck, must not extend below the top of the collar when standing erect." Another states:

> After obtaining previous supervisory approval, a wig may be worn by a Hostess if it enhances her uniform appearance. A wig may not be worn to disguise any non-conformity with standard hair regulations. A wig will be subject to inspection and must comply with standard hair regulations. The wig must be of good quality natural hair, regulation hair style, length and color and maintained in a good, clean condition. The decision as to whether the wig enhances the Hostess' uniform appearance, and complies with regulations, shall be made solely by the Supervisor.

X — , scheduled out for a flight on February 15, 1964, had not yet gone through the Hostess grooming appearance inspection. She was summoned to Hangar 12 at JFK, after her pre-flight briefing, by Hostess Supervisor Elizabeth Connelly. Miss Connelly found X — 's general appearance — complexion, weight, uniform and hands — satisfactory. However, Miss Connelly knew that X — had had approval as required by the regulations to wear a wig; had been told by another supervisor that she had been seen in Rome with her hair beyond regulation length; and had a year or more before flown and roomed with X — and knew that in the past she had had long hair.

Against this background Miss Connelly asked X — if she was wearing a wig. X — said no, whereupon the supervisor asked her to lift her hair at the back of her neck in order to verify if a wig was being worn or whether, on the other hand, she was in fact observing the hostess' natural hair. It appears that if a wig was being worn, X — would have been asked to remove it so that compliance with the requirement that her natural hair nonetheless not exceed regulation length could be verified.

X — , however, refused to demonstrate in the manner asked that she was wigless. She left on her flight, but on February 17 was interviewed by Alexander Rossi, Assistant Transportation Manager of Hostesses and Pursers, International, in the presence of Supervisor Connelly. Again she was asked if she was wearing a wig; again she said no; and again she was asked to, but refused to verify her answer in the manner described earlier.

Further efforts to persuade X — to submit to verification of her statement that she was not wearing a wig were unavailing. She was asked by Rossi to come in by February 21 for this purpose. When she did not do so she was placed on off-duty status and told to report to H. H. Brown, Rossi's superior. She did not so report whereupon Brown, by letter, told her to report to his office in complete uniform by March 3. When she did not appear by that date she was terminated for willful insubordination.

X — 's refusal to verify her claim that she was not wearing a wig, it appears, was based on her feeling that it was humiliating to be asked to raise the back of her hair; that she was being treated like a child; that she had not before been asked to make such a demonstration; that her appearance had been deemed satisfactory; and that she "did not feel it was necessary for a hostess to have to comply with these requests." She regarded the request as undignified, an invasion of privacy and personally obnoxious. She deemed the repeated requests that she reappear for inspection harassment and of the two grievances filed, one protests such harassment while the second protests her subsequent discharge.

X — is a long-service hostess with an otherwise good record and while her annoyance at having to supply verification of compliance with uniform and appearance regulations is understandable, it fails to take into account the fact that human nature being what it is, such regulations are not self-enforcing. While the great majority of hostesses are mature enough to comply with regulations regarding hair length or other matters of personal appearance not observable at a glance, in a work force of 2,200 there will inevitably be a few who will try to beat the rules. If successful, they imperil the very existence of the rules for each case of successful noncompliance breeds disrespect for the rule and undermines the will of others to comply.

Hence management must be accorded the right to verify compliance with clothing, hair length and appearance regulations in a manner which imposes no unreasonable or undignified demands on the employee. To ask an employee to furnish such verification is neither improper nor unreasonable. On the contrary, it constitutes the kind of submission to the discipline of the workplace that all human beings inevitably encounter in a complex, closely knit economic society. To the extent that X — 's stance in this case was based on a refusal to submit to this kind of discipline associated with her job, it was in error.

X — 's supervisors plainly had a right to determine whether her natural hair was of the prescribed length, regardless of whether or not a wig was being worn. The regulations are clear on the point and they are in no sense unreasonable. In order to do so, the supervisors had to determine whether or not she was wearing a wig.

X — 's refusal to demonstrate that she was not wearing a wig by lifting the hair at the back of her head was based, at least in part, on the claim that such an act would subject her to an indignity. Here we enter into the realm of individual emotions. We venture to guess that many young ladies would think nothing of complying with such a request and would see in it no indignity. On the other hand, it is possible that some individuals might deem a request for such a demonstration in the impersonal surroundings of the workplace to be offensive or humiliating. And a third possibility exists — that someone who has no qualms in the matter might nonetheless invoke personal privilege to avoid verification of her natural hair length.

We are uncertain of X — 's motivation in her refusal to demonstrate that she was not wearing a wig. On the other hand, there is no evidence to show that she was in fact masking an evasion of the hair length rule. Hence we are constrained to accept her plea that her refusal arose out of her belief that the request offended the canons of good taste as she views them.

It might be argued that this leaves supervision in the position of being unable to verify whether a hostess authorized to wear a wig has natural hair of regulation length. We point out, however, that supervision has the right to require hostesses with approved wigs to appear at inspections. If requested, with the wig in hand so that both the wig and the natural hair may be viewed by the supervisor.

There remains the question, whether a supervisor may require a hostess to demonstrate that her natural hair is of regulation length. Since hair is sometimes curly or wavy this may not always be ascertainable by a glance. We hold that it is reasonable to infer from the regulation prescribing hair length that a supervisor may verify it by asking the hostess to demonstrate it in the course of an inspection.

As we have said, there is no evidence that X — 's refusal to demonstrate that she was not wearing a wig was designed to evade the hair-length rule. Inasmuch as her refusal appears to have stemmed from deeply held, though misplaced feelings in the matter, we hesitate to affirm the discharge penalty levied in her case. For this reason, all Board members concur in her reinstatement. However, we are unable to overlook her failure to accede to requests to appear for subsequent inspections on February 21 and later. Her failure to do so violated her obligations as an employee.

The Neutral Referee and the Company members are of the opinion that X — was insubordinate in failing to appear for inspections by Rossi and Brown as directed and that her insistence on complete freedom from verification of compliance with appearance regulations was misplaced. Hence the majority, with the Association members dissenting on this point only, voted to direct her reinstatement without back pay as a means of pointing up her errors in these areas.

DECISION

1. The Union's grievance protesting harassment of X — is denied.
2. X — shall be reinstated without back pay but with seniority unimpaired.

NOTES AND QUESTIONS

1. *Functions of the three-member panel*: The union representative on the arbitration panel usually votes for the employee, and the management representative usually votes for the employer. The deciding vote, then, is cast by the neutral member. Why do parties often want this arrangement rather than just a single arbitrator?

2. *Arbitration contrasted with adjudication*: Arbitration usually proceeds with much less precise procedures than adjudication. Often the union does not state the grievance very clearly at the outset, and the dispute only comes into focus as the case is heard. The parties may or may not be represented by lawyers, although there is a trend toward a more technical approach as unions have become established institutions staffed by professionals. The rules of evidence are not observed formally in arbitration. Furthermore, the process often is said to serve the "airing" functions of a Kpelle moot. It may be important that the parties are able to speak their piece in full. Arbitrators are not bound by precedent, but often produce written opinions and are likely to feel pressure to be consistent. Ideally, arbitration would produce quick answers, but usually the entire grievance process works slowly.

3. *Goals of labor arbitration*: There is some dispute about how far labor arbitrators should go beyond a rather literal interpretation of the language of the contract. How far should they bring a sense of the customs of the plant or industry with them in reading the language? How far should they fashion a result they think will further the ongoing relationship between the organized workers and management? Contrast the following views:

John Phillips, discouraged by results in four of his cases in which arbitrators reviewed, and reversed, employee discharges, argued[102] that arbitrators were abusing their authority and that more judicial review of arbitrator's decisions was necessary. After recounting the results in his own cases, Phillips summarized nine other published arbitration awards with results he found ridiculous. He acknowledged that the Supreme Court had announced in the "Steelworkers

---

[102] Phillips, Their Own Brand of Industrial Justice: Arbitrators' Excesses in Discharge Cases, 10 Employee Relations Journal 48 (1984). Reprinted with permission from Employee Relations Law Journal, V10N1, Summer 1984. Copyright 1984 by Executive Enterprises, Inc., 22 West 21st Street, New York, NY 10010-6904. All Rights Reserved.

Trilogy"[103] that judicial deference to arbitrator's decisions was appropriate but noted that in the same case the Court had cautioned that an arbitrator's award was legitimate only if grounded in the collective bargaining agreement. "When the arbitrator's words manifest an infidelity to this obligation, courts have no choice but to refuse enforcement of the award." Phillips concluded:

> ... A 1983 survey of arbitrators disclosed that nearly 60 percent equated a discharge to capital punishment in a criminal case....
>
> Awards such as those discussed above destroy confidence in the arbitration process and jeopardize industrial discipline. A recent Gallup Poll disclosed that "65 percent of Americans think the overall level of ethics in American Society has declined in the past decade." Arbitrators who reinstate employees guilty of violence, harassment, carelessness, or other misconduct promote disorder and anarchy in the work place. It is unfortunate that employers cannot replace such offenders with the many capable workers now on the nation's unemployment rolls. How can American businesses hope to rival domestic and foreign competition when hamstrung by such "industrial justice?" How do such awards contribute to the quality of America's work life? ...
>
> In the final analysis, this article is a plea to arbitrators to enforce contracts and work rules as they are written, to exhibit more common sense and concern themselves less with social reform, and, in the words of the Supreme Court, to demonstrate "some minimum level of integrity" in discharge cases.

Robert Coulson, a leading figure in the development of the American Arbitration Association, responded to Phillips.[104] *He* began by recounting seven instances in which arbitrators had confirmed *harsh* actions by management. He went on to argue that we should not be so quick to condemn the arbitrator. The arbitrator has seen not just the summary of testimony but the testimony itself. In addition, Coulson notes that quite often management itself has signaled to the arbitrator that it would be satisfied with a suspension rather than a discharge. Coulson closes with a statement representative of the view that arbitration is more likely to respect the realities of the workplace:

The contract is not simply a piece of paper signed by the parties. It is a living relationship, defined and redefined during its term by innumerable conversations, grievance conferences, and arbitration hearings. Harsh discipline may be equally

---

[103]Three 1960 Supreme Court cases dealing with judicial review of arbitration awards.

[104]Coulson, The Arbitrator's Role in Discharge Cases: Another Viewpoint, 10 Employee Relations Law Journal 61 (1984). Reprinted with permission from Employee Relations Law Journal, V10N1, Summer 1984. Copyright 1984 by Executive Enterprises, Inc., 22 West 21st Street, New York, NY 10010-6904. All Rights Reserved.

as destructive to the employer-employee relationship as the overabundance of equity that so troubles lawyer Phillips....

4. *Impact of reinstatement of an employee*: Malinowski[105] studied employees reinstated with or without back pay by labor arbitrators. Employers found that most employees returning to work were satisfactory and caused few disciplinary problems, but employers still viewed the arbitrator's order as unacceptable and wrong. Ten of the seventy-three employees ordered reinstated never returned to work, and six of them had over 11 years seniority. Some might have found it difficult to return after being accused of wrongdoing. Some found other jobs while waiting for the result of the grievance process, and the new job may have seemed better than the old one.

c. Judicial Review of Arbitration

Suppose either union or management is dissatisfied with a decision of an arbitrator. The disappointed party can appeal to the courts, but what will the courts do with such a case? Notice there are two issues: first, the parties may debate as to whether they agreed to submit a particular dispute to arbitration. Second, they may debate the correctness of an arbitrator's interpretation of the collective bargain as applied to a particular case. The Supreme Court of the United States announced three opinions on the same day concerning judicial review of labor arbitration — not surprisingly, labor lawyers call these cases "the trilogy." Essentially what the Court held in these cases is that even the question of whether or not the parties have agreed to submit a particular issue to arbitration is, except for a few instances, for the arbitrator to decide.[106]

Lawyers have not been content to accept the power of arbitrators which the *Trilogy* cases seem to grant to them. They have gone to court, looking for ways around the *Trilogy* decisions, and they have found just enough success to keep them coming back to the courts. We must leave the topic for courses in Labor Law, but Professor Gould suggests what has happened in the thirty years since the *Trilogy* decisions:[107]

> It is now almost thirty years since the United States Supreme Court in its landmark *Steelworkers Trilogy* decisions, promoted both the labor arbitration process itself and the finality to be given to labor arbitration awards. But the landscape of judicial review of labor arbitration is now more reminiscent of a thirty years' war than the substitute for strife once heralded....

---

[105]Malinowski, An Empirical Analysis of Discharge Cases and the Work History of Employees Reinstated by Labor Arbitrators, 36 Arbitration Journal 31 (1981).

[106]United Steelworkers of America v. Warrior & Gulf Navigation Co., 363 U.S. 574 (1960).

[107] See Gould, Judicial Review of Labor Arbitration Awards--Thirty Years of the Steelworkers Trilogy: The Aftermath of AT & T and Misco, 64 Notre Dame Law Review 464, 470-471, 472-475 (1989). Copyright reserved by William B. Gould IV.

Reaffirmance of *Steelworkers Trilogy*, and indeed *expansion* of the *Trilogy's* principles, albeit with new exceptions to the rule promoting finality of arbitration awards, has only invited more litigation and judicial contests....

Finally, it is particularly ironic that the labor arbitration process is becoming more reviewed and regulated in this decade, just as parties in other relationships are looking to the labor arbitration process as a model through which wasteful litigation can be diminished. As alternatives to the judiciary are found elsewhere, the incentive to utilize what has been the most successful method of dispute resolution appears to be diminishing in the field of labor-management relations.

3. EMPLOYMENT RELATIONS

To what extent does, or should, the law intervene in long term employment relationships? Here we are interested primarily in regulation of the employer's power to hire and fire employees. We will leave to other courses the study of the many legal provisions governing minimum wages, maximum hours and health and safety on the job, unemployment and worker's compensation, as well as federal and state laws prohibiting hiring and firing people because of their race, religion, sex or age.

a. Proving Employment Contracts and Gaining Meaningful Remedies

Reliance and the policies of form: Suppose an employee asserts reliance on an oral promise, either an express or an implied one, for employment for 367 days? Once again we would face the Statute of Frauds. In most states promises that by their terms cannot possibly be performed within one year must be in writing. In many states this means that a contract to work for 367 days must be in writing. Many employment agreements are oral and uncertain. If the job is to run more than a year, the arrangement does not meet the demands of the writing requirement. But does reliance outweigh the policies of form which are crystallized in the Statute of Frauds?

MCINTOSH v. MURPHY

59 Hawaii 29, 469 P.2d 177 (1970)

LEVINSON, J. This case involves an oral employment contract which allegedly violates the provision of the Statute of Frauds requiring "any agreement that is not to be performed within one year from the making thereof" to be in writing in order to be enforceable. HRS § 656-1(5). In this action the plaintiff-employee Dick McIntosh seeks to recover damages from his employer, George Murphy and

Murphy Motors, Ltd., for the breach of an alleged one-year oral employment contract.

While the facts are in sharp conflict, it appears that defendant George Murphy was in southern California during March, 1964 interviewing prospective management personnel for his Chevrolet-Oldsmobile dealerships in Hawaii. He interviewed the plaintiff twice during that time. The position of sales manager for one of the dealerships was fully discussed but no contract was entered into. In April, 1964 the plaintiff received a call from the general manager of Murphy Motors informing him of possible employment within thirty days if he was still available. The plaintiff indicated his continued interest and informed the manager that he would be available. Later in April, the plaintiff sent Murphy a telegram to the effect that he would arrive in Honolulu on Sunday, April 26, 1964. Murphy then telephoned McIntosh on Saturday, April 25, 1964 to notify him that the job of assistant sales manager was open and work would begin on the following Monday, April 27, 1964. At that time McIntosh expressed surprise at the change in job title from sales manager to assistant sales manager but reconfirmed the fact that he was arriving in Honolulu the next day, Sunday. McIntosh arrived on Sunday, April 26, 1964 and began work on the following day, Monday, April 27, 1964.

As a consequence of his decision to work for Murphy, McIntosh moved some of his belongings from the mainland to Hawaii, sold other possessions, leased an apartment in Honolulu and obviously forwent any other employment opportunities. In short, the plaintiff did all those things which were incidental to changing one's residence permanently from Los Angeles to Honolulu, a distance of approximately 2200 miles. McIntosh continued working for Murphy until July 16, 1964, approximately two and one-half months, at which time he was discharged on the grounds that he was unable to close deals with prospective customers and could not train the salesmen.

At the conclusion of the trial, the defense moved for a directed verdict arguing that the oral employment agreement was in violation of the Statute of Frauds, there being no written memorandum or note thereof. The trial court ruled that as a matter of law the contract did not come within the Statute, reasoning that Murphy bargained for acceptance by the actual commencement of performance by McIntosh, so that McIntosh was not bound by a contract until he came to work on Monday, April 27, 1964. Therefore, assuming that the contract was for a year's employment, it was performable within a year exactly to the day and no writing was required for it to be enforceable. Alternatively, the court ruled that if the agreement was made final by the telephone call between the parties on Saturday, April 25, 1964, then that part of the weekend which remained would not be counted in calculating the year, thus taking the contract out of the Statute of Frauds. With commendable candor the trial judge gave as the motivating force for the decision his desire to avoid a mechanical and unjust application of the Statute.

The case went to the jury on the following questions: (1) whether the contract was for a year's duration or was performable on a trial basis, thus making it terminable at the will of either party; (2) whether the plaintiff was discharged for just cause; and (3) if he was not discharged for just cause, what damages were due the plaintiff. The jury returned a verdict for the plaintiff in the sum of $12,103.40.... The ... ground of appeal is whether the plaintiff can maintain an action on the alleged oral employment contract in light of the prohibition of the Statute of Frauds making unenforceable an oral contract that is not to be performed within one year.

I. TIME OF ACCEPTANCE OF THE EMPLOYMENT AGREEMENT

The defendants contend that the trial court erred in refusing to give an instruction to the jury that if the employment agreement was made more than one day before the plaintiff began performance, there could be no recovery by the plaintiff. The reason given was that a contract not to be performed within one year from its making is unenforceable if not in writing.

[W]e base our decision in this case on the doctrine of equitable estoppel which was properly briefed and argued by both parties before this court, although not presented to the trial court.

II. ENFORCEMENT BY VIRTUE OF ACTION
IN RELIANCE ON THE ORAL CONTRACT

In determining whether a rule of law can be fashioned and applied to a situation where an oral contract admittedly violates a strict interpretation of the Statute of Frauds, it is necessary to review the Statute itself together with its historical and modern functions. The Statute of Frauds, which requires that certain contracts be in writing in order to be legally enforceable, had its inception in the days of Charles II of England. Hawaii's version of the Statute is found in HRS § 656-1 and is substantially the same as the original English Statute of Frauds.

The first English Statute was enacted almost 300 years ago to prevent "many fraudulent practices, which are commonly endeavored to be upheld by perjury and subornation of perjury." 29 Car. 2, c. 3 (1677). Certainly, there were compelling reasons in those days for such a law. At the time of enactment in England, the jury system was quite unreliable, rules of evidence were few, and the complaining party was disqualified as a witness so he could neither testify on direct-examination nor, more importantly, be cross-examined. Summers, *The Doctrine of Estoppel and the Statute of Frauds*, 79 University of Pennsylvania Law Review 440, 441 (1931). The aforementioned structural and evidentiary limitations on our system of justice no longer exist.

Retention of the Statute today has nevertheless been justified on at least three grounds: (1) the Statute still serves an evidentiary function, thereby lessening the danger of perjured testimony (the original rationale); (2) the requirement of a writing has a cautionary effect which causes reflection by the parties on the importance of the agreement; and (3) the writing is an easy way to distinguish enforceable contracts from those which are not, thus channeling certain transactions into written form.

In spite of whatever utility the Statute of Frauds may still have, its applicability has been drastically limited by judicial construction over the years in order to mitigate the harshness of a mechanical application. Furthermore, learned writers continue to disparage the Statute regarding it as "a statute for promoting fraud" and a "legal anachronism."

Another method of judicial circumvention of the Statute of Frauds has grown out of the exercise of equity powers of the courts. Such judicially imposed limitations or exceptions involved the traditional dispensing power of the equity courts to mitigate the "harsh" rule of law. When courts have enforced an oral contract in spite of the Statute, they have utilized the legal labels of "part performance" or "equitable estoppel" in granting relief. Both doctrines are said to be based on the concept of estoppel, which operates to avoid unconscionable injury....

Part performance has long been recognized in Hawaii as an equitable doctrine justifying the enforcement of an oral agreement for the conveyance of an interest in land where there has been substantial reliance by the party seeking to enforce the contract.... Other courts have enforced oral contracts (including employment contracts) which failed to satisfy the section of the Statute making unenforceable an agreement not to be performed within a year of its making. This has occurred where the conduct of the parties gave rise to an estoppel to assert the Statute....

It is appropriate for modern courts to cast aside the raiments of conceptualism which cloak the true policies underlying the reasoning behind the many decisions enforcing contracts that violate the Statute of Frauds. There is certainly no need to resort to legal rubrics or meticulous legal formulas when better explanations are available. The policy behind enforcing an oral agreement which violated the Statute of Frauds, as a policy of avoiding unconscionable injury, was well set out by the California Supreme Court. In *Monarco v. LoGreco*, 35 Cal. 2d 621, 623, 220 P.2d 737, 739 (1950), a case which involved an action to enforce an oral contract for the conveyance of land on the grounds of 20 years performance by the promisee, the court said:

> The doctrine of estoppel to assert the statute of frauds has been consistently applied by the courts of this state to prevent fraud that would result from refusal to enforce oral contracts in certain circumstances. Such fraud may inhere in the unconscionable injury that would result from denying enforcement of the contract after one party has been induced by the other seriously to change his position in reliance on the contract....

In seeking to frame a workable test which is flexible enough to cover diverse factual situations and also provide some reviewable standards, we find very persuasive § 217A of the Second Restatement of Contracts. That section specifically covers those situations where there has been reliance on an oral contract which falls within the Statute of Frauds. Section 217A states:

> (1) A promise which the promisor should reasonably expect to induce action or forbearance on the part of the promisee or a third person and which does induce the action or forbearance is enforceable notwithstanding the Statute of Frauds if injustice can be avoided only by enforcement of the promise. The remedy granted for breach is to be limited as justice requires.
>
> (2) In determining whether injustice can be avoided only by enforcement of the promise, the following circumstances are significant: (a) the availability and adequacy of other remedies, particularly cancellation and restitution; (b) the definite and substantial character of the action or forbearance in relation to the remedy sought; (c) the extent to which the action or forbearance corroborates evidence of the making and terms of the promise, or the making and terms are otherwise established by clear and convincing evidence; (d) the reasonableness of the action or forbearance; (e) the extent to which the action or forbearance was foreseeable by the promisor.

We think that the approach taken in the Restatement is the proper method of giving the trial court the necessary latitude to relieve a party of the hardships of the Statute of Frauds. Other courts have used similar approaches in dealing with oral employment contracts upon which an employee had seriously relied. See *Alaska Airlines, Inc. v. Stephenson*, 217 F.2d 295 (9th cir. 1954); *Seymour v. Oelrichs*, 156 Cal. 782, 106 P. 88 (1909). This is to be preferred over having the trial court bend over backwards to take the contract out of the Statute of Frauds. In the present case the trial court admitted just this inclination and forthrightly followed it.

There is no dispute that the action of the plaintiff in moving 2200 miles from Los Angeles to Hawaii was foreseeable by the defendant. In fact, it was required to perform his duties. Injustice can only be avoided by the enforcement of the contract and the granting of money damages. No other remedy is adequate. The plaintiff found himself residing in Hawaii without a job.

It is also clear that a contract of some kind did exist. The plaintiff performed the contract for two and one-half months receiving $3,484.60 for his services. The exact length of the contract, whether terminable at will as urged by the defendant, or for a year from the time when the plaintiff started working, was up to the jury to decide.

In sum, the trial court might have found that enforcement of the contract was warranted by virtue of the plaintiff's reliance on the defendant's promise. Naturally, each case turns on its own facts. Certainly there is considerable discretion for a court to implement the true policy behind the Statute of Frauds, which is to prevent fraud of any other type of unconscionable injury. We therefore affirm the judgment of the trial court on the ground that the plaintiff's reliance was such that injustice could only be avoided by enforcement of the contract.

Affirmed.

DISSENTING OPINION OF ABE, J., (with whom KOBAYASHI, J., joins). The majority of the court has affirmed the judgment of the trial court; however, I respectfully dissent....

As acknowledged by this court, the trial judge erred when as a matter of law he ruled that the alleged employment contract did not come within the Statute of Frauds; however, I cannot agree that this error was not prejudicial as this court intimates.

On this issue, the date that the alleged contract was entered into was all important and the date of acceptance of an offer by the plaintiff was a question of fact for the jury to decide. In other words, it was for the jury to determine when the alleged one-year employment contract was entered into and if the jury had found that the plaintiff had accepted the offer more than one day before plaintiff was to report to work, the contract would have come within the Statute of Frauds and would have been unenforceable....

This court holds that though the alleged one-year employment contract came within the Statute of Frauds, nevertheless the judgment of the trial court is affirmed "on the ground that the plaintiff's reliance was such that injustice could only be avoided by enforcement of the contract."

I believe this court is begging the issue by its holding because to reach that conclusion, this court is ruling that the defendant agreed to hire the plaintiff under a one-year employment contract. The defendant has denied that the plaintiff was hired for a period of one year and has introduced into evidence testimony of witnesses that all hiring by the defendant in the past has been on a trial basis. The defendant also testified that he had hired the plaintiff on a trial basis.

Here on one hand the plaintiff claimed that he had a one-year employment contract; on the other hand, the defendant claimed that the plaintiff had not been hired for one year but on a trial basis for so long as his services were satisfactory. I believe the Statute of Frauds was enacted to avoid the consequences this court is forcing upon the defendant. In my opinion, the legislature enacted the Statute of Frauds to negate claims such as has been made by the plaintiff in this case. But this court holds that because the plaintiff in reliance of the one-year employment contract (alleged to have been entered into by the plaintiff, but denied by the defendant) has changed his position, "injustice could only be avoided by enforcement of the contract." Where is the sense of justice?

Now assuming that the defendant had agreed to hire the plaintiff under a one-year employment contract and the contract came within the Statute of Frauds, I cannot agree, as intimated by this court, that we should circumvent the Statute of Frauds by the exercise of the equity powers of courts. As to statutory law, the sole function of the judiciary is to interpret the statute and the judiciary should not usurp legislative power and enter into the legislative field.... Thus, if the Statute of Frauds is too harsh as intimated by this court, and it brings about undue hardship, it is for the legislature to amend or repeal the statute and not for this court to legislate.

NOTES AND QUESTIONS

1. *Unspoken premises*: Why was it so important for the plaintiff in this case to prove he had a contract for a year? What do you suppose the plaintiff expected, in terms of job security? Suppose nothing explicit was said; should a court imply a promise of job security from the circumstances surrounding the hiring.

2. *The policies of the Statute of Frauds*: Undoubtedly, the dissenting opinion is right when it says that, had there been a written contract, the parties could have avoided all of the confusion about the nature of the deal. However, in light of the usual bargaining positions of the parties, why should courts place the burden of getting a written contract on the employee? Wouldn't the dissent's rule allow employers to promise anything to get employees to move to the location of the job and then use the Statute of Frauds to walk away from their promises without having to pay for any reliance losses? If the rule suggested by the dissenting opinion were law, could a lawyer properly advise an employer client how to use the Statute of Frauds to trick employees in this way? Is there any limitation on advising a client about his or her legal rights? Would you distinguish externally imposed limitations such as codes of professional responsibility from your own conscience? Can you properly withhold from a client information about his or her legal rights because you disapprove how the client is going to use them?

3. *The Jury and the Statute of Frauds*: Is your enthusiasm (or skepticism) about the Statute of Frauds linked to your attitude about juries? What if you thought that the employer in this case probably made no one-year employment promise, but that the jury simply was sympathetic with the plaintiff? If you believed juries systematically were too sympathetic to plaintiffs, would you support a more rigorous application of the Statute of Frauds?

4. EMPLOYMENT-AT-WILL

You have just read *McIntosh v. Murphy*. It was very easy to read the case without focusing on the assumption that, unless the plaintiff had a contract for a definite term he could be discharged at any time. It is important to realize, however, that job security in the United States is limited. Some employees, such as television personalities and presidents of major corporations, have individual employment contracts for specified terms. Other Americans are members of labor unions working under some degree of job security provided by collective bargains and our labor laws. Civil service or tenure provisions protect others. As we see in the next case, however, most Americans are "employees-at-will" and that job status provides very little in the way of job security. Before examining challenges to the employee-at-will doctrine, it is important to see a case in which that doctrine is directly applied. We also get the opportunity to see how the Wisconsin Supreme Court applied, in a subsequent case, the rule of law it embraced in *Hoffman v. Red Owl, supra.*

FORRER v. SEARS, ROEBUCK & COMPANY

36 Wis. 2d 388; 153 N.W.2d 587 (1967)

[Syllabus by the court: The plaintiff, appellant in this court, brought an action, which he now denominates as one founded upon promissory estoppel, against the defendant and respondent, Sears, Roebuck & Company. The defendant's demurrer to the complaint was sustained, and this appeal is from that order. The plaintiff bases his claim on the following facts

It appears that he had worked for Sears for almost eighteen years, when, due to ill health, he left its employment in 1963 and commenced operating a farm near Stoughton, Wisconsin. The defendant's agents thereafter attempted to induce him to return to work. In November of 1964, he was persuaded to become the manager of the hardware department on a part-time basis. During December of 1964, the general manager of the Madison store promised him "permanent employment" as manager of the hardware division of the Madison store in consideration of giving up his farming operations and working full time for the defendant. It is alleged that thereupon the plaintiff sold his stock of hogs and cattle and rented the barn to a neighbor — all at a loss, placed his acreage in the United States Department of Agriculture feed-grain program, and on February 1, 1965, commenced working full time for the defendant. He alleges that thereafter, despite the understanding with Sears, he was discharged without cause on June 1, 1965. He claims damages in excess of $11,000.

The trial court sustained the defendant's demurrer, holding that no cause of action was stated.]

HEFFERNAN, J. In *Hoffman v. Red Owl Stores, Inc.* (1965), 26 Wis. 2d 683, 696, 133 N. W. 2d 267, this court adopted the doctrine embodied in § 90 of Restatement, 1 Contracts ... We stated in *Hoffman* that we chose to use the phrase, "promissory estoppel" to describe this doctrine. It is promissory estoppel upon which the plaintiff, William E. Forrer, bases his action.

In *Hoffman* we stated that three questions must be answered affirmatively to support an action for promissory estoppel:

(1) Was the promise one which the promisor should reasonably expect to induce action or forbearance of a definite and substantial character on the part of the promisee?

(2) Did the promise induce such action or forbearance?

(3) Can injustice be avoided only by enforcement of the promise?" *Hoffman v. Red Owl Stores, Inc.*....

That all of these questions can be answered affirmatively is evident from the face of the complaint. Plaintiff alleged that he was promised full-time permanent employment in consideration of giving up his farming operations. He also alleges that he thereupon gave up his farming operations at great financial loss. It is apparent that the plaintiff alleges that his action was not only induced by the defendant's promise, but was the conduct that was specifically required as the condition of the defendant's promise. In light of all the circumstances, the sale of the livestock, the leasing of the barn, and putting the farm into the feed-grain program were all acts which the promisor should reasonably have expected that his promise would induce. We would not hesitate to apply the doctrine of promissory estoppel under these facts if justice required it. Justice, however, does not require the invocation of the doctrine, for the promise of the defendant was kept, and this court is not required, therefore, to enforce it.

The defendant's promise was that of "permanent employment."... Generally speaking, a contract for permanent employment, for life employment, or for other terms purporting permanent employment, where the employee furnishes no consideration additional to the services incident to the employment, amounts to an indefinite general hiring terminable at the will of either party, and a discharge without cause does not constitute a breach of such contract justifying recovery of damages.... The same is true where the contract of hiring specifies no term of duration but fixes compensation at a certain amount per day, week, or month.... Although not absolute, the above stated rule appears to be in the nature of a strong presumption in favor of a contract terminable at will unless the terms of the contract or other circumstances clearly manifest the parties' intent to bind each other. The presumption is grounded on a policy that it would otherwise be unreasonable for a man to bind himself permanently to a position, thus eliminating the possibility of later improving that position. Moreover, a contract of permanent employment is by its very nature indefinite, and thus any effort to interpret the duration of the contract and assess the amount of damages becomes difficult.... We thus conclude that the most that was promised by Sears was employment terminable at will. This promise was carried out when the plaintiff was hired as the defendant's full-time manager. The defendant's obligation was discharged when its promise was kept, and, hence, the doctrine of promissory estoppel is not applicable.

The plaintiff in his oral argument stated that he chose to rely on promissory estoppel only, and specifically stated that he abandoned any claim based upon contract law. Nevertheless, it should be stated that conceivably the plaintiff could state a cause of action if it were affirmatively shown that he furnished "additional consideration" in exchange for the defendant's promise of permanent employment.

Under circumstances where an employee has given consideration of benefit to the employer, additional to the services of employment, a contract for permanent employment is valid and enforceable and not against public policy and continues to operate as long as the employer remains in business and has work for the employee, and the employee is willing and able to do his work satisfactorily and does not give cause for his discharge.... We do not deem that the detriment to the plaintiff herein in giving up his farming operations at a loss constituted such additional consideration. We conclude that a permanent employment contract is terminable at will unless there is additional consideration in the form of an economic or financial benefit to the employer. A mere detriment to the employee is not enough.... In *Wright v. C. S. Graves Land Co.* (1898), 100 Wis. 269, 75 N. W. 1000, an employment contract was held not to be terminable at will when the employee had obligated himself to, and did, purchase land and furnish a horse for clearing of fields. The court pointed out that the plaintiff had bound himself for at least two years and, hence, the contract was not terminable at the will of the employer. In so doing, the court gave recognition to those acts of the plaintiff that resulted in a benefit to the employer, and not to those acts that were merely of a detriment to the employee.

We conclude, therefore, that the facts as set forth in the plaintiff's complaint fail to spell out a cause of action for the breach of a contract for permanent employment supported by additional consideration of benefit to the defendant-employer. The only benefit to the defendant was the plaintiff's rendering of services. There was nothing more.

We are therefore obliged to conclude that the permanent employment alleged was a relationship that could be terminated at will by either party. Hence, once the relationship was established, the promise, which plaintiff seeks to enforce by promissory estoppel, was fulfilled. This court need not enforce the promise. It has been carried out. Promissory estoppel is not applicable to this case. Nor is there evidence of additional consideration that would bind the employer to a period not terminable at his will. The demurrer must be sustained.

By the Court. — *Order affirmed.*

NOTES AND QUESTIONS

1. *A study in contrasts?* Compare the decisions in *McIntosh* and *Forrer*. Are they consistent? Does it depend on whether one takes a broad or a narrow view of the meaning of the word "consistent?" If you had been on the Wisconsin Supreme Court, would you have joined in the decision of the court? If you had decided to dissent, what would have been the basis for that decision, and what arguments might you have made?

In *Hunter v. Hayes*,[108] defendants offered plaintiff a job as a flag girl on a construction job which was to begin on June 14, 1971. Defendants' agent also told plaintiff to quit her position at the telephone company. She did so, but defendants failed to employ her, as they had promised. She was out of work for two months. Relying on *Hoffman v. Red Owl*, the Colorado Court of Appeals found for plaintiff on the basis of promissory estoppel. It upheld an award of two months wages. Is this case consistent with *Forrer v. Sears, Roebuck & Co.*?

2. *A review of the rule*: Most Americans are employees-at-will. They have jobs, and often they expect that these jobs will continue as long as they don't give their employers cause to fire them. They are hired, and the employer tells them the rate of pay or salary. They learn the rest of the details on the job as they gain experience. Others have written contracts with many provisions spelled out. But their contracts do not specify employment for particular numbers of days, months or years. The employer may even state that the employment is "permanent" or for "as long as the employee does the job." As we have just seen, courts have generally construed all of these arrangements as creating an employment-at-will. The American rule was, and in many states still is, that such an employee can leave at any time. Equality seemed to call for the rule to cut both ways. Thus, an employer can fire an employee at will for good reason, bad reason, or no reason.

Essentially, the doctrine assumes that employment is a private relationship subject to its own internal sanction system plus the discipline of the market. To recall Professor Chafee's policies — the relationship is a "living tree," better left unregulated. Employees who develop skills are free to sell them elsewhere. They can use the possibility of moving in bargaining with their present employer. Employees who just do not get along with fellow workers or supervisors can change jobs. Exit, whether voluntary or involuntary, is the solution to this kind of problem. Employers, also, are free to replace good employees with better ones. This creates a tacit threat which may motivate employees to work harder. Employers can lay off workers in bad times or even close profitable plants to move their capital to more productive uses.

The United States is almost the only industrialized nation without some form of job security guaranteed by law for most workers. Great Britain, continental Europe, South America and Japan all have very different systems today. Of course, it is possible that we are right and they are wrong. Or their total social, economic and legal systems may call for a different rule.

In England, the common-law rule was that a general hiring was presumed to be for a term of one year. However, according to an oft-repeated story, H. G. Wood formulated the American employment at will rule in his 1877 treatise on master and servant:[109]

---

[108]533 P.2d 952 (Colo. Ct. Ap. 1975).

[109] Wood, Master and Servant (1877).

> With us the rule is inflexible that a general or indefinite hiring is *prima facie* a hiring at will, and if the servant seeks to make it out a yearly hiring, the burden is upon him to establish it by proof. A hiring at so much a day, week, month, or year, no time being specified, is an indefinite hiring, and no presumption attaches that it was for a day even, but only at the rate fixed for whatever time the party may serve.

Wood made this statement without explanation, citing four cases, none of which supported him. Andrew Morriss, however, points out: "The at-will rule was adopted by seven states before Horace Wood published his 1877 treatise, was present in the first draft of the proposed New York Civil Code drafted by David Dudley Field in 1862, and was included in the National Currency Act of 1863 for bank officers, as well as in earlier state banking statutes."[110] Morriss sees attributing the rule to Wood as only a tactic used by its critics to delegitimate it.

By the beginning of the 20th century, the at will rule had been adopted by many American courts without much analysis. However, this position fit with prevailing assumptions about a limited role for government interference in private relationships. Jay Feinman argued:

> Educated, responsible, and increasingly numerous, the middle level managers and agents of enterprises might have been expected to seek a greater share in the profits and direction of enterprises as the owners had to rely more heavily on them with the increasing size of business organizations. But the employment at will rule assured that as long as the employer desired it (and as long as the employee was not irreplaceable, which was seldom the case) the employee's relation to the enterprise would be precarious.[111]

A good deal of Morriss' legal history of the rule[112] argues that Feinman is wrong. For example, he argues that the adoption of the rule spread from the West and South to the East. Moreover, the rule became that of the majority of the states only after the mid-1890s, "well after many of the significant industrial struggles between capital and labor."[113]

Morriss' own explanation focuses on institutional considerations. He argues that the at-will rule allows appellate courts to take a group of cases from juries. A trier of fact will have difficulty deciding whether cause to fire an employee

---

[110] Andrew P. Morriss, Exploding Myths: An Empirical and Economic Reassessment of the Rise of Employment At-Will, 59 Missouri Law Review 679 (1994).

[111] Jay M. Feinman, The Development of the Employment at Will Rule, 20 American Journal of Legal History 118, 133 (1976).

[112]Morriss, *supra* note 110.

[113]*Id.* at 703.

exists. Faced with this capability problem, Morriss sees the courts serving as a gatekeeper blocking access to the legal system. He continues:

> [I]t is clear that a substantial number, if not percentage, of employee trial court victories were appealed and a substantial number of those included claims that the evidence was insufficient to support the verdict and/or that the trial court had erroneously instructed the jury. One of the fundamental problems for the courts in evaluating these claims was the difficulty of setting a standard by which they could measure the employee's conduct. As a result, the appellate courts which developed the at-will rule realized that the ability of the courts to evaluate the termination decision was weak. The at-will rule offered a partial solution by shifting cases involving indefinite contracts.[114]

You may remember cases such as *Balfour v. Balfour* or Richard Danzig's explanation for *Hadley v. Baxendale*. We found similar explanations there. Of course, we can imagine many functions that a legal doctrine might serve, but we can only speculate about why particular courts accepted a particular rule long ago. Indeed, we must be cautious about fashioning instrumental explanations. The judges may only have been responding to the legal culture of the time. Employees should not be bound, but should be free to seek their fortune. If this is true, it only made sense that employers likewise should not be bound.

The at-will rule provoked judicial decisions in the past that would bother many today. For example, in *Comerford v. Int'l. Harvester*,[115] a worker alleged that he was fired after his wife had refused the sexual advances of his boss. The court held that he failed to state a cause of action. It explained:

> [D]efendant could have well decided that it would be in the interest of good management not to have both plaintiff and the guilty assistant sales manager working together under the circumstances. It could have concluded that the services of the sales manager were preferable and retained him without in the least ratifying or condoning his conduct toward plaintiff.

3. *A countertheme:* As commonly is true in America law, there has long been a countertheme to the employment-at-will rule. American courts held that a promise of permanent employment was enforceable if there was also an independent consideration other than just doing the work. For example, at the turn of the century, railroads often obtained releases of tort claims from their employees in exchange for small payments of money and promises of permanent employment. Employees occasionally made contributions of money to businesses

---

[114]Morriss, *supra* at 752-753.

[115]235 Ala. 376, 178 So. 894 (1938).

in exchange for such promises. These "added benefits" were an extra or independent consideration for the promise of permanent employment. In these cases the employer would have to show cause to fire the employee. Some decisions found that if an employee gave up something of value to gain a job with the employer, this would be a special consideration making a promise of permanent employment enforceable. For example, one might sell a business for money and a promise of permanent employment. This would be enough to offer protection. However, few courts have been willing to protect an employee who left a good job to take one with the employer, relying on a promise of permanent employment. Various statutes now also limit an employer's right to fire employees at will for good, bad or no reason. For example, statutes prohibit firing if it is part of an effort to discriminate against members of protected groups, or punishment for taking time off work to serve on juries, and retaliation for certain union activities.

During the decade of reform which stretched from the late 1960s to the late 1970s, employment-at-will became an important issue in the law of contracts and in business journals. Cases challenging the employment-at-will rule had increased tenfold between 1969 and 1983.[116]

Courts in many states searched for ways to limit absolute discretion on the part of employers without undertaking to review all firings of employees-at-will. A number of academic writers called for industrial due process.[117] After a few decisions limiting the absolute right to fire, courts have pulled back from requiring employers to be able to show cause for any firing. Today, the state of the law across the United States is unclear and inconsistent, as we shall see.

4. *A hypothetical*: Consider the tale of Ellen Vale. The story is based on an actual case. We changed all the names to protect the guilty.

Ms. Ellen Vale, until last week, sold plastics to industrial users for a famous multinational corporation. She worked for the corporation for five years. She quit a high paying job with another firm to work for the multinational. Officials of the multinational recruited her. They said that the multinational rewards merit and offers a bright future to those who can do the job. Her written contract with the multinational contained no provision defining its duration. She was given an employee handbook which provided for annual performance reviews, notice of deficiencies in her performance and a hearing before she would be fired. Copies of these handbooks were given to all employees.

Until recently Ellen Vale was on the fast track to success. A group of purchasing agents for companies that bought large amounts of plastics were "her accounts." She is noted for her aggressiveness and skill in closing hard-to-make

---

[116]Marrinan, Employment At-Will: Pandora's Box May Have an Attractive Cover, 7 Hamline Law Review 155, 201 (1984).

[117]See, *e.g.*, Blades, Employment at Will vs. Individual Freedom: On Limiting the Abusive Exercise of Employer Power, 67 Columbia Law Review 1404 (1967); Summers, Individual Protection Against Unjust Dismissal: Time for a Statute, 62 Virginia Law Review 481 (1976).

deals. She is one of the best sales people in the company. Her performance reviews state that she is an outstanding sales person. Two months ago two competing manufacturers of plastics offered her jobs at large raises in base salary and commission. She talked with her supervisor, and he assured her that her future was with the multinational corporation. She turned down both offers.

Last summer Ellen Vale complained to managers about the prostitutes that the multinational furnished salesmen at the corporation's annual convention in Las Vegas. She also complained about the antiwoman jokes which managers told at sales meetings. She objected to the corporation's "casting couch" road to success for less competent women. One of the managers told her that she was not "one of the boys." In addition, often she has told secretaries who work at the multinational's main offices that they should form a union.

A month ago she sold a very large order of plastics to a customer who wanted to deal with her. Her supervisor decided that the sale was out of her territory. The customer belonged to another sales person. One of the top officers in the sales department told her she would get the commission because the person assigned to the territory never could have closed the sale. However, Ellen Vale's immediate boss gave the commission to Ms. X, in whose territory the sale was made. Those who work with Vale, assume that the boss and Ms. X have a long term sexual relationship.

Ellen Vale complained to an executive of the multinational who worked at its home office. She mentioned the personal relationship between her boss and Ms. X. Within a week, Ellen Vale was fired. The company did not follow its own internal procedure calling for warning, notice and a hearing. A Vice President wrote a letter to Ellen Vale. He said that she was insubordinate and a source of dissension among her fellow employees. He stated that the usual procedures could not be followed in this emergency situation.

Vale called her friend who was one of the multinational's executives. He was angry and promised something would be done. Within a week, the firm offered her another job at her salary and commission rate. However, the job was in a division known as "corporate Siberia." This division makes poor products, and the firm probably will close it soon. She rejected this offer.

Vale comes to your law firm and asks what to do. While she has some resources, she cannot invest much in attorneys' fees, costs of investigation and the like. One of your firm's partners will investigate her claims under the various federal and state statutes prohibiting discrimination against women. You are asked to investigate possible causes of action based on common law theories. It is unclear which state's law governs the transaction. The corporation's home office is in California. Ms. Vale operated out of midwest headquarters in Michigan. She lives in Wisconsin and called on customers in Wisconsin, Illinois, Michigan and Minnesota. A corporate official came to her home in Wisconsin to recruit her when she originally joined the company. She agreed to work for the multinational in a conversation which took place in Wisconsin. Another member of the firm will work on arguments about which state's law applies. You are to consider the common law of all these possible states. (Once you discover which state's laws are most helpful to Ms. Vale's case, your colleague will pursue arguments that those laws control.)

a. Employment-at-Will in California

We begin with a sampling from the California courts. Decisions from that state have received wide publicity among both professional and lay audiences. Both proponents and opponents of limiting the power of employers to fire employees-at-will can draw lessons from the California experiences:

GORDON TAMENY v. ATLANTIC RICHFIELD COMPANY

27 Cal. 3d 167, 164 Cal. Rptr. 839, 610 P.2d 1330 (1980)

TOBRINER, J. — Plaintiff Gordon Tameny instituted the present action against his former employer, Atlantic Richfield Company (Arco), alleging that Arco had discharged him after 15 years of service because he refused to participate in an illegal scheme to fix retail gasoline prices. Plaintiff sought recovery from Arco on a number of theories, contending, inter alia, that Arco's conduct in discharging him for refusing to commit a criminal act was tortious and subjected the employer to liability for compensatory punitive damages under normal tort principles.

Arco demurred to the complaint, contending that plaintiff's allegations, even if true, did not state a cause of action in tort. Arco conceded that California authorities establish that an employee who has been fired for refusing to perform an illegal act may recover from his former employer for "wrongful discharge." Arco contended, however, that the employee's remedy in such cases sounds only in contract and not in tort. The trial court accepted Arco's argument and sustained a general demurrer to plaintiff's tort causes of action. Plaintiff now appeals from the ensuing judgment.

For the reasons discussed below, we have concluded that the trial court judgment must be reversed with respect to the issue of tort liability. As we shall explain, past cases do not sustain Arco's contention that an employee who has been discharged because of his refusal to commit an illegal act at his employer's behest can obtain redress only by an action for breach of contract. Rather, as we shall see, the relevant authorities both in California and throughout the country establish that when an employer's discharge of an employee violates fundamental principles of public policy, the discharged employee may maintain a tort action and recover damages traditionally available in such actions.

1. *The facts and proceedings below.*

Because this appeal arises from a judgment entered after the sustaining of a general demurrer, we must, under established principles, assume the truth of all properly pleaded material allegations of the complaint in evaluating the validity of the trial court's action....

According to the complaint, plaintiff was hired by Arco as a relief clerk in 1960, received regular advancements, merit increases and commendatory evaluations in his initial years with the company, and, in 1966, was promoted to the position of retail sales representative, the position he held when discharged by Arco in 1975. His duties as a retail sales representative included among other matters the management of relations between Arco and the various independent service station dealers (franchisees) in his assigned territory of Bakersfield.

The complaint alleges that beginning in the early 1970s, Arco, Arco's district manager McDermott, and others engaged in a combination "for the purpose of reducing, controlling, stabilizing, fixing, and pegging the retail gasoline prices of Arco service station franchisees." According to the complaint, defendants' conduct in this regard violated express provisions of the Sherman Antitrust Act (15 U.S.C. § 1 et seq.), the Cartwright Act (Bus. & Prof. Code, § 16720 et seq.), and a specific consent decree which had been entered in a federal antitrust prosecution against Arco.

The complaint further asserts that during the early 1970s, defendants increasingly pressured plaintiff to "threaten [and] cajole ... the so-called 'independent' service station dealers in [his] territory to cut their gasoline prices to a point at or below a designated level specified by Arco." When plaintiff refused to yield to his employer's pressure to engage in such tactics, his supervisor told him that his discharge was imminent, and soon thereafter plaintiff was fired, effective March 25, 1975. Although at the time of the discharge Arco indicated in its personnel records that plaintiff was being fired for "incompetence" and for "unsatisfactory performance," the complaint alleges that "the sole reason" for plaintiff's discharge was his refusal to commit the "grossly illegal and unlawful acts which defendants tried to force him to perform."...

On the basis of the foregoing allegations, plaintiff sought relief on five separate theories. The complaint alleged, in particular, three tort causes of action (wrongful discharge, breach of the implied covenant of good faith and fair dealing, and interference with contractual relations), an action for breach of contract, and an action for treble damages under the Cartwright Act. Defendants demurred to the complaint, and the trial court sustained the demurrer as to all counts except for the count alleging a breach of contract. Thereafter, plaintiff voluntarily dismissed the contract count and the trial court then dismissed the entire action and entered judgment in favor of Arco. Plaintiff appeals from the adverse judgment.

2. (1) *An employee discharged for refusing to engage in illegal conduct at his employer's request may bring a tort action for wrongful discharge.*

Under the traditional common law rule, codified in Labor Code § 2922,[118] an employment contract of indefinite duration is in general terminable at "the will" of either party. Over the past several decades, however, judicial authorities in California and throughout the United States have established the rule that under both common law and the statute an employer does not enjoy an absolute or totally unfettered right to discharge even an at-will employee. In a series of cases arising out of a variety of factual settings in which a discharge clearly violated an express statutory objective or undermined a firmly established principle of public policy, courts have recognized that an employer's traditional broad authority to discharge an at-will employee "may be limited by statute ... or by considerations of public policy." (*Petermann v. International Brotherhood of Teamsters* (1959) 174 Cal.App.2d 184, 188 [344 P.2d 25] ....)

Petermann v. International Brotherhood of Teamsters, supra, one of the seminal California decisions in this area, imposes a significant condition upon the employer's broad power of dismissal by nullifying the right to discharge because an employee refuses to perform an unlawful act. In *Petermann*, the plaintiff, who had been employed as a business agent by defendant union, brought a "wrongful discharge" action against the union alleging that he had been dismissed from his position because he had refused to follow his employer's instructions to testify falsely under oath before a legislative committee, and instead had given truthful testimony. Emphasizing that the employer's instructions amounted to a directive to commit perjury, a criminal offense, plaintiff maintained that the employer acted illegally in discharging him for refusing to follow such an order.

The *Petermann* court recognized that in the absence of contractual limitations an employer enjoys broad discretion to discharge an employee, but concluded that as a matter of "public policy and sound morality" the employer's conduct, as alleged in the complaint, could not be condoned. The court explained: "The commission of perjury is unlawful. (Pen. Code, § 118).... It would be obnoxious to the interests of the state and contrary to public policy and sound morality to allow an employer to discharge any employee, whether the employment be for a designated or unspecified duration, on the ground that the employee declined to commit perjury, an act specifically enjoined by statute.... The public policy of this state as reflected in the Penal Code sections referred to above would be seriously impaired if it were to be held that one could be discharged by reason of his refusal to commit perjury. To hold that one's continued employment could be made contingent upon his commission of a felonious act at the instance of his employer would be to encourage criminal conduct upon the part of both the

---

[118]Section 2922 provides in relevant part: "An employment, having no specified term, may be terminated at the will of either party on notice to the other...."

employee and employer and serve to contaminate the honest administration of public affairs...." (174 Cal.App.2d at pp. 188-189.)

Thus, *Petermann* held that even in the absence of an explicit statutory provision prohibiting the discharge of a worker on such grounds, fundamental principles of public policy and adherence to the objectives underlying the state's penal statutes require the recognition of a rule barring an employer from discharging an employee who has simply complied with his legal duty and has refused to commit an illegal act.

Arco concedes, as it must in light of *Petermann*, that the allegations of the complaint, if true, establish that defendants acted unlawfully in discharging plaintiff for refusing to participate in criminal activity. Arco maintains, however, that plaintiff's remedy for such misconduct sounds only in contract and not in tort. Accordingly, Arco asserts that the trial court properly sustained its demurrer to plaintiff's tort causes of action, and correctly precluded plaintiff from recovering either compensatory tort damages or punitive damages.

In support of its contention that an action for wrongful discharge sounds only in contract and not in tort, Arco argues that because of the contractual nature of the employer-employee relationship, an injury which an employer inflicts upon its employee by the improper termination of such a relationship gives rise only to a breach of contract action. California decisions, however, have long recognized that a wrongful act committed in the course of a contractual relationship may afford both tort and contractual relief, and in such circumstances the existence of the contractual relationship will not bar the injured party from pursuing redress in tort.

Sloane v. Southern Cal. Ry. Co. (1896) 111 Cal. 668 [44 P. 320] illustrates the early application of these principles. In *Sloane*, a passenger who had purchased a railroad ticket to San Diego and had been wrongfully ejected from the train before her destination sued the defendant railroad for damages in tort. In response, the railroad contended that the passenger's "only right to action is for breach of the defendant's contract to carry her to San Diego, and that the extent of her recovery therefor is the price paid for the second ticket, and a reasonable compensation for the loss of time sustained by her...." (111 Cal. at p. 676.)

The *Sloane* court rejected the defendant's contention, declaring that "[t]he plaintiff's right of action ... is not ... limited to the breach of [the] contract to carry her to San Diego, but includes full redress for the wrongs sustained by her by reason of the defendant's violation of the obligations which it assumed in entering into such a contract ... [S]he could either bring an action simply for the breach of the contract, or she could sue ... in tort for [defendant's] violation of the duty ... which it assumed upon entering into such a contract." (111 Cal. at pp. 676-677.)

Numerous decisions decided in the 80 years since *Sloane* confirm that it [is] well established in this state that if the cause of action arises from a breach of a promise set forth in the contract, the action is ex contractu, *but if it arises from a breach of duty growing out of the contract it is ex delicto....* In conformity with this principle, recent decisions have held that a month-to-month tenant who is wrongfully evicted for exercising the statutory "repair and deduct" remedy may maintain a tort action for compensatory and punitive damages against his landlord. (See, *e.g.*, *Aweeka v. Bonds* (1971) 20 Cal.App.3d 278, 281 [97 Cal.Rptr. 650].) ...

[W]e conclude that an employee's action for wrongful discharge is ex delicto and subjects an employer to tort liability. As the *Petermann* case indicates, an employer's obligation to refrain from discharging an employee who refuses to commit a criminal act ... reflects a duty imposed by law upon all employers in order to implement the fundamental public policies embodied in the state's penal statutes. As such, a wrongful discharge suit exhibits the classic elements of a tort cause of action. As Professor Prosser has explained: "[Whereas] [c]ontract actions are created to protect the interest in having promises performed," "[t]ort actions are created to protect the interest in freedom from various kinds of harm. The duties of conduct which give rise to them are imposed by law, and are based primarily upon social policy, and not necessarily upon the will or intention of the parties...." (Prosser, Law of Torts (4th ed. 1971) p. 613.)

Past California wrongful discharge cases confirm the availability of a tort cause of action in circumstances similar to those of the instant case. In *Kouff v. Bethlehem-Alameda Shipyard* (1949) 90 Cal.App.2d 322 [202 P.2d 1059], for example, the court held that an employee who had been improperly discharged from his job for acting as an election poll official could maintain a tort cause of action against his employer for compensatory and punitive damages. Similarly, in *Glenn v. Clearman's Golden Cock Inn, Inc., supra*, 192 Cal.App.2d 793, *Wetherton v. Growers Farm Labor Assn., supra*, 275 Cal.App.2d 168, 174-175 and *Montalvo v. Zamora, supra*, 7 Cal.App.3d 69, the courts sanctioned the right of employees, who had been discharged for joining unions or otherwise exercising their statutory right to choose a bargaining representative, to maintain tort causes of action against their employers for wrongful discharge.[119]

Although Arco attempts to distinguish these past wrongful discharge cases from the instant action on the ground that the discharges in the former cases were specifically barred by statute, the suggested distinction does not withstand analysis. In *Glenn, Wetherton* and *Montalvo*, as in *Petermann* and the instant

---

[119]Contrary to the defendant's contention, the Petermann case in no way conflicts with the numerous California decisions sustaining a tort remedy for wrongful discharge. Although the employee in Petermann sought only back wages, a traditional contract remedy, nothing in that court's decision suggests that a wrongfully discharged employee may not maintain a tort action. Rather, after concluding that the allegations of the complaint in the case demonstrated the unlawfulness of the discharge, the Petermann court stated simply that the employee was "entitled to civil relief as a consequence thereof." (174 Cal.App.2d at p. 190.) Subsequent decisions, both in California and in other jurisdictions, have interpreted the Petermann decision as approving a tort cause of action in instances in which a discharge contravenes public policy....

case, no statute expressly prohibited an employer from discharging an employee on the stated ground; instead, the courts simply recognized that the general statute affording employees the right to join a union or choose a bargaining representative articulated a fundamental public policy which the employer's discharge clearly contravened. As the court observed in *Glenn*: "It would be a hollow protection indeed that would allow employees to organize and would then permit employers to discharge them for that very reason, unless such protection would afford to the employees the right to recover for this wrongful act." (192 Cal.App.2d at 798.)

Moreover, California courts have not been alone in recognizing the propriety of a tort remedy when an employer's discharge of an employee contravenes the dictates of public policy. In *Nees v. Hocks* (1975) 272 Ore. 210 [536 P.2d 512], for example, the Oregon Supreme Court upheld an employee's recovery of compensatory damages in tort for the emotional distress suffered when her employer discharged her for serving on a jury. Similarly, in *Harless v. First Nat. Bank in Fairmont* (1978) — W. Va. — [246 S.E.2d 270], the Supreme Court of West Virginia upheld a wrongful discharge action by a bank employee who was terminated for attempting to persuade his employer to comply with consumer protection laws, reasoning that "where the employer's motivation for [a] discharge contravenes some substantial public policy principle, then the employer may be liable to the employee for damages occasioned by the discharge," and concluding that the employee's cause of action "is one in tort and it therefore follows that rules relating to tort damages would be applicable." (*Id.*, at p. 275, fn. 5.)

Indeed, the *Nees* and *Harless* decisions are merely illustrative of a rapidly growing number of cases throughout the country that in recent years have recognized a common law tort action for wrongful discharge in cases in which the termination contravenes public policy. (See, *e.g.*, *Frampton v. Central Indiana Gas Co., supra*, 260 Ind. 249, [297 N.E.2d 425, 63 A.L.R.3d 973]; *Kelsay v. Motorola, Inc.* (1979) 74 Ill.2d 172 [384 N.E.2d 353, 358, 370]; *Jackson v. Minidoka Irrigation Dist.* (1977) 98 Idaho 330 [563 P.2d 54, 57-58]; *Sventko v. Kroger Co.* (1976) 69 Mich.App. 644 [245 N.W.2d 151]; *Reuther v. Fowler & Williams* (1978) 255 Pa. Super. 28 [386 A.2d 119]; see also *Pierce v. Ortho Pharmaceutical Corp.* (1979) 166 N.J. Super. 335 [399 A.2d 1023, 1025-1026].)

These recent decisions demonstrate a continuing judicial recognition of the fact, enunciated by this court more than 35 years ago, that "[t]he days when a servant was practically the slave of his master have long since passed." (*Greene v. Hawaiian Dredging Co.* (1945) 26 Cal.2d 245, 251 [157 P.2d 367].) In the last half century the rights of employees have not only been proclaimed by a mass of legislation touching upon almost every aspect of the employer-employee relationship, but the courts have likewise evolved certain additional protections at common law. The courts have been sensitive to the need to protect the individual employee from discriminatory exclusion from the opportunity of employment whether it be by the all-powerful union or employer....

We hold that an employer's authority over its employee does not include the right to demand that the employee commit a criminal act to further its interests, and an employer may not coerce compliance with such unlawful directions by discharging an employee who refuses to follow such an order. An employer engaging in such conduct violates a basic duty imposed by law upon all employers, and thus an employee who has suffered damages as a result of such discharge may maintain a tort action for wrongful discharge against the employer.

Accordingly, we conclude that the trial court erred in sustaining the demurrer to plaintiff's tort action for wrongful discharge.[120]

The judgment is reversed and the case is remanded to the trial court for further proceedings consistent with this opinion. Bird, C. J., Mosk, J., Richardson, J., Newman, J., concurred.

CLARK, J. I dissent. The role of this court does not include overseeing — then overruling — legislatively declared policy. (Cal. Const., art. III, § 3.) In the belief we know better the needs of society, we again substitute our policy judgment for that of the Legislature, not even attempting to act under constitutional or other than personal compulsion. (See ... *Marvin v. Marvin* (1976) 18 Cal.3d 660, dis. opn. at pp. 686-687 [134 Cal.Rptr. 815, 557 P.2d 106]; ...).

The legislative policy at issue in this case is declared in Labor Code § 2922 providing that employment without a particular term may be terminated *at will* by either employee or employer.

The Legislature went on to declare limited exceptions to the right of an employer to terminate an employment relationship. An employee may proceed in tort if dismissed because of absence from work to fulfill an obligation as an

---

[120]In light of our conclusion that plaintiff's complaint states a cause of action in tort under California's common law wrongful discharge doctrine, we believe it is unnecessary to determine whether a tort recovery would additionally be available under these circumstances on the theory that Arco's discharge constituted a breach of the implied-in-law covenant of good faith and fair dealing inherent in every contract. We do note in this regard, however, that authorities in other jurisdictions have on occasion found an employer's discharge of an at-will employee violative of the employer's "good faith and fair dealing" obligations (see Fortune v. National Cash Register Co. (1977) 373 Mass. 96 [364 N.E.2d 1251, 1257]; cf. Monge v. Beebe Rubber Company (1974) 114 N.H. 130 [316 A.2d 549, 62 A.L.R.3d 264]), and past California cases have held that a breach of this implied-at-law covenant sounds in tort as well as in contract....

Since neither plaintiff nor defendants suggest that the elements of a cause of action for breach of the implied covenant in this context would differ from the elements of an ordinary wrongful discharge action, however, we believe that a separate discussion of the "good faith and fair dealing" covenant in this case is unnecessary.

In a similar vein, we think that the count of the complaint seeking recovery for intentional interference with contractual relations should not be viewed as stating a cause of action distinct from the wrongful discharge claim....

election officer (see Elec. Code, § 1655; *Kouff v. Bethlehem-Alameda Shipyard* (1949) 90 Cal.App.2d 322 [202 P.2d 1059]), or because of participation in labor activities encouraged and authorized by the Legislature....

These are legislatively created exceptions giving rise to causes of action in tort. The majority improperly rely on such legislative exceptions to justify their own new exception. We err because the Legislature, by stating the general rule and *expressly* making exceptions thereto, must be deemed to intend no other exception for now. This court should — as others will — recognize not only a lack of legislative authorization for our new cause of action, but also recognize a legislative intent to reject such cause of action.

The California cases on which the majority rely either fall within the legislatively declared exceptions or are substantively distinguishable. The majority attempt to rely on *Petermann v. International Brotherhood of Teamsters*, noting "the present case closely parallels *Petermann* in a number of essential respects."... It doesn't work. *Petermann* holds only that the alleged discharge of an employee for refusal to commit perjury constitutes a breach of contract; the case doesn't hint of tort liability....

The majority also attempt to rely on cases wherein the negligent or intentional breach of a duty arising out of contract constitutes grounds for action in tort, as in the case of wrongful ejection of a ticketed passenger by a railway company.... There is no question that as a matter of general law a duty originating in contract, as well as a duty owing generally to all persons, may be breached in a manner giving rise to an action ex delicto. However, this does not mean every breach of a contractual duty is delictual.

The cases relied on by the majority wherein causes of action ex delicto arise out of breach of contractual duty are clearly distinguishable. The actionable conduct in each case constituted both contractual and tortious breaches, whereas in the instant case the breach — if termination of a no-term employment contract is a breach (see *Petermann v. International Brotherhood of Teamsters, supra,*) — is contractual only....

In the instant case the alleged actionable conduct is only contractual, that is, the alleged wrongful termination of an employment contract. In terminating that contract defendant did not *also* breach a duty giving rise to a cause of action in tort. (See *Petermann v. International Brotherhood of Teamsters, supra*, 174 Cal.App.2d 184.) As in *Petermann* there is no delictual breach in the termination itself, although it is alleged that defendants' *reason* for the termination — plaintiff's refusal to cooperate with defendants in committing acts contrary to public policy — was improper. There does not exist in the instant case, ... the least connection between defendants' actionable conduct (breach of contract) and *any* tort. The alleged wrongs — solicitations to violate or to conspire to violate the Cartwright and other acts — constitute no element of the termination as, according to the Legislature, an employer needs no reason to terminate.... [W]here the contractual breach itself constitutes a tortious breach, the wronged party can elect his remedy, whereas here the alleged unlawful termination of employment gives rise to only a cause of action for breach of contract. If defendants are independently guilty of Cartwright Act violations, independent proceedings may be taken against them.

The majority's further reliance on decisions in sister states totally without reference to governing statutory schemes ..., and our court's declaration that we are "sensitive to the need to protect the individual employee from discriminatory exclusion from the opportunity of employment whether it be by the all-powerful union or employer" ... reveals a rank insensitivity to our judicial role. Today's court judgment is a legislative judgment better left to the Legislature where, properly, public policy is declared. The Legislature has spoken; if the system is to work, the Legislature will redeclare its position.

The judgment of the trial court should be affirmed.

NOTES AND QUESTIONS

1. *Cost barriers and vindication of rights*: Why does it matter whether the California courts characterize an employee's claim as a contract or as a tort as long as it gives the employee a right limiting the employer's discretion?

2. *The implications of the Tameny case*: In *Cleary v. American Airlines, Inc.*,[121] plaintiff alleged that American Airlines purported to fire him because of theft, leaving his work area without authorization and threatening a fellow employee with bodily harm. It failed to afford him a fair hearing of his appeal from this discharge as called for by its own regulations. Actually, plaintiff alleged, American discharged him for his union organizing activities. Plaintiff had worked for American Airlines for 18 years under an oral contract for an unspecified term. The trial court sustained a demurrer, but the appellate court reversed. Two factors were of paramount importance: The court saw discharge after 18 years of apparently satisfactory performance as offending the implied-in-law covenant of good faith and fair dealing. Moreover, American Airlines had recognized its obligation by its specific procedures for adjudicating situations such as the one involved in this case. The court said that these factors operated "as a form of estoppel, precluding any discharge of such an employee without good cause." It continued, saying:

> Should plaintiff sustain his burden of proof, he will have established a cause of action for wrongful discharge that sounds in both contract and in tort. He will then be entitled to an award of compensatory damages, and, in addition, punitive damages if his proof complies with the requirements for the latter type of damages....

---

[121]111 Cal.App.3d 443, 168 Cal.Rptr. 722 (1980).

In *Pugh v. See's Candies, Inc.*,[122] the court required fairly clear evidence that an employer had fired an employee for refusing to do something illegal in order for the *Tameny* rule to come into play. Pugh had refused to serve on a management negotiating team, allegedly because he suspected a "sweetheart" deal had been made between the union and management which would favor some employees and sacrifice the interests of others. But the court noted he had nothing other than suspicions to go on, and held he was not entitled to protection on a public policy theory.

The court *did*, however, find an implied contract limitation on termination at will since Pugh had been an employee for 32 years, and See's had promoted and praised him in the organization. See's had never directly criticized him, and he had reason to rely on See's announced policies of job security for those who did their work. The court allowed both compensatory and punitive damages for breach of the implied contract limitation.

3. *The impact of the California rule*: A 1988 Rand Institute study[123] looked at the consequences of the changes in the rules concerning wrongful discharge in California. The study looked at 120 jury trials in California between 1980 and 1986. Plaintiffs were victorious in 68 percent of the cases. The average initial jury verdict was over $650,000, although some very large awards inflated this figure; the median verdict was $177,000. Except for the smallest awards, 40 percent of the award was for punitive damages.

As a result of post-trial motions, appeals and settlements the final payments to plaintiffs were approximately half of the amount initially awarded. A typical case cost $80,000 to defend. The larger the case, the higher the defense costs were likely to be. A 1987 case involving a potential award of $1.5 million would cost almost $250,000 to defend. Plaintiff's lawyers typically charged a 40% contingency fee. The total legal fees, including the fees of both plaintiff and defendant, averaged $160,000 per case. What this means is that the lawyers' fees constituted more than half of the money changing hands as a result of the litigation.

The median employee bringing suit could expect to recover only $30,000 once losing cases, post-trial reductions and contingency fees have been taken into account.

b. Employment-at-Will in States Other than California

Before we return to California to explore a significant retrenchment in California's pro-employee development, we should look at what was happening in other states.

---

[122]116 Cal.App.3d. 311, 171 Cal.Rptr. 917 (Ct.Ap. 1st Dist. 1981).

[123]Dertouzos, Holland and Ebener, The Legal and Economic Consequences of Wrongful Termination, Rand Institute for Civil Justice Report R-3602-ICJ (1988).

Implied covenants and public policy: Many other states have modified their employment-at-will doctrine to some extent. The Supreme Court of New Hampshire decided *Monge v. Beebe Rubber Co.*[124] The plaintiff was an assembly line night shift worker. Her foreman said that if she were "nice" to him, he would promote her. She refused. Then she was denied overtime, ridiculed and ultimately fired. She brought an action for damages, and the jury awarded $2500. On appeal the court found there was a breach of the promise of good faith and fair dealing implied in all contracts.[125] It held: "a termination by the employer of a contract of employment at will which is motivated by bad faith or malice or based on retaliation is not in the best interest of the economic system or the public good and constitutes a breach of the employment contract." In light of the rise of feminist consciousness, the *Monge* decision involved the kind of situation likely to prompt a court to make some new law. Marrinan[126] says "[a]lthough *Monge* resembles a traditional sexual harassment suit, it was filed at a time when there was no available statutory remedy for harassment. Sexual harassment was not interpreted as a form of sex discrimination under Title VII of the Civil Rights Acts of 1964 until 1981. The applicable state law, the New Hampshire 'Law Against Discrimination,' was amended to prohibit sex discrimination in 1971 but was not effective until August 22, 1975."

The *Monge* decision was followed by *Fortune v. National Cash Register Co.*[127] Here NCR fired a salesman, who had worked for the company for twenty-five years, a day after he placed a customer order that would have entitled him to a large bonus. He brought an action for damages to recover the bonus. The Supreme Judicial Court of Massachusetts cited the *Monge* decision in sustaining the wrongful discharge claim. The employer's motive for firing the plaintiff was to avoid paying the bonus and was in bad faith. However, the court was careful to avoid adopting the full theory of the *Monge* case, saying:

> [i]n the instant case, we need not pronounce our adherence to so broad a policy nor need we speculate as to whether the good faith requirement is implicit in every contract for employment at will. It is clear, however, that, on the facts before us, a finding is warranted that a breach of the contract occurred. Where the principal seeks to deprive the agent of all compensation by terminating the contractual relationship when the agent is on the brink of successfully completing the sale, the principal has acted in bad faith and the ensuing transaction between the principal and the buyer is to be regarded as having been accomplished by the agent.

---

[124]114 N.H. 130, 316 A.2d 549 (1974).

[125]Compare Uniform Commercial Code, § 1-203.

[126]Marrinan, Employment At-Will: Pandora's Box May Have an Attractive Cover, 7 Hamline Law Review 155 n.63 (1984).

[127]373 Mass. 96, 364 N.E.2d 1251 (1977).

The California cases and the first decisions elsewhere suggested that the courts might provoke a major change in employment practices in the United States. However, in the early 1980s, courts began to pull back. They searched for a way to handle outrage cases but not go too far in burdening employers. For example, in *Pierce v. Ortho Pharmaceutical Corp.*,[128] the Supreme Court of New Jersey stated that it "has long recognized the capacity of the common law to develop and adapt to current needs." As a result, it concluded that "[t]he interests of employees, employers, and the public lead to the conclusion that the common law of New Jersey should limit the right of an employer to fire an employee at will."

Balancing the interests of employer, employee, and the public, the New Jersey Supreme Court stated its "rule,":

> We hold that an employee has a cause of action for wrongful discharge when the discharge is contrary to a clear mandate of public policy. The sources of public policy include legislation; administrative rules, regulations or decisions; and judicial decisions. In certain instances, a professional code of ethics may contain an expression of public policy. However, not all such sources express a clear mandate of public policy. For example, a code of ethics designed to serve only the interests of a profession or an administrative regulation concerned with technical matters probably would not be sufficient. Absent legislation, the judiciary must define the cause of action in case-by-case determinations. An employer's right to discharge an employee at will carries a correlative duty not to discharge an employee who declines to perform an act that would require a violation of a clear mandate of public policy. However, unless an employee at will identifies a specific expression of public policy, he may be discharged with or without cause.

The court then applied its rule to the *Pierce* case and upheld the discharge of Dr. Pierce, who had refused to assist the pharmaceutical company that employed her in testing a drug which contained what she believed to be an unreasonably large amount of saccharin. Saccharin was believed by some at the time to be a carcinogen. The majority said, "Chaos would result if a single doctor engaged in research were allowed to determine, according to his or her individual conscience, whether a project should continue." The dissent pointed out the FDA's very poor history in monitoring dangerous drugs. This history justified professionals acting on their ethical beliefs.[129]

---

[128]84 N.J. 58, 417 A.2d 505 (1980).

[129]See Halbert, The Cost of Scruples: A Call for Common Law Protection for the Professional Whistleblower, 10 Nova Law Journal 1 (1985).

In *Brockmeyer v. Dun & Bradstreet*,[130] the Supreme Court of Wisconsin adopted an even narrower public policy exception to the rules governing at-will employment:

> Courts should proceed cautiously when making public policy determinations. No employer should be subject to suit merely because a discharged employee's conduct was praiseworthy or because the public may have derived some benefit from it.
>
> A plaintiff-employee alleging a wrongful discharge has the burden of proving that the dismissal violates a clear mandate of public policy. Unless the employee can identify a specific declaration of public policy, no cause of action can be stated. The determination of whether the public policy asserted is a well-defined and fundamental one is an issue of law which the trial court should decide. Once the plaintiff has demonstrated that the conduct that caused the discharge was consistent with a clear and compelling public policy, the burden of proof then shifts to the defendant employer to prove that the dismissal was for just cause.[131]
>
> We believe that the adoption of a narrowly circumscribed public policy exception properly balances the interests of employees, employers and the public. Employee job security interests are safeguarded against employer actions that undermine fundamental policy preferences. Employers retain sufficient flexibility to make needed personnel decisions in order to adapt to changing economic conditions. Society also benefits from our holding in a number of ways. A more stable job market is achieved. Well-established public policies are advanced. Finally, the public is protected against frivolous lawsuits since courts will be able to screen cases on motions to dismiss for failure to state a claim or for summary judgment if the discharged employee cannot allege a clear expression of public policy.

The court went on to label the cause of action as one in contract since "[w]e believe that the reinstatement and back pay are the most appropriate remedies for public policy exception wrongful discharges since the primary concern in these actions to make the wronged employee 'whole.'" Thus, punitive damages which could be awarded in a tort action would not be allowed. Also, "damages are limited by the concepts of foreseeability and mitigation."

---

[130]113 Wis.2d 561, 335 N.W.2d 834 (1983).

[131]Notice that the Supreme Court of Wisconsin leaves open the question of what to do with cases where the employer's reasons for discharge were both a desire to retaliate that violates a clear mandate of public policy and also just cause. For example, an employee refuses to murder a competitor as the employer demands and then the employer fires her, relying on her regular late arrival at work. Under the Wisconsin rule is the lesson for employers to wait and collect an employee's transgressions until enough pile up to constitute "cause"?

The court then turned to the facts of the case and applied its test, sustaining the dismissal of an employee who had alleged that he had been pressured not to testify in a sex discrimination suit in a way that would injure his employer. Brockmeyer contended that he was asked to commit perjury by Dun & Bradstreet. The Supreme Court of Wisconsin responded:

> The record is devoid of any evidence demonstrating that Dun & Bradstreet asked Brockmeyer to lie. Admittedly, an inference can be drawn from this record that Dun & Bradstreet was concerned over the fact that Brockmeyer would tell the truth if asked to testify at proceedings concerning his former secretary's sex discrimination claim. This inference is a far cry from the allegation that Dun & Bradstreet wanted Brockmeyer to commit perjury. There is no clearly defined mandate of public policy against discharging an employee because his testimony may be contrary to an employer's interests. Such behavior may be indicative of bad faith, but is not contrary to established public policies.

The Supreme Court then affirmed the Court of Appeals which had reversed a judgment in favor of Brockmeyer.

In *Bushko v. Miller Brewing Co.*,[132] Bushko, an employee at will, alleged that he was fired because he had complained about "Miller's policies in three areas — plant safety, hazardous wastes and 'honesty.'" The majority said that Bushko failed to allege that Miller had required him to violate a constitutional or statutory provision. Thus, he failed to state a claim under the *Brockmeyer* doctrine. The majority said, "the public policy exception may not be used to extend constitutional free speech protection to private employment." Are there likely to be many employees at will who will be able to make use of the Wisconsin rule? Indeed, is the Wisconsin position an exercise in empty symbolism?

The effect of the employer's own rules and policies: Some larger employers create their own private "legal system" to deal with employees. They provide for some type of annual review of performance and an evaluation, hearings, and review of decisions to fire an employee by someone other than an immediate supervisor. In material distributed to employees they talk about opportunities with the company and make representations that they will not fire people except for cause after warnings and an opportunity to remedy problems. What is the effect of such internal regulations on an employer's power to fire employees? Must the employer follow the procedures? Some courts have said they must.

For example, the Supreme Court of Michigan, in *Toussaint v. Blue Cross & Blue Shield of Michigan*,[133] said that provisions in a personnel manual voluntarily

---

[132]134 Wis.2d 136, 396 N.W.2d 167 (1986).
[133]408 Mich. 579, 292 N.W.2d 880 (1980).

adopted by an employer after it hired the employee, became part of an employment contract. The employee had legitimate expectations of job security. Toussaint asked about job security when he was hired. He testified that he was told he would be with the company "as long as I did my job." Later, he asked again about job security, and the employer gave him a copy of the personnel manual. It provided for discharge "for just cause only" after warnings, notice, hearings and procedures. However, he offered no proof that he had relied on the manual in any substantial way. The employer fired Toussaint because its officials suspected him of dishonesty. However, the employer did not follow the procedures in the manual. It is unlikely that the employer could have proved dishonesty, but Toussaint's supervisors had lost confidence in him.

Justice Levin, in an opinion concurred in by three other judges, wrote:

> While an employer need not establish personnel policies and practices, where an employer chooses to establish such policies and practices and makes them known to its employees, the employment relationship is presumably enhanced. The employer secures an orderly, cooperative and loyal work force, and the employee the peace of mind associated with job security and the conviction that he will be treated fairly. No pre-employment negotiations need take place and the parties' minds need not meet on the subject; nor does it matter that the employee knows nothing of the particulars of the employer's policies and practices or that the employer may change them unilaterally. It is enough that the employer chooses, presumably in its own interest, to create an environment in which the employee believes that, whatever the personnel policies and practices, they are established and official at any given time, purport to be fair, and are applied consistently and uniformly to each employee....
>
> An employer who establishes no personnel policies instills no reasonable expectations of performance. Employers can make known to their employees that personnel policies are subject to unilateral changes by the employer. Employees would then have no legitimate expectation that any particular policy will continue to remain in force. Employees could, however, legitimately expect that policies in force at any given time will be uniformly applied to all. If there is in effect a policy to dismiss for cause only, the employer may not depart from that policy at whim simply because he was under no obligation to institute the policy in the first place....
>
> The employer's standard of job performance can be made part of the contract. Breach of the employer's uniformly applied rules is a breach of the contract and cause for discharge. In such a case, the question for the jury is whether the employer actually had a rule or policy and whether the employee was discharged for violating it.

Justice Ryan wrote a dissenting opinion, joined in by two other justices. He thought that Toussaint might recover on a Restatement of Contracts, § 90 theory.

This theory required him to prove that he had relied justifiably on the personnel policy procedures. Justice Ryan concluded there was no evidence of such reliance.

In *Pine River State Bank v. Mettille*,[134] the Supreme Court of Minnesota reached a conclusion similar to the *Toussaint* decision in Michigan. The Pine River State Bank distributed an employee handbook some months after it had hired Mettille. The handbook guaranteed performance appraisals, discussed the lack of fluctuation of jobs in the banking industry, and described a four-step progressive disciplinary system. An audit revealed a number of errors for which Mettille was responsible. The bank discharged Mettille without following the progressive disciplinary system. Mettille did not show that he had relied in any definite and substantial way on the handbook. The court found an offer to contract when the manual was disseminated to all employees. Mettille accepted it by continuing to work at the bank. In effect, there was an offer for a unilateral contract which the bank could not withdraw once the employee started to perform. The court said that firms had to follow procedures announced to employees but did not have to follow those set out in internal documents. Furthermore, the Minnesota court said that employers could reserve discretion by language in an employee handbook. However, it is not clear how far the *Pine River State Bank* case can be put aside by drafting.[135]

In *Ferraro v. Koelsch*,[136] the Supreme Court of Wisconsin found that an employee's acceptance of a handbook with detailed dismissal provisions converted the relationship from one at-will into one that the employer could end only by following its own rules. The employer promised to follow the procedures in the handbook. In exchange, the employee promised to have the relationship governed by those procedures and to give a two-week notice before leaving the employment. The court said:

> To question whether an employees' handbook containing express promises by the employer, which handbook asks an employee for express responsive promises, can in Wisconsin ripen into something other than an employment relationship terminable at will is like asking whether contracts will be enforced in this state.... To ask the question is to answer it.

The court found that the employer had followed the procedures detailed in its handbook.

---

[134]333 N.W.2d 622 (Minn. 1983).

[135]The net impact of these cases may be prompt the revision of employee handbooks to ward off or limit liability. See, *e.g.*, Combe, Employee Handbooks: Asset or Liability, 12 Employee Relations Journal 5 (1984); Johnston & Taylor, Employee Handbooks: A Selective Survey of Emerging Developments, 11 Employee Relations Law Journal 225 (1985).

[136]124 Wis.2d 154, 368 N.W.2d 666 (1985).

What have courts in the various states done with exceptions to the employment-at-will doctrine? John F. Buckley, Ronald M. Green, William A. Carmell and Jerrold F. Goldberg categorized the decisions in the fifty states and the District of Columbia as of 1993.[137] Montana has a detailed statute, and so it is not included in the data that follow. Totals are given here only for states that have decided an issue. In each instance, the rest of the states either have no cases in point or their position is unclear.

First, the authors look at *contracts theories*. 42 states require employers to follow the procedures in their employment handbooks and manuals. Five do not. 18 states give effect to provisions that employers put in manuals and handbooks that create exceptions to termination procedures, and no state that has considered the point has refused to give effect to such disclaimers. 17 states recognize a cause of action based on the implied covenant of good faith and fair dealing; nineteen states do not. 25 states recognize the doctrine of promissory estoppel in an employment at will situation; six refuse to do so.

Second, 39 states recognize a *tort cause of action* for firing an employee in a situation that would violate public policy; seven do not. 21 states allow an employee who has won under the public policy tort theory to recover punitive damages; ten do not. 31 states recognize that an employer can commit the tort of defamation when it fires an employee; two refuse to allow such a cause of action. 31 states also recognize that an employer can commit the tort of inflicting emotional distress when it fires an employee; four do not. Thus, the old employment at will rule has been significantly qualified in the last twenty years. Of course, it is one thing to recognize a cause of action; it is another thing to apply its requirements in such a way that employees are likely to recover.

Trying a termination case: Springer, The Wrongful Discharge Case,[138] offers suggestions for lawyers engaged in employment litigation. He stresses the need for careful preparation and pretrial discovery. A plaintiff's lawyer should look for "(1) documents that reveal illogic or lack of thoroughness; (2) trivial reasons; (3) documents that give a sense that the employer was 'out to get' the employee because the paper case against him is too thorough or too recent; (4) examples of the employer's stated standards being applied differently to others; (5) important deviations from standard procedures, policies, or practices; and (6) a history of satisfactory performance and commendations." Employers seek to examine the fired employee in a lengthy pretrial deposition. They want to freeze an employee's case to particular claims. They want to get the employee to take extreme positions. They want the employee to sound unfair to the employer or coworkers. "A consistent theme employers are likely to use at trial is that the employee was not a team player." At trial, plaintiffs' attorneys do best when they emphasize themes of the company as aloof, callous, and indifferent and of the

---

[137]1994 State by State Guide to Human Resources Law (1994).
[138]21 Trial 38 (June 1985).

supervisor as arbitrary and uncaring. Defense lawyers do best when they show the plaintiff as obstinate and self-interested. "A successful cross-examination of a contentious plaintiff may well leave a juror thinking, 'Now I understand why the company got rid of him.'" What is the likely impact of these employment-at-will trial strategies on employment practices?

c. Legislative Solutions?

From the very beginning, many have suggested that legislation was necessary to strike a proper balance between contending values — security, market efficiency, and freedom in employment matters, to name just three — or to enhance clarity.

The Commissioners on Uniform State Laws have offered a Model Uniform Termination of Employment Act,[139] but, as of 1994, no state has passed it. Professor Peck[140] describes the Model Act:

> [S]ection 2(a) of the Act provides that an employer may not terminate the employment of an employee without good cause.[141] The ... [Model Act] ... offers three options for enforcement: arbitration, administrative proceedings, and judicial proceedings.... [I]f the employee alleges that a termination was without good cause, the employer must proceed first to present its case. The employee, however, has the ultimate burden of proving that the termination was prohibited. A written agreement signed by an employer and employee may authorize the employer to discharge the employee without good cause if severance payments are provided at specified rates of monthly pay for various years of service.

The Model Act has been attacked by both representatives of employers and lawyers who represent terminated employees. The employers' representatives do not accept the requirement that an employer must show cause for firing an

---

[139]The text of the proposed statute is printed at Daily Labor Report, No. 156, at D-1 (August 13, 1991).

[140]Peck, Penetrating Doctrinal Camouflage: Understanding the Development of the Law of Wrongful Discharge, 66 Washington Law Review 719, 750-751 (1991).

[141]Section 1(4) defines "good cause" as:

(i) a reasonable basis for termination of an employee's employment in view of relevant factors and circumstances, which include the employee's duties and responsibilities; the employee's conduct, job performance, and employment record; and the appropriateness of termination for the conduct involved, or (ii) the good faith exercise of business judgment by the employer as to the setting of economic goals and determining methods to achieve those goals, organizing or reorganizing operations, discontinuing or divesting operations or parts of operations, determining the size and composition of the work force, and determining and changing performance standards for positions.

employee — even under the broad definition of cause used in the act. Plaintiffs' lawyers, despite the Act's provisions calling for lawyers' fees if a violation is shown, do not like the Act's limitation on an employee's remedies. The Act calls for reinstatement and back pay or

> if reinstatement is not ordered, a lump-sum severance payment at the employee's rate of pay in effect before the termination, for a period not exceeding [36 months] from the date of the order, together with the value of fringe benefits lost during that period, reduced by likely earnings and benefits from employment elsewhere, and taking into account such equitable considerations as the employee's length of service with the employer and their reasons for the termination...

In reviewing the question of legislative solutions, Marrinen argued:

> If ... legislation is to resolve the uncertainties in this area as well as be a workable tool to solve factual problems in the workplace, it is paramount that such legislation specify a standard against which dismissals may be judged as well as establish a mechanism for handling disputes. An appropriate standard is the "employer judgment rule," an analogue of the business judgment rule. Under this standard employers would be liable for mistakes of judgment in dismissing employees when there is evidence of bad cause or other corrupt motive. This rule might assure that employers are not subject to causes of action in tort for no cause dismissals, but it would be inapplicable to a contract action in the event an employer undertook an obligation to dismiss only for cause. Therefore, this standard would provide fairness to both the employer and employee.[142]

Perritt, another author who addressed the likelihood of comprehensive legislative solutions said:[143]

> The strongest argument for legislation is an essentially conservative argument arising from the need for more order and predictability. It will be difficult to improve the uniformity of common law rules of decision for dismissal challenges without legislation, although the common law produces reasonably uniform "majority rules" over time. It would not be possible to consolidate the law of wrongful discharge into a single body of law, utilizing

---

[142]Marrinan, Employment At-Will: Pandora's Box May Have an Attractive Cover, 7 Hamline Law Review 155, 197-199 (1984).

[143]Perritt, Employee Dismissals: An Opportunity for Legal Simplification, 35 Labor Law Journal 407, 412-413 (1984). From the 1984 Labor Law Journal, published and copyrighted 1984 by Commerce Clearing House, Inc., 4025 W. Peterson Avenue, Chicago, Ill. 60646. Reprinted with permission.

efficient adjudicatory mechanisms, without legislation, because much of the existing law is statutory in origin.

Perritt noted that few states were actively considering legislative changes, and that only three had already enacted wrongful dismissal statues.

> The lack of legislative action on these measures is not surprising, considering the positions of major interests. Employers are opposed. The plaintiffs' bar probably prefers the common law status quo. Organized labor fears enactment of individual employee rights legislation that may reduce incentives to organize. Individual employees do not possess significant lobbying power.
>
> The balance of political power is likely to shift in favor of wrongful discharge legislation only if employers and the defense bar react against expanded common law liability for wrongful discharge. If these two groups decide that legislation is the only feasible alternative to continued expansion of common law liability, they may become powerful proponents of legislative action. If political realignment occurs in this fashion, wrongful discharge legislation could be an essentially conservative proposal, also having intuitive appeal for civil libertarians and others with sympathy for individual workers.[144]

Unemployment Compensation — A Partial Solution: Cases involving wrongful discharge should be considered in a context which includes the unemployment compensation system. The fact that a discharged employee may have a claim to unemployment compensation may mitigate the effects of the employee-at-will rules. The unemployment compensation system is largely the creation of state law (though partially regulated under the Social Security Act of 1935) and so the details of the system vary from state to state. The amount of the benefit normally depends on the duration of employment. Employer contributions, based on the history of claims against particular employers, play a major role in funding the system.

Eligibility for benefits depends on several factors. First, benefits are generally not available for an employee who leaves voluntarily, in the absence of "good cause" for leaving the job. Second, an employee discharged for "misconduct" is not entitled to benefits. "Misconduct" is generally defined as the "wanton or wilful disregard of the employer's interests." Third, discharge which was "due to the existence of a labor dispute" impairs eligibility. Fourth, benefits are payable for a limited period of time, with six-months being the most common

---

[144]See Note, Reforming At-Will Employment Law: A Model Statute, 16 University of Michigan Journal of Law Reform 389, 406 (1983). This proposal calls for a combination of mediation and arbitration to maximize the possibility of settlement. "The mediator-arbitrator's role is that of a catalyst; an award is imposed only when parties have clearly manifested their intransigence."

maximum. Finally, an employee is entitled to claim benefits only if they are able to work and actively seeking employment. Benefits are lost if the employee refuses to accept "suitable" work.

d. Growing Trend or an Odd Bit of History?

We've seen many courts make bold declarations but frame doctrines so that only the victims of atrocity cases not cleverly covered up can recover. Until 1988 California could be used as a test case of the consequences of a very pro-employee rule. But in *Foley v. Interactive Data Corp.*,[145] the Supreme Court of California revised that state's law concerning employees-at-will. Many believe the revision materially eroded the pro-employee changes won over the years.

Foley had worked for Interactive Data Corporation (IDC) for seven years. He did not have an express employment contract which specified a term. He had received regular promotions and superior performance evaluations. IDC had "Termination Guidelines" which set forth a seven-step procedure for firing an employee.

In January of 1983, Foley told Richard Earnest, an IDC official, that Kuhne, a man hired to become Foley's supervisor, was under investigation by the FBI for embezzling from Kuhne's former employer. Earnest told Foley not to discuss rumors.[146] In March, Kuhne transferred Foley from Los Angeles, California to Waltham, Massachusetts. A week after the transfer, Earnest told Foley that he was not doing a good job. Seven days later Earnest fired Foley.

Foley sued asserting three claims: (1) a tort claim for a discharge which violated public policy; (2) a contract action for breach of an implied-in-fact contract to terminate only for good cause; and (3) a tort cause of action for breach of the implied covenant of good faith and fair dealing.[147] The trial court sustained the employer's demurrer to Foley's entire complaint. The Court of Appeal upheld the trial court's dismissal of each of Foley's claims.

> In 1986, the California Supreme Court granted a hearing in the case. Given the composition of the court at that time, it is likely that the case was granted review in order to reverse the extremely narrow approach of the appellate court, which was at odds with most of the decisions of California's appellate courts in the area of wrongful termination. The case was argued

---

[145]47 Cal.3d 654, 765 P.2d 373 (1988).

[146]In September 1983, about six months after Foley's discharge, Kuhne pleaded guilty in federal court to a felony count of embezzlement.

[147]Foley did not base a claim on the failure to follow the Interactive Data's seven-step termination procedure. However, he did allege that defendant maintained written "Permanent Guidelines" that set forth express grounds for discharge and a mandatory seven-step pretermination procedure. This was a factor, he claimed, supporting his reasonable belief that defendant would not discharge him except for good cause.

in November 1986. However, before a decision could be rendered, the California electorate removed three of the justices from the court. The case was reargued before a more conservative court under the stewardship of Chief Justice Malcolm Lucas in April 1987, and a badly divided court [the court split four to three on some of the issues decided] rendered its decision on December 29, 1988.[148]

The California Supreme Court acknowledged the existence of a tort cause of action for the termination of an employee in a situation where the termination would violate public policy. The court provided little guidance about what constitutes a public policy for purposes of this cause of action. "We do not decide in this case whether a tort action alleging a breach of public policy under *Tameny* may be based only on policies derived from a statute or constitutional provision or whether nonlegislative sources may provide the basis for such a claim." However, it said that the policy had to be "substantial," "fundamental," and "basic." Moreover, relying on the Wisconsin decision in the *Brockmeyer* case, the court said it had to be a *public policy*. Foley claimed that he had a duty to communicate to his employer information that a prospective employee might be an embezzler. The court responded, saying "[w]hen the duty of an employee to disclose information to his employer serves only the private interest of the employer, the rationale underlying the *Tameny* cause of action is not implicated." Thus, it upheld the trial court's ruling sustaining the employer's demurrer to this count in Foley's complaint.

The Supreme Court of California next decided that Foley had pleaded facts which, if proved, might be sufficient for a jury to find an implied-in-fact contract limiting defendant's right to discharge him arbitrarily. Foley's implied contract claim was not barred by the Statute of Frauds since it could have been performed within one year: "[P]laintiff could have terminated his employment within that period, or defendant could have discharged plaintiff for cause." The court accepted the reasoning of *Pugh v. See's Candies, Inc.*, and found that Foley's allegations of facts were sufficient to establish a cause of action for breach of an implied contract.

> First, defendant overemphasizes the fact that plaintiff was employed for "only" six years and nine months. Length of employment is a relevant consideration but six years and nine months is sufficient time for conduct to occur on which a trier of fact could find the existence of an implied contract.... Plaintiff here alleged repeated oral assurances of job security and consistent promotions, salary increases and bonuses during the term of his

---

[148]Levine, Judicial Backpedaling: Putting the Brakes on California's Law of Wrongful Termination, 20 Pacific Law Journal 993, 1011-1012 (1989).

employment contributing to his reasonable expectation that he would not be discharged except for good cause.

Second, an allegation of breach of written "Termination Guidelines" implying self-imposed limitations on the employer's power to discharge at will may be sufficient to state a cause of action for breach of an employment contract....

Finally, ... plaintiff alleges that he supplied the company valuable and separate consideration by signing an agreement whereby he promised not to compete or conceal any computer-related information for one year after termination.

The majority of the court refused to recognize a wrongful termination action based on tortious breach of the implied covenant of good faith and fair dealing.[149] Such an implied covenant gives rise only to a contract action because the implied covenant does not protect a generalized public interest. This meant that the remedy for breach of this covenant was limited to contract damages. The court said that recovery for breach of the implied covenant should be limited to contractual remedies because there is a need for predictability to promote commercial stability. The court rejected the approach taken in *Cleary v. American Airlines, Inc.*; it was highly critical of this Court of Appeal decision.

The majority said that it was not "unaware of nor unsympathetic to claims that contract remedies for breaches of contract are insufficient because they do not fully compensate due to their failure to include attorney fees and their restrictions on foreseeable damages." However, it noted that there are many remedies which could better be provided by legislation such as increasing the amounts of contract damages, awarding attorney fees, establishing arbitration or providing tort remedies.

Thus, the Supreme Court affirmed the trial court's dismissal of Foley's tort claim based on the implied covenant of good faith and fair dealing. Furthermore, in *Newman v. Emerson Radio Corp.*,[150] a majority of the court decided that the *Foley* decision was to be applied to all claims filed both before and after *Foley*; that is, *Foley* was to be applied retroactively.

The Supreme Court of California decided *Rojo v. Kliger*,[151] in 1990. Plaintiffs were physicians' assistants. They alleged that the physician continually subjected them to sexual harassment and demands for sexual favors. Their refusal to tolerate the harassment or acquiesce to the demands prompted their wrongful discharge. The court said that the trial court should allow plaintiffs to amend

---

[149]The court distinguished insurance cases where it recognizes that breaches of the implied covenant give rise to a tort action. "[T]he employment relationship is not sufficiently similar to that of the insurer and insured."

[150]48 Cal.3d 973, 772 P.2d 1059 (1989).

[151]52 Cal.3d 65, 801 P.2d 373 (1990).

their complaint to state a cause of action for a wrongful discharge for refusing to act against public policy. "Regardless of the precise scope of its application, article I, § 8 [of the California Constitution] is declaratory of this state's fundamental public policy against sex discrimination, including sexual harassment.... No extensive discussion is needed to establish the fundamental public interest in a workplace free from the pernicious influence of sexism. So long as it exists, we are all demeaned."

In 1992, in *Gantt v. Sentry Insurance Corp.*[152], the Supreme Court of California found for the plaintiff employee but reaffirmed the directions charted in the *Foley* case. Gantt, a former district sales manager sued Sentry, his former employer, for wrongful discharge. He recovered a jury verdict of $1.34 million that the Supreme Court affirmed. A female employee, Ms. Bruno, complained to Gantt about being sexually harassed by her supervisor. Gantt told her to report the matter to higher levels in the company. The woman did, but the harassment continued. Gantt raised the issue again with his superiors. The woman was fired.

The woman then filed a complaint with the Department of Fair Employment and Housing (DFEH). Sentry's counsel in charge of labor-related matters investigated the situation. She talked with Gantt. He thought that she was pressuring him to change his story and testify that he had not told Sentry's higher management about the incident. "She repeatedly reminded him that he was the only management employee supporting Ms. Bruno's claim that she had notified management about the harassment." Later Gantt met with the DFEH investigator in charge of the case. The investigator testified that Gantt had been pressed to change his story and was afraid of retaliation. The DFEH hearing took place the day after Gantt talked with the Sentry lawyer. At this hearing, the lawyer asked the DFEH investigator why he was not investigating sexual harassment charges against Gantt. She suggested that Gantt had harassed Ms. Bruno and was trying to deflect attention from himself. The investigator was surprised. It was the first time that a company lawyer had ever suggested that charges be brought against one of its employees. Less than two months after the hearing, Gantt was demoted and a month later he left for another job.

Although the Sentry lawyer disputed Gantt's and the investigator's testimony about her actions and statements, the jury found that the lawyer had told the investigator that Gantt had sexually harassed Ms. Bruno, that the statement was false, and that the lawyer had acted with malice, oppression or fraud.

The Supreme Court of California found that the case fit within the wrongful discharge doctrine of the *Petermann* and *Tameny* decisions. The California statute creating the administrative agency specifically prohibits obstruction of its investigations. It said that any attempt to induce or coerce an employee to lie to an agency investigator "plainly contravenes the public policy of this state." The plaintiff had established his right to tort damages.

---

[152] 1 Cal.4th 1083, 824 P.2d 680 (1992).

A Sentry lawyer said that the *Gantt* decision would be "devastating to employers, inviting employees to seek multimillion-dollar damage awards any time they believed they were being pressured to refuse to support a harassment claim." He denied that a company attorney had acted in an improper manner. "It was a standard practice for attorneys in such situations to interview witnesses such as Gantt, testing inconsistencies in their stories and advising them when being questioned by investigators not to volunteer information...."[153]

We can note that the sexual harassment took place in 1980, Gantt was demoted in 1983, he won before the jury in 1986, and the Supreme Court of California affirmed his case at the end of 1992. In 1992, he was 50 years old and working as a junior high school math teacher. Gantt said that "co-workers accused him of betraying the company when he reported the harassment to his supervisors... [E]xecutives and co-workers shrugged off the sexually offensive conduct with comments like, 'He doesn't mean anything by it.'" Sentry argued that Gantt was fired because of poor job performance.[154]

In an amicus brief, the California Merchants and Manufacturers Association asked the court to tell employers where the line was to be drawn in claims of violations of public policy.[155] The Supreme Court of California responded in a long essay on the subject. It said that in a wrongful discharge case, courts could declare public policy only based upon constitutional or statutory provisions — not on judicial opinions nor on codes of ethics or general ideas of morality. The employee's discharge must affect the public and not be merely a matter of fairness to the individual. The court said:

> [S]o limited, the public policy exception presents no impediment to employers that operate within the bounds of the law. Employees are protected against employer actions that contravene fundamental state policy. And society's interests are served through a more stable job market, in which its most important policies are safeguarded.[156]

The court also decided that workers' compensation provides the exclusive remedy for claims for intentional infliction of emotional distress. A fired employee could not seek a tort remedy based on such a claim.

In *Hunter v. Up-Right, Inc.*,[157] the Supreme Court of California further limited employees' ability to transform contracts into torts. In this case, the employee alleged that the employer said that the employee's job was going to be eliminated and if he did not resign, he would be fired. The employee resigned. There had

---

[153]Los Angeles Times, Feb. 28, 1992, Part A, at 34, col. 1.

[154]San Francisco Chronicle, June 16, 1992, at A1.

[155]The Recorder, February 28, 1992, at 1.

[156]824 P.2d at 688.

[157]6 Cal.4th 1174, 864 P.2d 88 (1993).

been, however, no decision to eliminate employee's position. The court said that an employee can recover for misrepresentation only if it is separate from the termination of the employment contract so that plaintiff's damages cannot be said to result from the termination itself. It explained that misrepresentation claims are hard to defend and few could be thrown out at the demurrer or summary judgment stage. "The resultant costs and inhibition of employment decision making are precisely the sort of consequences we cited in *Foley* in disapproving tort damages for breach of the implied covenant of good faith and fair dealing."

e. The Impact of Almost Two Decades of Attack on Employment-at-Will

A. The Impact in California: What has been the impact of the *Foley* decision? Gregory S. Lemmer[158] surveyed reactions in the press, collected letters sent by large California law firms to their clients, and interviewed several corporate personnel managers in May of 1989. His conclusions follow:

Initial Reaction

The day after *Foley* was handed down, newspaper accounts portrayed the decision as a substantial victory for California employers and management attorneys.[159] Cliff Palefsky, a plaintiff's lawyer from Oakland, complained, "This is a major step backwards. Without the effect of punitive damages, there's no economic deterrent to wrongful termination anymore." Palefsky also told the New York Times that "people who get wrongfully terminated — fired for a motive that is improper — are simply not going to be able to use the courts for a remedy." Another plaintiff's lawyer was equally adamant about the "overwhelming effect" *Foley* would have on wrongful discharge cases in California. Guy Saperstein suggested, "[*Foley*] takes away the incentive for employers to clean up their act and treat employees fairly. So the bottom line is that this decision is a great loss inflicted by Governor Deukmejian and his four justices." Initially, management lawyers were also convinced that *Foley* would have a major impact on wrongful discharge

---

[158]Mr. Lemmer did the research while a law student at the University of Wisconsin. Before attending law school, Mr. Lemmer worked in the personnel department of a world-famous California corporation. What follows is from an unpublished summary of his research. We have omitted many of his footnotes.

[159]See "California Ruling Curtails Damages in Dismissal Suits," Wall Street Journal, Dec. 30, 1988, at B1, col. 5 (In the article, the writer incorrectly concluded, "[After *Foley*] most individuals suing their employers for wrongful dismissal cannot ask for punitive damages"). Similarly, the New York Times mistakenly suggested, "In a major victory for employers, the California Supreme Court today sharply narrowed the right of dismissed employees to bring suits on the basis of wrongful discharge. The [*Foley*] court ruled 4 to 3 that an employee dismissed without good cause may sue only on the basis of breach of an expressed or implied contract." (citations omitted)

cases in the state. Frank Cronin, a Los Angeles attorney, declared, "The decision relieves the defendant employer in most of these cases from the tremendous risk of punitive damage claims, which cannot be estimated or really evaluated before trial. It eliminates the guessing game that management has to know what their real exposure is in the majority of wrongful termination cases."

Just days after the *Foley* decision was released, however, newspapers were backing away from earlier statements that painted the decision as an overwhelming win for employers. On January 8, 1989, the Los Angeles Times published a piece written by an attorney from Paul, Hastings, Janofsky & Walker, California's largest management law firm. In the article, William Waldo explained, "Many pundits declared that employers won a big victory last month when the California Supreme Court limited damages that workers in most circumstances can claim in wrongful dismissal cases. Don't believe it. For everyone involved — employers, employees and lawyers alike — the impact of the ruling probably will be limited." Likewise, the San Francisco Chronicle warned readers, "At first glance [*Foley*] appeared to some to close the door on most lawsuits by employees who claim to have been unfairly dismissed from their jobs. At second glance, the ruling may mean a far less dramatic change than many predicted." Robert Kuenzel, the attorney who represented IDC in *Foley*, also tried to put the case in perspective when he said, "It has to be viewed as a significant victory for the employer community in the state, but certainly not an unreserved, total victory."

Wrongful Discharge Litigation after Foley

Public policy

The *Foley* court explicitly held that an employee may recover emotional distress and punitive damages if his or her dismissal was in violation of substantial public policy. The definition of "substantial public policy," however, remains unclear after the decision and the court expressly declined to decide whether "public policy" has to be declared by the legislature in the form of a statute or constitutional provision. Therefore, until the courts provide further guidance in this area, many attorneys predict that plaintiff's counsel will place greater reliance on "public policy" claims since no tort damages are now recoverable for bad-faith breach of the covenant of good faith and fair dealing.

Attorneys are also anticipating more litigation in this area as plaintiff's lawyers try to broaden public policy grounds for wrongful discharge to include actions based on job safety issues, smoking in the workplace, and exposure to hazardous substances. (footnote omitted) One law firm also told clients, "Employers functioning in highly regulated industries such as banking, insurance and defense can expect close scrutiny of regulatory limitations which could serve as a public policy springboard for former employees."

Implied-in-fact contracts

In *Foley*, the California Supreme Court, for the first time, held that an employment contract may be implied, thus protecting employees from discharge where there is no evidence of "good cause." Further, the court held that the parties' intent to contract for employment terminable only for good cause may be implied from the totality of circumstances. By adopting this "totality of circumstances" standard, *Foley* requires juries to consider numerous factual issues when breach of an implied contract is plead. Therefore, the decision will sharply limit those instances when management lawyers can defeat such claims before trial using summary judgment motions or other pretrial motions.

The elimination of the statute of frauds defense in implied contract cases will likely increase the number of plaintiffs alleging express oral contracts at the time of hire as well as oral assurances of continued employment after the employee joins the company. (footnote omitted) One management firm, taking an obviously biased view of the validity of implied contract claims, warned clients: "Experience has shown that plaintiff's frequently identify long-departed personnel as the source of such [assured employment] representations, making it difficult if not impossible to counter their testimony absent an express written at-will standard and a consistently applied hiring procedure."

It should be noted that the *Foley* court's refusal to decide what length of employment gives rise to a cause of action for breach of an implied contract will also result in continued litigation in this area.

Covenant of good faith and fair dealing

Although early media coverage of *Foley* predicted that the decision would put an end to causes of action based on a bad-faith breach of the covenant of good faith and fair dealing, many believe that such causes of action will still be plead by plaintiffs. While only contract damages are now available upon a breach of the covenant, in cases involving middle and upper level managers such damages may amount to hundreds of thousands, possibly millions of dollars. Contract damages are often that large in cases involving well paid employees who sue to recover salaries, bonuses, stock options, pensions and other employee benefits. (footnote omitted) Even in cases involving lower-paid employees, plaintiffs often argue that they should be able to recover losses from the date of their discharge until their retirement date, normally age 65. Thus, a terminated employee in her mid 40's earning

$25,000 a year could ask a jury to award contract damages exceeding $500,000 (assuming no opportunity to mitigate damages).[160]

Other causes of action

Although the *Foley* majority held that punitive damages are no longer available in bad-faith breach of covenant cases, the decision left unaffected numerous tort claims that provide for such damages. To fill the void left by *Foley*, plaintiffs' attorneys are expected to rely to a greater extent on common law tort theories such as fraud,[161] defamation,[162] intentional or negligent infliction of emotional distress,[163] invasion of privacy,[164] — all of which may result in emotional distress and punitive damages.[165] As one attorney explained, however, to the extent that plaintiff's counsel have used wrongful discharge as a "springboard" to establish a tort action, based on a special relationship between an employer and employee, *Foley* has taken that option away. (footnote omitted) Since *Foley* holds that there is no special relationship between employers and employees, it is unlikely an argument that the discharge itself will be grounds for a tort action such as intentional infliction of emotional distress will succeed. But, as management

---

[160]*Id.* See also "Fired Worker Suits Limited in California," The National Law Journal, Jan. 16, 1989, at p. 3, col. 1. (In the article, Sharon Lowsen, a sole practitioner who represents both employers and employees said, "Lost wages sometimes aren't chicken feed. Attorneys are going to make the most money from those big punitive cases, but sometimes really the best thing you can do for your client is to get in and out quickly"); Letter from Gibson, Dunn & Crutcher warning clients, "Contract remedies for breach of covenant or an implied in fact contract not to terminate absent good cause are not necessarily restricted to recovery of back pay and benefits as asserted in several press accounts. Substantial arguments can be made that future earnings and benefits which would have been earned but for the breach of employment contract have been made in the past. Large jury awards have been made in the past."

[161]Employees must prove that the employer knew the representation [of continued employment] was false at the time it was made, that the employer made the statement in order to induce the employees to take certain action, and that the employees reasonably relied upon the false information to their detriment.

[162]Employees must prove the publication by an employer of information that is false and injurious to their reputation. Intra-office communication can constitute "publication"; however, truth is an absolute defense.

[163]Employees must show that the conduct of the employer amounted to extreme and outrageous conduct by which the employer intentionally or recklessly caused employees severe emotional distress.

[164]Employees must prove one of the four types of this tort: (1) an unauthorized appropriation of the employees' name or likeness for monetary gain; (2) public disclosure of private facts; (3) placing the employees in a false light in the public eye; or; (4) unauthorized intrusion into the employee's seclusion (living space or personal life).

[165]According to one attorney, more than three-fourths of the wrongful discharge lawsuits filed in California in recent years already included one of these types of claims.

attorney Alan Berkowitz explained, "... if you take the termination out of the picture, and there's other conduct which would support a claim for intentional or negligent infliction, that will still stand. For example, if an employer in some way treats an employee outrageously and it causes the employee emotional distress, that's not affected by *Foley*."

Attorneys are also predicting that there will be a number of cases that, prior to *Foley*, would have been filed alleging breach of the implied covenant that will now be filed as federal[166] or California[167] discrimination cases — particularly under federal and state statutes that permit punitive damages. Attorney David Bacon of Adams, Duque & Hazeltine told the Los Angeles Daily Journal, "I think we'll see really a transmutation there, with some of the civil rights theories — especially age, race and sex theories which were not pursued very vigorously in the past — they will come back as avenues of punitive damage redress."

Personnel Practices and Policies after Foley

Given the media's initial treatment of *Foley* as a so-called "significant employer victory," most law firms were quick to remind clients that the decision should not be seen as an opportunity to discharge employees without fear of future litigation. Sharon Grodin, a management attorney with a San Francisco firm, warned employers, "*Foley* is a victory for employers. However, it is not a license to act arbitrarily or unfairly. We expect there will be attempts in the Legislature and in the courts to attack the *Foley* case. Employers should still proceed with caution in terminating any highly paid, longterm or potentially litigious employees." (footnote omitted) Similarly, an attorney told San Diego employers not to become complacent about hiring and firing practices even after *Foley*, noting, "Some people feel that because of the court decision, employers can now fire anyone for any reason. This is just not so. Employers have to be more careful than ever before in dealing with termination situations that could rise to punitive damages."

While management lawyers continue to remind employers not to make any sweeping changes in their termination procedures after *Foley*, many attorneys are encouraging employers to take a more preventive approach to termination so that the risk of employee litigation is reduced. Given the *Foley* court's adoption of a totality of circumstances standard in determining

---

[166]Federal discrimination statutes include: Title VII of the Civil Rights Act of 1964 (42 U.S.C. § 2000e-2000e-17); The Pregnancy Discrimination Act of 1978 (42 U.S.C. § 200e(k)); The Age Discrimination in Employment Act of 1967 (29 U.S.C. §§ 621-634); and The Rehabilitation Act of 1973 (38 U.S.C. §§ 793, 794).

[167]For example, California's Fair Employment and Housing Act (FEHA) prohibits employment discrimination on the basis of sex, race or national origin.

whether an implied contract exists between employers and employees, a number of attorneys are recommending that at-will clauses be inserted in all employment documents. According to these attorneys, California courts will not permit implied contract claims to be asserted if such claims contradict an express written term of the contract, that is, an at-will clause. Therefore, they are suggesting that "employers should be careful to continue to include such clauses in as many documents [i.e., applications, offer letters, personnel policy manuals, stock options] that their employees sign as possible, as well as handbooks which under *Foley* may set forth the contractual employment relationship." Employers are also being counseled to develop integration clauses including restrictions on subsequent oral modifications since they "may prove important in subsequent litigation."

Several management attorneys, however, dismiss at-will clauses as a "quick fix" that may not provide protection to employers during wrongful discharge litigation. These attorneys point out that the court did not explicitly rule on the validity of at-will language in implied contract claims and predict that plaintiff's lawyers will argue that such language is merely part of the evidence that should be considered by the triers of fact as they consider the "totality of the circumstances." They also expect that the enforceability of "boilerplate" at-will language in employment documents will be seriously questioned by courts. Although at-will disclaimers are appealing on the surface, one attorney notes that reliance on them may be unrealistic because personnel policies are often undermined by the actions of managers and line supervisors.

Instead of using at-will clauses, these attorneys are recommending that employers take advantage of *Foley*'s support for employment contracts and establish explicit standards for employee discharge. Using this approach, there would still be an at-will employment period, albeit of unknown length, and employers could define the standards for termination, rather than leaving it for the judge or jury after a claim is filed by a former employee. Victor Schacter, a management attorney, contends that more employers are turning to a "cause" standard as a means of managing employee terminations. The standard provides that employees may be discharged for poor performance, economic or business changes, bad conduct, and can specify arbitration as the remedy to settle termination disputes, rather than litigation.

Over the past several years, a number of management attorneys have suggested that arbitration clauses may provide the means to slow down the number of wrongful termination cases filed in California. In fact, five years ago a California State Bar committee, appointed by the Bar's Labor and Employment Law Section, issued a report that recommended arbitration be substituted for litigation and that more limited traditional labor law remedies such as back pay, reinstatement (where appropriate), attorney fees and costs be provided to employees that prevail in arbitration. Alan Berkowitz, a management attorney, has said that a reasonably drawn provision requiring any terminated employee to submit to arbitration will likely stand up to judicial scrutiny and that courts will not "second guess" an arbitration provision, unless the provision itself is unreasonable in its terms. Berkowitz also notes that arbitration clauses are most likely to appear first in employment contracts covering high-level employees rather than hourly employees. On the other hand, plaintiff's lawyers argue that the use of arbitration clauses would not have a significant effect on the number of wrongful discharge cases filed and that the clauses themselves might be actionable if the provision is not carefully tailored to ensure reasonable treatment of the employee.

Proposed Legislation

In light of the *Foley* court's invitation to the California legislature to develop statutory protections against wrongful discharge, several bills were introduced in the legislature dealing specifically with the issue. For example, Senate Industrial Committee Chair Bill Greene (D-Los Angeles) introduced SB 282. Under the bill, employees could seek mandatory and binding arbitration decisions that would determine whether their discharge was "wrongful." On the employer side, Senator Robert Beverly (R-Redondo Beach) introduced a bill, SB 222, which would provide for mediation of wrongful discharge claims, and if both sides agreed, binding arbitration. The bill also calls for a "just cause" standard that employers would have to meet to justify termination of any employees who earn less than $15,000 a year. Under the bill employees who earn between $15,000 and $100,000 would be protected by a less demanding "good cause" provision. Finally, employees earning over $100,000 a year would be provided no protection under the bill. Critics of SB 222, however, contend that it actually diminishes protection that even *Foley* gave [employees]. *Foley* said just cause for everybody and upheld implied contracts. [SB 222] eliminates implied contracts and even oral contracts.

In addition, Senator Art Torres (D-Los Angeles) introduced SB 181, which would essentially reverse *Foley*'s holding that emotional distress and punitive damages are not available in bad-faith breach of covenant claims. According to Torres, "This [*Foley*] decision in short, rewards bad conduct by the few unscrupulous employers in the state while undermining those well-intentioned businesses who have spent time and money developing fair employment practices documenting workers' performance."

Finally, another Los Angeles lawmaker, Senator Herschel Rosenthal (D-Los Angeles), introduced SB 115 that would prohibit California employers from requiring employees to sign documents containing at-will clauses. In support of his proposal, Rosenthal said "More and more employers are using 'termination at will' clauses as a way to insulate themselves from any legal repercussions after dismissing an employee. Unfortunately this practice has left many workers with no recourse, even in the case of a blatant violation of contract."

None of these statutes passed the California legislature.

B. The General Impact of Restrictions on Management Control Over Employees: Professor Lauren B. Edelman and several collaborators have studied the impact of equal opportunity and affirmative action laws as well as the limitations on employment at will.[168] Their study shows how corporate lawyers and officials in personnel departments in major corporations interpreted the limitations on employment at will.

If the employment at will cases have done nothing else, they have put the problem on the agenda of business people and lawyers. There is a vast literature about coping with the uncertainty created by the debate, and many training programs are offered. For example, Condon and Wolff, *Procedures that Safeguard Your Right to Fire,*[169] suggests avoiding any suggestion that passing a probationary period leads to lifetime job security, following disciplinary procedure to the letter in all cases, and setting up an internal review mechanism for any employee who wants to question termination. Markowich and Bartello,[170] suggests keeping personnel files current and auditing them regularly. Employers can document a case so their decisions are harder to challenge. Some employers, of course, will clean their files of embarrassing items before they fire employees.

Enterprising entrepreneurs have sold elaborate programs designed to train employees about how to deal with these new legal requirements. However, Edelman, Abraham and Erlanger point out that many entrepreneurs, lawyers and personnel officials exaggerated the real threat posed by the new rules. They argue:

> [P]ersonnel professionals and practicing lawyers have a shared interest in constructing the threat of wrongful discharge in such a way that employers perceive the law as a threat and rely upon those professions to curb the threat. That threat — and the proffered solution — would help both professions to gain a symbiotic jurisdiction over corporate response to the legal environment.

In an earlier article, Edelman asked why "a growing number of employers have implemented due process protections for their nonunion employees in the

---

[168]Lauren B. Edelman, Steven E. Abraham and Howard S. Erlanger, Professional Construction of Law: The Inflated Threat of Wrongful Discharge, 26 Law & Society Review 47 (1992).

[169]63 Harvard Business Review 16 (Nov.-Dec. 1985).

[170]Employee File Audits Can Reduce Discharge Conflicts, 64 Personnel Journal 80 (August 1984).

absence of any direct [legal] mandates to do so."[171] Many large firms changed their procedures and limited managerial discretion so that employees could not be discharged without hearings, warnings and the like. She explained this in terms of "legal environment theory." Law creates important indirect effects, influencing "the normative environment." She argues that the civil rights movement and the legal requirements of the 1960s "created a normative environment in which legitimacy was conditioned on fair governance. Pressure from that normative environment led employers to create formal protections of due process rights." The civil rights laws opened organizations to public scrutiny, and many managers and employees generalized these laws to a right of all employees to fair treatment. The personnel profession was the engine that drove the process. Personnel offices became an internal constituency for formal protection of employee rights because personnel department officials sought to ensure the survival and increased importance of their own positions and functions. She cautions, however,

> [i]t is important to recognize that the formalization of due process rights does not guarantee substantive justice in the workplace.... [D]ue process protections may reinforce employers' control over labor by giving the appearance of fair governance while channeling conflict into a forum that, especially in the nonunion context, is unlikely to produce significant reform.[172]

One means of coping with the threat raised by having to defend firing employees in court has been for large corporations to turn to arbitration. Arbitration clauses can be written into employment agreements so that this form of dispute resolution will be accepted by employees as they are hired. The process is quicker and less costly, and the awards from arbitrators with business experience are much lower than those made by juries. While some employees are worse off under arbitration, those whose claims do not raise the possibility of large awards of damages may not be able to find lawyers willing to go to court. Arbitration may offer something to such employees. However, there is concern that arbitration can be structured to unfairly benefit employers. Remedies can be limited and short time limits imposed. Employers have access to records and witnesses, and if the process limits discovery, an employee may be at a great disadvantage.[173]

---

[171]Edelman, Legal Environments and Organizational Governance: The Expansion of Due Process in the American Workplace, 95 American Journal of Sociology 1401, 1402 (1990).

[172]Edelman, *supra* at 1436.

[173]See ADR Techniques Gaining Favor in Non-Traditional Settings, Daily Labor Report (BNA), No. 48, March 15, 1993.

f. Conclusions About the Struggle Over Employment-at-Will

1. *What does it all mean? I:* What goals do the courts seem to be pursuing in the employment for an indefinite term area? Are they attempting to carry out the expectations of employees for which employers are responsible? Are they attempting to promote the mobility of labor and competition for jobs to keep job performance up and wages down? Are they following a policy of judicial restraint to leave the area to the power configuration found in American employment relations, promote "living trees," and avoid "dismal swamps?"

2. *What does it all mean? II*: After studying a great deal about employment at will, what do you think of the following comments about the area?

(a) In an article entitled "The Job as Property Right"[174] Peter F. Drucker writes:

> In every developed non-Communist country, jobs are rapidly turning into a kind of property. The mechanism differs from culture to culture; the results are very much the same.
>
> In Japan there is "lifetime employment" for the "permanent" (that is, primarily, male) employee in government and large businesses. This means, in effect, that short of bankruptcy the business is run primarily for the employee, whose right to the job has precedence over outside creditors and legal "owners" alike.
>
> In Europe, increasingly, employees cannot be laid off; they have to be bought out with "redundancy payments." In a few countries, such as Belgium and Spain, these payments are equivalent to a full salary or wage over the remainder of an employee's lifetime, for a worker with a few years of seniority. And the High Court of the European Community, in a decision which is considered binding for all member countries, has ruled that the claim to redundancy payments survives even an employer's bankruptcy and extends to the other assets of the owners of the employing firm.
>
> In the U.S. recent legislation has given the employee's pension claim a great deal of the protection traditionally reserved for property. Indeed, in the event of bankruptcy or liquidation of the employing firm, employee pension claims take precedence over all other claims (except government taxes) for up to 30% of the employing firm's net worth.
>
> The various fair-employment regulations in the U.S., whether on behalf of racial minorities, women, the handicapped or the aged, treat promotion, training, job security and access to jobs as a matter of rights. It's getting harder to dismiss any employee except "for cause."...

---

[174]Peter Drucker, The Job As Property Right, Wall Street Journal, March 4, 1980, at 18, cols. 4-6. Reprinted with permission of The Wall Street Journal c 1980 Dow Jones & Company, Inc. All rights reserved.

Jobs, in effect, are being treated as a species of property rather than as contractual claims. Historically there have been three kinds of property: "real" property such as land; "personal" property such as money, tools, furnishings and personal possessions; and "intangible" property such as copyrights and patents. It is not too far-fetched to speak of the emergence of a fourth — "property in the job" — closely analogous to property in the land in premodern times....

For the great majority of people in most developed countries, land was the true "means of production" until well in this century, often until World War II. It was property in land which gave access to economic effectiveness and with it to social standing and political power. It was therefore rightly called by the law "real" property.

In modern developed societies, by contrast, the overwhelming majority of the people in the labor force are employees of "organizations" — in the U.S. the figure is 93% — and the "means of production" is therefore the job. The job is not "wealth." It is not "personal property" in the legal sense. But it is a "right" in the means of production.... Today the job is the employee's means of access to social status, to personal opportunity, to achievement and to power.

For the great majority in the developed countries today, the job is also the one avenue of access to personal property. Pension claims are by far the most valuable assets of employees over 50, more valuable, indeed, than all his other assets taken together — his share in his house, his savings, his automobile and so on. And the pension claim is, of course, a direct outgrowth of the job, indeed part of the job.

The evolution of the job into a species of property can be seen as a genuine opportunity. It might be the right, if not the only, answer to the problem of "alienation" which Marx identified a century and a quarter ago as resulting from the divorce of the "worker" from the "means of production."

But as the long history of land tenure abundantly proves, such a development also carries a real danger of rigidity and immobility. In Belgium, for instance, the system of redundancy payments may prevent employers from laying off people. But it also keeps them from hiring workers they need, and thus creates more unemployment than it prevents or assuages. Similarly, lifetime employment may be the greatest barrier to the needed shift in Japan from labor intensive to knowledge intensive industries.

How can modern economies cope with the emergence of job property rights and still maintain the flexibility and social mobility necessary for adapting quickly to changes? At the very least, employing organizations will have to recognize that jobs have some of the characteristics of property rights and cannot therefore be diminished or taken away without due process. Hiring, firing, promotion and demotion must be subject to pre-established, objective, public criteria. And there has to be a review, a pre-established right to appeal to a higher judge in all actions affecting rights in and to the job.

Standards of review will, paradoxically, be forced on employers in the United States by the abandonment of fixed-age retirement. For companies to be able to dismiss even the most senile and decrepit oldster, they will have to develop impersonal standards of performance and systematic personnel procedures for employees of all ages.

The evolution of jobs into a kind of property also demands that there be no "expropriation without compensation," and that employers take responsibility to anticipate redundancies, retraining employees about to be laid off and finding and placing them in new jobs. It requires redundancy planning rather than unemployment compensation.

In the emerging "employee society," employees, through their pension funds, are beginning to own — and inevitably will also control — the large businesses in the economy. Jobs are becoming a nexus of rights and a species of property. This development is surely not what people mean when they argue about "capitalism," pro or con. But it is compatible with limited government, personal freedom and the rational allocation of resources through the free market. It may thus be the effective alternative to the "state capitalism" of the totalitarians which, under the name of "communism," makes government into absolute tyranny, and suppresses both freedom and rationality.

(b) In *Kumpf v. Steinhaus*[175] the 7th Circuit reviewed a jury verdict in a case in which Kumpf alleged that Steinhaus had wrongfully interfered with his prospects for receiving certain fees. In affirming the trial court decision Judge Frank Easterbrook, formerly a professor at the University of Chicago Law School, took the opportunity to comment about employment-at-will:

> The privilege to manage corporate affairs is reinforced by the rationale of employment at will. Kumpf had no tenure of office. The lack of job security gave him a keen motive to do well. Security of position may diminish that incentive. See Richard A. Epstein, In Defense of the Contract at Will, 51 University of Chicago Law Review 947 (1984). Employment at will, like the business judgment doctrine, also keeps debates about business matters out of the hands of courts. People who enter a contract without a fixed term know there is some prospect that their business partners may try to take advantage of them or simply make a blunder in deciding whether to continue the relationship. Yet people's concern for their reputation and their ability to make other advantageous contracts in the future leads them to try to avoid both mistakes and opportunistic conduct. Contracting parties may sensibly

---

[175]779 F.2d 1323 (7th Cir. 1985).

decide that it is better to tolerate the risk of error — to leave correction to private arrangements — than to create a contractual right to stay in office in the absence of a "good" reason. The reason for a business decision may be hard to prove, and the costs of proof plus the risk of mistaken findings of breach may reduce the productivity of the employment relation.

Many people have concluded otherwise; contracts terminable only for cause are common. But in Wisconsin, courts enforce whichever solution the parties select. A contract at will may be terminated for any reason (including bad faith) or no reason, without judicial review; the only exception is a termination that violates "a fundamental and well-defined public policy as evidenced by existing law." *Brockmeyer v. Dun & Bradstreet....* Greed — the motive Kumpf attributes to Steinhaus — does not violate a "fundamental and well-defined public policy" of Wisconsin. Greed is the foundation of much economic activity, and Adam Smith told us that each person's pursuit of his own interests drives the economic system to produce more and better goods and services for all....

The contention that businesses should be more considerate of their officers should be addressed to the businesses and to legislatures. Some firms will develop reputations for kind treatment of executives, some will be ruthless. Some will seek to treat executives well but find that the exigencies of competition frustrate their plans. The rule of *this* game is that Kumpf was an employee at will and had no right to stay on if his board wanted him gone.... Kumpf did not bargain for legal rights against Lincoln Life, and the judge properly declined to allow the jury to convert moral and ethical claims into legal duties.

(c) Peter Linzer, writing in the Georgia Law Review,[176] commented on Professor Ian Macneil's critique of the idea of "consent" in forming employment relationships. He went on to observe:

Macneil is not a believer in the state as curer of all ills, and he expressed doubt about my conclusions in no small part because he has a firm belief that no one is truly powerless, and that what we are really dealing with are degrees of relative power.

... the thrust of the cases, the longevity cases most clearly, but also the retaliatory discharge and personnel handbook cases, is that the employee's relation to a business enterprise is more complex than just a barter of his services for pay. The employee is becoming a part-owner of the business....

One cannot draw an exact parallel between employees and franchises, since employees are paid for their services, do not make a cash investment

---

[176]Linzer, The Decline of Assent: At-Will Employment as a Case Study of the Breakdown of Private Law Theory, 20 Georgia Law Review 323, 394-395, 408-409 (1986).

and do not normally expect to share directly in the firm's profits. Nonetheless, the employee's investment is in many ways similar to the franchisee's. The longer the employee has worked for a company, the more specific his job skills have become, the less mobile he is, and the more his investment in the firm becomes his only means of livelihood and self-respect. And the more courts are justified in hobbling the at-will doctrine because of the transaction-specific investment and the relationship that has accrued, however unconsciously, between the worker and the firm.

(d) Farber and Matheson[177] propose "[a] promise is enforceable when made in furtherance of an economic activity." Under this doctrine, they would enforce promises which employers make to employees. They contend:

> [A] mutual interest in a long-term and amicable relationship is part of the explanation that [economists] Okun and Thurow give for the behavior of the market. For example, classical economics suggests that if someone were to come along and offer to perform an employee's job at a reduced rate, the employer would fire the existing employee and replace him by the lower cost employee. Yet in reality this never happens. The reason is that the employer cannot afford to take action that will discourage employees from making long-term investments in their jobs. For example, much on-the-job training is actually given by older employees, who will have little incentive to provide such training if they fear their own jobs may be at stake. To maximize the benefits of their relationship, both sides need a certain amount of trust....
>
> Because trust is essential to our basic economic institutions, it is a public good. One individual breaking trust in a dramatic way, or many individuals breaking trust less dramatically, can lead to short-run benefits for those individuals but create negative externalities. The willingness of others to trust is impaired, requiring them to invest in precautions or insure themselves against the increased risk of betrayal. Such externalities exist because of asymmetrical information: the promisor necessarily has better information about his own trustworthiness than does the promisee. For example, in the short run employers can profit by making commitments to employees, obtaining the resulting benefits, and then reneging. But in the long run, enforcement benefits promisors as a group by fostering the reliance from which they seek to benefit. Conversely, trustworthy individuals confer a social benefit by increasing the general perception of trust, thereby allowing others to decrease such costs.

---

[177] Farber and Matheson, Beyond Promissory Estoppel: Contract Law and the "Invisible Handshake," 52 University Chicago Law Review 903, 927, 928-929, 935-936 (1985). Copyright © University of Chicago. Reprinted with permission.

Seen in this light, the cases in which courts have pushed the doctrine of promissory estoppel beyond its stated justification and technical limitations are characterized by a strong need both by the parties and society for a high level of trust. They involve relationships in which one party must depend on the word of the other to engage in socially beneficial reliance. In the employee cases, the socially beneficial reliance takes the form of higher job performance and lower turnover....

[E]conomic actors are free to make any statements they desire without fear of liability, so long as the other party understands that they are not committing themselves, are stating only their current intentions, and may change their mind at any time. In other words, where potential promisors are less than confident of their future conduct, the proposed rule fosters better information transmission by encouraging them to reveal their uncertainties. This information will help to insure that promisors will be trusted only insofar as they are worthy of trust.

Assume that we accept Farber and Matheson's argument about the value of trust for society. Does it follow that all promises by employers to employees must be enforceable to preserve that trust? I face many other-than-legal sanctions if I break my word. Why aren't these sanctions enough to defend the degree of trust needed by society?

During the past two decades many middle managers and professionals have lost their jobs as large corporations have "down-sized." Should we conclude that this experience has undercut whatever assumptions employees once had about their employment tenure or about how much to rely on promises made by their employers?

(e) A note in the Harvard Law Review[178] offers the following argument:

The public policy exception, as it now exists, represents a very limited attempt to control employer misconduct. It chiefly benefits employees constituting the most privileged third of the United States labor market — employees who already enjoy protection from the sorts of arbitrary and abusive treatment that the public policy exception is supposed to deter. Moreover, because courts have restricted its reach to only a narrow range of employer misconduct, the public policy exception reaffirms the legitimacy of the employer's otherwise unquestioned authority to fire employees at will.

Yet even when law plainly serves the goal of preserving the existing arrangement of economic and social interests, there may lie within it a kernel of emancipatory power. This potential is present in the public policy exception to the at will rule. Dual labor market theory has shown that the

---

[178]Note, Protecting Employees at Will Against Wrongful Discharge: The Public Policy Exception, 96 Harvard Law Review 1931, 1950-1951 (1983).

extension of job security to employees in the secondary market [these jobs are generally not sheltered from competition, are often found in smaller, less stable firms, and involve short promotional ladders] may reduce labor market stratification by improving the working conditions of women, minorities, and other disfavored groups in the secondary labor market. Moreover, the concept of public policy as a limit on employer discretion can raise the expectations of employees who might otherwise believe their rights to be unworthy of vindication. A more expansive application of the public policy exception may thus operate at the levels of both corrective justice and political consciousness to effectuate a change in labor relations that, as commentators have almost unanimously agreed, is long overdue.

(f) Finally, taking a still different tack, Catler argues:[179]

[T]he proposed modifications [of the at-will doctrine], doomed at best to provide little advantage to employees, could actually harm those who, absent such changes, would have sought and obtained better job protection.... The only way that employees can insure continued job security is by organizing themselves.

Do you agree that small reforms should sometimes be resisted because their enactment destroys support for larger, and more meaningful changes?

E. LONG-TERM RELATIONSHIPS IN COMMERCIAL TRANSACTIONS

In this section we turn from family and employment to buying and selling goods and dealing with ownership and control. These are settings in which we might expect contract law to be central, and the situations brought before the courts should fit neatly into contract rules. However, most behavior in commercial settings is relatively unaffected by the legal enforceability of contracts. Moreover, lawyers often must twist classical contract doctrine in these settings, just as in family cases, to produce results that seem appropriate. Contract law may be vital in some situations, but often its role, if any, is indirect and subtle.

Other-than-legal sanctions channel business behavior in most cases. Many transactions reflect what the economist Arthur Okun called "the invisible handshake."[180] One has a long-term relationship with a particular trading partner or one is part of a group of traders. These relationships benefit business people.

---

[179]Catler, The Case Against Proposals to Eliminate the Employment at Will Rule, 5 Industrial Relations Law Journal 471 (1983).

[180]Okun, Prices & Quantities: A Macroeconomic Analysis (The Brookings Institution 1981).

For example, relationships create sanctions. Those who depart from acceptable practices risk losing a relationship or position within the group of traders. Typically, relationships are left relatively unstructured — people order from their supplier or they make a deal on an exchange. In some situations parties structure arrangements in great detail, but usually the concern is with business needs rather than legal enforceability. Even where lawyers prepare elaborate contract documents, often the business people who carry out the transaction follow conventional practices rather than reading the written contract.

The law stands at the margin of these situations. In the next chapter we shall see that in business settings courts may police the procedures for making contracts. However, they seldom will look at the fairness of deals as such. Nonetheless, problems can occur in business settings that resemble disputes in families. Indeed, business partners who fall out resemble divorced former spouses who bitterly fight over any pretext. In some circumstances, those in business attempt to build their own private adjudication systems — commercial arbitration. There is a question as to how far the public legal system will support such private governments.

1. RELATIONAL SANCTIONS AND ENFORCEABLE CONTRACTS

The core transaction for academic contract law — what scholars assume to be the typical contract dispute before the courts — is a discrete sale of goods or services between two commercial enterprises. We have suggested that this kind of transaction is not as common as we might expect in view of the millions of transactions taking place each business day in this country. We might think that lawmakers should reshape contract law so it would be more useful to businesses engaged in long term continuing relations. Or we might decide that the system as it stands works well enough. People always can structure elaborate systems of private government for their business relationships if they think it worth the time and effort.

There is considerable evidence many other-than-legal sanctions prompt people to perform their promises in most cases. There are also reasons not to plan in too great detail in advance. Most of the following are excerpts from research notes of interviews with business people and their lawyers. They were interviewed when the economy was in good condition, and they might see matters differently in troubled times.

a. Business Views on Other-Than-Legal Sanctions

Interview with the Sales Manager of a manufacturer of machine tools:

> One cannot spell out terms and conditions in a contract which will govern responsibility for a machine that cannot do what a customer wants it to do. A lawyer would have to look over the shoulder of the sales department at

every point in every sales transaction. We would have to pay lawyers a lot of money to do this, and we would never get any business done — we'd be negotiating forever. Lawyers come into a transaction only when customers want an unusual financing arrangement that we will have to sell to some bank. Of course, one can get drastic problems in selling machines. For example, when a machine fails to work, a customer is likely to be subject to a great deal of delay. He will refuse to pay for the machine, and he may bill us for down time. He will be out of production and want the profits he could have made with our machine. But this is not something any lawyer could handle without putting you out of business. This must be handled on a business basis by a salesman and the man who bought the machine. We don't look for legal loopholes to avoid obligations like this. After all, you are selling reliability and your reputation gets around.

Interview with the Vice President in Charge of Sales of a manufacturer of paper:

The company has no written contracts with any of its customers although large amounts are involved on most of its sales. In the 1930s there were some contracts with publishers and printers. These contracts involved a commitment on the company's part to supply a certain amount of paper. Practically, the contracts were all one sided. They bound us but provided nothing in return. We could not make the publishers or printers eat the excess paper and take it when they could not use it. Moreover, when a publisher or printer cancels an order for paper, he has just lost a big order or his magazine is in trouble. He is a difficult man to hold for damages then. On the other hand, we do not need contracts with our big accounts — they will take the paper and pay for it. Thus a contract gives us nothing but reduces our flexibility in allocating paper to customers we want to favor.

Interview with the General Attorney of a large nationally known corporation that does a great deal of advertising:

In television everything seems to be left wide open except the amounts to be paid, the number of weeks the show is to run and the time for the commercials. For example, we were the sponsor of [a famous comedian's] show. Negotiations went on for over a year while the program was on the air. The show was canceled finally as its ratings dropped, but still a contract had not been signed. Finally, six months later a signed contract came through. This can be done since the interests of the parties are not adverse. NBC, CBS, and ABC know us as large advertisers. Perhaps contracts are not really needed here.

There is considerable evidence that when a contract is breached, the aggrieved party often does not obtain or expect "benefit of the bargain" damages to protect the expectation interest. For example, there is a widespread practice of canceling orders for goods or services when the buyer no longer needs what it ordered. As the following interviews show, rarely do sellers expect lost profits as damages when a buyer cancels an order although in most instances the seller would have a legal right to a judgment based on this measure.

Interview with a partner in a large law firm with a commercial practice:

> Mr. X noted that businessmen often do not feel they have a "contract" — rather there is an "order." They speak of canceling the order and not of breaching the contract. When he began practice he referred to cancellation of a purchase order as a breach of contract. He no longer talks in these terms as his clients do not think of cancellation this way. In heavy industry, at least, most clients believe that a cancellation right is part of the business relationship between buyer and seller. This attitude is widespread although the limits are vague. Clients expect to pay some cancellation charges if the seller has done anything substantial toward filling the order. However, few businessmen would think of the full lost anticipated profit as a proper item in a cancellation charge. The seller will often pad his costs in computing cancellation charges to cover some of this though.

Interview with the vice president in charge of sales of a manufacturer of die castings:

> At times customers do cancel orders. They then must pay for all of the items completed. If the customer has absolutely no use for the items, we will melt down the metal and allow a metal credit. The customer will be charged labor, burden and profit on the parts that have been made. He is not being charged just cost. If cancellation comes in the middle of producing a die, we have a per-hour rate. Of course, customers are free to cancel orders without charge before we've done anything toward production. We would never charge our anticipated profit on the entire job. Most people would not think this reasonable. However, things might be different in another type of business. Suppose 90% of a firm's operation depended on a particular order which was canceled. Then the company might be able to say it had turned down other business in reliance on this large order. It might seek its full lost profit in that case although this would depend on the reaction of the buyer and how badly the seller needed to do business with that buyer in the future.

Letter from the vice president of a manufacturer of women's hosiery:

> In my 40 years' experience with our company I do not believe that we have ever held a customer to the merchandise he ordered, whether it be on one

of our own order forms or on the customer's order form confirming that which our salesman has written up. We have been most liberal with our customers and more or less adopt the policy that if they play fair with us, we bend over backwards to play fair with them.

Being a manufacturer of perishable consumer goods, we are most liberal in making good defective merchandise returned by a customer to our dealers or where the dealer finds defective merchandise that we have shipped to him. We also are very liberal in our policy of exchange of unsalable colors and sizes, being ready to exchange old season colors for new season colors, but then with a reprocessing charge of 10% to cover our cost.

b. Form Contract Provisions

The provisions found on business forms used for buying and selling in manufacturing industry reinforce these ideas about easy cancellation. Forms used by *buyers* often contain provisions allowing them to cancel orders. Typically, the effect of these contract clauses is that the buyers can change their mind after they have made a contract. They can back out with little or no liability if they do it quickly enough. In many instances, they can wait a fairly long time. Larger companies often include a cancellation-for-convenience provision on their purchase orders — the document they use to buy materials, parts and services. Some buyers merely assert that they may cancel if they want to. Others concede they will pay cancellation charges in some situations if they want to back out. The amount of these charges specified varies widely:

(1) Some firms do not specify what they will pay. They say only that they will pay such charges as shall result from "an equitable adjustment."

(2) Many cancellation clauses agree to pay the contract price for items completed before cancellation (some require that the seller complete items and deliver them). Then the buyer also will pay only the costs allocatable solely to the order for work in process and materials purchased for the order which the seller cannot salvage. They pay no profit on items the seller has not completed. They can back out without charge before the seller orders special materials or starts work.

(3) Many agree to pay the contract price for items completed, the percentage of completion multiplied by the unit price under the contract for work in process, and the cost of materials which the seller cannot salvage. They pay only a percentage of profit on work in process, and they can back out without charge before the seller orders special materials or starts work.

(4) Only a very few buyers go so far as to agree to pay the lost anticipated profit on items before the seller starts production of them.

Sellers worry about buyers backing out of deals, but often contract damages rules do not help sellers very much. The provisions on *seller's* forms give another indication that cancellation is not uncommon. Cancellation for convenience provisions usually appear only on the buying forms of larger firms.

However, such provisions are common on the selling forms used by both large and small firms. (Of course, there are no provisions of any kind on the forms typically used by the very smallest manufacturers.) Some sellers ask for their full anticipated profit as well as their expenditures made in performing up to the time of cancellation. Yet many sellers ask only for some anticipated profit on items in process. "Reasonable estimated profits on the incomplete portion of the order multiplied by the percentage of completion of the incomplete portion of the order" is the way one firm put it. Some sellers are willing to demand only their expenditures which they cannot salvage on work not completed. Those who sell stock items to retailers usually are willing to accept returns from their customers upon payment of a restocking charge.

It also is rare for a buyer to recover full expectation damages if a seller breaches, and the buyer sues. There are several reasons for this. The formal legal rules themselves often make it difficult for aggrieved parties to gain protection of their expectation interest in a legal action. A person who wins a contract suit usually cannot recover attorneys' fees. If the difference between contract price and market or cover price is the appropriate remedy, usually the difference is not great enough to justify the costs of litigation. If it is enough, a buyer often has to worry about a seller's bankruptcy wiping out the claim. If lost profits are the appropriate measure of recovery, difficulty in proving the amount of anticipated profit with reasonable certainty, as well as the foreseeability rules of *Hadley v. Baxendale*, may prevent recovery. And specific performance seldom is available.

Moreover, many businesses operate under contracts which undercut even the relatively mild sanctions actually imposed by our legal system. On one hand, there is the "breach-proof bargain" which a lawyer structures so it is difficult for a seller to default on its obligation. Many sellers of machinery use a proposal form which almost makes no commitment or takes no risks. First, the seller makes it clear that its liability is limited to replacement or repair of the machine. It thus wards off claims for profit and scrapped raw material caused by defects in the machine. Then even liability for replacement and repair often is limited to claims filed within a limited time after delivery, often as short as 30 days. Some sellers word this type of clause so the time starts running as soon as the machine gets in the door at the buyer's plant. They do this although it may take over a month to set up the machine and get it running so defects could appear. Some sellers even start the time for claims running as soon as they deliver the machine to the trucking company or railroad for shipment. This further cuts down the time for discovering defects. We can debate whether such clauses would be valid under the Uniform Commercial Code. See § 1-102(3). Whether a seller that valued its reputation would hide behind such a clause is also debatable. A seller might make a grand gesture. Its officials could call the clause to the attention of the buyer and then put it aside as they offered what they considered a fair settlement.

Some sellers quote prices but guard against increases in manufacturing cost by using an escalator clause. If costs go up, the price to the buyer goes up too. The seller also guards against deterioration of the buyer's credit by providing that the seller can demand cash at any time the buyer's credit is no longer satisfactory.

c. Contract Litigation and Appeals

Contract litigation involves exceptional situations. The possible recovery in the contract action should exceed the possible loss of benefits from future business relationships. Furthermore, the defendant must be able to pay enough of any judgment to justify investing resources in litigating. One reason for breaching a contract, after all, is that a firm simply cannot perform because it no longer has the resources nor credit needed. If this is the reason for failing to perform, bankruptcy may discharge any judgment won.

Why, then, do we ever get contracts litigation and appeals? Often the background of litigated cases shows that the legal issues have little to do with the real reasons why the contractual relationship broke down. Rather, it often appears that sometime after relations turned sour, one party searched for some type of "out." This party relied on a technical interpretation of the law or the contract document to justify walking away from the deal.

We have seen an increase in the number of contracts cases filed in both state and federal courts over the last two or three decades. For example, in 1960, 8.5% of the cases filed in United States District Courts were contracts cases involving diversity of citizenship. The percentage had grown to 12.5% in 1987.

Interviews with business people and their lawyers show that not all of them express disdain for contract and the legal rules governing enforceability.

Interview with a partner in a large law firm with a commercial practice:

> Mr. X stated that he was impatient with businessmen who see contract as a scheme by lawyers designed to get fees. He is sick and tired of hearing that, "We can deal on the basis of good faith. We can trust old Max." Unsophisticated businessmen seem to need to be "burned" to understand the risks they are running. Just because your house has never burned down does not prove you do not need fire insurance. There is a great need for preventive law, and it could result in long-run savings. Questions do not arise from a lack of good faith. One simply has an honest misunderstanding, people tend to not admit that the other man's position is an honest misunderstanding, they argue and you have a dispute.
>
> In about ninety percent of the contracts involving the building industry you will have some kind of dispute before the building is up and paid for. One just doesn't know what he is getting. Here contracts are most important. Builders ought to know this because they are in court often enough trying to defend the job they have done. The number of disputes is in direct proportion to the size and complexity of the building. The parties simply cannot define everything called for in a contract to construct a twelve-story

building. The parties never seem to agree in advance on what kind of guarantee the builder is giving. Builders don't follow plans and specifications; they "interpret them." Owners just assume that roofs won't leak and that doors will close. Really, the concepts are more like negligence than contract since building plans are painted with such a broad brush. Then builders do not have as much money or as good accounting systems as manufacturers. They get over-extended, and then they try to cut corners. Residential building is worse than commercial building, but people are much more careful in adding a wing on a plant than in buying a machine which may cost just as much.

Interview with the general counsel of a nationally known manufacturing firm:

We negotiate overriding agreements to cover all our dealings with the aviation industry or subcontracts relating to it. We are extremely careful. An air frame manufacturer must negotiate with the airlines in great detail as to the warranty it will give them. Obviously, the air frame builders have a fantastic exposure to damage suits if anything goes wrong with the airplane. This exposure backs up to every one of their basic suppliers. The only way to handle this is by a carefully drafted contract defining responsibility and then by insurance to cover the responsibility undertaken. You will get careful contracts, if the businessman have any sense, whenever there is exposure to serious liability — products liability, the possibility of liability for patent infringement or the possibility of liability to workmen who come on the premises. Perhaps it is the influence of the insurance company.

Interview with the purchasing agent of a large utility:

Contractors do make mistakes in their bids. They might like to back out, but we hold them to the bids unless it would push the outfit into bankruptcy. A big contractor recently made an error that cost him $175,000. He underestimated the number of hours of labor he would have to put into the construction job for us. We held him to the contract. Someone else would have had the low bid and the job if he had not made the error, and we could not turn the job over to anyone else when the mistake was discovered. Here it was strictly a clerical error, and careful checking could have caught it. Contractors have to take the consequences of errors in order to learn not to make them. One must be reasonable, but one cannot let contractors off all the time. This would be throwing money down a rat hole and encouraging more sloppy practice. Contractors are careless enough as it is in their business methods.

While there are good reasons to avoid disputes or resolve those that do occur harmoniously, business transactions can turn sour. Sometimes suppliers do sue customers, particularly when the potential recovery outweighs possible loss of good will and reputation from the litigation.

NOTES AND QUESTIONS

1. *Explanations for wanting contracts*: Some of the business people and their lawyers quoted seem to see little need for legally enforceable contracts while others have a very different view. How would you account for the differing attitudes about enforceable contracts and contracts litigation? Is there anything about the types of transactions involved that might help explain some of the difference in attitude?

2. *Attitudes toward expectation damages*: Are expectation damages needed by business people? Would a rule limiting recovery to foreseeable reliance damages serve business better? In thinking about this question, remember that clauses allowing buyers to cancel for convenience while paying only a limited reliance recovery are very common in ordinary transactions.

3. *Litigation as an alternative to the normal means of dispute resolution*: Do business people need alternatives to litigation to resolve their disputes? Would mediation help? Would you expect to find arbitration schemes common in business? Is there a distinction between the lawyer's role and that of the counselor or psychologist?

2. COMMERCIAL RELATIONSHIPS AND PRIVATE GOVERNMENTS

Commercial arbitration is not a new idea but has a long history in the United States.[181] There is at least a little controversy about the merits of this means of resolving commercial disputes. Furthermore, if the parties do arbitrate, to what extent will the courts support the decisions of the arbitrators? Almost all states have arbitration acts. These direct courts to issue orders enforcing arbitration awards and to offer only limited judicial review of arbitrators' actions.

Soia Mentschikoff's article[182] is the classic study of commercial arbitration. She distinguishes three basic models. The *umpire* type stresses speed and economy. The parties or a trade association selects an expert who will be right, or at least will make decisions within a zone of reasonable judgment. In such situations a quick answer given by someone who knows the trade is more important than "the right answer." For example, in some areas lumber wholesalers and retail lumber yards settle disputes about the quality of lumber by calling in an expert lumber grader to decide whether a shipment complies with the contract. The expert looks

---

[181]See Horwitz, The Transformation of American Law 145-151 (1977); Note Commercial Arbitration in the Eighteen Century: Searching for the Transformation of American Law, 93 Yale Law Journal 135 (1983).

[182]Mentschikoff, Commercial Arbitration, 61 Columbia Law Review 846 (1961).

at the questioned lumber and announces its quality. The losing party pays the fee, which deters starting the procedure for trivial issues. Under the *adversary* model, the parties offer evidence and argument in hearings, and one or more arbitrators decide. It is roughly analogous to proceedings in court, but procedures can be quicker and less formal. In the *investigatory* model, representatives of an organization, such as a stock exchange, take responsibility for developing evidence and making a decision. We find this model where those who do business value membership in an association. Often the question is whether the association should allow a member to continue to participate in light of its actions.

a. Contrasting Views of Arbitration

Many people are enthusiastic about the potential for commercial arbitration as an answer to some of the problems involved in using courts to solve disputes.[183] They argue that a case which might take years to wend its way through the courts might be resolved in days in commercial arbitration.

> "The arbitration panel is there to give justice, not legal technicalities," says Michael Feiler, corporate attorney for the Continental Grain Company which will arbitrate 50 to 100 disputes a year, usually about weights or grades of grain. A case will take a few hours instead of years and sometimes it is even better to lose — "get the wrong decision," Mr. Feiler puts it — than "get litigated to death."...

Commercial arbitration may significantly reduce legal fees, and reduce the costs, in terms of fees and lost time, associated with depositions and other forms of discovery. The arbitrators, who usually serve without charge, are normally chosen from the business community and have an understanding of the issues. Architects would be chosen as arbitrators if the dispute involved architecture, and so on. In addition, the arbitration is usually final; there are few instances in which any kind of review is available. Finally, the arbitration process, unlike litigation, is secret. This means that people's business affairs are not exposed in public.[184]

Others, writing about arbitration, are less sanguine about its value.[185] They note that commercial arbitration, though usually cheaper than going to court can still be expensive and time-consuming. In addition, the procedures in arbitration

---

[183]See, for example, Flint, An Answer to Crowded Courts: Concerns Turn to Private Arbitration, New York Times, May 29, 1978, at D-1, col. 1.

[184]This might be counted as a disadvantage, from the point of view of the public, if the result were that business wrongdoing (like a price-fixing conspiracy, for example) were concealed.

[185]Greene, Flies in the Ointment, Forbes, June 20, 1983, at 141.

can become as rigid as litigation. In addition, there is a perception that arbitrators tend to "split the difference" rather than deciding the case in favor of either party. Such a compromise might work an injustice to someone whose claim is very strong. Many lawyers object to the use of arbitration. They argue that the lack of discovery procedures may deny claimants the opportunity to prevail on valid claims. They note that it is not that easy to find good commercial arbitrators, especially outside the fields (like the textile and construction industry) where arbitration is common. It may be especially difficult to find qualified arbitrators in big cases. Skeptics suggest that lawyers may object to arbitration because it impairs their chance to earn fees, and tends to reduce the chances for total victory.

Chapter 4

SOCIAL CONTROL OF FREE CONTRACT

We have already seen a number of limitations on free contract. The material in this chapter explores social control of contract in greater detail. The subject is controversial. Partisans fought political battles from the progressive era through the New Deal in the name of freedom of contract. These arguments, wearing slightly more modern dress, still are with us.

Taking a pure individualistic position, one can argue that because I have various abilities and rights and because society must support those abilities and rights rather than control them, I can make any contract I wish. If I make a good deal, I've won the game. If I make a bad one, that is just the price of freedom. Respect for me as an individual requires honoring my choices however they turn out. Relieving me of bad deals is an attack on my competence. There is no reason to assume that legislators, judges, or administrators know more than I do about what is best for me. Furthermore, I can learn from my own, or others, mistakes. We all benefit if people have reason to plan and deal with risk intelligently.

Most think that there is some truth in this position. Few, however, hold it without qualification. While most bargains may be a good thing, some are not. Suppose A and B make a contract to kill C. It could be a rational, cost effective, although immoral way for A to deal with problems caused by C. Nonetheless, performance of this contract would invade C's rights. It would injure C's friends, and those who are dependent upon C for economic support. Furthermore, everyone in a society has an interest in minimizing murder. There is no reason to allow A to sue B for breach of this contract. Indeed, we want to encourage B to breach it.

Insofar as we justify the institution of contract on the basis of choice, we may want to insist that people make real choices before they are bound to contracts. Suppose A drugs B so that B does not know what B is doing. A guides B's hand to sign a document labeled "Contract." Should the law enforce this bargain? An individualist defense of contract rests on choice. Despite his signature on the document, B's apparent choice was not a real one.[1] Some would want us to

---

[1] We wrote the sentence this way to make it easy to read. However, choices are not tangible things. What we want to call real choice is a mixture of facts and normative judgments. Our zombie hypothetical in the text seems a clear case. However, suppose A supplies a drug, whiskey for example. A suggests B have a drink. A keeps filling up B's glass. Under the norms of the community in which A and B live and work, one should not refuse the offer of a drink. B is very intoxicated when he signs the contract. Now is his choice real? If a court refuses to enforce this contract, is it because of B's lack of choice, A's bad conduct or a mixture of both?

examine B's conduct. If B could have avoided the problem, enforcing the transaction might offer an incentive for self reliance and care. It would be cheaper for B to avoid trouble than to have an official agency bail him out after A took advantage of him. Alternatively, A's fault might offend us enough to warrant denying him any advantage from drugging B.

How far can we push these ideas? Can we say that the legal system should refuse to enforce all contracts that impinge on the interests of those who are not parties to the transaction? Should the legal system refuse to enforce all deals in which the choice of one of the parties was not a real one? These are slippery slopes. Almost all contracts have impact on people who are not parties to the bargain. What kinds of impact warrant refusing to enforce deals? Also, we can view all choice as both free and constrained at the same time. How many constraints must there be before we see the consent in the transaction as flawed?

Writers and reformers also have advocated social control of contract based on other theories. Some call for making rules or applying them so that we redistribute wealth from the richer to the poorer in our society. Others advocate paternalism or maternalism. They say that legal agencies should take care of some, many or all people in the society. Rules should insure that bargains are fair. Some proposals focus on bargaining procedures to help people take care of themselves. Others seek to regulate particular terms or the content of entire contracts so that people do not make mistakes in entering disadvantageous or unfair transactions. Still others would have legal agencies intervene in particular transactions in the name of fairness.

Many of those taking these positions note that people are not equal in wealth, talent, or bargaining skill. A pure individualist contract law would allow the strong to prey on the weak. It would reward suspicion and penalize trust. It would magnify the advantages which the powerful already have. Distributional and paternal/maternal arguments usually oppose the virtues of individualism. These arguments also present their own slippery slope. How far should we go in trying to redistribute income? How far should we take care of what kinds of people? Must we just intuit that some interventions make sense while others do not?

Partisans in the free contract debate repeatedly make two other kinds of arguments. First, the costs of limiting free contract may be greater than the benefits of the regulation. For example, people in trouble may need to borrow money. It is not easy to find creditors willing to deal with people in economic trouble and regulation will make such loans even less attractive. Regulation in the form of usury laws, which limit the rate of interest lenders can charge, may actually create an illegal market. Some high risk debtors can't borrow money at the legal rate of interest. Loan sharks make loans at illegal rates of interest and since they cannot use the courts to aid in collecting their debts, they fashion their own private government, relying on threats of physical violence to encourage payment.

Second, it is not easy for legal agencies to regulate the process of making contracts or their content. Even assuming we want contracts policed, we must ask whether judges or administrators have the capability to regulate bargains. Suppose that a legislature passes a statute allowing courts to overturn bargains that are unfair. Standards such as fair, unreasonable or unconscionable are difficult to define. When we fashion working definitions they still are difficult to apply. Lawyers face difficulty in proving the circumstances surrounding a transaction and its impact. Some problems, perhaps, cannot be solved without basic structural changes in our society beyond the power of judges or administrators. Attempting to react on a case-by-case basis might distract us from seeing the need for these changes.

Whatever your initial reaction to these arguments, you must recognize that there is a great deal of social control of contract. Contracts to commit crimes may themselves be crimes. Courts have long refused to enforce most illegal contracts or those against public policy. Antitrust laws forbid contracts that limit competition. The law of fraud and duress limit bargaining tactics. Contracts with governmental units must contain promises not to discriminate on the grounds of race, sex, or religion. Employers may have to pay a minimum wage. Contracts to buy and sell insurance and corporate securities are subject to elaborate regulation. Obviously, we could offer many other examples.

In this chapter, we will look at two forms of social control of contract. First, we will consider contracts challenged because they adversely affect third parties. Usually, lawyers talk about illegal contracts and contracts against public policy. A party wanting out of a contract may argue that a court should not enforce the contract because it was socially undesirable. It has negative externalities. Some or all of us would be better off if people did not make such deals. It might be easier for courts if they said that contracts to do anything prohibited by criminal law were bad but all others were good, but they have not adopted this standard.

Second, we will consider contracts that a party challenges because something is wrong with his choice or consent. For example, a victim may have signed a document called a contract. However, the drafter of the document may have tricked the victim. The victim wouldn't have signed had he understood what the document said. Both the drafter and the person negotiating the contract may have taken steps which they hoped would mislead the victim. Should the law focus on the wickedness of the trickery or on the victim's failure to be self-reliant? Is all fair in love, war, and capitalism or should the legal system reinforce trust and demand altruism? Is it a matter of what's right or what's efficient?

We will spend a great deal of time on the many meanings of choice and consent. We will, however, watch carefully to see whether a choice analysis makes any sense in these cases. Perhaps some bargains are just too one-sided for courts to stomach whatever we conclude about choice. The classic example involves the criminal with a loaded gun who tells a person he finds on a lonely street, "give me your wallet or I'll shoot you." Sometimes we say that the victim didn't have a *real* choice. On the contrary, the choice offered the victim is all too real. Nonetheless, our courts do not want to give this choice any legal effect.

A. SOCIAL CONTROL AND THE INTERESTS OF OTHERS

1. ILLEGAL CONTRACTS

a. Introduction

Contracts to commit serious crimes are crimes themselves. Not surprisingly, the courts usually refuse to enforce these contracts. Furthermore, in most instances, a party to an illegal contract cannot recover restitution to get back what he has paid to have another break the law. Nonetheless, neither the criminal law nor the court's refusal to enforce illegal contracts deter all of these agreements. People do make deals to murder others. Illegal markets such as the drug trade involve all kinds of bargains. There are private governments offering sanctions that usually deter breaches of these contracts.[2] However, even if we think that few people will be deterred from making such deals by their legal unenforceability, courts' refusals to support them make an important symbolic statement.

b. Illegality: Form and Substance

Courts have long extended the illegal contract doctrine beyond contracts that state openly that their object is to commit crimes. *Everet v. Williams* is the celebrated "Highwayman's Case," decided by the Court of Exchequer in 1725. Apparently, the case involved an agreement between two highwaymen to share the expenses and the proceeds of crime. The pleadings, however, do not say this in so many words.

> [T]he Bill alleged that "the plaintiff was skilled in dealing in several commodities, such as plate, rings, watches, &c.; that the defendant applied to him to become a partner; and that they entered into partnership, and it was agreed that they should equally provide all sorts of necessaries, such as horses, saddles, bridles, and equally bear all expenses on the roads and at inns, taverns, alehouses, markets and fairs; that the plaintiff and the defendant proceeded jointly in the said business with good success on Hounslow Heath, where they dealt with a Gentleman for a gold watch; and afterwards the defendant told the Plaintiff that Finchley, in the County of Middlesex, was a good and convenient place to deal in, and that commodi-

---

[2]See Reuter, "Social Control in Illegal Markets," in Toward a General Theory of Social Control, Vol. II, at 29 (D. Black ed., Academic Press 1984). Two of Reuter's section headings are "The Mafia as a Dispute-Settlement System," and "The Mafia, Arbitration, and Extortion."

ties were very plenty at Finchley, and it would be almost clear gain to them; that they went accordingly, and dealt with several gentlemen for divers watches, rings, swords, canes, hats, cloaks, horses, bridles, saddles and other things; that about a month afterwards the defendant informed the plaintiff there was a Gentleman at Blackheath who had a good horse, saddle, bridle, watch, sword cane, and other things to dispose of, which he believe might be had for little or no money; that they accordingly went and met with the said Gentleman, and after some small discourse they dealt for the said horse, &c.; that the plaintiff and defendant continued their joint dealings together until Michaelmas, and dealt together at several places ... to the amount of 2000 pounds and upwards."... The rest of the Bill was in the ordinary form for a partnership account. The Bill is said to have been dismissed, with costs, to be paid by the Counsel who signed it; and the Plaintiff and the Defendant were, it is said, both hanged and one of the Solicitors for the Plaintiff was afterwards transported.

Another account is that the Solicitor was ordered to be led around Westminster Hall, when the Court was sitting, with the obnoxious Bill cut in strings and hung around his neck.[3]

The following case takes an approach different from that taken in *Everet v. Williams*. The plaintiff's lawyer wrote to us that "as far as I was concerned, this was purely a business transaction between two persons who had made a deal for the sale of property." The court agreed, refusing to look through the form of the transaction to its substance.

EDNA CARROLL v. AGNES BEARDON

381 P.2d 295 (Montana, 1963).

HARRISON, J. This is an appeal from a judgment ... in favor of plaintiff-respondent [Carroll] and against defendant-appellant [Beardon]....

On March 15, 1960, Edna Carroll ... and Agnes Beardon ... executed instruments in writing, one a warranty deed from respondent to appellant, and a note and mortgage back from appellant to respondent for the sale of a building and acreage in the amount of $42,000. A down payment of $8,000 was made at the time of the sale, and the note and mortgage provided that the appellant would pay to respondent monthly, the sum of $1,000 for the months of January through June and $2,000 for the months of July through December. The appellant paid one monthly payment. In September 1960, a mortgage foreclosure action was instituted by the respondent setting forth the ... facts, showing a sum due in the

---

[3]Riddell, A Legal Scandal Two Hundred Years Ago, 16 A.B.A.J. 422 (1930). Reprinted with the permission of the ABA Journal, the Lawyer's Magazine, published by the American Bar Association.

amount of $41,805.53 for the building, personal property and 50 acres of land located in Toole County.

So far the facts in the case set forth an ordinary real estate transaction with a default by the purchaser, and it is not until the appellant's answer is read that the court finds itself trying to settle a dispute of two madams over a house of prostitution. The appellant alleges by way of her answer that although she secured the deed for the property, gave the note and mortgage, and entered into possession, that the mortgage is absolutely void as contrary to express law, and public policy; that the alleged mortgage was entered into in furtherance of prostitution in violation of the laws of the State of Montana and intended by respondent Carroll and the appellant Beardon so to be, and was entered into by the parties hereto with the knowledge, intent and purpose on their part that the said property would be used for the purpose of prostitution in violation of the laws of the State of Montana; and that prior to, and on the date of the consummation of this illegal transaction, prostitution was the only activity at the so-called Hillside Ranch.

While neither counsel had the effrontery to parade these indignant madams before the court, their depositions speak for them, and are most enlightening. Both admit that they are madams, in the limited sense of the word, and have operated this valuable piece of property, known as the Hillside Ranch as a house of prostitution, the respondent some four years prior to the sale, and the appellant since that date. Both admit to the sale of liquor without a state license, but the respondent deposed she had a federal license, leaving the court to wonder whether she is a strong central government supporter, or a more careful business woman. The appellant's position concerning these lawful taxes seems to be that her payments going from $1,000 per month to $2,000 per month during the harvest months and the Christmas season, that she could not afford the luxury of taxation.

Counsel on both sides of the case dig deep in legal lore to convince the court of the righteousness of their client's cause.... Many courts refuse to aid either party to contracts where the transaction is illegal.... A review of the evidence put before the court in this case tempts this court to dismiss the appeal. However, there are many decisions to the effect that where the sale is of property that may or may not be used for an illegal purpose, that it is no defense that the seller knew the purpose of the buyer, without further evidence implicating the seller.... In the absence of active participation, the defense of illegality is ordinarily not available to the party who has breached the contract, where the fault and illegality are unilateral on her side of the transaction.... The bare knowledge of the purpose for which the property is sold is not enough to raise the valid defense of illegality....

It is also important to consider the fact that the defendant has had the benefit of this contract for several years. Her status naturally does not appeal to the favor of this court, and in order to sustain such a defense a party who has reaped its benefits must show more active participation by the seller than has been shown here....

[T]his same question, raising the illegality of the sale of gambling equipment was before the Supreme Court of Wyoming in the case of Fuchs v. Goe, 62 Wyo. 134, 163 P.2d 783, 166 A.L.R. 1329.... In the Fuchs case, as in this case, after the sale of the property, the seller had no connection with the business. The court, quoting from 32 Am.Jur. 68-69, 49, in the Fuchs case in this connection stated:

> ... in order to defeat a recovery for rent by the lessor it must be shown that he participated in some degree, however slight, in the wrongful purpose and intended the property be so used, and that mere indifference on his part as to the intended use of the premises is not sufficient to bar his recovery. Mere knowledge on the lessor's part that the lessee will use the premises for an unlawful purpose does not make the lessor a participant in that purpose; for mere knowledge that the lessee may or will use the premises for an unlawful purpose is not of itself sufficient to show that the lessor intended that they must or shall be so used....

Finding ample evidence in the record to sustain the trial court's findings and conclusions, *the judgment appealed from is affirmed....*

ADAIR, J. (concurring in part and dissenting in part): I concur in the result, but not in all that is said in the above opinion. This is a case of the pot calling the kettle black. However, the calling of names will not pay the promissory note nor discharge nor invalidate the mortgage upon which this action is brought. Each party to the contract is required to keep her promises and to perform her obligations thereunder....

NOTES AND QUESTIONS

1. *Explaining the court's decision: What is active participation?* Suppose in *Everet v. Williams*, the Highwayman's case, Joseph Williams had agreed to supply John Everet with "horses, saddles, bridles" and to "bear all expenses on the roads and at inns, taverns, alehouses, markets and fairs." Everet, in turn, promised to use his skill "in dealing in several commodities" on Hounslow Heath and in Finchley in the County of Middlesex to rob such people as the Gentleman at Blackheath. Would the approach of the Supreme Court of Montana call for the enforcement of their contract?

Suppose, instead, Williams sold Everet "horses, saddles and bridles" for cash, knowing what Everet planned to do with them. Would this contract be enforceable? The Supreme Court of Montana stresses that the vendor was not running the prostitution operation at the Hillside Ranch at the time of the suit. However, suppose the $42,000 price was greater than the value of the land had it been devoted to other purposes. Suppose, in other words, Agnes Beardon paid Edna Carroll for a going illegal business. Does "the active participation test" allow you to judge whether a court should refuse to enforce a contract in that event? Remember that Edna Carroll received more under the contract during the harvest and holiday seasons when business was likely to be better.

2. *Explaining the court's decision — "local option?"* To what extent, if at all, does the court's opinion reflect the judges' attitude about crimes such as gambling or prostitution? Justice Harrison seems to find the transaction amusing, and his opinion is playful. Both opinions seem concerned about "windfalls to the wicked." Madam Beardon is asking to keep a going business free of the obligation to pay for it. Everet and Williams "were, it was said, both hanged." What was likely to happen to Madam Beardon if the court accepted the defense of illegality?

Usually, we assume laws apply throughout a state. However, when many states repealed laws prohibiting the sale of alcoholic beverages, they expressly allowed counties or cities to exercise local option and continue prohibition. In many, if not all, states there is a tacit local option to apply state laws governing gambling and prostitution. Most law enforcement is in the hands of local officials. Both police and prosecutors have discretion concerning when to enforce which laws. If a community is at least indifferent to gambling and prostitution, police and prosecutors often will spend little effort trying to prosecute these crimes. When these crimes are prosecuted, sometimes juries refuse to convict.

We can guess from the court's opinion that the Hillside Ranch had been in business for at least five years. We can also guess that police and prosecutors knew of its existence and didn't enforce the law. In effect, the Supreme Court of Montana decided to leave matters to the discretion of law enforcement officials in Shelby, Montana. The citizens who influence affairs there may not find prostitution particularly objectionable when it is out of sight at the Hillside Ranch. This explanation is speculative since not a word in the opinion suggests anything of the sort. Although speculative, is it realistic or just cynical?

c. Comparative Fault

One of the problems with the defense of illegality is that the punishment may not fit the crime. The court leaves the parties where it finds them. It may reward one by leaving him with the fruits of the crime. It may penalize the other by leaving her out of pocket what she has contributed to the enterprise. This may provide an incentive to complete criminal transactions rather than back out before doing harm. Furthermore, courts long have recognized that a flat approach may be too blunt and unrefined. One party may have planned the criminal transaction while the other just went along. The maxim *in pari delicto potior est conditio defendentis vel possidentis* translates as "if (when) the parties are in equal guilt, the defendant or the possessor is in a better position." However, when the parties are not *in pari delicto,* then courts often make some adjustment.

Professor Leon Trakman[4] notes that New Zealand legislation authorizes a court to grant "relief to any party to an illegal contract ... as the Court in its discretion thinks just."[5] He says this standard reflects modern common law practice with or without express legislative authorization. Trakman makes a legal realist argument to defend this approach, saying:

> ... critics have contended that the exercise of judicial discretion will lead to unwarrantable capriciousness in the decision-making process. In reality, the risk of judicial arbitrariness is significantly reduced in view of the controls inherent within the common law system. Thus, the demand that judges give logical reasons for their decisions achieves both a public scrutiny of the decision-making process and the possibility that unsound judgments will be reversed on appeal. Judicial consistency is maintained by the requirement that courts reflect upon past experiences in the legal system.... [J]udicial arbitrariness is limited by rules of evidence and procedure which require courts to make determinations only after evaluating all relevant evidence, properly elicited and considered.
>
> Greater difficulty is posed by the suggestion that courts are insufficiently equipped to weigh normative public policy considerations which often contradict each other and fluctuate with time. Yet, even this criticism is rebutted by the attributes of the living common law. For, the fact that courts are constantly exposed to factual situations forces them to develop the "situation sense," necessary to make essentially "non-legal" decisions. In addition, judicial precedent compels common law judges to reflect upon the significance of previous fact situations. Finally, the rules of evidence require that courts give credence to party witnesses, including experts summoned to give testimony on issues of fact.
>
> However, the final fetter upon the judiciary lies in their capacity to develop meaningful methods of determining the effects of illegality through the evolutionary process of judicious experimentation and example.

Do you think the materials that follow support Professor Trakman's position? Or do they support the critics who are alarmed by what they see as judicial arbitrariness?

---

[4]Trakman, The Effect of Illegality in the Law of Contract: Suggestions for Reform, 55 Canadian Bar Review/La Revue du Barreau Canadien 627, 652-4 (1977). Contrast Professor Feinman's criticism of the discretionary approach called for by Restatement (Second) of Contracts § 90.

[5]See The Illegal Contracts Act, 1970, S.N.Z., 1970, c. 129, s.7(1).

JOHN G. GATES v. RIVERS CONSTRUCTION CO., INC.

515 P.2d 1020 (Supreme Court of Alaska, 1973)

BOOCHEVER, J. A contract of employment was entered into in Alaska by a Canadian alien. The trial court held it to be in violation of the immigration and nationality laws of the United States, and held that the alien was barred by the illegality of the contract from securing recovery of sums allegedly due. This appeal has been taken from that decision.

In late February or early March of 1969, John G. Gates traveled from his home in Alberta, Canada, to Fairbanks, Alaska. His expenses were paid by Guy Rivers, acting on behalf of Rivers Construction Co. and General Construction Co., Inc. Gates entered into discussions with Rivers and, as a result, agreed to engage in public relations work in order to obtain construction contracts for the two companies. The work was to be performed in Alaska, and Gates was to receive a salary of $1,400 or $1,600 per month,[6] commencing immediately; the funds were to be placed in trust for him in a bank in Alaska and were to be paid to him when, and only when, he obtained a visa to remain in the United States as a landed alien or permanent resident. The arrangement to withhold his salary was made for the reason that both Gates and Rivers believed that Gates could not lawfully remain in Alaska and perform services for a salary without first having received certification of permanent resident status.

Gates' employment was terminated by the companies on December 4, 1970. He became a landed alien or "permanent resident" on December 11, 1970. In February of 1971 he filed suit against the two corporations alleging that no payment of the salary which was to have been held in trust for him had been made. The companies answered admitting that services were performed and denying other allegations of the complaint.

At the conclusion of appellant's case in the court below, the companies moved to dismiss on the grounds that the contract of employment was in violation of the immigration laws. Section 1182(a)(14) of 8 United States Code provides in part:

(a) Except as otherwise provided in this chapter, the following classes of aliens shall be ineligible to receive visas and shall be excluded from admission into the United States.

... (14) Aliens seeking to enter the United States, for the purpose of performing skilled or unskilled labor, unless the Secretary of Labor has determined and certified to the Secretary of State and to the Attorney General that (A) there are not sufficient workers in the United States who are able, willing, qualified, and available at the time of application for a visa and admission to the United States and at the place to which the alien is

---

[6]The salary was fixed at $1,400 per month in July of 1969 when Gates filed an application for permanent residence.

destined to perform such skilled or unskilled labor, and (B) the employment of such aliens will not adversely affect the wages and working conditions of the workers in the United States similarly employed....

The court granted the motion to dismiss, concluding that the contract of employment was "in violation of law, and as such, is a contract contrary to public policy, is void, and is unenforceable." From the judgment of dismissal, this appeal has been taken.

Generally, a party to an illegal contract cannot recover damages for its breach. But as in the case of many such simplifications, the exceptions and qualifications to the general rule are numerous and complex. Thus, when a statute imposes sanctions but does not specifically declare a contract to be invalid, it is necessary to ascertain whether the legislature intended to make unenforceable contracts entered into in violation of the statute.

> Among the factors taken into consideration by the courts are the language of the statute; its nature, object, and purpose; and its subject matter and reach; the wrong or evil which the statute seeks to remedy or prevent; the nature of the prohibited act as malum in se or malum prohibitum; the class of persons sought to be controlled; the legislative history; the effect of holding contracts in violation of the statute void; and the later repeal of the statute by a new act which specifically provides that a contract in contravention thereof should be void. If, from all these factors, it is manifest that the statute was not intended to render the prohibited act void, the courts will construe the statute accordingly (footnotes omitted).[7]

Applying these considerations to this case, it is clear that the contract involved here should be enforced. First, it is apparent that the statute itself does not specifically declare the labor or service contracts of aliens seeking to enter the United States for the purpose of performing such labor or services to be void. The statute only specifies that aliens who enter this country for such purpose, without having received the necessary certification, "shall be ineligible to receive visas and shall be excluded from admission into the United States."

Second, that the appellee, who knowingly participated in an illegal transaction, should be permitted to profit thereby at the expense of the appellant is a harsh and undesirable consequence of the doctrine that illegal contracts are not to be enforced. This result, so contrary to general considerations of equity and fairness, should be countenanced only when clearly demonstrated to have been intended by the legislature. Third, since the purpose of this section would appear to be the safeguarding of American labor from unwanted competition, the appellant's contract should be enforced because such an objective would not be

---

[7] Annot., 55 A.L.R.2d 488-90.

furthered by permitting employers knowingly to employ excludable aliens and then, with impunity, to refuse to pay them for their services. Indeed, to so hold could well have the opposite effect from the one intended, by encouraging employers to enter into the very type of contracts sought to be prevented.

We find no such clear command indicated by the language or general purposes to be accomplished by the statute in question. Our conclusion in that regard is further bolstered by the fact that the predecessor to the present statute expressly made such contracts void and of no effect:

> All contracts or agreements, express or implied, parol, or special, which may hereafter be made by and between any person, company, partnership, or corporation, and any foreigner or foreigners, alien or aliens, to perform labor or service or having reference to the performance of labor or service by any person in the United States, its Territories, or the District of Columbia previous to the migration or importation of the person or persons whose labor or service is contracted for into the United States, *shall be utterly void and of no effect* (emphasis added).[8]

That provision was repealed by the Immigration and Nationality Act of 1952 and was replaced with what is now 8 U.S.C. § 1182(a)(14), which does not make such contracts void, but merely provides, as a deterrent, for ineligibility to receive visas and for exclusion from admission into the United States. The repeal of the former section coupled with the new enactment evinces an intent on the part of Congress that such contracts are no longer to be "void and of no effect." Apparently, Congress determined that the exclusion of certain aliens from admission to the United States was a more satisfactory sanction than rendering their contracts void and thus unjustifiably enriching employers of such alien laborers.

There are no cases construing § 1182(a)(14) with reference to this issue. Cases interpreting the former § 141 are obviously of little value in view of the material changes in its provisions.[9] Even under the former section, however, one court

---

[8]Act of Feb. 26, 1885, ch. 164, § 2, 23 Stat. 332 (formerly 8 U.S.C. § 141) (repealed 1952).

[9]See Coules v. Pharris, 212 Wis. 558, 250 N.W. 404 (1933), where it was held that an alien employed in a candy shop could not recover the wages he had earned. [Eds. Note: The Wisconsin court effectively overruled Coules in Arteaga v. Literski, 83 Wis.2d 128, 265 N.W.2d 148 (1978), noting that "... if the policy is to discourage illegal immigration, that policy is not furthered by refusing aliens access to the courts." But in Roberto v. Hartford Fire Ins. Co., 177 F.2d 811, 813 (7th Cir. 1949), the court wrote:

> We need not pause to consider whether the decision in the Coules case is sound law, except to say that we know of no case which has followed it or cited it with approval.

But see Tompkins v. Seattle Constr. & Dry Dock Co., 96 Wash. 511, 165 P. 384 (1917). An alien who had been paid for all services performed prior to the termination of his contract was prohibited

permitted an alien who had entered the United States illegally to recover for services rendered under a contract which, as here, was entered into after the alien had entered the United States.[10] The court stated:

> An examination of this enactment reveals that the contracts or agreements that are denounced and rendered unenforcible [sic] are only those made "previous" to the migration or importation into the United States of the person or persons whose labor or service is contracted for. It does not declare void or in any manner vitiate contracts or agreements made after their entry into the United States, even though such entry and continued presence is unlawful. The sole penalties prescribed for unlawful entry are deportation or fine and imprisonment; no civil rights or right to sue or seek redress in judicial tribunals is denied to an alien here under the circumstances mentioned, and I do not see how it can be read into the statute without violation basic rules of statutory construction.[11]

Because a subsequent harsher statute is at best a contemporary legislative interpretation of the former statute, the rationale for enforcing the contract is all the more compelling here, where the legislature which enacted the law being construed by us has expressly abrogated the harsher enactment. For the reasons set forth above, we therefore conclude that it was error to enter a judgment of dismissal, and the case is remanded for completion of the trial. Reversed and remanded.

NOTES AND QUESTIONS

1. *Repentance*: In *Greenberg v. Evening Post Ass'n*,[12] the court applied another qualification to the illegal contract doctrine based on a balancing of fault and a concern for incentives. The Hartford Post employed Fitch to run a contest to increase its circulation. One of the prizes was an automobile worth $2,500. Greenberg entered the contest. Fitch told him that only a person willing to put money into the contest could win. If Greenberg were willing to pay Fitch $300, Fitch would see that Greenberg won the automobile. Greenberg paid $300 to Fitch. Two weeks later, Fitch demanded another $100. Greenberg sought legal advice. His lawyer said that he was a party to a fraudulent scheme and should repudiate the whole transaction. Greenberg demanded his money and sued Fitch. Fitch left the state, and so Greenberg sued the publisher of the newspaper. A jury

---

from recovering for the alleged breach of that contract, due to illegality under former § 141. See also Valdez v. Viking Athletic Ass'n, 349 Ill.App. 376, 110 N.E.2d 680, 682-683 (1953).

[10]Dezsofi v. Jacoby, 178 Misc. 851, 36 N.Y.S.2d 672 (Sup.Ct.N.Y. 1942).

[11]*Id.* at 675.

[12]91 Conn. 371, 99 Atl. 1037 (1917).

found for Greenberg. The Supreme Court of Connecticut said, "we think the jury might reasonably have found that the defendant actually received the $300 paid by the plaintiff to Fitch, less Fitch's commission of 20 per cent — although it seems that the money was not received by the defendant in a lump sum, or with knowledge that it came from the plaintiff." The judgment was affirmed.

The court said that the "question is whether it is not quite as consistent with sound public policy to encourage the prompt repudiation of illegal and immoral contracts by permitting, under such circumstances, the recovery of money paid upon an illegal or immoral consideration, as to declare the money forfeit the moment it is paid, and thus discourage repentance in such cases." The court decided that the trial court had charged the jury correctly. A plaintiff may recover money paid to carry out an illegal or immoral design if the arrangement was repudiated with reasonable promptness. The plaintiff must back out before the other party acts to put into effect any part of the illegal or immoral design.

Is this an example supporting Professor Trakman's argument about judicial competence to make the necessary policy judgments in such cases?

JOHN KARPINSKI v. GENE COLLINS AND RUTH COLLINS

252 Cal. App. 2d 711, 60 Cal. Rptr. 846 (Ct. App. 1st Dist., 1967)

[If you are using Danzig, *The Capability Problem in Contract Law*, as a supplement to this text, you should read this case and associated materials at pp. 129-147 of those materials. For other students, the case is reproduced below.]

SHOEMAKER, J. Plaintiff John Karpinski brought this action against defendants Gene and Ruth Collins and the Santa Clara Creamery to recover secret rebates which plaintiff was allegedly compelled to pay defendants in order to secure and retain a Grade A contract for the sale of plaintiff's milk.

Plaintiff, the sole witness at the trial, was a dairyman. Prior to April 1962, he had sold his milk to a cheese factory under a contract entitling him to what in the business is called the Grade B price, which was established by the federal government and was approximately 60 percent of the Grade A price, which was established by the state. (The Grade A price was 44 cents per gallon and the Grade B price 27 cents per gallon.) Plaintiff testified that it was financially impossible for a dairyman in the Santa Clara Valley to remain in business without a Grade A contract.

Around April 1, 1962, defendant Gene Collins, the president of the Santa Clara Creamery, called on plaintiff and offered him a Grade A contract for the sale of his milk if plaintiff would pay him a rebate or "kickback" of 4 1/2 cents a gallon during the life of the contract. Plaintiff accepted the offer because no other Grade A contracts were available and he had no other choice.

On April 1, 1962, a formal contract was prepared whereby plaintiff agreed to sell the Santa Clara Creamery 51,600 pounds of Grade A milk per month, and the creamery agreed to purchase said milk at the Grade A price for the Santa Clara marketing area. The contract was terminable by either party upon 30 days' notice.

Thereafter, plaintiff furnished the milk and was paid the specified price. President Collins would then bill plaintiff for monthly "feeding charges" in an amount equal to the agreed rebate of 4 1/2 cents per gallon of milk delivered. No feeding services were ever performed by Collins or the Santa Clara Creamery.

Approximately one year after the contract had gone into effect, Collins informed plaintiff that he needed money to pay off a debt or he would lose the creamery; that if he did not loan him $6,500, Collins would terminate his contract and find another dairyman who could raise the money. Collins promised to repay the loan by reducing the rebate 1 1/2 cents per gallon during the life of plaintiff's contract.

Plaintiff obtained the $6,500 and gave it to Collins in exchange for a promissory note dated April 16, 1963, signed by Collins and his wife. Plaintiff thereafter paid Collins a rebate of only 3 cents per gallon of milk delivered.

Plaintiff subsequently fell behind in the payment of his monthly rebates, making no payments after October 1963. By letter of May 22, 1964, Collins advised plaintiff that his contract had been terminated. Plaintiff was unable to obtain another Grade A milk contract and ultimately disposed of his dairy.

Plaintiff testified that during the life of his contract with the Santa Clara Creamery, his payments to Collins had totaled $10,677.72, which sum consisted of the $6,500 loan and $4,177.72 in secret rebates.

Upon the facts, the court concluded that plaintiff was entitled to judgment against defendants Gene and Ruth Collins in the amount of $6,500 and against defendant Gene Collins in the additional amount of $4,177.72.

Judgment was accordingly entered, and defendants Collins appeal therefrom.

Defendants contend that the judgment must be reversed because the trial court erred in its findings that plaintiff was not *in pari delicto* with defendants; that he was a member of the class protected by § 4280, subdivision (a), of the Agricultural Code; and that he was entitled to recover from defendants the sums illegally paid to secure and obtain the Grade A milk contract.

Defendants point out that § 4280, subdivision (a), is applicable to milk producers as well as to milk distributors and prohibits the acceptance as well as the payment of secret rebates, and assert that the evidence in the instant case establishes as a matter of law that plaintiff violated the statute and was therefore *in pari delicto* with defendants. They rely upon ... (citations omitted) as authority for the general rule that an illegal contract furnishes no basis for an action either in law or in equity. However, in our case, the situation is not one in which the two parties, who were equally at fault, made the joint decision to enter into a transaction violative of § 4280, subdivision (a), of the Agricultural Code. The trial court found that "because of his position," plaintiff was not *in pari delicto* with defendants. It is obvious that by plaintiff's "position," the court had reference to the fact that plaintiff was a small dairyman whose economic survival was dependent upon his ability to obtain a Grade A milk contract in a locality where such contracts were extremely scarce and that he was therefore peculiarly vulnerable to the exertion of economic coercion by a person such as defendant, who was apparently unwilling to do business with any dairyman who would not agree to pay him unlawful rebates. Under these circumstances, we are satisfied that the court correctly determined that the case came within a well-recognized exception to the rule of *in pari delicto* and that since plaintiff was only slightly at fault and defendants were grievously at fault, plaintiff was entitled to recover what he had rendered as performance of the executed illegal transaction....

Defendants also point out that the purpose of the Milk Stabilization Act (Agr.Code, §§ 4200-4420) is to eliminate unfair, unjust, destructive and demoralizing trade practices in the producing, marketing, sale, processing or distribution of milk, which tend to undermine regulations and standards of the content and purity, and to insure a reasonable amount of stability and prosperity in the marketing of milk.... Defendants assert that § 4280, subdivision (a), and certain other provisions of the Milk Stabilization Act which prohibit unfair trade practices, are very similar to the Unfair Practices Act (Bus. & Prof.Code, §§ 17000-17101) and that both acts should be applied in the same manner. Since § 17051 of the Business and Professions Code provides that any contract made in violation of the Unfair Practices Act is illegal and affords no basis for recovery, defendants reason that the same rule should apply to contracts made in violation of § 4280, subdivision (a) of the Agricultural Code.

No provision similar to § 17051 of the Business and Professions Code is contained in the Milk Stabilization Act. Undoubtedly the Legislature in enacting the Milk Stabilization Act saw no necessity for including such a directive and being familiar with the doctrine of *in pari delicto* and the courts' application thereof, left the matters arising under the act to be dealt with by the courts as the facts of each case might warrant.

Judgment affirmed. Agee and Taylor, JJ., concur.

2. CONTRACTS AGAINST PUBLIC POLICY

a. Introduction

Courts have long asserted the power to refuse to enforce contracts or provisions in contracts which are against public policy. While the doctrine appears to call for judicial regulation of bargains, courts have used it primarily in limited well-defined areas. The Restatement (Second) of Contracts §§ 178-199 deals with the subject. In § 178 it sets a general standard, saying that a promise is unenforceable if "the interest in its enforcement is clearly outweighed in the circumstances by a public policy against the enforcement of such terms." It then sets out a complex balancing test. Courts are to weigh such things as the forfeiture resulting if they deny enforcement against the seriousness of any misconduct involved and the extent to which it was deliberate.

Contracts in restraint of trade (§§ 186-188) and contracts that impair family relations (§§ 189-191) are two long established areas subject to supervision on grounds of public policy. Other promises usually denied enforcement are promises to commit a tort (§ 192); promises to violate a fiduciary duty (§ 193); promises to interfere with the performance of a contract of another (§ 194); terms exempting from liability for harm caused intentionally, recklessly or negligently (§ 195); and terms exempting a party from the legal consequences of misrepresentation (§ 196). Restitution usually is also unavailable "unless denial of restitution would cause disproportionate forfeiture" (§ 197).

b. Covenants by Employees not to Compete

A classic application of the public policy doctrine involves covenants by employees not to compete if they resign. What is involved? On one hand, an employer does not have to hire anyone. It can choose to give up this freedom not to hire only if employees agree to particular terms. If it wants to demand such a promise, then, absent fraud or the like, we could view it as an application of free contract. Furthermore, employers seek to protect a real interest by demanding contract provisions against competition by former employees. Employers invest a great deal training employees, and they expect this investment to pay off in the future. Moreover, employees may learn trade secrets such as manufacturing processes, business strategy, and the characteristics of potential customers. Employees often establish long-term continuing relationships with customers who will follow them when they move to other employers or open their own businesses. Employees get the chance to create and develop these relationships through the investment of employers.

Nonetheless, courts, in the name of public policy, carefully police employee covenants not to compete. We must ask why they do this, and what the likely impact of their effort is?

FULLERTON LUMBER CO. v. ALBERT TORBORG

270 WIS. 133, 70 N.W.2D 585 (1955)

[If you are using Danzig, *The Capability Problem in Contract Law*, as a supplement to this text, you should read this case and associated materials at pp. 44-67. For other students, the case is reproduced below. Because the case has been edited somewhat differently for these materials, including portions of the opinion edited out in the Danzig materials, even students using the Danzig materials may get some benefit from reading the opinion in these materials.]

Action by plaintiff Fullerton Lumber Company, a foreign corporation, against defendant Albert C. Torborg, for an injunction restraining defendant from breach of contract. Upon findings of fact and conclusions of law filed by the trial court, judgment was entered dismissing plaintiff's complaint. From that judgment plaintiff appeals.

Plaintiff is a Minnesota corporation with its principal office in Minneapolis. It operates a number of retail lumber yards in Wisconsin and other states. Defendant began working for the plaintiff in a managerial capacity in 1938. In December 1942 he entered the military service and when he returned to civilian life in November 1945 he was rehired by the company and placed in charge of a yard at Gaylord, Minnesota. At the time of his rehiring he was advised that the pension plan provided for the company's employees had been made applicable to managers who had been employed five years; that the time spent in military service could be counted in the five-year period required to qualify; and that it was the company's policy to require employment agreements with employees who were eligible to participate in such plan. In March 1946 defendant was transfered to Clintonville, Wisconsin, as manager of the company's yard there. On April 15, 1946 he entered into an employment contract with the company which provided, in part:

> If, I cease to be employed by the company for any reason; I will not, for a period of ten years thereafter, work directly or indirectly for any establishment or on my own account handling lumber, building material or fuel at retail in any city, village or town, or within a radius of fifteen miles thereof, where I have served as manager for the company within a period of five years preceding the date of termination of my employment, unless first obtaining permission, in writing, from the company.

... In November 1953 [Torborg] voluntarily quit, advising plaintiff that he intended to open his own lumber yard in that city. He thereafter incorporated the Clintonville Lumber and Supply, Inc. and on December 1, 1953 commenced business in Clintonville, taking with him three other of the plaintiff's Clintonville yard employees.

Plaintiff thereafter brought this action to enjoin defendant from working for the Clintonville Lumber and Supply, Inc., for himself or for any other lumber and fuel business within a radius of fifteen miles of Clintonville during a period of ten years following the termination of his employment by the plaintiff, as provided in that portion of the contract set out above. The trial court found that the restraint as to time was unreasonably long and not reasonably necessary for the fair protection of plaintiff's business, and granted judgment dismissing the complaint....

MARTIN, J. ...There is no question that restrictive covenants of the type involved in this contract are lawful and enforceable if they meet the tests of necessity and reasonableness.

As stated in Restatement of the Law, Contracts, § 516 ...:

> The following bargains do not impose unreasonable restraint of trade unless effecting, or forming part of a plan to effect, a monopoly: ...
> (f) A bargain by an assistant, servant, or agent not to compete with his employer, or principal, during the term of the employment or agency, or thereafter, within such territory and during such time as may be reasonably necessary for the protection of the employer or principal, without imposing undue hardship on the employee or agent.

At § 515 ... of the same text it is stated:

> A restraint of trade is unreasonable, in the absence of statutory authorization or dominant social or economic justification, if it
> (a) is greater than is required for the protection of the person for whose benefit the restraint is imposed....

It is established that:

> The burden rests upon the employer to establish both the necessity for, and the reasonableness of, the restrictive covenant he seeks to enforce by enjoining the employee from violating its terms. Annotation, 52 A.L.R. 1364.

Cases such as ... (citations omitted), where this court has upheld restrictive covenants, are not very helpful in this instance because they grow out of the sale of a business rather than employment. As pointed out in the Restatement of the Law, Contracts, § 515, Comment (b):

> No identical test of reasonableness applies to bargains for the transfer of land or goods or of a business, on the one hand, and to bargains for employment on the other. The elements that must be considered in order to determine reasonableness differ in the two cases, especially where the employment is of a specialized character, and familiarity and skill in it are assets of the employee. Limitations of his use of these assets are less readily supported than limitations of the use of property or in carrying on a business. See, also, Annotation 9 A.L.R. 1456, *et seq.*

Our court has consistently recognized this difference with respect to applying the test of reasonableness, *Milwaukee Linen Supply Co. v. Ring,* 1933, 210 Wis. 467, 246 N.W. 567, and has allowed a much greater scope of restraint in contracts between vendor and vendee than between employer and employee. As there stated, 210 Wis. at 473, 246 N.W. at 569, "There is 'small scope for the restraint of the right to labor and trade and a correspondingly small freedom of contract.' " In all these cases the facts must be carefully scrutinized to determine whether the employee is restrained beyond the point where he could be reasonably anticipated to injure his employer's business. Where the facts warrant such a conclusion this court has held that the entire covenant must fall.

> ... if full performance of a promise indivisible in terms, would involve unreasonable restraint, the promise is illegal and is not enforceable even for so much of the performance as would be a reasonable restraint. Restatement, Contracts, § 518.

We agree with the trial court that the ten-year period of restraint imposed by the instant contract is unreasonably long. There is no case cited where this court has upheld a covenant in an employment contract restricting the employee from engaging in competitive activity for so long a time, and the evidence in this case does not establish that a ten-year restraint is necessary for the protection of plaintiff's business.

It cannot be seriously disputed, however, that defendant was plaintiff's key employee in the Clintonville yard. Being a foreign corporation with all its officers and supervisory employees outside of the state, the plaintiff necessarily depended for the growth and maintenance of good will in the Clintonville area upon the efforts and personal assets of the defendant. In the first three years of his employment as manager there he tripled the business of the yard and thereafter (with the exception of 1952 when the entire country experienced a building "boom") he maintained the sales at a level averaging well over $200,000 per year. He terminated his employment at the end of 1953 and immediately commenced operations in Clintonville in competition with the plaintiff. The sales of plaintiff's yard for 1954, based upon its business for the first five months of that year, were estimated at approximately $60,000, a decline of more than two-thirds of the average annual sales of the previous years (excluding the peak year 1952).

These facts conclusively show not only that the business of plaintiff's Clintonville yard depended largely on the efforts, and customer contacts of the defendant, but that it suffered an irreparable loss when defendant took those efforts and customer contacts, as well as three other employees of plaintiff's yard, into a competitive business immediately after he left its employ.

Defendant states in his brief:

> We concede at this point that plaintiff does have a legitimate interest in its business and good will which it is entitled to preserve by exacting a reasonable restrictive covenant from its manager. The testimony in this case clearly shows that defendant has been able to establish a business at Clintonville which has substantially cut into the business of plaintiff. This, of course, was possible because defendant started his business immediately after he quit plaintiff, while all of his connections with the customers of the

plaintiff were still strong. It is obvious that if defendant were removed from the scene for any extended period, and his place were taken by another Fullerton manager, the good will and trade of the plaintiff would be safe in the hands of the new manager.

There has been no case in this court where the facts presented such a clear need for the kind of protection plaintiff thought it was bargaining for when this contract was made. The facts show that it had every reason to anticipate its business would suffer if defendant, after developing and establishing personal relations with its customers in Clintonville, chose to leave its employ and enter into competition with it in that vicinity.

It is, of course, necessary to consider whether the legality of the covenant is open to objection on the ground of coercion or interference with individual liberty.

> ... injunctive relief will not be awarded against breach of a covenant the real purpose of which was to prevent the employee from quitting the employers' service. Annotation 52 A.L.R. 1363.

There is no evidence that such a purpose existed when this contract was drawn and the fact that defendant did in fact terminate the employment to carry on competitive operations shows that the restrictive covenant had no such deterring effect upon him. There is no showing that it had had that effect at any time while he was working for the plaintiff.

The evidence of irreparable damage to the plaintiff is so strong in this case that we have undertaken a thorough reconsideration of the rule that has obtained in Wisconsin — that a covenant imposing an unreasonable restraint is unenforceable in its entirety.

In *General Bronze Corporation v. Schmeling*, 1932, 208 Wis. 565, 243 N.W. 469, 470, where, in the sale of a business, the contract contained a restrictive covenant not to engage in a competitive business within certain states of the United States "or within the Dominion of Canada or the Republic of Mexico" the court found no evidence that the plaintiff had ever had any business in Canada and Mexico. It was held that to the extent that the covenant restricted competition in those countries it was broader than reasonably necessary to protect the good will sold. The plaintiff contended that the contract by its terms was divisible and that such portions as were void by reason of being in restraint of trade could be separated and the contract enforced as to the proper territory. This contention was held valid.

The Massachusetts court has applied the rule that if the restrictive agreement as to territory is unreasonable, even though it be indivisible in terms, it is nevertheless enforceable for so much of the performance as would be a reasonable restraint. In *Whiting Milk Companies v. O'Connell*, 1931, 277 Mass. 570, 179 N.E. 169, 170, where the covenant in question restricted an employee from interfering with the business of the employer or selling dairy products to any of its customers, and it was found that the plaintiff's business extended over a large area of the state, the court held that the covenant was too broad. Although the contract was not by its own terms divisible, since it specified the prohibited territory in general terms, the court enjoined its breach to the extent of the customers the defendant had served while in the plaintiff's employ....

In a later case, *Metropolitan Ice Co. v. Ducas,* 1935, 291 Mass. 403, 196 N.E. 856, 858, the rule was extended to the time limitation imposed in a restrictive covenant of an employment contract. Referring to the application of the rule in the *Whiting* case and others, the court said: "No reason presents itself why the rule of reasonable enforcement as to space should not be applicable to time." Whereas the agreement restriction was for a period of fifteen years, the court affirmed the decree of the lower court enjoining the defendant for eighteen months from the date of the decree.

In 5 Williston on Contracts (Rev. Ed.) §§ 1659 and 1660, the author discusses the divisibility of promises and states that the traditional test of severability is the "blue-penciling" test (which this court applied in the *General Bronze Corporation* case, *supra.*) But he points out that in England, which is the source of this rule ..., it has been held that:

> ... where a negative restrictive covenant, indivisible in terms, extended beyond a time that the court in its discretion thought appropriate for an injunction, it granted an injunction for the period during which it deemed that remedy reasonable. § 1659, p. 4683.

... Williston, referring to such authority (including most of the cases dealt with above), stated in Vol. 5, § 1660, p. 4683:

> Covenants, in terms, unlimited as to time, have sometimes been divided in the way suggested.... While the Restatement of Contracts, § 518, has accepted the rule laid down by the majority of American courts as stated in the preceding section [i.e., the blue-penciling test], the tendency of the late American cases has been toward the minority view, that the legality of contracts in restraint of trade should not turn upon the mere form of wording but rather upon the reasonableness of giving effect to the indivisible promise to the extent that would be lawful.

.... It is our considered opinion that this view should be adopted in Wisconsin. While we recognize that the rule of partial enforcement of indivisible promises is a departure from that which this court has adhered to in the past, there is no departure from the general principle that contracts in restraint of trade are void as against public policy if they deprive the public of the restricted party's industry or injure the party himself by precluding him from pursuing his occupation and thus prevent him from supporting himself and his family. Where the terms of a restrictive covenant, not otherwise invalid, restrain an employee beyond either the area or the time within which an employer needs protection from competition by him, it is that excess of territory or time that is contrary to public policy and void.

As set out above, this court has been willing to apply the "blue-pencil" test to area restrictions, *General Bronze Corporation v. Schmeling, supra*, but we do not see why the basic reason for such willingness to enforce a contract after removing terms which are literally divisible should not also exist in the case of indivisible promises where the evidence is ample to support a finding as to the extent the restriction would be necessary and valid. Territory limits are by their nature more susceptible to separate specification than time and are often so expressed, but we see no difficulty in making a finding as to time upon evidence which is available to show the necessity for restraint in that respect.

In considering this rule many authorities point to the danger that its application might tend to encourage employers and purchasers possessing superior bargaining power to insist upon oppressive restrictions. However, these contracts are always subject to the test of whether their purpose is contrary to public policy, and if there is any credible evidence to sustain a finding that they are deliberately unreasonable and oppressive, such covenants must be held invalid whether severable or not.

The judgment is reversed and the cause remanded for a determination by the trial court of the extent of time as to which the restrictive covenant with respect to defendant's operations in Clintonville is reasonable and necessary for plaintiff's protection, and for judgment enjoining defendant from a breach thereof. It appears to us that a minimum period of three years would be supported by the evidence. It was established that after defendant took over the managership of plaintiff's yard in 1945 he built the business to a fairly constant level in that period of time, and it must be assumed that any manager taking his place could accomplish the same thing if the restrictions of the contract were enforced against the defendant during that time. In view of the fact that defendant has engaged in continuous competitive activities since December 1, 1953, employing the advantage gained while he was in the service of the plaintiff, the injunction should run from the date of the judgment rather than the date the employment terminated.

We are not passing upon the reasonableness of the restrictive covenant with respect to competition by defendant in Arcadia and Gaylord, Minnesota. The record contains no evidence that restrictions are necessary for the plaintiff's protection in those areas, and a showing of necessity must be made before the covenant will be upheld as to those locations.

Judgment reversed and cause remanded for further proceedings in accordance with this opinion.

GEHL, JUSTICE (dissenting) ... It is true, as the majority say, that there has been a tendency on the part of some courts to ascertain whether a contract in restraint of trade is divisible and, if found to be, to hold it unreasonable only to the extent necessary for the protection of the covenantee. Unless that position is limited, however, as it has been by this court, it gives effect to the court's notion as to what should be included in the contract, rather than to the intent of the parties as expressed in the contract, the parties who, had they desired a narrower or a broader provision, should and could have expressed it in the writing. If the provision is to be treated as being divisible, such purpose must be found in the contract itself; that quality should not be supplied by the court simply because it might be considered that the parties should have made broader or narrower provision against possible competition than they did. That is the rule of this state.

General Bronze Corporation v. Schmeling ... was an action brought by a corporation to restrain former stockholders from competition. The defendants had been the principal stockholders of a manufacturing corporation which had sold its assets to the plaintiff. By the terms of the agreement it was provided that the defendants would not within fifteen years from the date of the transfer engage in competition with the plaintiff in the United States, the District of Columbia, the Dominion of Canada and the Republic of Mexico.... The action was brought to restrain the defendants from violating the provisions of the covenant. The court said:

> There is no evidence that the business of this company extended into Canada or Mexico, and to the extent that the covenant restricts competition in these countries, it is broader than is reasonably necessary to protect the good will sold. However, it is contended by the plaintiff that the contract by its own terms is divisible, and that the portions of the contract which are void by reason of being in restraint of trade may readily be separated and dropped, and the contract enforced as to the proper territory.... [Ed note: citations quoted by *Fullerton* court are omitted] We have concluded that this contention is valid. The parties have adopted as one unit of the restrictive agreement the states and territories of the United States and the District of Columbia, descriptive in a territorial sense of the entire United States; as a second unit the Dominion of Canada, and as a third unit the Republic of Mexico. These areas are disjunctively described and furnish a proper basis, under the doctrine of the foregoing cases, for dividing the covenant and enforcing it in the territory which is coextensive with the business of the old company.

It will be observed that the court said and pointed out very clearly that the contract "by its own terms is divisible." It could not be questioned that if the divisibility as to area should appear in the contract itself, the same requirement should apply as to time. This case is cited in the opinion of the majority, but the majority omits to refer to the fact that the court based its conclusion upon the fact that the contract was by its own terms divisible....

I have found no Wisconsin case which suggests that the court, rather than the parties who made the contract, should be permitted to substitute arbitrarily for the parties a provision making an indivisible covenant divisible. The citation of text authorities and of cases from other jurisdictions "is but misplaced industry." They are of no help to this court which has so clearly stated the rule that if a covenant is to be treated as being divisible and therefore enforceable to the extent that it is a reasonable restriction, the fact of divisibility must appear from the contract itself. If it can be said that a single provision as to time, ten years as is this case, is divisible and it is possible to read that quality out of the terms of the contract, then it is only reasonable to ask, how could a provision indivisible as to time be effectively expressed?

It is apparent that the majority have construed the contract and applied a rule in the light of what has taken place since its execution. It occurs to me to inquire: as of what time are we to determine that the terms of a contract are or are not unreasonable? Is it to be determined as of the time of its execution, or as of a later time? May we say that a contract is void and then, not because of its terms, but because of the manner in which one of the parties to it has subsequently construed its terms, or because he has violated its provisions to the loss of the other party, still hold it enforceable in whole or in part? I doubt it....

It would seem that if a provision of a contract valid when made cannot be rendered invalid even by legislative action, one invalid when made cannot be validated, in whole or in part, by action of the parties.

The mere fact that developments subsequent to the execution of the contract show that the parties, or one of them, should have made a better bargain for himself does not affect the situation.

I would affirm.

NOTES AND QUESTIONS

1. *Balancing the equities*: The Nebraska Supreme Court, in *Philip G. Johnson & Co. v. Salmen*,[13] listed factors to balance in judging whether or not to enforce a covenant not to compete. A court should consider: (1) the degree of inequality of bargaining power; (2) the risk of the employer actually losing customers as a result of the competition; (3) the extent of respective participation by the parties in securing and retaining customers; (4) the good faith of the employer; (5) the existence of general knowledge about the identity of customers; (6) the nature and extent of the business position held by the employee promising not to compete; (7) the employee's training, health, and education, and the needs of his or her family; (8) the current conditions of employment; (9) the necessity of the employee changing his calling or residence if the covenant is enforced; and (10)

[13]211 Neb. 123, 317 N.W.2d 900 (1982).

the correspondence of the restraint found in the contract with the need for protecting legitimate interests of the employer.

What are the consequences of standards that call for balancing so many intangible factors?[14]

2. *"Bad-boy" provisions*: Lawyers for employers who want covenants not to compete have shifted to a different technique. They use what writers call "bad-boy clauses." The employer creates a deferred compensation plan so key employees have future contingent claims to benefits. An employee who quits and competes with the employer loses all claim to accrued benefits. In this way, the employer does not have to seek an injunction to enforce the covenant. It just refuses to pay the deferred compensation. Then the burden is on the former employee to challenge the employer's decision.[15]

B. SOCIAL CONTROL, CONTRACT AND CHOICE

1. INTRODUCTION

Individual freedom turns on having a large degree of choice. Choice always is limited. We cannot choose to live forever or repeal the law of gravity. We bargain in the context of our experiences and social and economic situations. Nonetheless, those who value personal freedom celebrate maximizing choice. Ideally, contract coordinates choices so that both parties are better off. We are both free to choose whether or not to make a contract and what its terms should be. You seek the salary I will pay and find the tasks I wish performed enjoyable. I see you as a diligent and skillful employee well worth what I pay you. When we add a market with other employers and other employees, then I cannot pay you too little nor can you demand too much. Other potential contracts create a frame of reference affecting our satisfaction with our arrangement.

Perhaps paradoxically, the values of free choice and free contract demand some social control of the process. Suppose, for example, you did not want to make a contract with me. However, your words and actions caused me to think you had agreed to my proposals. We could honor free choice to the maximum and say that since there had been no meeting of the minds, there was no deal. However, this position would protect you at my expense if I had reasonably relied on what I had thought was our bargain. Moreover, since choice is a

---

[14]See generally, Grody, Partial Enforcement of Post-Employment Restrictive Covenants, 15 Columbia Journal of Law and Social Problems 181 (1979).

[15]In Post v. Merrill Lynch, Pierce, Fenner & Smith, Inc., 48 N.Y.2d 84, 397 N.E.2d 358 (1979). the court said that such forfeitures of accrued benefits would be more readily enforced than competition enjoined. A forfeiture does not bar a person from the right to earn a livelihood. However, in the Post case the employer terminated plaintiffs without cause, and so public policy prevented enforcement of the forfeiture clause.

subjective matter, you could back out if you were willing to lie about whether you had intended to contract. There are a number of possible solutions to these problems. A legal system could require people to make choices in a certain form so they are less likely to make mistakes. It could limit your freedom by requiring you to use reasonable care in communication to see that you do not cause harm to me. It could hold you responsible for my reasonable interpretations of your words and conduct. We have already touched on this problem in *Hawkins v. McGee*, and we will develop it further in the second volume of these materials. We mention it here only to remind you that even the objective theory of contracts is a form of social control of the process. Under it, a person may commit a contract which she did not intend to make.

A system designed to promote and protect free choice must go further. Some people cannot exercise choice and protect themselves. We may worry whether a contract between an adult and a five-year-old child is likely to produce the benefits of free contract. We may worry whether those who are mentally ill or insane can choose in their own best interests.

Once we start down this road, however, we encounter a problem. Children and those who are mentally ill are not the only people who may not be able to act in their own best interests. People have different capacities to choose what is prudent or best for themselves. Some are smarter than others. Some are honest and trusting and others may take advantage of these admirable qualities. Some like the thrill of taking unreasonable risks.

Moreover, contracts affect third parties who have no say in the negotiations. The late Frank H. Knight was a founder of the Chicago school of economics which celebrates free enterprise and challenges governmental regulation. Nonetheless, Knight often pointed out that people frequently do not act for themselves alone. Rather, their choices benefit or injure members of their families as well. In his words:

> [A] rather small fraction of the population of any modern nation enter into contracts on their own responsibility. Our "individualism" is really "familism"; all minors, the aged, and numerous persons in other classes, including for practical purposes the majority of adult women,[16] have their status-determining bargains made for them by other persons. The family is still the unit in production and consumption. It is hardly necessary to point out that all arguments for free contract are nullified or actually reversed whenever one person contracts on behalf of another.[17]

---

[16]This essay was published originally in 1923.

[17]Knight, The Ethics of Competition, in The Ethics of Competition and Other Essays 41, 49 (Allen & Unwin, 1951). Knight also said "[t]he family is the minimum effective social unit, and a vital part of the social problem is allocating responsibility for all those who cannot — or even will not — take adequate responsibility for themselves." Knight, Intelligence and Democratic Action 160 (Harvard University Press, 1960).

For example, a father's stupid business contract (just as his gambling debts) may limit his daughter's chances for education. While she is in no way responsible for her father's choices, the consequences of those choices may affect her life. In holding a father to the consequences of his choices, courts may deny the daughter's freedom to choose.

We might ask in every case whether the contracting parties had the capability of choosing wisely. There are two concerns with this approach. We may worry about allowing judges or jurors to decide whether your choices are reasonable. Some insist that you are the only one who can decide what you value. We may also worry about the burden on commerce and on the courts if we must examine the bargaining skill of all those who make contracts that turn out poorly. Some insist that as long as I do nothing illegal and commit no torts, the fruits of my bargaining skill belong to me. You got a bad deal, but I got a good one. There is debate about my obligation to consider your interests when we make a contract and when we perform it. Our responses may differ as context changes. For example, we may accept self interest as the only guide when two horse-traders wheel and deal. We may hesitate to allow self interest to govern in transactions between, say, an attorney and her client.

Freedom also implies that I cannot interfere with your choice. I may put a gun to your head and insist that you make a contract with me. I may trick you into making a choice. I may be able to influence your understanding of the transaction so you think it advantageous when in fact it is not. I may lie or I may deceive by half truths. Some find the situation harder to resolve when I do not coerce or trick you myself. Instead, I take advantage of a situation where your choices are constrained or where I know that you misunderstand the contract and its likely consequences. We can relieve the burden on courts and support the security of transactions by imposing a heavy burden of self reliance. However, the more the legal system moves in this direction, the harder it is to justify its actions in terms of freedom and choice.

As always, real problems involve conflicting values. Free choice may not be the only value involved. Some want to make it easier to run large organizations. Others may want to take care of the disadvantaged, either by fashioning rules in their favor or on a case-by-case basis.[18]

We will look at the idea of free choice and free contract, and at the degree of social control of contract implicit within it. The rules are sufficiently flexible to allow very different views to affect the results without changing the legal formula. Furthermore, views have changed one way and another over time.

---

[18]See Kennedy, Distributive and Paternalist Motives in Contract and Tort Law, with Special Reference to Compulsory Terms and Unequal Bargaining Power, 41 Maryland Law Review 563 (1982); Unger, The Critical Legal Studies Movement, 96 Harvard Law Review 561 (1983).

2. CAPACITY TO CONTRACT

A system championing free choice must face those people who cannot choose in their own best interests. Few would want to uphold contracts between a capable adult and someone who was clearly insane or a very young child. Granting this, the legal system then faces a typical line drawing problem with the typical difficulties. How do we define incapacity in an adult? When does one cease being a child subject to protection? Do we want to pay the price of case-by-case determination or can we have rules that make matters clear?

a. Mental Incapacity to Contract

The law of mental capacity to contract reflects changing views about mental illness. Courts based earlier decisions on ideas about mental capacity and personal responsibility which Freudians later attacked. If a person could understand what he was doing, his choices were binding. For example, in *American Granite Co. v. Kringel*,[19] a creditor sued on two promissory notes. The trial court found Kringel competent to do business when he signed the notes. The evidence showed Kringel was severely afflicted by "a disorder commonly affecting the mind." A short time after the notes were signed, he was placed under guardianship. He was declared insane and sent to a mental hospital where he died a few months after the notes had been executed.

Nonetheless, the Supreme Court of Wisconsin affirmed the trial court. It said "a person who, in general, is insane, may bind himself by contract made during a lucid interval rendering him capable of appreciating the nature of his acts and exercising judgment thereto." The Court said nothing about what the one receiving the notes knew about Kringel's condition nor the fairness of the transaction. Some today would question the reality of an apparent lucid interval during which he seemed capable of appreciating situations and exercising judgment. However, if I appear lucid and you know nothing about my mental problems, you have an interest in the benefit of your bargain with me.

Restatement (Second) of Contracts § 15 attempts to fashion a modern statement of the impact of mental illness on capacity to contract. Professor Robert Braucher of Harvard Law School was the Reporter for the Restatement (Second) of Contracts who drafted § 15. Later he became Justice Braucher of the Supreme Judicial Court of Massachusetts. In *Krasner v. Berk*,[20] the trial court found that when defendant entered a contract he was mentally incapable of making the agreement. The Appellate Division reversed. Justice Braucher wrote an opinion reinstating the decision of the trial court.

---

[19]156 Wis. 94, 144 N.W. 204 (1914).
[20]366 Mass. 464, 319 N.E.2d 897 (1974).

Plaintiff and defendant were doctors who shared equally the rent on a suite of offices. In April, 1969, they renewed their lease for three years beginning June 1, 1969. On May 22d, they agreed in writing that each would pay half the rent even if one of them moved out or was "unable to occupy his suite as a result of disability." Plaintiff's attorney drafted this agreement. In November, defendant was fifty-three. He was diagnosed as suffering from presenile dementia. (This involves loss of high intellectual function, memory, judgment.) In July 1970, he closed his office and moved out. Plaintiff sued to enforce the agreement to pay defendant's share of the rent.

In September of 1967, defendant had begun to be absent-minded and confused. He missed appointments with patients and records piled up in his office. He was unable to answer direct questions with direct answers, and he was forgetful and oversolicitous of everyone. At least once every two weeks he would forget his car at the office and hitchhike home. He would forget there were patients waiting for him. A neurologist examined defendant in June of 1969. He found that defendant was a friendly, cooperative man with a disorder of immediate recall. Defendant's mother had a presenile dementia beginning at the age of fifty. Defendant refused a definitive study because it might demonstrate a pathology of which he was afraid. Very probably, defendant could function at an adequate level in situations with which he was thoroughly familiar and where success depended simply on the use or reinstatement of earlier learned material. In situations demanding adaptation, he would probably do poorly. The neurologist advised defendant to give up practice.

Justice Braucher quoted § 15 of the Restatement. A person incurs only voidable duties "if by reason of mental illness or defect ... he is unable to understand in a reasonable manner the nature and consequences of the transaction." He noted that defendant's wife had discussed his condition with plaintiff, and plaintiff's attorney drew up a written agreement referring to the inability to occupy the suite "as a result of disability." "Perhaps it might be inferred that the plaintiff, contrary to his testimony, had reason to know of the defendant's condition." However, the court did not rest its decision on this ground.

> On the sufficiency of understanding, the case is a close one. We have little doubt that on a record like this one a finding that defendant had testamentary capacity, as distinguished from capacity to contract, would be upheld.... If the judge had found that the defendant was competent to contract, we would have no difficulty in upholding the finding.... There was evidence that the plaintiff and the defendant discussed the possibility of moving to other offices before deciding to renew the lease but could not find suitable office space, that the defendant read the agreement before he signed it and then said that it was fair, and that four months later he was able to dictate a letter of complaint to the landlord showing some understanding of the terms of the lease.

We think, however, that we would invade the province of the trial judge if we drew inferences as to capacity to understand from actions of the defendant which in the setting may have been equivocal.... The agreement was an improvident one for a doctor who was about to consider whether he should give up his practice. We think the judge could find that he was not competent to make it.

How, if at all, does the decision in *American Granite v. Kringel, supra,* differ from the decision in *Krasner v. Berk*?

Suppose you represented plaintiff in *Krasner v. Berk* at the April meeting concerning renewing the lease. What, if anything, could you do to deal with the problem of the lease renewal? Is it necessarily a favor to persons with mental disabilities to relieve them from liability for their contracts?

b. Contracts Made Under the Influence of Drugs

Alcohol and other drugs can affect our capacity to make the choices involved in free contract. We might wish to distinguish several situations. Suppose a person is under the influence of alcohol or other drugs that affect mental capacity. However, the other party either does not know this or does not realize the extent of the incapacity to make choices. Or suppose the other party is the one who has supplied the drug. For example, seller takes buyer to a restaurant. Seller suggests pre-dinner drinks, several bottles of wine with dinner, and an after-dinner drink. Then seller asks buyer to sign a contract.

Harlow v. Kingston,[21] suggests that courts have long overturned transactions in extreme cases. The court found that plaintiff had deeded his interest in real estate to defendant for $200. The fair value of the interest was $1,388. For ten days before the transaction, plaintiff had been on a prolonged spree and had been grossly intoxicated. When he signed the deed, he was not appreciably under the influence of liquor. However, he had been out of money for several days and had exhausted his credit. Plaintiff suggested the transaction. Immediately after he obtained the $200, he started on another drunken debauch that lasted two weeks. By reason of his debauch, plaintiff had such a consuming thirst for liquor that his mind did not act normally, and he did not appreciate what he was doing. The trial court ordered the property reconveyed after plaintiff had repaid $200 plus interest. The judgment was affirmed. The Supreme Court said "it is manifest that such disparity between value and consideration paid shows a grossly inadequate consideration, and the facts support the inference that defendant at the time of purchase fully realized that he was obtaining such a bargain. He acquainted himself with the nature of the property, and no doubt understood what was its actual value before the deal was consummated."

---

[21]169 Wis. 521, 173 N.W. 308 (1919).

Restatement (Second) of Contracts § 16 deals with intoxicated persons. Essentially, the text is the same as § 15(1) governing mental incapacity, but there is no provision analogous to § 15(2). Thus, in most instances the other party must have "reason to know that by reason of intoxication" he is unable to understand the nature and consequences of the transaction or act in a reasonable manner in relation to it.

c. Contracts Made with Minors — Infancy

Voidable Contracts: A contract made with a minor is voidable at the minor's election. (The defense is often called infancy, but it applies to anyone who has not reached the age of majority.) This is a flat rule. Intelligent and experienced people who are 17 years and 364 days old can disaffirm. Immature people who are 18 years and one day old cannot. This is true although the adult in the transaction has no reason to suspect the minor's age. Furthermore, the transaction is voidable, not void. If the minor wants to back out of the deal, he or she can do so. If the minor does not want to back out, the adult must go forward with the contract. The minor can bring an action to avoid the transaction and recover any money paid to the adult. The minor also can assert infancy as a defense when the adult sues on the contract.

In many instances minority is a surrogate for defenses such as fraud, duress, breach of warranty or unconscionability which we will study later. Unlike those defenses, the person seeking to get out of a contract need prove only his or her age. Usually, the matter is so clear that litigation can be avoided or any trial will be simple for the minor's lawyer to handle.

Professor Kronman explains the rule as working "to protect children from their own shortsightedness and lack of judgment." He notes "[h]owever great their eventual powers of autonomous self-control, persons have a natural history in which they undergo moral and psychological development along predictable lines and normally acquire the various capacities — including judgment or moral imagination — without which freedom in any meaningful sense is impossible."[22] He continues:

> [a] child's ability to harm himself through imprudent purchases is limited by the resources he happens to have at any given moment, resources that usually take time to accumulate. The time required to save for a substantial purchase itself functions as a kind of cooling-off period by providing an opportunity for reflection and by increasing the likelihood of parental intervention. If a child were allowed to make binding contracts, his spending power — and hence his capacity to harm himself by spending foolishly — would no longer be constrained by the limits of his present wealth. And

---

[22]Kronman, Paternalism and the Law of Contracts, 92 Yale Law Journal 763, 795-96 (1983).

since a contract can be made in an instant (unlike accumulation, which requires time), parents would have less control over the purchases their children make.[23]

How does this rule differ from those applicable to the mentally infirm? What might account for these differences?

Restitution: Suppose a minor makes a contract with an adult. The adult sues for breach, and the minor defends successfully on the ground of infancy. Is the adult entitled to restitution of any benefits conferred on the minor? *Halbman v. Lemke*,[24] suggests the sometimes harsh results of contracting with a minor.

In 1973, Michael Lemke agreed to sell a car to James Halbman, a minor, for $1250. Halbman paid Lemke $1,000 and promised to pay $25 a week until he paid the balance. Halbman took possession of the car. About five weeks later, a connecting rod in the engine broke and Halbman took the car to a garage where it was repaired at a cost of $637.40. Halbman did not pay the repair bill. The car remained at the garage. On October 15, 1973, Halbman wrote Lemke disaffirming the purchase contract. He demanded return of all the money he had paid. Lemke refused to return the money. In the spring of 1974, the garage removed the engine and transmission to satisfy its garageman's lien. It then towed the Oldsmobile to the residence of Halbman's father. Halbman asked Lemke to take the vehicle several times, but he refused. During the period the Oldsmobile was at the garage and later when it was at Halbman's father's home, it was vandalized, making it unsalvageable.

The Supreme Court of Wisconsin held that Halbman was entitled to the return of the money he had paid Lemke. In addition, a disaffirming minor need only return so much of the goods as is possible; Halbman did not have to make restitution for use of the car or depreciation in its value. Many other states also would reach this result. However, others have statutes that require restoration of any consideration received as a condition to disaffirming a contract.

In some states, minors are liable for misrepresenting their age to an adult. While they may disaffirm their contracts, they are still responsible for their torts. In these states, minors' claims for restitution are set off against adults' claims for tort damages. Automobile dealers often state on standard form contracts that the buyer represents that he or she is above 18 (or 21 if this is the age of majority.) When we consider misrepresentation later in this course, consider whether such a clause on a standard form should trigger tort liability in light of the requirements for establishing such a cause of action.

Necessaries: Minors cannot avoid liability on contracts they make for necessaries. Liability, however, is properly regarded as imposed to avoid unjust enrichment, and so grounded in the substantive law of restitution, and so should

---

[23]*Id*. at 788 n. 79.

[24]99 Wis.2d 241, 298 N.W.2d 562 (1980).

be for the fair market value of the necessaries, and not the contract price. Courts restrict seller's recovery pursuant to this exception to a few items such as clothing, food and shelter. They have not expanded it to include expensive things such as automobiles and stereo systems.

3. DURESS

a. The Search for a Standard

The doctrine of duress is sometimes approached as if it embodied the judicial definition of free choice. As the readings which follow demonstrate, it is probably more helpful to see it as an effort to establish the boundary between proper and improper advantage-taking. If I threaten to kill or injure you unless you make a contract, the resulting agreement is not an expression of free choice. The threat itself is a crime in most places. Not surprisingly, courts refuse to enforce such a contract. This is obvious but not very interesting. Those who extort money from others by making such threats have their own sanction system and do not worry about whether courts would give remedies for breach of their victims' promises.

At the other extreme, Professor Hale pointed out in 1923,[25] that we can view property as legally supported duress. You want my automobile. The law offers elaborate structures to make sure that you cannot have it unless you pay the price I demand. The car might serve your needs perfectly, and you may want it badly. In some situations, there may be no practical substitute for my car. You may be willing to pay what everyone would agree is a reasonable price for it. Nonetheless, the law gives me the privilege to keep the car from you. Or I can keep it unless you pay my unreasonable price. This protection — my property right — is a major part of my bargaining power.

The classic doctrine says that a threat to do what you are legally entitled to do cannot be duress. So, for example, it is not duress for me to refuse to contract with you except on terms that are very favorable to me and less favorable to you. This is true even though your situation, and my knowledge of it, allows me to "take advantage" of you. If you need a used car badly, and I own the only available used car, I can charge you double the market value of the car without being guilty of duress.

Common law judges in the late 19th and early 20th centuries solved a particular kind of duress problem through the doctrine of consideration. A and B make a contract. B refuses to perform unless he is paid more than the contract price. A promises to pay the added amount, and B performs. A then refuses to

---

[25]Hale, Coercion and Distribution in a Supposedly Non-Coercive State, 38 Political Science Quarterly 470 (1923). See also, Hale, Bargaining, Duress and Economic Liberty, 43 Columbia Law Review 603 (1943).

carry out his promise. A's promise would not be supported by consideration under the pre-existing obligation rule. In this way, Professor Gilmore tells us,[26] courts could apply an apparently objective rule and avoid having to deal with issues of fairness.

These cases seem to draw a sharp line. However, courts have branded as duress some threats of actions that would not be crimes or torts. Indeed, threats of inflicting some crimes and torts are less coercive than other threats.

R. L. MITCHELL v. C. C. SANITATION COMPANY, INC.

430 S.W. 2d 933 (Texas Ct. of Civ. App., 1968)

JOHNSON, J. This is a summary judgment case in which the appellant, R. L. Mitchell, brought action for personal injury damages against William W. Crane and C. C. Sanitation Co., Inc. Mitchell's damages were allegedly caused by the negligence of William W. Crane, while he, Crane, was driving a truck in the course and scope of his employment for  C. C. Sanitation Company. At the time of the accident in question, Mitchell was driving a truck in the course and scope of his employment for Herrin Transportation Company.

Subsequent to the collision in question, Mitchell signed two releases. The first was in favor of William W. Crane and C. C. Sanitation Company. It was signed by both Mitchell and Herrin Transportation Company and was for $388.65. The second release was also in favor of William W. Crane and C. C. Sanitation Company but it was signed only by Mitchell, and was for $62.12. Therefore the instant case was not only an action for damages but also an action to set aside the releases which the appellant had executed in favor of the appellees.

Appellees, defendants below, filed a motion for summary judgment asserting that the releases signed by Mitchell and the acceptance of the checks paid pursuant to the releases barred any recovery by him. The trial court, taking into consideration the depositions on file, the affidavits, the pleadings and other stipulations made by the parties, granted the motion for summary judgment denying all relief to the plaintiff. The essential question before this court is whether or not the record reveals a genuine issue of fact to have been raised which would enable the appellant to avoid the enforceability of such releases.

Being a case determined by summary judgment, we must resolve all doubts as to the existence of a genuine issue as to a material fact against the movant, appellees here.... Accepting as true that evidence which tends to support

---

[26]Gilmore, The Death of Contract 42, 48, 76 (1974).

appellant's position and viewing the evidence in the light most favorable to him, the following situation is presented.

Appellant alleged that at the time of the occurrence in question, he was driving a truck in the course and scope of his employment for Herrin Transportation Company. As he was in the process of passing another truck driven by the defendant, Crane, who was in the course and scope of his employment for the defendant C. C. Sanitation Company, the defendant's truck suddenly and without warning was negligently steered to the left by defendant, Crane, thus proximately causing the accident which resulted in serious and permanent injuries to him, the appellant. Numerous specific acts of negligence were alleged against the driver, Crane. The appellant alleged his damages to be in the sum of $40,000.00, which included damages for pain and suffering, lost wages, loss of earning capacity, and past and future medical expenses.

As to the releases, Mitchell alleged that they were signed by him because of duress and fraud imposed upon him by his employer, Herrin Transportation Company. Herrin handled its own claim service through one Ross C. Hall, under the name of Southwestern Claims Adjustment Company. After the accident, Hall advised C. C. Sanitation of the damages to Herrin's truck and to Mitchell, and placed C. C. Sanitation on notice of "Herrin's subrogation interest for all property damage inflicted upon its equipment and all workmen's compensation payments to or on behalf of its driver, Mr. Mitchell." By letter, Hall advised C. C. Sanitation and its insurance company, Maryland Casualty Company, of Herrin's truck damage of $281.65, that Herrin had paid Mitchell's physician, Dr. Cobb, $107.00, and that Herrin was therefore due $388.65. Thereafter Hall advised one Patrick Gorski, an adjuster for Maryland Casualty Company, that Mitchell was expecting to be paid $62.12 which he, Mitchell, had paid for his doctor out of his own pocket.

Maryland Casualty, acting by and through Gorski, prepared the proposed releases. The first was in the sum of $388.65 to be executed by Herrin and Mitchell, and the second was in the sum of $62.12 to be executed only by Mitchell. These were then transmitted from Gorski to Hall so that they might be signed by Herrin and by Mitchell. Hall apparently undertook the responsibility of obtaining Mitchell's signature on both releases. After the two releases were signed they were returned to Maryland Casualty Company who then issued the two checks. The first was mailed directly to Herrin and the second directly to Mitchell. At no time during the negotiations outlined did Maryland Casualty Company or its adjuster Gorski have any personal conversation with, or see Mitchell.

The allegations of duress and fraud find their primary support in the deposition and affidavit of the appellant, Mitchell. According to Mitchell, he was called to Hall's office and when he went there Hall had the two previously prepared releases in hand. Hall threatened that if Mitchell did not settle for the amounts stated in the releases and sign them that he, Mitchell, would be "through," that is that he would lose his job. Further, that "Ross Hall just told me that it was a release so they could get their money for the truck and I could keep my job." When asked if anyone for Herrin Transportation Company talked to him about the execution of the releases, Mitchell responded, "Well, before I signed them Ross Hall blew his stack because I refused to sign them. He had Eldon Brown call me and put pressure on me." He then testified that Eldon Brown was "second in command" for Herrin Transportation Company. He further testified, "Well, I was informed that I would either sign these releases or I wouldn't have a job." He was asked, "Now, were you told anything else that may have caused you to sign the releases?" He responded, "Nothing except if *they* didn't get *their* money I didn't have no job." (Emphasis added).

Mitchell stated that during this conversation and prior to signing the releases, Hall telephoned someone representing C. C. Sanitation and Crane and "What Mr. Hall said over the telephone was that he had finally convinced me that it would be better to sign it. In other words, it was either sign the release or not have a job." He continued, "Whoever he talked to on the phone, he said I prefer to sign the releases than lose my job." By affidavit, Mitchell identified Patrick Gorski, the adjuster for Maryland Casualty Company, as the person with whom Hall was speaking on the telephone. Mitchell also testified to Hall's statements that he, Hall, was handling the matter for C. C. Sanitation and William Crane, was working on behalf of them, was "taking care" of it for them, and was getting the releases signed for them.

Mitchell testified that he would not have signed the releases had Hall not told him that he was going to lose his job if he didn't sign, that he did not feel that he was being adequately compensated for the injuries he sustained in the accident and that the only reason he would sign releases like those that he did sign would be to keep his job. By affidavit Mitchell stated, "I told Mr. Hall nothing was being paid me for the pain and suffering I had experienced or for my future doctor's bills," but, "he was insistent that I sign the releases so that Herrin Transportation could get the money for their truck." Mitchell stated, "Had he not threatened me with my job I would not have signed the releases. His threat caused me to do something (sign the releases) which was against my own free will and accord."

Mitchell further alleged that at the time Hall made the threats against his job, he did so with the knowledge, consent and acquiescense of the insurance company for the appellees, Maryland Casualty Company, who was acting by and through Gorski, their insurance adjuster. Mitchell alleged that not only did Gorski know of the threats but after such threats were made, Maryland Casualty Company accepted the benefits arising therefrom by accepting the releases and attempting to enforce them. Mitchell alleged that Hall, at the time he procured the execution of releases, was acting as the agent of Maryland Casualty Company. Appellant alleged further, as the basis of the fraud and/or inadequate consideration, that the amount of the releases went solely to compensate Herrin Transportation Company for its expenses, and the appellant and Herrin Transportation Company, for the amount of the doctor bills to date; that no cash was paid to the appellant in addition to the above mentioned amounts. Lastly, appellant alleged that the appellees and his employer, Herrin Transportation Company, acted in a conspiracy coercing him into signing the releases.

It is a general rule that contracts obtained through duress or coercion are voidable and this rule is applicable to releases....

"Any coercion of another, either mental, physical, or otherwise, causing him to act contrary to his own free will or to submit to a situation or conditions against his own volition or interests constitutes 'duress.' " *Hailey v. Fenner & Beane,* (Tex.Civ.App.) 246 S.W. 412, no writ hist. However, there is authority stating, "There can be no duress unless there is a threat to do some act which the party threatening has no legal right to do." *Dale v. Simon* (Tex.Com.App.), 267 S.W. 467.... Appellee contends that duress cannot exist because Herrin Transportation Company was at liberty to discharge the appellant at any time and for any reason they so desired for he was not shown to be more than an employee at will. Stated another way, that the employer Herrin had the right to discharge the appellant at any time and the threat to do what they had the legal right to do cannot constitute duress or fraud.

As the disposition of the instant case was made on appellee's motion for summary judgment, applying the well known principles previously set forth, the following conclusions find support in the record and may be validly and helpfully made: (1) the employer Herrin had the right to discharge appellant at any time it desired; (2) there was a very real compulsion, economic and otherwise, here brought to bear on the appellant by his employer; (3) it was the force of this constraint alone, that caused appellant to do what he otherwise would not have considered doing; (4) this compulsion was brought to bear by the employer Herrin, working in concert with the defendant, C. C. Sanitation; (5) the employer Herrin did what it here did for its own economic benefit and advantage, and (6) the effect of such action was to effectively terminate and destroy a valid claim and otherwise good cause of action possessed by the appellant.

"Although an employer, acting singly, has the undoubted right to discharge an employee or one of his family, the coercion arising from a threat to do so, when employed as a means to force the employee to sign a release of an action which he has instituted against him or another employer is unlawful, and, under circumstances showing that such means in fact overcame the employee's resistance and will, may constitute duress." 20 A.L.R.2d 743, 751. We believe this reasoning is applicable to the instant case, and though no Texas cases directly in point are found, believe that substantial authority is otherwise available.

In *Wise v. Midtown Motors, Inc.,* 231 Minn. 46, 42 N.W.2d 404, 20 A.L.R.2d 735, the subject of the cited A.L.R. annotation, an employee brought an action against a prior employer who had discharged him. The prior employer arranged a meeting in the office of employee's present employer where the present employer told the employee that he would be "through" if his case was not then settled. Under these circumstances the employee signed a release which had been previously prepared by the prior employer. It was there held that, the employee being warranted in believing that his employer would discharge him if he did not sign the release, a question for the jury as to duress arose.

In *Holmes v. Industrial Cotton Mills Co.*, D.C., 64 F.Supp. 20, there had been an investigation by a representative of the wage and hour division of the defendant company. The employee was told by the company superintendent it looked as if he would lose his job, since the company would abolish the job if it had to pay overtime for over forty hours. The company president then called the employee into his office, read to him a previously prepared release, and told the employee that if he would sign the release it would clear the company and that he could then hold his job. It was there held as a matter of law that the employer had used duress in inducing the employee to sign the release of overtime pay.

In *Huddleston v. Ingersoll Co.*, 109 Colo. 134, 123 P.2d 1016, an employee lost his right hand as a result of alleged negligence of the employer in permitting unguarded farm machinery to be used. There the plaintiff testified that before he executed the release in question, the foreman urged him to sign it because the defendant company would not be liable in damages, had no compensation insurance, and that if he did not sign, he and others would lose their jobs. It was there held that there was sufficient evidence to warrant submission to the jury on the issue of whether or not the release of the employer signed for a consideration of $30.00, was signed as a result of fraud, mistake, or duress.

In *Perkins Oil Co. of Delaware v. Fitzgerald*, 197 Ark. 14, 121 S.W.2d 877, an employee who was an oiler at a cotton seed oil mill lost both arms in a machine accident at the mill. To induce the employee to release the company, the mill superintendent told him that if he consulted an attorney, or tried to sue the company, his step-father, the sole support of plaintiff's invalid mother, would be discharged, and the company would prevent his reemployment in any other like business. Such evidence was held sufficient to warrant submission to the jury on the question of whether the employee signed the release under duress or coercion.

In the case at bar there was obvious opportunity for employer oppression to be brought against the employee. The parties stood on no equal footing, there was great economic disparity between them, and there was no equality of bargaining positions. The appellant undoubtedly was the weaker party, the threat to discharge him was very real and he was fully justified in expecting that he would be immediately discharged.

In addition, the employer, Herrin Transportation Company, had a direct economic interest in their employee signing the releases, and this was the reason for doing what the company did. Absent the releases being signed by Mitchell, Herrin would not be paid the damages to its truck ($281.65) or the doctor's bills it had previously paid ($107.00). The major portion of the money received for signing the releases went to Herrin Transportation Company, with only $62.12

being paid to appellant. Even this sum was for doctor's bills that appellant had previously paid out of his own pocket as a result of the accident in question. There was no consideration of, nor compensation for, the most important elements of damages allegedly suffered by appellant, these being mental and physical pain and suffering and reduced capacity to work.

In addition there is evidence in the record from which it might properly be concluded that the defendant C. C. Sanitation not only knew of the constraint and compulsion that was applied to Mitchell by his employer, but participated in it, and later accepted its economic benefits.

It is the opinion of the majority of this court that even where the right of an employer to discharge an employee is unquestioned, duress and coercion may be exercised by the employer by threats to discharge the employee, where circumstances such as are here presented appear. We cannot conclude that an employer with the opportunity for oppression on an employee that here appears, may use such power for his own economic interest, and yet conclude that no question of duress or coercion arises. Where there is such an inequality in the terms, sacrifice of benefits, and rights on the part of the employer, inadequacy of consideration, and advantage taken of the weaker party, we cannot conclude that no fact situation of duress or coercion exists.

It is the opinion of the majority of this court that under the circumstances here presented the existence of duress and coercion sufficient for the avoidance of the releases was a genuine issue of fact, which was raised by the record. There being such issue of fact, under the law applicable to summary judgment, this cause must be reversed and remanded.

Reversed and remanded.

TUNKS, C.J., dissenting. I respectfully dissent.

The facts of this case are accurately stated in the majority opinion. Those facts show that the Maryland Casualty Company, insurer for the appellees, was confronted with two claims asserted by two different claimants growing out of one accident. The carrier declined to pay one claimant until the other claim was settled. Its conduct in that respect was not at all unreasonable. It is obvious that an important factor in the settlement of claims is the avoidance of possible expense to be incurred in defending suits. The carrier could not fully avail itself of the benefits in that respect by settling one claim and defending the other. Not only did the conduct of the carrier constitute a reasonable exercise of business judgment but it was conduct clearly within its legal rights.

The majority seems to place emphasis on the fact that it was to the financial interest of Herrin Transportation Company to get the plaintiff to release his claim. I would emphasize that fact as sustaining the validity and propriety of Herrin's conduct, rather than tainting it. It is uncontroverted that Herrin had the lawful right to terminate Mitchell's employment without any cause. It should follow, a fortiori, that they had a right to terminate his employment unless he would take such action as would permit them to recover on their claim. In my opinion their conduct would be more subject to attack if they, having no financial interest in the matter, had threatened to fire Mitchell because of personal spite or ill will or simply because they were permitting Maryland Casualty Company to avail itself of a lawful right to discharge which they, as employers at will, had.

As the two actors in this situation, the carrier and the employer, each acting individually, were acting within their legal rights, so were they, acting in concert, within the bounds of lawfulness. The majority opinion cites authorities for the proposition that an employer's threat to discharge an employee at will is not duress. Neither is any other threat to do any other lawful act duress. It may be assumed that the record supports a finding of fact to the effect that Maryland Casualty Company refused to pay Herrin until Mitchell had settled his claim for the purpose of inducing Herrin to exercise its influence in getting Mitchell to settle for the amount offered. At least Maryland Casualty Company got the benefit of Herrin's exercise of its influence. Maryland Casualty Company, however, did not induce Herrin to do or threaten to do something unlawful to influence Mitchell to settle.

Nor is the appellant's contention that his settlement was involuntary because it was made under economic compulsion sound. In *McKee, General Contractor v. Patterson*, 153 Tex. 517, 271 S.W.2d 391, it was held that a workman's acceptance or retaining employment in the face of known and appreciated dangers was voluntary though done under the economic necessity of earning a livelihood. Thus, Mitchell's settlement of his claim to avoid losing his job was, nevertheless, voluntary.

I would affirm the judgment of the trial court.

NOTES AND QUESTIONS

1. *What is a wrongful threat?* The *Mitchell* case expands the concept of duress past threats to commit crimes or torts. This poses the problem of, in Professor Dalton's words,[27] "isolating just those kinds of impairment [of bargaining power] that the law is prepared to redress without feeling that the whole structure of bargaining between unequals is put in jeopardy." Suppose the truck driver in the *Mitchell* case had been represented by a lawyer and had received some compensation for his injuries. Should the case then have come out the other way?

2. *Wrongful, but not illegal, threats*: Bargaining involves offering rewards and punishments. Lawyers are people who can cause trouble. Thus, when they offer to settle a dispute, there is at least the tacit threat of litigation if the other side refuses the offer. How far will courts attempt to police the negotiation tactics of the bar through the doctrine of duress?

---

[27]Dalton, An Essay in the Deconstruction of Contract Doctrine, 94 Yale Law Journal 997, 1031 (1985).

In *Wolf v. Marlton Corp.*,[28] a husband and wife sued to recover a down payment of $2,450. They had made this payment pursuant to a contract to buy a house to be built by Marlton Corporation. The plaintiffs sought to cancel their contract because they were having marital difficulties. Marlton sought to hold them to their bargain until the couple's lawyer threatened that, if the couple were forced to conclude the purchase they would arrange a subsequent resale to "a purchaser who would be undesirable in our tract, and that we would not be happy with the results." The lawyer also said "it will be the last tract that you will ever build in New Jersey, and it will be the last house that you will sell in this tract." Marlton then sold the house to a third party. Marlton sought to keep the downpayment, arguing that its failure to sue the couple for breach of contract was caused by their lawyer's threats which constituted duress. The appellate court, reversing a judgment for the plaintiffs, observed:

> Plaintiffs assert that, once they bought the house, they had a legal right to sell it to whomever they wished. They rely on the familiar general rule to the effect that a threat to do what one has a legal right to do does not constitute duress.... That proposition, however, is not an entirely correct statement of the law of duress as it has developed in this jurisdiction. Under the modern view, acts or threats cannot constitute duress unless they are wrongful; but a threat may be wrongful even though the act threatened is lawful. We have come to deal, in terms of the business compulsion doctrine, with acts and threats that are wrongful, not necessarily in a legal, but in a moral or equitable sense....
>
> The sale of a development home to an "undesirable purchaser" is of course, a perfectly legal act regardless of any adverse effect it may have on the fortunes of the developer's enterprise. But where a party for purely malicious and unconscionable motives threatens to resell such a home to a purchaser, specially selected because he would be undesirable, for the sole purpose of injuring the builder's business, fundamental fairness requires the conclusion that his conduct in making this threat be deemed "wrongful," as the term is used in the law of duress.

Was the Wolfs' lawyer vindicating the policy of the fair housing laws that attempted to end residential segregation? What were the Wolfs trying to achieve?

The court said that a threat may be wrongful, even though the act threatened is lawful. If this is true, by what standard do we measure wrongfulness? Suppose a borrower has fallen behind on payments on a loan to provide working capital for a business. The bank "threatens" to refuse to renew the loan unless the borrower gives a mortgage on her home. The bank subsequently seeks to foreclose the mortgage on the residence. Can the borrower argue that it gave the

---

[28] 57 N.J.Super. 278, 154 A.2d 625 (1959).

mortgage only under duress? Suppose a homeowner signs a note to pay an extremely high price for a pump to try to save property from the Mississippi River floods of 1993? Can the homeowner argue that it signed the note under duress? How can this be distinguished from *Wolf v. Marlton*?

3. *The Restatement's Approach*: Study Restatement (Second) of Contracts §§ 175-176.

Professor Clare Dalton[29] criticizes the Restatement's approach. She comments that the American Law Institute used the "no reasonable alternative" standard rather than the more traditional standards that talked of fear overcoming either the victim's free will or that of a person of ordinary firmness. She notes "[i]n comparison to 'fear,' 'reasonable alternatives' has a reassuringly rational and objective ring." It says that a victim should look for reasonable alternatives before he yields to a threat. This seems to be an objective test. However, although a judge thinks that a victim had reasonable alternatives, a victim actually may have signed a contract because he was afraid of a threat being carried out. The Restatement also tells a court to ask whether the victim's assent was induced by the threat. But this provokes the problem of knowledge. "We cannot directly know or ascertain the subjective intent of the disfavored party." Then we slide into focusing on the other party's behavior and the terms of the deal that resulted. "The interplay of subjective and objective creates a framework in which the decisionmaker can readily justify either finding or not finding a coerced assent in a given situation."

The Restatement then turns to "a focus on the prohibition of some types of coercive behavior, and a focus on the equivalence of the resulting exchange." But it does not tell us how judges should make these decisions. Dalton argues that threats to commit crimes or torts do not necessarily influence a person more than other threats not singled out. Many crimes and torts involve very serious injuries, but others involve less serious or even trivial injuries. "The only advantage of this strategy is that it displaces the problem of identifying unacceptable behavior over to some other area of the law, leaving the law of contract apparently free of the need for making such controversial normative choices." She looks at the other kinds of threats covered by the Restatement. She finds the tests turn on "unfair exchange," and highly uncertain measures of appropriate conduct such as "unfair dealing" or "the use of power for illegitimate ends." "These raise the very questions they were supposed to answer: What uses of power *are* illegitimate, what kinds of pressure *are* unfair, in the contractual context."[30]

Compare Dalton's criticism with Professor Kronman's statement: "[o]ne who believes, as Mill did and I do, that some paternalistic restrictions on contractual freedom are not only permissible but morally required, must supply a standard

---

[29]Dalton, An Essay in the Deconstruction of Contract Doctrine, 94 Yale Law Journal 997, 1032-36 (1985).

[30]*Id.* at 1035.

or principle for evaluating paternalistic arguments in particular cases; only in this way can the legitimacy of paternalism be established and its limits defined."[31] Contrast both Dalton's and Kronman's positions with Professor Trakman's praise ... of an open-ended approach in the areas of illegality and public policy.

Can we do better than telling judges to make ad hoc judgments about fairness with a presumption that contracts should be upheld? Professor Duncan Kennedy advocates a cautious ad hoc paternalism.[32] He tells us:

> To be an ad hoc paternalist is to admit that one has no powerful overarching test that will allow one anything more than intuitive confidence (either before or after one acts) that one is on the right side of this line.... [I]n fear and trembling you approach each case determined to act if that's the best thing to do, recognizing that influencing another's choice — another's life — in the wrong direction, or so as to reinforce their condition of dependence, is a crime against them.... Principled anti-paternalism is a defense mechanism. One way to deal with the pain and fear of having to make an ad hoc paternalist decision — one way to deny the pain and fear — is to claim that you "had" to do what you did because principle (say, the principle of incapacity) required it. That the principle doesn't really work is less important than that it anesthetizes.... The truth of the matter is that what we need when we make decisions affecting the well-being of other people is correct intuition about their needs and an attitude of respect for their autonomy. Nothing else will help. And even intuition and respect may do no good at all. There isn't any guarantee that you'll get it right, but when it's wrong you're still responsible.... What he's [a decision maker] doing, if he tries to be a systematic anti-paternalist in public life, is denying his knowledge of the relative incapacity of groups, of their characteristic mistakes. He is acting to deepen their incapacity by treating them as entitled to their mistakes, and then bringing to bear the apparatus of the state to evict them from their subcode apartments, exclude them under the law of trespass from power over the means of production they created through their labor, and leave them to beg for crumbs when accidents they didn't provide for befall them after all.

Does the Restatement approach serve to carry out Kennedy's ad hoc paternalism? At what cost? Is the *Mitchell* case, discussed above, an example of Kennedy's approach?

---

[31]Kronman, Paternalism and the Law of Contracts, 92 Yale Law Journal 763, 765 (1983).

[32]Kennedy, Distributive and Paternalist Motives in Contract and Tort Law, with Special Reference to Compulsory Terms and Unequal Bargaining Power, 41 Maryland Law Review 563, 638-49 (1982). Reprinted with permission.

b. A Better Approach?

The following student-written law review article suggests a new approach to duress cases. The article has provoked more discussion than most student work in law reviews. A Wisconsin Court of Appeals adopted its approach. The Supreme Court of Wisconsin reversed this decision on other grounds, neither accepting nor rejecting the Iowa Law Review's approach to duress. However, dicta in the supreme court opinion suggests that the court will continue to follow the old religion based on overcoming free will.

Note, Economic Duress After the Demise of Free Will Theory: *A Proposed Tort Analysis*[33]

When one party wrongfully threatens another with severe economic loss if he does not enter a proposed contract, and the threatened party acquiesces solely because of the wrongful threat, the injury to the threatened party may be redressed through the legal doctrine of economic duress. This doctrine may be used as an affirmative defense in an action to enforce the coerced contract, as the basis for a restitution suit to recover payments made under the coerced contract, or as support for a tort action for damages resulting from the coerced contract. The limits of the doctrine, however, are not clear, and the courts have not used consistent standards for a finding of duress. It is the function of this Note to investigate the purpose of the economic duress doctrine and to formulate analytical criteria applicable to all economic duress cases.

I. DEVELOPMENT OF THE DOCTRINE OF ECONOMIC DURESS

Duress arose at common law as an adjunct to tort law. Relief was initially restricted to cases in which a transfer of property resulted from threats of physical violence or the actual imprisonment of the victim. The courts further required that the threats or pressures be sufficient to overcome the will of a man of "ordinary firmness." These restrictions were gradually relaxed, and the doctrine of duress was extended into the area of economic pressure, although its relationship to tort law was maintained. The first economic pressure recognized as duress was the wrongful detention of another's property. This crude economic pressure, independently wrongful as a tort, was labelled "duress of goods," and it represented a great advance in the development of economic duress.

American courts in the nineteenth century expanded the concept of duress to invalidate transfers induced by more subtle economic pressure. Guided by the rationale of equity courts in undue influence cases and by the prevailing

---

[33]53 Iowa Law Review 892 (1968). Copyright © 1968 by The University of Iowa (Iowa Law Review). Reprinted by permission.

subjective will theory of contracts, the courts eventually rejected the "ordinary firmness" test in favor of a subjective test for duress. Under this test, agreements were held to be voidable for lack of free contractual consent if the court determined that the threats or actions of the stronger party actually overcame the victim's will. Since the early twentieth century, most American courts have used this subjective test in cases of both economic and physical duress.

The free will concept, however, has serious shortcomings. Because both normal contracts and those formed under duress result from a choice between alternative evils, it is impossible to distinguish one situation from another on the basis of any difference in the freedom of the consent. The free will test, therefore, has little analytical value in itself, and many writers have begun to equate a finding of duress to a moral judgment on the fairness of the alternatives presented by the threatening party. These writers have presented many different standards for determining whether the pressures exerted rise to the level of duress. One authority [John Dalzell] focused on the "essential and sufficient" elements of duress, which he found to be the wrongfulness of the threats and the inadequacy of alternative legal remedies open to the threatened party at the time of the threats. Another writer [John Dawson] rejected these factors and argued that the requisites for a finding of duress should be unequal bargaining positions of the parties and a disproportionate exchange resulting in unjust enrichment to the stronger party.

The theoretical confusion surrounding the duress area is reflected in the judicial decisions. Courts appear to give controlling weight to a variety of factors, including relative bargaining positions of the parties, adequacy of alternative legal remedies, gravity of the threatened evil, wrongfulness or illegality of the threats, fairness of the resulting bargain, and ratification by the allegedly coerced party. Some courts have held that there can be no duress if the victim had an opportunity to consult with a lawyer, if he had time for deliberation and reflection between the time of the threats and the time of the agreement, if he had knowledge of all the facts, or if the overwhelming pressure was the result of external circumstances. A few courts have decided duress cases without resort to any theoretical or analytical framework, and others, recognizing the fluidity and vagueness of the duress doctrine, have concluded that each case must be decided solely on its own facts. These discrepancies in decisional factors employed, together with the ambiguity of the common free will test, have contributed to lack of predictability, inaccurate use of precedents, confusion between the functions of judges and jury, and timidity in the extension of the duress doctrine.

PURPOSE AND CLASSIFICATION OF DURESS DOCTRINE
A. Purpose

The analytical confusion in the duress area reflects a confusion concerning the purpose of the duress doctrine. Clarification of this purpose will facilitate classification of duress as a tort, contract, or quasi-contract action, and allow the use of an established analytical scheme for dealing with duress cases....

A complete description of the purpose of economic duress doctrine ... should properly describe the interest to be protected, accounting for the requirement that the coercing pressure be wrongful, and distinguish the duress doctrine from antitrust law. It has been established that the duress doctrine does not protect the personal interest in the exercise of free will. [This is because normal and coerced contracts result from a choice between alternative evils, and all contracts involve some degree of coercion. Most courts require a showing that the pressure exerted was wrongful, independent of a showing of its tendency to deprive the victim of his free will.] Two possible protectable economic interests, however, can be isolated: the economic interest which is threatened by the threatened alternative to the agreement, and the economic interest which is damaged by the coerced agreement. It is clear that the doctrine of economic duress protects only the latter economic interest, because the threat is never carried out where the duress is effective. The compensation is measured by the degree of injury caused by the coerced agreement.

The wrongfulness of the coercer's conduct derives from the fact that the threatened party was forced to accept the contract, not from any inherent wrongfulness of the act threatened. Ordinarily a party may threaten to do what is lawful; however, a coercer's threats may be wrongful even though the threatened action would have been legal. The key factor, therefore, must be the fact that the threatened action is an unreasonable alternative to an injurious contractual demand in a bargain situation. The wrongfulness of the coercer's conduct must be related to the unreasonableness of the alternatives which he presents to the weaker party in a bargaining situation. The inherent wrongfulness of either alternative is relevant only insofar as it shows the unreasonableness of the alternatives. The purpose of the duress doctrine, therefore, is to prevent a stronger party from offering an unreasonable choice of alternatives to a weaker party in a bargain situation....

B. Classification

Recognition of the purpose of the economic duress actions permits a classification of the doctrine into its proper form of action, tort or quasi-contract....

The duty in duress cases should be defined by reference to the discovered purpose of the duress doctrine — to protect a party's economic interests from the abuse of superior economic power by another who presents unreasonable alternatives in a bargain situation. A more coherent description of that duty would be *an obligation to use superior economic power reasonably in bargain situations*. This obligation is general in that it is owed to any party in an inferior bargaining position. The wrongful conduct is the coercive means used to obtain a benefit by injuring another, not the situation of a benefit innocently received....

It may be argued that the classification of economic duress as a tort is unnecessary. Quasi-contract is a flexible category which seems to be tailored to achieve substantial justice in duress cases, and therefore, it is arguable that the classification of duress as a tort is a superfluous academic exercise, regardless of the technical similarities between duress and tort doctrines. Quasi-contract, however, has suffered from a lack of clear analytical guidelines. The courts rely on concepts of "equity and natural justice" to determine whether retention of a benefit is just. This vagueness in quasi-contractual doctrine has contributed to the analytical confusion surrounding the duress area. Tort law, on the other hand, has developed reasonably well-defined concepts for dealing with wrongful acts which injure innocent parties. The concepts of duty, breach of duty, cause in fact, and damages focus attention of the relevant issues in tort cases. Consequently, use of a tort analytical scheme should lead to a more precise analysis, and a better reasoned and more consistent line of decisions.

An intermediate appellate court in Wisconsin sought to apply the new approach in 1979.

WURTZ v. FLEISCHMAN

89 Wis.2d 291, 278 N.W.2d 266 (Ct. Ap. 1979)

[Paul Wurtz owned the hotel Luzern on the shores of Lake Geneva, Wisconsin. He wanted to sell, and he hired William Fleischman, a real estate broker to represent him. However, after a year they had received no serious offers. Fleischman suggested turning the hotel into a Hilton Inn, but Wurtz wanted to sell outright. Fleischman was the president of Lakeside Habitat, Inc. He organized, and invested in, a limited partnership to develop a new hotel on the Wurtz property.

Wurtz decided that he wanted to exchange the hotel property for real estate with a value equal to $300,000. By trading real property, Wurtz would receive a tax advantage. Fleischman, representing Lakeside Habitat, Inc., agreed to exchange real estate with Wurtz. Wurtz was to tell Fleischman what property he wanted in exchange, and Fleischman was to buy it. They were then to exchange real estate. Wurtz selected, and Fleischman bought, a McDonald's restaurant in New Mexico and a warehouse in Delavan, Wisconsin.

The written contract called for the closing to take place on October 10, 1973. The document contained a typical "time is of the essence" clause. The parties extended the closing date to March 31, 1974, and then postponed it again. Fleischman could not get the financing needed to complete the transaction. Both Wurtz and Fleischman continued to act as if they were bound by the transaction. Wurtz accepted a credit at the closing equaling the monthly rental payments earned during the postponement period from the property Fleischman held to exchange for Wurtz's hotel. Finally, they agreed that the closing would take place on March 24, 1975.

Fleischman contended that, in a telephone conversation on March 23rd, Wurtz threatened not to close the deal unless Fleischman paid him an additional $50,000. Fleischman thought he had to agree or face financial ruin. He had no cash available because he had committed all his assets to the project. He offered Wurtz his interest in Lakeside Habitat which was worth $47,500. Wurtz accepted this offer, and the closing took place. Fleischman later refused to transfer his interest to Wurtz. Wurtz sued, asserting that he had been induced to close the transaction by Fleischman's promise which Fleischman had no intention of performing. The trial judge agreed and awarded Fleischman's interest in Lakeside Habitat to Wurtz. The judge said there was no duress because Fleischman had an adequate legal alternative to agreeing to Wurtz' demand. He could have refused to meet it and brought a legal action. Fleischman appealed.]

BROWN, J. Wurtz claimed at trial and he claims on appeal that the $50,000 demand was first made two or three months before the actual closing date and not the night before as is alleged by Fleischman. Wurtz professes that since time was of the essence and the clause was not expressly waived at the time of the second postponement, he was under no obligation to go through with the closing. Wurtz asserts, therefore, that he was legally justified in seeking a modification of the contract calling for an increased consideration. He argues that there was no economic duress and maintains that he is entitled to specific performance as ordered by the trial court.

In discussing the doctrine of economic or business compulsion, we note that Wisconsin has adopted the doctrine as a viable defense to a contract. In *Minneapolis, St. Paul & Sault Ste. Marie Railway Co. v. Railroad Commission*, 183 Wis. 47, 197 N.W. 352 (1924), the court stated:

> The old rule that there could be duress only where there was a threat of loss of life, limb, or liberty has been so changed that duress may sometimes be implied when a payment is made or an act performed to prevent great property loss or heavy penalties when there seems no adequate remedy except to submit to an unjust or illegal demand and then seek redress in the courts. 183 Wis. at 56, 197 N.W. at 355.

As late as 1960, the supreme court reaffirmed the adoption of the modern view which recognizes the existence of the doctrine. While the court has adopted the doctrine of business or economic compulsion, the criteria to be used in determining whether a cause of action or defense exists for economic duress has not been specifically set forth by any court in this state. However, analysis of the criteria to be examined in economic duress has been the subject of a number of law review articles. As the writer of an Iowa Law Review Note states, the courts which have adopted the modern view of economic duress have used many different formulas to determine whether or not a contract is voidable for economic or business compulsion. These formulas include the relative bargaining positions of the parties, the adequacy of alternative legal remedies, the gravity of the threatened evil, the wrongfulness or illegality of the threats, the fairness of the resulting bargain, and the ratification by the allegedly coerced party.

Some of these criteria sound in quasi-contract and others sound in tort. There has been much discussion by academicians about the proper analytical framework into which economic duress falls. One thing is clear — when one party wrongfully threatens another with severe economic loss if he does not enter a proposed contract, and the threatened party acquiesces solely because of the wrongful threat, the injury to the threatened party may be redressed under the doctrine of economic duress. It is the application of a more consistent duress theory which we seek, and as a result of our research we hereby adopt the analytical formula as suggested in the Iowa Law Review Note. This formula involves the tort criteria of duty, breach, causation and damages.

Before we may analyze the elements of economic duress, we must determine the burden of proof Fleischman must meet in order to establish a defense. In cases involving intentional torts, the supreme court has adopted and applied a middle burden of proof. See *Kuehn v. Kuehn*, 11 Wis.2d 15, 26-30, 104 N.W.2d 138, 145-47 (1960). Therefore, Fleischman must prove to a reasonable degree of certainty, by evidence that is clear, satisfactory and convincing, that the portion of the contract requiring that he deed his interest in the Lakeside Habitat development was a product of economic duress. Damages, however, need only be proven by the greater weight of the credible evidence. *Lang v. Oudenhoven*, 213 Wis. 666, 669, 252 N.W. 167, 168 (1934); Wis J I — Civil, Part 1, 1705.

DUTY

The duty in economic duress cases is the duty to exercise superior economic power reasonably in a bargain situation. Relative bargaining position should be determined from the entire context of the bargaining relation if it is to be meaningful in the duress analysis. A party has a superior bargaining position if he is the sole effect or source of something needed by the other party to avoid a severe economic loss and the relationship is not reciprocal. The origin of the unequal bargaining power should be irrelevant. Once the superior bargaining position is established, the party has a duty to use the position reasonably to assure the weaker party a reasonable choice of alternatives.

In the case before us, Wurtz, at the time of his demand for increased consideration, was in the good bargaining position while Fleischman was in an inferior one. Wurtz knew that Fleischman had spent a considerable amount of time and money putting the project together. In fact, Wurtz, being in daily contact with Fleischman, knew that Fleischman and his partners had spent $150,000 for the McDonald's and Delavan properties on Wurtz' behalf. Further, it was evident that if the closing did not take place as scheduled, Fleischman would not be able to sell the properties. The $150,000 would have been defaulted and reverted to the lender. Thus, Fleischman would have been bereft of $150,000.

Wurtz also knew that Fleischman had spent in excess of $35,000 in architectural fees to design a building to specifically fit the Hotel Luzern property. Had the closing not taken place, Fleischman would have spent $35,000 for naught. Fleischman had also spent $4,750 to bring the title up to date for closing, a cost which he, as buyer, had agreed to incur even though it is a cost that is normally undertaken by the seller. Fleischman further paid $1,500 in surveying fees, $10,500 in attorney fees for the necessary documents to close on the date scheduled and other attorney fees. In addition, Fleischman had a construction contract for $1,580,000 as well as $2,500 in other incidental expenses.

Fleischman contends that his whole financial well-being was dependent on successfully closing by the scheduled date and that failure to do so would have placed him in a situation of probable bankruptcy. Wurtz knew this. In his trial testimony, he characterized Fleischman's consent to the $50,000 demand as "involuntary."

Wurtz, on the other hand, had nothing to lose. First, he had another possible buyer available. Second, his lawyer was counseling him not to go through with the transaction for reasons unclear in the record. Third, during the life of the agreement and prior to closing, Wurtz was still able to run his Hotel Luzern business.

We conclude, therefore, that Fleischman had relied upon the contract to such an extent that the failure of Wurtz to perform would cause a disproportionate economic loss to him. Further, we do find that there was neither genuine negotiation between the parties, nor a counterthreat from Fleischman which might have forced Wurtz, as the allegedly coercing party, to make a concession. Wurtz had a superior bargaining position and was subject to the duty to use his economic power reasonably to assure Fleischman a reasonable choice of alternatives in his effort to avert serious economic loss.

BREACH OF THE DUTY

In order to find a breach of duty in cases of economic duress, one must be found to have used his superior bargaining position unreasonably. Generally, courts have required a finding that there were threats which were wrongful. To be wrongful, however, the threats need not be unlawful. They merely need to be unreasonable or unjustifiable. The standard of justifiability used by the courts in economic duress cases should be a standard of commercial reasonableness. Several criteria are contained in the Uniform Commercial Code for determining commercial reasonableness. Section 401.203, Stats., imposes an obligation of good faith in the performance or enforcement of a contract or duty. Section 402.103(1)(b), Stats., defines good faith in a commercial transaction as "honesty in fact and the observance of reasonable commercial standards of fair dealing in the trade."

Applying these standards to the present case, we find that there was sufficient evidence to show that Wurtz' actions did not meet the standards of commercial reasonableness.

At trial, Wurtz claimed that he demanded the additional $50,000 as compensation for lost profits from the McDonald's and Delavan properties as a result of the delay in closing. However, the closing statement gave Wurtz a credit for $19,200 which represented the amount of money Fleischman had agreed to pay for lost profits as a result of the delay. This credit was in addition to the $50,000 demanded by Wurtz. Wurtz' justification for the $50,000 demand is, therefore, highly suspect and indicates that his concern for lost profits was not the reason for the additional demand. Furthermore, Wurtz admitted at trial that he possibly had another buyer for his property. This fact, taken together with the fact that Fleischman had already paid for lost profits, indicates that the $50,000 demand was made in bad faith with the intent to either scuttle the deal so he could sell the property to someone else or get an additional $50,000 above that by which he was equitably entitled. We find, therefore, that Wurtz' demand for the additional $50,000 above and beyond the payment already made for lost profits was unjustifiable.

In addition, Wurtz testified that the demand for the additional $50,000 was made two to three months prior to closing. However, the closing statement, signed by Wurtz shortly before the closing, made no reference to the additional $50,000. The evidence, therefore, supports Fleischman's assertion that the demand was made the night before the closing. Even assuming the demand was made two months before the closing, we believe this conduct does not meet the commercial standards of fair dealing in the trade. The trade involved is commercial real estate. As a general rule, commercial sales involve a great deal of money, involve complicated financing arrangements and require a longer period of time to close. The offer to purchase, once accepted, is a contract on which both the buyer and the seller must rely to avoid financial difficulties. The buyer often makes other financial commitments in order to close the deal. Likewise, the seller may rely on the offer to purchase in making future investments. To permit either the buyer or the seller to change the terms of the contract at the last minute for an unjustified reason places commercial sales contracts in jeopardy. The purpose of the contract is to create certainty and stability in the commercial real estate trade. To permit last minute changes creates uncertainty and instability in a trade that demands certainty and stability. Therefore, we find that Wurtz' last minute, unjustified demand for the additional $50,000 did not meet reasonable commercial standards of fair dealing. Thus, he breached his duty to exercise his superior economic power reasonably in a bargaining situation.

CAUSATION

In order to establish tort liability, it is necessary to show that the wrongful act of the tort-feasor caused the injury to the victim. In economic duress cases, the causation issue is reduced to the question of whether the victim would have acquiesced in the absence of the wrongful threat. Thus, a factual finding that the wrongful threat was communicated and understood is, of course, a prerequisite for a finding that the threat was the reason for the victim's acquiescence. In the present case, there is no dispute over the fact that the demand for the additional $50,000 was made by Wurtz and understood by Fleischman. The only real factual question is whether Fleischman would have acquiesced but for the wrongful threat of Wurtz.

Fleischman testified that he would not have acquiesced, but the testimony of the person alleging he was coerced is self-serving. To allow an opportunity for effective rebuttal of self-serving contentions, the court must rely heavily on indirect evidence of causation. Any test to determine causation in duress cases must, therefore, be primarily objective.

The primary criteria to be used in applying an objective test for causation is whether the victim had an adequate legal remedy available to protect his interest at the time it was threatened. If there was an adequate legal remedy, the victim's failure to use it is strong evidence that acquiescence was caused by factors other than the wrongful threat. The victim has the duty to show either that there was no legal remedy available or that, if there was a legal remedy, it was inadequate. To prove inadequacy of the legal remedy, he must show one of two things. He must prove that the availability of the remedy was not clearly apparent at the time of the threat or that the remedy would not clearly protect his interest. It is obvious that in some instances, the legal remedy available may be inadequate to protect the threatened interest for a variety of reasons. For example, the threatened action may cause irreparable harm before any legal steps would be effective, or the compensatory legal remedy may fail to compensate the projected injury effectively.

Using this criteria, we have no doubt that the evidence shows Fleischman acquiesced solely because of Wurtz' threat to refuse to close the deal. There was no adequate remedy available to Fleischman at the time the threat was made that would have protected him from financial disaster. The only possible remedy was for Fleischman to sue for specific performance, but this remedy was inadequate. Assuming Wurtz would have been ordered to close the transaction under the terms of the purchase contract, the delay in obtaining the judgment for specific performance would have forced Fleischman into financial ruin. Furthermore, any financial loss suffered by Fleischman as a result of the delay could not have been returned to him in a suit for specific performance. He, therefore, had no adequate legal remedy.

Even assuming, arguendo, that specific performance was an adequate remedy, Wurtz admitted at trial that Fleischman's acquiescence was involuntary. Since there is no other evidence to support a finding that Fleischman acquiesced for reasons other than Wurtz' threat, the only reasonable conclusion is that Wurtz' threat to refuse to close without the additional $50,000 caused Fleischman's acquiescence.

Based on the record and the foregoing analysis, we find that Fleischman has proven a defense of economic duress by the greater weight of the credible evidence.

DAMAGES

Fleischman has claimed economic duress as a defense to a suit requesting that he be ordered to deed his interest in the Lakeside Habitat development to Wurtz. His interest was valued at $47,500. Having proven the defense of economic duress, Fleischman is entitled to his restitutionary remedy of invalidating that portion of the contract which requires that he deed the property to Wurtz. However, we note that economic duress is not only available as a defense to a suit on a contract, but also may be a separate cause of action or counterclaim. In such cases, the damages shall be the damages generally available for intentional torts. Damages may be awarded in such a sum as will compensate the injured party for his full pecuniary loss. This is the loss which is proven to a reasonable certainty to have flowed directly and necessarily from the acts of duress.... In appropriate cases, punitive damages may also be awarded.

By the Court. — Judgment reversed and cause remanded with directions to enter judgment in favor of the defendant.

Concurring Opinion of Judge Moser omitted.

The Wisconsin Supreme Court reviewed the case the next year.

WURTZ v. FLEISCHMAN

97 Wis.2d 100, 293 N.W.2d 155 (Wis. 1980)

[Justice Heffernan wrote an opinion for a unanimous court. The court decided that the court of appeals had exceeded its authority as an appellate court in making factual determinations in lieu of and in addition to the trial court's findings. The court of appeals was reversed, and the case was remanded for further proceedings consistent with the Supreme Court's opinion.]

The court of appeals said that, although this court has recognized the doctrine of economic or business duress as a valid defense to a contract, we have not, as yet, specifically articulated the criteria to be used in determining whether a cause of action or defense exists for economic duress.... To fill this perceived need, the court of appeals adopted the analytical formula proposed in a student law review note, *Economic Duress after the Demise of Free Will Theory: A Proposed Tort*

Analysis, 53 Iowa Law Review 892 (1968), and applied it to the facts of the case....

Neither party to this review challenges the criteria adopted by the court of appeals for determining duress. Nor is there any contention that the various factual determinations made by the court of appeals are without at least arguable support in the record. The question on review is limited to whether the court of appeals exceeded its authority by making factual determinations, based on conflicting evidence, in lieu of, and in addition to, the findings made by the trial court. We conclude that it clearly did....

Because we agree with the unstated assumption underlying the court of appeals' decision that the trial court did not make all the findings necessary for appellate review, we remand the cause to the trial court for it to make the necessary findings. If the trial judge concludes, upon reviewing the record, that there is an inadequate basis for making the necessary findings, he may reopen the case and take additional testimony. He may enter a judgment on the basis of the existing record or upon the basis of additional proceedings.

Among the basic elements of economic duress which the trial court should expressly consider on remand are those listed by *Williston* ... § 1617 at 704:

> 1. The party alleging economic duress must show that he has been the victim of a wrongful or unlawful act or threat, and
>
> 2. Such act or threat must be one which deprives the victim of his unfettered will.
>
> As a direct result of these elements, the party threatened must be compelled to make a disproportionate exchange of values or to give up something for nothing. If the payment or exchange is made with the hope of obtaining a gain, there is not duress; it must be made solely for the purpose of protecting the victim's business or property interests. Finally, the party threatened must have no adequate legal remedy. (Citations deleted.) *Accord*, 25 Am.Jur.2d, ... at 353-56; *Annot. — Economic Duress of Business Compulsion in Execution of Promissory Note,* 79 ALR3d 598 (1977); Hillman, *Policing Contract Modifications under the U.C.C.: Good Faith and the Doctrine of Economic Duress,* 64 Iowa Law Review 849 (1979).

Williston emphasizes that merely driving a hard bargain or taking advantage of another's financial difficulty is not duress. *Williston,* ... at 708. As Judge Robert W. Warren noted recently in a decision from the Eastern District of Wisconsin holding there was no economic duress because there was no wrongful act:

> Duress involves "wrongful acts ... that compel a person to manifest apparent assent to a transaction without his volition or cause such fear as to preclude him from exercising free will and judgment in entering into a transaction."

Restatement of Contracts, § 493 (1932). See *T.F. Pagel Lumber Co. v. Webster*, 231 Wis. 222, 285 N.W. 739 (1939)." *Federal Deposit Ins. Corp. v. Balistreri*, 470 F.Supp. 752, 758 (E.D.Wis. 1979).

Applying these authorities to the present case will require the trial court to consider whether Wurtz's refusal to close the deal unless Fleischman consented to modifying the agreement was wrongful. This determination will depend, in part, on whether Wurtz was under any legal obligation to close the deal after March 31, 1974 on the terms originally contemplated.... As *Pagel, supra*, states at 225, "Threats to do what the threatening person has a legal right to do, do not constitute duress."

Finally, it should be added that for the defendant to successfully defend on the ground of duress all the essential elements must be proved by clear and convincing evidence — the same burden that is imposed upon the plaintiff in asserting his cause of action for fraud.

Decision of the Court of Appeals reversed; and cause remanded to the trial court with directions to vacate the judgment and for further proceedings consistent with this opinion.

NOTES AND QUESTIONS

1. *The effect of the Supreme Court opinion*: Justice Heffernan states in his opinion "[t]he question on review is limited to whether the court of appeals exceeded its authority by making factual determinations, based on conflicting evidence, in lieu of, and in addition to the findings made by the trial court." Did the Supreme Court of Wisconsin limit its decision to this question of appellate procedure? Did it also examine and reject the legal standards used by the Court of Appeals in its review of the case? Neither party in its brief mentioned the material from Williston discussed at the end of Justice Heffernan's opinion, and neither discussed the tort analysis in the Iowa Law Review.

2. *The retrial of the case*: One of the attorneys who participated in the case told us that the case was retried before a different judge. This judge found there was economic duress and refused to award Fleischman's interest to Wurtz. Wurtz had no claim to extra money. Wurtz received rent from the property that had been bought for him during the delay in closing. The judge did not see Wurtz' conduct as justified. Wurtz did not appeal "because Wurtz would have lost." The Hilton Inn was built in Lake Geneva. Does the case on retrial represent an application of the approach of the Iowa Law Review, Justice Heffernan's opinion for the Supreme Court of Wisconsin, the Restatement (Second) of Contracts § 175, or still another test for duress?

c. Yet Another Standard?

Sometimes, as we have seen, cases raising essentially issues of state law are brought in federal courts, requiring the federal courts to determine what state law is on the issues of the case. Does the 7th Circuit in this case correctly divine the law of Wisconsin?

THE SELMER COMPANY v. BLAKESLEE-MIDWEST COMPANY

704 F.2d 924 (7th Circuit, 1983)

POSNER, J. This appeal by the plaintiff from summary judgment for the defendants in a diversity case requires us to consider the meaning, under Wisconsin contract law, of "economic duress" as a defense to a settlement of a contract dispute.

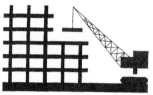

On this appeal, we must take as true the following facts. The plaintiff, Selmer, agreed to act as a subcontractor on a construction project for which the defendant Blakeslee-Midwest Prestressed Concrete Company was the general contractor. Under the contract between Blakeslee-Midwest and Selmer, Selmer was to receive $210,000 for erecting prestressed concrete materials supplied to it by Blakeslee-Midwest. Blakeslee-Midwest failed to fulfill its contractual obligations; among other things, it was tardy in supplying Selmer with the prestressed concrete materials. Selmer could have terminated the contract without penalty but instead agreed orally with Blakeslee-Midwest to complete its work, provided Blakeslee-Midwest would pay Selmer for the extra costs of completion due to Blakeslee-Midwest's defaults. When the job was completed, Selmer demanded payment of $120,000. Blakeslee-Midwest offered $67,000 and refused to budge from this offer. Selmer, because it was in desperate financial straits, accepted the offer.

Two and a half years later Selmer brought this suit against Blakeslee-Midwest (the other defendants' liability, being derivative from Blakeslee-Midwest's, does not require separate consideration), claiming that its extra costs had amounted to $150,000 ($120,000 being merely a settlement offer), and asking for that amount minus the $67,000 it had received, plus consequential and punitive damages. Although Selmer, presumably in order to be able to claim such damages, describes this as a tort rather than a contract action, it seems really to be a suit on Blakeslee-Midwest's alleged oral promise to reimburse Selmer in full for the extra costs of completing the original contract after Blakeslee-Midwest defaulted. But the characterization is unimportant. Selmer concedes that, whatever its suit is, it is barred by the settlement agreement if, as the district court held, that agreement is valid. The only question is whether there is a triable issue as to whether the settlement agreement is invalid because procured by "economic duress."

If you extract a promise by means of a threat, the promise is unenforceable. This is not, as so often stated, see, *e.g.*, *Totem Marine Tug & Barge, Inc. v. Alyeska Pipeline Serv. Co.*, 584 P.2d 15, 22 (Alaska 1978), because such a promise is involuntary, unless "involuntary" is a conclusion rather than the description of a mental state. If the threat is ferocious ("your money or your life") and believed, the victim may be desperately eager to fend it off with a promise. Such promises are made unenforceable in order to discourage threats by making them less profitable. The fundamental issue in a duress case is therefore not the victim's state of mind but whether the statement that induced the promise is the kind of offer to deal that we want to discourage, and hence that we call a "threat." Selmer argues that Blakeslee-Midwest said to it in effect, "give up $53,000 of your claim for extras [$120,000 minus $67,000], or you will get nothing." This has the verbal form of a threat but is easily recast as a promise innocuous on its face — "I promise to pay you $67,000 for a release of your claim." There is a practical argument against treating such a statement as a threat: it will make an inference of duress inescapable in any negotiation where one party makes an offer from which it refuses to budge, for the other party will always be able to argue that he settled only because there was a (figurative) gun at his head. It would not matter whether the party refusing to budge was the payor like Blakeslee-Midwest or the promisor like Selmer. If Selmer had refused to complete the job without being paid exorbitantly for the extras and Blakeslee-Midwest had complied with this demand because financial catastrophe would have loomed if Selmer had walked off the job, we would have the same case. A vast number of contract settlements would be subject to being ripped open upon an allegation of duress if Selmer's argument were accepted.

Sensitive — maybe oversensitive — to this danger, the older cases held that a threat not to honor a contract could not be considered duress. See, *e.g.*, *Sistrom v. Anderson*, 51 Cal.App.2d 213, 124 P.2d 372, 376 (Cal.App.1942); cf. *Batavian Bank v. North*, 114 Wis. 637, 645-46, 90 N.W. 1016, 1019 (1902). But the principle was not absolute, as is shown by *Alaska Packers' Ass'n v. Domenico*, 117 Fed. 99 (9th Cir. 1902). Sailors and fishermen (the libelants) "agreed in writing, for a certain stated compensation, to render their services to the appellant in remote waters where the season for conducting fishing operations is extremely short, and in which enterprise the appellant had a large amount of money invested; and, after having entered upon the discharge of their contract, and at a time when it was impossible for the appellant to secure other men in their places, the libelants, without any valid cause, absolutely refused to continue the services they were under contract to perform unless the appellant would consent to pay them more money." *Id.* at 102. The appellant agreed, but later reneged, and the libelants sued. They lost; the court refused to enforce the new agreement. Although the technical ground of decision was the absence of fresh consideration for the modified agreement, it seems apparent both from the quoted language and from a reference on the same page to coercion that the court's underlying concern was that the modified agreement had been procured by duress in the form of the threat to break the original contract. Cf. Farnsworth, Contracts 271 (1982).

Alaska Packers' Ass'n shows that because the legal remedies for breach of contract are not always adequate, a refusal to honor a contract may force the other party to the contract to surrender his rights — in *Alaska Packers' Ass'n*, the appellant's right to the libelants' labor at the agreed wage. It undermines the institution of contract to allow a contract party to use the threat of breach to get the contract modified in his favor not because anything has happened to require modification in the mutual interest of the parties but simply because the other party, unless he knuckles under to the threat, will incur costs for which he will have no adequate legal remedy. If contractual protections are illusory, people will be reluctant to make contracts. Allowing contract modifications to be voided in circumstances such as those in *Alaska Packers' Ass'n* assures prospective contract parties that signing a contract is not stepping into a trap, and by thus encouraging people to make contracts promotes the efficient allocation of resources.

Capps v. Georgia Pac. Corp., 253 Or. 248, 453 P.2d 935 (1969), illustrates the principle of *Alaska Packers' Ass'n* in the context of settling contract disputes. The defendant promised to give the plaintiff, as a commission for finding a suitable lessee for a piece of real estate, 5 percent of the total rental plus one half of the first month's rent. The plaintiff found a suitable lessee and the lease was signed. Under the terms of the commission arrangement the defendant owed the plaintiff $157,000, but he paid only $5,000, and got a release from the plaintiff of the rest. The plaintiff later sued for the balance of the $157,000, alleging that when requesting payment of the agreed-upon commission he had "informed Defendant that due to Plaintiff's adverse financial condition, he was in danger of immediately losing other personal property through repossession and foreclosure unless funds from Defendant were immediately made available for the purpose of paying these creditors." 253 Or. at 252, 453 P.2d at 937. But "Defendant, through its agent ..., advised Plaintiff that though he was entitled to the sums demanded in Plaintiff's Complaint, unless he signed the purported release set forth in Defendant's Answer, Plaintiff would receive no part thereof, inasmuch as Defendant had extensive resources and powerful and brilliant attorneys who would and could prevent Plaintiff in any subsequent legal proceedings from obtaining payment of all or any portion of said sums." *Id.* We can disregard the reference to the defendant's "powerful and brilliant attorneys" yet agree with the Oregon Supreme Court that the confluence of the plaintiff's necessitous financial condition, the defendant's acknowledged indebtedness for the full $157,000, and the settlement of the indebtedness for less than 3 cents on the dollar — with no suggestion that the defendant did not have the money to pay the debt in full — showed duress. The case did not involve the settlement of a genuine dispute, but, as in *Alaska Packers' Ass'n*, an attempt to exploit the contract promisee's lack of an adequate legal remedy.

Although *Capps* is not a Wisconsin case, we have no reason to think that Wisconsin courts would reach a different result. Cf. *Mendelson v. Blatz Brewing Co.*, 9 Wis.2d 487, 494, 101 N.W.2d 805, 809 (1960); *Wurtz v. Fleischman*, 97 Wis.2d 100, 109-11, 293 N.W.2d 155, 160 (1980). But the only feature that the present case shares with *Capps* is that the plaintiff was in financial difficulties. Since Blakeslee-Midwest did not acknowledge that it owed Selmer $120,000, and since the settlement exceeded 50 percent of Selmer's demand, the terms of the settlement are not unreasonable on their face, as in *Capps*. Thus the question is starkly posed whether financial difficulty can by itself justify setting aside a settlement on grounds of duress. It cannot. "The mere stress of business conditions will not constitute duress where the defendant was not responsible for the conditions." *Johnson, Drake & Piper, Inc. v. United States*, 531 F.2d 1037, 1042 (Ct.Cl.1976) (per curiam). The adverse effect on the finality of settlements and hence on the willingness of parties to settle their contract disputes without litigation would be great if the cash needs of one party were alone enough to entitle him to a trial on the validity of the settlement. In particular, people who desperately wanted to settle for cash — who simply could not afford to litigate — would be unable to settle, because they could not enter into a *binding* settlement; being desperate, they could always get it set aside later on grounds of duress. It is a detriment, not a benefit, to one's long-run interests not to be able to make a binding commitment.

Matters stand differently when the complaining party's financial distress is due to the other party's conduct. Although Selmer claims that it was the extra expense caused by Blakeslee-Midwest's breaches of the original contract that put it in a financial vise, it could have walked away from the contract without loss or penalty when Blakeslee-Midwest broke the contract. Selmer was not forced by its contract to remain on the job, and was not prevented by circumstances from walking away from the contract, as the appellant in *Alaska Packers' Ass'n* had been; it stayed on the job for extra pay. We do not know why Selmer was unable to weather the crisis that arose when Blakeslee-Midwest refused to pay $120,000 for Selmer's extra expenses — whether Selmer was undercapitalized or overborrowed or what — but Blakeslee-Midwest cannot be held responsible for whatever it was that made Selmer so necessitous, when, as we have said, Selmer need not have embarked on the extended contract.

[Eds. Note: We have deleted two paragraphs from the opinion in which the court rejects Selmer's argument that Blakeslee-Midwest's witholding of "retainage" constituted "duress of goods." The argument, though an interesting one, was discussed in a passage more confusing than illuminating.]

Affirmed.

NOTES AND QUESTIONS

1. *Judge Posner and law and economics*: Judge Posner is a former professor of law at the University of Chicago. He was appointed to the United States Court

of Appeals for the Seventh Circuit by President Reagan. A Wall Street Journal article[34] tells us something of Judge Posner:

CHICAGO — Judge Richard A. Posner has little use for words like fairness and justice. "Terms which have no content," he calls them. What America's lawyers and judges need, he says, is a healthy dose of free-market thinking.

From the bench of the U.S. Court of Appeals for the Seventh Circuit here, Judge Posner applies a standard of economic efficiency in cases where many others fail to see markets at play. He calibrates social costs and benefits on questions of religious expression and privacy.

In a highly controversial 1983 dissent, he argued against the widespread practice of appointing free counsel to represent prisoners who bring civil-rights suits. If the prisoner can't retain a lawyer on a contingency-fee basis, he wrote, "the natural inference to draw is that he doesn't have a good case."

Such opinions are part of what the 47-year old judge calls his self-assumed mission to "raise the level of economic literacy" in the federal judiciary. They have also drawn attention to "Law and Economics," an intellectual movement of which Judge Posner is a leading theorist and tireless booster....

Judge Posner is a tall, thin man whose friendly manner contradicts a reputation for bullying attorneys in the courtroom. Slumped casually on a green leather couch in his spacious Chicago chambers, the judge answers questions while flipping through a copy of his best-known book, the encyclopedic "Economic Analysis of Law." The text, a common sight on law campuses, sweeps all legal doctrine into the orderly economists world....

... In writing his judicial opinions — he has published some 450 in five years — Judge Posner says he resorts only sparingly to the "provocatively overt use of economics." But sometimes, he says, he can't resist the urge to shake things up....

... Judge Posner scoffs at criticism of his technique. "Many of my opinions would be more likely to use a word like 'costs' than other judges' opinions," he says, "but to the extent that it's this simple common-sensical balancing approach, it's nothing new."

He also welcomes controversy. "People don't bother to be hostile to things unless they fear them," he says. Much resistance to Law and Economics, he adds, comes from lawyers and judges who don't understand

---

[34]Barrett, Influential Ideas: A Movement Called "Law and Economics" Sways Legal Circles, (c) Wall Street Journal, August 4, 1986, at 1, col. 1. Reprinted by permission of Wall Street Journal, c 1986 Dow Jones & Company, Inc. All Rights Reserved Worldwide.

it and may feel threatened with "intellectual obsolescence." As recent law-school graduates move into influential firms and onto the bench, acceptance of Law and Economics will grow, he predicts.

For one response to some law and economics writing, including Posner's, see Kennedy and Michelman, Are Property and Contract Efficient?, 8 Hofstra Law Review 711 (1980). Arthur Leff reviewed Posner's *Economic Analysis of Law*.[35] He said that the closest analogue to Posner's approach was the picaresque novel such as *Tom Jones*. In such novels the "hero sets out into a world of complexity and brings to bear on successive segments of it the power of his own particular personal vision. The world presents itself as a series of problems; to each problem that vision acts as a form of solution; and the problem having been dispatched, our hero passes on to the next adventure." Posner's hero, of course, is economic analysis. It solves any and all problems. Leff asks "what pressures in contemporary legal scholarship might be responsible for the appearance, now, of four hundred pages of tunnel vision...." He concludes, "[s]ince its basic intellectual technique is the substitution of definitions for both normative and empirical propositions, I would call it American Legal Nominalism."

2. *The nature of Judge Posner's approach*: Does Judge Posner apply a will theory test? Is his approach consistent with the Restatement (Second) of Contracts § 175? Judge Posner is considering a case brought to federal court under diversity of citizenship jurisdiction. He says he is applying Wisconsin law. Is he applying the doctrine of the *Wurtz* case correctly?

4. Undue Influence

The doctrine of undue influence is another instance of social control of the contracting process. Undue influence can play a role in relational contracts when judges see the situation as falling outside an impersonal market setting. The rule is hardly precise. There must be something other than an impersonal market relationship. People can use bargaining power, but not too much. The court must see the weakness of the one wanting out of a deal as excusable. While we might see it as a special case of duress, often courts treat it as a distinct way to attack some types of contracts.

The doctrine plays its major role in gifts and wills. For example, an elderly person becomes attached to his doctor and alienated from his children and grandchildren. The person changes his will, leaving a large bequest to the doctor and then dies. The children and grandchildren contest the will. They claim that the doctor exercised undue influence to gain a bequest. A doctor often has a special relationship with an older person. It is not an arms-length sale of services

---

[35]Leff, Economic Analysis of Law: Some Realism About Nominalism, 60 Virginia Law Review 451 (1974).

in an impersonal market. The patient sees the doctor as the only one trying to make things better. Unlike the patient's adult children, the doctor pays attention to an older person. But the children will claim that the doctor poisoned the mind of the older person against the family. Courts struggle with many of these cases every year.[36] The chance of a will contest, of course, prompts many settlements under which doctors, lawyers, nurses and friendly neighbors share the bequest with family members.

Consider the following case and contrast its approach to that of courts judging claims of duress where one party drove a hard bargain.

ODORIZZI v. BLOOMFIELD SCHOOL DISTRICT

246 Cal.App.2d 123, 54 Cal.Rptr. 533 (2d Dist. 1966).

FLEMING, J. Appeal from a judgment dismissing plaintiff's amended complaint on demurrer.

Plaintiff Donald Odorizzi was employed during 1964 as an elementary school teacher by defendant Bloomfield School District and was under contract with the District to continue to teach school the following year as a permanent employee. On June 10 he was arrested on criminal charges of homosexual activity, and on June 11 he signed and delivered to his superiors his written resignation as a teacher, a resignation which the District accepted on June 13. In July the criminal charges against Odorizzi were dismissed ... [under a statute calling for dismissal where a person "has been indicted without reasonable or probable cause"] and in September he sought to resume his employment with the District. On the District's refusal to reinstate him he filed suit for declaratory and other relief.

Odorizzi's amended complaint asserts his resignation was invalid because obtained through duress, fraud, mistake, and undue influence and given at a time when he lacked capacity to make a valid contract. Specifically, Odorizzi declares he was under such severe mental and emotional strain at the time he signed his resignation, having just completed the process of arrest, questioning by the police, booking, and release on bail, and having gone for forty hours without sleep, that he was incapable of rational thought or action. While he was in this condition and unable to think clearly, the superintendent of the District and the principal of his school came to his apartment. They said they were trying to help and had his best interests at heart, that he should take their advice and immediately resign his position with the District, that there was no time to consult an attorney, that if he did not resign immediately the District would suspend and dismiss him from his position and publicize the proceedings, his "aforedescribed

---

[36]See Shaffer, Undue Influence, Confidential Relationship, and the Psychology of Transference, 45 Notre Dame Lawyer 197 (1970). Compare McClamroch v. McClamroch, 476 N.E.2d 514 (Ct.Ap. Indiana 1985), where the person unsuccessfully charged with undue influence was a second wife.

arrest" and cause him "to suffer extreme embarrassment and humiliation"; but that if he resigned at once the incident would not be publicized and would not jeopardize his chances of securing employment as a teacher elsewhere. Odorizzi pleads that because of his faith in their representations they were able to substitute their will and judgment in place of his own and thus obtain his signature to his purported resignation. A demurrer to his amended complaint was sustained without leave to amend....

No duress or menace has been pleaded.... [A] threat to take legal action is not unlawful unless the party making the threat knows the falsity of his claim.... The amended complaint shows in substance that the school representatives announced their intention to initiate suspension and dismissal proceedings under Education Code ... at a time when the filing of such proceedings was not only their legal right but their positive duty as school officials.... Although the filing of such proceedings might be extremely damaging to plaintiff's reputation, the injury would remain incidental so long as the school officials acted in good faith in the performance of their duties....

Nor do we find a cause of action for fraud ... [because the amended complaint] failed to assert the elements of knowledge of falsity, intent to induce reliance, and justifiable reliance.... As to mistake, the amended complaint fails to disclose any facts which would suggest that consent had been obtained through a mistake of fact or law....[37]

However, the pleading does set out a claim that plaintiff's consent to the transaction had been obtained through the use of undue influence.

Undue influence, in the sense we are concerned with here, is a shorthand legal phrase used to describe persuasion which tends to be coercive in nature, persuasion which overcomes the will without convincing the judgment.... The hallmark of such persuasion is high pressure, a pressure which works on mental, moral, or emotional weakness to such an extent that it approaches the boundaries of coercion. In this sense, undue influence has been called overpersuasion.... While most reported cases of undue influence involve persons who bear a confidential relationship to one another, a confidential or authoritative relationship between the parties need not be present when the undue influence involves unfair advantage taken of another's weakness or distress.

We paraphrase the summary of undue influence given the jury by Sir James P. Wilde in *Hall v. Hall*, L.R. 1, P & D 481, 492 (1891): To make a good contract a man must be a free agent. Pressure of whatever sort which overpowers the will without convincing the judgment is a species of restraint under which no valid contract can be made. Importunity or threats, if carried to the degree in which the free play of a man's will is overborne, constitute undue influence, although no force is used or threatened. A party may be led but not driven, and

---

[37]Apparently, the plaintiff alleged that both sides were mistaken when they thought plaintiff would be prosecuted for homosexual activity.

his acts must be the offspring of his own volition and not the record of someone else's.

In essence undue influence involves the use of excessive pressure to persuade one vulnerable to such pressure, pressure applied by a dominant subject to a servient object. In combination, the elements of undue susceptibility in the servient person and excessive pressure by the dominating person make the latter's influence undue, for it results in the apparent will of the servient person being in fact the will of the dominant person....

[T]his first element of undue influence resolves itself into a lessened capacity of the object to make a free contract.... Plaintiff declares he was under severe mental and emotional strain at the time because he had just completed the process of arrest, questioning, booking, and release on bail and had been without sleep for forty hours. It is possible that exhaustion and emotional turmoil may wholly incapacitate a person from exercising his judgment.... [P]laintiff has pleaded that possibility and sufficient allegations to state a case for rescission.

Undue influence in its second aspect involves an application of excessive strength by a dominant subject against a servient object.... Whether a person of subnormal capacities has been subjected to ordinary force or a person of normal capacities subjected to extraordinary force, the match is equally out of balance. If will has been overcome against judgment, consent may be rescinded.

The difficulty, of course, lies in determining when the forces of persuasion have overflowed their normal banks and become oppressive flood waters. There are second thoughts to every bargain, and hindsight is still better than foresight. Undue influence cannot be used as a pretext to avoid bad bargains or escape from bargains which refuse to come up to expectations. A woman who buys a dress on impulse, which on critical inspection by her best friend turns out to be less fashionable than she had thought, is not legally entitled to set aside the sale on the ground that the saleswoman used all her wiles to close the sale. A man who buys a tract of desert land in the expectation that it is in the immediate path of the city's growth and will become another Palm Springs, an expectation cultivated in glowing terms by the seller, cannot rescind his bargain when things turn out differently. If we are temporarily persuaded against our better judgment to do something about which we later have second thoughts, we must abide the consequences of the risks inherent in managing our own affairs....

However, overpersuasion is generally accompanied by certain characteristics which tend to create a pattern. The pattern usually involves several of the following elements: (1) discussion of the transaction at an unusual or inappropriate time, (2) consummation of the transaction in an unusual place, (3) insistent demand that the business be finished at once, (4) extreme emphasis on untoward consequences of delay, (5) the use of multiple persuaders by the dominant side against a single servient party, (6) absence of third-party advisers to the servient party, (7) statements that there is no time to consult financial advisers or attorneys. If a number of these elements are simultaneously present, the persuasion may be characterized as excessive....

[For example, in *Weger v. Rocha*, 138 Cal.App. 109, 32 P.2d 417] [p]laintiff, while confined in a cast in a hospital, gave a release of claims for personal injuries for a relatively small sum to an agent who spent two hours persuading her to sign. At the time of signing plaintiff was in a highly nervous and hysterical condition and suffering much pain, and she signed the release in order to terminate the interview. The court held that the release had been secured by the use of undue influence....

The difference between legitimate persuasion and excessive pressure, like the difference between seduction and rape, rests to a considerable extent in the manner in which the parties go about their business.[38] For example, if a day or two after Odorizzi's release on bail the superintendent of the school district had called him into his office during business hours and directed his attention to those provisions of the Education Code compelling his leave of absence and authorizing his suspension on the filing of written charges against him, had pointed out the alternative of resignation available to him, had informed him he was free to consult counsel or any adviser he wished and to consider the matter overnight and return with his decision the next day, it is extremely unlikely that any complaint about the use of excessive pressure could ever have been made against the school district.

But, according to the allegations of the complaint, this is not the way it happened, and if it had happened that way, plaintiff would never have resigned. Rather, the representatives of the school board undertook to achieve their objective by overpersuasion and imposition to secure plaintiff's signature but not his consent to his resignation through a high-pressure carrot-and-stick technique — under which they assured plaintiff they were trying to assist him, he should rely on their advice, there wasn't time to consult an attorney, if he didn't resign at once the school district would suspend and publicize the proceedings, but if he did resign the incident wouldn't jeopardize his chances of securing a teaching post elsewhere.

Plaintiff has thus pleaded both subjective and objective elements entering the undue influence equation and stated sufficient facts to put in issue the question whether his free will had been overborne by defendant's agents at a time when he was unable to function in a normal manner....

We express no opinion on the merits of plaintiff's case, or the propriety of his continuing to teach school.... We do hold that his pleading, liberally construed, states a cause of action for rescission of a transaction to which his apparent consent had been obtained through the use of undue influence.

The judgment is reversed.

---

[38]Students have objected to this sentence. They argue that rape and seduction differ fundamentally and not just in degree. The sentence is a quotation from the court's opinion. In context, is the judge's sentence objectionable?

NOTES AND QUESTIONS

1. *An application of the Odorizzi doctrine*: *Keithley v. Civil Service Bd. of Oakland*,[39] involved a situation very similar to the Odorizzi case. A woman charged a police officer with rape. The victim was a woman who had been staying with the officer and his wife. He admitted to having sexual relations with the woman but claimed she had consented. The officer's wife became hysterical when she learned of the charges against him. The officer stayed up all night with his wife. The next day, the officer reported to Deputy Chief Brown. Brown advised him that the district attorney had not issued a complaint and the rape charges were dropped. Then Brown read a provision in the police manual that said officers were to conduct their private affairs so as not to bring the department into disrepute. He asked the officer what he intended to do about the matter. The officer asked for a few hours to think over the matter, but the Deputy Chief refused. The officer then wrote a letter of resignation.

The court noted "there are no fixed definitions or inflexible formulas. Rather, we are concerned with whether from the entire context it appears that one's will was overborne and he was induced to do or forbear to do an act which he would not do, or would do, if left to act freely." It found enough evidence of undue influence to support a finding by a civil service board.

> Of particular significance is the evidence that Liquori [the officer] was called to police headquarters on three successive days, was kept waiting for long periods of time, was interrogated by a member of the homicide squad, and on the third day was ordered to appear before Brown, who, although already advised that the charges had been dropped, proceeded to read the statements regarding the charges and asked Liquori what he was going to do, emphasizing simultaneously that the charges should not be made public and suggesting that Liquori was guilty of unofficer-like conduct. Liquori was not given any time to consider what he wanted to do and was repeatedly asked what he was going to do about the situation. There was also evidence that at the time he signed his resignation Liquori was emotionally upset and that he was physically fatigued because he had not slept for 24 hours. These facts reasonably lend themselves to the inference that excessive pressure was used to persuade Liquori, who was vulnerable to such pressure by Brown, a dominant person, so as to overcome Liquori's will without convincing his judgment.

Suppose the officer had alleged that his resignation was the result of duress? Did the Deputy Chief threaten to do anything he didn't have a legal right to do? If he did not, what did he do to cause the court to overturn the transaction? The

---

[39]11 Cal. App. 3d 443, 89 Cal. Rptr. 809 (1st Dist. 1970).

court did not seem concerned about whether the Deputy Chief knew of the officer's situation or state of mind. Should this matter?

2. *Undue influence and duress*: Professor E. Allan Farnsworth, of the Columbia Law School, was the Reporter for the second half of the Restatement (Second) of Contracts. He discusses the relationship between undue influence and duress.[40] He notes that a court could have reached much the same result in the *Odorizzi* case using an expanded doctrine of duress rather than undue influence.

> The liberalization of the requirement that the threat be one that the law condemns would permit the court to find that the school board's threat to publicize any proceedings against Odorizzi and hurt his chances of obtaining another job was an improper one on the ground that doing so would harm Odorizzi and would not significantly benefit the school board. And the liberalization of the requirement that the threat be sufficiently grave to justify the victim's assent would permit the court to conclude that Odorizzi had no reasonable alternative but to resign in the fact of the improper threat.
>
> It is therefore a likely consequence of the liberalization of the requirements of duress that courts and litigants will place more emphasis on the coercive nature of transactions that were previously subject to attack only on the grounds of undue influence. The doctrine of duress may, in the long run, swallow up much of what has previously been considered to be undue influence.

5. Misrepresentation

Most people agree that the state should intervene in the contracting process to prevent and remedy fraud. Even those who want a wide area in which bargainers are free to exercise choices and power accept some limitations on dishonesty. We can provoke controversy, however, when we consider how far to carry this idea.

Those who believe in choice and individualism could view the law of misrepresentation in a number of ways. The virtues of free contract flow from situations where both understand the facts and risks. Then they fashion a deal responding to them. If I trick you into signing a contract, I have robbed you of free choice. The formal deal will be but an empty shell. It will not reflect your assumptions and expectations. Moreover, I know that it does not. I am trying to impose my will on you by trickery and cheating. My conduct has little, if any, social value. There is no reason to encourage it.

Nonetheless, the legal system may insist that you take care of yourself. It may deny remedies for fraud that you could have avoided. This may serve several functions. Courts lighten their work load by turning you away. Courts can give

---

[40]See Farnsworth, Coercion in Contract Law, 5 U. Arkansas at Little Rock Law Journal 329 (1982).

you incentives to use care and be suspicious. If you respond to these incentives, your behavior will help the market work better at less cost.[41]

Furthermore, courts seek to protect transactions from invalid claims of fraud made by dishonest people seeking to get out of a bad deal. When I discover I've made a bad deal, I may want to get out. I may lie about what you said, charging you with misrepresentations you did not make. They can impose hard to prove requirements and demand clear proof. Moreover, one faced with a bad deal may go through a very human process of self-deception. I may convince myself that you must have said certain things that, in fact, you did not say. Courts may wish to avoid having to search for truth by imposing heavy self-reliance rules.

We should recognize the practical consequences of the choices being made. If courts impose a high burden of proof to establish difficult to prove requirements, few law suits will succeed. If they accept the ordinary civil burden of proof and demand only easy-to-prove requirements, those asserting misrepresentation will win more cases. Who benefits from making misrepresentation hard to establish? Who benefits from making it easier to establish? The impact of these choices will benefit some and hurt others. This impact may not be random.

Fraud often is an orphan in the law school curriculum. Contracts teachers see it as part of torts. Torts teachers see their mission as exploring negligence and auto accidents. They either omit the subject or teach it very quickly. Nonetheless, dealing with misrepresentation is an important part of social control of contract.

The classic tort of fraud — the core doctrine — grants relief where the defendant (a) fraudulently has made (b) a material misrepresentation of (c) fact on which (d) the plaintiff had a right to rely. Then plaintiff must prove (e) reliance on the misrepresentation which (f) caused (g) injury. Until the mid-twentieth century, plaintiffs faced serious difficulties dealing with all of these ideas. For example, the statement must be false, and this can be the subject of debate. Defendant must intend to deceive plaintiff to induce making a contract. An honest mistake would not be fraudulent. It is not easy to prove that defendant knew her statement was false. Moreover, the false statement must be material. The legal system judges its significance in the transaction. It must be a statement of fact. Opinions and predictions normally were not enough. Of course, often it is not easy to distinguish between assertions of fact and opinions.

Those claiming fraud faced even greater difficulty under the classic law. Plaintiff must have a right to rely. The rule was *caveat emptor* — let the buyer beware. On one hand, a buyer could not rely on seller's talk or puffing. Buyers had to ignore statements such as "this is the finest used car available in this town." On the other hand, plaintiff had to take reasonable steps toward self-

---

[41]In the words of Judge Posner, "Even in the case of deliberate misrepresentations, a requirement that the plaintiff prove reasonable reliance ... serves a healthy purpose. Legal proceedings are costly, and it is cheaper for a potential victim of misrepresentation to take very inexpensive precautions than to allow him to shut his eyes to the obvious and then sue." Amoco Oil Co. v. Ashcraft, 791 F.2d 519 (7th Cir. 1986).

protection. She had to inspect the subject of the contract and find flaws for herself. She could not trust a seller's statements. She had to read and understand all documents. She had to discover clauses that offset oral representations. Finally, a plaintiff had to prove that her reliance caused injury of a tangible kind. The common law added to all this difficulty by requiring that a plaintiff prove fraud by clear and convincing evidence. This is a heavier burden than courts impose on plaintiffs in most civil cases.

By the 1990s, courts have questioned, softened or even abandoned almost all the elements of the classic tort. Sellers are sometimes responsible today for innocent misrepresentations. Buyers have much less duty to inspect and discover fraud. Why has the law changed? What virtues are there in holding sellers of goods, services and houses responsible for the truth of their statements and opinions expressed to buyers?

It is very difficult to state a general law of fraud that would hold true today across all states. Some jurisdictions are far more favorable to buyers than others. Even in a particular state, the cases may be inconsistent or difficult to reconcile.

We can only introduce this area. There are many cases dealing with aspects of misrepresentation as a tort, as a basis for restitution, and as a defense to a suit on a contract. We will look at one topic that provokes sharp differences of opinion. Over one hundred years ago, Lord Justice Cairns said, "[m]ere non-disclosure of material facts, however morally censurable ... would in my opinion form no ground for an action in the nature of ... misrepresentation."[42] About thirty years ago, Harper and James, both professors then at the Yale Law School, said, "the exceptions have gone far toward becoming the rule. Business is still business and the law does not yet require adversary parties, dealing at arm's length in a business transaction, to put all their cards on the table, face up. Nevertheless, business ethics, community standards and judicial practice have gone a long way from the caveat emptor norms of the nineteenth century."[43] After the years of the consumer movement, we have to consider today's situation carefully. Not only have courts changed the common law requirements, but statutes and administrative regulations often offer new forms of protection against misrepresentations.

OBDE v. SCHLEMEYER

56 Wash.2d 449, 353 P.2d 672 (1960).

FINLEY, J. — Plaintiffs, Mr. and Mrs. Fred Obde, brought this action to recover damages for the alleged fraudulent concealment of termite infestation in an apartment house purchased by them from the defendants, Mr. and Mrs. Robert Schlemeyer. Plaintiffs assert that the building was infested at the time of

---

[42]Peek v. Gurney, L.R. 6 H.L. 377, 403 (1873).

[43]Harper and James, The Law of Torts 590 (1956).

the purchase; that defendants were well apprised of the termite condition, but fraudulently concealed it from the plaintiffs.

After a trial on the merits, the trial court entered findings of fact and conclusions of law sustaining the plaintiffs' claim, and awarded them a judgment for damages in the amount of $3,950. The defendants appealed. Their assignments of error may be compartmentalized, roughly, into two categories: (1) those going to the question of liability, and (2) those relating to the amount of damages to be awarded if liability is established.

First, as to the question of liability: The Schlemeyers concede that, shortly after they purchased the property from a Mr. Ayars on an installment contract in April 1954, they discovered substantial termite infestation in the premises. The Schlemeyers contend, however, that they immediately took steps to eradicate the termites, and that, at the time of the sale to the Obdes in November 1954, they had no reason to believe that these steps had not completely remedied the situation. We are not convinced of the merit of this contention.

The record reveals that when the Schlemeyers discovered the termite condition they engaged the services of a Mr. Senske, a specialist in pest control. He effected some measures to eradicate the termites, and made some repairs in the apartment house. Thereafter, there was no easily apparent or surface evidence of termite damage. However, portions of the findings of fact entered by the trial court read as follows:

> Senske had advised Schlemeyer that in order to obtain a complete job it would be necessary to drill the holes and pump the fluid into all parts of the basement floors as well as the basement walls. Part of the basement was used as a basement apartment. Senske informed Schlemeyer that the floors should be taken up in the apartment and the cement flooring under the wood floors should be treated in the same manner as the remainder of the basement. Schlemeyer did not care to go to the expense of tearing up the floors to do this and therefore this portion of the basement was not treated.
>
> Senske also told Schlemeyer even though the job were done completely, including treating the portion of the basement which was occupied by the apartment, to be sure of success, it would be necessary to make inspections regularly for a period of a year. Until these inspections were made for this period of time the success of the process could not be determined. Considering the job was not completed as mentioned, Senske would give Schlemeyer no assurance of success and advised him that he would make no guarantee under the circumstances.

No error has been assigned to the above findings of fact. Consequently, they will be considered as the established facts of the case.... The pattern thus established is hardly compatible with the Schlemeyers' claim that they had no reason to believe that their efforts to remedy the termite condition were not completely successful.

The Schlemeyers urge that, in any event, as sellers, they had no duty to inform the Obdes of the termite condition. They emphasize that it is undisputed that the purchasers asked no questions respecting the possibility of termites. They rely on a Massachusetts case involving a substantially similar factual situation, *Swinton v. Whitinsville Sav. Bank* (1942), 311 Mass. 677, 42 N. E. (2d) 808, 141 A. L. R. 965. Applying the traditional doctrine of *caveat emptor* — namely, that, as between parties dealing at arms length (as vendor and purchaser), there is no duty to speak, in the absence of a request for information — the Massachusetts court held that a vendor of real property has no duty to disclose to a prospective purchaser the fact of a latent termite condition in the premises.

Without doubt, the parties in the instant case were dealing at arms length. Nevertheless, and notwithstanding the reasoning of the Massachusetts court above noted, we are convinced that the defendants had a duty to inform the plaintiffs of the termite condition. In *Perkins v. Marsh* (1934), 179 Wash. 362, 37 P. (2d) 689, a case involving parties dealing at arms length as landlord and tenant, we held that,

"Where there are concealed defects in demised premises, dangerous to the property, health or life of the tenant, which defects are known to the landlord when the lease is made, but unknown to the tenant, and which a careful examination on his part would not disclose, it is the landlord's duty to disclose them to the tenant before leasing, and his failure to do so amounts to a fraud."

We deem this rule to be equally applicable to the vendor-purchaser relationship. See 15 Tex. Law Review (December 1936) 1, 14-16, Keeton: *Fraud — Concealment and Non-Disclosure*. In this article Professor Keeton also aptly summarized the modern judicial trend away from a strict application of *caveat emptor* by saying:

It is of course apparent that the content of the maxim 'caveat emptor,' used in its broader meaning of imposing risks on both parties to a transaction, has been greatly limited since its origin. When Lord Cairns stated in *Peek v. Gurney* that there was no duty to disclose facts, however morally censurable their non-disclosure may be, he was stating the law as shaped by an individualistic philosophy based upon freedom of contract. It was not concerned with morals. In the present stage of the law, the decisions show a drawing away from this idea, and there can be seen an attempt by many courts to reach a just result in so far as possible, but yet maintaining the degree of certainty which the law must have. The statement may often be found that if either party to a contract or sale conceals or suppresses a material fact which he is in good faith bound to disclose then his silence is fraudulent.

The attitude of the courts toward non-disclosure is undergoing a change and contrary to Lord Cairns' famous remark it would seem that the object of the law in these cases should be to impose on parties to the transaction a duty to speak whenever justice, equity, and fair dealing demand it. (page 31.)

A termite infestation of a frame building, such as that involved in the instant case, is manifestly a serious and dangerous condition. One of the Schlemeyers' own witnesses, Mr. Hoefer, who at the time was a building inspector for the city of Spokane, testified that "... if termites are not checked in their damage, they can cause a complete collapse of a building, ... they would simply eat up the wood." Further, at the time of the sale of the premises, the condition was clearly latent — not readily observable upon reasonable inspection. As we have noted, all superficial or surface evidence of the condition had been removed by reason of the efforts of Senske, the pest control specialist. Under the circumstances, we are satisfied that "justice, equity, and fair dealing," to use Professor Keeton's language, demanded that the Schlemeyers speak — that they inform prospective purchasers, such as the Obdes, of the condition, regardless of the latter's failure to ask any questions relative to the possibility of termites.

... Schlemeyers' final contentions, relating to the issue of liability, emphasize the Obdes' conduct after they discovered the termite condition. Under the purchase agreement with the Schlemeyers, the Obdes paid $5,000 in cash, and gave their promissory note for $2,250 to the Schlemeyers. In addition, they assumed the balance due on the installment contract, under which the Schlemeyers had previously acquired the property from Ayars. This amounted to $34,750. After they discovered the termites (some six weeks subsequent to taking possession of the premises in November 1954), the Obdes continued for a time to make payments on the Ayars contract. They then called in Senske to examine the condition — not knowing that he had previously worked on the premises at the instance of the Schlemeyers. From Senske the Obdes learned for the first time that the Schlemeyers had known of the termite infestation prior to the sale. Obdes then ceased performance of the Ayars contract, and allowed the property to revert to Ayars under a forfeiture provision in the installment contract.

The Schlemeyers contend that by continuing to make payments on the Ayars contract after they discovered the termites the Obdes waived any right to recovery for fraud. This argument might have some merit if the Obdes were seeking to rescind the purchase contract.... However, this is not an action for rescission; it is a suit for damages, and thus is not barred by conduct constituting an affirmance of the contract. *Salter v. Heiser, supra.*

Contrary to the Schlemeyers final argument relative to the question of liability, the Obdes' ultimate default and forfeiture on the Ayars contract does not constitute a bar to the present action. The rule governing this issue is well stated in 24 Am. Jur. 39, Fraud and Deceit, § 212, as follows:

> Since the action of fraud or deceit in inducing the entering into a contract or procuring its execution is not based upon the contract, but is independent thereof, although it is regarded as an affirmance of the contract, it is a

general rule that a vendee is entitled to maintain an action against the vendor for fraud or deceit in the transaction even though he has not complied with all the duties imposed upon him by the contract. His default is not a bar to an action by him or fraud or deceit practiced by the vendor in regard to some matter relative to the contract....

... For the reasons hereinbefore set forth, we hold that the trial court committed no error in determining that the respondents (Obdes) were entitled to recover damages against the appellants (Schlemeyers) upon the theory of fraudulent concealment. However, there remains the question of the proper amount of damages to be awarded. The trial court found that:

"... because of the termite condition the value [of the premises] has been reduced to the extent of $3950.00 and the plaintiffs have been damaged to that extent, and in that amount."

As hereinbefore noted, judgment was thereupon entered for the respondents in that amount.

The appellants concede that the measure of damages in a case of this type is the difference between the actual value of the property and what the property would have been worth had the misrepresentations been true....

The judgment awarding damages of $3,950 is well within the limits of the testimony in the record relating to damages. The Obdes have not cross-appealed. *The judgment of the trial court should be affirmed* in all respects. It is so ordered.

Weaver, C. J., Rosellini, and Foster, JJ., concur. Hill, J., concurs in the result.

NOTES AND QUESTIONS

1. *The law of termites*: Judge Finley of the Supreme Court of Washington begins his opinion in *Hughes v. Stusser*,[44] as follows:

Of the forms of animal life known to modern science, few, if any, classifications other than Homo sapiens have been the subject of as much legal controversy as the members of the order *Isoptera*. The species involved in this particular lawsuit does not appear in the record, but it is likely it was from the genus *Reticulitermes* of the family of *Rhinotermitidae*, known to the nonbiologically oriented as "termites." The wooden edifices of man represent nothing more to these despicable insects than an abundant source of cellulose, which is their principal food.

---

[44] 68 Wash.2d 707, 415 P.2d 89 (1966).

There is an annotation in 22 ALR3d 972 on "Duty of Vendor of Real Estate to Give Purchaser Information as to Termite Infestation." The annotation and the 1985 supplement list 37 cases decided between 1952 and 1984. This annotation, of course, does not cover all reported cases involving termites but only those where a duty to give accurate information about them was in issue. The courts in the deep South seem less likely to give relief to a buyer than those elsewhere. Why might this be the case?

2. *Silent misrepresentation in Washington*: The Supreme Court of Washington clarified its *Obde* decision in *Hughes v. Stusser*.[45] Purchasers of a house sued vendors for damages, alleging fraudulent failure to disclose a concealed dry rot and termite condition. There was enough evidence to support the trial judge's finding that the Stussers had no knowledge of the condition at the time of sale. Thus, "there could be no affirmative duty to disclose to Mr. and Mrs. Hughes the conditions of which the Stussers had no knowledge! Correlatively, the Stussers could not *conceal* a condition unknown to them."

In *Mitchell v. Straith*,[46] the court interpreted the *Obde* case also to require proof that "the undisclosed fact was a material fact to the extent that it substantially affected adversely the value of the property or operated to materially impair or defeat the purpose of the transaction." It also pointed out that the *Obde* case "relied on a finding that the purchaser had no knowledge of the alleged defect and that it was a defect a reasonable inspection would not disclose."

However, in *House v. Thornton*,[47] the court found that a builder *impliedly warrants* that a new house's foundations are firm and secure so the house is structurally safe for occupation. An implied warranty is a promise read into a contract[48] by a court, guaranteeing some minimum quality of an item. Thus, the buyer of the house could recover damages without proof that the builder knew of the defective condition or made any affirmative statements about it. In a sense, when a builder offers to sell a new house it impliedly represents that the building is placed on adequate foundations to keep it from sinking or sliding down a hill. A structure on inadequate foundations isn't a new house.

While a number of states have taken this step, warranties in sales of houses remain an open question in most jurisdictions. The Washington Court limited its rule in *Klos v. Gockel*.[49] The court explained that the essence of the *House* doctrine was "the vendor-builder be a person regularly engaged in building, so that the sale is commercial rather than casual or personal in nature." It noted that

---

[45] 68 Wash.2d 707, 415 P.2d 89 (1966).

[46] 40 Wash.App. 405, 698 P.2d 609 (1985).

[47] 76 Wash.2d 428, 457 P.2d 199 (1969). See Brown, The Implied Warranty of Habitability Doctrine in Residential Property Conveyances: Policy-Backed Change Proposals, 62 Washington Law Review 743 (1987).

[48] This is a nice but misleading way of saying imposed.

[49] 87 Wash.2d 567, 554 P.2d 1349 (1976).

the sale must be of a new house. The sale must be nearly contemporaneous with completion. An intervening tenancy must not interrupt the transaction unless the builder-vendor created such an intervening tenancy for the primary purpose of promoting the sale of the property.

Thus, in Washington, an individual selling a house must disclose known defective conditions such as termites. However, the buyer must prove that the vendor knew of them. An owner selling an older house does not impliedly promise it to be free from defects. A builder selling a new house, however, is liable for structural defects even without proof of knowledge. Why did the court draw these lines? Are they based on choice, paternalism or something else?

As of 1994, about 8 states had regulated implied warranties imposed on builders in new residential construction by legislation.[50] Professor Jeff Sovern is very critical of these statutes.[51] "The law has focused more on implying warranties and less on disclosure or enforcement than is desirable." Several of the statutes, for example, do not require that a builder disclose the warranty to the consumer, and warranties can be disclaimed in form contracts.

3. *Seller's disclosure forms*: The precise problem raised by *Obde v. Schlemeyer* is less likely to come up in many states today. Sellers of used residential property often deal through real estate agents. The National Association of Realtors estimated that two-thirds of all suits filed after a real estate transaction allege misrepresentation or a failure to disclose defects in the property. Buyers who think that they have been misled about a house often are not satisfied to sue the seller. Indeed, often the seller has moved to another state and is hard to sue or the seller may no longer have sufficient assets to satisfy a judgment. Buyers, as a result, almost always sue the real estate agent for alleged misrepresentations or failures to disclose what they knew or ought to have known. As a result, a number of large real estate brokerages began requiring sellers who engaged their services to fill out elaborate disclosure forms. Sellers would check boxes on the forms indicating that they knew of a defect in the house. Copies were given to potential buyers. Real estate agents then could ward off suits or defend those that were brought. They could prove that buyers had been told about defects, and sellers no longer could remain silent. If a seller did not indicate that there was a defect, the seller was making a positive representation about the quality of the house. Real estate agents could defend against claims

---

[50]See Conn. Gen. Stat. Ann. §47-118 (West 1991); Ind. Code Ann. §34-4-20.5 (Burns Supp. 1992); Md. Real Prop. Code Ann. §10-203 (1991); Minn. Stat. Ann. §327B.02 (West Supp. 1992); N.J. Stat. Ann. §46:3B-3 (West Supp. 1991); N.Y. Gen. Bus. Law §777-a (Consol. 1992); Va. Code Ann. §55-70.1 (Michie Supp. 1992).

[51]Sovern, Toward a Theory of Warranties in Sales of New Homes: Housing the Implied Warranty Advocates, Law and Economics Mavens, and Consumer Psychologists Under One Roof, 1993 Wisconsin Law Review 13, 101-102.

of misrepresentation or failure to disclose by asserting that they only had passed along the seller's claims about his or her house.

In 1985, California passed legislation requiring sellers to make such disclosures. California Civil Code §§1102-1102.15. Since 1991, the National Association of Realtors has lobbied the state legislatures seeking laws requiring sellers to complete mandated forms. As of late 1994, about 26 states had passed such laws, including Alaska, California, Delaware, Illinois, Indiana, Iowa, Kentucky, Maine, Maryland, Michigan, Mississippi, New Hampshire, Ohio, Oregon, Rhode Island, South Dakota, Tennessee, Texas, Virginia, Washington and Wisconsin.[52]

Suppose a seller makes a false statement in a required disclosure statement. What are the consequences? Wisconsin's statute, for example, says no more than that real estate brokers must use forms approved by a state commission. These forms include the required disclosures. Presumably buyers are left to their remedies for fraud or innocent misrepresentation based on a seller's answers on the disclosure form. Vance A. Fisher, A Closer Look at Michigan's Seller Disclosure Act,[53] finds the Michigan statute unclear. The act calls for disclosures, but fails to provide the consequences of a seller's failure to disclose or of an erroneous statement. "Presumably, the Legislature meant to relegate the result to the case law of Michigan concerning misrepresentation and nondisclosure." The statute provides that no transfer shall be invalidated because of noncompliance with the act. Apparently, a buyer must assert rights based on misrepresentation before the closing when a deed is signed.

Other statutes limit the time in which a buyer may assert any remedy. Usually in real estate transactions a seller quotes an asking price, buyers make offers and the seller concludes a contract for sale by accepting an offer. Then time is allowed so that the buyer can obtain financing and the seller can take any steps necessary to convey a clear title. At the closing a deed is exchanged for money. Disclosure statutes differ as to when a seller must give the buyer the form with his or her answers. Some give the buyer only a few days after receiving the disclosure form to rescind the contract for sale.

California Civil Code §1102.6 provides that the seller provide a completed form that provides: "This Statement Is a Disclosure of the Condition of the Above Described Property ... It is not a Warranty of Any Kind by the Seller(s).... This Information is a Disclosure and Is Not intended to Be Part of Any Contract Between the Buyer and Seller." In *Alexander v. McKnight*,[54] a

---

[52]See, *e.g.*, Michigan Stat. Ann. §§26.1286(51) et seq.; Wis.Stat. §§452.05(1)(b); 452.14(3)(m).

[53]Michigan Lawyers Weekly, March 21, 1994, at 2.

[54]7 Cal.App.4th 973, 9 Cal.Rptr.2d 453 (Ct.Ap. 1992).

California intermediate appellate court said: "Failure to disclose a negative fact when it can reasonably be said to have a foreseeably depressing effect on the value of property is tortious."

4. *Professor Kronman on the duty to disclose*: Professor Kronman notes that the common law features inconsistent rules.[55] On one hand, I cannot snap up your offer, knowing you have made a mistake. For example, you write me, offering to sell goods for $1.25 a unit. Suppose any reasonable person in my position would know that you meant the price to be $2.15 a unit. Your typist just transposed the 1 and 2 in writing the price. My attempted acceptance would not create a contract at $1.25 a unit. However, if all I said in my letter responding to your offer was "I accept," my acceptance might create a contract at $2.15 a unit. I might be responsible for leading you to believe we had a deal at that price.

On the other hand, there is great inconsistency about my duty to disclose material facts likely to affect your decision to enter a contract. For example, I know my house is infested with termites or roaches. I should be aware that you would not buy it if you were aware of the condition. Can I conclude a binding contract with you if I fail to tell you about the termites or roaches? The law is uncertain.

Suppose a buyer thinks there is oil on seller's land. It buys the property at a price that does not reflect its value as a source of oil. Is there a duty to disclose? Does it matter if the seller is a farmer with little wealth and the buyer is a multinational oil company with great assets?

Kronman suggests: "where the knowledgeable party's contract rights are enforced despite his failure to disclose a known mistake, the knowledge involved is typically the product of a costly search. A rule permitting nondisclosure is the only effective way of providing an incentive to invest in the production of such knowledge."[56] Buyers often spend a good deal of money, for example, searching for land that might contain valuable minerals. Kronman offers an example of this. Texas Gulf Sulfur conducted expensive aerial surveys revealing a geological anomaly associated with valuable ore deposits. Texas Gulf Sulfur paid the estate of Murray Hendrie $500 for a 2-year option to buy the mineral rights for $18,000 plus 10 per cent of the profits made on exploitation. When the optioned property proved to be extremely valuable, the estate sued, alleging that Texas Gulf Sulfur had intentionally misled the seller by failing to disclose the promising geological information. (The case was settled). Kronman notes that buyers in such cases would be less likely to invest in costly searches for information if they were required to disclose that information to the seller. Buyers expect to recover the search costs, in part at least, from the increase in value of the land

---

[55]Kronman, Mistake, Disclosure, Information, and the Law of Contracts, 7 Journal of Legal Studies 1 (1978).

[56]*Id*. at 9.

attributable to the discovery of minerals on it. [It is important to remember that the searchers must also recover the costs of unsuccessful searches from the proceeds of those that prove successful.]

Kronman discusses *Obde v. Schlemeyer*.[57] He argues that requiring disclosure of latent defects such as those involved there makes sense from an economic perspective. Where a seller knows of a defect that the buyer does not, the seller is the party best able to avoid the buyer's mistake at least cost. "A disclosure requirement is unlikely to have a substantial effect on the level of investment by homeowners in the detection of termites.... In most cases a homeowner will have an adequate incentive to check for termites even if the law requires him to disclose what he discovers." He will want to protect his own investment in the house. Kronman finally notes "[e]ven where neither party has knowledge of the defect, it may be efficient to allocate to the seller the risk of a mistaken belief that no defect exists, on the grounds that of the two parties he is the likely to be the cheapest mistake-preventer [because of his superior access to information]."

5. *Professor Scheppelle's study of Kronman's theory*: Professor Scheppelle studied "[c]onsciously withholding information in order to get others to do something they would not have otherwise done."[58] She calls this the problem of "strategic secrets." She subjected Kronman's theory to the test of a sample of about 100 reported cases drawn from the legal encyclopedias, American Jurisprudence 2d and Corpus Juris Secundum, supplemented by those cases frequently cited in the secondary literature.

She reports:

> I located seven features of disputes which were emphasized in deciding these secrecy-as-fraud cases. These facts show that the law is not primarily concerned with promoting efficiency, as Kronman suggests. Rather the law values equality of opportunity to acquire the information at issue. This "equal access" rule directs judges to examine the relative costs of acquiring the information for both of the parties to the transaction. Where those costs are roughly equal, the parties may be said to have equal access, and no disclosure is required. But where the parties face highly unequal search costs, the law requires the actor with the superior access (cheaper search costs) to disclose information to the disadvantaged actor.

Scheppelle argues, "[i]nformation which the law allows to remain secret is, in virtually every case, information which could be obtained with roughly equal efforts by both parties. This principle helps explain why sellers have to disclose

---

[57]*Id*. at 24-25.
[58]Scheppelle, Legal Secrets: Equality and Efficiency in the Common Law (U. of Chicago Press, 1988)

latent but not obvious defects, as well as why buyers rarely have obligations to disclose." She concludes that the law requires equality of opportunity to gain potentially useful information. It recognizes only limited status-based differences. Thus, the common law's goals seem primarily egalitarian and redistributive rather than promoting efficient production of information. However, these egalitarian and redistributive goals are severely limited. Courts do not recognize inequality of resources at the parties' command. Large oil companies can buy land from small landowners without disclosing the results of research. The courts reason that the information about subsurface oil is available to anyone who chooses to look. They refuse to consider that some can afford the costs of looking far better than others.

Professor Scheppelle concludes:

> What is most likely ... is that the common law is not reduceable to a single value, although there may be a rather small set. This small set of values, of which efficiency is probably one and egalitarianism and communitarianism are others, is probably quite internally inconsistent with limits on each being set by each of the others. From this investigation, it should be apparent that it is not possible to develop a positive theory of the common law reasoning from first principles. Instead, more investigation of the sort done here will probably begin to show rather soon just what the small core of values is and how they are traded off against each other.

To what extent has Scheppelle destroyed Kronman's theory explaining the duty to disclose cases? Insofar as she has, can we revive Kronman by revising his theory? Could we argue that whatever its power to describe what courts have done in the past, it suggests what they should do in the future? Would you go further than either Scheppelle or Kronman and argue that large oil companies should not be able to buy land from small landowners without disclosing the results of research? The courts may reason that the information about subsurface oil is available to anyone who chooses to look. However, this position ignores the actual situations of the parties.

Why should courts benefit society by rewarding production of information by large corporations at the expense of small landowners? Is allowing large companies to buy their land without disclosure likely to delegitimate our economic and social system in the eyes of small landowners, for example?

6. *Innocent misrepresentation*: Classic fraud doctrine required *scienter*, a guilty mind. Typically, a buyer had to prove that a seller intentionally made a false statement to mislead the buyer. Often it is easy enough to prove that a statement is false. However, it may be almost impossible to show that a seller knew that it was false. The Obdes were fortunate to find the specialist in pest control. He could establish what the Schlemeyers knew about the termites in their house.

Many states allow rescission but deny damages for innocent misrepresentation.[59] For example, the Supreme Court of Rhode Island recognized a right to rescind and recover what was paid when a vendor and her agent told the buyers there was no termite problem. See *Halpert v. Rosenthal.*[60] It explained that simple justice demands that when both vendor and vendee are innocent, the one making the false statement should bear the loss of the benefits of the transaction. "The speaker who uses the unqualified statement does so at his peril. The risk of falsity is his." He is strictly accountable for his words. It is an absolute liability to achieve certain goals.

Not all states limit the remedy to rescission. For example, in *Maser v. Lind*[61] the vendors represented that buildings were in sound condition. Termites had damaged the buildings seriously. The court allowed the purchasers to recover damages although they could not prove the vendors knew there were termites. It did not limit the purchasers to rescinding the transaction.

In many situations, rescission for innocent misrepresentation is a welcome remedy. However, often it has a major defect. Rescission may not create a fund large enough so that a successful vendee can pay an attorney. The purchaser may recover what she paid. However, after she pays her lawyer, she will not be where she was before she bought a house infested with termites.

7. *Remedies for misrepresentation*: Victims of knowing misrepresentation often have many remedies. They can sue for the tort of fraud. Most jurisdictions will protect the victim's expectation interest in fashioning remedies. The victim is entitled to the benefit of the bargain. Suppose the $54,000 contract price in the *Halpert* case was the fair value of the house if it were termite free. Assume, further, that given the termite infestation, the market value of the house was only $35,000. The buyer would be entitled to $19,000, the difference in value. However, suppose the house could be repaired for $10,000. Would this be the appropriate remedy? Of course, this situation is opposite to that found in *Peevyhouse v. Garland Coal Co.*, where the costs of repair were more than the difference in value. Courts may be affected by the wrongdoing of the defendant in fraud cases and be more willing to award greater damages. Indeed, in some cases, punitive damages are awarded to deter fraud. A few jurisdictions limit recovery in tort actions to "out of pocket" damages, roughly a measure of the plaintiff's reliance losses. For a discussion of this point, see *Beardmore v. T.A. Burgess Co.*[62]

---

[59]In practice, this means the victim can bring an action to declare that the transaction has no legal effect. She can also gain restitution of what she paid. She also can defend against a suit brought by the one making the misrepresentation. However, she cannot sue to be put where she would have been had the defrauder performed the contract. She cannot recover the benefit of her bargain without proving an intentional, or perhaps negligent, misrepresentation.

[60]107 R.I. 406, 922, 267 A.2d 730 (1970).

[61]181 Neb. 365, 148 N.W.2d 831 (1967).

[62]245 Md. 387, 226 A.2d 329 (1967).

8. *State statutory remedies for innocent misrepresentation*: Many states have statutes which provide greater remedies for misrepresentations than the common law. Some of these statutes are limited to cases involving consumers while others can be used by businesses complaining about the practices of other businesses. Some states model their statutes on the Federal Trade Commission Act, prohibiting "unfair methods of competition and unfair or deceptive practices." Others broadly prohibit consumer fraud or unconscionable consumer practices. Still others, based on the Uniform Deceptive Trade Practices Act, specifically prohibit 11 deceptive practices and contain, in addition, a catch-all prohibition against "any other conduct which similarly creates a likelihood of confusion or misunderstanding."[63]

Most of these statutes are enforced by the state attorney general or by administrative agencies.[64] However, individual plaintiffs often can bring private lawsuits based on these statutes. Sometimes it is said that they are private attorneys general, helping enforce the law against deceptive practices.

The elements of a statutory cause of action are much easier to establish than the classic tort of fraud. Many state courts have followed the United States Supreme Court's interpretation of the Federal Trade Commission Act. In *FTC v. Sperry & Hutchinson Co.*,[65] it said an unfair act is defined by considering the following factors:

> (1) whether the act or practice is within at least the penumbra of some common law, statutory or other established concept of unfairness; (2) whether it is immoral, unethical, oppressive or unscrupulous; or (3) whether it causes substantial injury to consumers or competitors or other businessmen.

However, most courts require more than just a breach of contract. Furthermore, often a plaintiff who wins her case can recover reasonable attorney's fees. Nevertheless, in many cases the lawyers consulted by plaintiffs find the amounts involved fail to justify attempting to assert these statutory rights. Many members of the bar, however, are unaware of the possibilities under these statutes.

Texas has a *Deceptive Trade Practices Act*.[66] It attacks twenty-three deceptive acts or practices. Consumers also have actions for breach of warranty, insurance violations or an unconscionable act that takes advantage of a consumer's lack of

---

[63]For a discussion of these statutes, see Sebert, State Government: Consumer Protection in the States and Local Communities, in State Studies Prepared for the National Institute for Consumer Justice (1973).

[64]For a statute-by-statute analysis of the unfair and deceptive acts and practices statutes of all 50 states and the District of Columbia, see National Consumer Law Center, Unfair and Deceptive Acts and Practices, 1985 Cumulative Supplement, Appendix B, at 237-51.

[65]405 U.S. 233, 244 (1972).

[66]See Vernon's Texas Code Annotated Secs. 17.41-17.63.

knowledge or results in gross disparity between what a consumer paid and received. There are many appellate cases interpreting the statute. In *Pennington v. Singleton*,[67] a Texas court of appeals found that the statute authorized damages for innocent misrepresentation. It stressed that the statutory purposes were to encourage consumers to litigate under the Act and deter sellers from violating it. In mid-1979, after lower court decisions suggested that a consumer could get treble her actual damages on the basis of an innocent misrepresentation, the Legislature amended the statute. Thereafter, treble damages were in the discretion of the trier of fact in cases involving knowing violations of the Deceptive Trade Practices Act.

Nonetheless, the statute offers treble damages to many disappointed buyers. In *Jim Walter Homes, Inc. v. Valencia*,[68] a builder represented to a buyer that a house was constructed in good workmanlike manner when the builder released the completed house to the buyer. The Supreme Court of Texas affirmed a finding of a knowing violation of the DTPA. It said:

> The act or practice giving rise to the Valencias' cause of action was not the misrepresentations made to them at the time they entered into the contract; it was the act of building the house defectively after representing that the house would be built in a good and workman like manner.... The record contains evidence from which the jury could have inferred that Jim Walter Homes knew that the house was defective at the time of construction. For example, two building inspectors testified that the piers supporting the house were improperly poured and that Jim Walter Homes attempted to cover up these defects with plaster. From this and other evidence in the record the jury could have inferred that Jim Walter Homes committed a knowing violation of the DTPA.[69]

Obviously, the text and interpretations of these statutes and administrative regulations will differ from state to state. All we can do in these materials is alert you to the existence of these alternatives to difficult actions based on misrepresentation. You should never consider a misrepresentation action without first reading the applicable statutes and administrative regulations to see whether they provide better tools than the common law.

---

[67] 606 S.W.2d 682 (1980).

[68] 690 S.W.2d 239 (1985).

[69] The Supreme Court of Texas requires more than just a breach of contract for treble damages under the DTPA. See Jim Walter Homes, Inc. v. Reed, 711 S.W.2d 617 (1986), where the jury found the builder to have been grossly negligent in its supervision of construction. The court said, "[g]ross negligence in the breach of a contract will not entitle an injured party to exemplary damages because even an intentional breach will not." There was no finding of a knowing misrepresentation in the Reed case.

Furthermore, the statutes and regulations we discussed should provoke policy debate. They involve a good deal of social control of contract. Few of them set precise standards. Professor Trakman's arguments about judicial capacity which we discussed with the materials on illegality come back on stage once more.

9. *Federal RICO and misrepresentations*: The Racketeer Influenced and Corrupt Organizations Act[70] provides that it "shall be unlawful for any person employed by or associated with any enterprise engaged in, or the activities of which affect, interstate or foreign commerce, to conduct or participate, directly or indirectly, in the conduct of such enterprise's affairs through a pattern of racketeering activity or collection of unlawful debts." The statute imposes criminal sanctions, but those injured by reason of racketeering activity can bring civil actions for treble damages, costs and attorneys' fees.

The statute calls certain racketeering activities "predicate acts." Securities fraud, mail fraud, and wire fraud as defined by federal statutes are predicate acts. The mail and wire fraud statutes require "a scheme or artifice with intent to defraud" and the use of the mails or wires to carry out the scheme. These schemes include a wide range of deceptive plans. They do not have to fit common law fraud or misrepresentation. A pattern of activity under RICO involves the commission of at least two predicate acts within a ten year period.

The New York Times[71] reports that in 1986 and 1987, about 1,000 civil RICO cases were filed by private plaintiffs seeking to recover triple their actual damages from business competitors, investment swindlers, employers and unions. Most RICO suits have been dismissed, but plaintiffs in a few RICO cases have won multimillion dollar verdicts. Half of the 22 private civil racketeering cases that were decided in 1985 and 1986 were dismissed, and only 13 resulted in damage awards from final judgments. Courts have fined law firms or their clients more than $247,000 for bringing frivolous racketeering claims.

This note can only alert you to a complex and fast developing area of law. It may be a major example of social control of contract.[72] It may be only a legislative mistake with a short life. Groups ranging from the American Civil Liberties Union to business lobbying organizations have attacked civil RICO. There is a campaign to repeal or amend the statute. Until the law is changed, the prospect of treble damages and attorneys' fees will tempt lawyers to transform breaches of contract into schemes with intent to defraud. If this alchemy works,

---

[70]18 USC § 1961, *et seq.*

[71]August 1, 1988, at 1, col. 5.

[72]See Strafer, Massumi and Skolnick, Civil RICO in the Public Interest: Everybody's Darling, 19 American Criminal Law Review 655 (1982); Vaca, Arbitrating Civil Rico and Implied Causes of Action Arising Under Section 10(b) of the Securities Exchange Act of 1934, 36 Catholic University Law Review 455 (1987).

usually they will have no trouble finding a letter or telegram to bring the case under the mail or wire fraud statutes.

6. RELATIONSHIPS OF TRUST AND SOCIAL CONTROL

Introduction: A great part of the common law of contracts rests on assumptions of discrete transactions conducted at arm's length. Buyers and sellers must take care of themselves. However, much human interaction rests on long-term continuing relations. In light of experience and expectations about the future, I may come to trust you. Our dealings will be cooperative rather than antagonistic. I may assume that we both value our relationship and we will do what is necessary to maintain it. How far does, or should, the law reflect our expectations about trust and cooperation? When will I have a duty to consider your interests before I assert my rights?

Classic doctrine recognizes at least three distinct relationships between contracting parties: (1) The rules assume the typical situation is at arms length. Your interests are not my concern. (2) Then there are relations of "trust and confidence." The courts relax many of the requirements for relief based on misrepresentation. I may have to disclose all I know relevant to your decisions, and you may be justified in relying on my opinions.[73] (3) Finally, there are fiduciary relationships where I must act for your benefit. If I hold fiduciary obligations to you (for example, I am your lawyer and you are my client), you may be able to challenge many of the contracts we might make. The fiduciary must prove that the contract is fair and the product of a full understanding of facts and legal rights.[74]

The important question, of course, is how do courts decide whether a relationship involves trust and confidence or fiduciary duties? Professor Unger criticizes the current law.[75] He says it "consists largely of a list of special circumstances, often defined by signs that have only an oblique connection with the facts that engender trust or justify self-restraint." We can look at some of the special circumstances and ask about the modern process of deciding that one party had special obligations to the other.

Confidential relationships: Three decisions that respond to assertions that a confidential relationship was present illustrate some of the difficulties of the present approach. In *Lucas v. Frazee*,[76] Adrian Lucas and Emma Frazee were adult sisters. Adrian was in ill health, and her husband had died just before the transaction in question. She stayed with Emma for about three weeks after her husband's death. Emma often had cared for Adrian, and the sisters enjoyed a

---

[73]See Restatement (Second) of Contracts Secs.161(d), 169(a).

[74]See Restatement (Second) of Contracts Sec.173.

[75]See Unger, The Critical Legal Studies Movement, 96 Harvard Law Review 561 (1983).

[76]471 N.E.2d 1163 (Ind.App. 1984).

good relationship. Other family members suggested that Adrian leave her property to Emma who never had much money. Adrian said she wanted to convey her home to Emma and herself as joint tenants. Emma and her husband had agreed to move to Adrian's home and care for her. Emma heard the conversation but said nothing. Accompanied by Emma, Adrian consulted a lawyer. Adrian's lawyer warned her that there could be problems if she changed her mind later, but Adrian wanted to carry out the transaction. After Adrian executed the deed, Emma and her husband stayed with Adrian for one night. However, they then left for reasons unclear in the record. Adrian sued to rescind the deed. After a trial to the court,[77] the trial court judge denied rescission and upheld the transfer.

Adrian argued that a confidential relationship had existed between the sisters. Thus, Emma had the burden of proving that the arrangement was fair and the product of full disclosure. The appellate court said this would be the rule governing traditional fiduciary relationships such as attorney and client, guardian and ward, principal and agent, pastor and parishioner, husband and wife, and parent and child. However, brothers and sisters do not have fiduciary duties to each other just because they are siblings. They may in fact have a confidential relationship. The law does not presume undue influence or fraud in a confidential relationship. The one seeking to overturn a transaction must prove them. The relationship serves only to justify trust and reliance that would not be justified in an arms length transaction. The majority found there was no evidence of overreaching and affirmed the trial court. The dissent said that Emma knew that the arrangement was one requiring her to live with Adrian. In view of her relationship with her sister she could not accept the deed and remain silent to avoid making a promise.

Vargas v. Esquire, Inc.[78] involved an illustrator's challenge to a contract produced by his relationship with the president of a magazine publisher. Vargas had been born in Peru but had lived in the United States for 25 years. He read English very well. Vargas and Smart, the President of Esquire, were close friends. Smart advised Vargas about where to live in Chicago and how to furnish his apartment. Smart did what he could to satisfy the wants and desires dictated by Vargas' artistic temperament. Smart advanced sums to bring Vargas' mother and sister to the United States from Peru, to buy Vargas' wife a ring and a coat, to decorate and furnish apartments, and to rent a studio. The trial court found a confidential relationship existed, and Esquire did not prove that the contract between Vargas and Esquire was fair. The Court of Appeals reversed by a two to one vote.

---

[77] The phrase "trial to the court" is used to indicate that there was no jury. Sometimes lawyers or judges refer to these as "bench trials."

[78] 166 F.2d 651 (7th Cir. 1948).

The majority said that belief in the honesty and integrity of a close and intimate friend is not enough to establish a fiduciary or confidential relationship. Vargas understood he was signing a contract under which he was to furnish drawings to Esquire. "There are but six paragraphs in the contract. It is written in plain and ordinary language and is readily understandable."[79] Smart read part of the contract to Vargas and handed it to Vargas to check. Vargas looked at the salary, the number of pictures and the percentage Esquire would pay on sales of calendars, but he did not read the document carefully. The evidence leads "inescapably to the conclusion that Vargas was making an independent examination of the terms ... of the contract and that Vargas placed no reliance on what Smart had said or might have said."

The dissent said, "[i]f this record does not support the finding that a relation of special trust and confidence existed between plaintiff and Smart, it would be futile to attempt to make such a record.... [Vargas] was an artist and his time and energy were confined to that field. It is doubtful if he had any inclination and certainly no reason to do otherwise, because he had often been assured by Smart that he need not worry or concern himself with financial matters but that they would be taken care of by Smart."

In *Frowen v. Blank*,[80] the vendor sought to rescind the sale of a farm because of a breach of the duties involved in a confidential relationship. The trial court denied rescission, but the Supreme Court of Pennsylvania reversed. The vendor was an 86 year old woman suffering from loss of hearing and sight. She had only two or three years of formal education and little business education. The purchaser and his wife bought the adjoining farm in the early 1960s. A close social relationship developed between the older woman and the young couple. The vendor taught the young couple farm-related crafts. The couple helped her with farm chores and often drove her to local social events.

The couple drafted a one page document that stated that the vendor agreed to sell the farm to them for $15,000. Vendor signed. About a year later, the purchasers drove the vendor to their lawyer's office where she signed a formal document without reading it. The fair market value of the farm was $35,000. There was "dependence or trust justifiably reposed." The case was remanded to give the purchasers an opportunity to establish that the transaction was "fair, conscientious and beyond the reach of suspicion."

Can we put these three cases together to suggest the meaning of the confidential relationship doctrine? Vargas was an artist, unconcerned with business. He trusted a close friend, but he could have, and perhaps did, read the contract before signing it. It is unclear what Vargas' objection to the contract was. A lawyer cautioned Adrian, but she went ahead anyway, trusting her sister. She

---

[79] The contract is reprinted in a footnote to the court's opinion. We could debate whether it is written in plain and ordinary language and is readily understandable.

[80] 493 Pa. 137, 425 A.2d 412 (1981).

was in poor health and recently widowed. However, she was the moving party. As far as the record shows, all her sister did was drive her to the lawyer's office and watch silently. The couple who bought the farm developed a relationship with a weak woman who had no independent advice. The price the couple agreed to pay seems grossly unfair. The court protected her trust in the couple. Do these distinctions establish that these cases reflect adequate social control of contract?

Fiduciary relationships: Courts impose fiduciary duties in some classic business situations. For example, a lawyer who buys a client's house might be challenged to prove that the deal was fair and nothing was concealed from the client. A stock broker who has discretion to buy and sell for a customer's account also is a fiduciary.[81] However, a fiduciary duty is not imposed on a broker-customer relationship where a sophisticated investor-customer makes all investment decisions.[82] As a result, the broker has no duty to keep the customer informed of market information about political, economic, weather or price changes.

Courts do sometimes impose fiduciary duties on companies that enter into "joint ventures."[83] This means that joint venturers must fully disclose material facts to their co-venturers. But whether or not someone is in a joint venture can itself be a controversial question. There generally must be a sharing of profits and joint control of property. Absent those features, there is no joint venture, and no fiduciary duty.[84]

Unger argues[85] that the typical approach is flawed. Instead of asking whether a joint venture is present, he advocates asking whether the situation is appropriate for constraints on self-interest. "A contractual arrangement ... may involve a close, difficult, and long-term collaboration that calls for the exercise of prudent discretion without being directed toward an uncertain profit [as in a joint venture]. Such an undertaking may well be viewed by the participants as one demanding from each of them the most scrupulous regard to mutual loyalty. Conversely, a contract that looks to an undefined reward rather than to an exchange of predetermined performances may require, and be understood to require, only a minimum of actual cooperation."

Of course sometimes courts can find, in the situation, a contractual duty (either expressed or implied) which prohibits one party from taking advantage of another. This may arise even if no fiduciary duty is found. For example, the Uniform Commercial Code § 1-203 provides, "[e]very contract or duty within

---

[81]See Leib v. Merrill Lynch, Pierce, Fenner & Smith, Inc., 461 F.Supp. 951 (E.D.Mich. 1978).

[82]See Robinson v. Merrill Lynch, Pierce, Fenner & Smith, Inc., 337 F.Supp. 107 (N.D.Ala. 1971); Merrill Lynch, Pierce, Fenner & Smith, Inc. v. Boeck, 120 Wis.2d 591, 357 N.W.2d 287 (1984).

[83]See, *e.g.*, Witter v. Torbett, 604 F.Supp. 298 (W.D.Va. 1984).

[84]See, *e.g.*, Stratford Group, Ltd. v. Interstate Bakeries Corp., 590 F.Supp. 859 (1984).

[85]Unger, The Critical Legal Studies Movement, 96 Harvard Law Review 561, 642 (1983).

this Act imposes an obligation of good faith in its performance or enforcement."
§ 2-103(b) provides " '[g]ood faith' in the case of a merchant means honesty in
fact and the observance of reasonable commercial standards of fair dealing in the
trade." Note, too, that § 1-102(3) bans disclaiming the obligation of good faith
by contract. It does allow parties to "by agreement determine the standards by
which the performance of such [an] obligation ... is to be measured if such
standards are not manifestly unreasonable." Is the obligation of good faith
substantially different from the duties imposed on a relationship of trust and
confidence or a fiduciary?

Expansion of fiduciary duties? Should courts expand the fiduciary doctrine or
the requirement of good faith beyond the current uncertain approach? Frankel[86]
identifies three types of relationships: status, contract, and fiduciary. The law
creates status relationships such as parent and child. Contractual duties rest on
choice. Fiduciary duties arise out of expectations associated with relationships.
Frankel sees modern society as more and more becoming one based on fiduciary
relationships. She says:

> [W]e are witnessing the emergence of a society predominantly based on
> fiduciary relations. This type of society best reflects our contemporary social
> values.... A fiduciary society attempts to maximize both the satisfaction of
> needs and the protection of freedom.
>
> Unlike status and contract societies, a fiduciary society emphasizes not
> personal conflict and domination among individuals, but cooperation and
> identity of interest pursuant to acceptable but imposed standards. It permits
> government to moderate between altruistic goals and individualistic, selfish
> desires, as well as between the social goal of increasing the common welfare
> and the individual desire to appropriate more than a "fair share."[87]

Unger[88] seeks to develop a countervision of legal doctrine as part of a
necessary transformation of "the institutional framework of economic and
political action." He looks at the law of fiduciary relations and its place within
the main corpus of contract law. Its expansion would have great transformative
potential. He says:

> One of the more remarkable features of classical contract theory is its
> oscillation between an ideal of strict altruism in a confined range of
> situations and a tolerance for unrestrained self-interest in the great majority
> of contracts. Thus, in fiduciary relations one party may be required to
> confer upon the other party's interests a weight greater than upon his own

---

[86]Frankel, Fiduciary Law, 71 California Law Review 795 (1983).

[87]*Id.* at 802.

[88]See Unger, The Critical Legal Studies Movement, 96 Harvard Law Review 561 (1983).

(or, in any event, at least equal to his own). In the ordinary commercial contract, however, the other party's interests can be treated as of no account as long as the rightholder remains within his zone of discretionary action.... This license merely restates the approach to the nature of rights and to the sources of obligations that characterizes mainstream contract theory. The higher standard of solidarity — the one that gives primacy to the other party's interests — is necessarily exceptional. Any attempt to insist upon it in the generality of dealings would depart so radically from the standards by which people ordinarily deal with each other that it would merely encourage massive circumvention and hypocrisy coupled with a stifling despotism of virtue. It does not follow, however, that ordinary contracts and human encounters should be surrendered to the notion that one may treat other people's interests as if they were nonexistent. In fact, the parties to continuing or recurrent contractual relations, and often even to one-shot transactions, seem generally to adhere to a far stricter standard.

... [D]octrine might develop a series of distinguishing criteria to characterize situations suitable for the application of a more limited solidarity constraint, a constraint requiring each party to give some force to the other party's interests, though perhaps less than to his own....[89]

7. MOST OF THE THEORIES AT ONCE: A REVIEW

So far, we have presented various approaches to social control of contract as distinct legal categories. A lawyer can ask whether her client lacked capacity, agreed under duress or undue influence, or made a decision on the basis of misrepresentation. As so often is true, common law categories are not bounded by bright distinct lines. A particular case may almost fit in a number of them. The following case should prompt reflection and review of the material presented in the preceding sections of this chapter.

Professor Kronman[90] offers an argument for paternalism based on the goal of promoting efficiency by reducing transaction costs. He says:

When a fraud has been committed, but cannot be proven, the agreement will be enforced. This is an inefficient result. Of course, if this happens only rarely — if fraud can be established in almost every case in which it occurs — the inefficiency of enforcing a few fraudulent bargains may be justified by some other, more desirable, consequences of a strict proof system (for example, its tendency to discourage vexatious lawsuits brought only to harass or blackmail the defendant). But if a large number of fraudulent bargains are enforced, the efficiencies of a strict proof system may be

---

[89]*Id.* at 641-642.
[90]Paternalism and the Law of Contracts, 92 Yale Law Journal 763, 768-69 (1983).

outweighed by its inefficiencies. One way of remedying this situation, of course, is to lower the proof requirements. But if fraud is widespread, if it can be concealed with sufficient ease, and if the victims of fraud typically lack the resources to prosecute their legal claims, lowering the proof requirement may not be enough. A more radical solution — but one that is nevertheless justifiable from an economic point of view, at least under certain conditions — is to give the victims an inalienable entitlement they cannot waive and therefore cannot be fraudulently induced to abandon. This solution has the obvious defect of preventing the parties from modifying the entitlement, even when it would be efficient for them to do so and neither has practiced fraud upon the other. But if the entitlement can be waived, and if the fraud can rarely be proven, the inefficiencies of a no-waiver rule may be outweighed by the greater inefficiency of enforcing too many fraudulent bargains....

For the argument to have merit in ... [a] particular case, there must be some reason for believing that fraudulent deception is more likely and less easily provable here than in general. One factor that may make the danger of unprovable fraud especially great in certain situations ... is the existence of a significant asymmetry in the parties' access to relevant information.

Consider whether Professor Kronman's argument applies to contracts for lessons at a dancing or martial arts studio or a health club.

VOKES v. ARTHUR MURRAY, INC.

212 So.2d 906 (DCA Fla.1968).

PIERCE, J. This is an appeal by Audrey E. Vokes, plaintiff below, from a final order dismissing with prejudice, for failure to state a cause of action, her fourth amended complaint, hereinafter referred to as plaintiff's complaint.

Defendant Arthur Murray, Inc., a corporation, authorizes the operation throughout the nation of dancing schools under the name of "Arthur Murray School of Dancing" through local franchised operators, one of whom was defendant J. P. Davenport whose dancing establishment was in Clearwater.

Plaintiff Mrs. Audrey E. Vokes, a widow of 51 years and without family, had a yen to be "an accomplished dancer" with the hopes of finding "new interest in life." So, on February 10, 1961, a dubious fate, with the assist of a motivated acquaintance, procured her to attend a "dance party" at Davenport's "School of Dancing" where she whiled away the pleasant hours, sometimes in a private room, absorbing his accomplished sales technique, during which her grace and poise were elaborated upon and her rosy future as "an excellent dancer" was painted for her in vivid and glowing colors. As an incident to this interlude, he sold her eight 1/2-hour dance lessons to be utilized within one calendar month therefrom, for the sum of $14.50 cash in hand paid, obviously a baited "come-on."

Thus she embarked upon an almost endless pursuit of the terpsichorean art during which, over a period of less than sixteen months, she was sold fourteen "dance courses" totalling in the aggregate 2302 hours of dancing lessons for a total cash outlay of $31,090.45, all at Davenport's dance emporium. All of these fourteen courses were evidenced by execution of a written "Enrollment Agreement — Arthur Murray's School of Dancing" with the addendum in heavy black print, "No one will be informed that you are taking dancing lessons. Your relations with us are held in strict confidence," setting forth the number of "dancing lessons" and the "lessons in rhythm sessions" currently sold to her from time to time, and always of course accompanied by payment of cash of the realm.

These dance lesson contracts and the monetary consideration therefor of over $31,000 were procured from her by means and methods of Davenport and his associates which went beyond the unsavory, yet legally permissible, perimeter of "sales puffing" and intruded well into the forbidden area of undue influence, the suggestion of falsehood, the suppression of truth, and the free exercise of rational judgment, if what plaintiff alleged in her complaint was true. From the time of her first contact with the dancing school in February, 1961, she was influenced unwittingly by a constant and continuous barrage of flattery, false praise, excessive compliments, and panegyric encomiums, to such extent that it would be not only inequitable, but unconscionable, for a Court exercising inherent chancery power to allow such contracts to stand.

She was incessantly subjected to overreaching blandishment and cajolery. She was assured she had "grace and poise"; that she was "rapidly improving and developing in her dancing skill"; that the additional lessons would "make her a beautiful dancer, capable of dancing with the most accomplished dancers"; that she was "rapidly progressing in the development of her dancing skill and gracefulness," etc., etc. She was given "dance aptitude tests" for the ostensible purpose of "determining" the number of remaining hours instructions needed by her from time to time.

At one point she was sold 545 additional hours of dancing lessons to be entitled to award of the "Bronze Medal" signifying that she had reached "the Bronze Standard," a supposed designation of dance achievement by students of Arthur Murray, Inc.

Later she was sold an additional 926 hours in order to gain the "Silver Medal," indicating she had reached "the Silver Standard," at a cost of $12,501.35.

At one point, while she still had to her credit about 900 unused hours of instructions, she was induced to purchase an additional 24 hours of lessons to participate in a trip to Miami at her own expense, where she would be "given the opportunity to dance with members of the Miami Studio."

She was induced at another point to purchase an additional 126 hours of lessons in order to be not only eligible for the Miami trip but also to become "a life member of the Arthur Murray Studio," carrying with it certain dubious emoluments, at a further cost of $1,752.30.

At another point, while she still had over 1,000 unused hours of instruction she was induced to buy 151 additional hours at a cost of $2,049.00 to be eligible for a "Student Trip to Trinidad," at her own expense as she later learned.

Also, when she still had 1100 unused hours to her credit, she was prevailed upon to purchase an additional 347 hours at a cost of $4,235.74, to qualify her to receive a "Gold Medal" for achievement, indicating she had advanced to "the Gold Standard."

On another occasion, while she still had over 1200 unused hours, she was induced to buy an additional 175 hours of instruction at a cost of $2,472.75 to be eligible "to take a trip to Mexico."

Finally, sandwiched in between other lesser sales promotions, she was influenced to buy an additional 481 hours of instruction at a cost of $6,523.81 in order to "be classified as a Gold Bar Member, the ultimate achievement of the dancing studio."

All the foregoing sales promotions, illustrative of the entire fourteen separate contracts, were procured by defendant Davenport and Arthur Murray, Inc., by false representations to her that she was improving in her dancing ability, that she had excellent potential, that she was responding to instructions in dancing grace, and that they were developing her into a beautiful dancer, whereas in truth and in fact she did not develop in her dancing ability, she had no "dance aptitude," and in fact had difficulty in "hearing the musical beat." The complaint alleged that such representations to her "were in fact false and contrary to the plaintiff's true ability, the truth of plaintiff's ability being fully known to the defendants, but withheld from the plaintiff for the sole and specific intent to deceive and defraud the plaintiff and to induce her in the purchasing of additional hours of dance lessons." It was averred that the lessons were sold to her "in total disregard to the true physical, rhythm, and mental ability of the plaintiff." In other words, while she first exulted that she was entering the "spring of her life," she finally was awakened to the fact there was "spring" neither in her life nor in her feet.

The complaint prayed that the Court decree the dance contracts to be null and void and to be cancelled, that an accounting be had, and judgment entered against the defendants "for that portion of the $31,090.45 not charged against specific hours of instruction given to the plaintiff." The Court held the complaint not to state a cause of action and dismissed it with prejudice. We disagree and reverse.

The material allegations of the complaint must, of course, be accepted as true for the purpose of testing its legal sufficiency. Defendants contend that contracts can only be rescinded for fraud or misrepresentation when the alleged misrepresentation is as to a material fact, rather than an opinion, prediction or expectation, and that the statements and representations set forth at length in the complaint were in the category of "trade puffing," within its legal orbit.

It is true that "generally a misrepresentation, to be actionable, must be one of fact rather than of opinion." *Tonkovich v. South Florida Citrus Industries, Inc.*, Fla.App.1966, 185 So.2d 710; *Kutner v. Kalish*, Fla.App.1965, 173 So.2d 763. But this rule has significant qualifications, applicable here. It does not apply where there is a fiduciary relationship between the parties, or where there has been some artifice or trick employed by the representor, or where the parties do not in general deal at "arm's length" as we understand the phrase, or where the representee does not have equal opportunity to become apprised of the truth or falsity of the fact represented. 14 Fla.Jur. Fraud and Deceit, § 28; *Kitchen v. Long*, 1914, 67 Fla. 72, 64 So. 429. As stated by Judge Allen of this Court in Ramel v. Chasebrook Construction Company, Fla.App.1961, 135 So.2d 876:

> ... A statement of a party having ... superior knowledge may be regarded as a statement of fact although it would be considered as opinion if the parties were dealing on equal terms.

It could be reasonably supposed here that defendants had "superior knowledge" as to whether plaintiff had "dance potential" and as to whether she was noticeably improving in the art of terpsichore. And it would be a reasonable inference from the undenied averments of the complaint that the flowery eulogiums heaped upon her by defendants as a prelude to her contracting for 1944 additional hours of instruction in order to attain the rank of the Bronze Standard, thence to the bracket of the Silver Standard, thence to the class of the Gold Bar Standard, and finally to the crowning plateau of a Life Member of the Studio, proceeded as much or more from the urge to "ring the cash register" as from any honest or realistic appraisal of her dancing prowess or a factual representation of her progress.

Even in contractual situations where a party to a transaction owes no duty to disclose facts within his knowledge or to answer inquiries respecting such facts, the law is if he undertakes to do so he must disclose the *whole truth*. *Ramel v. Chasebrook Construction Company, supra; Beagle v. Bagwell*, Fla.App.1964, 169 So.2d 43. From the face of the complaint, it should have been reasonably apparent to defendants that her vast outlay of cash for the many hundreds of additional hours of instruction was not justified by her slow and awkward progress, which she would have been made well aware of if they had spoken the "whole truth."

In *Hirschman v. Hodges*, etc., 1910, 59 Fla. 517, 51 So. 550, it was said that

> ... what is plainly injurious to good faith ought to be considered as a fraud sufficient to impeach a contract,

and that an improvident agreement may be avoided

> ... because of surprise, or mistake, *want of freedom, undue influence, the suggestion of falsehood, or the suppression of truth.*" (Emphasis supplied.)

We repeat that where parties are dealing on a contractual basis at arm's length with no inequities or inherently unfair practices employed, the Courts will in general "leave the parties where they find themselves." But in the case sub judice, from the allegations of the unanswered complaint, we cannot say that enough of the accompanying ingredients, as mentioned in the foregoing authorities, were not present which otherwise would have barred the equitable arm of the Court to her. In our view, from the showing made in her complaint, plaintiff is entitled to her day in Court.

It accordingly follows that the order dismissing plaintiff's last amended complaint with prejudice should be and is reversed.

Reversed. Liles, C. J., and Mann, J., concur.

NOTES AND QUESTIONS

1. *Review*: Counsel for Arthur Murray argued that Mrs. Vokes was "not justified in relying upon statements of a dancing instructor to the effect that she has good dancing aptitude and is progressing well in the development of her dancing skills where she continually has difficulty in hearing the musical beat, is therefore unable to acquire any ability to learn different dance steps, and does not in fact develop in her dancing ability." What, if anything, is wrong with this argument? Could Mrs. Vokes' lawyer argue plausibly that she lacked capacity to make this contract? That she was the victim of duress?

Compare *Parker v. Arthur Murray, Inc.*[91] Plaintiff was a 37 year-old college-educated bachelor who lived alone in a one-room attic apartment. His instructors regularly praised and encouraged him, despite his lack of progress. He executed contract extensions and new contracts with Arthur Murray. An automobile accident severely injured plaintiff. At that time he had contracted for a total of 2,734 hours of lessons, for which he had paid $24,812.80.

The trial judge dismissed plaintiff's cause of action for fraud and his demand for punitive damages. The appellate court affirmed. It said that statements that plaintiff had "exceptional potential to be a fine and accomplished dancer" and was a "natural born dancer" were not fraud. These were only opinions, and plaintiff did not have a right to rely. The court took into account the business relationship of the parties as well as the educational background of plaintiff. However, the court affirmed the trial court's finding excusing plaintiff from

---

[91]10 Ill.App.3d 1000, 295 N.E.2d 487 (1973).

performance because of his injury.[92] This prompted rescission of the contracts and restitution of all amounts paid.

How does the *Parker* case differ from the *Vokes* decision? What are the courts assuming about Mr. Parker and Mrs. Vokes? Why did the court consider Parker's educational background?

2. *Dance studios versus gullible lonely people*: While it may seem hard to believe, the legal problem in the *Vokes* case is not uncommon. New York City attempted to deal with the problem by developing an "ethics code." See New York Times, Oct. 15, 1959, at 47, col. 3. We asked *Lexis* to list all cases with Arthur Murray in the title.[93] Ten cases decided between 1960 and 1973 involved roughly the situation in the *Vokes* case — people had bought long-term contracts for dance lessons promising to pay thousands of dollars and alleged fraud. Buyers won 6 of these cases, Arthur Murray won 3, and in one the court reversed buyer's award of summary judgment and remanded the case for trial. Two subsequent cases involved similar allegations but the plaintiffs were unable to get personal jurisdiction over Arthur Murray (the parent corporation). In addition, the five cases decided under the California statute discussed below all seem to involve something resembling the *Vokes* situation, and the plaintiff buyers won all of these decisions.

3. *The Federal Trade Commission attacks the Vokes poblem*: In 1960, the Federal Trade Commission brought a deceptive practices complaint against Arthur Murray, Inc., and its officers. It noted that Murray was the licensor of some 450 studios throughout the world. The complaint charged that the respondents had employed the following techniques to sell courses, which were sometimes used to mislead and coerce purchasers:

> 1. The use of "relay salesmanship," involving a number of Arthur Murray representatives who sign up a lone prospect by force of numbers and unrelenting sales talks, sometimes aided by hidden listening devices monitoring the conversation with the pupil;
> 2. The use of so-called "analyses," "studio competitions," and similar purported objective methods of judging dancing ability, which actually are to get the "winner" or "successful candidate" to buy future lessons;

---

[92]A party to a contract may be, in some circumstances, excused from performance when circumstances have so changed that the purpose of the performance can no longer be achieved, and achievement of that purpose was clearly central to the agreement. This is sometimes referred to as the "frustration of purpose" doctrine. It means, for example, that I might not be liable to pay rental for a racing car which I had rented for purposes of driving it in the Indianapolis 500 if the Indianapolis 500 was cancelled because of a natural disaster. This excuse for non-performance is the subject of investigation as part of Volume II of these materials.

[93]We also found five cases raising the *Vokes* problems involving other dance studios. Apparently, Arthur Murray, Inc. does not have a patent on these practices. However, it is the most litigious.

3. The use of blank or partially filled out contract forms, and by refusing to answer or evading questions as to amount due or payable so that pupils are misled as to the amount of their financial obligations;

4. By falsely assuring prospects that a given course will enable him to achieve a certain "standard" of dancing proficiency when it is planned that the prospects will be subjected to further coercive sales efforts before both the given course is completed and the "standard" reached.[94]

The FTC and Arthur Murray, Inc. settled the proceeding by a consent order. See CCH Trade Reg. Rept. Par. 28,965 (1961); New York Times, Aug. 3, 1960, at 14, col. 3.

What difference does a consent order make? The FTC can go to court and seek remedies for its violation. However, in such a proceeding the FTC must prove that the order is being violated. This raises a major problem in the Arthur Murray, Inc. situation. While the FTC might show that particular local Arthur Murray studios were violating the order, it would have to attribute these actions to the national corporation. Arthur Murray, Inc. argued vigorously that the questionable practices were those of local studios or even those of particular employees of local studios. Some courts ruled that Arthur Murray, Inc. so controlled its local licensees that their actions should be attributed to the national corporation; other courts were unwilling to ignore the formal structure that Arthur Murray, Inc.'s lawyers had drafted which denied relationships of agency.

The Court of Appeals, in *Arthur Murray Studio of Washington, Inc. v. Federal Trade Commission*,[95] noted:

> The record is replete with trick advertisements to draw prospects, sham dancing analysis tests, relay salesmanship, some secret electronic supervision by management, promises of social status and companionship, psychological sales techniques based on unpleasant experiences (described as X-Factor or "past is black" technique). In many instances these tactics added up to cajolery and coercion. Many were reduced to tears. One woman begged from her knees to be allowed to contract. Another woman testified:
>
>> The constant battering, it never let up. Two weeks at a time was about all they would let you go without being approached for some little additional something, not a big one, the big ones were about every two months and the little ones were about every two weeks. I was a nervous wreck there most of the time.

---

[94]Federal Trade Commission, Annual Report 60 (1960).
[95]458 F.2d 622 (5th Cir. 1972).

It was commonplace for contracts to be outstanding for several hundred hours of lessons which would take several years to complete. In one case, an elderly woman was signed up over a period of slightly more than a year for 696 hours of lessons. One of her contracts was in excess of $6,000. Many of the customers were placed in financial straits due to the contracts.

[In this case the court upheld a FTC finding that the respondent had violated an existing consent order and ordering that henceforth the respondent not enter into contracts providing for payment of more than $1500 in dance lessons in advance.]

4. *Statutory solutions*: In the early 1960s, the California Assembly Interim Committee on the Judiciary studied dance and health studios. It found,

> The opportunity to make a quick dollar at the expense of the lonely, credulous or impressionable customer has led to practices which form a pattern of overreaching and misrepresentation seriously close to fraud and extortion....
>
> They [long-term contracts] offer an irresistible temptation to the fraudulent operator to use high-pressure salesmanship, sign up all the customers he can for the largest amounts and longest terms that can be extracted, then close the studio or curtail services enough to discourage his newly acquired clientele.

The Committee then recommended the passage of what is now the California Dance Studio Act.[96] California Civil Code §§ 1812.50-1812.68 (1985). The statute provides:

> (a) Lessons must begin within 12 months from the date the contract is entered into, and no contract for dance studio lessons shall require payment of more than $2,500;
>
> (b) Contracts may be canceled within 180 days after receipt by the customer of a copy of the contract. The customer may recover all sums paid less compensation for any lessons actually given;
>
> (c) Contracts may be canceled after 180 days. The studio must refund all the customer paid except for compensation for lessons actually given and 10% of the unpaid balance;
>
> (d) Contracts must provide for relief as a result of death or disability so that the customer cannot use the lessons. The customer or the estate is entitled to a full refund of all paid less compensation for lessons actually given;

---

[96]A draft of the act was prepared for the Committee by students at the Stanford Law School.

(e) Contracts which do not comply with statutory requirements are void as contrary to public policy, and the requirements cannot be waived by the buyer;

(f) Any contract for dance studio lessons and other services entered into in reliance upon any willful and false, fraudulent, or misleading information, representation, notice or advertisement of the seller shall be void and unenforceable.

(g) Any buyer injured by a violation of this title may bring an action for the recovery of damages. Judgment may be entered for three times the amount at which the actual damages are assessed plus reasonable attorney fees. [However, a dance studio may correct any contract not in compliance within thirty days of execution and avoid the penalty.]

(h) The Attorney General, district attorneys or any city attorney has power to bring proceedings to restrain and enjoin violations. Any person who violates the act shall be guilty of a misdemeanor.

(i) Dance studios must post bonds from which damages may be paid unless a studio receives less than $50 in advance payments from each student and payments are not required more than once every 30 days.

The statute survived challenges by Arthur Murray, Inc.[97]

5. *Regulation by the market*: Most national corporations guard their reputation. In theory, at least, those who fail to satisfy their customers will suffer the penalties of the impersonal market. Whatever the merits of the allegations, there are a great many cases similar to the *Vokes* decision involving Arthur Murray dance studios. Why did the old and the lonely continue to go to the dance studios and buy expensive long-term courses of dancing instruction? Professor Gordon says "our sense of experience is always pushing up against the

---

[97]In People v. Arthur Murray, Inc., 238 Cal.App.2d 333, 47 Cal.Rptr. 700 (1965), the court upheld an injunction against selling lifetime contracts and doing other acts prohibited by the act. The court found that Murray's method of doing business "is calculated to aid and abet the violations which are committed by the dance studios." It also found that the statute was constitutional. In Beck v. Arthur Murray, Inc., 245 Cal.App.2d 976, 54 Cal.Rptr.328 (1966), Murray had its licensees post a sign saying they were responsible for "all obligations of any kind respecting the business of this studio." The court found that this did not avoid Arthur Murray, Inc.'s liability for violating the Dance Studio Act. See, also, Nichols v. Arthur Murray, Inc., 56 Cal.Rptr. 728 (1967); Staples v. Arthur Murray, Inc., 253 Cal.App.2d 507, 61 Cal.Rptr. 103 (1967). In Porter v. Arthur Murray, Inc., 249 Cal.App.2d 410, 57 Cal.Rptr. 554 (1967), Arthur Murray, Inc. changed its contract with those who were running local studios. Nonetheless, the court found that Arthur Murray, Inc. was still responsible for the violations of the Dance Studio Act by those licensed to run a studio with the Arthur Murray name. Finally, in Holland v. Nelson, 5 Cal.App.3d 308, 85 Cal.Rptr. 117 (1970), Arthur Murray's lawyers argued unsuccessfully that a one year statute of limitations applied to claims under the Dance Studio Act. The court added attorneys' fees of $1,500 for the appeal to those awarded for the trial.

legal categories, and potentially forcing alternative understandings of what is going on." He continues,

> Through the briefly sketched images of the court, our rational consumer has been transformed into a lonely, vulnerable woman in search of excitement and companionship — the dance studio, from a seller of dancing skills, into a sort of surrogate lover. A 51-year-old widow who would not dream of going, for example, to a singles bar wants safe and respectable ways to find male companionship. Learning how to dance is such a way. The dance studio becomes not just a way of getting there, but the destination itself: a place where attractive and charming instructors discover in her unsuspected graces and talents, and encourage her to feel desirable and at home among friends. They put her in a hierarchy of achievement and reward her efforts with medals and promotions. Was she really misled by being told how graceful and talented she was? Would things have been better, and she happier, if she had been given a coldly critical appraisal of her dancing ability? Perhaps the flattery and attention, even the lies if one must label a seducer's compliments as such, were not a distortion of the service the studio should have been rendering her, but an essential part of the service itself. The commodity the studio men are supplying is much more than dancing skills; it is the sensation of being alive and exciting....[98]

Younger people often enter similar long-term contracts with health or exercise studios. Both California and New York specifically regulate these contracts by statute.[99]

6. *Vulnerable young entertainers*: Young entertainers are sometimes eager to sign a contract with anyone promising to give them a chance to exploit their talents. Later, some become big stars and regret having signed a contract which no longer seems fair. For example before she became a well-known signer, Donna Summer signed contracts with Casablanca Records and Neil Bogard, Casablanca's President. Summer became very successful; she was known as the Queen of Disco. She had two triple-platinum double albums, a pair of platinum LPs and five gold albums to her credit.

Three years before the end of her contracts, she sued to have them revoked, alleging undue influence, misrepresentation and fraud, and breach of fiduciary obligation. She claimed that she had been physically and emotionally ill when she entered the contracts, and too inexperienced to know about business. She claimed that Joyce Bogard had managed her affairs primarily to benefit Casablanca

---

[98]Gordon, Unfreezing Legal Rationality: Critical Approaches to Law, 15 Florida State University Law Review 195, 205 (1987).

[99]See, *e.g.*, Faer v. Vertical Fitness & Racquet Club, Ltd., 119 Misc.2d 295, 462 N.Y.S.2d 784 (Civ.Ct.City of N.Y. 1983).

Records. Summer then signed a contract with Warner Brothers Records. Casablanca countersued, demanding that Summer complete the term of her contract.

The case was settled three years later, after a trial court had ruled that a "key man" clause had excused Summer from further performance when Bogard left Casablanca Records. The settlement provided that Summer deliver an album to Polygram (which had purchased Casablanca). Though the undue influence, misrepresentation and fraud, and breach of fiduciary obligations were never tried, they undoubtedly played a role in the negotiations which led to the settlement.[100]

C. SOCIAL CONTROL IN THE GUISE OF SEEKING CHOICE

1. CHOICE AND FORM CONTRACTS

Private Legislation and the Duty to Read — Business Run by
IBM Machine, the Law of Contracts and Credit Cards
Stewart Macaulay[101]

"It will not do for a man to enter into a contract, and, when called upon to abide by its conditions, say that he did not read it when he signed it, or did not know what it contained."[102] This rallying cry often is sounded in contracts and restitution opinions. Sometimes it makes such good sense that it is axiomatic. Yet in common with all grand slogans, there are situations where it just doesn't fit. For example, where the one who signs cannot read and has reason to trust another who tricks him by misreading the document, most courts have thought that the limits of the duty to read and understand have been reached. Undoubtedly courts would find other boundaries to the principle, if asked to do so. Imagine, for example, a purchase order form printed on gray paper. On the back are a number of terms and conditions printed in such light gray ink that they can be seen only by holding the paper at an angle to the light. Clearly, if a court ever were to enforce any of these terms and conditions, it would be marching to some ideology other than "choice." More difficult are the cases where the words are more easily read and understood but where it is probable that only the most suspicious will discover and understand them. This describes many form contracts. Organizations often attempt to use such forms and contract ideology

---

[100]See Billboard, February 9, 1980, at 3, June 28, 1980 at 3, July 5, 1980 at 4, and September 20, 1980 at 4.

[101]19 Vanderbilt Law Review 1051 (1966).

[102] Sanger v. Dun, 47 Wis. 615, 3 N.W. 388, 389 (1879).

to legislate privately. Sometimes this is successful. How then should we decide what effect to give the seldom-read form contract?

[The following case is a decision of the House of Lords, the highest court of the United Kingdom. Usually five Law Lords hear the case and each issues an opinion. Only three opinions (or "speeches," as they are called) are reproduced here.]

MCCUTCHEON v. DAVID MACBRAYNE, LTD.

[1964] 1 W.L.R. 125

This was an appeal against an interlocutor[103] of the Second Division of the Court of Session dated November 7, 1962, recalling an interlocutor of the Lord Ordinary (Lord Walker) dated March 23, 1962. The proof was taken before the Lord Ordinary[104] on March 8, 1962. On March 23, 1962, the Lord Ordinary held that the respondents, David 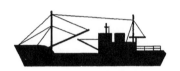 MacBrayne Ltd., the defenders in the action, had failed to prove that the contract of carriage, with which the case was concerned, was subject to conditions absolving them from liability and decerned[105] against them for payment to the appellant, Alexander McCutcheon, the pursuer in the action, of the sum sued for. The respondents reclaimed[106] and the case was heard before the Second Division on October 18 and 19, 1962. On November 7, 1962, the Second Division allowed the reclaiming motion and assoilzied[107] the respondents.

The facts are set out in their Lordships' opinions.

Their Lordships took time for consideration.

LORD REID. My Lords, the appellant is a farm grieve in Islay. While on the mainland in October, 1960, he asked his brother-in-law, Mr. McSporran, a farmer in Islay, to have his car sent by the respondents to West Loch Tarbert. Mr. McSporran took the car to Port Askaig. He found in the respondent's office

---

[103]Eds. Note: This paragraph contains a number of legal terms peculiar to English legal practice. An "interlocutor" is, in Scottish practice, the name given to the judicial order disposing of all, or part of, a case. It is the operative part of the decision, as contrasted to the "opinion" in which the judge gives reasons for the entry of the interlocutor.

[104]Eds. Note: The Lord Ordinary is a single judge of the Court of Session of Scotland, sitting as a trial judge.

[105]Eds. Note: In Scottish law, to decree.

[106]Eds. Note: Once again, a term used in Scottish procedure, meaning to appeal.

[107]Eds. Note: In Scots law, to find a defendant not liable. Such a finding may also be called "granting absolvitor."

there the purser of their vessel *Lochiel*, who quoted the freight for a return journey for the car. He paid the money, obtained a receipt and delivered the car to the respondents. It was shipped on the *Lochiel* but the vessel never reached West Loch Tarbert. She sank, owing to negligent navigation by the respondents' servants, and the car was a total loss. The appellant sues for its value, agreed at 480 Pounds.

The question is, what was the contract between the parties? The contract was an oral one. No document was signed or changed hands until the contract was completed. I agree with the unanimous view of the learned judges of the Court of Session that the terms of the receipt, which was made out by the purser and handed to Mr. McSporran after he paid the freight, cannot be regarded as terms of the contract. So the case is not one of the familiar ticket cases where the question is whether conditions endorsed on or referred to in a ticket or other document handed to the consignor in making the contract are binding on the consignor. If conditions not mentioned when this contract was made are to be added to or regarded as part of this contract it must be for some reason different from those principles which are now well settled in ticket cases. If this oral contract stands unqualified there can be no doubt that the respondents are liable for the damage caused by the negligence of their servants.

The respondents' case is that their elaborate printed conditions form part of this contract. If they do, then, admittedly, they exclude liability in this case. I think I can fairly summarise the evidence on this matter. The respondents exhibit copies of these conditions in their office, but neither the appellant nor his agent, Mr. McSporran, had read these notices, and I agree that they can play no part in the decision of this case. Their practice was to require consignors to sign risk notes which included these conditions before accepting any goods for carriage, but on this occasion no risk note was signed. The respondents' clerkess, knowing that Mr. McSporran was bringing the car for shipment, made out a risk note for his signature, but when he arrived she was not there and he dealt with the purser of the *Lochiel*, who was in the office. He asked for a return passage for the car. The purser quoted a charge of some 6 Pounds. He paid that sum and then the purser made out and gave him a receipt which he put in his pocket without looking at it. He then delivered the car. The purser forgot to ask him to sign the risk note.

The Lord Ordinary believed the evidence of Mr. McSporran and the appellant. Mr. McSporran had consigned goods of various kinds on a number of previous occasions. He said that sometimes he had signed a note, sometimes he had not. On one occasion he had sent his own car. A risk note for that consignment was produced signed by him. He had never read the risk notes signed by him. He said: "I sort of just signed it at the time as a matter of form." He admitted that he knew he was signing in connection with some conditions but he did not know what they were. In particular, he did not know that he was agreeing to send the goods at owner's risk. The appellant had consigned goods on four previous occasions. On three of them he was acting on behalf of his employer. On the other occasion he had sent his own car. Each time he had signed a risk note. He also admitted that he knew there were conditions but said that he did not know what they were.

The respondents contend that, by reason of the knowledge thus gained by the appellant and his agent in these previous transactions, the appellant is bound by their conditions. But this case differs essentially from the ticket cases. There, the carrier in making the contract hands over a document containing or referring to conditions which he intends to be part of the contract. So if the consignor or passenger, when accepting the document, knows or ought as a reasonable man to know that that is the carrier's intention, he can hardly deny that the conditions are part of the contract, or claim, in the absence of special circumstances, to be in a better position than he would be if he had read the document. But here, in making the contract neither party referred to, or indeed had in mind, any additional terms, and the contract was complete and fully effective without any additional terms. If it could be said that when making the contract Mr. McSporran knew that the respondents always required a risk note to be signed and knew that the purser was simply forgetting to put it before him for signature, then it might be said that neither he nor his principal could take advantage of the error of the other party of which he was aware. But counsel frankly admitted that he could not put his case as high as that.

The only other ground on which it would seem possible to import these conditions is that based on a course of dealing. If two parties have made a series of similar contracts each containing certain conditions, and then they make another without expressly referring to those conditions it may be that those conditions ought to be implied. If the officious bystander had asked them whether they had intended to leave out the conditions this time, both must, as honest men, have said "of course not." But again the facts here will not support that ground. According to Mr. McSporran, there had been no constant course of dealing; sometimes he was asked to sign and sometimes not. And, moreover, he did not know what the conditions were. This time he was offered an oral contract without any reference to conditions, and he accepted the offer in good faith.

The respondents also rely on the appellant's previous knowledge. I doubt whether it is possible to spell out a course of dealing in his case. In all but one of the previous cases he had been acting on behalf of his employer in sending a different kind of goods and he did not know that the respondents always sought to insist on excluding liability for their own negligence. So it cannot be said that when he asked his agent to make a contract for him he knew that this or, indeed, any other special term would be included in it. He left his agent a free hand to contract, and I see nothing to prevent him from taking advantage of the contract which his agent in fact made. "The judicial task is not to discover the actual intentions of each party; it is to decide what each was reasonably entitled to conclude from the attitude of the other" (Gloag on Contract, 2nd ed., p.7). In this case I do not think that either party was reasonably bound or entitled to conclude from the attitude of the other, as known to him, that these conditions were intended by the other party to be part of this contract. I would therefore allow the appeal and restore the interlocutor of the Lord Ordinary.

LORD DEVLIN. My Lords, when a person in the Isle of Islay wishes to send goods to the mainland he goes into the office of MacBrayne (the respondents) in Port Askaig which is conveniently combined with the local post office. There he is presented with a document headed "conditions" containing three or four thousand words of small print divided into 27 paragraphs. Beneath them there is a space for the sender's signature which he puts below his statement in quite legible print that he thereby agrees to ship on the conditions stated above. The appellant, Mr. McCutcheon, described the negotiations which preceded the making of this formidable contract in the following terms: "Q. Tell us about that document; how did you come to sign it? A. You just walk in the office and the document is filled up ready and all you have to do is to sign your name and go out. Q. Did you ever read the conditions? A. No. Q. Did you know what was in them? A. No."

There are many other passages in which Mr. McCutcheon and his brother-in-law, Mr. McSporran, endeavor more or less successfully to appease the forensic astonishment aroused by this statement. People shipping calves, Mr. McCutcheon said (he was dealing with an occasion when he had shipped 36 calves), had not much time to give to the reading. Asked to deal with another occasion when he was unhampered by livestock, he said that people generally just tried to be in time for the boat's sailing; it would, he thought, take half a day to read and understand the conditions and then he would miss the boat. In another part of his evidence he went so far as to say that if everybody took time to read the document, "MacBrayne's office would be packed out the door." Mr. McSporran evidently thought the whole matter rather academic because, as he pointed out, there was no other way to send a car.

There came a day, October 8, 1960, when one of the respondents' vessels was negligently sailed into a rock and sank. She had on board a car belonging to Mr. McCutcheon which he had got Mr. McSporran to ship for him, and the car was a total loss. It would be a strangely generous set of conditions in which the persistent reader, after wading through the verbiage, could not find something to protect the carrier against "any loss ... wheresoever or whensoever occurring"; and condition 19 by itself is enough to absolve the respondents several times over for all their negligence. It is conceded that if the form had been signed as usual, the appellant would have had no case. But, by a stroke of ill luck for the respondents, it was upon this day of all days that they omitted to get Mr. McSporran to sign the conditions. What difference does that make?

If it were possible for your Lordships to escape from the world of make-believe which the law has created into the real world in which transactions of this sort are actually done, the answer would be short and simple. It should make no difference whatever. This sort of document is not meant to be read, still less to be understood. Its signature is in truth about as significant as a handshake that marks the formal conclusion of a bargain.

Your Lordships were referred to the dictum of Blackburn J. in *Harris v. Great Western Railway Co.*[108] The passage is as follows: "And it is clear law that where there is a writing, into which the terms of any agreement are reduced, the terms are to be regulated by that writing. And though one of the parties may not have read the writing, yet, in general, he is bound to the other by those terms; and that, I apprehend, is on the ground that, by assenting to the contract thus reduced to writing, he represents to the other side that he has made himself acquainted with the contents of that writing and assents to them, and so induces the other side to act upon that representation by entering into the contract with him, and is consequently precluded from denying that he did make himself acquainted with those terms. But then the preclusion only exists when the case is brought within the rule so carefully and accurately laid down by Parke B., in delivering the judgment of the Exchequer in *Freeman v. Cooke,*[109] that is, if he 'means his representation to be acted upon, and it is acted upon accordingly: or if, whatever a man's real intentions may be, he so conduct himself that a reasonable man would take the representation to be true, and believe that it was meant that he should act upon it, and did act upon it as true.' "

If the ordinary law of estoppel was applicable to this case, it might well be argued that the circumstances leave no room for any representation by the sender on which the carrier acted. I believe that any other member of the public in Mr. McCutcheon's place — and this goes for lawyers as well as for laymen — would have found himself compelled to give the same sort of answers as Mr. McCutcheon gave; and I doubt if any carrier who serves out documents of this type could honestly say that he acted in the belief that the recipient had "made himself acquainted with the contents." But Blackburn J. was dealing with an unsigned document, a cloakroom ticket. Unless your Lordships are to disapprove the decision of the Court of Appeal in *L'Estrange v. F. Graucob Ltd.*[110] — and there has been no suggestion in this case that you should — the law is clear, without any recourse to the doctrine of estoppel, that a signature to a contract is conclusive.

This is a matter that is relevant to the way in which the respondents put their case. They say that the previous dealings between themselves and the appellant, being always on the terms of their "risk note," as they call their written conditions, the contract between themselves and the appellant must be deemed to import the same conditions. In my opinion, the bare fact that there have been previous dealings between the parties does not assist the respondents at all. The fact that a man has made a contract in the same form 99 times (let alone three or four times which are here alleged) will not of itself affect the hundredth contract in which the form is not used. Previous dealings are relevant only if they

---

[108](1876) 1 Q.B.D. 515, 530.

[109](1848) 2 Ex. 654.

[110][1934] 2 K.B. 394, C.A.

prove knowledge of the terms, actual and not constructive, and assent to them. If a term is not expressed in a contract, there is only one other way in which it can come into it and that is by implication. No implication can be made against a party of a term which was unknown to him. If previous dealings show that a man knew of and agreed to a term on 99 occasions there is a basis for saying that it can be imported into the hundredth contract without an express statement. It may or may not be sufficient to justify the importation, — that depends on the circumstances; but at least by proving knowledge the essential beginning is made. Without knowledge there is nothing.

It is for the purpose of proving knowledge that the respondents rely on the dictum of Blackburn J. which I have cited. My Lords, in spite of the great authority of Blackburn J., I think that this is a dictum which some day your Lordships may have to examine more closely. It seems to me that when a party assents to a document forming the whole or a part of his contract, he is bound by the terms of the document, read or unread, signed or unsigned, simply because they are in the contract; and it is unnecessary and possibly misleading to say that he is bound by them because he represents to the other party that he has made himself acquainted with them. But if there be an estoppel of this sort, its effect is, in my opinion, limited to the contract in relation to which the representation is made; and it cannot (unless of course there be something else on which the estoppel is founded besides the mere receipt of the document) assist the other party in relation to other transactions. The respondents in the present case have quite failed to prove that the appellant made himself acquainted with the conditions they had introduced into previous dealings. He is not estopped from saying that, for good reasons or bad, he signed the previous contracts without the slightest idea of what was in them. If that is so, previous dealings are no evidence of knowledge and so are of little or no use to the respondents in this case.

I say "of little or no use" because the appellant did admit that he knew that there were some conditions, though he did not know what they were. He certainly did not know that they were conditions which exempted the respondents from liability for their own negligence, though I suppose, if he had thought about them at all, he would have known that they probably exempted the respondents from the strict liability of a carrier. Most people know that carriers exact some conditions and it does not matter in this case whether Mr. McCutcheon's knowledge was general knowledge of this sort or was derived from previous dealings. Your Lordships can therefore leave previous dealings out of it and ask yourself simply what is the position of a man who, with that amount of general knowledge, apparently makes a contract into which no conditions are expressly inserted?

The answer must surely be that either he does not make a contract at all because the parties are not ad idem, or he makes the contract without the conditions. You cannot have a contract subject to uncommunicated conditions the terms of which are known only to one side.

It is at this point, I think, that their Lordships in the Second Division fell into error. The Lord Justice-Clerk said:[111] "It is, I think, well settled that, if A contracts with B for the carriage by B of A's goods in the knowledge, gained through previous experience of similar transactions, that B carries goods subject to conditions, A is bound by these conditions under this later contract, if it is of a similar nature to those which have gone before, in the absence of agreement or information to the contrary. This applies even if A, knowing that there are conditions, does not take the trouble to ascertain precisely what these conditions are." Similarly Lord MacIntosh said:[112] "In these circumstances, I am of opinion, following what I understand to be the law as laid down in *Parker v. South Eastern Railway Co.*,[113] and particularly by Baggallay L.J., that the pursuer being aware, by reason of his own previous experience and of that of the agent who happened to be acting for him in the present transaction, that goods were carried on the defenders' vessels subject to certain conditions, and having been given no reason to think that these conditions were not still operative on October 8, 1960, was bound by the conditions, although, as was proved to have been the case, he had never at any time acquainted himself with their purport."

My Lords, I think, with great respect, that this is to introduce a new and fundamentally erroneous principle into the law of contract. There can be no conditions in any contract unless they are brought into it by expression, incorporation or implication. They are not brought into it simply because one party has inserted them into similar transactions in the past and has not given the other party any reason to think that he will not want to insert them again. The error is based, I think, on a misunderstanding of what are commonly called the ticket cases; I say this because the single authority cited for the proposition is one of the leading ticket cases, *Parker v. South Eastern Railway Co.*[114] The question in these cases is whether or not the passenger has accepted the ticket as a contractual document. If he knows that it contains conditions of some sort, he must know that it is meant to be contractual. If he accepts it as a contractual document, then prima facie (I am not dealing with questions of reasonable notice) he is bound by the conditions that are printed on it or incorporated in it by sufficient reference to some other document, whether he has inquired about them or not. That is all that Baggallay L.J. is saying in *Parker v. South Eastern Railway Co.*[115]

In the present case there is no contractual document at all. There is not so much as a peg on which to hang any terms that are not expressed in the contract nor a phrase which is capable of expansion. It is as if the appellant had been

[111]1962 S.C. 506, 512.
[112]*Ibid.* 516.
[113]2 C.P.D. 416, 425.
[114]2 C.P.D. 416, 425.
[115]2 C.P.D. 416, 425.

accepted as a passenger without being given a ticket at all. There is, then, no special contract and the contract is the ordinary one which the law imposes on carriers. As Baggallay L.J. said: "This clearly would be the nature of the contract if no ticket were delivered, as occasionally happens."

If a man is given a blank ticket without conditions or any reference to them, even if he knows in detail what the conditions usually exacted are, he is not, in the absence of any allegation of fraud or of that sort of mistake for which the law gives relief, bound by such conditions. It may seem a narrow and artificial line that divides a ticket that is blank on the back from one that says "For conditions see time-tables," or something of that sort, that has been held to be enough notice. I agree that it is an artificial line and one that has little relevance to everyday conditions. It may be beyond your Lordships' power to make the artificial line more natural: but at least you can see that it is drawn fairly for both sides and that there is not one law for individuals and another for organisations that can issue printed documents. If the respondents had remembered to issue a risk note in this case, they would have invited your Lordships to give a curt answer to any complaint by the appellant. He might say that the terms were unfair and unreasonable, that he had never voluntarily agreed to them, that it was impossible to read or understand them and that anyway if he had tried to negotiate any change the respondents would not have listened to him. The respondents would expect him to be told that he had made his contract and must abide by it. Now the boot is on the other foot. It is just as legitimate, but also just as vain, for the respondents to say that it was only a slip on their part, that it is unfair and unreasonable of the appellant to take advantage of it and that he knew perfectly well that they never carried goods except on conditions. The law must give the same answer: they must abide by the contract they made. What is sauce for the goose is sauce for the gander. It will remain unpalatable sauce for both animals until the legislature, if the courts cannot do it, intervenes to secure that when contracts are made in circumstances in which there is no scope for free negotiation of the terms, they are made upon terms that are clear, fair and reasonable and settled independently as such. That is what Parliament has done in the case of carriage of goods by rail and on the high seas.

I have now given my opinion on the main point in the case and the one on which the respondents succeeded below. On the other points on which the respondents failed below and which they put forward again as grounds for dismissing the claim, I have nothing to add to what your Lordships have already said. In my opinion, the appeal should be allowed.

LORD HODSON. My Lords, the decision of the Second Division of the Inner House in favour of the defenders seems to me to involve an extension of the application of the doctrine of "course of dealing" which is not warranted by the facts of this case.

... The law as it stands appears hard on the holders of tickets who, unless they are exceptional persons, will not take pains to make an examination of a ticket offered to them to see if any conditions are imposed. It would be scarcely tolerable to take the further step of treating a contracting party as if he had signed and so bound himself by the terms of a document with conditions embodied in it, when, as here, he has done no such thing but may be supposed, having regard to his previous experience, to have been willing to sign what was put before him if he had been asked....

NOTES AND QUESTIONS

1. *The background of the case*: A map of the Inner Hebrides shows the isolation of Islay. It is about a 2 hour and 10 minute boat trip from Port Askaig to West Tarbert. West Tarbert is about 150 miles from Glasgow on a road around a loch. Indeed, although Port Askaig, West Tarbert and Glasgow are about on the same latitude, one must drive about 85 miles north of West Tarbert before one can turn southeast for Glasgow. Islay is almost directly north of Ballycastle in Northern Ireland.

Others who had signed the risk note doubtless lost valuable property when MacBrayne's boat sank.[116] Isn't it capricious to allow Mr. McCutcheon to recover for his lost car but deny recovery to all the others who suffered such severe losses when the boat sank? Would it make more sense to hold a lottery and allow the winner to recover his or her loss? Or is the case itself an odd form of lottery?

2. *Discovering one is making a contract and its important terms*: American courts probably begin just as the English courts do — with a presumption that a person knows the contents of a document which he executes, understands the literal meaning of its terms, and so is bound by those terms. Some American courts have tempered this principle in a number of ways however. For example, in *Henningsen v. Bloomfield Motors, Inc.*[117] a woman was injured driving a new Plymouth two days after taking delivery. There was a small-print limitation of liability, which the court refused to enforce, on the back of the signed purchase order. The clause was a standard one drafted by the Automobile Manufacturers Association and used by all American manufacturers. The court held it was invalid because it was inimical to the public good. One reason was that the "type of print itself was such as to promote lack of attention rather than sharp scrutiny." Another was that even if the court charged a buyer with awareness of the language, "can it be said an ordinary layman would realize what he was relinquishing in return for what he was being granted?" The court noted that the "draftsmanship is reflective of the care and skill of the Automobile manufacturers

---

[116]We know, for example, that one farmer lost four years' savings when his forty sheep drowned. See John McPhee's The Crofter and the Laird 32-3 (© Farrar, Straus & Giroux 1970).

[117]32 N.J. 358, 161 A.2d 69 (1960).

Association in undertaking to avoid warranty obligation without drawing too much attention to its effort in that regard."[118]

The court stated, contrary to the holdings of the English ticket cases discussed in *McCutcheon* as well as the holdings in many American cases,

> [c]lauses on baggage checks restricting the liability of common carriers for loss or damage in transit are not enforceable unless the limitation is fairly and honestly negotiated and understandingly entered into. If not called specifically to the patron's attention, it is not binding. It is not enough merely to show the form of a contract; it must appear also that the agreement was understandingly made.... The same holds true in cases of such limitations on parcel check room tickets ... and on storage warehouse receipts ... on automobile parking lot or garage tickets or claim checks....

Statutes or administrative regulations change many of the traditional rules as well. For example, the Indiana Code, § 32-8-28-1, addresses the limited liability of hotel keepers for guests' property. The hotel may offer a safe in which guests may place valuable property. If it conspicuously posts a notice in each room of the availability of the safe and that the hotel is not liable unless articles are tendered for safekeeping, then it is not liable. Furthermore, maximum liability for goods accepted for safekeeping is $600.

3. *Disclaimers in instruction books:* Often sellers print disclaimers of liability in instruction booklets or other material that the customer obtains only after she buys the product and takes delivery. These attempts to limit liability may come too late to be part of the contract. The contract may be formed on the basis of the transaction between the sales representative and the buyer. The time for negotiations has passed when the buyer opens the box at her home. Instruction books do not seem to be part of the contract process. Their function is instruction

---

[118]The case is of largely historical interest today. The practices of automobile manufacturers as regards warranties are very different. The law, too, has changed significantly. We will see some of the newer law in the next section.

The Henningsen case was an early victory of the consumer movement. The Supreme Court of New Jersey on its own motion declared the standard automobile warranty to be against the public policy of the state. Mrs. Henningsen's lawyer made no such argument. Indeed, the briefs and record on appeal show that the debate between Chrysler and Mrs. Henningsen concerned the trial court's refusal to admit a record into evidence. Chrysler offered the record made by the nurse on duty who had admitted Mrs. Henningsen to the emergency room of the hospital where she had been taken after her new Plymouth had crashed into a wall. Mrs. Henningsen's lawyer tried the case on the theory that part of the steering had snapped causing the car to leave the road at almost a right angle. The document, however, said that Mrs. Henningsen had told the nurse that her hand had slipped on the steering wheel.

and not negotiation.[119] Compare *Monsanto Agricultural Products Co. v. Edenfield*.[120] A farmer sued a herbicide manufacturer for damage to his soybean crop when weeds choked his soybean plants and stifled their growth. The farmer bought Lasso in sealed five gallon cans. On both the labels of the cans and in the instruction booklets affixed to the tops, there was "limit of warranty and liability." The instruction booklet stated:

> Read "LIMIT OF WARRANTY AND LIABILITY" before buying or using. If terms are not acceptable, return at once unopened.

The farmer admitted he had read the instructions, but he said "I don't remember reading anything about the warranty." The court found he was charged with knowledge of a conspicuous disclaimer. The court does not explain why the farmer is bound by terms on a label and in an instruction booklet that he received after he had concluded a contract to purchase the herbicide.[121]

Contrast *Marion Power Shovel v. Huntsman*, 246 Ark. 152, 437 S.W.2d 784 (1969). An express warranty, which included a disclaimer of implied warranties, was included in the instruction manuals, which were not delivered to the buyer until the equipment was delivered. Documents signed and given to the buyer at the time the sale was concluded made no mention of either an express warranty or a disclaimer of implied warranties. Relying on *Hunt v. Perkins Machinery Co.*, *supra*, the court held that the disclaimer was not conspicuous and hence ineffective under the U.C.C.

4. *Reading and understanding form contracts*: Suppose that McSporran had both read and signed the contract before consigning McCutcheon's automobile on that fateful day. No doubt the House of Lords would have held McCutcheon bound to the terms of the contract and denied recovery. However, often many people would be unable to understand the contract if they did read it. Contract terms frequently concern technical matters. In addition, the language used in form contracts may be antiquated and legalistic and may violate principles of clear writing.

---

[119]Many people do not read instructions that come with products or they look at them only when they have a specific question. Drafting information for consumers so that it conveys information is a difficult technical task. Often instruction books and labels are so poorly written that people are discouraged from reading them. See, generally, Wright, The Instructions Clearly State.... Can't People Read? 12 Applied Ergonomics 131 (1981).

[120]426 So.2d 574 (DCA Fla. 1983).

[121]Those familiar with computer software will recognize the common technique. Many suppliers of software attempt to make removing the wrapping on the package or the disks a token of assent to various disclaimers and promises not to copy the software. Again, we can ask whether this step comes too late in the process to include the action in the formation of the contract.

New York and several other states have responded to the problems of incomprehensible forms by adopting a "Plain English Law."[122] The statute requires that a consumer contract must be drafted in a "clear and coherent manner using words with common and everyday meanings," and "appropriately divided and captioned by its various sections." A study[123] done a year after the statute's passage suggests relatively widespread compliance. Most firms surveyed revised their forms because of the law. Most also were pleased with the results. The note concludes:

> The benefits of contracts written in plain English are undeniable. For the consumer, the obvious benefits are the avoidance of frustration and unfair surprise. The benefits to business, while not so obvious, are equally worthwhile. Most importantly, the use of plain English is fundamental to good business. The movement should generate good will and foster confidence and trust in business. Consumers are much more likely to abide by terms which they understood from the beginning. Businessmen and employees will spend less time explaining clauses, answering complaints and defending themselves in lawsuits. Businesses will be in a much stronger position to enforce contracts when the consumer's obligations have been clearly spelled out.

A leading printer of legal forms revised them to follow the New York and New Jersey plain language laws. He said that New York's law "has not been an instrument of social change. It works for the middle-class consumers who realize the system works for them." A lawyer who drafted plain language form contracts argues, however, that the law "has helped people without their realizing it." We can get a flavor of the differences by comparing an older form with a new one drafted after the plain language laws. Both clauses are designed to sell a house "as is." The seller is not responsible for defects. The older traditional provision reads:

> This contract is entered into with the purchaser's full knowledge as to the value of the land the buildings and improvements thereon, and not upon any representations as to the value, character, quality or condition thereof, other than as may be expressly provided herein.

---

[122]See N.Y. Gen. Obligation Law § 5-702 (McKinney Supp. 1984-85).

[123]Note, New York's Plain English, 8 Ford. Urb. L.J. 451 (1980). See also Davis, Protecting Consumers from Overdisclosure and Gobbledygook: An Empirical Look at the Simplification of Consumer-Credit Contracts, 613 Virginia Law Review 841 (1977).

The plain language version of the same clause states:

> The Buyer has inspected the Property or has had the Property inspected by others. Except for any rights of inspection reserved elsewhere in this Contract, the Buyer accepts the property "as is." The Seller makes no claim or promise about the condition or value of the Property.[124]

In *Gross v. Lloyds of London Ins. Co.*,[125] the Wisconsin Supreme Court applied a statute requiring that insurance policies be "written in commonly understood language, legible, appropriately divided and captioned by its various sections and presented in a meaningful sequence."[126] The Supreme Court of Wisconsin reversed a trial court decision which had given effect to a term in an insurance policy. The term provided that the insurance company could concede it was liable for the maximum amount payable under the policy and then refuse to pay for the defense of the claim. The case report consists of a majority and three concurring opinions.

The majority opinion stated "an insurer cannot rely on a standard form for its protection when the provisions relied upon are not made clear to the insured." The language freeing the insurance company from a duty to defend the case was just one clause among many in a printed form. The majority said that for an insured to be relieved of its duty to defend upon tendering the policy limits "language must be highlighted in the policy and binder by means of conspicuous print, such as bold, italicized, or colored type, which gives clear notice to the insured that the insurer may be relieved of its duty to defend by tendering the policy limits for settlement." It concluded "once insureds have been given notice by the insurer of a limited duty to defend, they may choose to afford themselves greater protection in the defense of claims by increasing the amount of their policy limits or seek a policy which provides for unlimited defense."

Justice Abrahamson concurred but refused to join the majority's adoption of a readability and notice rule. She thought "prescribing the form of insurance policies is not a matter for this court," and would have left the matter to the Commissioner of Insurance.

Can we expect plain language and bold type to make much of a difference? Is this likely to be an effective type of regulation? Professor Whitford argues:

> [P]recontract disclosure is most often required only in the written document called the contract. Sellers have long known that it is precisely in the contract, and only in the contract, that information consumers are *not*

---

[124]See New York Times, Nov. 7, 1981, at 31, cols. 1-4. See also Leete, Plain Language Legislation: A Comparison of Approaches, 18 American Business Law Journal 511 (1981).

[125]121 Wis.2d 78, 358 N.W.2d 266 (1984).

[126]Wis.Stat. § 631.22(2)

supposed to notice is to be put. Admittedly, sellers have often buried unfavorable information in small type. But the use of large, bold type, commonly required by disclosure regulations, will rarely communicate information prior to the signing of the contract unless the consumer is searching for the information and has reason to expect it to be in the contract. In nearly all consumer transactions — and to a very great extent in all contractual transactions — the effective agreement, an oral one, is made before the buyer ever sees the written contract. To the parties, the signing of the written contract is usually only a ritual, roughly equivalent to a handshake. The written contract is likely to be read carefully enough to be understood at some time subsequent to its signing, if at all. Even in the rare case in which a consumer actually reads the contract before signing, it must be remembered that he usually views himself as already morally committed. If he comes across information in the written contract which ordinarily would persuade him not to sign, it puts him in a conflict situation and one which, in accordance with the theory of cognitive dissonance, he may resolve by discounting the disclosed information. Certainly in this situation, unless the information pertains to a buying desire valued very highly by the consumer, he is likely to be receptive to a conflict-resolving suggestion by a salesman that the disclosed information is not really significant and is only included because the law so requires.[127]

Whitford distinguishes a predictive from a normative model of buyer behavior. If those seeking to aid consumers accept *people as they are*, they must seek information about how people make decisions and whether items that might be put in bold type would be significant to most people. If those drafting regulations are operating on the basis of a normative model, they base their decisions about what items to be put in bold type on how they think buyers *ought to behave*. He notes that a great deal of disclosure regulation seems based on a normative model of behavior and seems to have but little impact on actual behavior.

Some have argued that, insofar as form contracts are concerned, the law should place the burden of justifying any departures from "background law" — the law that would apply in the absence of agreement — on the drafter of the agreement.[128] The following case arguably takes at least a small step in that direction. Do you find this approach promising?

---

[127]Whitford, The Functions of Disclosure Regulation in Consumer Contracts, 1973 Wisconsin Law Review 400.

[128]Rakoff, Contracts of Adhesion: An Essay in Reconstruction, 96 Harvard Law Review 1174, 1229, 1235, 1243 (1983).

C & J FERTILIZER, INC. v. ALLIED MUT. INS. CO.

227 N.W.2d 169 (Iowa 1975)

REYNOLDSON, J. This action to recover for burglary loss under two separate insurance policies was tried to the court, resulting in a finding plaintiff had failed to establish a burglary within the policy definitions. Plaintiff appeals from judgment entered for defendant. We reverse and remand.

Trial court made certain findings of fact in support of its conclusion reached. Plaintiff operated a fertilizer plant in Olds, Iowa. At time of loss, plaintiff was insured under policies issued by defendant and titled "BROAD FORM STOREKEEPERS POLICY" and "MERCANTILE BURGLARY AND ROBBERY POLICY." Each policy defined "burglary" as meaning,

> ... the felonious abstraction of insured property (1) from within the premises by a person making felonious entry therein by actual force and violence, of which force and violence there are visible marks made by tools, explosives, electricity or chemicals upon, or physical damage to, the exterior of the premises at the place of such entry....

On Saturday, April 18, 1970, all exterior doors to the building were locked when plaintiff's employees left the premises at the end of the business day. The following day, Sunday, April 19, 1970, one of plaintiff's employees was at the plant and found all doors locked and secure. On Monday, April 20, 1970, when the employees reported for work, the exterior doors were locked, but the front office door was unlocked.

There were truck tire tread marks visible in the mud in the driveway leading to and from the plexiglas door entrance to the warehouse. It was demonstrated this door could be forced open without leaving visible marks or physical damage.

There were no visible marks on the exterior of the building made by tools, explosives, electricity or chemicals, and there was no physical damage to the exterior of the building to evidence felonious entry into the building by force and violence.

Chemicals had been stored in an interior room of the warehouse. The door to this room, which had been locked, was physically damaged and carried visible marks made by tools. Chemicals had been taken at a net loss to plaintiff in the sum of $9,582. Office and shop equipment valued at $400.30 was also taken from the building.

Trial court held the policy definition of "burglary" was unambiguous, there was nothing in the record "upon which to base a finding that the door to plaintiff's place of business was entered feloniously, by actual force and violence," and, applying the policy language, found for defendant.

Certain other facts in the record were apparently deemed irrelevant by trial court because of its view [that] the applicable law required it to enforce the policy provision. Because we conclude different rules of law apply, we also consider those facts.

The "BROAD FORM STOREKEEPERS POLICY" was issued April 14, 1969; the "MERCANTILE BURGLARY AND ROBBERY POLICY" on April 14, 1970. Those policies are in evidence. Prior policies apparently were first purchased in 1968. The agent, who had power to bind insurance coverage for defendant, was told plaintiff would be handling farm chemicals. After inspecting the building then used by plaintiff for storage he made certain suggestions regarding security. There ensued a conversation in which he pointed out there had to be visible evidence of burglary. There was no testimony by anyone that plaintiff was then or thereafter informed [that] the policy to be delivered would define burglary to require "visible marks made by tools, explosives, electricity or chemicals upon, or physical damage to, the exterior of the premises at the place of ... entry."

The import of this conversation with defendant's agent when the coverage was sold is best confirmed by the agent's complete and vocally-expressed surprise when defendant denied coverage. From what the agent saw (tire tracks and marks on the interior of the building) and his contacts with the investigating officers "...the thought didn't enter my mind that it wasn't covered...." From the trial testimony it was obvious the only understanding was that there should be some hard evidence of a third-party burglary vis-à-vis an "inside job." The latter was in this instance effectively ruled out when the thief was required to break an interior door lock to gain access to the chemicals.

The agent testified the insurance was purchased and "the policy was sent out afterwards." The president of plaintiff corporation, a 37-year-old farmer with a high school education, looked at that portion of the policy setting out coverages, including coverage for burglary loss, the amounts of insurance, and the "location and description." He could not recall reading the fine print defining "burglary" on page three of the policy....

Extrinsic evidence that throws light on the situation of the parties, the antecedent negotiations, the attendant circumstances and the objects they were thereby striving to attain is necessarily to be regarded as relevant to ascertain the actual significance and proper legal meaning of the agreement....

The question of *interpretation, i.e.*, the meaning to be given contractual words, is one to be determined by the court unless the interpretation depends on extrinsic evidence or on a choice among reasonable inferences to be drawn from extrinsic evidence.... *Construction* of a contract means determination of its legal operation — its effect upon the action of the courts.... "[C]onstruction [of a contract] is always a matter of law for the court." 3 Corbin on Contracts § 554, p. 227. "[C]ourts in construing and applying a standardized contract seek to effectuate the reasonable expectations of the average member of the public who accepts it." Restatement (Second) of Contracts § 237, comment e, p. 540....

Trial court never made a finding [that] there was or was not a burglary. We have noted its examination of the evidence was tailored to fit the policy "definition" of burglary: " 'Burglary' means the felonious abstraction of insured property (1) from within the premises by a person making *felonious entry therein by actual force and violence*, of which force and violence there are visible marks...." (Emphasis supplied.).

Nor did trial court consider the evidence in light of the layman's concept of burglary (who might well consider a stealing intruder in his home or business premises as a burglar, whether or not the door was entered by force and violence) or the legal definition of burglary, hereinafter referred to. Trial court made no determination regarding burglary in those contexts.

Insofar as trial court was construing the policy — that being a matter of law for the court — we are not bound by its conclusions.... Neither are we bound by trial court's rule [that] this case is controlled by the fineprint "definition" of burglary, if that rule was erroneously applied below....

And if the definition of "burglary" in defendant's policy is not enforceable here, then trial court's finding [that] there was no evidence of forcible entry through an outside door is not controlling in the disposition of this case.

Plaintiff's theories of recovery based on "reasonable expectations," implied warranty and unconscionability must be viewed in light of accelerating change in the field of contracts.

I. *Revolution in formation of contractual relationships*

Many of our principles for resolving conflicts relating to written contracts were formulated at an early time when parties of equal strength negotiated in the historical sequence of offer, acceptance, and reduction to writing. The concept that both parties assented to the resulting document had solid footing in fact.

Only recently has the sweeping change in the inception of the document received widespread recognition:

> Standard form contracts probably account for more than ninety-nine percent of all contracts now made. Most persons have difficulty remembering the last time they contracted other than by standard form; except for casual oral agreements, they probably never have. But if they are active, they contract by standard form several times a day. Parking lot and theater tickets, package receipts, department store charge slips, and gas station credit card purchase slips are all standard form contracts.
>
> ... The contracting still imagined by courts and law teachers as typical, in which both parties participate in choosing the language of their entire agreement, is no longer of much more than historical importance.

W. Slawson, Standard Form Contracts and Democratic Control of Lawmaking Power, 84 Harvard Law Review 529 (1971).

... It is generally recognized the insured will not read the detailed, cross-referenced, standardized, mass-produced insurance form, nor understand it if he does. 7 Williston on Contracts § 906B, p. 300 ("But where the document thus delivered to him is a contract of insurance the majority rule is that the insured is not bound to know its contents"); 3 Corbin on Contracts § 559, pp. 265-66 ("One who applies for an insurance policy ... may not even read the policy, the number of its terms and the fineness of its being such as to discourage him"); Note, Unconscionable Contracts: The Uniform Commercial Code, 45 Iowa Law Review 843, 844 (1960) ("It is probably a safe assertion that most involved standardized form contracts are never read by the party who 'adheres' to them. In such situations, the proponent of the form is free to dictate terms most advantageous to himself")....

The concept that persons must obey public laws enacted by their own representatives does not offend a fundamental sense of justice: an inherent element of assent pervades the process.

But the inevitable result of enforcing all provisions of the adhesion contract, frequently, as here, delivered subsequent to the transaction and containing provisions never assented to, would be an abdication of judicial responsibility in face of basic unfairness and a recognition that persons' rights shall be controlled by private lawmakers without the consent, express or implied, of those affected.... A question is also raised whether a court may constitutionally allow that power to exist in private hands except where appropriate safeguards are present, including a right to meaningful judicial review. See W. Slawson, *supra* at 553.

The statutory requirement that the form of policies be approved by the commissioner of insurance, § 515.109, The [Iowa] Code, neither resolves the issue whether the fineprint provisions nullify the insurance bargained for in a given case nor ousts the court from necessary jurisdiction.... In this connection it has been pertinently stated:

> Insurance contracts continue to be contracts of adhesion, under which the insured is left little choice beyond electing among standardized provisions offered to him, even when the standard forms are prescribed by public officials rather than insurers. Moreover, although statutory and administrative regulations have made increasing inroads on the insurer's autonomy by prescribing some kinds of provisions and proscribing others, most insurance policy provisions are still drafted by insurers. Regulation is relatively weak in most instances, and even the provisions prescribed or approved by legislative or administrative action ordinarily are in essence adoptions, outright or slightly modified, of proposals made by insurers' draftsmen.

> Under such circumstances as these, judicial regulation of contracts of adhesion, whether concerning insurance or some other kind of transaction, remains appropriate.

Keeton, Insurance Law Rights At Variance With Policy Provisions, 83 Harvard Law Review 961, 966-67 (1970).

The mass-produced boiler-plate "contracts," necessitated and spawned by the explosive growth of complex business transactions in a burgeoning population left courts frequently frustrated in attempting to arrive at just results by applying many of the traditional contract-construing stratagems. As long as fifteen years ago Professor Llewellyn, reflecting on this situation in his book "The Common Law Tradition — Deciding Appeals," pp. 362-71 wrote,

> What the story shows thus far is first, scholars persistently off-base while judges grope over well-nigh a century in irregular but dogged fashion for escape from a recurring discomfort of imbalance that rests on what is in fact substantial *non*agreement despite perfect semblance of agreement. (pp. 367-368).
> ... The answer, I suggest, is this: Instead of thinking about 'assent' to boiler-plate clauses, we can recognize that so far as concerns the specific, there is no assent at all. What has in fact been assented to, specifically, are the few dickered terms, and the broad type of transaction, and but one thing more. That one thing more is a blanket assent (not a specific assent) to any not unreasonable or indecent terms the seller may have on his form, which do not alter or eviscerate the reasonable meaning of the dickered terms. The fine print which has not been read has no business to cut under the reasonable meaning of those dickered terms which constitute the dominant and only real expression of agreement, but much of it commonly belongs in. (p. 370)

In fairness to the often-discerned ability of the common law to develop solutions for changing demands, it should be noted appellate courts take cases as they come, constrained by issues the litigants formulated in trial court — a point not infrequently overlooked by academicians. Nor can a lawyer in the ordinary case be faulted for not risking a client's cause on an uncharted course when there is a reasonable prospect of reaching a fair result through familiar channels of long-accepted legal principles, for example, those grounded on ambiguity in language, the duty to define limitations or exclusions in clear and explicit terms, and interpretation of language from the viewpoint of an ordinary person, not a specialist or expert....

Plaintiff's claim [that] it should be granted relief under the legal doctrines of reasonable expectations, implied warranty and unconscionability should be viewed against the above backdrop.

II. *Reasonable expectations*

This court adopted the doctrine of reasonable expectations in *Rodman v. State Farm Mutual Ins. Co.*, 208 N.W.2d 903, 905-908 (Iowa 1973). The *Rodman* court approved the following articulation of that concept:

> The objectively reasonable expectations of applicants and intended beneficiaries regarding the terms of insurance contracts will be honored even though painstaking study of the policy provisions would have negated those expectations.

At comment *f* to § 237[129] of Restatement (Second) of Contracts, ... we find the following analysis of the reasonable expectations doctrine:

> Although customers typically adhere to standardized agreements and are bound by them without even appearing to know the standard terms in detail, they are not bound to unknown terms which are beyond the range of reasonable expectation. A debtor who delivers a check to his creditor with the amount blank does not authorize the insertion of an infinite figure. Similarly, a party who adheres to the other party's standard terms does not assent to a term if the other party has reason to believe that the adhering party would not have accepted the agreement if he had known that the agreement contained the particular term. Such a belief or assumption may be shown by the prior negotiations or inferred from the circumstances. Reason to believe may be inferred from the fact that the term is bizarre or oppressive, from the fact that it eviscerates the non-standard terms explicitly agreed to, or from the fact that it eliminates the dominant purpose of the transaction. The inference is reinforced if the adhering party never had an opportunity to read the term, or if it is illegible or otherwise hidden from view. This rule is closely related to the policy against unconscionable terms and the rule of interpretation against the draftsman.

Nor can it be asserted the above doctrine does not apply here because plaintiff knew the policy contained the provision now complained of and cannot be heard to say it reasonably expected what it knew was not there. A search of the record discloses no such knowledge.

The evidence does show, as above noted, a "dicker" for burglary insurance coverage on chemicals and equipment. The negotiation was for what was actually expressed in the policies' "Insuring Agreements": the insurer's promise "To pay for loss by burglary or by robbery of a watchman, while the premises are not

---

[129][Eds. note: This citation is to the Tentative Draft of the Restatement (Second). Section 237 became § 211 in the final version, and this comment was re-written, though to the same effect.]

open for business, of merchandise, furniture, fixtures and equipment within the premises...."

In addition, the conversation included statements from which the plaintiff should have understood defendant's obligation to pay would not arise where the burglary was an "inside job." Thus the following exclusion should have been reasonably anticipated:

Exclusions

This policy does not apply: ... (b) to loss due to any fraudulent, dishonest or criminal act by any Insured, a partner therein, or an officer, employee, director, trustee or authorized representative thereof....

But there was nothing relating to the negotiations with defendant's agent which would have led plaintiff to reasonably anticipate defendant would bury within the definition of "burglary" another exclusion denying coverage when, no matter how extensive the proof of a third-party burglary, no marks were left on the exterior of the premises. This escape clause, here triggered by the burglar's talent (an investigating law officer, apparently acquainted with the current modus operandi, gained access to the steel building without leaving any marks by leaning on the overhead plexiglas door while simultaneously turning the locked handle), was never read to or by plaintiff's personnel, nor was the substance explained by defendant's agent.

Moreover, the burglary "definition" which crept into this policy comports neither with the concept a layman might have of that crime, nor with a legal interpretation. See *State v. Murray*, 222 Iowa 925, 931, 270 N.W. 355, 358 (1936) ("We have held that even though the door was partially open, by opening it farther, in order to enter the building, this is a sufficient breaking to comply with the demands of the statute"); *State v. Ferguson*, 149 Iowa 476, 478-479, 128 N.W. 840, 841-842 (1910) ("It need not appear that this office was an independent building, for it is well known that it is burglary for one to break and enter an inner door or window, although the culprit entered through an open outer door...."); see *State v. Hougland*, 197 N.W.2d 364, 365 (Iowa 1972).

The most plaintiff might have reasonably anticipated was a policy requirement of visual evidence (abundant here) indicating the burglary was an "outside" not an "inside" job. The exclusion in issue, masking as a definition, makes insurer's obligation to pay turn on the skill of the burglar, not on the event the parties bargained for: a bona-fide third party burglary resulting in loss of plaintiff's chemicals and equipment.

The "reasonable expectations" attention to the basic agreement, to the concept of substance over form, was appropriately applied by this court for the insurer's benefit in *Central Bearings Co. v. Wolverine Insurance Company*, 179 N.W.2d 443 (Iowa 1970), a case antedating *Rodman*. We there reversed a judgment for the insured which trial court apparently grounded on a claimed ambiguity in the policy. In denying coverage on what was essentially a products liability claim where the insured purchased only a "Premises-Operations" policy (without any misrepresentation, misunderstanding or overreaching) we said at page 449 of 179 N.W.2d:

> In summation we think the insured as a reasonable person would understand the policy coverage purchased meant the insured was not covered for loss if the 'accident' with concomitant damage to a victim occurred away from the premises and after the operation or sale was complete.

The same rationale of reasonable expectations should be applied when it would operate to the advantage of the insured. Appropriately applied to this case, the doctrine demands reversal and judgment for plaintiff.

[The court went on to consider, and apply, doctrines of implied warranty and unconscionability. Both of these doctrines will be discussed later in these materials. After you have read the materials on implied warranty and unconscionability you should return to this case and consider how you believe they might be applicable.]

We reverse and remand for judgment in conformance herewith....

LeGRAND, JUSTICE (dissenting). I dissent from the result reached by the majority because it ignores virtually every rule by which we have heretofore adjudicated such cases and affords plaintiff ex post facto insurance coverage which it not only did not buy but which it *knew* it did not buy....

While it may be very well to talk in grand terms about "mass advertising" by insurance companies and "incessant" assurances as to coverage which mislead the "unwary," particularly about "fine-print" provisions, such discussion should somehow be related to the case under review. Our primary duty, after all, is to resolve *this* dispute for *these* litigants under *this* record.

There is total silence in this case concerning any of the practices the majority finds offensive; nor is there any claim plaintiff was beguiled by such conduct into believing it had more protection than it actually did.

The record is even stronger against the majority's fine-print argument, the stereotype accusation which serves as a coup de grace in all insurance cases. Except for larger type on the face sheet and black (but not larger) print to designate divisions and sub-headings, the entire policies are of one size and style of print....

Nor can the doctrine of reasonable expectations be applied here. We adopted that rule in *Rodman v. State Farm Mutual Automobile Insurance Company,* 208 N.W.2d 903, 906, 907 (Iowa 1973). We refused, however to apply it in that case, where we said:

> The real question here is whether the principle of reasonable expectations should be extended to cases where an ordinary layman would not misunderstand his coverage from a reading of the policy and where there are no

circumstances attributable to the insurer which foster coverage expectations. Plaintiff does not contend he misunderstood the policy. He did not read it. He now asserts in retrospect that if he had read it he would not have understood it. He does not say he was misled by conduct or representations of the insurer. He simply asked trial court to rewrite the policy to cover his loss because if he had purchased his automobile insurance from another company the loss would have been covered, he did not know it was not covered, and if he had known it was not covered he would have purchased a different policy. Trial court declined to do so. We believe trial court correctly refused in these circumstances to extend the principle of reasonable expectations to impose liability.

Yet here the majority would extend the doctrine far beyond the point of refusal in *Rodman*. Here we have affirmative and unequivocal testimony from an officer and director of the plaintiff corporation that he knew the disputed provision was in the policies because "it was just like the insurance policy I have on my farm."

I cannot agree plaintiff may now assert it reasonably expected from these policies something it knew was not there....

[The dissent went on to reject the majority's application of both the implied warranty and unconscionability theories.]

NOTES AND QUESTIONS

1. *Applications to areas other than insurance*: Can we apply the approach of the *C & J Fertilizer* case to form contracts in areas other than insurance? In *Elliott Leases Cars, Inc.*,[130] the Supreme Court of Rhode Island extended it to a lease of an automobile. John Quigley, in his capacity as president of Rhode Island Buckle, Inc., leased an automobile from Elliott. The wife of an officer of the corporation drove the car with her husband's permission. She had an accident caused by her negligence. Elliott Leases Cars sued her for the total cost of repairing the car. She denied liability, asserting that the lease required Elliott to provide collision insurance for her benefit. The trial court, relying on an explicit provision in the contract, ruled there was no obligation to provide collision insurance for her benefit. Defendant was found liable. The Supreme Court of Rhode Island reversed. Two justices dissented.

Elliott Leases Cars used two forms for its leasing. One was an "Automobile Leasing Order." It was a single page summary of the transaction. It contained a list of 18 items which were followed by a check mark in one of two columns. The first was headed "HERE IS WHAT ELLIOTT PROVIDES," and the second, "HERE IS WHAT CUSTOMER PAYS FOR." Included in items to be paid for by Elliott was "ACCIDENT REPAIRS — 100/deduct — Due to

---

[130]373 A.2d 810 (Rhode Island 1977).

Collision (or Upset) per Accident." The second document was the formal lease. It consisted of 28 provisions in small print covering two full pages. Clause 2 required the lessee to pay for any loss or damage to the automobile caused by negligence.

The majority said that courts construe ambiguous or conflicting provisions against the author of those provisions. Its opinion said:

> [i]t is common knowledge, and so should have been known to plaintiff, that the detailed provisions of insurance contracts are seldom read by consumers. *C & J Fertilizer, Inc. v. Allied Mut. Ins. Co....* The plaintiff should have known that the leasing order, which was a simple, highly readable summary of the transaction, would be relied upon by its customers. The plaintiff could easily have avoided any ambiguity in the contract, and hence avoided creating a reasonable expectation of coverage, by noting the exclusion of negligence on the face of the leasing order.

The dissent argued that the rule of construction against the drafter was a rule of last resort. There was no reason to extend the rules governing insurance to routine form contracts in common everyday use. The opinion continued,

> ... the majority's expressed solicitude for consumers is irrelevant to the resolution of this case. In particular, their statement that "the detailed provisions of insurance contracts are seldom read by consumers" ... is strikingly inapposite to the present context. I repeat that this is not an insurance contract. It is a commercial automobile lease, signed by a businessman — who presumably had his eyes open when he signed it — in his capacity as a corporate president. I would hold him to his bargain....

There are many cases where a business person has failed to read a contract provision. Courts seldom are sympathetic. For example, the court in *Phillips Machinery Co. v. LeBlond, Inc.*,[131] commented "[w]hile it is true that the term was not 'conspicuous' or 'negotiated,' neither was it hidden in fine print, and the few pages involved could have been easily read by a man of Mr. Raskin's business experience."

In *Stanley A. Klopp, Inc. v. John Deere Co.*,[132] the plaintiff was a John Deere dealer from 1936 to 1978. The arrangement was renewed yearly. Language prohibiting the recovery of lost profits upon termination of the dealership was introduced in the contract in 1965. Plaintiff alleged that he had not read the contract because he had assumed that the agreements were similar in substance to the standard agreements long in use. The court said "[t]he general rule which

---

[131]494 F.Supp. 318, 324 (N.D. Okla. 1980)

[132]510 F.Supp. 807 (E.D.Pa. 1981).

imposes a duty to read, the clear language used in the clause, and the plaintiff's own neglect for thirteen years to inform itself lead me to conclude that as a matter of law the plaintiff's lack of knowledge cannot be said to be an unfair surprise worked by the defendant." Was the plaintiff's behavior unreasonable? Did the lawyers for John Deere have reason to think that many of their dealers would not read and understand changes in a lengthy franchise written in legal terms? Should this matter?

2. *Is regulation really necessary?* Schwartz and Wilde,[133] argue that regulation of standard form contracts is unnecessary if certain conditions prevail. A market of substantial size will contain a significant number of buyers who will read and understand the implications of the terms and conditions offered by the seller. If the market is sufficiently competitive, and if the sellers cannot customize their forms only for the sophisticated buyers, sellers will have to write their forms to benefit all buyers; if they do not, they will lose sales to those who read and understand. Thus, all buyers gain the terms that informed buyers want. This result is likely better than one produced by courts or other legal agencies.

Slawson,[134] responds:

> The firm of which I was a member when I was a practicing lawyer represented three corporate clients that used standard forms which, it happened, I drafted. One of the clients was a bank which used a wide variety of forms for different aspects of its business. To the best of my recollection, no one in any of the corporations or in the law firm ever suggested that the forms should be drafted other than as one-sidedly in the interests of the corporate client as possible. Nor did anyone ever report a customer or other business firm with which any of the corporations had dealt as objecting to anything in any of their forms or wanting to change them. In no case in which special arrangements were made with a very large buyer or borrower were the favorable terms extended to other dealings of the same kind. Moreover, I cannot even conceive of a situation in which it would have been profitable for the corporations we represented to make their forms more favorable to the interests of all customers merely because special arrangements occasionally had to be made for some.

Does Slawson convince you that Schwartz and Wilde are wrong by this argument? Whether or not you are willing to concede that this kind of market pressure produces the best results possible, would you accept that it could have some influence? Do you know of examples of competition on the terms of

---

[133]Intervening in Markets on the Basis of Imperfect Information: A Legal and Economic Analysis, 127 University of Pennsylvania Law Review 630 (1979).

[134]The New Meaning of Contract: The Transformation of Contracts Law by Standard Forms, 46 University of Pittsburgh Law Review 21, 44 (1984).

standard form contracts? Does Schwartz and Wilde's position seem more plausible to you than it does to Slawson?

3. *Reaching the desired result by construction of the meaning of contracts*: Even if we assume that particular provisions in a contract are valid, courts then must determine what those provisions mean. The proper interpretation frequently is not obvious. Where contract terms are deemed ambiguous, then there may be room for a court to favor the interpretation that produces what it sees as the fair result. Sometimes, when courts want to avoid a particular result, they strive mightily to find ambiguity where none would seem evident. Then they construe the "ambiguous" provision in the contract so as to avoid the result they wish to avoid.

The classic illustration of creative interpretation to avoid an undesired result is in Shakespeare's *Merchant of Venice*. We left the story hanging in Chapter Two of these materials. As you will recall, Shylock sued to enforce his bond. It called for Antonio to forfeit one pound of flesh upon non-payment of his debt. Shylock rejected the Court's plea to be merciful. Then Portia appeared on the scene, disguised as a doctor of laws. She was the newly won wife of Bassanio, Antonio's good friend. She was, however, so effectively disguised that nobody recognized her. The Court permitted her to conduct the proceedings, assuming her to be an expert in such matters.

> *Shylock.* My deeds upon my head! I crave the law.
> The penalty and forfeit of my bond.
> *Portia.* Is he not able to discharge the money?
> *Bassanio.* Yes, here I tender it for him in the court;
> ...
> Wrest once the law to your authority:
> To do a great right, do a little wrong,
> And curb this cruel devil of his will.
> *Portia.* It must not be. There is no power in Venice
> Can alter a decree established:
> 'Twill be recorded for a precedent,
> And many an error by the same example
> Will rush into the state. It cannot be.
> *Shylock.* A Daniel come to judgment! yea, a Daniel!
> O wise young judge, how I do honor thee!
> *Portia.* I pray you, let me look upon the bond.
> *Shylock.* Here 'tis, most reverend doctor; here it is.
> ...
> *Portia.* Why, this bond is forfeit;
> And lawfully by this the Jew may claim
> A pound of flesh, to be by him cut off
> Nearest the merchant's heart. Be merciful:
> Take thrice thy money; bid me tear the bond.

Shylock. When it is paid according to the tenour,
It doth appear that you are a worthy judge;
You know the law, your exposition
Hath been most sound: I charge you by the law,
Whereof you are a well-deserving pillar,
Proceed to judgment: by my soul I swear
There is no power in the tongue of man
To alter me. I stay here on my bond.

...

Portia. For, the intent and purpose of the law
Hath full relation to the penalty,
Which here appeareth due upon the bond.
Shylock. 'Tis very true! O wise and upright judge!
How much more elder art thou than thy looks!
Portia. Therefore lay bare your bosom.
Shylock. Ay, 'his breast:'
So says the bond: — doth it not, noble judge? —
'Nearest his heart: those are the very words.
Portia. It is so. Are there balance here to weigh
The flesh?
Portia. A pound of that same merchant's flesh is thine:
The court awards it, and the law doth give it.
Shylock. Most rightful judge!
Portia. And you must cut this flesh from off his breast:
The law allows it, and the court awards it.
Shylock. Most learned judge! A sentence! come, prepare!
Portia. Tarry a little: there is something else.
This bond doth give thee here no jot of blood;
The words expressly are 'a pound of flesh:'
Take then thy bond, take thou thy pound of flesh:
But in the cutting it, if thou dost shed
One drop of Christian blood, thy lands and goods
Are, by the laws of Venice, confiscate
Unto the state of Venice.
Gratiano. [a friend of Antonio] O upright judge!
Mark, Jew: O learned judge!
Shylock. Is that the law?
Portia. Thyself shalt see the act:
For, as thou urgest justice, be assur'd
Thou shalt have justice, more than thou desir'st.

[At this point Shylock abandoned his suit for enforcement of the bond, but the judicial proceeding transformed from a civil suit into a criminal prosecution of Shylock and led to his impoverishment and forced conversion. For these further developments of the story you will have to see or read the play. We confine ourselves here to the "contract" aspect of the proceeding.]

Portia purports to interpret the contract provision, and her reading of the bond is literal. However, if the purpose of contract interpretation is to discern the intention of the parties at the time the contract was made, she misinterpreted it. Bassanio beseeched Portia "To do a great right, do a little wrong." Portia responded: "It must not be." But did it be? Was the result consistent with the expectations of Antonio and Shylock when they arranged the loan? Would Shylock have given Antonio credit on the security of a pound of flesh without the right to draw blood? Did Antonio have any reason to think Shylock would?[135]

If Portia misinterpreted the contract, then courts have followed her example many times since. This is particularly true when the contract is a printed standard form and a court sees the parties as unequal in bargaining power. Professor Karl Llewellyn wrote vividly about such contract reading, grouping it with a number of other techniques for reaching the right result. He wrote that:

> First, since they [such techniques] all rest on the admission that the clauses in question are permissible in purpose and content, they invite the draftsman to recur to the attack. Give him time, and he will make the grade. Second, since they do not face the issue, they fail to accumulate either experience or authority in the needed direction: that of making out for any given type of transaction what the *minimum decencies* are which a court will insist upon as essential to an enforceable bargain of a given type, or as being inherent in a bargain of that type. Third, since they purport to construe, and do not really construe, nor are intended to ... they seriously embarrass later efforts ... to get at the true meaning of those wholly legitimate contracts and clauses which call for their meaning to be got at instead of avoided....
> ... [c]overt tools are never reliable tools.[136]

When Llewellyn drafted Article II of the Uniform Commercial Code, he sought to provide reliable tools to deal with problems such as those posed by standard form contracts. In the next sections we will have occasion to judge his skill as a tool maker.

---

[135]See von Jhering, The Struggle For Law 76-78, 86-88, 1-1ii (Lalor trans. 1915) ("[T]he Jew is cheated out of his legal right . . . True it is done in the interest of humanity, but does chicanery cease to be chicanery because it is practiced in the name of humanity?").

[136]Llewellyn, Book Review, 52 Harvard Law Review 700, 702-703 (1939).

2.   WARRANTY, DISCLAIMERS AND REMEDY LIMITATIONS: THE U.C.C. PATTERN

a. Warranties as a Tool to Guard Expectations

Courts regulate the quality of goods or services supplied by sellers through the legal device called warranty. Sometimes sellers make detailed promises about the quality of the goods they will deliver under a contract. For example, a seller may explicitly promise that a machine will produce a given number of units per hour or is free from defects in workmanship and materials. More often, however, contracts for the sale of goods have few, if any, express provisions about quality. Furthermore, they say nothing about the buyer's rights and the seller's duties if there are problems with the goods. What happens then? The law could say that it is up to the buyer to bargain for express guarantees. It could rule that in the absence of express provisions concerning quality, the buyer takes the product "as is" and "with all faults." However, whatever the virtues of this hard-line position, it would fly in the face of ways sellers promote their products. The seller works hard to create the buyer's expectation that seller produces high quality goods. Advertisements and sales persons' statements attempt to affect buyers' views of quality. Expectations arise, though they differ depending on the circumstances and are not the same with respect to new, as opposed to used, goods.

While we find warranties elsewhere, their usual territory is sales of goods. Courts have long held sellers of goods to some duty to provide products of at least minimal quality. Often judges talked of implied promises flowing from the buyer's reasonable expectations in a particular transaction. More skeptical writers argue that warranties are imposed promises, enforced for reasons of policy. Social control of contract is still the topic before us. Traditionally, courts did not hold sellers of real estate to warrant the quality of the buildings involved. As we've noted in the materials on misrepresentation, courts in some states at least hold commercial sellers of real estate to warrant a minimum quality. Judges may be imposing regulation on transactions between professionals and amateurs. Services contracts usually do not involve warranties as such. Nonetheless, courts often must interpret the obligations assumed when the parties dispute whether the one providing services has defectively performed. In this section, we will focus on warranties in sales of goods.

You can best understand what follows by trying to solve a problem. What do the materials in this section say about the solution of the *XYZ v. ABC* case? (This is a difficult problem. You should read U.C.C. §§ 2-312, 2-313, 2-314, 2-315, 2-316, 2-317, 2-714(2), and 2-719.)

ABC Manufacturing Company manufactures production machinery ordered by its customers. XYZ Widget Co., Inc. negotiated with ABC, seeking a contract to buy a production machine capable of converting "R" grade steel into widget frames. Representatives of the firms reached agreement. An ABC engineer wrote the order on a form document written by ABC's lawyers. On the form he described the machine sold as a "widget frame stamping machine capable of using "R" grade steel, produced according to the plans and specifications attached to this document." ABC's engineers prepared these plans and specifications for this contract after lengthy negotiations with XYZ's engineers. At the bottom of the form document, just above the line for XYZ's signature, the following printed language appeared: "ABC agrees to replace all defective parts for 30 days, without charge for parts or labor, which shall be the exclusive remedy if any part is defective. There are NO OTHER REPRESENTATIONS OR WARRANTIES, express or implied, accompanying this sale. This contract is the final and complete expression of the parties' agreement." Authorized representatives of both ABC and XYZ signed the form.

ABC manufactured the machine and delivered it to XYZ within the time specified in the contract. XYZ paid the full purchase price upon delivery. XYZ installed the machine properly and attempted to stamp widget frames using "R" grade steel. It soon discovered that the machine was not capable of stamping acceptable widget frames from "R" grade steel. XYZ cannot use a different grade of steel in its product. XYZ immediately notified ABC that the machine was defective, and it explained the problem in detail. XYZ asked ABC to honor its warranty. ABC sent a representative to XYZ's factory, and she inspected the machine. Based on her report, ABC refused to accept return of the machine or to repair it. ABC explained that it had built the machine according to plans and specifications (which nowhere contained a requirement that the machine be capable of using "R" grade steel), and there were no defective parts. Both parties now agree that a machine manufactured according to the plans and specifications attached to their contract cannot stamp acceptable widget frames from "R" grade steel.

XYZ sued ABC for the price of the machine. XYZ also claimed as damages its lost profits for the time it had taken a third company to manufacture a widget frame stamping machine that would meet its needs. How likely is it that XYZ will win the remedies it seeks? What will it argue? How will ABC defend?[137]

b. Warranties, Express and Implied

The Uniform Commercial Code attempts to balance the expectations of buyers with the freedom of sellers to limit the risks they assume in putting products on the market. Several sections deal with creating express and implied warranties.

---

[137]One of the authors of these materials sketched some notes on this problem. His answer ran seven single-spaced typed pages. Much is concealed in these three innocent paragraphs.

These focus on the buyer's expectations. Nonetheless, you may detect some social control of contract as well. Then the Code attempts to regulate how a seller can disclaim warranties or limit the remedies a buyer may have for any defect in the goods. Lawyers must work with many interrelated Code sections in order to make a technically adequate argument.

1. The buyer's expectations and fair dealing: creating warranties: Sellers may make express or implied warranties when they sell goods. First, § 2-313(1) says sellers create *express warranties* in a number of ways:

> (a) Any affirmation of fact or promise made by the seller to the buyer which relates to the goods and becomes part of the basis of the bargain creates an express warranty that the goods shall conform to the affirmation or promise.
> (b) Any description of the goods which is made part of the basis of the bargain creates an express warranty that the goods shall conform to the description.
> (c) Any sample or model which is made part of the basis of the bargain creates an express warranty that the whole of the goods shall conform to the sample or model.

On the other hand, subsection (2) says "an affirmation merely of the value of the goods or a statement purporting to be merely the seller's opinion or commendation of the goods does not create a warranty."

What does this mean? If seller states that the car gets better than 35 miles per gallon on the highway, it has breached a warranty if the car gets only 25 miles per gallon. If seller promises to deliver a 1978 Chevrolet Nova 4 door sedan, it cannot perform by delivering a 1975 Chevrolet station wagon. The Code makes it clear that this liability does not turn on the use of the word "warranty" or the intention of the seller to back its goods. However, statements such as "I could sell this car for more than I'm asking," "I think the car ought to get around 35 miles per gallon," or "this is a fine automobile" do not create express warranties. Absent effective disclaimers, sellers are bound by affirmations of fact, promises and descriptions of the goods. They are not bound by opinions and statements commending the goods.

The Code goes further and says sellers can make *implied warranties* too. Under § 2-314, *merchant* sellers impliedly warrant that goods are *merchantable*. The definition of merchantability has six factors. Perhaps the first is the most important. Merchantable goods are such as "pass without objection in the trade under the contract description."

The other important implied warranty is *fitness* for particular purpose. Section 2-315 tells us that sellers who know "any particular purpose for which the goods are required and that the buyer is relying on the seller's skill or judgment to select or furnish suitable goods" make such a warranty.

Again, all this seems designed to protect the likely expectations of a reasonable buyer. However, we might also justify imposing warranties to police the fairness of transactions. Courts may preserve the integrity of the market by allowing buyers to trust sellers rather than demanding to have everything spelled out in detail. For example, suppose a used car dealer contracts to sell a 1988 Chevrolet Nova sedan. The implied warranty of merchantability allows buyer to rely on getting whatever "passes without objection in the trade under that description." Suppose the Nova tendered lacked effective brakes. A court might hold that the Nova does not comply with the implied merchantability warranty because it believes it is undesireable for cars in unsafe condition to be sold without explicit warning to the buyer. A court might so hold even though a typical buyer might have no opinion about whether a used car with unsafe brakes "passes without objection in the trade." In other words, more may be happening than protecting the buyer's expectations.

2. *The seller's free contract and fair dealing — warranty disclaimers and remedy limitations*: So far, so good. Sellers must honor their buyers' reasonable expectations. But the Code's drafters also wanted to honor free contract. Sellers ought to be able to limit their obligations so they can control costs and Buyers should be able to accept risks in exchange for lower prices. And what of those sellers who create expectations that the goods were of high quality and then hide clauses in form contracts contradicting those understandings. Again, we face the problem of the conflict between the real deal and the paper deal. The drafters tried to balance the competing interests by saying that sellers could tailor their liability, but they had to do so "conspicuously," so buyers had to have a fighting chance to understand just what they were buying. Whether the drafters succeeded in the latter objective is the subject of debate. In addition, the drafters may have introduced some direct regulation, restricting some remedy limitations no matter how conspicuously disclosed by the seller.

How did the authors of the U.C.C. attempt to regulate limiting liability? First, they distinguished *disclaiming warranties* from granting warranties but *limiting remedies*. Many find this distinction confusing. But the difference is critical to understanding the Code's regulation of the risks of selling goods. Section 2-316 governs exclusion or modification of warranties. Section 2-719 deals with modification or limitation of remedies. *The tests differ*. As a result, a lawyer must first classify a contract clause as either a disclaimer or a remedy limitation to consider whether it is valid.

For example, suppose a farmer sells a 1938 Packard, which has been in the barn for years, to a buyer who restores old cars. The farmer has been to law school. He tells the buyer that the Packard is being sold "as is," and "with all flaws and faults." Furthermore, he makes clear that he does not know anything about its mechanical condition. In the Code's terms, the seller has *disclaimed all warranties*. He is refusing expressly to guarantee anything about the quality of the remains of the Packard. The farmer has disclaimed any warranties under U.C.C. § 2-316(3)(a).

Alternatively, suppose a buyer purchases a new Chevrolet from a dealer. General Motors makes a number of promises about the quality of the automobile.

These are warranties, and GM does not try to disclaim them. However, it provides in the contract that within 50,000 miles or 5 years it will replace or repair defective parts or workmanship on the drive train of the car. After the car has been driven for that distance or time, General Motor's obligations cease. The contract also provides that buyer may not recover consequential damages for loss of the use of the car. GM has made a warranty, but it has *limited the remedy* for its breach. Whether courts would enforce this limitation would turn on all three subsections of U.C.C. § 2-719.

Just to make things more confusing, lawyers often draft remedy limitations in the form of warranty disclaimers. For example, a fairly common clause provides "seller will replace or repair defective items for one year from the date of delivery. There are no other warranties, either express or implied." Technically the first clause says nothing about warranty.[138] Promising to replace and repair defective goods for a year is a statement about remedy. This language attempts to say that the buyer gets one remedy for a limited time *and no other*. Yet the seller called the clause a warranty and said there were no *other* ones. Could a court interpret such a clause as not disclaiming any warranties?

3. *The necessary steps*: We can summarize this discussion by stressing the logical structure of these provisions of the U.C.C. There are a series of steps and lawyers must take them *in order*. Sections or subsections of the Uniform Commercial Code do not exist in isolation. We repeat to emphasize the point — there are a series of steps and you must take them *in order*:

First, lawyers must decide whether, absent disclaimers, the seller gave any warranty. If there is a warranty, they must classify it. Is it an express or an implied warranty? If it is an implied warranty, is it one of merchantability or fitness for particular purpose? (Express and implied warranties also may overlap or conflict. We sort this out by applying § 2-317).

Second, they must consider whether the type of warranty given has been disclaimed successfully. We test disclaimers of express warranties against § 2-316(1). Sections 2-316(2) and (3) control disclaimers of implied warranties.

Finally, lawyers must ask whether a seller has effectively limited remedies for the breach of any warranties not successfully disclaimed, under § 2-719.

As you might expect after some experience with the Code, this outline of simple steps conceals many difficult issues. To resolve them, lawyers must refer to many other Code sections that we have not discussed here.[139] If matters were not difficult enough, warranties in *consumer transactions* add other layers of

---

[138] We could read the language as promising impliedly that the goods are not defective. If a court accepts this interpretation, there is an express warranty that the goods are not defective.

[139] One of the most important issues omitted in this discussion is the parole evidence rule, codified in § 2-202. This issue is covered extensively in chapter 7, *infra*. For an indication of the complexity and challenges, see Special Project, Article Two Warranties in Commercial Transactions: An Update, 72 Cornell Law Review 1159 (1987), a 167 page analysis of U.C.C. warranty problems.

complexity. There are federal and state statutes and regulations that add to and subtract from the U.C.C.'s approach.

You may find much of this discussion abstract and difficult to follow. It should make more sense after you consider some cases that present actual transactions and try your hand at the XYZ v. ABC problem.

c. Conspicuous Disclaimers and Conscionable Remedy Limitations

HUNT v. PERKINS MACHINERY CO., INC.

352 Mass. 535, 226 N.E.2d 228 (1967)

CUTTER, J. Hunt, an experienced commercial fisherman, got in touch with the defendant (Perkins), a distributor of Caterpillar Tractor Company's products. He was considering the purchase of a diesel engine for his fishing boat. In the fall of 1960, Perkins's sales manager, one Rideout, went to Hunt's house in Orleans to acquaint him with the various Caterpillar diesel engines available. At Rideout's suggestion, Hunt went to Maine to look at a boat equipped with such an engine. In January, 1961, Hunt signed a purchase order for one Caterpillar Model D330 engine with a 1.2 to 1 reduction gear (instead of one reduction gear ordinarily supplied by the manufacturer) and certain specified accessories. The written portion of the purchase order was prepared (except for the signatures) by Rideout. It was on a "pad of paper containing several copies separated by carbon paper."

Hunt did not read anything on the back of the order when he signed it. "The original and all ... copies of the ... [o]rder were taken by Rideout ... for signature by an official" of Perkins. Hunt received a fully executed copy of the order by mail a few days later.

The face of the purchase order contains a statement of the property sold, acknowledgment of a $500 deposit, a statement of the balance ($4,095) due, and certain miscellaneous information. In the center of the face of the order in bold face type capitals appears the statement **"BOTH THIS ORDER AND ITS ACCEPTANCE ARE SUBJECT TO 'TERMS AND CONDITIONS' STATED IN THIS ORDER."** On the reverse side of the order at the top in the same bold face type capitals appear the words **"TERMS AND CONDITIONS."** Underneath those words there are eleven numbered paragraphs. Included among the numbered paragraphs are those set out in the margin.[140]

---

[140]The relevant terms and conditions are the following: "1. *Acceptance.* This order is subject to acceptance by Seller only at Seller's place of business in Massachusetts and shall become a binding contract only when a copy has been accepted in writing and ... returned to Buyer. 2. *All Agreements.* This written order when accepted by Seller shall be the ... exclusive statement of all terms of the agreement between the parties other than such additional agreements as may be contained in any contracts, notes or other documents specified herein. No representations of any

After Hunt had received his executed copy of the order, he took his boat to Plymouth Marine Railway (Marine) to have it prepared for the new engine. Seven or eight days later Hunt by telephone learned from Rideout that there would be a delay in delivery. Rideout then told Hunt that he could tear up the contract and forget the engine if he wanted to do so. Hunt decided to go through with the purchase because his boat was already at Marine and the old engine had been removed.

The engine was delivered to Marine on March 6, 1961, and was thereafter installed in the boat by Marine. This installation work included everything that was necessary to connect the engine, with the exception of the initial starting. That was done by employees of Perkins. Marine was not connected with, nor acting for, Perkins at any time. Its work was not controlled by Perkins. It was engaged by and paid by Hunt.

After the engine was installed a series of mechanical problems arose, each of which was corrected by Perkins at no expense to Hunt other than the time involved while the repairs were being made. The engine, when running, gave off excessive quantities of heavy black smoke, which caused the boat to become dirty, inside and out, and rendered Hunt's work on the boat unpleasant. This condition persisted until the removal of the engine. At Hunt's request Perkins, on several occasions and by a variety of means, attempted without success to curtail the smoking.

About July 20, 1961, the engine was removed by Hunt and put on the dock at Marine's plant. Hunt called Perkins and reported that he had removed the engine and advised Perkins to get it. The engine is still on Marine's premises.

In July, 1961, Hunt purchased a new engine from another manufacturer. This new engine has performed satisfactorily.

Hunt's evidence of damages consisted of a showing of cash payments to Marine of $761.49 for installation work and testimony that he lost $250 each day when he was prevented from fishing as a result of Perkins' work on the boat. Perkins worked on the boat on about ten different occasions between the installation of the engine and June, 1961.

The trial judge denied motions for directed verdicts in this action in two courts, count 1 for breach of an implied warranty of merchantability and count 2 for breach of an implied warranty of fitness for a particular purpose. The jury returned verdicts for $5,357. Perkins brings before us exceptions to the denial

---

kind have been made except as set forth in this order or in the other documents specified herein. 3. WARRANTIES. SELLER MAKES NO WARRANTIES (INCLUDING ... ANY WARRANTIES AS TO MERCHANTABILITY OR FITNESS) EITHER EXPRESS OR IMPLIED WITH RESPECT TO THE PROPERTY UNLESS ENDORSED HEREON IN WRITING. BUYER SHALL BE LIMITED TO THE WARRANTIES OF THE RESPECTIVE MANUFACTURERS OF THE PRODUCTS SOLD.... 6. *Limitation of Liability*. Seller shall not be liable for any property damage or for any ... injuries ... suffered in connection with the operation or installation of the [p]roperty...."

of directed verdicts and to the judge's refusal to order verdicts entered for Perkins under leave reserved. There was evidence from which the facts stated above could have been found.

1. This case presents issues under the Uniform Commercial Code ... concerning excluding or modifying (a) the implied warranty of merchantability under ... § 2-314, and (b) the implied warranty under ... § 2-315, that goods shall be fit for a particular purpose. Section 2-316(2) reads, in part: "(2) ... [T]o exclude or modify the implied warranty of merchantability or any part of it the language must mention merchantability *and in case of a writing must be conspicuous*, and to exclude or modify any implied warranty of fitness the exclusion must be by a writing and *conspicuous*. Language to exclude all implied warranties of fitness is sufficient if it states, for example, that 'There are no warranties which extend beyond the description *on the face hereof* '" (emphasis supplied). Section 2-316(2) must be read with § 1-201(10) which provides, in part: " Conspicuous': A term ... is conspicuous when it is so written that a reasonable person against whom it is to operate *ought to have noticed it*. A printed heading in capitals (as: NON-NEGOTIABLE BILL OF LADING) is conspicuous. Language in the body of a form is 'conspicuous' if it is in larger or other contrasting type of color.... Whether a term or clause is 'conspicuous' ... is for decision by the court" (emphasis supplied). The first question for decision is whether the disclaimer of the warranties on the back of this purchase order was "conspicuous."

Some light is shed upon the meaning of "conspicuous" in § 1-201(10) by the official comment on the subsection, which says in part, "This is intended to indicate some of the methods of making a term attention-calling. But the test is whether attention can reasonably be expected to be called to it."

Under § 2-316(2) read with the last sentence of § 1-201(10), it is a question of law for the court whether a provision is conspicuous. We are in as good a position to decide that issue as the trial judge, for a photographic copy of both sides of the purchase order is before us. We decide the issue by applying the statutory test under § 1-201(10) of what is conspicuous, viz. whether "a reasonable person against whom ... [the disclaimer] is to operate ought to have noticed it."

In the language of the official comment the bold face printing on the front of the purchase order (although adequate in size and contrast with the rest of the printing on the form) was not in words sufficient to call attention to the language on the back of the form. That language would naturally be concealed because the forms were part of a pad of paper when Hunt signed the paper. There was no reference whatsoever on the front of the order to the "Terms and Conditions" as being on the back of the order, and the quoted words "Terms and Conditions" might have been thought to apply to other small type provisions on the front of the order unless Hunt had happened to turn over the form and look at the back of the order. His first reasonable opportunity to do this was when the executed form was returned to him.

In the opinion of a majority of the court, the provisions on the front of the purchase order did not make adequate reference to the provisions on the back of the order to draw attention to the latter. Hence the provisions on the back of the order cannot be said to be conspicuous although printed in an adequate size and style of type. The disclaimer was not effective.

2. Upon the evidence, the jury could reasonably conclude that the continued smoking of the engine was caused by a condition which constituted a breach both of the warranty of merchantability and of the warranty of fitness for a particular purpose. A smoking marine engine can hardly be regarded as of merchantable quality when sold by a distributor of such engines who is unable to cure the defect after persistent efforts. It could be found that Perkins, through Rideout, was fully aware of Hunt's requirements and his purpose in buying the engine and that Hunt relied on Perkins to guide him in its selection.... No evidence summarized in the bill of exceptions suggests that any injury to the engine may have been caused by Marine's work in installing it in Hunt's boat. Verdicts could not have been directed for Perkins.

Exceptions overruled.

NOTES AND QUESTIONS

1. *Conspicuousness*: Suppose a court in another state considered a case with facts similar to *Hunt v. Perkins Machinery Co., Inc.*. The lawyers for the seller argue that the Supreme Judicial Court of Massachusetts was wrong. They point out that the Massachusetts court recognized that the bold face printing on the front of the purchase order was "adequate in size and contrast with the rest of the printing on the form." Though the front of the form did not specifically direct attention to the back, it did mention "terms and conditions stated in this order." The disclaimer of a warranty of merchantability on the back is printed in bold face larger type. The text of § 1-201(10) says,"[l]anguage in the body of a form is 'conspicuous' if it is in larger or other contrasting type or color." This sentence is unambiguous. As a result, there is no reason to turn to the Official Comment to interpret it.

Furthermore, a literal reading of the text of § 1-201(10) serves familiar contract policies. In most cases the test is the qualitative "reasonable person ought to have noticed it" one. However, the parties will not have to debate this issue if material is printed in "larger or other contrasting type or color." The issue is not factual but normative. A *"reasonable* person *ought* to" notice "larger or other contrasting type or color." In most situations, it is not worth listening to people who claim they did not see "larger or other contrasting type or color." They are either irresponsible or telling lies.

The court in *Armco, Inc. v. New Horizon Development Co. of Va., Inc.*,[141] said "[b]ecause the excluding language in the contract is in larger type, we hold as a matter of law that it is conspicuous." Seller's lawyers urge the court to follow the Virginia approach and reject the Massachusetts decision. Does this argument undercut the authority of *Hunt v. Perkins Machinery Co., Inc.*?

Suppose a reasonable person ought to have noticed a disclaimer using the word "merchantability." Would most business people understand the meaning of that word? Would most consumers? Could a court, relying on the comment to § 1-210 emphasized in *Hunt*, hold that a disclaimer using the word "merchantability" was not conspicuous?

2. *"As is" disclaimers*: A seller can disclaim the implied warranty of merchantability or fitness for particular purpose without meeting all the tests of § 2-316(2). Under subsection (3)(a) a seller can exclude all implied warranties "by expressions like 'as is,' 'with all faults' or other language which in common understanding calls the buyer's attention to the exclusion of warranties and makes plain that there is no implied warranty." Notice, too, that subsection (3)(c) allows exclusion or modification of warranties by course of dealing (§ 1-205), course of performance (§ 2-208) or usage of trade (§ 1-205). That is, the risk could be placed on a buyer by the way the parties have dealt in the past, by the way they have performed the particular contract or by methods of dealing "having such regularity of observance" as to justify an expectation that it will be observed with respect to this transaction. Nonetheless, most sellers draft their implied warranty disclaimers to comply with § 2-316(2) rather than rely on § 2-316(3). Few sellers of new products want to offer them "as is." Many see their warranty as a selling tool.

3. *"As is" disclaimers and conspicuousness*: In *Gindy Mfg. Corp. v. Cardinale Trucking Corp.*,[142] seller's printed form contract used in a sale of goods contained an invalid disclaimer of implied warranties under § 2-316(2); the clause intended as a disclaimer did not mention merchantability and was not conspicuous. The issue considered by the court was whether 2-316*(3)* requires an "as is" disclaimer to be conspicuous. U.C.C. 2-316(3) does not expressly say so. The court said:

> It does not make sense to require conspicuous language when a warranty is disclaimed by use of the words "merchantability" or "fitness" and not when a term like "as is" is used to accomplish the same result.... Nor does it make sense to require conspicuous language to disclaim the implied warranties of merchantability and fitness and not impose a similar requirement to disclaim other implied warranties that arise by course of dealing or usage of trade. The expectations of the buyer need as much protection in one

---

[141]331 S.E.2d 426 (Va. 1985).
[142]11 N.J.Super. 383, 268 A.2d 345 (1970).

case as in another. My preference, therefore, is to find that there is a requirement of conspicuousness when terms like "as is" are used to exclude an implied warranty of merchantability or fitness. It seems reasonable to say that to avoid these implied warranties the requirements of subsection (2) must be met, except that expressions like "as is" will be given effect in addition to the expressions specified in subsection (2). This interpretation, nevertheless, would still leave intact the exclusion of implied warranties arising from a course of dealing or usage of trade by expressions like "as is," whether conspicuous or not....

4. *Limited remedies that fail of their essential purpose*: Sellers frequently warrant their goods but limit the remedy for any defects to replacement or repair at their option. If they take this step, almost certainly they will also provide that they are not liable for consequential damages. U.C.C. §§ 2-719(2) & (3) regulate these clauses.

Many of the first cases to interpret these provisions involved consumers who had purchased defective automobiles or other expensive goods. They took their vehicles to dealers for repair again and again. The dealers kept the vehicles for a long time and could not successfully repair them. For example, in *Murray v. Holiday Rambler, Inc.*,[143] plaintiffs purchased a 22-foot 1973 Avenger motorhome for $11,007.15. They took possession in January of 1974 and by July the vehicle had been returned to the dealer nine or ten times. In July, they took a trip to Colorado and experienced more difficulty, including a brake failure on a mountain road. When they returned home, they complained. Arrangements were made to take the vehicle to the factory in Indiana for repairs. The manufacturer, however, told the plaintiffs they would have to pick up the vehicle in Indiana themselves. Plaintiffs consulted a lawyer and brought a lawuit to recover the cost of the vehicle, and damages for loss of use.

The trial court found that when a buyer gives a seller reasonable opportunity to repair but the vehicle fails to operate as a new vehicle free of defects should, the limited remedy of replacement or repair fails of its essential purpose under § 2-719. This meant that the buyers could revoke their acceptance under § 2-608 and recover what they had paid. They also recovered $2,500 for loss of use of the vehicle.

The Supreme Court of Wisconsin found that the recovery for loss of use was an award of consequential damages. It then said "although an express warranty excludes consequential damages, when the exclusive contractual remedy fails, the buyer may recover consequential damages under § 402.715, Stats., as though the limitation had never existed."

---

[143] 83 Wis.2d 406, 265 N.W.2d 513 (1978).

Consumers seldom have significant consequential damages.[144] Business purchasers, however, often have claims for the profits they would have made had a machine not been defective. Sellers of commercial products usually disclaim liability for consequential damages. When courts encountered commercial cases where a seller could not repair defective goods within a reasonable time, many declined to follow the reasoning in cases such as *Holiday Rambler*. For example, in *Chatlos Systems, Inc. v. National Cash Register Corp.*,[145] NCR sold a computer system to a manufacturer. It was to be "up and running" by March of 1975. About a year and a half later, only one of the six promised functions had been implemented and there were difficulties even with it. Chatlos demanded that NCR remove the computer, and NCR refused. Chatlos sued, seeking lost profits as consequential damages. The trial court awarded this. The Court of Appeals reversed.

It agreed that the limited remedy had failed of its essential purpose. However, it said:

> The limited remedy of repair and a consequential damages exclusion are two discrete ways of attempting to limit recovery for breach of warranty.... The Code, moreover, tests each by a different standard. The former survives unless it fails of its essential purpose, while the latter is valid unless it is unconscionable. We therefore see no reason to hold, as a general proposition, that the failure of the limited remedy provided in the contract, without more, invalidates a wholly distinct term in the agreement excluding consequential damages.

The court then looked at the situation in the case. It stressed that this was a commercial case between substantial business concerns. There was no great disparity in the parties' bargaining power or sophistication. Chatlos engineers had some appreciation of the problems in installing a computer system. "Some disruption of normal business routines, expenditure of employee time, and impairment of efficiency cannot be considered highly unusual or unforeseeable in a faulty computer installation." There was no element of surprise since the contract expressed the limitation in a short and easily understood document. The seller did not act unreasonably or in bad faith. Thus, there was no reason not to enforce the parties' allocation of risk.[146]

Chatlos could recover a buyer's remedy under § 2-714(2). This remedy was not the subject of the disclaimer of consequential damages. The limited remedy of repair had failed of its essential purpose, making available to the plaintiff other

---

[144]An exception is when a consumer suffers personal injury as a result of a defect in, or the failure of, some potentially dangerous product.

[145]635 F.2d 1081 (3d Cir. 1980), cert. dismissed, 457 U.S. 1112 (1982).

[146]For a very similar approach, see Xerox Corp. v. Hawkes, 475 A.2d 7 (N.H. 1984).

remedies not separately disclaimed. Thus, Chatlos could recover the difference "between the value of the goods accepted and the value they would have had if they had been as warranted...." The court remanded the case for a finding on the difference in values.[147]

d. Regulating Warranties in Consumer Transactions

Many reformers and scholars think that the Uniform Commercial Code's provisions on warranties, disclaimers and remedy limitations are inadequate to protect consumers. The United States Congress has taken steps to further regulate some or all warranties in consumer transactions.

The Magnuson-Moss Act.

Under the Magnuson-Moss Act,[148] a "supplier" of a "consumer product" need not give any "written warranty."[149] However, if a business is a supplier offering a consumer product, and if it does offer a written warranty, then it must "clearly and conspicuously designate" that warranty as either a "full" or a "limited" one.[150] The drafters of the statute hoped to create simple terms that consumers would understand. If a supplier wanted to offer an attractive full warranty to gain market share, it would have to meet federal requirements.[151] For example, a supplier giving a full warranty must remedy any defect within a reasonable time without charge to the customer. If the supplier cannot do this after a reasonable number of attempts, then the customer can elect a refund of what she paid or a replacement of the product. Furthermore, if a supplier gives full warranties, it cannot disclaim implied warranties nor limit their duration unreasonably. Any exclusion of consequential damages must appear conspicuously on the face of the written full warranty.

---

[147]The trial court found that the system delivered was worth $6000, but if it had been as warranted, it would have been worth $207,826.50. Another appeal followed and in a second opinion (670 F2d 1304 (3rd Cir. 1982)) the court affirmed the trial court's verdict. The principle issue in the second appeal arose from the fact that the *price* for the system was less than $50,000. Apparently the NCR salesforce had been extravagant in representing its virtues!

Another commercial case raising a similar issue is Fiorito Bros. v. Fruehauf Corp., 747 F.2d 1309 ((th Cir.,1984). On the facts of that case the court found that the invalidation of alimited remedy provision under § 2-719(2) also invalidated the disclaimer of consequential damages. The court stressed, however, that this conclusion wasbased on the facts of the specific case and would not necessarily apply to all cases.

[148]15 U.S.C. Secs. 2301-12.

[149]The statute defines all of these terms. In addition, there are regulations which amplify and explain. For example, the content regulations with respect to the warranty apply only to consumer goods costing more than $10 (excluding tax).

[150]Section 2303.

[151]Section 2304 lists these requirements.

If a supplier is unwilling to grant all of these rights to consumers, it must call its warranty a "limited" one. Those who drafted the statute hoped that competition would push manufacturers to offer full warranties rather than those stigmatized as limited ones. Originally, the proposed statute required sellers to identify warranties less than full ones by words showing that they were second rate. However, the suppliers' lobbyists battled and changed the term to the neutral phrase "limited warranty."

Most suppliers have offered only limited warranties. Suppliers have wide freedom to write almost any kind of warranty they desire if they call it a limited warranty. However, a supplier of a consumer product cannot disclaim any implied warranty imposed by statutes such as the Uniform Commercial Code.[152] A supplier, however, may limit the duration of implied warranties to that "of a written warranty of reasonable duration, if such limitation is conscionable and is set forth in clear and unmistakable language and prominently displayed on the face of the warranty."[153]

The Magnuson-Moss Act says nothing about *limiting the remedies* offered for implied warranties.[154] On first impression, we might think that remedy limitations are still governed only by the Uniform Commercial Code. The Federal Trade Commission (which has rule-making powers) has indicated it interprets the Act to require exclusions or limitations of consequential damages to be conspicuous.

Thus, the Magnuson-Moss Act, and the FTC's administrative regulations, grant consumers a number of rights beyond those found in the Uniform Commercial Code.[155] But how are consumers to enforce them? The Magnuson-Moss Act creates a federal cause of action for "a consumer who is damaged by the failure of a supplier ... to comply with any obligation under this title, or under a written warranty, implied warranty, or service contract...." However, the statute grants the federal courts jurisdiction to hear claims under its provisions only if the amount in controversy is more than $50,000. Congress did not intend to burden the federal courts with claims based on defective automobiles, recreational vehicles, and appliances.

Most consumers must sue for breach of warranty in state courts.[156] In the state courts consumers will proceed under the Uniform Commercial Code's provisions

---

[152]See § 2308(a).

[153]Section 2308(b).

[154]Remember that manufacturers can offer attractive warranties but limit remedies to replacement or repair at their option.

[155]For example, Checker Taxi Co., Inc. v. Checker Motors Sales, Corp., 376 F.Supp. 997 (D.Mass. 1974), says that a remedy limitation need not be conspicuous under U.C.C. § 2-719(2). Remedy limitations must be conspicuous under the FTC Regulations.

[156]15 U.S.C. § 2310(d)(1) says that a consumer who is damaged by the failure of a supplier to honor any obligation under the statute, or under a written warranty, implied warranty, or service contract, may bring suit for damages and other legal and equitable relief in any court of competent jurisdiction in any state.

on warranties, disclaimers and remedy limitations, as well as the Magnuson-Moss Warranty Act. Lawyers for consumers will have to educate state trial judges in the requirements of the federal statute.

Furthermore, the Magnuson-Moss Act provides that a court may award attorney's fees to a consumer who prevails. Several courts have found that this part of the federal statute applies in an action brought in a state court where part of the case was based on the federal act.[157] Often these decisions involve a basic U.C.C. warranty, disclaimer and remedy limitation analysis with the Magnuson-Moss Act occupying only a minor role. Nonetheless, the federal statute serves as a springboard for attorneys fees.[158]

We can raise a number of questions about the coverage and impact of Magnuson-Moss Warranty Act. The statute applies only where a seller gives a "written warranty" covering a "consumer product." The definition of written warranty is not as broad as that of an express warranty under the Uniform Commercial Code.

The statute has had some impact. Though there are few reported cases of individuals having brought claims under the Act, there have been several class actions brought representing all the buyers of particular products. Litigation may be a poor measure of the success or failure of the statute. Almost all consumer products come with written warranties drafted by lawyers who have read the statute. Many, if not most, warranties are easier to read and understand today than before Congress passed the statute. Many firms have tried to communicate to consumers what is and is not covered by the warranty.

Nonetheless, the statute calls for disclosure regulation. Its underlying theory assumes the behavior of informed rational consumers in a competitive market. We suspect that not many consumers in fact consider details of warranty coverage in making purchasing decisions. Is it enough that manufacturers fear that a small group of consumers will read, understand, and refuse to buy if warranties are unsatisfactory? Perhaps in a mass market it will be difficult for manufacturers to make special deals for these few fully-informed rational consumers, and their diligence will prompt suppliers to offer better warranties to everyone.

In the view of many consumer advocates who struggled to regulate consumer product warranties, the Magnuson-Moss Act stands as a strong example of symbolic legislation. Congress wanted to cool out the consumer advocates pressing for action when consumer protection was a popular issue. At the same time, many Representatives and Senators did not want to offend big business. Congress solved its problem by passing a statute that required suppliers of

---

[157]See, *e.g.*, Volkswagen of America, Inc. v. Harrell, 431 So.2d 156 (Ala. 1983); Sherer v. DeSalvo, 634 S.W.2d 149 (Ark.App. 1982); Black v. Don Schmid Motor, Inc., 232 Kan. 458, 657 P.2d 517 (1983).

[158]Sherer v. DeSalvo, 634 S.W.2d 149 (Ark. App. 1982).

consumer products to redraft their warranties. This benefited corporate lawyers by making more work for them. Nonetheless, it offered most consumers little benefit. Suppliers advertise and market products proclaiming their virtues. They create expectations of quality. At the same time, they undercut these expectations by warranty disclaimers and remedy limitations. All the redrafting demanded by Magnuson-Moss will not offset the expectations created by advertising and marketing strategies.

Furthermore, while the statute seems to grant individuals private rights, few situations will involve enough money to make it worth trying to use the rights created by the statute. To what extent, if at all, is this argument unfair?

Lemon laws and automobile warranties.

Another example of an attempt to regulate warranties to benefit consumers are the "lemon laws" passed by many states. Typically, automobile manufacturers offer warranties of a specified duration but limit remedies to replacement or repair of defective parts. Representatives of the manufacturers talk of the interchangeability of parts and insist all cars can be repaired. Consumer advocates view this as a comforting fantasy. As of 1985, 37 states had passed lemon laws. Most of these laws provide the consumer with remedies, including the right to return the car, if the dealer's repeated efforts to solve recurring problems prove to be ineffective. Rights under "lemon laws" are in addition to rights granted under the U.C.C., or pursuant to the terms of the contract of sale. Vogel[159] surveyed their provisions and expressed doubt as to their value. A consumer must exhaust any remedies possible under a manufacturer's private consumer dispute mechanism. Private government often prevents litigation by providing meaningless steps for consumers. As a result, they are cooled out and lump it. She says "[i]n many respects, they [lemon laws] simply restate the present law. In other respects they are more restrictive than alternative legal remedies." She continues,

> If lawmakers wish to provide increased protection to purchasers of automobiles, there are certain modifications which would make the lemon laws more effective: (1) clear rules or standards; (2) presumptions which ease the burden of proof, (3) a minimum of technicalities; and (4) a choice between refund and other damages or a replacement vehicle. They could also publicize consumers' rights under the improved laws.

---

[159]Vogel, Squeezing Consumers: Lemon Laws, Consumer Warranties, and a Proposal for Reform, 1985 Arizona State Law Journal 589.

Braucher[160] criticizes consumer product warranty law based on a legal rights model. These disputes must be resolved informally and settled outside of court. Thus, the law should be framed to encourage and assist consumers bargaining in the shadow of the law. A statute should encourage complaining to the seller. It must make clear what the product should do for how long. Warranties should be required to contain instructions to consumers about how to complain, a description of what consumers can expect from the product, and clear and specific remedies for product quality defects. Doesn't any proposal for mediation and settlement rest on power created by the chance of costly litigation? Why should manufacturers mediate seriously when there is no real threat of sanctions for not settling a dispute? Could Professor Braucher answer this objection? How?

Have lemon laws had an impact? In January of 1993, Consumer Reports said: "Weak laws, including many that allow auto manufacturers to run the arbitration process; poor oversight by the states; and miles of red tape have stymied consumers at every turn."[161] Its study showed that consumers win much more often in states where there are government-run lemon law arbitration programs than in states where the auto makers run the arbitration programs. Nonetheless, those who run lemon law programs claim great benefits for consumers. For example, New York's Attorney General said that in 1992, 715 consumers won refunds, replacement vehicles and settlements worth $9.29 million. From 1989 to 1993, New Jersey consumers received almost $7.4 million in reimbursement and more than 400 replacement vehicles. From 1989 to 1992, Florida consumers recovered more than $37 milllion worth of lemon law relief. A Wisconsin appellate court upheld a judgment of $74,371 when Chrysler failed to replace a defective mini-van within 30 days after a consumer's demand. The van cost about $15,000 and the judgment included lawyer's fees and twice the consumer's pecuniary loss. See *Hughes v. Chrysler Motors Corp.*[162]

The Secretary of Consumer Affairs in Massachusetts suggested that the lemon laws were an important influence on how manufacturers treated customers. Only 46 consumers requested arbitration under the Massachusetts lemon law in 1993 as compared to about 800 in 1987. Several American automobile companies have worked hard to minimize lemon law claims. For example, the Wall Street Journal reported:

> [General Motors] is going nationwide with a program to satisfy disgruntled customers before they file complaints under state lemon laws. The move comes after a year-ong xperiment in Massachusetts during which the auto maker opted to settle most lemon-law claims, rather than fight them as in the

---

[160]Braucher, An Informal Resolution Model of Consumer Product Warranty Law, 1985 Wisconsin Law Review 1405.

[161]58 Consumer Reports, January, 1993, at 40.

[162]1994 Wisc. App. LEXIS 1202.

past. The results: Only one Chevrolet owner has been accepted for arbitration under the Massachusetts lemon law so far this year. That compares with 180 Chevy owners for all of 1988.[163]

Consumers who must go through a lemon law process are unlikely to buy another car from the manufacturer whose dealers could not repair their car. Moreover, in many states an agency publishes rankings on lemon law claims adjusted for the number of a particular make and model sold in the state. A Texas official commented: "It's quite possible one reason that manufacturers such as General Motors, Chrysler and Ford are settling a lot of cases is that they want to have a low lemon index. They have a tendency to be more proactive... Some of them [other manufacturers] are slower to catch on."[164] Lemon laws, of course, are not the only reason that manufacturers have worked harder in recent year than in the past to improve the service offered by their dealers. Repeated unsuccessful trips to a dealer's service department produce only unhappy buyers who are unlikely to buy the same brand of car again.

Regulation of warranties — costs and benefits: Are all these attempts to regulate warranties wise? Disclosure regulation rests on the idea that consumers will be able to make better choices. Undoubtedly, redrafting forms and making material available to consumers costs money. However, we can wonder whether the law forces manufacturers to waste most of this effort. How often which consumers read disclaimers and remedy limitations before making a purchase decision? Perhaps manufacturers are influenced by the chance that a few prospective purchasers might read the warranty coverage. Perhaps they fear that consumer activists might publicize what they viewed as substandard warranty coverage.

Substantive regulation of warranties raises a number of other issues. Many states have adopted lemon laws to regulate the performance of automobile warranties. The goal is to force dealers to repair automobiles successfully and promptly. Consumers may expect this, and manufacturers may be responsible for creating these expectations. Nonetheless, the obligation adds to the cost of distributing automobiles. Manufacturers face the threat of having to repair cars successfully and promptly or suffering penalties. As a result, they may invest in better quality control at their factories and better service management and technology. Manufacturers may keep stocks of parts available, and offer consulting services to dealers on difficult-to-solve repair problems. This may raise the price of automobiles for everyone. Those consumers willing to gamble

---

[163]Wall Street Journal, August 31, 1990, at B1, col. 2. See also Kahn, Ford Steers Clear of Arbitration: Washington Lemon Law Stats Show Trend to Earlier Solutions, Automotive News, April 29, 1991, at 30.

[164]The Houston Post, November 24, 1994, at A52.

that their car might nota lemon would no longer be able to choose lower prices for bigger risks.

Consumers face many bureaucratic or administrative problems in enforcing warranty rights. Manufacturers reward officials for keeping down warranty costs. It is difficult for the manufacturers to reward them for retaining consumer good will. Delays often result from difficulties in running a parts system. Manufacturers strive to reduce the costs of maintaining large inventories of parts that they may never sell. Shipping a small part of little value to a dealer may be very expensive, and manufacturers try to combine shipments of various orders to dealers to cut these costs. Some problems are extremely difficult to diagnose. For example, some malfunctions come and go. Unless the dealer can see the product while it is experiencing the problem, it is almost impossible to uncover the cause of these intermittent difficulties.

Finally, manufacturers seek to police the way dealers administer warranties. Dealers must fill out forms justifying certain repairs before the manufacturers will reimburse them. Dealers must obtain approval from a manufacturer's agent before they do certain costly warranty work. While these steps hold down costs, they do create incentives to deny warranty claims or to minimize efforts to solve consumers' problems.[165]

Any successful reform would have to deal with these bureaucratic incentives to minimize warranty expenses. However, if a reform did succeed, it might increase warranty expenses. Manufacturers would deal with these increased costs in some way. Suppose the public learned more about consumer complaints dealing with particular products and their defects. For example, statistics on problems with products could be gathered and published. Would this be a better way to deal with the problem compared to considering individual cases one by one?

3. UNCONSCIONABILITY AND THE LOW-INCOME CONSUMER: CAN WE REGULATE CONTRACTUAL TRANSACTIONS EFFECTIVELY AT ACCEPTABLE COST?

More people are comfortable with a liberal theory of free contract when the bargainers have some rough equality of bargaining power. Indeed, the theory works better if both have some measure of resources beyond those needed to purchase a minimum of food, clothing and shelter. Suppose seller and buyer are both wealthy people. Seller offers what she thinks is her rare violin to buyer. Buyer examines the violin carefully. Then buyer agrees to purchase it for about the current market value of a rare instrument. The violin is an old copy of a rare violin, worth much less. Courts could decide that both made mistakes and rescind

---

[165]See Whitford, Law and the Consumer Transaction: A Case Study of the Automobile Warranty, 1968 Wisconsin Law Review 1006.

the sale. They could, on the other hand, decide that buyer assumed the risk and hold him to the bargain. While the losing party will be unhappy, the court's decision is unlikely to change very much the way the parties live. The loser's material situation will be much the same as before.

Things are different when one of the parties is poor. Seller may be trying to convert her one asset into cash so she can command food and shelter. If the transaction is rescinded, she may face a desperate situation. Or a wealthy seller may offer a poor buyer food, shelter, clothing or some of the things that make life more enjoyable. Poor buyers may have few choices about who to buy from or sell to. They may lack skill and experience in appraising the quality and value of goods. Their continuing good will may be worth little, and so others can exploit them in a particular transaction without concern about future business.

The idea that bargains should be fair is not new. For example, Konig describes Essex County, Massachusetts between 1629 and 1692.[166] He tells us "[i]n a Puritan Community, charges of oppression or exceeding a just price were serious matters that could harm a merchant whether he was guilty or not. So fearful were Essex merchants of rumors about their integrity that they were quick to sue for defamation in order to vindicate their reputations to all who might think of dealing with them."

On the other hand, many also have defended charging "all the traffic will bear." Most of us know the lyrics of this song. Market forces deflect at least the worst instances of exploitation. Price control and regulation have high costs. Even if they were free, they seldom work well.

During the late 1950s and early 1960s, Americans discovered the poor. President Lyndon Johnson even waged a "war on poverty." By the 1980s, many Americans had found the poor boring or offensive. Some choose simply to ignore the poor, or segregate them so that they can be more effectively ignored. The privileged often justify their good fortune by accepting comforting fantasies. For example, candidates for office often charge that most of the poor are unworthy because they refuse to take the many available jobs and cheat the welfare system; self effort and sacrifice by the poor would end any problem.

Nonetheless, efforts to do something to aid those on the bottom of the income distribution are an important part of recent history and can teach us much about our society and its legal system. Again we note that the law of contract reflects social context. When Americans want to help the poor, contract is a tool, for better or worse, in that effort. When we need to rationalize denying that the poor have any claim to our sympathies, contract theory also comes to the rescue. And again we note that a contracts teacher cannot offer a course dealing with the reality of the subject without pushing you to consider your politics.

Public interest lawyers were some of the important warriors against poverty during the 1960s and 1970s. They used many bodies of law as tools to attack

---

[166]Konig, Law and Society in Puritan Massachusetts: Essex County, 1629-1692.

what they saw as wrong in American society. One important tool was the doctrine of unconscionability, found in § 2-302 of the Uniform Commercial Code. We will look at the cases and the reactions of scholars. We will ask what one can say for and against attacking important social problems by attacking particular contracts. We will contrast class actions and administrative action of various levels of government. Whatever our politics teaches us about ends, as lawyers we must be concerned with means as well. There are no cost-free magic solutions.

a. Retailing and the Poor

Federal Trade Commission Economic Report
on Installment Credit and Retail Sales Practices
in the District of Columbia (1968)
Summary and Conclusions

This report presents the results of a survey of installment credit and sales practices involving household furnishings and appliances in the District of Columbia. The purpose of the survey was to obtain a factual picture of the finance charges, prices, gross margins and profits, legal actions taken in collecting delinquent accounts, and the assignment relationships between retailers and finance companies. The survey covered those D.C. retailers of furniture and appliances having estimated sales of at least $100,000 for the year 1966. The 96 retailers providing data had combined sales of $226 million, which represented about 85 percent of the sales of furniture, appliance, and department store retailers in the District of Columbia.

USE OF INSTALLMENT CREDIT BY D.C. RETAILERS

Sixty-five retailers with combined sales of $151 million indicated regular use of consumer installment sales contracts. The remainder sold only for cash or on a regular or revolving charge account basis. This report focuses primarily on retailers using installment contracts. These retailers were classified into two groups: those appealing primarily to low-income customers and those appealing to a more general market.

D.C. stores varied widely in their use of installment credit. Some general market discount appliance stores made very few sales on credit. At the other extreme, a number of low-income market retailers sold entirely on installment credit.

Installment credit was used much more extensively by retailers selling to low-income consumers than by retailers selling to other consumers. Low-income market retailers used installment credit in 93 percent of their sales. The comparable figure for general market retailers was 27 percent.

CUSTOMER CHARACTERISTICS OF LOW-INCOME MARKET RETAILERS

A sample of installment sales contracts and credit applications was analyzed to identify the customer characteristics of low-income market retailers. The analysis revealed substantial differences between customers of the low-income market retailers and all residents of the District of Columbia. The average family size was larger — 4.3 persons compared to an average of 3.5 persons for the District of Columbia. Almost half of the families of customers in the sample had five or more members. The median family income during 1966 of the sample customers was $348 per month. This is very low considering the larger than average size of the families. The Bureau of Labor Statistics recently estimated that the maintenance of a moderate standard of living for four in Washington, D.C., requires a monthly income of $730.

Most customers were engaged in low-paying jobs. The largest proportion, 28 percent, were Service Workers, such as waitresses and janitors. Second in importance were Operatives (including such occupations as taxi drivers and laundry workers). Laborers and Domestic Workers also represented a significant share of the sample. Together, these 4 major occupational groups accounted for 75 percent of the customer sample. In comparison, only 36 percent of the general population in the District was classified in these low-paying occupational groups. There were 31 welfare recipients in the sample, accounting for 6 percent of all customers in the sample. There were also a number of customers in the sample dependent on social security, alimony, support payments, and income received from relatives.

A review of credit references noted in the 486 contracts subject to detailed analysis revealed that 70 percent indicated no credit references or references with low-income market retailers only. Only 30 percent of the customers of this retailer, therefore, had established credit with general market retailers.

GROSS MARGINS AND PRICES OF LOW-INCOME MARKET RETAILERS

The survey disclosed that without exception low-income market retailers had high average markups and prices. On the average, goods purchased for $100 at wholesale sold For $255 in the low-income market stores, compared with $159 in general market stores.

Contrasts between the markup policies of low-income and general market retailers are most apparent when specific products are compared. Retailers surveyed were asked to give the wholesale and retail prices for their two best-selling models in each product line. These price data are typical of the large volume of products sold by each class of retailer.

For every product specified, low-income market retailers had the highest average gross margins reported. When similar makes and models are compared, the differences are striking. For example, the wholesale cost of a portable TV set was about $100 to both a low-income market and a general market retailer. The general market retailer sold the set for $129.95, whereas the low-income market retailer charged $219.95 for the same set. Another example is a dryer, wholesaling at about $115, which was sold for $150 by a general market retailer and for $300 by a low-income market retailer.

OPERATING EXPENSES AND NET PROFITS OF RETAILERS SURVEYED

Despite their substantially higher prices, net profit on sales for low-income market retailers was only slightly higher and net profit return on net worth was considerably lower when compared to general market retailers. It appears that salaries and commissions, bad-debt losses, and other expenses are substantially higher for low-income market retailers. Profit and expense comparisons are, of course, affected by differences in type of operation and accounting procedures. However, a detailed analysis was made for retailers of comparable size and merchandise mix to minimize such differences.

Low-income market retailers reported the highest return after taxes on net sales, 4.7 percent. Among the general market retailers, department stores had the highest return on net sales, 4.6 percent. Furniture and home furnishings stores earned a net profit after taxes of 3.9 percent; and appliance, radio, and television retailers were the least profitable with a net profit of only 2.1 percent on sales.

Low-income market retailers reported an average rate of return on *net worth* after taxes of 10.1 percent. Rates of return on net worth varied considerably among various kinds of general market retailers. Appliance, radio, and television retailers reported the highest rate of return after taxes, 20.3 percent of net worth. Next in order were furniture and home furnishings retailers with 17.6 percent and department stores with 13 percent on net worth.

ASSIGNMENT OF INSTALLMENT CONTRACTS

Low-income market retailers typically held their installment contracts and did not assign them to finance companies or banks. Only one-fifth of the total contracts were assigned by low-income market retailers. Among general market retailers, appliance stores assigned almost all (98 percent) of their contracts to finance companies and banks. General market furniture stores assigned somewhat more than half their contracts (57 percent). Among the retailers surveyed, only the department store category involved no contract assignment.

FINANCE CHARGES ON INSTALLMENT CONTRACTS

There is considerable variation in the finance charges of D.C. retailers of furniture and appliances, particularly among the low-income market retailers. Most of the retailers surveyed determined finance charges in terms of an "add-on" rate based on the unpaid cash balance. When calculated on an effective annual rate basis, finance charges of general market retailers varied between 11 percent and 29 percent, averaging 21 percent when contracts were assigned and 19 percent when retailers financed their own contracts. Finance charges by low-income market retailers imposing such charges ranged between 11 and 33 percent per annum, averaging 25 percent on contracts assigned to finance companies and 23 percent on contracts the retailers held themselves.

One low-income market retailer made no separate charge for installment credit. All of his finance charges were, in effect, included in the purchase price. Other low-income market retailers kept finance charges below the actual cost of granting credit. This practice of absorbing credit costs can give the illusion of "easy" credit, but the customer may be paying a great deal for such installment credit in the form of much higher prices.

JUDGMENTS, GARNISHMENTS AND REPOSSESSIONS BY RETAILERS

One of the most notable facts uncovered by the study relates to the frequency with which a small group of retailers utilized the courts to enforce their claims with respect to installment contracts. Eleven of the 18 low-income market retailers reported 2690 judgments in 1966. Their legal actions resulted in 1,568 garnishments and 306 repossessions. For this group, one court judgment was obtained for every $2,200 of sales. In effect, low-income market retailers make extensive use of the courts in collecting debts. While general market retailers may take legal action as a last resort against delinquent customers, some low-income market retailers depend on legal actions as a normal order of business.

CONCLUSIONS

Installment credit is widely used in marketing appliances and home furnishings to low-income families. Often these families purchase durable goods, such as furniture, television sets, and phonographs, through the mechanism of "easy" credit. Low-income market retailers specialize in granting credit to consumers who do not seek or are unable to obtain credit from regular department, furniture, or appliance stores. As a group, low-income market retailers made about 93 percent of their sales through installment credit.

The real cost of this "easy" credit is very dear, however. Primarily it takes the form of higher product prices. Credit charges, when separately stated, are not notably higher than those imposed by general market retailers. Though some low-income market retailers imposed effective annual finance charges as high as 33 percent, others charged much less or nothing at all. Markups on comparable products, however, are often two or three times higher than those charged by general market retailers.

The findings of this study suggest that the marketing system for distribution of durable goods to low-income consumers is costly. Although their markups are very much higher than those of general market retailers, low-income market retailers do not make particularly high net profits. They have markedly higher costs, partly because of high bad-debt expenses, but to a greater extent because of higher salaries and commissions as a percent of sales. These expenses reflect in part greater use of door-to-door selling and expenses associated with the collection and processing of installment contracts.

The high prices charged by low-income market retailers suggest the absence of effective price competition. What competition there is among low-income market retailers apparently takes the form of easier credit availability, rather than of lower prices. Greater credit risks are taken to entice customers. Insofar as the problem for low-income consumers is availability of credit, merchants who sell to them focus on this element.

The success of retailers who price their merchandise on such a high markup in selling to low-income families leads inevitably to the conclusion that such families engage in little comparative shopping. It would appear that many low-income customers lack information or knowledge of their credit charges and credit source alternatives, or of the prices and quality of products available in general market retailing establishments. To the extent that door-to-door sales techniques are utilized, such families frequently make crucial purchases without leaving the home and without seeing the products they commit themselves to buy. The fact that low-income market retailers emphasize the use of door-to-door salesmen both reflects and encourages such behavior. The Commission is well aware that door-to-door selling, as well as home-demonstration selling, provides an opportunity for deceptive and high pressure sales techniques. Moreover, such selling methods are also very high-cost methods of distribution. It would appear, therefore, that the low-income consumers who can least afford mistakes in their buying decisions face two serious problems when they are confronted with a door-to-door or home-demonstration sales approach — (1) the high costs of this sales technique will ultimately be borne by the purchaser, and (2) the opportunity for high pressure or deceptive selling is great, thus discouraging comparative shopping and enhancing the probability that the consumer will agree to purchases he would otherwise not want.

While public policy can help solve the problems of low-income consumers, legislation alone may not be sufficient. Legislation aimed at disclosure and regulation of finance charges will help low-income as well as other consumers make more rational buying decisions. Intensified programs on both state and federal levels to eliminate all deceptions and frauds in the advertising and oral representations of the terms of sale and credit charges will also help to ensure that their money is spent advantageously. The poor, to a considerable extent, however, are not sophisticated shoppers. Many cannot afford the luxury of "shopping around" because their potential sources of credit are limited. Others, because of inadequate consumer education or lack of mobility, simply do not engage in comparison shopping.

Thus, in attempting to deal with the phenomenon of the poor paying more for consumer goods, every effort should be made to improve consumer counseling. Many customers continue to buy from low-income market retailers even though they have sufficient income to qualify for credit at stores selling for less. Greater community effort in consumer education is needed.

Beyond the matter of education is the question of credit availability. Many low-income families are quite capable of making regular payments. They should have the option of making payments on reasonably priced merchandise. Local community effort in the development of effective credit sources could contribute materially to freeing individuals from dependence on "easy" credit merchants.

Moreover, perhaps general market retailers can take steps to make it easier for low-income families to apply for and receive credit. Some retailers have already found that they can do so economically. Various community business organizations might consider ways of more actively encouraging low-income families to seek credit from retailers selling for less.

Increased competition for the patronage of low-income consumers would go a long way toward resolving many of the problems confronting them in the low-income market. Public policy should consider the various ways by which new entrants could be encouraged into these markets to increase the competitive viability of these markets.

While the availability of credit is perhaps the major reason why low-income families purchase from the low-income market retailers, it is only logical to conclude that the sales techniques of these retailers are also an important factor. Low-income market retailers have every incentive to continue these techniques since their risk of loss is substantially reduced by their virtually unopposed access to judgment and garnishment proceedings to enforce payment or secure repossession. The 2,690 actions taken by 11 low-income market retailers in 1966 suggest a marketing technique which includes actions against default as a normal matter of business rather than as a matter of last resort. At present, in the face of default, creditors can seek both repossession and payment of the deficiency, including various penalties. It may be appropriate to require creditors to choose one or the other of these legal remedies, and not to have the option of pursuing both courses simultaneously. Repossession would then fully discharge the merchant's claim. It is equally necessary to ensure that purchasers receive *actual* notice of any such proceedings and have legal counsel available to defend them in court. Perhaps, consideration should also be given to some form of negotiation before a court-appointed neighborhood referee as a compulsory prelude to a default judgment.

It is apparent that the solution to the problem of installment credit for the poor requires a variety of actions. A requirement that finance charges be clearly and conspicuously stated is a necessary but not a sufficient solution to the problem of installment credit for those consumers who are considered poor credit risks and are unsophisticated buyers. Among the complementary steps which might be considered are the following: (1) make reasonable credit more accessible; (2) provide counseling services which will encourage customers to practice comparison shopping; (3) equalize the legal rights of buyers and creditors in installment credit transactions; (4) encourage additional businesses to enter the low-income market; (5) intensify consumer protection activities on both federal and local levels to eliminate all fraud and deceptions in the advertising and offering of credit.

NOTES AND QUESTIONS

1. *Time for a new study?* The FTC Study you just read was published in 1968. Do you expect that another study, if conducted today, would discover significant changes? If you were a policy-maker, what do you do when faced with data which you believe may be dated, or the result of imperfect collection techniques? How often do you suppose trial and appellate judges face such problems? What should they do about it?

2. *The middle class goes shopping*: Ross and Littlefield[167] studied complaint handling at Western TV and Appliance Co., a major store in Denver. They found that perceived problems were relatively infrequent, but that high status people were more likely to report problems to the store. Those who perceived problems complained. The response to their complaint satisfied most. Most got repairs, but when they insisted on replacement of a nonfunctioning appliance, they got it. Finally, if a customer insisted, Western refunded his or her money for virtually any reason.

Ross and Littlefield point out that these middle class customers often received far more than their legal rights. Assertive customers exchanged appliances and got refunds although U.C.C. § 2-508 gives sellers the right to cure defects. The authors speculate that Sears' policy of customer satisfaction may create expectations that other stores must meet. In the appliance business, stores such as Western can push many of the costs of a very liberal complaint policy back on the manufacturers.[168] Customers are repeat players who buy many kinds of appliances. Their good will is very valuable, and the cost of handling complaints is very low if a store is willing to repair or replace appliances or give refunds without question. The authors note that the present system may supply the public with the highest quality appliances at the lowest costs. They point out, however, "the factors producing generous responses to their complaints may be absent for economically disadvantaged consumers and other special groups."

3. *Another country — the poor go shopping*: Greenberg studied Walker-Thomas Furniture Co.'s operations.[169] The store was located on 7th Street in the "easy credit" corridor of downtown Washington, D.C. It sold appliances and furniture, but its customers and operation differed greatly from the store in Denver studied by Ross and Littlefield.

---

[167]Ross and Littlefield, Complaint as a Problem-Solving Mechanism, 12 Law & Society Review 199 (1978).

[168]They caution "[i]f there is less consumer satisfaction with distributors of automobiles, this is more understandable when one compares the effect of replacing a washing machine on the finances of Sears Roebuck with that of replacing a Chevrolet on Jones Motors." *Id*. at 213.

[169]Greenberg, Easy Terms, Hard Times: Complaint Handling in the Ghetto, in Laura Nader (ed.) No Access to Law: Alternatives to the American Judicial System at 379 (N.Y.: Academic Press 1980).

Walker-Thomas marketed through about 30 door-to-door people who were both sales representatives and collection agents. They had from 15,000 to 20,000 working accounts. The store had an average yearly sales volume of $4 million. Its business derived almost completely from welfare, Social Security, and Supplemental Security Income recipients as well as segments of the working poor. Few of these people could obtain credit for major purchases in normal retail stores.

Walker-Thomas found it profitable to deal with its customers. It offered credit to them, and it had a means of collecting a high percentage of what was due. Since its customers' prime source of income was the monthly benefit check, its salespeople scheduled collection for days when checks were likely to arrive. These salespeople carried money, and cashed the check while deducting the required payment. This benefited the poor, who had difficulty cashing checks.

The salespersons provided intangible psychological rewards for customers by personalizing interaction. Low income customers may be misunderstood at retail stores because of language difficulties. Security guards watch them suspiciously. Clerks ignore them or indicate that they are worthless customers. The Walker-Thomas person who came to the apartment, however, was friendly, helpful and willing to simplify procedures. However, Greenberg argues that the salesperson controlled the interaction. The salesperson would not tell these customers the total price, emphasizing the amount of the monthly payment. The salesperson knew the income of the customer and saw the apartment. The salesperson could suggest that the customer needed a new television set or a new couch. Often the customer signed a contract and the salesperson selected the particular appliance or item of furniture for them.

When time for collection came, the salesperson could allow extra time when there was good reason for the delay. However, if Walker-Thomas thought a customer should pay, it was expert in many debt collection techniques. It used a series of letters with increasing threats. They telephoned debtors, calling very early in the morning or late in the evening. They called friends and relatives and asked why payments are not being made.

Walker-Thomas seldom gave warranty service on the goods. The salesperson would attempt to fix various items, adding the cost of repairs to the monthly payments where it would not be seen. Often the salesperson kept the payment booklet and revised it to add charges. Those who paid on time got things fixed as a reward. The salespersons blamed the customer; the children were rough on the item; the customer failed to operate the item properly. However, they told good customers that the salesperson could do a favor and get the item fixed.

If a customer complained to a legal services or social agency, Walker-Thomas responded using its power. It threatened to end the customer's access to credit. It threatened to be inflexible about prompt payments in the future. Walker-Thomas employed six people, called the pimps, to assemble information about customers who might present problems. For example, a customer complained to the Federal Trade Commission about Walker-Thomas practices. The management called the customer and threatened to tell her social worker that her husband was working on a construction site in Virginia. The customer's status could change from "husband's whereabouts unknown" to that of an ex-welfare recipient. While the husband was not contributing anything to her, she would have to establish this by going through procedures at the welfare office. Welfare kept down its case load by being arbitrary so those facing any new hearing ran the risk of a wrong decision. The customer withdrew the complaint.

Greenberg's conclusion warns about focusing on Walker-Thomas. It is worth remembering as we work though the following cases:

> Consider that labor and insurance costs, shoplifting, inability to secure lines of credit, and bad debts combine to push business out of the ghetto and make profit a virtually impossible goal except for ... [a] firm like Walker-Thomas.... The complaints of poor people ... represent a "trickle down" from the choices made by the politically and economically powerful. The complaints of the poor therefore derive from the same sources as their poverty. To castigate Walker-Thomas ... is ultimately to criticize the political and economic choices we make as a society.

b. Judicial Review of Retailing and the Poor

WILLIAMS v. WALKER-THOMAS FURNITURE CO.

350 F.2d 445 (D.C.Cir. 1965)

J. SKELLY WRIGHT, J. Appellee, Walker-Thomas Furniture Company, operates a retail furniture store in the District of Columbia. During the period from 1957 to 1962 each appellant in these cases purchased a number of household items from Walker-Thomas, for which payment was to be made in installments. The terms of each purchase were contained in a printed form contract which set forth the value of the purchased item and purported to lease the item to appellant for a stipulated monthly rent payment. The contract then provided, in substance, that title would remain in Walker-Thomas until the total of all the monthly payments made equaled the stated value of the item, at which time appellants could take title. In the event of a default in the payment of any monthly installment, Walker-Thomas could repossess the item.

The contract further provided that "the amount of each periodical installment payment to be made by [purchaser] to the Company under this present lease shall be inclusive of and not in addition to the amount of each installment payment to be made by [purchaser] under such prior leases, bills or accounts; *and all payments now and hereafter made by [purchaser] shall be credited pro rata on all outstanding leases, bills and accounts* due the Company by [purchaser] at the time each such payment is made." Emphasis added.) The effect of this rather obscure provision was to keep a balance due on every item purchased until the balance due on all items, whenever purchased, was liquidated. As a result, the debt incurred at the time of purchase of each item was secured by the right to repossess all the items previously purchased by the same purchaser, and each new item purchased automatically became subject to a security interest arising out of the previous dealings.

On May 12, 1962, appellant Thorne purchased an item described as a Daveno, three tables, and two lamps, having total stated value of $391.10. Shortly thereafter, he defaulted on his monthly payments and appellee sought to replevy all the items purchased since the first transaction in 1958. Similarly, on April 17, 1962, appellant Williams bought a stereo set of stated value of $514.95.[170] She too defaulted shortly thereafter, and appellee sought to replevy all the items purchased since December, 1957. The Court of General Sessions granted judgment for appellee. The District of Columbia Court of Appeals affirmed, and we granted appellants' motion for leave to appeal to this court.

Appellants' principal contention, rejected by both the trial and the appellate courts below, is that these contracts, or at least some of them, are unconscionable and, hence, not enforceable. In its opinion in *Williams v. Walker-Thomas Furniture Company*, 198 A.2d 914, 916 (1964), the District of Columbia Court of Appeals explained its rejection of this contention as follows:

> Appellant's second argument presents a more serious question. The record reveals that prior to the last purchase appellant had reduced the balance in her account to $164. The last purchase, a stereo set, raised the balance due to $678. Significantly, at the time of this and the preceding purchases, appellee was aware of appellant's financial position. The reverse side of the stereo contract listed the name of appellant's social worker and her $218 monthly stipend from the government. Nevertheless, with full knowledge that appellant had to feed, clothe and support both herself and seven children on this amount, appellee sold her a $514 stereo set.
>
> We cannot condemn too strongly appellee's conduct. It raises serious questions of sharp practice and irresponsible business dealings. A review of the legislation in the District of Columbia affecting retail sales and the pertinent decisions of the highest court in this jurisdiction disclose, however, no ground upon which this court can declare the contracts in question contrary to public policy. We note that were the Maryland Retail Installment Sales Act, Art. 83 §§ 128-153, or its equivalent, in force in the District of Columbia, we could grant appellant appropriate relief. We think Congress should consider corrective legislation to protect the public from such exploitive contracts as were utilized in the case at bar.

---

[170]At the time of this purchase her account showed a balance of $164 still owing from her prior purchases. The total of all the purchases made over the years in question came to $1,800. The total payments amounted to $1,400.

We do not agree that the court lacked the power to refuse enforcement to contracts found to be unconscionable. In other jurisdictions, it has been held as a matter of common law that unconscionable contracts are not enforceable. While no decision of this court so holding has been found, the notion that an unconscionable bargain should not be given full enforcement is by no means novel. In *Scott v. United States*, 79 U.S. (12 Wall.) 443, 445, 20 L.Ed. 438 (1870), the Supreme Court stated:

> ... If a contract be unreasonable and unconscionable, but not void for fraud, a court of law will give to the party who sues for its breach damages, not according to its letter, but only such as he is equitably entitled to....

Since we have never adopted or rejected such a rule, the question here presented is actually one of first impression.

Congress has recently enacted the Uniform Commercial Code, which specifically provides that the court may refuse to enforce a contract which it finds to be unconscionable at the time it was made. 28 D.C. Code § 2-302 (Supp. IV 1965). The enactment of this section, which occurred subsequent to the contracts here in suit, does not mean that the common law of the District of Columbia was otherwise at the time of enactment, nor does it preclude the court from adopting a similar rule in the exercise of its powers to develop the common law for the District of Columbia. In fact, in view of the absence of prior authority on the point, we consider the congressional adoption of § 2-302 persuasive authority for following the rationale of the cases from which the section is explicitly derived. Accordingly, we hold that where the element of unconscionability is present at the time a contract is made, the contract should not be enforced.

Unconscionability has generally been recognized to include an absence of meaningful choice on the part of one of the parties together with contract terms which are unreasonably favorable to the other party.[171] Whether a meaningful choice is present in a particular case can only be determined by consideration of all the circumstances surrounding the transaction. In many cases the meaningfulness of the choice is negated by a gross inequality of bargaining power.[172] The manner in which the contract was entered is also relevant to this consideration.

---

[171]See Henningsen v. Bloomfield Motors, Inc.; Campbell Soup Co. v. Wentz.

[172]See Henningsen v. Bloomfield Motors, Inc., 161 A.2d at 86, and authorities there cited. Inquiry into the relative bargaining power of the two parties is not an inquiry wholly divorced from the general question of unconscionability, since a one-sided bargain is itself evidence of the inequality of the bargaining parties. This fact was vaguely recognized in the common law doctrine of intrinsic fraud, that is, fraud which can be presumed from the grossly unfair nature of the terms of the contract. See the oft-quoted statement of Lord Hardwicke in Earl of Chesterfield v. Janssen, 28 Eng. Rep. 82, 100 (1751):

> [Fraud] may be apparent from the intrinsic nature and subject of the bargain itself; such as no mean in his senses and not under delusion would make....

Did each party to the contract, considering his obvious education or lack of it, have a reasonable opportunity to understand the terms of the contract, or were the important terms hidden in a maze of fine print and minimized by deceptive sales practices? Ordinarily, one who signs an agreement without full knowledge of its terms might be held to assume the risk that he has entered a one-sided bargain. But when a party of little bargaining power, and hence little real choice, signs a commercially unreasonable contract with little or no knowledge of its terms, it is hardly likely that his consent, or even an objective manifestation of his consent, was ever given to all the terms. In such a case the usual rule that the terms of the agreement are not to be questioned, should be abandoned and the court should consider whether the terms of the contract are so unfair that enforcement should be withheld.

In determining reasonableness or fairness, the primary concern must be with the terms of the contract considered in light of the circumstances existing when the contract was made. The test is not simple, nor can it be mechanically applied. The terms are to be considered "in the light of the general commercial background and the commercial needs of the particular trade or case." Corbin suggests the test as being whether the terms are "so extreme as to appear unconscionable according to the mores and business practices of the time and place." 1 Corbin, § 128 (1963). We think this formulation correctly states the test to be applied in those cases where no meaningful choice was exercised upon entering the contract.

Because the trial court and the appellate court did not feel that enforcement could be refused, no findings were made on the possible unconscionability of the contracts in these cases. Since the record is not sufficient for our deciding the issue as a matter of law, the cases must be remanded to the trial court for further proceedings.

So ordered.

DANAHER, CIRCUIT JUDGE (dissenting):

The District of Columbia Court of Appeals obviously was as unhappy about the situation here presented as any of us can possibly be. Its opinion in the *Williams* case, quoted in the majority text, concludes: "We think Congress should consider corrective legislation to protect the public from such exploitive contracts as were utilized in the case at bar."

My view is thus summed up by an able court which made no finding that there had actually been sharp practice. Rather the appellant seems to have known precisely where she stood.

There are many aspects of public policy here involved. What is a luxury to some may seem an outright necessity to others. Is public oversight to be required of the expenditures of relief funds? A washing machine, *e.g.*, in the hands of a relief client might become a fruitful source of income. Many relief clients may well need credit, and certain business establishments will take long chances on the sale of items, expecting their pricing policies will afford a degree of protection commensurate with the risk....

I mention such matters only to emphasize the desirability of a cautious approach to any such problem, particularly since the law for so long has allowed parties such great latitude in making their own contracts. I dare say there must annually be thousands upon thousands of installment credit transactions in this jurisdiction, and one can only speculate as to the effect the decision in these cases will have.

I join the District of Columbia Court of Appeals in its disposition of the issues.

NOTES AND QUESTIONS

1. *Walker-Thomas' goals in the law suit*: The writ of replevin issued in the *Williams* case sought to seize the following: 1 wallet, 2 pairs of draperies, 1 apron set, 1 pot holder set, 1 set of rugs, 1 pair of draperies, 1 2 x 6 folding bed, 1 chest, 1 9 x 12 linoleum rug, 2 pairs of curtains, 4 sheets, 1 WS20 portable fan, 2 pairs of curtains, 1 Royal portable typewriter, 2 gun and holster sets (presumably toys), 1 metal bed, 1 inner spring mattress, 4 chrome kitchen chairs, 1 bath mat set, shower curtains, 1 Speed Queen washing machine and 1 Admiral stereo.[173]

Many of these items seem to have little resale value. Why did Walker-Thomas structure its security provisions in the standard form contract so it maintained a security interest in them? Why was Walker-Thomas interested in repossessing such things as used shower curtains and children's toys?

2. *Cross collateral clauses*: The type of security arrangement used by Walker-Thomas and challenged in the *Williams* cases now is regulated by statute in many states. For example, the Arizona Retail Installment Sales Transactions Act (A.R.S. § 44-6002(6)) provides "goods purchased under the previous contract or contracts may be security for the goods purchased under the subsequent contract, but only until such time as the total of payments under the previous contract or contracts is fully paid."

3. *Conscionability and warranty disclaimer*: Is the doctrine of unconscionability available to check possible abuses of disclaimers of warranty? Before reading further, you might see if you can construct for yourself, out of the provisions of the U.C.C. and Comments, the arguments on both sides of this question.

Many argue that warranty disclaimers are *not* vulnerable to application of the unconscionability doctrine because 2-316(2) indicates what is necessary for a warranty disclaimer to be valid, and the requirement that it be "not unconscionable," which was inserted in 2-719(3) dealing with limitations on consequential

---

[173]See Dostert, Appellate Restatement of Unconscionability: Civil Legal Aid at Work, 54 A.B.A.J. 1183 (1968).

damages, is conspicuously absent. Some courts have accepted this view.[174] Other courts have rejected the same arguments, finding unconscionability to be a limitation on warranty disclaimers.[175] Even if the warranty disclaimer might survive the challenge of 2-302, plaintiffs might still prevail either on a theory of strict product liability (if the claim is for other than economic loss), or under the terms of consumer legislation, either state or federal.

JONES v. STAR CREDIT CORP.

59 Misc.2d 189, 298 N.Y.S.2d 264 (Special Term 1969)

WACHTLER, J. On August 31, 1965 the plaintiffs, who are welfare recipients, agreed to purchase a home freezer unit for $900 as the result of a visit from a salesman representing Your Shop At Home Service, Inc. With the addition of the time credit charges, credit life insurance, credit property insurance, and sales tax, the purchase price totalled $1,234.80. Thus far the plaintiffs have paid $619.88 toward their purchase. The defendant claims that with various added credit charges paid for an extension of time there is a balance of $819.81 still due from the plaintiffs. The uncontroverted proof at the trial established that the freezer unit, when purchased, had a maximum retail value of approximately $300. The question is whether this transaction and the resulting contract could be considered unconscionable within the meaning of § 2-302 of the Uniform Commercial Code
....

There was a time when the shield of "caveat emptor" would protect the most unscrupulous in the marketplace — a time when the law, in granting parties unbridled latitude to make their own contracts, allowed exploitive and callous practices which shocked the conscience of both legislative bodies and the courts.

The effort to eliminate these practices has continued to pose a difficult problem. On the one hand it is necessary to recognize the importance of preserving the integrity of agreements and the fundamental right of parties to deal, trade, bargain, and contract. On the other hand there is the concern for the uneducated and often illiterate individual who is the victim of gross inequality of bargaining power, usually the poorest members of the community.

Concern for the protection of these consumers against overreaching by the small but hardy breed of merchants who would prey on them is not novel. The dangers of inequality of bargaining power were vaguely recognized in the early English common law when Lord Hardwicke wrote of a fraud, which "may be apparent from the intrinsic nature and subject of the bargain itself; such as no man in his senses and not under delusion would make." The English authorities

---

[174]Avery v. Aladdin Prod. Div., 128 Ga. App. 266, 196 S.E.2d 357 (1973); Tacoma Boatbldg. Co. v. Delta Fishing Col, 28 U.C.C. Rep. 26 (U.S. Dist. Ct., W.D. Wash. 1980).

[175]A & M Produce Co. v. FMC Corp. 135 Cal. App.3d 473, 186 Cal. Rptr. 114 (4th App. Dist., 1982). See also Martin v. Joseph Harris Co., 767 F.2d 296 (6th Cir. 1985).

on this subject were discussed in Hume v. United States, 132 U.S. 406, 411, 10 S.Ct. 134, 136, 33 L.Ed. 393 (1889) where the United States Supreme Court characterized (p. 413, 10 S.Ct. p. 137) these as "cases in which one party took advantage of the other's ignorance of arithmetic to impose upon him, and the fraud was apparent from the face of the contracts."

The law is beginning to fight back against those who once took advantage of the poor and illiterate without risk of either exposure or interference. From the common law doctrine of intrinsic fraud we have, over the years, developed common and statutory law which tells not only the buyer but also the seller to beware. This body of laws recognizes the importance of a free enterprise system but at the same time will provide the legal armor to protect and safeguard the prospective victim from the harshness of an unconscionable contract.

Section 2-302 of the Uniform Commercial Code enacts the moral sense of the community into the law of commercial transactions. It authorizes the court to find, as a matter of law, that a contract or a clause of a contract was "unconscionable at the time it was made," and upon so finding the court may refuse to enforce the contract, excise the objectionable clause or limit the application of the clause to avoid an unconscionable result. "The principle," states the Official Comment to this section, "is one of the prevention of oppression and unfair surprise." It permits a court to accomplish directly what heretofore was often accomplished by construction of language, manipulations of fluid rules of contract law and determinations based upon a presumed public policy.

There is no reason to doubt, moreover, that this section is intended to encompass the price term of an agreement. In addition to the fact that it has already been so applied (State by *Lefkowitz v. ITM, Inc.*, 52 Misc.2d 39, 275 N.Y.S.2d 303; *Frostifresh Corp. v. Reynoso*, 52 Misc.2d 26, 274 N.Y.S.2d 757, revd. 54 Misc.2d 119, 281 N.Y.S.2d 964; *American Home Improvement, Inc. v. MacIver*, 105 N.H. 435, 201 A.2d 886, 14 A.L.R.3d 324), the statutory language itself makes it clear that not only a clause of the contract, but the contract in toto, may be found unconscionable as a matter of law. Indeed, no other provision of an agreement more intimately touches upon the question of unconscionability than does the term regarding price.

Fraud, in the instant case, is not present; nor is it necessary under the statute. The question which presents itself is whether or not, under the circumstances of this case, the sale of a freezer unit having a retail value of $300 for $900 ($1,439.69 including credit charges and $18 sales tax) is unconscionable as a matter of law. The court believes it is.

Concededly, deciding the issue is substantially easier than explaining it. No doubt, the mathematical disparity between $300, which presumably includes a reasonable profit margin, and $900, which is exorbitant on its face, carries the greatest weight. Credit charges alone exceed by more than $100 the retail value of the freezer. These alone, may be sufficient to sustain the decision. Yet, a caveat is warranted lest we reduce the import of § 2-302 solely to a mathematical ratio formula. It may, at times, be that; yet it may also be much more. The very limited financial resources of the purchaser, known to the sellers at the time of the sale, is entitled to weight in the balance. Indeed, the value disparity itself leads inevitably to the felt conclusion that knowing advantage was taken of the plaintiffs. In addition, the meaningfulness of choice essential to the making of a contract, can be negated by a gross inequality of bargaining power. (*Williams v. Walker-Thomas Furniture Co.*, 121 U.S.App.D.C. 315, 350 F.2d 445.)

There is no question about the necessity and even the desirability of installment sales and the extension of credit. Indeed, there are many, including welfare recipients, who would be deprived of even the most basic conveniences without the use of these devices. Similarly, the retail merchant selling on instalment or extending credit is expected to establish a pricing factor which will afford a degree of protection commensurate with the risk of selling to those who might be default prone. However, neither of these accepted premises can clothe the sale of this freezer with respectability.

Support for the court's conclusion will be found in a number of other cases already decided. In *American Home Improvement, Inc. v. MacIver, supra*, the Supreme Court of New Hampshire held that a contract to install windows, a door and paint, for the price of $2,568.60, of which $809.60 constituted interest and carrying charges and $800. was a salesman's commission was unconscionable as a matter of law. In State of *Lefkowitz v. ITM, Inc., supra*, a deceptive and fraudulent scheme was involved, but standing alone, the court held that the sale of a vacuum cleaner, among other things, costing the defendant $140 and sold by it for $749 cash or $920.52 on time purchase was unconscionable as a matter of law. Finally, in *Frostifresh Corp. v. Reynoso, supra*, the sale of a refrigerator costing the seller $348 for $900 plus credit charges of $245.88 was unconscionable as a matter of law....

Having already paid more than $600 toward the purchase of this $300 freezer unit, it is apparent that the defendant has already been amply compensated. In accordance with the statute, the application of the payment provision should be limited to amounts already paid by the plaintiffs and the contract be reformed and amended by changing the payments called for therein to equal the amount of payment actually so paid by the plaintiffs.

PATTERSON v. WALKER-THOMAS FURNITURE CO., INC.

277 A.2d 111 (D.C. Ct. App. 1971)

KELLY, J. According to an agreed statement of proceedings and evidence the appellant, Mrs. Bernice Patterson, bought merchandise from appellee in three separate transactions during 1968. In January she bought an 18-inch Emerson portable television, with stand, for $295.95, signing an installment contract which obligated her to pay appellee $20 a month on

account. In March she bought a five-piece dinette set for $119.95, increasing her monthly payments to $24. In July she purchased a set of wedding rings for $159.95 and the payments rose to $25 per month. The total price for all the goods, including sales tax, was $597.25. Mrs. Patterson defaulted in her payments after she had paid a total of $248.40 toward the agreed purchase price.

Appellant answered[176] Walker-Thomas' action to recover the unpaid balance on the contracts by claiming, in pertinent part, that she had paid an amount in excess of the fair value of the goods received and that the goods themselves were so grossly overpriced as to render the contract terms unconscionable and the contracts unenforceable under the Uniform Commercial Code as enacted in the District of Columbia.

Objections to interrogatories addressed to appellee in an effort to establish her defense that the goods were in fact grossly overpriced were sustained, the court ruling in part that the information sought was outside the scope of discovery "because the defense of unconscionability based on price is not recognized in this jurisdiction." It ruled further "that certain information sought was readily obtainable to defendant by resort to the contracts admittedly in her possession and that certain of the interrogatories amounted to 'harassment of the business community.'"

Appellant persisted in her efforts to present the defense of unconscionability by issuing a subpoena *duces tecum* for the production of appellee's records, and, alleging indigency, by moving for the appointment of a special master or expert witness to establish the value of the goods, the price Walker-Thomas paid for them, and their condition (whether new or secondhand) when she purchased them. The pretrial judge quashed the subpoena *duces tecum* on the ground that appellant was precluded from obtaining the same information by means of the subpoena that she had been denied through the use of interrogatories. The motion to appoint a special master or expert witness was also denied.

A trial judge subsequently held that the prior rulings of the motions judge and the pretrial judge established the law of the case. Inasmuch as appellant's then sole defense was that the goods were grossly overpriced and no proof on this issue was presented, the court entered judgment for appellee.[177] We affirm.

---

[176]Originally, appellant filed a pro se answer stating she was behind in her payments because of illness and that Walker-Thomas had refused to accept a partial payment on account. She was later allowed to file an amended answer.

[177]The agreed statement of proceedings and evidence says (R. 79, 80) that "[d]efendant [appellant], not present in Court, proferred [sic] testimony through counsel and over objection of plaintiff [appellee] that in January 1968 defendant had bad credit at Montgomery Ward, the store at which she previously made her household purchases; defendant did not have credit lines established at any other retail store; defendant met a salesman of Walker-Thomas who, understanding defendant's credit situation, encouraged her to go to plaintiff's store and represented to defendant that credit would be available to her at Walker-Thomas; and relying on this representation defendant went to plaintiff's store, was extended credit and executed the first of the series of three contracts upon which plaintiff sues." The proffered testimony, of course, is not

Suggested guidelines for deciding whether or not a contract is unconscionable appear in *Williams v. Walker-Thomas Furniture Co.,* 121 U.S.App.D.C. 315, 319-320, 350 F.2d 445, 449-450, 18 A.L.R.3d 1297, 1301-1303 (1965), as follows:

> Unconscionability has generally been recognized to include an absence of meaningful choice on the part of one of the parties together with contract terms which are unreasonably favorable to the other party. Whether a meaningful choice is present in a particular case can only be determined by consideration of all the circumstances surrounding the transaction. In many cases the meaningfulness of the choice is negated by a gross inequality of bargaining power....
>
> In determining reasonableness or fairness, the primary concern must be with the terms of the contract considered in light of the circumstances existing when the contract was made. The test is not simple, nor can it be mechanically applied. The terms are to be considered "in light of the general commercial background and the commercial needs of the particular trade or case." Corbin suggests the test as being whether the terms are "so extreme as to appear unconscionable according to the mores and business practices of the time and place." (Citation omitted.) We think this formulation correctly states the test to be applied in those cases where no meaningful choice was exercised upon entering the contract. (Footnotes omitted.)

Later, citing *Williams* in another context, this court said that "two elements are required to exist to prove unconscionability; i.e., 'an absence of meaningful choice on the part of one of the parties together with contract terms which are *unreasonably favorable to the other party.*'" *Diamond House Corp. v. Robinson,* D.C. App., 257 A.2d 492, 493 (1969). (Emphasis in original.)

On the basis of these authorities we conclude that in a proper case gross overpricing may be raised in defense as an element of unconscionability. Under the test outlined in *Williams* price is necessarily an element to be examined when determining whether a contract is reasonable. The Corbin test mentioned in the opinion specifically deals with the "terms" of the contract and certainly the price one pays for an item is one of the more important terms of any contract. We emphasize, however, that price as an unreasonable contract term is only one of the elements which underpin proof of unconscionability. Specifically, therefore, in the instant case the reasonableness of the contracts is not to be gauged by an examination of the price stipulation alone or any other terms of the contract

---

evidence in this case. An offer of proof is made when testimony to be given by a witness in court is, upon objection, excluded by the court. It is not made through counsel when the witness is not present to testify.

without parallel consideration being given to whether or not appellant exercised a meaningful choice in entering into the contracts.

We conclude also that because excessive price-value may comprise one element of unconscionability, discovery techniques may be employed to garner information relevant to that issue for purposes of defense. By statute, upon a claim of unconscionability, the court determines as a matter of law whether a contract or any clause thereof is unconscionable *only* after the parties have been given a reasonable opportunity to present evidence as to its commercial setting, purpose and effect. Certainly, therefore, interrogatories may be used to develop evidence of the commercial setting, purpose and effect of a contract at the time it was made in order to assure an effective presentation of the defense at an evidentiary hearing.

In our judgment, however, appellant here was not erroneously precluded from developing evidence through the use of interrogatories by the ruling of the trial court. Having said that under proper circumstances excessive price may be a component of the defense of unconscionability and that discovery techniques may be used to develop that defense, we are nevertheless of the opinion that a sufficient factual predicate for the defense must be alleged before wholesale discovery is allowed. An unsupported conclusory allegation in the answer that a contract is unenforceable as unconscionable is not enough. Sufficient facts surrounding the "commercial setting, purpose and effect" of a contract at the time it was made should be alleged so that the court may form a judgment as to the existence of a valid claim of unconscionability and the extent to which discovery of evidence to support that claim should be allowed.

Admittedly, appellant neither alleged nor attempted to prove the existence of any fraud, duress or coercion when she entered into the instant contracts. Her verified complaint alleges only that the goods she purchased and still retains were grossly overpriced and that she has already paid appellee a sum in excess of their fair value. These are conclusions without factual support. It cannot be said that the goods were grossly overpriced merely from an examination of the prices which appear on the face of the contracts. No other terms of the contract is alleged to be unconscionable, nor is an absence of meaningful choice claimed.[178] We hold that the two elements of which unconscionability is comprised; namely, an absence of meaningful choice and contract terms unreasonably favorable to the other party, must be particularized in some detail before a merchant is required to divulge his pricing policies through interrogatories or through the production of records in court.[179] An answer, such as the one here, asserting the affirmative

---

[178]The proffered testimony at trial is the first mention of any purported facts surrounding these transactions.

[179]The same reasoning applies to a request for appointment of a master or expert witness.

defense of unconscionability only on the basis of a stated conclusion that the price is excessive is insufficient.

Accordingly, the judgment of the trial court is affirmed.

NOTES AND QUESTIONS

1. *Excessive-price unconscionability*: Cases involving allegations that excessive prices in a consumer contracts are unconscionable under U.C.C. § 2-302 appear much less often today in appellate reports. What might explain this? It may be important that many of these problems now fall under various state deceptive trade practices or consumer protection statutes, and hence get resolved on bases other than unconscionability. There are also fewer public interest lawyers representing poor consumers today than there were in the 1960s and early 1970s. Furthermore, when price unconscionability cases do arise, courts often uphold the contract. See *Remco Enterprises v. Houston,* 9 Kan. App. 2d 296, 677 P.2d 567 (1984) (upholding a 108% markup of a television set as non unconscionable). Perhaps consumers or their lawyers realize that the prevailing public sentiments about what ought to happen in price unconscionability cases are different today than they were in the 1960's and hence they are less likely to pursue price unconscionability litigation.

2. *The relevance of a party's financial position*: In the previous cases the plaintiffs all had limited income. Should prosperous consumers also be able to invalidate their consumer contracts on the grounds of unconscionability? Suppose, for example, that Article 2 applied to the fact situation in *Vokes v. Arthur Murray*. Should Ms. Vokes be able to assert successfully that her contracts were invalid as unconscionable? In what ways can Ms. Vokes claim that she had an absence of meaningful choice?

In *Gladden v. Cadillac Motor Car Div., General Motors Corp.*,[180] the plaintiff had purchased a new Cadillac. She claimed that a one car accident that had "totalled" the car resulted from a blowout on a defective tire. A separate tire warranty that came with the car disclaimed all consequential damages resulting from tire defects. The court found this disclaimer unconcionable in the circumstances of that case, but held open the possibility that with better drafting and more forthright disclosure the seller could validly disclaim consequential damages.

---

[180]83 N.J. 320, 416 A.2d 394 (1980). Study of this case is an excellent way to review all the Code's provisions pertaining to warranties and unconscionability.

c. Remedies for Victims of Unconscionable Contracts

FROSTIFRESH CORP. v. REYNOSO

52 Misc.2d 26, 274 N.Y.S.2d 757 (D.Ct., Nassau Co. 1966)

Action by seller to recover from buyer amount allegedly due under a contract for a refrigerator-freezer, together with attorney's fees and a late charge. The District Court, Second District, Francis J. Donovan, J., held that installment contract entirely in English, executed by Spanish speaking buyers, wherein a cash sales price was set forth at $900, and a credit charge of $245.88 was added thereto, making a total of $1,145.88 to be paid for the appliance which seller admitted cost it $348, was "too hard a bargain," and under the circumstances, court would not permit enforcement of the contract as written, and seller would be limited to recovery of its cost without allowance for commissions, legal fees, service charges or other matters of overhead.

Judgment for plaintiff in accordance with opinion.

DONOVAN, J. Plaintiff brings this action for $1364.10, alleging that the latter amount is owed by the defendants to the plaintiff on account of the purchase of a combination-refrigerator-freezer for which they agreed to pay the sum of $1145.88. The balance of the amount consists of a claim for attorney fees in the amount of $227.35 and a late charge of $22.87. The only payment made on account of the original indebtedness is the sum of $32.00.

The contract for the refrigerator-freezer was negotiated orally in Spanish between the defendants and a Spanish speaking salesman representing the plaintiff. In that conversation the defendant husband told the salesman that he had but one week left on his job and he could not afford to buy the appliance. The salesman distracted and deluded the defendants by advising them that the appliance would cost them nothing because they would be paid bonuses or commissions of $25.00 each on the numerous sales that would be made to their neighbors and friends. Thereafter there was submitted to and signed by the defendants a retail installment contract entirely in English. The retail contract was neither translated nor explained to the defendants. In that contract there was a cash sales price set forth of $900.00. To this was added a credit charge of $245.88, making a total of $1145.88 to be paid for the appliance.

The plaintiff admitted that cost to the plaintiff corporation for the appliance was $348.00.

No defense of fraud was set forth in the pleadings and accordingly such defense is not available.

However, in the course of the trial, it did appear to the court that the contract might be unconscionable. The court therefore continued the trial at an adjourned date to afford a reasonable opportunity to the parties to present evidence as to the commercial setting, purpose and effect of the contract.

The court finds that the sale of the appliance at the price and terms indicated in this contract is shocking to the conscience. The service charge, which almost equals the price of the appliance is in and of itself indicative of the oppression which was practiced on these defendants. Defendants were handicapped by a lack of knowledge, both as to the commercial situation and the nature and terms of the contract which was submitted in a language foreign to them.

The question presented in this case is simply this: Does the court have the power under § 2-302 of the Uniform Commercial Code to refuse to enforce the price and credit provisions of the contract in order to prevent an unconscionable result....

In the instant case the court finds that ... it was "too hard a bargain" and the conscience of the court will not permit the enforcement of the contract as written. Therefore the plaintiff will not be permitted to recover on the basis of the price set forth in the retail installment contract, namely $900.00 plus $245.85 as a service charge.

However, since the defendants have not returned the refrigerator-freezer, they will be required to reimburse the plaintiff for the cost to the plaintiff, namely $348.00. No allowance is made on account of any commissions the plaintiff may have paid to salesmen or for legal fees, service charges or any other matters of overhead.

Accordingly the plaintiff may have judgment against both defendants in the amount of $348.00 with interest, less the $32.00 paid on account, leaving a net balance of $316.00 with interest from December 26, 1964.

FROSTIFRESH CORP. v. REYNOSO

54 Misc. 2d 119, 281 N.Y.S.2d 964 (S. Ct., App. Term 1967)

PER CURIAM. Judgment unanimously reversed, without costs, and a new trial ordered limited to an assessment of plaintiff's damages and entry of judgment thereon.

While the evidence clearly warrants a finding that the contract was unconscionable (Uniform Commercial Code, § 2-302), we are of the opinion that plaintiff should recover its net cost for the refrigerator-freezer, plus a reasonable profit, in addition to trucking and service charges necessarily incurred and reasonable finance charges.

PEARSON v. NATIONAL BUDGETING SYSTEMS, INC.

31 App. Div. 2d 792, 297 N.Y.S.2d 59 (S. Ct. App. Div. 1969)

PER CURIAM. Order entered on September 15, 1968 denying motion for a protective order unanimously reversed, on the law and the facts, without costs or disbursements, the motion granted and the notice is vacated.

The plaintiffs seek to recover punitive damages from defendant asserting a complaint based on Uniform Commercial Code § 2-302 in that plaintiffs were induced to buy a refrigerator freezer at an "unconscionable" price within the meaning of the said statute. The defendant, a finance company, purchased the said installment sales contract from the seller.

Section 2-302 ... does not provide any damages to a party who enters into an unconscionable contract. This section gives the court the power to refuse to enforce ... an unconscionable contract or ... clause....

The documents called for under the notice of inspection are neither material nor necessary to plaintiffs' cause of action and their production would be an undue harassment of defendant.

Under the circumstances, it was an improvident exercise of discretion not to grant the motion.

DEVLIN v. KEARNY MESA AMC/JEEP/RENAULT, INC.

155 Cal.App.3d 381, 202 Cal.Rptr. 204 (4th Dist. 1984)

WIENER, J. Defendant Kearny Mesa AMC/ Jeep/Renault, Inc. (Kearny Mesa) appeals a second time from the judgment in favor of plaintiffs Frank L. and Helen B. Devlin (Devlins).

 ... [What follows is the court's summary of the facts, which we have moved to the beginning of our edited version of the opinion. The action in this case alleged fraud, and not a violation of U.C.C. 2-302.] In October 1980 the Devlins visited Kearny Mesa to look at new cars. They wanted merely to look, not to buy. At that time, Mr. Devlin was 84 years old and only 5 years retired from his job as a cement finisher. He was in poor health and unable to drive, having just undergone a cataract operation. Mrs. Devlin was 66 years old. She could drive but was suffering from cancer and had recently had a kidney removed.

A Kearny Mesa salesman showed the Devlins a used 1980 AMC Spirit. Lee Johnson, Kearny Mesa's sales manager, told them the vehicle had never been owned and was used only as a demonstrator for the dealership. Johnson stated and the odometer showed the vehicle had been driven only 8,462 miles. After indicating an interest in buying the car, the Devlins were taken to a small room to negotiate terms. On occasion as many as five salesmen were in the room with them. The Devlins finally signed a purchase agreement.

Several weeks later Mr. Devlin found a Department of Motor Vehicles (DMV) form in the glove compartment of the Spirit which showed the vehicle had been driven 20,689 miles. He also discovered from the DMV the vehicle had been previously owned and then repossessed by Kearny Mesa. After driving the car about 5,500 miles it needed substantial repairs consistent with actual mileage in excess of 20,000 miles.

[The court noted that] ... The pressures applied and the misrepresentations made to defraud this elderly couple were unconscionable. As expressed by the lower court, the case represented "a glaring example of what consumer fraud cases are all about." Protection of unwary consumers from being duped by unscrupulous sellers is an exigency of the utmost priority in contemporary society....

The Punitive Damages Are Not Excessive as a Matter of Law

Punitive damages are not a new phenomenon. They have been part of our common law tradition for more than two centuries.... Allowed in almost every state in certain cases, they have been part of our Civil Code since 1872. Civil Code § 3294 allows plaintiffs to recover punitive damages in cases of "oppression, fraud, or malice." The legislative purpose is primarily to punish wrongdoers and deter the commission of wrongful acts. (*Neal v. Farmers Ins. Exchange, supra,* 21 Cal.3d at p. 928, fn. 13, 148 Cal.Rptr. 389, 582 P.2d 980.) Civil Code § 3294 expresses these twin goals.

Whether punitive damages should be awarded and the amount of such an award are issues for the jury and for the trial court on a new trial motion. All presumptions favor the correctness of the verdict and judgment.... While the trial court's determination is not binding upon a reviewing court, it must be accorded great weight.... An award of punitive damages will be reversed as excessive "only when the entire record viewed most favorably to the judgment indicates the award was rendered as the result of passion and prejudice. [Citation.]" (*Walker v. Signal Companies, Inc.* (1978) 84 Cal.App.3d 982, 997, 149 Cal.Rptr. 119; ...

The process through which a factfinder finds punitive damages is somewhat contradictory. On the one hand, the court or jury must be sufficiently disturbed to conclude the defendant must be punished. On the other hand, although outraged, the factfinder cannot be vindictive. The channeling of just the correct quantum of bile to reach the correct level of punitive damages is, to put it mildly, an unscientific process complicated by personality differences. Conduct which one person may view as outrageous another may accept without feeling, depending on such diverse characteristics as an individual's background, temperament and societal concerns. The process is further complicated by the lack of objective criteria from either the Legislature or the courts as to "how much" is necessary to punish and deter.

We have examined a number of appellate decisions in an effort to determine whether we could discern from the cases a single formula for calculating punitive damages.... Frankly, we are unable to find that formula. Instead of making a mathematical breakthrough we discovered what everyone probably already knows: the formula does not exist. And, we have concluded, that is properly so.

Although we may now live in a highly computerized society, it is important to recognize the justice system need not and should not mirror a mechanistic view of life. The life of the law should continue to be experience. The concept of justice connotes a human process, performed by judges and juries in good faith, exercised with compassion, still tinged with sufficient subjectivity to conform the rules of law to the realities of life. Accordingly, we examine the usual factors recited by appellate courts when reviewing punitive damages awards, applying those factors in the customary manner to reach what we believe is a decision consistent with precedent.

The factors to be considered in assessing a punitive damages award are the nature of the defendant's acts, the amount of compensatory damages awarded and the wealth of the defendant....

In *Neal v. Farmers Ins. Exchange, supra*, we acknowledged punitive damages should bear a reasonable relationship to actual damages suffered ... but also noted there is no fixed ratio by which to determine the reasonableness of that relationship.... In light of the circumstances of this case, we could not say as a matter of law that punitive damages equal to almost 27 times the award of compensatory damages were unreasonable. As concluded above, the calculation of punitive damages does not involve strict adherence to a rigid formula. It involves, instead, "a fluid process of adding or subtracting depending on the nature of the acts and the effect on the parties and the worth of the defendants. Juries within this framework have a wide discretion in determining what is proper. [Citation.]" (*Walker v. Signal Companies, Inc., supra*, 84 Cal.App.3d at p. 998, 149 Cal.Rptr. 119.) Courts have affirmed punitive damage awards with a ratio of as high as 2000 to 1. (*Finney v. Lockhart, supra*, 35 Cal.2d at pp. 162, 165, 217 P.2d 19...)

Kearny Mesa directed its most strenuous argument to the applicability of *Neal*'s third factor, the wealth of the defendant. There can be no question but that wealth is an important consideration.... Because the purposes of punitive damages are to punish the defendant and to make an example of him, "the wealthier the wrongdoing defendant, the larger the award of exemplary damages need be in order to accomplish the statutory objective" (*Bertero v. National General Corp.* (1974) 13 Cal.3d 43, 65, 118 Cal.Rptr. 184, 529 P.2d 608), from which "[i]t also follows that the poorer the wrongdoing defendant the smaller the award of punitive damages need be in order to accomplish the statutory objective." (*Merlo v. Standard Life & Acc. Ins. Co.* (1976) 59 Cal.App.3d 5, 18, 130 Cal.Rptr. 416.) We reversed and remanded for a redetermination of punitive damages because evidence of Kearny Mesa's wealth was totally absent from the record.... The Devlins have since closed that gap. Ample evidence of Kearny Mesa's wealth was presented at the second judgment hearing.

Net worth generally is considered the best measure of a defendant's "wealth" for purposes of assessing punitive damages.... Here, the lower court considered net worth plus a variety of other figures relating to Kearny Mesa's wealth....

While the function of punitive damages will not be served if the wealth of the defendant allows him to absorb the award with little or no discomfort, the function also will not be served by an award which is larger than necessary to properly punish and deter....

In light of the fluid process involved in determining the proper amount of punitive damages, the amount awarded here is not excessive as a matter of law. Looking at the entire record in the light most favorable to the judgment, the court below properly concluded Kearny Mesa's conduct was highly reprehensible and involved a calculated attempt on its part to take advantage of the Devlins. Accordingly, the relatively large $80,000 award was necessary to properly punish and deter. There is nothing in the financial data presented which suggests the award will unduly interfere with or hamper Kearny Mesa's future operations. Although the award, representing 17.5 percent of Kearny Mesa's annualized net worth or almost four months' net profit, is somewhat greater than comparable ratios contained in the reported cases ... , we cannot say these numerical differences mandate a finding of excessiveness. The lesson we learned from parsing the cases is that the reason why there is no simple formula for calculating punitive damages is that there is no particular sum which represents the *only* correct amount for such damages in any given case. Instead, there is a range of reasonableness for punitive damages reflective of the factfinder's human response to the evidence presented. In light of the evidence in this case, $80,000 certainly falls within the range of reasonableness.

Viewed in absolute terms, the Devlins' $80,000 award does not appear to be the product of passion or prejudice. To say, relative to the reported cases, the 17.5 percent net worth award must be reduced by a certain percentage (compare *Zhadan v. Downtown Los Angeles Motor Distributors, Inc.* (1979) 100 Cal.App.3d 821, 835-836, 161 Cal.Rptr. 225) or the excess over three months net profit must be excised (compare *Schomer v. Smidt* (1980) 113 Cal.App.3d 828, 836, 170 Cal.Rptr. 662) is merely to substitute the factfinding of appellate judges for that of trial courts in the guise of mathematical semantics. In the context of this case, shaving the percentages would give the reported cases a sacrosanct quality without reason. This is not a case where an unreasonable award was rendered by a runaway jury. Rather, the award was the result of measured deliberation by a conscientious judge. Deference to the trial court function requires appellate restraint.... We therefore hold that in light of the relevant factors, the punitive damages award of $80,000 is not excessive as a matter of law.

Disposition: *Judgment affirmed.* Gerald Brown, P.J., and WORK, J., concur.

NOTES AND QUESTIONS

1. *When can a plaintiff get punitive damages?*: Courts have hesitated to award punitive damages in contract cases. In *Walker v. Sheldon*,[181] the court said:

> [p]unitive or exemplary damages have been allowed in cases where the wrong complained of is morally culpable, or is actuated by evil and reprehensible motives, not only to punish the defendant but to deter him, as well as others who might otherwise be so prompted, from indulging in similar conduct in the future.

An ordinary breach of contract does not involve moral culpability, and we would not expect punitive damages to be awarded. Some courts have found that nonperformance of a contract might involve an independent tort which can serve as the basis for punitive damages. Some courts, for example, find that insurance companies have a duty to settle claims in good faith. An insurer that resists claims in bad faith has committed a tort and can be charged with punitive damages.

Not all courts are willing to allow punitive damages even in fraud cases. For example the New York Court of Appeals in the *Walker* case said, "[a]lthough they have been refused in the "ordinary" fraud and deceit case ..., we are persuaded that, on the basis of analogy, reason and principle, there may be a recovery of exemplary damages in fraud and deceit actions where the fraud, aimed at the public generally, is gross and involves high moral culpability."

Can one who has been the victim of an unconscionable contract recover punitive damages? Nothing in U.C.C. § 2-302 mentions any kind of damages. The language of the section offers only defenses. However, many of the consumer fraud and deceptive trade practices acts do allow punitive damages. One might be able to find unconscionable conduct a violation of one of those statutes and then turn to its remedies provisions for such an award.

2. *The pros and cons of punitive damages*: The risk of punitive damages could deter some outrageous fraudulent behavior. The chance of collecting them could prompt a lawyer to take a consumer fraud case on a contingent fee in a situation where the amounts involved otherwise would not warrant action. Perhaps we want a jury to express our collective outrage at certain behavior in extreme cases. Indeed, a jury is likely to do this whatever they are instructed if the case is outrageous enough. Perhaps it is better to allow them to label part of their award as compensatory and part as punitive. This way, the trial judge and appellate courts can review the sums awarded as a penalty.

On the other hand, the dissent in *Walker v. Sheldon*, expressed concern about allowing a jury to award punitive damages:

---

[181]10 N.Y.2d 401, 179 N.E.2d 497 (1961).

The reasons against extending the coverage of punitive or exemplary damages are manifold, and many of them are patent under the facts of this case. McCormick on Damages (1935 ed. p. 276) says that it is probable that, in the framing of a model code of damages today, for use in a country without previous legal tradition, "the doctrine of exemplary damages would find no place." His reasons are the double jeopardy involved in subjecting a defendant to both criminal prosecution and to punishment in the form of civil punitive damages for the same act, in violation of the spirit, if not the letter, of the constitutional prohibitions against punishing a man twice for the same offense, and the limitation of exemplary damages "only by the caprice of jurors, subject to a review by the judges only in a rare case where the judge can find impropriety of motive or gross disproportion, and that this want of a guiding measure leads to excess and injustice." Other reasons against extending the coverage of punitive damages in tort cases are stated in a learned article (44 Harvard Law Review, pp. 1173-1209). Among these objections are the difficulty of apportioning punitive damages where, as in this case, there are several defendants possibly guilty of moral turpitude in varying degrees, and also that in the prosecution of such actions the proper admonition of a defendant need not involve the payment of money in as large an amount as can be obtained by a plaintiff by inflaming the passions of the jury. The motivation of plaintiffs in prosecuting such suits is likened to the situation which would exist if a District Attorney were paid according to the number of convictions that he was able to secure. The plaintiff profits more by heavy punishment than by light, even in instances where light punishment might have better admonitory value. The injustice is, of course, mentioned of lining the pocket of a plaintiff with money taken from a defendant in the interest of society, in addition to any loss which the plaintiff may have actually sustained. If it be thought that such a plaintiff should be recompensed not only for his damages but also for the expense of prosecuting a lawsuit for fraud, then the allowance of punitive damages is an inept manner of doing so. The jury are not instructed that the plaintiff's expenses of suit are a measure of the exemplary damage, but, rather, that whatever amount be awarded should be computed in such sum as would represent the payment of a defendant's debt to society. All of this is more properly the function of the criminal law.

3. *Punitive damages and the litigation explosion*: Punitive damages became controversial in the 1980s. Insurance companies and manufacturers tried to convince the public that America was in the midst of a litigation explosion. Jury sympathy and punitive damages ran up costs so individuals and firms could not get insurance. Many withdrew from activities because they could not take the risks of high verdicts. Remedial legislation was introduced in Congress and many state legislatures. Some of these proposals were passed in the states.

These claims prompted researchers to study what was happening. Many are skeptical about whether there has been a litigation explosion. Two investigators from the American Bar Foundation traced jury awards of punitive damages in the courts of 42 counties in 10 states in the early 1980s. They found that some 4.9% of the 25,627 reported verdicts in cases seeking money damages included a punitive award. This was 8.8% of the verdicts in which plaintiff was successful.

Almost one-half of the punitive damage awards were in cases involving intentional torts; 18.9% of them were in personal injury cases; 31.7% of the punitive damage awards were in business/contract cases. The rate of punitive damages awards was highest in intentional tort cases (22.8% of verdicts studied) and lowest in personal injury cases (1.5%). Punitive damages were awarded in 9.2% of verdicts in business/contract cases.

Another study of punitive damages traces awards in Cook County, Illinois and San Francisco County, California from 1960 to 1984. These investigators found that in Cook County, 5% of the business/contract trials from 1960-79 led to punitive damages and from 1980-84 they were awarded in 7% of these cases. In San Francisco 11% of business/contract trials ended with punitive awards from 1960-79 and from 1980-84 they were awarded in 20% of these cases. There was a dramatic upward trend in the size of punitive awards in business/contracts cases. In Cook County the average award in constant 1984 dollars rose from a median of $9,000 in 1960-64 to $149,000 in 1980-84. In San Francisco County the median rose from $13,000 in 1960-64 to $101,000 in 1980-84.

These studies examine jury verdicts. They do not consider any reduction of such damages by way of settlement or post-verdict motion or on appeal. The Cook and San Francisco Counties study report that awards were reduced in 32 of the 68 cases in which they could generate data. Overall, defendants in all 68 cases paid only fifty percent of the total amount awarded by the juries.

4. *The constitutionality of punitive damages*: In *Browning-Ferris Industries of Vermont, Inc. v. Kelco Disposal, Inc.*, the Supreme Court of the United States decided that the excessive fines clause of the Eighth Amendment to the Constitution does not apply to punitive damages awards in civil cases. That Amendment provides: "Excessive bail shall not be required, nor excessive fines imposed, nor cruel and unusual punishments inflicted." The Court declined to decide whether the award of punitive damages in the *Browning-Ferris* case was unconstitutional under the Due Process Clause of the Fourteenth Amendment.

The Court subsequently considered three cases making just such a challenge. In the first case the Court sustained a jury award of punitive damages even though the jury instruction was widely seen as offering little meaningful guidance to the jury. In the second case[182] the Court again upheld a jury award of $10 million in punitive damages, though the compensatory damages were only

---

[182]TXO Production Corp. v. Alliance Resources Inc., 113 S.Ct. 2711, 125 L.Ed.2d 366 (1993).

$19,000. In each of these cases the Court refused to "draw a mathematical bright line between the constitutionally acceptable and the constitutionally unacceptable that would fit every case."[183] In the most recent case the Court reversed a state court's affirmation of a $5 million punitive damage award as unconstitutional, holding that a state constitutional provision precluding judicial review of punitive damages awarded by a jury "unless the [reviewing court] can affirmatively say there is no evidence to support the verdict" violated the Due Process Clause.[184]

The Court seems committed to leaving the matter of regulation of punitive damages to state courts and legislatures. Those who were optimistic about the Court's acting to limit punitive damages have once again directed their attention to legislative action.

d. Evaluating Unconscionability

Many scholars question granting judges power to regulate contracts in the name of unconscionability. Others defend using the concept. We will look at some of the debate. The late professor Arthur Leff wrote often about unconscionability. All of his writing is worth reading, and much of it is fun as well! The first article by Professor Leff reprinted here responds to one written by Professor John Murray in which Murray proposed an elaborate definition of unconscionability. Leff both praises and criticizes Murray's argument. You would have to read Murray to understand all of Professor Leff's comments, but you can understand the main points of the Murray-Leff debate from the following excerpt. In fairness to Professor Murray, you should read Leff's description of Murray's position critically.

---

[183]*Pacific Mutual, supra*, at 18.

[184]Honda Motor Co. v. Oberg, 114 S.Ct. 2331, 129 L.Ed.2d 336 (1994). In this case, unlike its predecessors, the Court did not explore the character of the standard that would identify unconstitutionally excessive awards. Instead the case confronted the question of what procedures were necessary to ensure that punitive damages were not imposed in an arbitrary manner.

*Unconscionability and the Crowd — Consumers and
the Common Law Tradition*
Arthur Leff[185]

Professor Murray[186] and I[187] agree on so many things. We are both dreadfully disappointed by what the Code's unconscionability clause[188] has spawned in the way of case law.[189] Neither of us has much good to say about the learned writing about the section.[190] A strong lack of enthusiasm informs both our discussions of the section's Official Comments.[191] In fact, there is even a subtle hint that Professor Murray thinks as I do, that the job of drafting § 2-302 itself might have been improved upon.[192]

But more important than all of that is our basic agreement that in the vast majority of instances, examination of the *way* the consumer "contract" was made is a not very helpful step in attempting to decide whether, under the rubric of unconscionability, to grant or deny it judicial enforcement. In the typical consumer-adhesion-contract case, people sign the proferred forms without reading them or bothering to attempt to understand them — except for the particular dickered terms. As Professor Murray clearly recognizes, what I have called "procedural unconscionability" is, therefore, typically irrelevant to the merchant's form-pad sale. Either the whole contract is valid, or it is all (except for the dickered terms) *potentially* invalid as unconscionable. Oh, one can imagine instances of some sort of super-disclosure by a seller, coupled with some sort of super-assent by a consumer, which might validate an otherwise "unconscionable" provision, but we both know that not very frequently in the real mercantile world would such a rarity show up. Thus Professor Murray devotes most of his essay to discussing which provisions, assuming no such super-assent, ought to be stricken as unconscionable when they are part of a typical form-pad

---

[185]31 University of Pittsburgh Law Review 349 (1969), c University of Pittsburgh Law Review, Reprinted with Permission.

[186]Murray, Unconscionability: Unconscionability, 31 University of Pittsburgh Law Review 1 (1969) [hereinafter cited as Murray].

[187]Leff, Unconscionability and the Code--The Emperor's New Clause, 115 University of Pennsylvania Law Review 485 (1967) [hereinafter cited as Leff].

[188]Uniform Commercial Code § 2-302 (1962) [hereinafter cited as U.C.C.].

[189]Murray, at 37, 44, 55-66, 69-72; Leff, at 547-58. Of course, Professor Murray has many more cases to deplore than I had in 1967.

[190]Leff, at 528, 558; Murray, at 2: "[T]he writers have done little beyond deplore the Delphic nature of the concept of any codification thereof." Here again, of course, Professor Murray had a greater number of efforts by which to be unimpressed than I. See Murray, at 1 n.1 for his list.

[191]Leff, at 489-528; Murray, at 39-41.

[192]*See* Murray, at 38 n.110: "What is alarming is his [Leff's] failure to recognize the need for the kind of provision which § 2-302 is, notwithstanding successful criticisms of the language of the section as it exists."

contract. He does that job with thus far unparalleled care and thoroughness. And since his essay says what it says better than I could resay it (even if I were trying to be fairly fair) I will not try to summarize it. Let it suffice to say here that I find Professor Murray's attempt to explain unconscionability an admirable job, one which carefully considers almost all of the subtle difficulties involved in such a definitional struggle. Or to be brief, I cannot help but prefer Professor Murray's unconscionability clause to the Code's.

In fact, our dispute, such as it is, has little to do with the "meaning" of unconscionability at all. It involves instead a difference of opinion over the importance of the concept to any system for the control of unfair retailing practices.

What is the function of an unconscionability concept or clause? Briefly, it appears to be one technique for controlling the quality of a transaction when free market control is considered ineffective. It is one method for substituting government regulation for regulation by the parties. The theory of classical contract, paralleling classical economics, was that ordinarily the market mechanism should maximize the welfare of the parties. With the coming of the mass distribution of mass-produced goods via equally mass-produced "contracts," many observers of the contract scene became convinced that one could not rely on the bargaining process to protect certain individuals and classes against harsh contracts. That does not mean, and did not mean to those commentators, that the end of individual bargaining between roughly equal contending parties (assuming that ever really existed) necessarily meant a net decrease in human welfare, not, at least, if any reasonably materialistic definition of welfare were used. For it is arguable that mass production is the source of a vast total increase in economic welfare, and that successful mass production requires mass distribution by documents also inalterably mass-produced, or briefly, that one can no more efficiently customize contracts than customize goods for a mass market without losing all of the economic gains of non-customized production.

Even if that is true, however, it is also true that the welfare gain, if any, is in the net only; that is, not all graphs work perfectly in an imperfect market. Now, no market is perfect, but the consumer market may be more imperfect than others. First, there may be monopolistic or oligopolistic powers in that market, either "natural," conspiratorial, or government sanctioned. Second, the information necessary for market choice may not be available at reasonable cost with respect to any particular consumer product, especially when a consumer has to process information about a vast array of goods; consumers notably lack the expertise that comes from buyer specialization. Third, with respect to consumer "contracts," most of the boiler plate is about contingencies, things that will become important only if the product or deal breaks down. It is hard to focus attention on what should not ordinarily happen, or at least to focus as carefully as upon what will happen for sure; *i.e.*, the price and the nature of the goods. In any event, for these and other reasons, it has been persuasively argued that the market bargaining process will not protect consumers from a large variety of injuries in a huge array of transactions. And if not, some other device to supply that protection may have to be designed. The natural step is to look to government intervention; *i.e.*, to invoke the political "market" instead of the economic due to correct the latter's alleged imperfections.

In any event, let us *assume* that the distribution of goods and services to consumers via essentially inalterable forms is an area of national economic life requiring governmental intervention for the maximization of social welfare. Even having made that decision, however, one has barely begun the intellectual struggle such an apparent insight should set off. If the government is to intervene, what form should that intervention take? Should it be legislative and administrative, legislative and judicial? Should the directive to the relevant bureaucracy (administrative or litigative) be express and detailed, or open-ended and open-textured? Should the regulatory scheme focus on those market breakdowns the source of which is a lack of market-supplied relevant information, or should the approach instead be direct governmental quality control, akin to the government's forays into the milk, auto and, most interestingly, life-insurance-policy fields.

As for this last choice, between government regulation of information, and regulation of deal-quality regardless of information, Professor Murray and I are, as previously noted, more or less in accord. I may have a little more faith in the regulatory powers of government-mandated disclosure than he, but I think we agree that to attempt to regulate the consumer contracting process is frequently to attempt to regulate a process that not only does not take place, but perhaps one which, as a matter of economic efficiency, ought not to take place.[193] As I said,

---

[193] *See* Leff, *supra* note 10, for a more detailed discussion of this particular trade-off. My own starting place there is to argue that we should all stop thinking about these consumer adhesion "contracts" as contracts altogether, and think about them as products, just like the products sold pursuant to them. Once having established that outlook, one is better able to discuss *what* governmental regulatory decisions ought to be made about the quality of these "products." For when one says that a particular contract or portion of it is "unconscionable," what one is really deciding is that the contract ought not be allowed to fall below a certain minimum quality. The chief advantage of this particular mind-set is that it makes unavoidable the consideration of factors which Professor Murray found perhaps too easy to avoid, the various costs of direct bureaucratic quality control, be it of goods or "contracts." When you focus on something as a "contract," it is too easy to assume that what doesn't fall on one party will fall on the other, thus, if the shift of a risk is held by the court bureaucracy to be "unconscionable," it will somehow come to rest on the party whose attempted shift was frustrated. When, however, one thinks of the situation as involving a directive to a manufacturer not to sell risky or defective "goods" to the public, one is more likely to recognize that the risk has not been bounced back permanently to the maker-seller, but has been lobbed back temporarily, so that he can slip it into his price base and allocate it ratably to the whole class of buyers. Thus, the net effect of a series of decisions following Henningsen v. Bloomfield Motors, Inc., 32 N.J. 358, 161 A.2d 69 (1960), which both Professor Murray and I admire (I because it did not facilely rely on the unconscionability clause of the Code, *see* Leff, at 558 n.300, and he as if it did, *see* Murray, at 50-54), would be that all buyers of automobiles would eventually automatically "buy" from the manufacturers an insurance policy

it is here that Professor Murray makes his most significant contribution to unconscionability comentary. *If* one assumes that the minimum quality of consumer contracts ought to be regulated by the government via the judicial bureaucracy, on an *ad hoc* case-by-case basis essentially unrestrained by legislative or administrative guidance, then the heart of Professor Murray's essay carefully, at great length, and with considerable intellectual acuity, sets out the relevant criteria and their application.

But what if one does not so assume? That, I think, is where Professor Murray and I really part company. He seems to feel that with something like fatality: "The obligation to develop a viable concept of unconscionability falls upon the judicial process in our legal system." If all he means by that is that since § 2-302 is in the Code, the courts will have to do something about it, then of course one can't disagree. The damn thing *is* there; one can't just ignore it. Indeed, as I said several years ago, it is likely that the courts will eventually get to some not-too-grotesque end-position. But I can't believe that that's all Professor Murray means. Rather, it seems to me he thinks that the nation *needs* something like the unconscionability clause of the Code in order to achieve substantial consumer justice. Or, to put it another way, he appears to believe that regulation of the quality of mass-distribution contracts requires some open-textured directive to courts to strike naughty provisions, and that the proper governmental quality-control agency is an unguided court. I don't.

Professor Murray's model is a litigation model. In order to establish the unenforceability of any particular provision, in any particular jurisdiction, there will have to be at least one lawsuit, with the relatively high transaction costs (especially relative to the amount at issue) of that law-reform technique. Now, what happens after that first lawsuit? Take a case like *Williams*.[194] In that case the court remanded for a finding whether a cross-collateral clause, allowing the seller to repossess all items ever bought from it by the buyer, upon default in payment for the most recently purchased item, was "unconscionable." Let us assume that on remand that it is decided that, at least where the buyer is a lady on relief with seven children, such a clause is unenforceable. What's the seller's next move? Why to "distinguish the case," of course. Perhaps the next thing to do is make the clause clearer, maybe to make it read: "Caution: if you don't pay for what you just bought we may be able to take back whatever we ever sold you." Well,

---

covering any personal injuries which might arise from manufacturing defects in the cars they bought. I suppose it is possible to believe that one can buy insurance policies without having to pay premiums; it's just that I can't.

That does not mean that such spreading of risk is an evil. In the Henningsen situation, for instance. I would guess that having an oligopolistic industry sell insurance against its own defective equipment to its customers might actually minimize the premium paid. In other words, I am not balking at the charge but only trying to scotch any odd idea that such protection might be cost-free.

[194]Williams v. Walker-Thomas Furniture Co., 350 F.2d 445 (D.C. Cir. 1965); *see* Leff, at 551-56; *see* Murray, at 54-59.

now, we've got a new case for case-by-case development. O.K., let's assume that the seller loses that one too, perhaps because the apparent assent was not "verified" (in Professor Murray's terms) because the buyer did not have, in the "relevant geographic market," any alternative to such a clause when buying what he bought, or any functional equivalent of it (to make which finding the court must also decide, under Professor Murray's approach, what the "relevant product market" is). Fine. We've just had two little internal antitrust suits, (under § 2-302(2), I assume), one on relevant geographical markets and one on functional equivalence, and the seller has lost again. But, of course, the next seller who wants to use a clause like the first seller ought not be daunted. After all, if his neighborhood or product is different, it's a whole new ball game — or so it seems under Professor Murray's honest and careful approach.

But let us say that over the course of many such cases it is pretty well settled by the court in that jurisdiction that with respect to almost any kind of goods sold in any one of the poor neighborhoods in town, the clause which figured in *Williams* is unconscionable. Now, that does not mean that seller would necessarily stop using it. After all, under the common-law tradition they lose only if the other party chooses to litigate, and most consumers don't. But let us say that the sellers' lawyers (assuming they have lawyers, and the kind who go over their forms too, not just the kind who procure default judgments) insist as a matter of ethics that the clause not appear as a trap for the unwary consumer. Does that mean it's gone? Not necessarily. How about a change that reads: "Caution: if you do not pay for what we just sold you, we may be able to take back everything we ever sold you which is not protected from execution under state law." Is that unconscionable? It gets the seller priority over other creditors, which is one of its major purposes. But it also saves the seller the transaction costs of post-judgment execution, thereby increasing the chance that the buyer will *indeed* lose some of the things he previously bought. And that loss, because of the difference between "value" to the possessor and "value" when sold as used goods, might still be scarifying. Is that risk still "material"? Is the assent not "validated" because every other seller has such a clause or worse, even though it would make no *formal* difference (except between creditors) if there were no clause at all? Well, all we know now is that now we've got ourselves another lawsuit.

Let us say that the seller loses this one too, perhaps on the ground that the actual risk from self-help repossession is much greater than the actual risk from judgment execution, and the buyer could not have recognized that. Is the seller class finally finished with respect to cross-collateral clauses? Most likely not, if it wants to fight. For there is still another not unethical method of operations. Change the clause again ("... and the chance we will perhaps take them back is better than if we had to sue and ask the sheriff to take them back for us") and maybe put in a spot for initialling in the margin. Would that do it? Back to the old courtroom.

And, winning there, let's all start up again with new parties in a new jurisdiction.

To cut this short, the problem is not with Professor Murray's criteria, but with the common-law tradition itself when sought to be used to regulate the quality of transactions on a case-by-case basis, each one of which is economically trivial (so that you need free legal help for the consumer, and the seller can almost always avoid nasty precedent by an early surrender or settlement), and each one of which depends upon several doses of "the total context of the fact situation" and "copious examination of the manifestations of the parties and the surrounding circumstances followed by a balancing effort." It is as if there were some breakdown in the competitive structure which permitted, even fostered, the production of shoddy goods — not dangerous, just crummy — and one sought to have an impact upon that disutility by encouraging individual suits by individual buyers for individual product insufficiencies on (often) very individual factual patterns. One cannot think of a more expensive and frustrating course than to seek to regulate goods or "contract" quality through repeated lawsuits against inventive "wrongdoers." Wouldn't it be easier and far more effective, *if* one finds these cross-collateral clauses, or some others, offensive in consumer transactions, just to face one's conclusion and regulate them out of existence, in a manner no lawyer could conscientiously avoid? Wouldn't it be better, finally, to face the political problems and pass a statute that deals with cross-collateral clauses, negotiable-note and waiver-of-defense financing, abusive collection devices, a wide panoply of quasi-crooked marketing devices and so on, and maybe even gross overpricing (on analogy to the civil-law *laesio enormis* progeny) and tuck in, along with private causes of action for the victims, an administrative enforcement arm to police these repetitive nasty practices (and perhaps get compensation for the whole class of bilked consumers theretofore identifiably bilked)? Isn't there some economy of scale in that approach? Remember, the idea is to change as many nasty forms and practices as possible, not merely to add to the glorious common law tradition of eventually coping. Wouldn't more be changed by explicit positive law, administratively interpreted and enforced, than by the feed-back from easily distinguishable, easily stallable, exceedingly expensive *cases*?[195]

Well, I really don't know. It kind of depends on whether facile devices like § 2-302 will stall the hard thinking and lobbying that has to be done. If not, I suppose there is some marginal need for some provision to deal with particularly egregious consumer-contract horrors not yet reached by any statute. The key factor I suppose, is that in dealing with mass vices in mass contracts, administra-

---

[195]Of course, I may seem to be missing the point that one may not be able openly to convince the legislatures to do that which ought to be done, and thus the proper course is to slip by them an open-textured provision, and then have the courts exploit its ambiguities. Well, maybe. But, goddammit, maybe not. *See* Leff, *passim*, Professor Murray, to my fair surprise and substantial spiritual oppression, refers to that theme in my article as "legislative history." See Murray, at 35.

tion by way of the litigation bureaucracy is likely to have only trivial impact, for good or evil. One does not cure any serious breakdown in a theoretically competitive market system by case-to-case sniping, but one doesn't do much harm either. As I have said before, the court *will* adjust; the trouble is that the economic system most certainly will not have to, and will not, I think, until more than this cute litigation game is played.

So now our dispute is at least open. Professor Murray wonders, I assume rhetorically, what I would have done with "a statute providing that one should not be unjustly enriched at the expense of another," or with "Section 5 of the Federal Trade Commission Act which merely proscribes unfair methods of competition." Well, if you must know, pretty much what I would do with § 2-302 of the Uniform Commercial Code, with considerable enthusiasm and some historical justification too. Or, once more to quote myself (to whom, I am sure, the last word will not belong): "Subsuming problems is not as good as solving them, and may in fact retard solutions instead. Or, once more to quote Karl Llewellyn (to whom, after all, the last word justly belongs), 'Covert tools are never reliable tools.' "[196]

The following piece by Leff provides other ideas about why a precise definition of unconscionability has proven so elusive.

Thomist Unconscionability
Arthur Leff[197]

... [W]e worry and are worried about the question of unconscionability as much as we are because it is a spectacular example of an attempt to give a legal-technological answer to a question really posed by a fundamental ambivalence over values, that is, by a problem which has no technical solution.

It seems to me that the real question underlying and masked by "the unconscionability problem" is this: ought one be allowed by the law to reap material gain from some advantage for which one is not responsible, that is, which one did not, commendably or evilly, cause? To put it another way, should a person be allowed to arrogate to himself the fruits of being just smarter, or just stronger, or just luckier than the someone else with whom he is doing a deal?

Notice, this is a question about unachieved advantages. About those that are the product of the possessor's efforts, there is some cultural unanimity. It is, for example, widely accepted that a person is entitled to be paid for work, and to be paid more for superior work. If a person makes a better product, or distributes

---

[196]Leff, at 559, quoting Llewellyn, The Common Law Tradition 265 (1960), quoting Llewellyn, Book Review, 52 Harvard Law Review 700, 703 (1939).

[197]4 Canadian Business Law Journal 424 (1979).

it more conveniently, so that people want it more and want more of it, it is generally conceded that if he takes advantage of his advantage he is entitled to do so, even if he makes an above-normal profit, even, indeed, if he grows stinking rich. And, this includes the "work" of acquiring superior information — about products, production, or markets. There is some cultural uneasiness about some natural advantages (Wilt Chamberlain's height, for instance) and the extent to which they justify extraordinary returns — but not much.

Similarly, it is pretty well accepted that a man cannot be allowed to take advantage of achieved advantages which were achieved through force or fraud. If a man has better information than the other party to the deal because he lied to that other, or if he finds himself with a strong market position because he forcibly bars the other party from getting to his competitors, then "we" disapprove — strongly enough to render deals made under those conditions void, voidable, or unenforceable. The law will deny to defrauder and thug his above-normal profit; in the more pallid language of the law, common law fraud and knife-at-the-throat duress are valid defenses to actions upon a contract.

Nor indeed, when it comes to "achieved" commercial advantages, has our law gotten stuck at these crude species of lying and forcing. The law, developing through the centuries, has given pejorative juridical significance to modes of "achievement" beyond pure intentional and knowing lies and business propositions in the form "buy my widgets or I'll cut your throat." One can in fact display quite a large number of contract defences so that things would look (in descending order of clear moral naughtiness) something like this:

Comparative Defects in Complainant's Information	*Comparative Defects in Complainant's Freedom*
Common Law Fraud	Common Law Duress
Intentional Misrepresentation	Duress by Imprisonment
Negligent Misrepresentation	Duress of Goods
Innocent Misrepresentation	Conspiratorial Monopoly
Duty to Volunteer Material Information	Inequality of Bargaining Power

Now note, in both columns, until one reaches the last term in the progression, the law is making the source of the defence some action on the part of the party to the transaction who would like to uphold it. By and large it is possible to describe that action as in some comprehensible way "wrongful." Admittedly, the wrongfulness is often stretched; the real locus of "innocent misrepresentation" in the common law of commerce is, after all, "express warranty, and the most pervasive form of "duty to volunteer material information" is "implied warranty." But by and large, at least historically, before the law would step in it was required that the guy with the better competitive position in a deal be found to have gotten that position in some sneaky or otherwise unfair way. (Remember, all you have to "volunteer" under implied warranty is a lack of title, a declination below "fair average quality" or a misfit with a "particular purpose" known to you.)

But now look at the last term in each column. The "fraud" line first. If there were indeed a general duty to volunteer to the other party in a deal *all* relevant information that you have and he does not, then there could be no pay-off for investment in superior information — or training or skill *a fortiori* there could be no profit from mere accidental information advantages, or lucky guesses, or a better natural business head.

And what if one took seriously the last entry in the "duress" line, and actually made "inequality of bargaining power" a contract defence? If withholding information were in general a defence, that would remove from capitalist profit any return to search and training. But if inequality of bargaining power were taken seriously, then no one could be allowed to profit from any market deformation, any momentary declination of any market from textbook perfection, even if it were the product of forces over which neither party had any control. When demand outran supply for a time, one could not increase one's prices so as to take advantage of the temporary misfit of desire and satisfaction. But that is one of the most common states of any reasonably competitive market, and one not ordinarily caused by any anticompetitive conspiracy at all.

One can see how dramatic an effect actual widespread application of these last items on each chart would have by asking for a moment how one would *know* if a party had failed to disclose material information, or was profiting from an inequality of bargaining power. Simple: any differentiation of the price from that normally charged would conclusively prove either superior information or superior power; if both parties had equal knowledge and equal freedom there would be only one price, the normal market price. So (if the last lines were taken seriously) any deal at any higher price would be unenforceable under the law.

Moreover, it is by now pretty well understood that every term in a contract is part of the price, in the sense that every term is part of the total deal, and thus every changed term will have to be reflected some place in the total exchange ratio. Hence, every abnormal contract *is* a contract at a non-normal price, and it would be, under the above reasoning, legally unenforceable.

What follows is this: both a general duty to volunteer all information material to a transaction, and a general concept of inequality of bargaining power are, in fact, not the culminations of the fraud and force lines of contract defences at all. They belong, instead, to that grand old third line of historic contract-control legal devices, the line in the middle so to speak, the line of illegality (and its little brother "against public policy"). It is here that we find those defences that have nothing really to do with information or freedom defects, that have nothing to do with trying to create efficient markets, that operate instead without proof of any fraud-like or force-like activities. It is here that today we find usury, but usury is just the last pale left-over emanation from that great monument of medieval commercial law, the fair price doctrine.

And that is where we find unconscionability, or rather, that is what unconscionability means: a bad deal not brought about by any determinable bad conduct (the finding of which would render the use of unconscionability superfluous), but rather bad only because of its intrinsic badness: its out of the ordinary "price." It is what one uses when one wants to say "you cannot take advantage of any advantage you have, no matter how, or how innocently, your advantage was brought about."

That then, I think, is why the unconscionability doctrine continues to fascinate and torment us. It is not an extension of market-perfecting, capitalism facilitating law, but its covert enemy. The other contract defences — fraud and all the little "fraudlets," duress and all the lesser pressures — are market-process oriented; in the economist's terms, they look to *efficiency of allocation*. But the "middle line" — usury, fair price and, yes, unconscionability — is result oriented; in economic terms, it looks toward *fairness of distribution*. Our problem is that we want *simultaneously* to produce and protect market efficiency *and* to achieve non-exploitative market results. But (given individual differences among people, and innocently achieved superior information, market power, and pure luck) *we cannot have both at the same time*.

In effect, we want to have the world so arranged that everyone will be motivated to get as good a deal for himself as possible by being as informed and efficient as he can be, but that no one will have to get a bad deal in the process. But the payoff for the former necessitates, indeed entails, the latter. Hence doing both is not a technical problem — how do you define unconscionability, how do you specify unfairness in a short statute — but a cultural one: we cannot have perfect freedom and perfect fairness at once. What we have, instead, is "unconscionability," a legal device that allows us, inconsistently and with only symbolic impact, an occasional evasive bow in the direction of our incoherent hearts' desires.

NOTES AND QUESTIONS

1. *The impact of the Williams case*: Shortly after the Court of Appeals released its opinion in the *Williams* case, Mrs. Williams' lawyer commented on what he saw as the impact of the decision.

The best effect of the decision lies in the fact that it is a dormant threat to unconscionable conduct which could become very active with little or no notice. In other words, sheer existence of Judge Wright's majority opinion has encouraged a greater degree of "conscionability" in my opinion. When the case enters the defense at trial level, plaintiffs seem to be much more disposed towards settlement, rather than risk an adverse finding under a decision with a possible trial memorandum opinion applying the reasoning of Judge Wright.[198]

Mrs. Williams's lawyer also said,

> The United Planning Organization, which had recently established a number of neighborhood legal offices, began to make extensive use of Judge Wright's opinion in defending indigent persons at the trial level....
>
> The corporation counsel evidently concluded that the language of the Uniform Commercial Code (§ 2-302), coupled with the opinion of Judge Wright, was sufficient to protect the consumer; legislation covering consumer protection was not presented to Congress as had been planned.[199]

If we assume these comments accurately reflect the impact of *Williams v. Walker-Thomas*, do they support or undercut Professor Leff's analysis?

2. *The cost of the benefits gained*: Mrs. Williams' lawyer worked for the Legal Assistance Office of the Bar Association of the District of Columbia. He commented,

> I decided to take the two cases as far as necessary to achieve a precedent which would afford some protection to the lesser members of the community ... Trial, appeal to the D.C. Court of Appeals, and then to the U.S. Circuit Court of Appeals took 210 man hours of legal time, for which the appellants were not obligated to pay.[200]

If Mrs. Williams had paid for this legal work at $25 per hour (a not unreasonable fee in 1965), her legal fees would have been $5,250. She could have paid all she owed Walker-Thomas if she had about $1,200. Does this support or undercut Professor Leff's analysis? What might be other costs of the *Williams v. Walker-Thomas* case?

It is important to note that although the general rule is that parties pay their own attorney fees, legislatures in many states provide, in a not-very-systematic way for the recovery of attorney fees in some kinds of cases. It is not uncommon for an act passed in the interests of consumers to contain an attorney fee provision. For example, the Wisconsin Consumer Act provides, at § 425.308 if the customer prevails in an action for violation of the act, the customer is entitled to recover costs and expenses, "... together with a reasonable amount for

---

[198]Helstad and Skilton, Protection of the Installment Buyer of Goods Under the Uniform Commercial Code, 65 Michigan Law Review 1465, 1480 (1967).

[199]Dostert, Appellate Restatement of Unconscionability: Civil Legal Aid at Work, 54 American Bar Association Journal 1183 (Dec. 1968).

[200]Helstad and Skilton, *supra*, at 1480 n. 38.

attorney's fees." Often the presence or absence of an attorney fee provision may determine whether or not a claim can be made, and the nature of the claim.

3. *Professor Duncan Kennedy on unconscionability*: Professor Duncan Kennedy first commented on *Williams v. Walker-Thomas* in 1976. Then he said:

> How should a person committed to altruism ... assess the significance of informality in our actual law of contracts, for example? I have only a little confidence in my own answer, which is that the case for standards is problematic but worth making. There is a strong argument that the altruist judges who have created the modern law of unconscionability and promissory estoppel have diverted resources available for the reform of the overall substantive structure into a dead end. There is an argument that individualist judges are restrained from working social horrors only by a mistaken faith in judicial neutrality that it would be folly to upset. It might be better to ignore contract law, or to treat it in an aggressively formal way, in order to heighten the level of political and economic conflict within our society.
>
> Nonetheless, I believe that there is value as well as an element of real nobility in the judicial decision to throw out, every time the opportunity arises, consumer contracts designed to perpetuate the exploitation of the poorest class of buyers on credit. Real people are involved, even if there are not very many whose lives the decision can affect. The altruist judge can view himself as a resource whose effectiveness in the cause of substantive justice is to be maximized, but to adopt this attitude is to abandon the crucial proposition that altruistic duty is owed by one individual to another, without the interposition of the general category of humanity.
>
> Further, judges like Skelly Wright are important actors in a symbolic representation of the conflict of commitments. Given the present inability of altruism to transform society, it is only a dramatic production, ancillary to a hypothetical conflict that would be revolutionary. As such, the judge is a cultural figure engaged in the task of persuading adversaries, in spite of the arbitrariness of values. More, he is at work on the indispensable task of imagining an altruistic order. Contract law may be an ideal context for this labor, precisely because it presents problems of daily life, immediate and inescapable, yet deeply resistant to political understanding. It seems to me that we should be grateful for this much, and wish the enterprise what success is possible short of the overcoming of its contradictions.[201]

---

[201]Kennedy, Form and Substance in Private Law Adjudication, 89 Harvard Law Review 1685, 1178 (1976).

In 1982, Kennedy[202] offered a different reaction:

> To understand the doctrine of unequal bargaining power, one must understand that the liberal position is ... that reform of exceptional cases and intelligent response to abuses are all that is needed to meet the just demands of the disadvantaged and thereby to relegitimate the overall system of distribution and the overall quality of life.... [W]hatever one may think of this or that transaction, one sees the basic allocation of power between capitalists, workers, managers, and government bureaucrats, along with the basic cultural underpinnings of family and social life, as beyond the scope of political action....
>
> This implicit message of equality conveyed by appealing to inequality is a classic example of the apologetic functions of doctrine. The equality is of "power," so that though we willingly interpolate terms favoring the buyer into an insurance contract, we don't see that as committing us in any way to equalizing peoples' actual enjoyment of the material things everyone is struggling over. Eliminating inequality of bargaining power, as liberals conceive it, has nothing to do with eliminating factual inequalities.... It nonetheless gives a very good feeling....
>
> Courts using the doctrine of unconscionability like to put their decisions on grounds of unequal bargaining power (in spite of the comment to § 2-302 of the U.C.C.). But it's often obvious that they are concerned not with power but with naivete, or with lack of ability to make intelligent calculations about what one can afford on one's budget. People make mistakes about how much pleasure they will get out of a product — a deep freeze — and about how likely it is that they will be able to find five other people to whom to sell deep freezes in a pyramid scheme.

What is Kennedy's reaction to attempting to aid the poor through applications of U.C.C. § 2-302? Remember, this is the same article in which Kennedy suggests "cautious ad hoc paternalism."[203] What does it mean to be an ad hoc paternalist in the context of the application of 2-302?

Why don't we solve the problems more directly? The United States Government runs special stores for certain people. Both government employees overseas and military personnel can shop at a post exchange or PX. The government could supply appliances and furniture to welfare recipients by creating a PX system for them too. It could increase their welfare payments so they could have stereos and microwave ovens or it could deduct the price from welfare checks. The

---

[202]Kennedy, Distributive and Paternalist Motives in Contract and Tort Law, with Special Reference to Compulsory Terms and Unequal Bargaining Power, 41 Maryland Law Review 563, 620-21 (1982).

[203]The extract of Kennedy's article in which this approach was presented is in the part of these materials dealing with duress.

government could buy in large quantity to hold down the cost of these products. Its volume buying would give it leverage to see that manufacturers honored warranties. The system would end ghetto merchants as well as the need for investing great amounts of lawyer time from legal aid offices. Would Kennedy advocate a system something such as this PX proposal? Do you see any problems with establishing PX's for welfare recipients or just supplying these people with appliances and furniture?

4. *Collective efforts to assert consumer rights*: Professor Leff suggests that a major problem in using U.C.C. § 2-302 to vindicate consumer rights is that the costs of litigation frequently exceed the small amounts at stake in any particular case. Courts could remedy that problem by increasing the amounts collectible in a § 2-302 suit. If, for example, they allowed punitive damages, this would make litigation economically possible. Lawyers would have reason to take these cases on a contingent fee. This, in turn, might deter merchants from using unconscionable contracts.

We could reduce consumers' costs of litigation through economies of scale. Merchant creditors frequently do this by using collection agencies which use form complaints, have their attorneys handle many cases in a single court appearance, and litigate on a mass production basis. This enables them to litigate for fairly small amounts such as $50 or $100. This may secure an even greater number of settlements as consumers pay the merchant's claims to avoid trouble.

Could government or a private organization create a collection agency for consumers with unconscionability claims? One reason merchant collection agencies are successful is that consumer debtors default in over 90% of the cases brought against them. Merchant defendants would be unlikely to default in many unconscionability cases, particularly if they risked publicity. Still, a somewhat analogous problem confronts composers of music. Each performance without the composer's permission creates a claim under the composer's copyright. However, each claim is for such a small sum that litigation by each composer is not possible. Organizations such as the American Society of Composers, Authors and Publishers (ASCAP) solve this problem. Composers license their copyrights to ASCAP. ASCAP then licenses large users of music such as broadcasters and juke box operators to use the music in exchange for payment of a fee. The Society is able to use economies of scale to detect unauthorized performances and sue. A large user violating copyrights is likely to have violated many at the same time.[204] Can you imagine consumers assigning claims to an organization in exchange for the rights to share in any proceeds of litigation?

Another possible solution to the small claim problem is to aggregate them and sue on them in one large lawsuit. Essentially, this is the idea behind the *class action*. In a class action, one or a few representative plaintiffs are permitted to

---

[204]See Finkelstein, The Composer and the Public Interest — Regulation of Performing Rights Societies, 10 Law & Contemporary Problems 275 (1954).

assert claims for all those similarly situated. If the action is successful, a method is devised for distributing the damages recovered to all members of the plaintiffs' class. For example, a court might appoint a master to locate potential members of the class and then to determine the extent of their damages. Total damage awards in class actions often are in the millions of dollars. Methods have been devised to award attorneys fees large enough to tempt lawyers to handle these cases.

Consumer class actions have attracted attention since the 1960s. Consumer groups have had limited success in pushing for legislation eliminating jurisdictional and procedural barriers to such suits. Some actions have been successful. One of the most famous is *Vasquez v. Superior Court of San Joaquin Co.*, 484 P.2d 964 (Calif. 1971). However, unconscionability claims do not fit into the class action structure in many situations. A class action involves many people who are similarly situated so at least the question of liability to the entire group can be decided in a single trial. However, if a merchant's liability turns on facts particular to each consumer, there may not be sufficient "commonality" or "community of interest" among the merchant's customers to support a class action. If a claim turns on what a salesperson said when the contract was made, a class action may be impossible unless the salesperson used a standard script in dealing with everyone. If a claim turns on the income of the buyers, a class action would be possible only if all the members of the class had roughly the same income.

Both federal and state government agencies sue to protect consumer interests in many ways. The Federal Trade Commission directs most of its enforcement activities at national advertising and product labeling. The FTC has seldom attempted to regulate the ghetto merchandising that lawyers for the poor have attacked by using U.C.C. § 2-302. (The FTC has taken action in the District of Columbia where it has special authority and duties.) Since the late 1960s, state consumer protection agencies have initiated cases against door-to-door sellers and others operating in low-income neighborhoods.

It is tempting to see administrative regulation such as the *Kugler* case to be the solution to problems of the poor consumer. Although administrative agencies have won important victories, they are not always successful. Defendants often can delay proceedings for years after an agency files its initial complaint. See Schrag, On Her Majesty's Secret Service: Protecting the Consumer in New York City, 80 Yale L.J. 1529 (1971). See also the *Allen v. Quality Furniture* essay at p. 205 of Danzig, The Capability Problem in Contract Law (Foundation Press 1978).

Government agencies may fail to act in the interests of consumers for many reasons. They may lack resources. There is debate about the effectiveness of hard and soft law enforcement tactics. And then government agencies are actors in the political process and not disinterested experts. Those who administer agencies live in a political world in which aggressive prosecution of consumer claims may be politically unpopular.[205] While there may be political capital in supporting general legislation to protect consumers, there may be little incentive to actually prosecute individual cases, especially when the defendants in such cases are part of the business establishment.

Even when the Attorney General does elect to press a case, they do not always succeed, however, as the next case shows.

STATE v. AVCO FINANCIAL SERVICE OF N.Y., INC.

50 N.Y.2d 383, 406 N.E.2d 1075 (1980)

FUCHSBERG, J. The Attorney-General, acting on a consumer complaint, instituted this special proceeding under subdivision 12 of § 63 of the Executive Law to enjoin respondent Avco's use of a security clause in a loan agreement form. The petition alleged that the clause was illegal and void as against public policy on the theory that it constituted an impermissible waiver of the personal property exemption afforded a judgment debtor under CPLR 5205 (subd. [a]). Special Term summarily declared the clause invalid for this reason. Although the Appellate Division, over a single dissent, affirmed the order and judgment, it did so on the ground that the provision was unconscionable (70 A.D.2d 859, 418 N.Y.S.2d 52). We now reverse, holding that it is not illegal and that the determination of unconscionability was improperly made without any opportunity for an evidentiary presentation as to the commercial and bargaining context in which the clause appears.

The clause at issue is one regularly inserted by Avco, a finance company, in its loan agreements. Its terms unmistakably provide: "This loan is secured by ... all household goods, furniture, appliances, and consumer goods of every kind and description owned at the time of the loan secured hereby, or at the time of any refinance or renewal thereof, or cash advanced under the loan agreement secured hereby, and located about the premises at the Debtor's residence (unless otherwise stated) or at any other location to which the goods may be moved."

It is not denied that this language must be understood to create a security interest in items of personal property which include the ones made exempt from the reach of a judgment credit by CPLR 5205 (subd. [a]). From its inception, this statute — along with its venerable antecedents — has embodied the humanitarian policy that the law should not permit the enforcement of judgments to such a point that debtors and their families are left in a state of abject deprivation.

It is well recognized, however, that simply because the law exempts such property from levy and sale upon execution by a judgment creditor does not

---

[205]The New York Times carried a story in 1973 (April 22, 1973, at 39, col. 1) about the head of the Arizona Consumer Protection Division who was apparently forced to resign because of his "over-zealous" prosecution of cases under the state's Consumer Fraud Act.

mean that the exemption statute was intended to serve the far more paternalistic function of restricting the freedom of debtors to dispose of these possessions as they wish.... No statute precludes exempt property from being sold; nor is there any which expressly interdicts the less drastic step of encumbering such property. So, for example, while contractual waivers of a debtor's statutory exemptions are usually held to be void ... the law has not forbidden a debtor to execute a mortgage upon the property so protected and thus create the lien which may be foreclosed despite the property's exempt status.... The clause here permits no more and, hence, cannot be said to contravene the exemption statute.

The Attorney-General nevertheless argues that the clause should be invalidated under the doctrine of unconscionability. The contention, as accepted by the majority of the Appellate Division, is that "the inequality of bargaining position and the granting to the creditor of enforcement rights greater than those which the law confers upon a judgment creditor armed with execution, lead inevitably to the conclusion that the absence of choice on the part of the debtor left him with no recourse but to grant to his creditor rights which, in good conscience, the law should not enforce" (70 A.D.2d 859, 860, 418 N.Y.S.2d 52). The clause is also alleged to be unconscionable in that its broad terms create security interests even in items not sold or financed by Avco and function mainly as an *in terrorem* device to spur repayment.

In this connection, we note initially that the statute under which this proceeding was brought (Executive Law, § 63, subd. 12) lists "unconscionable contractual provisions" as a type of "fraudulent" conduct against which the Attorney-General is authorized to move. Furthermore, an application for injunctive or other relief under this provision is one which may properly look to the exercise of a sound judicial discretion ... But the petition here provided no opportunity for the operation of such discretion on the issue of unconscionability since it alleged only that the clause per se was "illegal" and "void as against public policy and contrary to law," theories which, as we have seen, are not consonant with established law. Indeed, the only ground presented to nisi prius was that the clause violated CPLR 5205 (subd. [a]); the petitioner never raised an unconscionability argument until it arrived at the Appellate Division.

As a general proposition, unconscionability, a flexible doctrine with roots in equity ... requires some showing of "an absence of meaningful choice on the part of one of the parties together with contract terms which are unreasonably favorable to the other party" (*Williams v. Walker-Thomas Furniture Co.*, D.C.Cir., 350 F.2d 445, 449). The concept, at least as defined in the Uniform Commercial Code — which both parties seem to agree governs the transactions at issue here — is not aimed at "disturbance of allocation of risks because of superior bargaining power" but, instead, at "the prevention of oppression and unfair surprise" ... To that extent at least it hailed a further retreat of *caveat emptor*.

By its nature, a test so broadly stated is not a simple one, nor can it be mechanically applied (see White and Summers, Handbook on the Uniform

Commercial Code [2d ed], p. 151). So, no doubt precisely because the legal concept of unconscionability is intended to be sensitive to the realities and nuances of the bargaining process, the Uniform Commercial Code goes on to provide: "When it is claimed or appears to the court that the contract or any clause thereof may be unconscionable the parties shall be afforded a reasonable opportunity to present evidence as to its commercial setting, purpose and effect to aid the court in making the determination" (Uniform Commercial Code, § 2-302, subd. 2).

That such evidence may be crucial is made plain too by the drafters' own explication of unconscionability as "whether ... the clauses involved are so one-sided as to be unconscionable under the circumstances existing at the time of the making of the contract" ... And, in the light of this dependency upon the particular circumstances surrounding a transaction, courts and commentators have consistently construed subdivision 2 of § 2-302 to mandate at least the opportunity for an evidentiary hearing ... But as indicated, here a case on unconscionability was not presented to Special Term either in form or substance. Nor was that issue available when raised on appeal for the first time ... Specifically, at no point did the Attorney-General by affidavits from borrowers or otherwise make any factual showing as to such matters as, for instance, deception of borrowers as to the clause's content or existence ... or the presence of language difficulties or illiteracy affecting its execution, or any other reasons that would have made it unlikely that consent was freely and knowingly given (see *Frostifresh Corp. v. Reynoso*, 52 Misc.2d 26, 274 N.Y.S.2d 757), all within the embrace of what is sometimes referred to as "procedural unconscionability" ... Nor, for that matter, in light of the limited scope of its petition, was there occasion to delve into, much less attempt to prove, the now belated assertion of so-called "substantive unconscionability" (see, generally, Leff, Unconscionability and the Code — The Emperor's New Clause, 115 University of Pennsylvania Law Review 485, 487; cf. *Jones v. Star Credit Corp.*, 59 Misc.2d 189, 298 N.Y.S.2d 264 [Wachtler, J.]).

Accordingly, the order of the Appellate Division should be reversed and the petition should be dismissed, without costs, with leave to the petitioner to commence a new proceeding, if it be so advised.

Cooke, C. J., and Jasen, Jones, Wachtler and Meier, JJ., concur. Gabrielli, J., taking no part. Order reversed, etc.

NOTES AND QUESTIONS

1. *Other battles with Avco*: The Attorney General of New York continued to attempt to regulate Avco's collection practices. On June 13, 1980, the New York Times reported:

Avco Financial Services of New York, the state's third largest consumer loan company, was charged by the State Attorney General with illegally abusing and threatening debtors to collect delinquent loans.

Announcing the lawsuit filed in State Supreme Court in Manhattan for recovery of damages for some 200 complainants, Attorney General Robert Abrams said one debtor had been told, "How would you like to be dragged behind a building and killed?"

Avco, which made 50,000 loans totaling $2 million through 50 offices in the state last year, said in response that it met the standards of the State Banking Department and other regulators.[206]

Later it was reported that Avco Financial Services had agreed to pay $85,000 to settle a conflict with the state of New York Attorney General's office over alleged violations of state debt collection laws. If every complainant had an equal claim, $85,000 divided by 200 would yield $425 for those who had appealed to the Attorney General. Does this suggest that the recovery is so trivial as to be not worth the effort?

---

[206]N.Y. Times, June 13, 1980, § II, at 4, col. 6.

Chapter 5

FORMATION OF CONTRACT

With this chapter, our focus shifts to performing contracts. We consider questions such as the effect of a seller's only slightly defective performance. Must the buyer accept it with, perhaps, an offset for its flaws? Or does close count only in horseshoes and hand grenades? Suppose a seller tenders defective goods. Can it have a second chance and cure its performance or does the buyer have a right to call off the deal? Should courts consider whether the buyer really was hurt by the defective tender or whether it wants out only because it can get the goods cheaper? Suppose a seller is almost certain that buyer will not be able to pay for the goods when the day for performance comes. Must seller continue performance or can seller stop unless buyer can offer assurances that it will pay when the time comes?

Before confronting such questions, however, we need to establish familiarity with two opposed models of the contracting process; judicial answers to questions of performance often reflect assumptions about how deals are made. The first model sees the parties' contract as a blueprint for performance. It is assumed that buyers and sellers do or should attempt to fashion an agreement in which they specify obligations very precisely and allocate all the risks of possible contingencies. Contract drafters bring the future back to the present. Since we cannot know the future in advance, the drafter deals with the possibility of a war, a depression, a strike, and so on. Ideally, if something goes wrong as parties perform a contract, all the parties, lawyers, and judges need do is read a written document and discover what is to happen in this event.

The second model acknowledges that many contracts reflect long-term continuing relationships with a rich history that take place in a business and social context. Instead of a magic moment when everything is defined, the contours of the parties' bargain emerge as they perform it through time. While they may have agreed to terms at the outset, everything is always subject to formal or tacit renegotiation. Moreover, those accepting this second model of bargaining processes understand that a written document signed by the parties is not necessarily their bargain-in-fact. For example, the contract may be drafted by elite lawyers at the home office, but the actual agreement is negotiated and performed by people in the field. In this world, we should be surprised when there is no gap between the real deal and the paper deal.

Those who feel more comfortable with the first image of bargaining are likely to solve questions concerning performance by looking to what the parties agreed at the point they made their deal. They will be uneasy when the parties left too much unprovided for. Those who are more comfortable with relational contracts will view written documents signed by the parties as but one factor to consider in solving problems. They will seek fair results in light of the way things turned out, with risk assumption being just one factor among many which are relevant to what is fair.

Because questions of performance often turn on whether the parties made a deal and what its terms were, we must begin with some of the classic dilemmas concerning how courts know whether the parties closed a deal and how they discover what the bargain means. People often communicate in a sloppy fashion. They sign documents that say things that they don't mean. While every bargain rests on what the parties assume about the world, at times buyer and seller assume very different things, or things that turn out to be wrong. Courts must respond to all these situations.

Thus, we turn to issues involving formation and interpretation of contracts. Then we consider performance questions. As we do, we discover that formation and interpretation issues influence the solutions. Finally, we return to unpleasant surprises in a different context. One party discovers she has made a very bad deal and seeks relief, arguing that she shouldn't be required to absorb the losses associated with what has happened.

Formation of Contract: Choice Versus Imposed Liability and Regulation

How does the American legal system legitimates holding people bound to what judges, lawyers, and scholars call contracts. Why do we care? The reasons judges accept as common sense may influence how they decide cases. Judges and lawyers form a community with a common language. Judges want to explain their decisions so that lawyers will understand and accept them. Sometimes other audiences may respond to a judge's explanations. For example, newspapers and television may attack a decision. Judges, as the rest of us, do not like to appear foolish or stupid before any audience.

The relationship between law and legitimacy is unclear. Law contributes something to our view that we live in a just, decent, or tolerable society. Americans tend to regard their legal system as at least acceptable, particularly when they compare it with those found in totalitarian states. It is less clear that Americans honor the results in particular cases. Nonetheless, the legal system itself may have enough prestige so that any norms applied by legal officials seem just. In part, this claim rests on our assumption that the legal system is autonomous enough from other centers of power so that it can apply its procedures, make decisions, and enforce them impartially. Both the King and the Chase Manhattan Bank are under the law. Moreover, legal officials are selected in ways Americans find acceptable. They are experts, selected by Presidents or governors in recognition of their skill or, alternatively, elected and seen as expressing the will of the people. This view suggests that politics should play no role in judicial selection.

Finally, some see particular norms as the law because they naturally flow from legal science, reflect common sense, and are dictated by wise policy choices. We should not, under this view, question the result in a particular case. Experts removed from power and politics have decided. Their decisions reflect legitimate rules.

You probably noticed a few problems with this account. Many, if not most, Americans do not believe that the legal system is autonomous and free from the influence of those who hold power in society. On one hand, some think that legal officials use their power to favor the wealthy and influential. On the other hand, some think those with wealth can play the legal game better even if the rules are applied evenly and fairly by officials. Then, too, some think that a judge is a lawyer who knew the governor. Some see nothing wrong with having a Catholic, a Jew, a Black, and a Woman sit on the highest courts. It is a way of symbolizing that a particular group is both worthy and powerful.

We face a major problem in specifying the link between a claim to legitimacy and the attitude of a particular audience. Most people, after all, know very little about particular laws or the legal system. We can wonder whether those who lose when they come before the courts are impressed by the majesty of the law. Few convicted murderers, for example, comment favorably on the skill with which the judge instructed the jury. Indeed, perhaps the major audience for the law's claims to legitimacy are lawyers. Whatever the impact of law on our views about legitimacy, do these attitudes affect our behavior? Do people obey or disobey law because they think it just or unjust?

Having said all this, we can observe that lawyers and judges do make legitimacy claims. Much of the business of law school consists of studying this rhetoric. Although the legitimacy claim often is assumed, law professors, lawyers and judges exert great effort to show that a rule or procedure reflects some version of the good, the true, and the beautiful. The problem comes when we recognize that each side usually can claim plausibly that a decision in its favor will carry out an important value. If this is true, how do we persuade judges and legislators? How do we predict what they will do? If both sides had equally able lawyers, would all cases end in ties?

We will look at explanations offered for holding or refusing to hold people to obligations which might be called contracts, selecting problems important to modern business. We will also set the stage for the consideration of problems of performing contracts. We will see that the two questions are closely related. Whether or not I have performed my promise often turns on what, if anything, the courts will say that I promised to do.

A. CHOICE, FAULT, OR SOMETHING ELSE?

EMBRY v. HARGADINE, McKITTRICK DRY GOODS CO.

127 Mo.App. 383, 105 S.W. 777 (St. Louis Ct. App. 1907)

GOODE, J.... The appellant was an employee of the respondent company under a written contract to expire December 15, 1903, at a salary of $2,000 per annum. His duties were to attend to the sample department of respondent, of which he was given complete charge. It was his business to select samples for the traveling salesmen of the company, which is a wholesale dry goods concern, to use in selling goods to retail merchants. Appellant contends that on December 23, 1903, he was re-engaged by respondent, through its president, Thos. H. McKittrick, for another year at the same compensation and for the same duties stipulated in his previous written contract. On March 1, 1904, he was discharged, having been notified in February, that on account of the necessity of retrenching expenses, his services and that of some other employees, would no longer be required. The respondent company contends that its president never re-employed appellant after the termination of his written contract and hence that it had a right to discharge him when it chose. The point with which we are concerned requires an epitome of the testimony of appellant and the counter-testimony of McKittrick, the president of the company, in reference to the alleged re-employment. Appellant testified that several times prior to the termination of his written contract on December 15, 1903, he had endeavored to get an understanding with McKittrick for another year, but had been put off from time to time; that on December 23d, eight days after the expiration of said contract, he called on McKittrick, in the latter's office, and said to him that as appellant's written employment had lapsed eight days before, and as there were only a few days between then and the first of January in which to seek employment with other firms, if respondent wished to retain his services longer he must have a contract for another year or he would quit respondent's service then and there; that he had been put off twice before and wanted an understanding or contract at once so that he could go ahead without worry; that McKittrick asked him how he was getting along in his department, and appellant said he was very busy as they were in the height of the season getting men out — had about 110 salesmen on the line and others in preparation; that McKittrick then said: "Go ahead, you're all right; get your men out and don't let that worry you;" that appellant took McKittrick at his word and worked until February 15th without any question in his mind. It was on February 15th that he was notified his services would be discontinued on March 1st. McKittrick denied this conversation as related by appellant and said that when accosted by the latter on December 23d, he (McKittrick) was working on his books in order to get out a report for a stockholders' meeting and when appellant said if he did not get a contract he would leave, that he (McKittrick) said:

Mr. Embry, I am just getting ready for the stockholders' meeting tomorrow, I have no time to take it up now; I have told you before I would not take it up until I had these matters out of the way; you will have to see me at a later time. I said: 'Go back upstairs and get your men out on the road.' I may have asked him one or two other questions relative to the department; I don't remember. The whole conversation did not take more than a minute.

Embry also swore that when he was notified he would be discharged, he complained to McKittrick about it, as being a violation of their contract, and McKittrick said it was due to the action of the board of directors and not to any personal action of his and that others would suffer by what the board had done as well as Embry. Appellant requested an instruction to the jury setting out in substance the conversation between him and McKittrick according to his version and declaring that those facts, if found to be true, constituted a contract between the parties that defendant would pay plaintiff the sum of $2,000 for another year, provided the jury believed from the evidence that plaintiff commenced said work believing he was to have $2,000 for the year's work. This instruction was refused but the court gave another embodying in substance appellant's version of the conversation, and declaring it made a contract "if you (the jury) find both parties thereby intended and did contract with each other for plaintiff's employment for one year from and including December 23, 1903, at a salary of $2,000 per annum." Embry swore that on several occasions when he spoke to McKittrick about employment for the ensuing year, he asked for a renewal of his former contract and that on December 23d, the date of the alleged renewal, he went into Mr. McKittrick's office and told him his contract had expired and he wanted to renew it for a year, having always worked under year contracts. Neither the refused instruction nor the one given by the court embodied facts quite as strong as appellant's testimony, because neither referred to appellant's alleged statement to McKittrick, that unless he was re-employed he would stop work for respondent then and there. It is assigned for error that the court required the jury, in order to return a verdict for appellant, not only to find the conversation occurred as appellant swore, but that both parties intended by such conversation to contract with each other for plaintiff's employment for the year from December, 1903, at a salary of $2,000. If it appeared from the record that there was a dispute between the parties as to the terms on which appellant wanted re-employment, there might have been sound reason for inserting this clause in the instruction; but no issue was made that they split on terms; the testimony of McKittrick tending to prove only that he refused to enter into a contract with appellant regarding another year's employment until the annual meeting of stockholders was out of the way. Indeed, as to the proposed terms McKittrick agrees with Embry; for the former swore as follows: "Mr. Embry said he wanted to know *about the renewal of his contract*; said if he did not have the contract made he would leave." As the two witnesses coincided as to the terms of the proposed re-employment, there was no reason for inserting the above mentioned clause in the instruction in order that it might be settled by the jury whether or not plaintiff, if employed for one year from December 23, 1903, was to be paid $2000 a year. Therefore it remains to determine whether or not this part of the instruction was a correct statement of the law in regard to what was necessary to constitute a contract between the parties; that is to say, whether the formation of a contract by what, according to Embry was said, depended on the intention of both Embry and McKittrick. Or, to put the question more precisely, did what was said constitute a contract of re-employment on the previous terms irrespective of the intention or purpose of McKittrick? Judicial opinion and elementary treatises abound in statements of the rule that to constitute a contract there must be a meeting of the minds of the parties and both must agree to the same thing in the same sense. Generally speaking this may be true; but it is not literally or universally true. That is to say, the inner intention of parties to a conversation subsequently alleged to create a contract, cannot either make a contract of what transpired or prevent one from arising, if the words used were sufficient to constitute a contract. In so far as their intention is an influential element, it is only such intention as the words or acts of the parties indicate; not one secretly cherished which is inconsistent with those words or acts....

In view of those authorities we hold that though McKittrick may not have intended to employ Embry by what transpired between them according to the latter's testimony, yet if what McKittrick said would have been taken by a reasonable man to be an employment, and Embry so understood it, it constituted a valid contract of employment for the ensuing year.

The next question is whether or not the language used was of that character; namely, was such that Embry, as a reasonable man, might consider he was re-employed for the ensuing year on the previous terms, and act accordingly. We do not say that in every instance it would be for the court to pronounce on this question, because, peradventure, instances might arise in which there would be such an ambiguity in the language relied on to show an assent by the obligor to the proposal of the obligee, that it would be for the jury to say whether a reasonable mind would take it to signify acceptance of the proposal.... In *Lancaster v. Elliott*, 28 Mo. App. 86, 92, the opinion, as to the immediate point, reads:

> The interpretation of a contract in writing is always a matter of law for determination by the court, and equally so, upon like principles, is the question what acts and words, in nearly every case, will suffice to constitute an acceptance by one party, of a proposal submitted by the other, so that a contract or agreement thereby becomes matured.

The general rule is that it is for the court to construe the effect of writing relied on to make a contract and also the effect of unambiguous oral words.... However, if the words are in dispute, the question of whether they were used or not is for the jury.... With these rules of law in mind, let us recur to the conversation of December 23d between Embry and McKittrick as related by the former. Embry was demanding a renewal of his contract, saying he had been put off from time to time and that he had only a few days before the end of the year in which to seek employment from other houses, and that he would quit then and there unless he was re-employed. McKittrick inquired how he was getting along with the department and Embry said they (i.e., the employees of the department) were very busy getting out salesmen; whereupon McKittrick said: "Go ahead, you are all right; get your men out and do not let that worry you." We think no reasonable man would construe that answer to Embry's demand that he be employed for another year, otherwise than as an assent to the demand, and that Embry had the right to rely on it as an assent. The natural inference is, though we do not find it testified to, that Embry was at work getting samples ready for the salesmen to use during the ensuing season. Now when he was complaining of the worry and mental distress he was under because of his uncertainty about the future, and his urgent need, either of an immediate contract with respondent, or a refusal by it to make one, leaving him free to seek employment elsewhere, McKittrick must have answered as he did for the purpose of assuring appellant that any apprehension was needless, as appellant's services would be retained by the respondent. The answer was unambiguous, and we rule that if the conversation was according to appellant's version and he understood he was employed, it constituted in law a valid contract of re-employment, and the court erred in making the formation of a contract depend on a finding that both parties intended to make one. It was only necessary that Embry, as a reasonable man, had a right to and did so understand....

The judgment is reversed and the cause remanded. All concur.

NOTES AND QUESTIONS

1. *Individual choice and freedom:* Some see the legitimacy of contract resting on its connection with individual choice. People have rights, and they do not lose them unless they freely choose to do so. However, the court in the *Embry* case abridges Thos. H. McKittrick's freedom. It exposes his business to liability even if, upon retrial, a jury were to find he did not intend to make a contract. Does this mean that assertions about contract and free choice are largely mystification?

Tiersma[1] argues for a different idea of intention. He relies on speech act theory, a widely used approach to the philosophy of language. Offer and acceptance are not matters of expression or manifestation of intent. They are acts that commit a speaker to a particular course of content. Thus, "[l]oosely stated, the speaker must intend to create in the hearer the perception that in saying the words, the speaker is committing himself to a particular proposal." Under this

---

[1]Comment, The Language of Offer and Acceptance: Speech Acts and the Question of Intent, 74 California Law Review 189 (1986).

theory, would the *Embry* case be decided differently? Tiersma asserts it would not. He bases this on the conversational maxims of Grice, a philosopher of language. Most parties will interpret an utterance as being relevant to what went before. Considering the *Embry* case, Tiersma says,

> The primary reason that "Don't worry about it" can constitute acceptance of the employee's implicit offer has to do with Grice's conversational maxim of relevance. A literal interpretation of the employer's statement would not be a relevant answer to the employee's concern. Therefore, this possible interpretation can be eliminated. All that remains is the more idiomatic meaning of the phrase as a promise to dispose of the employee's concern. The employer's response was relevant only as an acceptance.

Does Tiersma's analysis just quoted establish that the employer intended to create in the employee the perception that the employer was committing himself to a year's renewal of the contract?

2. ***Contract as a variety of tort: committing contracts***: In *Hotchkiss v. National City Bank*,[2] Judge Learned Hand said,

> A contract has, strictly speaking, nothing to do with the personal, or individual intent of the parties. A contract is an obligation attached by the mere force of the law to certain acts of the parties, usually words, which ordinarily accompany and represent a known intent. If, however, it were proved by twenty bishops that either party, when he used the words, intended something else than the usual meaning which the law imposes upon them, he would still be held, unless there were some mutual mistake, or something else of the sort. Of course, if it appear by other words, or acts, of the parties, that they attribute a peculiar meaning to such words as they use in the contract, that meaning will prevail, but only by virtue of the other words, and not because of their unexpressed intent.

Hand is expressing what Professor Grant Gilmore called the Holmes-Williston construct. Holmes offered the idea in the late 19th century, and Williston developed it in the early 20th century. It certainly had great influence on the vocabulary of generations of law students. Often they talked about the objective theory of contracts.

> The theory seems to have been ... that, ideally, no one should be liable to anyone for anything. Since the ideal was not attainable, the compromise solution was to restrict liability within the narrowest possible limits. Within these limits, however, liability was to be absolute....

---

[2]200 Fed. 287, 293 (S.D.N.Y. 1911).

[T]he "objective theory of contract" became the great metaphysical solvent — the critical test for distinguishing between the false and the true.... [T]he post-Holmesian "objectivists," led by Williston, made no attempt to argue that their principle had any common law past. Perhaps the attempt would have overtaxed even their own very considerable ingenuity. On the contrary, the emergence and triumph of the "objective theory" was put forward as one of the great accomplishments of recent times — the apprehension of a fundamental truth which had long been hidden in a deep morass of error....

The effect of the application of the objective theory to such areas of law as mistake was of course to narrow the range within which mistake could be successfully pleaded as a defense. That is, it is no longer enough that I was subjectively mistaken, even with respect to a fundamental term of the contract.... With the narrowing of the range of availability of such excuses as mistake, we move toward the ideal of absolute liability which ... was one of the basic ideas of the great theory.[3]

3. *A theory about the rise of objective theory*: Holmes' lectures, "The Common Law," were first published in 1881; Williston's great treatise on the American law of contracts was first published in 1920. Why did an objective theory of contracts appeal to men such as Holmes and Williston? Why were they able to sell it to the elite of the American bar at this period? Professor Morton Horwitz, a legal historian on the Harvard Law School faculty, argues that Holmes and Williston merely reflected a battle largely won earlier. This battle served distinct social ends. Horwitz tells us,

For seventy or eighty years after the American Revolution the major direction of common law policy reflected the overthrow of eighteenth century precommercial and antidevelopmental common law values. As political and economic power shifted to merchant and entrepreneurial groups in the postrevolutionary period, they began to forge an alliance with the legal profession to advance their own interests through a transformation of the legal system.

By around 1850 that transformation was largely complete. Legal rules providing for the subsidization of enterprise and permitting the legal destruction of old forms of property for the benefit of more recent entrants had triumphed. Anticommercial legal doctrines had been destroyed or undermined and the legal system had almost completely shed its eighteenth century commitment to regulating the substantive fairness of economic exchange. Legal relations that had once been conceived of as deriving from

---

[3]Grant Gilmore, The Death of Contract, 14, 42-44, copyright 1974 by the Ohio State University Press. Reprinted by permission.

natural law or custom were increasingly subordinated to the disproportionate economic power of individuals or corporations that were allowed the right to "contract out" of many existing legal obligations. Law, once conceived of as protective, regulative, paternalistic and, above all, a paramount expression of the moral sense of the community, had come to be thought of as facilitative of individual desires and as simply reflective of the existing organization of economic and political power.

This transformation in American law both aided and ratified a major shift in power in an increasingly market-oriented society. By the middle of the nineteenth century the legal system had been reshaped to the advantage of men of commerce and industry at the expense of farmers, workers, consumers, and other less powerful groups within the society. Not only had the law come to establish legal doctrines that maintained the new distribution of economic and political power, but, whenever it could, it actively promoted a legal redistribution of wealth against the weakest groups in the society.

The rise of legal formalism can be fully correlated with the attainment of these substantive legal changes. If a flexible, instrumental conception of law was necessary to promote the transformation of the postrevolutionary American legal system, it was no longer needed once the major beneficiaries of that transformation had obtained the bulk of their objectives. Indeed, once successful, those groups could only benefit if both the recent origins and the foundations in policy and group self-interest of all newly established legal doctrines could be disguised. There were, in short, major advantages in creating an intellectual system which gave common law rules the appearance of being self-contained, apolitical, and inexorable, and which, by making "legal reasoning seem like mathematics," conveyed, "an air ... of ... inevitability" about legal decisions....

Contract law provides another excellent illustration of the deep pressure toward formalism in nineteenth century law. During the first half of the century, legal writers and judges were largely successful in banishing fair price conceptions from the law of contract and in shifting the focus of contract law to the determination of whether there had been a "meeting of the minds." As a result, one of the central problems of the "new" contract law was the development of supposedly nonpolitical criteria for distinguishing between "free" and "unfree" wills, while at the same time barring any substantive inquiry into the equivalency of an exchange, which now had come to be regarded as "subjective" and "political." This proscription against examining "consequences" or "outcomes" eventually led to the creation of a disembodied conception of "unfree" states of mind which measured the impairment of "will" by criteria entirely detached from concrete social or economic forms of coercion....

These efforts during the first half of the nineteenth century to disengage the contract system from substantive criteria of fairness produced internal pressures to generate "objective" and "nonpolitical" doctrinal measures of "free will" and "meeting of the minds." These pressures were generalized still further beginning in the 1850s into an "objective" theory of contract. What most distinguished the "objective" theory was its insistence upon establishing uniform and general rules of law with reference to which contracting parties would be required to shape their conduct. With this change, contract law was no longer conceived of as simply implementing the parties' "wills," but rather its categories were often treated as existing somehow prior to individual bargains.

I discussed earlier how economic pressures toward uniformity and predictability, as well as efforts to restrict the scope of jury discretion, also ultimately contributed to this shift toward formal and objective legal rules. But it is important to see as well that this trend toward uniformity necessarily required doctrines of greater abstraction and generality, which in turn had the effect of detaching contract doctrine from the particularities of individual cases and of creating internal logical pressure to conceive of the law of contract as a system of disembodied logical interrelationships. This tendency throughout the second half of the nineteenth century to seek higher levels of generality and inclusiveness of legal doctrine is one of the more important characteristics associated with the development of legal formalism. One of the most important results of this trend in thought was to prevent particularized equitable inquiries into the circumstances of individual cases and to destroy more particular legal rules in the name of promoting the "rule of law."...

There were, in short, extremely deep and powerful currents which moved American law to formalism after 1850.... A scientific, objective, professional, and apolitical conception of law, once primarily a rhetorical monopoly of a status-hungry elite of legal thinkers, now comes to extend its domain and to infiltrate into the every day categories of adjudication.... For the paramount social condition that is necessary for legal formalism to flourish in a society is for the powerful groups in that society to have a great interest in disguising and suppressing the inevitably political and redistributive functions of law.[4]

Horwitz' positions on many issues have been criticized sharply. For example, Professor A.W.B. Simpson responds,

No doubt certain aspects of contract law pressed on the poor — imprisonment for debt is surely the principal villain here. But ... it was their

---

[4]Morton J. Horwitz, The Rise of Legal Formalism, 19 American Journal of Legal History 251-52, 254, 259, 261-262, 264 (1975).

misfortune to be outside the world in which such luxuries as legal actions at common law or bills in equity much mattered.[5]

Scheiber also questions interpretations that ignore what he sees as the complexities of American history.

> The courts *did not* inexorably devolve advantage upon industrial interests at the expense of agrarian interests (the very dichotomy is inapplicable in the West except on fundamentally different terms). Nor did the courts predictably mobilize either "instrumentalist" or "formalist" doctrine to defend and advance large-scale industrial aggregates. Both judicial defenses of "rights of the public" and judicial surprises, in choosing between contending economic interests, are prominent enough to cast doubt on any simplistic model of unilinear and monolithic doctrinal innovation. There is ample room for agreement that law was often, if not to say usually, mobilized to provide effective subsidies and immunities to heavily-capitalized special interests without leaping to the simplistic corollaries that some scholars have advanced.[6]

Remember that an application of the objective theory favors an employee over an employer in the *Embry* case. Does this, combined with Simpson's and Scheiber's comments, suggest that Horwitz's position can be ignored safely?

4. *Value conflict in contract law*: Modern contract law contains many inconsistent goals. If we accept Horwitz's explanation for the appeal of the objective theory, we also must explain legal realism and its attacks on formalism that began about World War I. We then would have to turn to reactions to realism. Scholars searched for neutral principles for decision in the early 1960s. Law and economics offers another attack on appeals to fairness and case-by-case reactions to situations in the 1970s.

The following excerpts from Professor Macaulay's article attempt to sketch some of the conflicting goals set for contract law. Notice that Macaulay's discussion is empirical and descriptive. Unlike Horwitz, Macaulay does not link any of the approaches he identifies with the interests of particular classes or groups. Nonetheless, do some of the approaches he identifies seem to serve some interests more than others? Might an approach serve manufacturers at one time but, say, consumers at another?

---

[5]Simpson, The Horwitz Thesis and the History of Contract, 46 University of Chicago Law Review 533 (1979).

[6]Harry N. Scheiber, Regulation, Property Rights, and Definition of "The Market": Law and the American Economy, 41 Journal of Economic History 103, 109 (1981). Published by Cambridge University Press.

Private Legislation and the Duty to Read — Business Run by IBM
Machine, the Law of Contracts and Credit Cards
Stewart Macaulay[7]

[A]n analytical scheme I find helpful calls for first separating out the substantive policies that contract and restitution may serve and then identifying at least some of the goals related to the proper or efficient operation of the legal system. For example, we might want our legal system to aid the operation of the insurance industry in order to minimize premium costs (a substantive policy), but we also might want our legal system, insofar as reasonably possible, to reflect the policy choices of a community consensus or those made by an elected legislature rather than those of an appointed judge (a system policy).

Substantive policies primarily can be classified on two dimensions. The first concerns a choice of a market or non-market orientation, in which contract law and restitution can either (a) be tools to facilitate the operation of a market economy — focusing on the needs of those exchanging goods, services, labor and capital or (b) serve to blunt the impact of the unregulated market by refusing to recognize some socially undesirable business practices or by giving aid to people or groups seeking to get out from under onerous contracts. The second dimension concerns the approaches by which contract law and restitution can proceed, tending *toward* either (a) relatively precise general rules or (b) a case-by-case approach. This classification yields four primary categories which must be explained in some detail. The categories, and their somewhat arbitrary names, can be represented as follows:

	Market Goals	Other than Market Goals
Generalizing approach ("rules")	a. market functioning policy	c. social or economic planning policy
Particularistic approach ("case-by-case")	b. transactional policy	d. relief-of-hardship policy

a. *Market functioning policy* calls for rules of general application in relatively specific terms which minimize (but never eliminate) the creative role of judge and jury or administrators. Predictable law is to be preferred to results that satisfy in particular cases. Thus the parties can consider the impact of contract law both in planning their bargains and in settling disputes. Legal results will not turn on vague abstractions such as "good faith" but on specific conduct such as signing a contract. In addition to certainty, the rules should tend to reward

---

[7] 19 Vanderbilt Law Review 1051, 1056-65 (1966)

rational assessment of risks in the market and penalize unbusiness-like conduct. One can usefully identify at least three products of market functioning policy: increased self-reliance, rewards to the crafty, and advantages to the operation of bureaucratic organizations.

The duty to read in a fairly strict form carries out the substantive goal. The legal system should enforce contracts "as written" and ignore pleas that one party did not read or understand, that the parties agreed that some of the written terms would not apply or that additional ones which were never reduced to writing would apply, and that the words used should be read in some unusual fashion, or in light of some general abstraction such as "reasonableness." On the basis of common sense but not much evidence, some have assumed that this tack will promote self-reliance. If one knows he will be legally bound to what he signs, he will take care to protect himself (or so it is said). And this would be a good thing. People will recognize risks, allocate them in their bargains and plan to deal with them rationally. As a result, more bargains will approach the economists' ideal where both leave the bargaining table in a better position than when the negotiations began. Moreover, disputes during the life of the transaction should tend to be minimized since the process of reading and understanding should make clear who is to do what and who is to take what loss if a particular risk occurs. Also where the legal result is clearly that documents will mean what they say, there is less chance that in settlement negotiations one party's rights must be discounted because of the risk of what a jury might do or because of delay.

Such rules reward those who plan and are careful. In one view those who can drive the best bargains, short of gross fraud, are entitled to their winnings. Perhaps one who can slip into a contract with terms highly favorable to himself which are undetected by the other party, is to be praised for his skill rather than censured. This is just good salesmanship. In this view, a bargain is not an exchange of mutual advantage but a game where each party is to maximize his own gains at the expense of the other. Some may feel that the ability to do well in this game is a skill to be rewarded. A strict duty-to-read rule often will help supply this reward.

Another product of market functioning policy — advantages to the operation of bureaucratic organizations — often derives from people being treated as if they had read and understood a written contract even when it is probable they have not done so. Large economic organizations frequently promulgate rules to govern their exchanges with other organizations and individuals. Typically these rules are cast, or can be cast, in the form of a contract. The other unit's representative or the other individual signs a printed form document or accepts a contractual symbol (say, delivery of a document or goods) although he has little chance or incentive to read, understand, bargain to change the rules or do any or all of these things. Larger firms operate this way for a number of reasons. They must deal through a corps of agents in a myriad of transactions. As a result, there is a need to standardize and formalize procedures. On one hand, the large organization must control its agents who deal with the outside world and limit their power to "give the company away." These agents are under many pressures to treat their customers as individuals and tailor the particular deal to suit their customers' needs; most obvious is the pressure to make sales to earn commissions or promotions. Also, "the customer is always right" in the salesman's world. A rigid form contract which the customer must sign without alteration often is thought to be an efficient way to exercise control over salesmen. The customer is "on notice" of the salesman's limited authority, and the firm wants to avoid being legally bound to expectations its salesman has created by his conduct that are inconsistent with company policy. On the other hand, the written document signed by the customer becomes the obligation within the larger organization because of the problems of internal communication. It specifies what must be produced or shipped, and it indicates the full extent of future payments to be received and contingent obligations assumed. If a salesman has made a promise inconsistent with the formal written contract which is highly standardized, it is difficult to communicate this to those who must perform and to those who must make plans based on cash flow and risk assumption. Even if the inconsistent promise is communicated, it poses a problem for a rational bureaucratic organization which tends to thrive on routine. Large organizations are helped if they can control and plan their exposure to risks; if they can do so, their accounting and pricing will be more accurate, and they will not have to set up large reserves to cover a host of unpredictable contingencies. Arguably, this kind of certainty will foster their activities in the market which in turn should yield more jobs and more products at lower prices. A rather strict duty to read, rather than attacking the balance of economic power in the society, supports the operations of large organizations that have this power. This tends to promote rational business affairs, whatever the impact on the individual who assumed he could rely on what he was told rather than what he signed....

Usually these bureaucratic considerations are coupled with the self-reliance idea — the large organization can deal through standardized forms and the prudent individual will protect himself by reading and taking appropriate action — although at times the likelihood of self protection is slim indeed. Occasionally, bureaucratic policy is coupled with a requirement designed to help self-reliance. For example, a Virginia statute demands that a written contract be set in a certain size type to be legally enforceable, the Uniform Commercial Code requires some warranty disclaimers to be conspicuous to be effective.

b. *Transactional policy*, the second policy category, also seeks to aid the operation of the market, but with a case-by-case strategy rather than by rules that ignore particular circumstances. The courts ought to take steps to carry out the particular transaction brought before them — they should discover the bargain-in-fact and enforce it with appropriate remedies cut to fit the facts of the case. If this discovery is not possible, the court should work out a result involving the least disruption of plans and causing the least amount of reliance loss in light of the situation at the time of the dispute. In short, courts should seek to implement the "sense of the transaction," and thus solve the problem in the particular case in market terms — assumption of the risk, reasonable reliance, and so on.

Transactional policy calls for a duty to read and understand only where the one who has failed to do this is responsible for misleading the other into believing that the document has been read and approved or that the careless one is willing to sign and assume the risk of whatever might be found in the document. Suppose seller sends buyer an offer quoting a price in a letter which also very clearly spells out a number of conditions the seller says are most important to him. The buyer reads the first few sentences of the letter and the price quoted but not the seller's important conditions. The buyer writes on the bottom margin of the seller's letter, "We accept your offer," and signs it; he then mails this back to the seller who begins production of the items in question. The buyer later wants to back out and asserts he did not read the seller's conditions and would not have agreed to them if he had. The buyer has been negligent in conveying his agreement resulting in disappointed plans and at least the probability of a good deal of reliance loss. A court following a transactional approach would treat the buyer *as if* he had read and understood the seller's letter. But the decision would turn on the rather extreme facts of the case — the buyer's communication was careless and caused either very probable or actual injury.

Perhaps more often transactional policy will call for overturning or modifying a written document (by reforming or construing it) in the light of the bargain-in-fact of the parties. While a case can be made for self-reliance, part of decent social and business conduct is trust. In many negotiation situations all of the pressures push for friendly gestures rather than a suspicious line-by-line analysis of the writing. The buyer of home siding can believe the president of the home remodeling company when he says his siding will not rust or crack; the buyer does not have to parse the text of the lengthy and technical printed form and spot the integration clause at his peril. In cases such as this, the writing was drafted to run counter to the likely agreement-in-fact. If a court is seeking the actual sense of the transaction, it will not let such a writing get in its way....

c. *Social planning policies* can be reflected in contracts and restitution, as well. In one sense, rather than enforcing the bargain that was made, in this third type of policy the courts will enforce the bargain which the parties should have made. Conversely, the courts may refuse to take any action when the actual bargain is found offensive. This policy is something of a catchall, as social planning can call for a variety of things ranging from wealth redistribution to the regulation, or even promotion, of particular types of people, industries or transactions. The most obvious examples involve a change in the market context by removing certain types of bargains from the kinds that will be enforced by the legal system or by requiring or prohibiting particular terms in some bargains. Again, this is a generalizing approach stressing specific rules, so it parallels market functioning policy in strategy — but the goals of the two are very different since social planning policies, by definition, seek to blunt the impact of the market.

A social planning rule relevant to our topic would be one that said certain classes of people could not be held to contracts they signed or accepted, despite their careless failure to read and protect themselves. One could conceive of a rule protecting such people as consumers, illiterates, those of limited mental ability or minors. In effect, the power of a minor to disaffirm even contracts that he has read and understood is such a rule. Since, in theory, the minor cannot guard his own interests, the legal system protects him from his own carelessness and improvident bargains. Consumers may get some of the same treatment under Uniform Commercial Code § 2-719's provisions on limiting remedies for breach of warranty; perhaps consumers need not read and protect themselves since limitations of liability for personal injury caused by a breach of warranty are prima facie unconscionable. It is difficult to offer many examples of this kind of social planning rule since the legal system has preferred a more case-by-case (relief of hardship) approach, rather than letting a whole class of people out of certain kinds of contracts. On the other hand, social planning goals often enter as the price for following the bureaucratic type of market functioning policy. For example, the standard fire insurance policy is set by statute in many states. One side of the coin involves the setting of terms deemed fair to the consumer by the legislature — removing the insurance contract from the area of self-reliance and the exercise of market power. The other side of the coin, however, involves telling insurance companies that if they follow the statute, certain practices have been validated. An insurance company can know where it stands, and this certainty may be extremely important to it. The insurers get certainty at the cost of following fair terms imposed by the legal system.

d. *Relief-of-hardship* is the fourth policy. It calls for the legal system to let one party out of his bargain in exceptional cases where enforcement would be unduly harsh, or, where the content of the bargain is in doubt, to place the burden on the party best able to spread the loss or absorb it. This case-by-case approach is based not upon considerations of market functioning or protecting actual expectations but upon ethical ideals and emotional reactions to the plight of the underdog, to pressing an advantage too far, to making too much profit, or to inequality of resources. To a great extent, this is the policy that is not expressed openly in contract doctrine, but courts can construe language and stretch the innocent misrepresentation or mistake doctrines to help out when the facts are particularly appealing. When done with a deft hand, a relief-of-hardship approach will leave little trace of a precedent to embarrass the court in the next case, where the facts are not quite so appealing.

It is hard to offer a pure example of this policy in operation, but it can be suggested that a good deal of it lurks in the insurance release cases where a duty to read and understand sometimes is and sometimes is not applied. Also the Supreme Court of Wisconsin in several cases has stressed the lack of education of the person seeking to be relieved from a written contract he signed or accepted. On one hand, this factor tracks with transactional policy and the degree of care one could expect from a particular individual. Arguably, an illiterate is not responsible for misleading one who knows the illiterate cannot read the document he signed. But on the other hand, the party seeking to uphold the contract, especially the home office of a corporation that deals through salesmen in the field, may have no way accurately to gauge the education and literacy of the man who signed the printed form. Its expectations and potential reliance remain despite the literacy of the man it dealt with. Still the factor may lead to the overthrow of the written treaty. We can speculate that the inability to read and understand is correlated with a generally low socio-economic status, and such people may be the best candidates for relief-of-hardship in the eyes of many.

B. THE RISK OF AMBIGUITY OR MISUNDERSTANDING

People make a number of different kinds of mistakes in entering contracts. Sometimes the law lets a mistaken party back out. Sometimes it doesn't. A true Holmes-Williston objective theory draws sharp lines. The cases, however, are blurred.

Suppose I write a letter saying that I will sell my house to you for $200,000. You accept my offer. However, I own two houses. One is located in the city where I work. The other is located about 100 miles away in a resort area. I always refer to the house in the city as "my house." I call the one in the resort area "my cottage." However, the cottage is an architect designed large house built on the shore of a beautiful lake. I thought I was selling my house in the city. You, however, thought you were buying my house in the resort area. You did not know that I usually called one the house and the other the cottage. If courts are concerned with my free choice, they will hesitate before deciding that I sold a house I did not want to sell. Of course, I did use language that could refer to two different structures, but this is not the same thing as choosing to sell my house. Nonetheless, you also made a choice, and my letter prompted you to create certain expectations. A court cannot simultaneously protect both my choice and yours.

Suppose, to change the case, both of us correctly understand my letter to refer to my house in the city. You accept my offer to sell the house for $200,000. Later you discover that the house is worth no more than $150,000. If you had known this, you would not have bought it. Is this kind of error different from that suggested by our conflicting interpretations of the term "house"?

Suppose, instead, I submit a bid to you. I propose to do all the electrical work involved in constructing a large building which you are erecting. When I was compiling the information needed to make my bid, the piece of paper on which my assistant had calculated the cost of wiring the third floor fell into my wastebasket. I did not notice this. As a result, I neglected to take the cost of the work on the third floor into my calculations. My bid is much lower than it would have been had I not made a mistake. Is this a kind of mistake different from those involved in the examples about ambiguity and value of an asset?

Suppose we applied an objective theory of contract to all of these cases. A reasonable person hearing or reading the offer and acceptance would assume a deal had been closed. Outward manifestations look as if there were a deal. All of the mistakes are subjective. To recognize them, a court would have to look past the form of bargain to the actual situation. We can defend holding seller and buyer to a contract in all three cases. Such a rule promotes reliance and protects reasonable expectations. Such a rule punishes mistakes and thus offers an incentive for care to avoid them. The person making an error will be taught a lesson. Moreover, others learning of the result will shape up or take the consequences. Not insignificantly, this rule makes the court's job much easier too. We will often hear this song played loudly in the cases. However, there also is a powerful countertheme which we cannot ignore, reflecting our sensitivity to the harsh consequences of applying such an approach.

1. CHOICE AND THE CARELESS USE OF LANGUAGE

What is the relation between what is ethical and what is legal? Keep this question in mind as you consider the legal rules in the materials that follow. We begin with one of the classics of contracts folklore. Remember as you read the opinion, the objective theory is still largely in the future.

RAFFLES v. WICHELHAUS[8]

2 Hurl. & C. 906, 159 Eng. Rep. 375 (Ct. of Exchequer 1864)

[The plaintiff sued the defendant for failing to accept delivery of 125 bales of Surat cotton, pursuant to a contract which specified that defendant was to buy cotton "to arrive ex 'Peerless' from Bombay." Defendant argued for dismissal of the claim on the ground that there were two ships named Peerless, both bringing cotton from Bombay, and that it appeared that the plaintiff intended to *sell* the cotton which was on a Peerless which was to leave Bombay in December, while the defendant intended to *buy* cotton on a Peerless which was to sail in October. The defendant had refused to accept the cotton tendered by the plaintiff.]

[The report of the case begins with Milward arguing for the plaintiff.] ...

The contract was for the sale of a number of bales of cotton of a particular description, which the plaintiff was ready to deliver. It is immaterial by what ship the cotton was to arrive, so that it was a ship called the "Peerless." The words "to arrive ex 'Peerless,'" only mean that if the vessel is lost on the

---

[8]English opinions can be difficult to read. In order to focus your attention on the substantive issue, we offer an edited version of the opinion, with some clarifications in [...] which don't appear in the original report. Purists may consult the original.

voyage, the contract is to be at an end. [At this point, Lord Chief Baron Pollock interrupted: "It would be a question for the jury whether both parties meant the same ship called the 'Peerless.'"] That would be so if the contract was for the sale of a ship called the "Peerless"; but it is for the sale of cotton on board a ship of that name. [Pollock interrupted again: "The defendant only bought that cotton which was to arrive by a particular ship. It may as well be said, that if there is a contract for the purchase of certain goods in warehouse A., that is satisfied by the delivery of goods of the same description in warehouse B.] In that case there would be goods in both warehouses; here it does not appear that the plaintiff had any goods on board the other "Peerless." [At this point, Baron Martin chimed in: "It is imposing on the defendant a contract different from that which he entered into." Baron Pollock added: "It is like a contract for the purchase of wine coming from a particular estate in France or Spain, where there are two estates of that name."] The defendant has no right to contradict by parol evidence a written contract good upon the face of it. He does not impute any misrepresentation or fraud, but only says that he fancied the ship was a different one. Intention is of no avail, unless stated at the time of the contract. [Baron Pollock again:. "One vessel sailed in October and the other in December."] The time of sailing is no part of the contract.

[Mellish, who was arguing the case for the defendant, then began to argue for defendant.] There is nothing on the face of the contract to shew that any particular ship called the "Peerless" was meant; but the moment it appears that two ships called the "Peerless" were about to sail from Bombay there is a latent ambiguity, and parol evidence may be given for the purpose of shewing that the defendant meant one "Peerless," and the plaintiff another. That being so, there was no *consensus ad idem*, and therefore no binding contract. [At this point, apparently the Court had heard enough, and Mellish was instructed he need not continue.]

PER CURIAM. *There must be judgment for the defendants....*

NOTES AND QUESTIONS

1. *Legal history*: Professor A.W.B. Simpson, in his paper "Contracts for Cotton to Arrive," concluded that traditional contracts scholarship has misinterpreted the *Raffles* case. Accepting Simpson's research and conclusions, the conventional interpretation of the case has a life of its own (like *Hadley v. Baxendale*). It is a part of American, and probably common law, legal culture. You can talk to most lawyers and judges about the two ships named *Peerless*, and they will know what you are talking about; most would not remember that there was no opinion in the case.

2. *Holmes' explanation of the Raffles case*: Melish's argument, which seems to have been accepted by the court, was that subjectively plaintiff and defendant were thinking of different ships although they used the same word. Thus, there

was "no consensus ad idem," or meeting of the minds. Holmes, as we have seen, was the great advocate of objective approaches in the common law. He struggled to explain *Raffles v. Wichelhaus*. Does his explanation seem convincing?

> The defendant agreed to buy, and the plaintiff agreed to sell, a cargo of cotton, "to arrive ex Peerless from Bombay." There were two such vessels sailing from Bombay, one in October, the other in December. The plaintiff meant the latter, the defendant the former. It was held that the defendant was not bound to accept the cotton. It is commonly said that such a contract is void, because of mutual mistake as to the subject matter, and because the parties did not consent to the same thing. But this way of putting it seems to me misleading. The law has nothing to do with the actual state of the parties' minds. In contract, as elsewhere, it must go by externals, and judge parties by their conduct. If there had been but one "Peerless," and the defendant has said "Peerless" by mistake, meaning "Peri," he would have been bound. The true ground of the decision was not that each party meant a different thing from the other, as is implied by the explanation which has been mentioned, but that each said a different thing. The plaintiff offered one thing, the defendant expressed his assent to another.[9]

Professor Eisenberg[10] says,

> Holmes had it precisely backward; the result in *Peerless* is correct, not because the parties *said* different things, but because they *meant* different things. Where the parties subjectively attach materially different but equally reasonable meanings to their expressions, the governing rule should be that neither is liable for the other's expectation damages. This rule does not conflict with the principle of fault, because either both parties are fault-free or both are equally at fault. Nor does it significantly impair the security of transactions, because its application rests on the existence of two meanings of an expression that are equally reasonable under all the circumstances — a condition that is objective, relatively unusual, and difficult to prove.

Do you find Justice Holmes or Professor Eisenberg more convincing?

3. *The Restatement (Second) of Contracts and the Raffles case*: The modern statement of the rule follows neither the 1864 opinion nor Holmes. You should consult, at this point, § 20 (Effect of Misunderstanding) and § 201 (Whose Meaning Prevails) of the Restatement (Second) of Contracts in the statutory supplement.

---

[9]O.W. Holmes, Jr., The Common Law 309 (Little, Brown and Co., 1881).

[10]Eisenberg, The Responsive Model of Contract Law, 36 Stanford Law Review 1107, 1123 (1984).

In *Lamb Plumbing & Heating Co. v. Kraus-Anderson of Minneapolis, Inc.*,[11] Lamb sued a general contractor for the value of work done on a large project which Lamb said was not covered by its bid but which the general contractor had demanded Lamb do. The general contractor learned of a problem in the specifications before bids were submitted. Another subcontractor pointed out that different interpretations of the specifications were possible concerning which the subcontractor was to furnish and install certain valves. The general contractor notified several mechanical subcontractors it knew were likely to bid on the job that the mechanical contractor must supply and install the valves. Plaintiff had obtained the plans and specifications on its own, and the general contractor did not know it would bid. Plaintiff reasonably interpreted the contract documents as not requiring it to supply and install the valves. Its officials did not see the ambiguity in the contract documents. It submitted a bid on this basis, and the general awarded it the contract. The general demanded Lamb install the valves, Lamb did this, and now sues for extra compensation for work beyond that required by the contract. Under the Restatement (Second) of Contracts §§ 20, 201, how should a court decide this case? What more, if anything, do you need to know to answer this question?

4. *Professor Sharp and carelessness in communication*: Professor Malcolm Sharp offered an explanation for the position later taken in the Restatement (Second) of Contracts. Essentially, he argued that a promise is a dependable statement about the statement-maker's future behavior that may predictably lead to reliance by the person to whom it is made. The actual intentions of the maker are not important. What is important is that language be used carefully, and that losses resulting from the careless use (or understanding) of language be shifted to the person who has been careless. Since our social system is largely built on the protection of private property interests, one must protect those whose business interests suffer as the result of the carelessness of others. Analogizing losses arising from confusion in business situations to losses arising from automobile accidents, Sharp suggests that loss can intelligibly be allocated in terms of fault. That is, one can analyze contractual liability in terms of fault rather than consent. One can rely on an analysis of the meaning of the language used measured against what is "more or less normal in the business community" rather than against the actual intentions of either party to the communication.

> It will be noted that we have now said that care must be used by both parties to communications. If the promisor is careful and the promisee careless, the promisor's understanding will control, in the event of misunderstanding. If both are careful or both careless, neither understanding

---

[11]296 N.W.2d 859 (S. Ct. Minn. 1980).

will control, and there will be no effective communication in the event of misunderstanding.[12]

Does Professor Sharp's explanation of promissory liability support Professor Horwitz' position? Does it make a substantial change in the claim for legitimacy one puts forward for contract law? Has Sharp reduced contract to a specific application of tort — liability for the negligent use of language? Does this matter?

Part of Sharp's position is that a person hearing or relying on what she thinks is a promise must be justified or reasonable. Barnett[13] asserts that this does no more than pose the crucial question it is supposed to answer. He says,

> ... whether a person has "reasonably" relied on a promise depends on what most people would (or ought to) do. We cannot make this assessment independently of the legal rule in effect in the relevant community, because what many people would do in reliance on a promise is crucially affected by their perception of whether or not the promise is enforceable....
>
> Unlike the subject of the prediction required by foreseeability analysis in tort law — the physical consequences that follow from physical actions — the subject of the prediction required by foreseeability analysis in contract law is the actions of a self-conscious person. A prediction that a promise can reasonably be expected to induce reliance by a promisee or a third party will unavoidably depend upon whether the promisee or third party believes that reliance will be legally protected. The legal rule itself cannot be formulated based on such a prediction, however, without introducing a practical circularity into the analysis....
>
> In short, a person, rather than being entitled to legal enforcement because reliance is justified, is justified in relying on those commitments that will be legally enforced.

Does Barnett's objection require us to disregard Sharp's position? What does Barnett assume about bargaining? Where does he get his data?

5. *Other theories of liability*: Choice and fault are not the only possible principles for decision in contracts cases. We could frame rules designed to support the market or the process of contracting. Is the following case an illustration of such a rule?

---

[12]Malcolm Pitman Sharp, Promissory Liability I, 7 University of Chicago Law Review 1, 4-7 (1939).

[13]Barnett, A Consent Theory of Contract, 86 Columbia Law Review 269, 275 (1986).

2. FLAT RULES TO ALLOCATE LOSSES

WPC ENTERPRISES, INC. v. UNITED STATES

323 F.2d 874 (Ct.Claims 1964)

DAVIS, J. This is a study in the toils of ambiguity. The parties put their names to a contract which, on the point crucial to this lawsuit, could reasonably be read in two conflicting fashions. Each signatory seized in its own mind upon a different one of these contradictory versions. Compounding that confusion, they discussed the issue with each other in such a way that each thought, but this time without good reason, it had obtained the other's acquiescence in its chosen reading. The impasse became unmistakably plain when it was too late. Our task is to determine on whom should fall the risk of such mutually reinforced obscurity.

The Government set out to procure, through bids, a large number of complex generator sets — called the MD-3 set — used to calibrate the electronic systems of the B-47 and other aircraft and to start the engines when an electric starter is required. Beech Aircraft Corporation, which had previously made these elaborate devices for the Air Force on a negotiated basis, had prepared specifications and drawings of various of the component parts which the Government acquired and incorporated in the bid invitations. Plaintiff was the low bidder, lower than Beech and another company which had also provided the sets under a negotiated contract. After a period of consideration and some discussion, the award was made to plaintiff and it performed the contract as required by the Government.

The only dispute now before us is whether five components of these generator sets had to be manufactured by (or with the authorization of) certain named companies, as the Government urges, or whether plaintiff was entitled under the contract to furnish identical components made by other firms (presumably at lower prices). After the award, defendant insisted that the products of the specified companies had to be furnished. Plaintiff complied but, claiming that this directive constituted a contractual change, sought review by the Board of Contract Appeals under the Changes and Disputes articles. The Board turned down the appeal on the ground that plaintiff had been told before the award of the defendant's position and had acquiesced.

For the five components now involved, the textual provisions of the specifications (borrowed from Beech) gave general descriptions, without naming any manufacturer; however, the drawings (also from Beech) listed the part numbers given to the item by a particular firm and declared that manufacturer was the "approved source," or that the component "may be purchased" from that company, or indicated "make from" a part furnished by a particular company, or simply said that the component was a certain part number of a specific firm. There are also other, slighter, indications of contractual meaning on which the parties rely; the details are set forth in the findings.

Each side urges that its position is sustained by the invitation as a whole — without any need to go beyond the bounds of the contractual instruments. The defendant stresses the references to specific part numbers, designated by particular fabricators, as necessarily showing that only parts made under the aegis of that manufacturer would be acceptable; this use of exact part numbers is said to be equivalent to a mandatory direction to incorporate only those very items. Defendant also points out that: (i) the drawings and specifications for the five components were not adequate for a new manufacturer to make those articles in the relatively short time allotted for completion of the procurement; (ii) the defendant was satisfied with components made from parts supplied by the named manufacturers (because they had been fully tested in the past), but would be required before acceptance to test components made by others; and (iii) this burdensome and time-consuming testing would not be practicable within the scheduled period of delivery. It should have been clear, defendant concludes, that the contract called for items supplied by or through the specific companies named in the drawings. (Defendant's witnesses testified to this effect before the Board and at the trial in this court.)

The plaintiff, on the other hand, emphasizes the lack of express mandatory language in the references to particular manufacturers for the five disputed components — in contrast to certain other components which the specifications very plainly declared "shall be" or "shall consist of" an identified part made by a named manufacturer. A command to use only materials or elements made by a specific firm is not frequent in government procurement; it can be expected to be phrased explicitly and not left to inference. Moreover, the references to particular part numbers are not read as mandatory because of a specification provision (labeled "Identification of Parts") which stated:

> *Beech and vendor part numbers will be shown on all items except those items supplied by other than Beech Aircraft Corporation or vendors to Beech. On items supplied by other than present sources Beech part numbers will be used with a suffix to indicate a different supplier.*

To plaintiff, this clause implicitly authorized the use of identical components made by other companies than those named in the Beech drawings. It thought that it could obtain such qualified substitutes by combining the knowledge gained from three sources: the drawings and specifications (insufficient though they might be); a careful break-down of the sample models supplied plaintiff by the defendant; and general engineering competence. Plaintiff was satisfied that the proper components could be produced in this way within the time allowed. (The contractor's position was likewise supported by evidence before the Board of Contract Appeals.)

This summary of the opposing contentions is enough to show that no sure guide to the solution of the problem can be found within the four corners of the contractual documents. As with so many other agreements, there is something for each party and no ready answer can be drawn from the texts alone. Both plaintiff's and defendant's interpretations lie within the zone of reasonableness; neither appears to rest on an obvious error in drafting, a gross discrepancy, or an inadvertent but glaring gap; the arguments, rather, are quite closely in balance. It is precisely to this type of contract that this court has applied the rule that if some substantive provision of a government-drawn agreement is fairly susceptible of a certain construction and the contractor actually and reasonably so construes it, in the course of bidding or performance, that is the interpretation which will be adopted — unless the parties' intention is otherwise affirmatively revealed....

This rule is fair both to the drafters and to those who are required to accept or reject the contract as proffered, without haggling. Although the potential contractor may have some duty to inquire about a major patent discrepancy, or obvious omission, or a drastic conflict in provisions ... he is not normally required (absent a clear warning in the contract) to seek clarification of any and all ambiguities, doubts, or possible differences in interpretation. The Government, as the author, has to shoulder the major task of seeing that within the zone of reasonableness the words of the agreement communicate the proper notions — as well as the main risk of a failure to carry that responsibility. If the defendant chafes under the continued application of this check, it can obtain a looser rein by a more meticulous writing of its contracts and especially of the specifications. Or it can shift the burden of ambiguity (to some extent) by inserting provisions in the contract clearly calling upon possible contractors aware of a problem-in-interpretation to seek an explanation before bidding....

If there were nothing more, the case would end here with a ruling for the plaintiff. But the defendant argues, and the Board of Contract Appeals found, that before the award was made or the contract signed the plaintiff learned the Government's view of the disputed point and accepted that position....

At the trial in this court, Commissioner McConnaughey had the benefit, with respect to the pre-award meetings between the parties, of testimony by Sugarman (who did not appear before the Board) and of other representatives of both sides, as well as of certain documentary materials (notably an internal memorandum by a Government contracting official made after the December 19, 1956 meeting with Sugarman). He also had the evidence before the Board.... [W]e agree with the Trial Commissioner that (i) both parties became aware of the other's interpretation; (ii) neither acquiesced knowingly in the other's interpretation; (iii) both thought, however, that the other had acquiesced; (iv) without either having reasonable grounds for so thinking; and, finally, that (v) neither took the proper steps to clarify the pertinent terms of the transaction until after the award was made. On both sides ambiguous utterance was piled on unwarranted assumption and laced together by unspoken premise. In the end, the Government officials thought they had made it quite clear that the named manufacturers would have to be used for all components, while the plaintiff's people felt that they had successfully stood their ground at least as to these five components. Both were wholly wrong in their understanding of the other's understanding. The discussions had been one prolonged minuet of cross-purposes.

In these circumstances should the onus of the original ambiguity in the specifications still rest on the defendant? We can see no other conclusion. As the author of the defect in the drafting which led plaintiff to the reasonable supposition that it could obtain the five components elsewhere than from the named companies, the Government was under the affirmative obligation (if it wished its own view to prevail) to clarify the meaning of the contract in definitive fashion before the plaintiff was bound. It did make such an attempt, and it did reveal its own view. But when the plaintiff demurred the Government did not adequately indicate that it stood steadfast by its announced opinion. There was a fatal insufficiency in the defendant's effort to communicate to plaintiff that the contract was to be interpreted as the Government understood it. Largely because of this lapse, the plaintiff was left with the mistaken impression that the defendant, rather than insisting, would accept plaintiff's rendering of the contract. The Government, in a word, was very lax in seeing the matter through. Since the burden of clarification was the defendant's, it must bear the risk of an insufficient attempt, even though the plaintiff's obtuseness likewise contributed to the continuance of the misunderstanding. If there had been no communication by defendant to plaintiff between the receipt of the bids and the making of the award, the defendant would have had to suffer the consequences of its poorly drafted specifications. The ineffective attempt to put things right does not place the defendant in a better position. Only an adequate effort to reach the plaintiff's mind could have that result.

Two objections may be made to our taking this ground. The inconclusive discussions between the parties show, it may be said, that there was no "meeting of the minds" on the issue which concerns us, and therefore no valid contract. There was no subjective coming-together, it is true, but an enforceable agreement came into being nevertheless. The design of the contract can be picked from the terms and words of the invitation, objectively read with the aid of rules of contract construction (which are distillates of the common experience and the common sense of justice). It is a normal characteristic of the class of cases in which the courts have held ambiguities against the drafter that the parties' minds have failed to meet on the specific point in dispute. That gap has not been permitted to swallow the whole contract except perhaps where the gulf is far closer to the bounds of the entire consensual perimeter than here. For a contract to exist there does not have to be, and rarely is, a subjective "meeting of the minds" all along the line....

The other objection is that the plaintiff is bound by the opposing view of the contract because it twice extended the defendant's time to make the award (on February 8 and 18, 1957) after the Air Force's representatives had told plaintiff of their attitude. This contention must be rejected for the reason given above. Although it had the burden, the defendant simply did not make it clear enough that it stood by its position despite the plaintiff's disagreement. When the latter extended the time for the award it did not comprehend that the Government was insisting on its own construction. This state of affairs was attributable, in substantial measure, to defects in the defendant's course of communication to plaintiff on the subject of the source of the five components. Plaintiff was also at fault, but the risk of a failure to clarify lay largely upon the Government and could have been averted only by a more sufficient effort than was made.

We hold, therefore, that the defendant was wrong in demanding that only products of (or authorized by) the named manufacturers could be used for the five components. The contract did not so require. The issue of the amount of damages or recovery has not been tried and we are not called upon to pass upon any aspects of that question. We leave all such problems to the trial under Rule 38(c), including the issue of which party has the burden of showing that the components plaintiff planned to use would or would not have been available, and would or would not have qualified under this contract.

The plaintiff is entitled to recover and judgment is entered to that effect....

NOTES AND QUESTIONS

1. *Limits on the rule of thumb*: The Court of Claims has been unwilling to resolve all ambiguities in favor of the contractor. In *National By-Products, Inc. v. United States*,[14] the Court refused to apply the rule of the *WPC* case, even though the parties had "two contrary understandings of the 'deal' [which] were both objectively reasonable in the totality of the circumstances." The court noted that, "Here, there was no root fault on the part of the Government from which the later misunderstanding flowered." The Court commented,

> The truth is, we suppose, that, here as in so many dealings, both parties talked in too-vague generalities and refrained from putting the precise, pointed queries which would have exposed the unresolved ambiguity. Each may have been reluctant to ask the exact question or to detail meticulously his own understanding for fear that precision would be detrimental to his interest or would destroy the whole transaction. In any event, their words flew across the room without ever colliding. Both were responsible for the failure to clarify, but even so we are inclined to see the plaintiff as the party with the greater responsibility since it was seeking to pin a contractual obligation on another. The company's understanding is not flatly contradicted by the documents, but neither is it at all spelled out in those writings. In would be natural to tie down through explicit inquiry that those unclear papers embodied the large-scale undertaking plaintiff envisaged.

---

[14]405 F.2d 1256 (Ct. Claims 1969).

2. *Another rule of thumb*: Suppose a seller offers goods for $2.10 each in a telegram. An employee of the telegraph company mistakenly sends the offer as one for $2.00 each. Buyer accepts the offer of items at $2.00 each. Neither seller nor buyer can hold the telegraph company because of federal regulations governing its liability. Nonetheless, is there a contract between seller and buyer? If so, what are the terms? In *Ayer v. Western Union Tel. Co.*,[15] the court noted "[i]t would be hard, that the negligence of the telegraph company, or an error in transmission resulting from uncontrollable causes, should impose upon the innocent sender of a message, a liability he never authorized, nor contemplated. It would be equally hard that the innocent receiver, acting in good faith upon the message as received by him, should, through such error lose all claim upon the sender." The court created a rule and offered an explanation based neither on choice nor fault:

> ... It is evident that in case of an error in the transmission of a telegram, either the sender or receiver must often suffer loss. As between the two, upon whom should the loss finally fall? We think the safer and more equitable rule, and the rule the public can most easily adapt itself to, is, that, as between sender and receiver, the party, who selects the telegraph as the means of communication, shall bear the loss caused by the errors of the telegraph. The first proposer can select one of many modes of communication, both for the proposal and the answer. The receiver has no such choice, except as to his answer. If he cannot safely act upon the message, he receives through the agency selected by the proposer, business must be seriously hampered and delayed. The use of the telegraph has become so general, and so many transactions are based on the words of the telegram received, any other rule would now be impracticable.
>
> Of course the rule above stated, presupposes the innocence of the receiver, and that there is nothing to cause him to suspect an error. If there be anything in the message, or in the attendant circumstances, or in the prior dealings of the parties, or in anything else, indicating a probable error in the transmission, good faith on the part of the receiver, may require him to investigate before acting. Neither does the rule include forged messages, for in such case, the supposed sender did not make any use of the telegraph.

Professor Sharp saw the rule as "an aberration." "This appears to be comparable to a rule that everyone who drives a car takes the risk of all accidents which the car may occasion. One who drives knowing of his defective brakes, may indeed assume the risks of accidents. But one who uses an ordinary car, though he knows well that accidents may result, is not, therefore, held to have

---

[15] 79 Me. 493, 10 A. 495 (1887).

assumed the risk of all accidents."[16] Does the court in the *Ayer* case answer Sharp's objection?

3. WHEN IS IT TOO LATE TO DISCOVER A MISTAKE, AND AVOID THE CONTRACT?

a. Introducing the Problem of the Mistaken Bid

People often make offers based on mistakes. When should we let them back out of contracts formed when the other party accepted the mistaken offer? Professor Fuller, in his classic article exploring the reliance and expectation interests,[17] justified holding people to contracts and protecting their expectation interests because of the difficulty of proving reliance. For example, when I think I have a deal with you, I am likely to stop looking for other suppliers of the same item. At the least, your failure to perform costs me the chance to find other bargains. This explanation for holding people to promises suggests several problems. On one hand, buyer may rely on seller's promise even before they make a legally binding contract. Seller, however, wants to withdraw because it made a mistake. Should buyer's reliance be protected? On the other hand, the injury actually or likely caused by buyer's reliance after the parties made a legally binding contract may be very small as compared to the burden on the seller if it is held to its mistaken promise. Should this matter?

Legal formalism would ignore both situations. Under this theory, a bargainer was free to back out of any transaction before the magic moment of closing the deal took place. Conversely, once a deal was closed, absent fraud or a *mutual* mistake going to the essence of the transaction, a bargainer had to live with any mistakes. However, the solutions offered by legal formalism fail to track with much of business life. Many transactions involve an incremental process of give and take. It is hard to find any magic moment of bindingness that matters to the parties. After parties work together, either may suffer losses if the other backs out. Expectations of fairness and good faith grow as the transaction progresses.

Should the law recognize these business practices or should judges demand that parties go through formalities that mark when the parties make a contract? Alternatively, how much weight should courts give to contract formalities? Suppose a seller submits an offer that the buyer accepts. This creates a legally binding contract. Shortly afterward, the seller discovers he made a substantial mistake in calculating the price he quoted. The buyer has done little in reliance. Should the law offer relief from the mistake?

We must keep several questions distinct. First, we might ask as a matter of ethics whether a person who has made a promise based on a mistake should stand

---

[16]Sharp, Promissory Liability I, 7 University of Chicago Law Review 1, 6-7 (1939).
[17]The Reliance Interest in Contracts Damages, 46 Yale Law Journal 52 (1936).

behind it. Would the good person back out if her lawyer told her that no legally binding agreement was made under the rules of contract law? Second, we might ask whether the ethical person would hold another to a contract once she discovers their agreement was based on the other's mistake? Third, we can ask whether legal rules should reflect whatever moral decisions we reach. We might conclude that most people will offer to stand behind their promises based on mistakes. Most who might benefit from such errors may refuse to accept the benefits of these promises. Most people are ethical or they are subject to private sanction systems that offer all the regulation that is needed.

We will look at several situations in which one party makes a promise based on a mistake. In each situation, the other party has no reason to know that a mistake has been made. In some cases, courts enforce the agreement; in other cases, enforcement is denied. In some cases relief is given to a party even though the formalities of a contract were not met. Can we formulate a principled and coherent explanation of these cases?

Buyers of goods or services often use competitive bidding. Statutes may require governmental units to operate this way to save money and minimize favoritism and kick-backs. Plans and specifications are drawn by architects and engineers and owners make them available to interested general contractors. General contractors then ask subcontractors and suppliers to make bids. A bid is a statement that the firm making it will do some part of the project for a certain amount. Typically, subcontractors and material suppliers give general contractors bids shortly before the generals must submit their prime bids to the corporation or governmental unit having the work done. Though some bids may be submitted in writing, more typically the bidder telephones them to the general contractors just before the deadline. Often the process is hectic and chaotic.

Each general contractor then takes the best bids, adds its own estimates for work its crew will do, and then includes a sum to cover the expense of coordinating the work and taking the risks involved. A general must both keep the amount of the bid as low as possible to get the job and keep it high enough to make money on the project. The owner then makes a contract with the lucky general contractor. Then the general usually makes contracts with selected subcontractors and material suppliers to assure itself of getting the goods and services at guaranteed prices.

Clearly, there is a great deal of room for error in this process. Some building contractors, subcontractors and material suppliers are highly professional and use the most advanced methods of preparing bids. Others operate in a more seat-of-the-pants fashion, scorning paperwork. A general or a subcontractor may misread plans and specifications. These documents may be ambiguous or conflict with one another. A contractor may assume that it may make something in a customary way, but an owner's architect may demand a special and more costly procedure in a clause buried in lengthy and poorly organized specifications. A contractor may fail to add a column of figures correctly or a number can be transposed when copied. A component (sometimes a room, or a whole floor) can be inadvertently omitted during the last minute calculations.

Mistakes can hurt everyone involved. If a subcontractor must perform a mistaken bid, it may go broke. But a general may have relied on that bid in computing its offer to the owner and if the subcontractor backs out, the general contractor must cope with the loss. If the owner calls for new bids because of the mistakes, this may increase the price of the building. Ideally, bidders would avoid mistakes; however, this is easier said than done.

We will explore the range of choices open to courts in these cases, and the advantages and disadvantages of each. The cases will expose the eternal tension between a desire for orderly, clear, certain rules and the urge to give relief when those clear rules seem to work a hardship. We begin with the war-horses of traditional contract courses — the mail-box rule, and the firm offer — and then move to other rules which implicate the same policies. Throughout, we will ask whether courts are protecting free choice, holding people to the consequences of their negligence, or making decisions based on ideas of social engineering or sympathy. Keeping in mind Professor Horwitz' arguments, we will ask whether developments in these areas favor general or subcontractors systematically.

b. The Mail Box Rule

The classic common law "mail box rule" closes deals quickly without requiring communication. Acceptances create legally binding contracts when they are mailed. Nothing happening between the time of mailing and receipt affects the formation of the contract. (All *other* communications — offers, rejections, and revocations — take effect only when they are received.)

Suppose, for example, after a bid, a governmental unit sends the low bidder a purchase order. The purchase order is an offer to be accepted by the contractor that made the bid. The contractor signs the acknowledgement of order copy of the purchase order form. This document is an acceptance. The contractor then deposits it in the mail. Then the contractor discovers a major error. Its representative telephones a government official, saying the government should ignore the acceptance because of the mistake. Under the common law rule, it would be too late. One cannot withdraw an acceptance after the parties' actions create a contract.

The common law is clear. The attempted revocation is too late. The rule has been rationalized in terms of protecting an offeree's likely reliance. Once it mails a letter of acceptance, it must take that contract into account in its planning from that point onward. It will not seek other contracts to fill the needs involved in the one created by mail. The mail-box rule means that the offeree need not wait for the offeror to learn of the acceptance before the offeree can begin to rely on the contract's existence. The offeror knows that it is in an uncertain situation once it makes an outstanding offer. Its possible reliance is a necessary part of making contracts by correspondence. Notice that the rule applies and there is a contract although the offeree cannot show that it suffered any reliance loss. As you might expect, in many situations offerees will not assert their contract rights. Buyers often allow sellers to back out when they believe that the reason for the attempted revocation is a mistake rather than a desire to sell to another buyer at a higher price.

Notwithstanding the venerability and widespread acceptance of the mailbox rule, in 1949 the Court of Claims announced an acceptance-when-received rule. *Dick v. United States*,[18] involved the following sequence of communications:

(1) After an extended exchange of telegrams, a manufacturer sent the Coast Guard a bid to supply propellers for an ice-breaking vessel.

(2) The Coast Guard mailed its purchase order to the manufacturer, offering to buy the propellers.

(3) The manufacturer mailed its acceptance of the order to the Coast Guard.

(4) While the letter of acceptance was in transit, the manufacturer discovered that the order was for two *sets* of two propellers and not one set of two propellers as it had assumed. (That is, the Coast Guard ordered four propellers while the manufacturer's representatives thought they were agreeing to supply only two for the price they quoted.) The manufacturer telegraphed the Coast Guard, informing it of the mistake and saying that the price quoted should be doubled. This telegram arrived *before* the Coast Guard received the letter of acceptance.

(5) The Coast Guard's contracting officer told the manufacturer that they would make a new contract. Relying on this, the manufacturer supplied the four propellers (two sets) the Coast Guard wanted. However, the Comptroller General ruled that the contracting officer had no authority to give away the government's rights. A contract was formed when the manufacturer placed a letter of acceptance in the mail. As a result, the government paid the manufacturer only the price set forth in the purchase order. This was the price the manufacturer mistakenly had calculated for only one set of propellers instead of the two sets ordered.

On these facts, the United States Court of Claims changed its rule to acceptance-when-received. It found that the Government should pay the manufacturer for both sets of propellers supplied. We are almost certain there was no reliance by the offeror on the letter of acceptance. The first thing the Coast Guard received in response to its offer was a communication telling it to disregard the earlier mailed acceptance because of a mistake. Thus, the *Dick* case

---

[18]82 F.Supp. 326 (Ct. Claims 1949).

reached the right result in terms of protecting expectations and reliance, but violated the mailbox rule.

Six years later, the Court of Claims decided *Rhode Island Tool Co. v. United States*.[19] It applied its acceptance-when-received rule and found no contract. An offeror tried to revoke its offer after the offeree had mailed a letter of acceptance but before the offeror had received it. The court assumed there could be but one rule covering both the *Dick* and *Rhode Island Tool* situations. It had to adopt an acceptance-when-mailed or an acceptance-when-received rule for all situations.

Several writers suggest that we need different rules for different situations. To oversimplify, in the *Dick* situation the rule should be acceptance-when-received. In the *Rhode Island Tool* situation, it should be acceptance-when-mailed. This makes sense if the primary goal is to protect likely reliance. In the *Dick* situation, the Coast Guard's officials did not know that the manufacturer had mailed an acceptance before they learned it had made a mistake. An offeror cannot rely on an acceptance its officials have never seen or heard of. In the *Rhode Island Tool* case, however, an offeree who deposits a letter of acceptance in the mail is entitled to start relying from that point on. Other writers worry about binding one party to a contract when the other party is not bound. However, they concede that perhaps courts should give relief in the *Dick* situation on the ground of mistake. Consider the mistake possibility after we have studied traditional and modern views about such relief.

c. The Firm Offer

Another change in traditional contract rules affects responsibility for mistaken bids and offers. In the last thirty years, courts and legislatures have created more liability where parties have not followed procedures for forming contracts. Again we must understand the consequences and ask who benefits and who suffers by the changes.

Suppose Seller offers to sell goods to Buyer at a specified price. Buyer neither accepts nor rejects the offer. Seller, eager to make a sale, says, "Take your time and think about this deal. You'll find it is a good price for goods of this quality." Seller leaves. Buyer then gets another offer for the same type of goods from Competitor, but the price is higher. Buyer rejects Competitor's offer, planning to accept Seller's proposal. However, before Buyer can communicate, Seller revokes its offer. (Seller may have found another customer for the goods it has or may have discovered an error in its calculations upon which it quoted a price or may simply have changed its mind.) Buyer has lost its possible deal with Competitor. May Buyer recover from Seller? The traditional common law rule was clear. Offers are revocable until they are accepted. Buyer had no right to

---

[19]128 F.Supp. 417 (Ct. Claims 1955).

rely on an unaccepted offer. It should have known it did not have a contract. Thus, Buyer could not recover.

Suppose Seller was very eager to make a sale. She says, "Take your time and think about this deal. You'll find it is a good price for goods of this quality. I promise not to revoke this offer for one week." Under the common law rules, the case for Buyer is no stronger. Seller's promise not to revoke lacks consideration. It would not be enforceable, and Seller could revoke without liability to Buyer. Buyer could make a promise not to revoke enforceable by paying for an "option."

There have been changes in these rules. Section 2-205 of the Uniform Commercial Code offers a very limited change in the rules. It provides,

> An offer by a merchant to buy or sell goods in a signed writing which by its terms gives assurance that it will be held open is not revocable, for lack of consideration, during the time stated or if no time is stated for a reasonable time, but in no event may such period of irrevocability exceed three months; but any such term of assurance on a form supplied by the offeree must be separately signed by the offeror.

Notice that the rule applies only to merchants. The promise to hold open an offer must be in writing and signed. The statute limits the duration of the option. Moreover, the Code imposes a special rule for a form contract supplied by the offeree.

This cautious relaxation of the consideration doctrine stands in contrast to the court-fashioned rule applicable to subcontractor bids in building construction. Recall bidding in building construction. Typically, an owner invites bids on the plans and specifications for a project. Several general contractors plan to bid on the job. They calculate their bids from their own estimates of the costs of that part of the work they plan to carry out with their own crew, as well as sub-bids from subcontractors and suppliers of machinery and materials. Sub-bids may be written, but often they are transmitted at the last minute by telephone.

The owner usually awards a contract to construct the building to the low-bidding general contractor. Suppose one of the subcontractors refuses to stand behind its bid and enter a contract. Assume the subcontractor revokes its offer (its bid) before the general contractor accepts it and forms a contract. The common law rule would allow subcontractors to back out if they did it before their bids were accepted.

The general contractor relied on the subcontractor's bid. The general used this sub-bid in calculating its bid on the contract. Moreover, this reliance is foreseeable and reasonable. Can general contractors find a theory of liability to hold subcontractors or suppliers? Soon after the first Restatement of Contracts was published, a lawyer for a general contractor sued a supplier of materials that had submitted a bid based on mistaken calculations. The lawyer tried to use § 90. It provides "a promise which the promisor should reasonably expect to induce action or forbearance of a definite and substantial character on the part of the promisee and which does induce such action or forbearance is binding if injustice can be avoided only by enforcement of the promise." It was not clear whether it applied to reliance on bids.

Judge Learned Hand of the United States Court of Appeals for the Second Circuit was a member of the American Law Institute. He helped draft the Restatement of Contracts. He wrote the opinion in this first attempt to use § 90 in a bidding case. He refused to apply it to block withdrawal of a bid. "[A]n offer for an exchange is not meant to become a promise until a consideration has been received.... In the case at bar the defendant offered to deliver the linoleum in exchange for the plaintiff's acceptance, not for its bid, which was a matter of indifference to it.... There is no room in such a situation for the doctrine of 'promissory estoppel.'"[20]

There were a number of cases suggesting that Judge Hand was wrong. However, the major break-through came in an opinion of Justice Roger Traynor of the Supreme Court of California in 1958. His opinion in *Drennan v. Star Paving Co.*[21] is cited often. In the *Drennan* case, a paving subcontractor telephoned an oral bid to a general contractor. The subcontractor's representative did not promise to keep the bid open. There was no finding that this was the custom among subs and generals in that area. The subcontractor refused to enter a contract based on its bid to the general. Justice Traynor found an implied secondary promise in the bid that the subcontractor would keep its offer open for a reasonable time. This implied promise became irrevocable under § 90 once the general relied on it by using the sub-bid in its prime bid.

Was Justice Traynor's decision based on choice or fault? Is liability imposed for some purpose? While some suppliers of materials have more bargaining power than the general contractors with whom they deal, in the usual situation a large general contractor is seeking to hold a smaller subcontractor to its bid. Subcontractors as a group have a stake in the bidding process. Most will stand behind their bids and eat their losses when they make mistakes. Generals may not ask subcontractors who refuse to honor their bids to submit them in future transactions. However, there is no guarantee that the general who receives the prime contract will award a contract to the subcontractor with the lowest bid. Even if a general does offer the contract to the low bidding subcontractor, the general may seek to bargain for an even lower price.

Is the firm offer rule just another example of the law being twisted in the interests of the powerful behind apolitical-seeming abstractions? None of the judges writing opinions applying Restatement § 90 to subcontractor bids explain why "injustice can be avoided only by enforcement of the promise." Scholars and politicians tell us that judges should not make major political choices but

---

[20]See James Baird Co. v. Gimbel Bros., 64 F.2d 344 (2d Cir. 1933).

[21]51 Cal.2d 409, 333 P.2d 757 (1958).

should leave them to the legislature. Why don't they leave this choice to legislation? Organized lobbying groups represent many general contractors, subcontractors and material suppliers. Isn't their failure to seek legislation significant? If courts can hold subcontractors to their bids under § 90, they must then consider whether to offer relief for mistake under other provisions. Wouldn't it be easier just to continue the common law position? Are subcontractors who back out and refuse to honor bids likely to hurt general contractors often? How do we know that reputational sanctions are not enough?

How should jurists answer questions such as these? Most of these questions are normative, but they rest on assumptions about the likely consequences of various rules courts could adopt. Facts alone cannot answer normative questions. Nonetheless, data can sharpen normative issues when they let us see how various proposals might operate.

In 1967 the Virginia Law Review conducted and published a survey addressing bidding practices in Virginia.[22] While it represents, at best, a snapshot of the situation in Virginia in the mid 1960s, and is subject to the usual caveats concerning whether the sample surveyed was representative, the quality of the questions, whether practices in Virginia were typical of practices in other states, and so forth, it *does* offer far more information than legal decision-makers usually have about a problem.

The Virginia survey involved questionnaires to 100 general contractors, and 94 subcontractors. About two thirds of both groups responded. Some relatively clear patterns were revealed in the answers:

a. Few subcontractors submitted their bids more than 24 hours before the general was required to submit *its* bid. Most subs said that they submitted their bid from one to four hours before the general's bid was due. The general contractors also noted that subcontractor's bids were submitted at very nearly the last minute -- a practice apparently designed to prevent bid-shopping by general contractors. None of the generals would admit to bid shopping, but half or more indicated that they did not always accept the lowest bid by a subcontractor; they indicated that they often had concerns about the reliability of subcontractors based either on reputation, or past experience. Some general contractors admitted that they sometimes used a subcontractor's bid as a way of estimating what some portion of the job would cost, and then chose to do that portion of the job themselves; other generals said they believed this was unethical, and pointed out that it was specifically defined as unethical conduct under the AGC code of ethics.

b. Less than 20% of the submitted bids were in writings which contained reassurances that the bid would not be withdrawn for some specified time. 40% of subcontractors indicated that they made oral bids which contained such an

---

[22]Note, Another Look at Construction Bidding and Contracts Formation, 35 Virginia Law Review 1720 (1967).

assurance. It appears that many bids (the subcontractors had a lower estimate of the actual percentage than the generals did) contained no statement at all concerning whether the bids would remain open. Apparently, then, U.C.C. § 2-205 (the firm offer provision) does not cover a large percentage of the bids of subcontractors.

c. A majority of the subcontractors indicated that they had trouble with generals who engaged in bid shopping. They generally believed that it was unethical for a general to bid shop either before, or after, the award of the prime contract. They were concerned not only with the bargaining advantage the practice of bid shopping gave generals, but also with the potential disclosure of their bids to competing subcontractors. Most subcontractors indicated they would try to take steps to discourage bid shopping. This included refusing to submit bids to generals who shop bids, publicizing the general's behavior, "trapping" the general by making a low bid and then withdrawing it, and late bids. No subcontractor mentioned the possibility of suing the general contractor as a likely course of action.

d. Subcontractors were united in saying that they would feel bound to go ahead and perform the work at the original bid price if it was discovered that an error had been made in computing the bid, but that the general had used their mistaken bid in making its own bid. None of the subs felt that they were free to withdraw their bid -- although it must be remembered that the subs here were merely answering questions on a questionnaire, and not absorbing substantial financial losses. Several general contractors indicated that they had faced just these circumstances in the past. Of the sixty-six generals who responded, 15 said that they considered the sub bound once the bid had been used by the general, 5 indicated that neither party should be bound, and the majority believed that *both* parties became bound when the general used the sub's bid in making its own bid on the prime contract. In considering the question of whether a sub is bound or not, neither subs nor generals seemed to attribute significance to whether or not the bid was "firm." The important factor was the extent to which the general was in an exposed position once it had used the bid. Subs felt that preserving their reputations required that they perform according to their bids. Generals suggested that it would be unfair for subs to withdraw after the general had been awarded the prime contract. It wasn't always clear that the parties distinguished between legal and ethical obligations in these circumstances.

e. Generals did not usually notify subs that their bids would be used in computing the general's own bid. A more common practice was for subs to be notified once the general had in fact submitted a bid made in reliance on that subcontractor's bid. The majority of the time, subcontractors were not notified until after the prime contract was awarded. Generals gave a number of different reasons for delaying notifying subs, including that it was "accepted practice," that it helped prevent mistakes, and that it allowed them time to review the materials which had been submitted in the rush of bidding.

f. Generals and subs were both asked what objection they would have, if any, to a legal rule which provided that a contract was formed, binding on both parties, if a sub's bid was used and the general was subsequently awarded the contract. This question, of course, is really at the heart of the survey. Not surprisingly, the subcontractors almost unanimously approved of this idea. Interestingly, 28 of the generals also agreed, with 35 voicing either reservations, or opposition. In fact, the Virginia editors suggested that some of the reservations were sufficiently minor that one could responsibly count 50 of the generals as not objecting, and only 13 as objecting.

g. Three objections, or reservations, seemed to be voiced concerning the proposed rule. First, it is sometimes difficult to determine whose bid was actually used. Several bids might have been in the same range, or a general may have had to revise submitted bids in order to meet contract requirements. Second, some of the bids are uncertain, to varying degrees. Some of this uncertainty is a product of the time pressures involved. The bids may be oral, and consist of a substantial number of subsidiary components. Some of the bids refer to specifications in the contract, while others do not. Some fail to specify important details. Some may even prove to be unresponsive to the general's request. Finally, and perhaps most importantly, general's were concerned about being obligated to do business with the "unknown" bidder. Generals expressed substantial concern about remaining free to evaluate a bidder's reliability, and qualifications to actually complete the work *after* being awarded the prime contract. It was not possible to make this evaluation during the hectic course of the bidding process. Sometimes a general may conclude that a low bidder doesn't have a large enough labor force to do the job, or is too inexperienced. This led some generals to suggest that bids which had been solicited from subcontractors could be treated differently from bids which were unsolicited.

At about the same time, Lewis did a study of the firm offer problem in England, in connection with an effort by the Law Commission for England and Wales.[23] He concluded by noting, "The refinement of the general principles of contract has been the concern of lawyers steeped in classical contract theory. The working paper [of the Commission] rests on an assumption of classical theory that formally available legal opportunities will be exploited in practice. This article together with earlier empirical studies has suggested in the particular areas investigated such an assumption is not warranted." Does this suggest that things in the United Kingdom are not too different from things in Virginia?

Consider the following decision in light of the Virginia study. How does the court know that the Wisconsin courts would hold that a subcontractor cannot

---

[23]Richard Lewis, Contracts Between Businessmen: Reform of the Law of Firm Offers and an Empirical Study of Tendering Practices in the Building Industry, 9 Journal of Law & Society p. 152 (1982).

withdraw a mistaken bid once the general contract has used that bid in computing its bid on the prime contract?

JANKE CONSTRUCTION CO. v. VULCAN MATERIALS CO.

386 F. Supp. 687 (W.D. Wis. 1974),
aff'd, 527 F.2d 772 (7th Cir. 1976)

ROSENSTEIN, J. In this action, plaintiff, a general contractor, alleges that defendant, a producer of construction materials, including reinforced concrete pipe, agreed to provide plaintiff with pipe and fittings at a per-unit cost, for a marine construction project at the University of Wisconsin at Milwaukee, Wisconsin; that defendant expressly warranted and represented to plaintiff that defendant's products would meet the specifications required for that project; that plaintiff, in reliance thereon, used defendant's prices in bidding on the marine project and was awarded the contract; that following the award, defendant proposed to provide plaintiff with pipe and fittings which did not meet the specifications and which were rejected by the project engineers; and that plaintiff was thereby compelled to purchase the specified materials from another supplier at a higher cost, sustaining damages of $40,442.40....

Plaintiff, a Wisconsin corporation with its principal offices near Wausau, Wisconsin, has been engaged in various types of construction work, including highway, sewer, airport and marine projects. Defendant, a New Jersey corporation, operates quarries and has sand, gravel, aggregate, and redi-mix concrete plants in several states. In 1970, it also operated a concrete pipe plant located in Illinois which produced only AWWA (American Water Works Association) Specification C302 pipe.

In February 1970, the State Bureau of Engineering, on behalf of the Regents of the University of Wisconsin, publicly invited submission of sealed bids for the construction of condenser water transmission lines, lake piping, and a pumping station for the University of Wisconsin-Milwaukee campus.

....The materials required for marine piping included concrete subaqueous pipe in full compliance with either AWWA Specification C300 or AWWA Specification C301. The main contract also contained an "or equal" clause, permitting use of nonspecified materials of equal quality to those specified if they were considered equally acceptable to and approved by the project engineers.

Plaintiff, intending to bid on the marine work, obtained price quotations from suppliers of the various materials required for that portion of the project. On March 5, 1970, Jerry Janke, then vice-president of plaintiff, received by telephone from a Vulcan representative price quotations for the various concrete pipe items to be used in the marine work. Janke made a memorandum of the prices quoted, but did not inquire during this conversation whether defendant proposed to supply C300 or C301 pipe, nor did the caller specify the quality or type of pipe Vulcan intended to furnish. Defendant's prices were $40,000 below that quoted by Interpace, another subaqueous concrete pipe supplier.

[At a meeting on March 9, the plaintiffs met briefly with a representative of Vulcan. The parties agreed that there was no discussion, during this meeting, of the specifications of the pipe which Vulcan proposed to provide. The next day, after James Janke met the Vulcan representative, and expressed concern about Vulcan's low bid, he was reassured that Vulcan could furnish the pipe for the project. The Vulcan representative testified that the conversation concerned only whether Vulcan could lower its price even further. Janke relied on Vulcan's bid in calculating its own bid, and was awarded the prime contract.]

Within the week after the bid opening plaintiff received a written quotation from Vulcan setting forth the same prices that were quoted to Jerry Janke over the telephone on March 5, but stating that the quotation was for AWWA C302 pipe. [Meetings were held between Janke and Vulcan and engineers representing the state in order to discuss the suitability of using C302 pipe under the "or equal" clause; the state refused to accept the substitution.]

Plaintiff was then forced to buy the specified pipe from Interpace at a cost of $197,093.50, which was $39,942.40 over the $157,101.10 it would have paid for Vulcan's pipe in accordance with the latter's quotation. James Janke considered $150 to $200 per day to be the reasonable and fair value of his time spent in attending the meetings at Madison and Milwaukee with the state engineers on Vulcan's pipe....

[Normal bidding practices in the construction industry include the publication of requests for bids in a construction news service, "Dodge Reports". Plans are then available for review by potential bidders in "Dodge plan rooms."]

An interested materials supplier checks the plans and specifications to determine if he can supply any of the required materials. He then submits a quotation by telephone, mail, or both to the contractors interested in bidding on the project. These quotations are used by the contractors to estimate their own costs in preparing their bids. Normally, the twenty-four-hour period preceding the prime bid deadline is one of great activity, with the subcontractors and suppliers making the rounds of the contractors who are still preparing their bids. By this time, the first quotations have generally become known, and the prices are often revised downward at the last minute, with the prime contractors revising their bids accordingly.

The contractor usually purchases the materials from the supplier whose prices he relied upon in preparing his bid. However, the contract is not entered into until the contractor has been awarded the contract and the project engineers have approved the material, if such approval is needed. The supplier then prepares the shop drawings for the project after the successful bidder signs a letter of intent to purchase the material.

The Janke brothers testified that the supplier normally submits a price on material that will meet the specifications. However, Jerry Janke stated, if the supplier were offering non-specified material under the "or equal" clause he would, in the normal course of trade, alert the contractor to that fact so that the latter, if he relies upon this quotation, would note on his [the general's] bid that he proposed to supply alternate material under the "or equal" clause and that his bid is based on the substitute material....

Plaintiff views this action as one grounded in contract and governed by the Uniform Commercial Code which was adopted by Wisconsin (Wis.Stat. chs. 401-409). It contends that (1) defendant breached an alleged contract to furnish suitable and acceptable materials for the project, and (2) knowing that plaintiff relied upon its skill and judgment in furnishing the materials for the project, defendant had impliedly warranted their fitness for that particular purpose.

I agree with defendant that no binding contractual obligation existed under the Code. The mere use of Vulcan's bid was not an acceptance in law which gave rise to a contract with plaintiff. *N. Litterio & Company v. Glassman Construction Company*, 115 U.S. App.D.C. 335, 319 F.2d 736 (1963);... *Drennan v. Star Paving Company*, 51 Cal.2d 409, 333 P.2d 757 (1958);...

Defendant had not offered to make its bid irrevocable, nor was there an option supported by consideration. Thus its bid does not meet the "firm offer" requirement of § 402.205 Wis.Stat., which states:

> An offer by a merchant to buy or sell goods in a signed writing which by its terms gives assurance that it will be held open is not revocable, for lack of consideration, during the time stated or if no time is stated for a reasonable time,...

However, the absence of a contractual basis to plaintiff's claim is not fatal to its action. The facts which plaintiff has pleaded and relied upon to support its claim and to which defendant has responded in entering its defense give rise to the application of the doctrine of promissory estoppel. This doctrine is expressed in the Restatement of the Law of Contracts § 90 as follows:

> A promise which the promisor should reasonably expect to induce action or forbearance of a definite and substantial character on the part of the promisee and which does induce such action or forbearance is binding if injustice can be avoided only by enforcement of the promise.

In *Hoffman v. Red Owl Stores, Inc.*, 26 Wis.2d 683, 696, 133 N.W.2d 267, 274 (1965), the Supreme Court of Wisconsin, in a significant and what may prove to be far-reaching opinion, expressly adopted the doctrine of promissory estoppel, stating:

> Because we deem the doctrine of promissory estoppel, as stated in § 90 of Restatement, 1 Contracts, is one which supplies a needed tool which courts may employ in a proper case to prevent injustice, we endorse and adopt it.

The opinion is significant in that the Court clearly distinguished between an action on a promise based on promissory estoppel and one based on breach of contract. The Court further held that a promise actionable under § 90 need not have all the elements of an offer that would result in a binding contract between the parties if the promisee were to accept the same....

Although the Wisconsin authorities have not had occasion to consider the applicability of promissory estoppel to construction bidding cases, the doctrine has found increasing acceptance in other jurisdictions as a basis for a cause of action in litigation involving construction bids....

There is no logical reason, particularly in light of the language used in *Hoffman*, why § 90 of the Restatement should not apply to the situation herein.

The rationale for application of promissory estoppel to construction bidding cases is perhaps best expressed in *Drennan v. Red Star Paving Company, supra.* That case involved an oral bid by a subcontractor for certain work at a school project on which plaintiff, the general contractor, was about to bid. As defendant's bid was the lowest, plaintiff computed his own bid on the basis of defendant's bid price. Plaintiff was the successful bidder, but was informed the next day by defendant that it would not do the work at its quoted price. The California Supreme Court, applying the promissory estoppel rule to prevent defendant's revocation of its bid stated (333 P.2d at 760):

> ... The very purpose of § 90 is to make a promise binding even though there was no consideration 'in the sense of something that is bargained for and given in exchange.'" (See 1 Corbin, Contracts 634 et seq.) Reasonable reliance serves to hold the offeror in lieu of the consideration ordinarily required to make the offer binding....
>
> When plaintiff used defendant's offer in computing his own bid, he bound himself to perform in reliance on defendant's terms. Though defendant did not bargain for this use of its bid neither did defendant make it idly, indifferent to whether it would be used or not. On the contrary, it is reasonable to suppose that defendant submitted its bid to obtain the subcontract. It was bound to realize the substantial possibility that its bid would be the lowest, and that it would be included by plaintiff in his bid. It was to its own interest that the contractor be awarded the general contract; the lower the subcontract bid, the lower the general contractor's bid was likely to be and the greater its chance of acceptance and hence the greater defendant's chance of getting the paying subcontract. Defendant had reasoned not only to expect plaintiff to rely on its bid but to want him to. Clearly defendant had a stake in plaintiff's reliance on its bid. Given this interest and the fact that plaintiff is bound by his own bid, it is only fair that plaintiff should have at least an opportunity to accept defendant's bid after the general contract has been awarded to him.

It bears noting that a general contractor is not free to delay acceptance after he has been awarded the general contract in the hope of getting a better price. Nor can he reopen bargaining with the subcontractor and at the same time claim a continuing right to accept the original offer.

Under the guidelines set down in *Hoffman*, if plaintiff is to prevail in an action under § 90 of the Restatement, it must establish that a definite promise was made by defendant with the reasonable expectation that it would induce action of a definite and substantial character on plaintiff's part; that plaintiff had acted in justifiable reliance upon the promise to its detriment; and that injustice can be avoided only by enforcement of the promise.

I find substantial evidence to support each of the afore-described elements of promissory estoppel.

Jerry Janke received a definite offer by telephone on March 5, 1970.... At no time prior to the awarding of the contract was plaintiff informed that defendant was proposing to furnish anything other than the pipe specified in the project plans....

The Janke brothers, not unreasonably, had relied upon the representations of Vulcan's Wisconsin representative, ... who continued to assure them up to the bid deadline that Vulcan could and would supply the required pipe. Accordingly, the Jankes, men of limited formal education and with no engineering or technical experience in concrete subaqueous piping, were never alerted to the fact that they were relying upon a bid which was based on non-specified material....

Plaintiff suffered substantial detriment by acting in reliance upon defendant's bid. It was compelled to go forward on the contract and supply the specified pipe when defendant's products were rejected as unsuitable. Upon defendant's refusal or inability to furnish the required material, plaintiff had to purchase it from Interpace, the other pipe supplier, at a price which was $39,992.40 over defendant's bid. Injustice can be avoided only by enforcement of the promise; accordingly, plaintiff is entitled to reliance damages.

[The court found that Barry had both real and apparent authority to make representations on behalf of Vulcan. It is worth noting that the "apparent authority rule in agency law seens to embody an objective theory of contract formation."]

One question remains. Can the statute of frauds, raised by defendant as a defense in the context of plaintiff's contractual claim, be raised as a defense to a claim for damages based on the theory of promissory estoppel? The issue has not been raised in the Wisconsin courts, and there is a split of opinion in other jurisdictions where this question has been considered.

[The court noted that some courts, like New York, have declined to use promissory estoppel to defeat a statute of frauds defense. Other states, like Hawaii, in the *McIntosh v. Murphy* case (included in Volume I of these materials), have no such reservations. The District of Columbia, in the *Litterio* case, *supra*, held that promissory estoppel could be used in cases of oral promises.]

I agree with the statement in *Litterio* as to the inapplicability of the statute. The statute of frauds relates to the enforceability of *contracts*; promissory estoppel relates to *promises* which have no contractual basis and are enforced only when necessary to avoid injustice. The Wisconsin Supreme Court clearly stated in *Hoffman* that a promise which could not meet the requirements of an offer that would ripen into a contract if accepted by the promisee is nonetheless enforceable to avoid injustice if the other elements of promissory estoppel are present. To allow defendant to raise the statute of frauds herein as a defense to prevent enforcement of a promise that is actionable under § 90 of the Restatement would defeat the spirit and intent of *Hoffman*. Accordingly, I find the statute is not applicable in an action based on promissory estoppel.

Turning now to plaintiff's claimed damages, the rule in Wisconsin is that "Where damages are awarded in promissory estoppel instead of specifically enforcing the promisor's promise, they should be only such as in the opinion of the court are necessary to prevent injustice." *Hoffman, supra*, 26 Wis.2d at 701, 133 N.W.2d at 276. I find that the sum of $39,992.40, which represents the difference between what would have been paid for the pipe under defendant's bid and the actual cost to plaintiff in purchasing it from Interpace is a proper item of damages. However, the damages claimed for the time James Janke spent in attending meetings with the state engineers after the contract was awarded and with the knowledge that defendant would not supply the required pipe are not recoverable under the promissory estoppel doctrine. These actions were not taken in reliance upon defendant's promise, but were part of an effort to get the State to accept defendant's nonspecified pipe. In other words, they were not induced by defendant's bid.

It is hereby ordered that judgment be entered in favor of plaintiff in the amount of $39,992.40 plus costs.

NOTES AND QUESTIONS

1. *The Restatement (Second) of Contracts solution*: At this point, you should consult § 87 of the Restatement (Second) of Contracts. Those drafting the Restatement (Second) of Contracts were aware of cases such as *James Baird Co. v. Gimbel Bros.* and *Drennan v. Star Paving Co.* They adopted neither a rule that all, nor one that no, firm offers were enforceable against a bidder but instead fashioned an intermediate position embodied in § 87. Consider the adequacy of the Restatement's solution in light of the Virginia survey.

2. *The legislative decision*: Suppose you were a legislator considering a bill to deal with the legal enforceability of bids by subcontractors submitted to general contractors. Thus, you are free to decide how to vote entirely on the merits of the proposal. In light of the Virginia survey, would you have adopted the solution of the court in the *Janke Construction* case, the Restatement of Contracts, or something else?

California has passed such a statute, the Subletting and Subcontracting Fair Practices Act. The Supreme Court of California, in *Southern California Acoustics Co., Inc. v. C.V. Holder, Inc.*,[24] considered the consequence of listing a subcontractor on a contract with the State of California, in light of the statute. The court found that this statute was passed "to protect the public and subcontractors from the evils attendant upon the practices of bid shopping and bid peddling subsequent to the award of the prime contract for a public facility." Under the statute, the prime contractor could not substitute another subcontractor unless the listed subcontractor "becomes insolvent or fails or refuses to perform a written contract for the work or fails or refuses to meet the bond requirements of the prime contractor." The court decided that a listed subcontractor who was not given the job could sue for damages.

3. *Equality and the subcontractor's rights*: Suppose a general contractor uses a subcontractor's bid, and under cases such as *Janke Construction Co., Inc. v. Vulcan Materials Co., Inc.* the subcontractor cannot withdraw it. The general contractor then receives the award from the state agency or owner. Now can the subcontractor successfully sue the general contractor if it does not award the subcontractor the contract? The Minnesota Supreme Court, which had followed *Drennan v. Star Paving Co.*, decided that symmetry did not require that the subcontractor gain rights. In *Holman Erection Co. v. Orville E. Madsen & Sons, Inc.*,[25] a general contractor declined to award a contract to a subcontractor whose bid it had used (and had listed on its own winning bid). In a suit brought by the disappointed sub, the court directly addressed the apparent unfairness of allowing the general to choose another sub, while at the same time refusing to allow subs to refuse to accept contracts at the general's option. The court reasoned that the general has (and must) rely on the subcontractors, while the subs have no reciprocal need to rely on getting a contract. In addition,

> [t]he bidding process puts the subcontractor and the general in very different positions as to the context of the subcontract. The subcontractors have the luxury of preparing their bids on their own timetable, subject only to the deadline for submitting their bids to the general contractors. The same bid goes to all the general contractors and covers the same work. The generals, on the other hand, are dealing with all the various construction aspects of the project and with numerous potential subcontractors. They compile their bids, as the various subcontractor bids are received, within a few hours of the deadline for submission of the prime bid. Specifics are necessarily given less than thorough consideration and are left for future negotiations....

---

[24] 79 Cal.Rptr 319, 456 P.2d 975 (1969).

[25] 330 N.W.2d 693 (Minn. 1983).

Although supplying some certainty and symmetry to the construction industry, ... a decision [in favor of subcontractors whose bids have been used by generals] would also impose a rigidity on the process and result in greater cost to awarding authorities and potential detriment to general contractors. If such a change is to take place, it is one properly brought before the legislature.

4. *Representing the bidder who wants out*: Suppose you are retained to represent a bidder who does not want to perform under the terms and conditions of the bid it made. First, you establish that the general contractor seems willing to sue your client. In other words, the damages claimed are substantial, and your client has sufficient assets to make it worth seeking a judgment. Second, the other-than-legal sanctions are not strong enough to prompt your client to perform and swallow its losses. Third, your client probably made a mistake in preparing its bid so that it is far too low.

What can you do to defend your client? Of course, you would like to win a total victory, but remember that if you can fashion a plausible theory, you might be able to settle the case for far less than the general's total damages. The following strategies are worth considering.

A. *Attack the firm offer rule*: You might try to persuade the court in your state to reject the firm offer rule reflected in Restatement (Second) of Contracts § 87. This would be playing a long shot. Court after court has adopted the rule. Many of these decisions fail to offer convincing arguments justifying holding bidders once generals have used their bids. Nonetheless, you would have to be very persuasive to convince a court that Justice Traynor's *Drennan v. Star Paving* opinion, the Restatement (Second) of Contracts, almost all writers in the law reviews and the great weight of authority were wrong.

B. *Construe the bid*: Lawyers, seeking a way out for clients caught in contracts that have turned out unfavorably, know that they may find legal ammunition if they read written documents or carefully consider testimony about the deal. If the case can be made, it always is nice to say that your client is ready, willing and able to perform its side of the bargain. However, it never promised to do A, B, and C, as the plaintiff contends. Rather, it only promised to do A, B, and D. (This tactic is feasible only if your client is willing to perform A, B, and D.) Plans and specifications for building construction often are ambiguous, if not contradictory.

A few cases have said that the bidder can reserve a right to withdraw the bid after a general has used it. However, if you want to use such language, you face all the fine-print problems. For example, in *Lyon Metal Products, Inc. v. Hagerman Construction Corp.*,[26] a general contractor sued a manufacturer of athletic lockers which had made a mistaken bid. The manufacturer's bid was

---

[26]391 N.E.2d 1152 (Ct.Ap. Ind. 1979).

submitted on its quotation form. On the reverse side, a clause printed in very small type stated "this quotation may be withdrawn and is subject to change without notice after 15 days from date of quotation." The general relied on the supplier's bid, but it did not make a contract with the manufacturer before 15 days had passed. The manufacturer attempted to withdraw its quotation, arguing that it was entitled to withdraw the bid unless it was accepted within 15 days. Nonetheless, the court found the general's reliance reasonable and held the manufacturer to the bid. It noted that the bid was in small print on the back of the quote, was not brought to the attention of the general, and was arguably inconsistent with terms in the specifications.

C. *Use the rules of mistake and Restatement § 90*: To trigger Restatement § 90, reliance must be reasonable. If a general knew or should have known that a bid was based on a mistake, then it cannot reasonably rely on it. For example, in *Maurice Electrical Supply Co., Inc. v. Anderson Safeway Guard Rail Corp.*,[27] the court found that "plaintiff's reliance was not reasonable because of the great difference in price quotes received from defendant and the other two potential suppliers.... While the price quotes obtained from the other two suppliers were quite similar to each other, they were anywhere from 50 to almost 100 percent higher than the price quotes given by defendant. In such circumstances, plaintiff's reliance was not justifiable." The court noted "[w]hile a party may reasonably rely on an unusually low price quote if it reconfirms the price quote prior to reliance, here the Court found plaintiff did not reconfirm the price quote prior to bidding on the resale contract."

To similar effect, the Supreme Court of Utah, in *Tolboe Construction Co. v. Staker Paving & Construction Co.*,[28] found that a general contractor's reliance was not reasonable, although its estimator telephoned the subcontractor and asked it to review its bid. Defendant's bid was 290 percent below that of the next lowest bid and 350 percent below the other bid submitted. Experts testified that they had never seen a disparity in bids for asphalt paving as large as the one in this case. Another general contractor who bid on the project received the same erroneous bid from defendant and rejected it, assuming that it must be mistaken. The telephone call did not alert defendant to the problem.

In an earlier decision, *Union Tank Car Co. v. Wheat Bros.*,[29] the Utah Supreme Court described the firm offer rule as one involving a balancing of the equities. Wheat Brothers bid $22,500 to paint four steel tanks, based on the erroneous assumption that they could use ordinary paint, which cost $6/gallon. Their bid was $6,000 lower than any others because in fact the specifications required "phenoline" paint which cost $26/gallon. Union Tank's representative had called John Wheat to invite a bid and Wheat had phoned in a bid later in the

---

[27]632 F.Supp. 1082 (D.D.C. 1986).

[28]682 P.2d 843 (1984).

[29]15 Utah 2d 101, 387 P.2d 1000 (1964).

day. A document subsequently sent to Wheat described the job, listed the Wheat Brother's price, and noted that the job was to be done "as per attached specifications"; the specifications referred to "phenoline" paint, but there was no indication that the paint was extraordinarily expensive. Wheat Brothers signed the document. They then discovered the cost of the paint and sought to withdraw the offer. However, Union Tank had used the Wheat Brothers bid, and had been awarded the contract. The Utah court found that the balance of equities favored Wheat Brothers. Union Tank was in control of the situation. It could have warned Wheat Brothers about the high cost of phenoline paint; it was obvious that Wheat Brothers' bid was based on the price of ordinary paint. Union Tank called twice to verify the bid, but did nothing to alert Wheat Brothers to the high cost of phenoline paint.

D. *Try to prove bid shopping and chopping*: Most of the states that have adopted the position of Justice Traynor's *Drennan* decision have followed his suggestion that a general contractor loses the right to hold a sub to its bid if the general engages in bid shopping or chopping. That is, the general cannot negotiate with other subcontractors for a cheaper offer after it gets the award and still hold the sub whose bid the general used. Nor can the general negotiate with the sub whose bid the general used and still hold the sub to the original bid.

E. *Assert the Statute of Frauds*: Often, bids of subcontractors and material suppliers are made orally by telephone at the last minute before a general must submit its bid. Contracts for the sale of services need not be in writing unless they cannot be performed within one year. Contracts for the sale of goods for a price of $500 or more, however, come under § 2-201 of the Uniform Commercial Code. Furthermore, § 2-205 provides that merchants can make firm offers "in a signed writing which by its terms give assurance that it will be held open."

Remember that the *Janke Construction Co.* case finds that the Statute of Frauds applies to enforcing contracts, but not to recovery based on promissory estoppel. Thus, Restatement (Second) of Contracts § 90 makes an oral bid of a supplier of goods irrevocable once a general has used it. The court notes in a footnote that Restatement (Second) of Contracts § 217A[30] provides that a court can enforce a promise because of reliance to avoid injustice despite the Statute of Frauds. This provision calls for a case-by-case balancing of factors.

But the court in *C.R. Fedrick, Inc. v. Borg-Warner Corp.*,[31] came to a different result. The federal court decided that the Supreme Court of California would not apply promissory estoppel in a case involving a bid to supply goods for a price of $500 or more. While California had recognized that equitable estoppel might be used to overcome the provisions of the Statute of Frauds, the court declined to apply the doctrine in this case. It decided that equitable estoppel required either a promise not to assert the Statute of Frauds or a representation

---

[30]This section is now § 139 in the published version of the Restatement.

[31]552 F.2d 852 (9th Cir. 1977).

that a writing was not required; mere reliance on the alleged oral contract was not enough. The Court of Appeals further decided that equitable estoppel to assert the Statute of Frauds requires a greater degree of detrimental reliance than does promissory estoppel. Finally, the Court of Appeals found that the California legislature had resolved the policy questions by passing § 2-201 of the Uniform Commercial Code. Section 2-201(3) itself offers limited exceptions to the writing requirements of subsections (1) and (2) and it was not proper for the court to create new exceptions.

While firm offers and consideration may have been the issue of the 1950s and 1960s, today oral firm offers and the Statute of Frauds provoke more dispute. Slightly more courts have followed the *Fedrick* approach than the one found in the *Janke Construction Co.* case. The argument in many of these decisions refusing to apply promissory estoppel is very simple: U.C.C. §§ 2-201 and 2-205 demand writings and make only limited exceptions. Thus, there is no room for Restatement § 90 to apply to oral bids to supply goods. If this doctrine were recognized, the U.C.C. provisions would be meaningless. If there are to be any further exceptions, it is for the legislature to create them.

How should courts reconcile the competing goals of protecting the reliance of generals on bids from material suppliers and the Statute of Frauds' demand for writings? It is clear that oral bids are common in the construction industry. However, notice that U.C.C. § 2-201 applies only to transactions in goods and not to bids to supply services mixed with goods incidental to the transaction. Thus, if promissory estoppel does not override the U.C.C. Statute of Frauds, bids from suppliers of materials such as the Borg-Warner Corporation will not be enforced unless they are in writing. Oral bids from small asphalt paving contractors, as in Justice Traynor's *Drennan* case, will be enforced since they are not governed by the U.C.C.

Does this distinction make sense? On one hand, large corporations are bureaucratic, and they typically deal through written documents as a way for those at the top of the chain of command to control salespeople and others who deal with outsiders. From this perspective, is it reasonable for a general contractor bidding on a job to rely on oral bids from a salesperson representing a large corporation? Even if it is reasonable, perhaps the courts are trying to make it easier to run large bureaucratic corporations. On the other hand, the position of the *Fedrick* case means that large corporations need not stand behind their bids, while small contractors must.

Carlson[32] and Steinberg[33] both argue that promissory estoppel and U.C.C. § 2-201 can be reconciled if courts award only restitution or reliance damages for an

---

[32]Carlson, Promissory Estoppel and the Statute of Frauds in California, 66 California Law Review 1219 (1978).

[33]Note, Promissory Estoppel as a Means of Defeating the Statute of Frauds, 44 Fordham Law Review 114 (1975).

oral promise enforced because of reliance. This would mean that a general contractor who relied on an oral bid to furnish goods could recover limited compensation, but not full expectation damages. Does this compromise appeal to you? Why?

Mistakes, bids, and government contracts: Governmental agencies cannot give away the taxpayer's money. Contracting officers seldom are authorized to be sympathetic, or to compromise to preserve a relationship. If contracting officers are given too much discretion, some might sell it for bribes. Hard and fast rules may also help ward off political influence. These reasons suggest governments could justifiably have the benefit of different rules than commercial enterprises. However, bidding mistakes are a recurrent problem and seem to call for some relief. Cases and statutes have attempted to deal with it by creating standards for relief. How should the balance be struck? The following case provides one court's effort.

MARANA UNIFIED SCHOOL DIST. NO. 6 v. AETNA CASUALTY AND SURETY CO.

144 Ariz. 159, 696 P.2d 711 (1985).

BIRDSALL, C.J. This appeal arises from a complaint filed by the appellee, Marana Unified School District, seeking judgment on a bid bond given by appellants, L.G. Lefler, Inc., doing business as Defco Construction Company, principal, and the Aetna Casualty and Surety Company, surety. The bond was provided pursuant to A.R.S. § 34-201(A)(3) because Defco submitted a bid proposal to construct a junior high school building for the appellee. The statute provides:

3. That every proposal shall be accompanied by a certified check, cashier's check or a surety bond for five per cent of the amount of the bid included in the proposal as a guarantee that the contractor will enter into a contract to perform the proposal in accordance with the plans and specifications, or as liquidated damages in event of failure or refusal of the contractor to enter into the contract. The certified check, cashier's check or surety bond shall be returned to the contractors whose proposals are not accepted, and to the successful contractor upon the execution of a satisfactory bond and contract as provided in this article.

Although Defco was the low bidder, it refused to enter into a contract with the appellee because it had made a mathematical mistake in its proposal.

The trial court entered summary judgment in favor of the Marana District.... The appellants' cross-motion for summary judgment was denied.

The facts considered in the light most favorable to the appellants may be summarized as follows. The appellee gave notice of its intent to receive sealed bids for the construction of the school pursuant to A.R.S. § 34-201. The bids were required to be submitted by 4 p.m., February 2, 1982, at which time they were opened. The appellant's bid was for $4,890,000 together with alternates, all of which totalled $5,936,500. The bid bond attached to the proposal was "in the sum of five per cent of contract bid." No actual figures were set forth on the bond but the proposal referred to the required bid bond amount as five per cent of the "base bid" which would have been $244,500. Nine other contractors submitted bids. Defco's was the lowest base bid. The next lowest base bid was $5,447,000. The architect's estimated cost for the construction without alternates was $4,900,000. Defco's bid was within two-tenths of one per cent of that estimate.

After all bids were opened, the architect and school district officials reviewed them and a written recommendation was made that day to accept Defco's base bid together with two alternates totalling $5,253,080.

At about the same time, Defco personnel were rechecking their figures since it appeared that a mistake may have been made. The employee who had tabulated Defco's bid sheet then discovered that she had used $42,000 as the bid for the structural steel when the correct figure was $412,000, a mistake of $370,000.

According to the employee's affidavit attached to the appellants' cross-motion for summary judgment, she was still receiving telephone bids from subcontractors and suppliers and working on Defco's bid up until 3:30 on February 2; she found a mistake in her first tabulation of some 170 items on the bid sheet and did a second tabulation, then added the figures six times. Since this brought her so close to the time the bid had to be submitted, there was no time to have another employee check her figures.

Defco advised appellee by telephone within one and one-half hours of the bid opening of the mistake which came to $398,752 with the addition of other items based on percentages of the $370,000 error. A letter containing the same information was delivered to the school within three hours after the bid was opened at 4 p.m. In the letter Defco asked to meet with the school officials to show them the calculator tapes and bid sheet which revealed how the error had occurred.

[After 2 school board meetings, and confirmation that Defco was unwilling to perform if awarded the contract, the architect was instructed to re-bid the job.]

The important issue presented by this appeal is whether a low bidder for a public contract may refuse to enter into a contract because of a mistake in the bid without forfeiting the bid bond. Although this question has never been decided in Arizona, it has been the subject of numerous opinions in our sister states and federal courts....

It is the appellee's position that the statute permits no escape from forfeiture. There is authority to support such a result. These decisions are cited by the appellants: *Board of Edn. v. Sever-Williams Co.*, 22 Ohio St.2d 107, 258 N.E.2d 605, cert. denied, 400 U.S. 916, 91 S.Ct. 175, 27 L.Ed.2d 155 (1970), and *A.J. Colella, Inc. v. County of Allegheny*, 391 Pa. 103, 137 A.2d 265 (1958).... The reasoning in these decisions is generally the same, that this is the purpose of the statute and to permit exceptions would materially weaken the purpose of the bidding procedure for public contracts and make the bid bond requirement meaningless. In *Colella* the court opines that plea of a clerical mistake would make the system of sealed bids a mockery. *Sever-Williams* speaks of possible abuse of the bidding procedure, i.e., favoritism or fraud....

We do not agree with the reasoning or result in those cases. Nor do we believe that the Arizona legislature intended that there be no relief from forfeiture of the bid security for equitable reasons. We agree with the appellants that unless the legislature clearly indicates an intention to do so, its enactments shall not be construed so as to change established common law....

We believe the trial court erred in granting summary judgment in favor of the appellee. We follow those decisions which hold that when relief from the forfeiture is legally justifiable, statutes like Arizona's do not mandate the forfeiture. The cases upon which we rely all arise under a statute or bid solicitation which, on its face, prohibits a withdrawal of bids.... In these cases the bidder notified the public authority of the mistake prior to acceptance of the bid. Clearly this notice was promptly given by Defco before the appellee had accepted the bid. [The Arizona statute also prohibited bidders from withdrawing their bids for 45 days.]

A starting point is the decision in *Moffett, Hodgkins, & Clarke Co. v. City of Rochester, supra*. The mistake in *Moffett* resulted from mathematical errors committed by an extremely nearsighted engineer working in great haste with a voluminous number of specifications. Affirming a decree in favor of the contractor, the Supreme Court said that the contractor was not endeavoring to withdraw or cancel a bid or bond in contravention of the city charter, since the contractor was proceeding upon the theory that the bid read at the meeting of the board was one which it had never intended to make, and that the minds of the parties had never met. The Court added that if the city was correct in its contention that the charter provision barred any remedy, then there would be no redress for a bidder on a public work, no matter how aggravated or palpable his blunder. A material mistake of fact in a bid justifies a conclusion that there has been no meeting of the minds because the bidder did not intend to make the erroneous bid....

What appear to be the majority decisions rely upon the equitable remedy of rescission. In these decisions the courts have held or recognized that the bidder who had notified the public authority of the mistake prior to acceptance of the bid was entitled to a decree rescinding the bid, or to similar equitable relief, despite a statute similar to A.R.S. § 34-201(A)(3)....

These cases generally set forth certain criteria to be satisfied before a forfeiture can be avoided. The criteria are summarized in yet another especially comprehensive decision, *City of Baltimore v. De Luca-Davis Construction Co.*, 210 Md. 518, 524, 124 A.2d 557, 562 (1956).

> 1, the mistake must be of such grave consequences that to enforce the contract as made or offered would be unconscionable; 2, the mistake must relate to a material feature of the contract; 3, the mistake must not have come about because of the violation of a positive legal duty or from culpable negligence; 4, the other party must be put in status quo to the extent that he suffers no serious prejudice except the loss of his bargain.

... Other cases have added as an additional reason for permitting rescission that the public body knew or had reason to know that a mistake had been made....

We do not understand that to be a requirement for rescission. It is indeed difficult to envisage a fact situation where the public body would know that a sealed bid contained a mistake prior to its opening unless the bidder discovered and gave notice of the mistake. After that, unless the bid is accepted and a contract made, it seems immaterial whether upon opening the bid the public body knew or should have known. At least in the instant case, where the appellant notified the appellee within three hours and before any attempted acceptance of the bid, it does not appear to be material.

Other courts admonish that a bidder should not be able to withdraw a bid under circumstances profitable to the bidder or which would permit any collusion or connivance among bidders to the detriment of the public....

Nothing suggests any such problems in the record before us.

Turning to the four conditions required by *DeLuca* and other decisions, we believe they are all satisfied by the undisputed evidence before the trial court. We consider them in order.

First, was the mistake of such consequence as to make enforcement of the contract unconscionable? From our analysis of the reported decisions this refers not to the bid bond, since it contains no mistake, but to the mistake in the bid. That mistake was in the amount of almost $400,000. This was approximately eight per cent of the base bid of $4,890,000. Although we believe this to be unconscionable on its face, we compare it to the amounts involved in other reported cases. Thus we find: [The court then cited 10 cases finding mistakes of unconscionable size. Rounding off the amounts, they can be summarized as follows: Mistake of $34,000 on bid of $464,000; mistake of 14% on bid of $141,000; mistake of $150,000 on bid of $883,000; mistake of $590,000 on bid of $1,769,000; mistake of $100,000 on bid of $1,367,000; mistake of $301,800 on bid of $780,000; mistake of $35,000 on bid of $173,000; mistake of $50,000 on bid of $145,000; mistake of $145,000 on bid of $1,242,000 and mistake of $182,000 on bid of $3,547,000.]

Although some of these are proportionately greater than the mistake of Defco, some are smaller in proportion to the bid, and we believe the amount of the mistake was of such grave consequence that it would be unconscionable to enforce it.

The appellee argues, however, that forfeiture of the 5 per cent bid bond is not unconscionable because it is the very bid contract which was bargained for and made by the parties. This argument does not go to the issue of unconscionability but rather to the principal issue, i.e., must the bid bond be forfeited despite the presence of legal justification for the refusal to enter into the contract. In all of the cases cited above, the discussion of unconscionability concerns the amount of the mistake in the bid and not the bid security. In each case it appears that the bid security sought to be forfeited was required by statute or by the bidding documents. Thus if unconscionability was to be determined by reference to the fact that the parties knew the amount of the penalty to be exacted, we believe that would have been decisive in many of those cases. We find no such holding. Assuming, arguendo, that we should look to the forfeiture of the bid bond rather than the amount of the mistake, one quarter of a million dollars is still, in the vernacular, a lot of money, and we believe it would be unconscionable to require even this forfeiture in the instant case.

The second condition, that the mistake must relate to a material feature of the contract, cannot be disputed. The amount to be paid for the construction is clearly a material feature of the contract.

The third condition concerns the question of whether the mistake constituted culpable negligence or the violation of a positive legal duty. If either, then this third requirement is unsatisfied. Since there is no contention that the appellant violated any legal duty, we must determine only whether there was "culpable negligence." Generally a mechanical, clerical, or mathematical error satisfies this condition whereas an error in judgment does not. *Kemper, supra.* In fact this distinction highlights the inequitable result of the trial court's decision in this case. The mistake was not one of judgment, as for example, underestimating the cost of labor or materials. It was not intended. We believe this distinction also serves to show the real purpose for the statute requiring forfeiture of the security. The bidder who makes an error in judgment should be penalized if he then refuses to execute the contract. On the other hand, the bidder who submits a bid which is different than that which he intended to make is entitled to relief.... The type of mistake satisfying this condition has been variously referred to as resulting from some reasonable excuse, ... based upon an erroneous omission and not involving gross negligence, ... and honest and not gross negligence, ...

We agree with the rationale appearing in the comment to § 157 of the Restatement, Second, Contracts. Section 157 concerns the effect of the fault of the party seeking relief from a mistake and provides:

A mistaken party's fault in failing to know or discover the facts before making the contract does not bar him from avoidance or reformation under the rules stated in this Chapter, unless his fault amounts to a failure to act in good faith and in accordance with reasonable standards of fair dealing.

The comment to the section states:

The mere fact that a mistaken party could have avoided the mistake by the exercise of reasonable care does not preclude either avoidance or reformation. Indeed, since a party can often avoid a mistake by the exercise of such care, the availability of relief would be severely circumscribed if he were to be barred by his negligence. Nevertheless, in extreme cases the mistaken party's fault is a proper ground for denying him relief for a mistake that he otherwise could have avoided. Although the critical degree of fault is sometimes described as "gross" negligence, that term is not well defined and is avoided in this Section as it is in the Restatement, Second, of Torts. Instead, the rule is stated in terms of good faith and fair dealing.

Defco's burden of showing good faith and fair dealing is satisfied and not in dispute. No facts are suggested by affidavit, deposition, or otherwise from which it could be inferred that there was a lack of good faith or fair dealing.

Thus we are left with the question of whether the appellee has been placed in status quo so that it suffers no serious prejudice except loss of bargain.

The minutes of the Marana school board meeting of February 4 show that the board rejected all bids and instructed the architect to prepare to rebid the construction contract. All of the rejected bids including the bid the appellant intended to make exceeded the architect's estimate by over $350,000. Obviously the board decided to try again. These facts were before the court for its consideration on the cross-motions for summary judgment. The appellants contend that they established that the school had been put in status quo. The appellee offered nothing to refute this conclusion. No evidence shows that the appellee contends that it suffered serious prejudice, or, in fact, any prejudice except the loss of a bargain which was never intended by the appellants.

We reverse the judgment and direct the trial court to enter judgment in favor of the appellants. HATHAWAY, J., and WILLIAM N. SHERRILL, Superior Court Judge, concur.

NOTES AND QUESTIONS

1. *Mistaken bids on public projects*: Notice that the bid bond statute creates something similar to a firm offer. Absent excuse, the general will forfeit its bid bond if it refuses to enter a contract. The bid is an offer, and in the usual case involving a mistake the general wants to back out after the bids are opened but before its own offer has been accepted by the governmental unit. As the *Marana*

Unified School District case indicates, some courts require the bond to be forfeited despite clerical errors. Others offer relief under a number of theories with many qualifications. The Arizona court, along with many others, refuses to require that the public body knew or should have known of the mistake. Thus, we are considering a remedy for a unilateral mistake of the bidder not shared by the public body.

2. *Private construction and mistaken bids*: Suppose the owner seeking bids for construction is not a unit of government, but a business corporation. Would the doctrine of *Marana Unified School District v. Aetna* offer relief for bidding mistakes in such a case? If not, are there any avenues open to a bidder who has made a serious error? Many cases say that I cannot snap up your offer, knowing it to be mistaken. The difficulty, of course, comes in deciding that I knew or should have known of your error. It is not necessarily enough that your bid is the lowest one I received. It is not necessarily enough that it is entirely out of the range of the other bids. Your very low bid might rest on a mistake, but also it might rest on efficiency or competitive conditions. Assuming that you cannot show that I knew or should have known your bid to rest on a mistake, can you recover for your mistake that I did not share?

d. Unilateral Mistakes in Communicating: I Meant X but Said Y

A note on unilateral mistake: Courts have always been reluctant to grant relief to a bargainer who makes a mistake in entering a contract. In part, this reflects our view that a deal is a deal. A court will not relieve a life insurance company of liability because it did not expect the insured to die so soon. A trader on a commodities exchange cannot claim an excuse because he thought the market would go up, but it went down. A consumer may want a red car instead of the black one he bought, but has no right to insist that the seller exchange automobiles. You have a right to rely on the deal, even if I made a mistake. Furthermore, taking responsibility for my errors should give me reason to be careful and avoid them.

Nonetheless, many writers have advocated more relief for bargainers' mistakes — at least when relief would not hurt the other party. In recent years courts have moved in this direction. However, most of the cases where they have been willing to grant relief involve different kinds of mistakes than the ones we've mentioned.

Section 503 of the first Restatement of Contracts reflects the common law core rule. It says a "mistake of only one party that forms the basis on which he enters into a transaction does not of itself render the transaction voidable...." The comment says "[t]here is a contract formed by the acceptance of an offer even though the offer is made under a mistake or fails to express what the offeror intends. The objective appearance of his acts is controlling...." Under this classic view, my mistake would be the basis for relief only if my error was caused by your fault or where you know or have reason to know of my error.

The first Restatement reflects an objective theory of contracts: I am bound by my actions and not my intentions. You have a right to rely on what a reasonable person would think I meant. My errors in judgment and communication are no excuse unless you caused or should have known of them. If, however, we share a mistake, then there is a chance for relief.

This core position is much less forgiving than the results of the cases. Few would state the law this way in the mid-1990s without a long list of exceptions. While we still think a deal is a deal, we want to be sure what the deal really was. People constantly make mistakes in calculation and communication. We are more willing to ask whether there is good reason to give one party the benefit of another's error. We can see some of the problems with unilateral mistake by tracing the struggles of the Supreme Court of Wisconsin with the issue.

In *Miller v. Stanich*,[34] the Supreme Court of Wisconsin found a unilateral mistake warranted reworking a lease. In 1922, Michael Stanich leased a butcher shop for $75 a month. The term of the lease was five years and there was an option to renew the lease at the same rent for an additional five years. In 1926, S. Miller bought the property from Stanich's lessor, subject of course to the lease to Stanich.

As the first five-year term was coming to an end, Stanich went to his lawyer to talk about negotiating an extended renewal of his lease. Stanich wanted to renew the lease at $75 a month for five years from 1927 to 1932 and wanted another option to renew the same rent for a third five-year term (from 1932 to 1937). Stanich's lawyer drafted a lease reflecting his client's wishes, sending two copies of this lease to Miller's building manager. The manager telephoned Stanich's lawyer and told him "I don't think that Mr. Miller will sign those leases." Stanich's lawyer responded that to save time, he would also send Miller two copies of a lease which ran from 1927 to 1932, but which had no option to renew for the third term. Stanich's lawyer drafted such a lease. The two leases were the same, except one contained twenty-three additional words granting an option to renew from 1932 to 1937. Both sets of leases (two copies of each version) were sent to Miller, at his home in Marshfield, Wisconsin.

Although Miller was the president of a wholesale fruit and cold storage business, he could neither read nor write English. His son read the leases to him. They discovered that one set contained an additional five-year renewal option while the other did not. Miller did not want to renew Stanich's lease at all because he thought that the $75 a month rent was far too low, and he clearly did not want to give Stanich an option to renew for an additional five years at that rent.

Miller drove to Wisconsin Rapids to see his lawyer, R. B. Graves. Miller asked if he had to renew the lease. Graves told him that Stanich had a right to

---

[34]202 Wis. 539, 230 N.W. 47, 233 N.W. 753 (1930). Much of our description of the case is taken from the briefs and record on appeal.

renew the lease from 1927 to 1932. There was no discussion about granting Stanich a right to renew again from 1932 to 1937. Apparently, Graves read only one copy of the lease — one that did not have the additional twenty-three words granting Stanich an option to renew from 1932 to 1937. Apparently, he assumed there were four copies of the same lease. Graves dated two copies of the lease and gave them to Miller. Miller took all four copies back to Marshfield. He signed the two copies Graves had dated and sent them to his building manager who passed them along to Stanich. Graves, of course, had dated the wrong set. As a result, Miller had mistakenly signed the copies that gave Stanich an option to renew for the third five-year term.

In late June of 1927, Miller had a chance to sell the building. To make the sale, he had to buy out Stanich's lease. Miller and Stanich met in Milwaukee. Stanich asked $9,000 to surrender his rights under the lease. Miller said that this was too much for only a five-year term. Stanich said, "No, it is not five. It is ten." Miller and Graves then tried to persuade Stanich that a mistake had been made. However, Stanich insisted that he had a lease for five years with an option to renew at the same rent for another five.

Miller then sued to have a court reform the lease and cancel the option to renew for an additional five years from 1932 to 1937. The trial court reformed the lease, striking out the option to renew. It found "at no time was there a meeting of the minds ... to execute a lease for five years with the privilege to renew the same for another period of five years."

On appeal, the Supreme Court of Wisconsin *first* issued an opinion by Justice Fritz, joined by four other justices. Justice Fritz stated:

> Although plaintiff may have made a mistake in signing and sending to defendant the copies of the lease which contained the provision giving defendant an option for a further renewal, nothing had occurred because of which defendant had reason to believe that plaintiff did not intend to agree to that provision, or that plaintiff had made a mistake. Defendant, in good faith, had submitted two forms. Without being misled by any trick or artifice on the part of any one, plaintiff signed and sent the two copies, containing the clause for another option, to defendant for his signature. When defendant also signed those copies he was entitled to assume that the minds of the parties had met as to all terms embodied in the signed instruments, and that the plaintiff, by signing, had evidenced his intention to agree to all of those terms. Nothing had been done by plaintiff, of which defendant had knowledge, that indicated an intention of plaintiff's part not to consent to the option for the additional extension. Nothing had occurred which can be said to evidence a meeting of the minds to another contract, which plaintiff is now entitled by reformation to have expressed in the lease which he voluntarily signed. There was no mutual mistake. At best it was merely a unilateral mistake, without any fraud on the part of the defendant. Under the circumstances there was no ground for reformation.

Justice Fowler, joined by Justice Stevens, dissented:

> The case is so simple that to my mind the mere statement of it proves the decision of the court wrong.... [P]laintiff, promptly and before defendant had taken any steps whatever in reliance upon the provision for a five-year extension, comes into a court of equity and asks relief on the ground of mistake.... There was ... no meeting of the minds of the parties in respect to the extension.... Mere inadvertence in signing the wrong lease is not such negligence as should bar plaintiff from relief.... Where no one is injured by a mistake except the party making it, and no one has changed his position in consequence of it, relief may be granted although a high degree of care was not exercised....
>
> It is true ... that equity does not reform instruments for mistake unless the mistake is mutual, and the mistake here involved is not mutual but unilateral. But equity rescinds written instruments for unilateral mistakes.... The complaint in terms erroneously asks for reformation of the lease by striking out the clause for extension. The plaintiff, strictly speaking, is not entitled to the particular form of relief he asks for, because the defendant did not by signing the lease returned to him agree to a lease without the extension. But the fact is proved and found by the court that entitles plaintiff to rescission of the lease signed by him. Striking from that lease the provision for extension and letting the lease stand as so changed, affords the plaintiff precisely the same relief that he would have were the lease declared canceled and the defendant adjudged to have the right to hold the premises for the extended term provided for by the original lease. Strictly speaking, that is the relief that should have been adjudged. But the error of decreeing reformation instead of rescission did not affect the substantial rights of the defendant....

The Supreme Court granted a motion for rehearing, and the case was reargued. This time Justice Fowler wrote an option for the new majority, and Justice Fritz dissented. The court changed its decision. It ordered a judgment cancelling the lease if plaintiff executed and filed with the clerk of the court a lease with the terms he had intended to sign and deliver.

Miller v. Stanich could have marked a real retreat by the Wisconsin court from an objective theory of contract or the beginning of a general relief-of-hardship doctrine. However, viewed 50 years later, it seems but an odd instance in Wisconsin jurisprudence — since one could argue that it has been overruled implicitly, or at least limited to a very narrow exception. On the other hand, it is an available resource in the event a future court chooses to use it.

The Supreme Court of Wisconsin first cited its *Miller v. Stanich* decision eight years later in *Willett v. Stewart*.[35] The facts of the *Willett* case are complicated because of the tangled relationships among the parties. In June of 1929, Mr. and Mrs. Willett, both of whom then were in their seventies, owned property mortgaged to Mr. Garland. About ten acres of this land were referred to as the Bristol Tile Works, consisting of a factory, machinery and land from which workers took clay as a raw material. The Willetts' home occupied another acre or more and was part of the same tract of land. The description in the Willetts' deed covered both the Bristol Tile Works and their home.

The Willetts wanted to convey the portion of their land which contained the Bristol Tile Works to John and Zelba Runge. Zelba was the Willetts' daughter and John was her husband. William Runge, John's brother, practiced law in the same office as Calvin Stewart; Stewart was the Municipal Judge for Kenosha County. An associate in their law office drafted the conveyance from the Willetts to John and Zelba. He mistakenly used the same description of the property he found on the original deed. The Willetts signed the conveyance which they were not aware conveyed *both* the Bristol Tile Works *and their home* to their daughter and son-in-law.

Judge Stewart had some money to invest. William Runge suggested that Stewart loan John and Zelba about $7,000, secured by a mortgage on the Bristol Tile Works. Judge Stewart agreed. The same associate drafted the mortgage securing Judge Stewart's loan to John and Zelba and used the same mistaken description of the property he had used in the original conveyance. This subjected the Willetts' home to Judge Stewart's mortgage.

John and Zelba Runge failed to make payments and failed to keep the Bristol Tile Works insured. In 1936, Judge Stewart began foreclosure procedures. The Willetts sued for reformation so that the mortgage would not apply to their home.

The trial court reformed the mortgage to exclude the Willetts' home. It relied on Judge Stewart's testimony,

> William Runge did not tell me there were any buildings on the property used for residential purposes. I was not told that anyone lived in any of the buildings on the land that was mortgaged to me. At the time I loaned the money, ... I didn't have the Willett home in my mind. The first time I knew the Willett home was included in the description was after we started to foreclose. Prior to that time I never thought anything about whether or not the Willett home was included in my mortgage.

Stewart did not see the premises before making the loan. The trial court said "if the defendant Calvin Stewart was in any way misinformed as to the extent or

---

[35]227 Wis. 303, 277 N.W. 665 (1938). Again, we have taken much of the information about the case that follows from the briefs and record on appeal.

value of the property on which he was to be given a mortgage to secure the loan he was making to the defendants, John and Zelba Runge, it was because of statements made to him by William Runge, a brother of John Runge, an attorney sharing an office with Mr. Stewart at the time...." While some of the proceeds of the loan had gone to pay off the Garland mortgage on the home, Mr. and Mrs. Willett were not responsible for anything said by William Runge.

The case was appealed to the Supreme Court of Wisconsin. Neither side mentioned *Miller v. Stanich* in its briefs. Both sides offered rather weak legal analyses. Both attorneys tried to convince the Supreme Court that the equities favored their clients. Judge Stewart's lawyer pointed out that if the Willetts gained reformation of the mortgage, they would own their home free and clear of security interests while Judge Stewart would have loaned over $7,000 on the property now valued at no more than $2,500. His brief spoke of a conspiracy between William Runge, Judge Stewart's former associate in practice, and Runge's relatives. The Willetts' lawyer responded that the low value of the Bristol Tile Works was caused by the depression and not by any fault of the Willetts. Moreover, he objected to the expression of personal anger "against a young lawyer who had the moral courage to testify against his former office associate, who at the time happened to be a judge before whom the lawyer would have occasion to appear from time to time."

The Supreme Court of Wisconsin reversed the decree reforming the mortgage. It said "no doubt, there was a mutual mistake as between the Willetts and the Runges." However, Judge Stewart loaned money on the representation that it would be secured by a mortgage on about 11 1/2 acres of land. Without the Willetts' homestead, there would be less than 11 acres included. The court quoted language from *Jentzch v. Roenfanz*:[36] "[I]f the mistake has not been mutual but has been made inadvertently on one side and yet in good faith by the other, if any amendment or reformation of the contract can, under any circumstances, be made, it cannot be made so as to make the agreement conform merely to the views of the party seeking reformation, but only to the original views of both parties." The court then cited *Miller v. Stanich* as supporting this proposition, but it did not discuss the case. Finally, the court concluded "there was no mutual mistake such as is necessary for reformation on the part of the Stewarts."[37]

How does the *Willett* case differ from *Miller v. Stanich*? Both involve drafting mistakes made by lawyers concerning documents related to real estate. It is likely that neither Stanich nor Judge Stewart relied on a literal reading of the rights

---

[36] 185 Wis. 189, 201 N.W. 504 (1924).

[37] We can notice another odd fact about the case. Judge Stewart benefits from a mistake made by a lawyer working in Stewart's law office. Today we might consider fiduciary duty and agency theories if we were representing the Willetts. Indeed, Judge Stewart's firm seems to have represented both sides to the transaction. Lawyers cannot benefit from such a conflict of interest. None of this was raised at trial or on appeal.

granted to them by the documents in a way related to their economic interests. Stanich thought he had a five year renewal plus an option to renew for five more years at a very favorable rent. Judge Stewart thought he had a mortgage on 11 1/2 acres of land, but he did not think he had a mortgage on any residential property. Stanich lost only his expected gain as a result of the decision in his case.[38] Judge Stewart would have found himself with security worth only $2,500 to cover a $7,000 debt if the Willetts had won.

Does the distinction between the *Miller* and the *Willett* cases turn on the remedy? In *Miller*, the court could rescind and rely on the option to renew contained in the original lease to put the parties where they should have been. In *Willett*, rescission would have ended Judge Stewart's security interest in the Bristol Tile Works as well as the Willett home. Reformation to exclude the home was needed. However, why can't judges rewrite legal documents to arrive at what they see as appropriate results? In the *Willett* case, would reformation of the mortgage be anything more than making the paper deal conform to the real deal? Or to the deal Judge Stewart would have made had he known the facts in 1929?

The Supreme Court of Wisconsin had cited *Miller v. Stanich* in only four other Wisconsin decisions concerning mistake as of 1994. The most recent Supreme Court decision distinguishes, but does not repudiate, it.[39] A recent[40] Court of Appeals decision dismissed an appellant's argument that Wisconsin had adopted the Restatement view of unilateral mistake, finding no evidence of this. It commented on the appellant's citation to *Miller v. Stanich*, by observing in a footnote that "The [appellant] offers only a 1930 case, *Miller v. Stanich*...." Other than that case, the court found no evidence that Wisconsin had adopted a liberalized view of unilateral mistake.

Why has *Miller v. Stanich* had such a limited application? If we read the decision narrowly, it may be that it applies only to a situation very unlikely to occur. One can get relief for a unilateral mistake which a court views as innocent only when a court can be almost certain there has been no reliance. In addition,

---

[38]However, consider Fuller and Perdue's comment in light of Stanich's position:

> The difficulties in proving reliance and subjecting it to pecuniary measurement are such that the business man knowing, or sensing, that these obstacles stood in the way of judicial relief would hesitate to rely on a promise in any case where the legal sanction was of significance to him. To encourage reliance we must therefore dispense with its proof. For this reason it has been found wise to make recovery on a promise independent of reliance, both in the sense that in some cases the promise is enforced though not relied on (as in the bilateral business agreement) and in the sense that recovery is not limited to the detriment incurred in reliance.

Fuller and Perdue, The Reliance Interest in Contracts Damages: Pt.1, 46 Yale Law Journal 52, 62 (1936).

[39]Dept. of Transportation v. Transportation Commission, 330 N.W.2d 159 (1983).

[40]Erickson by Wrightman v. Gunderson, 515 N.W.2d 293 (Wis. App. 1994).

perhaps it must be a situation in which a court can bring about a proper result by rescission rather than reformation. If a court calls off the mistaken transaction, some other transaction must exist that defends the rights of both parties.

In the *Miller* case, an illiterate could not protect himself by reading the lease, and he relied on his lawyer. The lawyer made an error that anyone might make. (Indeed, Stanich's lawyer has some responsibility for creating a situation in which it was easy to make a mistake. He drafted two detailed and complex commercial leases that differed only in twenty-three words which were easy to overlook.) Stanich could not argue that he had relied in any substantial way on a lease to begin five years in the future. Stanich clearly wanted to renew for five years whether he got an option to renew for an additional five beyond that. Finally, since the original lease stood, all a court had to do was rescind the mistaken renewal.

In the *Willett* case, however, the Supreme Court of Wisconsin could not be sure that Judge Stewart had not relied on representations about the total number of acres of land that would be security for his loan. Moreover, rescission of the mortgage would have left Judge Stewart without any security. Reformation was needed, but the court was unwilling to write a contract for the parties that they ought to have written.

There is another, although very speculative, explanation for the history of *Miller v. Stanich*. Professor William Herbert Page was the University of Wisconsin Law School's expert on contracts through the 1920s and 1930s. Page knew many of the Justices of the Supreme Court of Wisconsin personally. His views influenced many lawyers who graduated from the Law School before the Second World War. The late Professor William Gorham Rice was a young contracts teacher at Wisconsin shortly after the court decided the *Miller* case. Rice reported that Page annually singled out *Miller v. Stanich* in his contracts class for a major attack. He used it as an example of a foolish decision which ignored the objective theory of contracts in favor of some vague ideas about the meeting of the minds. We can never be sure, but perhaps *Miller v. Stanich* became an embarrassment to the Supreme Court of Wisconsin. It was better ignored than even distinguished. Moreover, Wisconsin lawyers who had taken Page's class were taught that the case was unsound. They might hesitate to raise it before the courts.

Was Page right? Or is there reason to have an expansive unilateral mistake doctrine which would allow reworking of contracts and other legal documents to achieve good ends? Consider the following, and ask how Sharp, Kessler and Fine, and the authors of the Restatement would have dealt with *Miller* and *Willett*. As you read the selections, ask yourself how easy the criteria they suggest would be to apply.

Promissory Liability. II
Malcolm Pitman Sharp[41]

The extreme and simple case of unilateral mistake is indeed the case where one signs the wrong paper and sends it off to his correspondent by way of the acceptance of an offer already made; discovering the mistake at once, and notifying the correspondent before the communication has in any way affected his conduct. Here it appears persuasively that the same reasons which require relief in cases of mutual error may also require relief in any case of unilateral mistake.

The objective theory of contracts is not really threatened by such a suggestion, for relief from the consequences of the transaction will be allowed subject only to equitable limitations. Thus it is commonly said that change of position on the part of the person relying on the transaction will defeat relief for mistake. The mistaken person has perhaps merely by making a promise assumed some risk. He seems, however, in no worse a position than one who negligently misstates a fact. Apart from odd decisions about the measure of damages for deceit, a consistent treatment of liability would, it seems, require the mistaken party at most to make good the loss of the other party from the transaction as a whole, as a condition of relief against other consequences of the transaction. The mistaken party would thus of course make restitution and compensate the other party normally for expenses incurred in reliance on the promise as made, but the mistaken person would be relieved from liability for expectation damages.

Culpa in Contrahendo?

In an important article entitled *Culpa in Contrahendo*, Bargaining in Good Faith, and Freedom of Contract: A Comparative Study,[42] Friedrich Kessler and Edith Fine advanced some important ideas concerning pre-contractual, or non-contractual, liability. They argued that the German doctrine of *Culpa in Contrahendo* had important functional analogs in U.S. law, and that a study of the German doctrine could help inform our understanding of problems faced in our own legal system.

The German doctrine provides that parties engaged in negotiating a contract have a duty to negotiate in good faith. If the parties fail to reach an agreement, and if one of the negotiating parties has failed to act in good faith, then that party can be held responsible for the expenses incurred by the other in relying on ultimate formation of the contract. American contract law, at least formally, fails to recognize any pre-contractual duty, but the law of preliminary agreements,

---

[41]7 University of Chicago Law Review 250, 267 (1939).

[42]77 Harvard Law Review 401 (1964).

firm offers, mistake, and misrepresentation, as well as rules of negligence, estoppel and implied contract give some of the same protections.

The German doctrine arose as a way of dealing with the problem of unilateral mistake. Civil law countries, like Germany, had endorsed the subject theory of contract formation. In some cases, however, especially in cases of unilateral mistake, the application of the subject theory might create too broad a right of avoidance. *Culpa in contrahendo* emerged as a way of creating an incentive to avoid careless promise-making, as well as giving some protection to those who might rely on those promises. Some U.S. commentators had been critical of the German doctrine, and had urged that the objective theory, which would often protect the full expectation interest, provided a stronger, and more suitable incentive for parties to avoid careless manifestations of assent.

The first Restatement of Contracts, which can be taken to represent the conventional view of the matter in the United States, states that the mistake of one party does not automatically render a transaction voidable even when the mistake formed the basis for the mistaken party to enter into the contract. But there is a growing body of case law that offers relief for mistake, and which emphasizes some of the same factors that are important under the doctrine of *culpa in contrahendo*. Exceptions in the American law have been carved out for fraud and misrepresentation. Courts are also increasingly considering notions of good faith and fair dealing even at the expense of creating unpredictability in the market place. This has led to exceptions being made for unconscionability and for mistakes of which the other party should have been aware. Relief is also available for material mistakes as to essential terms. Usually when relief is denied, the unilateral nature of the mistake is only one of a number of factors considered. Often courts, in denying relief, stress the immateriality of the mistake, the fact that parties could not be restored to their prior positions and negligence on the part of the mistaken party. Also while miscalculations of price, or errors as to quantity, are generally sufficient, several decisions denying relief in such cases have emphasized the fact that the goods had already changed hands or the parties had materially altered their positions. As Kessler and Fine put it:

> To sum up, in attempting to find acceptable solutions mediating between the legitimate interests of both promisor and promisee, traditional doctrine in this country has been redefined by a body of case law too large to be ignored. In this process of refinement of our law of contract, *culpa in contrahendo* and notions of unjust enrichment have played a significant role. While in the civil law countries *culpa in contrahendo* has been used in large measure to mitigate the will theory, the common law starting from the other end has employed it as one of its weapons to soften the rigor of the objective theory of contracts. In this country the process of mitigation has found further manifestation in the notion that a mistaken party should be protected against oppressive burdens when rescission would impose no substantial hardship on the party seeking enforcement of the contract. Thus a link has

been established between operative mistake and unjust enrichment. Here is an instance where the common law will look into adequacy of consideration. This variance from the general rule is not surprising, since the ordinary interest in protecting a price mutually arrived at is not present here.[43]

The Restatement's Synthesis of Common Law Rules

The Restatement (Second) of Contracts contains a number of rules dealing with unilateral mistakes. Those who drafted it were influenced by cases such as *Miller v. Stanich* and the Kessler and Fine article. Remember, as a way to give some content to the Restatement's abstractions, ask how a court adopting the Restatement (Second) would decide the *Miller* and *Willett* cases. You also should ask what the likely impact of the Restatement (Second) on bargaining to settle cases might be. At this point you should consult §§ 153, 154, 157, 158 and 204 of the Restatement (Second) of Contracts in the statutory supplement.

The following case does not cite the Restatement (Second) of Contracts provisions on unilateral mistake. Nonetheless, does it take the approach advocated by the second Restatement?

S.T.S. TRANSPORT SERVICE, INC. v. VOLVO WHITE TRUCK CORP.

766 F.2d 1089 (7th Cir. 1985)

CUDAHY, J. Plaintiff appeals from a finding of unilateral mistake and rescission of a contract of sale. We affirm the judgment of the district court....
Plaintiff-appellant S.T.S. Transport Service, Inc., ("S.T.S.") is an Illinois corporation whose principal place of business is located in Alsip, Illinois. Since its incorporation in 1978, S.T.S. has leased tractor trucks and trailers to other companies and has also hauled freight for customers. Volvo White Truck Corporation ("Volvo White") is a Virginia corporation with its principal place of business in Greensboro, North Carolina. There is a branch dealership of Volvo White in Alsip, Illinois. In 1979 and 1980 S.T.S. bought trucks and heavy equipment from White Motor Company ("White Motor"), a truck manufacturer whose assets were purchased in 1981 by Volvo White.

Early in 1981 S.T.S. expressed an interest in purchasing eight new tractor trucks from White Motor in Alsip. In order to avoid a down payment, S.T.S.

---

[43]Kessler and Fine, *supra*.

wanted to trade in trucks it already owned and use its equity in those trucks as a down payment. After appraising the trucks S.T.S. intended to trade in, and after some negotiations concerning the appraised value, White Motor offered to sell S.T.S. eight 1981 Road Commander trucks on the following terms:

(a) The 1981 Road Commander trucks would be sold to S.T.S. for a price of $58,749 each;

(b) S.T.S. would trade White Motor one used truck for each new truck purchased;

(c) S.T.S. would continue to make payments (to financing companies) on the used trucks through July, 1981;

(d) White Motor would value six of the used trucks at the same amount that S.T.S. would owe on them in July, 1981; $26,560 each;

(e) White Motor would give S.T.S. a credit of $25,000 on another of the trucks;

(f) White Motor would arrange financing for S.T.S.

Provision (d) meant that S.T.S. would receive no credit for any equity in six of the trucks it owned, but that White Motor would simply pay off the amount still owed by S.T.S. on those trucks. The list price of the Road Commander trucks was $80,784. The offer price of $58,749 was reached by adding a profit of $2,200 to the Alsip branch's base cost of $56,549 for the trucks. These terms were confirmed in a March 10, 1981 letter from White Motor to S.T.S. Apparently they were not satisfactory to S.T.S., and negotiations were suspended.

In August, 1981, while White Motor [remember — the assets of White Motor were later bought by Volvo-White] was the subject of bankruptcy proceedings, S.T.S. solicited a new offer from them. White Motor recalculated its costs and sent a letter, dated August 17, 1981, which set out the specifications of the eight Road Commander Trucks, and which concluded with the following paragraphs:

Net delivered price F.O.B. Alsip, including preparation, but excluding state/local taxes is ... $273,176.00.

We will pay off balance due to White Motor Credit Corporation on the (6) 1979 Western Stars. We assume you will make your payment to White Motor Credit Corporation on December 14, 1981, and then begin a new note with White Motor Credit Corporation effective January 30, 1982, as your first payment on the new equipment. There will be no prepayment return to you, that figure ($9,035) is included in the above figures.

We will also pay off the "estimated" money owed to I.T.T. of $31,755 once your trades are turned in. This is the estimated balance after your November 30, 1981 payment to I.T.T. We will receive the 1978 Freightliner and 1977 Peterbilt as trades and we will also receive the 1979 Western Stars.

> *Hope this isn't confusing. I just net'd everything out and gave you the bottom line. It's a good deal for you for 2 reasons, there is a $3,500.00 U.T.A. on this deal, and we expect 6% 1982 increase by September 1, 1981. You are actually purchasing 1982 units at 1981 prices with $3,500 off on top.*
>
> *What do you think!!!!!!!*

A moment's calculations makes clear how widely the price suggested in the August 12 letter diverges from the earlier price. Eight trucks at the March 10 price of $58,749 would total $469,992; there was to be no credit for the equity of any of the trucks traded in, except for one, and the credit for that one was to be $25,000. Subtracting that credit from the total for the eight trucks would result in a net price of something just under $445,000. The new net price named in the August letter is some $170,000 — over $20,000 a truck — less.

Appellee Volvo White claims that the August figure was the result of a miscalculation. Intending to offer the eight new trucks for the lower price of $56,530 each, for a total of $452,240, White Motor subtracted from that figure not only $42,000 in credit that it was now willing to allow on the trade-in of two trucks, but the $137,064 in assessed value on six other trucks, an amount which equalled the outstanding debt on the trucks. Since S.T.S. was to be credited with no equity on those six used trucks, the assessed value should not have been subtracted from the price of the new trucks. White Motor merely intended to wipe out S.T.S.'s remaining debt on those trucks. By subtracting the amount they did from the price of the new trucks, White Motor in effect offered to credit S.T.S. with an amount equal to the amount of the debt remaining on each truck.

In response to further inquiries by S.T.S, White Motor sent out a second letter on September 2, 1981. This letter was in all respects identical to the August 17 letter, except that in place of the last line of the August letter the September 2 letter contained the following paragraph regarding interest rate charges:

> *If prime rate increases from todays [sic] rate of 20.5%, your rate to be charged will be 2.5% below the existing prime on date of delivery. If prime decreases, your rate will be the then existing add on rate charged by White Motor Credit Corporation.*

Both letters were sent out by Joseph LaSpina, manager of the Alsip branch. LaSpina admitted at trial that he did not review the August 17 letter before it went out, and that he did not review or sign the September 2d letter; his name was signed on the first page by his secretary.

S.T.S. accepted the offer. In December, 1981, S.T.S. turned over to Volvo White all of the trade-in vehicles. S.T.S. also entered into a new lease agreement with Suburban Truck & Trailer, under the terms of which Suburban would lease five of the new trucks from S.T.S. for three years. S.T.S. expected the lease to produce gross income before expenses of $37,876.49 per truck per year.

In January, 1982, [before the 8 new trucks were delivered to S.T.S.] the parties became aware of the problem. Volvo White informed S.T.S. that the net purchase price for the new trucks was $452,000, and S.T.S. insisted that under the contract the purchase price was $273,176. On January 15, 1982, Volvo White sent a letter admitting that it had made a clerical error in the contract. It offered to go ahead at the $452,000 price or to call off the transaction, and it confirmed that the eight trade-ins, now in Volvo White's lot, would remain the property of S.T.S. until the deal was closed. Maintaining that it could not use the trade-in vehicles in its new leasing contract with Suburban, and maintaining that under the terms of the contract Volvo White should have taken over payments of the used trucks, S.T.S. neither reclaimed the trucks nor kept up payments on them. They were repossessed and sold later in the year for approximately $20,000 per truck.[The 8 new trucks were never delivered to S.T.S.]

S.T.S. claims that it lost an equity of $70,900 which it had built up in those trade-in units. It also claims that it lost a profit of $372,352 that it would have earned under its lease with Suburban.

S.T.S. had apparently been experiencing some financial difficulty in the latter half of 1981. In January and February, 1982, it sold its remaining tractor trucks. This lawsuit was commenced on June 11, 1982. A trial in the Northern District of Illinois was held during the week of June 13, 1983. S.T.S. sought as damages its lost profits under the Suburban lease. Volvo White counterclaimed for an unpaid balance on parts and materials Volvo White had provided to S.T.S.

The district court found first that S.T.S. had a duty to mitigate its damages. It found that S.T.S. should have gone ahead with the purchase at the higher price, so that it might fulfill its own commitment to provide trucks for Suburban, reserving the right to sue Volvo White for the difference under the U.C.C. It found that since the plaintiff did not mitigate in that way, it could not realize any of the damages it claimed.

But the district judge also found that the contract contained a mistake with respect to the price term, a mistake that would not have been discovered by merely proof-reading the document. Since she found a mistake, she also found that the mistake could be excused and the contract rescinded if the plaintiff could be returned to the *status quo ante*. She found that the costs of the parts and labor which were the subject of Volvo White's counterclaim were incurred in the process of getting the trucks ready for the trade-in, so that the *status quo* could be restored with respect to those obligations by excusing them. On the other hand, she was persuaded by the testimony of witnesses that S.T.S. intended to go out of business at the end of 1981, and that "there is nothing really to restore it to in that regard." Accordingly, she entered judgment for the plaintiff on the counterclaim [denying Volvo-White's claim for parts and materials] but against the plaintiff on its principal claim. [The S.T.S. claim for lost profits and equity on trade-in trucks.]

On the question of equity, the district judge found that the used trucks probably could have been sold by S.T.S. for more than they were sold for after repossession, but that since S.T.S. had not taken advantage of the opportunity to reclaim the trucks, it was stuck with the price the trucks had actually been sold for. At that price, there was no equity, since the trucks were sold for less than the amount owed on them....

If the contract is void because of a mistake, then there is no question of mitigation, since the duty to mitigate (if there is such a duty) arises out of the breach of a valid contract. Where the court applies the doctrine of mistake, the parties are excused from the contract and consequently there is no breach. Thus, if the district court properly found a mistake concerning the price term and properly voided the contract, we need not reach the issue of mitigation.

The parties have stipulated that Illinois law governs. The sale of the trucks would be governed by the Uniform Commercial Code, chapter 26 of the Illinois Revised Code; but under § 1-103 of the Code, mistake and certain other questions are governed by the common law. 26 Ill.Rev.Stat. § 1-103.

Although the traditional case in which a contract is found to contain a mistake is one in which the parties understand a key term differently (hence, a case in which the mistake is mutual), the cases have also voided contracts — though more reluctantly — where only one party is mistaken as to the facts. In the typical case of this sort, a seller or contractor will miscalculate in adding up a list of items. Under the appropriate circumstances courts will now recognize a right to avoidance of this sort of mistake.

[The court excludes errors of judgment from the kinds of errors which may permit avoidance of the contract.]

As the law now stands, three conditions must be fulfilled before a contract can be rescinded: (1) the mistake must relate to a material feature of the contract; (2) it must have occurred despite the exercise of reasonable care; and (3) the other party must be placed in the position it was in before the contract was made....

The mistake in this case relates to the price, which must be conceded to be material. The mistake must also have occurred in spite of the exercise of reasonable care. Although reasonable care is as difficult to be precise about in this sort of case as it is elsewhere, there are some fairly clear groupings of mistake cases that can serve as guideposts. Most helpful is the knowledge that Illinois courts will generally grant relief for errors "which are clerical or mathematical." ... The reason for the special treatment for such errors, of course, is that they are difficult to prevent, and that no useful social purpose is served by enforcing the mistaken term. No incentives exist to make such mistakes; all the existing incentives work, in fact, in the opposite direction. There is every reason for a contractor to use ordinary care, and, if errors of this sort — clerical or mathematical — slip through anyway, the courts will generally find it more useful to allow the contract to be changed or rescinded than to enforce it as it is. Naturally there are cases of extreme negligence to which this presumption should not apply; and there is an exception of sorts where the contract has been relied upon. We will have something to say about this last at a later point.

Although it would be wrong to suppose that "merely" mathematical or clerical errors are easily distinguished from other errors such as those of judgment — a miscalculation about the economic climate, say — the distinction is clear enough for ordinary purposes. A merely mathematical or clerical error occurs when some term is either one-tenth or ten times as large as it should be; when a term is added in the wrong column; when it is added rather than subtracted; when it is overlooked.

The error involved here is of that sort, but if anything more difficult to detect. The Alsip manager, LaSpina, made the crucial calculations. The assessed value of the used trucks was subtracted from the price of the new trucks. Such a procedure is perfectly appropriate, ordinarily; whoever buys a new car expects to have the price reduced by the value of the trade-in. Here, however, the assessed value was set so as to match the outstanding debt on the trucks. Even so, had the offer been for S.T.S. to pay off the remaining debt on the trucks before they were traded in, the calculation would have been correct. But that was not the offer; Volvo White offered to take over the remaining debt on the trade-ins, so that there was nothing in the way of trade-in value to be subtracted from the purchase price. The assessed value was completely offset by the outstanding debt.

However foolish this mistake, once made it would not easily have been detected. S.T.S. points out that Volvo White conceded in testimony that neither of the two letters containing the term in question were reviewed by LaSpina before going out. But such an omission ought to bar rescission only if it would have resulted in the error's being detected. Here, the mistaken calculations were made by LaSpina, and there is little reason to suppose that he would have detected the error had he proof-read the errors before they went out. The error involved, therefore, was not one that would have been detected by the exercise of ordinary care, and we do not think that the trial judge erred in rejecting the defense of negligence.

The question of reliance is no different from the question whether the parties can be put into the position they were in at the time the contract was signed. Here, S.T.S. claims that it lost the equity it had in the trucks traded in. If it did in fact lose those trucks because of reliance on the contract; and if in fact there was equity in the trucks — that is, if the market value of the trucks exceeded the remaining debt; then S.T.S. is entitled to claim that equity as the price of putting it back into the position it would have been in had it not relied on the contract.

The district court found that S.T.S. could have reclaimed its trucks at any time. At the time it became apparent that Volvo White was not going to honor the contract as written, sometime in January, 1982, S.T.S. could have arranged to sell the trucks on its own. A party to a contract cannot be allowed to create damages by continuing to rely on a contract which has either been breached, or been void from the start. As of January, 1982, S.T.S. was on notice that one of those two situations applied....

Instead, S.T.S. refused to make further payments, and the trucks were repossessed and sold for amounts less than the amounts still owed on each. S.T.S. might have complained of the reasonableness of these sales, but it did not; in any case the sales do not appear to have been unreasonable.[44] The district court therefore correctly found that any loss of equity — if there was equity to begin with — was due to conduct of S.T.S., and that restoring S.T.S. to the *status quo* did not require payment for lost equity.

S.T.S. also incurred certain obligations in preparing the trucks for the trade-in; Volvo White has counterclaimed for repayment of approximately $9500 for parts and services priced during this period. The district judge found that these obligations were legitimately incurred in reliance on the contract and that before the contract can be rescinded those obligations must be excused. She therefore dismissed the counterclaim and rescinded the contract. Volvo White does not reassert its counterclaim on appeal.

Since the district court properly rescinded the contract, the question of mitigation does not arise. The judgment of the district court is affirmed.

NOTES AND QUESTIONS

1. *Mistaken calculations*: The Volvo White dealer's initial offer was calculated as follows:

Price for 8 at $58,748 each:	469,992
Less credit for 1 used truck:	*25,000*
Total to be paid by S.T.S.:	444,992
[*6 trucks traded in and dealer pays off amounts due*]	

The second mistaken offer was calculated as follows:

Price for 8 at $56,530 each:	452,240
Less credit for 2 used trucks:	*42,000*
Subtotal:	410,240 [correct amt.]
Less assessed value of 6 trucks:	*137,064* [MISTAKE]
Mistaken total:	273,176

2. *The buyer's interest*: Why does the buyer lose the benefit of the bargain? Should it have seen the mistaken calculation? At the time the second offer was made, the court tells us "White Motor was the subject of bankruptcy proceedings." Could the buyer reasonably assume that it was getting a great deal as part

---

[44]The trucks were sold for $20,000 each. Volvo White had appraised the trucks at $22,000-23,000; testimony for S.T.S. would have set the value at $30,000. Considering the conditions under which the trucks were sold, the selling price does not appear unreasonable, whichever estimate of market value we choose.

of clearing out the inventory of an almost bankrupt manufacturer? However, the next to last sentence of the second offer says "You are actually purchasing 1982 units at 1981 prices with $3,500 off on top." Was this enough to alert the buyer that the calculations were mistaken?

C. UNENFORCEABLE CONTRACTS, RESTITUTION, AND RELIANCE

People can make mistakes about whether they made a contract or if they did, what its terms are. If the mistake is discovered soon enough, all that is lost is the chance that they might have made as good, or better, a bargain elsewhere. However, in some situations reliance losses may be much greater. You will not be surprised when we tell you that restitution serves to clean up the mess in some cases. Suppose that buyer and auto dealer think they have made a contract, but are mistaken. Dealer delivers the car to buyer before discovering that there was no contract. When the mistake is discovered, the buyer won't go through with the deal. The buyer has been unjustly enriched, and the seller can recover the car in a restitution action. Things are less clear when there has been a reliance loss that does not create an economic benefit for the other party. Furthermore, even where there is a benefit, there are problems when the buyer reasonably thought she was buying something else or that the deal had not yet been closed. The seller has suffered a loss, but it may not be clear that the buyer should pay for it.

We have placed this material here for teaching reasons. It relates both backwards and forwards. That is, we considered situations where people have been mistaken about whether they made contracts or what the terms were. The material in this section suggests that the question is more than contract or no contract.

This material also forms part of the context within which problems in the coming sections occur. Up to this point, we did not want to raise restitution and reliance questions because we thought you had enough on your plate. However, we do not want to wait until the end of the course to look at this material either. Those who accept realist jurisprudence insist that judges and lawyers do not decide (1) is there a contract or can it be rescinded for mistake?, and then (2) if there is no contract, can some or all of the reliance losses be recovered? Rather, anyone considering a close question concerning whether a contract was formed may be influenced by the consequences of deciding one way or the other. Judges and lawyers may approach things backwards, asking whether the best solution to a tangled transaction may be to allow expectation or reliance damages, reformation, restitution for benefits conferred or some combination of these forms of relief.

VICKERY v. RITCHIE

202 Mass. 247, 88 N.E. 835 (1909)

KNOWLTON, C.J. This is an action to recover a balance of $10,467.16, alleged to be due the plaintiff as a contractor, for the construction of a Turkish bath house on land of the defendant. The parties signed duplicate contracts in writing, covering the work. At the time when the plaintiff signed both copies of the contract, the defendant's signature was attached, and the contract price therein named was $33,721. When the defendant signed them the contract price stated in each was $23,200. Until the building was completed the plaintiff held a contract under which he was to receive the larger sum, while the defendant held a contract for the same work, under which he was to pay only the smaller sum. This resulted from the fraud of the architect who drew the contracts, and did all the business and made all the payments for the defendant. The contracts were on typewritten sheets, and it is supposed that the architect accomplished the fraud by changing the sheets on which the price was written, before the signing by the plaintiff, and before the delivery to the defendant. The parties did not discover the discrepancy between the two writings until after the building was substantially completed. Each of them acted honestly and in good faith, trusting the statements of the architect. The architect was indicted, but he left the Commonwealth and escaped punishment.

The auditor found that the market value of the labor and materials furnished by the plaintiff, not including the customary charge for the supervision of the work, was $33,499.30, and that their total cost to the plaintiff was $32,950.96. He found that the land and building have cost the defendant much more than their market value. The findings indicate that it was bad judgment on the part of the defendant to build such a structure upon the lot, and that the increase in the market value of the real estate, by reason of that which the plaintiff put upon it, is only $22,000. The failure of the parties to discover the difference between their copies of the contract was caused by the frequently repeated fraudulent representations of the architect to each of them.

The plaintiff and the defendant were mistaken in supposing that they had made a binding contract for the construction of this building. Their minds never met in any agreement about the price. The labor and materials were furnished at the defendant's request and for the defendant's benefit. From this alone the law would imply a contract on the part of the defendant to pay for them. The fact that the parties supposed the price was fixed by a contract, when in fact there was no contract, does not prevent this implication, but leaves it as a natural result of their relations. Both parties understood and agreed that the work should be paid for, and both parties thought that they had agreed upon the price. Their mutual mistake in this particular left them with no express contract by which their rights and liabilities could be determined. The law implies an obligation to pay for what has been done and furnished under such circumstances, and the defendant, upon whose property the work was done, has no right to say that it is not to be paid for. The doctrine is not applicable to work upon real estate alone. The rule would be the same if the work and materials were used in the repair of a carriage, or of any other article of personal property, under a supposed contract with the owner, if, through a mutual mistake as to the supposed agreement upon the price, the contract became unenforceable....

The principle has often been applied when the ground for an implication of an agreement to pay was much less strong than in the present case. In *Butterfield v. Byron*, 153 Mass. 517, ... where the owner was to do a part of the work in the erection of a building, and a contractor was to do the rest under an express contract for an agreed price, it was held that, when the building was destroyed by lightning, so that the contract became impossible of performance, the contractor might recover, on a *quantum meruit* the fair value of the labor and materials that he had furnished. This was on the ground that, when the contract came to an end without the fault of either party, there was an implication that what was furnished was to be paid for, and if it could not be paid for under the contract it should be paid for on a *quantum meruit*....

If the law implies an agreement to pay, how much is to be paid? There is but one answer. The fair value of that which was furnished. No other rule can be applied. Under certain conditions the price fixed by the contract might control in such cases. In this case there was no price fixed.

The defendant contends that because the erection of a Turkish bath house on Carver Street was not a profitable investment, and therefore, through a seeming error of judgment on the part of the defendant, the building did not add to the value of the land so much by a large sum as it cost, the plaintiff must suffer the consequences of the defendant's mistake and be precluded from recovery.... [N]owhere, so far as we have been able to discover, does the law, as applied to such cases in other jurisdictions, make the right of the contractor depend in any degree upon the profit or loss to the owner, arising from his wisdom or folly, or good fortune or bad fortune, in erecting the building upon his land....

In this case there was no express contract. The plaintiff's right is to recover upon an implied contract of an owner to pay for labor and materials used upon his [owner's] property at his [owner's] request.... [I]n cases of the class to which the present one belongs the right does not depend upon the ultimate benefit received by the owner....

In all cases to which this general principle has been applied, the recovery has been upon a *quantum meruit* for that which was furnished, subject to diminution of the amount by the price named in the contract, if that was very low. The right of recovery depends upon the plaintiff's having furnished property or labor, under circumstances which entitle him to be paid for it, not upon the ultimate benefit to the property of the owner at whose request it was furnished....

NOTES AND QUESTIONS

1. *The AIA treatment of the problem*: Architects, builders and owners make many building contracts today using standard forms drafted by the American Institute of Architects. Under the 1987 version of the A.I.A. Standard Form of Agreement Between Owner and Architect § 2.4.2, "[t]he Architect shall assist the Owner in the preparation of the necessary bidding information, bidding forms, the Conditions of the Contract, and the form of Agreement between the Owner and Contractor." Section 2.5.1 provides: "[t]he Architect, following the Owner's approval of the Construction Documents and of the latest preliminary estimate of Construction Cost, shall assist the Owner in obtaining bids or negotiated proposals, and assist in awarding and preparing contracts for construction." Section 2.6.4 provides: "The Architect shall be a representative of and shall advise and consult with the Owner (1) during construction until final payment to the Contractor is due, and (2) as an Additional Service at the Owner's direction from time to time during the correction period described in the Contract for Construction. The Architect shall have authority to act on behalf of the Owner only to the extent provided in this Agreement unless otherwise modified by written instrument."[45]

In almost all building contracts, the owner and not the builder selects the architect. Principals usually are liable for contracts made by their agents acting within the scope of their actual or apparent authority. They are liable also for their agents' torts committed in the scope of their employment. In light of all this, shouldn't a rule similar to that of the *Ayer* case apply in *Vickery v. Ritchie*? That is, shouldn't the owner who selected the architect be responsible for the architect's fraud and mistakes?

2. *Calculating the amount of restitution*: If liability is based on restitution, how much should the builder in *Vickery v. Ritchie* be able to recover? Consider the possibilities, rounding off the sums:

(a) Increased value of owner's land	$22,000
(b) Owner's contract price	$23,000
(c) 1/2 the difference between construction cost and the added value to the land, or ($32,750 -$22,000 = 10,750; 1/2 10,750 = 5,375 + 22,000)	$27,375
(d) Cost of construction	$32,750
(e) Market value of labor & material, but not including supervision	$33,500
(f) Builder's contract price	$33,721

---

[45]AIA Document B141, Owner-Architect Agreement, 14th ed. © The American Institute of Architects.

Does your answer turn on choice, fault, benefit, loss sharing or some form of social engineering?

3. *The Restatement of Restitution's solution*: Section 155 of the Restatement of Restitution offers still another solution to the *Vickery v. Ritchie* problem:

(1) Where a person is entitled to restitution from another because the other, without tortious conduct, has received a benefit, the measure of recovery for the benefit thus received is the value of what has been received, limited, if the recipient was not at fault or was no more at fault than the claimant, to its value in advancing the purposes of the recipient, except as limited by the statement in Subsection (2).

(2) Where a transaction is rescinded solely because of a mistake as to price, the recipient's duty of restitution is to pay not less than he expected to pay nor more than the claimant expected to receive.

Thus, the Restatement of Restitution would award the "value of what was received, limited ... to its value in advancing the purposes of the recipient ..." or $22,000. However, under Subsection (2), the recipient must "pay not less than he expected to pay ..." or $23,000. Does this solution appeal to you? Given the difficulty in establishing the values in question, shouldn't we just presume that the builder's cost is the owner's benefit? Is the cost of establishing the facts worth the effort?

4. *Recovering for reliance expenses and calling it restitution*: The *Vickery* case deals with the situation in which the work done by the builder in the mistaken belief that there was a contract was clearly received by the landowner. The *Vickery* case is interesting because the cost incurred by the builder so substantially exceeded the increase in the value of the land — which we might expect to be an unusual occurrence. (Do you see why?) Nevertheless, it is undeniable that plaintiff's work had really enriched the defendant; the question was, how much, and whether to focus on increases in asset value or the imputed value of work done at one's request. This undeniable fact of enrichment apparently provides the justification for a recovery on a restitution theory. But the court seems candid in admitting that the benefit recovered by the defendant, though the ground for the claim, is not the measure of the recovery. In contrast, the Restatement of Restitution suggests that the award cannot exceed its "... value in advancing the purposes of the recipient." The measure of recovery seems more clearly constrained by the substantive rationale for the claim, which is said to be the avoidance of unjust enrichment.

But what happens when a person, mistakenly believing themselves to be party to an enforceable contract, incurs expenses which seem not to benefit the other party to the *un*enforceable contract at all? Remember the next to the last paragraph in *S.T.S. Transport, Inc. v. Volvo White Truck Corp.*? It appears that in preparing the used trucks to be traded in, S.T.S. repaired them, buying parts and services from Volvo White on credit. Volvo White had asked to be paid for these parts and services. The trial court had dismissed Volvo White's claim (for reasons that are either ill-considered or unclear), and Volvo White had not pressed the claim on appeal. But what if Volvo White *had* insisted that the court address its counterclaim?

First, it is not clear that the delivery of parts and services to S.T.S. should even have been regarded as part of the ill-fated transaction involving the sale of the 8 new trucks. Second, even if S.T.S. was obliged to repair the trucks, and to buy services and parts from Volvo White, S.T.S. may have received the benefit of those parts and services when the used trucks were subsequently resold after being repossessed. The repairs and parts may have increased the liquidation value of the trucks. *But lets assume* that, perhaps because the trucks sat unused on the Volvo White lot for several months, the parts and services were never of any measurable economic benefit to S.T.S.? Should Volvo White receive nothing? Or should it be paid something because it provided goods and services to another upon the request of that other? Is this like *Vickery*?

The 1928 Connecticut case of *Kearns v. Andre*[46] allowed recovery of reliance expenses. In *Kearns* the seller incurred expenses in remodeling a house to suit the tastes of a buyer who then refused to complete the transaction. The buyer was held to be entitled to refuse, since the court held the contract to be insufficiently definite. The court concluded, however, that the disappointed seller was entitled to recover expenses it had incurred "... in good faith and in the honest belief that the agreement was sufficiently definite to be enforced," subject to a deduction to the extent that any of those expenses were of any benefit to the seller. The court said, "He has performed those services at the request of the other party to the contract, and in the expectation, known to the other, that he would be compensated therefore. Here is a sufficient basis in law that reasonable compensation would be made...." The court disallowed a claim for additional remodeling to meet the needs of a second buyer, on the ground that to allow such recovery would be to permit recovery upon an unenforceable contract. *Kearns v. Andre* was distinguished in 1941 in *R.F. Baker & Co. v. P. Ballentine & Sons*.[47] Finally, in *Automobile Insurance Co. v. Model Family Laundries*[48] the Connecticut court asserted that the true ground for recovery in cases like *Kearns v. Andre* was quasi contract for unjust enrichment, and that quasi contract required that defendant receive a benefit.

The courts in these cases seem conflicted. There seems to be an urge to allow some recovery. The problem is that the theory available to them is apparently grounded in the retention of a benefit by a defendant in circumstances where to retain that benefit without some payment for it is unjust. But if the defendant has received no benefit ... ?

---

[46]107 Conn. 181, 139 A. 695 (1928).

[47]127 Conn. 680, 20 A.2d 82 (1941).

[48]133 Conn. 433, 52 A.2d 137 (1947).

The paradox was addressed head on in the California case of *Earhart v. William Low Co.*,[49] Earhart Construction Co. made a contract with William Low Co. to construct the Pana Rama Mobile Home Park. The contract was subject to the conditions that William Low Co. obtain the needed financing and that Earhart Construction Co. secure a performance bond. Neither condition ever was fulfilled. The park was to be built on land owned by William Low Co. and an adjoining tract owned by Ervie Pillow. There was a special use permit altering the zoning regulations that allowed a mobile home park to be built on Pillow's land. However, it would expire on May 27th, without possibility of renewal unless work on the property was "diligently underway" by that date. William Low Co. made a contract to buy the Pillow tract subject to financing. On May 25th, William Low's representative telephoned Fayette L. Earhart and said it had obtained the necessary financing. It urged Earhart to move the necessary equipment onto the property and begin work immediately to save the special use permit. Earhart's crew began work at once. It worked for a week, often in the presence of William Low. On June 1st, Earhart Construction Co. submitted a request for a progress payment. Fayette Earhart then learned that William Low Co. had not obtained the needed financing. William Low Co. refused the bill, and it later signed a contract with another construction company to build the park.

The trial court awarded Earhart Construction Co. the reasonable value of the work done on William Low Co.'s tract but refused to award anything for the work done on the land owned by Ervie Pillow. It explained, "[a]ll he pays for is the value of what he got, notwithstanding how much it cost the plaintiff to produce it." In other words, work done on the Pillow land at the request of the William Low Co. was not a benefit to it. The trial court followed several California decisions. They held that there must be a direct benefit to justify restitution and the satisfaction of obtaining compliance with a request was not enough.

The Supreme Court of California reversed. Justice Tobriner relied on a dissenting opinion of former Chief Justice Roger Traynor that "urged we abandon the unconscionable requirement of 'benefit' to the defendant and allow recovery in quantum meruit whenever a party acts to his detriment in reliance on another's representation that he will give compensation for the detriment suffered." Traynor argued that benefit conferred was a pure fiction. Allowing recovery would place the loss where it belongs — on the party whose requests induced performance in justifiable reliance on the belief that the requested performance would be paid for. It was enough that plaintiff performed the work on the Pillow property at the urgent request of defendant. Plaintiff reasonably relied, believing that defendant would pay for the work.

---

[49]158 Cal.Rptr. 887, 600 P.2d 1344 (1979).

Justice Clark dissented on this point. He said, "[a]bsent promise of payment, a person who does no more than request an attorney to consult with a potential client does not incur an obligation to pay the attorney for the consultation." Justice Clark said that William Low Co. might have benefited from saving the special use permit. This increased the time William Low Co. had to obtain financing. However, "[b]y commencing work to maintain the permit, thereby increasing the time to obtain financing, plaintiff also increased the likelihood that his contract would be effective. Because the benefits to plaintiff are substantially similar to those to defendant company, there is no unjust enrichment, and no basis for finding an implied in fact promise to pay."

5. *Same result — different theory*: Is there another way in which one could provide relief to those who rely on unenforceable contracts? If there is, it might be possible to apply it, and avoid the potentially unfortunate effects of stretching the concept of benefit in restitution cases (if not, as some might assert, eliminating it altogether). What about using Restatement § 90? The Wisconsin Supreme Court held in *Hoffman v. Red Owl*[50] that Hoffman was entitled to recover the losses he had reasonably incurred in relying on Red Owl's promise even though that promise was not definite enough to support a contract. Should cases of indefiniteness be treated differently than cases of unilateral mistake? Would the utilization of § 90 as a theory allow courts to get to just outcomes without doing violence to existing restitutionary doctrines? Or doesn't it matter? What difference does it make so long as the courts are able to arrive at results which square with our sense of justice?

DUNNEBACKE v. PITTMAN

216 Wis. 305, 257 N.W. 30 (1934)

NELSON, J. ... Did the court err in permitting Pittman to recover from the defendants Gilligan upon quasi contract for work performed and materials furnished by him in erecting a breakwater upon certain premises belonging to defendant Lena B. Gilligan?

... The defendants Gilligan were residents of Chicago. Mrs. Gilligan taught school there. She owned a parcel of real estate in Kenosha county which abutted upon Lake Michigan. It extended about 140 feet along the lake. The side of the property which sloped abruptly toward the lake was subject to erosion. The defendant Pittman was a local contractor. Prior to the fall of 1932 he had been employed at various times by the Gilligans to perform small jobs in and upon the premises. One of such jobs was the erection of a concrete wall across the slope of the bank for the purpose of protecting it from erosion. That wall as constructed did not extend very far into the soil, and the Gilligans feared that it might give

---

[50]26 Wis.2d 683, 133 N.W.2d 267 (1965).

way and fall down unless it was in some manner protected. The Gilligans talked to Pittman at different times about building another wall to protect it. In the spring of 1932 the Gilligans and Pittman met on the beach of the property and at that time discussed what could be done to protect the existing wall. Mr. Pittman testified that at that conference Mrs. Gilligan stated that she would like to put in a wall to protect the first wall; that at that time she walked out to the water's edge, extended her arms, and indicated where the wall which she had in mind should be located; that she asked him whether it should run straight along the bank parallel with the water's edge; that he expressed the opinion that it should not, but should be constructed in the form of a V; that he marked a point near the water's edge to which the end of the proposed wall should reach; that he told her it was his opinion that the structure should be 7 feet high, 4 feet thick at the bottom and 3 or 3½ feet thick at the top; that he told Mrs. Gilligan that it would cost her 25 cents per cubic foot; and that Mrs. Gilligan told him to go ahead and get it in as quickly as he could.

Mrs. Gilligan testified that in the spring of 1932 she discussed with Mr. Pittman the advisability of constructing a wall; that she then told him that she would like to have something constructed about 12 feet in front of the existing wall that would extend into the soil four feet and be level with the bank, for the purpose of protecting the first wall; that she asked him to give her a figure on it and that he promised to do so; that she talked about a wall which would extend across the bank, parallel with the first wall, and that Pittman suggested a V-shaped wall; that Mr. Pittman judged that the wall proposed by him would be about 40 feet from the ends of the old wall to the apex of the triangle; that she asked him how much that would cost; that he said he did not just know, but that he would figure it up and let her know. She further testified that during the summer of 1932 several other conversations regarding the proposed wall were had; that she saw Mr. Pittman upon the property on September 25 and talked to him about finishing up the different jobs that he had not completed; that she never gave Mr. Pittman orders to go ahead with the construction of the V-shaped wall, but told him to go ahead and finish the things that he had already begun; that thereafter she and her husband went back to Chicago and did not again visit the property until two weeks later, when she discovered that Mr. Pittman had erected a massive V-shaped wall extending from the bank across the beach, a distance of about fifty feet, to the water's edge (the wall is about 7 feet high, 4 feet thick at the bottom, and about 3 feet thick at the top); that upon discovering the wall she was greatly excited because she had never given him any orders to build it; that she told him that the structure was a monstrosity and that she wanted it removed from her property; that after a heated discussion he told her that, if she would pay his workmen, he would blow the damn thing into the lake; that she told him to go ahead and do it as it did not do her any good. The testimony of Mrs. Gilligan was in all respects corroborated by her husband. The breakwater, as constructed, completely blocked travel along the beach and made it impossible to go from one side of the property to the other along the beach without stepping into the water. Testimony was adduced to show that the structure as completed was a benefit to the property and also to the effect that the erection of the wall had greatly damaged it.

At the conclusion of the testimony the court said: "I do not think I can find under the evidence here that the minds of these parties ever met on this subject, there was never more than a discussion about it. I do not believe the plaintiff was warranted in doing the work he did there. That is the way it impresses me. In important work like this the minds of the parties certainly should meet as to what it is to be and the payments and everything. It illustrates a careless way of doing business, that is what it is, very careless. I cannot see how a contractor would go ahead and do a piece of work like this without having something more, something to show for it. It seems he did it. I cannot imagine why he did it if he did not suppose he was doing what he should do. But the evidence is not satisfactory. The burden is on them to show that there was a contract entered into here with the owner of the property as what it was to be."

Pittman's attorney thereupon asked leave to amend the cross-complaint to conform to the proof so that it would state a cause of action based upon the theory of unjust enrichment.... The court allowed the amendment. The court said: "These parties had business dealings with one another and it is undisputed that they talked about some improvement of this kind being made. The mistake is that the defendant went ahead with this great expense without getting specification and contract, of course, as it should have been done; but it cannot be said that he did not go in there and make all of this expenditure in good faith."

... The real question therefore is whether the judgment entered may be upheld under the law of quasi contracts.

... Quasi contracts "Are legal obligations rather than equitable in the sense that they originated in the courts of law and are enforced by means of so-called legal as distinguished from equitable remedies." They rest "solely upon the universally recognized moral obligation of one who has received a benefit, the retention of which would be unjust, to make restitution." Woodward, The Law of Quasi Contracts, § 6(4)....

In this case, although the court found that the property was benefited, it appears that the breakwater was constructed during the absence of the Gilligans; that they had not contracted with Pittman to build it; that they had never contemplated building that kind of structure; that they did not desire to retain it, but insisted rather that it should be removed from the property. The only sense in which it may be said that the Gilligans are retaining the breakwater is that it continues to exist upon the property against their will. It therefore appears that there is no unjust or inequitable retention of a benefit by them. Had the Gilligans been present during the time that the construction work was going on and had they made no protest, we should have a different situation with which to deal. If, after the breakwater was constructed, the Gilligans had in some manner manifested an intention to retain it, a recovery on the basis of quasi contract might be sustained. It is our opinion that neither the evidence, the findings of fact, nor the conclusions of law sustain a recovery based on the law of quasi contracts.... *Reversed.*

NOTES AND QUESTIONS

1. *Distinctions*: How is *Dunnebacke* different from *Vickery v. Richie*? How is it different from *Kearns v. Andre* (discussed in note 4, above)? In all three cases construction work is done in the apparent good faith belief that the one doing it will be fairly compensated according to a contract, and in all three cases courts find that no contracts arose. Can you rationalize the no-recovery result in *Dunnebacke* with the recoveries in the other two cases? If not, which one reaches the better result?

2. *Material from the briefs and record*: The trial judge said that he did "not believe the plaintiff was warranted in doing the work he did there.... In important work like this the minds of the parties certainly should meet as to what it is to be and the payments and everything. It illustrates a careless way of doing business, that is what it is, very careless. I cannot see how a contractor would go ahead and do a piece of work like this without having something more, something to show for it." Given the relationship between Pittman and the Dunnebackes, was Pittman likely to await plans, specifications and a written contract? Should courts follow ordinary patterns of behavior or impose their own notions of how business ought to proceed? Is the court doing this or is it just applying the burden of proof?

3. *The real party in interest*: While the case appears to be a suit between the builder of the wall and the property owners, the record indicates that the supplier of the cement used in the wall was never paid. It was attempting to assert the builder's rights. Pittman, the builder of the wall, did not have sufficient assets to pay for the cement. He was a small handy-man builder, and the case took place in the middle of the great depression. The supplier was seeking to assert Pittman's claim, if any, against the property owner. We can wonder whether the case might have been decided differently had Pittman himself been the real party in interest. As between a supplier of materials and an owner who received little tangible benefit who should take the loss of the value of the cement?

Those who work on the property of others or supply materials often are protected by statutes giving them liens on property that has been improved. However, these statutes require the mechanic or materialman to follow certain procedures. For example, Wis. Stat. § 289.41(1) provides, "Every mechanic and every keeper of a garage or shop, and every employer of a mechanic who transports, makes, alters, repairs or does any work on personal property *at the request of the owner* ... thereof, shall have a lien thereon for his just and reasonable charges therefor, ... and may retain possession of such property until such charges are paid." They also protect those who have a recorded security interest. Several cases involve attempts by those who otherwise would have been protected by these statutes but who failed to follow procedures to assert a right to recover for unjust enrichment. The Supreme Court of Wisconsin has been unsympathetic to attempts to get around the statutory requirements for liens. The restitutionary end-run has not worked.[51]

---

[51]See, *e.g.*, Gebhardt Bros., Inc. v. Brimmel, 31 Wis.2d 581, 143 N.W.2d 479 (1966); Industrial Credit Co. v. Inland G.M. Diesel, Inc., 51 Wis.2d 520, 187 N.W.2d 157 (1971).

Chapter 6

INCOMPLETE PLANNING, FLEXIBILITY, AND ENFORCEABILITY

A. SPECIFYING ENDS BUT NOT MEANS: "WE CAN WORK IT OUT!"

1. BUILDING CONSTRUCTION AND ORDINARY PEOPLE

KLIMEK v. PERISICH

231 Or. 71, 371 P.2d 956 (1962)

PERRY, J. This is an action brought by the plaintiff to recover damages from the defendant for breach of contract to remodel an old dwelling house into a rooming house.

The jury returned a verdict for the plaintiff which was set aside and judgment entered notwithstanding the verdict for the defendant. The plaintiff has appealed.

[Much of the court's opinion consists of extracts from the trial court testimony. We offer a summary of it here, At the beginning of the opinion, the court observed that "[b]oth plaintiff and defendant were born in Yugoslavia, and while they now speak and understand English, the record discloses limitations in this regard." It seems that Mrs. Klimek, the plaintiff, had purchased an old building with hopes of turning it into a boarding house. She had conversations with Mr. Perisich, a builder, about the remodeling. Apparently, Mr. Perisich told Mrs. Klimek that he was not sure how many rooms she could get out of the house but that the cost of refurbishing would run $8,000, $9,000 or at the most $10,000.

Blueprints for the remodeling were obtained but no specifications covering materials to be used were ever drafted. The parties did not enter into a formal contract; Mr. Perisich simply began remodeling the building. Although, Mr. Perisich was supervising the job, he was paid the same as the other carpenters. Mr. Perisich received no compensation for helping Mrs. Klimek obtain plans and building permits. Mrs. Klimek herself testified that no arrangements were made between the parties as to who would do the required plumbing, heating or electrical wiring, but as these items became necessary both she and Mr. Perisich would search for the most reasonable price. Mrs. Klimek took care of paying bills for materials, services and the workmen's wages. Mrs. Klimek ran out of money before the work was done, was unable to get financing, and sued Mr. Perisich to recover damages.]

1. We have set forth only the evidence of the plaintiff, as this is an action at law, and if there is substantial evidence of the formation of a contract, as sued upon, the finding of the jury must be sustained.

3. To constitute a contract such as here present, there must be an offer and an acceptance.

4-6. An offer must be certain so that upon an unqualified acceptance the nature and extent of the obligations of each party are fixed and may be determined with reasonable certainty ... As to an acceptance of an offer:

> It is well settled that when a contract is to be founded on offer and acceptance, it must be shown that the latter coincides precisely with the former. Unless this appears, there is no agreement.... *Northwestern Agencies v. Flynn*, 138 Or. 101, 106, 5 P.2d 530.

In other words, there must be a meeting of the minds as to the obligations each assumes under the contract before it can be said that a contract exists.

In the matter before us the plaintiff agreed to pay money and the defendant agreed to render services, therefore both the amount to be paid and the services to be rendered must be reasonably certain.

As stated by ... Corbin on Contracts, § 100, p 315:

> It is not always the price in money that is left uncertain in an agreement; sometimes it is that for which the price is to be paid. If no method is agreed upon for rendering this subject matter sufficiently definite for enforcement, the agreement must nearly always fail of legal effect; it is not customary for courts to fill the gap by finding that a reasonable amount of goods or land or labor has been agreed upon as the exchange for the money.

8. The trial court, in granting judgment for the defendant, notwithstanding the verdict of the jury, based its opinion upon the indefiniteness of the subject matter of the offer. The plaintiff contends that the subject matter of the offer is sufficiently definite in that the parties agreed upon a maximum amount to be paid by the plaintiff for the remodeling of a certain building; that the extent and requirements for remodeling were certain, although no specifications were agreed upon; that the minimum requirements of the building code of the city of Portland required certain materials to be used, and this supplied the lack of specifications as to the work to be done and the material to be used by the defendant. Defendant contends that no agreement existed other than to perform labor at an hourly rate and there was no agreement as to the extent of remodeling or the materials to be used, and therefore no contract existed between the parties.

The difficulty with plaintiff's contentions that the minimal requirements of the city building code are sufficiently definite as a substitute for specifications is that there is no evidence that the parties agreed that compliance with the minimal requirements of the building code would constitute a satisfactory execution of the purported contract, and also there is no evidence that the building code specifies the extent of the remodeling, or the kinds or types of materials that could be satisfactorily used in the remodeling of this particular. Also there is no evidence of what the parties agreed was necessary to constitute a remodeling of the structure.

The building code of the city of Portland was not introduced into evidence, and therefore the jury could not determine whether the building code covered these requirements.

The plaintiff cites and relies upon a number of cases, such as *Helm v. Speith*, 298 Ky. 225, 182 S.W.2d 635. [There] the parties agreed that the building should be contracted to comply with the minimal requirements of the Federal Housing Administration, and the Federal Housing Administration requirements were introduced into evidence. [Here] ... as previously stated, there is no evidence that the parties agreed that the minimal requirements of the Portland building code were agreed upon as a basis of their negotiations, nor was it introduced into evidence.

The trial court correctly held that there was no contract.

There is additional reason why the judgment of the trial court should be affirmed. An examination of the evidence of the plaintiff, in our opinion, is such that reasonable minds could reach only the conclusion that at all times the plaintiff knew that the statements made by the defendant with relation to the cost of remodeling of the structure were only estimates and that the plaintiff knew this to be such, therefore the words and actions of the defendant could only be construed as not an offer to remodel the building to the satisfaction of the plaintiff at a fixed maximum amount, nor as an acceptance of such an offer.

The judgment of the trial court is affirmed.

NOTES AND QUESTIONS

1. *An additional argument from defendant's brief*: In his brief, defendant argued that a promise to guarantee the cost of a construction project is enforceable only if there is consideration for it. In this case, the defendant received only a carpenter's wages for the work that he did. There was no mechanism by which defendant could share in any cost-savings on component parts of the project.

> There is no question but what a contractor can guarantee a maximum cost of construction, but before that is done there must be an allegation and proof that the agreed figure which is the ceiling price must be a guaranteed maximum cost. In the case at bar, it is clear that the parties merely agreed that this "would be the cost." There is no allegation or proof that the defendant guaranteed this to be the maximum cost and there is no allegation

or proof that defendant agreed to be liable for any costs in excess of $10,000. Nor is there any consideration for the alleged guarantee.

2. *The building code as a gap filler*: Should the Supreme Court of Oregon have found that the contract was too indefinite to be enforced in view of the jury's verdict for the plaintiff? Plaintiff argued in her brief that the parties impliedly agreed that the building code provided minimum specifications. Apparently, the jury was not charged that it needed to decide this issue. If we assume that plaintiff had raised this question at trial and in her request for jury instructions, should the appellate court have remanded the case for a new trial on this question? Would this depend on the degree to which the Portland building code specifies what is required in a rooming house?

3. *The real consequences of the case*? What can you say for and against the following statement?

> The *Klimek* case illustrates the poverty of our legal system in dealing with real human problems. It is likely that neither party came away from their adventure before the Oregon courts with a sense that justice had been done. Of course, Mrs. Klimek could have gone to an architect and a large construction company. They would have given her a firm price as part of a form contract which would have protected their interests and few of hers. Mr. Perisich could have hired a lawyer to draft an agreement limiting his liability so he would never have been sued. However, these solutions ignore the real situations of people such as Mrs. Klimek and Mr. Perisich. These solutions reward education, experience, wealth and social status. They also serve the economic interests of middle class professionals.

Suppose that you agree with the preceding statement? What consequence? What program for change?

2. THE U.C.C. AND INDEFINITENESS: TRANSACTIONS IN GOODS BETWEEN MAJOR CORPORATIONS

BETHLEHEM STEEL CORP. v. LITTON INDUSTRIES, INC.

321 Pa. Super. 357, 468 A.2d 748 (Pa. Super. 1983)

WICKERSHAM, J. The central issue in this case is whether a certain written option agreement is a contract. [The trial judge, sitting without a jury, had ruled that the plaintiff-appellant had failed to meet its burden to show the parties intended to be contractually bound.]

Basically the complaint alleged that on or about April 25, 1968 Litton entered into an agreement with Bethlehem whereby Litton would construct and deliver and Bethlehem would purchase a one thousand foot self-unloading ore vessel.

The vessel constructed under the agreement was delivered, accepted, and the price paid therefor.

The complaint further alleged that Litton extended to Bethlehem by letter dated April 25, 1968 "a written offer good until December 31, 1968 for the entry into an option agreement for five vessels." Furthermore, it was alleged that on or about December 31, 1968 Bethlehem accepted Litton's offer to enter into an option agreement under which Bethlehem was granted the right for a period of five years after the execution of the option agreement to obtain from Litton from one to five vessels for prices varying between $22,400,000 and $18,400,000 each. Further, the complaint alleged that Bethlehem, pursuant to the option agreement, by letter dated November 16, 1973 exercised its option for two vessels and thereby ordered the first and second vessels in accordance with the option agreement. On December 26, 1973 Bethlehem, pursuant to the option agreement, exercised its option for an additional (third) vessel.

Finally, the complaint alleged that Litton expressly and unequivocally refused to perform in accordance with its obligations under the option agreement; that Litton demanded the payment of a price for each vessel many millions of dollars in excess of the price provided for in the option agreement and indicated delivery dates substantially later than the delivery provided in the option agreement. Damages were sought in a sum in excess of $95,000,000.00 together with interest and costs ...

In its defense, Litton responded, *inter alia*: (1) PX-1 (the letter of December 31, 1968) was never intended to be and was not a contract; (2) no contract was formed in any event because the vital terms left for later negotiation could not be filled by the court on a reasonably certain basis; (3) any purported "option agreement" had been rejected prior to exercise by Bethlehem's assertions that it would "never" order another vessel from Litton; (4) since an "option" unsupported by consideration is revocable at will, any purported "option agreement" had been revoked prior to exercise by Litton's notice to Bethlehem that the Erie shipyard was to be closed; (5) any purported "option" had never been properly exercised; and (6) Litton had never breached or repudiated any "agreement" which might have existed.

On June 28, 1978 a non-jury trial began and Judge Louik filed his adjudication on June 6, 1979 which provided, in part, as follows:

[Beginning of an extended excerpt from the *trial court opinion*.]

After a protracted trial of approximately nine months with over 12,000 pages of testimony and some 500 exhibits, this matter is now before the Court for determination. The claim in excess of 95 million dollars, together with a counterclaim, is based on a two-page letter between two giant corporations.

For background purposes, it should be noted that on April 25, 1968, at a formal signing ceremony, the plaintiff and defendant entered into a ship-construction contract for a newly designed 1,000 foot self unloading ore vessel. This vessel, known as Hull 101, was commissioned "The Cort."

In addition, there is in evidence as PX-4 a document which was executed on that very same day, April 25, 1968, together with a document dated December 31, 1968, in evidence as PX-1. These are the documents in issue in the instant case.

The primary and fundamental question now before the Court is whether or not there has been an option contract. The plaintiff's claim is based upon the following two-page letter:

ERIE MARINE, INC.
ERIE, PENNSYLVANIA

April 25, 1968

Bethlehem Steel Corporation
Bethlehem, Pennsylvania
Attn: Ralph K. Smith

Gentlemen:

Reference is made to the ship construction contract signed by our companies this date for the construction by us of a 1,000 self-unloading ore vessel for you. Reference is also made to my letter to you of this date extending to you an option to purchase either one or two additional vessels upon the terms therein set forth.

We hereby extend to you an offer to enter into an option agreement to have us construct for you from one to five additional vessels in accordance with "Specifications covering the Construction of a Self-Unloading Bulk Carrier for Bethlehem Steel Corporation" (Number Y 917) dated March 1968, addendum number 1 thereto dated March 28, 1968 and addendum number 2 thereto dated April 17, 1968. This offer to enter into an option agreement shall be firm and irrevocable until December 31, 1968 at 5:00 P.M. E.S.T.

The terms of the option agreement are to be as follows:

(a) The specifications for the vessels shall be the specifications referred to above, except for mutually agreeable reduced test schedules of the vessels, if the testing of the vessel to be delivered under the contract executed this date proves successful.

(b) Bethlehem to have the right at any time within five years after the effective date of the option agreement to order from one to not more than a total of five vessels, for delivery within 24 months from the date of the order for the first vessel ordered and for delivery within 24 months plus 4 months for each additional vessel ordered within any one calendar year; provided however no vessel shall be scheduled for delivery between November 31 and March 31.

c) The price of the vessel shall be as follows:

1st vessel ordered	*$22,400,000.00*
2nd " "	*$21,400,000.00*
3rd " "	*$20,400,000.00*
4th " "	*$19,400,000.00*
5th " "	*$18,400,000.00*

(d) The vessel prices are subject to escalation for both labor and material for a base price of $20,400,000.00 for each vessel and based upon Fourth Quarter 1968 mutually agreed upon index such as:

Material — "Material index for Bureau of Ships steel vessel contracts" furnished to the Naval Ship Systems Command by the Bureau of Labor Statistics of the U.S. Department of Labor.

Labor — "Index of changes in straight-time average hourly earnings for selected shipyards" (June 1962 = 100) for steel ship construction, furnished to the Naval Ship Systems Command by the Bureau of Labor Statistics of the U.S. Department of Labor.

At the time of exercise of the option for any vessel, the escalation shall be computed to the date of contract execution, and an appropriate contract clause will be included therein providing for quarterly escalation thereafter. We will furnish you the labor and material percentages subject to escalation by May 15, 1968.

(e) The terms and conditions of the ship construction contracts to be in accordance with the attached terms and conditions and any other mutually agreed to terms and conditions and shall contain a clause giving to Bethlehem the right to cancel at any time upon the payment of all of our costs incurred to date of cancellation, including similar vendor and subcontractor cancellation charges, plus 15% of such costs.

> *Very truly yours,*
> *George K. Geiger*

In response to this letter, a letter dated December 31, 1968 was sent by Bethlehem to Erie which stated in part 'We hereby accept your offer of an option to have you construct for us from one to five additional vessels.' In all other respects, the letter of December 31, 1968 is merely identical repetition of the language in the letter of April 25, 1968.

On November 16, 1973, plaintiff sent a letter to defendant stating that it exercises its option to order two vessels and then on December 26, 1973, plaintiff sent another letter to defendant stating that it exercises its option to order a third vessel.

Defendant did not enter into any ship construction contract with plaintiff and did not construct any vessels under the letters of November 16, 1973 and December 26, 1973.

CONCLUSION OF LAW

1. Bethlehem has not sustained its burden of proof, either in law or in fact, of imposing liability on Litton-Erie, and a finding accordingly will be entered in favor of Litton-Erie on Bethlehem's claim.

[End of excerpt from trial court opinion.]

SCOPE OF REVIEW

It is quite clear that the scope of appellate review of a finding on contractual intent is limited — indeed narrowly circumscribed.

The "intent to contract" is a question of fact for the trier-of-fact. It is axiomatic that a trial judge's findings of fact, sustained by the Court *en banc*, have the weight of a jury verdict and cannot be disturbed on appeal if supported by competent evidence in the record.

We have reviewed the entire trial record and viewing the evidence in the light most favorable to the victorious party below, a fair distillation of the evidence would indicate the following scenario.

This controversy arose out of ship construction on the Great Lakes. Litton, a newcomer to the Lakes, tried unsuccessfully through its subsidiary, Erie, to develop a market for a unique and revolutionary supertanker-type ore vessel, 1,000 feet long with novel self-unloading features. In seven years of effort (from 1967 to 1973), however, Litton sold only one ore vessel ("Hull 101" [the Cort]) — to Bethlehem.

In 1968, Litton and Bethlehem exchanged two incomplete letters, one dated April 25, 1968 (PX-4) and the other dated December 31, 1968 (PX-1), concerning an offer to negotiate a long-term option agreement for construction of up to five novel multimillion dollar vessels at Litton's new shipyard. In the words of Judge Louik: "If anything, there is one matter that is absolutely clear, and that is that the writing provides that further agreements between the parties are necessary." (Ad 13.) During the ensuing years, Litton repeatedly attempted to interest Bethlehem in commencing the negotiations contemplated. These efforts were in vain, however, and from late 1972 through early 1973 Litton repeatedly informed Bethlehem of its intention to close the Erie shipyard unless ship construction orders were immediately forthcoming. When Bethlehem disclaimed interest in purchasing any additional ships and no other contracts were obtained, Litton began closing its Erie yard and disbanding its workforce.

Thereafter, however, Bethlehem notified Litton that it wished to negotiate a ship construction contract pursuant to PX-1. When the parties were unable to agree on contractual terms, Bethlehem commenced this action, contending that despite the parties's failure to agree upon the myriad terms explicitly left for future negotiations, the mere exchange of the letters in 1968 bound the parties to a "contract" for the construction of novel ships worth millions of dollars.

The April 25, 1968 Letter (PX-4)

After four months of careful negotiation and drafting and redrafting of contract terms, representatives of Litton and Bethlehem met on April 25, 1968 for the ceremonial exchange of a contract for the immediate construction of Hull 101, the only 1,000-foot vessel actually sold by Litton, for the firm fixed price of $17,994,138.00 ("Hull 101 Contract"). Bethlehem's Board of Directors had insisted upon "great precision" in every aspect of the sale, especially price. The Hull 101 Contract was fully performed and is not at issue here.

During the two to three hours that the parties were together on April 25, 1968, primarily for the exchange of the Hull 101 contract, they jointly drafted a two-page letter (PX-4), extending a last minute sales promotional offer to negotiate a long-term option agreement for up to five additional Hull 101 type vessels. The parties clearly understood that PX-4 was not part of the consideration for the Hull 101 Contract. With one exception, none of the representatives at the April 25 meeting even was aware before that meeting that such an offer was to be made or drafted that day. On its face, PX-4 clearly was not an option agreement; rather, it expressly provided for future negotiations which, if successfully completed, would have resulted in an option agreement which, in turn, if properly exercised, would have resulted in formal execution of a formal written ship construction contract.

In hurriedly drafting PX-4 during a part of their short meeting on April 25, the parties explicitly agreed that price escalation would be included in any long-term option agreement and ship construction contract upon which they might subsequently agree. The parties further expressly acknowledged, however, that because escalation was so critical and so complex, they would postpone the negotiations necessary for agreement upon that vital subject.

PX-4 thus was jointly drafted during the less than three-hour meeting on April 25 in the form of a two-step offer to enter into a future option agreement in order to provide until the end of the year for the parties to investigate and develop the terms of an appropriate escalation clause and the other important matter intentionally left for future negotiation and agreement.

Having taken more than four months to negotiate a contract for a single vessel (Hull 101), on which construction was to begin immediately for a fixed price with no escalation, the parties recognized that negotiation of a long-term option agreement for up to five novel multimillion dollar vessels providing for price escalation would be infinitely more complex and time consuming.

On several occasions from May through November of 1968, Litton sought to negotiate the terms of an option agreement. On each occasion, Bethlehem replied that it was not yet willing to spend the time and effort required for such negotiations, since it would not even consider additional 1,000 foot ore vessels until the revolutionary Hull 101 had been successfully operated for at least one season.

By December of 1968, aware that the PX-4 offer was about to lapse, but still unwilling to devote the time necessary to negotiate the terms essential for a definitive option agreement and ship construction contract, Bethlehem sought to preserve the status quo.

Between April 25 and December 31, 1968, there were no discussions, negotiations or agreements between the parties with respect to any of the terms, including escalation, expressly left for future negotiation and mutual agreement under PX-4.

In short, whatever the parties had intended by drafting PX-4 was unchanged by PX-1. In PX-4 the parties had explicitly contemplated negotiations and agreements necessary to create a binding option contract. PX-1 did not resolve any of the substantive terms left open for negotiation in PX-4; as the record clearly reveals, it was adopted as an accommodation to Bethlehem's request for a "holding pattern."

From 1968 through 1973, Litton attracted no other customers to its Erie shipyard. Indeed, by early 1973, Litton officials warned Bethlehem that the Erie yard would be closed unless Bethlehem ordered additional ships. Bethlehem officials had previously stated, however, that they were "disgusted" by the "slow" construction of Hull 101, and by 1973, rather than express any objection to the closing of the Erie yard, repeatedly insisted that they would never order any additional ships from Litton. Thus, without any hope of future business from Bethlehem, Litton "mothballed" its Erie yard.

Thereafter, in full knowledge of the fact that the Erie Shipyard had dismissed most of its labor force for lack of business, Bethlehem notified Litton by letter that it was planning to "exercise its options" for ore vessels. Significantly, however, Bethlehem expressly acknowledged that the terms of an option agreement had to be negotiated before Bethlehem could exercise any option.

At subsequent meetings, Litton advised Bethlehem that although it had closed down its shipyard in reliance upon Bethlehem's representations, it was willing to build vessels if the parties could reach agreement on a ship construction contract (Ad-9), which Litton was at all times willing to negotiate. The parties, however, never agreed on any of the material terms left open in PX-4 and PX-1, including escalation — found by the trial judge to be "one of the most critical provisions of a ship construction contract" (Ad-26). Nor would Bethlehem accept any of Litton's alternative proposals.

Judge Louik carefully considered all the relevant factors under the common law and under the Uniform Commercial Code — the letters themselves, the discussions at the time of the exchange of the letters, the surrounding circumstances, subsequent conduct, the nature of the contemplated construction contract, and the parties's prior dealings and found that the parties did not intend to enter a binding agreement until they mutually agreed on the critical terms intentionally deferred, including the terms of a price escalation clause, and reduced those terms to a formal ship construction contract. The Court alternatively found that under § 2-204(3) of the U.C.C., no contract had been formed — because the Court simply could not, on "a reasonably certain basis," fill in the price escalation terms and other missing contract provisions in order to provide for "an appropriate remedy." ...

Returning now to relevant portions of the adjudication of Judge Louik dated June 6, 1979, our review of the record supports the correctness of the court's conclusions, as follows:

[The court again quotes from the trial court opinion.]

...One of the contentions of Bethlehem is that these agreements come within the Uniform Commercial Code and, therefore, gaps, (if any appear in the documents), may be filled in by the Court.

Even if the Uniform Commercial Code is applicable, the Court must first find that there was intent to enter into a contract by the two letters (PX-4 and PX-1). The same criteria has to be used in this regard as is used in determining whether or not there is a contract at common law. Even if the Court had found that there was such an intent, there then arises the matter of ability of the Court to fill in the gaps because, if anything is clear in PX-4 and PX-1, it is that gaps exist which must be filled in.

If a contract did exist, there are three general areas in which gaps appear which would require the Court's intervention to fill.

The first term obviously left open was the original escalation index which would be used to calculate the increase in cost per vessel over the time between PX-1 to the date of contract execution.

The only aspect of this stage of escalation that the documents provided is that an index method of escalation shall be used for this portion of escalation, and that the index shall be mutually agreed upon, as evidenced by the language "mutually agreed upon index such as." Because the parties established the method of arriving at the index as mutual agreement, and because of the complexity of negotiations of escalation clauses in the shipbuilding industry, the Court cannot fill in such a gap in light of Code § 2-305(4)...

The second gap relates to "second stage escalation" which PX-4 and PX-1 establishes as the escalation from the execution of the construction contract to the end of the escalation period:

an appropriate contract clause will be included therein providing for quarterly escalation thereafter.

An escalation clause is a complex, detailed contractual provision negotiated between parties to provide a means necessary to calculate and pay escalation. It is an equitable concept that escalation clauses must be such as not to give the builder a windfall nor to have the builder suffer losses due to inflation. Because of inflation since the middle 1960s, the escalation clauses became one of the most critical provisions of a ship construction contract. There are many essential elements to be negotiated in an escalation clause, some of which are very critical, such as the indexes to be used, the escalatable amount, the amount escalatable each computation period, the duration of escalation, payment, and the method of computation. These elements can have numerous possible variations resulting from negotiations between the parties. One of the most critical elements and perhaps the heart of an escalation clause is the amount escalatable each computation period. This is called the "apportionment" which can have an infinite number of possible variations and will vary from ship to ship depending upon the time of construction, the place of construction, needs and desires of the parties.

The third gap which the Court would have to fill if it found a contract otherwise existed, arises from the language indicated that the terms and conditions were to be in accordance with the sample contract and "any other mutually agreed upon terms and conditions." In view of the fact that the sample form of contract was for a fixed price contract, there must of necessity be changes required since the writings clearly indicate that the parties contemplated an escalation contract. Such a contract would require additional terms and conditions from those that appear in the sample form.

In addition, there are numerous other terms which might be expected to be in a ship construction contract of this magnitude. Evidence of this can be found in the contract (DX-12) proposed by the plaintiffs at the September 24, 1973 meeting with defendants. This proposed contract varied substantially from the sample contract in at least twelve separate items (See Finding 28). These altered or added terms strongly suggest that, at least in the mind of Bethlehem, there were many items left out of the sample contract, or left to be negotiated at a later time....

All of the expert testimony indicated that such clauses could not be materialized from the air by the Court. Because of the nature of negotiations in shipbuilding and the extreme complexity of the undertaking, such a clause would require careful negotiations between the parties and would need to be custom tailored to fit the project.... Because these gaps are so wide, the Court cannot make a new contract for the parties....

[End of second extended extract from trial court opinion.]

In summary, we agree with the finding of the lower court that there was no enforceable contract between the parties. Order affirmed.

[JUDGE HESTER's dissent follows. Rowley and Wieand, JJ. joined in it.]

For the reasons that follow, I would reverse and remand to the lower court for further proceedings consistent with this Opinion.

The threshold issue to be resolved in the instant appeal concerns the contractual intent of the parties. Unlike the majority, which views this issue as a question of fact, I believe the issue of contractual intent is a question of law or ultimate fact.

Undeniably, the basic findings of fact of the lower court should not be disturbed if these findings are based upon competent evidence, unless the lower court committed an abuse of discretion or error of law in admitting the evidence from which the findings of fact were derived. However, the contractual intent of the parties as an ultimate fact or conclusion of law is subject to independent appellate scrutiny....

It is clear that the Code applies to the instant case. The issue, as refined by the language of the Code, thus becomes, "Did the parties intend to enter into a contract for sale, whereby Bethlehem would have the right to exercise its option to order specially-manufactured future goods from Litton, resulting in a contract to sell future goods?"

The Code states: [under the heading: Options and cooperation respecting performance]

> (a) Specifying particulars of performance — An agreement for sale which is otherwise sufficiently definite (§ 2204(c)) to be a contract is not made invalid by the fact that it leaves particulars of performance to be specified by one of the parties. Any such specification must be made in good faith and within limits set by commercial reasonableness. 13 Pa. C.S.A. § 2311(a).

In the instant case, the time of performance, and whether performance would be required, at all, was specifically left to Bethlehem as an option. The time within which Bethlehem was required to exercise its option was specified, so there is no issue concerning "commercial reasonableness."

The lower court did not specifically decide whether the Code applies. Rather, the trial court improperly relied upon numerous pre-Code decisions and other authority not involving a contract for the sale of goods.

[The court then summarizes a pre-Code case which had been cited "repeatedly" by the trial court, and argues that the pre-Code principles of the case with respect to definiteness have been specifically displaced by provisions in the Code.]

From § 2204 of the Code, it is clear that the existence of a contract is initially dependent upon the intent of the parties. If the parties have intended to contractually obligate and benefit each other, their contract is enforceable even if certain terms are left open or are left to be agreed upon in the future. In other words, the Code specifically contemplates that the parties may "agree to agree" with respect to certain terms. The comment to § 2204 acknowledges that, depending upon how many terms are uncertain, an agreement may be defeated due to "indefiniteness" if there is no reasonably certain basis for granting an appropriate remedy. However, the Code specifically provides "gap-filling" so as to avoid defeating a contract which the parties otherwise intended....

Under the Code, parties can expressly agree to be contractually bound, even though certain terms are left open to be negotiated or agreed upon at a future time. It does not matter whether the original agreement is "a preliminary accord," "an agreement to agree," or "an agreement to negotiate." The crucial inquiry is whether the parties intended to enter into an agreement; and, if the parties left certain terms to be negotiated at a future time, then those parties contemplate that those terms will be filled in, on a reasonable basis, through the mutual good-faith negotiations of the parties....

The Code also states "Every contract or duty within this title imposes an obligation of good faith in its performance or enforcement." 13 Pa.C.S.A. § 1203. Therefore, if parties agree to agree concerning certain open contractual terms, then both parties must attempt to negotiate those terms, on a reasonable basis and in good faith.

As evinced by the letter of April 25 and December 31, 1968, as well as other discussions, negotiations, communications and "course of dealing" between the parties, it is clear that the parties intended to enter into an agreement which would give Bethlehem the right to exercise its option to order as many as five one thousand foot, self-unloading ore vessels from Litton at any time during a five year period.

The letter of April 25, 1968, from Litton to Bethlehem states, *inter alia*:

> We hereby extend to you an offer to enter into an option agreement to have us construct for you from one to five additional vessels ... this offer to enter into an option agreement shall be firm and irrevocable until December 31, 1968 at 5 p.m. E.S.T.

This correspondence expressly represents itself to be "an offer to enter into an option agreement," which is "firm and irrevocable." See 13 Pa.C.S.A. § 2205.

The letter of December 31, 1968, from Bethlehem to Litton states "We hereby accept your offer of an option to have you construct for us from one to five additional vessels." Said letter of December 31, 1968, was executed by George K. Geiger on behalf of Litton and Erie under a heading "AGREED TO."

These two letters are "sufficient to show agreement" for the purposes of 13 Pa.C.S.A. § 2204(a). The letter of December 31, 1968, operated as an acceptance of Litton's offer to enter into an option agreement, for the purposes of 13 Pa.C.S.A. § 2206(a).

Furthermore, the conduct of the parties manifests that they both recognized the existence of such a contract. [Judge Hester then enumerated several letters in which representatives of Litton and Bethlehem seemed to acknowledge that a binding agreement was in force.]

In determining that the parties had not intended to create a legally-binding option agreement, the lower court heavily relied on "the fact that the parties involved here are two of the largest corporations in this country, and [the letter of April 25, 1968] is only a two-page letter," citing *Essner v. Shoemaker*, 393 Pa. 422, 143 A.2d 364 (1958).

I cannot agree with the majority that this reasoning is supported by the evidence. The letters of April 25 and December 31, 1968, incorporate by reference the detailed specifications concerning the construction of the self-unloading ore carrier for Bethlehem Steel Corporation, which were used by the parties in connection with the construction of the Cort. These specifications serve the purposes of identifying the specially-manufactured vessels, as contemplated by the parties at the inception of their agreement.

Furthermore, both letters incorporated by reference the *pro forma* Ship Construction Contract which consists of 26 pages and 21 articles and which was also used as the basis of the agreement between the parties for the construction of the Cort....

As stated in the letters of April 25 and December 31, 1968, "... the terms and conditions of the ship construction to be in accordance with the attached terms and conditions and any other mutually agreed to terms and conditions...." Thus, the parties specifically agreed that any ship construction contract concerning any vessel ordered by Bethlehem pursuant to its option would be based upon the detailed *pro forma* contract as drafted by Mr. Davis, an attorney for Litton.

[Judge Hester then catalogued certain additional terms which supplemented the *pro forma* agreement.]

The use of the *pro forma* contract by the parties as the basis of the Ship Construction Contract of April 25, 1968, sharply brings into focus the relevancy of the "course of dealing" between the parties. 13 Pa.C.S.A. § 1205. It is apparent from the documentation of the transaction between the parties which occurred on April 25, 1968, that Litton's offer to Bethlehem to enter into an option agreement was part of this overall transaction, perhaps a contract "sweetener." The course of dealing between the parties with respect to the construction of the Cort amplifies the intentions of the parties to be legally bound to each other on the basis of the option agreement. Litton obviously desired to enter the shipbuilding industry as evinced by its construction of a ship for Bethlehem. Clearly Litton was hopeful that it would be able to build additional vessels for Bethlehem in the future and granted options to Bethlehem accordingly. As part of the ship construction contract for the Cort, Litton specifically gave Bethlehem a right of first refusal to purchase any of the ships described in its quarterly shipbuilding schedule.

By letter of July 10, 1968, Litton gave notice to Bethlehem of its projected ship-building schedule, offered Bethlehem the right of first refusal on projected Hull 102, and submitted to Bethlehem a proposed form of contract which was identical to the *pro forma* contract referenced in the letters of April 25, 1968, and December 31, 1968. The suitability of these basic contractual terms was therefore repeatedly recognized by Litton. The fact that the letters of April 25 and December 31, 1968, specified that the ship construction contract might also contain "any other mutually agreed to terms and conditions." does not indicate that the parties did not intend to be legally bound *unless* such additional terms were agreed upon. The parties were obviously able to agree to terms concerning the construction of the Cort and consented to similarly negotiate in good faith at some future time regarding any additional terms.

This "course of dealing" between the parties was not considered by the court below. However, Litton itself recognized the relevancy of this course of dealing and interrelationship between the construction of the Cort and the option agreement. The letter of April 25, 1968, which was drafted by Litton, began as follows:

> Reference is made to the ship construction contract signed by our companies this date for the construction by us of a one thousand self-unloading ore vessel for you. Reference is also made to my letter to you of this date extending to you an option to purchase either one or two additional vessels upon the terms therein set forth.

Thus did Litton make references to the "course of dealing" between the parties. This evidence cannot be ignored, for under the Code, "course of dealing" is always relevant....

As author of the letter of April 25, 1968, Litton was in control of the terms of the offer. Litton also offered and controlled the attached *pro forma* contract. I cannot understand how Litton, as a large corporation, could conceivably have delivered the letter of April 25, 1968, to Bethlehem without intending to be legally bound by the terms stated herein. The letter of April 25, 1968, created a power of acceptance by Bethlehem, which was exercised by the jointly-executed letter of December 31, 1968, was prepared by both the parties and was intended to be a final expression of the terms included therein. "The official commentary to [13 Pa.C.S.A. § 2203] recognizes that the parties may condition their assent on formalities, but must do so expressly. Official Commentary to § 203, 1 Uniform Laws Annotated, Uniform Commercial Code 107 (West, 1968)."...

In addition to the previously mentioned course of dealing between the parties, the following conduct by both parties additionally supports the existence of a contract, for the purposes of 13 Pa.C.S.A. § 2204(a):

[Judge Hester then catalogued 16 instances in which, in letters or corporate documents, either Litton or Bethlehem or both seemed to acknowledge the existence of a contract.]

Finally, and perhaps most importantly, my review of the record does not indicate a single instance whereby Litton denied Bethlehem's right to exercise its option, nor did Litton ever deny that the letter of December 31, 1968, was intended to be a legally-binding agreement, prior to the expiration of the option period on December 31, 1973.

Having concluded that the parties intended to make a contract, the next question to be addressed is whether "there is a reasonably certain basis for giving an appropriate remedy." 13 Pa.C.S.A. § 2204(c).

[Judge Hester argues that since the trial court held there was insufficient evidence of intent to be bound, it never engaged in the fact-finding necessary to decide the question of whether there was an appropriately certain basis for providing a remedy. Judge Hester, therefore, concluded that reversal, and fact finding on those issues was called for.]

NOTES AND QUESTIONS

1. *The end of the appellate story*: Bethlehem Steel Corporation appealed to the Supreme Court of Pennsylvania. Three justices of that court did not participate in the case. The remaining four justices were evenly divided, and so the order of the Superior Court was affirmed. Eleven appellate judges considered the case. Six found enough evidence in the record to support the trial court's conclusion that no contract was formed while five would have reversed. We can only speculate about what might have happened if some or all of the three Pennsylvania Supreme Court Justices who did not consider the case had participated in the decision. How would you have voted?

2. *Relationship to the Klimek case*: Instead of a woman seeking to run a rooming house and a builder, the *Bethlehem Steel* case involves two of the largest corporations in the world. The parties in each case intended some commitment to one another. Do the Supreme Court of Pennsylvania's opinions serve the interests of Bethlehem Steel and Litton Industries any better than the opinion of the Supreme Court of Oregon served Klimek and Perisich?

3. *A different court, a different contract, a different result: Oglebay Norton Co. v. Armco, Inc.*, 52 Ohio 3d 232, 556 N.E.2d 515 (1990) concerned a 1957 contract for shipping iron ore on the Great Lakes. Oglebay was to provide ore boats if and when Armco wished to transport ore from Lake Superior to the lower Great Lakes. Armco was to pay "the regular net contract rates for the season in which the ore is transported, as recognized by the leading iron ore shippers in such season for the transportation of iron ore." If there was no recognized regular net contract rate, "the parties shall mutually agree upon a rate for such transportation by the leading independent vessel operators engaged in transportation of iron ore from The Lake Superior District." The contract was modified four times during the period from 1957 to 1980. In 1980 the contract was amended so that Oglebay Norton was require to provide vessels with self-unloading capability. Armco was to pay an extra twenty-five cents per ton shipped in self-unloading ore boats. Oglebay Norton began a $95 million capital improvement program to meet this provision of the amended contract.

The parties had a complex long-term continuing relationship. Armco held a seat on Oglebay Norton's Board of Directors and owned Oglebay Norton stock. They were partners, owning and developing the Eveleth iron ore mine in Minnesota.

From 1957 to 1983, the parties established shipping rates by referring to those indicated in "Skillings Mining Review." After 1983, such information was no longer available from this source. The parties failed to negotiate mutually acceptable rates in 1984 and 1985 — Oglebay Norton billed at one rate but Armco paid at a much lower rate which Oglebay Norton was forced to accept.

In 1986, Oglebay Norton filed a declaratory judgment action, asking the court to declare the rate demanded in its 1985 invoices as the contract or to declare a reasonable rate for its services. The trial court found that the parties intended to be bound to a contract even if they could not agree on a price for Oglebay Norton's services. It then set a reasonable rate based on expert testimony, Oglebay Norton's past charges for carrying Armco's iron ore, and evidence of what others were charging for those services. Finally, the trial court ordered that "if the parties were unable to agree upon a rate for the upcoming seasons, then the parties must notify the court immediately. Upon such notification, the court, through its equitable jurisdiction, would appoint a mediator and require the parties' chief executive officers ... to meet for the purposes of mediating and determining the rate for such season by mutual agreement."

The Ohio Supreme Court affirmed the judgment. It relied on Restatement of Contracts Second § 33. Section 33 provides that if the parties intend to conclude a contract and the pricing mechanism fails, the contract will be enforced and the price will be a reasonable one. (This section, in substance, applies U.C.C. § 2-305 to contracts that are not transactions in goods). The Ohio court rejected old cases that found agreements to agree to be unenforceable. It said that there was sufficient evidence to support the trial court's findings of fact about the intent to be bound and the reasonable price. The court said that the trial court's order for mediation "neither added to nor detracted from the parties' significant obligations under the contract." Its order "would merely facilitate in the most practical manner the parties' own ability to interact under the contract." A trial court "may exercise its equitable jurisdiction and order specific performance if the parties intend to be bound by a contract where determination of long-term damages would be too speculative." The court stressed the "unique and long-lasting business relationship between the parties."

Suppose you agree with the dissenting judges in *Bethlehem Steel Corp. v. Litton Industries, Inc.*, and conclude that the parties in that case intended to be bound whether or not they agreed on an escalator clause. Would the mediation approach taken by the Ohio trial court have solved the problem of fashioning an appropriate escalator clause? Suppose the mediator fails to lead the parties to an agreement on a reasonable price or reasonable escalator clause. Then what happens?

4. *The U.C.C. and indefiniteness*: The fact that the parties did not agree to a term that most of us think essential to a deal is some evidence they had yet to make a commitment. However, the U.C.C. says that is all it is — some evidence. The two-page signed letter may have been drafted at the last minute, but which party is responsible for that? The long-term continuing relationship between the two firms was not last minute and casual. Why wasn't Bethlehem's reliance on the option reasonable and foreseeable? The U.C.C. tells courts to work things out if there is enough so that a court can fashion a remedy. The standard is no more than that the courts should fashion reasonable terms. How

should they do this? Must the remedy reflect risk assumption and choice or can judges engage in rate making when the parties have failed to do it?

The late Professor Edwin W. Patterson, a distinguished contracts scholar at the Columbia Law School, studied Article II of the Uniform Commercial Code for the New York Law Revision Commission. In reviewing § 2-305, he wrote,

> The last sentence of subsection (4) provides for restitution in case the "agreement" fails to be a contract. It is well to have this sentence to show that an alleged buyer and seller may *think* they have a contract and *act* as if they had one, and yet not have one. The "buyer" is, in such a case, required to make *specific* restitution if able to do so. Perhaps this is the simplest solution; yet the *remedy* of specific restitution is limited in other cases to *unique* chattels. While this sentence does not cover all the problems of restitution, it will serve as a guidepost to the case law on that subject.

Does or should the adequacy of available restitutionary remedies have any bearing on a court's determination as to whether the parties have made a contract enforceable under U.C.C. § 2-305?

5. *Letters of intent*: Business people, particularly in international trade, often deal on the basis of letters of intent. Lake says,

> In general, letters of intent can be classified into four types: letters designed to provide information; framework agreements intended to govern only the negotiation process; memorializations of partial agreements during a negotiation process; and documents erroneously entitled letters of intent that are, in actuality, legally enforceable contracts.[1]

Why write a letter of intent? Lake, who is the Europe and Middle East Legal Counsel of Holiday Inns, Inc., says that modern business transactions are becoming increasingly complex. Contracts contain hundreds or thousands of pages.

> The negotiation of such contracts can be a lengthy process and often requires the resolution of numerous details. Participation of financial institutions, government agencies, subcontractors, consultants, and other professionals is essential. Therefore, precontractual agreements that have moral, if not legal effect, are useful in bringing order to the complexity.

Also, letters of intent serve to exclude lawyers from the negotiation process until the final stages. Writers of letters of intent sometimes believe they will incur no obligations but obtain a commitment from the other party. Lake tells us,

---

[1]Lake, Letters of Intent: A Comparative Examination Under English, U.S., French, and West German Law, 18 George Washington Journal of International Law and Economics 331-332 (1984).

generally, English law does not recognize precontractual liability. United States courts have the doctrine of promissory estoppel at their disposal and increasingly impose an obligation to negotiate in good faith. French law imposes liability in tort for actions prior to contractual execution. West German law uses the doctrine of *culpa in contrahendo* to impose precontractual liability.

6. *Judicial enforcement of agreements to agree*: Classic doctrine dismisses agreements to agree as illusory and unenforceable. What about an obligation to bargain in good faith? In *Thompson v. Liquichimica of America, Inc.*,[2] the parties stated "[i]t is understood that all parties will exercise their best efforts to reach an agreement on or before May 15, 1979." The court found an obligation to negotiate in good faith. "Such an agreement does not require that the agreement sought be achieved, but does require that the parties work to achieve it actively and in good faith." Compare *Reprosystem, B.V. v. SCM Corp.*[3] The Second Circuit found that since no contract was formed, there was no obligation to act in good faith. If the United States District Courts' analyses were accepted as the law, how, if at all, would it affect the result in the *Bethlehem Steel* case? On one hand, Bethlehem attempted to exercise its option after it knew that Litton had taken significant steps to close its shipyard. Moreover, Litton had told Bethlehem that the shipyard would close unless it got more orders for the self-unloading ore carriers. On the other hand, Litton's construction of the first ore carrier was long delayed, and Bethlehem's officials doubted Litton's ability to produce these ore carriers efficiently.

B. FLEXIBLE PRICE AND QUANTITY: "I'LL BUY WHAT I WANT AT A FAIR PRICE"

From the 1920s to the 1960s, a classic problem in the contracts courses involved what business people call flexibility. Buyer and seller make what they see as a contract. However, their agreement gives Buyer discretion as to how much it will order. Seller, in turn, has discretion as to the price which it will charge. Many judges and legal scholars saw such bargains as offending contract theory because the parties had not made specific commitments to buy a specified amount for a stated price. Nonetheless, despite questions about legal enforceability, business people continued to make these arrangements. Since almost every state has adopted Article II of the U.C.C., the classic problems about flexibility have been transformed. Some of the old struggles remain, but we must discuss them with a new vocabulary. However, since the U.C.C.'s provisions are a response to older law, we must consider a little history to understand the statutory scheme.

---

[2]481 F.Supp. 361 (S.D.N.Y. 1979).

[3]522 F. Supp. 1257 (S.D.N.Y. 1981), rev'd 727 F.2d 257 (2d Cir. 1984).

While much legal thought assumes discrete transactions between strangers, many important economic transactions involve long-term continuing relationships, almost bordering on joint-ventures or partnerships. For example, Sellerco is Buyerco's supplier; Buyerco is Sellerco's account. There may be no document establishing and regulating their relationship. When Buyerco needs to restock its inventory, it simply orders from Sellerco. Both parties often assume some obligation to each other. In times of shortage, Sellerco will take care of Buyerco as best it can. Buyerco may cancel orders for goods it cannot use. However, its officials feel some obligation to place additional orders later or to be reasonable when Sellerco is late on deliveries of future orders. There are advantages to dealing this way. Buyers can cut the costs of finding reliable high quality performance at an acceptable price by dealing with a small group of suppliers whose reputation cements the relationship. The loss of the status of regular supplier would be costly, and so the threat of turning elsewhere serves as a sanction pressing for good performance.

As long as parties leave matters to customary patterns, it is unlikely that they will create a legally binding contract until the buyer orders goods and the seller accepts the order. While parties may feel ethical obligations to continue to place and fill orders, most lawyers would think the parties are legally free to walk away at any time. They do not make definite commitments for the future. They assume tacitly that their relationship will continue.

Instead of leaving matters to custom or practice, parties may draft what they call contracts covering their long-term relationship. However, the world of business involves fluctuating demand and rising prices. Business people are likely to seek flexibility. Buyers cannot be sure how many parts #123 they will use in the coming quarter or year. Sellers, in turn, hesitate to promise to fill all orders for part #123 at 50 cents each for several months or more. If the price of the special type of steel needed to make part #123 jumps 20% during the course of the year, a fixed price contract could be disastrous.

There are a number of techniques for dealing with these risks. A seller may make a continuing offer subject to a series of acceptances by the buyer. For example, suppose the seller promises to supply all the #123's that buyer orders at 50 cents each. Each time buyer orders this would close a contract for the amount ordered at that price. If the seller made a promise in writing to hold such an offer open for a specific term, it might be enforceable under U.C.C. § 2-205. However, absent such a firm offer, seller could withdraw the offer as to future deliveries. Sellers also may promise to fill all orders at a specified price, but reserve the right to withdraw their offer at any time. Buyers may order their projected needs for, say, the first quarter of the year, but reserve the right to cancel their order for convenience — perhaps agreeing to pay a specified cancellation charge. Sellers also may promise to supply part #123 for six months as ordered by the buyer but at "seller's price in effect at the time and place of shipment" or at "market price." The parties may use elaborate price escalation clauses so that the contract price tracks some index of prices in the trade. Buyers may agree to buy all or part of their requirements from seller. They can draft this clause to limit the obligation — for example, buyer may promise to take "33% of the requirements of its Janesville, Wisconsin plant, but no less than 1,000 units and no more than 10,000 units." We will consider these and other techniques to gain flexibility in the materials that follow.

Flexible quantity and price terms created problems for courts applying the common law of contracts. For example, some judges asked whether a seller who had the power to change the price had really promised to do anything. Seller might want to back out of the deal to serve another preferred customer. Seller then could set a price at $1 million per item, forcing Buyer to back out. On the other hand, many courts found requirements contracts to lack mutuality of obligation. It was not certain that a buyer would have any requirements, and the amount of requirements were largely within the control of the buyer. Some courts adopted a middle position: they would enforce contracts calling for a seller to supply the requirements of an existing business, but they would not enforce new business requirements contracts since the needs of a new business offered no standard by which to measure a commitment.

The jobber or distributor requirements contract was particularly troublesome. Suppose a producer agrees to supply all of a distributor's requirements of the producer's product. The distributor makes no promise to have any requirements of that product. If the distributor's customers want the product, then the distributor will order some from the producer. If a producer had to fill orders but a distributor did not have to place any, the arrangement seemed to lack mutuality.

For example, before the days of mass marketing of beer by television, there were many local or regional brewers. Suppose Ace Beer Co. agreed to supply Acme Distributors with all of its requirements of Ace Beer. Acme also distributed King, Queen, and Jack beers which were made by Ace's competitors. On one hand, if Ace beer were not very popular, Acme's sales people would spend their time promoting King, Queen, and Jack beers. They would do little more than take any orders for Ace which tavern and liquor store owners wanted to place. Indeed, Acme might not order any Ace beer under this contract. On the other hand, if Ace beer suddenly became the rage with drinkers, Acme could make almost unlimited demands on the brewer to supply the needed product. To make matters worse, suppose that Ace had agreed to supply Acme with beer at $1.00 per case. Because of unanticipated increases in prices of raw materials, the cost to all brewers to produce a case of beer jumped to at least $1.25 a case. Acme Distributors had no requirements contracts with the other breweries, and they all increased their prices to cover the increase in their costs. Acme then might offer Ace beer to taverns and liquor stores at an extremely favorable price. Now they would promote it with great efforts. The demand could grow for a product on which the brewer lost at least 25 cents a case. Courts in many states refused to enforce jobber or distributor requirements contracts, saying they lacked mutuality.

Many writers, notably Yale's Professor Arthur Corbin, attacked the refusal of courts to keep up with modern business practices. These writers noted that sellers could not name just any price they pleased — "seller's price in effect at time and place of shipment" meant the price the seller was quoting to the trade. This was at least influenced, if not controlled, by the market. Moreover, the mutuality requirement was an unnecessary addition to the requirement of consideration. A promise to buy one's requirements satisfied the consideration doctrine whatever the likelihood there would be any requirements. The buyer gave up its freedom to buy elsewhere whatever the likelihood that it would buy anything. Courts said they were interested in the existence and not the adequacy of consideration. If a seller thought a promise to buy requirements had value, why should courts refuse to enforce the contract when the buyer was a new business? The seller's business judgment may have been poor, but courts seldom recognize this as a reason for relief. Moreover, courts could push jobber or distributor requirements contracts into the consideration mold simply by implying a promise to use reasonable efforts to promote and sell the product.

The Uniform Commercial Code changed the common law response to flexibility in long term contracts. Its drafters were aware of the academic criticism of the case law and modern business practices. Rather than asking whether a contract was formed when the parties left issues of quantity and price open, the Code usually finds a binding contract and then directs courts to interpret the obligation assumed in light of standards such as commercial reasonableness or good faith. First, we will look at flexible pricing and then we will consider flexible quantity. However, we must recognize that often both go together. A seller may agree to supply the buyer's requirements only if there is a clause in the contract protecting the seller against rising costs of production.

1. FLEXIBLE PRICING

We can consider arrangements under which the price fluctuates from the perspective of the policy maker considering a legal response or that of a lawyer drafting an escalator clause. First, to what extent, if at all, are flexible pricing clauses socially desirable? Should the likely or possible consequences of these clauses affect the judgments of courts about whether a particular clause is legally enforceable?

Escalator clauses may increase prices beyond actual increases in costs. For example, some sellers may be able to set high base prices that reflect estimates of increasing costs. Then on top of this amount, they provide for an increased price if certain costs increase. Thus, they may be able to justify increasing prices beyond an amount that reflects their actual costs. Other sellers have substantial control over their costs of labor and materials. An escalator clause may weaken their resistance to cost increases that they can pass along directly to their customers without renegotiation. Sellers' escalator clauses may have an "upward bias" as well. A drafter must weigh components of cost in the formula used.

How does she deal with items drawn from old inventories purchased at lower prices or from fixed costs that do not increase? How does the clause deal with changes in methods of production that may, at least in part, offset increased raw material costs? How does the clause deal with an industry-wide index of costs which fits a particular seller's costs poorly?

Of course, sellers may have little freedom to draft escalator clauses or to put into effect the prices called for by such clauses in their contracts. In a highly competitive market, buyers may be able to negotiate for fixed prices based on the threat to take their business elsewhere. Or buyers may refuse to honor contracts if sellers exercise the option to raise prices. Of course, a seller always could sue, but this threat is often a paper tiger. Suing a customer jeopardizes future sales. Such litigation is costly, and uncertain.

Professor Daniel A. Farber[4] argues that there are high costs when businesses rely on flexible long-term continuing relationships. He says:

> [T]hese informal incentives are costly; to the extent that inadequate legal incentives cause excessive use of informal incentives, economic efficiency suffers ... Customers will tend to deal with sellers with whom they have dealt before and will tend not to engage in a widespread search for sellers. As a result, their willingness to shop for better prices can decrease. Furthermore, entry by new sellers becomes more difficult, because a reputation for reliability cannot be immediately established. Although these effects on behavior are difficult to quantify, they nevertheless represent real costs, because they impede the market's movement toward equilibrium.

Farber is obviously right when he suggests that not all markets are highly competitive, but do the costs of flexible long-term relationships outweigh the benefits? The late Dr. Arthur Okun was the Chairperson of President Lyndon Johnson's Council of Economic Advisors and a scholar at the Brookings Institution. He suggested that long-term continuing relationships are a major part of why we can have falling demand and rising prices at the same time.[5] Structures fashioned by lawyers such as flexible pricing clauses and requirements contracts can foster these relationships.

Okun points out there are a number of "auction markets" where supply and demand affect prices directly. Stocks and bonds, agricultural commodities, some primary metals, and things such as cotton and lumber are sold this way. However, most product transactions take place in *customer markets* rather than *auction markets*. Okun explains, "[a]s long as there are costs associated with shopping and limited information about the location of the lowest price in the

---

[4]Farber, Reassessing the Economic Efficiency of Compensatory Damages for Breach of Contract, 66 Virginia Law Review 1443, 1465-66 (1980).

[5]Okun, Prices & Quantities: A Macroeconomic Analysis (The Brookings Institution 1981).

marketplace, buyers do not find it worthwhile to incur all the costs required to find the seller offering the lowest price."

Firms discourage customers from shopping by convincing them of the continuity of their policies on price, quality and service. Buyers rely on the experience of their last shopping venture. Even professional buyers prefer continuing relationships with suppliers and will pay premiums for dependability. Sellers who have adopted this customer market strategy are inhibited from exploiting increases in demand by raising prices. This commitment introduces upward stickiness of prices. These sellers limit price increases to certain periods, give notice before they act, and often promise to meet competition. Furthermore, when firms raised prices often they tell customers that higher costs have forced them to do so. This legitimates their action and makes it seem inevitable rather than exploitative of their customers' situations.

Dr. Okun notes that prices are more responsive to changes in costs than to shifts in demand. "I suggest that the asymmetry stems, in part, from implicit contracts or conventions that introduce a concept of fairness in the relations between suppliers and customers whereby price increases based on cost increases are generally accepted as fair, but many that might be based on demand increases are ruled out as unfair." The customer-market view "does not regard the inflexibility of prices as necessarily an adverse consequence of oligopoly. On the contrary, it accepts the attachment between buyer and seller as an inherently desirable institutional arrangement that economizes on the expenses of shopping, trying out products, and otherwise engaging in transactions...."

Whether or not these clauses are socially desirable, lawyers often are asked by clients to draft them. It is difficult to write a contract which parties are to perform over time if the drafter anticipates inflation. The following law review articles discuss many of the problems.

Drafting Contracts in an Inflationary Era
Thomas R. Hurst[6]

[In periods of inflation the] climate of economic uncertainty poses significant risks for the businessman who has contracted to supply goods or services without allowing for the effects of such instability. A large rise in the cost of labor or materials required to fulfill a contractual commitment could easily turn a contract that was apparently profitable at the time of execution into

---

[6]28 University of Florida Law Review 879 (1976). Reprinted with permission of the University of Florida Law Review, Copyright 1976.

Eds. Note — We have removed many of the footnotes from this article, leaving only those that we thought served a teaching purpose.

a losing proposition. Similarly, these adverse effects could also result from a change in currency values.

Even more serious problems may result if the materials necessary to fulfill the contractual commitment are unavailable at any price because of an embargo or shortages resulting from price controls. In such a situation, the seller's liability may include the difference between the contract price and the market price on the date of delivery as well as substantial consequential damages.

In some of these situations, the law provides relief to the seller either through the doctrine of frustration of purpose or through the doctrine of impossibility of performance. The doctrines of impossibility and frustration, as codified in § 2-615 of the Uniform Commercial Code, discharge the seller from his obligation if performance becomes "commercially impracticable" as the result of the "occurrence of a contingency, the nonoccurrence of which was a basic assumption" on which the contract was made. Nonetheless, exclusive reliance on the impossibility doctrine as a tool to cope with inflationary disruptions is undesirable for two reasons. First, the impossibility defense will not operate to release the promisor from his contractual obligation in every situation in which changed circumstances might conceivably warrant a discharge. Second, the doctrine operates to release the seller or buyer from his obligation of performance entirely. In many situations the parties would prefer to modify the contract so that performance would become feasible despite changed circumstances. Thus, drafting sufficient flexibility into the contract to allow for prevailing economic realities is preferable to exclusive reliance on the impossibility doctrine.[7]

---

[7]In many situations, of course, whether the contract contains provisions that either excuse or modify the promisor's duty in a situation in which performance as originally called for would be burdensome is of little consequence. In the context of an ongoing business relationship in which the parties to the contract anticipate doing business with one another over a period of years, the buyer's long term interests will not be best served by insisting on strict enforcement of his contractual rights in situations in which the contract has become unduly burdensome on the seller. Thus, regardless of whether the contract contains any provisions exculpating or modifying the seller's obligations, it is likely that the parties will voluntarily agree on a modification of the seller's duty of performance in such situations. See generally L. Friedman, Contract Law in America (1965). Nevertheless, for a variety of reasons, there will be situations in which voluntary renegotiation may not occur. First, the contract in question may be an isolated transaction in which there is no incentive for the buyer to behave leniently toward the seller. Second, the possible windfall resulting to the buyer from insisting on full performance of the contract may be so great that the buyer is willing to risk alienating the seller by insisting on full performance of the contract as written. Third, even if a voluntary renegotiation of the contract is likely, the contract may contain some exculpatory language that places the party seeking modification or termination in a stronger bargaining position. Finally, even if voluntary negotiation of a contract seems likely in the event of unexpected occurrences, there inevitably will be some cases in which the parties simply will fail to reach a satisfactory renegotiation of the agreement; thus, litigation will result. Since the defenses of impossibility of performance and frustration of purpose have been raised frequently in recent litigation, the parties to the contract should, for the above reasons, provide at the outset for discharge or modification of an agreement in the event that performance becomes impossible or unduly burdensome.

The balance of this article examines the techniques that may be utilized within the confines of existing contract law to protect the parties to a contract from various changes resulting from economic instability. The article briefly describes the history of the development of each technique, the situations in which each technique is most appropriately used, and the dangers or problems involved in its use.

Protecting Against Changes in Price or Cost of Performance

The Open-Price Contract. Perhaps the most obvious means by which the parties to an executory contract can protect themselves against changes in the cost of performance between the time the agreement is made and the time performance is called for is to postpone the determination of the contract price until the time of performance. This technique, which is known as the open-price contract, is advantageous to the seller when inflation is anticipated and to the buyer when deflation is feared.[8]

In the past, courts have been hostile to the open-price contract and seldom, if ever, have enforced an executory contract that did not contain a specified price. The courts have generally justified this hostility on the grounds that a mere "agreement to agree" is unenforceable or that the Statute of Frauds bars enforcement of an open-price contract.

This judicial reluctance to enforce open-price contracts is curious, especially when it is contrasted with the willingness of the courts to imply an obligation of reasonableness into contracts in other contexts. For example, in one well-known case in which defendant gave plaintiff the exclusive right to market dresses and millinery under her trademark, the court upheld the agreement over defendant's claim that it lacked mutuality of obligation by reading into the contract an implied obligation of reasonable effort on the part of the plaintiff to promote and market dresses under plaintiff's trademark. Similarly, in situations in which contracts have appeared to give the defendant the absolute right to personal satisfaction, courts have upheld such contracts against the defense of lack of consideration on the grounds that the "personal satisfaction called for is that of a reasonable man and that such approval cannot be unreasonably withheld."

---

[8]There are various categories of open-price contracts. Among the more commonly used are the following: (1) Nothing whatsoever is said about price. (2) A provision stipulates that the price is "to be agreed upon" by the buyer and seller at the time of performance. (3) The price shall be the market price at the time of performance. (4) The price shall be the seller's cost plus a specified percentage or absolute dollar markup. (5) The price shall be no more than that charged by the seller's competitors at the time of performance. (6) The price shall be that charged by the seller to other buyers on the date of performance. (7) The price shall be determined by one of the previous methods but with specified maximum and minimum limitations. (8) The price shall be the buyer's resale price less a specified absolute or percentage discount. (9) The price shall be determined by an impartial third party or by reference to a specified trade journal or formula.

In a similar vein, a strong argument can be made that an open-price contract should be sustained by reading into the agreement an implied obligation of the parties to agree to a reasonable price. Few courts, however, have found this argument persuasive. Instead, the majority of jurisdictions appears to regard the contract price as an extremely critical provision and thus feels that judicial reconstruction of the parties's presumed intent should not extend to the determination of the price. Also, the courts frequently find difficulty in determining exactly how the parties intended to establish the price; therefore, any judicial interference would run the risk of contravening the intent of the parties.

Notwithstanding such reluctance, the courts have been willing generally to enforce executory open-price contracts that contained a formula by which the price could be determined at the time of performance. Typically, such formula would be the price established in the market place, or the price published in some specified trade journal, or the price charged by some competitor, or a price based on the seller's cost. By presently agreeing on the formula to be applied in determining the contract price, any future agreement of the parties is not required.

Section 2-305 of the Uniform Commercial Code has further encouraged the use of the open-price contract by providing that "if they so intend," the parties can conclude a contract even if nothing is said about the price and no means is provided by which the price can be determined. The comments accompanying § 2-305 provide that the intent of the section is to overrule prior case law to the effect that an agreement to agree is unenforceable and that a contract with an open-price term is void for indefiniteness. The comments also indicate that § 2-305 is not intended to give the seller unfettered discretion to establish any price that he may wish but that the price must be reasonable. Comment 3 states that the "posted price," "market price," "price in effect," or "given price" would all be considered to be a reasonable price for purposes of § 2-305.

The usefulness of § 2-305, however, is extremely limited. As with all of article 2 of the Uniform Commercial Code, § 2-305 is only applicable to contracts for the sale of goods. Therefore, contracts other than for the sale of goods may continue to be held unenforceable for want of mutuality or for indefiniteness if they do not contain a price or a definite formula for agreeing on a price.

Despite the increasing acceptance of the open-price contract evidenced by Uniform Commercial Code § 2-305 and, to a lesser extent, by the courts at common law, its usefulness is mitigated by the following considerations. First, the open-price contract may be unsatisfactory to the buyer if his main purpose in entering into the contract is to protect himself against future increases in price or to the seller if he wishes to lock into a sale at the prevailing market price to protect himself against future price declines. Thus, to the extent that a contract provides for *future* determination of the price, it fails to accomplish these objectives. If, however, the major purpose for entering into a contract for future delivery is to assure the buyer a supply of an essential product or the seller a market for his output and the parties are content that the contract price be determined at the time of delivery, then the open-price contract should be satisfactory.

Second, the open-price contract is of limited utility when it is difficult to find a formula by which the price will be determined. For this reason, open-price contracts are most commonly used in agreements for the sale of homogeneous commodities or for services that are regularly bought and sold in an active market. Conversely, a contract for a manufactured product involving a variety of materials and substantial labor costs in its production will not normally be suitable for an open-price contract.

Third, in using an open-price contract, considerable care should be exercised in specifying the manner in which the price is to be determined. For example, if the contract specifies that the price is to be the "market price," there is often considerable room for argument as to just what is the market price. Disputes that may arise include what price is meant when trading is inactive, whether customary discounts from listed market prices should be taken into account, and whether the prices of one or two sellers who habitually undercut the majority of sellers in a given market should be taken into account.

Finally, in some situations a contract calling for payment of the current "market price" or a "reasonable price" at the time of delivery might be subject to challenge if the market is severely distorted by shortages, strikes, or price-wars. Hence, if the parties decide that the use of the open-price contract is desirable, they should specify as precisely as possible the manner in which the price is to be determined and the circumstances, if any, that would render the formula inapplicable.

Cost-Plus Contracts. Another method by which the seller may protect himself against inflationary increases in his cost of materials or labor is through the use of the cost-plus contract. In this type of contract, the contract price is computed by determining the seller's cost of production and adding to that the seller's profit, which may be either a fixed sum agreed on in advance or a percentage of the total cost of production.

The cost-plus contract has been used most commonly in the defense industry. Rather than protecting against inflation, this contract has been used in the defense industry because of the inability of contractors to estimate accurately the cost of developing new weaponry. Since most contractors would refuse to enter into a fixed-price contract in this situation, the cost-plus contract has become virtually a necessity. Although cost-plus contracts, as such, have not met with the hostility that has been accorded open-price contracts, they have on occasion been held unenforceable because of uncertainty in situations in which the court was not able to determine what the parties meant by "cost."

While use of the cost-plus contract may be a necessity in research and development contracts, it is not the most desirable contractual device when the parties' main concern is protecting against inflation or deflation. First, the cost-plus clause is not likely to be viewed with favor by the buyer because it removes the incentive for the seller to minimize his costs of production; indeed, if the seller's profit is to be determined by taking a specified percentage of the total cost, the seller actually has an incentive to *maximize* his cost of production. Theoretically, the buyer could guard against this possibility by providing in the contract that only those costs that are "reasonable and necessary" to perform the contract shall be allowed in computing the contract price. In practice, however, the buyer inevitably encounters difficulty in establishing that a particular item claimed by the contractor was not reasonable and necessary.

In addition, it is extremely difficult to draft a cost-plus contract that contains a definition of "cost" that will be sufficiently clear to avoid controversy in its application. A glance at the extensive provisions of the Armed Services Procurement Regulations dealing with the determination of cost illustrates the magnitude of this problem. If the contract involves the sale of goods in their present state — for example, a contract between a wholesaler and a retailer — the problem may be relatively simple since the seller's cost will consist of the cost of goods purchased plus associated incidental costs of transportation, storage, and insurance. By contrast, however, the determination of "costs" for a manufacturing contract will require the parties to resolve many complex problems of cost accounting. Overhead expenses must be allocated to the contract. The hiring of additional labor to perform the contract may be a source of controversy as may be the employment of workers at overtime wages. The hiring of additional managerial and front office personnel may be even more difficult to allocate to a particular contract, and the decision on the valuation of inventory on a LIFO or FIFO basis is open to question.

In summary, the cost-plus contract should be used only as a last resort when other methods of protecting against economic fluctuations are unavailable. In situations in which the parties' primary concern is providing protection against price changes in critical costs of production, a much simpler solution than the cost-plus contract is to include a price-adjustment clause providing for the contract price to be increased in proportion to any increases in the costs of materials and labor above the current market price for such materials and labor. This technique avoids the complex cost determination problems that are involved in the cost-plus contract; furthermore, it provides some protection for the seller's profit margin in times of economic uncertainty. In any event, the attorney who decides to draft a cost-plus contract would be wise to consult the Armed Services Procurement Regulations for guidance in drafting the agreement.

Price Indexing and Price Escalator Clauses. One of the most commonly employed methods of protecting against inflation and deflation in contracts is the use of price indexing or price escalator clauses. Generally, these clauses provide for periodic adjustments in the contract price based on the change in a price index or the change in the price of materials or labor that constitutes a significant portion of the seller's cost of performance. Both indexing clauses and escalator clauses are commonly found in such diverse types of contracts as collective bargaining agreements, Social Security and other pension benefits, various government welfare programs, long-term bank loans, residential mortgage loans by savings and loan associations, commercial office leases and shopping center leases, insurance policies, and long-term commercial purchase contracts. Several foreign countries have even indexed personal income tax rates and government bond interest rates.

In contrast to the judicial reluctance to enforce open-price contracts, the courts generally have had no difficulty in upholding contracts containing indexing provisions.... As long as the indexing formula is drafted so that the method of price calculation can be determined by the courts with reasonable certainty, the contract will likely withstand judicial scrutiny. This conclusion is strengthened by the adoption of Uniform Commercial Code § 2-305, which relaxes the common law requirements of definiteness and certainty.

While the use of the price indexing clause presents no serious conceptual difficulties, a number of practical problems must be surmounted if an indexing clause is to be acceptable and fair to both parties. The first problem is the selection of an appropriate price index for use in a given contract. Most parties contemplating the use of an indexing clause automatically turn to the Department of Labor's Consumer Price Index (CPI) or Wholesale Price Index (WPI). In many contexts, however, neither of these indices will provide an accurate measure of the effect of inflation on a particular contract. The CPI is designed to measure the effects of inflation on the income of urban, blue-collar wage earners. It does so by measuring monthly the price changes of approximately 400 goods and services. The WPI measures the monthly changes in the wholesale prices of a representative group of 2700 industrial and agricultural commodities. While providing a reasonably accurate overall picture of inflation, both of these indices are too broad to accurately measure the effect of inflation on many types of contracts. For example, use of the CPI as an indexing tool in a commercial office lease or a contract for the sale of farm machinery would be inappropriate since the Index will not accurately measure the change in the promisor's costs. Despite these limitations, many persons appear to be utilizing the CPI in precisely those situations because of the lack of knowledge of what the CPI does measure or because of the lack of a more accurate index.

Fortunately, a multitude of other, more accurate indices are readily available. In addition to the CPI and WPI, the Department of Labor's Bureau of Labor Statistics also publishes specific price indices for the output of selected Standard Industrial Classification Industries. The Department of Agriculture publishes an Index of Prices Paid by Farmers and an Index of Prices Received by Farmers. In addition, various indices dealing with prices in particular industries are published by trade associations.

In short, indexing is an accurate means of compensating for inflation only if the indexing device is an accurate measure of the changes in the cost of performing a contract. To the extent that such an index is unavailable and cannot be calculated by the parties, indexing may not be a satisfactory answer to the problem at hand.

The problem of finding a suitable index that will accurately represent the true change in the contract price can be solved at least partially by including in the index only those elements of the total contract price that can be accurately measured. Although the formulation of an index that would accurately measure the change in rental value of commercial real estate over a long period of time would be difficult and impractical, a long-term commercial lease can provide for an automatic adjustment of the rent on the basis of certain changes in the landlord's costs that can be easily measured, such as property taxes, utility expenses, and custodial fees. Similarly, in the case of a contract for the manufacture of goods, the price could be indexed to labor costs or to the cost of one or more crucial commodities involved in the manufacturing process.

The second problem confronting potential users of a price indexing clause is to be certain that the index is carefully and accurately compiled, preferably by an impartial source. A trade association publishing an index may have a vested interest in making prices appear as high as possible, which would render such an index unfair to the buyer. For this reason, indices compiled by impartial sources, such as the government or an independent business publication, are generally more desirable.

The third problem lies in attempting to assess the reliability and continuity of the index. Litigation has occasionally resulted when the index on which a contract was based was no longer compiled. Again, government indices would generally seem to be the most reliable, although even these are occasionally changed. To guard against drastic modification or termination of an index, the contract should contain a provision designed to protect the parties from this contingency. An arbitration clause, for example, would be one solution to the problem. Finally, to enable appropriate adjustments in the contract price to be timely made, the parties should take care to select an index that will be published with reasonable speed.

Assuming the seller is able to find an appropriate index that satisfies the above criteria, he may encounter problems in using such an index. Although the seller's cost of production may increase in a given situation, the seller may find the buyer reluctant to agree to an open-ended indexing clause. In the case of a labor contract, although the cost of living may have increased so that the wage earner feels himself entitled to a wage adjustment, the employer's revenues may not have increased sufficiently to enable him to pay the increase.

Another problem with indexing in a period of constantly changing prices is that it may necessitate frequent and inconvenient revision of the contract price. This problem may be minimized by including a triggering clause providing that adjustments in the contract price shall be made only if the index increases by a certain specified minimum percentage in a given time period. Furthermore, the indexing clause can provide for adjustments to be made semi-annually or yearly rather than monthly.

To summarize, indexing is perhaps the most useful device that can be employed to safeguard the parties from the effects of changes in the price level.

Price indexing clauses are well accepted by the judiciary, can be tailored to suit the needs of the particular parties involved, and can provide near total protection to the parties against changes in the price level. On the other hand, because it eliminates the certainty provided by a fixed-price contract, indexing may not always be acceptable to both parties. When utilized, indexing clauses must be carefully drafted to avoid problems in application and to fairly represent actual, relevant changes in costs and prices.

NOTES AND QUESTIONS

1. *Some more thoughts on techniques for drafting "inflation-guard" provisions:* (This note is a short summary of some of the arguments made by Stephen A. Chaplin in his article, Redistributing the Cost of Inflation;[9] all of the quotations are from that article and the balance is paraphrase.) Chaplin begins by explaining that lawyers should gain a proper understanding of inflation in order to advise their clients of the risk of a "decrease in the value of performance in a contractual relationship before it is rendered," due to inflation. Lawyers should understand how this risk can be shifted or shared in a contractual relationship.

The risk of receiving a decreased value of performance when it is actually rendered is a type of risk that is rarely shifted in the negotiation process. Usually the risk is borne by the party that has agreed to postpone the receipt of the other's performance. Thus "it has been said that one party to an agreement bears the entire risk of fluctuation in the value of performance because he has agreed to bear it." This commonly occurs when "money, goods or services are transferred in exchange for a promise· of future payment. By agreeing to discharge the obligation in a fixed number of dollars with knowledge that the purchasing power of those dollars will probably change, the contracting parties implicitly agree that the recipient of those dollars bears the risk that they may decease in value due to inflation." However, "the risk of changes in the value of promised future performance is by no means limited to decreases in the value of money owed. A contracting party who agrees to deliver goods or render services in the future, in exchange for present payment, bears the similar risk that the cost of future performance may increase substantially before it is due. Thus, because so many variables affecting the value of future performance are out of the parties's control, it seems unfair that the entire burden of losses due to value fluctuations should fall arbitrarily on one of the parties."

"Parties may redistribute the risk of changes in the value of performance in a number of ways." In long-term relationships, one of the most effective ways of redistributing the risk of inflation is through "periodic revaluation of the goods, services or money bargained for, to reflect their value to the party receiving them. In this end, index clauses are one of the most effective ways of dealing

___

[9] 34 University of Miami Law Review 301 (1980).

with significant fluctuations in prices over the long term. This is because "[i]ndex clauses link the price of goods and services to their current market values." Yet, the use of an index clause which is not appropriate to the particular needs of the parties can have grave consequences.

For an indexing clause to be useful to the parties it should be appropriate to their needs, but also, it must be reliable and easily accessible. Currently, there are a wide variety of indices which are published regularly by government and private institutions. Particular indices may be published in a number of different versions. For example, some indexes have both a regional and a national version. Others are composite indexes with various subgroups which could be used separately if desired. Some indices also have seasonally and nonseasonally adjusted versions. With all of the possible variations available, it is vital for the lawyer to specify the exact form of the index which is being used. Moreover, the lawyer should check to see what the lag time is in the publishing of a particular index to see that it is current when it is published.

The most common method of indexing is where "one party bears the risk of value fluctuations up to an agreed point, and the other party bears the risk over and above that point." Thus no adjustments would be made in the obligation unless "the index moves more than a certain number of points within a specified period." For this method to work, it is important to clearly specify what event triggers adjustment and how often the adjustment is supposed to be made. One of the purposes of having a trigger is to maintain the administrative costs. Thus, the parties will have to consider the administrative costs of the clause in the context of the overall agreement.

It is also important that the index formula is not amenable to multiple interpretations. Thus, the formula should be as simple and as clear as is possible under the circumstances. The clause should also stipulate which parts of the agreement are subject to the clause and which items are excluded.

Provisions should be made for all reasonably foreseeable contingencies. Even when the probability of a particular event occurring seems small, the event may have a large impact on performance. The index clause should account for events which affect the goods and services bargained for as well as events which affect the index itself. Many of the contingencies such as changes in price controls or taxes are government related. Others are controlled by general market forces. In the case of governmental or market changes that significantly affect the value of the agreement, the clause should allow for renegotiation or arbitration of the price structure or the agreement.

The way in which the index clause works can also be significantly affected by events which affect the index itself. For example, the meaning of the terminology used in the index clause could change. Changes could also occur in the way in which the index is calculated. And most importantly, the clause should be drafted to protect against the discontinuation of the index. Oftentimes a successor index will replace an index which is discontinued. In this case, the parties may specify that they will use the replacement index as long as it is substantially similar to the original. Otherwise, again the parties may wish to protect against the discontinuation of an index by providing for renegotiation or arbitration of the contract.

Whenever the agreement involves security, the secured party should insist that the security agreement and the index clause grant them an interest in the amount including adjustments which may be made under the index clause.

2. *Specific examples of flexible pricing:* Consider the following examples of flexible pricing clauses. As to each, ask first whether the clause is legally enforceable under the Uniform Commercial Code.[10] Ask also whether the clause creates a workable governance structure so that the parties can perform under the contract.

— Acknowledgment of order form of a major American producer of steel:

Our base prices, together with related lists of Extras and Deductions, are subject to changes without notice, and all orders and contracts are accepted subject to price in effect at time of shipment.

— Requirements contract between a major American producer of aluminum and a major American automobile manufacturer:

The price for primary aluminum pig, ingot and billet sold by [the aluminum company] and purchased by Buyer [the automobile company] hereunder shall be [the aluminum company's] current published price (including transportation allowance, if any) in effect at the date of delivery for the products involved, unless the price as quoted in "American Metal Market" (or, in the event that "American Metal Market" quotations shall be unavailable or inapplicable, as quoted in some other recognized trade publication) is lower, in which case the price quoted in the "American Metal Market" shall apply.

If buyer receives a legitimate offer from some other domestic United States supplier source to sell to Buyer aluminum of the same quality as sold by [the aluminum company], Buyer may communicate to [the aluminum company] the quantity, price and terms so offered to Buyer and if [the aluminum company] is unable or unwilling to meet such price and terms for such quantity, Buyer may, without such action constituting a breach of this agreement, purchase from such other source such quantity at the price and terms so quoted.

---

[10]Consider U.C.C. §§ 2-204; 2-305; 2-311. Do not overlook § 204(3) and the first official comment to § 2-305.

— Purchase order of a manufacturer of automobile components such as brakes and transmissions:

> Buyer may at any time make changes in writing relating to this order including changes in the drawings or specifications, method of shipment, quantities, packing, or time, or place of delivery. If such changes result in an increase or decrease in cost of, or time required for, the performance of this contract, an equitable adjustment shall be made in the contract price, delivery schedule or both.

Consider the following comments, made in the course of an interview with a partner in a large law firm with a business practice.

> Many courts are hostile to clauses calling for negotiation or settlement on a fair basis. Yet this is just what the parties want at the time they draft the contract, and a lawyer often cannot get them to be more specific. They are unwilling to work out standards for settlement since there are too many facts that are uncertain and too much remains that cannot be foreseen. Businessmen do not like to deal with hypothetical cases.

What is a lawyer to do in a situation in which the client wants more flexibility than the rules seem to permit?

2. FLEXIBLE QUANTITY

a. Blanket Orders

Major American automobile manufacturers and some other firms with a great deal of bargaining power use blanket order purchasing. The arrangement allows a buyer to separate two functions of contract: an elaborate document drafted by a team of lawyers helps parties plan their transaction, but the buyer makes the minimum commitment possible to purchase anything from the seller. The following article describes practices as of the early 1970s. As automobile manufacturers attempt to follow Japanese methods of management in the 1980s, they often deal with far fewer suppliers and give them real commitments so they can invest in new technology. Also, this way they are able to hold much smaller inventories and count on suppliers delivering just enough to keep the assembly lines moving. Nonetheless, blanket order purchasing continues to be used widely.

The Standardized Contracts of United States Automobile Manufacturers
Stewart Macaulay[11]

... 21. The automobile industry in the United States is large, very complex and has great economic power. The major manufacturers are run as bureaucratic structures designed to operate efficiently at all levels. Those people and organizations that deal with the manufacturers have patterned their conduct to accommodate this model of economic efficiency. However, new models of automobiles must be designed several years before they are offered to the public and the demand for new automobiles fluctuates significantly. Bureaucratic operation in the service of economic efficiency, time-span and fluctuating demand are all critical factors which are reflected in many different kinds of exchange transactions found in this industry. In this paper we will consider some of the exchange relationships between the manufacturers, and their suppliers, their dealers and their customers in order to generalize about contract as it is found in this kind of large scale industry.

A. CONTRACTS TO BUILD AND SELL CARS

i. *The Manufacturers and Their Suppliers*

a. Description of the Relationship

22. Although the manufacturers can and do make in their own plants some of almost all of the parts which go into an assembled automobile, they also buy many of these parts from suppliers. There are a number of reasons why they purchase from outside suppliers. First, the manufacturer gets a product without investing additional capital in buildings, machines and a trained work force. Second, the manufacturer gets a yardstick which can be used to measure the efficiency of its own division making the same item. If a division making grease seals can produce them at 2 cents each, but an outside supplier can make them for 1 1/2 cents each, the manufacturer knows he must reexamine the efficiency of his internal operation. Third, the manufacturer increases the chance that he may benefit from technological innovation. The supplier's designers and engineers may be able to suggest a different design or an improved manufacturing process. On the other side, most businesses, but not all, that can produce parts for automobiles want to sell their output to the automobile manufacturers because of the possibilities for extremely high volume production which, in an efficiently managed firm, can be highly profitable.

---

[11]7 International Encyclopedia of Comparative Law, Ch. 3, 3-21 to 3-30, 3-51 (1973).

There are three additional factors influencing the course a manufacturer-supplier relationship takes: First, the mass production techniques of American automobile manufacturing require that the assembly line not be stopped. When, for example, a particular Ford sedan arrives at a certain point on the assembly line, four hubcaps must be there ready to be installed. It would be extremely costly to the manufacturer if the line had to be stopped because the supplier's machines that stamp out hubcaps broke down, because a supplier's inventory was not great enough to meet the demand or because the parts were lost in shipment. However, demand for automobiles and even for particular types of automobiles fluctuates. To a great extent, this second factor offsets the first. The easiest way to avoid stopping assembly lines would be to produce large quantities of parts far in advance of need. Yet this approach increases costs because of the possibility of waste and the loss of the use of funds thus devoted to inventories. If, for example, the demand for station wagons declines during the year, exhaust pipes that fit only station wagons that will never be produced are mere scrap metal. Third, component parts can be defective, the defect can cause injury to property or person, and in United States law the injured party in such cases has increasingly been gaining rights against manufactures. Not surprisingly, one finds that manufacturers wish to hold suppliers responsible for such claims, and the suppliers must defend themselves against the costly results of seemingly minor defects in the parts they make.

b. The Blanket Order System

aa. The System Described

23. The *manufacturers* have accommodated all of these economic and legal factors in an imaginative piece of transaction architecture which is usually called a "blanket order." Coupled with the suppliers's great desire to do business with the automobile manufacturers, the blanket order system almost always insures that parts will arrive at the assembly plants at the right time, that the suppliers will take the risk of scrapped parts caused by fluctuations in demand, and that the suppliers will be responsible for claims caused by defects. Moreover, the system gives the manufacturers great leverage to ward off price increases caused by the suppliers's increased costs.

This is how it works: Some time before the beginning of the model year, the manufacturer will issue a blanket order to a supplier of, for example, tail pipes designed specifically for one of the manufacturer's station wagons. The blanket order states a number of "agreements." One of the most important is the price per unit. This price is computed on the basis of an estimated number of units to be ordered, and it will not be increased if fewer are actually ordered. Thus, the manufacturer has made the supplier run the risk that he will not even recover his cost of producing the items actually shipped to the manufacturer in the event that the manufacturer uses substantially fewer than the estimated number. And the blanket order does not oblige the manufacturer to take and pay for *any* of the parts described in it. That obligation comes only when the manufacturer sends the supplier documents called "releases." The idea seems to be that the blanket order creates a force which is held back until released little by little.

Each month, sometimes more often, the manufacturer sends the supplier a release, ordering him to manufacture and ship a specified number of the parts each week. On the release form, the manufacturer also will estimate the number of parts he will require for the next two or three months, but this estimate, to quote one manufacturer's form, "is for planning purposes only and does not constitute a commitment." Typically, manufacturers do not send releases calling for more parts than they will need in a month since their monthly estimates of sales are fairly accurate. However, sometimes they do order too few or too many parts. If there is an increase in public demand for a particular model, the blanket order allows the manufacturer to send another release form to the supplier calling for increased deliveries. Such sudden increases may be a great strain on the supplier if he does not have unused capacity for production. Moreover, a supplier must always guard against a break-down of his machinery, which temporarily destroys his ability to meet the manufacturer's demands. As a result, the supplier usually makes more than the number of parts ordered by the manufacturer so that the supplier will have an inventory to cover anticipated future demands. He builds this inventory at his own risk since the blanket order clearly provides that "Seller shall not fabricate any articles covered by this order, or procure materials required therefor, or ship any articles to Purchaser, except to the extent authorized by ... written releases ... Purchaser will make no payments for finished work, work in process or raw material fabricated or produced by Seller in excess of Purchaser's written releases."

If a manufacturer has "released" too many parts in light of a sudden decrease in demand, the blanket order gives it the right to cancel the amount ordered in whole or in part. It then is obligated to pay the contract price for each part finished and "the cost to Seller (excluding profit or losses) of work in process and raw material, based on any audit Purchaser may conduct and generally accepted accounting principles." ·

bb. Blanket Orders and American Contract Law

(1) Legal Enforceability

24. American contract law would likely support the manufacturer's plan for the transaction so that, when the law is combined with the market situation, the manufacturer's interests would be favored. Under the law there must be an exchange of promises or of performances to create a legally enforceable contract. In a blanket order, the manufacturer makes no promise until it sends a "release," and so until then there has been no exchange and contract rights have not been created. In effect, at the manufacturer's request, the supplier makes an offer - a

promise to supply certain goods if they are ordered - which the manufacturer accepts every time it sends a release. The continuing offer and the many acceptances create a series of contracts. It is possible that two developing doctrines in the Common Law of the United States might be applied in the future to offer remedies despite the absence of a contract. Reliance by the manufacturer on the supplier's promise to fill all orders might receive legal protection, in the unlikely event it were needed, by the growing "firm offer" doctrine. Reliance by the supplier on any assurances (most likely implied ones) of the manufacturer that it would order a reasonable quantity might be protected by the development of rules requiring fairness in negotiations.

25. One can only speculate about the legal situation in light of general principles of contract law and the Uniform Commercial Code, since litigation testing these conclusions is unlikely. The large automobile manufacturers try to avoid placing total reliance on any one supplier, and other suppliers usually can increase production so that a manufacturer's assembly line is not stopped for lack of an item. Thus manufacturers tend to avoid injury rather than litigate for compensation. On the other hand, no automobile parts supplier is likely to bring a case against a manufacturer; the loss on any one order is very unlikely to be large enough to justify jeopardizing future business. Of course, the trustee of a bankrupt supplier would be free of this constraint. However, in light of the uncertainty of the supplier's legal position, many trustees would think it unwise to risk the cost of legal action against a manufacturer.

26. What are the consequences of the legal situation? If we assume that the developing reliance and fairness doctrines would not apply, the parties get legal rights only after the manufacturer has issued a release and only as to the goods ordered in that release. This means that there can be a great deal of reliance by the supplier which is unprotected by contract rights. On the other hand, legally the supplier would be free to refuse to continue the relationship by revoking his outstanding offer to supply the parts as ordered by the release forms. As we have said previously, few suppliers who were not going out of business could afford to exercise such a right; very few situations short of bankruptcy would justify losing the good will of General Motors, Ford, Chrysler or American Motors. Most importantly for the manufacturer, it does get legal rights once a release is issued. As a result, it manages to avoid any question that the supplier will bear liability for injuries caused by defective parts which it ships. Once the parts are ordered by a release there is a contract which the manufacturer has written, and the disclaimers and limitations of remedy so typically found in documents drafted by sellers are thus avoided. As between Chrysler and its suppliers, the responsibility for compliance with federal safety and air pollution regulations is also clearly placed on the supplier.

(2) Remedies

27. The standard blanket order documents drastically limit the remedies to which a supplier would otherwise be entitled under American contract law once a legally binding contract is created by the issuance of a release. Typically, the manufacturer reserves a right to cancel the goods ordered by its release, either in whole or in part. Under American contract law such a cancellation would be a breach if not authorized by the agreement, and, absent a contract provision to the contrary, the seller would be entitled to recover what he had spent in performance before the buyer's notice of cancellation plus the profit he would have made had he been allowed to complete his performance. Most blanket order cancellation clauses, however, exclude a right to profit except as to those parts which have been completed before cancellation. Thus even when a contract is formed by a release, the supplier's rights in most situations will be minimal. The manufacturer gains a practical commitment from the supplier to meet the demands of its assembly line. It retains maximum flexibility by making no commitment to buy any parts until a release is given and making only a very limited payment if it wishes to cancel after one is sent.

c. The Absence of a Reform Movement

28. There are no statutes attempting to regulate this relationship, and no movement seeking such legislation has been discovered. Insofar as statutes in the United States are the result of pluralistic struggle and compromise, one essential element of pluralism seems lacking. It would be hard to form a group of suppliers to seek legislation. Supplying the manufacturers is very profitable for a firm that can accept all of the risks allocated to it by the blanket order system. Such successful firms would hesitate to jeopardize their standing with the manufacturers by supporting an organization taking a stand antagonistic to the manufacturers' interests. Without the most successful firms, such a group would lack political power. Firms that do not wish to assume the risks of the blanket order system can easily seek other customers since their facilities are not limited to producing original-equipment automobile parts. "Exit" is a relatively cheap remedy for dissatisfaction in this case. The facilities devoted to producing original-equipment parts can be converted readily to producing parts for repairing automobiles — the so-called "after market" — or to supplying related industries such as truck or industrial engine manufacturers which, generally, do not have the bargaining power to use the blanket order system. "Voice" — using private or legal power to change the allocation of risks — would entail high costs and the chances of success would not be great in light of the many resources of the manufacturers.

Moreover, insofar as statutes flow from the efforts of those with access to the communications media attempting to enhance their status and power by acting as champions of the deserving underprivileged, this seems an unpromising area. The auto parts suppliers typically are not small businessmen but only smaller organizations than the giant auto manufacturers. The image of the suppliers is that of junior partners who are well-paid for taking large but acceptable risks: it would be hard for an ambitious United States Senator to champion them as the exploited victims of the corporate system.

Finally, insofar as one explains United States legislation as an instrument of the powerful to further their interests, no statutory action is needed in this area. The Common Law of contracts serves to legitimate and support the manufacturers's procedures by minimizing or denying rights to the suppliers.

29. In summary, the manufacturers have tailored a relationship whereby they get most of the advantages of producing parts in a division of their own firms while preserving most of the advantages of dealing with an outside organization. The suppliers are offered a chance to make high profits in exchange for assuming great risks. Most suppliers are eager for the chance to play the blanket order game. The public may get better automobiles at a lower price as a result of the system, but one cannot be sure. There are important parallels to the contract system used by the United States government to procure military equipment such as tanks and aircraft. Since experience may change the need for a weapon or call for a modification in its design, the government retains great power to change or terminate its orders to private industry while paying less than the damages specified in general contract law... It is thought that the risks in dealing with the United States government are reflected in higher prices paid to the weapons industry on government contracts. The automobile manufacturers may also pay for the flexibility in the blanket order system. However, unlike the United States government, the manufacturers make some of their own needs of each type of part. They can turn to their own divisions if prices are too high, and they can negotiate about prices with suppliers in the light of detailed knowledge about what it costs to make the item. Moreover, unlike the government's, the manufacturers's decisions and negotiations are not directly subject to a political process.

ii. *Evaluation: Benefits at What Price?*

a. The Balance of Gains and Costs

51. Undoubtedly, this kind of rationalized planning has advantages. It is not an insignificant part of a system which has produced great wealth for executives of automobile manufacturers, stockholders in these companies, automobile dealers, parts suppliers, and even, to some extent, for workers employed by this industry and its satellites. The high demand for automobiles produces opportunities for profit and jobs in many related industries and has a major impact on the total American economy. The system may have produced less expensive automobiles than could be made by any other, since one can assume that if the manufacturers had had to assume all of the risks they avoid by these contracts,

they would have passed on these costs to buyers in the form of higher prices for new cars.

NOTES AND QUESTIONS

1. *Understanding the arrangement's functions*: Creating a blanket order system costs major buyers something. Why don't they avoid these costs by buying their needs on the market? Why are suppliers interested in blanket orders? Why don't they sell on the market to those who want to buy rather than accept arrangements under which buyers make so little commitment to them? Does the blanket order system help minimize the costs of production or does it increase those costs and contribute to inflation when they are passed along to consumers by higher prices?

2. *Blanket orders when a seller has superior bargaining power*: Sellers with superior bargaining power will use a different structure for blanket orders than those of the automobile manufacturers described by Macaulay. For example, in *Franklin v. Demico, Inc.*,[12] Demico, Inc. contracted to supply electronic circuit boards to Python Corporation under the "Demico Blanket Order Policy." Python agreed to purchase large quantities of circuit boards. However, it could give 90 days notice and increase or decrease the amounts called for. If it decreased the amounts called for, there would be a "bill back" to reflect a higher price per unit. This arrangement, of course, reflects the usual practice of charging less per unit when goods are ordered in large quantities. Under the Demico policy, it bills a buyer on the assumption that it will order enough units in the future to qualify for a quantity discount. If it does not, it owes additional amounts for those units it has received and paid for. The Georgia court upheld this arrangement. It found that the supplier had proved its damages with reasonable certainty under the bill back system.

b. Requirements and Output Contracts

Requirements and output contracts are one of the places where classic contracts scholarship touches modern business practices. A requirements contract is one under which a seller agrees to supply all the part #123 that buyer requires, and buyer agrees to buy all its requirements of that part from seller. An output contract is one under which a seller agrees to deliver to buyer all the output of a particular factory or farm. These contracts raise a number of practical and legal questions. Most were recognized in a classic article written over sixty years ago. Havighurst and Berman[13] dealt with the problems of mutuality and enforceability found in the common law cases. The Uniform Commercial Code solves or

---

[12]347 S.E.2d 718 (Ct. App. Ga. 1986).

[13]Requirement and Output Contracts, 27 Illinois Law Review 1 (1932).

transforms most of these problems. We will survey the transformation of the requirements and output contract problem from mutuality to U.C.C. interpretation.

Havighurst and Berman also pointed out that lawyers and judges had to interpret the risks taken by each side as a result of promises to supply all the buyer's requirements. The seller risks that the buyer will have either no requirements or too many requirements. In a falling market for seller's goods, buyer can get them elsewhere cheaper. Thus, buyer has an incentive to look for ways out of the requirements contract. First, buyer may change the design of the product in which it used what seller was to supply so buyer no longer has any requirements for seller's goods. Also, suppose buyer had a contract to buy its requirements of fuel oil from seller. Can a buyer switch to natural gas to heat and power its factory? Second, mergers and consolidations can affect requirements contracts. Suppose a contract calls for buyer to purchase "all requirements for the Racine, Wisconsin plant" from seller. Buyer then is merged into a multinational corporation which closes the Racine plant. However, multinational makes the same product at its Deep South Plant, free of labor unions and state regulation. Has seller any rights against multinational? Third, suppose buyer goes bankrupt and ceases doing business. Has seller a claim in the bankruptcy proceedings on the theory of an implied promise to have requirements?

Suppose, on the other hand, the requirements contract calls for a fixed price and the market price for the goods in question increases rapidly. Now the buyer may demand too many goods from the seller. Suppose buyer ordered the goods for use in buyer's own manufacturing process. Once the market takes off, may buyer order additional items and resell them at a higher price? Suppose buyer is merged into a multinational corporation which uses its marketing skills and capital to double the demand for buyer's product. Must seller supply these additional requirements at the lower contract price?

Those who drafted Article II of the U.C.C. were well aware of Havighurst and Berman's article. Sections 2-306; 1-201; 2-103(1)(b) and the Official Comments to these sections tell us something about how the Code proposes to solve these problems. (Of course, those drafting requirements and output contracts can and do deal with these problems explicitly. Indeed, we raise them, in part, so that you will see them if you are ever called on to draft such documents.[14]) However, what are the requirements and output contracts problems of the 1970s and 1980s which are likely to extend into the 1990s? We will look at a case considering the Code's resolution of one of the problems raised by Havighurst and Berman. Then we will study two of the most common problems involving requirements contracts today — whether a distributorship is a requirements contract governed by the U.C.C. and the impact of U.C.C. § 2-201(1) on provisions for flexible

---

[14]See Note, Requirements Contracts: Problems of Drafting and Construction, 78 Harvard Law Review 1212 (1965).

quantity. That section, you may recall, says that a "writing is not insufficient because it omits or incorrectly states a term agreed upon but the contract is not enforceable under this paragraph beyond the quantity of goods shown in such writing." How does U.C.C. § 2-306 track with this apparent demand that parties show the quantity in writing?

EMPIRE GAS CORP. v. AMERICAN BAKERIES CO.

840 F.2d 1333 (7th Cir. 1988)

POSNER, CIRCUIT JUDGE. This appeal in a diversity contract case presents a fundamental question — surprisingly little discussed by either courts or commentators — in the law of requirements contracts. Is such a contract essentially a buyer's option, entitling him to purchase all he needs of the good in question on the terms set forth in the contract, but leaving him free to purchase none if he wishes provided that he does not purchase the good from anyone else and is not acting out of ill will toward the seller?

Empire Gas Corporation is a retail distributor of liquefied petroleum gas, better known as "propane." It also sells converters that enable gasoline-powered motor vehicles to operate on propane. The sharp rise in gasoline prices in 1979 and 1980 made American Bakeries Company, which operated a fleet of more than 3,000 motor vehicles to serve its processing plants and bakeries, interested in the possibility of converting its fleet to propane, which was now one-third to one-half less expensive than gasoline. Discussions between the companies resulted in an agreement in principle. Empire Gas sent American Bakeries a draft of its standard "Guaranteed Fuel Supply Contract," which would have required American Bakeries to install a minimum number of conversion units each month and to buy all the propane for the converted vehicles from Empire Gas for eight years. American Bakeries rejected the contract and Empire Gas prepared a new one, which was executed on April 17, 1980, and which was "for approximately three thousand (3,000) [conversion] units, more or less depending upon requirements of Buyer, consisting of Fuel Tank, Fuel Lock Off Switch, Converter & appropriate Carburetor & Small Parts Kit," at a price of $750 per unit. American Bakeries agreed "to purchase propane motor fuel solely from EMPIRE GAS CORPORATION at all locations where EMPIRE GAS has supplied carburetion and dispensing as long as EMPIRE GAS CORPORATION remains in a reasonably competitive price posture with other major suppliers." The contract was to last for four years.

American Bakeries never ordered any equipment or propane from Empire Gas. Apparently within days after the signing of the contract American Bakeries decided not to convert its fleet to propane. No reason has been given for the decision.

Empire Gas brought suit against American Bakeries for breach of contract and won a jury verdict for $3,254,963, representing lost profits on 2,242 conversion units (the jury's estimate of American Bakeries' requirements) and on the propane fuel that the converted vehicles would have consumed during the contract period.

The heart of this case is the instruction concerning American Bakeries's obligation under the contract. If there were no legal category of "requirements" contracts and no provision of the Uniform Commercial Code governing such contracts, a strong argument could be made that American Bakeries agreed to buy 3,000 conversion units or *slightly* more or *slightly* less, depending on its actual needs, and hence that it broke the contract by taking none. This is not only a semantically permissible reading of the contract but one supported by the discussions that the parties had before the contract was signed (and these discussions are admissible to explain though not to change the parties's undertakings), in which American Bakeries assured Empire Gas that it was planning to convert its entire fleet. American Bakeries insisted on adding the phrase "more or less depending upon requirements of Buyer" just in case its estimate of 3,000 was off, and this is quite different from supposing that the phrase was added so that American Bakeries would have no obligation to buy any units at all.

The parties agree, however, that despite the negotiating history and the inclusion in the contract of a specific estimate of quantity, the quoted phrase sorted the contract into the legal bin labeled "requirements contract" and thereby brought it under the governance of § 2-306(1) of the Uniform Commercial Code ... Over American Bakeries' objection the judge decided to read the statute to the jury verbatim and without amplification ... [However,] the law is [not] what a jury might make out of statutory language. The law is the statute as interpreted. The duty of interpretation is the judge's. Having interpreted the statute he must then convey the statute's meaning, as interpreted, in words the jury can understand. If § 2-306 means something different from what it seems to say, the instruction was erroneous.

The interpretive question involves the proviso [in § 2-306(1)] dealing with "quantity unreasonably disproportionate to any stated estimate." This limitation is fairly easy to understand when the disproportion takes the form of the buyer's demanding more than the amount estimated. If there were no ceiling, and if the price happened to be advantageous to the buyer, he might increase his "requirements" so that he could resell the good at a profit ... This would place him in competition with the seller — a result the parties would not have wanted when they signed the contract. So the "unreasonably disproportionate" proviso carries out the likely intent of the parties. The only problem is that the same result could easily be reached by interpretation of the words "good faith" in the preceding clause of § 2-306(1), thus making the proviso redundant. But redundancies designed to clarify or emphasize are common in legal drafting, and anyway the Uniform Commercial Code has its share of ambiguities, see *Wisconsin Knife Works v. National Metal Crafters*, 781 F.2d 1280, 1288 (7th Cir. 1986).

The proviso does not distinguish between the buyer who demands more than the stated estimate and the buyer who demands less, and therefore if read literally it would forbid a buyer to take (much) less than the stated estimate. Since the judge did not attempt to interpret the statute, the jury may have read it literally, and if so the judge in effect directed a verdict for Empire Gas. The stated estimate was for 3,000 units; American Bakeries took none; if this was not unreasonably disproportionate to the stated estimate, what buyer shortfall could be?

So we must decide whether the proviso should be read literally when the buyer is demanding less rather than more than the stated estimate. There are no cases on the question in Illinois, and authority elsewhere is sparse, considering how often (one might think) the question must have arisen. But the clearly dominant approach is not to construe the proviso literally, but instead to treat the overdemanding and underdemanding cases differently.... We think this is right.

Granted, there is language in the Official Comments (not official in Illinois, be it noted) which points to symmetrical treatment of the overdemanding and underdemanding cases: "the agreed estimate is to be regarded as a center around which the parties intend the variation to occur." U.C.C. § 2-306, Comment 3. But there is no elaboration; and the statement is in tension with the statement in Comment 2 that "good faith variations from prior requirements are permitted even when the variation may be such as to result in discontinuance," for if that principle is sound in general, why should it cease to be sound just because the parties included an estimate of the buyer's requirements? A tiny verbal point against the symmetrical interpretation is the last word of the proviso — "demanded." The statement that "no quantity unreasonably disproportionate to any stated estimate ... may be ... demanded" is more naturally read as applying to the case where the buyer is demanding more than when he is reducing his demand below the usual or estimated level.

More important than this verbal skirmishing is the fact that the entire proviso is in a sense redundant given the words "good faith" in the main clause of the statute. The proviso thus seems to have been designed to explicate the term "good faith" rather than to establish an independent legal standard. And the aspect of good faith that required explication had only to do with disproportionately *large* demands. If the buyer saw an opportunity to increase his profits by reselling the seller's goods because the market price had risen above the contract price, the exploitation of that opportunity might not *clearly* spell bad faith; the proviso was added to close off the opportunity. There is no indication that the draftsmen were equally, if at all, concerned about the case where the buyer takes less than his estimated requirements, provided, of course, that he does not buy from anyone else. We conclude that the Illinois courts would allow a buyer to reduce his requirements to zero if he was acting in good faith, even though the contract contained an estimate of those requirements.

This conclusion would be greatly strengthened — too much so, as we shall see — if the only purpose of a requirements contract were to give the seller a reasonably assured market for his product *by forbidding the buyer to satisfy any of his needs by buying from another supplier....* The buyer's undertaking to deal exclusively with a particular seller gives the seller some, although far from complete, assurance of having a market for his goods; and of course he must compensate the buyer for giving up the opportunity to shop around for a better deal from competing sellers.

There was no breach of *this* obligation ... If the obligation were not just to refrain from buying a competitor's goods but to buy approximately the stated estimate (or, in the absence of any estimate, the buyer's "normal" requirements), the contract would be altogether more burdensome to the buyer. Instead of just committing himself not to buy from a competitor even if the competitor offered a better product or terms of sale, he would be committing himself to go through with whatever project generated the estimate of required quantity, no matter what happened over the life of the project save those exceptional events that would excuse performance under the related excuses of *force majeure*, impossibility, impracticability, or frustration. This would be a big commitment to infer from the inclusion in the contract of an estimated quantity, at least once the parties concede as they do here that their contract really is a requirements contract and not a contract for the estimate itself — not, in other words, a fixed-quantity contract.

Both extreme interpretations — that the buyer need only refrain from dealing with a competitor of the seller, and that the buyer cannot go significantly beneath the estimated quantity except in dire circumstances — must be rejected, as we shall see. Nevertheless the judge should not have read the "unreasonably disproportionate" proviso in § 2-306(1) to the jury. The proviso does not apply, though the requirement of good faith does, where the buyer takes less rather than more of the stated estimate in a requirements contract.

This error in instructions requires reversal and a new trial on liability unless it is clear either that American Bakeries acted in good faith or that it acted in bad faith, since the statute requires the buyer to take his "good faith" requirements from the seller, irrespective of proportionality. The Uniform Commercial Code does not contain a definition of "good faith" that seems applicable to the buyer under a requirements contract. Compare § 2-104(1) with § 2-103(1)(b). Nor has the term a settled meaning in law generally; it is a chameleon ... Clearly, American Bakeries was acting in bad faith if during the contract period it bought propane conversion units from anyone other than Empire Gas, or made its own units, or reduced its purchases because it wanted to hurt Empire Gas (for example because they were competitors in some other market). Equally clearly, it was not acting in bad faith if it had a business reason for deciding not to convert that was independent of the terms of the contract or any other aspect of its relationship with Empire gas, such as a drop in the demand for its bakery products that led it to reduce or abandon its fleet of delivery trucks. A harder question is whether it was acting in bad faith if it changed its mind about conversion for no (disclosed) reason. There is no evidence in the record on why it changed its mind beyond vague references to "budget problems" that, so far as appears, may have been nothing more than a euphemism for a decision by American Bakeries not to allocate funds for conversion to propane.

If no reason at all need be given for scaling back one's requirements even to zero, then a requirements contract is from the buyer's standpoint just an option to purchase up to (or slightly beyond, i.e., within the limits of reasonable proportionality) the stated estimate on the terms specified in the contract, except that the buyer cannot refuse to exercise the option because someone offers him better terms. This is not an unreasonable position, but it is not the law. Among the less important reasons for this conclusion are that option contracts are dealt with elsewhere in the Code, see § 2-311, and that the Official Comments to § 2-306 state that "a shut-down by a requirements buyer for lack of orders might be permissible where a shut-down *merely to curtail losses* would not." U.C.C. § 2-306, Comment 2 (emphasis added). More compelling is the Illinois Code Comment to § 2-306 which states that "this section ... is but a codification of prior Illinois decisional law," which had made clear that a requirements contract was more than a buyer's option. "By the original agreement, appellant was entitled to order all the coal which was required or needed in its business for the season named; by the modified contract, appellant was restricted to the privilege of ordering twelve thousand tons. It was not the intention here to contract for the mere option or privilege of buying coal at a future time, but simply to limit the quantity to be bought ... [I]t was not intended to be an option contract." *Minnesota Lumber Co. v. Whitebreast Coal Co.*, 160 Ill. 85, 96-97, 43 N.E. 774 (1896). "Requirements" are more than purely subjective "needs," which would be the equivalent of "wants." [citations omitted].

These cases are old, but nothing has happened to sap their strength.... The statement of an estimate invites the seller to begin making preparations to satisfy the contract, and although no reliance expense was incurred by the seller in this case, a seller is entitled to expect that the buyer will buy something like the estimated requirements unless it has a valid business reason for buying less. More important than the estimate (which was not a factor in the Illinois cases just cited) is the fact that ordinarily a requirements contract is terminated after performance has begun, rather than before as in the present case. Whether or not the seller can prove reliance damages, the sudden termination of the contract midway through performance is bound to disrupt its operations somewhat. The Illinois courts interpret a requirements contract as a sharing of risk between seller and buyer. The seller assumes the risk of a change in the buyer's business that makes continuation of the contract unduly costly, but the buyer assumes the risk of a less urgent change in his circumstances, perhaps illustrated by the facts of this case where so far as one can tell the buyer's change of mind reflected no more than a reassessment of the balance of advantages and disadvantages under the contract. American Bakeries did not agree to buy conversion units and propane for trucks that it got rid of, but neither did Empire Gas agree to forgo sales merely because new management at American Bakeries decided that its capital would be better employed in some other investment than conversion to propane.

The general distinction that we are trying to make is well illustrated by *Southwest Natural Gas Co. v. Oklahoma Portland Cement Co.*, 102 F.2d 630 (10th Cir. 1939), which to the drafters of the Uniform Commercial Code exemplified "reasonable variation of an extreme sort" (at least in the absence of an estimate, but that is irrelevant, for reasons we have explained). U.C.C. § 2-306, Comment 2. A cement company agreed to buy all of its requirements of gas from the seller for 15 years. Seven years later, the cement company replaced its boiler, which had worn out, with more modern equipment; as a result its need for gas fell by 80 percent. The court deemed this a bona fide change in the cement company's requirements. It would have been unreasonable to make the company replace its worn-out plant with an obsolete facility.

It is a nice question how exigent the buyer's change of circumstances must be to allow him to scale down his requirements from either the estimated level or, in the absence of estimate, the "normal" level. Obviously it need not be so great as to give him a defense under the doctrines of impossibility, impracticability, or frustration, or under a *force majeure* clause. Yet, although more than whim is required, ... how much more is unclear. There is remarkably little authority on the question. This is a good sign; it suggests that, while we might think it unsatisfactory for the law to be unclear on so fundamental a question, the people affected by the law are able to live with the lack of certainty. The reason may be that parties linked in an ongoing relationship — the usual situation under a requirements contract — have a strong incentive to work out disagreements amicably rather than see the relationship destroyed by litigation.

The essential ingredient of good faith in the case of the buyer's reducing his estimated requirements is that he not merely have had second thoughts about the terms of the contract and want to get out of it ... Whether the buyer has any greater obligation is unclear, ... but need not be decided here. Once it is decided (as we have) that a buyer cannot arbitrarily declare his requirements to be zero, this becomes an easy case, because American Bakeries has never given any reason for its change of heart. It might seem that once the district judge decided to instruct the jury in the language of the statute, American Bakeries was foreclosed from arguing that it had scaled down its requirements in good faith; a reduction to zero could never be proportionate if, as the instruction implied, the proviso on disproportion applies to reductions as well as increases in the buyer's takings. But the judge did not make this decision until the instructions conference. Until then American Bakeries had every opportunity and incentive to introduce evidence of why it decided not to convert its fleet to propane. It introduced none, and even at the argument in this court its counsel could give no reason for the change of heart beyond a hint that it was due to a change in management, which would not be enough by itself to justify a change in the buyer's requirements.

Even though Empire Gas had the burden of proving breach of contract and therefore (we may assume) of proving that American Bakeries acted in bad faith in reducing its requirements from 3,000 conversion units to zero ... , no reasonable jury could have failed to find bad faith, and therefore the error in instructing the jury on proportionality was harmless. Empire Gas put in evidence, uncontested and incontestable, showing that American Bakeries had not got rid of its fleet of trucks and did have the financial wherewithal to go through with the conversion process. After this evidence came in, American Bakeries could avoid a directed verdict only by introducing some evidence concerning its reasons for reducing its requirements. It not only introduced no evidence, but as is plain from counsel's remarks at argument it has no evidence that it would care to put before the jury — no reasons that it would care to share with either the district court or this court. It disagrees with the standard of good faith, believing that so long as it did not buy conversion units elsewhere or want to hurt Empire Gas it was free to reduce its requirements as much as it pleased. It does not suggest that it has a case under the standard we have adopted, which requires at a minimum that the reduction of requirements not have been motivated solely by a reassessment of the balance of advantages and disadvantages under the contract to the buyer.

The jury's finding of liability must stand; but was there error in the assessment of damages? American Bakeries objects violently to the assumption made by Empire Gas's expert witness that the vehicles converted by American Bakeries, had it honored what Empire Gas contends were its obligations under the contract, would have run 100 percent on propane. The conversion units would have been dual units, which permit the driver by a flick of a switch in the engine to run his vehicle on either gasoline or propane. But since the parties agree that the price of propane was lower than that of gasoline throughout the entire contract period, a driver would have switched his conversion unit to gasoline only when he was low on propane and too far away from a propane station to reach it before he ran out. This factor was not big enough to upset the expert witness's calculations significantly. The calculation of damages is estimation rather than measurement, and it is foolish to prolong a lawsuit in quest of delusive precision.

The other complaints about the damage assessment are equally inconsequential, and do not require discussion. A great weakness of American Bakeries's case was its failure to present its own estimate of damages, in the absence of which the jury could have no idea of what adjustments to make in order to take account of American Bakeries's arguments. American Bakeries may have feared that if it put in its own estimate of damages the jury would be irresistibly attracted to that figure as a compromise. But if so, American Bakeries gambled double or nothing, as it were; and we will not relieve it of the consequences of its risky strategy.

The judgment is affirmed ... [Judge Kanne's dissent is omitted.]

NOTES AND QUESTIONS

1. *Practical problems*: A seller faces some real difficulty in determining just when requirements have become "unreasonably disproportionate." Parties face similar practical problems in asserting that demands are not made in good faith. Guttenberg[15] asserts:

> [t]he distinction between good and bad faith reductions in requirements that the Seventh Circuit adopted in *Empire Gas* is of no ... practical use ... The court stated that seller assumes the risk of changes in buyer's circumstances that make continuation of the contract unduly costly, but does not assume the risk of less urgent changes. It is unclear when a change in circumstances makes performance of a contract unduly costly and when a change is less urgent. The court offered no guidelines other than that something more than whim is required ... [T]his distinction leaves an expansive middle ground where a court's application of the distinction would be wholly unpredictable.

She advocates a business reason rule: "[i]t would define good faith as buyer providing seller with a business reason for a reduction. 'Business reason's means an economic reason, such as business losses or a more profitable alternative investment." She asserts this rule "would provide contracting parties with definite guidelines." This would be efficient because the parties will not have to expend resources bargaining for a more explicit allocation of risk.

2. *A contrasting idea:* Contrast Judge Posner's explanation of why there are few cases construing § 2-306(1):

> There is remarkably little authority on the question. This is a good sign; it suggests that, while we might think it unsatisfactory for the law to be unclear on so fundamental a question, the people affected by the law are able to live with the lack of certainty. The reason may be that parties linked in an ongoing relationship — the usual situation under a requirements contract — have a strong incentive to work out disagreements amicably rather than see the relationship destroyed by litigation.

c. Distributorships — Is a Distribution Contract a Requirements Contract?

As you know, a very common commercial arrangement involves a manufacturer who contracts with a distributor to promote and deliver the manufactured goods within a defined territory. The distributors often provide warehousing and delivery services, as well as acting as a sales force. A distributor may carry

---

[15]And Then There Were None: Requirements Contracts and the Buyer Who Does Not Buy, 64 Washington Law Review 871 (1989).

several "lines" from several different manufacturers. A distributor generally prefers to be the exclusive source for a manufacturer's product in the region. Only if the distributor "has an exclusive" can the distributor be sure of capturing all of the value of its promotional efforts, and developing long-term loyal customers. The distributor acts as a conduit for the goods. The contracts between manufacturers and distributors involve duties that make the distributors look, for some purposes, as if they were the part-time employees or agents for the manufacturer, but for other purposes as if they were buyers of goods for resale. What difference does the characterization of the agreement make? One important difference is that if the transaction between a manufacturer and a distributor is characterized as a sale of goods, the U.C.C. applies. And the application of the U.C.C. may yield different results from the application of common law.

An example of such a question arose in the case of *Famous Brands, Inc. v. David Sherman Corp.*[16] In the course of Famous Brands's purchase of a liquor wholesaler (Midland), Famous sought reassurance that Sherman would continue to supply it with Everclear, and other liquor brands. Sherman's representative replied that, "[If the proposed sale] happens, I want you to know that we will be more than happy to have you distribute Everclear alcohol and any other brands that Midland will be selling for us." Later, Sherman said that Famous could "count on" Sherman. Shortly thereafter, Sherman terminated the distributorship, apparently because Famous refused to carry a full line of Sherman's products. Famous sued to enforce the distributorship agreement. The trial court granted Sherman's motion for summary judgment on the grounds that (1) the terms of the contract were too indefinite, and (2) there was no mutuality of obligation.

The 8th Circuit reversed, finding that since the parties had operated under the agreement for over a year there was a jury issue as to whether an implied contract had arisen. In addition, the court found that the "no mutuality" objection was not well founded. First, the arrangement could be regarded as a "requirements" contract, recognized as valid in South Dakota's adoption of § 2-306 of the U.C.C. In addition, the plaintiff had a plausible promissory estoppel argument, based on reliance by Famous on Sherman's reassurance that it could continue as a distributor.

In *Famous Brands*, characterizing the contract as governed by the U.C.C. imposes an obligation of good faith, and since the U.C.C. validates requirements contracts, arguably avoids some common law challenges which are based on the more demanding standard of definiteness which may apply if the common law rule applies.

The U.C.C., however, is a two-edged sword.

In *Lorenz Supply Co. v. American Standard, Inc.*[17] a distributor sought to *avoid* the application of the Code, since the Code may require signed writings in

---

[16] 814 F.2d 517 (8th cir. 1987).
[17] 419 Mich 610, 358 N.W.2d 845 (1984).

cases in which the common law would not. The *Lorenz* court ruled that the distributorship was *not* a sale of goods, in order to avoid the application of U.C.C. 2-201, the Code's statute of frauds section, to the contract. The court noted that *if* the distributorship were a sale of goods it would run afoul of the requirement in 2-201 that quantities be specifically stated. The court observed, "Because many distributorship agreements are not requirements or output contracts and in such cases the quantity term is generally uncertain, we conclude that the drafter's of the Uniform Commercial Code did not intend that all distributorship agreements be regarded as 'contract[s] for the sale of goods.' " Justice Brickley, in a concurrence, argued that most courts had applied the Code to distributorship contracts, and that the statute of frauds requirement could be satisfied, in the case of distributorships, by implying that the distributor was to be provided with that quantity of goods sufficient to meet the requirements of a distributor; this, according to Brickley, would satisfy the definiteness requirements.

In *Cox Caulking & Insulating Co. v. Brockett Distributing Co.*,[18] a case that embodies the concern of the majority in the *Lorenz* case, Cox Caulking & Insulating Co. was the insulation subcontractor on a construction project. It made an oral agreement to buy the needed insulating material from Brockett Distribution Co. A Brockett official wrote a letter saying that it had "submitted a price of $2.62 a bag for the above project." The letter earlier defined the project as the "Cardinal and Hunt Joint Venture in Hinesville, Georgia." The Court of Appeals of Georgia acknowledged "the quantity need not be designated numerically where the memorandum evidences a requirements or output contract." However, it said, "we reject appellant's contention that the phrase, 'for the above project,' was sufficient as a term of quantity. We conclude, instead, that the phrase merely designated the project which was the subject of the letter and that the letter contained no such 'term which measure[d] the quantity by the output of the seller or the requirements of the buyer. Code § 109A-2-306(1)." As a result, the court affirmed summary judgment in favor of Brockett Distributing Co.

Professor Caroline N. Bruckel writes that the *Cox Caulking & Insulating Co.* case "is perhaps the most notorious example of § 2-201's potential for thwarting the effects of the Code sections that approve open quantity contracts."[19] She continues, "the difficulty was the omission of such a magic word as 'all's or 'requirements's which would allow a *certain* quantitative determination by reference to the project." She notes that U.C.C. § 2-306 does not require these magic words. Professor Bruckel says,

---

[18]150 Ga.App. 424, 258 S.E. 51 (1979).

[19]Bruckel, The Weed and the Web: Section 2-201's Corruption of the U.C.C.'s Substantive Provisions — The Quantity Problem, 1993 University of Illinois Law Review 811, 820, 822, 856-57. Copyright 1984 by the Board of Trustees of the University of Illinois.

The cornerstone of the difficulty concerning quantity lies in the initial determination that the statute requires quantity to "appear." This rule is almost universally accepted, despite the absence of any clear statutory direction to that effect. As construed in cases like *Cox Caulking*, the test imposed for quantity is stricter than the test recognized for the writing's sufficiency to show that the asserted transaction is genuine. The sufficiency requirement which is clearly *central* to the purpose and language of the statute, may be satisfied by merely an "indication." Quantity, on the other hand, must "appear," according to the language of the Official Comment to § 2-201. The court in *Cox Caulking* apparently took this language to mandate that the quantity term be mechanically ascertainable solely from the face of the writing (together with any reference indicated as necessary to quantify it). In accordance with many courts, the *Cox Caulking* court effectively ruled that if *any* inferences must be drawn from circumstances outside the writing to establish quantity, the memorandum is insufficient.

This standard is highly inappropriate, for it subordinates the central issue of sufficiency to the peripheral one. It can, and does, result in a refusal of recovery to a plaintiff who clearly establishes a legitimate agreement. This plaintiff will lose even after producing a written memorandum sufficient to "indicate" quantity as well as the agreement's legitimacy, if the written term requires even an obvious inference to give it substance.

The Official Comment to § 2-201 ... begins by echoing the drafters's primary concern to reverse the prior rule requiring all essential terms to be stated; it then notes that the only goal of the writing requirement is to establish a credible evidentiary basis for a real transaction. Two sentences later, however, the comment falls into confusion, seeming to recognize a requirement that quantity be stated.

[T]he *single* statutory standard to determine the sufficiency of a memorandum should be its indication of a real transaction. No quantity term need be shown or even indicated in the writing; thus, the only standards affecting quantity are the Code's substantive standards. Consequently, the quantity term may be established by an unsigned writing or by oral allegations sufficient to satisfy the trier of fact, or supplied by implication from usage or conduct, or by law under § 2-306.

When the writing *does* contain a quantity term, § 2-201(1) directs that it serve as a ceiling on enforceability. Even this limitation, however, should give way to avoid manifest injustice when no statutory purpose is served by maintaining it. In cases where granting the plaintiff relief seems especially compelling, the statutory guideline properly yields to the overriding purpose of avoidance of fraud. Safety for the defendant *must* be weighed against injustice to the plaintiff before any coherent place for § 2-201 may be discovered in the Code....

Can you defend the courts against Professor Bruckel's attack? Can you answer her arguments? As she notes, there are many cases involving the relationship between U.C.C. § 2-306 and § 2-201, and most courts have insisted that the quantity term be stated in writing. In answering Professor Bruckel, assume that it is not enough to argue that her position does not follow the majority view.

This is not the only time we will consider a substantive doctrine alongside the statute of frauds. Compare, for example, *Janke Construction Co. v. Vulcan Materials Co.*, *supra*. Might judges comfortable with classic contract law seek to reach the old results by using the statute of frauds to offset legal realist innovations such as the firm offer and the enforceability of requirements contracts? Professor Henderson, for example, in his article on promissory estoppel, discussed those decisions that denied "any basis whatsoever for the operation of the doctrine [of promissory estoppel] in opposition to the Statute of Frauds." He said "these decisions surely reflect some lingering doubts about the general legitimacy of the reliance ground of enforcement of promises."[20] Could the same thing be said about the judicial reaction to oral flexible quantity terms?

C. BUSINESS DOCUMENTS AND FORMING CONTRACTS

Businesspeople often sign written agreements. Sometimes a business contract is signed with a formal ceremony. The signatures of high officials of both sides are symbolic acts of commitment, marking a sharp line between being free to back out and being bound. However, on other occasions a deal is closed by a handshake or phone call. Papers are signed to keep accountants and lawyers happy. The parties may be in the midst of performing before anyone thinks about a formal ceremony.

Even where written documents are used, the situation may be unclear. For example, a letter may convey information with no intention of commitment. "I wouldn't think of selling for less than $500,000, and I might get more if I put the property on the market. Furthermore, unless you are thinking of buying for cash, I would need adequate security for your obligation." Contrast this with a letter saying, "I am willing to sell the Jones Farm to you for $500,000, payable in cash now." On the other hand, we may have a single commitment but too many documents. Seller may send its proposal and Buyer may respond with its purchase order. However, the two forms contain terms that do not match. Often the parties do not notice the inconsistency and start to perform. Is there a legally enforceable contract? If so, what are its terms?

Business patterns do not always neatly fit the categories of contract law. Judges and legislators could demand that businesspeople change their ways, and sometimes they do. However, generally judges, lawyers and law professors see

---

[20]Henderson, Promissory Estoppel and Traditional Contract Doctrine, 78 Yale Law Journal 343, 381-82 (1969).

contract law as facilitative and supportive of the market. When business reality does not fit into legal categories, many think that the legal categories should be changed. As we have noted before in these materials, Professor Duncan Kennedy points out that older teachers of common law subjects explained many problems in terms of the core and a periphery of exceptions to deal with hard cases. In the core situations, many lawyers assume the theories work, but there always will be a few peripheral situations that cause difficulty. Kennedy, however, asserts that the periphery tends to swallow the core in area after area. We are about to consider an area where we can ask about the status of core and periphery. Once again we encounter our familiar questions: Is liability based on choice, responsibility for careless use of language, social planning to serve the market or something else? Furthermore, do the rules favor larger, more bureaucratically organized businesses, the underdog consumer or small business, or are the impacts random?

Should the law insist on a signed written document as a kind of magical symbol dividing obligation from freedom or should it try to give effect to the understandings of the parties? Two Uniform Commercial Code provisions indicate conflicting views. U.C.C. § 2-204(1) says "a contract for the sale of goods may be made in any manner sufficient to show agreement, including conduct by both parties which recognizes the existence of such a contract." Subsection (2) says "an agreement sufficient to constitute a contract for sale may be found even though the moment of its making is undetermined." Nonetheless, if the price of the goods is $500 or more, U.C.C. § 2-201 requires some writing sufficient to indicate that a contract for sale has been made between the parties and signed by the party against whom enforcement is sought." While these provisions can be reconciled, they point in different directions. How do business people regard the practice of documenting transactions?

— Interview with the Purchasing Agent of a large manufacturer of small electric appliances:

Mr. X does make orders at times by telephone, but he always confirms them later by a written purchase order. For example, recently he was buying a complete new appliance to be marketed under his firm's brand name and to be manufactured by one of the large well-known appliance manufacturers. So far only an order to buy the tooling necessary to make the appliance has been issued. In order to have the manufacturer ready to go, Mr. X has called and told it to begin buying materials. He has given them the number of the purchase order which will be sent to the manufacturer, over the telephone. The formal purchase order for the materials is now in the process of being written and approved. Mr. X is sure that the manufacturer has gone ahead and started buying materials at this point because once it has a purchase order number it is safe.

— Interview with the General Counsel of an automobile parts manufacturer:

Mr. Y remarked that, unless something is unusual about a transaction, the house counsel is seldom called in until after a contract has been made and problems develop in performance. People in this corporation often write "letters of intent" in purchasing situations without going through either the purchasing department or the house counsel. In his view these letters of intent often go far towards creating binding offers or contracts. In one case, Mr. Y found that nothing was in the file indicating any commitment on the part of a manufacturer as to how a $50,000 machine would perform, and his company's engineers seemed to have made a binding contract through a fairly vague letter of intent. The engineers said they had intended to refer the matter to the purchasing department to have a formal contract drafted but had overlooked the matter as they were anxious to get started.

— Interview with the General Counsel of a manufacturer of a well-known small consumer item:

Most people would rather not put things in writing. It is amazing how in casual conversations people will agree to one thing after another and will reach almost complete agreement. Then one asks for a signature on a document embodying that agreement. That seems to be a very disruptive act. At this point, many people back out and say, "No, I'd better think about that before I sign," even though they have orally agreed to everything in the written contract.

— Interview with the Vice President in Charge of Merchandising of a firm in the textile industry:

Things can be worked out informally, you decide to close and do, and then something comes up and you change your mind. You look for something that has been omitted, argue that things really hadn't been closed but there was another point remaining for negotiation, and then you back out. You just simply refuse to go through with things. It is more just to end things at this point, if you change your mind, than to string the other guy along or to maneuver in your performance of the contract to minimize what he gets out of it. At times it is better to break off. It is nice to find a subject of negotiation which has not been completed to save a little face when you do this. Of course, it is not absolutely necessary.

1. BUSINESS DOCUMENTS AND COMMERCIAL PRACTICES

People can make contracts many ways, but those who repeatedly make agreements often follow patterns. Lawyers for larger firms attempt to structure these patterns so that they fit into the models favored by the legal system. Some businesspeople, however, pay little attention to lawyer's advice. Usually, business agreements are carried out well enough so that commercial life goes on.

Now and again, however, deals collapse. Businesspeople and their lawyers may then look in their files to determine their legal position — assuming enough is involved to make an inquiry, or a struggle, worthwhile. Sometimes business practices have offset all or most of what the lawyers who drafted the documents tried to achieve.

People can draft detailed blueprints of their transactions. While we may wish that parties would do this in all situations, human behavior is flexible and sloppy. Businesspeople write letters that cover some, but usually not all, of the terms of their deal. The provisions in my letter may not match those in your letter. We may not notice this or we may ignore it. Businesses may use printed form documents designed for routine transactions for complex and unusual bargains. Lawyers may attempt to create careful procedures which businesspeople find cumbersome and ignore. We will review some of the forms frequently used and then turn to the legal problems created by business behavior and business forms.

Business forms: The documents for exchanges serve both business and legal functions. When these functions conflict we should not be surprised that the commercial function usually wins out. First, let's look at *documents used by sellers*. Price lists and catalogs usually give information to potential customers about standard items (often called "shelf goods"). A firm's sales department usually has a *proposal or quotation form*. Sellers use this form to state that they will supply some item at an indicated price. Proposals tend to be made for sales of specially made items or large orders of standard items. A proposal form serves as a checklist so that a seller will not fail to cover important matters by oversight and usually must be signed so that someone in the seller's organization will take responsibility for the transaction.

A sales department also may use an *acknowledgment of order form*. Buyers place orders after they have looked at a seller's price list or catalog, talked with a salesperson, or asked for a formal proposal. Most sellers routinely acknowledge these orders for a number of reasons. The form is to control the sale within the seller's organization. Some copies go to the seller's production or shipping department. Some go to the financial department so that the buyer will be billed. The *acknowledgement of order* copy goes to the customer. It serves to tell the buyer that the order was received and what the seller thinks should be shipped, and how much it will charge.

A sales department also may use a sales representative's *order form*. Salespeople visit potential customers and talk with them. If they get an order, they fill in the blanks on this form. This serves as a checklist. The sales representative must determine such things as the necessary sizes, speeds, where the product will be shipped and how the customer will pay for it.

Buyers, if their organizations are big enough, also have form documents. Purchasing departments may have a *request for quotation form* which is sent to sellers asking for bids. If sellers fill out the form, the buyer gains information needed to choose between competitors. Obviously, the functions of this form and sellers' forms overlap. Both buyer and seller may prefer their own forms. A buyer's form, for example, is likely to demand more precise specifications of delivery dates than will be given on a seller's form.

A company big enough to have a purchasing department is likely to have a printed *purchase order*. This form commits the company to buy and gives the transaction an internal control number. It tells the financial department that the company will be billed by the seller, and tells the buyer's receiving department to accept the shipment when it arrives. Some buyers send with their purchase orders their own *acknowledgment of order form*, asking sellers to sign and return it. Obviously, the functions of this form and sellers' acknowledgments overlap.

Selling and buying patterns: If any of several patterns of behavior are followed, there will be little question about when or whether the parties have agreed to sell and buy and what is to be supplied at what price. For example,

(A) The engineers and purchasing agents of the buyer may negotiate with the seller's engineers and sales representatives for a machine made for the buyer's purposes — for example, the buyer wants a machine that automatically cleans, fills, and seals glass jars at a given rate per hour. Preliminary ideas are exchanged. Seller drafts a proposal, either in a letter or on a proposal form, which contains detailed specifications, prices for alternatives and a delivery date and two lines for signatures. Authorized representatives of both seller and buyer sign the form. While engineers, corporate officers, and even lawyers might have to interpret the terms, it is likely that the parties have a deal and they can determine what it is.

(B) The purchasing agent of a corporation seeking to buy glass jars wants to discover which manufacturer will furnish them at the best price with the best delivery date. The purchasing agent sends a request for quotation form to several manufacturers. The form states "THIS IS NOT AN ORDER." Each manufacturer fills in the blanks that ask for a description of the product, prices, delivery schedules and the like, and signs it. The purchasing agent selects a lucky supplier. The purchasing department prepares a purchase order and sends it to that seller. Again, the parties have a deal and they probably can determine what it is.

(C) A purchasing agent seeking to buy glass jars may study products and prices from catalogs. She selects a supplier and sends a purchase order which has an acknowledgment of order copy. The supplier's authorized agent signs the acknowledgment of order copy and returns it. There is a deal.

(D) A sales representative calls on a purchasing agent, and they discuss the price of glass jars. The salesperson fills out an order form, and the purchasing agent signs it. Typically, this form states, "this order is subject to acceptance at Seller's home office." Sellers may want to check a buyer's credit, inventory, or production capacity. Sales representatives seldom are given power to make these decisions. The home office personnel approve the order. The seller may send the buyer an acknowledgment of order form or it may just ship the goods. Again, there is a deal.

Often businesspeople follow these patterns. If the buyer is a large corporation, its suppliers may be smaller organizations. Large corporations with many employees with the power to make contracts may insist that their employees follow standardized procedures. The small suppliers often go along with a large buyer's procedures since a good customer is always right!

Life does not always run smoothly. Anyone who has worked for a major corporation knows there always is some give in the rules. Moreover, while those at the lower levels may follow routines, those higher in the organization often assert their independence and discretion. For example, lawyers and others may plan and draft careful procedures which both serve business procedures and limit liability for breach of warranty. Sales representatives use the proper forms and get buyers' signatures. Then a Vice President writes a letter to one of a buyer's officials. The Vice President explains the meaning of the deal or says that his firm never would use its rights against a customer such as the buyer.

Suppose a seller sends buyer a quotation form, stating a price for a particular product. The buyer immediately sends a purchase order back to the seller. Does this create a legally enforceable contract? The answer turns in large part on whether a court would classify the quotation as an offer or only a preliminary negotiation. Catalogs and advertisements directed at the world usually are not offers. Buyers are held to understand that sellers do not guarantee to have sufficient inventory or productive capacity to supply the world at the listed price. Catalogs and advertisements are useful ways to convey information, but some of this usefulness would be lost if sellers had to proofread them with great care to avoid being held to mistaken prices. Finally, a seller may be willing to supply the item subject to a credit check.

Some price quotations are similar to advertisements. A quotation, however, which is directed to a particular buyer and is for a specified quantity is another matter. If the quotation is sent in response to a buyer's inquiry, the seller can foresee that the buyer is likely to rely. Clearly, the surrounding circumstances and the words used in the quotation will be important. Many proposal forms attempt to answer the question by their express terms. For example, the proposal form used by one major corporation states in large print, "This proposal will become a binding contract when signed by the purchaser and thereafter accepted by an officer of the ... [seller corporation] at its home office in Milwaukee, Wisconsin, U.S.A."

a. The Battle of the Forms: Magic Through Contract Drafting

The "Battle of the Forms" has been a pet of contracts scholars for thirty years. Casebook authors dwell on it, and scholars write articles about it. You should ask whether it is a sufficiently large problem for businesspeople to justify all the attention. The Uniform Commercial Code has an elaborate section designed to solve these problems; you should ask whether it does so.

The business versus the legal model of contract. Many business transactions follow patterns which involve the exchange of inconsistent business forms. In some instances a lawyer will have to determine whether any contract has been made or what its provisions are. An all too common transaction would proceed as follows:

(A) Buyer has a seller's catalog. Buried in the back, along with tables of equivalent weights and measures and other handy bits of information, are the seller's terms of sale. They are written in legal language and printed in small type. Buyer's purchasing agent has dozens, if not hundreds, of catalogs issued by her suppliers. She has never read the terms and conditions in seller's particular catalog, although she has a general idea of what most sellers put on their forms. She finds the item she wants in the catalog, notes its price, and telephones seller's office to ask if the item is available at the catalog price. Seller's agent says "Yes."

(B) The purchasing agent tells a typist to prepare a purchase order. He types it, she checks it, and may or may not sign it. Buyer's purchase order form is a printed set of documents. There are many terms and conditions on the reverse side of the copy that is sent to the seller. The purchasing agent has read these terms and conditions in the past, but she now has only a general idea of what they say and mean. Buyer's purchase order protects its interests; its terms almost certainly add to or conflict with any seller's conditions of sale for example, buyer may demand a broad warranty while sellers will offer a narrow warranty. The second copy of the purchase order is an acknowledgment form. Sellers are asked to sign and return it, thus "agreeing" to all of buyer's terms and conditions.

(C) The purchase order and acknowledgment copy are sent to seller.

(D) An assistant sales manager receives the purchase order and acknowledgment copy from buyer. He reads only the face of the document, ignoring the fine print on the back as is customary. He decides to fill the order. (Of course, his decision is based on seller's capacity to make the items, its inventory, its backlog of orders and, importantly, buyer's credit rating.)

(E) The assistant sales manager tells a secretary to write up the order. She types a description of the item ordered, the price, an estimated delivery date, and any other necessary information on a set of business forms. Several copies from this set will go to the accounting or billing department for use as an invoice and for financial records. Several will go to production or shipping to get the item ordered, made, and shipped. One copy of this set is marked "Customer's Acknowledgment." On the reverse side of this document all of the seller's terms and conditions of sale are restated — which are not necessarily the same as those stated in seller's catalog! The document reads, "We accept your order subject to the terms and conditions on the face and reverse side of this acknowledgment." Of course, the sales manager has not read his firm's terms and conditions for a number of years, but he has a general idea of what is covered.

(F) Seller sends the acknowledgment copy of the seller's set of business forms to buyer. Buyer's acknowledgment of order copy of its purchase order is not signed and returned. It is filed with buyer's purchase order. (Or, to really complicate matters, seller sends *both* its acknowledgment form and buyer's acknowledgment form back to buyer.)

(G) When buyer receives seller's acknowledgment, the material typed on its face is checked against the face of the purchase order to see that the order has been interpreted correctly. No one at the buyer's office reads the fine print on the reverse side of seller's form.

(H) The purchase order and the seller's acknowledgment copy are filed away by buyer.

(I) One of two things happens:

(1) Most commonly, the goods are delivered on time, seller is paid in full, and the goods work perfectly, OR

(2) The goods are not delivered at all or arrive late, buyer does not pay seller, or the goods prove to be defective.

In most instances the inconsistent or additional terms and conditions on buyer's and seller's forms will not matter to anyone. The seller may not deliver the goods at all, they may arrive late, be defective, or the buyer may not pay on time. Nonetheless, buyer and seller negotiate a settlement without reading what is said on the faces or backs of business forms. They will not involve lawyers. However, in the few instances where there is a major problem that cannot be resolved easily, someone may begin to read purchase order clause 1(a)(ii)(cc)(5) and wonder whether it is part of a binding contract. The traditional common law answer seemed easy. As was said in *Clark v. Burr*,[21] "The acceptance of an offer upon terms varying from those of the offer, however slight,[22] is a rejection of the

---

[21]85 Wis. 649, 55 N.W. 401 (1893).

[22]There are dicta suggesting that a purported acceptance with a "slight," "insubstantial," or "immaterial" variation would not defeat the formation of a contract and make the purported acceptance a counter-offer. However, the point is not considered in any of these cases. See, *e.g.*, Hess v. Holt Lumber Co., 175 Wis. 451, 185 N.W. 522 (1921); Russell v. The Falls Mfg. Co., 106 Wis. 329, 82 N.W. 134 (1900). In light of § 2-207 of the Uniform Commercial Code, a lawyer seeking to overcome or limit the common law rule in non-Code situations might draw on this dicta as the basis for arguing that the Code only restates and clarifies the common law rule in Wisconsin. The lawyer would have to overcome the phrase "however slight" in the Clark case and

offer."[23] The Wisconsin court further explained that "[a]n attempted acceptance of an offer, if coupled with any condition that varies or adds to the offer, is not an acceptance, but a counter-proposition or counter-offer ... [T]here must be an acceptance of the counter-offer in order to complete the contract ... [A]cceptance of a counter-offer can be inferred from any conduct on the offeree's part indicative thereof, but ... mere silence bears no such significance."

Exemplifying the traditional common law approach is *Russell v. The Falls Mfg. Co.*,[24] the buyer ordered flour to be shipped between May 27th and July 1st on buyer's request. Payment was due 30 days after shipment. Seller accepted the order but stated that the deal was for shipment "sometime" in June of 1898, apparently at seller's option. Furthermore, the terms were stated as "30 days acceptance without interest, and if longer time wanted 8% interest after thirty days." About twelve days after the order was placed, buyer canceled it. Seller resold the flour at a $267 loss and sued for this amount. The court denied recovery. The seller's response contained substantial modifications and thus it was a rejection of the buyer's offer and a counter-proposal. Buyer's silence was not an acceptance. However, "had [buyer] ordered any of the flour after receiving plaintiff's letter, that would have sufficed" to accept the counter-offer.

These common law rules are substantially modified by § 2-207 of the Uniform Commercial Code. However, Article II of the Code applies only to "transactions in goods." The common law rules may still apply to all other kinds of transactions such as sales of real estate and services. These kinds of transactions are less likely to be conducted by the exchange of forms with inconsistent terms, but the problem can arise here as well as in sales of goods. For example, in *Leuchtenberg v. Hoeschler*,[25] the buyer offered to buy a lot with a depth of "about 150 feet." The owner tried to accept the offer but drew a line through the number 150 and substituted "120." The purported acceptance was a counter offer and no contract was formed.

The common law solution to the battle of the forms meant that even after an exchange of documents which both buyer and seller assumed formed a contract, either might be able to back out without legal liability. Thus, there was a chance that the law would leave reliance unprotected, which contracts scholars assumed was a significant problem. If we assume the opinions expressed by businesspeople and their lawyers in the excerpts which follow are typical, is there a problem? Does the U.C.C. solve it? Keep your answers to these questions in mind. After you have studied § 2-207 of the U.C.C., consider whether the

---

some of the discussion in Leuchtenberg v. Hoeschler, 271 Wis. 151, 72 N.W.2d 758 (1955).

[23]See also Morris F. Fox & Co. v. Lisman, 208 Wis. 1, 237 N.W. 267, 240 N.W.. 809, 242 N.W. 679 (1932).

[24]106 Wis. 329, 82 N.W. 134 (1900).

[25]271 Wis. 151, 72 N.W.2d 758 (1955).

problems with that section are worse than those which businesspeople faced under the common law.

— Interview with the purchasing agent of a manufacturer of nationally advertised electrical appliances:

The purchasing department is too busy getting the items needed to spend its time reading and checking terms and conditions. The company does not need legal sanctions since in every case it gets what it wants. We have never referred to the back of a buying or selling form to get performance from a supplier. A telephone call stressing the agreed schedule for delivery and the specifications is far more effective. All of the company's vendors have been doing business with the firm for years.

— Interview with the purchasing agent of a large manufacturer of industrial and residential electrical equipment:

The purchasing department will review all of a vendor's terms of acceptance, and if it finds any disagreement with the company's way of doing business, it will take the matter up with the vendor. It does not mind if the vendor simply adds items as long as they are not contrary to the usual way of doing business. This is true although additional items might prevent the formation of a legally binding contract. It is interested in a legally binding contract only in the case of building construction or large capital items such as automation machinery. In normal business one does not pay any attention to the problem of legal enforceability.

— Interview with the sales and production managers of a manufacturer of packaging machinery:

The company has recently redrafted its standard contract for selling its machines. It now insists that its contract be signed or any modifications be carefully approved. Before these forms were drafted and this procedure was installed, the company often was on the edge of trouble. It is easy to fail to deliver on time when you are manufacturing machinery engineered for the customer's product and his factory. It takes five months, or more, to design and build this machinery. You cannot always predict how long it will take to solve some special problem. Yet customers' purchase orders tend to demand firm delivery dates. At present, a competitor is being sued for $600,000 for missing a delivery date on a packaging machine. The customer had arranged a TV presentation to promote a packaging idea that was to be produced on the machine. He had committed his production to the machine and had torn his plant down to install it. Our competitor did not get the machine there on time. The customer had to put his factory back together again and use the old machinery. The customer claims it suffered a loss of reputation when it could not supply its distributors with the item it had advertised. This suit has caused a lot of rethinking in this industry.

— Interview with the purchasing agent of a manufacturer of machine tools:

Terms and conditions might have significance in 1 or 2 percent of all cases. We do not read them. I have been purchasing agent for 11 years and with the company for 16. During that time we've had only 3 or 4 disputes on terms and conditions, and we've never lost much money. Our experience shows that elaborate procedures to check the 8,000 to 15,000 purchase orders and acknowledgments which pass through here each year would not be justified.

— Interview with the General Counsel of a manufacturer of machinery which puts products into containers. He supplied letters written by him to be sent out by his firm's sales manager to indicate how the company takes exception to a customer's conditions of purchase:

The sales manager first acknowledges "your most valued purchase order." Then he states, "we have followed the practice for years of selling our machinery under a uniform type of contract under which our liabilities are limited. For those liabilities for which we are responsible under the contract, we purchase insurance so that our annual cost can be anticipated and our selling prices adjusted accordingly." He goes on to discuss the warranties demanded by the customer. Next he states, "we are certain that we can arrange an acceptable contract that will protect you. Our insurance companies, however, have asked us to obtain additional information so that they can advise us whether our present coverage is sufficient and what costs would be involved in acquiring additional protection." Then he states, "in making such comments we want you to know that we are desirous of meeting every reasonable request and that our only objection will be to situations where insurance protection is not reasonably available or the cost thereof was not anticipated in the selling price of the equipment, or where the condition is contrary to a long established and desirable policy of the company." He next makes a show of accepting as many of the customer's conditions as he can. He objects to conditions dealing with warranty, excuses for failure to perform and inspections. He makes, in the course of his argument, several references to the fact that his terms and conditions have been accepted by the customer's major competitors. He ends his letter by saying, "we regret the length of this discussion and hope that we have not in any manner indicated an intention to avoid reasonable responsibility to provide and install a first class unit of equipment. However, it becomes impossible for us to operate under a different contract in the plant of each customer and we have, therefore, established our selling prices on the basis of our uniform contract provisions."

In another letter, the sales manager argues that if the extensive guaranties demanded by the customer are given, it will only be a bonanza for the insurance companies and an additional cost for the seller and its customers. "This kind of protection is not necessary when dealing with a company of our standing. We fear that making an exception in a few cases will lead to a general breakdown of our rule."

— Interview with a partner in a law firm in a large city with a corporate practice:

I can think of many disputes where it was wonderful to find that the back of the documents protected my client and not the other party although perhaps there was no enforceable contract. You need arguments for negotiating a settlement. What are you going to say on the telephone?

— Interview with the General Counsel of a large manufacturer of paper and paper products:

The important thing about a contract is not its legal enforceability but its meaning when read by the other side. There is a moral sanction. You can look at the man on the other side of the table and say, "you have agreed to this. Are you going to back out and not honor your word?" But this is a business where buyers and sellers know each other very well.

Before the Uniform Commercial Code was passed, many lawyers relied on "the last shot principle" in planning for their firm in its role as seller. Normally, the last document sent in a battle of the forms situation is a seller's acknowledgment of a buyer's order. Under pre-Code law, if a seller sent an acknowledgment with additional or different terms from those on the buyer's purchase order, it would be a counter-offer rather than an acceptance. No contract would be formed at this point. However, if the seller shipped goods and the buyer accepted them, the buyer's action also accepted the counter-offer and formed a contract on the seller's terms. Of course, the buyer might get the last shot. Suppose a seller offered goods on a proposal form, the buyer sent a purchase order with inconsistent terms and conditions, and the seller responded by shipping the goods. Now the shipment probably would be the acceptance of buyer's counter-offer.

Lawyers drafting forms for buyers and sellers tried to cope with the common law's last shot approach. For example, the selling forms of the Anaconda American Brass Company provided that "seller's failure to object to provisions contained in any communications from buyer will not be deemed as an acceptance of such provisions or as a waiver of the provisions hereof." On the other hand the purchase order of the Pabst Brewing Company provided that "you accept all the terms and conditions on the front and reverse sides of this order ... by failing to make prompt written objection to these terms and conditions, even if you fail to sign or return the acknowledgment copy to us." Several major corporations used clauses on their purchase orders that read "buyer recognizes that seller may for operating convenience desire to utilize its own form of acknowledgment, contract, or other document in connection with this transaction. Therefore, it is agreed that any provisions in the form of acceptance used, which modify, conflict with, or contradict any provision of this contract or order, shall be deemed waived." Of course, the legal effect of these clauses is debatable, but they gave lawyers something to argue about as part of negotiations.

b. Section 2-207 of the Uniform Commercial Code

Section 2-207 of the Uniform Commercial Code purports to wipe out the common law approach to the battle of the forms and start over. We begin by looking at the text of the statute. As always, one must consider the structure of the legislation and touch all the bases rather than rip a phrase or paragraph out of context. Then we'll turn to some appellate opinions to highlight problems.

Subsections (1) and (2) of § 2-207 go together. If a case does not fit within them, then you must go on to subsection (3). Subsection (1) deals with whether a contract has been formed. If a contract has been formed under subsection (1), then we look to subsection (2) to determine its terms. If a contract has not been formed under subsection (1), then we turn to subsection (3) and not the common law or the last shot doctrine.

Subsection (1) asks whether there is a contract. It says that a "definite and seasonable expression of acceptance" closes a deal and creates a contract. Notice that we must have a communication which a court will classify as an acceptance. Reading the statute literally, a preliminary negotiation, an offer or a counteroffer does not come under U.C.C. § 2-207(1). However, if we have an acceptance, it creates a contract although it states "terms additional to or different from those offered or agreed upon." Clearly, this overturns much of the common-law rule. Under the common law, a purported acceptance that stated "terms additional to or different from those offered or agreed upon," is only a counter-offer. Under the U.C.C., it can close a contract. However, it does not have this effect if "acceptance is expressly made conditional on assent to the additional or different terms." Courts have had great difficulty interpreting this last clause.

What are the terms of a contract created under sub (1)? Additional terms are proposals for additions to the contract. In effect, the Code says that we treat the communication as if it said, "I accept your offer and we have a deal now. However, I propose we also add term XYZ to our contract." Between merchants these proposals become part of the contract unless any of the three qualifications in sub (2) apply. Notice that the "materially alter it" provision goes to the terms of a deal formed under sub (1) and not to whether there is a contract formed under sub (1).

Suppose instead of additional terms, the acceptance contains different terms that do not alter the contract materially and to which there is no objection. Do added terms become part of the deal while different terms drop out? Courts and writers have struggled with this question.

Assume the buyer's and seller's forms do not create a contract under sub (1). Now we turn to sub (3). "Conduct by both parties which recognizes the existence of a contract is sufficient to establish a contract for sale although the writings of the parties do not otherwise establish a contract." Suppose the seller offered goods on its proposal form. The buyer accepted the offer by sending a purchase order to seller, but the terms printed on the purchase order expressly made acceptance conditional on assent to the additional or different terms found there. Thus, under U.C.C. § 2-207(1) the writings of the parties would not create a contract. However, seller then ships the goods ordered, and buyer accepts and pays for them. This seems to be conduct by both of them which "recognizes the existence of a contract." If a court finds it does, a contract is established.

What are its terms? Sub (3) says that they are those on which the writings of the parties agree "together with any supplementary terms incorporated under any other provisions of this Act." The proposal and purchase order are likely to agree on the description of the goods and their price. Often the seller's form disclaims warranties and limits remedies while the buyer's form claims these rights. The warranty and remedy provisions found in these documents would drop out of the deal. The U.C.C. provisions on warranties and remedies would fill the gap. Notice that this is not the last shot principle where the one which last submitted a document gets its terms and conditions as the contract.

MCCARTY v. VERSON ALLSTEEL PRESS CO.

80 Ill. App. 3d 498, 411 N.E.2d 936 (1980)

ROMITI, J. [A Nash Bros. employee was injured using a machine manufactured by Verson. The employee sued Verson, who settled. Verson then sued Nash Bros. for indemnification under a clause in the form which accompanied its price quotation.] The trial court, after a bench trial, found that the clause was part of the contract and entered judgment for [Verson] in the amount of $322,745.44. We disagree and reverse.

In early 1971, Nash Bros. Co. (hereinafter called buyer), and Verson Allsteel Press Company (hereinafter called seller), entered into oral negotiations regarding the sale of a punch press from the seller, Verson, as a manufacturer, to Nash, the buyer. These negotiations centered almost completely around the technical specifications of the subject punch press. At no time during this period of oral negotiation were any discussions had regarding the indemnification of seller by buyer for injuries caused by defects in seller's presses.

On May 19, 1971, seller sent buyer a document entitled Proposal No. 5575-1-RB. It stated: "In accordance with your request, we are pleased to offer the following press brake equipment for your consideration...." A detailed list of "General Specifications" and "Items Included" followed. The proposal concluded,

> Point of operation guards are not included with this equipment. It is the employer's responsibility to provide guards, devices, tools, or other means to effectively protect all personnel from serious injury which may otherwise occur as a result of any particular machine use or activity. Thank you for this opportunity to offer our equipment. Should you require any additional information, please let us know.

This offer was subject to thirty days' acceptance.

At the foot of the first page of the proposal was the legend: "All quotations, orders and contracts are subject to acceptance of home office."

Enclosed with the May 19th proposal was a copy of seller's form "Conditions of Sale — Machinery." In pertinent part, these provided:

> ...
> 7. WARRANTY-WARRANTY LIMITATIONS-INDEMNITY, ...
> (c) Customer assumes and shall bear all responsibility for providing adequate and sufficient safeguards, work handling tools and safety devices to protect fully the operator and any other users of the goods at all times, in accordance with the prevailing federal, state, and local codes and industry-accepted standards. Verson shall bear no liability whatsoever for the failure of customer to order, install, or use such safeguards, work handling tools or safety devices.
> Customer shall establish and use, and require all persons operating the equipment to use, all proper and safe operating procedures, including but not limited to procedures set forth in any manuals or instructions sheets relating to the equipment. Customer shall not remove or modify any devices, warning sign, or manual furnished with, or installed upon or attached to the goods.
>
> NOTWITHSTANDING ANY PROVISION OF THESE TERMS AND CONDITIONS, THE WARRANTY CONTAINED IN THIS PARAGRAPH, AS LIMITED HEREIN, IS THE ONLY WARRANTY EXTENDED BY VERSON IN CONNECTION WITH ANY SALE BY IT AND IS IN LIEU OF ALL OTHER WARRANTIES, EXPRESS OR IMPLIED, INCLUDING WARRANTIES OF MERCHANTABILITY AND FITNESS FOR PURPOSE.
>
> 8. INDEMNITY, Customer hereby (1) waives, releases and discharges any and all claims of any and every kind (including but not limited to injury to or death of any person or damage to property), which it may have at any time against Verson, its agents or employees, by reason of or arising out of any claimed improper design, specifica-

tions or manufacture of the goods sold hereunder, or of
devices; and (2) covenants to indemnify and hold-harmless
Verson, its agents and employees of, from and against any
and all loss, damage, expense, claims, suits or liability
which Verson or any of its employees may sustain or incur
at any time for or by reason of any injury to or death of
any person or persons or damage to any property, arising
out of any claimed improper design or manufacture of the
goods sold hereunder, or of any claimed inadequate or
insufficient safeguards or safety devices ...

14. ACCEPTANCE-WHOLE AGREEMENT,

**ALL ORDERS ARE VALID AND BINDING UPON VERSON ONLY UPON
ACKNOWLEDGEMENT BY A DULY AUTHORIZED OFFICER OR DEPARTMENT
MANAGER OF VERSON, BY ANY ACKNOWLEDGMENT OR ACCEPTANCE BY
CUSTOMER IN ANY MANNER OF VERSON'S PROPOSAL, OR BY THE
SUBMISSION OR ISSUANCE OF CUSTOMER'S OWN PURCHASE ORDER
BASED ON SUCH PROPOSAL, CUSTOMER UNCONDITIONALLY ACCEPTS
AND AGREES TO BE BOUND BY THE TERMS AND CONDITIONS HEREIN,
SUCH TERMS AND CONDITIONS SHALL CONSTITUTE THE COMPLETE
AGREEMENT BETWEEN CUSTOMER AND VERSON AND SHALL NOT BE
SUPERSEDED BY ANY CONDITIONS OR PROVISIONS IN CUSTOMER'S
ORDER WHICH MAY CONFLICT WITH, BE CONTRARY TO OR OTHERWISE
VARY FROM THOSE HEREIN CONTAINED. ALL PREVIOUS COMMUNICA-
TION BETWEEN THE PARTIES HERETO, WHETHER VERBAL OR
WRITTEN, WITH REFERENCE TO THE SUBJECT MATTER HEREOF, IS
HEREBY ABROGATED, IT BEING UNDERSTOOD THAT THERE ARE NO
OTHER AGREEMENTS, UNDERSTANDINGS, GUARANTEES OR WARRANTIES
WHATEVER, EXPRESS OR IMPLIED, EXCEPT AS CONTAINED IN
VERSON'S PROPOSAL, AND THESE CONDITIONS.**

Verson Allsteel Press Co.

On or about May 28, 1971 seller sent buyer its Proposal No. 5575-1-RB
Revised. This document contained language almost identical to the May 19, 1971
proposal in its opening and conclusion. It also provided that the prices were
subject to thirty days' acceptance and that all quotations, orders and contracts
were subject to the acceptance of the home office. The enclosures included
another copy of seller's "Conditions of Sale — Machinery." Various changes
were made, however, in the "General Specifications" and "Included Items."

On June 8, 1971, seller sent buyer a letter, on its own stationery, reducing the
price of the press which was the subject of its proposals. On the face of this letter
was printed:

All quotations, orders and contracts are subject to acceptance of home office and are contingent upon strikes,
fires or other causes beyond our control.

Seller's "Conditions of Sale" were not included with this document and did not
appear therein.

On June 16, 1971, buyer sent seller its form PURCHASE ORDER. On its face was typed:

```
IN ACCORDANCE WITH YOUR QUOTATION PROPOSAL NO. 5575-1-RB
REVISED AND LETTER DATED 6-8-71, WE WISH TO PURCHASE THE
FOLLOWING:
```

A detailed list of "General Specifications" and "Included Items" was then typed on each of 7 pages. On the front of each page was printed the following:

```
This Purchase Order Is Subject To The Terms and Conditions
Below and On The Reverse Side.

PLEASE ACKNOWLEDGE THIS ORDER AT ONCE UPON ATTACHED COPY.
This order is not binding until accepted. This order shall
become a binding contract when Vendor executes and returns
the attached Acknowledgment copy or ships any of the
items, or renders any of the services, ordered herein.
When accepted, the terms and conditions on the face and
reverse sides of this order will constitute the complete
agreement between Purchaser and Vendor. No additional or
different terms that may be contained in Vendor's forms or
otherwise proposed by Vendor will be binding upon Purchas-
er unless accepted in writing signed by Purchaser.
```

On the back of each page were buyer's "Terms and Conditions." In pertinent part these provided:

```
                        PURCHASE ORDER
                      Terms and Conditions
1. ACCEPTANCE OF ORDER. This order is an offer to purchase
upon the conditions and terms below and on the reverse
side hereof and at the prices stated herein and may be
withdrawn at any time prior to the actual receipt by
Purchaser of Vendor's unconditional, written acceptance
hereof. No modifications of, or exceptions to, any of the
terms, conditions, or provisions of this order by Vendor
shall be of any effect unless and until accepted in
writing by Purchaser. Any delivery (complete or partial)
by Vendor pursuant hereto prior to actual receipt of
Vendor's unconditional, written acceptance hereof, shall
constitute Vendor's acceptance of this order in accordance
with all terms, conditions, and provisions thereof ...
```

On June 25, 1971, seller responded to the buyer's Purchase Order by returning a copy of the buyer's Acknowledgment form, signed by Walter C. Johnson, Vice-President of Verson, as follows:

ACCEPTED:

Verson Allsteel Press Company
(Vendor)

_____
Date
/s/ Walter C. Johnson
Walter C. Johnson
Vice-President — Marketing
Industrial Products

The cover letter accompanying the Acknowledgment provided:

Gentlemen:

We acknowledge and express our sincere gratitude for your subject order, covering a # B-1110 — 250 and a # B-3010 Verson Major Series Press Brakes. The order has been entered in our production schedule for shipment of the B-1110-250 during the month of October, 1971, and the B-3010 during the month of November, 1971.

Based upon the previous correspondence, our formal proposal and your purchase order, the enclosed acknowledgment copies of our production orders give our terms, specifications, and pricing.

Point of operation guards are not included with these equipments. It is the employer's responsibility to provide guards, devices, tools, or other means to effectively protect all personnel from serious injury which may otherwise occur as a result of any particular machine use or activity. Again, please accept our thanks for your purchase order.

The maintenance manual delivered with the machine also stated that "Providing safe working conditions and safety devices are the sole responsibility of the user."

In 1974 an employee of the buyer was injured while operating the press, allegedly because of defects in the sufficiency of safety guards and warning devices on the press. He collected workmen's compensation benefits from the buyer and then sued the seller which settled for $300,000. Seller in turn sued buyer on the alleged indemnification agreement.[26]

_____

[26]Prior to 1977 Illinois did not permit a manufacturer held liable for a products liability injury to a buyer's employee to seek common-law indemnification from the employer of the employee for its negligence in maintaining or altering the machine. This rule was overturned in 1977 by the Illinois Supreme Court in Stevens v. Silver Manufacturing Co. (1977), 70 Ill.2d 41, 374 N.E.2d 455, 15 Ill. Dec. 847, which held, however, that its ruling was prospective only. Accordingly, since the injury occurred in 1974, the seller cannot recover from the buyer unless it can prove a contractual right to indemnification.

At trial Johnson, seller's vice-president, testified the price of the machinery did not vary with the inclusion or exclusion of the indemnification agreement. He also volunteered the statement that they would not sell the machine without such an agreement. Buyer's contracting officer testified that he was familiar with the purchase of this type of machine and that when some other press manufacturer had wanted a similar indemnification agreement, they refused. He could recall no other occasion in his eight and one half years of employment at buyer's where a manufacturer had required an indemnification agreement as a condition of sale.

The trial court held that the buyer was bound by the indemnification agreement.

I.   The rights of the parties are governed by § 2-207 of the Commercial Code.

The seller, relying on *Alan Wood Steel Co. v. Capital Equipment Enterprises, Inc.* (1976), 39 Ill. App. 3d 48, 349 N.E.2d 627, contends that the price quotation was an offer, although any contract was subject to approval by the home office; that since the price quotation was an offer the order must have been an acceptance of the offer; and that, therefore, the terms in the price quotation are binding.

We are not convinced, however, that *Alan Wood* is controlling. It is true that that case stated that the price quotation, which, like the price quotation in the present case, provided that no order was binding until acceptance by the seller, was an offer. However it does not appear from the case that this question had been litigated by the parties. Furthermore, the court in *Alan Wood* stated that the buyer orally accepted the offer by telephone before mailing the purchase order. Obviously, therefore, both parties in that case were treating the price quotation, not the purchase order, as the offer.

A price quotation, if sufficiently detailed as was the price quotation in the present case, may constitute an offer ... It does not follow, however, that a price quotation which is not binding when accepted by a buyer but only becomes binding if and when accepted by the seller, who is under absolutely no obligation to accept it, can by itself be treated as an offer ... It follows that where the so-called offer is not intended to give the so-called offeree the power to make a contract there is no offer ...

In *West Penn Power Co. v. Bethlehem Steel Corp.* (1975), 236 Pa. Super. 413, 348 A.2d 144, *allocatur refused*, the court refused to treat a proposal requiring acceptance by its home office as an offer since the clause was clearly intended to prevent formation of a contract by the unilateral action of the other party, saying at 236 Pa. Super. 426, 427, 348 A.2d 152:

> The first legal issue involved in this conclusion concerns the validity of the "Acceptance" clause. There can be no doubt about appellee's right to include this clause in its proposal to appellants, nor about the effect of the clause. The clause kept the proposal in effect for seven days but precluded

the formation of a contract except upon approval by appellee's home office....

II.   Even if we were to treat the seller's price quotation as an offer and the buyer's purchase order as an acceptance ... it does not follow under the facts in the present case that the provisions in the seller's proposal would control. The seller unconditionally signed the buyer's acknowledgment form sent with the purchase order. The purchase order retained by the seller provided on its face above the purchaser's signature, in fairly large sized print, that when the order was accepted, the terms and conditions on the face and reverse sides of this order would constitute the complete agreement between the purchaser and vendor and that no additional or different terms contained in the vendor's forms would be binding on the purchaser. Where the seller signs the buyer's acknowledgment without expressly conditioning that signature, the seller accepts the conditions in the buyer's forms ... even though the price quotation contained a provision that the buyer by ordering any of the listed merchandise agreed to the enumerated conditions of sale ... The seller could, of course, have avoided this result by not signing the acknowledgement at all or by expressly conditioning the signature as did the seller in *Lincoln Pulp & Paper Co., Inc. v. Dravo Corp.* (D. Me.1977), 445 F. Supp. 507 where the seller said on the acknowledgment that it was accepted in accordance with the accompanying letter and the letter said conditions on back of form were not acceptable.

III.   Furthermore, even if we were to treat the price quotation as an offer, it does not follow that the purchase order was necessarily an acceptance of that offer, despite the provision in the seller's condition of sale which, apparently, attempts to make any purchase order, regardless of its terms, an acceptance of all of the seller's terms. (Absent proper punctuation, it is impossible to decipher the precise meaning of paragraph 14.) While it is true that the offeror has total control over its own offer and may condition *acceptance* to the terms of the offer (Ill. Rev. Stat. 1969, ch. 26, par. 2-207(2)(a)), as apparently the seller did here, nevertheless, it is not true that the first party to a sales transaction will always get his own terms. In most commercial transactions which party processes its terms first is purely fortuitous ... and "it must be recognized that the offeree should not be compelled to accept the terms of the offer if he does not want them, and he ought also to be free to respond with a counteroffer." 3 R. Duesenberg & L. King, Uniform Commercial Code Service (MB) (1977) § 3.06[3].

Under § 2-207(1) of the Commercial Code ... any definite and seasonable expression of acceptance operates as an acceptance even though it is not a mirror image of the offer unless the acceptance is expressly made conditional on assent to the additional or different terms. However that section still requires a definite expression of acceptance and does not change the basic common law requirement that there must be an objective manifestation of mutual assent. ...

No contract can be found where the offeror could not reasonably treat the response of the offeree as an acceptance (*Air Products and Chemicals, Inc. v. Fairbanks Morse, Inc.* (1973), 58 Wis. 2d 193, 206 N.W.2d 414), and parties may initially exchange printed forms which differ so radically that the second cannot be treated as an acceptance of the first. (*Koehring Co. v. Glowacki* (1977), 77 Wis. 2d 497, 253 N.W.2d 64.) Here the purchase order clearly, expressly and repeatedly stated that it was an offer to be accepted by the seller and that no contract existed until it was accepted by the seller. We cannot distort this definite expression of an offer into a "definite and seasonable expression of acceptance."

IV. Seller's signing of the purchase order acknowledgment acted as an acceptance of the order. Indeed, the seller admitted this in its request to admit that "Verson Allsteel Press Company by Walter C. Johnson, Vice-President, accepted the purchase order and signed it on Page 1." Nor did seller dispute this point in its brief although it was raised by the buyer. The mere fact that the seller enclosed its "Conditions of Sale" with the accompanying letter merely stating that enclosed copies gave its terms, specifications and pricing was not sufficient to make the acceptance a counteroffer instead of an acceptance since to prevent such an assent from being an acceptance under § 2-207(1) it must be *expressly* made conditional on assent to the additional or different terms. This provision is construed narrowly to apply only to an acceptance which clearly reveals that the offeree is unwilling to proceed without agreement to the additional terms....

[See] *Dorton v. Collins & Aikman Corp.* (6th Cir. 1972), 453 F.2d 1161, which held that even a statement that acceptance subject to all the terms and conditions on reverse side was not "expressly made conditional on assent to [the additional or different] terms."

Under § 2-207(2) of the Commercial Code the terms enclosed with the letter were merely to be construed as proposals for additions to the contract. They did not, however, become part of the contract since, as the seller admits, they materially altered it....

V. If we were to assume, contrary to the cases, that seller's acceptance was expressly made conditional on assent to the conditions set forth in its "Conditions of Sale," the result would still be the same. In that case, under § 2-207(1) of the Commercial Code the acknowledgment would act as a counteroffer not an acceptance ... Following this reasoning, since the only contract formed would be that formed by the parties' conduct, their rights would be controlled by § 2-207(3) of the Code ... This section provides that the terms of the particular contract consist of those on which the *writings* of the parties agree and the code provisions. It is well established that under this provision terms contained only in one of the party's forms are not part of the contract....

VI. The seller argues, however, that the court's finding was proper because the parties intended to make the indemnity clause part of the contract, pointing to the testimony of seller's marketing vice-president that seller would never have sold the press without the indemnity provision. There is absolutely no evidence in the record that this intent was communicated to the buyer. To the contrary, the only evidence in the record is that there was no discussion between the parties regarding the indemnification of the seller....

Seller, however, contends that the terms of the "Conditions of Sale" were incorporated into the buyer's order by the language "in accordance with your quotation Proposal No. 5575-1-RB Revised and letter dated 6-8-71," relying on the well-established axiom that typewritten provisions prevail over printed ones. This rule is applicable only where there is a conflict between typed and printed portions of a document ... A contract must be read as a whole ... and neither the printed portion nor the typewritten portion should be disregarded unless there is a conflict between the two. Rather, a typewritten provision of a contract should prevail over inconsistent printed stipulations only as far as it is apparent that the parties intended to modify or disregard such printed stipulations, and where the antagonism is merely apparent, the difference should be reconciled, if possible, by any reasonable interpretation....

Reading the purchase order as a whole it is clear the general phrase "in accordance with" was intended only to identify the pertinent price quotations and not to incorporate the "Conditions of Sale" attached to only one of those quotations in direct conflict with the many provisions of the purchase order specifically stating that the seller's conditions were not binding.

The seller also contends that the buyer is bound by the indemnity provision because it failed to object to it. The indemnity provision only appeared in the "Conditions of Sale" which, as we have already determined, did not become part of the contract. The other notices sent to the buyer repeatedly informed the buyer that the responsibility for installing safety devices was on the buyer but did not contain an indemnification clause. Such unobjected-to notice might be construed as modifying the contract so as to remove any warranties relating to the safety of the machine, but obviously could not be considered to change the contract to add an indemnification clause never referred to in such notice. To the contrary, an indication that the seller was not relying on any indemnification clause is the fact that while the notices reaffirmed the buyer's duty to install safety devices, a duty first mentioned in the "Conditions of Sale," they failed to make any reference to the indemnification clause also in the same conditions. Since the accident occurred before the decision in *Stevens v. Silver Manufacturing Co.* (1977), 70 Ill. 2d 41, 374 N.E.2d 455, 15 Ill. Dec. 847, the claim does not and cannot arise out of the buyer's failure to install effective devices. It can arise only if the buyer did in fact agree "to indemnify ... Verson ... against any and all loss, damage, expense, claims, suits or liability which Verson ... may sustain or incur at any time for or by reason of any injury to or death of any person or persons or damage to any property, arising out of any claimed improper design or manufacture of the goods sold hereunder, or any claimed, inadequate or insufficient safeguards or safety devices."

Since we believe it is clear as a matter of law that the indemnification clause cannot be found to be part of the contract agreed upon by the parties, the judgment of the trial court is reversed.

Reversed.

NOTES AND QUESTIONS

1. *Section 2-207 and substantive policy concerning the clauses in question*: The seller tried to convince the court that the safety obligation was that of the buyer who was to use the machine in a particular setting for a particular purpose. It said that the buyer's "safety device obligation was not an overlooked item in a 'battle of forms,' but a prime point expressly reiterated at least 10 different times in the documents exchanged between the parties."

2. *The buyer's views about indemnity*: The buyer responded that the case "remains one in which Verson, as seller, is attempting to foist a hold harmless clause (which is contrary to the policies embodied in the Uniform Commercial Code) on its buyer, Nash, after the fact of sale, and without procuring any agreement, written or otherwise, from Nash with respect to the clause." The buyer pointed out that the parties had never discussed the clause during negotiations. It continued,

> This court is asked to decide whether the manufacturer of an unreasonably dangerous machine can attempt to enforce a hold-harmless clause in the "contract" of sale of the machine, and, thereby, escape liability for its failure to equip the machine with safety devices. It is submitted that to allow such a practice would be to effectively remove a manufacturer's obligation to create its products safely. Certainly, if one realizes that he will be reimbursed for any damages he may be required to pay on account of his responsibility for another's injuries, he will no longer be as inclined to take precautions which will prevent the injury. It is the prevention of this injury with which the law of products liability is concerned....
>
> Thus, Verson has marketed a product which is unreasonably dangerous due to its lack of safety devices, and has, simultaneously attempted to transfer its liability for injuries caused thereby to Nash. A minute clause on the back of Verson's printed form is the means by which Verson seeks to effectuate this transfer. Verson's attempted transfer of the financial responsibility for its violation of a duty which it could not delegate cannot, and should not, be tolerated if the policies embodied in the doctrine of strict tort liability are to be preserved.

3. *Sneaking provisions into deals*: Professor John E. Murray asserts "[i]f a party would not reasonably understand that certain terms were included in the

contract ab initio, they will not be included, because their inclusion would unfairly surprise and oppress the party against whom they would have operated. Section 2-207, therefore, may be viewed as addressing incipient unconscionability — its philosophy is identical to that of § 2-302's."[27] Suppose the seller's representative had called the attention of buyer's officials to the hold-harmless clause and to the problem of installing safety devices on the machine. Is it likely that this would have made a difference in the negotiations or other behavior of the parties?

STEINER v. MOBIL OIL CORP.

20 Cal. 3d 90, 569 P.2d 751 (1977)

TOBRINER, J. — In this case, over one year after apparently accepting plaintiff's offer, the Mobil Oil Corporation sought to impose upon plaintiff the very contractual terms which plaintiff expressly rejected in his offer. As justification for its conduct, Mobil asserted that the crucial provision of plaintiff's offer was lost in the labyrinth of the Mobil bureaucracy, and thus that Mobil decisionmakers had no opportunity to pass on plaintiff's offer as such. As we shall see, however, the trial court correctly concluded that § 2207 of the California Uniform Commercial Code bars Mobil from in this way converting its own error into plaintiff's misfortune.

Section 2207, subdivision (1), provides that parties may form an agreement, even if the terms of offer and acceptance do not entirely converge, if the offeree gives a definite expression of acceptance, and if the terms of acceptance do not explicitly condition agreement upon the offeror's consent to the offeree's new proposed terms. In this case, as the trial court found, defendant Mobil did not condition its acceptance of plaintiff's offer upon plaintiff's agreement to Mobil's alteration of plaintiff's offer and thus a contract was formed. Section 2207, subdivision (2), provides in turn that, if the terms of the offer and acceptance differ, the terms of the offer become part of a contract between merchants if the offer expressly limits acceptance to its own terms, or if the varying terms of the acceptance materially alter the terms of the offer. As the trial court found, under either of these clauses, the terms of Steiner's offer must prevail, because Steiner's offer was expressly conditional upon Mobil's agreement to provide a guaranteed discount, and Mobil's substitution of a discount terminable at its discretion materially affected Steiner's interests.

Accordingly, the trial court did not err in granting judgment for plaintiff, and we shall thus affirm its judgment.

---

[27]Murray, The Chaos of the "Battle of the Forms": Solutions, 39 Vanderbilt Law Review 1307, 1322 (1986). Permission to reprint granted by the Vanderbilt Law Review. All rights reserved.

[Facts: Steiner was an independent service-station operator. He leased a station from a third party, and bought gasoline from Mobil. In 1971 Steiner was informed that the lessor wanted to sell the property. Steiner contacted Mobil, and Mobil indicated that though they were not interested in buying the property, they would help Steiner to do so. Steiner negotiated with Chenen, Mobil's area manager. They tentatively worked out a deal whereby Mobil would supply a $30,000 down payment on the property which would be treated as a "repaid competitive allowance," amortized over a ten year period. Steiner would also get an additional 1.4 cents/gallon "competitive allowance" (a discount) from the "tank wagon price." Basically this meant that, over the ten years of the deal, Steiner would get a substantial subsidy from Mobil to enable him to buy and operate the station. Steiner was convinced that discounts were essential to making the transaction a viable one.

Chenen explained that neither he, nor his immediate supervisor (Dalbec) had the authority to actually commit Mobil; that power lay with Pfaff, the division general manager. Chenen and Steiner, using several standard Mobil forms, put together the proposal, modifying Mobil's forms where necessary. Steiner signed the forms. One of the forms that Steiner received, but that did not require his signature, contained a statement to the effect that the 1.4 cents per gallon competitive allowance could be changed or discontinued at any time by Mobil. When Steiner called this to Chenen's attention, Chenen and Dalbec responded with a letter which sought to reassure Steiner that unless Mobil accepted all of Steiner's terms, which was understood to include a *guaranteed* competitive allowance, the deal was off. The trial court found that Chenen was authorized to write Steiner, and that Chenen's actions and knowledge were attributable to Mobil.

In fact, however, neither Chenen nor Dalbec informed Pfaff of the letter sent to Steiner and the assurance that the discount would be irrevocable. The bundle of documents sent to Pfaff for his approval included the form that made revocable the 1.4 cents per gallon competitive allowance. Early in 1972, several months after it had been sent to him, Pfaff approved the proposal as submitted. Chenen informed Steiner by telephone of Pfaff's approval. Chenen told Steiner that Mobil had a check for him, and that the next thing for Steiner to do was to open an escrow account and proceed with purchase of the property. Subsequently Steiner received a manila folder containing the documents approved by Pfaff. He was not alerted to the fact that among the documents was the one which contained a clause making the competitive allowance revocable at Mobil's option.

By April 1972 Steiner had completed purchase of the service-station property. Beginning in March, Mobil began to extend the 1.4 cents per gallon allowance. On July 16, however, Chenen informed Steiner by letter that Mobil was reducing the allowance to 0.5 cents per gallon. Steiner brought suit and the trial court ruled in favor of Steiner. The court found that Mobil had reason to know that Steiner would not enter the agreement unless the competitive allowance was non-cancelable, that in returning the documents to Steiner Mobil intended to accept

Steiner's offer and not to make a counteroffer, and that in the exercise of good faith Mobil was required to specifically bring to Steiner's attention the statements concerning the revocability of the competitive allowance. Mobil appealed.]

Under California Uniform Commercial Code § 2207, Steiner's contract with Mobil grants Steiner a 1.4 cents per gallon discount for the duration of the contract.

[The California U.C.C. applies to this dispute, and § 2-207 (2207 in the Cal. Code) is the critical section.]

Under traditional common law, no contract was reached if the terms of the offer and the acceptance varied ... This "mirror image" rule of offer and acceptance was plainly both unfair and unrealistic in the commercial context, ... [since it ignored the parties mutual and reasonable understandings that there was a deal.]

Section 2207 rejects the "mirror image" rule. (See, *e.g., Roto-Lith, Ltd. v. F. P. Bartlett & Co.* (1st Cir. 1962) 297 F.2d 497, 500.) "This section of the Code recognizes that in current commercial transactions, the terms of the offer and those of the acceptance will seldom be identical." (*Dorton v. Collins & Aikman Corp.* (6th Cir. 1972) 453 F.2d 1161, 1166.)

Under § 2207, for example, the parties may conclude a contract despite the fact that, after reaching accord, they exchanged forms which purport to memorialize the agreement, but which differ because each party has drafted his form "to give him advantage." [citations omitted] Similarly, the parties may form a contract even if the terms of offer and acceptance differ because one or the other party, in stating its initial position, relies upon "forms drafted to cover the majority of [its] transactions in a uniform, standard manner" [citations omitted] and subsequently fails to amend its form to reflect the deal which the other party claims was actually negotiated. [citations omitted]

In place of the "mirror image" rule, § 2207 inquires as to whether the parties intended to complete an agreement ... If the parties intend to contract, but the terms of their offer and acceptance differ, § 2207 authorizes a court to determine which terms are part of the contract, either by reference to the parties' own dealings (see § 2207, subds. (1), (2)), or by reference to other provisions of the code. (See § 2207, subd. (3).)

Section 2207 is thus of a piece with other recent developments in contract law. Instead of fastening upon abstract doctrinal concepts like offer and acceptance, § 2207 looks to the actual dealings of the parties and gives legal effect to that conduct. Much as adhesion contract analysis teaches us not to enforce contracts until we look behind the facade of the formalistic standardized agreement in order to determine whether any inequality of bargaining power between the parties renders contractual terms unconscionable, or causes the contract to be interpreted against the more powerful party, § 2207 instructs us not to *refuse* to enforce contracts until we look below the surface of the parties' disagreement as to contract terms and determine whether the parties undertook to close their deal. Section 2207 requires courts to put aside the formal and academic stereotypes of traditional doctrine of offer and acceptance and to analyze instead what really happens. In this spirit, we turn to the application of § 2207 in this case.

Section 2207, subdivision (1), provides: "A definite and seasonable expression of acceptance or a written confirmation which is sent within a reasonable time operates as an acceptance even though it states terms additional or different from those offered or agreed upon, unless acceptance is expressly made conditional on assent to the additional or different terms."

In this case, as the trial court found, Mobil provided "[a] definite and seasonable expression of acceptance." Steiner offered to enter into a 10-year dealer contract with Mobil only if Mobil, among other things, agreed to advance Steiner $30,000, and to give Steiner a 1.4 cents per gallon competitive discount on the price of Mobil gasoline for the duration of the contract. When Steiner telephoned Chenen, Mobil's employee, to inquire as to the fate of Steiner's offer, *Chenen told Steiner that Mobil had a check for him, that he should open an escrow account, and that he should go ahead with the purchase of the service station property* — in context a clear statement that Mobil had approved the deal.

Moreover, through Montemarano, another Mobil employee, Mobil returned to Steiner various executed documents in an envelope unaccompanied by any cover. The documents provided written confirmation of the deal. The fact that Mobil returned the documents without in any way calling Steiner's attention to them is further evidence that Mobil regarded the process of negotiation as over and the deal as complete.

As the trial court also found, Mobil did not in any way make its acceptance "expressly ... conditional" on Steiner's "assent to the additional or different terms." Chenen, in telling Steiner to go ahead with the purchase, did not suggest that Mobil had conditioned its acceptance. In returning the executed documents, Mobil enclosed no cover letter; again, it did not use the occasion in any way to condition expressly its acceptance.

Thus, neither of the restrictions which limit § 2207, subdivision (1)'s application are relevant in this case. Despite the fact that the terms of Mobil's acceptance departed partially from the terms of Steiner's offer, Mobil and Steiner did form a contract. To determine the terms of this contract, we turn to § 2207, subdivision (2).

Section 2207, subdivision (2), provides: "... additional terms are to be construed as proposals for addition to the contract. Between merchants such terms become part of the contract unless: [¶] (a) The offer expressly limits acceptance to the terms of the offer; [¶] (b) They materially alter it; or [¶] (c) Notification of objection to them has already been given or is given within a reasonable time after notice of them is received."

Under § 2207, subdivision (2), Mobil's revocable discount provision does *not* become part of the agreement between Steiner and Mobil. In order to become part of the agreement, Mobil's provision must not fall within *any* of the categories defined by § 2207, subdivision (2), subsections (a), (b), and (c). Mobil's term, however, clearly comes within subsections (a) and (b).

Subsection (a) provides that no additional term can become part of the agreement if Steiner's offer "expressly limit[ed] acceptance to the terms of the offer." (§ 2207, subd. (2)(a).) Mobil concedes that Steiner's offer provided that the competitive allowance of 1.4 cents per gallon would run for the full length of the 10-year dealer contract. Chenen's December 2 letter to Steiner explicitly acknowledges Mobil's awareness that "[i]f Mobil management does not accept in full the above conditions outlined in your competitive offer, the above mentioned contract is void."

Moreover, Mobil's acceptance falls within subsection (b) since without question the acceptance "materially alter[ed]" the terms of Steiner's offer. (See § 2207, subd. (2)(b).) The Uniform Commercial Code Comment notes that a variation is material if it would "result in surprise or hardship if incorporated without express awareness by the other party ... " (§ 2-207, U. Com. Code, com. 4.) Here, Steiner clearly indicated to Mobil in the course of the negotiations that, without the 1.4 cents per gallon discount, he could not economically operate the service station. Mobil's alteration, therefore, amended the terms of the offer to Steiner's significant detriment; accordingly, the alteration was necessarily "material."

To reiterate, subsections (a), (b), and (c) of § 2207, subdivision (2), operate in the alternative. If any one of the three subsections applies, the variant terms of an acceptance do not become part of an agreement. Here, as we have seen, the provisions of both subsections (a) and (b) are met. Mobil's declaration that the 1.4 cents per gallon discount was terminable at Mobil's discretion did not become part of the contract. Instead, Steiner and Mobil formed a contract incorporating the terms of Steiner's offer: Under this contract, Steiner was guaranteed a 1.4 cents per gallon discount throughout the 10-year period of the dealer contract.

Thus, on their face, subdivisions (1) and (2) of § 2207 confirm the trial court's conclusion that Mobil breached its agreement with Steiner. We now turn to Mobil's opposing argument that we should adopt an interpretation of § 2207 which conflicts with the trial court's conclusion.

Contrary to Mobil's argument, California Uniform Commercial Code §§ 2204 and 2207 do not incorporate the traditional rule that parties to a contract must mutually assent to all essential terms.

We set forth Mobil's contentions, which, although elaborately developed, can be simply stated. Section 2207 does not apply if the general contract formation rules of § 2204 are not met. Section 2204 does not change the traditional rule that, in order to create an enforceable contract, the parties must mutually assent to all essential terms of the supposed agreement. In order to square § 2207 with § 2204, Mobil argues, we must construe § 2207, subdivision (1), to provide that there is no "definite" acceptance unless the parties agree to all essential terms. Moreover, Mobil contends, we must also hold that, under the same section, an acceptance which alters an essential term of an offer is an acceptance "expressly made conditional on assent" to the variant term. Finally, Mobil concludes that, since its acceptance, in changing the duration of the discount, modified an essential term of Steiner's offer, i.e., price, we must find that Steiner cannot claim a continued discount.

As we shall explain, Mobil's arguments do not survive scrutiny. The Official Comments accompanying § 2204, other provisions of the code, and the case law interpreting § 2204, all support the conclusion that § 2204 does not require mutual assent to all essential terms. Mobil's interpretations of the definite agreement and conditional acceptance provisions of § 2207, subdivision (1), likewise conflict with other subdivisions of § 2207.

[As to § 2-204] Section 2204, subdivision (3), does not, by its terms, require parties to a contract to assent to *all* essential terms. Instead, this provision states that a court, if it is to enforce a contract, must first make two findings. Initially, the court must find some basis for concluding that the parties engaged in a process of offer and acceptance, rather than inconclusive negotiations. Second, the court must find that it possesses sufficient information about the parties' incomplete transaction to apply the provisions of the California Uniform Commercial Code which fill in the gaps in parties'contracts.[28] As we have already seen, both of these minimal requirements are met in this case: the parties did not engage in inconclusive negotiations, and § 2207 readily fills in the terms of their contract....

The case law interpreting § 2204 reinforces the interpretation offered by the code comment and the implication of other code provisions: the rules of contract formation under the California Uniform Commercial Code do not include the principle that the parties must agree to all essential terms in order to form a contract. Courts have held that, under § 2204, subdivision (3), parties may form a contract even though they do not agree as to the terms of payment ..., the time or place for performance ..., or the quantity of the goods sold ... — all terms which might appear to be "essential" to an agreement.

More significantly, in view of Mobil's emphasis on the essential character of price terms, a number of courts have held that, under § 2204, subdivision (3), the parties may frame a contract without fully agreeing as to price ... Concededly, one court has suggested in dictum that § 2204, subdivision (3), incorporates the requirement of assent to essential terms....[29]

---

[28]These provisions, of course, include § 2207; they also include, for example, § 2305, which deals with open price terms, § 2307, which fixes otherwise open delivery provisions, and § 2309, which sets a duration for otherwise indefinite contracts.

[29]In the instant case, Steiner and Mobil, at Mobil's instigation, arranged their dealings in a way that clearly distinguished preliminary bargaining from the process of offer and acceptance as such. As we have seen, Steiner and Chenen initially negotiated the terms of Steiner's offer. Chenen and

California Uniform Commercial Code § 2207, subdivision (1), should not be narrowly read to conform to the principle of mutual assent to all essential terms.

As we have seen, § 2204 quite clearly does *not* incorporate the rule that parties must mutually assent to all essential terms. Mobil has thus failed to establish the premise that it would postulate as justifying a narrow reading of § 2207, subdivision (1). We shall, however, briefly consider Mobil's other and further arguments concerning the construction of § 2207, and show that these arguments, taken in isolation, are consistent neither with the language of § 2207, subdivision (1), nor with the logic of § 2207 as a whole.

Initially, Mobil focuses on § 2207, subdivision (1)'s requirement of a "definite … expression of acceptance." Mobil would define "definite" by reference to the extent of the difference between offer and acceptance: the more significant the divergence, the less definitely a response is an acceptance. This construction suffers from two flaws. First, in § 2207, subdivision (1), "definite" modifies "expression" and not "acceptance," and thus refers to the *process* of offer and acceptance and not to the *terms* of the acceptance itself. Second, in any event, § 2207 as a whole bars any interpretation of "definite" which, as Mobil urges, would exclude from the ranks of acceptances all but collateral variations on the terms of offers. Section 2207, subdivision (2)(b)'s concern with material variations necessarily implies that acceptances incorporating such variations can satisfy the requirements of subdivision (1).

Mobil would also construe the final clause of § 2207, subdivision (1), which provides that, if acceptance "is expressly made conditional on assent to … additional or different terms," the "acceptance" does not operate as an acceptance but as a counteroffer. Specifically, Mobil argues that we should read this provision broadly, by adopting the interpretation advanced in *Roto-Lith, Ltd. v. F. P. Bartlett & Co., supra*, 297 F.2d at page 500: "a response which states a condition materially altering the obligation solely to the disadvantage of the offeror is an 'acceptance … expressly … conditional on assent to the additional … terms.' "

Dalbec then submitted the offer to Pfaff, who accepted it on Mobil's behalf. Other Mobil employees treated Pfaff's decision as terminating negotiations: Chenen told Steiner to go ahead with the service station purchase; Montemarano delivered the contract documents to Steiner without comment or cover letter. Thus, because of the hierarchical structure which Mobil imposed on the bargaining, the trial court could conclude, as it did, that Mobil intended to accept Steiner' offer and not merely to continue negotiations.

In this case, thus, the serious nature of the contract provision in dispute does not preclude a finding that they intended to conclude a contract; the parties'negotiating procedure itself reveals their intent. In other cases, in which negotiations are not so well organized, the importance of a term which the parties leave open may very well be a decisive measure of whether the parties intended to enter into a contract….

Again, however, Mobil's construction does not accord with the language of the section. Such an interpretation of the conditional acceptance clause would transform acceptances into counteroffers without regard to whether the acceptance is in fact, as § 2207, subdivision (1), requires, "expressly made conditional on assent to ... additional or different terms." Moreover, under Mobil's reading, the conditional acceptance clause of § 2207, subdivision (1), would largely duplicate the function of the material variation clause of § 2207, subdivision (2)(b).

As Mobil concedes, courts and commentators alike have repeatedly criticized the *Roto-Lith* interpretation of § 2207, subdivision (1) ... Most courts have rejected *Roto-Lith*, and have instead interpreted the conditional acceptance clause literally, as we did earlier ... Recognizing the superiority of the majority view, we reject Mobil's attempt to advance the *Roto-Lith* interpretation of § 2207, subdivision (1).

Conclusion.

In this case, as we have seen, the trial court correctly concluded that under § 2207 the guaranteed discount included in the terms of Steiner's offer, and not Mobil's standard revocable discount provision, became part of the agreement between Mobil and Steiner. Mobil cannot assert as a defense the failure of its own bureaucracy to respond to, or even fully recognize, Steiner's efforts to modify the standard Mobil dealer contract.

The judgment is affirmed. [Bird, C. J., Mosk, J., Clark, J., Richardson, J., Manuel, J., and Jefferson, J., concurred.]

NOTES AND QUESTIONS

1. *Of offers and acceptances*: Suppose the court had found that the package of forms created by Chenen and Steiner and submitted to Pfaff was a proposal and not an offer. Then assume the court found that the manila folder containing the documents approved by Pfaff was an offer. Finally, assume that Steiner's actions in acquiring the service station property and running the business under the competitive allowance was deemed an acceptance. Would a court decide the case for Mobil?

Remember that U.C.C. § 2-207(1) applies only to a "definite and seasonable expression of acceptance." However, does anything of substance turn on whether a court classifies Mobil's documents in the manila folder as the offer or as an acceptance of Steiner's offer? Justice Tobriner said "[i]nstead of fastening upon abstract doctrinal concepts like offer and acceptance, § 2207 looks to the actual dealings of the parties and gives legal effect to that conduct ... § 2207 requires courts to put aside the formal and academic stereotypes of traditional offer and acceptance and to analyze instead what really happens." Can a court put aside the "formal and academic stereotype" of an acceptance when § 2-207(1) says it applies to an acceptance? Should the section be amended to avoid this problem?

2. *Why did the middle managers create the mess*? Unfortunately, the briefs cast no light at all on the most interesting question raised by the case: Why did the middle managers of Mobil create the problem by not telling their supervisor about the competitive allowance provision? Compare the role of the architect in *Vickery v. Ritchie, supra.*

3. *The interpretation of 2-207(2) — "additional vs. different" terms*: In one of the omitted footnotes in the preceding case the court addresses an argument which arises in the course of interpreting 2-207(2). The question is whether there is an important distinction between "different" and "additional" terms; the *Steiner* court concludes that there is none. The question arises because 2-207(1) refers to acceptances in which terms are either "additional to or different from" the offered terms, whereas 2-207(2) seems to concern itself only with "additional" terms. The court mentions, in that footnote, the case of *Air Products & Chemical, Inc. v. Fairbanks Morse, Inc.*,[30] the facts of which may serve not only to illuminate that issue, but as a useful review and drill concerning the difficulties of applying 2-207.

It seems that Air Products wanted to buy some large electric motors from Fairbanks Morse. After discussions about the specifications of the motors, Air Products verbally agreed to buy several. Air Products then submitted a purchase order. Fairbanks Morse returned an executed copy of the purchase order *together with Fairbanks Morse's acknowledgment of order form.* Air Products asserted that the motors failed to perform properly, and brought suit against Fairbanks Morse. (The complaint alleged 43 causes of action; they must have been really mad!) Fairbanks Morse interposed as a defense a limitation of liability term contained on its acknowledgment of order form. The front of the Fairbank's form contained the following language, which the Wisconsin Supreme Court described as being printed "in reasonably bold face type at the bottom." [We have tried, as nearly as we could, to reproduce the type size of the form itself. You might note that 2-207 contains no explicit requirement of conspicuousness. Does this mean the appearance of the clause is irrelevant?]

WE THANK YOU FOR YOUR ORDER AS COPIED HEREON, WHICH WILL RECEIVE PROMPT ATTENTION AND SHALL BE GOVERNED BY THE PROVISIONS ON THE REVERSE SIDE HEREOF UNLESS YOU NOTIFY US TO THE CONTRARY WITHIN 10 DAYS OR BEFORE SHIPMENT WHICHEVER IS EARLIER.
BEFORE ACCEPTING GOODS FROM TRANSPORTATION COMPANY SEE THAT EACH ARTICLE IS IN GOOD CONDITION. IF SHORTAGE OR DAMAGE IS APPARENT REFUSE SHIPMENT UNLESS AGENT NOTES DEFECT ON TRANSPORTATION BILL. ACCEPTANCE OF SHIPMENT WITHOUT COMPLYING WITH SUCH CONDITIONS IS AT YOUR OWN RISK.
THIS IS NOT AN INVOICE. AN INVOICE FOR THIS MATERIAL WILL BE SENT YOU WITHIN A FEW DAYS.

ACKNOWLEDGMENT OF ORDER

---

[30] 58 Wis.2d 193, 206 N.W.2d 414 (1973).

The reverse side of the "acknowledgment of order" contained six printed provisions which were immediately preceded by the following statement:

> The following provisions form part of the order acknowledged and accepted on the face hereof, as express agreements between Fairbanks, Morse & Co. ('Company') and the Buyer governing the terms and conditions of the sale, subject to modification only in writing signed by the local manager or an executive officer of the Company:

Provision 6, which became the subject of the dispute between the parties, provided:

> 6. — The Company nowise assumes any responsibility or liability with respect to use, purpose, or suitability, and shall not be liable for damages of any character, whether direct or consequential, for defect, delay, or otherwise, its sole liability and obligation being confined to the replacement in the manner aforesaid of defectively manufactured guaranteed parts failing within the time stated.

Fairbanks Morse asserted that Paragraph 6 became part of the contract, and effectively limited its liability. Air Products asserted that Paragraph 6 did NOT become part of the contract and, therefore, that Air Products was entitled to rely on the Code's provisions governing the implied warranties of merchantability, fitness for a particular purpose, and providing for recovery of consequential damages. The trial court had concluded, apparently without thoroughly considering U.C.C. 2-207(2)(b) that, since the terms limiting damages were completely new and additional proposed terms, and since the parties were merchants, the terms became part of the contract.

Air Products advanced two arguments to seek to avoid Paragraph 6. They first argued that 2-207(2) only applies to "additional" terms; that is, that only terms which can be characterized as "additional" can become part of the contract by reason of the application of 2-207(2). Air Products then, of necessity, argued that Paragraph 6 was a "different, as opposed to an "additional" term, and so was not included *via* 2-207(2). They argued that terms are "additional" if they concern a subject matter not addressed in the offer, and that they are "different" if they concern a subject matter which was covered and deal with it in a variant way. Air Products then argued that their offer must be regarded as including the terms expressly included AND the terms implied by law — such as the implied warranty and damages claims. *Voilà!* By this logic the Fairbanks Morse confirmation contains a "different" term because it is at variance with the terms of the offer, which included the implied terms concerning warranty and liability.

Fairbanks Morse sought to parry the thrust of this argument by asserting that recovery of consequential damages is not included in every contract by implication, since they are only recoverable "in a proper case" (2-714(3)). As a result, even if you accept the first steps of the Air Products' argument, Paragraph 6 is OK because recovery of consequential damages is not among the terms which could fairly be implied in a contract otherwise silent on the topic.

The Court expressed doubt about the basic premise of the entire debate, suggesting that the Code should not be interpreted as creating an important distinction between "different" and "additional" terms. But in addition to suggesting the argument was perhaps irrelevant, the Court rejected Fairbanks Morse counterargument by carrying it one step farther. The Court noted that the comment to 2-715 observes that seller's are liable to buyers for consequential damages in cases in which the seller "had reason to know of the buyer's general or particular requirements at the time of contracting." In this case Fairbanks Morse was aware of the needs of Air Products, making it a "proper case" for recovery of consequential losses — and so a recovery of consequential loss was implicit in the contract.

Air Products' second argument was more direct, since it was not based in the argument that "additional" terms and "different" terms should be treated differently — an argument which has been widely criticized. Air Products argued that the disclaimer in the Fairbanks Morse acknowledgment was a material alternation of the agreement and could become a part of the contract only if expressly agreed to. To quote from the Court's decision,

> Hartford and Air Products contend that the eradication of a multimillion dollar damage exposure is per se material. Fairbanks bases its argument on the ground that consequential damages may not be recovered except in "special circumstances" or in a "proper case." (2-714(2) and (3)). As already stated, these "special circumstances" would seem by Comment 3 to § 2-715 to be referring to situations which concern instances where the seller [had] reason to know of buyer's general or particular requirements at the time of contracting. "Consequential damages resulting from the seller's breach include (a) any loss resulting from general or particular requirements and needs of which the seller at the time of contracting had reason to know and which could not reasonably be prevented by cover or otherwise; ... " U.C.C. § 2-715(2)(a).
>
> While Comment 4 clearly indicates that a disclaimer of an implied warranty of merchantability is material, there is no good reason to hold that a disclaimer that has the effect of eliminating millions of dollars in damages should become a part of a contract by operation of law.
>
> We conclude that the disclaimer for consequential loss was sufficiently material to require express conversation between the parties over its inclusion or exclusion in the contract.

4. *An additional argument in Air Products v. Fairbanks Morse*: The lawyers for Fairbanks Morse made an argument in their brief which seems not to have been confronted in the Court's opinion. The argument, essentially, was that the

Code, in § 2-719(3), provides that limitations on consequential damages are valid unless unconscionable. This goes to whether a limitation on consequential damages should be regarded as a material alteration of the offer. In the commercial world in which Air Products and Fairbanks Morse were resident, such limitations were, allegedly, quite common, and, in the words of the Fairbanks Morse brief, "effectuate the very purpose of § 2-719 which is to encourage and facilitate the allocation of risks associated with the sale of goods, particularly those occurring in a commercial setting."

Suppose Fairbanks Morse's lawyers commissioned a survey of machinery manufacturers and purchasers, and this survey showed that in, say, 92.66% of all contracts for the sale of machinery consequential damages were ruled out. Would, or should, this information change the court's decision? Suppose the clause was found in 60% of all contracts? 40%? Would an attitude survey be better? Suppose businesspeople were asked whether they expected to be able to recover consequential damages. 85% said that they would not in the ordinary case. Would this be relevant to the application of § 2-207 to the Fairbanks Morse situation? How does the Supreme Court of Wisconsin get its data on whether the remedy limitation materially alters the contract created by F-M's acceptance? Or is it a question of data?

5. *Once burned, twice shy*: You might be interested to learn that as a result of the litigation with Fairbanks Morse, Air Products adopted the following language in its purchase order form. This is the fifteenth clause printed in small type on the back of the form:

> This Order shall be binding upon the parties either upon receipt of Seller's acknowledgment of its acceptance hereof or commencement of its performance of the work contemplated by this Order. No terms or conditions in Seller's order acknowledgment form or in any other form of acceptance of this Order, shall bind Buyer or modify Seller's obligations hereunder, unless accepted in writing by Buyer.

C. ITOH & CO. (AMERICA) INC. v. JORDAN INTERNATIONAL CO.

552 F.2d 1228 (7th Cir. 1977)

SPRECHER, J. The sole issue on this appeal is whether the district court properly denied a stay of the proceedings pending arbitration under § 3 of the Federal Arbitration Act, 9 U.S.C. § 3.

I. C.Itoh & Co. (America) Inc. ("Itoh") submitted a purchase order dated August 15, 1974 for a certain quantity of steel coils to the Jordan International Company ("Jordan"). In response, Jordan sent its acknowledgment form dated August 19, 1974. On the face of Jordan's form, the following statement appears:

Seller's acceptance is, however, expressly conditional on Buyer's assent to the additional or different terms and conditions set forth below and printed on the reverse side. If these terms and conditions are not acceptable, Buyer should notify seller at once.

One of the terms on the reverse side of Jordan's form was a broad provision for arbitration.[31] Itoh neither expressly assented nor objected to the additional arbitration term in Jordan's form until the instant litigation.

Itoh also entered into a contract to sell the steel coils that it purchased from Jordan to Riverview Steel Corporation, Inc. ("Riverview"). The contract between Itoh and Riverview contained an arbitration term, which provided in pertinent part:

> Any and all controversies arising out of or relating to this contract, or any modification, breach or cancellation thereof, *except as to quality*, shall be settled by arbitration....

After the steel had been delivered by Jordan and paid for by Itoh, Riverview advised Itoh that the steel coils were defective and did not conform to the standards set forth in the agreement between Itoh and Riverview; for these reasons, Riverview refused to pay Itoh for the steel. Consequently, Itoh brought the instant suit against Riverview and Jordan. Itoh alleged that Riverview had wrongfully refused to pay for the steel; as affirmative defenses, Riverview claimed that the steel was defective and that tender was improper since delivery was late. Itoh alleged that Jordan had sold Itoh defective steel and had made a late delivery of that steel.

Jordan then filed a motion in the district court requesting a stay of the proceedings pending arbitration under § 3 of the Federal Arbitration Act, 9 U.S.C. § 3. The district court concluded that, as between Itoh and Riverview, the issue of whether the steel coils were defective was not referable to arbitration because of the "quality" exclusion in the arbitration provision of the contract between Itoh and Riverview. Since arbitration would not necessarily resolve all the issues raised by the parties, the district court, apparently assuming *arguendo* that there existed an agreement in writing between Jordan and Itoh to arbitrate their dispute, denied the stay pending arbitration. In the district court's opinion, sound judicial administration required that the entire litigation be resolved in a single forum; since some of the issues — those relating to quality between Itoh

---

[31]The arbitration clause provides:

> Any controversy arising under or in connection with the contract shall be submitted to arbitration in New York City in accordance with the rules then obtaining of the American Arbitration Association. Judgment on any award may be entered in any court having jurisdiction....

and Riverview — were not referable to arbitration, this goal could only be accomplished in the judicial forum.

It is from this denial of a stay pending arbitration that Jordan appeals ...

III. Having concluded that the district court had no discretion under § 3 of the Federal Arbitration Act, 9 U.S.C. § 3, to deny Jordan's timely application for a stay of the action pending arbitration *if* there existed an agreement in writing for such arbitration between Jordan and Itoh, the remaining issue is whether there existed such an agreement....

In support of its contention that there exists an agreement in writing to arbitrate, Jordan places some reliance on certain New York decisions interpreting § 2-201 of the Uniform Commercial Code, the U.C.C. Statute of Frauds provision. That section provides in pertinent part:

> (1) Except as otherwise provided in this section a contract for the sale of goods for the price of $500 or more is not enforceable by way of action or defense unless there is some writing sufficient to indicate that a contract for sale has been made between the parties and signed by the party against whom enforcement is sought....
>
> (2) Between merchants if within a reasonable time a writing in confirmation of the contract and sufficient against the sender is received and the party receiving it has reason to know its contents, it satisfies the requirements of subsection (1) against such party unless written notice of objection to its contents is given within ten days after it is received.

Several New York lower court decisions have apparently held that under § 2-201, where there has been an oral offer or agreement followed by a written confirmation containing an additional arbitration term and where the merchant recipient of the confirmation has reason to expect that a provision for arbitration would be included in any written confirmation of an oral offer or agreement, the arbitration provision becomes a part of the parties' agreement unless notice of objection is given within the prescribed period ....

These decisions are premised on a fundamental misconception of the purpose and effect of § 2-201. See generally Duesenberg & King, Sales and Bulk Transfers Under the Uniform Commercial Code § 308[1] at 97-99 (1976). The *only* effect of a failure to object to a written confirmation of an oral offer or agreement under § 2-201 is to take away from the receiving merchant the defense of the Statute of Frauds.... Although § 2-201 may make *enforceable* an oral agreement which was in fact reached by the parties, it does not relieve the party seeking enforcement of the alleged oral agreement of the obligation to prove its existence. Official Comment 3 to § 2-201. Section 2-201 obviously cannot be relied on to make a particular term, such as a provision for arbitration, binding on a party if that section does not even serve to establish the *existence* of an agreement.

The Official Comments make clear that, while under § 2-201 the failure to object to a written confirmation of an oral agreement has the limited effect of removing the Statute of Frauds as a bar to the enforceability of an oral agreement, under § 2-207 a failure to object to a term in a written confirmation may, *under the circumstances specified by that section*, have the effect of making that term a part of whatever agreement is proved to have been reached by the parties. Official Comment 3 to § 2-201. Hence, once the existence and terms of an alleged oral agreement have been established, it is necessary to refer to § 2-207, Additional Terms in Acceptance *or Confirmation*, not § 2-201, to ascertain whether a term included in a written confirmation but not in the parties' oral agreement is binding on the recipient of the written confirmation....

However, even if we assume that New York's highest court would adhere to those lower court decisions and their extremely questionable application of the Statute of Frauds to situations where a party has added an arbitration term to a written *confirmation of* an *oral offer* or agreement, this is not such a situation. Jordan does not suggest that its acknowledgment form was simply a *confirmation of* a prior *oral* offer or agreement. Rather, Jordan's argument is that *the exchange of forms* between itself and Itoh *created* a contract, which includes the additional arbitration term in Jordan's form.

The instant case, therefore, involves the classic "battle of the forms," and § 2-207, not § 2-201, furnishes the rules for resolving such a controversy. Hence, it is to § 2-207 that we must look to determine whether a contract has been formed by the exchange of forms between Jordan and Itoh and, if so, whether the additional arbitration term in Jordan's form is to be included in that contract....

· IV. ... Under § 2-207 it is necessary to first determine whether a contract has been formed under § 2-207(1) as a result of the *exchange of forms* between Jordan and Itoh.

At common law, an acceptance which contained terms additional to those of the offer constituted a rejection of the offer and thus became a counter-offer. Thus, the mere presence of the additional arbitration term in Jordan's acknowledgment form would, at common law, have prevented the exchange of documents between Jordan and Itoh from creating a contract, and Jordan's form would have automatically become a counter-offer.

Section 2-207(1) was intended to alter this inflexible common law approach to offer and acceptance....

However, while § 2-207(1) constitutes a sharp departure from the common law "mirror image" rule, there remain situations where the inclusion of an additional term in one of the forms exchanged by the parties will prevent the consummation of a contract *under that section*. Section 2-207(1) contains a proviso which operates to prevent an exchange of forms from creating a contract where "acceptance is expressly made conditional on assent to the additional ... terms."

In the instant case, Jordan's acknowledgment form contained the following statement:

> Seller's acceptance is ... *expressly conditional* on Buyer's *assent* to the additional or different terms and conditions set forth below and printed on the reverse side. If these terms and conditions are not acceptable, Buyer should notify Seller at once.

The arbitration provision at issue on this appeal is printed on the reverse side of Jordan's acknowledgment, and there is no dispute that Itoh never expressly assented to the challenged arbitration term.

The Court of Appeals for the Sixth Circuit has held that the proviso must be construed narrowly:

> Although ... [seller's] use of the words "subject to" suggests that the acceptances were conditional to some extent, we do not believe the acceptances were "expressly made conditional on [the buyer's] assent to the additional or different terms," as specifically required under the Subsection 2-207(1) proviso. In order to fall within this proviso, it is not enough that an acceptance is expressly conditional on additional or different terms; rather, an acceptance must be expressly conditional on the offeror's *assent* to those terms (emphasis in original).

[I]t is clear that the statement contained in Jordan's acknowledgment form comes within the § 2-207(1) proviso.

Hence, the exchange of forms between Jordan and Itoh did not result in the formation of a contract under § 2-207(1), and Jordan's form became a counteroffer. "[T]he consequence of a clause conditioning acceptance on assent to the additional or different terms is that *as of the exchanged writings, there is no contract.* Either party may at this point in their dealings walk away from the transaction." Duesenberg & King, *supra*, § 3.06[3] at 73. However, neither Jordan nor Itoh elected to follow that course; instead, both parties proceeded to performance — Jordan by delivering and Itoh by paying for the steel coils.

At common law, the "terms of the counteroffer were said to have been accepted by the original offeror when he proceeded to perform under the contract without objecting to the counteroffer."

... Thus, under pre-Code law, Itoh's performance (*i.e.*, payment for the steel coils) probably constituted acceptance of the Jordan counteroffer, including its provision for arbitration. However, a different approach is required under the Code.

Section 2-207(3) of the Code first provides that "[c]onduct by both parties which recognizes the existence of a contract is sufficient to establish a contract for sale although the writings of the parties do not otherwise establish a contract." ... Thus, "[s]ince ... [Itoh's] purchase order and ... [Jordan's] counter-offer did not in themselves create a contract, § 2-207(3) would operate to create one because the subsequent performance by both parties constituted 'conduct by both parties which recognizes the existence of a contract.' " ...

What are the terms of a contract created by conduct under § 2-207(3) rather than by an exchange of forms under § 2-207(1)? As noted above, at common law the terms of the contract between Jordan and Itoh would be the terms of the Jordan counter-offer. However, the Code has effectuated a radical departure from the common law rule.[32] The second sentence of § 2-207(3) provides that where, as here, a contract has been consummated by the conduct of the parties, "the terms of the particular contract consist of those terms on which the writings of the parties agree, together with any supplementary terms incorporated under any other provisions of this Act." Since it is clear that the Jordan and Itoh forms do not "agree" on arbitration, the only question which remains *under the Code* is whether arbitration may be considered a supplementary term incorporated under some other provision of the Code.

We have been unable to find any case authority shedding light on the question of what constitutes "supplementary terms" within the meaning of § 2-207(3) and the Official Comments to § 2-207 provide no guidance in this regard. We are persuaded, however, that the disputed additional terms (*i.e.*, those terms on which the writings of the parties do not agree) which are necessarily excluded from a Subsection (3) contract by the language, "terms on which the writings of the parties agree," cannot be brought back into the contract under the guise of "supplementary terms." This conclusion has substantial support among the commentators who have addressed themselves to the issue. As two noted authorities on Article Two of the Code have stated:

> It will usually happen that an offeree-seller who returns an acknowledgment form will also concurrently or shortly thereafter ship the goods. If the responsive document [sent by the seller] contains a printed assent clause, and the goods are shipped and accepted, Subsection (3) of § 2-207 comes into play... [T]he terms on which the exchanged communications do not agree drop out of the transaction, and reference to the Code is made to supply necessary terms.... Rather than choosing the terms of one party over those of the other... it compels supplying missing terms by reference to the Code....

---

[32]Jordan relies on Roto-Lith [Ltd. v. F.B. Bartlett & Co., 297 F.2d 497 (1st Cir. 1962)], in support of its contention that Itoh's payment for the steel coils constituted acceptance of all the terms in Jordan's counteroffer. In *Roto-Lith* the court ignored § 2-207(3) and simply applied the common law rule.... We adopt the consensus of the courts and commentators that *Roto-Lith*, in reading § 2-207(3) out of the Code, evidences an incorrect interpretation and application of § 2-207.

Duesenberg & King, *supra*, § 3.06[4] at 73-74. Similarly, Professors White and Summers have concluded that "contract formation under subsection (3) gives neither party the relevant terms of his document, but fills out the contract with the standardized provisions of Article Two." White & Summers, *supra*, at 29.

Accordingly, we find that the "supplementary terms" contemplated by § 2-207(3) are limited to those supplied by the standardized "gap-filler" provisions of Article Two. See, *e.g.*, § 2-308(a) ("Unless otherwise agreed ... the place for delivery of goods is the seller's place of business or if he has none his residence"); § 2-309(1) ("The time for shipment or delivery or any other action under a contract if not ... agreed upon shall be a reasonable time"); § 2-310(a) ("Unless otherwise agreed ... payment is due at the time and place at which the buyer is to receive the goods even though the place of shipment is the place of delivery"). Since provision for arbitration is not a necessary or missing term which would be supplied by one of the Code's "gap-filler" provisions unless agreed upon by the contracting parties, there is no arbitration term in the § 2-207(3) contract which was created by the conduct of Jordan and Itoh in proceeding to perform even though no contract had been established by their exchange of writings.

We are convinced that this conclusion does not result in any unfair prejudice to a seller who elects to insert in his standard sales acknowledgment form the statement that acceptance is expressly conditional on buyer's assent to additional terms contained therein. Such a seller obtains a substantial benefit *under § 2-207(1)* through the inclusion of an "expressly conditional" clause. If he decides after the exchange of forms that the particular transaction is not in his best interest, Subsection (1) permits him to walk away from the transaction without incurring any liability so long as the buyer has not in the interim expressly assented to the additional terms. Moreover, whether or not a seller will be disadvantaged *under § (3)* as a consequence of inserting an "expressly conditional" clause in his standard form is within his control. If the seller in fact does not intend to close a particular deal unless the additional terms are assented to, he can protect himself by not delivering the goods until such assent is forthcoming. If the seller does intend to close a deal irrespective of whether or not the buyer assents to the additional terms, he can hardly complain when the contract formed under Subsection (3) as a result of the parties' conduct is held not to include those terms. Although a seller who employs such an "expressly conditional" clause in his acknowledgment form would undoubtedly appreciate the dual advantage of not being bound to a contract under Subsection (1) if he elects not to perform and of having his additional terms imposed on the buyer under Subsection (3) in the event that performance is in his best interest, we do not believe such a result is contemplated by § 2-207. Rather, while a seller may take advantage of an "expressly conditional" clause under Subsection (1) when he elects not to perform, he must accept the potential risk under Subsection (3) of not getting his additional terms when he elects to proceed with performance without first obtaining the buyer's assent to those terms. Since the seller injected ambiguity into the transaction by inserting the "expressly conditional" clause in his form, he, and not the buyer, should bear the consequence of that ambiguity under Subsection (3)....

Accordingly, for the reasons stated in this opinion, *the decision of the district court is affirmed.*

NOTES AND QUESTIONS

1. *The real dispute and making a case*: The briefs and record suggest that the legal proceedings were a game far removed from the assumptions and understandings of the real parties to the dispute. Itoh, the buyer, submitted a purchase order for steel coils. Jordan, the seller, confirmed the order on its own form. The terms on this confirmation included a standard American Arbitration Association clause calling for arbitration of disputes. Itoh then contracted to sell the steel coils to Riverview. Riverview submitted a purchase order, and Itoh accepted the order on its form that included the same standard American Arbitration Association clause calling for arbitration of disputes. Jordan pointed out that arbitration clauses are the custom in the steel brokerage industry, Itoh regularly used them, and Itoh knew that Jordan regularly used them. Moreover, the exact arguments based on U.C.C. § 2-201 (the Statute of Frauds section) asserted here by Jordan, had been asserted successfully by Itoh in *Klockner, Inc. v. Itoh & Co.*[33] to bring an arbitration clause into a bargain on the same facts as were before the court in this case. Is such a triumph of legal technicality justified? Or does the case represent a failure of legal technique?

2. *"[O]ther provisions" of this Act*: The court in the *Itoh* case says that § 2-207(3) governs, and that if the parties' documents fail to create a bargain but their conduct recognizes the existence of one, then the terms are those upon which they agree, plus all of the gap-filling provisions of Article II. Furnish,[34] argues that the terms of a § 2-207(3) contract should be based on agreement plus Article I as well as Article II. If this view were accepted, then a court could look to sections such as 1-205 which deals with course of dealing and usage of trade. If arbitration could be shown to be the usage of the steel brokerage trade, then it could "supplement or qualify terms of an agreement." For this approach to change the result in the *Itoh* case, the seller would have had to show "any practice or method of dealing having such regularity of observance in a place, vocation or trade as to justify an expectation that it will be observed with respect to the transaction in question." Official Comment 5 provides:

---

[33] 17 U.C.C. Rep. Serv. 915 (N.Y. Sup. Ct. 1975).

[34] Commercial Arbitration Agreements and the Uniform Commercial Code, 67 California Law Review 317 (1979).

5. A usage of trade ... must have the "regularity of observance" specified. The ancient English tests for "custom" are abandoned in this connection. Therefore, it is not required that a usage of trade be "ancient or immemorial," "universal" or the like.... [F]ull recognition is thus available for new usages and for usages currently observed by the great majority of decent dealers, even though dissidents ready to cut corners do not agree.

We will consider course of dealing, usage of trade, and course of performance under § 2-208 in some detail later in this course.

Many modern § 2-207 cases deal with arbitration clauses. On one hand, the Court of Appeals of New York almost never will use U.C.C. § 2-207 to add an arbitration clause to a contract.[35] On the other hand, other courts have found an obligation to arbitrate as a result of the battle of the forms.[36]

c. Lawyers Cope with § 2-207: Business Procedures and Drafting Practices

Lawyers have struggled with the problems posed by the need to anticipate the application of § 2-207. For every controversy which has ripened into a lawsuit, requiring lawyers to figure out how to apply § 2-207 after a transactional breakdown, there are many instances in which lawyers have struggled to draft forms which will either avoid problems, or give their clients an edge if a problem arises. We can set the stage with an interview with the General Counsel of a manufacturer of heating and cooling equipment:

> The battle of the forms is the most important contracts problem the firm faces. Our ordering and billing processes still are back in the days of the Uniform Sales Act when the last shot decided which set of terms and conditions governed. In the process we will fire our terms and conditions

---

[35]In Matter of Marlene Industries Corp., 45 N.Y.2d 327, 380 N.E.2d 239 (1978),the court stressed its long standing policy that one should not be subject to arbitration in the absence of an express, unequivocal agreement to arbitrate. Receiving a form and doing nothing would not be enough. In Schubetex, Inc. v. Allen Snyder, Inc., 49 N.Y.2d 1, 399 N.E.2d 1154 (1979), the court conceded that an agreement to arbitrate could be implied from a prior course of dealing or usage of trade. However, it demanded clear evidence that the parties agreed to arbitrate their disputes. In the Schubetex case the buyer had retained without objection seller's forms containing arbitration clauses in a number of transactions. The court found this not enough to show a course of dealing. It said that repeated use of an ineffective form does not show an agreement to arbitrate.

[36]For example, in Schulze and Burch Biscuit Co. v. Tree Top, Inc., 831 F.2d 709 (7th Cir. 1987), the court noted "Tree Top's agent Brady had sent a confirmation form containing the same arbitration provision to Schulze in each of the previous nine transactions he brokered between the two parties. Schulze had ample notice that the tenth confirmation would be likely to include an arbitration clause." Thus, Schulze could not claim "unfair surprise" when its past course of dealing created an obligation to arbitrate. See also Genesco, Inc. v. T. Kakiuchi & Co., Ltd., 815 F.2d 840 (2d Cir. 1986).

more than our customers or vendors, but the other party may have objected under U.C.C. § 2-207.

When we order goods, our form has an acknowledgment copy. When we sell goods we acknowledge purchase orders from our customer or sign their acknowledgment copies, but we stamp their acknowledgment saying that we accept the order in accordance with our terms. There is no real working out of each contract. It would be a hard task since there are 100s if not 1000s of orders passing through the office daily. We have never tried to sit down and negotiate a deal on a routine basis with each customer. It would be impossible.

However, we face special problems in one air conditioning application. We produce what we call a "computer room air conditioning unit." It is a top of the line system with a sophisticated humidity control. It costs a great deal more than a normal installation, but its very name and the way we sell it involves express if not implied warranties that it will protect computers and their software. Suppose one of our units were to fail without a backup available. Someone could lose an entire computer program and all the data. We can foresee this — indeed, the point of our expensive air conditioning installation is to avoid just this. I understand that in an as yet unreported case, a major airline lost 60 days of reservations when an auxiliary power unit for its computer went out. It sued the manufacturer and was successful. We must be concerned because our liability insurance does not cover this. It would cover a case where the unit blew up and the explosion damaged the property of a customer or it would cover water leaking from our unit that caused damage. But "passive" damage isn't covered and cannot be at a reasonable cost.

Our practice with this machine is as follows: if the customer's purchase order has no inconsistent terms, we will treat the situation as one where there is no notice of objection to our disclaimer which will be on our acknowledgment of the order. If the customer's document has an inconsistent requirement, then our sales representative must go to the customer and get a document that says our remedy limitation governs. The sales rep must do this personally and explain that the customer must get its own insurance. Even though there are a lot of equities in our favor since we are warning customers and who can expect us to guarantee a unit forever against any defect, we have had a lot of trouble getting these agreements. As a result of all this trouble, we are now offering an option to our customers. They can buy consequential damages protection. Our approach is to introduce this matter into the negotiations for the contract itself because the exposure is just too great. If the customer does not want to pay for insurance, great, but then don't expect us to underwrite a machine forever.

However, an important problem may remain. Suppose we sell our air conditioner to a mechanical contractor who then installs it in a building. Does the limitation and the opportunity to buy insurance help us now? We had a lawyer in our office work several days at a major university law library, but he could not find a case on the impact of the chance to buy insurance on a third party purchaser. How do you ward off liability to third parties you cannot negotiate with? As a practical matter, you cannot control how your machine is used and maintained, but it is hard to prove that the third party buyer's own fault produced the breakdown that destroyed a computer program and data being processed or stored.

Purchasing agents for mechanical contractors object to our attempts to negotiate contracts since they must bid on terms that come down the chain to them which they cannot modify. Many of them are thinly capitalized, and they will sign anything to get the job. If a job goes bad, they will go bankrupt and lose only a minute book and a corporate seal. As a result, they pay little attention to things that are vital to us.

Matters usually are different when you are dealing with industrial users of our equipment. They are used to being careful, and they see liability as just a simple business problem. You buy just as much warranty as you want. Moreover, typically if air conditioning fails, all that happens is that people get hot. Usually, all that results is unhappiness and not monetary damages. However, if one of our heat exchangers is used in a process where a great deal of money is involved, we try hard to negotiate questions of liability. Then we are careful.

In our role as purchaser, usually we get what we want without question. Our purchase order form is fairly innocuous. We feel that we will get plenty of rights under the U.C.C. if we ever have to look for them. We are a good customer, and other firms treat us well. Generally, all of our suppliers sign our acknowledgment of order form, and this binds them to our terms. In one case, we settled an argument with the president of a supplier by sending him a photocopy of our form with his signature on the bottom. On the other hand, we buy a lot of motors from General Electric, but GE won't just sign our acknowledgment of order form.

The following is taken from a major corporation's acknowledgment of order form, drafted in response to U.C.C. § 2-207:

If your order is an acceptance of a written proposal on the regular Company proposal form without the addition of any other terms and conditions of sale or any other modification, this document shall be treated solely as an acknowledgment of such order. If your order is not such an acceptance, then this document is not intended as an acceptance on the part of our Company, but an offer to provide the goods ordered solely in accordance with the following terms and conditions of sale. If we do not hear from you within two weeks from the date hereof, we shall rely upon your silence as an acceptance therewith. Your acceptance of goods shipped

by our Company on this order will in any event constitute an acceptance by
you of these terms and conditions of sale.

The drafting effort in the selling form attempts to solve the 2-207 dilemma by
making the buyer's silence an acceptance of the seller's terms and conditions.
Will this work? It introduces another constraint into the mix. In most situations
I cannot force you to speak to avoid making a contract with me. You can ignore
my letters and demands. However, this is not always true. The Restatement
(Second) Contracts § 72 states its version of the rule as follows:

> (1) Where an offeree fails to reply to an offer, his silence and inaction
> operate as an acceptance in the following cases and in no others:
>> (a) Where an offeree takes the benefit of offered services with reasonable
>> opportunity to reject them and reason to know that they were offered with
>> the expectation of compensation.
>> (b) Where the offeror has stated or given the offeree reason to understand
>> that assent may be manifested by silence or inaction, and the offeree in
>> remaining silent and inactive intends to accept the offer.
>> (c) Where because of previous dealings or otherwise, it is reasonable that
>> the offeree should notify the offeror if he does not intend to accept.
>
> (2) An offeree who does any act inconsistent with the offeror's ownership
> of offered property is bound in accordance with the offered terms unless
> they are manifestly unreasonable. But if the act is wrongful as against the
> offeror it is an acceptance only if ratified by him.

Does the Restatement validate the approach used in the selling forms quoted
above? Would the attempt to use silence, or the act of accepting goods, overcome
the provisions of U.C.C. § 2-207(3)? Recall § 2-206(1)(b). We will encounter
another aspect of the "silence as acceptance" rule in just a few pages, when we
discuss the "subject to approval of the home office" clause.

Sometimes, aggressive drafting by a merchant can backfire. Is the drafting
suggested by Lipman always a good idea? In *Salt River Project Agricultural
Improvement & Power District v. Westinghouse Electric Corp.*,[37] such drafting
caused problems for a buyer.

In the early 70's Westinghouse sold power plant equipment to SRP. In May
of 1976, there was an explosion causing $1,900,000 damage to the SRP power
plant. SRP alleged that the damage was caused by a malfunction of a $15,000
control device it had purchased from Westinghouse in 1973. It sued Westinghouse, alleging causes of action in strict products liability, breaches of express
and implied warranties, and negligence in design, manufacture and installation

---

[37]143 Ariz. 437, 694 P.2d 267 (Ct. App. 1983), *modified en banc*, 143 Ariz. 368, 694 P.2d
198 (1984).

of control device. Westinghouse moved for summary judgment on the strict products liability and warranty theory and partial summary judgment on the negligence theory which would limit SRP's recovery to $15,000, the price of the control device. The Court of Appeals affirmed the grant of summary judgment to Westinghouse.

The transaction under which the control unit was purchased involved a battle of the forms. SRP's purchase order stated:

> This Purchase Order becomes a binding contract, subject to the terms and conditions hereof, upon receipt by Buyer at its Purchasing Department of the acknowledgment copy hereof, signed by Seller, or upon commencement of performance by Seller, whichever occurs first. Acceptance of this Purchase Order must be made on its exact terms and if additional or different terms are proposed by Seller such response will constitute a counter-offer, and no contract shall come into existence without Buyer's written assent to the counter-offer. Buyer's acceptance of or payment for material shipped shall constitute acceptance of such material subject to the provisions herein, only, and shall not constitute acceptance of any counter-offer by Seller not assented to in writing.

Westinghouse returned an acknowledgment form. On its face it said "SEE REVERSE SIDE FOR TERMS AND CONDITIONS." There Westinghouse gave a warranty that the goods would be as described in the acknowledgment and would be free of defects in workmanship and materials. All other warranties were disclaimed in a provision printed in capital letters. It also limited its liability, stating that it would not be liable for consequential damages nor for more than the price of the product sold in this transaction.

The Court of Appeals found "as a matter of law that the exclusions of warranty and limitation of liability set forth in Westinghouse's Acknowledgment form are enforceable against SRP." It explained,

> Paragraph I of the "Terms and Conditions of [SRP's] Purchase Order" dictated how the SRP order could or could not ripen into a binding contract by expressly providing: (1) that it could only be accepted on its "exact terms"; (2) that any contrary document would constitute only a "counter-offer," and (3) that no contract would result from such an exchange unless SRP assented to the counter-offer in writing.
>
> The Westinghouse Acknowledgment did not accept SRP's Purchase Order on its "exact terms." The Acknowledgment's warranty exclusions and limitation of liability clauses are substantially different from those contained in the SRP Purchase Order; therefore, the Acknowledgment became a "counter-offer" as was contemplated by the express terms of SRP's Purchase Order. The pivotal question before use then is whether SRP accepted the Westinghouse counter-offer.

The record reveals that SRP failed to object to the changed terms contained in the Acknowledgment. SRP took delivery of the LMC, paid for it and made extended use of it.... A contract for the sale of goods may be made in any manner sufficient to show agreement, including *conduct* by both parties which recognizes the existence of a contract ... U.C.C. § 2-204(1). Furthermore, an offer to make a contract shall be construed as inviting acceptance in any manner and by any medium reasonable in the circumstances ... U.C.C. § 2-206(1). The "counter-offer" embodied in the Westinghouse Acknowledgment was accepted by SRP's conduct manifested through SRP's acceptance, payment for, and use of the LMC. This was true even in the absence of SRP's express assent. Where, as here, an offeree uses a seller's goods for his own purposes, that action will be deemed to constitute an acceptance of the terms of the counter-offer or offer.... While SRP's Purchase Order specifically states that any counter-offer can only be accepted by SRP when that acceptance is in writing, the SRP Purchase Order terms concerning the acceptance of the counter-offer do not control. Because SRP's original offer was rejected, the rejected offer could not govern how the new Westinghouse "counter-offer" could or would be accepted. Absent any limiting language in the counter-offer which would restrict the manner of acceptance, the acceptance of the counter-offer would be governed by the general provisions of the U.C.C....

We find no support for SRP's argument that ... U.C.C. § 2-207, the so-called "battle of the forms" provision, applies in this case because SRP's own Purchase Order rejected in advance its possible application. The SRP order distinctly stated that a responsive document containing any different or additional terms would operate as a counter-offer and could not be an acceptance of the SRP offer ... [§ 2-207] comes into play when there has in fact been a "definite and seasonable expression of acceptance." The Westinghouse Acknowledgment was not such an "expression of acceptance" because the SRP Purchase Order would not permit it to be one. Thus, the exchange of documents which occurred in this case is wholly outside the scope of ... [§ 2-207].

Professor Murray comments,

The first reaction to this bizarre situation may be to regard the buyer's draftsman as a classic illustration of one who, in Llewellyn's words, tried to "draft to the edge of the possible" and was hoisted on his own excessively drafted petard. Further reflection, however, reveals a more troubling analysis.... In *Salt River* the seller's form is not a counter-offer by its own language. Instead, it becomes a counter-offer by *unread* language in the buyer's purchase order. Section 2-207 has no application. *Salt River* thus provides the most recent example of the "last shot" principle.... [T]his kind of analysis may appear at any time because of chaotic judicial interpretations in this area.[38]

Would a careful application of § 2-207(3) produce a different result in the *Salt River* case? See Official Comment 7 to that section. Moreover, could we say that in this case a remedy limited to the amount of the purchase price "failed of its essential purpose" under § 2-719(2) because it "operates to deprive ... [the buyer] of the substantial value of the bargain?"

Assuming a good technical argument could be made for liability under §§ 2-207(3) and 2-719(2), did the court, nonetheless, reach the right result? Consider the policies sought by the courts in *McCarty v. Verson Allsteel Press Co.*, *Steiner v. Mobil Oil Corp.*, *Air Products & Chemicals, Inc. v. Fairbanks Morse, Inc.*, and *C. Itoh & Co. v. Jordan Intl. Co.* Would they favor Westinghouse in this case? Make a case that they would and that they would not. Remember the policies justifying the *Hadley v. Baxendale* rule in carrying out this exercise.

Should lawyers drafting form contracts be able to fashion forms which they know will protect their clients whatever the actual negotiations between representatives of the parties? In seeking the actual expectations of the parties, does U.C.C. § 2-207 undercut a lawyer's ability to structure transactions?

A large and distinguished law firm sends the following memorandum to its clients who are concerned about the battle of the forms and § 2-207:

> To distill a few rules ... your company *as a seller of goods* should do the following to the extent feasible:
>
> 1. DO NOT sign and return a copy of the buyer's purchase order.
>
> 2. Use your printed quotation and acknowledgment forms containing standard terms and conditions prepared or reviewed by your attorneys; makeshift forms and oral agreements not confirmed in writing may not provide your company with the substantial protections which it paid its attorneys to draft.
>
> 3. Obtain the buyer's acceptance to your company's terms by having the buyer sign and return a copy of your quotation or acknowledgment form, and refuse to proceed with the order until the signed form is received.
>
> 4. Use the quotation form as an offer. Even if the buyer does not sign and return a copy of it, you may receive a "clean" purchase order which does not object to your company's standard quotation terms and is consistent with the negotiated terms. Make sure, however, that the quoted terms are terms you can live with; *e.g.*, do not understate price or delivery dates.

---

[38]Murray, The Chaos of the "Battle of the Forms": Solutions, 39 Vanderbilt Law Review 1307 (1986).

5. Acknowledge in writing promptly all oral or written orders you intended to accept with the acknowledgment form. Promptly object to those which are unacceptable.

6. On telephone orders obtain the buyer's oral acknowledgment to your standard terms as part of the order. With the permission of the buyer, record the telephone conversation.

7. If objection is received to your company's terms and conditions, either expressly or by an inconsistent or conditional order form, do not proceed with the order until the objection is resolved to your satisfaction.

8. Flag all conditional purchase orders and notify the buyer promptly in writing that its order is not accepted and that buyer must sign and return the order on your company's form.

9. For repeat customers, enter into a signed override agreement which supersedes printed terms on the buyer's standard printed forms used for each other.

10. On large orders or orders fraught with undue risks in which the buyer's order form is well-drafted, conditional, and/or inconsistent with your company's terms of sale, negotiate compromise terms which will afford your company basic liability protections such as limiting warranties to your standard warranty, disclaiming implied warranties, avoiding consequential damages, and reducing the statute of limitations. If the buyer refuses to negotiate in good faith, consider rejecting the business or be prepared for the risks.

11. When in doubt about the conditional nature of a purchase order or confirmation form, treat it as such or seek advice of counsel.

Does this memorandum indicate that lawyers are able to fashion sound advice for clients despite all the questions we've raised about the applications of § 2-207?

d. Remember the United Nations Convention on Contracts for the International Sale of Goods

You should, at this point, have a fair appreciation for the difficulties both with the perceived problem which the Code sought to "solve" in § 2-207, and the problems with the solution. A certain measure of consternation would not be an unusual reaction upon a first reading of the previous pages. Unfortunately, the picture is just slightly more confusing still. Though you might face a dispute concerning your domestic client's purchase or sale of goods, requiring an analysis of incomplete or contradictory paperwork, the answer might not be in the Uniform Commercial Code. Another body of law might apply, such as the CISG.

The manner in which the CISG deals with the battle of the forms is different from the U.C.C. solution. Article 19(1) of the Convention is analogous to the common law "mirror image" rule. It provides that "a reply to an offer which purports to be an acceptance but contains additions, limitations or other modifications is a rejection of the offer and constitutes a counter offer." But, paragraph (2) states that unless the offeror objects, a reply is an acceptance if the additional or different terms do not materially alter the terms of the offer. The terms of a contract thus formed would incorporate the modifications included in the acceptance of the offer. Paragraph (3) goes on to furnish a non-exclusive list of terms that are considered material. These relate to price, quality and quantity of goods, place and time of delivery, means of settling disputes, and the extent of a party's liability. The impact of Article 19 is likely to be that fewer enforceable contracts will result under the Convention than under the U.C.C., so long as the parties have not performed. If there is performance, Article 18 provides that the "conduct of the offeree indicating assent to an offer is an acceptance." Therefore when one party has met its contractual obligation, the "last shot" doctrine would indicate what the terms of the contract are.

D. CLOSING THE DEAL BUT LEAVING A WAY OUT

Bargainers often want to close a deal but, at the same time, leave a way out. I want you committed, but I want to be able to call things off. I may not be sure whether it is a good deal, and I may want some time to think about it. I may want to control my salespeople who dealt with you. I may want to investigate your credit or my ability to perform. I may want time to seek financing to pay for my purchase, but I may not be sure I can find a lender willing to put up the money on acceptable terms.

If the parties are willing to put their cards on the table and have good legal advice, legally enforceable contracts can be created that achieve these purposes. An *option* is perhaps the easiest way to preserve a business opportunity while buying time. For example, a TV producer thinks she may want to fashion a television show or series based on a novel. She can buy an option from the novelist or the publisher. In exchange for money, the novelist or publisher agrees not to sell the rights to anyone else for a specified time. On the other hand, a bargainer can make its performance *subject to a condition*. We can agree we have a contract provided I am awarded a government contract.

As always, things can be more complicated. A common problem is created by a practice sellers have long used to limit the authority of their salespeople to close contracts.[39] The sales person calls on a customer and writes an order on the seller's standard form. The customer and the sales person sign, and the customer is likely to think that the deal is closed. However, the form states "[a]ny quotation by Seller on the face hereof or on any attachment hereto is merely an invitation for an offer from potential customer(s). All resulting customer offers

---

[39]See Cole-McIntyre-Norfleet Co. v. Holloway, 141 Tenn. 679, 214 S.W. 817 (1919).

(orders) are thus subject to acceptance at Seller's offices at the address shown on the face here, before any contract is formed." The customer, thinking there is a deal, is not likely to back out, but the seller can decide whether or not to accept the order. We can view this as a condition, but it is a condition that goes to creating a contract. Furthermore, it is a condition left in the hands of the seller. It has said no more than it will perform if it wants to.

Such clauses usually work as their drafters plan. There are many cases saying that if an order is subject to acceptance at the home office, no contract is formed until such acceptance is given.[40] However, these clauses raise all the problems of duty to read fine print, and even the battle of the forms. Can the buyer reasonably rely on such a transaction when the seller has not accepted its order? In some situations sellers try to have it both ways. They want buyers to think they are bound, but they want the power to back out if it suits their purposes. Do sellers have a duty to approve or reject orders within a reasonable time? Can the seller's conduct create an obligation even when it has not accepted the order?

HILLS v. WILLIAM B. KESSLER, INC.

41 Wash. 2d 42, 246 P.2d 1099 (1952)

MALLERY, J. The plaintiff, Hill's, Inc., ordered thirty-four men's suits from the defendant, using a printed form supplied by defendant through its salesman.

The printed form provided that the order would not become a binding contract until it had been accepted by an authorized officer of the defendant at its office in Hammonton, New Jersey.

The defendant's salesman procured the order on May 16, 1950, and on May 23, 1950, the defendant, by form letter, advised the plaintiff that "You may be assured of our very best attention to this order." What occurred next is shown by the trial court's finding of fact:

> ... but notwithstanding, on or about July 18, 1950, defendant intentionally and deliberately, at the instigation of a large retail store selling defendant's clothing in the downtown Seattle area, wrongfully cancelled said order and breached its agreement with plaintiff to deliver said suits as ordered, or at all. That at the time defendant cancelled said order and breached its agreement, the period for placing orders for delivery of fall suits had passed, and it was impossible for plaintiff to thereafter procure comparable suits from any other source to meet its fall trade....

---

[40]See, *e.g.*, Foremost Pro Color, Inc. v. Eastman Kodak Co., 703 F.2d 534 (9th Cir. 1983); Meekins-Bamman Prestress, Inc. v. Better Construction, Inc., 408 So.2d 1071 (Fla. App. 1982).

Thereupon, plaintiff brought this action for loss of profits in the amount of a 66⅔ percent markup aggregating $815.83.

From a judgment in favor of the plaintiff, the defendant appeals.

The defendant contends that its letter of May 23, 1950, in which it said "You may be assured of our very best attention to this order," was not an acceptance of the plaintiff's order.

In *Bauman v. McManus*, 75 Kan. 106, 89 P. 15, 18, 10 L.R.A.,N.S., 1138, the court said:

> ... The promise that the order shall receive prompt and *careful* attention seems to imply something more than that the manufacturers will quickly and cautiously investigate the advisability of accepting it. The care they might expend in that direction — in looking up the defendants' financial standing, for instance — is not presumably a matter in which any one but themselves would be greatly interested. The engagement to use care seems more naturally to relate to the manner of filling the order than to the settling of a doubt whether to fill it at all. The expression of thanks for the favor has some tendency in the same direction. We incline strongly to the opinion that the letter standing by itself was as effectual to close a contract as though in set phrase it had said that the goods would be shipped; that to permit any other construction to be placed upon it would be to countenance the studied use of equivocal expressions, with a set purpose, if an advantage may thereby be derived, to keep the word of promise to the ear and break it to the hope.

Notwithstanding that the *Bauman* case is exactly in point, it is not necessary to rely upon it exclusively, for the reason that the intention of the defendant to accept the offer is shown by subsequent correspondence with the plaintiff in this case.

On July 18, 1950, defendant wrote plaintiff the following letter:

> *This is to inform you we find it will be impossible to ship the Fall order which you placed with Mr. Jacobus on May 16, order #8585. We dislike very much having to inform you of this, but we trust that you will understand when we say that because of previous commitments to other stores in town it is necessary to cancel this order.*
>
> *We are certainly sincerely sorry if this action on our part inconveniences you at all.*

This letter recognizes the existence of a contract, which it undertakes to cancel.

The defendant contends that the correspondence in this case was not signed by an authorized officer of the defendant corporation. The treasurer of the corporation testified that Glenda Fitting was a clerk in the office; was not an officer of the corporation; was not authorized to accept orders; and that the only persons who were authorized to accept orders were the president, the secretary, and the treasurer.

From a large amount of correspondence in this record, all signed by Glenda Fitting, which the trial court examined, it was justified in not believing the foregoing testimony. The testimony does not go so far as to make out that Glenda Fitting intruded herself into the affairs of the defendant corporation without its knowledge or over its protest.

In such a case, " ... where a principal has, by his voluntary act, placed an agent in such a situation that a person of ordinary prudence conversant with business usages and the nature of the particular business is justified in assuming that such agent has authority to perform a particular act and deals with the agent upon that assumption, the principal is estopped as against such third person from denying the agent's authority; he will not be permitted to prove that the agent's authority was, in fact, less extensive than that with which he apparently was clothed.... " 2 Am.Jur. 86, Agency, § 104.

The defendant contends that the court erred in allowing loss of profits as the measure of damages, in this case, and complains that the plaintiff made no effort to procure similar suits elsewhere by way of mitigating the damages. The plaintiff, however, showed that the cost of going east to fill such an order would have been greater than his lost profits, and, hence, would not have been justified.

We think that the defendant understood that the plaintiff was purchasing the thirty-four suits for resale at a 66 2/3 per cent markup; that the order was specifically placed for the plaintiff's fall trade; and that the suits, of the defendant, were of a quality that was unobtainable in the west. Loss of profits, in such a case, is a correct measure of damages....

The judgment is affirmed. [Concurrence by Donworth, J. omitted.]

NOTES AND QUESTIONS

1. *Background from the briefs*: The briefs submitted to the court clarify the parties' arguments and some facts in the case. The lawyers for the manufacturer (William B. Kessler, Inc.) argued that the "letter is merely a courteous acknowledgment of the order, and an assurance to respondent that its order will receive attention." They continued, saying,

> This letter was apparently written immediately upon receipt of the order without any time having elapsed which would have permitted appellant to consider the order and to decide whether it should be accepted or rejected. Mr. Chester Kessler, the treasurer and sales-manager of appellant, testified that the above letter was a form letter which was sent to each customer upon receipt of an order before the order was processed through the Credit, Manufacturing, Sales and other departments for the purpose of making a decision as to the acceptance or rejection of the order. He further testified that it usually takes about two weeks to process an order and arrive at a

decision as to the acceptance or rejection of same in the case of appellant's regular accounts, or where there are special problems, it would take a considerable length of time to assemble the information on which the decision would be based.

The order, among other things, constituted a request for the extension of credit by the provision "terms net 30 days." It is inconceivable that appellant would have accepted the order immediately upon its receipt without having had an opportunity to investigate the credit of respondent.

What argument(s) was appellant making? Why is it relevant that it is "inconceivable that appellant would have accepted the order immediately upon its receipt without having had an opportunity to investigate the credit of respondent"?

2. *A cross reference to agency law*: Much of the debate in the briefs concerned the power of Glenda Fitting to bind William B. Kessler, Inc. to contracts. Agents can be given express authority to make contracts, but they also can have apparent authority if the principal is responsible for putting them in a position where others reasonably will assume that they have this power. The reasons for the rule are similar to those underlying an objective theory of contract; in an exchange-based society, people find it easier to deal in light of reasonable assumptions and appearances.

The trial court found that Chester Kessler, the manufacturer's treasurer and sales-manager, had testified falsely in several respects. The judge said "and then the question is whether he told the truth or not in regard to the authority of Glinda Fitting. And it is my opinion that he didn't tell the truth under oath in that respect." Notice that the court could have found that Fitting had apparent authority since she signed a wide variety of correspondence directed to William B. Kessler's customers and there was no indication on the letter of her position in the company.

3. *Silence as acceptance*: "Subject to approval at the home office" clauses raise the classic problem of "silence" as acceptance of an offer. The older black letter rule was that silence could not be taken as an acceptance. This position seems to have been an over-generalization of the idea that I cannot force you to act to ward off a contract. Suppose I park my 1978 Chevrolet Nova in your driveway and send you the keys with a letter saying that unless you reject my offer within three days, I will deem you to have agreed to buy the car for $1,000. Individualistic contract law refused to allow me to force you to act; your inaction would not taken by courts to be an agreement to buy the car.

However, courts were never easy with a rule saying that "silence" never could be an acceptance. On the one hand, a person receiving such an offer could rely on it and get hurt. On the other hand, a person receiving such an offer could try to play it both ways. If she or he desired to enforce the contract, inaction could be called an acceptance. If she or he desired not to be bound, inaction could be called a rejection. The cases cannot be explained in terms of whether silence was a manifestation of acceptance — one must turn to other factors.

For example, in *Kukuska v. Home Mutual Hail-Tornado Ins. Co.*,[41] a farmer filed an application for insurance on July 3; the insurance company gave notice of rejection of the application at 11:00 a.m. on August 1st; and the crops were destroyed by a storm later that afternoon. The Court found the insurance company liable. It said that three theories support such a conclusion: silence as acceptance; an implied contract to act promptly; and a duty arising from the franchise created by being licensed as an insurance company in the state. The Court observed that, "[i]f the insurer is under such a duty and fails to perform the duty within a reasonable time and, as a consequence, the applicant sustains damage, it is not vastly important that the legal relationship be placed in a particular category."

Later, in *Sell v. G.E. Supply Corp.*,[42] the same court found that inaction had not created liability. The plaintiff applied to become a distributor for Hotpoint refrigerators and ordered five. The order, written on a G.E. Supply Corporation form, was "subject to approval" by G.E. Supply. Seventeen days later, General Electric Contracts Corporation notified plaintiff that it would purchase his customers' installment payment contracts. However, nineteen days later plaintiff received a telegram saying that the application to become a distributor had been disapproved. It explained that there was a shortage of refrigerators, and it had decided to allocate production to the existing distributors rather than add new ones. The Supreme Court of Wisconsin, finding no liability, pointed out that there was a good reason for rejecting the application, the decision was relatively prompt, and plaintiff's reliance was not particularly great.

The "silence cannot be acceptance" rule was further shaken in *Morris F. Fox & Co. v. Lisman*.[43] Here plaintiff made an offer on a form drafted by defendant which stated that a contract was "subject to approval at home office." Defendant considered the deal and plaintiff's credit and made a note on plaintiff's offer indicating that defendant had accepted the contract. However, this letter was filed away, and no notice of acceptance was ever given to plaintiff. While other things were communicated by defendant to plaintiff, the court stressed that the letter showed defendant's intention to accept and found that a contract had been made. Compare *International Filter Co. v. Conroe Gin, Ice and Lt. Co.*,[44] reaching a similar result.

All in all, cases such as *Hills v. Wm. B. Kessler, Inc.* and the three Wisconsin decisions just discussed suggest that some courts have been willing to regulate the reservation of a right of approval after the business adopting the practice creates

---

[41] 204 Wis. 166, 235 N.W. 403 (1931).

[42] 227 Wis. 242, 278 N.W. 442 (1938).

[43] 208 Wis. 1, 237 N.W. 267, 240 N.W. 809, 242 N.W. 679 (1932).

[44] 277 S.W. 631 (Tex. Civ. App. 1925).

a situation where an applicant can be hurt by reliance, particularly when the one reserving the right does not use it for legitimate business purposes or, as in the *Morris F. Fox & Co.* case, where the legitimate business purposes of the procedure have been served. Compare Restatement (Second) Contracts § 72, *supra.*

4. *Estoppel and good faith in bargaining*: In *Iacono v. Toll Brothers*,[45] the plaintiffs sued for specific performance of a contract to purchase real property. Defendants were developers. They listed units in Colts Neck Estates with a real estate broker. The broker sold buyers a house to be built by the developers on a contract form provided by the developers. This form provided:

> This Agreement has been obtained by Seller's salesman or agent who has no authority to bind Seller to this Agreement. This Agreement shall not be binding upon Seller unless signed by Seller within thirty (30) calendar days from the date below. Otherwise, the deposit money will be returned to the Buyer without interest....

Buyers conceded that they were aware of the clause and understood it. They paid a deposit, but defendants never signed the form. Almost two months after buyers signed the contract, defendants notified them there was no deal. The trial court found that a binding contract had been formed. The appellate court reversed this judgment. However, it remanded the case for findings necessary to determine whether the defendants were equitably estopped. The defendants had not returned the deposit, and they had waited almost two months before writing plaintiffs rejecting the agreement of sale. Plaintiffs requested several modifications in the design of the house defendants were to build, and defendants agreed to these changes. Plaintiffs tendered checks in partial payment for construction charges which defendants accepted and deposited. The defendants' construction superintendent referred to the house as "your home" or "your new home." Plaintiffs were not in the real estate market looking for another house at a time of sharply rising real estate values.

The court said there were a number of unresolved issues:

> [W]hether Toll Brothers' [the defendants] silence or conduct or both following April 13, 1985 [30 days after the agreement was signed by the buyer] induced reliance by plaintiffs that Toll Brothers had accepted the agreement of sale; whether such reliance, if found factually, was reasonable and in good faith in the light of plaintiffs' concessions that they knew of and understood the import of the home office acceptance clause in the agreement of sale; whether plaintiffs, relying upon Toll Brothers' silence or conduct or both, changed their position to their detriment by staying out of the rising

---

[45]217 N.J.Super. 475, 526 A.2d 256 (1987).

real estate market as purchasers for a significant time interval after April 13, 1985.

Plaintiffs would be entitled to judgment on remand only if the determination of all the foregoing fact questions is in the affirmative. If so, there should be a further factual determination as to whether the Statute of Frauds was met.

Notice that while the buyers and the developers may not have entered a binding contract, they did enter a continuing relationship. Can we explain the court's decision in terms of a duty of good faith in negotiations? That is, the developers would have several acceptable reasons for not wanting real estate brokers to have the power to bind them to contracts. For example, the developers had only a certain number of lots, and various brokers might sell more than the total available. Developers might want to investigate the credit of buyers or institutions providing financing for buyers. However, developers also might want to be able to reject buyers in order to discriminate on the grounds of race or religion. In the *Iacono* case, the buyers argue that the developers tried to back out so they could benefit from a rapid rising housing market. Can we view these cases finding at least a possible liability despite subject to approval clauses as American versions of *culpa in contrahendo*? See Kessler and Fine, *supra*.

Chapter 7

THE DEAL IS CLOSED — BUT WHAT IS IT?

A. INTRODUCTION: WHAT'S COMING?

A great many judicial opinions deal with giving meaning to contracts. This suggests there are two important lawyering tasks that students should know something about: first, you should know how to write contracts that are sufficiently clear to avoid unnecessary disputes about their meaning. Second, you should know something about how courts give meaning to those contracts that come before them. Obviously, these questions are related.

Law schools have not done well teaching about either of these problems. Teaching contract drafting is difficult.[1] Many, if not most, Americans are not skilled writers or speakers of English. Few students come to law school able to state what they mean and no more or less. Probably we have to play the game to learn how. That is, we have to write, have our drafts ripped apart, redraft in light of criticism and so on. This requires individual instruction which is not generally available — certainly not in most introductory contract courses. Law schools are funded largely on the assumption that a single teacher armed only with a case book can instruct 50 to 100 students or more. Legal writing classes, which tend to be underfinanced, rarely devote their resources to contract drafting.

Law school contracts courses do not do much better in teaching how courts give meaning to contracts. The rules of construction are vague. While students might draw analogies, each case turns on its own facts. Furthermore, many cases involving interpretation age poorly. Lawyers draft around a problem in later contracts so that the original case offers solutions to a problem unlikely to occur again.

While some lawyers are masters at contract drafting, many do a poor job. For example, Suchan and Scott[2] studied 196 collective bargaining agreements between managements and unions. They used three formulas to test how understandable these documents were — Rudolph Flesch's Reading Ease Formula, Robert Gunning's Fog Index, and Farr-Jenkins-Patterson's Reading Ease Index. These tests use sentence and clause length as well as the number of single-and polysyllabic words in a passage as variables to measure readability. According

---

[1]See Felsenfeld and Siegel, Writing Contracts in Plain English (West Publishing Co. 1981) for an excellent collection of materials.

[2]Suchan and Scott, Unclear Contract Language and Its Effect on Corporate Culture, 29 Business Horizons 20 (1986).

to the Flesch and Farr-Jenkins-Patterson formulas, 95 to 99 percent of these collective bargaining agreements would be "difficult" or "very difficult" to understand. The Gunning Fog Index indicated that these contracts had an average score of 18.73. "What this figure means is that the rank and file would need more than 18 years of education — a college degree plus two years of graduate school — to unscramble a typical union-management agreement."

Suchan and Scott seek to explain why collective bargaining agreements are so hard to read. They suggest that those who draft the contracts may inhabit different semantic worlds from rank and file workers. "Accustomed to reading drawn-out sentences filled with passive constructions and polysyllabic, Latin-based words, negotiators have little trouble translating the 'cognizants,' 'as-certains,' and 'hereinafters' into language they can understand." Those who draft contracts also may take the easy way out and copy stock clauses from form books. The legalese and convoluted sentences of earlier contracts set the standard for appropriate style. People may want these documents to look legal so others will honor them.[3] Few drafters consider the audience for the agreements and ask if they can understand them. At times, drafters deliberately use unclear language. Those negotiating may want to avoid being pinned down on an issue or may think it is better to agree to something rather than not agree at all. If I'm too clear about a point, the other side may object or may call off the entire transaction. On the other hand, those negotiating may not be clear on what they are trying to say. Contracts often reflect the rushed and confused thinking of fatigued negotiators. Skilled negotiators may not be skilled drafters. Those who are insecure about their writing ability often try to hide behind jargon, complicated sentences, and endless paragraphs. People write "to *impress* rather than *express*, often with disastrous results."

Collective bargaining agreements may be extreme examples of a common problem. While we think that labor negotiations are conducted between management and the union, many different people are involved. For example, the Vice President for Labor Relations may negotiate the contract, working under guidelines set by the Chief Executive Officer and the Board of Directors. The actual drafting will be done by management lawyers. Workers are represented by their union. They, too, will have their lawyers. To make matters more complicated, the lawyers for one or both sides may write primarily for officials of regulatory agencies or judges who might review the document in the future.

---

[3]Lawyers know that some clients, even sophisticated ones, are disappointed if a lawyer drafts a contract or will in simple and clear language. They wonder what they got for their money. They mistakenly think that anyone could have written a clear document in simple language. They want "whereas clauses," and "parties of the first part" along with a dash of legal Latin so that the document will have magical properties. Of course, in some situations the client may be right. If others honor a document because it looks legal and thus is something out of the ordinary, then this is a form of power. As always, a major part of a lawyer's stock in trade is judgment about when to do what.

Furthermore, labor negotiations are more adversarial than many business bargains. There is some incentive to try to slip things past the other side.

When a question arises during the life of the collective bargain, the document may be read by a foreman, a shop steward or a rank and file worker. Many times these people will ignore the text and work matters out on a common sense basis. This will create expectations and working interpretations of the real deal which may or may not reflect what is written on paper.

Commercial contracts between business people may share many features of collective bargains. Those who perform a deal often are not the ones who wrote it. People often copy form clauses to save time. Businesspeople dictate documents and don't revise them. They use vague words to deal with problems they think are unlikely to occur, or don't want to call attention to, or to avoid upsetting the other side. Language which makes sense in one context may be ambiguous when it is applied to a problem the drafter did not foresee. Furthermore, English is not a precise language. It is filled with synonyms with different shades of meaning. Ordinary conversation relies heavily on context and common patterns. There often is a wide gap between what I said and what I meant.

This is the reality lawyers and judges confront when they have to give meaning to words and phrases in contracts. Remember what you know about communication when you read that courts interpret contracts to find "the intention of the parties" or to find the "plain meaning" of a writing. Remember to ask who is going to read what *you* write and what they are likely to make of it. It is not always easy to communicate to judges and lawyers. It is harder to communicate to those unaccustomed to reading legal documents.

As you will see, there are two related issues in all this material. First, we can ask how judges give meaning to words. Second, we must confront rules that define what judges can look at in this process. We can think of the issues as how do judges interpret contracts and what are the boundaries of the communications to be interpreted? For example, suppose buyer and seller sign a written contract. Seller tells buyer that clause 28 doesn't apply to him. Will courts read only the written document or will they take account of this inconsistent statement? For now, all we can say is that it depends. This problem is put in the category called the parol evidence rule.[4] Long ago, Professor Thayer commented, "[f]ew things are darker than this [the parol evidence rule], or fuller of subtle difficulties."[5] We will try to shed some light on this dark subject, but the subtle difficulties remain.

We begin our discussions of interpretation, and of the parol evidence rule, by reproducing excerpts from several articles. A first reading should give you an idea about the nature of the problems involved in giving meaning to words in a written document. You also should begin to recognize common judicial responses

---

[4]Do not spell parol "parole."

[5]Thayer, A Preliminary Treatise on Evidence 390 (1898).

to these problems and difficulties with them. Cases are offered to serve as examples of what you have read.

B. INTERPRETATION AND CONSTRUCTION OF CONTRACTUAL LANGUAGE

The Interpretation and Construction of Contracts
Edwin W. Patterson[6]

I. Interpretation, Construction, and Inference Distinguished

A. *Interpretation* What is interpretation? It is the process of endeavoring to ascertain the meaning or meanings of symbolic expressions used by the parties to a contract, or of their expressions in the formative stage of arriving at the creation of one or more legally obligatory promises. Since most contracts are temporary in their effects, the process of interpretation often consists merely of the direct application  of the symbols used to the factual situation that gives rise to controversy. For example, if *S*, a farmer, has agreed for a stated price to sell and deliver to *B*, a grocer, four dozen egg-plants, and on the appointed day *S* tenders as his performance to *B* four dozen eggs, an objective observer could, without formulating any *general* conception of the genus and species of "egg-plant," give a *particular* interpretation that the tender was not within the terms of the contract; and this interpretation might well support a *particular* legal evaluation that *B* was under no duty to accept the eggs in performance, and possibly that *S* has breached his contractual duty. Interpretation, then, goes on without the framing of *generalities* about the symbols, such as the definitions one finds in a dictionary of the Anglo-American language. These "definitions" are synonyms (logical equivalents) of the terms defined, expressed in other words (*i.e.*, other than the word to be defined) that are, in turn, to be defined elsewhere, or, as "primitive terms," left undefined (in a particular realm of discourse).

However, the process of interpretation of a contract may be used to establish a *general* meaning of the symbols used. This may occur in the case of a long-term contract (*e.g.*, a 99-year lease) or a contract affecting the interests of many people, such as a collective labor agreement, or a standardized contract used by a large number of individuals or corporations. Among the oldest examples of the

---

last is the British marine insurance contract, the quaint language of which has been judicially interpreted often enough to establish a body of esoteric meanings familiar only to specialists....

The process of interpretation may be applied to the spoken words or other symbolic utterances expressed by the party, or his authorized agent, as terms of an oral contract, or it may be applied to the written (handwritten, typed, printed, or otherwise inscribed) words of a written contract, or to an offer or purported acceptance, in the formative stage of contracting. Interpretation may be aided by the nonverbal conduct of one or both parties, as, for example, the depositing in a United States mailbox of a written, signed, addressed, and stamped letter which expressly states an acceptance of an offer. The offeree's conduct in mailing the letter is a "manifestation of intent" to make a contract, which, coupled with the terms of the letter and of the previous offer, may constitute the formation of a contract. Mailing is a manifestation of intent, under the circumstances sketched above, yet it is not by itself a *symbolic* act, as that term is commonly understood. It is not symbolic in the same way that the fall of the auctioneer's hammer is symbolic of the words "offer accepted." We shall need to explore further the distinction between symbolic conduct and nonsymbolic conduct from which a legally significant *inference* may be drawn.

B. *Construction* Construction, which may, in this writer's opinion, be usefully distinguished from interpretation, is a process by which legal consequences are made to follow from the terms of the contract and its more or less immediate context, and from a legal policy or policies that are applicable to the situation. Construction may be applicable along with interpretation, or it may take over when interpretation wholly or partly fails. Take three possible cases:

1. An action has been brought upon an alleged contract which has vague and meaningless expressions of what would normally be important terms; *e.g.*, the quality and quantity of goods are vague, and so is the price. In such a case the symbolic conduct will ordinarily be adjudged to be too indefinite to be enforced. "The court cannot make a contract for the parties," is the basic policy. Yet if goods have been delivered and accepted, the context may show that no gift was intended, as the recipient knew, and the court will construe (imply) a duty to pay the reasonable value of the goods. The policy seems to be to prevent unjust enrichment, yet the duty construed is contractual, not quasi-contractual.

2. An action has been brought by *P* upon a written contract, partly printed and partly typed, the terms of which are chosen and drafted by *D* defendant. On interpretation of the terms it appears that a crucial term, such as a condition precedent of *D*'s promise, is ambiguous, that is, has two possible meanings, one of which is more favorable in its effect to *D*, and the other of which is more favorable to *P*. If the latter interpretation will signify that *P* has fulfilled the condition, then the court will usually construe the crucial term *contra proferentem*, that is, unfavorably to the party drafting the contract, *D*, and favorably to the other party, *P*. This construction may be based upon the

inference that D in drafting the instrument intended only the meaning favorable to P, otherwise it would have excluded that meaning by more explicit drafting; or it may be based upon a policy of equalizing the inequality of the one-sided bargain. This principle of construction is frequently applied to insurance contracts (where sometimes, it seems, the court conjures up the ambiguity) and to other "contracts of adhesion."

3. An action is brought by P upon a contract which contains an unconscionable condition of D's contractual duty or an unconscionable limitation or extension of the measure of damages for a breach by D. In such a case the court may, under exceptional circumstances, and in direct denial of the meaning that interpretation properly would give, construe the unconscionable term to be unenforceable in this action and in this sense "void." Here construction overrides interpretation. Such uses of construction are exceptional.

Other examples of construction of conditions will be given below; yet the process is inexhaustible.

Can we say that interpretation is a matter of "pure fact" and construction a matter of "pure law"? No, because interpretation (of a *legal* instrument) is meaningless without some one or more possible legal consequences as ends-in-view; and because construction does not operate without regard to some facts, including not only the terms of the contract but also its transactional context. The latter, be it noted, is properly available for use in the process of construction, but part of it is ordinarily excluded in the process of interpretation of a contract embodied in a single written memorial by a legal doctrine known as the "parol evidence" rule. Aside from the utterances of the parties that are not expressed in the written memorial, the "surrounding circumstances," it is commonly said by courts, may be considered by the court in interpreting the written contract. Since all circumstances are "surrounding," we avoid tautology by referring to the transactional circumstances or, more broadly, the transactional context.

C. *Inference* Inference of fact plays an important part in the interpretation and construction of contracts. An example was given above — the inference of intent to accept from the offeree's dropping in the mailbox a letter expressing an acceptance. The act of mailing is not a symbolic expression, yet is a part of a sequence of conduct which manifests an intention to accept. Another example is the process by which the court infers some purpose or purposes of the parties and then interprets the language of the contract in such a way as to be consistent with the purpose or purposes. Still another example is the so-called "practical construction" of the parties; that is, their conduct during the course of performance may support inferences as to the meaning of language in the contract, or as to their intentions with respect to gaps and omissions in the contract. Here inference may aid either a genuine interpretation, or a policy of avoiding unjust enrichment or of favoring the creation of a contract, or it may aid both.

D. *Court and Jury* Even in a case in which a jury is the trier of issues of fact, the interpretation and construction of a written contract is within the exclusive province of the judge. While the judge may be called upon, in this process, to determine several issues of "fact," such as those inferences referred to above, the relevant dictionaries, and relevant circumstances, yet the meaning of a written instrument is often called "a question of law." This characterization of the rule is a surviving fiction (or semi-fiction). The continuance of the rule is justified by the judge's superior equipment — his education and legal experience — to interpret written instruments and to give them reliability. As a determination of law, the trial judge's interpretation of the meaning of a written contract is not as conclusive upon an appellate court as his "findings of fact" would be and hence may be set aside as an "error of law."

Where the contract is partly oral and partly written, the judge may instruct the jury as to the meaning of the written part and, with other instructions, leave the remaining issues of interpretation to be determined by the jury. If the jury is directed to bring in a general verdict (*i.e.*, for the plaintiff or for the defendant), it may in so doing exercise its views of jury equity and thus impair the reliability of written instruments. This possibility may account for the reluctance of courts to admit parol evidence and other extrinsic aids to interpretation, and for their adherence to the "plain meaning" of the contract.

E. *Reasons for Distinction* The distinction between interpretation and construction of contracts has been doubted or rejected, principally, it is believed, for two reasons: First, because it is difficult or impossible to draw the line between the two in many problematic cases, and secondly, because many courts in many cases have ignored the distinction. However, as exemplified in the three illustrations given above it is believed by the present writer to be a workable and useful distinction for the following reasons, among others:

1. To say that all determinations by a judge of the meaning of a contract are *merely* his legal evaluations is at least a gross exaggeration. The judge (or judges) must start with the symbols (and other manifestations of intention) expressed by the parties in order to arrive at a proper judicial determination. If every "contract" were "interpreted" as if it were a (signed) blank sheet of paper, the usefulness of contract would vanish. The careful drafting of contracts is commonly rewarded by smooth performance, or by an expected and justified judicial interpretation. When the court knows what the symbols mean but regards this meaning as "unconscionable," they go beyond the meaning of symbols and enforce a special kind of legal policy. Of this, too, the canny draftsman should be aware. In ordinary cases the meanings of symbols and the manifestations of intention provide the operative facts upon which the legal consequences depend.

2. An expert witness may be called to testify to the meaning of a term in a trade or technical dictionary. But no expert can be called to tell the court when it should find a term or a clause unfair or unconscionable. That is the court's exclusive function.

3. A trial court's construction of a contract may be set aside by an appellate court as an error of law; yet its finding as to the meaning of a trade or technical term would more likely be deemed conclusive on appeal.

II. "Plain Meaning" and the Several Dictionaries

The ideal result that legal draftsmen seek to attain and that judicial interpreters commonly seek to find in a written contract is that a judge should be able, by reading the contract without lifting his eyes from the page, to determine its one and only "true" meaning in relation to the issues being litigated. Once this "true" meaning has been ascertained, no other evidence should be permitted to fritter away the meaning and thus make written contracts unreliable. What I have called the "true" meaning is transformed into "plain meaning" in the standard set of maxims of interpretation. In accordance with this ideal, if the court finds a "plain meaning" of the relevant terms of the writing, it will exclude various kinds of proof, discussed in this and the next two sections, which would contradict or qualify the plain meaning. If, however, the written contract on its face contains an ambiguity, then evidence extrinsic to the contract will be admitted....

How seriously ... should one take the "plain meaning" rule that is stated in many judicial opinions? Seriously enough to induce the counselor to draft every contract as clearly as he knows how and as the other party (or perhaps his own client) will let him. While he can not always foresee the contingencies that will arise to frustrate his best efforts, he may still be able to state clearly the rights and duties, powers and privileges, risks and immunities that will arise under the terms of the contract. He cannot exclude all latitude of interpretation of terms, yet, to quote the words of a brilliant judge, [Learned Hand] "there is a critical breaking point ... beyond which no language can be forced...." This breaking point is the limit of "plain meaning." It serves to fulfill one or more of the basic purposes of the law of contracts.

Yet the plain meaning rule must be taken with reservations. The first one is that it does not apply in case of an "ambiguity," which may be cleared up by extrinsic aids; only the courts can say when there is an ambiguity. A second one, less important, is that a "plain meaning" provision may be deemed unconscionable and thus unenforceable. A third one is more important than either of these: the term of a contract that at first sight seems to have only one "plain" meaning may have two to a dozen meanings in a standard or universal dictionary of the vernacular. From among these the court, if it looks at the universal dictionary, has to *select* the one meaning that is "plainly" *appropriate* in this case. Usually, however, the crucial interpretation is not dependent on a single word but is dependent upon a phrase or a sentence which is not listed in a dictionary and to which the court gives its own interpretation.

A fourth reservation to the "plain meaning" rule is that a local, trade, or other special usage may give to a term a meaning very different from that given to it by the common or universal dictionary, and when one reads the contract terms with the proof of the usage, of which both parties knew or should have known, the appropriate meaning is no longer merely the "plain" one. A striking example is the old English case involving a suit by a lessee of a rabbit warren against his lessor, who by the terms of the written lease agreed to pay the lessee, at the expiration of the lease, "£60 per thousand" of rabbits left in the warren, and the lessor proved that by local usage, of which the lessee had reason to know, the term "thousand" meant "1,200," so that for 19,200 rabbits, the lessee was entitled to recover just 16 times £60. It is not easy to match this case with one in which the contract term, unaided by a special usage, had as "plain" a meaning as "thousand," and the special usage had a "plain" and plainly contradictory meaning. Does the admission of the usage for such a purpose contradict the late Judge Learned Hand's statement that there is a "breaking point" beyond which no language can be forced? And what of the famous dictum of Judge Oliver Wendell Holmes, Jr.? "It would open too great risks if evidence were admissible to show that when they [the parties] said "five hundred feet" they agreed that it should mean "one hundred inches," or that "Bunker Hill monument" should signify the "Old South Church."

The late Professor John H. Wigmore, who first developed the notion that there are several "dictionaries," besides the ordinary lexicon, in which symbols may have meaning (*e.g.,* trade or technical usages), apparently thought there was a contradiction. Yet Learned Hand certainly, and Holmes probably, was referring to the latitude of discretionary interpretation of words taken in their "ordinary dictionary" sense. This restrictive view would, it is believed, be appropriate if, as in the case of a recorded deed to land, third persons had innocently relied upon the ordinary meaning. If a trade or local usage can be proved and if it was known to both parties at the time when the written instrument was signed, then a different case is presented and the special usage should control.... [For example] a promise by *R*, a seller of books by subscription, was to pay his salesman, *E*, a commission on "every order," yet *R* was allowed to prove that "every order" meant, in the subscription book business, "every order where five volumes were taken and paid for by the subscriber." In such cases there is a substantial variance between the contract term in its ordinary sense and the usage meaning; yet the contract term does not manifest an intention not to be "bound" by the usage. On the other hand, an extreme case, such as the "1,000 rabbits" case, might be taken to express such an intention, and the court should require stricter than usual proof that there was such a linguistic usage, that the objector may fairly be charged with knowledge of it, and that the contract term was not intended to exclude it.

If the interpretation of the contract requires ascertainment of the meaning of a scientific or technical term that the court cannot find in any standard dictionary, the scientific or technical linguistic usage as to the meaning of the term may be proved by the testimony of expert witnesses who are familiar with it. For instance, a contract in litigation contained a promise to purchase dyes, "Amacid Blue Black KN," and expert testimony was admissible to prove the meaning of the quoted term. Here the term had no "plain meaning" to the court, and not even ambiguous meanings — it was meaningless. Hence the "plain meaning" rule was not applicable. Cases of this type give no difficulty.

Despite numerous dicta that a "plain meaning" cannot be explained by a special usage, it is believed that the law as laid down in judicial precedents is otherwise. A contract to sell 125,000 "chickens, 2 1/2-3 lbs." was, by the aid of expert testimony and of terminology derived from the U.S. Department of Agriculture, interpreted by the court to include "stewing chickens," as the seller interpreted it, and not limited to "broilers or fryers," as the buyer argued it should be. The *Restatement*, which does not recognize the "plain meaning" rule, states as the standard of interpretation of a contract contained in a single written instrument ("integrated") "the meaning that would be attached to the ... [instrument] by a reasonably intelligent person acquainted with all operative usages...."

The term, "operative usages," includes the linguistic usages here referred to and also the additive usages that add to the terms of a contract. The latter are discussed below.

Still another kind of dictionary may be used to interpret the terms of a contract: a private code agreed upon by the parties, in advance of making the contract, as their means of communication with each other. Such private codes are used by and between persons who frequently have dealings with each other, in order to prevent others from learning valuable business information. They are used, for instance, by and between stockbrokers trading on the various stock exchanges and brokers on commodity exchanges. If litigation arises over a contract made in this way, the code book may be produced in evidence to translate the apparently meaningless language, or the language whose "plain" meaning would be at variance with its code meaning. To emphasize his position that one can not reliably determine the meaning of a contract in the way described above, Wigmore told of a young man who, before going on a pleasure trip to Europe, agreed with his father to use a certain code book in cabling. Later the father was startled to receive from his son by cable the single word, "laugh," which he found, on looking it up in the code book, to mean, "send $500."

Besides all these dictionaries there is the law dictionary, which gives the established meanings of legal terms or phrases. If an instrument embodying a contract has been drafted by a lawyer or lawyers, a legal term in it would presumably be interpreted in its legal sense, and in the absence of fraud or mistake this meaning would be given it regardless of the unfamiliarity of the term to one or both parties. Such terms are most often found in our archaic vocabulary of real property law. However, this interpretation is not conclusive; by the transactional context it may be shown that the established legal meaning was not intended. Thus where two laymen draw up their contract and use words having a technical-legal and also an ordinary meaning (such as, for instance, "consideration," "condition") they are not to be entrapped by this inadvertent use of legal lingo.

The "plain meaning" rule serves as a last resort, to guide a court that has found no aids to interpretation nor signs of intention in the transactional context and no basis for an "equitable construction," and thus falls back upon the literal wording of the contract for which the court does not see any rational basis. Either poor drafting of the contract or supervening unforeseen circumstances have made the contract scarcely intelligible, and the court refuses, under the guise of "equitable interpretation," to make a new contract for the parties.

III. Extrinsic Aids: Relevant Circumstances

An extrinsic aid is anything outside of the written instrument in which the terms of a contract are embodied ("integrated") and which may be used in ascertaining the meaning of these terms. The ideal process of interpretation outlined in Part II can rarely, if ever, be realized: the contra-document usually does not "speak for itself." In suggesting that such a document *may* carry its own meaning I refer only to the *interpretation* of the contract, not to its validity or to the proof of its performance. In case of dispute as to the genuineness of the signatures, the authority of agents to sign on behalf of their principals, or the identity of agents and principals, extrinsic proof may be used. So, if a claim is made that the contract was induced by fraud or duress and is therefore voidable, proof of conduct of the parties and other facts outside the contract are admissible. The same is true when a dispute arises as to the facts of performance of the contract. A written contract *may* be so carefully drawn with explicit provisions, definitions of terms, and recitals of fact, that, as to some disputes that *do* arise (but not as to all disputes that *might* arise) its meaning is clear in relation to the particular dispute without the aid of extrinsic proof.

Yet proof of many of the circumstances of the transaction that would tend to show how the contract came to be made, the motivation or purposes of the parties in making it, the particular characteristics of the subject matter, and the like, are admissible to show its meaning. Even courts which profess to follow the "plain meaning" rule generally recognize an exception for "relevant circumstances." For instance, in an action by a railroad company against a motor-vehicle manufacturer the court first said the switch-track agreement between them was so clear that there could be no "right of construction," and then said:

> The greatest latitude should be given in developing the surrounding situations and conditions attending the negotiations for the consummation of a contract, and the language employed in a contract should be construed in the light of circumstances surrounding the contracting parties at the time. Circumstantial evidence is as competent to prove a contract as it is to prove a crime.

A. *Course of Performance* The conduct of both parties to a contract in the course of its performance is, if it indicates that they gave a particular meaning to its terms, provable as evidence of that meaning. This kind of proof is frequently called the "practical construction" of the parties. The basis of inference in such cases is often an admission by one party, by his conduct, that the contract has a certain meaning. For instance, the fact that *P*, a trucking company, did not in its monthly billings to the other party, a freight forwarder, make any claim for certain alleged "receiving charges" referred to in the contract, was deemed sufficient evidence of the meaning of the provision concerning "receiving charges" to justify a denial of a later claim for such charges....

A party's course of performance in a manner against his interest, as he now claims it to be, is primarily an admission by that party, and as such it is not conclusive or legally binding on that party, but may be withdrawn or corrected by him. Mere forgetfulness or ignorance of a claim does not discharge the claim. However, the position taken by one party in the course of performance may signify to the other a representation or a promise on which he relies and acts to such an extent as to create an estoppel, and when this occurs the representation can not be corrected nor the promise revoked. An example appears in an action by *S*, a subcontractor for painting, against *G*, a general contractor for the erection of 175 dwelling units at an airforce base. After *S* had completed the exterior and interior painting in accordance with contract specifications, weather damaged the outside paint and defective lumber spoiled the interior paint. *G* told *S* that he would be paid for repainting the houses; *S* did so and then sought recovery of 96,000 dollars for this additional work. In affirming a judgment for *S* the court treated the conduct of the parties as a "practical construction" of the contract. The decision might, it seems, have been based on estoppel, or on a new and independent contract.

One party's performance in accordance with his interpretation, favorable to his own interests, may, if the other party consents to or acquiesces in this interpretation, create a practical construction unfavorable to the latter. If the latter gives an *express* assent to the former, who afterward acts in reliance on it, an estoppel may be created. Hence practical construction may entrap a party who is not alert to detect and repudiate practical interpretations with which he disagrees. "Self-serving" interpretations by one party are not often given effect. At least they should be limited to cases of knowledge and acquiescence by the other party.

For contracts to sell goods the Uniform Commercial Code gives a clearer and more restrictive meaning of course of performance than can be found in judicial opinions: [§ 2-208(1)]

> Course of Performance or Practical Construction.... Where the contract for sale involves repeated occasions for performance by either party with knowledge of the nature of the performance and opportunity for objection to it by the other, any course of performance accepted or acquiesced in without objection shall be relevant to determine the meaning of the agreement.

This language avoids the pitfalls of the doctrine.

B. *Prior Utterances and Thoughts* [We have omitted Patterson's brief summary of the parol evidence rule, since we take up that topic somewhat later, in more detail.]

C. *Recitals* Recitals are statements of a factual character inserted in written contracts for the purpose of explaining and clarifying their terms. They are frequently worded as "whereas" clauses, and are useful aids to interpretation.

IV. Extrinsic Aids: Course of Dealing and Trade Usages

"Custom conquers all" is a maxim that had somewhat greater reliability in previous centuries than in this one. Still, it may serve to remind us that the transactions with which lawyers and judges have to deal take place in an ordered and established society for the most part, and that the social matrix envelops every word that the parties may utter, or every sentence that they may sign. What is this social matrix? It includes, above all, the common or universal language of the community, for which no dictionary is ordinarily needed by parties, lawyers, judge, or jury. It includes the vocabulary of lawyers when relevant. It includes a previous course of dealing (if any) between these same parties to this contract. It includes the linguistic usages discussed in Part III above that give meaning to special terms in the contract, and also those *additive* usages which may add terms to the contract where the contract itself is silent and does not exclude such usages.

A. *Course of Dealing* A prior course of dealing between the parties to a contract has long been recognized by courts as relevant to the interpretation of their contract. A contract by *D* to supply *P* with chemicals at "ruling market rates" was followed by deliveries, monthly rendition of accounts by *D* to *P*, and payment by *P*. Then *P* discovered he had been paying jobber's rates, rather than the lower exporter's rates, and sued for the difference. Prior dealings between *P* and *D* (and also their prior conversations) were relied on by the court to show that *P* had not been overcharged. A course of dealing may, it seems, consist of a repeated practice of one party that was known to the other, which the jury might find helpful in determining their rights — here a buyer's belated claim for breach of warranty. Yet one party's practice, unknown to the other, can not establish a course of dealing. The regular accounts rendered by one party to another and acquiesced in by failure to object within a reasonable time may be held effective against the latter on the basis of two older doctrines, estoppel, or account stated. Course of dealing, sometimes confused with "custom" or "usage," has seldom been relied upon in reported case law.

The Uniform Commercial Code defines the term: [§ 1-205(1)]

A course of dealing is a sequence of previous conduct between the parties to a particular transaction which is fairly to be regarded as establishing a common basis of understanding for interpreting their expressions and other conduct.

This definition, far superior to any previous judicial attempts, gives some objectivity ("sequence of conduct establishing") to the term, yet the requirement of knowledge of the sequence, "between the parties," is left to "fairly" and "common basis of understanding." The trier of fact will, it seems, have considerable discretion; yet it is somewhat limited by the hierarchy of persuasiveness discussed below.

B. *Additive and Linguistic Usages* American case law as to customs and usages shows a good deal of confusion. To the present writer it seems that some clarification results from distinguishing *linguistic* or translative usages from *additive* usages. The former merely give special meanings to the words or other expressions or symbols of a contract, as explained in Part II above. The latter add something to the terms of the contract, some regular practice in a trade, locality, or class which implies an obligation to do or not to do something in a particular way. For instance, a theatrical producer by a telegram offered an actor employment, on the road and in stock, with some terms specified but no mention of the period of employment. The actor accepted by telegram. After four months the producer gave the actor two weeks notice of termination and paid him accordingly. The actor claimed he was employed according to an oral agreement with the producer's agent for a year. The producer's proof that in the theatrical profession a usage, well understood by both parties, was to the effect that either party had a right to terminate the contract on two weeks notice was excluded by the trial court. On appeal it was held error not to let this evidence go to the jury. A trade usage may prescribe what should be done by one party with respect to a matter not mentioned in the contract. Thus, whether a buyer of fine granulated sugar had inspected it within a reasonable time was determined partly by proving a usage that a buyer who resold the sugar in the original containers would not inspect it until he received some complaint from his customers. A usage in this sense has two elements: (1) a pattern of prevailing human conduct, and (2) a conviction or belief that the pattern *ought* to be followed. This was shown in a case in which a contract between a congregation and a rabbi-cantor of Orthodox Jewish faith was said to have "read into it" the ancient custom and belief that the men and the women should be seated separately in the synagogue. The failure of the congregation to observe this old usage was deemed to justify the rabbi-cantor in his refusal to perform and to give him a right to recover damages for breach of contract.

Although a trade or class usage resembles a custom, such usages are not required to have existed "from time immemorial," as are English local customs. The original of a trade usage need not be veiled in mystery. It may be embodied in regulations adopted by a trade association, of which one party is a member, if the regulations are known to the other party. However, if the nonmember was not aware of the trade rule when the contract was made, he is not bound by it. American courts have been less careful than English courts in requiring proof from which it might be inferred that one party knew, or had reason to know, of a usage relied on by the other. Under a contract by a seller to deliver potatoes f.o.b. railroad cars in Virginia, a jury found that the seller was aware of a usage by which payment by the New York buyer was to be deferred until after the potatoes arrived in New York and were inspected by him. On the other hand, a court in Arkansas held that a remote nonresident, dealing with a New York buyer, was not charged with knowledge of a New York usage, and a New York court held a usage of fruit buyers in New York was not so long and well established as to be imputed to a fruit-grower shipping fruit from Oregon to the New York market. Ordinarily the "insider" tries to impute knowledge of his group's usage to the "outsider." However, on the principle of reciprocity, the "outsider" should not be allowed to claim the benefit of the "insider's" usage if the "outsider" was not aware of it when the contract was made, and in Virginia it was so held. With respect to *knowledge* by a party of a trade usage so as to make it binding upon him the Uniform Commercial Code seems to provide three categories: (1) parties engaged in the vocation or trade, (2) parties who are aware, and (3) parties who should be aware are deemed to have knowledge....

C. *"Unreasonable" Usages and the Hierarchy of Authority* While usage may often be used to smooth the channels of commercial transactions, yet parties to contracts sometimes seek to prove usages with which their lawyers may mislead juries. There has thus grown up the judicial doctrine that a court will not permit proof of an "unreasonable" or an unlawful usage. [For example, a] Missouri court held that a usage of used-car dealers to turn back the speedometer mileage on used cars, after making "improvements" on them, was deceptive and contrary to the public good. On the whole judicial supervision of usages has been salutary.

The Commercial Code seeks to express the requirement of reasonableness along with a statement as to which source of interpretation prevails when they are in conflict with each other: "The express terms of an agreement and an applicable course of dealing or usage of trade shall be construed wherever reasonable as consistent with each other; but when such construction is unreasonable express terms control both course of dealing and usage of trade and course of dealing controls usage of trade." An alleged usage which contradicts express terms of the contract is to be rejected. A course of dealing between these two parties is more likely to express their expectations than a conflicting usage that may be the practice of other persons.

D. *Notice of Intention To Prove Usage* As another safeguard against the false usage as an escape hatch for delinquents the Uniform Commercial Code provides that one party's evidence of a usage shall not be admissible "unless and until he has given the other party such a notice as the court finds sufficient to prevent unfair surprise to the latter." The Code will, it is believed, have good effects in two ways: in clarifying the legitimate role of usage in commercial contracts, and in preventing some of the abuses of usage-evidence that prior case law revealed.

V. Secondary Maxims of Interpretation and Construction

In addition to or in conjunction with the principles of interpretation and construction of contracts set forth above, courts rely upon and purport to use a number of maxims of interpretation some of which are very broad but most of which are applicable only to special situations. There is some doubt whether they have reliable guidance value for judges, or are merely justifications for decisions arrived at on other grounds, which may or may not be revealed in the opinion. This rather cynical view is supported by two observations. One is that for any given maxim that would persuade a judge to a certain conclusion a contrary maxim may be found that would persuade him to the opposite (or contradictory) conclusion. For instance, the courts often quote the maxim, "the court cannot make a contract for the parties," and, somewhat less frequently, they make statements such as: "The law does not favor, but leans against, the destruction of contracts because of uncertainty; and it will, if feasible, so construe agreements as to carry into effect the reasonable intentions of the parties if that [sic] can be ascertained."

[The author then provides other possibly contradictory maxims.]

The second reason, referred to above, for believing that the maxims of interpretation are ceremonial rather than persuasive is that in many instances the court will set forth in its opinion the whole battery of maxims and then proceed to decide the case on the basis of an analysis of the terms of the contract and the facts of the dispute, without indicating which maxim or maxims, if any, were applied or invoked in reaching that decision. In a system of law based on judicial precedents, a clear statement of the operative facts and the legal reasons is a part of judicial responsibility. However, the court's awareness of the quoted maxims is a part of the context of its reasoning. Moreover, the lawyers on each side of a controversy would do well to quote to the court the relevant maxims for their positions....

In this brief treatment we can only quote a list of standard maxims, which may not be complete. The ones most often phrased in Latin are given first:

1. *Noscitur a sociis.* The meaning of a word in a series is affected by others in the same series; or, a word may be affected by its immediate context. The example for the next maxim may be taken to illustrate this one.

2. *Ejusdem generis.* A general term joined with a specific one will be deemed to include only things that are like (of the same genus as) the specific one. This one if applied usually leads to a restrictive interpretation. For example, *S* contracts to sell *B* his farm together with the "cattle, hogs, and other animals."

This would probably not include S's favorite house-dog, but might include a few sheep that S was raising for the market.

3. *Expressio unius exclusio alterius.* If one or more specific items are listed, without any more general or inclusive terms, other items although similar in kind are excluded. For example, S contracts to sell B his farm together with "the cattle and hogs on the farm." This language would be interpreted to exclude the sheep and S's favorite house-dog.

4. *Ut magis valeat quam pereat.* By this maxim an interpretation that makes the contract valid is preferred to one that makes it invalid.

5. *Omnia praesumuntur contra proferentem.* This maxim states that if a written contract contains a word or phrase which is capable of two reasonable meanings, one of which favors one party and the other of which favors the other, that interpretation will be preferred which is less favorable to the one by whom the contract was drafted. This maxim favors the party of lesser bargaining power, who has little or no opportunity to choose the terms of the contract, and perforce accepts one drawn by the stronger party. Such "contracts of adhesion" are discussed below. However, the maxim is commonly invoked in cases that do not reveal any disparity of bargaining power between the parties.

6. *Interpret contract as a whole.* A writing or writings that form part of the same transaction should be interpreted together as a whole, that is, every term should be interpreted as a part of the whole and not as if isolated from it. The maxim expresses the contextual theory of meaning, which is, perhaps, a truism.

7. *"Purpose of the parties."* "The principal apparent purpose of the parties is given great weight in determining the meaning to be given to manifestations of intention or to any part thereof." This maxim must be used with caution. In fact, the two parties to a (bargain) contract necessarily have different purposes, and if these are apparent, then the court can construe a principal or common purpose from the two as a guide to the interpretation of language or the filling of gaps. Thus a contract to sell, buy, and export scrap copper was construed to make the buyer's obtaining of an export license a condition of the seller's promise to deliver. However, if the purposes of the parties are obscure the court may well fall back upon "plain meaning."

8. *Specific provision is exception to a general one.* If two provisions of a contract are inconsistent with each other and if one is "general" enough to include the specific situation to which the other is confined, the specific provision will be deemed to qualify the more general one, that is, to state an exception to it. A lease of a truck-trailer provided that the lessee should be absolutely liable for loss or damage to the vehicle, yet another clause stated that no party's liability should be increased by this contract. It was held that the former was more specific and therefore controlled the general provision, hence the lessee was liable. A careful draftsman would have stated the former as an exception to the latter, and the court in effect does it for him.

9. *Handwritten or typed provisions control printed provisions.* Where a written contract contains both printed provisions and handwritten or typed provisions,

and the two are inconsistent, the handwritten or typed provisions are preferred. This maxim is based on the inference that the language inserted by handwriting or by typewriter for this particular contract is a more recent and more reliable expression of their intentions than is the language of a printed form. While this maxim is used in interpreting insurance contracts and other contracts of adhesion, it is also applicable to all contracts drawn up on a printed form.

10. *Public interest preferred.* If a public interest is affected by a contract, that interpretation or construction is preferred which favors the public interest. The proper scope of application of this rule seems doubtful. It may have some appropriate uses in construing contracts between private parties. However, as applied to government contracts it would, if applied, be used to save the taxpayers' money as against those contracting with the government. But this is not, it is believed, a standard of interpretation or construction uniformly applied to government contracts.

This battery of maxims is never fired all together. The judge or other interpreter-construer of a contract may, by making prudent choices, possibly obtain some useful guides for his reasoning and justifications for his conclusion.

VI. Contracts of Adhesion and Compulsory Contracts

[We have omitted Patterson's treatment of this topic. Briefly, Patterson notes that if the drafter of a contract was in a stronger bargaining position than the other signer, a court under the influence of twentieth-century views might favor the weaker party whenever possible. This is consistent with the general rule of interpretation which suggests construction against the drafter, but is an extension of it. The origins of the idea that there are some contracts — contracts of adhesion — which are in some respects "pretended contracts" seemed to originate in France. The French scholar suggested that those contracts in which are the expression of the intentions of only one party (the drafter) should be treated, in a sense, as private legislative enactments. There may be sound reasons, grounded in efficiency concerns, to enforce such contracts, but they do threaten the assumptions about contract as the expression of two or more parties sharing some common intention. Whether the adhesion contract is subject to different interpretive rules is a question which neither courts nor scholars have answered with any clarity.]

NOTES AND QUESTIONS

1. *Another Patterson, another view*: Professor Edwin Patterson's article is written in what we might call the "authoritative" voice. But we must always remember that there can be more than one side to nearly any assertion. In IV. C. *supra*, Professor E. Patterson asserts that, under the Code, "An alleged usage which contradicts express terms of the contract is to be rejected." This statement is a part of the argument which he presents concerning the hierarchies of

authority which bear on interpretation. Professor Dennis Patterson, in an article which seeks, in part, to examine the jurisprudence of Code-architect Karl Llewellyn,[7] suggests that at the very least Edwin Patterson's assertion was antithetical to Llewellyn's purpose, if not the presumed purpose of the Code's drafters; he labels the assertion we have just quoted as "simply fantastic." He first notes that Llewellyn was seeking, in the Code, to integrate trade usage and course of dealing with the written terms of the parties, giving effect to each. Dennis Patterson argues:

> Llewellyn's conceptual revolution was not universally embraced. After completion of the New York Law Revision Commission hearings, Professor Edwin Patterson of the Columbia University Law School prepared a report recommending "amendment of § 1-205(4) to insure that express terms would always dominate usage of trade and course of dealing." No published discussion of Patterson's recommendation exists; however, neither the New York Law Revision Commission nor the Code Editorial Board adopted the recommendations.
>
> Having failed in his attempt to influence the Law Revision Commission in New York to adopt a totem-pole approach to § 1-205, Professor Patterson never gave up in his attempt to reorient judicial thinking to the classical model. In 1964, fully eight years after having his perspective rejected by the New York Law Revision Commission, Patterson wrote the following:
>
> [Dennis Patterson then quotes from a paragraph from the article you have just read which includes the contested assertion concerning the hierarchy of express terms and trade usage.]
>
> Patterson's assertion ... [that trade usages must be rejected if they contradict express terms] is simply fantastic. It represents an unabashed attempt to subjugate Llewellyn's creation, the Code concept of agreement, to the classical model of contract. Lest one think that the classical orthodoxy has been eclipsed, a review of current treatises on the Code reveals that at least one influential authority proffers the argument that the proper interpretation of § 1-205 results in a totem-pole approach in the analysis of the meaning of agreement.... [Dennis Patterson then quotes Chancellor Hawkland as supporting the view that express terms control course of performance, which in turn dominates course of dealing, which trumps usage of trade, which triumphs over statutory terms.]
>
> Hawkland's methodological approach to § 1-205 is sure to mislead initiates to the Code. This flatly literal reading of § 1-205 is completely at odds with Llewellyn's concept of agreement and with the overall architecture of the Code.... Instead the logic of § 1-205 is that "if a contract can be

---

[7]Good Faith, Lender Liability, and Discretionary Acceleration: Of Llewellyn, Wittgenstein, and the Uniform Commercial Code, 68 Texas Law Review 169, 192 (1989).

defined by shared expectations, and if those expectations were created by trade usage, then the contract should be defined by trade usage."

At the risk of opening the door to a deconstructionist debate, should we accept the proposition that the Code means what Llewellyn intended it to mean, because he wrote it?

"Meaning" in the Law of Contracts
E. Allan Farnsworth[8]

"Interpretation" will be used here ... to refer to the process by which courts determine the "meaning" of the language. We are not concerned with overriding legal rules which may render contract language ineffective after it has been interpreted. Nor are we concerned with "gap filling" by which the absence of contract language is remedied. Our concern is exclusively with contract language and its "meaning."

The object of contract law is to protect the justifiable expectations of the contracting parties themselves, not those of third parties, even reasonable third parties.

"Meaning" for the purpose of contract interpretation should therefore be defined as: (1) that to which either party refers, where it can be determined and where it can be established that it is the same as that to which the other party refers, or believes or has reason to believe the first party to be referring; and, only failing this, (2) that to which either party has reason to believe the other to be referring. Interpretation then becomes the process applied to the language of the parties by which this meaning is determined. It is sometimes supposed, however, that language can be so clear that no recourse need be had to external circumstances to determine its meaning. Are there circumstances under which the meaning of language is so "plain" that some other definition of that term is appropriate?

The Search for Plain Meaning

In Semantics. The very concept of plain meaning finds scant support in semantics, where one of the cardinal teachings is the fallibility of language as a means of communication. Waismann lamented that,

> Ordinary language simply has not got the "hardness," the logical hardness, to cut axioms in it. It needs something like a metallic substance to carve a deductive system out of it such as Euclid's. But common speech? If you

---

[8]Reprinted by permission of The Yale Law Journal Company and Fred B. Rothman & Company from The Yale Law Journal, Vol. 76, pp. 939-957.

begin to draw inferences it soon begins to go "soft" and fluffs up somewhere. You may just as well carve cameos on a cheese *soufflé.*

Much of this softness of language comes from the differing ways in which we
learn to use words, for the use of a symbol for communication is ordinarily
preceded by an elaborate process of conditioning which may vary greatly with
the individual.... [E]ach person learns words on the basis of different sets of
stimuli. To borrow Quine's example of the word "red," some will have learned
this word in situations where red was sharply contrasted with other colors that
differ greatly; others will have learned it by being rewarded for distinguishing
red from other reddish colors. It seems clear that the former group will use
"red" more freely than the latter group. Second, the abilities of people to group
stimulations into sets differ somewhat. Thus, some children will simply respond
"red" when either a red object or a crimson object comes into view and will
remain incapable of distinguishing them.

Quine has built upon Skinner's theory of language learning to explain the
concept of vagueness. According to Quine, "stimulations eliciting a verbal
response, say 'red,' are best depicted as forming not a neatly bounded class but
a distribution about a central *norm*." The idea of a central norm is useful in
explaining the concept of vagueness, for a word is vague to the extent that it can
apply to stimuli that depart from its central norm.

Contract language abounds in perturbing examples of vagueness. The parties
provide for the removal of "all the dirt" on a tract; may sand from a stratum of
subsoil be taken? An American seller and a Swiss buyer agree upon the sale of
"chicken"; is stewing chicken "chicken"? Vagueness may even infect a term that
has an apparently precise connotation. The parties contract for the sale of
horsemeat scraps "Minimum 50% protein"; may evidence be admitted to show
that by trade usage scraps containing 49.5% or more conform?

Ambiguity, properly defined, is an entirely distinct concept from that of
vagueness. A word that may or may not be applicable to marginal objects is
vague. But a word may also have two entirely different connotations so that it
may be applied to an object and be at the same time both clearly appropriate and
inappropriate, as the word "light" may be when applied to dark feathers. Such
a word is ambiguous.

Whether an ambiguity arises may depend upon the medium of communication.
Some ambiguities (ordinarily homonyms), such as "beer" and "bier" arise only
in speech and disappear in writing; others such as "tear" (a rip or a drop), arise
only in writing and disappear in speech. Speech will do much to remove the
ambiguity from sentences such as, "Do you think that one will do?" which can
be read aloud in a variety of ways by stressing a different word each time.
Gestures also play a part in normal face-to-face conversation, and habits of
speech have been shown to change when conversation is over a telephone and
normal gesture reinforcement is lost. Ambiguity may arise in a telegram because
of the lack of punctuation which would ordinarily be supplied in a letter. And

even given an ambiguity, it may be resolved by its context: one drinks a beer, not a bier, and sheds a tear (drop) not a tear (rip).

Ambiguities may be classified into those of term and those of syntax. As Young has pointed out, true examples of ambiguity of term are rare in contract cases. A contract specifies "tons"; are they to be long or short tons? A charter party provides that a vessel must be "double-rigged," which by usage can refer to either two winches and two booms per hatch, or four of each per hatch; how many must the vessel have? An important variety of ambiguity of term, for our purposes, is proper name ambiguity, the kind of ambiguity that plagued Shakespeare's Cinna,[9] the kind of ambiguity that we deliberately create when we name a child after someone. It was this kind of ambiguity that was involved in the celebrated case of the ships "Peerless."

An ambiguity of syntax is, in the strictest sense, an ambiguity of grammatical structure, of what is syntactically connected with what. A classic example is, "And Satan trembles when he *sees* / The weakest saint upon his knees," in which the ambiguity is that of pronominal reference.

Ambiguity of syntax is probably a more common cause of contract disputes than is ambiguity of term. An insurance policy covers any "disease of organs of the body not common to both sexes"; does it include a fibroid tumor (which can occur on any organ) of the womb? A contract provides that, "Before the livestock is removed from the possession of the carrier or mingled with other livestock, the shipper ... shall inform in writing the delivery carrier of any visible injuries to the livestock"; is it enough that he notify before mingling although after removal?

Syntactical ambiguity is often the result of inadequate punctuation. Note, for example, the confusion that sometimes results from contracts concluded by an unpunctuated telegram. Sometimes the ambiguity is caused by the dropping of words to make shorthand expressions. A contract for the sale of "approx. 10,000" heaters adds "All in perfect condition"; is this, as buyer contends, an express warranty ("All *to be* in perfect condition") or, as seller contends, a limitation on the quantity ("All *that are* in perfect condition")?

Particularly hazardous as a source of ambiguity for the contract draftsman are the words "and" and "or."

Ambiguity in contracts may also result from inconsistent or conflicting language. A buyer agrees to pay "at the rate of $1.25 per M" for all the timber on a designated tract, and that "the entire sale and purchase price of said lumber is $1400.00"; how much must he pay for 4,000 M feet? In many of these cases the conflict is between language in a form contract and that added by the parties for the particular transaction. A printed warranty in the sale of a house requires

---

[9](Cinna): "I am Cinna the poet ... I am not Cinna the conspirator!" (Second Plebeian): "It is no matter, his name's Cinna; pluck but his name out of his heart and turn him going." Julius Caesar, III, iii.

the owner to give notice of breach "within one year from ... the date of initial occupancy" and also provides that "notice of nonconformity must be delivered no later than January 6, 1957," the date having been inserted by hand; when must the buyer give notice if he moves in on May 16, 1955?

It would be wrong to assume that the failure of contract language to dispose of a dispute that later arises is invariably due to some inherent fallibility of language as a means of communication. The parties may simply not have foreseen the problem at the time of contracting. An insurance contract on a motor vessel covers "collision with any other ship or vessel"; is a collision with an anchored flying boat included? Or one or both may have foreseen the problem but deliberately refrained from raising it during the negotiations for fear that they might fail — the lawyer who "wakes these sleeping dogs" by insisting that they be resolved may cost his client the bargain. An elderly lady enters a home for the aged, paying a lump sum, to be returned to her "if it should be found advisable to discontinue her stay" during a two-month probationary period; must the home refund her money if she dies within that time? Or both may have foreseen the problem but chosen to deal with it only in general terms, delegating the ultimate resolution of particular controversies to the appropriate forum. A contract for the sale of wool requires "prompt" shipment from New Zealand to Philadelphia; does shipment in 52 days conform? It is interesting to note that while either ambiguity or vagueness may result from the other causes just suggested, only vagueness is suitable for use in such a conscious attempt at delegation....

[We have omitted Farnsworth's discussion of the parol evidence rule, but you should keep his discussion of ambiguity and vagueness in mind, since parts of the parol evidence rule require characterizations of a contractual term as ambiguous, or not ambiguous.]

FEDERAL EXPRESS CORP. v. PAN AMERICAN WORLD AIRWAYS, INC.

623 F.2d 1297 (8th Cir. 1980).

MCMILLIAN, J. Appellant Federal Express Corporation, which operates an air express cargo service, appeals from a judgment of the district court dismissing its claim of damages for breach of contract in a diversity action against appellee Pan American World Airways, Inc. For the reasons stated below, we affirm.

This case involves contracts for the sale of a particular kind of jet aircraft called the Falcon 20 Jet, manufactured by Avions Marcell Dassault and marketed at the time of the contracts in the United States by the Business Jets division of appellee. The controversy is over a provision in the sales contracts calling for appellee to provide to appellant (the buyer) "initial training" for flight personnel on a "flight simulator," a machine designed to recreate conditions that might be encountered in flight and to test the responses of the trainee. While we do not attempt to detail the facts of the case, which are admirably set forth in the district court's opinion, some background is required for an understanding of the parties' dispute.

Appellant Federal Express came into existence after Frederick W. Smith, a young but experienced pilot and aircraft industry businessman, sought to set up a new kind of air express delivery service. He planned to use Falcon 20 Jets for this purpose, an inventive idea which created a new function for what had been primarily a "corporate jet," normally used by large enterprises for transportation of personnel. Smith took his plan to Mr. C. C. Flemming, an executive officer of the Business Jets division of appellee, who was supportive, and the parties arranged in 1971 for a sale of a total of twenty-five jets, two at once and the other twenty-three for future delivery. After some delays while appellant obtained financing and while regulatory changes were made which enabled appellant to go into business, the twenty-three aircraft were delivered between October, 1972, and May, 1973.

The contracts called for delivery of the aircraft in a "green" condition, that is, without modifications for appellant's particular needs and without finished instruments or interiors. Appellant subsequently modified the aircraft as they were delivered, with the modifications on the last aircraft completed by December, 1974.

The contracts also called for appellee to provide certain training for appellant's personnel, including the "initial training" for aircraft crews on the flight simulator which is at issue in this case. In regard to this training, the schedule provided by appellee with the first two aircraft purchased in 1971 varied from that provided under the contract for the twenty-three aircraft delivered in 1972-73. The training schedule covering the first two aircraft provided,

> Seller shall arrange to provide, at its expense, initial training of flight and maintenance personnel of buyer as follows: ... Flight Simulator Training.... Up to 30 hours per crew....

A similar printed training schedule was appended to the subsequent contract for the twenty-three with a typed alteration in the first sentence to read,

> Seller shall arrange to provide, at its expense, for each Aircraft, initial training of flight and maintenance personnel....

A modification of this provision occurred in September, 1972, when appellant had encountered delays in obtaining financing which postponed the delivery dates envisioned under the contract, and the parties negotiated a letter agreement under which appellant agreed to waive all rights to training under the original contract except the simulator time.

The only flight simulator for the Falcon 20 aircraft in existence at the time of the contract was owned by a firm called Flight Safety, Inc., which had purchased the simulator from appellee. Under terms of the simulator sale, Flight Safety agreed upon notice of appellee to supply to customers of the Business Jets division who purchased Falcon 20 aircraft "initial training" of flight personnel, "including use of the Simulator as necessary," without charge to Business Jets or the customer. Business Jets, however, apparently did not notify Flight Safety, Inc., of the sale to appellant.

Nor did appellant request training until July, 1975. In the meantime, appellant made certain other arrangements for training. It set up a Veterans Administration approved school for veterans who could make use of federal training funds and trained about 400 Falcon Jet pilots, about 200 of whom appellant employed. In 1973, it ordered its own Falcon simulator, a $1.25 million machine, but its financial sources balked and appellant transferred the simulator to Flight Safety, Inc., where it was installed in early 1975. On July 3, 1975, having sold its flight school, appellant contracted with Flight Safety, Inc. to provide simulator training for flight personnel on a continuing basis, allowing appellant 1,000 hours of training a year and covering Falcon Jets as well as other aircraft.

A week later, on July 10, 1975, appellant requested from appellee the "30 hours per crew, per aircraft, for initial flight simulator training" appellant considered itself entitled to under the sales contracts. Appellee refused, and this lawsuit ensued.

The result below hinged upon the meaning of "initial training" of flight personnel in the sales contracts. Appellant urged that the meaning of "initial training" must be taken from the Federal Aviation Administration regulations covering training of flight crew members, which defines "initial training" as that "required for crew members" in order to qualify them for service on a type of aircraft. 14 C.F.R. § 121.400(c)(1) (1979). Under appellant's interpretation, therefore, the phrase "initial training" refers to the status of the crew to be trained, and the "initial training" for pilots provided under the contracts would be available to appellant to train two crew members per aircraft at appellee's expense at any reasonable time upon appellant's demand. The district court found that, under the contracts for the first two aircraft, this interpretation would be proper.

The court also found, however, that the phrase, "for each aircraft, initial training," which appeared in the contract for the additional twenty-three aircraft, was on its face susceptible of a second interpretation which appellee advanced: whatever training of crew the buyer needed at the time of the purchase to put the aircraft into its initial operation. Under appellee's interpretation, therefore, "initial training" refers to the status of the aircraft, and under the contract training would be available for two crew members per aircraft only as required at the time of purchase to provide an initial crew for appellant to operate the aircraft.

The court concluded that the phrase "initial training" was ambiguous. Applying the law of New York, which has adopted the Uniform Commercial Code, New York Uniform Commercial Code Annotated (McKinney 1964) (hereinafter NYUCC), the court resolved the ambiguity by interpreting the writing in light of trade usage. NYUCC §§ 1-205(4), 2-208(2). Finding that the trade usage was for the seller of this kind of aircraft to provide only initial training for an original crew to put a particular aircraft into service for a buyer, the court interpreted the writing as consistent with this usage....

Appellant argues that the district court erred on three points, each of which requires reversal: (1) appellant contends that the contract was not ambiguous and clearly referred to initial training in the sense of the training required to qualify any crew member; (2) appellant contends that trade usage for sale of a single aircraft as a "corporate jet" does not apply to this sale of a fleet of aircraft intended to be used as cargo vehicles; ... [We omit discussion of appellant's third point.]

Turning to the ambiguity issue, appellant's own argument suggests that the contract was ambiguous. Although appellant contends that the regulation of the Federal Aviation Administration controls the meaning of the parties' written agreement, there is a facial difference between the regulation which defines "initial training" of flight crew and *dispatchers*, 14 C.F.R. § 121.400(c)(1) (1979), and the written sale agreement which calls for "initial training" of flight crew and *mechanics*. On this basis alone, we would consider some doubt justified that the contract phrase referred to the same thing the FAA regulations referred to. Furthermore, we think it would do violence to the plain sense of the words to read the phrase "for each aircraft, initial training" without understanding the phrase to refer at least ambiguously to the training required for initial use of the aircraft. We therefore fully agree with the district court's conclusion that the contract was ambiguous....

Next, appellant asserts that usage of trade in sales of "corporate jets" was inapplicable to this case, because sale of a whole fleet of aircraft for cargo service is unique and fundamentally different than other sales of single aircraft for personnel transport purposes. In particular, appellant urges that when used as a "corporate jet" the Falcon would only require one flight crew for relatively infrequent use, while the use of Falcons in a cargo business required five or six different flight crews for each aircraft because of much more frequent use. Therefore different training provisions would be anticipated under this sale.

Whatever the validity of this distinction, it does not avail appellant. The critical point is that this transaction involved the same aircraft and virtually the same written agreement as the "corporate jet" sales. The usage in those cases therefore had some relevance to this transaction, and the trial court clearly was correct in considering it. NYUCC § 1-205, ... The existence and scope of trade usage is a matter of fact. NYUCC § 1-205(2); 1 R. Anderson, Uniform Commercial Code § 1-205-6. "In case a dominant pattern has been fairly evidenced, the party relying on the usage is entitled to go to the trier of fact on the question of whether such dominant pattern has been incorporated into the agreement." Draftsmen's Comment 9, NYUCC § 1-205. The dominant pattern in this case was the pattern that buyers of Falcon aircraft had a contract right to certain training for the first crew to fly the aircraft. We find no error in the conclusion of the trial court that usage of trade shown by other sales of Falcon Jets was applicable to this contract to explain the meaning of the indefinite term "initial training," and we certainly see no reason to find this conclusion clearly erroneous. Fed.R.Civ.P. 52(a).

Appellant argues that in any event New York law requires construction of ambiguities in a writing against the drafting party. It is true that New York courts have shown some tendency to do so where the party who drafted the agreement takes a position which has little support outside some verbal ambiguity....

But the Uniform Commercial Code specifically requires the written language of the parties' agreement to be construed consistently with applicable trade usage, and this statutory rule of construction must prevail. NYUCC § 1-205....

Accordingly, the judgment of the district court is affirmed.

NOTES AND QUESTIONS

1. *Usage of trade*: Judge McMillian says "[w]e find no error in the conclusion of the trial court that usage of trade shown by other sales of Falcon Jets was applicable to this contract to explain the meaning of the indefinite term 'initial training .'" He points to no evidence that Frederick W. Smith (the CEO of Federal Express) knew of the usage of the executive jet trade. Under the U.C.C. does this matter? Remember Professor Patterson's discussion of this point.

The Federal Express brief did not raise the question of Mr. Smith's knowledge of the usage. Indeed, it does not deal with the U.C.C. in any way.[10] However, Mr. Smith was asked whether airline crews flew only particular aircraft. He responded,

> A. No. In that regard, it would probably be the most dramatic difference between corporate and airline-type flying, and *I am very familiar with both of those fields.* In the case of corporate aviation, with a few notable exceptions of some major companies ... generally the business operate has a specific crew for a specific aircraft, and as long as these people are employed, they fly the aircraft.... In the airline business, on the other hand, because of the considerably higher utilization of the aircraft ... the crews are never married to the aircraft. They rotate among all of the given aircraft of a given type in the airline's fleet. So the unusual nature of this contract [between Federal and Pan Am] ... was the fact that the Falcon aircraft for the first time was going to be put into the regime of airline operations.

---

[10]It cites the Code only once. The brief relies entirely on pre-U.C.C. cases and a legal encyclopedia. The U.C.C. was adopted in New York in 1964.

Does the underlined sentence solve the problem of Mr. Smith's knowledge of trade usage? Until this sale, there had never been a purchase of more than five Falcon jets by one corporation. Federal Express ordered 23, and its crews rotated among them. Does this suggest that there was no usage in the trade of selling Falcon jets for airline use? Suppose we agreed with Federal Express' argument on this point. How, then, would the case have been decided?

All of the questions in this note address the reasons why usage of trade is relevant to finding giving meaning to contract language. How many reasons are there? Is trade usage relevant because I am so likely to know of the trade usages that the usages are evidence of my actual intentions? Or is it because it is reasonable for you to assume that these usages form the context of my words and conduct? Or is it because if courts hold people to the usages of their trades, this lowers the cost of transacting business, and saves valuable court time? All of these reasons? Are the reasons consistent? Are there other reasons for believing trade usage relevant?

2. *Proof of usage*: How do you prove a usage of trade? Does this require a social science survey? Would the testimony of an expert witness be enough? How would a person qualify as an expert on the usages of a particular trade? Notice that Mr. Smith testified about his knowledge of practices in corporate and commercial aviation. Pan American did not question his qualifications to do this.

How common must an understanding be to qualify as a usage? Suppose people in the trade usually understand expressions in a certain way, but occasionally they do not. Can you defeat a claimed usage by showing it does not hold in every case? Mr. Smith qualified his observations about corporate aviation. He used the word "generally" and said "with a few notable exceptions of some major companies." Can you have a usage "with a few notable exceptions?" What does U.C.C. § 1-205(2) say about this?

3. *Construction against the drafter*: Judge McMillian refuses to construe the contract against Pan American, the firm that drafted it. He says "[b]ut the Uniform Commercial Code specifically requires the written language of the parties' agreement to be construed consistently with applicable trade usage, and this statutory rule of construction must prevail." Does Official Comment 6 to § 1-205 indicate that this particular maxim of construction should no longer be applied but that tests of good faith and unconscionability must be used? Does it make any difference?

4. *Course of performance*: The opinion addresses the question of trade usage, but does not discuss whether or not the behavior of the parties themselves was relevant to the contract's interpretation. Read U.C.C. § 2-208, and ask whether such an argument could have been made. What facts would have been relevant to such a claim? Which of the parties could profitably have asserted it?

C. THE PAROL EVIDENCE RULE

The parol evidence rule is not easy to understand. This short note and the next essay should help sort the cases that follow. While the rule may be difficult for judges, lawyers and law students, it is clear that it is an important doctrine in modern contract law.

Let's begin with the easiest case. Seller and Buyer are negotiating a complicated contract. They have been exchanging oral and written communications for weeks. As a result, both have file folders filled with formal drafts of provisions, scraps of paper with hand written proposals, notes and letters. They have tried to consider matters one by one. However, the bargaining about, say, point five has reopened their tentative agreement about point three. Of course, also there have been oral concessions and proposals. Some of these are reflected in the notes in the files and some remain only imperfectly in the memories of the parties.

Finally, Seller confesses that she is uncertain just where they stand. She says she thinks they really have agreed on everything and have a contract. However, it is not written down anywhere from beginning to end. She proposes that she draft a clean text from which they can work. Buyer thinks this is a good idea. Two days later, Seller and Buyer met again. Seller presents Buyer with a detailed written contract. She says, "I think this is our deal. Look it over. If I've left out anything, tell me. If I've got something wrong, we can change it. If there's more to negotiate, at least we'll know where to start." A day later Buyer returns and says, "You've done a remarkable job in capturing just what we have agreed. I have one small problem in clause 2, but, if we can solve that, we have a contract." Together they work out the problem in clause 2. Seller then says to Buyer, "Now, you are sure that this writing expresses your understanding of our deal? We haven't left anything out? I don't want any misunderstandings or mistakes." Buyer responds, assuring Seller that the writing reflects perfectly his understanding of their agreement. He says, "My lawyer and I have been through all of the earlier material. Of course, you made some changes to harmonize the entire deal, but I can live with them in order to close a contract. The document is our deal." They have the document retyped to reflect the few corrections to clause 2. Then they both sign it.

A year later, Buyer sues Seller for breach of contract. Buyer offers as evidence the text of a preliminary draft of clause 23 which both Buyer and Seller had initialed. This draft is dated a week before Buyer and Seller signed the writing to close their deal. Clause 23 in the preliminary draft declares that if X occurs, then Buyer shall have right Y. Clause 23 in the writing they signed to create a contract declares, on the other hand, if X occurs, then Buyer shall not have right Y but only right Z.

The parol evidence rule would bar admission of evidence of the preliminary draft of clause 23. Here, it is just a matter of free contract. Buyer and Seller agreed that their entire agreement was expressed in the writing they signed to create a contract. Implicitly, they also agreed that the final writing superseded and overturned all prior inconsistent agreements — after all, this was the point of starting with a clean draft. If parties agree that a particular document states their entire agreement and amends or repeals all prior bargains, then courts will give effect to their choice. In short, if we agree that version 2 of our written agreement repeals version 1, then it does. We can wipe the slate clean and start over. This is not a rule of evidence, but simply a rule of contract law calling for courts to enforce parties agreements.

However, our story, while understandable, is atypical. People seldom agree expressly that a writing they sign is the final crystallization of their contract.[11] They just sign written documents called contracts. We could presume that everyone understands, or should understand, any writing which s/he signs. However, we know this will not be the case in many instances. Whatever the wisdom of doing business this way, people do assume that *both* a formal writing labeled "CONTRACT" and their prior oral statements and letters *together* constitute the deal. If clause 23 in a prior letter and clause 23 in the written contract conflict, it is likely to be the product of mistake. Courts could approach the situation much as the British judges did in *Raffles v. Wichelhaus*. On the other hand, perhaps it is just easier for courts to presume that formal later writings supersede whatever is said in earlier correspondence and conversations. Many people see writings as a form of magic, and it may help bureaucratically run organizations to ignore choice and hold people to whatever they signed.

A more typical case is even more difficult. Buyer offers in evidence a letter from Seller. It was written before their final contract was signed. In it, Seller agrees to something which is not covered in the final document. Should courts view the omission of this provision as an implied agreement that there should be no such clause in the contract? Should courts recognize that people may put some but not all of their bargain in a final writing? Should courts seek the actual intentions of the parties or create presumptions to protect writings?

Matters get more uncertain. Suppose Buyer offers a preliminary draft of clause 23 in evidence. Buyer does not seek to have it enforced as part of the contract. Rather Buyer argues that the preliminary draft is relevant to interpreting the meaning of clause 23 in the final agreement. The written document says that if X occurs, Buyer shall have right Z. However, what are the boundaries of right Z? Buyer argues that it should be interpreted in light of the definition of right Y in the preliminary draft — in effect, what is not Y is Z. Should courts consider this evidence? Must they first determine that the scope of right Z is ambiguous?

Suppose, on the other hand, Buyer wants to show that clause 23 never was supposed to be effective. Rather, it was written into the contract to comply with

---

[11]Lawyers drafting form contracts may sneak clauses saying this into documents which they should understand are not likely to be read. Is this a type of fraud? Should you feel a personal sense of guilt if you use guile, and legal knowledge, to take advantage of the trusting or unwary?

requirements of the Mexican government. Buyer and Seller agreed in a prior letter that the clause was to have no effect. Should this evidence be admitted? Suppose, instead, Buyer wants to show that Buyer and Seller agreed in a side agreement that clause 23 would be effective only if the Mexican government could not be persuaded to waive its regulation in the case of this transaction. Should this evidence be admitted?

Finally, suppose Buyer wants to have the court *reform* the final written contract to change the term "right Z" to "right Y." Buyer wants to offer evidence of prior agreements to show that Seller's word processor was mistakenly programmed so that it produced the wrong clause when a typist entered "ALT 25." "ALT 25" should have produced language giving Buyer "right Y." Instead, it produced language giving the Buyer "right Z." Neither Buyer nor Seller discovered the error before they signed the document. Is an action for reformation different than one for damages for breach of contract? Can Buyer contradict the writing in a reformation action? Is the claim really different than the original case where Buyer wanted to contract a final writing with a preliminary draft?

Obviously, a great deal turns on whether courts seek to carry out real choices. They may seek other goals without announcing them openly. We can now turn to consider what courts have done with such cases.

A Plea for a Uniform Parol Evidence Rule and Principles of Contract Interpretation
John D. Calamari & Joseph M. Perillo[12]

Any reader of advance sheets is well aware that most of the contract decisions reported do not involve offer and acceptance or other subjects usually explored in depth in a course in contracts but rather involve the parol evidence rule and questions of interpretation, topics given scant attention in most courses in contracts. Although a number of articles have appeared recently on these subjects, for the most part they tend to express the individual view of the writer as to what the law should be. While the authors of this paper will state their views, their principal purpose is to set forth the basic problems involved and to offer a guide for comprehending the reasons for the many contradictory decisions in these areas. Much of the fog and mystery surrounding these subjects stems from the fact that there is basic disagreement as to the meaning and effect of the parol evidence rule and as to the appropriate goals to be achieved by the process of contractual interpretation. The cases and treatises of the contract giants tend to conceal this conflict. While frequently masking disagreement by using the same terminology, Professors Williston and Corbin are often poles apart in the meaning they attach to the same term. Often starting from what superficially

---

[12]42 Indiana Law Journal 333 (1967).

appear to be the same premises, they frequently advocate different results in similar fact situations. The polarity of their views reflects conflicting value judgments as to policy issues that are as old as our legal system and that are likely to continue as long as courts of law exist. Although many writers and courts have expressed their views on the subject and have made major contributions to it, concentration on the analyses of Professors Williston and Corbin will point up the fundamental bases upon which the conflicting cases and views rest.

I. The Parol Evidence Rule

The Area of Substantial Agreement

There is a rule of substantive law which states that whenever contractual intent is sought to be ascertained from among several expressions of the parties, an earlier tentative expression will be rejected in favor of a later expression that is final. More simply stated, the contract made by the parties supersedes tentative promises made in earlier negotiations. Consequently, in determining the content of the contract, the earlier tentative promises are irrelevant.

The parol evidence rule comes into play only when the last expression is in writing. Professor Corbin states the rule as follows: "When two parties have made a contract and have expressed it in a writing to which they have both assented as the complete and accurate integration of that contract, evidence, whether parol or otherwise, of antecedent understandings and negotiations will not be admitted for the purpose of varying or contradicting the writing." Professor Williston's formulation is not to the contrary: "Briefly stated," he writes, "this rule requires, in the absence of fraud, duress, mutual mistake, or something of the kind, the exclusion of extrinsic evidence, oral or written, where the parties have reduced their agreement to an integrated writing." Both agree that this, too, is a rule of substantive law that also operates as an exclusionary rule of evidence merely because prior understandings are irrelevant to the process of determining the content of the final contract. The similarity between the parol evidence rule and the rule stated in the preceding paragraph is obvious. The main and important difference is that where the last expression is not in writing the jury determines whether the parties intended the second expression to supersede the first. This is to say that this question of intention is determined as is any other question of intention stemming from oral transactions. Where the later expression is in writing, however, this question is usually determined by the trial judge. At an early date it was felt (and the feeling strongly remains) that writings require the special protection that is afforded by removing this issue from the province of unsophisticated jurors.[13]

---

[13]It is often assumed that the parol evidence rule protects the "haves" against the "have nots," since it is the former who ordinarily draft written contracts and the latter who receive the sympathy of the jury.... Surprisingly, however, a substantial number of the reported cases dealing with the rule involve sizable transactions between persons with apparently strong bargaining power.

While it is unanimously agreed that the parol evidence rule applies to *prior* expressions, and has no application to an agreement made *subsequent* to the writing, there is no unanimity as to expressions *contemporaneous* with the writing. Williston and the *Restatement* take the position that contemporaneous expressions should be treated the same as prior expressions except that contemporaneous writings should be deemed to be a part of the integration. Corbin appears to argue that expressions are either prior or subsequent to the writing and that therefore the word "contemporaneous" merely clouds the issue. Everyone agrees that the parol evidence rule does not apply to a separate agreement; that is, an agreement that has a separate consideration.

A distinction is drawn between a total and a partial integration. Where the writing is intended to be *final* and *complete*, it is characterized as a total integration and may be neither contradicted nor supplemented by evidence of prior agreements or expressions. But where the writing is intended to be *final* but *incomplete*, it is said to be a partial integration; although such a writing may not be *contradicted* by evidence of prior agreements or expressions, it may be *supplemented* by evidence of consistent additional terms. Thus, in approaching a writing, two questions must be asked: (1) Is it intended as a final expression? (2) Is it intended to be a complete expression?

Is the writing intended as a final expression? Writings that evidence a contract are not necessarily "final" embodiments of the contract. Exchanges of letters or memoranda that show the conclusion of a contract may have been intended to be read in the light of more far-ranging conversations and documents. Or, the parties may have intended their writing to be tentative and preliminary to a final draft. In these cases, the parol evidence rule does not bar enforcement of the entire agreement as proved by the writing read in the context of prior and contemporaneous expressions. It is agreed that any relevant evidence is admissible to show that the writing was not intended to be final. Although the question of finality is frequently characterized as one of law in order to remove it from the province of unsophisticated jurors, it is actually a question of fact — one of intention — which the trial judge determines. To be considered final the writing need not be in any particular form and need not be signed. The crucial requirement is that the parties have regarded the writing as the final embodiment of their agreement.

Sometimes confused with this question of finality, but clearly distinguishable, is the frequently raised question of whether parties who have made a tentative written agreement intended that no contract would exist until a final writing was executed. On this issue of the existence of the contract, the parol evidence rule is even more clearly inapplicable. This question is treated as a normal question of intention…. The determination is frequently made by the jury.

Is the writing a complete or partial integration? Once it is determined that the writing is intended to be final and therefore an integration, it becomes necessary to ascertain whether the integration is complete (so that it cannot be contradicted or supplemented) or only partial (so that it cannot be contradicted but may be supplemented by evidence of consistent additional terms). It seems to be generally agreed that this is a question of law in the sense that it is determined by the trial judge.

The Parol Evidence Rule: The Major Area of Conflict

Apparent agreement by Professors Williston and Corbin, except as noted, on the rules stated above conceals real conflict. The battleground upon which they express disagreement is a major one: the concept of total integration. This, of course, is the area in which most of the cases arise. Both assert that the existence of a total integration depends on the intention of the parties. Williston does so primarily in a section entitled, "Integration Depends Upon Intent." Corbin's emphasis on intent runs throughout his entire discussion of the rule. It appears, however, that in this context they use the term "intent" in ways that are remarkably dissimilar. A typical fact situation will illustrate this. *A* agrees to sell and *B* agrees to purchase Blackacre for $10,000. The contract is in writing and in all respects appears complete on its face. Prior to the signing of the contract *A*, in order to induce *B*'s assent, orally promises him in the presence of a number of reputable witnesses that if *B* will sign the contract, *A* will remove an unsightly shack on *A*'s land across the road from Blackacre. May this promise be proved and enforced? This depends upon whether the writing is a total integration.

Williston argues that if the intention to have a total integration were to be determined by the ordinary process of determining intention, the parol evidence rule would be emasculated. He points out that the mere existence of the collateral oral agreement would conclusively indicate that the parties intended only a partial integration and that the only question that would be presented is whether the alleged prior or contemporaneous agreement was actually made. This would be a question of fact for the jury, thus eliminating the special protection which the trial judge should afford the writing.

Williston, therefore, suggests that the issue of partial or total integration should be determined according to the following rules.

(1) If the writing expressly declares that it contains the entire agreement of the parties (what is sometimes referred to as a merger clause), the declaration conclusively establishes that the integration is total unless the document is obviously incomplete or the merger clause was included as a result of fraud or mistake or any other reason exists that is sufficient to set aside a contract. As previously indicated, even a merger clause does not prevent enforcement of a separate agreement supported by a distinct consideration.

(2) In the absence of a merger clause, the determination is made by looking to the writing. Consistent additional terms may be proved if the writing is obviously

incomplete on its face or if it is apparently complete but, as in the case of deeds, bonds, bills and notes, expresses the undertaking of only one of the parties.

(3) Where the writing appears to be a complete instrument expressing the rights and obligations of both parties, it is deemed a total integration unless the alleged additional terms were such as might naturally be made as a separate agreement by parties situated as were the parties to the written contract.

Thus in the hypothetical case given, Williston's view is that the collateral promise to remove the unsightly shack could not be enforced. The writing was apparently complete on its face and contracting parties would ordinarily and naturally have included such a promise in the writing. Many might agree with this result, but can it be seriously argued that this result is based on the parties' intent that the agreement be integrated? How can a rule based on the intention of the parties be emasculated by seeking to determine their actual expressed intent? It is quite clear that the expressed intent shown by overwhelming evidence is at variance with an intent to have the writing serve as their complete agreement.

Professor Corbin takes a contrary view as to the proper result in our hypothetical case: "It can never be determined by mere interpretation of the words of a writing whether it is an 'integration' of anything, whether it is 'the final and complete expression of the agreement' or is a mere partial expression of the agreement." Elsewhere, he states: "Since the very existence of an 'integration' ... is dependent on what the parties thereto say and do (necessarily extrinsic to the paper instrument), at the time they draw that instrument 'in usual form,' are we to continue like a flock of sheep to beg the question at issue, even when its result is to 'make a contract for the parties,' one that is vitally different from the one they made themselves?" When Professor Corbin speaks of the intent of the parties he emphatically means their actual expressed intent.

Thus, two schools of thought are on the scene, one determined to seek out the intent of the parties, the other speaking of intent but refusing to consider evidence of what the intent actually was....

Fictions have been enormously important in the development of our law. In an era when the law was deemed unchangeable and eternal, they provided almost the only mechanism for avoiding the impact of rules deemed unwise. Their use today serves only to obfuscate what should be clear. Shorn of language indicating a fictitious search for intent, the courts and writers who adopt a Willistonian approach are saying this: *When parties adopt a written form that gives every appearance of being complete and final, they are required to incorporate in that form their entire agreement. If they fail to do so, unincorporated agreements relating to the same subject matter are void.*

That the intention of the parties is not relevant in courts adopting the same approach as Williston has been recognized in a number of opinions. In a California case, testimony in violation of the parol evidence rule was admitted without objection. The question presented was whether the rule could be invoked despite the lack of objection. The court held that the rule could be invoked, stating that the parol evidence rule did not merely prohibit the proof of contemporaneous oral agreements; rather it prohibited the making of such agreements.

Professor Corbin has an easy task in demolishing the Willistonian approach. In treating the matter of integration as a question of intent, as Professor Williston purports to do, he shows the absurdity of excluding all relevant evidence of intent except the writing itself. But, as we have seen, Williston ... [is] unconcerned about the true intention of the parties. Rather, shorn of rote language of fiction indicating a search for intention ... [he is] advocating and applying a rule of form. Since (and even before) the common law had its genesis, there has been a deeply felt belief that transactions will be more secure, litigation will be reduced, and the temptation to perjury will be removed, if everyone will only use proper forms for his transactions. The Statute of Wills and the Statute of Frauds are but examples of this belief. Professor Corbin, by attacking the apparent arguments of Williston's position has not expressly come to grips with the substance of his position. This is not to suggest that either he or Professor Williston have been unaware of the true nature of their disagreement. Rather, they seem for the most part to have been content not to make explicit the basis of their differing views. The purpose of the above discussion is to bring their differences into bold relief so that the debate on this matter can break away from the bland assumption that everyone agrees as to the statement of the parol evidence rule and that there is merely some confusion as to its application.

The debate involves the question: is the public better served by giving effect to the parties' entire agreement written and oral, even at the risk of injustice caused by the possibility of perjury and the possibility that superseded documents will be treated as operative, or does the security of transactions require that, despite occasional injustices, persons adopting a formal writing be required, on the penalty of voidness of their oral and written side agreements, to put their entire agreement in the formal writing.

The conflict is an old one. Rules excluding evidence on the ground that it is likely to be false are not strangers to the law. Formerly, parties and interested third persons were incompetent to testify on the ground that their testimony would be unworthy of belief. The Statute of Frauds and Statute of Wills embody similar considerations. The authors believe, however, that the possibility of perjury is an insufficient ground for interfering with freedom of contract by refusing to effectuate the parties' entire agreement.

The whole thrust of our law for over a century has been directed to the eradication of exclusionary rules of evidence in civil cases. Thus parties may now testify, their interest in the outcome affecting only the weight and not the admissibility of the evidence. Dissatisfaction with rigid application of the parol evidence rule has resulted in the strained insertion of fact situations into the categories where the parol evidence rule is inapplicable. Thus, to circumvent the rule fraud has been found and reformation has been granted in situations where these concepts are not ordinarily deemed applicable. Moreover, whole categories of exceptions have been carved out; for example, a deed absolute may be shown to be a mortgage. Professor Thayer's summation of the parol evidence problem warrants repetition: "Few things are darker than this, or fuller of subtle difficulties." When any rule of law is riddled through with exceptions and applications difficult to reconcile, it is believed that litigation is stimulated rather than reduced. If the policy of the parol evidence rule is to reduce the possibility of judgments predicated upon perjured testimony and superseded documents, it may be effectuated to a large extent by continuing to leave control over determining the question of intent to integrate in the hands of the trial judge. Finally, the trend of modern decisions, as Williston suggests, "is toward increasing the liberality in the admission of parol agreements." This tendency of the courts is in no small measure due to the influence of Professor Corbin's treatise.

It is of little moment whether the views of the authors of this article as to what the law should be are convincing. The essential point being made here is that there is no uniform parol evidence rule. Rather, there are at least two rather dissimilar rules which, for convenience, may be denominated the Corbin Rule and the Williston Rule. In view of the confusion engendered by having two contradictory rules expressed in the same terminology, it is remarkable that a few states have shown a degree of consistency. New York, despite some inconsistent cases, generally maintains a rigorously Willistonian approach. Rhode Island seems recently to have adopted the Corbin approach with a Willistonian touch, admitting extrinsic evidence out of the presence of the jury to determine whether a total integration exists; the trial judge decides this question on the Willistonian test of whether the alleged collateral agreement "is such that the parties would naturally or normally" have included it in the writing. This seems to be a sound indicia of intent, but not a conclusive one. If the norm is that of the "reasonable man," this good citizen would probably insist that the entire agreement be reduced to writing. The end result would seem to be pure Williston. Some states, such as Connecticut, reach results consistent with Corbin's test, while utilizing the most varied reasoning. Perhaps most states are consistently erratic. Such is the confusion that in any state a decision may be reached which is ludicrous in result and analysis or sensible in result but strained in analysis.

It is hoped that once the source of confusion is comprehended, courts will achieve a greater degree of consistency by consciously choosing one of the competing rules. The widespread adoption of the Uniform Commercial Code may give impetus to a consistent and enlightened approach if it is applied to cases not specifically under its coverage. An Official Comment to § 2-202 states:

> [C]onsistent additional terms, not reduced to writing, may be proved unless the court finds that the writing was intended by both parties as a complete and exclusive statement of all terms. If the additional terms are such that, if agreed upon, they would *certainly* have been included in the document in the view of the court, then evidence of their alleged making must be kept from the trier of fact. (Emphasis added.)

Thus, the Code requires the court to ascertain the intention of the parties, and it can be assumed that the codifiers meant a true expressed intention and not a fictitious intention. The trial judge has an important function in making this determination. If he finds that it is certain the parties would have incorporated the additional term into the writing if they had agreed upon it, he excludes evidence of the alleged term from the jury's consideration. If it is merely improbable that the parties would have agreed to the term without incorporating it into the writing, the jury must determine whether the additional term was agreed upon. The Code, of course, does not propose to affect the power of the court to set aside or direct a verdict where the evidence supporting an alleged supplementary term is flimsy. Thus, the writing is protected at two stages. First, there is a preliminary finding, based on an external standard, as to whether any evidence will be heard by the jury. Second, the court contains its control over the quality and quantity of evidence required to support a verdict....

III. The Relationship Between the Parol Evidence Rule and Rules and Standards of Interpretation

Before the parol evidence rule may be invoked, the judge must determine that the parties intended the writing to be final. The question of intent is determined according to the standards and rules of interpretation discussed above. Conversely, the parol evidence rule should have no effect on the question of interpretation — the *meaning* of language. Stated otherwise, before the parol evidence rule can be invoked to exclude evidence, the *meaning* of the writing must be ascertained since one may not determine whether a writing is being contradicted or supplemented until one knows what the writing means.

This should mean that evidence of prior and contemporaneous expressions is always admissible to aid in determining the meaning of the integration, and Corbin so states. Williston is cautiously in accord. Such evidence may be introduced, he grants, but not to prove that the intention of the parties is at variance with the appropriate local meaning of the words. The evidence may be considered only on the question of whether the parties contracted with reference to a local or trade usage or, if this local or trade meaning is ambiguous, on the question of what meaning the parties attached to the words. Even accepting his premise that the true intention of the parties is usually irrelevant, there are two difficulties with Williston's position on the admissibility of this evidence. First, it assumes that the court can successfully ignore the parties' real intention when it is shown by the evidence. Second, it involves a great deal of tension with the exclusionary aspects of his version of the parol evidence rule. If evidence of prior and contemporaneous expressions is not admissible to prove terms supplementary to or at variance with a total integration, but is admissible to show the meaning of the integration, the astute trial lawyer will characterize his evidence on what are really supplementary or contradictory terms as evidence on the true meaning of the contract. Although the function of this evidence is to demonstrate the "meaning of the writing," once it is admitted the court may find it difficult (and unjust) to disregard what may be clear and convincing proof that the writing is not the complete agreement of the parties. Williston's grand structure meticulously separating the parol evidence rule, standards of interpretation, and primary and secondary rules of interpretation seems to collapse into this procedural pitfall.

It is little wonder, then, that many courts that share Williston's concern for the "security of transactions" have retreated even further from the intention of the parties to the almost universally condemned "plain meaning rule," holding that if a writing appears clear and unambiguous on its face, its meaning must be determined from the four corners of the instrument without resort to extrinsic evidence of any nature. This approach excludes evidence of trade usage and prior dealings between the parties as well as evidence of surrounding circumstances and prior and contemporaneous expressions. The latest legislative ruling on the matter, the Uniform Commercial Code, explicitly condemns the plain meaning rule and explicitly allows use of evidence of a course of dealing or course of performance to explain the agreement "unless carefully negated."

1. THE PAROL EVIDENCE RULE: SEARCH FOR TRUTH ... OR DEFENSE OF FORM?

BINKS MANUFACTURING CO. v. NATIONAL PRESTO INDUSTRIES, INC.

709 F.2d 1109 (7th Cir. 1983)

COFFEY, J. This appeal involves a contractual dispute concerning the manufacture and sale of an "industrial spray finishing and baking system." Binks Manufacturing Company, the System's manufacturer, brought an action in federal district court to collect the purchase price of the System. Presto Manufacturing Company, counterclaimed alleging damages resulting from defective design and manufacture of the System as well as late delivery. The jury returned verdicts in favor of Binks on its purchase price claim and against Presto on its counterclaims. *We affirm.*

I.   Presto is engaged in the manufacture and sale of electrical appliances, including hamburger cookers. Binks Manufacturing Company is a leading manufacturer of industrial spray finishing equipment. In 1975, Presto management decided to increase its production capacity of electric hamburger cookers and as part of its expansion plan, determined to purchase an automatic system designed to coat aluminum castings (the principal components of hamburger cookers) with a non-stick "teflon-like" coating for installation at its Alamogordo, New Mexico plant. Presto entered into negotiations with Binks Manufacturing Company for the design and manufacture of the system.

The negotiations between Binks and Presto continued from October 1975 through March 1976, resulting in a contract with Binks agreeing to manufacture "a custom designed, custom built automatic spray application and oven curing system intended to apply coatings to various Presto products" (hereinafter the "System"). The System was to consist of one continuous conveyor 858 feet long, designed to carry an aluminum casting through a six-step manufacturing process: (1) a booth in which the castings would be sprayed with a primer; (2) an oven where the primer would be baked on to the aluminum castings; (3) a cooling area; (4) a booth where the castings would be sprayed with a non-stick coating; (5) three progressively hotter ovens in which the non-stick coating would be based on to the aluminum castings over the primer; and (6) a final cooling area....

[The contract provided for delivery of the system not later than June 2, 1976; the contract contained a clause providing that "time is of the essence." In fact, due to unforeseeable and apparently unavoidable problems encountered by a Binks' subcontractor (Radiant Products), delivery was not accomplished until July 19, 1976.]

Binks offered to supervise installation of the System, but Presto chose not to accept the offer and hired their own local independent contractors to install the System. According to Binks, Presto's independent contractors committed installation errors of major proportions, including a failure to properly align and anchor the conveyor equipment. Binks further contends that Presto insisted upon initially operating the System at maximum capacity, thereby ignoring Binks' advice that the System be brought up to full capacity only gradually.

After installation of the System had been completed, Presto personnel made several unsuccessful attempts to operate the System's conveyor. In the ensuing weeks representatives of Presto, Binks and Radiant [the oven subcontractor] made other attempts to operate the System, but experienced a myriad of problems. Binks contends that Presto's independent contractors failed to properly synchronize the electric motors used to run the conveyor causing the conveyor to run sporadically and jam. These problems in conveyor synchronization continued for some two months causing the System to operate at less than half capacity.

Binks and Presto disagree as to the underlying cause of the System's faulty performance. Presto alleges that the System was defectively manufactured in that the conveyor, contrary to the contract specifications, was totally enclosed in the System's ovens, causing the conveyor components to overheat, contributing to the twisting, bending, and eventually breakage of the conveyor chain.

Binks, on the other hand, contends Presto: (1) improperly installed the System; (2) inadequately lubricated the conveyor; (3) operated the System's oven at excessive temperatures; (4) ignored Binks' advice in initially operating the System at maximum capacity; and (5) ran defective castings through the System, resulting in pieces breaking off the castings and jamming the conveyor.

Binks also asserts that Presto abused the System by "double loading" the castings used to make upper components of the hamburger cookers, thereby exceeding the System's maximum capacity set forth in the contract. According to Binks, "double loading" the System resulted in twice as many upper burger castings being loaded into the System per hour as specified in the contract (2,250 "upper double burger" castings per hour instead of the 1,125 castings per hour outlined in the contract and 4,500 "upper square burger" castings per hour rather than 2,250 castings per hour set forth in the contract)....

Binks and Presto made several unsuccessful attempts to reach a negotiated settlement and failing to achieve this, on November 4, 1977, Binks filed a complaint seeking recovery under the contract for the balance of the purchase price. Presto answered by filing a $9.5 million counterclaim against Binks alleging late delivery of the System, breach of contractual warranties, breach of implied warranties, negligence and misrepresentation in connection with the design, manufacture and sale of the spraying and baking system.

The case came to trial on March 1, 1982, and after the four-week jury trial, judgment was entered in favor of Binks on its claim for the balance of the purchase price and [against Presto's counterclaims].

[One of the crucial issues involved determining the "maximum capacity" of the system.] The parties agree that the following provision of the contract sets forth the System's maximum capacity:

> One Item of Equipment designed to coat any one of the following parts on one and/or both sides in quantities, as listed at the conveyor rate of 25 fpm with either 16 or 18 inch spindle spacing:
>
> | | | |
> |---|---|---|
> | #60-001* | Upper Double Burger at (13 oz.) | 1,125 pcs./hr. |
> | #60-002* | Lower Double Burger at (24 oz.) | 1,125 pcs./hr. |
> | #60-003* | Upper Square Burger (9.5 oz.) | 2,250 pcs./hr. |
> | #60-004* | Lower Square Burger (12 oz.) | 2,250 pcs./hr. |
> | #60-121* | Upper Round Burger (7 oz.) | 2,250 pcs./hr. |
> | #60-120 | Lower Round Burger (5 oz.) | 2,250 pcs./hr. |
> | #28-006 | Fry Pan at 3.8# — Quantities as later established. | |

> *Asterisk to indicate item coated on both sides. Hinges on 60-001 and 60-003 coated both sides.

> The maximum capacity of the system is limited to the above parts or parts of similar size and cross section with a maximum loading of 4,500 pounds per hour and 4,500 #/hr. of work holders, which would pass through each oven.

Based on the foregoing contractual language, Binks takes the position that the "maximum capacity" of the System for the castings specified in the contract is defined in terms of the *number* of castings that the System can handle per hour consistent with the design of the machine. Presto, however, contends that extrinsic evidence concerning negotiation and performance of the contract demonstrates that the parties intended the maximum capacity of the System to be defined in terms of *pounds* of castings run through the System per hour; i.e., 4,500 pounds of castings per hour. Presto further argues, and Binks concedes, that Presto never loaded the System with more than 4,500 pounds of castings per hour.

Presto, in support of its contention that the parties intended the System's maximum capacity to be defined in *pounds* per hour, sought to introduce extrinsic evidence pertaining to the negotiation and performance of the contract.[14] On February 25, 1976, four days before trial, Binks presented a motion in limine seeking an order precluding Presto from presenting extrinsic evidence to show that the parties intended to define the maximum capacity of the System in terms of pounds per hour rather than number of castings per hour. After hearing arguments, the court ruled in favor of Binks on the motion in limine and stated:

> I conclude that so far as the six identified parts are concerned, the specified maximums of the system are those numbers appearing opposite each of the items [in the contract provision quoted above] and not the number of items which would aggregate 4,500 pounds.

Presto contends the court committed reversible error in ruling that Presto could not introduce extrinsic evidence to show that the parties intended to define the System's maximum capacity in pounds per hour.

In evaluating Presto's challenge to the district court's ruling, we must bear in mind that our role as an appellate court is not to consider a case *de novo*. Rather, our role in reviewing the district court's ruling on the motion in limine is limited as "decisions regarding the admission and exclusion of evidence are peculiarly within the competence of the district court and will not be reversed on appeal unless they constitute a clear abuse of discretion." *Ellis v. City of Chicago*, 667 F.2d 606, 611 (7th Cir. 1981)....

Guided by these principles, we turn to the issue of whether the court abused its discretion by precluding Presto from introducing extrinsic evidence to establish that the parties intended the System's maximum capacity for "Upper Double Burger" and "Upper Square Burger" castings to be defined in pounds per hour, rather than number of castings per hour. The admissibility of extrinsic evidence to interpret the contract in this case is governed by Ill.Rev.Stat. ch. 26, § 2-202 [Uniform Commercial Code § 2-202] ...

---

[14]This extrinsic evidence included *inter alia*: (1) a quotation submitted by Binks several days prior to formation of the contract stating "approximately 4,500 pounds of aluminum work pieces ... will pass through each oven per hour"; (2) a March 9, 1976 letter from Binks' project engineer to Presto reciting "The System capacity increased from 1500 to 4500 #/Hr."; and (3) that Binks participated in designing the work holders in which castings were placed, and allowed for "double loading" of castings.

Thus, it is evident that under U.C.C. § 2-202, evidence of a prior agreement or a contemporaneous oral agreement must be excluded if (1) the writing (here the contract between the parties) was intended as the final expression of the parties agreement with respect to the maximum capacity term; *and* (2) the proffered evidence *contradicts* or is *inconsistent* with the terms of the written contract. See Nordstrom, Law of Sales 161-66 (1970). It is evident from the record that both Binks and Presto agree that their written contract was intended to be the final expression of their agreement; therefore, the crucial question is whether the interpretation urged by Presto (i.e., that the parties intended the System's maximum capacity for "Upper Square Burger" and "Upper Double Burger" castings to be a function of pounds of castings per hour) contradicts or is inconsistent with the terms of the written contract.

Although the Uniform Commercial Code itself fails to delineate or set forth when extrinsic evidence contradicts or is inconsistent with written terms of a contract, this court recently defined "inconsistency" for the purpose of U.C.C. § 2-202 as "the absence of reasonable harmony in terms of the language and respective obligations of the parties." *Luria Bros. & Co. v. Pielet Bros. Scrap Iron*, 600 F.2d 103, 111 (7th Cir. 1979). Applying this definition of "inconsistency" to this case, it is clear that if the court were to allow the admission of extrinsic evidence tending to show that the maximum capacity of the System for "Upper Square Burger" and "Upper Double Burger" castings was defined in terms of pounds per hour it would necessarily lead to an "absence of reasonable harmony" between the terms of the written contract and the proffered extrinsic evidence of the parties' purported intent. Presto's theory that the System's maximum capacity for the upper burger castings was defined as 4,500 pounds of such castings per hour would render almost meaningless the express language of the written contract which, after reciting a specified number of each particular casting, states "the maximum capacity of the System is limited to the above parts...." On the other hand, the district court's well reasoned interpretation of the written contract gave meaning to each and every provision of the contract; for each of the six castings listed, the maximum capacity of the System was defined in number of parts per hour, while for other unspecified castings which Presto might decide to run through the System in the future, the maximum capacity was defined in pounds of castings per hour. Thus, the court's decision to exclude the extrinsic evidence of the parties intent is amply supported by the basic principles of contract interpretation that a written contract should be given a construction that "harmonizes all the various parts" of the contract so that no provision is "conflicting with, or repugnant to, or neutralizing of any other." *Zannis v. Lake Shore Radiologists, Ltd.*, 73 Ill.App.3d 901, 29 Ill.Dec. 569, 392 N.E.2d 126, 129 (1979).

Furthermore, the district court's decision to preclude Presto from introducing extrinsic evidence regarding the maximum capacity issue pays credence to the policy underlying the parol evidence rule as set forth in U.C.C. § 2-202....

This policy of upholding the integrity of written contracts and favoring written terms over extrinsic evidence is particularly relevant in cases of this nature involving a written contract between two large corporations presumably represented by competent counsel. Such parties should be held to the terms of their written contract whenever it is reasonable to do so, as it is incumbent upon courts to uphold the dignity of a contract whenever possible by preventing parol evidence from being used to negate the terms of written contracts....

> ... when ... understandings purporting to be comprehensive are solemnized by documents which both parties sign and concede to be their agreement, such documents are not easily bypassed or given restrictive interpretations.

Additionally, as this lawsuit involved a lengthy and complicated fact situation, admitting extrinsic evidence would have increased the possibility of unnecessarily confusing the jury, a possibility § 2-202 is designed to avoid:

> But the way [§ 2-202] is worded, the trial is certainly not to be a freewheeling affair in which the parties may introduce before the jury all evidence of terms, including the writing, with the jury then to decide on terms. Rather, it is plain from the rule and from prior history of similar rules that some of the evidence is to be heard initially only by the judge and that he may invoke the rule to keep this evidence from the jury.

White & Summers, The Law Under the Uniform Commercial Code 77 (2d ed. 1980).

Conclusion

We agree with the rulings of the trial court and hold that: (1) the district court did not err in precluding Presto from introducing extrinsic evidence to attempt to prove that the parties intended the maximum capacity of the System to be defined solely in terms of pounds of castings per hour....

NOTES AND QUESTIONS

1. *Interpretation as a surrogate for the real dispute*: Presto's small hamburger cookers were very successful, and a large Christmas market was anticipated in 1976. Seller's delivery was six weeks late. The trial court ruled that it was excused by the delay of an oven subcontractor caused by a supplier's strike and an injury to a key employee. The trial court also suggested that Presto had waived any damages from late delivery by accepting delivery, not terminating the contract, and not making a written claim at that time. Presto was in a tough spot once Binks announced it would be late. What should they have done? What are the risks of complaining, and threatening a suit? On the other hand, what are the

risks of remaining silent? The minutes of a November 15, 1976 meeting of the seller's officials, said that "Presto has made commitments on their products and they cannot make their commitments. Presto is desperate. Their frying pans are a commitment to Sears for the Christmas rush." We will return to the issue of what victims of breach can do when we look at waiver and the required notices of an intention to hold a seller for damages under the Uniform Commercial Code. Notice that in this case, however, the issue of the interpretation of the contract as to the capacity of the unit is largely a surrogate for the responsibility for the delay and the efforts made to overcome the lost time. For example, the seller's brief tells us,

> Binks and its suppliers recommended that Presto break in the System gradually after installation. Presto started up the system "full bore" and thereby increased the chance that the conveyor later would drag and the ovens would not seal properly. When the contract was made, the parties assumed the ovens would run 8 hours a day 5 days a week, but Presto decided to operate it 24 hours per day 6 days a week. Presto had no program of preventive maintenance until 6 months after installation.

2. *The excluded parol evidence*: The key item of parol evidence excluded by the trial court was the second of three quotations submitted to Presto by Binks. This quotation provided that:

> The equipment is designed to process approximately 2250 work pieces per hour on 8" centers at a conveyor speed of 25 fpm or the same number of pieces held two per work holder on 16" centers.
>
> Approximately 4500 pounds of aluminum work pieces and 4500 pounds of steel work holders will pass through each oven per hour.

Binks' letter of a day after the second proposal said that under it "the system capacity increased from 1500 to 4500#Hr." The third proposal which became the contract was written within four days after this letter.

Presto also argued that the trial court should have looked at the course of performance to indicate the proper construction of the contract. The work holder was designed to allow two parts per holder and thus a load more than what the trial court found to be the maximum weights under the contract. The system was operated with Binks' knowledge, and Presto double loaded the system at the 24-hour test run, and Binks' officials did not object.

3. *Explaining the way the contract was drafted*: Binks responded, arguing,

> There was an important reason for expressing the maximum capacity of the System in terms of specific hourly quantities for the identified parts. The ovens in the System baked Presto's coatings by "impinged high velocity hot air" — jets of hot air directed at the parts as they progressed through the ovens. An increase in the number of parts passing back and forth through

the ovens would obstruct the impinged air and, therefore, decrease the efficiency of the ovens. On the other hand, the "maximum loading" provision in the contract established the weight above which the loading of the parts (4500 pounds) and the workholders (4500 pounds) would exceed the weight-bearing tolerances of the entire System, including the conveyor and conveyor drives....

Binks has never contended that it was improper to load 2 parts per workholder, so long as the applicable pieces-per-hour limitation was not exceeded. These overall limits could have been observed even when workholders were being doubleloaded simply by doubling the distance between workholders.

2. OF PARTIAL INTEGRATIONS AND SIDE AGREEMENTS

MITCHILL v. LATH

247 N.Y. 377, 160 N.E. 646 (1928)

Appeal, by permission, from a judgment of the Appellate Division of the Supreme Court in the second judicial department, entered May 27, 1927, unanimously affirming a judgment in favor of plaintiff entered upon a decision of the court on trial at Special Term in an action to compel specific performance of an alleged contract to remove an ice house....

ANDREWS, J. In the fall of 1923 the Laths owned a farm. This they wished to sell. Across the road, on land belonging to Lieutenant-Governor Lunn, they had an ice house which they might remove. Mrs. Mitchill looked over the land with a view to its purchase. She found the ice house objectionable. Thereupon "the defendants orally promised and agreed, for and in consideration of the purchase of their farm by the plaintiff, to remove the said ice house in the spring of 1924." Relying upon this promise, she made a written contract to buy the property for $8,400, for cash and a mortgage and containing various provisions usual in such papers. Later receiving a deed, she entered into possession and has spent considerable sums in improving the property for use as a summer residence. The defendants have not fulfilled their promise as to the ice house and do not intend to do so. We are not dealing, however, with their moral delinquencies. The question before us is whether their oral agreement may be enforced in a court of equity.

This requires a discussion of the parol evidence rule — a rule of law which defines the limits of the contract to be construed. (*Glackin v. Bennett*, 226 Mass. 316.) It is more than a rule of evidence and oral testimony even if admitted will not control the written contract (*O'Malley v. Grady*, 222 Mass. 202), unless admitted without objection. (*Brady v. Nally*, 151 N.Y. 258.) It applies, however, to attempts to modify such a contract by parol. It does not affect a parol collateral contract distinct from and independent of the written agreement. It is, at times, troublesome to draw the line. Williston, in his work on Contracts (§ 637), points out the difficulty. "Two entirely distinct contracts," he says, "each for a separate consideration may be made at the same time and will be distinct legally. Where, however, one agreement is entered into wholly or partly in consideration of the simultaneous agreement to enter into another, the transactions are necessarily bound together.... Then if one of the agreements is oral and the other is in writing, the problem arises whether the bond is sufficiently close to prevent proof of the oral agreement." That is the situation here. It is claimed that the defendants are called upon to do more than is required by their written contract in connection with the sale as to which it deals.

The principle may be clear, but it can be given effect by no mechanical rule. As so often happens, it is a matter of degree, for as Professor Williston also says where a contract contains several promises on each side it is not difficult to put any one of them in the form of a collateral agreement. If this were enough written contracts might always be modified by parol. Not form, but substance is the test.

In applying this test the policy of our courts is to be considered. We have believed that the purpose behind the rule was a wise one not easily to be abandoned. Notwithstanding injustice here and there, on the whole it works for good. Old precedents and principles are not to be lightly cast aside unless it is certain that they are an obstruction under present conditions. New York has been less open to arguments that would modify this particular rule, than some jurisdictions elsewhere. Thus in *Eighmie v. Taylor* (98 N.Y. 288) it was held that a parol warranty might not be shown although no warranties were contained in the writing.

Under our decisions before such an oral agreement as the present is received to vary the written contract, at least three conditions must exist, (1) the agreement must in form be a collateral one; (2) it must not contradict express or implied provisions of the written contract; (3) it must be one that parties would not ordinarily be expected to embody in the writing; or put in another way, an inspection of the written contract, read in the light of surrounding circumstances must not indicate that the writing appears "to contain the engagements of the parties, and to define the object and measure the extent of such engagement." Or again, it must not be so clearly connected with the principal transaction as to be part and parcel of it.

The respondent does not satisfy the third of these requirements. It may be, not the second. We have a written contract for the purchase and sale of land. The buyer is to pay $8,400 in the way described. She is also to pay her portion of any rents, interest on mortgages, insurance premiums and water meter charges. She may have a survey made of the premises. On their part the sellers are to give a full covenant deed of the premises as described, or as they may be described by the surveyor if the survey is had, executed and acknowledged at their own expense; they sell the personal property on the farm and represent they own it; they agree that all amounts paid them on the contract and the expense of examining the title shall be a lien on the property; they assume the risk of loss or damage by fire until the deed is delivered; and they agree to pay the broker his commissions. Are they to do more? Or is such a claim inconsistent with these precise provisions? It could not be shown that the plaintiff was to pay $500 additional. Is it also implied that the defendants are not to do anything unexpressed in the writing?

That we need not decide. At least, however, an inspection of this contract shows a full and complete agreement, setting forth in detail the obligations of each party. On reading it one would conclude that the reciprocal obligations of the parties were fully detailed. Nor would his opinion alter if he knew the surrounding circumstances. The presence of the ice house, even the knowledge that Mrs. Mitchill thought it objectionable, would not lead to the belief that a separate agreement existed with regard to it. Were such an agreement made it would seem most natural that the inquirer should find it in the contract. Collateral in form it is found to be, but it is closely related to the subject dealt with in the written agreement — so closely that we hold it may not be proved.

Where the line between the competent and the incompetent is narrow the citation of authorities is of slight use. Each represents the judgment of the court on the precise facts before it. How closely bound to the contract is the supposed collateral agreement is the decisive factor in each case....

Attention should be called also to *Taylor v. Hopper* (62 N.Y. 649), where it is assumed that evidence of a parol agreement to remove a barn, which was an inducement to the sale of lots, was improper.

We do not ignore the fact that authorities may be found that would seem to support the contention of the appellant.... But the fixed form of a deed makes it inappropriate to insert collateral agreements, however closely connected with the sale. This may be cause for an exception. Here we deal with the contract on the basis of which the deed to Mrs. Mitchill was given subsequently, and we confine ourselves to the question whether its terms may be modified.

Finally there is the case of *Chapin v. Dobson* (78 N.Y. 74, 76). This is acknowledged to be on the border line and is rarely cited except to be distinguished. Assuming the premises, however, the court was clearly right. There was nothing on the face of the written contract, it said, to show that it intended to express the entire agreement. And there was a finding, sustained by evidence, that there was an entire contract, only part of which was reduced to writing. This being so, the contract as made might be proved.

It is argued that what we have said is not applicable to the case as presented. The collateral agreement was made with the plaintiff. The contract of sale was with her husband and no assignment of it from him appears. Yet the deed was given to her. It is evident that here was a transaction in which she was the principal from beginning to end. We must treat the contract as if in form, as it was in fact, made by her.

Our conclusion is that the judgment of the Appellate Division and that of the Special Term should be reversed and the complaint dismissed, with costs in all courts.

LEHMAN, J. (dissenting). I accept the general rule as formulated by Judge Andrews. I differ with him only as to its application to the facts shown in the record. The plaintiff contracted to purchase land from the defendants for an agreed price. A formal written agreement was made between the sellers and the plaintiff's husband. It is on its face a complete contract for the conveyance of the land. It describes the property to be conveyed. It sets forth the purchase price to be paid. All the conditions and terms of the conveyance to be made are clearly stated. I concede at the outset that parol evidence to show additional conditions and terms of the conveyance would be inadmissible. There is a conclusive presumption that the parties intended to integrate in that written contract every agreement relating to the nature or extent of the property to be conveyed, the contents of the deed to be delivered, the consideration to be paid as a condition precedent to the delivery of the deeds, and indeed all the rights of the parties in connection with the land. The conveyance of that land was the subject-matter of the written contract and the contract completely covers that subject.

The parol agreement which the court below found the parties had made was collateral to, yet connected with, the agreement of purchase and sale. It has been found that the defendants induced the plaintiff to agree to purchase the land by a promise to remove an ice house from land not covered by the agreement of purchase and sale. No independent consideration passed to the defendants for the parol promise. To that extent the written contract and the alleged oral contract are bound together. The same bond usually exists wherever attempt is made to prove a parol agreement which is collateral to a written agreement. Hence "the problem arises whether the bond is sufficiently close to prevent proof of the oral agreement." See Judge Andrews' citation from Williston on Contracts, § 637....

I have conceded that upon inspection the contract is complete. "It appears to contain the engagements of the parties, and to define the object and measure the extent of such engagement;" it constitutes the contract between them and is presumed to contain the whole of that contract. (*Eighmie v. Taylor*, 98 N.Y. 288.) That engagement was on the one side to convey land; on the other to pay the price. The plaintiff asserts further agreement based on the same consideration to be performed by the defendants after the conveyance was complete, and directly affecting only other land. It is true, as Judge Andrews points out, that "the presence of the ice house, even the knowledge that Mrs. Mitchill thought it objectionable, would not lead to the belief that a separate agreement existed with regard to it;" but the question we must decide is whether or not, *assuming* an agreement was made for the removal of an unsightly ice house from one parcel of land as an inducement for the purchase of another parcel, the parties would ordinarily or naturally be expected to embody the agreement for the removal of the ice house from one parcel in the written agreement to convey the other parcel. Exclusion of proof of the oral agreement on the ground that it varies the contract embodied in the writing may be based only upon a finding or presumption that the written contract was intended to cover the oral negotiations for the removal of the ice house which lead up to the contract of purchase and sale. To determine what the writing was intended to cover "the document alone will not suffice. What it was intended to cover cannot be known till we know what there was to cover. The question being whether certain subjects of negotiation were intended to be covered, we must compare the writing and the negotiations before we can determine whether they were in fact covered." (Wigmore on Evidence [2d ed.], § 2430.)

The subject-matter of the written contract was the conveyance of land. The contract was so complete on its face that the conclusion is inevitable that the parties intended to embody in the writing all the negotiations covering at least the conveyance. The promise by the defendants to remove the ice house from other land was not connected with their obligation to convey, except that one agreement would not have been made unless the other was also made. The plaintiff's assertion of a parol agreement by the defendants to remove the ice house was completely established by the great weight of evidence. It must prevail unless that agreement was part of the agreement to convey and the entire agreement was embodied in the writing.

The fact that in this case the parol agreement is established by the overwhelming weight of evidence is, of course, not a factor which may be considered in determining the competency or legal effect of the evidence. Hardship in the particular case would not justify the court in disregarding or emasculating the general rule. It merely accentuates the outlines of our problem. The assumption that the parol agreement was made is no longer obscured by any doubts. The problem then is clearly whether the parties are presumed to have intended to render that parol agreement legally ineffective and non-existent by failure to embody it in the writing. Though we are driven to say that nothing in the written contract which fixed the terms and conditions of the stipulated conveyance suggests the existence of any further parol agreement, an inspection of the contract, though it is complete on its face in regard to the subject of the conveyance, does not, I think, show that it was intended to embody negotiations or agreements, if any, in regard to a matter so loosely bound to the conveyance as the removal of an ice house from land not conveyed.... *Affirmed.*

Cardozo, Ch. J., Pound, Kellogg and O'Brien, JJ., concur with Andrews, J.; Lehman, J., dissents in opinion in which Crane, J., concurs.

Judgment accordingly.

NOTES AND QUESTIONS

1. *Background from the briefs and record*: The buyers sued for specific performance. On December 20, 1926, the trial court issued a degree ordering the seller to remove the ice house by December 25th or to pay buyers $8,000. The court found that the sellers orally promised to remove the ice house by the spring of 1924. Relying on this promise, buyers bought the farm for $8,400. The deed was delivered on December 19, 1923. Buyers made extensive repairs and improvements, spending over $23,000, "during the course of some of which the defendants were employed." The presence of the ice house and the operation of the ice business decreased the value of the property by $8,000.

2. *The likely impact of the decision*: What lessons might the decision teach the rest of us? Are future buyers in Mrs. Mitchill's position likely to learn that they cannot trust sellers but must get these promises in writing? Can we count on real estate brokers and lawyers to tell her? What is likely to happen in cases where parties deal without brokers or lawyers? To what extent is a demand to put promises such as this one in writing an attack on the integrity of the other party?

3. *Is the Mitchill standard still good law in New York?*: Judge Andrews' opinion spoke of additional terms "that parties would not ordinarily be expected to embody in the writing." Official Comment 3 to U.C.C. § 202 talks of "additional terms ... such that, if agreed upon, ... would certainly have been included in the document...." Is the difference between these two formulations of the standard significant? In what setting? To whom?[15]

4. *A way around Mitchill?*: In *Plum Tree, Inc. v. N.K. Winston Corp.*,[16] a commercial tenant sued the lessor of space in a large shopping center. The tenant alleged oral promises to advertise, select other tenants whose businesses would complement those of existing lessees, provide security measures, and maintain and clean the center. It also alleged that these were fraudulent misrepresentations. The court applied *Mitchill v. Lath* and ruled that the tenant could not offer evidence of the oral promises. It said, "[o]ne would expect the promise if made to be written down along with the other written promises." However, the court said that making promises with no intention to perform would be fraud. The parol evidence rule does not bar proof of fraudulent statements that prompt a

---

[15]A lower New York court suggested in George v. Davoli, 91 Misc.2d 296, 397 N.Y.S.2d 895 (City Ct. Geneva 1977) that the Mitchill case "does not apply herein as its application to the instant case [a transaction in goods covered by Article 2 of the U.C.C.] has been changed by legislative enactment (Uniform Commercial Code § 2-202, sub (b)) which took effect in 1964." In the case of Braten v. Bankers Trust Co., 60 N.Y.2d 155, 456 N.E.2d 802 (1983). The Court of Appeals indicated that the Mitchill case is alive and well, at least outside the area covered by Article 2 of the U.C.C., finding in that case that evidence of an oral promise to delay enforcing foreclosure rights contradicted the document since it did not appear in the writing and "Such a fundamental condition would hardly have been omitted."

[16]351 F. Supp.2d 80 (S.D.N.Y. 1972).

person to enter a contract. The court allowed the tenant to amend its complaint to proceed on this theory. While this allowed the tenant to survive a motion for summary judgment, the tenant faced real problems proving such a case.

MASTERSON v. SINE

68 Cal.2d 222, 436 P.2d 561 (1968)

Action for declaratory relief to establish plaintiff's right to enforce an option to repurchase certain real property. Judgment declaring plaintiff's right to exercise the option reversed.

TRAYNOR, C.J. — Dallas Masterson and his wife Rebuke owned a ranch as tenants in common. On February 25, 1958, they conveyed it to Medora and Lu Sine by a grant deed "Reserving unto the Grantors herein an option to purchase the above described property on or before February 25, 1968" for the "same consideration as being paid heretofore plus their depreciation value of any improvements Grantees may add to the property from and after two and a half years from this date." Medora is Dallas' sister and Lu's wife. Since the conveyance Dallas has been adjudged bankrupt. His trustee in bankruptcy and Rebuke brought this declaratory relief action to establish their right to enforce the option.

The case was tried without a jury. Over defendants' objection the trial court admitted extrinsic evidence that by "the same consideration as being paid heretofore" both the grantors and the grantees meant the sum of $50,000 and by "depreciation value of any improvements" they meant the depreciation value of improvements to be computed by deducting from the total amount of any capital expenditures made by defendants grantees the amount of depreciation allowable to them under United States income tax regulations as of the time of the exercise of the option.

The court also determined that the parol evidence rule precluded admission of extrinsic evidence offered by defendants to show that the parties wanted the property kept in the Masterson family and that the option was therefore personal to the grantors and could not be exercised by the trustee in bankruptcy.

The court entered judgment for plaintiffs, declaring their right to exercise the option, specifying in some detail how it could be exercised, and reserving jurisdiction to supervise the manner of its exercise and to determine the amount that plaintiffs will be required to pay defendants for their capital expenditures if plaintiffs decide to exercise the option.

Defendants appeal. They contend that the option provision is too uncertain to be enforced and that extrinsic evidence as to its meaning should not have been admitted. The trial court properly refused to frustrate the obviously declared intention of the grantors to reserve an option to repurchase by an overly meticulous insistence on completeness and clarity of written expression.... It properly admitted extrinsic evidence to explain the language of the deed ... to the end that the consideration for the option would appear with sufficient certainty to permit specific enforcement.... The trial court erred, however, in excluding the extrinsic evidence that the option was personal to the grantors and therefore nonassignable.

When the parties to a written contract have agreed to it as an "integration" — a complete and final embodiment of the terms of an agreement — parol evidence cannot be used to add to or vary its terms.... When only part of the agreement is integrated, the same rule applies to that part, but parol evidence may be used to prove elements of the agreement not reduced to writing....

The crucial issue in determining whether there has been an integration is whether the parties intended their writing to serve as the exclusive embodiment of their agreement. The instrument itself may help to resolve that issue. It may state, for example, that "there are no previous understandings or agreements not contained in the writing," and thus express the parties' "intention to nullify antecedent understandings or agreements." (See 3 Corbin, Contracts (1960) § 578, p. 411.) Any such collateral agreement itself must be examined, however, to determine whether the parties intended the subjects of negotiation it deals with to be included in, excluded from, or otherwise affected by the writing. Circumstances at the time of the writing may also aid in the determination of such integration....

California cases have stated that whether there was an integration is to be determined solely from the face of the instrument, ... and that the question for the court is whether it "appears to be a complete ... agreement...." ...

Neither of these strict formulations of the rule, however, has been consistently applied. The requirement that the writing must appear incomplete on its face has been repudiated in many cases where parol evidence was admitted "to prove the existence of a separate oral agreement as to any matter on which the document is silent and which is not inconsistent with its terms" — even though the instrument appeared to state a complete agreement....

Even under the rule that the writing alone is to be consulted, it was found necessary to examine the alleged collateral agreement before concluding that proof of it was precluded by the writing alone. (See 3 Corbin, Contracts (1960) § 582, pp. 444-446.) It is therefore evident that "The conception of a writing as wholly and intrinsically self-determinative of the parties' intent to make it a sole memorial [*227] of one or seven or twenty-seven subjects of negotiation is an impossible one." (9 Wigmore, Evidence (3d ed. 1940) § 2431, p. 103.) For example, a promissory note given by a debtor to his creditor may integrate all their present contractual rights and obligations, or it may be only a minor part of an underlying executory contract that would never be discovered by examining the face of the note.

In formulating the rule governing parol evidence, several policies must be accommodated. One policy is based on the assumption that written evidence is more accurate than human memory.... This policy, however, can be adequately served by excluding parol evidence of agreements that directly contradict the writing. Another policy is based on the fear that fraud or unintentional invention by witnesses interested in the outcome of the litigation will mislead the finder of facts....

McCormick has suggested that the party urging the spoken as against the written word is most often the economic underdog, threatened by severe hardship if the writing is enforced. In his view the parol evidence rule arose to allow the court to control the tendency of the jury to find through sympathy and without a dispassionate assessment of the probability of fraud or faulty memory that the parties made an oral agreement collateral to the written contract, or that preliminary tentative agreements were not abandoned when omitted from the writing. (See McCormick, Evidence (1954) § 210.) He recognizes, however, that if this theory were adopted in disregard of all other considerations, it would lead to the exclusion of testimony concerning oral agreements whenever there is a writing and thereby often defeat the true intent of the parties. (See McCormick, *op. cit. supra*, § 216, p. 441.)

Evidence of oral collateral agreements should be excluded only when the fact finder is likely to be misled. The rule must therefore be based on the credibility of the evidence. One such standard, adopted by § 240(1)(b) of the Restatement of Contracts, permits proof of a collateral agreement if it "is such an agreement as might *naturally* be made as a separate agreement by parties situated as were the parties to the written contract." (Italics added; see McCormick, Evidence (1954) § 216, p. 441; see also 3 Corbin, Contracts (1960) § 583, p. 475, § 594, pp. 568-569; 4 Williston, Contracts (3d ed. 1961) § 638, pp. 1039-1045.) The draftsmen of the Uniform Commercial Code would exclude the evidence in still fewer instances: "If the additional terms are such that, if agreed upon, they would *certainly* have been included in the document in the view of the court, then evidence of their alleged making must be kept from the trier of fact." (Com. 3, § 2-202, italics added.)[17]

The option clause in the deed in the present case does not explicitly provide that it contains the complete agreement, and the deed is silent on the question of assignability. Moreover, the difficulty of accommodating the formalized structure of a deed to the insertion of collateral agreements makes it less likely that all the terms of such an agreement were included. (See 3 Corbin, Contracts (1960) § 587; 4 Williston, Contracts (3d ed. 1961) § 645; 70 A.L.R. 752, 759 (1931);

---

[17]Corbin suggests that, even in situations where the court concludes that it would not have been natural for the parties to make the alleged collateral oral agreement, parol evidence of such an agreement should nevertheless be permitted if the court is convinced that the unnatural actually happened in the case being adjudicated. (3 Corbin, Contracts, § 485, pp. 478, 480; cf. Murray, The Parol Evidence Rule: A Clarification (1966) 4 Duquesne Law Review 337, 341-342.) This suggestion may be based on a belief that judges are not likely to be misled by their sympathies. If the court believes that the parties intended a collateral agreement to be effective, there is no reason to keep the evidence from the jury.

68 A.L.R. 245 (1930).) The statement of the reservation of the option might well have been placed in the recorded deed solely to preserve the grantors' rights against any possible future purchasers, and this function could well be served without any mention of the parties' agreement that the option was personal. There is nothing in the record to indicate that the parties to this family transaction, through experience in land transactions or otherwise, had any warning of the disadvantages of failing to put the whole agreement in the deed. This case is one, therefore, in which it can be said that a collateral agreement such as that alleged "might naturally be made as a separate agreement." *A fortiori*, the case is not one in which the parties "would certainly" have included the collateral agreement in the deed.

It is contended, however, that an option agreement is ordinarily presumed to be assignable if it contains no provisions forbidding its transfer or indicating that its performance involves elements personal to the parties.... The fact that there is a written memorandum, however, does not necessarily preclude parol evidence rebutting a term that the law would otherwise presume....

Moreover, even when there is no explicit agreement — written or oral — that contractual duties shall be personal, courts will effectuate a presumed intent to that effect if the circumstances indicate that performance by a substituted person would be different from that contracted for....

In the present case defendants offered evidence that the parties agreed that the option was not assignable in order to keep the property in the Masterson family. The trial court erred in excluding that evidence.

The judgment is reversed....

BURKE, J. — I dissent. The majority opinion:

(1) Undermines the parol evidence rule as we have known it in this state since at least 1872 by declaring that parol evidence should have been admitted by the trial court to show that a written option, absolute and unrestricted in form, was intended to be limited and nonassignable;

(2) Renders suspect instruments of conveyance absolute on their face;

(3) Materially lessens the reliance which may be placed upon written instruments affecting the title to real estate; and

(4) Opens the door, albeit unintentionally, to a new technique for the defrauding of creditors.

The opinion permits defendants to establish by parol testimony that their grant to their brother (and brother-in-law) of a written option, absolute in terms, was nevertheless agreed to be nonassignable by the grantee (now a bankrupt), and that therefore the right to exercise it did not pass, by operation of the bankruptcy laws, to the trustee for the benefit of the grantee's creditors.

And how was this to be shown? By the proffered testimony of the bankrupt optionee himself. Thereby one of his assets (the option to purchase defendants' California ranch) would be withheld from the trustee in bankruptcy and from the bankrupt's creditors. Understandably the trial court, as required by the parol evidence rule, did not allow the bankrupt by parol to so contradict the unqualified language of the written option.

The court properly admitted parol evidence to explain the intended meaning of the "same consideration" and "depreciation value" phases of the written option to purchase defendants' land, as the intended meaning of those phrases was not clear. However, there was nothing ambiguous about the granting language of the option and not the slightest suggestion in the document that the option was to be nonassignable. Thus, to permit such words of limitation to be added by parol is to *contradict* the absolute nature of the grant, and to directly violate the parol evidence rule.

Just as it is unnecessary to state in a deed to "lot X" that the house located thereon goes with the land, it is likewise unnecessary to add to "I grant an option to Jones" the words *"and his assigns"* for the option to be assignable. As hereinafter emphasized in more detail, California statutes expressly declare that it *is* assignable, and only if I add language in writing showing my intent to withhold or restrict the right of assignment may the grant be so limited. Thus, to seek to restrict the grant by parol is to *contradict* the written document in violation of the parol evidence rule.

The majority opinion arrives at its holding via a series of false premises which are not supported either in the record of this case or in such California authorities as are offered....

To support further speculation that "the reservation of the option might well have been placed in the recorded deed solely to preserve the grantors' rights against any possible future purchasers, and this function could well be served without any mention of the parties' agreement that the option was personal," the majority assert that "There is *nothing in the record* to indicate that the parties to this family transaction, through experience in land transactions or otherwise, had any warning of the disadvantages of failing to put the whole agreement in the deed." (Italics added.) The facts of this case, however, do not support such claim of naivete. The grantor husband (the bankrupt businessman) testified that as none of the parties were attorneys "we wanted to contact my attorney ... which we did.... The wording in the option was obtained from [the attorney].... I told him what my discussion was with the Sines [defendant grantees] and he wanted ... a little time to compose it.... And, then this [the wording provided by the attorney] was taken to the title company at the time Mr. and Mrs. Sine and I went in to *complete the transaction.*" (italics added.) The witness was an experienced businessman who thus demonstrated awareness of the wisdom of seeking legal guidance and advice in this business transaction, and who did so. Wherein lies the naive family transaction postulated by the majority? ...

Comment hardly seems necessary on the convenience to a bankrupt of such a device to defeat his creditors. He need only produce parol testimony that any options (or other property, for that matter) which he holds are subject to an oral "collateral agreement" with family members (or with friends) that the property is nontransferable "in order to keep the property in the family" or in the friendly group. In the present case the value of the ranch which the bankrupt and his wife held an option to purchase has doubtless increased substantially during the years since they acquired the option. The initiation of this litigation by the trustee in bankruptcy to establish his right to enforce the option indicates his belief that there is substantial value to be gained for the creditors from this asset of the bankrupt. Yet the majority opinion permits defeat of the trustee and of the creditors through the device of an asserted collateral oral agreement that the option was "personal" to the bankrupt and nonassignable "in order to keep the property in the family"![18]

It also seems appropriate to inquire as to the rights of plaintiff wife in the option which she holds with her bankrupt husband. Is her interest therein also subject to being shown to be personal and not salable or assignable? And, what are her rights and those of her husband in the ranch land itself, if they exercise their option to purchase it? Will they be free to then sell the land? Or, if they prefer, may they hold it beyond the reach of creditors? Or can other members of "the family" claim some sort of restriction on it in perpetuity, established by parol evidence?

And if defendants sell the land subject to the option, will the new owners be heard to assert that the option is "personal" to the optionees, "in order to keep the property in the Masterson family"? Or is that claim "personal" to defendants only?

These are only a few of the confusions and inconsistencies which will arise to plague property owners and, incidentally, attorneys and title companies, who seek to counsel and protect them.

I would hold that the trial court ruled correctly on the proffered parol evidence, and I would affirm the judgment. [McComb, J., concurred.]

NOTES AND QUESTIONS

1. *Justice Traynor*. Roger Traynor was a member of the University of California at Berkeley Law Faculty when he was appointed to the Supreme Court of California in 1940. He served on that court until his retirement in 1970. Henry Friendly, a much respected judge, wrote a tribute on the occasion of Justice Traynor's death. He said, "Roger Traynor was the ablest judge of his generation in the United States. I say this without hesitation, qualification, limitation, or fear of successful contradiction."[19]

---

[18]As noted at the outset of this dissent, it was by means of the bankrupt's own testimony that defendants (the bankrupt's sister and her husband) sought to show that the option was personal to the bankrupt and thus not transferable to the trustee in bankruptcy.

[19]Friendly, Ablest Judge of His Generation, 71 California law Review 1039 (1983).

Walter Schaefer, another famous appellate judge, wrote,[20]

> "Roger Traynor is a law professor's judge," said the late Professor Harry
> Kalven, pointing out that his own case book on torts used eight Traynor
> cases and that "we would be well advised to have used more.... "
>
> That Roger Traynor was also a judge's judge is obvious from the frequent
> citation of his opinions. A Traynor opinion is always sound currency,
> always to be reckoned with. His influence on judges was enhanced by his
> warm personal relationships with so many of them. Over a span of just short
> of ten years, he served on the faculty of the Appellate Judge's Seminar at
> New York Law University Law School. There he met for two weeks each
> year with twenty to twenty-five judges of top state courts and federal courts
> of appeals. The atmosphere was informal; common problems were discussed
> frankly and lasting friendships resulted.

Justice Traynor's opinions in cases such as *Drennan v. Star Paving*, *supra*, and
in areas such as the conflict of laws and products liability have had great
influence on courts in other states. Although it has been cited in Alaska,
Colorado, Idaho, North Carolina, Oregon, Rhode Island, Utah, Washington,
Wisconsin, and Wyoming, *Masterson v. Sine* has not had great influence outside
of California. Why not?[21]

2. **Justice Traynor on construction of documents**: *Masterson v. Sine* is but
one of several decisions written by Justice Traynor concerning interpreting and
construing written documents. Roughly, he adopts Professor Corbin's approach.
For example, in *Pacific Gas & Elect. Co. v. G.W. Thomas Drayage & Rigging
Co.*,[22] there was a contract for repairs on a steam turbine. It provided that G.W.
Thomas was to indemnify PG & E "against all loss ... resulting from ... injury
to property ... in any way connected with the performance of this contract." PG
& E sued to recover damages for an injury to the turbine itself. G.W. Thomas
offered evidence that the parties intended the indemnity clause to cover only
injury to the property of third parties. The trial court refused to consider this
evidence because the contract had a "plain and clear" meaning. The Supreme
Court of California reversed. The question was the credibility of this evidence
and not its admissibility.

Justice Traynor reinforced (and perhaps even extended?) this view in *Delta
Dynamics, Inc. v. Arioto*.[23] In a case in which the trial court refused to hear
evidence that the parties intended that cancellation of the contract was the

---

[20]Schaefer, A Judge's Judge, 71 California Law Review 1050 (1983).

[21]For a discussion of Justice Traynor's opinions, see Macaulay, Mr. Justice Traynor and the
Law of Contracts, 13 Stanford Law Review 812 (1961).

[22]69 Cal.2d 33, 442 P.2d 641 (1968).

[23]69 Cal.2d 525, 446 P.2d 785 (1968).

exclusive remedy for a failure by a distributor to sell a specified number of safety devices, the Supreme Court of California reversed.

Justice Traynor said "[t]he test of admissibility of extrinsic evidence to explain the meaning of a written instrument is not whether it appears to the court to be plain and unambiguous on its face, but whether the offered evidence is relevant to prove a meaning to which the language of the instrument is reasonably susceptible."[24] However, Justice Traynor also suggests that credible evidence does not necessarily mean evidence conforming to an objective standard. That implies that all credible evidence should be admitted provisionally to prove the intentions of the parties. Indeed, he even suggests that the evidence may be credible and establish a meaning to which the language of the document is not reasonably (objectively?) susceptible. If this is the case, then it could be argued that courts must look at all the offered evidence to see if this interpretation is believable.[25]

Contrast Justice Traynor's approach with that of the Seventh Circuit's approach in *Binks Manufacturing Co. v. National Presto Industries, Inc.* What are the advantages and disadvantages of each approach?

3. *Later developments*: *Masterson v. Sine* has been cited by California appellate courts 111 times up to October of 1992. To a great extent, the California courts have followed the approach sketched by Justice Traynor.[26] It is certainly an important case if one asks about which opinions appear in law school casebooks. Both it, and the cases which followed it, have provoked criticism of its supposed undermining of market certainty and the sanctity of documents. One of the most colorful attacks occurred in *Trident Center v. Connecticut Gen. Life Ins. Co.*[27] In that case a partnership consisting of an insurance company and two of Los Angeles' largest and most prestigious law firms brought an action in federal court for a declaratory judgment. California law governed the transaction. The partnership asserted that it had the right to prepay a loan of more than $56 million. The 12¼ percent rate that had seemed reasonable in 1983 compared unfavorably with 1987 market rates and Trident [the partnership plaintiff] started looking for ways of refinancing the loan to take advantage of the lower rates. The defendant lender brought a motion to dismiss, claiming that the loan documents clearly and unambiguously precluded prepayment during the first 12 years of the loan. The trial court granted the motion and dismissed the plaintiff's

---

[24]Pacific Gas & Elec. Co. v. G.W. Thomas Drayage & Rigging Co., 69 Cal.2d at 37, 442 P.2d at 644.

[25]For a discussion, see West, Chief Justice Traynor and the Parol Evidence Rule, 22 Stanford Law Review 547 (1970).

[26]But see Riley v. Bear Creek Planning Committee, 17 Cal.3d, 500, 551 P.2d 1213 (1976), which could be interpreted as a retrenchment and suggests a move in the direction of granting more protection to formal written documents.

[27]847 F.2d 564 (9th Cir. 1988).

complaint. Moreover, the trial court also sanctioned the plaintiff for filing a frivolous lawsuit.

The United States Court of Appeals reversed. Judge Kozinski said,

> The contract documents are lengthy and detailed; they squarely address the precise issue that is the subject of this dispute; to all who read English, they appear to resolve the issue fully and conclusively.
>
> Plaintiff nevertheless argues here, as it did below, that it is entitled to introduce extrinsic evidence that the contract means something other than what it says. This case therefore presents the question whether parties in California can ever draft a contract that is proof to parol evidence. Somewhat surprisingly, the answer is no.

Judge Kozinski analyzed Justice Traynor's opinion in the *Pacific Gas & Electric Co.* case. He was highly critical:

> We question whether this [Justice Traynor's] approach is more likely to divulge the original intention of the parties than reliance on the seemingly clear words they agreed upon at the time....
>
> *Pacific Gas* casts a long shadow of uncertainty over all transactions negotiated and executed under the law of California. As this case illustrates, even when the transaction is very sizeable, even if it involves only sophisticated parties, even if it was negotiated with the aid of counsel, even if it results in contract language that is devoid of ambiguity, costly and protracted litigation cannot be avoided if one party has a strong enough motive for challenging the contract. While this rule creates much business for lawyers and an occasional windfall to some clients, it leads only to frustration and delay for most litigants and clogs already overburdened courts.
>
> It also chips away at the foundation of our legal system. By giving credence to the idea that words are inadequate to express concepts, *Pacific Gas* undermines the basic principle that language provides a meaningful constraint on public and private conduct. If we are unwilling to say that parties, dealing face to face, can come up with language that binds them, how can we send anyone to jail for violating statutes consisting of mere words lacking "absolute and constant referents"? How can courts ever enforce decrees, not written in language understandable to all, but encoded in a dialect reflecting only the "linguistic background of the judge"? Can lower courts ever be faulted for failing to carry out the mandate of higher courts when "perfect verbal expression" is impossible? Are all attempts to develop the law in a reasoned and principled fashion doomed to failure as "remnant[s] of a primitive faith in the inherent potency and inherent meaning of words"? ...

By holding that language has no objective meaning, and that contracts mean only what courts ultimately say they do, *Pacific Gas* invites precisely this type of lawsuit. With the benefit of 20 years of hindsight, the California Supreme Court may wish to revisit the issue. If it does so, we commend to it the facts of this case as a paradigmatic example of why the traditional rule, based on centuries of experience, reflects the far wiser approach.

Judge Kozinski noted that the defendant could move for summary judgment after completion of discovery. He said that the motion would succeed "unless Trident [the plaintiff] were to come forward with extrinsic evidence sufficient to render the contract reasonably susceptible to Trident's alternative interpretation, thereby creating a genuine issue of fact resolvable only at trial."

Did Judge Kozinski read Justice Traynor's opinions correctly or plausibly? Two months after the *Trident* decision was announced, another panel of judges on the United States Court of Appeals for the Ninth Circuit raised this question very politely. In *A. Kemp Fisheries, Inc. v. Castle & Cooke, Inc.*,[28] the court said:

> The broad language in *Trident* suggests that under California law courts must always admit extrinsic evidence to determine the meaning of disputed contract language. *Trident* held only that courts may not dismiss on the pleadings when one party claims that extrinsic evidence renders the contract ambiguous. The case must proceed beyond the pleadings so that the court may consider the evidence. If, after considering the evidence, the court determines that the contract is not reasonably susceptible to the interpretation advanced, the parol evidence rule operates to exclude the evidence. The court may then decide the case on a motion for summary judgment.

Does it matter whether a court can dismiss a case on the pleadings when it thinks documents are unambiguous or whether it must allow the parties to develop evidence by discovery and otherwise before considering a motion for summary judgment? Even if allowing the case to go on past the initial pleadings has some costs, does Justice Traynor's position "chip ... away at the foundations of our legal system"?

4. *The parol evidence rule and the intentionally misleading document.* In *Masterson v. Sine,* Rebuke Masterson sought to introduce evidence of an unexpressed limitation on a term in a contract. She sought, in a sense, to prove its private meaning. This private meaning may have arisen innocently, with no intention of creating a document that purported to be something which failed to express the parties' true intentions. Sometimes, however, the parties have an interest in creating a document which deliberately misdescribes the "true"

---

[28]852 F.2d 493 n. 2 (9th Cir. 1988).

transaction. Then later, for some reason, one of the parties (or an assign, or successor) decides to assert that the document should be taken to mean what it (apparently) says. The other seeks to prove the private meaning. Sometimes the misdescriptive document was intended to deceive a regulatory agency of the government, a bank, creditors, or others who might have an interest in the contractual affairs of the parties.

Should the parol evidence rule be used as a device for sanctioning parties who create misleading documents by giving literal effect to their lies? Or should the parties be entitled to prove the "real" deal and then be subject to whatever sanction might be appropriate for their effort to mislead? In other words, should the parol evidence rule serve a regulatory purpose, like rules governing illegal contracts, or contracts against public policy, or should it be treated as a neutral rule which, in general and over the long term, will have a tendency to enhance the quality of contractual documents, and will have a tendency to prevent the use of unreliable evidence of contractual intention?

In re Spring Valley Meats, Inc.: Dairyland Equipment Leasing, Inc. v. Bohen, 94 Wis.2d 600, 288 N.W.2d 852 (1980) may be an example of a misleading document case. In 1976 Dairyland Equipment Leasing and Spring Valley Meats executed two documents which, on their face, appeared to be leases of equipment to be used by Spring Valley. By 1977 Spring Valley had experienced financial trouble and was not making its payments on the "lease." Dairyland asked that the "leased" property be returned to it, and uncontradicted testimony was introduced to the effect that the real transaction had been a lease-purchase agreement which would give Spring Valley ownership of the equipment upon completion of the payment schedule. The only evidence that it was NOT a lease-purchase agreement consisted of the words of the standard form contract. The trial court ruled that the written agreements were not in fact leases, but rather security agreements, and so Dairyland was not entitled to the return of the equipment. A lessor is entitled to the return of the property when the lessee stops making lease payments. A secured creditor's right to the property turns on whether it recorded its security agreement.

On appeal, the court held first that, since the parol evidence rule is a substantive rule and not a rule of evidence, the consideration of the evidence could be raised on appeal even if not raised below. Second, the court held that the agreements contained no merger clauses. Third, the court said that it was proper to permit evidence to be introduced on the question of whether or not the parties had intended the document to be a complete, or partial, integration. But the court then held that even if the contract was intended as a partial integration, the offered evidence could not be considered because the offered evidence directly contradicted that part of the agreement which had been reduced to writing — apparently the word "lease." The document which announced itself as a lease could not, by parol evidence, be proven to be a non-lease.

Does the decision effectuate the intentions of the parties? Or is the court seeking to protect someone against fraudulent claims? The Spring Valley Meats brief suggested that it was common for equipment sales to be drafted as leases " ... so that the seller would be able to secure his tax advantage [Eds. note -- presumably depreciation] in the meantime." Does this suggest that the paperwork was part of a scheme to illegitimately reduce tax payments? Should that matter? If we see the case as a battle between the creditors of a failed business, does that affect the purpose of the parol evidence rule?

Compare *Kergil v. Central Oregon Fir Supply Co., Inc.*[29] A truck owner sued a wholesale lumber dealer for breach of an equipment lease. At the trial, the defendant introduced evidence that the lease was a sham transaction designed to assist plaintiff in avoiding federal taxes. The trial court gave judgment for the defendant. The Supreme Court of Oregon reversed on the ground that parol evidence should not be admitted to show that a written document was executed to defraud a third party. The court said,

> The courts are not of a single mind on this issue. We confess, the majority of jurisdictions at the present time, based upon pure logic, admit the evidence on the basis that such testimony is offered, not to vary the terms of the written instrument within the letter of the parol evidence rule, but only to show the parties never intended the written instrument to be a binding agreement.
>
> The difficulty with this view is that it overlooks the moral aspects of the situation. It permits the law to be used to lend its aid to those who would mislead or defraud third parties without providing any restraining penalty upon their immoral actions.

How does the court's decision reflect "the moral aspects of the situation"? Who planned the transaction and benefited from it? Is a deterrence argument convincing? Doesn't any rule which deters one party, in some sense, encourage the other? Remember the complexity and uncertainty of illegality as a defense to contract formation; isn't this an illegality case in disguise?

Parties may think that a perfectly legal bargain might offend others. For example, in *Zell v. American Seating Co.*,[30] plaintiff Zell was hired by American Seating. He was to attempt to procure contracts for American Seating, from the United States Government. Zell was to be paid $1,000 a month for three months. If he were successful, he was to be paid a percentage of the price paid by the United States. The parties executed a written contract that omitted any mention of the agreement to pay a contingent fee, in order to "avoid any possible stigma which might result" from using such a term. Such contingent fee contracts had been criticized in Congress, but were not illegal. Zell got the contracts for American Seating which then refused to pay the agreed contingent fee. Zell sued,

---

[29]213 Ore. 186, 323 P.2d 947 (1958).
[30]138 F.2d 641 (2d Cir. 1943).

the District Court granted summary judgment, but the Second Circuit reversed. Judge Jerome Frank wrote:

> [i]t has been held virtually everywhere ... that ... in the absence of any fraudulent or illegal purpose ... a purported written agreement, which the parties designed as a mere sham, lacks legal efficacy, and that extrinsic parol or other extrinsic evidence will always be received on that issue.... [W]hile it may be undesirable that citizens should prepare documents so contrived as to spoil the scent of legislators bent on proposing new legislation, yet such conduct is surely not unlawful and does not deserve judicial castigation as immoral or fraudulent; the courts should not erect standards of morality so far above the customary ...
>
> The rule, then, does relatively little to deserve its much advertised virtue of reducing the dangers of successful fraudulent recoveries and defenses brought about through perjury. The rule is too small a hook to catch such a leviathan. Moreover, if at times it does prevent a person from winning, by lying witnesses, a lawsuit which he should lose, it also, at times, by shutting out the true facts, unjustly aids other persons to win lawsuits they should and would lose, were the suppressed evidence known to the courts ...
>
> We are asked to believe that the rule enables businessmen, advised by their lawyers, to rely with indispensable confidence on written contracts unimpeachable by oral testimony. In fact, seldom can a conscientious lawyer advise his client, about to sign an agreement, that, should the client become involved in litigation relating to that agreement, one of the many exceptions to the rule will not permit the introduction of uncertainty-producing oral testimony.

In *American Seating v. Zell*,[31] the Supreme Court of the United States reversed Judge Frank's decision by a vote of 7 to 2. The District Court decision was affirmed. Four justices thought that proof of the contract was precluded by the applicable state parol evidence rule, and three thought that the contract was contrary to public policy and void. The Supreme Court wrote only a two sentence *per curiam* opinion. Do you understand the views of the four justices who thought the evidence was barred by the parol evidence rule? Do you think they understood the rule? Suppose instead of omitting the contingent fee term, the parties wrote the contract in code. Most courts would allow parol evidence admitted to interpret the code. Would this situation differ significantly from that in the *Zell* case? From *Spring Valley Meats*? "When I say *lease*, you know I mean *sale*. (Nudge ... wink)"

5. *Misleading documents*: People may sign what appears to be a written contract but not intend it to take effect immediately, or at all. For example, in

---

[31]322 U.S. 709 (1944).

Merritt v. Walter Pocock Associated Brokers, Inc.,[32] Pocock asked Merritt, one of the owners of a building, to sign a listing contract. The document set forth the terms on which the owners would sell the building and called for an $8,000 broker's commission to be paid by the seller. Pocock, the broker, and Merritt agreed that the listing contract was subject to the approval of the other owners of the building although they failed to mention this in the writing. Pocock sued to enforce his rights under the writing. Merritt tried to prove that Pocock and he had agreed that the approval of the other owners was a condition to the writing taking effect. The trial court refused to allow Merritt to prove the alleged condition and granted summary judgment in favor of the broker. The Supreme Court of Arizona reversed and remanded the case for trial. It said "[p]roof of such a condition precedent is clearly not a violation of the Parol Evidence Rule since it is not introduced to vary the terms of the writing but rather is intended to show that the contract never came into existence."

This is one of the classic exceptions to the parol evidence rule. Why is proof of this kind of oral agreement allowed? Doesn't it vary the express terms of the written contract?

3. THE PAROL EVIDENCE RULE, MISREPRESENTATION, AND PROMISSORY ESTOPPEL

ENRICO FARMS, INC. v. H.J. HEINZ CO.
PALLADINO v. CONTADINA FOODS, INC.[33]

629 F.2d 1304 (9th Cir. 1980)

PER CURIAM: ... Palladino sought to prove the breach ... [by Contadina] of two written contracts for the sale and purchase of processing tomatoes by means of parol evidence to interpret or explain the contracts. [The District Court entered a partial summary judgment in favor of defendant Contadina Foods, Inc. The 9th Circuit affirmed.]

Palladino is a California grower, harvester, and seller of processing tomatoes. [Contadina] buys and processes tomatoes. The first written contract between Palladino and [Contadina] is for the sale and purchase of tomatoes. The second written contract is for the sale of tomatoes by Edward Pippo to [Contadina]; and Palladino, as a harvester, is a third-party beneficiary of the Pippo contract.

The gist of Palladino's claim is that although both contracts contain written provisions allowing ... [Contadina], in time of glut, to place quotas on the quantity of tomatoes it would accept, he, Pippo and ... [Contadina]'s field agent

---

[32]105 Ariz. 392, 465 P.2d 585 (1970).

[33]The caption for this case is explained by virtue of the fact that Palladino was an intervenor in an antitrust case involving Enrico Farms and Heinz.

made oral modifications striking these provisions and providing instead that ... [Contadina] would purchase Palladino's and Pippo's entire outputs.

The District Court dismissed the claim under the Palladino- [Contadina] contract for the reason parol evidence cannot be received to contradict the terms of the written agreement and the Statute of Frauds requires that this agreement be in writing. The District Court dismissed the claim on the Pippo contract because Palladino could not reasonably rely on an oral statement made by Contadina to Pippo since he knew Pippo had also signed a written contract containing the provision for proration of the crop. The District Court was right.

"Parol evidence may be admitted to prove elements of an agreement not reduced to writing so long as the parties have not intended the writing to be a complete and final embodiment of their agreement and the parol evidence does not contradict the terms of the writing." *James G. Freeman & Associates, Inc. v. Tanner*, 56 Cal.App.3d 1, 9, 128 Cal.Rptr. 109, 114 (1976). We realize that an integration clause in the written agreement is not necessarily conclusive as to the parties' intent to include their entire agreement in the writing. *Masterson v. Sine*, 68 Cal.2d 222, 436 P.2d 561, 65 Cal.Rptr. 545 (1968). Nevertheless, ... the intent not to embody the complete agreement in the writing is only one condition that must be met before parol evidence may be admitted. The parol evidence must also "not contradict the terms of the writing." We, therefore, need not actually determine to what extent the written contract was integrated. The "threshold integration issue" referred to in *Royal Industries v. St. Regis Paper Co.*, 420 F.2d 449, 452 (9th Cir. 1969), need only be resolved in order to decide whether or not the parol evidence rule precludes admission of oral evidence that would add to or vary the terms of a written agreement. Similarly, *Masterson* is of no help to Palladino; it held that when a writing is not intended to embody the complete agreement of the parties, parol evidence may be admitted to prove a matter "on which the document is silent and which is not inconsistent with its terms." 65 Cal.Rptr. at 548, 436 P.2d at 564. We find no support for and reject Palladino's contention that, absent an integration, parol evidence may be admitted to directly contradict a written agreement.

Palladino's reliance upon this Court's decision in *Bell v. Exxon Co., U.S.A.*, 575 F.2d 714 (9th Cir. 1978), is misplaced. The written contract in *Bell* contained a provision for prorating the agreed gallonage supply of gasoline in the event of a shortage of the defendant-seller's supply of gasoline. Bell claimed that he was fraudulently induced to enter into the contract by relying upon sales representations of Exxon's sales representative "that despite the anticipated fuel supply shortage appellee would supply appellant's gasoline requirements if he entered into the new agreement." ...

Here Palladino's complaint did not allege that the appellee's field agent's oral statements were fraudulent. At best, he claimed only that the quota purchase provision in time of glut was "waived" and the written contract modified.

We are firm in the conclusion that under the facts here, the parol evidence sought to be introduced by Palladino is in direct contradiction to the terms of the written contract.

The other issues presented by Palladino are without merit.

The Partial Summary Judgment entered by the District Court on October 3, 1977 is ... *affirmed*.

KILKENNY, CIRCUIT JUDGE, dissenting:

I would allow the petition for rehearing and remand the case to the district court for a decision on whether the contracts in question were integrated as required by the decisions in *Masterson v. Sine*, 436 P.2d 561 at 563, 65 Cal.Rptr. 545 at 547 (1968); *In re Wm. Rakestraw Co.*, 450 F.2d 6 (CA9 1971), ...

I find nothing in the record which would lead me to believe that the district court passed on the issue dealing with the integration of the contract or contracts....

NOTES AND QUESTIONS

1. *A first mention of 3rd Party Beneficiary rules*: You might have been puzzled by the fact that Palladino, the harvester, is apparently complaining about the breach of a promise that Contadina made to Pippo. The court assumes, perhaps merely for the sake of argument in this case, that Palladino has a right to complain about Contadina's failure to keep its promise to Pippo. It is clear that since apparently Pippo has arranged for Palladino to harvest the Pippo tomatoes, Palladino has a financial interest in the harvesting of those tomatoes. Courts sometimes allow those who will benefit from a performance of a promise to sue for its enforcement. The rules governing just when non-parties can sue to enforce promises will be taken up in a later section. When we *do* take it up, you might come back to this case and reflect on whether it is a strong case for the acknowledgment of third-party rights.

2. *Authority to modify the contract*: Contadina Foods' brief raises an issue never decided by the court but which might explain the result of the case. Palladino and Pippo were members of the California Tomato Growers' Association (CGTA), a grower's cooperative. As members, Palladino had given CGTA the exclusive right to negotiate the terms of a standard "Approved Contract" which was to be used by all of the members; the only exception was for additional clauses which were subject to CGTA approval. The standard contract which CGTA had negotiated contained the proration clause. Contadina complained that Palladino should be estopped from claiming an oral agreement at variance with the collectively bargained contract that it had use. To allow Palladino to prevail would give it the benefit of a contract preferential to all of the other tomato growers in the Association.

3. *Misrepresentations that contradict a written contract*: Notice the court's discussion of *Bell v. Exxon*. Parol evidence generally can be admitted to prove misrepresentations. Palladino alleged that Sal Lucchesi, a field agent for Contadina, had assured Palladino and Pippo that all of their tomatoes would be accepted and they "would not lose a single tomato." He said that it was not necessary to put this in writing and they could trust him to treat them as well as they had been treated in the past. Is this sufficient to raise a claim of fraud in the inducement? Contadina's brief suggests the problem with a fraud approach in the *Enrico Farms* case:

> Palladino, for the first time in his memorandum of law in opposition to Contadina's motion for summary judgment, claimed "fraud in the inducement." There is no allegation of fraud in the complaint or in Palladino's affidavit, nor is there evidence to support such an allegation....
>
> It is just this type of unsupportable assertion of "fraud" that the leading commentators on the U.C.C. warn against permitting to be used in an attempt to avoid the Parol Evidence Rule.... [The brief then quotes White and Summer's treatise on the U.C.C., where they say "A party should not be allowed to introduce his evidence of an alleged extrinsic term merely by alleging fraud."] Allowing introduction of parol evidence on the basis of unsupportable arguments of counsel, such as presented here, would undermine the policy behind the parol evidence rule and the integrity of written contracts.

4. *Parol evidence and estoppel*: In *Ehret Co. v. Eaton, Yale & Town, Inc.*,[34] Ehret, a former manufacturer's sales representative, sued Eaton for breach of contract. Ehret often had to adapt Eaton's products so they would work with customers' finished products or their manufacturing equipment. Ehret often had to work as long as ten years before a sale became final. Eaton proposed a contract under which either party could terminate the relationship upon thirty days' notice. This contract provided that commissions would be paid on orders accepted before termination, provided purchasers would take delivery within three months from the date of cancellation. Ehret objected. Eaton could cancel after Ehret had expended considerable time and money procuring a sale but before its customer placed an order. Eaton refused to change the written contract. One of its officials wrote a letter which said,

> [In] those few cases where the contract has been canceled by us we have always been much more liberal than provided for in the contract.... [W]e cannot alter the terms of the contract — the same contract must exist with

---

[34]523 F.2d 280 (7th Cir. 1975).

you as with all of our other representatives and in the very unlikely event of cancellation, you will have to rely on receiving extremely fair treatment.

Ehret signed the contract.

About two years later, Eaton canceled the contract. It first applied the written contract literally and refused to pay commissions on sales to be shipped after three months from termination. Later it agreed to pay commissions on orders received before termination no matter when the goods were shipped. Ehret sued, contending it was entitled to better treatment than called for by the written contract. It relied on the letter which stated that it would receive "extremely fair treatment." Eaton's motion for summary judgment was denied.

The Court of Appeals affirmed. Eaton was estopped to set up the clause in the written document. Ehret was induced to sign the writing by Eaton's representation that Ehret would receive "extremely fair treatment" in the unlikely event of termination. The court quoted an Illinois decision which said "[f]raud is a necessary element [of estoppel] but it is not essential that there be a fraudulent intent. It is sufficient if a fraudulent effect would follow upon allowing a party to set up a claim inconsistent with his former declarations." The theory of equitable estoppel relied on by the court in this case is a close cousin to promissory estoppel à la Restatement 90. The court noted that if Eaton could disclaim its representations after receiving the benefits of them, "this would have the fraudulent effect that an estoppel was designed to prevent." As a result, the trial court did not err in admitting the letter written and received before the written contract was signed. This letter "is not in conflict with the parol evidence rule as the defendant contends. An estoppel is an equitable remedy which has its own independent force."

Next the court interpreted the phrase "extremely fair treatment." This phrase is susceptible to numerous interpretations. Thus parol evidence could be considered to give it meaning. "There was sufficient evidence to establish that it took up to ten years for the plaintiff to develop a customer prior to an order being placed. It was this concern of the plaintiff that prompted the defendant's promise of 'extremely fair treatment' and it was on this basis that the jury awarded damages."

Suppose Palladino had argued that Contadina was estopped to deny the field agent's statements in the *Enrico Farms* case. Might Palladino have won on this theory? See generally, Metzger, The Parol Evidence Rule: Promissory Estoppel's Next Conquest?[35]

5. *More on the relationship between the parol evidence rule and the statute of frauds*: Contadina argued that if the parol evidence striking the glut clause were admitted, Palladino's alleged oral contract would be unenforceable under the Statute of Frauds. U.C.C. § 2-201 states that "[a] writing is not insufficient

---

[35]36 Vanderbilt Law Review 1383 (1983).

because it omits or incorrectly states a term agreed upon but the contract is not enforceable under this paragraph beyond the quantity of goods shown in such writing." Striking the glut clause would have obligated Contadina to take a greater quantity than the writing, and so this provision of § 2-201 would bar enforcement of the oral modification. Palladino, in reply, says that the written contract provides that Contadina agreed to take 875 tons of tomatoes grown from 25 acres at $53.50 per pound, and this is the provision that it was seeking to enforce. The rider provision "has nothing to do with quantity but only specifies the terms of delivery in the event that all plants are glutted." The Ninth Circuit's decision on the parol evidence rule made it unnecessary to decide this issue. However, you should recognize that the parol evidence rule and the statute of frauds *both* must be satisfied, and in some instances one may be able to jump the parol evidence hurdle but fail to clear that of the statute of frauds.

NANAKULI PAVING AND ROCK CO. v. SHELL OIL CO.

664 F.2d 772 (9th Cir. 1982)

Hoffman, J. Appellant Nanakuli Paving and Rock Company (Nanakuli) initially filed this breach of contract action against appellee Shell Oil Company (Shell) in Hawaiian State Court in February, 1976. Nanakuli, the second-largest asphaltic paving contractor in Hawaii, had bought all its asphalt requirements from 1963 to 1974 from Shell under two long-term supply contracts; its suit charged Shell with breach of the later 1969 contract. The jury returned a verdict of $220,800 for Nanakuli on its first claim, which is that Shell breached the 1969 contract in January, 1974, by failing to price protect Nanakuli on 7200 tons of asphalt at the time Shell raised the price for asphalt from $44 to $76. Nanakuli's theory is that price-protection, as a usage of the asphaltic paving trade in Hawaii, was incorporated into the 1969 agreement between the parties, as demonstrated by the routine use of price-protection by suppliers to that trade, and reinforced by the way in which Shell actually performed the 1969 contract up until 1974. Price-protection, appellant claims, required that Shell hold the price on the tonnage Nanakuli had already committed because Nanakuli had incorporated that price into bids put out to or contracts awarded by general contractors and government agencies. The District Judge set aside the verdict and granted Shell's motion for judgment n. o. v., which decision we vacate. We reinstate the jury verdict because we find that, viewing the evidence as a whole, there was substantial evidence to support a finding by reasonable jurors that Shell breached its contract by failing to provide protection for Nanakuli in 1974....

Nanakuli offers two theories for why Shell's failure to offer price-protection in 1974 was a breach of the 1969 contract. First, it argues, all material suppliers to the asphaltic paving trade in Hawaii followed the trade usage of price-protection and thus it should be assumed, under the U.C.C., that the parties intended to incorporate price-protection into their 1969 agreement. This is so,

Nanakuli continues, even though the written contract provided for price to be "Shell's Posted Price at time of delivery," F.O.B. Honolulu. Its proof of a usage that was incorporated into the contract is reinforced by evidence of the commercial context, which under the U.C.C. should form the background for viewing a particular contract. The full agreement must be examined in light of the close, almost symbiotic relations between Shell and Nanakuli on the island of Oahu, whereby the expansion of Shell on the island was intimately connected to the business growth of Nanakuli. The U.C.C. looks to the actual performance of a contract as the best indication of what the parties intended those terms to mean. Nanakuli points out that Shell had price protected it on the two occasions of price increases under the 1969 contract other than the 1974 increase. In 1970 and 1971 Shell extended the old price for four and three months, respectively, after an announced increase. This was done, in the words of Shell's agent in Hawaii, in order to permit Nanakuli to "chew up" tonnage already committed at Shell's old price.[36]

Nanakuli's second theory for price-protection is that Shell was obliged to price protect Nanakuli, even if price-protection was not incorporated into their contract, because price-protection was the commercially reasonable standard for fair dealing in the asphaltic paving trade in Hawaii in 1974. Observance of those standards is part of the good-faith requirement that the Code imposes on merchants in performing a sales contract....

Shell presents three arguments ... First, it says, the District Court should not have denied Shell's motion *in limine* to define trade, for purposes of trade usage evidence, as the sale and purchase of asphalt in Hawaii, rather than expanding the definition of trade to include other suppliers of materials to the asphaltic paving trade. Asphalt, its argument runs, was the subject matter of the disputed contract and the only product Shell supplied to the asphaltic paving trade. Shell protests that the judge, by expanding the definition of trade to include the other major suppliers to the asphaltic paving trade, allowed the admission of highly prejudicial evidence of routine price-protection by all suppliers of aggregate. Asphaltic concrete paving is formed by mixing paving asphalt with crushed rock, or aggregate, in a "hot-mix" plant and then pouring the mixture onto the surface to be paved. Shell's second complaint is that the two prior occasions on which it price protected Nanakuli, although representing the only other instances of price increases under the 1969 contract, constituted mere waivers of the contract's price term, not a course of performance of the contract. A course of performance of the contract, in contrast to a waiver, demonstrates how the parties understand the terms of their agreement. Shell cites two U.C.C. comments in support of that argument: (1) that, when the meaning of acts is

---

[36]Price-protection was practiced in the asphaltic paving trade by either extending the old price for a period of time after a new one went into effect or charging the old price for a specified tonnage, which represented work committed at the old price. In addition, several months' advance notice was given of price increases.

ambiguous, the preference is for the waiver interpretation, and (2) that one act alone does not constitute a relevant course of performance. Shell's final argument is that, even assuming its prior price-protection constituted a course of performance and that the broad trade definition was correct and evidence of trade usages by aggregate suppliers was admissible, price-protection could not be construed as reasonably consistent with the express price term in the contract, in which case the Code provides that the express term controls.

We hold that the judge did not abuse his discretion in defining the applicable trade, for purposes of trade usages, as the asphaltic paving trade in Hawaii, rather than the purchase and sale of asphalt alone, given the unusual, not to say unique, circumstances: ... Additionally, we hold that, under the facts of this case, a jury could reasonably have found that Shell's acts on two occasions to price protect Nanakuli were not ambiguous and therefore indicated Shell's understanding of the terms of the agreement with Nanakuli rather than being a waiver by Shell of those terms.

Lastly we hold that, although the express price terms of Shell's posted price of delivery may seem, at first glance, inconsistent with a trade usage of price-protection at time of increases in price, a closer reading shows that the jury could have reasonably construed price-protection as consistent with the express term.... Our decision is reinforced by the overwhelming nature of the evidence that price-protection was routinely practiced by all suppliers in the small Oahu market of the asphaltic paving trade and therefore was known to Shell; that it was a realistic necessity to operate in that market and thus vital to Nanakuli's ability to get large government contracts and to Shell's continued business growth on Oahu; and that it therefore constituted an intended part of the agreement, as that term is broadly defined by the Code, between Shell and Nanakuli.

I. History of Nanakuli-Shell Relations Before 1973

Nanakuli, a division of Grace Brothers, Ltd., a Hawaiian corporation, is the smaller of the two major paving contractors on the island of Oahu, the larger of the two being Hawaiian Bitumuls (H.B.). Nanakuli first entered the paving business on Oahu in 1948, but it only began to move into the largest Oahu market, Honolulu, in the mid-1950's.... In the early sixties Nanakuli owner Walter Grace began to negotiate a mutually advantageous arrangement with Shell whereby Shell, which had a small market percentage and no asphalt terminals in Hawaii, would sign a long-term supply contract with Nanakuli that would commit Nanakuli to buy its asphalt requirements from Shell. On the other hand, Nanakuli would be helped to expand its paving business on Oahu through a guaranteed supply and a discount on its asphalt prices. Nanakuli's growth would expand the market for Shell's asphalt on the island, which would justify Shell's capital investment of a half a million dollars on Oahu, to which asphalt would be brought in heated tankers from Shell's refinery in Martinez, California.

Shell signed two five-year contracts in 1963: a supply contract with Nanakuli itself and a distributorship with Grace, which provided for a $2 commission on all Nanakuli's sales. In fact, almost all Nanakuli's sales were to itself and thus the commission operated, according to Shell's Hawaiian representative, Bohner, primarily as a discount mechanism. Lennox, who succeeded Grace as president in 1965 at Grace's death, testified that its purpose was "to make us competitive in our paving operation with our competitor [H.B.] who is much larger than ourselves because they were a distributor for the Standard Oil Company's asphalt operation." Lennox and Smith, who joined Nanakuli as vice-president in 1965 and eventually succeeded Lennox, both saw Nanakuli's and Shell's relationship as that of partners. That characterization was not denied by Bohner, Shell's Hawaiian representative from 1964 to 1978, who, in fact, essentially corroborated their description of the close relations between the two companies. As a symbol of that relationship, Nanakuli painted its trucks "Shell white," placed Shell's logo on those trucks, chose the same orange as used by Shell for its own logo, and put the Shell logo on its stationery.

In 1966 Pacific Cement and Aggregates (P.C. & A.), Nanakuli's landlord at its rented rock quarry at Halawa, was bought by Lone Star Cement Corporation, which later became Lone Star Industries. Lone Star requested that Nanakuli upgrade its plant facilities at the quarry, which Nanakuli estimated would cost between $250,000 to $300,000. Nanakuli, knowing Shell was eager to build up its paving business on Oahu, approached Shell for direct financing of the plant, an idea to which Shell was initially receptive.... Shell management philosophy later changed and it was decided not to finance the plant directly but rather to offer Nanakuli an additional $2 volume discount on all sales over five thousand tons to help finance the plant, according to Bohner.... In 1968 two top Shell asphalt officials came from the mainland to discuss Nanakuli's expansion.... Together with Bohner and Nanakuli's Lennox and Smith, they met with officials of Nanakuli's bank to discuss the loan and repayment schedule. The three contracts were finally signed after long negotiations on April 1, 1969. They were to parallel the amortization schedule of the bank loan for the plant: a supply contract, a distributorship contract, and volume discount letter, all three to last until December 31, 1975, at which point each would have the option to cancel on six-months' notice, with a minimum duration of over seven years, April 1, 1969, to July 1, 1976. Such long-term contracts were certainly unusual for Shell and this one was probably unique among Shell's customers, at least by 1974.

Lennox' testimony, which was partially stricken by the court as inadmissible, was that Shell's agreement with Nanakuli in 1969 included a commitment by Shell never to charge Nanakuli more than Chevron charged H.B., in order to carry out the underlying purpose of the agreement to make Nanakuli competitive with H.B. and thus expand its and Shell's respective businesses on Oahu. This testimony was ruled inadmissible as parol evidence. Shell, itself at the end of the trial, read in parts of Smith's earlier deposition in which he made a similar point. Smith's deposition testimony was that, although no written provision was included on price-protection, he was led to believe by Shell's Bohner that he would get price-protection.... He said Nanakuli understood the price term to mean that Shell would not increase prices without advance notice and would hold the price on work bid for enough time to allow Nanakuli to use up the tonnage bid at the old price. Smith's testimony backed up that of Lennox: the price was to be "posted price as bid as was understood between the parties," further explaining that it was to be Shell's price at time and place of delivery, except for price increases, at which point the price was time and place of bid for a period of time or a specified tonnage.[37]

Much information relevant to the "commercial context" of the agreement, essential to an understanding of the meaning of the terms, was contained in the testimony of Smith and Lennox. See Haw.Rev.Stat. § 490:2-202, Comment 2. None of it was flatly contradicted by the evasive responses of Bohner to such inquiries. Smith testified that Bohner was in Nanakuli's offices at least weekly, sometimes was involved in the preparation of bids, and knew when a bid had been submitted or a contract awarded, at times attending the awards himself. The amount of time he spent following Nanakuli's progress was understandable; as he explained, in the 1960's and 1970's Nanakuli "was basically ... our only customer at this time." Thus Nanakuli felt it had no need to notify Shell in writing of projects awarded; Lennox testified he was only told to do so on one occasion, the award of its first big contract on August 17, 1970. Due to the long shipping time from California, Bohner had to know well in advance Nanakuli's supply needs. Lennox testified that Bohner was "as close to us as any person could be as far as the asphalt supply was concerned. He had to know what we were doing...." Lennox said Bohner was not only aware of Nanakuli's day-to-day progress but knowledgeable about the broader asphaltic paving marketplace in which Nanakuli was competing....

---

[37]The principal reason the judge initially refused to allow any such testimony and one major reason for his inclination to grant the defendant's motion for a directed verdict, was his belief that there was no ambiguity in the express price term of "posted price at time of delivery." He was reluctantly persuaded to allow the evidence because of Shell's answer to interrogatory 11, asking its understanding of the contract term, that it never had a posted price although it did have a list price. The court stated its doubts about Nanakuli's case at the time it denied Shell's directed verdict motion: lack of ambiguity in the express term and inconsistency between the trade usage of that term. When first requested to allow evidence of prior dealings the judge asked, "Can you point out what terms [in the written contract] are supposed to be ambiguous?" However, the Code lets in evidence of prior dealings, usage, and performance under § 2-202(a) *even if* the contract terms are clear: "This section definitely rejects: ... (c) The requirement that a condition precedent to the admissibility of the type of evidence specified in paragraph (a) is an original determination by the court that the language used is ambiguous." Haw.Rev.Stat. § 490:2-202, Comment 1.

II. Trade Usage Before and After 1969

The key to price-protection being so prevalent in 1969 that both parties would intend to incorporate it into their contract is found in one reality of the Oahu asphaltic paving market: the largest paving contracts were let by government agencies and none of the three levels of government — local, state, or federal — allowed escalation clauses for paving materials. If a paver bid at one price and another went into effect before the award was made, the paving company would lose a great deal of money, since it could not pass on increases to any government agency or to most general contractors. Extensive evidence was presented that, as a consequence, aggregate suppliers routinely price protected paving contractors in the 1960's and 1970's, as did the largest asphaltic supplier in Oahu, Chevron. Nanakuli presented documentary evidence of routine price-protection by aggregate suppliers.... The smallness of the Oahu market led to complete trust among suppliers and pavers....

[The court summarized evidence that Chevron had given price-protection to H.B., and that there was no mention of price-protection in the written contract between H.B. and Chevron.]

In addition to evidence of trade usages existing in 1969 when the contract at issue was signed, the District Judge let in evidence of the continuation of that trade usage after 1969, over Shell's protest. He stated that, giving a liberal reading to § 1-205, he felt that later evidence was relevant to show that the expectation of the parties that a given usage would be observed was justified. The basis for incorporating a trade usage into a contract under the U.C.C. is the justifiable expectation of the parties that it will be observed. That later evidence consisted here of more price-protection by the aggregate companies on Oahu, as well as continued asphalt price-protection. Chevron after 1969 continued price protecting H.B. on Oahu and, on raising prices in 1979, price protected Nanakuli on the island of Molokai, where Nanakuli purchased its asphalt from Chevron. Additionally, Shell price protected Nanakuli in 1977 and 1978 on Oahu.[38]

III. Shell's Course Of Performance Of The 1969 Contract

The Code considers actual performance of a contract as the most relevant evidence of how the parties interpreted the terms of that contract. In 1970 and 1971, the only points at which Shell raised prices between 1969 and 1974, it price protected Nanakuli by holding its old price for four and three months,

---

[38]We do not need to decide whether usage evidence after a contract was signed is admissible to show that a party's reliance on a given usage was justifiable, given its continuation, because part of that evidence dealing with asphalt prices was admissible to show the reasonably commercial standards of fair dealing prevalent in the trade in 1974 and the part dealing with the continuation of price-protection by aggregate suppliers, after 1969 was not so extensive as to be prejudicial to Shell.

respectively, after announcing a price increase.... In addition, Bohner volunteered on direct the information that Shell price protected Nanakuli on the only two occasions of price increases after 1974 by giving 6 months' advance notice in 1977 and 3 or 4 months' advance notice in 1978, a practice he described as "in effect carryover pricing," his term for price-protection. By its actions, Bohner testified, Shell allowed Nanakuli time to make arrangements to buy up tonnage committed at the old price, that is, to "chew up" tonnage bid or contracted. [Shell offered the evidence to show it acted in good faith, but the jury may have taken it to show what constituted commercially reasonable behavior.]

IV. Shell-Nanakuli Relations, 1973-74

Two important factors form the backdrop for the 1974 failure by Shell to price protect Nanakuli: the Arab oil embargo and a complete change of command and policy in Shell's asphalt management. The jury was read a page or so from the World Book about the events and effect of the partial oil embargo, which shortened supplies and increased the price of petroleum, of which asphalt is a byproduct. The federal government imposed direct price controls on petroleum, but not on asphalt. Despite the international importance of those events, the jury may have viewed the second factor as of more direct significance to this case. The structural changes at Shell offered a possible explanation for why Shell in 1974 acted out of step with, not only the trade usage and commercially reasonable practices of all suppliers to the asphaltic paving trade on Oahu, but also with its previous agreement with, or at least treatment of, Nanakuli.

Bohner testified to a big organizational change at Shell in 1973 when asphalt sales were moved from the construction sales to the commercial sales department. In addition, by 1973 the top echelon of Shell's asphalt sales had retired. Lewis and Blee, who had negotiated the 1969 contract with Nanakuli, were both gone. Their duties were taken over by three men: Fuller in San Mateo, California, District Manager for Shell Sales, Lawson, and Chippendale, who was Shell's regional asphalt manager in Houston. When the philosophy toward asphalt pricing changed, apparently no one was left who was knowledgeable about the peculiarities of the Hawaiian market or about Shell's long-time relations with Nanakuli or its 1969 agreement, beyond the printed contract.

Shell had begun rethinking its asphalt pricing policies several years before. This rethinking apparently led to a November 25, 1970, letter setting out "Shell's New Pricing Policy" at its Honolulu and Hilo terminals. The letter explained the elimination of price-protection: "In other words, we will no longer guarantee asphalt prices for the duration of any particular construction projects or for the specific lengths of time. We will, of course, honor any existing prices which have been committed for specific projects for which we have firm contractual commitments." The letter requested a supply contract be signed with Shell within 15 days of the receipt of an award by a customer.

The District Judge based his grant of judgment n. o. v. largely on his belief that, had Nanakuli desired price-protection, it should have complied with Shell's request in that 1970 letter, by which we assume he meant Nanakuli should have made a firm contractual commitment with Shell for each project on which its bid was successful within 15 days of award. That conclusion, however, ignores several facts. First, compliance by Nanakuli with the letter's demand that a contract be signed within 15 days of an award would have offered Nanakuli little, if any, protection. Nanakuli still would have been stuck with only charging the government the price incorporated into its bid if Shell raised its price between bid and award. The purpose of price-protection was to guarantee the price in effect when a paver made a bid because of the often lengthy time span between bid and award. Second, if price-protection was a part of Nanakuli's 1969 agreement with Shell, Shell had no right to terminate unilaterally that protection. Third, the letter was addressed to "Gentlemen" with Nanakuli's name typed in at the top; it was apparently addressed to all Shell's Hawaiian customers. Fourth, Nanakuli officials testified that they did not believe the letter was applicable to its unusual situation of already having a long-term contract with Shell.... Nanakuli ... already had a supply contract with all the terms of sales set forth, a point its two officials made repeatedly at trial. For example, Smith testified he saw no need to notify Shell because Bohner knew of each project and because the supply contract was a firm contractual commitment with Shell.[39] Shell had added in the 1970 letter: "All previous contractual commitments made prior to the date of this letter will, of course, be honored." Smith's reading of this was that Nanakuli's supply contract with Shell *was* a firm contractual commitment by Shell and that no further contract was needed.... There is an additional reason why Nanakuli might have felt that the letter did not apply to its particular situation. The letter announced that Shell would charge "from this date forward ... the posted selling price on the date of purchase." This was different from the express term of Nanakuli's contract with Shell, which was the price in effect at time of *delivery*. Either Shell's agreement with Nanakuli embraced price-protection, in which case Shell could not unilaterally abrogate Nanakuli's rights by this letter, or, as Shell argues, only the words on the written contract counted, in which case the price to Nanakuli was Shell's price at delivery. In the latter case, Nanakuli could safely ignore any attempt by Shell to change the price to that at purchase....

Nanakuli's strongest argument as to its failure to comply with the letter was that there was no need to notify Shell, as Bohner already knew of each project as it was bid and each award as it was made. Lennox testified, "The Shell Oil representative was in our office frequently and knew what jobs we had successfully bid." At another point Lennox said, "The Shell representative was

---

[39] "We already had a supply contract. Why would we need another supply contract?" Smith asked. "There was no need to write. We had our supply contract. We didn't need to enter a new contract with the Shell Oil Company with every successful project."

in the office and was fully aware of what we were doing and what jobs we had gotten. He was familiar and was more or less a partner in this thing; he even attended the bid openings at times. He was fully aware and congratulated us every time we got a nice big job because it was more for Shell." ...

After Shell's December 31, 1973, letter arrived on January 4, 1974, Smith called Bohner, as he had done before at times of price increases, to ask for price-protection, this time on 7200 tons. Bohner told Smith that he would have to get in touch with the mainland, but he expected that the response would be negative. Smith wrote several letters in January and February asking for price-protection. After getting no satisfaction, he finally flew to California to meet with Lawson, Fuller, and Chippendale. Chippendale, from the Houston office, was acknowledged by the other two to be the only person with authority to grant price-protection. All three Shell officials lacked any understanding of Nanakuli and Shell's long, unique relationship or of the asphaltic trade in Oahu. They had never even seen Shell's contracts with Nanakuli before the meeting. When apprised of the three and their seven-year duration, Fuller remarked on the unusual nature of Nanakuli's relations with Shell, at least within his district. Chippendale felt it was probably unique for Shell anywhere. Smith testified that Fuller admitted to knowing nothing, beyond the printed page of Nanakuli's agreement with Shell, of the background negotiation or Shell's past pricing policies toward Nanakuli. Chippendale could not understand why Nanakuli even had a distributorship contract giving it a $2 commission on sales; he thought Nanakuli had been paid "illegally." No one had ever heard about Shell giving price-protection to Nanakuli before. Instead of asking Bohner directly, Chippendale told Fuller to search the files for something on paper. Fuller testified that Shell would not act without *written* proof of Shell's past price-protection of Nanakuli. He admitted he was unable to find anything in the files before 1972 because the departments had been reorganized in that year, about which he informed Chippendale. Chippendale accordingly decided to deny Nanakuli any price-protection and wrote a draft of a letter for Fuller to send Nanakuli. He wrote a note to Fuller that he should adopt the "least said" approach with Nanakuli and check any letters with the legal department. When asked at trial if he had ever simply asked Bohner about Shell's past pricing practices toward Nanakuli, Fuller answered, "No, I didn't know we had it, other than the standard policy if we had one which we didn't." Chippendale told Smith in the California meeting that, although 7200 tons represented an infinitesimal amount for Shell, it would set a bad precedent for Shell, since price-protection was not Shell's "*current* policy." (emphasis supplied)....

We conclude that the decision to deny Nanakuli price-protection was made by new Houston management without a full understanding of Shell's 1969 agreement with Nanakuli or any knowledge of its past pricing practices toward Nanakuli. If Shell did commit itself in 1969 to price protect Nanakuli, the Shell officials who made the decisions affecting Nanakuli in 1974 knew nothing about that commitment. Nor did they make any effective effort to find out. They acted instead solely in reliance on the 1969 contract's express price term, devoid of the commercial context that the Code says is necessary to an understanding of the meaning of the written word. Whatever the legal enforceability of Nanakuli's right, Nanakuli officials seem to have acted in good faith reliance on its right, as they understood it, to price-protection and rightfully felt betrayed by Shell's failure to act with any understanding of its past practices toward Nanakuli.

V. Scope of Trade Usage

The validity of the jury verdict in this case depends on four legal questions. First, how broad was the trade to whose usages Shell was bound under its 1969 agreement with Nanakuli: did it extend to the Hawaiian asphaltic paving trade or was it limited merely to the purchase and sale of asphalt, which would only include evidence of practices by Shell and Chevron? Second, were the two instances of price-protection of Nanakuli by Shell in 1970 and 1971 waivers of the 1969 contract as a matter of law or was the jury entitled to find that they constituted a course of performance of the contract? Third, could the jury have construed an express contract term of Shell's posted price at delivery as reasonably consistent with a trade usage and Shell's course of performance of the 1969 contract of price-protection, which consisted of charging the old price at times of price increases, either for a period of time or for specific tonnage committed at a fixed price in non-escalating contracts? Fourth, could the jury have found that good faith obliged Shell to at least give advance notice of a $32 increase in 1974, that is, could they have found that the commercially reasonable standards of fair dealing in the trade in Hawaii in 1974 were to give some form of price-protection?

We approach the first issue in this case mindful that an underlying purpose of the U.C.C. as enacted in Hawaii is to allow for liberal interpretation of commercial usages. The Code provides, "This chapter shall be liberally construed and applied to promote its underlying purposes and policies." Haw.Rev.Stat. § 490:1-102(1). Only three purposes are listed, one of which is "[t]o permit the continued expansion of commercial practices through custom, usage and agreement of the parties;...." *Id.* § 490:1-102(2)(b). The drafters of the Code explain:

> This Act is drawn to provide *flexibility* so that, since it is intended to be a semipermanent piece of legislation, it will provide its own machinery for *expansion of commercial practices*. It is intended to make it possible for the law embodied in this Act to be *developed* by the courts in the light of *unforeseen and new circumstances and practices....*

> ... The text of each section should be *read in the light of the purpose and policy* of the rule or principle in question, as also of the Act as a whole, and

the application of the language should be *construed narrowly or broadly*, as the case may be, in *conformity with the purposes and policies* involved. ... [t]he Code seeks to *avoid ... interference with evolutionary growth....*

This principle of *freedom of contract is subject* to specific *exceptions* found elsewhere in the Act.... [An example being the bar on contractual exclusion of the requirement of good faith, although the parties can set out standards for same.] ... *In this connection*, § 1-205 incorporating into the agreement *prior course of dealing and usages of trade is of particular importance.*

Id., Comments 1 & 2 (emphasis supplied). We read that to mean that courts should not stand in the way of new commercial practices and usages by insisting on maintaining the narrow and inflexible old rules of interpretation. We seek the definition of trade usage not only in the express language of the Code but also in its underlying purposes, defining it liberally to fit the facts of the particular commercial context here.

The Code defines usage of trade as "any practice or method of dealing having such regularity of observance in a *place, vocation or trade* as to justify an expectation that it will be observed with respect to the transaction in question." *Id.* § 490:1-205(2) (emphasis supplied). We understand the use of the word "or" to mean that parties can be bound by a usage common to the *place* they are in business, even if it is not the usage of their particular vocation or trade. That reading is borne out by the repetition of the disjunctive "or" in subsection 3, which provides that usages "in the vocation or trade in which they are entitled *or* of which they are or should be aware give particular meaning to and supplement or qualify terms of an agreement." *Id.* § 490:1-205(3). The drafters' comments say that trade usage is to be used to reach the "... commercial meaning of the agreement ..." by interpreting the language "as meaning what it may fairly be expected to mean to parties involved in the particular transaction *in a given locality or* in a given *vocation or trade." Id.*, Comment 4 (emphasis supplied). The inference of the two subsections and the comment, read together, is that a usage need not necessarily be one practiced by members of the party's own trade or vocation to be binding *if* it is so commonly practiced in a locality that a party should be aware of it. Subsection 5 also shows the importance of the place where the usage is practiced: "An applicable usage of trade in the place where any part of performance is to occur shall be used in interpreting the agreement as to that part of the performance." The validity of this interpretation is additionally demonstrated by the comment of the drafters: "Subsection (3), giving the prescribed effect to usages of which the parties 'are or should be aware', reinforces the provision of subsection (2) requiring not universality but only the described 'regularity of observance' of the practice or method. This subsection also reinforces the point of subsection (2) that such usages may be either *general to trade or particular to a special branch of trade." Id.*, Comment

7 (emphasis supplied). This language indicates that Shell would be bound not only by usages of sellers of asphalt but by more general usages on Oahu, as long as those usages were so regular in their observance that Shell should have been aware of them. This reading of the Code, in our opinion, achieves an equitable result. A party is always held to conduct generally observed by members of his chosen trade because the other party is justified in so assuming unless he indicates otherwise. He is held to more general business practices to the extent of his actual knowledge of those practices or to the degree his ignorance of those practices is not excusable: they were so generally practiced he should have been aware of them.

No U.C.C. cases have been found on this point, but the court's reading of the Code language is similar to that of two of the best-known commentators on the U.C.C.:

> Under pre-Code law, a trade usage was not operative against a party who *was not a member of the trade unless* he actually knew of it or *the other party could reasonably believe he knew of it.*

J. White & R. Summers, *Uniform Commercial Code*, § 12-6 at 371 (1972) (emphasis supplied).... White and Summers add (emphasis supplied):

> This view has been carried forward by 1-205(3), ... [U]sage of the trade is only binding on *members of the trade* involved *or persons* who knew or *should know about it*. Persons who should be aware of the trade usage doubtless *include those who regularly deal with members of the relevant trade*, and also members of a second trade that commonly deals with members of a relevant trade (for example, farmers should know something of seed selling).

White & Summers, *supra*, § 12-6 at 371. Using that analogy, even if Shell did not "regularly deal" with aggregate supplies, it did deal constantly and almost exclusively on Oahu with one asphalt paver. It therefore should have been aware of the usage of Nanakuli and other asphaltic pavers to bid at fixed prices and therefore receive price-protection from their materials suppliers due to the refusal by government agencies to accept escalation clauses. Therefore, we do not find the lower court abused its discretion or misread the Code as applied to the peculiar facts of this case in ruling that the applicable trade was the asphaltic paving trade in Hawaii. An asphalt seller should be held to the usages of trade in general as well as those of asphalt sellers and common usages of those to whom they sell. Certainly, under the unusual facts of this case it was not unreasonable for the judge to extend trade usages to include practices of other material suppliers toward Shell's primary and perhaps only customer on Oahu....

Shell argued not only that the definition of trade was too broad, but also that the practice itself was not sufficiently regular to reach the level of a usage and that Nanakuli failed to show with enough precision how the usage was carried out in order for a jury to calculate damages. The extent of a usage is ultimately a jury question. The Code provides, "The existence and scope of such a usage are to be proved as facts." Haw.Rev.Stat. § 490:1-205(2).[40] The practice must have "such regularity of observance ... as to justify an expectation that it will be observed...." *Id.* The comment explains:

> The ancient English tests for "custom" are abandoned in this connection. Therefore, it is not required that a usage of trade be "ancient or immemorial," "universal" or the like.... [F]ull recognition is thus available for new usages and for usages currently observed by the great majority of decent dealers, even though dissidents ready to cut corners do not agree.

Id., Comment 5. The comment's demand that "not universality but only the described 'regularity of observance'" is required reinforces the provision only giving "effect to usages of which the parties 'are or should be aware'...." " *Id.*, Comment 7. A "regularly observed" practice of protection, of which Shell "should have been aware," was enough to constitute a usage that Nanakuli had reason to believe was incorporated into the agreement.[41]

Nanakuli went beyond proof of a regular observance. It proved ... that price-protection was probably universal practice by suppliers to the asphaltic paving trade in 1969.[42] It had been practiced by H.C. & D. since at least 1962, by P.C. & A. since well before 1960, and by Chevron routinely for years, with the last specific instance before the contract being March, 1969, as shown by documentary evidence. The only usage evidence missing was the behavior by Shell, the only other asphalt supplier in Hawaii, prior to 1969. That was because its only major customer was Nanakuli and the judge ruled prior course of dealings between Shell and Nanakuli inadmissible. Shell did not point in rebuttal to one instance of failure to price protect by any supplier to an asphalt paver in Hawaii before its own 1974 refusal to price protect Nanakuli....

Shell next argues that, even if such a usage existed, its outlines were not precise enough to determine whether Shell would have extended the old price for

---

[40]Written trade codes, however, are left to the court to interpret. *Id.*

[41]White and Summers write that Code requirements for proving a usage are "far less stringent" than the old ones for custom. "A usage of trade need not be *well known*, let alone 'universal.'" It only needs to be regular enough that the parties expect it to be observed. White & Summers, *supra*, § 3-3 at 87 (emphasis supplied). "Note particularly [in 1-205(1) & (2)] that it is not necessary for both parties to be consciously aware of the trade usage. It is enough if the trade usage is such as to 'justify an expectation' of its observance." *Id.* at 84.

[42]All evidence was that trade usage continued to be universally practiced after 1969, even by Shell.

Nanakuli for several months or would have charged the old price on the volume of tonnage committed at that price. The jury awarded Nanakuli damages based on the specific tonnage committed before the price increase of 1974. [The court considers code sections and comments which eliminate the need to prove usages and related damages with "mathematical accuracy.] The manner in which the usage of price-protection was carried out was presented with sufficient precision to allow the jury to calculate damages at $220,800.

VI. *Waiver or Course of Performance*

Course of performance under the Code is the action of the parties in carrying out the contract at issue, whereas course of dealing consists of relations between the parties *prior* to signing that contract. Evidence of the latter was excluded by the District Judge; evidence of the former consisted of Shell's price-protection of Nanakuli in 1970 and 1971. Shell protested that the jury could not have found that those two instances of price-protection amounted to a course of performance of its 1969 contract, relying on two Code comments. First, one instance does not constitute a course of performance. "A single occasion of conduct does not fall within the language of this section...." Haw.Rev.Stat. § 490:2-208, Comment 4. Although the comment rules out one instance, it does not further delineate how many acts are needed to form a course of performance. The prior occasions here were only two, but they constituted the only occasions before 1974 that would call for such conduct. [The court discusses another occasion Shell seemed in discussions to have recognized Nanakuli's right to price-protection.]

Shell's second defense is that the comment expresses a preference for an interpretation of waiver.

> 3. Where it is difficult to determine whether a particular act merely sheds light on the meaning of the agreement or represents a waiver of a term of the agreement, the preference is in favor of "waiver" whenever such construction, plus the application of the provisions on the reinstatement of rights waived ..., is needed to preserve the flexible character of commercial contracts and to prevent surprise or other hardship.

Id., Comment 3. The preference for waiver only applies, however, where acts are ambiguous. It was within the province of the jury to determine whether those acts were ambiguous, and if not, whether they constituted waivers or a course of performance of the contract. The jury's interpretation of those acts as a course of performance was bolstered by evidence offered by Shell that it again price protected Nanakuli on the only two occasions of post-1974 price increases, in 1977 and 1978.

VII. Express Terms as Reasonably Consistent With Usage in Course of Performance

Perhaps one of the most fundamental departures of the Code from prior contract law is found in the parol evidence rule and the definition of an agreement between two parties. Under the U.C.C., an agreement goes beyond the written words on a piece of paper. "'Agreement' means the bargain of the parties in fact as found in their language or by implication from other circumstances including course of dealing or usage of trade or course of performance as provided in this chapter (§§ 490:1-205 and 490:2-208)." *Id.* § 490:1-201(3). Express terms, then, do not constitute the entire agreement, which must be sought also in evidence of usages, dealings, and performance of the contract itself. The purpose of evidence of usages, which are defined in the previous section, is to help to understand the entire agreement.

> [Usages are] a factor in reaching the commercial meaning of the agreement which the parties have made. The language used is to be interpreted as meaning what it may fairly be expected to mean to parties involved in the particular commercial transaction in a given locality or in a given vocation or trade.... Part of the agreement of the parties ... is to be sought for in the usages of trade which furnish the background and give particular meaning to the language used, and are the framework of common understanding controlling any general rules of law which hold only when there is no such understanding.

Id. § 490:1-205, Comment 4. Course of dealings is more important than usages of the trade, being specific usages between the two parties to the contract. "[C]ourse of dealing controls usage of trade." *Id.* § 490:1-205(4). It "is a sequence of previous conduct between the parties to a particular transaction which is fairly to be regarded as establishing a common basis of understanding for interpreting their expressions and other conduct." *Id.* § 490:1-205(1). Much of the evidence of prior dealings between Shell and Nanakuli in negotiating the 1963 contract and in carrying out similar earlier contracts was excluded by the court.

A commercial agreement, then, is broader than the written paper and its meaning is to be determined not just by the language used by them in the written contract but "by their action, read and interpreted in the light of commercial practices and other surrounding circumstances. The measure and background for interpretation are set by the commercial context, which may explain and supplement even the language of a formal or final writing." *Id.*, Comment 1. Performance, usages, and prior dealings are important enough to be admitted always, even for a final and complete agreement; only if they cannot be reasonably reconciled with the express terms of the contract are they not binding on the parties. "The express terms of an agreement and an applicable course of dealing or usage of trade shall be construed wherever reasonable as consistent with each other; but when such construction is unreasonable express terms control both course of dealing and usage of trade and course of dealing controls usage of trade." *Id.* § 490:1-205(4).

Of these three, then, the most important evidence of the agreement of the parties is their actual performance of the contract. *Id.* The operative definition of course of performance is as follows: "Where the contract for sale involves repeated occasions for performance by either party with knowledge of the nature of the performance and opportunity for objection to it by the other, any course of performance accepted or acquiesced in without objection shall be relevant to determine the meaning of the agreement." *Id.* § 490:2-208(1). "Course of dealing ... is restricted, literally, to a sequence of conduct between the parties previous to the agreement. However, the provisions of the Act on course of performance make it clear that a sequence of conduct after or under the agreement may have equivalent meaning (§ 2-208)." *Id.* 490:1-205, Comment 2. The importance of evidence of course of performance is explained: "The parties themselves know best what they have meant by their words of agreement and their action under that agreement is the best indication of what that meaning was. This section thus rounds out the set of factors which determines the meaning of the 'agreement' ... " *Id.* § 490:2-208, Comment 1. "Under this section a course of performance is always relevant to determine the meaning of the agreement." *Id.*, Comment 2.

Our study of the Code provisions and comments, then, form the first basis of our holding that a trade usage to price protect pavers at times of price increases for work committed on nonescalating contracts could reasonably be construed as consistent with an express term of seller's posted price at delivery. Since the agreement of the parties is broader than the express terms and includes usages, which may even add terms to the agreement, and since the commercial background provided by those usages is vital to an understanding of the agreement, we follow the Code's mandate to proceed on the assumption that the parties have included those usages unless they cannot reasonably be construed as consistent with the express terms.

Federal courts usually have been lenient in not ruling out consistent additional terms or trade usage for apparent inconsistency with express terms....

Numerous state courts have interpreted their own state's versions of the Code in line with the weight of federal authority on the U.C.C. to admit freely evidence of additional terms, usages, and prior dealings and harmonize them in most instances with apparently contradictory express terms. The only Hawaiian case on the subject dealt with the parol evidence rule in dicta....

Some guidelines can be offered as to how usage evidence can be allowed to modify a contract. First, the court must allow a check on usage evidence by demanding that it be sufficiently definite and widespread to prevent unilateral post-hoc revision of contract terms by one party. The Code's intent is to put usage evidence on an objective basis[43]....

Although the Code abandoned the traditional common law test of nonconsensual custom and views usage as a way of determining the parties' probable intent, *id.* at 1106-07, thus abolishing the requirement that common law custom be universally practiced, trade usages still must be well settled, *id.* at 1113....

Evidence of a trade usage does not n

C.eed to be protected against perjury because, as one commentator has written, "an outside standard does exist to help judge the truth of the assertion that the parties intended the usage to control the particular dispute: the existence and scope of the usage can be determined from other members of the trade."...

Here the evidence was overwhelming that all suppliers to the asphaltic paving trade price protected customers under the same types of circumstances. Chevron's contract with H.B. was a similar long-term supply contract between a buyer and seller with very close relations, on a form supplied by the seller, covering sales of asphalt, and setting the price at seller's posted price, with no mention of price-protection. The same commentator [Kirst] offers a second guideline:

> Because the stock printed forms cannot always reflect the changing methods of business, members of the trade may do business with a standard clause in the forms that they ignore in practice. If the trade consistently ignores obsolete clauses at variance with actual trade practices, a litigant can maintain that it is reasonable that the courts also ignore the clauses.

---

[43]White and Summers write that usage and dealings evidence "may not only supplement or qualify express terms, but in appropriate circumstances may even override express terms." White & Summers, *supra*, § 3-3 at 84. "[T]he provision that express terms control inconsistent course of dealing and [usages and performance evidence] really cannot be taken at face value." *Id.* at 86. That reading, although at odds with the actual wording of the Code, is a realistic reading of what some of the cases allow. A better formulation of the Code's mandate is offered by R. W. Kirst, Usage of Trade and Course of Dealing: Subversion of the U.C.C. Theory, 1977 Law Forum 811:

> The need to determine whether the parties intended a usage ... to be part of the contract does not end if the court finds that the commercial practice is inconsistent with or contradicts the express language of the writing. If an inconsistency exists, the intention of the parties remains unclear. The parties may have intended either to include or exclude the practice. Determining the intent of the parties requires that the court attempt to construe the written term consistently with the commercial practice, if that is reasonable. If consistent construction is unreasonable the Code directs that the written term be taken as expressing the parties' intent. Before concluding that a jury could not reasonably find a consistent construction, the judge must understand the commercial background of the dispute.

Id. at 824.

> Similarly, members of a trade may handle a particular subset of commercial transactions in a manner consistent with written terms because the writing cannot provide for all variations or contingencies. Thus, if the trade regards an express term and a trade usage as consistent because the usage is not a complete contradiction but only an occasional but definite exception to a written term, the courts should interpret the contract according to the usage.

Kirst, supra, at 824. *Levie* [another commentator], *supra*, at 1112, writes, "Astonishing as it will seem to most practicing attorneys, under the Code it will be possible in some cases to use custom to contradict the written agreement.... Therefore usage may be used to 'qualify' the agreement, which presumably means to 'cut down' express terms although not to negate them entirely." Here, the express price term was "Shell's Posted Price at time of delivery." A total negation of that term would be that the buyer was to set the price. It is a less than complete negation of the term that an unstated exception exists at times of price increases, at which times the old price is to be charged, for a certain period or for a specified tonnage, on work already committed at the lower price on nonescalating contracts. Such a usage forms a broad and important exception to the express term, but does not swallow it entirely. Therefore, we hold that, under these particular facts, a reasonable jury could have found that price-protection was incorporated into the 1969 agreement between Nanakuli and Shell and that price-protection was reasonably consistent with the express term of seller's posted price at delivery.

VIII. Good Faith in Setting Price

Nanakuli offers an alternative theory why Shell should have offered price-protection at the time of the price increases of 1974. Even if price-protection was not a term of the agreement, Shell could not have exercised good faith in carrying out its 1969 contract with Nanakuli when it raised its price by $32 effective January 1 in a letter written December 31st and only received on January 4, given the universal practice of advance notice of such an increase in the asphaltic paving trade. The Code provides, "A price to be fixed by the seller or by the buyer means a price for him to fix in good faith," Haw.Rev.Stat. § 490:2-305(2). For a merchant good faith means "the observance of reasonable commercial standards of fair dealing in the trade." *Id.* 490:2-103(1)(b). The comment to § 2-305 explains, "[I]n the normal case a 'posted price' ... satisfies the good faith requirement." *Id.*, Comment 3. However, the words "in the normal case" mean that, although a posted price will usually be satisfactory, it will not be so under all circumstances. In addition, the dispute here was not over the amount of the increase — that is, the price that the seller fixed — but over the manner in which that increase was put into effect. It is true that Shell, in order to observe the good faith standards of the trade in 1974, was not bound by the practices of aggregate companies, which did not labor under the same disabilities as did asphalt suppliers in 1974. However, Nanakuli presented evidence that Chevron, in raising its price to $76, gave at least six weeks' advance notice, in accord with the long-time usage of the asphaltic paving trade. Shell, on the other hand, gave absolutely no notice, from which the jury could have concluded that Shell's manner of carrying out the price increase of 1974 did not conform to commercially reasonable standards. In both the timing of the announcement and its refusal to protect work already bid at the old price, Shell could be found to have breached the obligation of good faith imposed by the Code on all merchants. "Every contract or duty within this chapter imposes an obligation of good faith in its performance or enforcement," *id.* § 490:1-203, which for merchants entails the observance of commercially reasonable standards of fair dealing in the trade. The comment to 1-203 reads:

> This section sets forth a basic principle running throughout this Act. The principle involved is that in commercial transactions good faith is required in the performance and enforcement of all agreements or duties. Particular applications of this general principle appear in specific provisions of the Act.... It is further implemented by § 1-205 on course of dealing and usage of trade.

Id. § 490:1-203, Comment. Chevron's conduct in 1974 offered enough relevant evidence of commercially reasonable standards of fair dealing in the asphalt trade in Hawaii in 1974 for the jury to find that Shell's failure to give sufficient advance notice and price protect Nanakuli after the imposition of the new price did not conform to good faith dealings in Hawaii at that time. Because the jury could have found for Nanakuli on its price-protection claim under either theory, we reverse the judgment of the District Court and reinstate the jury verdict for Nanakuli in the amount of $220,800, plus interest according to law.

Reversed and remanded with directions to enter final judgment. [Special concurrence by Kennedy omitted]

NOTES AND QUESTIONS

1. *Expectations versus bureaucratic control*: Once again the person in the field made a deal with a customer. As often is true, their deal was inconsistent with the "legislation" of the organization, as announced in its printed form contracts. The people in Shell's home office knew little about what was going on in Hawaii. Shell's managers in corporate headquarters wanted to control agents in the field. Their lawyers fashioned lengthy documents protecting Shell's interest, warding off liability, and claiming maximum flexibility.

At the same time, Shell's agents in the field dealt with their own problems. They worked in specific business contexts influenced by the competitive situation. They did not go by the book. They created expectations inconsistent with the literal language of Shell's standard form contracts.

Should courts honor the "real deal" or the "paper deal?" A strict parol evidence rule helps officials of large corporate bureaucracies. They rely on what they find in their files. The court's approach in the *Nanakuli* case places real burdens on the home office. They cannot know for sure what their agents have said and done. Nonetheless, Nanakuli's people were likely to be less cautious about reading and understanding written documents than people in more distant relationships. Nanakuli and Shell were not in an arms-length relationship. They were quasi-partners, and officials of Nanakuli and Shell's local representative worked together for mutual benefit for a long time. In short, we are suggesting that the case reflects far more than a technical construction of the provisions of the Uniform Commercial Code. The court looked to the relationship rather than to the abstractions of formal contract law.[44]

2. *Price-protection in the asphalt trade*: The *Nanakuli* case isn't the only dispute arising out of the custom of price protecting distributors of asphalt. When OPEC caused petroleum prices to rise drastically in the early 1970s, the United States government regulated prices charged by major oil companies. Asphalt, however, was largely unregulated. Thus, the oil companies could make up on asphalt pricing some of what they lost under the regulations controlling other petroleum products. When the major oil companies withdrew price-protection, their distributors suffered losses on bids outstanding which they had calculated at the old prices.

3. *CISG and parol evidence*: A court applying the Convention on Contracts for the International Sale of Goods will have the authority to consider extrinsic evidence which contradicts the "paper deal"; the Convention contains no parol evidence rule. There would be no need to struggle, as the court seemed to in *Nanakuli*, to justify consideration of evidence which it regarded as relevant and probative. In Article 8(3) the Convention states that "in determining the intent of a party ... due consideration is to be given to all relevant circumstances of the case including negotiations, any practices which the parties have established between themselves, usages and any subsequent conduct of the parties."

---

[44]For discussions of the problems raised by the Nanakuli case, see Kastely, Stock Equipment for the Bargain in Fact: Trade Usage, "Express Terms," and Consistency Under § 1-205 of the Uniform Commercial Code, 64 North Carolina Law Review 777 (1986); Goetz and Scott, The Limits of Expanded Choice: An Analysis of the Interactions Between Express and Implied Contract Terms, 73 California Law Review 261 (1985); Hadjiyannakis, The Parol Evidence Rule and Implied Terms: The Sounds of Silence, 54 Fordham Law Review 35 (1985).

a. Merger and No Representations Clauses

ANDERSON v. TRI-STATE HOME IMPROVEMENT CO.

268 Wis. 455, 67 N.W.2d 853 (1955)

[Plaintiffs, the Andersons, were husband and wife. He was a machinist with thirty years' experience. She had no business experience. Spector, the President of Tri-State, called on the Andersons. He persuaded them to sign a contract  calling for the installation of Perma-loy siding on their home. The jury found that Spector told the Andersons that Tri-State guaranteed the siding against chipping, cracking, rusting, or peeling for at least thirty years. He said that the siding had been tested under all climatic conditions in their area, and the paint on the siding was not affected by snow, ice, or salt water. These statements were false, which Spector did not know but should have known. He made the statements recklessly, having no knowledge about testing. The written contract did not mention a thirty year guarantee nor did it contain statements about testing and the impact of snow, ice or salt water. The writing did contain a "no representations" clause.]

CURRIE, J. The contract entered into between plaintiffs and defendant company under date of April 6, 1950, contained the following clause:

"The company prohibits the making of any promises, or representations, unless it is inserted in writing in this agreement before signing...."

The first question which faces us on this appeal is whether such clause is effective to bar plaintiffs' cause of action grounded upon the alleged false representations of defendant's president and agent which induced the plaintiffs to enter into the contract.... We conclude that it is not.

An excellent statement of the policy reasons which have caused courts to refuse to construe so-called "integration" clauses, and contract clauses attempting to bar liability for false representations, as being effective to bar causes of action based upon fraudulent representations inducing a contract, is set forth in *Bates v. Southgate* (1941), 308 Mass. 170, 182, 31 N.E.2d 551, 558, as follows:

As a matter of principle it is necessary to weigh the advantages of certainty in contractual relations against the harm and injustice that result from fraud. In obedience to the demands of a larger public policy the law long ago abandoned the position that a contract must be held sacred regardless of the fraud of one of the parties in procuring it. No one advocates a return to outworn conceptions. The same public policy that in general sanctions the avoidance of a promise obtained by deceit strikes down all attempts to circumvent that policy by means of contractual devices. In the realm of fact it is entirely possible for a party knowingly to agree that no representations have been made to him, while at the same time believing and relying upon representations which in fact have been made and in fact are false but for which he would not have made the agreement. To deny this possibility is to ignore the frequent instances in everyday experience where parties accept, often without critical examination, and act upon agreements containing somewhere within their four corners exculpatory clauses in one form or another, but where they do so, nevertheless, in reliance upon the honesty of supposed friends, the plausible and disarming statements of salesmen, or the customary course of business. To refuse relief would result in opening the door to a multitude of frauds and in thwarting the general policy of the law.

1 Restatement, Agency, p. 579, § 260, states in effect that a principal, by inserting in a contract that he is not liable for the representations of his agent, may relieve himself from liability in an action for deceit to recover damages for the agent's fraudulent representations inducing the execution of the contract, but cannot by such a clause bar the other party's cause of action for rescission. However, 3 Williston, Contracts (rev. ed.), p. 2283, § 811A, points out that such rule, in so far as it relates to the barring of an action of damages for deceit, is not applicable where the fraud is attributable to the principal. In the case at bar, the defendant did not contend that Spector, its president, was not authorized to make the false representations claimed by the plaintiffs, but denied that any such representations were made by him. It seems to us that, where a corporation clothes its president with authority to execute a contract on its behalf, it is in no position to contend that such president was without authority to make representations of fact for the purpose of inducing the execution of the contract.

It appears that the authorities are divided on the question of whether an action to recover damages for deceit can be maintained against a principal for fraudulent representations of an agent, which induced the entering into of the contract, where the contract contains a clause negativing the existence of any representations not incorporated in the contract....

[D]efendant contends that the ... [false representation] constitutes merely an unfulfilled promise as to future events and, therefore, no liability can be grounded thereon....

[T]his court in *Alropa Corp. v. Flatley* (1938), 226 Wis. 561, 277 NW 108, adopted the position contended for by Mr. Justice FAIRCHILD ... [in a concurring opinion in *Beers*] recognizing ... an exception to the general rule, that an unfulfilled promise to perform a future act cannot be the basis of an action for deceit, and declared:

To amount to a fraud upon the purchaser the representations must relate to present or pre-existing facts, and it cannot ordinarily be predicated on unfulfilled promises or statements made as to future events. *Beers v. Atlas Assurance.*... One of the exceptions to this rule is that *when promises are made upon which the purchaser has a right to rely, and at the time of making them the promisor has a present intent not to perform them, the promises may amount to fraudulent representations and liability result."* (Emphasis supplied.)

... Furthermore, we believe a reasonable construction of the representation, that Spector and his company (the defendant) *"guaranteed the siding against chipping, cracking, rusting, or peeling for at least thirty years,"* to be that the defendant had a policy of so guaranteeing all Perma-loy siding installed on buildings of its customers for thirty years. In other words, the representation had reference to the existence of a general business policy of defendant rather than to a promise which was restricted to the siding to be installed on plaintiffs' home....

We conclude that, whether construed as an unfulfilled promise, which when made defendant had no intention of performing, or as a statement of an existing general business policy, the representation as to the guaranty is sufficient upon which to ground plaintiffs' cause of action for fraud and deceit....

NOTES AND QUESTIONS

1. *Merger clauses and warranty theory*: Suppose that the *Anderson* case had been tried as a breach of an express warranty under U.C.C. § 2-313. Do you see any problems in bringing the case under that section? What would have been the effect of the merger or integration clause in the seller's form contract? See U.C.C. §§ 2-316(1) and Comment 2; 2-721; 1-103.

2. *Merger clauses and the parol evidence rule*: A merger clause states that the parties agree that the written document is the final and complete expression of their agreement. If, in fact, the parties agreed that a written document should have this effect, the clause makes their choice clear, and insertion of the clause may serve to protect one, or the other, or both parties. Problems arise when a merger clause does not express the parties' bargain in fact but reflects the drafting skill, craft or even trickery of the lawyer for the more sophisticated party. Do even fairly experienced businesspeople realize that these clauses purport to cancel the legal effect of all a salesperson's representations and promises? Or is it the case that lawyers who insert such clauses in sales contracts to be used in transactions with unsophisticated consumers are structuring fraud? Is it ethically permissible for a lawyer to use his or her training to trick the unsuspecting? Or are lawyers entitled to assume that their clients are ethical people and will use the rights granted by form contracts only to ward off unjustified claims by those who want something for nothing? It could be argued

that clients who use clauses hidden in form contracts to injure their customers will be disciplined by the market. Moreover, some would assert that lawyers are hired to implement their clients not-unlawful wishes, and not to pass moral judgment on them. Lawyers, under this view, are expected to protect their clients by drafting such clauses, not to protect the interests of non-clients. What do you think? How would you respond if asked to draft a potentially crucial provision for a form contract, and were told to "make it as inconspicuous as the law will allow?"

3. *Using contract terms to limit responsibility for the actions of an agent*: To what extent can a company use language in form contracts to immunize itself from liability for responsibility for statements made by its sales force? This is a major problem both for buyers and sellers, as well as for the courts that are confronted with their disputes. First, if contract law seeks to hold people for the expectations they intentionally or negligently create, we need to consider the extent to which the clauses in form contracts serve as meaningful warnings to customers to discount advertising, the seller's reputation, and the "seller's talk" of salespeople and sales engineers. This would seem to be an empirical question. Next, with the answer to that question in hand, we could try to assess the advantages and disadvantages of the consequences we would bring about by enforcing the clauses.

We need to consider these consequences not only from the point of view of those whose potential claims are limited by the form provisions, but from the point of view of those seeking immunity as well. It is important to understand that salespeople deal with potential customers outside the direct supervision and control of the top officials of a corporation. The salespeople have incentives to oversell the product, and this is hard to control. The problem sometimes arises not because of what a salesperson literally said, but because of the impression they created, in combination with the assumptions made by the customers; a customer may be severely disappointed with a product which literally complies with the express promises made about it. Customers may lie about what salespeople said, or shade the truth either deliberately or innocently. In addition, juries may be more sympathetic with retailers or other small businesses than with the Fortune 500 companies that manufacture the products. If we give effect to the liability-denying provisions in form contracts, we may do an injustice to those who have innocently and in good faith relied on the impressions created by the sales force, and we may allow some companies to make sales by painting a rosy picture of their product's capacities, while avoiding the responsibility of living up to the promises implicit in the picture. On the other hand, if we deny to corporations the ability to use this tool, we weaken their control over their sales force, and permit victories by those who can convince a jury that promises were made that really weren't, or enforcement of promises that reasonable buyers should have realized were beyond the authority of the agent to make.

A brief look at some of the litigation involving Burroughs Corp. may serve to make the abstract problem described in the foregoing paragraph more concrete.

In the 1960's and 70's Burroughs was a profitable company selling, among other things, computers and installed software to small commercial users.[45] Many of its became dissatisfied, and they filed at least 190 cases against Burroughs customers. Although Burroughs emphasized that this represented only a small fraction of its installed base of users, and that other computer equipment companies had suffered similar problems leading to litigation, no other company faced as many cases as Burroughs did. Burroughs blamed the customers for inexperience in using computers, for neglecting to send operators to Burroughs' training sessions, and for having unrealistic expectations. The customers charged that Burroughs oversold its computers, put products on the market before they were developed properly, and either encouraged or allowed its salesforce to misrepresent what the machines could do. Though there is no doubt a fair amount of truth in both sides of the story, a computer consultant said, "Burroughs has a long and colorful history of announcing machines before they are fully developed, shipping them without software, and having hardware breakdowns in the user's shop." Some Burroughs' salespeople testified for plaintiffs, and suggested that they only said what they were instructed to say in the sales meeting.

Some of the other computer suppliers adopted a strategy of settling disputes with customers. Burroughs was more litigious. The chief weapon in its defensive strategy was the standard form contract which it required its customers to sign. The terms of the contract were described in *Badger Bearing Co. v. Burroughs Corp.*[46] A provision on the front page of the contract provided that there was a three-month warranty, governed by the terms on the reverse side of the form. On the reverse side were two clauses; the first was a limitation of remedy clause, and the second a merger clause:

> Seller ... shall not be held responsible ... in any event under this agreement for more than a refund of the purchase price, less reasonable rental for past use, upon return of the equipment to Seller with Seller's prior written consent. (Purchaser hereby expressly waives all incidental and consequential damages.)

> **There are no understandings, agreements, representations, or warranties, express or implied (including any regarding merchantability or fitness for a particular purpose), not specified herein, respecting this contract or the equipment hereunder. This contract states the entire obligation of seller in connection with this transaction.**

---

[45]In 1986 Burroughs merged with Sperry to form Unisys Corporation.

[46]444 F. Supp. 919 (E.D. Wis. 1977), aff'd without opinion, 588 F.2d 838 (7th Cir. 1978).

The express warranty offered by Burroughs was relatively narrow. In addition, the provisions were in many cases accompanied by a provision which cut the time for filing claims from the four or six years provided by most state statutes to just two years. Burroughs sometimes brought cross-actions against its customers, and some lawyers accused Burroughs of delaying the progress of litigation by extensive (and allegedly unnecessary) use of pre-trial procedures.

Burroughs won some, and it lost some. In the *Badger Bearing* case, in which the customer had experienced 76 service calls in 2 1/2 years on a $62,590 computer, Judge Gordon, (the trial judge) found that any warranties which might have been breached had been successfully disclaimed, and that Badger had not established that any material misrepresentations had been made. Although the outcome represented a victory for Burroughs, Judge Gordon did find that the sales agreement was not intended as a final expression of the contract, and so allowed Badger to try to prove the existence of terms which contradicted the sales form. Unfortunately for Badger, he then concluded that the plaintiff had failed to prove that the disclaimer language had been "negotiated out" of the contract. As a result the disclaimers stood. Judge Gordon also ruled that the contractual disclaimers could not be used to prevent Badger from proceeding on the tort theories of negligent misrepresentation or strict responsibility for misrepresentation. Again, it was just that Badger failed to prove those claims. And so in *Badger Bearing* the effort to use the parol evidence clause or merger clause proved ineffective, as it did for similar reasons in *Sierra Diesel Injection Service, Inc. v. Burroughs Corp.*[47] An Arizona court, however, found that "[s]ince the contract specifically negated the alleged misrepresentations, Kalil's [plaintiff] claims for negligent misrepresentations, fraud and consumer fraud, based upon statements made prior to the signing of the contract were not actionable because of the parol evidence rule."[48] The 5th Circuit seemed to follow the same approach in *Earman Oil Co. v. Burroughs Corp.*[49] Other cases, which turned on other factors and other U.C.C. sections, met with similarly mixed success for Burroughs.

(Parenthetically, what can we learn from the fact that different courts, faced with the same contractual language, seemed to come to different conclusions as to its legal effect? How big a problem is the inconsistency? If it is a big problem, what can be done about it? Is the existence of the inconsistency an indictment of the ability of the legal system to live up to its goal of objectivity and uniformity?)

To return to the Burroughs cases themselves, they could be described in at least two different ways. Some might suggest that they represent a situation in which a major company attempted to use its superior market power to abuse its customers, who were not in a position to evaluate the Burroughs' promises. The

---

[47]874 F.2d 653 (9th Cir. 1989).

[48]Kalil Bottling Co. v. Burroughs Corp., 127 Ariz. 278, 619 P.2d 1055 (Ct.App. Ariz. 1980).

[49]625 F.2d 1292 (5th Cir. 1980).

fact that the provisions were available to customers does not mean that the customers assented to them in any meaningful way, especially since they were inconsistent with all of the other signals being sent by the seller. If that is your view, you would probably be disappointed in those courts which seemed to permit Burroughs to use its forms and technical Code sections to escape justice.

On the other hand, some would paint a more benign picture. They would argue that if one wants companies like Burroughs to bring new and innovative products to market, they must be able to free themselves from the burden of claims for consequential damages or compensation for the misrepresentations of sales people. In the long, and even medium, term they would assert that we can rely on the desire to protect commercial reputation to prompt most companies to fix defective machines, or give refunds. Companies that fail to offer good products on fair terms will wither and disappear. In time, the market will correct the situation. In a sense, the relationship between Burroughs and its customers could be seen as a kind of partnership. By trial and error both producer and customer attempt to get a new product to operate properly, sharing the rewards and risks. If we impose liability, we can expect to increase the cost to everyone of spreading the benefits of computers. Much of any damages award will be siphoned off to pay lawyers fees and litigation costs. In the long run, this argument concludes, enforcing merger clauses and disclaimers is in the best interest of most people in society, even though in the short run firms like Badger Bearing must pay a price.

Do you find either argument convincing? Can you offer others? Strike the balance?

4. *Disclaiming the fraud of your employees*: In the Burroughs' cases, to give Burroughs the benefit of the doubt, we may have had a pattern of widespread corporate optimism, unwarranted by the operating characteristics of the computers. Sometimes, however, sellers make knowing misrepresentations. In *City Dodge, Inc. v. Gardner*,[50] the jury found that the seller's salesman had knowingly misrepresented that a used car sold to the buyer had never been wrecked and repaired. The buyer signed a sales agreement which stated, "no other agreement, promise or understanding of any kind pertaining to this purchase will be recognized." In addition, the sales agreement stated that the car was sold "as is." The buyer sued for fraud and deceit, and won a verdict which was affirmed on appeal.

The Supreme Court of Georgia found that U.C.C. § 2-202 was inapplicable to misrepresentation actions. Some earlier Georgia cases had found a disclaimer in a written contract defeated a fraud action because it prevented a buyer from justifiably relying on a misrepresentation. However, in the *City Dodge* case, the Georgia Court rejected this view, explaining that "[i]t is inconsistent to apply a disclaimer provision of a contract in a tort action brought to determine whether

---

[50]232 Ga. 766, 208 S.E.2d 794 (1974).

the entire contract is invalid because of alleged prior fraud which induced the execution of the contract. If the contract is invalid because of the antecedent fraud, then the disclaimer provision therein is ineffectual since, in legal contemplation, there is no contract between the parties. In this case ... [a]s the antecedent fraud was proven to the satisfaction of the jury, it vitiated the contract." ["Vitiate" means "to contaminate; spoil; corrupt; pollute; debase; pervert; or render ineffective."]

Suppose Salesman knowingly made a false representation that a used car had never been wrecked and repaired and then negotiated a price with Buyer. A form contract with the same provisions as found in the *City Dodge* case was filled out by Salesman. Then the Owner of the dealership talked with Buyer, telling him that "salesmen say a lot of things and buyers hear what they want to hear. You understand that I am selling this car 'as is,' and as this written contract says, I cannot be responsible for whatever Salesman said or you think he said about this car." Buyer said, "understood," and signed the written sales agreement. Under the reasoning of the *City Dodge* case, would Buyer be able to sue the dealership for misrepresentation despite the disclaimer and merger clause in the document? Should Buyer be able to sue even when the Owner gave him such a warning? Would Buyer be able to sue for misrepresentation in such a case under the rule in the *Anderson* decision?

5. *Conspicuousness of merger clauses*: In *Seibel v. Layne & Bowler, Inc.*,[51] there was a "merger clause" in a printed form contract, purporting to bar the buyer from showing representations and warranties not stated in the writing. The court found the merger clause to be inconspicuous. As a result, it said, the parol evidence rule did not prevent the buyer from offering testimony about oral warranties. Is there any requirement of conspicuousness in U.C.C. § 2-202? Such a requirement is stated, of course, in § 2-316(2) for an effective disclaimer in writing of the implied warranty of merchantability and for any disclaimer of the implied warranty of fitness for particular purpose. Can we argue with any chance of success that § 2-202 speaks of a writing "intended by the parties as a final expression of their agreement." U.C.C. § 1-201(3) defines "agreement" as "the bargain of the parties in fact as found in their language or by implication from other circumstances ..." If a merger clause in a printed form contract is not conspicuous, then this is evidence that this part of the writing is not "intended by the parties as a final expression of their agreement." Notice that the phrase from the Code is stated in the plural and not singular. It is not enough that the clause is intended by its drafter as a final expression of the deal.

Suppose a merger clause were found to be conspicuous under the tests in § 1-201(10). Would it necessarily then be effective? And what is the authority, in states other than Oregon, of the *Seibel* case? Can it be ignored safely elsewhere?

---

[51]56 Ore.App. 387, 641 P.2d 668 (1982).

b. Reformation and Parol Evidence

To what extent, if at all, can a party seeking to contradict a written contract *reform* the document and avoid the parol evidence rule? Classically, this could be done in a few limited situations. For example, suppose Vendor sells Purchaser the house at 123 Main Street. However, the typist made an error, and the written contract describes the house as located at 213 Main Street. Traditionally, courts of equity would reform legal instruments to cure such mistakes. Of course, when a court allows this mistake to be proved, it allows evidence that contradicts a writing that appears complete on its face. We can say that the parties did not intend the writing with the mistaken description to be the final and complete record of their bargain. However, we could say the same thing about the agreement to tear down the ice house in *Mitchill v. Lath*. Perhaps the willingness of courts to allow evidence of this kind of mistake rests on the absence of a jury in an equitable action. Perhaps it rests on the ease of proof in the usual situation — after all, the vendor usually owns the house at 123 Main and not the one at 213 Main.

How far can we go using reformation as a way around the parol evidence rule? If the party seeking to prove an oral agreement is willing to give up a jury, can she add prior agreements and contradict the language of the writing by casting the suit as one for reformation? Courts have been hesitant to attack the parol evidence rule this way, but the possibility remains.

JOHNSON v. GREEN BAY PACKERS

272 Wis. 149, 74 N.W.2d 784 (1956)

Action by the plaintiff Clyde Johnson against defendant the Green Bay Packers, Inc., for reformation of contract and to recover damages for breach of contract.

Plaintiff's complaint contained two causes of action stated in the alternative, the first of which prayed for reformation of the contract entered into between the parties on June 30, 1948, and for the recovery of damages by plaintiff for breach of the contract as so reformed; while the second cause of action prayed for recovery of damages by the plaintiff for breach of the contract as originally written without first being reformed. The answer interposed by the defendant ... contained denials of most of the material allegations of plaintiff's complaint. The action was tried to the court without a jury.... A summary of the testimony and evidence adduced at the trial follows.

Johnson, a professional football player, had a contract with the Los Angeles Rams for the 1947 season. This was a "season" contract under which Johnson could not be released during the season at the option of the Rams. The contract also provided that the Rams had the right to renew the contract for the 1948 season. At the end of the 1947 season the Rams informed Johnson that they would employ him for the 1948 season, but not on the basis of a season contract. This was not satisfactory to Johnson and the parties failed to agree on terms. The Rams then traded Johnson to the defendant Packers.

About June first, Lambeau, in behalf of the defendant Packers contacted Johnson by phone and arranged an appointment.... At the first meeting between Mr. and Mrs. Johnson and Lambeau at the latter's home contract terms were discussed for the employment of Johnson by the Packers. Johnson testified that he insisted on a "season" contract like he had had with the Rams and that Lambeau agreed thereto. This Lambeau denied.

Later, Lambeau and Johnson met at the Hotel Roosevelt in Hollywood on or about June 30, 1948. Lambeau produced a printed form of contract in blank which was in triplicate (one for the player, one for the Packers, and one for the commissioner of the National Football League). Lambeau wrote in longhand the figure "$7,000" on the face of the contract. Johnson then brought up the fact that a "season" contract had been agreed on, whereupon Lambeau turned over the contract and wrote in longhand on the back:

$7,000 season 1948	Season
	contracts
Minimum $7,000 1949	E. L. L.

Both Johnson and Lambeau signed the contract in triplicate and Lambeau retained all copies for the purpose of sending them in to the Packers to be typed and made to conform to the verbal understanding of the parties, after which one of the three would be returned to Johnson.

Johnson testified that at the time of these negotiations at the Hotel Roosevelt he asked Lambeau to strike out paragraph 6 on the printed forms of the contract, covering the power of the Packers to release the player, to which Lambeau replied that he would send the contracts in and have them "fixed" as agreed.

Several weeks later Johnson received his copy of the contract which bore the aforementioned notations in ink on the back made by Lambeau, but he noted that paragraph 6 had not been stricken. Such paragraph 6 reads as follows:

> The player represents and warrants that he is and will continue to be sufficiently highly skilled in all types of football team play to play professional football of the caliber required by the league and by the club, that he is and will continue to be in excellent physical condition, and agrees to perform his services hereunder to the complete satisfaction of the club and its head coach. (If in the opinion of the head coach the player does not

```
maintain himself in excellent physical condition or fails
at any time during the football seasons included in the
term of this contract to demonstrate sufficient skill and
capacity to play professional football of the caliber
required by the league and by the club, or if in the
opinion of the head coach the player's work or conduct in
the performance of this contract is unsatisfactory as
compared with the work and conduct of other members of the
club's squad of players, the club shall have the right to
terminate this contract upon written notice to the player
of such termination.)
```

As soon as Johnson received his copy, he called Lambeau and protested that the printed portion of the contract which gave the Packers the right to release Johnson during the season (paragraph 6) had not been stricken as agreed. Lambeau replied that Johnson should not worry, that the commissioner did not like the contracts to be cut up or have portions crossed out, that his (Lambeau's) word was as good as gold, and that Johnson had a two-year "season" contract. Johnson accepted this explanation by Lambeau, Johnson's testimony on this point being as follows:

"Well, as closely as I can remember, I took him at his word, plus the notation on the back of the contract that it was a two-year seasonal."

Johnson later came to Green Bay, went into training, and played two exhibition games. On or about September 16, 1948, the defendant Packers then terminated Johnson's employment by written notice sent by mail, reading as follows:

Notice of Termination
Attention of Clyde Johnson
Dear Sir: *Date: September 16, 1948*

You are hereby notified that the Green Bay Packers, Inc., a member of the National Football League, pursuant to paragraph 6 of its contract with you dated June 30, 1948, hereby terminates said contract, effective immediately, for the reason[s] checked below:

☐ In the opinion of the head coach, you are not and have not maintained yourself in excellent physical condition.

☒ In the opinion of the head coach, you are failing and have failed to demonstrate sufficient skill and capacity to play professional football of the caliber required by the league and by the club.

☒ In the opinion of the head coach, your work and conduct in the performance of your contract is unsatisfactory as compared with the work and conduct of other members of the club's squad of players.

Remarks:
Club
By /s/ E. L. Lambeau

The only compensation Johnson received from the Packers was $100 travel money for the trip to Green Bay. Johnson played the remainder of the 1948 season with the Los Angeles Dons and his earnings from such source were $6,000. Early in the spring of 1949, Johnson wrote to the Packers and informed them that he was ready, willing, and able to play for them in 1949, but received no answer. The total amount of his earnings and income for the period of August through December, 1949, was $1,007.25. The answer of the defendant raises no issue that Johnson should have attempted to earn more during such period, or to take other action to mitigate damages.

Following the trial, the trial court made and filed a memorandum decision in which he determined that the plaintiff Johnson was entitled to have his contract of employment with the defendant for the football seasons of 1948 and 1949 reformed by striking out paragraph 6 thereof, and that Johnson should recover from the defendant the agreed compensation for said two seasons less his earnings from other sources....

Judgment was ... rendered ... in favor of plaintiff and against the defendant. From such judgment the defendant has appealed.

CURRIE, J. The following issues are raised on this appeal:

(1) Whether reformation may be decreed to delete a provision in a contract, where such provision was left in the contract with the consent of the aggrieved party, even though such consent was obtained in reliance upon a contemporaneous oral promise which was not kept;

(2) Whether the judgment in behalf of Johnson can be affirmed on the ground set forth in plaintiff's second cause of action, i.e., that the trial court should have enforced the contract as written giving effect to the written portion over the conflicting printed paragraph 6;

... [Issues 3 & 4 deleted.]

Without dispute, it appears from the facts found by the trial court that, when Johnson in the summer of 1948 received back his copy of the contract of employment, he at once discovered that paragraph 6 thereof had not been deleted as agreed between the parties, and that he immediately called the matter to Lambeau's attention. Lambeau then explained to Johnson that paragraph 6 had not been deleted because the league commissioner did not like contracts with parts crossed out, but assured Johnson that the original agreement for a "season" contract for the years 1948 and 1949 would be lived up to. Upon such verbal assurance from Lambeau, Johnson did not renew his request that paragraph 6 be deleted but entered into employment with such paragraph still in the contract.

In *Touchett v. E Z Paintr Corp.* (1953), 263 Wis. 626, 630, 58 N.W. (2d) 448, 59 N.W. (2d) 433, this court had before it a cause of action for reformation of contract, and in its opinion stated [p. 630]:

There is a further rule of law that the court will not insert a provision in a contract which was omitted with the consent of the parties asking for reformation, although such consent was given in reliance on an oral promise of the other party that the omission would not make any difference.

We consider the above-quoted principle to be equally applicable to the facts in the instant case. The fact that here we are concerned with the failure to delete a clause necessary to conform the written contract to the prior verbal understanding of the parties, while in the *Touchett Case* the written contract failed to include a paragraph covering a matter previously agreed upon by the parties in parol, we deem to be of no significance. In both situations the aggrieved party accepted the contract as written and entered into performance thereof upon the oral promise of the other party that the failure of the contract to read as agreed would not make any difference. We, therefore, conclude that it was error for the trial court to decree reformation of the contract by ordering the deletion of paragraph 6.

Counsel for Johnson urge that, even if the contract be not reformed so as to delete paragraph 6 thereof, the written provisions indorsed in the back of plaintiff's copy of the contract by Lambeau, being in direct conflict with the printed provisions of paragraph 6, must prevail over such printed provisions. In other words, it is urged that the trial court should have reached the same result by a proper interpretation of the contract as written....

We deem that the point under consideration is ruled in plaintiff's favor by the case of *Tollefson v. Green Bay Packers, Inc.* (1950), 256 Wis. 318, 41 N.W. (2d) 201. Such case involved an action to recover damages for breach of contract of employment by Tollefson, a professional football player, against the same defendant as in the instant case. Most of the provisions of the contract were in printed form, as in the instant case, and Lambeau, manager of the Packers, wrote in longhand in paragraph 1, which covered the matter of Tollefson's compensation, "minimum $3,600 for season." Paragraph 7, one of the printed clauses of the agreement, provided that the contract might be terminated any time by the Packers giving notice in writing within forty-eight hours after the date of the last game in which Tollefson had participated. This court interpreted such words to mean that, unless discharged for cause, Tollefson was entitled to the full sum of $3,600 whether he participated in the games played by the Packers or not. In its opinion, this court stated (p. 322): ..."Where written provisions are inconsistent with printed provisions [of a contract], an interpretation is preferred which gives effect to the written provisions." Restatement, 1 Contracts, p. 328, § 236(e)....

Lambeau in the instant case testified on his adverse examination that if the provision contained in paragraph 6 of the printed form of the contract were deleted then the contract would have constituted that which is known "in the trade" as a "season contract." This corroborates Johnson's testimony that it was verbally agreed between him and Lambeau that he was to have a "season" contract for both years 1948 and 1949 under which the Packers would have no right to terminate the same except for cause, and that the notation placed on the back of Johnson's copy of the contract in longhand by Lambeau, and initialed by him, were in order to comply with Johnson's request that he have a "season" contract for such two years. As we view it, the only material difference in the facts of the *Tollefson Case* and the one at bar is that the governing provision written in longhand in the former was written on the face of Tollefson's contract, while in the instant case it was written on the back of the contract. However, inasmuch as the parties intended the provision in the instant case with respect to a "season" contract to be part of the contract, its location, whether on the face or back, is wholly immaterial....

Inasmuch as the provisions of paragraph 6 directly conflict with the provision in Lambeau's handwriting for "season" contracts for each of the years 1948 and 1949, the latter provision must govern....

NOTES AND QUESTIONS

1. *Relief for victims of the parol evidence rule*: Suppose the trier of fact believed Clyde Johnson's version of all of the events involved in the case. Suppose, however, that Lambeau had made no notation on the standard National Football League contract. Lambeau told Johnson that when the form came back from the League office with clause 6 still included that Johnson could trust Lambeau because his word was good as gold. Johnson could not get reformation. There would be no handwritten provision to override the printed form. Would Johnson have any remedy?

Today could Johnson assert Restatement (Second) of Contracts § 90 to offset the parol evidence rule? Few courts have faced the problem squarely. Professor Metzger argues that courts are likely to use promissory estoppel to undercut the parol evidence rule.[52] The same reasons for applying promissory estoppel to the Statute of Frauds also suggest its application to the parol evidence rule. He suggests that courts following a Willistonian parol evidence rule because of their desire to defend written documents will resist. Courts following a Corbin parol evidence rule might not need the doctrine. If one party has reasonably relied on a prior or contemporaneous promise or statement, then the parties did not intend the writing to be a final statement of their deal. Nonetheless, he argues:

> Estoppel could enhance the effectuation of the parties' true intent in a written contract, an objective shared by modern formulations of the parol evidence rule, and could minimize the injustice associated with mechanical

---

[52]See Metzger, The Parol Evidence Rule: Promissory Estoppel's Next Conquest? 36 Vanderbilt Law Review 1383, 1466 (1983).

applications of the rule. Estoppel also could provide a better doctrinal explanation for the results courts reach in many parol evidence cases than the traditional parol evidence rubric that courts currently employ affords. Such doctrinal clarity would result in the focusing of judicial attention in parol evidence cases on the real issues that ultimately will determine whether a court will give legal effect to an extrinsic promise, a consequence likely to provide a much needed measure of clarity and predictability in the administration of the parol evidence rule. Finally, promissory estoppel's application in parol evidence cases would be consonant with the tendency of twentieth century contract law to elevate substance over form in the pursuit of just results, a tendency of which the reliance principle is just one manifestation.

Compare Restatement (Second) of Contracts §§ 155, 158, *supra*.

D. CONCLUSIONS ABOUT THE PAROL EVIDENCE RULE

Professors Childres and Spitz[53] studied the 149 cases relevant to the parol evidence rule cited in volumes ten through fifteen of West's General Digest, Fourth Series.[54] They found they could order the apparent chaos of the parol evidence rule by classifying the cases in terms of the status of the parties to the contracts in question.

They divided the cases into categories they labelled as (a) formal contracts, (b) informal contracts, and (c) contracts involving an abuse of the bargaining process. Formal contracts are transactions between parties with some expertise and business sophistication. The parties can be regarded as professionals, and the agreements are negotiated fairly and in detail. Informal contracts are agreements between people who lack sophistication in business. Abuse of bargaining power cases include contracts of adhesion and unconscionable contracts as well as other contracts objectionable on public policy grounds.

Courts protect written documents in formal contract situations. They do not allow oral evidence to replace contract language with an alleged prior understanding. They will allow parties to show that the writing was not a complete statement of the contract. For example, parties may not have defined all their obligations because they deal under the assumption that usages of trade will govern. Businesspeople can prove side agreements. However, courts frequently ignored the parol evidence rule in informal contracts. About 27% of the cases in the sample involved these situations. Courts refused to hear extrinsic evidence in only three reported cases involving informal contracts. The approach here was

---

[53]Childres and Spitz, Status in the Law of Contract, 47 New York University Law Review 1 (1972).

[54]Roughly, these volumes reported cases decided during the decade of the 1960s.

obviously inconsistent with both that in the formal situation and the language of the rule itself. Often courts strain to find terms in the written document to be ambiguous so parol evidence can be admitted. In those cases where courts upheld the written document, the courts frequently indicated that they did not believe the alleged oral agreement had been made. Finally, any person who alleged inferior bargaining position or an abuse of bargaining power usually gets his evidence to the trier of fact. 33.5% of the cases in the sample involved an abuse of bargaining power, and the courts in all but seven of them allowed the evidence to be considered.

Childres and Spitz conclude "[o]nce it is made explicit that no single rule can be expected to operate across all status lines, we can get about the business of trying to create new categories and rules." The authors concede that their categories may be crude and imprecise. Their study tells us only about reported appellate cases. Furthermore, some might suspect that the reactions of courts in the 1960s might differ substantially from reactions in the 1990s. Interestingly, in 1991 Michael Lawrence[55] sought to replicate the Childres and Spitz analysis, using Wisconsin cases. He concluded that the outcomes in the cases supported the Childres and Spitz hypothesis with "striking frequency."

Professor Justin Sweet[56] argues,

> [T]rue integration should be the only basis for any rule that limits provability of prior oral agreements. The desirable objectives now sought through the parol evidence rule can be accomplished more directly through other accepted legal doctrines. To make the integration concept work, however, there is a need for workable and realistic methods of recognizing the objective trappings of a true integration. A model of a truly integrated contract should be created and criteria developed for identification of truly integrated writings....
>
> The hallmark of a truly integrated contract is that it is put together carefully and methodically. In this sense it resembles the creation of a statute or a treaty. A good deal has occurred before the act of integration. The person preparing the integration, usually the attorney, gathers all the evidence of what has transpired in order to prepare a draft. He will look at letters, wires, memoranda, agreements, contracts and any other data relevant to the final document.... Drafts are exchanged and revised. Provisions are traded, eliminated or modified. Each party uses its persuasiveness to support inclusion or deletion of specific clauses. Language is reviewed carefully with a view toward achieving phraseology satisfactory to both parties. Usually, a clause stating that the writing covers the entire transaction is included.

---

[55] 1991 Wisconsin Law Review 1071 (1991).

[56] Sweet, Contract Making and Parol Evidence: Diagnosis and Treatment of a Sick Rule, 53 Cornell Law Review 1036 (1968).

Attorneys look over the final draft and confer with the top negotiators in order to iron out final details. The final draft is prepared and the date set for execution. Top executives of the contracting parties and other interested persons gather to sign or to witness the execution of the agreement....

Obviously, the percentage of contracts made in this manner is small. It can be argued that if we protect only true integrations of this sort, we are in effect abolishing the parol evidence rule. But these are the only types of written agreements which can confidently be assumed to integrate the entire transaction in one repository....

Even a contract put together in a manner suggested by the above model would not invariably integrate everything relating to the transaction. Contracts which appear to be integrated contracts *may* not contain everything. Oral agreements may be made simultaneously with the execution of a complete and final-looking written agreement, and may nevertheless be enforceable.

Sweet then lists nine factors a court should consider in deciding whether a written document truly was intended as a final and complete expression of the parties' contract. Two important factors, he lists, are the "bargaining situation" and the "degree of standardization of the writing." He says "[t]he greater the onesidedness of the bargaining situation, the less likely it is that the bargain was concluded by an integrated writing." Furthermore, "[t]he greater the standardization of the writing, the less likely that the transaction was concluded by an integrated writing."

How might corporate lawyers respond to Childres and Spitz and to Sweet? Are there reasons for defending written documents these authors fail to consider? Professor Duncan Kennedy sees the parol evidence rule as hiding an important political position. How would you state the politics of the cases you have read in this section? Would you agree with Professor Patricia J. Williams. She says,

The body of private laws epitomized by contract, including slave contracts, for example, is problematic not only because it endows certain parties with rights, but because it denies the object of contract any rights at all.

The quintessential rule of contract interpretation, the parol evidence rule, illustrates the mechanics by which such construction is achieved.... If ... this rule is understood as a form of social construction, the words could as well read: "Terms with respect to which the constructed reality (or governing narrative) of a given power structure agree, may not be contradicted, but only supplemented or explained." ... One consequence of ... [a] broader reconfiguration of rights, again in the context of contract, is to give voice to those people or things which, by virtue of their object relation to the contract, historically had no voice.

We have been talking for much of this chapter about the problems associated with determining what a contract means. Much of this enterprise is linked to the doctrines of contract formation. Most of these contract formation rules imagine a single moment of formation. The question of the meaning of the contract, therefore, often focusses on the question of what the contract meant at the moment of its winking into existence. Courts frame the interpretive question as, "What did the parties mutually intend at the moment of the contract's formation." This idea, while theoretically appealing is, sometimes more and sometimes less, a fiction. As many have observed, (most stubbornly, perhaps, Ian MacNeil) contracts don't wink on. The truth of contractual behavior is to be found in the development, over the life of an often complicated relationship, of a set of mutually interlocking expectations. Nevertheless contract doctrine finds it convenient to imagine that there was a moment of no contract, followed by a moment when there was contract, with no intervening moment of uncertainty. As soon as there was a contract, all of the essential terms were determinable.

Sometimes, of course, one can look at the subsequent behavior of the parties as evidence of what their intentions were at the moment of formation, but theoretically at least that subsequent behavior was not seen as the filling in of some blank or void in the contract, but merely as confirmation of some already defined term; we know what they *meant* then by what they *did* later. Even in a case like the *Nanakuli* case, in which a great deal of the evidence concerns trade practices and the course of performance of the parties themselves in the months and years after the contract was created, that evidence is read back onto the terms which constituted the contract at the moment of creation. There are a whole host of legal rules which are designed to serve, and render administrable, the fiction that contracts wink on — that a contract has no infancy, but emerges from the union of the paries' intentions in its adult, mature form. The parol evidence rule is very much a rule born of the necessity of determining the meaning of a contract in the moment of its creation.

E. THE ADJUSTMENT OR MODIFICATION OF PERFORMANCE TERMS

It is hard to make a contract of any complexity that will continue to satisfy everyone concerned as it is performed over time. People often expect to make adjustments and changes during the course of performance. Often contracts are written with provisions designed to track with changing conditions. We have already seen flexible quantity and price arrangements.

At times, however, people will write what appears to be flat and absolute contracts with no provisions for changes, but they will understand that there is an implicit obligation to make adjustments as circumstances change. Some American lawyers are surprised to find that Japanese and Chinese negotiators often view an express contract as only the starting place for adjustments. However, the cultural differences are ones of degree and not kind. Americans in many fields recognize the necessity of altering deals as circumstances change.[57] It is not always easy to tell when business culture allows me to hold you to the letter of our bargain and when custom demands that I let you out of what you are literally obligated to do.

While often there are good reasons to adjust bargains to changing situations, sometimes people want out of contracts for opportunistic reasons. Beale, Bishop and Furmston[58] note:

> [a]n agreement running over a period of time may give a party the scope for "opportunism," by taking advantage of the other's circumstances to threaten a breach of contract unless the deal is renegotiated in his favor. Frequently the opportunity for such extortion arises from the operation of the contract itself. Even if the parties met on an equal footing originally, when the time for performance draws near one party may be heavily dependent on the other; he may face serious losses if he does not get the other's performance and has nowhere that he can readily obtain a substitute.

Contract law often is contradictory if not incoherent. This is particularly true in the area of adjustments, modifications and changes to an ongoing bargain. There are a number of issues that have troubled courts, legal scholars and law students. For example, how far can we control the future by clauses in contracts? Suppose we agree that we cannot modify a contract or that we can modify only by following certain procedures. Later can we agree to ignore the provisions of our earlier bargain concerning modifications? Do modifications of contracts require consideration or sufficient reliance to trigger promissory estoppel? Or can we just give up rights voluntarily? Suppose my failure to perform entitles you to certain remedies. However, you do not assert them but allow me to continue to perform. Can you lose some or all of your remedies? Does this require bad faith, consideration, reliance, writings or any other conduct or form? The answers to these questions are important but very unclear.

The following material serves as a transition between ideas about forming contracts and performing them. While in theory we can distinguish making and carrying out bargains, in practice often these things are intertwined.

---

[57]In some fields of business, form contracts provide that they may be cancelled for convenience and spell out a cancellation charge. Other clauses say that quantities ordered may be decreased subject to an equitable adjustment in the unit price.

[58]Beale, Bishop and Furmston, Contract: Cases and Materials 491 (Butterworths 1985).

1. "WRITTEN MODIFICATIONS ONLY" CLAUSES

UNIVERSAL BUILDERS, INC. v. MOON MOTOR LODGE, INC.

430 Pa. 550, 244 A.2d 10 (1968)

EAGEN, J. [This was an appeal from a final equitable decree ordering the defendant to pay the plaintiff the balance due on a construction contract, plus extras. The plaintiff had sued to have a real estate conveyance set aside on the ground that it was a fraudulent conveyance. Plaintiff also had asked to have a supplemental agreement declared void, alleging it was procured by fraud. Plaintiff also sought money damages for work done under both the basic and supplemental agreement. The defendant had denied the fraud, and had denied it owed plaintiff any money for work which had been done, claiming both a set off and damages for delay. Except for the decree for the balance due, the trial court had denied all of the claims and counterclaims.]

Briefly, the background facts of this case are as follows. On August 16, 1961, the plaintiff, Universal Builders, Inc. (hereinafter Universal), entered into a written contract with the defendant, Moon Motor Lodge, Inc. (hereinafter Moon), for the construction of a motel and restaurant in Allegheny County. The contract provides, inter alia, that all change orders must be in writing and signed by Moon and/or the Architect and that all requests for extension of time must be made in writing to the Architect. The contract specifications also required that a certain proportion of a reinforcing substance be used in the building walls. The masonry sub-contractor failed to use the specified proportion. When this defect was discovered, Moon magnified its importance, withheld from Universal a progress payment to which Universal was entitled, threatened to expel Universal from the job and thereby induced Universal to enter into the supplemental agreement. The supplemental agreement, dated March 27, 1962, provides, inter alia, that Universal will pay Moon $5000 as damages for the absence of the reinforcing material, that Universal will perform certain additional work at no additional cost to Moon, that the date for completion of the project is extended from April 1, 1962, to July 1, 1962, and that liquidated damages at a specified rate per day will be assessed for delay.

Universal substantially completed performance on September 1, 1962, and left the construction site on October 1, 1962. After filing this suit, Universal went into bankruptcy. The trustee prosecuted this action and won a final decree in the lower court....

... Moon urges that the lower court erred in several respects.

First Moon submits that the chancellor erred in not enforcing the contract provision that extras would not be paid for unless done pursuant to a written, signed change order.

Unless a contract is for the sale of goods, see the Uniform Commercial Code — Sales, the Act of April 6, 1953, P.L. 3, § 2-209(2), as amended, 12A P.S.

§ 2-209(2), it appears undisputed that the contract can be modified orally although it provides that it can be modified only in writing.... Construction contracts typically provide that the builder will not be paid for extra work unless it is done pursuant to a written change order, yet courts frequently hold that owners must pay for extra work done at their oral direction.... This liability can be based on several theories. For example, the extra work may be said to have been done under an oral agreement separate from the written contract and not containing the requirement of a written authorization.... The requirement of a written authorization may also be considered a condition which has been waived....

On either of the above theories, the chancellor correctly held Moon liable to pay for the extras in spite of the lack of written change orders. The evidence indicates that William Berger, the agent of Moon, requested many changes, was informed that they would involve extra cost, and promised to pay for them. In addition, Berger frequently was on the construction site and saw at least some of the extra work in progress. The record demonstrates that he was a keen observer with an extraordinary knowledge of the project in general and the contract requirements in particular. Thus it is not unreasonable to infer that he was aware that extra work was being done without proper authorization, yet he stood by without protesting while the extras were incorporated into the project. Under these circumstances there also was an implied promise to pay for the extras.

C.I.T. Corp. v. Jonnet, 419 Pa. 435, 214 A.2d 620 (1965), does suggest that such non-written modifications are ineffective unless the contract provision requiring modifications to be in writing was first waived. That case, however, is misleading. Although it involved a contract for the sale of movable bar and restaurant equipment, which is a contract for the sale of "goods" controlled by the Uniform Commercial Code — Sales, *supra*, § 2-101 et seq., as amended, 12A P.S. § 2-101 et seq., it overlooks that legislation, in particular § 2-209....

From subsection (5) it can be inferred that a provision in a contract for the sale of goods that the contract can be modified only in writing is waived, just as such a provision in a construction contract is waived, under the circumstances described by Restatement, Contracts, § 224 (1932), which provides: "The performance of a condition qualifying a promise in a contract within the Statute [of Frauds or in a contract containing a provision requiring modifications to be in writing (§ 407)] may be excused by an oral agreement or permission of the promisor that the condition need not be performed, if the agreement or permission is given while the performance of the condition is possible, and in reliance on the agreement or permission, while it is unrevoked, the promisee materially changes his position." Obviously a condition is considered waived when its enforcement would result in something approaching fraud.... Thus the effectiveness of a non-written modification in spite of a contract condition that modifications must be written depends upon whether enforcement of the condition is or is not barred by equitable considerations, not upon the technicality of whether the condition was or was not expressly and separately waived before the non-written modification.

In view of these equitable considerations underlying waiver, it should be obvious that when an owner requests a builder to do extra work, promises to pay for it and watches it performed knowing that it is not authorized in writing, he cannot refuse to pay on the ground that there was no written change order.... When Moon directed Universal to "go ahead" and promised to pay for the extras, performance of the condition requiring change orders to be in writing was excused by implication. It would be manifestly unjust to allow Moon, which mislead Universal into doing extra work without a written authorization, to benefit from non-performance of that condition.

Next Moon submits that the lower court erroneously dismissed its counterclaim for delay damages. The lower court denied Moon any recovery for the delay because it resulted from Moon's own acts in ordering many changes. There is authority for this position.... In this case, however, the contract expressly conditions the allowance of any time extension on the submission of a written request to the Architect. This condition specifically applies to delays caused by the owner's, i.e., Moon's, own acts. Article 18 of the General Conditions provides: "If the contractor be delayed at any time in the progress of the work by any act or neglect of the Owner or the Architect, or of any employee of either, or by any separate contractor employed by the Owner, or by changes ordered in the work ... then the time of completion shall be extended for such reasonable time as the Architect may decide. No such extension shall be made for delay occurring more than seven days before claim therefor is made in writing to the Architect...."

Consequently the case authority on which the lower court based its decision is not controlling.

The evidence that Universal conformed with the procedure required by Article 18 is slight; what evidence there is has been largely discredited. However a condition precedent such as the one contained in Article 18 can of course be waived ... and there is evidence to support at least a partial waiver.

By executing the Supplemental Agreement (which extends the time of substantial completion from April 1, 1962, to July 1, 1962) without reference to the procedure established by Article 18, Moon certainly waived Article 18 with reference to that extension. It is not apparent, however, that this waiver applies to subsequent delays. Apart from the execution of the supplemental agreement, there is no evidence that Moon expressly or impliedly promised that the condition precedent contained in Article 18 would not apply to subsequent delays. We think it does so apply....

Finally, we have carefully considered the record and we agree with the lower court that there was sufficient evidence to establish the amount of Universal's claim for extras and that there was not sufficient evidence to establish Moon's set-off claim for uncompleted work.

The decree of the lower court therefore was correct, except insofar as it failed to allow Moon's counterclaim for delay damages, as before indicated, for the period from July 1, 1962, to September 1, 1962.

Decree vacated and record remanded for entry of a decree consonant with this opinion. Each party to bear own costs.

Dissenting Opinion by MUSMANNO, J.:

I believe an injustice is being done the defendant in this case. The lower court awarded the plaintiff $42,283.29, for extras, but the record shows that only $900 of such extras was earned on two signed change orders agreed to in writing. Yet the agreement specifically provides that, except in an emergency endangering life or property, no claim for an addition to the contract price was to be valid unless the work was done pursuant to the owner's written, signed order, and after written notice given by the contractor before proceeding with the work. I am disturbed that the Majority could have reached its conclusion when the record shows that *there was no such writing*.

Even the plaintiff did not contend that the requirement in writing was waived by agreement of the parties.... The most that the plaintiff has shown are oral modifications of the work called for under the contract, which is exactly what is prohibited by the solemn agreement entered into between the parties. The oral modification certainly cannot be used as evidence of a waiver, for otherwise, a requirement of writing would become meaningless. This Court clearly pointed out this fundamental proposition of law in *C.I.T. Corp. v. Jonnet*, 419 Pa. 435, 438, where this writer, speaking for the Court, said: "Nowhere, however, do the defendants allege cancellation by the plaintiff of the express term of the original conditional sale contract that 'no waiver or change in this contract or related note, shall bind such assignee (in this case, the plaintiff) unless in writing signed by one of its officers.'

"This specific condition stands as a stone wall in the path of the defendants' contention. However, they believe they have found a way around this formidable barrier by citing the case of *Kirk v. Brentwood M.H., Inc.*, 191 Pa. Superior Ct. 488, 492 where the Superior Court said that 'Even where the written contract prohibits a non-written modification, it may be modified by subsequent oral agreement.' This is true but there must first be a waiver of the requirement which has been spelled out in the contract. Otherwise, written documents would have no more permanence than writings penned in disappearing ink. If this, the defendants' argument, were to prevail, contractual obligations would become phantoms, solemn obligations would run like pressed quicksilver, and the whole edifice of business would rest on sand dunes supporting pillars of rubber and floors of turf. Chaos would envelop the commercial world."...

It was the plaintiff's duty to support its claim for extras with competent evidence which in my opinion it wholly failed to produce. I cannot, therefore, go along with the Majority's conclusions as to recoveries to be permitted....

Mr. Chief Justice BELL joins in this dissenting opinion.

NOTES AND QUESTIONS

1. *Colorful language from the Wagner case*: Both opinions cited *Wagner v. Graziano Construction Co.*[59] There the court said "The most iron-clad writing can always be cut into by the acetylene torch of parol modification.... The hand that pens a writing may not gag the mouths of the assenting parties." The parol evidence rule itself does not apply to parol modifications of writing made *after* a writing is executed.[60] On one hand, we can agree that our written document cancels all prior agreements, and courts will apply the principles of free contract to enforce our choice. On the other hand, we can agree that our written contract cannot be modified or cannot be modified except by a specified procedure. Nonetheless, we remain free to change our minds and agree to make changes apart from this procedure.

The somewhat heated dispute between the majority and Justice Musmanno in *Universal Builders v. Moon Motor Lodge* does not involve this proposition. Rather they battle about whether an oral waiver of the required writing clause must be a distinct step in the process. Justice Musmanno would seem to want the builder to say to William Berger, Moon's agent, "if you want us to perform extras, then you must execute a written change order or tell me now that you are waiving that requirement." Then Berger would have to say, "go ahead. We hereby waive that requirement." The majority is willing to take the oral request for changes as enough to establish both a waiver and a promise to pay for the extras. Its opinion seems to rely on both the policies of choice and unjust enrichment. Moreover, the court could have talked about a duty of good faith in performing a contract. Berger seemed to be trying to trick the builder into doing work while hiding behind the formal requirement.

2. *Written modifications clauses in modern building contracts*: Building construction projects traditionally involve making detailed plans and specifications, getting bids from contractors, and finally executing a contract to build according to the plans and specifications. Building contracts often require all changes to be approved by the architect in writing.

Professor Halper comments:

---

[59]390 Pa. 445, 136 A.2d 82 (1957).

[60]Childres and Spitz, Status in the Law of Contract, 47 New York University Law Review 1, 16 (1972), studied the 149 cases applying the parol evidence rule found in West's General Digest during the 1960s. They tell us,

The parol evidence rule is not, at present, well understood. The depth of misunderstanding is indicated by the fact that eight of the fifty-nine cases in the formal category (more than 15%) were concerned with *subsequent* modifications of written documents. This is error at such an elementary level as to be astonishing.

>[T]he goal of limiting changes in the scope of the work to those memorialized in formal change orders is a laudatory but usually unattainable ideal. Developers and their field personnel often request changes on the spur of the moment, and they often find it impractical to wait until the architect can actually prepare formal drawings and specifications to describe the change. Thus, the contractor has a dilemma. Should he ignore a change order request until the architect gets around to preparing the formal documentation, or should he take a chance and immediately perform the work? A decision to wait may be wasteful because he may be proceeding with work that he will have to demolish or alter later in order to conform to the change order. Furthermore, delay might irritate the developer. On the other hand, a decision to go ahead might result in the developer's refusal to pay for the changed work.[61]

Under modern "design-build/fast track" construction methods, those involved in building complicated structures merge the design and performance steps to minimize delays and cut costs. For example, a builder may make a contract before the plans and specifications are final. Often these contracts contain the standard provisions calling for written change orders signed by the architect. Nonetheless, all involved understand that changes and adjustments to the preliminary plans and specifications will be made as work progresses, difficulties are encountered, and practical solutions found. There often will be a high volume of change orders, and frequently owners, project managers, architects and builders will shortcut procedures for changes written in contract documents and handle modifications informally to avoid delays and paperwork.

Can an owner assert the formal provisions calling for written modifications to be approved by the owner, architect or both to resist paying for extras? While there always is a risk that courts and arbitrators will find that there has not been a waiver of the formal procedure, courts and arbitrators have enforced "the real deal" rather than the "paper deal" in a number of cases.

3. *CISG and modification-in-writing clauses:* The Convention on International Sale of Goods provides in Article 29 that "a contract may be modified or terminated by the mere agreement of the parties." At the same time, the Article gives effect to contract clauses which require that modification be in writing. However, (and we might have expected the however) the Article goes on to provide that "a party may be precluded by his conduct from asserting such a provision to the extent that the other party has relied on that conduct." How different is the approach taken by the CISG from that advocated by Judge Posner in *Wisconsin Knife?*

---

[61]Halper, Negotiating Construction Contracts III, 18 Real Estate Review 45 (Summer 1988).

F. WAIVING CONDITIONS CONTRASTED WITH MODIFYING CONTRACTS

JOHN B. CLARK v. WEST

193 N.Y. 349, 86 N.E. 1 (1908)

[Plaintiff, an author, sued defendant, a publisher, for breach of contract. The trial court overruled defendant's demurrer to the complaint. The Appellate Division reversed this decision and sustained the demurrer. But the Court of Appeals reversed the Appellate Division, ruling that the complaint stated a cause of action.

Clark, the plaintiff, alleged that he had entered a contract with the West Publishing Company to write and prepare for publication a series of law books. Manuscripts were to be satisfactory to West. Clark promised "to totally abstain from the use of intoxicating liquors during the continuance of this contract, and the payment to him in accordance with the terms of this contract of any money in excess of $2 per page is dependent on the faithful performance of this as well as the other conditions of this contract." Clark was to be paid $2 a page for each manuscript accepted by West. The contract continued, stating that if Clark "abstains from the use of intoxicating liquor and otherwise fulfills his agreements, ... he shall be paid an additional $4 per page."

Clark's complaint alleged that West published Clark's three volume work on corporations. The book was successful, and West received large net receipts. The work contained 3,469 pages. West paid Clark at a rate of $2 per page ($6,938). It refused to pay Clark the additional $4 a page. Clark fully performed the contract, except he "did not totally abstain from the use of intoxicating liquor during the continuance of said contract, but such use by the plaintiff was not excessive and did not prevent or interfere with the due and full performance by the plaintiff of all the other stipulations in said contract."

The complaint stated that the intoxicating liquor condition had been waived. Long prior to the completion of the book, West had full knowledge that Clark drank intoxicating liquor. It did not then terminate the contract. It's agents failed to object. They continued to "exact and require of the plaintiff performance of all the other stipulations and conditions." West continued to receive installments of manuscript and continued to make advance payments. It published the book. At no time did West's agents "notify or intimate to the plaintiff that defendant would insist upon strict compliance, or that defendant intended to take advantage of plaintiff's said breach." "With full knowledge of plaintiff's said use of intoxicating liquors, defendant repeatedly avowed and represented to the plaintiff that he was entitled to and would receive said royalty payment (the full $6 a page), and plaintiff believed and relied on said representation, and in reliance thereon continued in the performance of said contract."]

WERNER, J. ... Briefly stated, the defendant's position is that the stipulation as to plaintiff's total abstinence is the consideration for the payment of the difference between $2 and $6 per page, and therefore could not be waived except by a new agreement to that effect based upon a good consideration; that the so-called waiver alleged by the plaintiff is not a waiver, but a modification of the contract in respect of its consideration. The plaintiff, on the other hand, argues that the stipulation for his total abstinence was merely a condition precedent, intended to work a forfeiture of the additional compensation in case of a breach, and that it could be waived without any formal agreement to that effect based upon a new consideration.

The subject-matter of the contract was the writing of books by the plaintiff for the defendant. The duration of the contract was the time necessary to complete them all. The work was to be done to the satisfaction of the defendant, and the plaintiff was not to write any other books except those covered by the contract unless requested to do so by the defendant, in which latter event he was to be paid for that particular work by the year. The compensation for the work specified in the contract was to be $6 per page, unless the plaintiff failed to totally abstain from the use of intoxicating liquors during the continuance of the contract, in which event he was to receive only $2 per page. That is the obvious import of the contract construed in the light of the purpose for which it was made, and in accordance with the ordinary meaning of plain language. It is not a contract to write books in order that the plaintiff shall keep sober, but a contract containing a stipulation that he shall keep sober so that he may write satisfactory books. When we view the contract from this standpoint, it will readily be perceived that the particular stipulation is not the consideration for the contract, but simply one of its conditions which fits in with those relating to time and method of delivery of manuscript, revision of proof, citation of cases, assignment of copyrights, keeping track of new cases and citations for new editions, and other details which might be waived by the defendant, if he saw fit to do so. This is made clear, it seems to us, by the provision that, "in consideration of the above promises," the defendant agrees to pay the plaintiff $2 per page on each book prepared by him, and if he "abstains from the use of intoxicating liquor and otherwise fulfills his agreements as hereinbefore set forth, he shall be paid an additional $4 per page in manner hereinbefore stated." The compensation of $2 per page, not to exceed $250 per month, was an advance or partial payment of the whole price of $6 per page, and the payment of the two-thirds, which was to be withheld pending the performance of the contract, was simply made contingent upon the plaintiff's total abstention from the use of intoxicants during the life of the contract....

It is obvious that the parties thought that the plaintiff's normal work was worth $6 per page. That was the sum to be paid for the work done by the plaintiff, and not for total abstinence. If the plaintiff did not keep to the condition as to total abstinence, he was to lose part of that sum.... This, we think is the fair interpretation of the contract, and it follows that the stipulation as to the plaintiff's total abstinence was nothing more nor less than a condition precedent. If that conclusion is well founded, there can be no escape from the corollary that this condition could be waived; and, if it was waived, the defendant is clearly not in a position to insist upon the forfeiture which his waiver was intended to annihilate. The forfeiture must stand or fall with the condition. If the latter was waived, the former is no longer a part of the contract. Defendant still has the right to counterclaim for any damages which he may have sustained in consequence of the plaintiff's breach, but he cannot insist upon strict performance....

The theory upon which the defendant's attitude seems to be based is that, even if he has represented to the plaintiff that he would not insist upon the condition that the latter should observe total abstinence from intoxicants, he can still refuse to pay the full contract price for his work. The inequity of this position becomes apparent when we consider that this contract was to run for a period of years, during a large portion of which the plaintiff was to be entitled only to the advance payment of $2 per page; the balance being contingent, among other things, upon publication of the books and returns from sales. Upon this theory the defendant might have waived the condition while the first book was in process of production, and yet, when the whole work was completed, he would still be in a position to insist upon the forfeiture because there had not been strict performance. Such a situation is possible in a case where the subject of the waiver is the very consideration of a contract ... but not where the waiver relates to something that can be waived. In the case at bar, as we have seen, the waiver is not of the consideration or subject-matter, but of an incident to the method of performance. The consideration remains the same. The defendant has had the work he bargained for, and it is alleged that he has waived one of the conditions as to the manner in which it was to have been done. He might have insisted upon literal performance, and then he could have stood upon the letter of his contract. If, however, he has waived that incidental condition, he has created a situation to which the doctrine of waiver very precisely applies.

The cases which present the most familiar phases of the doctrine of waiver are those which have risen out of litigation over insurance policies where the defendants have claimed a forfeiture because of the breach of some condition in the contract ..., but it is a doctrine of general application which is confined to no particular class of cases. A "waiver" has been defined to be the intentional relinquishment of a known right. It is voluntary and implies an election to dispense with something of value, or forego some advantage which the party waiving it might at its option have demanded or insisted upon.... In the recent case of *Draper v. Oswego Co. Fir R. Ass'n*, 190 N.Y. 12, 16, 82 N.E. 755, Chief Judge Cullen, in speaking for the court upon this subject, said: "While that doctrine and the doctrine of equitable estoppel are often confused in insurance litigation, there is a clear distinction between the two. A 'waiver' is the voluntary abandonment or relinquishment by a party of some right or advantage.... The doctrine of equitable estoppel, or estoppel in pais, is that a party may be precluded by his acts and conduct from asserting a right to the detriment of another party who, entitled to rely on such conduct, has acted upon it.... As already said, the doctrine of waiver is to relieve against forfeiture. It requires no consideration for a waiver, nor any prejudice or injury to the other party."...

... In the ... complaint, the plaintiff alleges facts and circumstances which we think, if established, would prove defendant's waiver of plaintiff's performance of ... [the] contract stipulation [calling for total abstinence]....

NOTES AND QUESTIONS

1. *Getting performance from a delinquent*: Suppose the West Publishing Co. editor in charge of Clark's book wanted to get the best book written as close to on time as possible. The editor knows Clark has a problem with alcohol. The editor becomes aware of Clark's drinking. What does the opinion in *Clark v. West* suggest that the editor should do to preserve West's rights to pay only $2 a page for the manuscript? Could the editor do anything less than give Clark formal notice that the publisher would not pay the added $4 a page? What might a reasonable editor fear would be the consequence of such a notice.

Furthermore, the court seems to see the case as one involving forfeiture. West has the book, but it won't now pay the contract price for it. Is the quality of the book necessarily the same as West had hoped for? Is it possible that Clark's book produced while drinking is acceptable but that he could have written an excellent one had he not taken a single drink? The court says West could sue for its damages caused by Clark's drinking. How would you compute them? Or, suppose West's editor discovered Clark's drinking. The editor then told Clark that he would be paid only $2 a page. Clark finished the book. It became a best seller, and West earned a great deal from its publication. Moreover, knowledgeable critics praised the book as well written and thought out. Should Clark then be able to recover the additional $4 a page?

2. *Consideration and waiver — some history I*: Suppose I owe you $1,000, and I am supposed to pay you today. I tell you that I am in financial trouble and have only $600. You agree to discharge the debt if I will pay you $600 now. Later you discover that I have plenty of money. You can sue me for $400 because your release was not supported by *consideration*. Or suppose I am the captain of a fishing boat. You agree to work on the boat during a trip for a certain wage. When we arrive at the fishing area, you refuse to work unless I double your wage. I agree to do this. When we return to port, I refuse to pay you the additional money. I can defeat your lawsuit for the additional money both because of duress and the lack of consideration for my promise to pay more for the services you promised me.

Of course, as you are aware, courts have sidestepped the pre-existing duty rule in many ways. Suppose, for example, you and I rescind our first contract. I give up my rights against you in exchange for your giving up your rights against me. Now we are free to walk away and have no dealings. However, we are also free to make a new contract under which you must pay me more to do what I promised to do for less under our original deal. Some courts have found that when we modify a contract we are impliedly rescinding our original deal. Thus, there is consideration for our new bargain. The doctrine of consideration is more than an exercise in abstract logic. The technical rules can be manipulated to reach desired results.

In classic contract theory, modifications of bargains required consideration. However, this did not apply to waivers of certain conditions to duties under contracts. Suppose, for example, a buyer accepts services a week after the contract called for them to be rendered. The buyer says nothing about the delay. Six months later the buyer wants to sue the seller for the delay. The seller argues that the buyer waived its rights by accepting the services a week late. The buyer argues that this would be a modification of the contract unsupported by consideration. Section 88 of the original Restatement of Contracts recognized that there could be a waiver of rights without consideration if, in our example, performance on time was "not a substantial part of what was to have been given in exchange for" the buyer's duty to pay money and if "the uncertainty of the happening of" performance on time "was not a substantial element in inducing the formation of the contract."

Professor Farnsworth explains the fondness courts have had for waiver. It "permits more flexibility in dealing with the conduct of the parties at the performance stage than would the rules of contract law that are designed for the negotiation stage. By characterizing the conduct as a 'waiver' rather than as a 'modification,' a court may avoid three requirements for a modification: the requirement of assent, the requirement of a writing under the statute of frauds, and the requirement of consideration or of detrimental reliance." He notes that "if the court asks whether the conduct amounted to a 'waiver,' it may give effect to more dubious manifestations of assent." "[I]f the court concludes that the conduct amounted to a 'waiver,' the statute [of frauds] is not relevant." Moreover, if there is a waiver that is effective without consideration or reliance, it can be retracted. "If a party, without consideration, has waived a condition that is within the other party's control *before* the time for occurrence of the condition has expired, he can retract the waiver and reinstate the condition unless the other party has relied to such an extent that retraction would be unjust."[62]

Waiver, then, is a useful tool. But why did courts want such a tool? Why did they want to turn off rules such as those dealing with mutual assent, consideration, the Statute of Frauds and the literal reading of conditions?

---

[62]Farnsworth, Contracts 561-563 (1982).

3. ***Consideration and waiver — some history II***: The opinion in *Clark v. West* tells us that much of the development of waiver came from judicial opinions dealing with insurance contracts. Spencer Kimball studied insurance regulation in a single jurisdiction from 1835 to 1959.[63] He found that courts regulated the administration of insurance claims. They attempted to balance two policies: they tried to give effect to the reasonable expectations of the parties while at the same time preserving the integrity of the insurance fund by preventing unwarranted raids on it by persons not entitled to share. Major fires destroyed large cities throughout the second half of the Nineteenth Century, and the insurance companies were faced with the threat of serious losses.

> [I]t became industry policy to tighten up loss settlement practices. Suspicion of arson seldom resulted in a defense frankly based on an allegation of criminal incendiarism; instead the companies used whatever technical defenses came to hand. Moreover, to protect the companies against fraudulent and exorbitant claims, and to give time for adequate investigation, it was industry policy to delay settlement as long as possible under the contract. Though insurance men were presumably actuated only by creditable motives, no device can be imagined more calculated to harm the industry's public relations than a set policy of arbitrary delay of loss settlement for the maximum period permitted by law.[64]

Loss settlement usually involved two steps which policies made conditions to recovery. First, the insured had to give notice within a certain time. Second, it had to submit proofs of the amount of loss within another specified time after that. Insureds often missed the deadlines. Kimball says "the judges were not willing to forfeit the insured's protection by reason of his failure to perform these technical conditions, so long as they could possibly rationalize a contrary result without overtly discarding the canon that freedom of contract was a basic value."[65] This provoked a game between the courts and insurance company lawyers.

> The industry men saw it as a game, the object of which for them was finding and using language so explicit that the court could find in it no latent ambiguity. Though in fact the courts were less hostile than company men supposed, industry committees frequently made drafting suggestions for making the contracts so airtight that even a judge with a strong bias against insurance companies could not misunderstand.... Occasionally someone expressed a more pessimistic view — that the courts were creating liability

---

[63]Kimball, Insurance and Public Policy (Wisconsin Press 1960).

[64]*Id*. at 215.

[65]*Id*. at 213.

arbitrarily outside the contract. If that were true, more careful drafting would help little.[66]

Lawrence Friedman[67] developed these ideas further. He argued first that classic contract law was grounded in abstraction; it assumed a system of doctrine that appears to be constructed by the deduction of rules from principles. The principles are universal. That is, they are applicable whether the parties are rich or poor, without regard to the subject matter of the transaction, and are unchanging over time. But, Friedman argued next, it is not really possible for a rapidly developing economy to cope with this abstract law which gave no regard to context and change. How was the idea of abstract contract law applied to serve the needs of a developing economy? Two of the tools which Friedman suggests the courts used to bridge this gap were waiver and estoppel. He notes:

> It might offend a purist to talk in one breath about estoppel, waiver, ratification, election of remedies, laches, and accord and satisfaction. These were all different concepts, with different histories and uses. They had in common, however, that they all related to particular acts of particular parties, subsequent to the formation of a contract but affecting the contract rights of the actors. And they were all ideas that could be used to bend rules of higher generality. Though they themselves could be expressed in terms of rules, they constituted statements of reasons (derived from the facts of particular cases) why some more general rule should not be applied.

> ... A concept like estoppel is in essence antithetical to pure contract abstraction. A party is "estopped" for reasons which are peculiar to his or her opponent's situation. Abstraction, however, abhors the special and the particular. [Friedman then notes that the use of these concepts was common throughout the period he was studying (1836 to 1958) but was perhaps more common at the end of the nineteenth century. The use of the doctrines to give relief in individual cases avoided the "bother or embarrassment" of making radical changes in the formal doctrine.]

> Waiver and estoppel were not used only on a case-by-case basis. if the court had a consistent bias of values in a given area of transactions, it sometimes applied one or more of these concepts consistently in handling such transactions. This warping and sliding process was characteristic of the way the common law developed. After a generation or two in which a court consistently found that not the general rule but the "exception" applied to

---

[66]*Id.* at 211-212.

[67]Friedman, Contract Law in America: A Social And Economic Case Study (Wisconsin Press 1965).

whatever cases was at hand, the original general rule turned into a mummified corpse. historically the insurance companies were on the losing end of such a process, which, by the use of "estoppel" and "waiver," created what amounted to a set of rules for construing insurance policies so as to aid the insured. This process of attrition took place frequently in the law; and in the twentieth century "legal realism" gave dead rules decent burial in many instances simply by pointing out that the old rules were no longer used even when legal literature still paid them lip service.

4. *Consideration and waiver — the Restatement (Second) of Contracts' provisions*: Modern courts have allowed parties to modify contracts without much concern about consideration. The Restatement (Second) of Contracts reflect this. It deals with both waiving conditions as in *Clark v. West* and modifying more central provisions of contracts. Section 84 provides,

[A] promise to perform all or part of a conditional duty under an antecedent contract in spite of the non-occurrence of the condition is binding, whether the promise is made before or after the time for the condition to occur, unless

(a) occurrence of the condition was a material part of the agreed exchange for the performance of the duty and the promisee was under no duty that it occur; or

(b) uncertainty of the occurrence of the condition was an element of the risk assumed by the promisor.

The section also allows a party to reinstate a condition that it has waived if a reasonable time to perform it remains, there has been so little reliance that reinstatement would not be unjust, and the promise is not enforceable on some other ground.[68]

---

[68] As we have noted several times in these materials, under the Restatement (Second) more significant changes in contracts also can be made without orthodox consideration. Section 89 provides,

A promise modifying a duty under a contract not fully performed on either side is binding
(a) if the modification is fair and equitable in view of circumstances not anticipated by the parties when the contract was made, or
(b) to the extent provided by statute; or
(c) to the extent that justice requires enforcement in view of material change of position in reliance on the promise.

See Lowey v. Watt, 684 F2d 957 (D.C.Cir. 1982) for a case in which, for reasons analogous to those covered by R. § 89, the court gave effect to a unilateral waiver even though there was neither consideration, nor notice.

5. *U.C.C. § 2-209(1) and bad faith modifications*: Section 2-209(1) overturns the pre-existing duty rule for modifications of transactions in goods. Official Comment 2 says

> modifications made thereunder [the section] must meet the test of good faith imposed by this act. The effective use of bad faith to escape performance on the original contract terms is barred, and the extortion of a 'modification' without legitimate commercial reason is ineffective as a violation of the duty of good faith. Nor can a mere technical consideration support a modification made in bad faith.

The Official Comment adds a good deal of substantive law to the text of the statute. Professor Robert Hillman[69] says that courts are reading the text of § 2-209(1) and ignoring the Official Comment. They are enforcing modifications without considering the issue of good faith.

He proposed an amendment to § 2-209(1) which would add two sentences to it: "An agreement modifying a contract made as a result of economic or other duress is not enforceable. The burden of establishing that a modification involving a material net loss to the party opposing its enforcement was not a product of duress is on the party seeking to enforce the modification." He would add to the Official Comment the following: "Factors relevant to determining whether a material net loss modification was entered into as a result of duress include the reasonableness of entering into the modification, the availability of market substitutes to the party seeking to avoid the modification, the manner of presentation of the modification, the reasons for seeking the modification, and the foreseeability of those reasons." Why haven't courts taken something such as this approach following the invitation in the U.C.C. comment?

6. *Elections contrasted with waivers*: An "election of remedies" may be seen as different from a "waiver" of right. For example, one of the most important remedies granted buyers by the U.C.C. is the right to reject or return defective goods and have no obligation to pay for them. However, under U.C.C. § 2-606(1)(a) a buyer "accepts" goods when "after a reasonable opportunity to inspect the goods," he signifies to the seller "that he will take or retain them in spite of their nonconformity." If the buyer has no "reasonable assumption that ... [the] ... non-conformity would be cured," then the buyer cannot return them. He has given up this remedy and *elected* to do nothing or seek damages. The seller need offer no new consideration nor prove that he relied on the statement. Does this kind of election of remedies significantly differ from a waiver of rights? The buyer's choice may be less than ideally free when confronted by a delivery of defective but usable goods. She may no longer have time to find

---

[69]Hillman, Policing Contract Modifications under the U.C.C: Good Faith and the Doctrine of Economic Duress, 64 Iowa Law Review 849 (1979).

substitutes. Of course, she can accept the goods and sue for damages, but often this will not provide an adequate remedy. Yet under the language of the Code read literally, this does not seem to matter.

Chapter 8

PERFORMANCE AND BREACH OF CONTRACT

A. THE MAIN THEMES — PROMISES, CONDITIONS, AND THE ROLE OF COURTS

1. THE LOGIC OF "CONDITIONS"

Suppose S and B make a legally enforceable contract under which S contracts to sell an antique car to B for $40,000. They agree in their written contract that S is to rebuild the engine before delivery of the car. After S and B close the deal, many things must happen before the transaction is completed. What happens to B's obligations if S does not perform some or all of his? Does it matter that S comes close to performing all his obligations but does not quite make it? Not surprisingly in a society that gives a high place to individual choice, courts and lawyers attempting to answer these questions give great weight to the parties' agreement. However, often the parties have said little about the details involved in carrying out their contract. In many instances, having just made a deal, they do not want to think about what will happen if one or both fails to perform. Courts often are called on to fill in gaps in planning.

Students may have difficulty with questions of performance and breach of contracts. Part of that difficulty comes from attempting to begin with complex issues before a number of simple matters are understood. Thus, it may help to consider some relatively easy examples in order to establish a vocabulary and see the logic of orthodox conditions analysis.

First, assume seller promises to deliver the car to buyer on April 7th if buyer is then ready, willing and able to pay $40,000 to seller. The buyer, in turn, promises to pay $40,000 on April 7th if seller is then ready, willing and able to deliver the car. Assume further that on April 7th, seller fails to deliver the goods and does not have a legally adequate excuse. Buyer, who was ready, willing and able to pay on April 7th, did not pay because seller failed to make delivery.

Suppose an unlikely event: seller sues buyer for failing to pay $40,000. *Seller would lose because buyer did not breach his promise.* Buyer did not make an unqualified promise to pay $40,000. He promised to pay ONLY IF seller was ready, willing and able to deliver the goods. Seller was not. Putting the matter in the vocabulary of contracts, a *condition precedent* to buyer's duty to perform was not fulfilled, and this failure serves to shield him from liability. Conditions precedent usually are "if" or "when" clauses qualifying promises to perform. If the qualifications are not met, then my promise literally does not bind me to do anything. I cannot be held liable for failing to do what I never promised to do.

Now assume the same contract and facts but add that buyer came to seller's place of business on April 7th with $40,000, asked for delivery of the goods and indicated clearly that he had the money and was ready to pay if seller was ready to deliver. As before, seller refused to deliver. Buyer could sue seller and win a judgment for damages because seller has failed to perform his promise — the conditions on that promise were fulfilled and so there was an obligation to perform.[1]

Notice that in the example, the *condition* to buyer's promise and seller's *promise* are almost the same. Buyer promises to pay *if and when seller delivers*. Seller promises to deliver *if and when buyer pays*. Paying is both a condition and promise; delivering, also, is both condition and promise. But paying is a condition to the promise to deliver and delivering is a condition to the promise to pay. These are simple ideas, but some students look for something subtle and complex. If you find this confusing, perhaps a diagram will help:

> Buyer *promises* to pay on *condition* that seller deliver.
> Seller *promises* to deliver on *condition* that buyer pay.

Keep one thing clear: *one always sues for breach of promise and not breach of condition*. Although it is not uncommon, the phrase breach of condition is misleading insofar as it connotes that someone did something she was not supposed to do — "failure of condition" is probably a more descriptive term. A failure of condition is a *defense* and often ends the obligation to perform a qualified promise.

Notice, as well, that an aggrieved party often gets rights based on both a breach of promise and a failure of a condition flowing from the same actions by the defaulting party. The buyer refuses to pay if seller refuses to deliver. The buyer can both sue the seller for breach and defend any suit brought by the seller claiming damages because buyer failed to pay the purchase price. When the promise on one side is the same as the condition on the other, lawyers often speak of *concurrent conditions*. While this may be a useful shorthand, it does not describe the situation very well. Paying the money is both promise and condition, as is delivering the goods. What we are talking about is a swap where I do not have to perform unless you do, but you do not have to perform unless I do. In our example, buyer is immune from a successful suit by seller based on the contract since seller failed to deliver and that was a condition on buyer's duty to

---

[1] Put aside for the moment the question of whether buyer could do anything less than engage in the elaborate ceremony we sketched and still meet the conditions of seller's promise. We will get to this later.

pay $40,000. Buyer can recover from seller because the condition on seller's duty was met.

Let's change the facts slightly to illustrate another possibility. Assume that seller promises to deliver the car on April 7th, (a) if buyer is then ready, willing and able to pay $40,000, and (b) if the components needed to rebuild the engine arrive from England on or before March 27th. Buyer promises to pay $40,000 on April 7th if seller then is ready, willing and able to deliver. The components fail to arrive from England on or before March 27th. Buyer is at seller's place of business on the 7th ready, willing and able to pay. Seller, of course, fails to deliver. Buyer sues seller for breach of contract. Buyer would lose her suit because seller did not breach the promise to deliver ONLY IF the components arrived on time. Seller did not promise that they would arrive on time, but he negotiated the contract so that he would not assume this risk. Here we have an express condition precedent to seller's duty to deliver *which is not also a promise*. Of course, seller could not sue buyer for failure to pay $40,000 since that promise to pay was still qualified by a condition that seller deliver the car. In this case, the conditions would give each party a defense to a suit by the other.

Sometimes lawyers talk of a "failure of consideration" in situations such as this one. Notice that this is not the same thing as an "absence" of consideration. Formation and performance of contracts are different things. Buyer and seller made a legally enforceable contract, supported by the consideration of their promises to pay and deliver. However, since seller failed to deliver goods, he cannot sue buyer, and since the components failed to arrive from England, buyer cannot sue seller. "Failure of consideration" is too easy to confuse with "absence of consideration," and so the term is not favored by contracts teachers. This does not stop courts from using it, and so you should both understand the phrase and be careful to avoid confusion.

Finally, let's illustrate a more complicated situation. Suppose buyer wants to purchase a car from a seller who needs first to borrow $30,000 to finance the acquisition of the car and the repair parts. X Bank agrees to provide the needed money. However, it demands that the transaction be structured as follows: seller expressly promises to deliver the car to buyer on April 7th. In exchange, buyer expressly promises to pay $30,000 to the X Bank on May 1st *in any event whether or not seller has delivered the car on April 7th.*[2] As a result of this contract, X bank on March 5th pays 30,000, less its charges for financing the deal, to seller. Seller, however, fails to deliver on April 7th without a legally sufficient excuse. Buyer refuses to pay X Bank on May 1st, asserting seller's non-delivery as a defense.

X Bank would win in a suit against Buyer. Buyer's promise to pay was not conditioned on delivery of the car by seller. The bank was not taking the risk of

---

[2] X Bank also is likely to keep a security interest in the goods until it is paid so that it can sell them to recover some or all of its money if B fails to pay.

problems in the seller-buyer transaction. It advanced money to seller and bargained for a right to be repaid by buyer even if seller failed to perform. Buyer's remedy would be to sue seller for failure to deliver the goods. Seller, in turn, might have a cause of action against buyer for any damages caused by buyer's failure to pay X Bank. X Bank likely would have reserved a right to hold seller responsible if buyer failed to pay. Of course, almost certainly suits involving buyer, seller and X Bank would involve setting off damages due one against the other; modern procedure offers devices to avoid multiple lawsuits. In this kind of case, lawyers often speak of *independent promises* — that is, promises that are unqualified by reference to performance by other parties. They are rare in two party situations, but they can serve a function when the deal involves more than two people.

Planning the Transaction to Minimize Risks: So far we've stated the obvious: courts usually enforce promises as made, and if a person puts a qualification on a promise, she hasn't promised to act unless or until something happens. But there is more to the matter than this. Conditions reflect assumptions of risk by the parties. On one hand, they can be geared to allocate risks of events external to the particular deal. For example, our seller promised to perform provided that component parts arrived from England by a certain date. Seller also might provide that it would perform only if its shop were not damaged by some natural disaster before it could do the work. Of course, if buyer had sufficient bargaining power, it might demand that seller *promise* to deliver goods whether or not component parts arrived from England. Under such a contract, seller would have to get parts from England, find substitutes elsewhere, or be liable to pay damages to the buyer for non-delivery of the goods.

Furthermore, conditions reflect a structuring of a relationship so that one person has sanctions to induce the other to perform. For example, often it is advantageous to arrange things so that the other person performs first before you must act (that is, the other's promise is unconditional and must be performed on a certain date. Your promise, however, is to be performed later and is conditioned on receiving the other's full performance). If you have the bargaining power and skill to negotiate such a contract, you take no risk of losing your performance if the other breaches the contract as you would if you had to pay in advance before he was to perform.

Of course, if the contract requires that you pay in advance but the other person fails to perform, you are likely to have a cause of action for breach of contract or restitution. However, you may have to hire a lawyer to evaluate your case, draft documents, gain personal jurisdiction over the other party, win a verdict, and defend it on appeal And *then* find some non-exempt assets owned by the other party to satisfy your judgment, and hope she isn't bankrupt. You avoid all this if you can make her go first.

If the other person must perform before you act, you may have another tactical advantage. If you think that the other person's performance is defective, you can deduct an allowance from your performance and offer it to her in full settlement.

(See U.C.C. § 2-717.) Since she has performed, she must accept the offer or take legal action against you to recover the balance. She must make the difficult choice. Moreover, since the other person wants to be sure that you perform after she does, she has some incentive to perform well and on time. Her interest in keeping you happy may grow as she invests more and more effort in her performance and seeks to guard that investment by making you a satisfied customer who feels some obligation to pay for the fine performance.

The person who must perform first may have some countervailing power. If you need her performance by a certain time, you may become more and more dependent on her completing the job as time passes. You no longer can turn elsewhere and get performance on time. In this case, she may ask you to modify the contract and make a payment in order to finance the completion of the performance.

Also certain psychological factors might operate to the disadvantage of the one who has arranged things so that the other person must perform a complex and lengthy task before getting paid. If the risks are out of balance, the other person may perceive the situation as coercive and feel that she was tricked or forced to accept an unfair deal. This may produce resentment and hostility. If it does, the person who holds the advantage in a hard bargain may lose any moral claim to first-class performance based on customary norms of reciprocity, craftsmanship or an obligation to help others. The one who has driven the hard bargain may get only performance to the letter of the contract most restrictively construed but not first class performance. Furthermore, the disadvantaged person may remember the situation when it comes time to deal again, and what is gained in one contract may be lost in the next. In short, at the bargaining stage it is possible to negotiate too good a deal for yourself when the performance stage arrives. This may not be a problem if the performance is to pay money and one has reasonably good security; it may be critically important if the performance involves judgment, discretion, technical skill or even artistic aspects.

We do not find too many contracts where all the risks in performance rest solely on one side.[3] Rather, leverage is used to provide incentives for both sides to perform.

For example, frequently an owner who wishes a building constructed agrees to pay a down payment and then installments at specified times as the building is erected. In this way, the owner helps the builder finance construction. The

---

[3]Employment contracts once tended to be out of balance. Today statutes, with some exceptions, require wages to be paid frequently rather than withheld for long periods of time. Still employees usually work first and then get paid. Compare performances of motion pictures, plays, rock concerts and the like. Typically, a member of the audience pays first and then sees the performance. Why is this order of performance customary? Imagine the consequences of a custom in which the audience saw the show and then paid on the way out. However, restaurants manage to collect in all but a few situations when they present the bill after their customers have eaten the food.

builder does not have to provide or borrow all the money needed to purchase labor and materials during the course of performance. The builder also minimizes the risk that she will not be paid for the work which she has done by limiting the amount put into the building before the owner pays. If one or more payments are missed or late, the builder may have the right to suspend working on the job until she is paid for what is due. On the other hand, an owner is likely to negotiate for the right to hold back, say, ten percent of the value of the work done at each installment and this "hold-back" is paid to the builder only upon full completion of the job. Thus, the builder is given an incentive to finish the work and do it well. All of this can be expressed in the language of conditional promises — the builder *promises* to perform *provided* that the down payment and installments are paid on time; the owner *promises* to pay the installments *provided* the builder is performing and *promises* to pay the amount held back *provided* the builder completes the structure on time according to plans and specifications.

People planning a transaction can rely on forms of leverage that only awkwardly conform to a conditions analysis. On one hand, if the transaction is part of a long-term continuing mutually advantageous business relationship, the other's continued satisfaction is a powerful sanction. If she becomes dissatisfied, there is a risk that she will end the relationship and turn to a competitor. On the other hand, where continuing relationships or the right to withhold one's own performance do not seem to offer enough leverage, there may be other things that can be done. One can insist that the other person buy a bond to guarantee his performance. One can insist that money be paid to a neutral third party who will hold it until the return performance is completed — an "escrow" arrangement. One selling goods can retain a security interest in them, thereby retaining some right to reclaim the goods if payment is not made as agreed (the threat of losing the machine, the T.V. or the car may induce performance, but a seller who repossesses may be hard pressed to gain much from a resale of used goods). Bonds, escrow arrangements and conditional sales provisions can be expressed in terms of conditions, but they are sufficiently different from the questions of the timing of performance and the right to withhold performance to warrant special mention.

Some Problems in Applying the Law of Conditions: Courts must interpret or construe contracts to determine whether promises are to be deemed subject to a condition, and, if so, what that condition is — as must lawyers planning transactions and lawyers engaged in salvage operations after transactions have collapsed.

Even where the parties spell out things, they are likely to leave a few questions unanswered by the express words of their agreement. In the examples we've considered, the parties expressly said that the seller would be ready, willing and able to deliver on April 7th if the buyer was ready, willing and able to pay $40,000 then. As a result, we know that if the buyer cannot pay, the seller need not deliver and cannot be sued for failing to do so.

But even in this simple case questions remain. Suppose buyer refuses to come to seller's place of business with the money but insists that seller bring the car to buyer's place of business and pick up the money there. The contract is silent about where money and goods are to be exchanged. U.C.C. § 2-308, following common law tradition, fills the gap in the contract and tells us that in most instances a buyer must go to a seller's place of business unless they agree otherwise.

Suppose buyer offers seller a personal check calling for a bank to pay seller $40,000. Has buyer met the condition on seller's promise to deliver so that the buyer is entitled to the goods? Or must a buyer tender cash? U.C.C. § 2-511(2) fills this gap and tells us that "tender of payment is sufficient when made by any means or in any manner current in the ordinary course of business unless the seller demands payment in legal tender and gives any extension of time reasonably necessary to procure it."

And suppose it is fairly clear by April 1st that the buyer will be unable to pay for the car on April 7th. Does the seller have to offer it to the buyer on the 7th to put the buyer in default as a necessary step in creating a cause of action? U.C.C. §§ 2-609, 2-610, 2-703(f) suggest that the seller may have other alternatives open.

Contracts frequently, if not typically, are less explicit than our example. People often neglect to spell out who is to do what and when in the event certain contingencies occur. A seller may offer to sell goods for a specified sum, and the buyer may sign a letter saying little more than "I accept your offer." Nothing is said about whether the buyer must pay in advance, whether the seller must deliver before the buyer pays or whether they must pay and deliver at the same time. And whatever order of performance we select, *when* are these things to take place?

Often courts must supply "constructive conditions" to fill such gaps in contracts, and the process is very much as that when they "imply" promises. Courts can look to the likely expectations of the parties; flat rules which are designed to serve the market; who ought to win, applying sympathy for the underdog; or rules based on achieving some other goal. In the simple situation given here as an example, there are a number of gap filling rules which probably would control. For example, U.C.C. § 2-511(1) says that "unless otherwise agreed tender of payment is a condition to the seller's duty to tender and complete any delivery." Section 2-507(1) says that "tender of delivery is a condition to the buyer's duty to accept the goods and, unless otherwise agreed, to his duty to pay for them. Tender entitles the seller to acceptance of the goods and to payment according to the contract." Section 2-310 says that unless otherwise agreed "payment is due at the time and place at which the buyer is to receive the goods even though the place of shipment is the place of delivery...." Section 2-309(1) provides that "the time for shipment or delivery ... if not ... agreed upon shall be a reasonable time." Section 2-503(1) provides that "the manner, time and place for tender are determined by the agreement and this

Article, and in particular (a) tender must be at a reasonable hour...." Thus, we can see that the Uniform Commercial Code, following common law tradition, fills the gaps by presuming a swap rather than a credit transaction.

However, there is a common law rule, implicit in the U.C.C., which pushes one party to go first. If a contract calls for one performance which by its nature takes time and another which can be done instantly, the one that takes time must be done first. For example, I promise to work for you for a month. You promise to pay me $1,000 for my services. Under this rule of construction, I must do the work before you must pay me. Why is there such a rule? Does it reflect custom? Does it protect wealth and power at the expense of the dominated? Does it prompt efficient behavior?

A second major problem faced by the courts in the area of performance and breach of contracts is that of fairness and the prevention of forfeitures. The parties, for example, may have provided in their contract that if one fails to perform, the other has no obligation to carry out his or her promise. The default may be relatively minor. Calling off the contract may cause extreme reliance losses, great forfeiture benefiting the one not in default or both reliance loss and forfeiture. For example, suppose a contract calls for a seller to manufacture and install a machine by April 7th which will do certain specified things. The buyer promises to pay $100,000 if the machine is installed by April 7th. The machine cannot be resold to anyone else since it is tailored to the buyer's special needs. The seller spends $85,000 to make and install the machine, and it is in place on April 7th. However, it will not quite do the things specified, but it comes close. On April 8th, seller could make adjustments which would cost $1,000, and they would make the machine perform as specified in the contract. While the buyer would lose the use of the machine for a day, it would be valuable to him on the 8th and thereafter. May the buyer refuse to allow these adjustments on the 8th and be free of any obligation under the contract since the condition to his promise was not met precisely?

On one hand, this could be seen as just a question of interpretation of the contract. We might doubt whether the seller had in fact assumed the risk without a clear showing from the facts that he was aware he was entering an $85,000 gamble. We might wonder whether the buyer's conduct was in good faith or only was serving as a pretext to bail out of what now seems to be a poor deal. On the other hand, suppose it is clear that the buyer has drafted the contract to put the risk of timely performance on the seller. Will courts accept this allocation of risk, or will they impose some standard of fairness and consider whether or not to enforce the contract as written? Suppose a court accepts the contractual allocation of risk in this example and finds that the condition to the buyer's promise to pay has not been met. Does this mean that the buyer gets a machine without an obligation to pay for it? Can a seller in default on a contract get restitution of any net benefits conferred? (See U.C.C. §§ 2-606; 2-602; 2-703; 1-103.)

2. CONDITIONS AND FORFEITURES: FREE CONTRACT VERSUS FAIRNESS AND SYMPATHY?

In the cases that follow, those drafting the written contracts attempted to structure the transactions to gain advantages for their clients. In some cases, the language used could be read one way or another; in others there were gaps; in still others the most plausible literal reading of the language would have produced results that the courts seemed not to want to reach. Consider the role of courts in these cases, and consider the lessons for those planning commercial transactions.

Jacobs Associates v. Argonaut Insurance Company[4] provides an example of a court struggling to accommodate freedom to structure contracts as one chooses, with the avoidance of injustice which may arise if the courts interpret contractual language literally, albeit consistently with the intentions of the drafter. In this case the plaintiff, Jacobs Associates, was an engineering firm which had provided services to a Target Dredging and Piledriving, a prime contractor that had been adjudicated bankrupt without paying the plaintiff nearly $11,000 under a subcontract. As a condition of obtaining the principal contract, Target Dredging had obtained a bond from Argonaut Insurance Company. The bond was artfully written. Its language provided that the bonding company was liable to the owner of the property, Portland General Electric Company, in the amount of $820,771 unless certain conditions occurred. The conditions which would discharge the obligation included Target's payment to those who provided labor or materials during the project.

The plaintiff argued that the contract between Target Dredging and Piledriving and Argonaut Insurance should be treated *as if* it contained a promise by Argonaut that the providers of material and services would be paid, and that plaintiff was entitled to sue to enforce the promise. The defendant had demurred, and the trial court had sustained the demurrer. The trial court and the defendant had relied on three earlier cases in which the Oregon Supreme Court had held that such language in a surety bond did not constitute a promise, but only a condition. Since it was not a promise, no action could be maintained for its breach. The plaintiff asked the Oregon Supreme Court to reconsider, and overrule its earlier cases.

The court overruled its earlier cases. It first noted that the problem arises because of the "archaic" form which is used in surety bonds, and quoted Corbin who urged that it was sound policy to liberally interpret the language of the bond.

> ... Words of "condition" are not words of "promise" in form; but in this class of cases it is sound policy to interpret the words liberally in favor of

---

[4] 580 P.2d 529 (S. Ct. Ore. 1978).

the third parties. In a majority of states, it is already done; and without question the surety's rate of compensation for carrying the risk is sufficiently adjusted to the law. The compensated surety has become an institution that is well suited to carry the risk of the principal contractor's default, whereas individual laborers and materialmen are frequently very ill prepared to carry the risk. The legislatures have recognized this fact, and in the case of public contracts have required surety bonds to protect the third parties. While this has not been done in the case of private construction, and while the courts should not on their own motion put such a provision into a private surety bond, they may well interpret a bond that is expressly conditioned on the payment of laborers and materialmen as being a promise to pay them and made for their benefit. The words reasonably permit it, and social policy approves it.... Corbin, *supra*, at 177-178....

The court buttressed its reliance on policy, however, by arguing that unless the conditional language was construed as a promise, it was surplus language, since other conditional language would have covered the situation.

The court also suggested that its earlier decisions should be overruled because they ran counter to developments both within the law of other jurisdictions, and the practices of bonding companies. In addition, the earlier cases gave insufficient weight to the principle of construing the writings of compensated surety's "most strongly against it." Additionally, the court noted that it had overestimated, in the most recent of its prior cases, the impact of changing the rule in question. Finally, the court suggested that the defendant and other sureties retain the authority to change the form of the bonds and "clearly provide that unpaid engineers ... have no right of action."

The opinion contains a strong dissent by Justice Holman, who argues that:

> ... In view of the quoted language from the agreement, I do not understand how the majority comes to the conclusion that the contracting parties intended that the bond should also run in favor of someone else. A contract is a matter of the intention of the parties, and there is no evidence here that this contract was intended to benefit anyone other than PGE. The contract, although drawn in an archaic form, is clear and unambiguous.... [Holman then remarks on the majority's citation of Corbin.] A reading of the text preceding and following the quoted material makes it apparent that his reason for such a statement is that he believes a better social result would follow if sureties were made responsible to all claimants--not because he believes the parties to such a contract usually intend to so agree.

Justice Linde concurred in the finding that a demurrer was improper, noting that the majority found the bond to contain a promise, while the dissent found the absence of such a promise to be "clear." To decide this case on the pleadings would be to suggest that "the parties clearly understood something, but we disagree on what they clearly understood."

A digression on third party beneficiaries: Once the court in the *Jacobs Associates* case found that Argonaut had *promised* the owner to pay all those who had worked on the Portland Headquarters Building, it then allowed *Jacobs Associates* to sue to enforce that promise as a "third party beneficiary."

Nineteenth and early Twentieth Century courts struggled with the idea of allowing a person who was not a party to a contract bring an action to enforce it. Today it is clear that beneficiaries of some contracts between others can sue in almost all states. Moreover, the parties to the contract may not be able to rescind it without the consent of beneficiaries in some circumstances.

As you might expect, there are a core of clear cases and a periphery of uncertain ones. The first Restatement of Contracts divided all beneficiaries of other people's contracts into three kinds: creditor, donee and incidental. Incidental beneficiaries could not sue. For example, owner and builder make a contract to construct a beautiful house on a vacant lot. If the house were built, it would increase the value of neighbor's adjoining property. Builder breaches the contract with owner, and the house is not built. Neighbor would be "an incidental beneficiary" and could not sue the builder.

Creditor and donee beneficiaries could sue. For example, A sells his painting to B for $1,000. Instead of paying the money to A, B is to pay it to C. This will satisfy a debt that A owes C. B fails to pay. C may sue B as a "creditor beneficiary." Or B buys A's painting for $1,000. A is to deliver it to C who is B's mother. It is a birthday gift. A fails to deliver the painting. C can sue A. She is a "donee beneficiary."

However, can A and B in either case rescind the contract without C's consent? The first Restatement distinguished donee and creditor beneficiaries. A donee's right vested immediately and could not be rescinded without the donee's consent. A creditor beneficiary's right vested only when the beneficiary had relied on the promise, and the deal could be rescinded before that. The courts have not always followed the Restatement's distinction between donee and creditor beneficiaries. Furthermore, they differ on whether the beneficiary's right vests when the contract is made, when the beneficiary learns of it or when the beneficiary relies.

Restatement (Second) of Contracts § 302 abandons the creditor, donee and incidental beneficiary scheme. It keeps the idea that incidental beneficiaries cannot sue. However, those who can sue are called "intended beneficiaries." To be one, a person must show that "recognition of a right to performance in the beneficiary is appropriate to effectuate the intention of the parties." In addition, one must show either that (a) the performance of the promise will satisfy some obligation of the promise maker to pay money to the beneficiary, or that (b) the circumstances show that the promise maker intended that the beneficiary would receive the benefit of the performance.

Restatement (Second) of Contracts § 311 states a general rule and some exceptions concerning the power of the original parties to change or end a beneficiary's rights. Generally, the parties who made the contract can modify it without the consent of the beneficiary. They do not have this power if their contract provides that the third party beneficiary's rights cannot be changed. Also, if a beneficiary "materially changes his position in justifiable reliance on the promise or brings suit on it or manifests assent to it at the request of the promisor or promisee," the beneficiary's rights cannot be changed.

RONALD D. DAVIS v. ALLSTATE INSURANCE CO.

101 Wis.2d 1, 303 N.W.2d 596 (1981)

DAY, J. ... The principal question on review is: Did the court of appeals err in overturning the trial court's finding that the Allstate Insurance Company (Allstate), exercised bad faith in the course of handling Ronald D. Davis' (insured's) claim under a contract of fire insurance?

The insured is an attorney who graduated from law school in 1974 and immediately entered the private practice of law in Milwaukee.

In 1975, insured obtained a standard "deluxe" business-owner's fire and extended coverage insurance policy from Allstate in the amount of $8,000. The policy coverage was based on Allstate's inspection of the insured's business personal property, which resulted in a written report placing an approximate value of $7,500 on the property in plaintiff's office. A second Allstate inspection in February, 1976, estimated the value of plaintiff's business property at $11,100. Based on this second estimate, the policy limit was increased to $15,000 on Allstate's recommendation. In October of 1976, Allstate conducted another inspection and recommended that the policy limits be raised to $25,000, however, the policy was not amended.

On February 22, 1977, a fire destroyed all of the contents of insured's law office, including invoices and receipts for purchases of the contents of the office. Allstate was notified of the loss on the day following the fire.

Bruce Piette, an Allstate claims adjuster, was assigned to the claim. He investigated the fire between February 24 and May 15, 1977, and recommended to Allstate a "cash out" settlement of $14,860.04, which was approved by Mr. Piette's supervisor, Larry Peterson, a commercial claims supervisor.

On May 15, 1977, the insured filed a sworn proof of loss statement detailing the property destroyed in the fire and the value of each item, claiming losses in excess of the policy limit of $15,000. Internal Allstate memoranda stated that both Piette and Peterson believed the proof of loss to be substantially completed in proper form.

In a separate internal memorandum, Mr. Piette stated he would offer the plaintiff a lower amount initially, and go up to $14,860 if necessary.

Jerome Mondl, Piette and Peterson's supervisor, rejected their recommendations. He advised Peterson to reject insured's proof of loss for lack of documentation of purchase of the individual items of property claimed. Mr. Mondl did authorize settlement of $4,148.53 which Piette offered the insured to satisfy the claim. This offer was rejected.

The insured then brought this action seeking damages for the fire loss and compensatory and punitive damages for bad faith. The case was tried before a jury. The jury returned a special verdict finding that the insured substantially performed the conditions required by the policy to recover his claim and found damages for losses to his personal property of $14,860.04. The jury also found that Allstate exercised bad faith in the course of its handling of the claim and awarded compensatory damages resulting from the defendant's bad faith of $12,103 and punitive damages of $30,000.

Allstate's motions after verdict were denied and the trial court affirmed the jury's verdict and judgment was entered in the amount of the jury's verdict plus costs and disbursements for a total of $57,306.54. [The defendant appealed.]

The court of appeals affirmed the jury's finding that the insured substantially performed his obligations under the insurance contract to recover his claim. The court rejected Allstate's contention that an insured must supply certified invoices or receipts establishing the cost of each item of lost property as a precondition to recover, characterizing that theory as "nonsense." The court of appeals found that an insured need only substantially comply with the proof of loss requirements in the insurance contract, which he had done....

Turning to the bad faith issue, the court of appeals found insured's claim to be "fairly debatable," thus shielding Allstate from charges of "bad faith."... and reversed the jury's findings on that issue....

The first question on review is: Did the insured satisfy the conditions of the standard fire insurance policy concerning proof of ownership and valuation of property lost in the fire?

The insurance policy was the standard form required by § 203.06, Stats. 1973.

It is clear that insured failed to comply with that part of the insurance contract providing that:

> The insured ... shall produce for examination all books of account, bills, invoices and other vouchers, or certified copies thereof if originals be lost....

He did, however, provide the company with a sworn proof of loss setting out in detail the items lost and the value of each.

The record shows that Allstate's employees did not demand certified copies of the invoices which were lost in the fire until June 10, 1977, nearly four months after the insured's loss occurred. In fact, the record amply supports the insured's contention that until that date, Allstate agreed to verify ownership and valuation by checking with the vendors of the lost property and later by referring to the insured's tax records. The record also shows that insured cooperated with the defendant in determining ownership and valuation of the property.

Substantial performance with the terms of the contract is necessary for insured to recover under the policy. Where a party has met the essential purpose of the contract, he has substantially performed under the contract....

We conclude that, on this record, the jury correctly found that the insured substantially performed his obligations under the contract....

The second question is: Did Allstate exercise bad faith in the handling of the insured's claim?

The controlling case on the law of bad faith is *Anderson v. Continental Ins. Co.*, 85 Wis.2d 675, 271 N.W.2d 368 (1978). Bad faith is an intentional tort "which results from a breach of duty imposed as a consequence of the relationship established by contract." *Anderson, supra*, 85 Wis.2d at 687. The duty imposed on an insurance company has been characterized as being analogous to that of a fiduciary. *Anderson, supra*, 85 Wis.2d at 688. "Bad faith" is defined as deceit, duplicity or insincerity. *Anderson, supra*, 85 Wis.2d at 692.

In order to show a claim for bad faith, this court has held that:

> ... a plaintiff must show the absence of a reasonable basis for denying benefits of the policy and the defendant's knowledge or reckless disregard of the lack of a reasonable basis for denying the claim. *Anderson, supra*, 85 Wis.2d at 691.

The insurer is, however, entitled to challenge the claim on the basis of debatable law or facts....

Allstate contends that no bad faith issue was presented because the failure of the insured to supply certified invoices or receipts showing the cost of each claimed item of property provided a reasonable basis for denying the claim.

The court of appeals found the issue of valuation to be fairly debatable as a matter of law. We disagree.

The insured submitted upon request a sworn proof-of-loss statement to Allstate, claiming damage to his property under the policy of $15,000. The proof of loss statement placed a value on each of nearly four hundred items destroyed by the fire. The testimony of two of defendant's claims personnel considered the statement to be substantially complete. The same Allstate employees recommended a cash payment to plaintiff of nearly $15,000. Allstate investigators had recommended an increase in coverage on plaintiff's property to $25,000 only four months before the fire. Allstate's claims adjuster confirmed the insured's purchase of many of the major items shown on the proof of loss statement. After recommending a cash settlement of nearly $15,000, Allstate's claims adjuster noted in his records that:

> *When I get authorization I will attempt to cashout insured for a complete loss. I will start at a low price and work my way up. I'm not going to offer*

the full amount at first. There is no harm in offering a lower amount at first. I can always go up.

The insured testified that he spoke with Allstate's Commercial Claims supervisor, after the claims adjuster offered only $4,000 to settle the claim. He testified that the supervisor told him:

> We know we owe the money but if you don't take the $4,000, we are not going to offer you anything else and if you don't take the settlement we'll just turn it over to our lawyers and we'll tie you up for the next two or three years in a [sic] litigation and you won't see a dime.

The claims adjuster also wrote to his supervisor stating that:

> *I don't feel we should drag this out to [sic] much longer. Insured is more than willing to supply us with tax records. [which had been requested by Allstate to verify ownership.]*

Allstate introduced evidence at trial showing that the insured had represented the value of his office property at $350 to $3,500 and in one case claimed the property was merely rented by him. These representations were not made to Allstate but in divorce and bankruptcy proceedings and on personal property tax returns.

But whatever the insured's motives were in those proceedings, it is apparent from its inter-office memos that Allstate was not misled as to the property's ownership or value, even if others may have been.

We conclude that the evidence before the trial court was sufficient to submit the bad faith question to the jury and find no error in submitting the question.

The jury was obviously persuaded that the property was worth what insured had claimed. That figure was almost identical to the amount recommended by Allstate's representatives to their superiors to settle the claim and $10,000 less than the coverage limits recommended by Allstate's underwriters four months before the fire. Accordingly, the jury determined that Allstate had no reasonable basis for denying the claim.

Because there is ample evidence to support that conclusion, we reverse that part of the court of appeals' decision overturning the award of damages for bad faith, and reinstate the award for bad faith of $12,103 in compensatory damages and $30,000 in punitive damages found by the jury and approved by the trial court. Accordingly, we uphold the entire judgment of the trial court for $57,306.54....

NOTES AND QUESTIONS

1. *Behavior of lawyers, clients, and insurance companies:* Given the amount involved, a great deal of legal work was devoted to Davis' claim. If courts insisted on literal rather than substantial compliance with the conditions in the insurance policy, we would get easy and quick answers. Why are courts and lawyers willing to spend so much effort on cases such as that of Mr. Davis?

In thinking about exact and substantial performance, consider the third paragraph of Justice Day's opinion carefully. Is it likely that the salespeople from Allstate explained to Mr. Davis the record keeping requirement and the risk that records would be destroyed in the very fire being insured against? What if they had done so? Moreover, consider Allstate's sales tactics in the transaction. What expectations did it create as it sold Davis more and more insurance? Finally, should the jury have been told to consider whether both parties were dealing in good faith?

What is the lesson of the Allstate loss for insurance companies? Would you expect Allstate to change its practices? In what way? Should Allstate be able to use technical defenses when they suspect that a policy holder is making a questionable claim? Should insurance companies be able to drive hard bargains when they question the merit of a policy holder's claim? Would this lead to desirable compromises rather than an all or nothing resolution of the problem? Should courts require lawyers to protect themselves more than other business-people? Should they be required to read policy terms and comply with them closely? Should they be left to their own skill and bargaining power?

2. *Regulation of insurance settlement*: Many courts recognize a tort of bad faith performance of an insurance contract. We will consider later how far courts will use this idea outside the insurance area. Why isn't an insurance company privileged to bargain to settle claims? What was wrong with taking advantage of Mr. Davis' need for money to continue his law practice? Suppose Mr. Piette had made an opening offer of $8,000 (twice the offer he did make). Would the situation have been different? Recall the history of judicial supervision of the insurance contract. Compare the discussions of waiver and estoppel in insurance cases by Kimball and Friedman, *supra*.

3. *Substantial performance in building contracts*: Insurance is not the only home of the substantial performance doctrine. Courts also often use substantial performance in contracts to erect or repair buildings. For example, suppose owner promises to pay when builder constructs the building according to plans and specifications. Courts generally read the builder's *promise* as building to plans and specifications. However, they read the *constructive condition* on the owner's promise to pay as requiring only substantial performance of the contract in good faith.

As a result, the owner must pay the full contract sum although he or she did not get exactly what was bargained for. The owner has a cause of action for damages for the builder's failure to perform the promise to meet plans and specifications. This might seem to approximate compensation for loss better than a forfeiture which might result if the condition were construed as full and complete performance. However, at least in some cases, the owner's damages are measured as the difference between the value of the house as it stands and as it would be had the contract been performed exactly. Often this produces only a token sum, leaving the owner's interest in having good craftsmanship unprotected insofar as it is not reflected in market values.

4. *Experts' certificates in building contracts and substantial performance*: Under many construction contracts, owners are to pay only when the builder obtains an *architect or engineer's certificate* that the work has been done. Suppose the architect or engineer refuses to grant the certificate. May the builder claim the contract price less a set-off for the owner's damages on the ground that the builder has substantially performed? We can contrast two views:

In *Coorsen v. Ziehl*,[5] the court found that the satisfaction of the architect "is a condition precedent to the right to sue for the contract price, unless the refusal to certify should be disregarded on the grounds of fraud or bad faith, or clear evidence of mistake, on the part of the architect." In *Wauwatosa v. Jacobus & Winding Concrete Construction Co.*,[6] the court said that the kind of mistake needed to overturn the requirement of an architect's certificate must be an "unintentional misapprehension or ignorance of some material fact, and it must be clearly established by the evidence, and so gross and palpable that it is equivalent in its effects to dishonest, fraudulent, or merely arbitrary action."

However, in the classic case of *Jacob & Youngs, Inc. v. Kent*,[7] Justice Cardozo found that a builder could recover despite his failure to obtain the required architect's certificate when the builder had substantially performed and where "the defect was insignificant in its relation to the project" and denial of recovery would result in a great forfeiture. One of the specifications for plumbing work provided that "all wrought iron pipe must be well galvanized, lap welded pipe of the grade known as 'standard pipe' of Reading manufacture." About nine months after occupying the country residence, the owner discovered that some of the pipe "instead of being made in Reading, was the product of other factories." $3,483 remained unpaid. The builder was directed by the architect to do the work anew. Carrying out the order would have meant the demolition at great expense of substantial parts of the completed structure. The omission of Reading pipe "was neither fraudulent or willful. It was the result of the oversight and inattention of the plaintiff's subcontractor." The builder sued for the unpaid balance.

---

[5] 103 Wis. 381, 79 N.W. 362 (1899).
[6] 223 Wis. 401, 271 N.W. 21 (1937).
[7] 230 N.Y. 239, 129 N.E. 889 (1921).

The trial court excluded evidence that the pipe installed was of the same quality, appearance and market value as Reading pipe, and it directed a verdict for the defendant owner. The Court of Appeals reversed and directed a judgment for Jacob & Youngs by a 4 to 3 vote.

The dissent said that Kent "had a right to contract for what he wanted." "It may have been a mere whim on his part, but even so, he had a right to this kind of pipe, regardless of whether some other kind, according to the opinion of the contractor or experts, would have been 'just as good, better, or done just as well.' He agreed to pay only upon condition that the pipe installed were made by that company and he ought not be compelled to pay unless that condition be performed."

Danzig,[8] studied the background of the *Jacob & Youngs* case. The contract was lengthy and detailed. It created a system whereby the builder was to be paid when it obtained architect certificates, but it did not expressly state the circumstances under which certificates should be granted or denied. All that was said was that the builder was entitled to a certificate when "in the Architect's judgment the work called for ... has been satisfactorily executed ..." Paragraph 22 of the General Conditions stated that "Where any particular brand of manufactured article is specified, it is to be considered as a standard. Contractors desiring to use another shall first make application in writing to the Architect, stating the difference in cost, and obtain their written approval of the change." Jacob & Youngs, of course, had made no such written application nor received written approval of a substitution of brands of pipe.

Kent was a successful New York lawyer, and there is no evidence that he had any connection with the Reading Pipe Company. There were four major brands of wrought iron pipe on the market, and an informant said that they were of the same quality and price. Wrought iron pipe cost 30% more than steel pipe, it was used in quality construction before World War I, but it is almost never used today. It was normal trade practice to assure wrought iron pipe quality by naming a manufacturer known not to use iron containing steel scrap. The specifications themselves were imprecise. Apparently, it was impossible to make lap welded wrought iron in all of the sizes necessary for the house as called for by the specifications.

Why did Kent object to the pipe? Danzig reports he was told "The old man would go all over town to save a buck." However, he may have used the substitution as an expression of his frustration with Jacob & Youngs' performance of the contract. Completion of the job was long delayed. Jacob and Youngs did additional work that added to Kent's bill.

---

[8]The Capability Problem in Contract Law (Foundation Press 1978).

5. *Free contract and excusing experts' certificates*: John Murray,[9] argues:

> A few courts have taken the position that the condition is excused if the architect's failure to grant the certificate resulted from his mere unreasonableness. Such holdings are unsound since they have the effect of nullifying the condition entirely. In every case in which the certificate is refused and the price not paid, the contractor will claim that the architect was unreasonable, with the result that the whole matter will have to be decided as a question of fact, just as it would be if no condition were stated in the contract. This is contrary to the obvious intent of the parties.

Is Murray right? What does Cardozo's approach do to the power of lawyers to control the future by contract drafting? Are there reasons why a disappointed contractor might accept an architect's determination rather than relitigate the matter in court even when it followed Justice Cardozo's approach?

However, is it realistic to say that the contractor made a choice to accept a private government subject to almost no meaningful review by public government? To what extent is the substantial performance doctrine a covert application of the ideas behind the unconscionability doctrine? Does a rule strictly enforcing the condition permit exploitation of the weak or unwary?

VAN IDERSTINE CO. v. BARNET LEATHER CO.

242 N.Y. 425, 152 N.E. 250 (1926)

LEHMAN, J.... On September 10th, 1920, the parties entered into another contract for the sale of 6,000 vealskins, delivery to be made in September, "to be received by Jules Star & Co. subject to their approval."...

... Jules Star & Co. rejected the entire quantity of 6,000 skins which the plaintiff tendered in attempted performance of its contract of September 10th, 1920, and defendant refused to accept them.

The plaintiff has brought this action to recover damages suffered because of the defendant's refusal to accept the skins which plaintiff offered to deliver....

... In the second cause of action as amended at the trial the plaintiff alleged that any condition for approval by a representative of Jules Star & Co. of the skins to be delivered under the contract of September 10th was waived and excused because the approval was unreasonably withheld, and because defendant prevented Jules Star & Co. from giving such approval and "because defendant and said Jules Star & Co. wrongfully and knowingly colluded to withhold that approval, with intent to avoid defendant's having to accept the said skins." The

---

[9]Copyright 1974, 1965, 1947 The Michie Company. Reprinted from Murray on Contracts, Second Edition, by John Edward Murray, Jr., with permission from The Michie Company, Charlottesville, Virginia.

issues raised by the denial to these allegations were submitted to the jury and decided in favor of the plaintiff....

We have pointed out that under both contracts sued upon, the seller agreed to make delivery subject to the approval of Jules Star & Co. The parties chose to stipulate that such approval must be given. It constitutes a condition which, unless waived or excused, must be fulfilled before the buyer can be compelled to accept skins that are tendered. Concededly approval of Jules Star & Co. has not been given....

... The condition was waived also in regard to the contract which forms the basis of the second cause of action if refusal of approval by Jules Star & Co. was the result of bad faith on the part of Jules Star & Co. in which the defendant had some share. If by its own interference and wrong the defendant prevented the plaintiff from obtaining the stipulated approval, then the plaintiff may recover without it. We have pointed out that in the second cause of action the plaintiff has pleaded that the condition was waived and excused not only because of wrongful act on the part of the defendant but because approval was "unreasonably withheld," and the serious question raised upon this appeal is whether the plaintiff may recover under its contract upon proof that it offered to deliver skins which in quality complied with the contract requirements, and that the representative of Jules Star & Co. unreasonably withheld its approval of these skins.

The trial judge charged that if "approval was unreasonably withheld, whether Barnet had anything to do with it or not, the plaintiff could recover. Star must have acted honestly. If he showed an honest judgment the defendant is entitled to a verdict." Though the parties have stipulated that the approval of Jules Star & Co. must be obtained for any skins delivered under the contract, under the rule laid down in the charge, the plaintiff may become liable for damages if he insists upon this stipulation being carried out. It places upon the buyer the risk of determining whether Jules Star & Co. have acted reasonably; it makes the buyer determine whether approval should reasonably have been given, though not he but Jules Star & Co. were to approve of the quality of the skins. In effect it makes the buyer a guarantor of both the honesty and the good judgment of Jules Star & Co.

It is said that authority for the rule laid down in the charge may be found in many cases in this and other jurisdictions where the courts have considered the effect of unreasonable or dishonest refusal of architect or engineer to approve of work done or materials furnished, under building contracts when such approval was made a condition precedent to payment.... In those cases it must be remembered that by the nature of the contracts, if failure to obtain approval deprived the contractor of the right to recover the agreed compensation, the result would be that the benefit of work actually performed and materials actually furnished could be appropriated by the owner without payment, though in other respects the contractor had fully complied with his contract. It would cause forfeiture of agreed price for agreed service without any fault on the contractor's part. In the same manner as the courts have evolved the rule that under contracts of that nature there may be recovery for substantial performance, they have evolved a rule which permits recovery without stipulated certificate of approval where the certificate has been wrongfully or unreasonably refused....

So, too, in some cases where the contract shows that the person whose approval is required under the contract is merely an agent of a buyer selected by the buyer to pass upon the goods in the buyer's place, wrong on the part of the agent is imputed to the principal....

... Here the contract is of different nature. The parties agree that a designated broker acting as expert and not simply as the buyer's agent must pass upon the goods and delivery must be made subject to the expert's approval. Refusal to approve by the expert does not enable the buyer to obtain property from the seller without payment. According to the terms of the contract it merely permits him to refuse to accept the goods because he stipulated not merely for goods of a certain quality but for goods of that quality approved by a particular expert. To compel him to accept and pay for the goods without such approval is to impose liability upon him which he had not agreed to assume, and gives compensation to the seller for goods not delivered in full compliance with contract. The theoretical soundness of the rule applied to building contracts has not escaped criticism. It rests upon the basis that enforcement of the contract according to its strict terms would cause forfeiture of compensation for work done or materials furnished. The rule should not be extended by analogy where the reason for the rule fails.... Unless the certificate has been withheld dishonestly and in bad faith, and the defendant is a party to that bad faith through control of the expert or collusion with him, there may be no recovery under the second cause of action.

There are cases where parties stipulate for the approval or certificate of a third person not as part of the contractual obligation of either party to the contract but rather as machinery for avoiding dispute between the parties as to whether these obligations have been properly performed. Question may then arise as to whether the stipulated approval or certificate constitutes in full sense a condition precedent to recovery, or whether there may be recovery based on substantial performance, upon proof that in other respects the contract has been fully complied with. Such question we do not now decide. Doubtless there are cases where such hardship would be imposed upon a party who performs work or manufactures goods at the special instance of another if payment were withheld merely because approval is wrongfully refused, that argument may well be made that such result was not intended by the parties. Here we have no such circumstances. The plaintiff's obligation is only to deliver certain goods, and by express stipulation there may be no delivery without approval of a third party. It has done nothing for which it might legally or equitably expect compensation until delivery is made. If approval is withheld the plaintiff cannot perform; it loses the profit which it might have otherwise made by delivery of goods at a contract price higher than the then prevailing market price. It assumed this risk. It still retains the goods and may sell them at market price. The defendant should not be required to pay the contract price unless the plaintiff performs according to contract "subject to the approval" of the third party....

The judgments should be reversed and a new trial granted, with costs to abide the event. Cardozo, Pound and Andrews, JJ., concur; Hiscock, Ch. J., McLaughlin and Crane, JJ., dissent.

NOTES AND QUESTIONS

1. *Material from the briefs and record — the buyer's story*: The briefs and record in the case disclose that the jury was presented with two conflicting stories about the transaction. It was agreed that calfskins from farmers and butchers outside of New York City were likely to be of lower quality than New York City skins. Those slaughtering calves in New York City exercised care so that the skins would not be marked, and it was customary in New York City to use a special salt that did not discolor in the tanning process. The Barnet Leather Company, the buyer, offered evidence that before the contract involved in the case was signed, representatives of the seller had tried to sell calfskins to Barnet. Barnet refused because Van Iderstine "does not handle skins that are satisfactory to us, on account of buying outside skins, and our experience has been such that we have refrained from buying from you since last year."

Jules Star & Co. was a broker handling calfskins. It offered seller's skins to buyer on the standard form contract in the industry. The contract provided that the skins were "to be received by Jules Star & Co.'s representative subject to their approval." Star told his employees to bend over backwards to find the skins acceptable if possible, but they found that the skins were not of acceptable quality. Van Iderstine's representatives asked that Jules Star himself look at the skins. He did, and he testified,

> I could not approve of that kind of skins, that is not what the contracts call for.... I found that the condition of the skins was very bad, they were ... in the worst shape I have ever been presented with New York City skins by anybody. I did not trust my eyes when I really saw this lot of poor stuff laying there coming out of that pack, and satisfying myself from all over that they were poor all the way through.... [The] custom of the trade is to reject a lot of skins if a proportion of these country and resalted and old outside city skins is mixed in with a supposedly first class New York City first salted skin.

Van Iderstine's representatives then contacted Mr. Barnet, the buyer, and complained about the rejection.

> So I told both of them that Mr. Star was our representative and the skins had been sold subject to his approval and that was final, as it had been final in every other transaction we had ever made through Star with them, or with

anybody else, and that we would not have inserted in our contract that they were subject to the approval of Jules Star if it did not mean something. They were not satisfied, nevertheless, with Star's rejection and they begged me to come over. I decided that I would go over in all fairness to determine whether these skins were as Star reported to us or not, but without any obligation of any kind on our part.... [It] was a shame to call that [material offered] a first salted New York City skin and try to force him [Star] to take that kind of stuff.

Finally, the buyer offered the testimony of a former Van Iderstine Company employee. He said that Van Iderstine collected many skins from farmers and others outside New York City, including people known in the business to offer lower quality goods. Then Van Iderstine would mix the best of the outside skins in with New York City skins, offering all of them at New York City prices.

2. *Material from the briefs and record — the seller's story*: Van Iderstine, the seller, offered evidence that told a very different story. The salesman who handled the deal testified that in fact the skins offered were clean, fresh New York City calfskins. After Barnet claimed that the skins were badly scored, dirty and not clean and bright as New York City's should be, the salesman said he responded "[t]he reason you do not want these skins, Mr. Barnet, is not because they are not New York City's, but due to the fact that the market has dropped badly."

Jules Star was a stockholder in the Barnet Leather Company. A telegram was introduced in evidence. It was sent by Star representing Barnet Leather Company in a transaction with another seller shortly after Star and Barnet had rejected the skins offered by Van Iderstine. It said "Barnet agrees to take quantity as per contract not exceeding two thousand. Take as few as possible make strict selection make sure skins sound not slipped salt stained or otherwise damaged." Van Iderstine argued that this showed Star and Barnet were raising the standard for skins to minimize losses in a falling market. In denying Barnet's motion for a new trial, the judge said that he regarded this telegram "to be perfectly competent, especially upon cross-examination, because it was sent so close to the transaction in suit as to give a valuable insight into the motives and actions of defendant's agent."

3. *The trial judge's view of the evidence*: The jury found for Van Iderstine, the plaintiff seller, based on the evidence and instructions quoted. The buyer moved for a new trial in part because it was against the weight of the evidence, but its motion was denied. The trial judge said "the court would not have disturbed the verdict whichever way it went, although its impressions upon the trial were distinctly in favor of the merit of the plaintiff's [seller's] claim, and the impression has not been changed by the further consideration of the testimony."

4. *Van Iderstine under the U.C.C.*: Would the *Van Iderstine* case be decided differently today now that such a transaction in goods is governed by the U.C.C.? Section 2-513 deals with a buyer's right to inspect goods, but it does

not mention inspections by experts. Would a sale of calfskins "to be received by Jules Star & Co.'s representative subject to their approval" be governed by § 2-515(b)? It provides:

> In furtherance of the adjustment of any claim or dispute ... the parties may agree to a third party inspection or survey to determine the conformity or condition of the goods and may agree that the findings shall be binding upon them in any subsequent litigation or adjustment.

Does this section cover only claims or disputes which have already arisen or would it apply to potential claims or disputes that might arise as well?

5. *A hypothetical question:* Imagine that the time is the present. You are a lawyer for a manufacturer who utilizes vealskins to make leather goods. Your client has a contract which obligates them to accept "suitable" vealskins from Seller. The market for veal skins has fallen to substantially below the contract price. Your client has refused to accept a shipment of vealskins, having characterized them as "unsuitable." what will be the standard by which your client's behavior will be judged, should Seller complain? Will it differ importantly from the standard in *Van Iderstine*? Is it relevant that the market price has fallen?[10]

6. *Can one bargain for discretion under the U.C.C.?* Suppose a buyer wanted to have the final judgment on the quality of the goods offered and avoid debate about the matter. Can its lawyer write a provision in the contract with the seller stating that the buyer's determination of quality cannot be challenged even on the ground of bad faith? U.C.C. § 1-102(3) is an important but often overlooked provision. It says:

> The effect of provisions of This Act may be varied by agreement, except as otherwise provided in this Act and except that the obligations of good faith, diligence, reasonableness and care prescribed by this Act may not be disclaimed by agreement but the parties may by agreement determine the standards by which the performance of such obligations is to be measured if such standards are not manifestly unreasonable.

Thus, a buyer could not contract out of an obligation to use good faith, but it could set "not manifestly unreasonable" standards by which the performance of that obligation was to be measured.

7. *Another condition of satisfaction example:* Conditions of satisfaction are also used in the publishing industry. (Can you see why?) Sometimes, as we might expect, problems arise. For example, in *Doubleday & Co., Inc. v. Curtis* a publisher sued for the return of an advance it had paid actor Tony Curtis, and he

---

[10]See, *e.g.*, Neumiller Farms, Inc. v. Jonah D. Cornett, 368 So.2d 272 (S.Ct.Ala. 1979).

counterclaimed for anticipated earnings. In 1976 Doubleday signed a two-book contract with Curtis. On the basis of this, Curtis prepared a draft manuscript for a novel entitled *Kid Andrew Cody and Julie Sparrow*. After examining the manuscript, Doubleday signed a standard publishing contract. It provided that Curtis was to be paid royalties provided that he could deliver a final manuscript which was "satisfactory to Publisher in content and form." A final draft, prepared by Curtis and Larry Jordan (a Doubleday editor) was accepted for publication.

Doubleday then agreed to renegotiate the contract governing the second book. It paid Curtis an advance on future royalties. The contract provided, once again, that the manuscript was to be "satisfactory to Publisher in content and form." Doubleday then made a contract with New American Library which provided for payment to Doubleday of $200,000 for the paperback rights in the second novel, if and when the second novel was accepted for publication by Doubleday.

Curtis delivered a partial first draft of a rags-to-riches story of a Hollywood starlet; the book was entitled *Starstruck*. The draft was assigned to Adrian Zackheim, a Doubleday editor who was a stranger to Curtis. Four months later Zackheim sent Curtis a seven-page letter which contained both praise and criticism of the manuscript. The letter said Zackheim was "charmed" with the "wonderful possibilities" of *Starstruck* and that he did not anticipate the need for substantial changes in the basic outlines of the novel. On the other hand, the letter noted numerous inconsistencies and inherent contradictions in the manuscript, and urged Curtis to tighten the plot. Curtis, who had worked closely with Larry Jordan on the first book, was pre-occupied with his divorce proceedings, and, apart from a few conversations, did not work with Zackheim on the revision of the book.

Curtis subsequently delivered what he characterized as a completed manuscript. He had paid little attention to the suggestions and criticisms contained in Zackheim's letter. Zackheim believed the book was unpublishable, but passed it along to Elizabeth Drew, his supervisor. Notwithstanding the fact that rejecting the book would cost Doubleday the NAL reprint arrangement, Drew wrote a memo in which she characterized *Starstruck* as "junk, pure and simple" and concluded that neither editing nor rewriting could make it publishable. Zackheim suggested to Curtis' agent that the manuscript be submitted to a "novel doctor," but this suggestion was rejected.

At the trial Curtis characterized Zackheim as an apathetic and incompetent editor, as compared to Larry Jordan. He also complained that he had not received any indication from Doubleday that *Starstruck* would be unacceptable until his agent, Lazar, informed him that Doubleday had made an irreversible decision not to publish it. Zackheim admitted at trial that his letter overstated the strengths of Curtis' first draft, and minimized the weaknesses. But both Zackheim and Drew testified that they sincerely believed the manuscript was irreparable, and that their decision not to publish was motivated by both ethical and artistic considerations.

The trial court judge began by finding that though New York decisions did not make it clear whether a "satisfactory to the publisher" clause required the publisher to offer editorial services, Doubleday had in fact offered such services. Next he concluded that Doubleday's rejection was animated by a genuine belief that the manuscript was unpublishable. But he then found that Doubleday had led Curtis to believe the book would be published, and that this constituted a waiver of the publisher's right to ask that the advance be returned.

There was an appeal and the Court of Appeals ruled that good faith honest dissatisfaction was a prerequisite to assertion of a "satisfaction" clause. It was appropriate to investigate the good faith and honesty of the publisher, since "to shield from scrutiny the already chimerical process of evaluating literary value would render the 'satisfaction' clause an illusory promise, and place authors at the unbridled mercy of their editors." On the other hand, it was important to realize that a requirement that publishers perform honestly was not the same as a requirement that they perform skillfully.

> The possibility that a publisher or an editor — either through inferior editing or inadvertence — may prejudice an author's efforts is a risk attendant to the selection of a publishing house by a writer, and is properly borne by that party. To imply a duty to perform adequate editorial services in the absence of express contractual language would, in our view, represent an unwarranted intrusion into the editorial process. Moreover, we are hesitant to require triers of fact to explore the manifold intricacies of an editorial relationship. Such inquiries are appropriate only where the contracts specifically allocate certain creative responsibilities to the publisher.

The Court of Appeals sustained the trial court finding that Doubleday had acted in good faith. Though Zackheim's revisions may have been offered somewhat belatedly, he did extend numerous offers to discuss the novel with Curtis, which Curtis refused. There is no reason to regard the encouraging notes in Zackheim's letter as prejudicial to Curtis. Doubleday did sacrifice the financial rewards of the NAL contract by choosing not to publish, and the decision could "hardly be said to constitute an act of bad faith."

The Court of Appeals then reversed the trial court on the waiver issue, and remanded with orders that a judgment be entered for Doubleday on that issue. The issue of waiver was not properly before the trial court. Curtis had not raised the issue at trial, and Doubleday had no notice that its claim was subject to challenge on the ground of waiver.

Having offered a brief summary of the controversy, we are left with questions. Why doesn't an obligation to produce a satisfactory manuscript impose a reciprocal obligation on the publisher to supply skillful editorial services? Doubleday editor Larry Jordan had apparently provided skillful services on the first book. Why couldn't Curtis reasonably expect Doubleday to provide the same level of editorial support on the second? Does this decision rest on a determination of what the likely expectations of the parties were? How does the United States Court of Appeals for the Second Circuit know what those expectations were? Does the decision rest on a judgment that the courts should not enter the dismal swamp of attempting to review editorial decisions? Should the Court have considered that the contracts with new authors are generally drafted by the publishers? Won't publishers be largely exempt from supervision when dealing with the works of unknown authors, since only successful authors will have the bargaining power to eliminate the "satisfactory to the publisher" clauses? If this is true, is it a good or bad thing?

B. MY RIGHT TO CALL OFF SOME OR ALL OF THE DEAL BECAUSE OF YOUR FAILURE TO PERFORM: "MATERIAL FAILURE OF PERFORMANCE"

1. A NOTE AND SOME PROBLEMS TO SET THE STAGE

What should a court do when one party fails to perform perfectly but comes close? Earlier in these materials we considered the remedial alternatives available to a victim of a breach. In the course of that inquiry, we looked at *Colonial Dodge v. Miller* in which the issue was whether a disappointed purchaser could walk away from the transaction when the seller had tendered a defective performance. We will be revisiting that issue here, but exploring it in greater detail, and emphasizing not only the question of the availability of remedy, but spending more time on the question of the qualitative assessment of performance. Where the seller is to supply a single tangible object, and the buyer is to pay the contract price when the object is delivered, one of the buyer's important rights is to walk away free and clear of obligations to the seller if there is anything wrong with the item. However, it is not so clear that the buyer should be able to walk away free and clear of obligations to the seller where the seller's performance was complex and a great deal but not all of it has been given to the buyer. In some situations, at least, it may make more sense to require the buyer to pay for the less than perfect performance but grant an offsetting claim for damages. In ordinary transactions, at least, buyers cannot expect extremes of perfection. Consider several examples:

(1) Suppose seller sells her car to buyer for $1,000, and they agree that seller will tender the keys and the title certificate to the buyer in front of the buyer's house between 9:00 and 11:00 a.m. on April 7th. Both are present on that morning at 10:00. Buyer takes the key and tries to start the car unsuccessfully. The battery is dead. A new battery of the type in the car can be purchased for $50 at the service station across the street from where the car is parked. Seller is a regular customer at the service station, and its owner is willing to bring the battery across the street and install it. Seller

explains this to the buyer, but he says that he is no longer bound to the contract since the seller failed to perform. Has buyer the right to back out of the deal free from contractual liability? What more, if anything, do you need to know?

(2) Suppose a singer of popular music of some fame agrees to perform at a night club. He promises to perform there on the night of April 7th, singing in shows to begin at 9:00 and 11:00 p.m. of no less than 30 minutes and no more than one hour. He is to be paid $10,000 for the performances. Suppose the singer performs for 45 minutes at the 9:00 show, and the audience is enthusiastic. However, the singer cuts the 11:00 show short and sings for only 20 minutes because the audience fails to respond to his act. Assume that the owner of the club is in no way responsible for the reaction of the audience at the 11:00 show. The owner asserts that since the singer did not perform for at least 30 minutes at the 11:00 show, he did not perform his part of the contract, and, as a result, the owner owes the singer nothing. Are the singer's lawyers likely to collect the $10,000? Anything? Could they assert with any real chance of success that since he performed the 9:00 show, he should be paid $5,000 for it? Since he also performed 20/30 of the 11:00 show, should he be paid 2/3 of $5,000 (or $3,333), making a total of $8,333 earned for the night of April 7? Of course, this would be subject to a set-off of any damages the club owner could prove had been caused by the failure to perform for ten minutes. Suppose the singer cut short the 9:00 show which annoyed many in the audience who might have stayed for the 11:00 show and did not. Would this make a difference?

(3) Suppose seller is to deliver an X, a Y, and a Z in exchange for buyer's payment of $250. Seller delivers the X and the Y, but fails to produce the Z. Can buyer refuse delivery or return the items and then be free of any obligation under the contract? Suppose the Z is a trivial part of the total contract as compared to the X and the Y. For example, X is an automatic turntable and tone arm for playing phonograph records; Y is a cartridge and stylus installed in the tone arm; Z is a level used to position the turntable properly. Suppose now that X and Y have little value to the buyer without Z. For example, X is a turntable and tone arm; Y is a stylus (the "needle" which touches the record); Z is a cartridge into which the stylus is inserted and without which records cannot be played. Suppose seller and buyer have made a single written agreement for the three items. Would it matter that they named separate prices for X, Y and Z rather than simply stating a total price for all three? Would it matter whether Z is readily available at many stores in town or is an item which only seller's store carries and which takes at least three months to obtain on order from Japan?

Courts could solve most of these problems by saying that because one party has not performed precisely, she or he cannot assert any rights under the contract. The one in default could be left to restitution for benefits conferred by partial performance. However, often the defaulting party would not think this a fair solution. Restitution for a party in default will cost the almost-performer his or her expectation interest as well as much of the reliance interest that does not produce tangible economic benefits. In some states, moreover, it is said that a party in default (or perhaps one in "willful" default) cannot recover restitution. The defaulting party may forfeit a great deal, and in some cases, at least, the punishment may be too great for the crime.

Rather than using a strict performance standard, courts have often adopted a test of materiality. If X has performed some but not all of his duties under a contract, Y may walk away free and clear of any obligation other than restitution only if the failure of performance is "material" or "substantial." In the first example which dealt with the delivery of a used car with a dead battery, a new battery could be installed quickly and the contract carried out. It seems unlikely that any failure of performance here would be material or substantial. Contrast a case where seller tenders the keys and the title, but buyer looks under the hood and discovers that there is no engine in the car. Almost certainly the seller's default would be material then; installing a new battery and a new engine are different matters, and we can wonder about the seller's good faith in one situation but not the other.

2. SOLUTIONS OFFERED BY THE RESTATEMENT (SECOND) OF CONTRACTS

So far we've talked about the consequences of finding a failure to give a complete performance to be material or immaterial. How does one decide how important the defect is? To a great extent, materiality seems to turn on whether or not the ultimate consequences of the classification seem appropriate, given the facts of the case. The late Professor Malcolm Sharp wrote that the "best statement of these ordinary tests [for materiality], and perhaps the best portion of the work, is § 275 of the Restatement of Contracts."[11] Section 275 is now § 241 in the second Restatement. How would you deal with our three examples (the car and battery; the singer who cut short a show; the delivery of an X, and a Y but not a Z) under the Restatement? To see the structure of the Restatement's approach, you will have to consider Restatement (Second) of Contracts §§ 225, 237, 240, 241 and 242 in the statutory supplement.

Professor Eric G. Anderson challenges the Restatement approach to material breach. He says "the relevant *Restatement* provisions seem enigmatic at best." They "resemble a list of ingredients rather than a recipe; no real guidance is

---

[11]Sharp, Promissory Liability II, 7 U. Chi. L. Rev. 250, 272 (1939).

provided on the order or proportions in which to combine the provisions." They "fail to identify an underlying, unifying principle more specific than 'fairness' or 'justice....'" Courts can apply these rules only through a "gut-level judgment about how a particular case should be decided."

Professor Anderson offers his solution. Materiality requires us to focus on the appropriateness of courts making cancellation available to the victim under the circumstances of the case. We must seek to protect the victim's expectation interest without imposing needless costs on the defaulting party. A party to a contract has two interests. One is her interest in *present performance*. The defaulting party promised to perform today, but he failed to do so. Usually, courts can protect this interest by allowing the victim to sue for damages. The other is her interest in *future performance* — an interest in the likelihood that the contract will be performed as agreed in the future despite the defaulting party's failure to perform as promised to date. In some cases courts must allow the aggrieved party to cancel to protect this interest. The victim must be sure that she is free of her original contract so she can seek her needs elsewhere. Thus, courts should ask whether it is necessary to allow cancellation to protect this interest and whether the victim could take reasonable steps to eliminate or avoid injury.

Anderson attacks the Restatement's balancing approach. He argues that we should not look at the burden on the defaulting party. Rather he advocates an expanded view of restitution for a party in default to protect any interest of the defaulting party. In this way, we can be sure that the victim will have the right to cancel when she must in order to turn elsewhere to protect her expectation interest.

Finally, Anderson asserts "[c]ancellation should be invoked only when a breach so impairs the interest in future performance that the victim has reasonable cause to bring the contract to an end, so that the bargained-for security [of performance], or its economic equivalent, may be acquired elsewhere." He concludes: "[w]hen the interest it protects is so understood and administered, the cancellation power is effectively harnessed."

Consider Professor Anderson's criticism of the Restatement's balancing test. Does it call for an intuitive approach? If so, why would anyone object to this? Does Anderson's approach significantly limit the amount of judgment and discretion necessary when a court considers whether to allow one party to cancel? To what extent, if at all, does it make a court's task easier?

3. TRANSACTIONS IN GOODS: THE BASIC SOLUTIONS OF THE U.C.C.

a. The General Pattern

To what extent does the Uniform Commercial Code follow the approach of the Restatement of Contracts for cases coming within Article II? Standing alone, § 2-601 appears to state what has been called "the perfect tender" rule. With some important qualifications, it says that "if the goods ... fail *in any respect* to conform to the contract, the buyer may ... reject the whole...." [Emphasis added]. For example, in the pre-U.C.C. case of *Frankel v. Foreman & Clark*,[12] the court permitted rejection of an entire shipment of coats although the jury found that there was a trivial or inconsequential failure to comply with the contract involving only one or two percent of the coats. Would a court be likely to reach this result under the U.C.C.? White and Summers[13] think not, saying,

> Close examination of the Code reveals that the Code well nigh abolishes the [perfect tender] rule. First of all, § 2-601 renders the perfect tender rule inapplicable to installment contracts, and 2-612 permits rejection in such contracts only if "the non-conformity substantially impairs the value of that installment...." Secondly, the seller's right to cure a defective tender, embodied in 2-508 ... is a further substantial restriction upon the buyer's apparent right to reject for insubstantial defects under 2-601. Additional restrictions upon the perfect tender rule in 2-601 may be found in 2-504 (an improper shipment contract which causes a late delivery is grounds for rejection only if "material delay or loss ensues")[14] and in the Code's general invitations to use trade usage, course of dealing, and course of performance in interpretation.... Finally, the courts have the power to deny rejection for what they regard as insubstantial defects by manipulating the procedural requirements for rejection. That is, if the court concludes that a buyer ought to be denied his right to reject because he has suffered no damage, the court might arrive at that conclusion by finding that the buyer failed to make an effective rejection (for example, because his notice was not timely).
>
> We conclude, and the cases decided to date suggest, that the foregoing changes have so eroded the perfect tender rule that little is left of it; the law would be little changed if 2-601 gave the right to reject only upon "substantial" nonconformity.

Turn back to the chart of remedial alternatives which followed the opinion in *Colonial Dodge v. Miller* in Chapter 2. It should help you see the pattern of the Uniform Commercial Code's sections related to tender, acceptance, rejection, cure, revocation of acceptance, notices and remedies. We will be exploring these issues in greater detail in the pages that follow.

The following decisions illustrate the U.C.C.'s basic approach to a buyer's right to reject or return a defective performance. Remember, however, that a seller may have a right to cure a defective performance under § 2-508.

---

[12]33 F.2d 83 (2d Cir. 1929).

[13]White & Summers, Uniform Commercial Code 304-305 (2d ed. 1980).

[14]See Monte Carlo Shirt, Inc. v. Daewoo Int'l (America) Corp., 707 F.2d 1054 (9th Cir. 1983).

Furthermore, under § 2-612 installment contracts are treated differently. We will consider these variations later.

b. Inspection and Acceptance of the Goods

You should re-read, at this point, the opinion in *Colonial Dodge, Inc. v. Miller* in Chapter 2 — the first of two opinions which the Court of Appeals wrote in the case. The second opinion, written after rehearing, follows.

It seems that Brennan must have had second thoughts. Why have we included the second opinion here? Ask yourself, as you read it, whether there are many new points of substantive contract law which are added. If not, why bother to read a rehash of the first opinion, even if the vote comes out differently? Before you read the decision after rehearing, ask what you believe the weak points of the first opinion are. If you were on the court, would you join one of the existing opinions, or write your own?

COLONIAL DODGE, INC. v. MILLER

328 N.W.2d 678 (1982)

Before CYNAR, P.J., and BRENNAN and DEMING, JJ. (On Rehearing of 116 Mich. App. 78, 322 N.W.2d 549)

PER CURIAM.[15] A judgment was entered on January 18, 1981, awarding damages in favor of plaintiff against defendant Clarence R. Miller in the amount of $1,000, together with costs entered in the amount of $342.31. Plaintiff, Colonial Dodge, Inc., appeals as of right.

... [P]laintiff sought damages for breach of a sales contract to purchase a new automobile. In a nonjury trial, the trial judge determined that plaintiff was entitled to the contract price of the motor vehicle less the amount plaintiff could have received from a resale of the vehicle within a reasonable period of time after the breach....

The issues ... concern whether plaintiff is entitled to the full contract price of the vehicle purchased by Miller and whether the trial court properly awarded damages to plaintiff. Miller did not file a cross-appeal.

On April 19, 1976, Miller executed a purchase order to buy a 1976 Dodge Royal Monaco station wagon from plaintiff for $5,677. The order was submitted to Chrysler Corporation (Chrysler) for special equipment, including a heavy trailer towing package with extra large tires. Plaintiff received an invoice from

---

[15]What is a per curiam opinion? Who do you suppose wrote it? Why was it issued as a per curiam opinion, do you think?

Chrysler pursuant to Miller's order; the invoice indicated that the spare tire was omitted from the delivery and would be shipped later.

On May 28, 1976, the specially-ordered station wagon was picked up by Miller. Miller drove the car to a nearby expressway and exchanged cars with his wife. He drove the old car to work, and she drove the new car home. Upon getting the new vehicle home, Mrs. Miller discovered that the spare tire was missing. Miller called plaintiff the next day and spoke to Donald Diem, a salesman, about the missing spare tire. Both persons were distraught at the time of the call. Diem was under stress due to the serious surgery his wife was about to undergo. Diem offered no explanation for the missing spare tire but offered his own spare tire which turned out to be the wrong size. Miller told Diem that he would stop payment on the money orders unless he received the tire. Miller stopped payment on the two money orders, parked the vehicle in front of his home, and advised Diem to pick up the vehicle.

The tire was not delivered with the vehicle when it was received by plaintiff from the manufacturer because of a national tire shortage due to a labor strike. When the tire arrived, a notice was sent to Miller informing him of the tire's arrival and requesting that he make an appointment for its mounting on the vehicle's spare wheel located in the vehicle. There was no dispute that Miller was entitled to five tires with the purchase of the car.

On the day Miller picked up the car, he executed an application for a Michigan title. Plaintiff made application to the Secretary of State for a new title, license plates and a certificate of registration in the name of the purchaser. After the parties executed the application for Michigan title, a temporary ten-day registration sticker was affixed to the vehicle. After the sticker had expired, the car was towed from in front of Miller's home by the St. Clair police department for storage in the Kuhn Bros. dealership in St. Clair. Defendant refused to accept the license plates when they were sent to him.

According to the trial court's opinion, the parties agreed that defendant Miller had made a valid acceptance of the station wagon under § 2606 of the Uniform Commercial Code (U.C.C.), M.C.L. § 440.2606; M.S.A. § 19.2606. Their dispute concerned whether Miller's revocation of acceptance was valid under M.C.L. § 440.2608; M.S.A. § 19.2608, the section providing that a buyer may revoke acceptance of a commercial unit where the nonconformity "substantially impairs its value to him."

The trial court noted, in interpreting this section of the code, that the court in *Fargo Machine & Tool Co. v. Kearney & Trecker Corp.*, 428 F.Supp. 364 (E.D. Mich., 1977), utilized a modified standard in determining substantial impairment by making it a factual question to be determined by objective evidence rather than the buyer's personal position. The trial court ruled that the missing spare tire did not substantially impair the value of a new automobile under either the objective or the subjective test in this case and that the defendant wrongfully revoked acceptance,....

In *Zabriskie Chevrolet, Inc. v. Smith*, 99 N.J.Super. 441, 240 A.2d 195 (1968), the automobile became inoperable 7/10 of a mile and minutes after leaving the dealer's showroom. The disposition of *Zabriskie* was premised on the finding that there was no acceptance. The facts in *Zabriskie* are clearly distinguishable on the basis that the car was inoperable; whereas here the sole nonconformity was the temporary absence of a spare tire due to a nationwide strike in the tire industry.

A buyer may properly revoke acceptance of a commercial unit where the nonconformity substantially impairs its value. The existence of such nonconformity depends on the facts and circumstances of each case. *Jorgensen v. Pressnall*, 274 Or. 285, 545 P.2d 1382 (1976). The determination of substantial impairment is made from an objective view or from the buyer's subjective view, considering the particular needs and circumstances. See White & Summers, Uniform Commercial Code (2d ed), § 8-3, p. 308, and M.C.L. § 440.2608, comment 2; M.S.A. § 19.2608, comment 2. The objective approach was utilized in *Fargo Machine & Tool Co.* In *Jorgensen*, both the objective and subjective tests were used in the determination.

The trial judge determined that the missing spare tire did not constitute a substantial impairment in value under either the subjective or objective test.

The purpose of the requirement of substantial impairment of value is to preclude revocation for trivial defects or defects which may be easily corrected. *Rozmus v. Thompson's Lincoln-Mercury Co.*, 209 Pa.Super. 120, 224 A.2d 782 (1966). [This case is in Volume I of these materials. Remember the misaligned drive shaft?]

The trial judge's determination that the temporarily missing spare tire did not constitute a substantial impairment in value under either the subjective or objective test was not clearly erroneous. We affirm the trial court's finding in that regard.

Having determined that Miller wrongfully revoked acceptance in this case, the trial court found that the vehicle could have been resold on or about September 1, 1976, for $1,000 less than the sales price to Miller, and, therefore, that this is the amount of damages plaintiff is entitled to recover....

The trial court stated that "an implied duty on the part of the seller arose to retain the property and hold it for resale." Miller stopped payment on the money orders, parked the vehicle in front of his home and advised plaintiff to pick up the vehicle. Plaintiff did not have a security interest or lien on the vehicle. The vehicle was registered and titled in Miller's name. Based on the record, plaintiff could not have transferred good title, contrary to the trial court's opinion.

M.C.L. § 440.2709; M.S.A. § 19.2709 provides:

> (1) When the buyer fails to pay the price as it becomes due the seller may recover, together with any incidental damages under the next section, the price ... (a) of goods accepted....

It is not disputed that plaintiff sold Miller a car for $5,697; that Miller paid for the car in full with two money orders; that Miller took delivery of the car; that Miller stopped payment on the money orders which were tendered in payment of the car; that Miller wrongfully revoked acceptance and breached his contract.

Because plaintiff is entitled to the full contract price of $5,697 for the vehicle purchased by Miller, the judgment of the trial court relating to damages is clearly erroneous and set aside, and plaintiff is awarded the contract price.

DEMING, JUDGE (dissenting).

I respectfully dissent....

I do not accept the finding by the trial court that Mr. Miller accepted the vehicle within the meaning of the Uniform Commercial Code. M.C.L. § 440.2606; M.S.A. § 19.2606. The parties certainly did not agree on this point and there is absolutely nothing in the record which would support such a finding.... Because acceptance is a term of art as it is used in the U.C.C., and because acceptance has broad legal ramifications, including the duty to pay for the goods, M.C.L. § 440.2607(1); M.S.A. § 19.2607(1), the finding of the trial court was clearly erroneous and should be reversed. As one notes, taking delivery is not acceptance, because the U.C.C. provides that the buyer has a reasonable time to inspect prior to accepting within the meaning of the code. M.C.L. § 440.2606(1)(a), (b); M.S.A. § 19.2606(1)(a), (b)....

The right to reject nonconforming goods prior to acceptance is nearly absolute. The U.C.C. plainly and unequivocally rejects the notion of substantial compliance by a seller, insisting on a rule of perfect tender. M.C.L. § 440.2601; M.S.A. § 19.2601. The U.C.C. limits the perfect tender rule only by express delineation found in §§ 2-612, M.C.L. § 440.2612; M.S.A. § 19.2612, pertaining to installment contracts and §§ 2-718, M.C.L. § 440.2718; M.S.A. § 19.2718, and 2-719, M.C.L. § 440.2719; M.S.A. § 19.2719, which allow contractual limitations on remedies.

In some cases, the U.C.C. also limits a buyer's right to reject for nonconformity. Section 2-508, M.C.L. § 440.2508; M.S.A. 19.2508, gives the seller a right to cure the nonconforming defect. Here the buyer asked for, then demanded a cure, but was met with refusal, then a claim that cure was not possible because of a tire strike. The U.C.C. places the burden of cure on the seller, not the buyer, M.C.L. § 440.2508(1); M.C.L. § 19.2508(1). Failure to cure within a reasonable time is a risk of the seller, not the risk of the buyer. I conclude that this risk is one the plaintiff chose to take.

Since the majority opinion speaks to the matter of an acceptance, this I will address. If there has been an acceptance, it may be revoked for reasons found in § 2-608, M.C.L. § 440.2608; M.S.A. § 19.2608. At issue is whether the missing spare tire constituted a substantial impairment to the value of the automobile. The majority cites *Rozmus v. Thompson's Lincoln-Mercury Co.*, 209 Pa.Super. 120, 224 A.2d 782 (1966), for the proposition that § 2-608 precludes revocation after acceptance for trivial matters that are easily corrected. I accept that as a valid statement of the law, however, in this case, the missing tire was not trivial or unimportant to defendant Miller. The dealer had specific knowledge of the buyer's requirement of a spare tire, and a specific good was ordered. Therefore, the lack of such tire was not trivial.

Functional tires, including an adequate spare, are an integral part of the safety equipment of every automobile purchased, anywhere. As I pointed out in my original opinion, one would be foolish or suicidal, in light of recent events on Detroit area expressways, to venture forth in an improperly equipped automobile....

Also at issue is the propriety of defendant's rejection. M.C.L. § 440.2602; M.S.A. § 19.2602 requires a nonmerchant buyer who has rightfully rejected goods to inform the seller of the fact of rejection. Thereafter, the buyer has no further obligation to goods rightfully rejected. M.C.L. § 440.2602(2)(c); M.S.A. § 19.2602(2)(c). The duty of the seller to remove or repossess the nonconforming goods is universally recognized.... I find that defendant's method of notice, the telephone, was appropriate under these circumstances. There is no dispute concerning the unequivocal nature of Mr. Miller's rejection of the automobile or the reason for the rejection. Moreover, there is no doubt that Mr. Miller did not use the car after he told the plaintiff's agent to come and pick it up. The cases holding that oral notice is not sufficient are not applicable here.... Rather, I would opt for the U.C.C. rule that any notice must be "reasonable" — a notice that reasonably tells the seller of the fact of rejection and the reason therefor....

I would hold that if there was an acceptance, and I think that there was not, then Miller's rejection was both appropriate and timely....

The majority concludes that the plaintiff-seller is entitled to the full purchase price of the automobile. This result is not only unconscionable on these facts but wrong as a matter of law. It was the seller who breached the contract. It has no right to damages whatsoever on its own breach because the law gives it no such right, absent a wrongful rejection on the part of the buyer....

I would reverse.

NOTES AND QUESTIONS

1. *Reaching a "fair" result*: Why did the court change its view on rehearing? In the second opinion, the court notes that Colonial Dodge's salesman "was under stress due to the serious surgery his wife was about to undergo." It also points out that the salesman offered his own spare tire which turned out to be the wrong size. Furthermore, the dealer had an understandable reason for delivering a car without a spare tire. Why is this information relevant to the buyer's rights under § 2-608? Suppose the salesman's tire had been the right size; would Miller have been obligated to accept it?

2. *Rejecting seller's tender when offered*: Suppose the buyer had noticed the lack of a spare tire before he took possession of the car and had refused to accept

delivery. Would the result have been different? If so, why? Would the legal standard be the same or different?

3. *Violence on the Detroit freeways*: Judge Deming thinks that "one would be foolish or suicidal, in light of recent events on Detroit area expressways, to venture forth in an improperly equipped automobile." Suppose the buyer had a spare tire. Would the risk of changing it by the side of the Detroit freeway be significantly less than the risk of waiting in the car for help or walking to a telephone or service station? How do we know?

4. *Subjective or objective defects*: If the buyer's lawyer could not rely on judicial notice of the "violent crime" on Detroit area freeways, what evidence might she or he offer to show that the lack of a spare tire substantially impaired the value of the car to the buyer? Suppose a reasonable person would not be afraid to drive those freeways without a spare tire but the buyer was in fact afraid to drive them without one. The final opinion in the case talks of some mixture of an objective and a subjective test. How can these tests be mixed? Is there language in the statute itself which warrants the use of a subject standard?

5. *Reasons for litigation*: Why did the dealer resist the buyers' claims? Usually reliable sources tell us that Chrysler Corporation urged Colonial Dodge, Inc. to fight, and the Chrysler legal staff participated in the litigation and appeals. Chrysler's officials thought that the Millers must have known that their car would be delivered without a spare tire. The Detroit newspapers and television gave great coverage to the tire workers' strike and the automobile industry's response to it. Newspapers and television reports discussed the industry's decision to deliver new cars with only four tires and a promise to deliver another when the strike ended. Moreover, Colonial Dodge tried to show that the car had been driven over 400 miles before the Millers called to complain.

Both Chrysler and Colonial Dodge officials saw the Millers' reasons for revoking acceptance as a mere pretext. Suppose Chrysler and Colonial Dodge could show that another Dodge dealer had offered Mr. Miller a similar Dodge station wagon at a lower price? Suppose they could show that the Millers could not afford to make the monthly payments on the station wagon and only realized this after they had promised to buy the car? Should a court insist that a seller resisting a revocation of acceptance prove some bad faith reason for trying to back out? In other words, to what extent does § 2-608 reflect ideas about good faith in settling contract disputes? Is the section related to the tort of bad faith settlement of disputes found in insurance cases such as *Davis v. Allstate*, *supra*?

6. *The last chapter in the story*: The Supreme Court of Michigan, by a four-to-three vote, reversed the Court of Appeals in *Colonial Dodge, Inc. v. Miller*, 420 Mich. 452, 362 N.W.2d 704 (1985). The Supreme Court first said "[w]e are not persuaded that, had the matter been contested in the trial court, a finding of acceptance would be warranted on this record. However, since defendant did not submit the question to the trial judge, but in effect stipulated to acceptance, we will treat the matter as though there was acceptance." It then found that the

failure to include the spare tire was a substantial impairment in value to Mr. Miller, and so he could properly revoke his acceptance. The court noted,

> The defendant's occupation demanded that he travel extensively, sometimes in excess of 150 miles per day on Detroit freeways, and often in the early morning hours. Mr. Miller testified that he was afraid of a tire going flat on a Detroit freeway at 3 a.m. Without a spare, he testified, he would be helpless until morning business hours. The dangers attendant upon a stranded motorist are common knowledge, and Mr. Miller's fears are not unreasonable.

The dissent argued that the impairment of value must be substantial. "It is not sufficient that the nonconformance be worrisome, aggravating, or even potentially dangerous. It must be a nonconformity which diminishes the value of the goods to the buyer to a substantial degree." It found the possibility of Mr. Miller being stranded in an unsafe area to be unlikely. Moreover, it was a temporary deficiency easily remedied.

The National Law Journal[16] reported that the 1976 Dodge station wagon had logged less than 400 miles when the Millers attempted to call off the transaction. Mr. Miller parked the car in front of his house and told the dealer to pick it up, the dealer refused, and the police towed the car to another dealership. Either the police or this second dealer placed the car in storage where it remained for nine years pending the course of the litigation. Miller's lawyer said that it was uncertain who would pay for the nine-year storage bill. Title remained in Mr. Miller's name.

We have no way of judging the merits of the Millers' claim. However, Chrysler's and Colonial Dodge's reading of the situation is a possible one. What does this suggest about the practical impact of the Code's legal standard?

7. *Drafting to limit the right of inspection*: Suppose that Colonial Dodge's form sales contract provided that "Buyer acknowledges that, by signing this document, they have accepted delivery of the car. The Buyer is encouraged to take some time to test drive the vehicle, and to inspect it, before executing this document." Would such a provision, coupled with actually encouraging buyers to test drive the car before signing the form, make a difference?

Sellers may sometimes want to limit their buyers' rights to inspect so that they can be sure when a deal is completed. Section 2-513(1) operates "unless otherwise agreed...." Furthermore, subsection (4) allows the contract to specify the "place or method of inspection," subject to adjustment in some circumstances "if compliance becomes impossible." See Official Comments 1, 6 and 7. All such provisions are regulated by § 1-102(3), an important and often overlooked statute. It provides that "the obligations of good faith, diligence, reasonableness

---

[16]National Law Journal, February 11, 1985.

and care prescribed by this Act may not be disclaimed by agreement but the parties may by agreement determine the standards by which the performance of such obligations is to be measured if such standards are not manifestly unreasonable." We can assume, for example, that if a seller's form stated that a short time for inspection began running when it shipped the goods rather than when buyer received them, such a clause might be challenged under § 1-102(3) as an attempt to trick buyers. Such attempts at trickery are used by some sellers. You should always check when time limitations begin when you review contracts.

8. *Giving the U.C.C. a bad name:* This is the kind of case that may cause lawyers, judges, law students, and law professors nervously to examine their nails when asked to explain. The facts seem so simple. Things like this must happen every day. Why is the legal analysis so complicated, and not only that, but so uncertain? Don't you imagine that Mr. Miller, and the folks at Colonial Dodge, were surprised to learn that it would take a trial and three appellate court decisions to decide the question, and that all of that legal analysis would yield nothing even approaching a consensus? Is it indefensible? Or just hard to understand and explain?

c. Cooperation and Good Faith

Section 1-203 is certainly one of the most elegant, and shortest, sections of the Uniform Commercial Code. It provides that, "Every contract or duty within this Act imposes an obligation of good faith in its performance or enforcement." We have encountered some cases in which it seems that this section could have been used to explain a result, since the policy and spirit of a duty of good faith and cooperation seemed central to a court's concern. One thinks of the case of *Bethlehem Steel Corp. v. Litton Industries, Inc., supra,* in which Bethlehem's failure to pursue negotiations with Litton with respect to the option seemed to concern the court, since that delay was arguably tactical, and certainly had the effect of putting Litton in a very difficult situation with respect to the decision to close, or keep open, its shipbuilding facilities. Would a failure to act in good faith been a more convincing ground for decision in *Bethlehem Steel* than the court's rationale, which is that the contract was insufficiently definite?

Increasingly, lawyers and the courts have utilized § 1-203 as the ground for decision, or have at least mentioned it as an alternative ground. In *Conoco, Inc. v. Inman Oil Co., Inc.,*[17] Conoco was found to have breached its implied obligation of good faith to one of its distributors. Inman Oil Co. obtained most of the products it sold from Sinclair Oil Co. and Shell Oil Co. from 1967 to 1972. St. Joe Minerals Corp., a lead mining company, was one of its major customers. Conoco had been unable to sell products to St. Joe Minerals. Conoco

---

[17]774 F.2d 895 (1985).

and Inman held a series of meetings in 1972. Their officials agreed to cooperate in Conoco's attempt to persuade St. Joe to switch from Sinclair products to Conoco products to be supplied by Inman as a distributor. The effort was successful, and there were no problems until 1980.

Conoco operates through two divisions. Conoco Wholesale and Commercial Operations (WCO) sells petroleum products directly to large commercial and industrial users. Conoco Branded Division sells to distributors such as Inman. In 1981, WCO decided to bid directly on the St. Joe Minerals account and bypass Inman Oil. It was successful. The loss of the lucrative, long-time St. Joe account was a significant factor in Inman Oil going out of business in 1982.

The Court of Appeals reversed the finding that Conoco had acted in good faith. It found the relationship governed by the U.C.C. It said,

> Conoco had earlier obtained St. Joe as an indirect Branded Division customer through the efforts and good will of Inman Oil. On the basis of its long-standing relationship with and confidence in Inman Oil, St. Joe had agreed to transfer much of its business from Sinclair to Conoco. However, Conoco evidently felt no obligation to repay this substantial favor by continuing to channel its St. Joe business through Inman Oil. Moreover, having acquired St. Joe as a direct customer [by submitting bids below its jobber price quotations], Conoco then refused to permit Inman Oil to serve as the delivery agent ...

The Court of Appeals remanded the case, directing a federal magistrate to find Inman Oil's damages as a result of Conoco's direct bids on the St. Joe account.

In another case, *Admiral Plastics Corp. v. Trueblood, Inc.*,[18] the 6th Circuit affirmed a decision of the trial court which had found that each party to a contract to build an injection molding machine had been guilty of a failure to act in good faith and a failure to cooperate. The result was that the contract was held to be void, and the buyer was entitled only to the return of its down payment. While the court did cite § 1-203, it also found that the parties had been guilty of mutual breaches of the contract. The court found that the Code does not provide remedies for mutual breach, which permitted the court to utilize § 1-103 (which incorporates non-preempted principles of law and equity) to gain access to the common law of Ohio. The rule in Ohio was that mutual delinquency creates a presumption of rescission. The court found that, in this case, the behavior of the parties was consistent with a mutual intention to rescind.

Why did the court feel the need to provide the alternative ground of mutual rescission, in addition to the finding of a violation of the duty of good faith? The court talks about a duty of good faith and cooperation. Are these words synonymous? Is there a duty of good faith, and a separate duty of cooperation?

---

[18] 436 F.2d 1335 (6th Cir. 1971).

Does it matter? Are both present in every contract? Do you believe that they provide meaningful standards against which to measure performance? Which interest groups would you expect to lobby for and against the inclusion, of a Code section providing for a duty of good faith? Are terms like "good faith" and "cooperation" good candidates for terms setting norms for commercial behavior? Some would question whether they would provide the certainty that those in commerce might like. Others would argue that the certainty provided by other terms is illusory, and that "good faith" and "cooperation" are exactly the terms that express the ideas which should be at the root of commercial and personal obligation. What do you think?

d. Notice: Section 2-607(3)(a) — and a Note on § 2-608(2)

The next case is an interesting, and instructive one. It raises several issues in addition to that involving the application of § 2-607(3). We say this only to alert you that we will return to the Eastern — McDonnell Douglas dispute later in these materials.[19]

EASTERN AIR LINES, INC. v. MCDONNELL DOUGLAS CORP.

532 F.2d 957 (5th Cir. 1976)

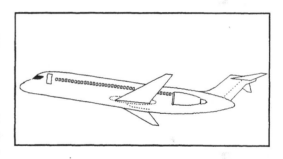

AINSWORTH, J. This important Florida diversity case involves an appeal from a judgment for damages for breach of contract in favor of Eastern Air Lines against McDonnell Douglas Aircraft, Inc. based on a jury verdict in Eastern's favor for the sum of $24,552,659.11 plus costs of $241,149.02 — one of the largest jury verdicts ever reviewed by this Court. Involved is a series of contracts covering the years 1965-1968 by which Douglas Aircraft, Inc. agreed to manufacture and sell to Eastern Air Lines nearly 100 jet planes for approximately a half billion dollars. Suit was filed by Eastern against Douglas on July 31, 1970, based on allegations that 90 of these planes were delivered a total of 7,426 days late. It was not until July 12, 1973, after almost three years of pretrial motions and discovery and four and one-half months of trial, that the jury's verdict was rendered in the District Court.

Our review of the case convinces us that the District Court made a diligent effort to resolve the many difficult matters before it. Nevertheless, we conclude that the trial judge committed substantial and prejudicial errors in a number of

---

[19]In connection with construing the impossibility clause in the contract.

his rulings and instructions to the jury, which require reversal of the judgment and a new trial. Accordingly, we reverse and remand.

I. *Background*

Eastern Air Lines decided in 1964 to replace what remained of its outmoded propeller-driven fleet in an effort to reverse a serious five-year financial decline. Ever since the advent of the commercial jet age in 1959, Eastern had lagged behind its competitors in the purchase of jet-powered planes. Consequently, the company's decision to order 100 new planes made it the last major trunk carrier to purchase a large number of jet aircraft.

Although Eastern is one of the largest passenger carriers in the world, its route system has historically been composed of relatively short segments. In 1964, only Boeing and Douglas could offer a small, twin-engine, short-range jet suited to Eastern's needs. Eastern's decision to purchase the Douglas DC-9 rather than Boeing's 737 was based in part on Douglas' offer to lease it a number of DC-9-14's as an interim plane until the larger "stretched" DC-9-31's were available. Boeing had been unable to provide Eastern with an equivalent aircraft as a substitute for its short-haul, twin-engine 737 which was not due to be delivered until a year after Douglas was to begin producing the DC-9-31. For its longer range flights, Eastern also ordered a number of DC-8-61 jets which are Douglas' equivalent of the Boeing 707.

Letters of intent providing for Eastern's lease or purchase of DC-9-14's and for its purchase of the "stretched" DC-9-31 and the DC-8 planes were signed in February of 1965. The following July, Douglas and Eastern entered into the first three of what was to be a series of eight contracts providing for the delivery of a total of 99 planes. Five of the eight contracts were amended, some a number of times, between 1965 and 1968.

Although varying in details, all the agreements are basically similar; each required Douglas to manufacture a number of planes at a stipulated price per aircraft to be paid upon the delivery of each plane at Douglas' California plant. Each jet was designated for delivery during a particular calendar month. In addition, every contract contained two provisions which are of special importance to these appeals. One clause is a choice of law provision which requires that the contracts' construction and performance be determined under California law. The other provision is an "excusable delay" clause which exempts Douglas from liability for delays beyond its control and not its fault.

Problems developed in the Douglas-Eastern relationship before even the first plane was scheduled to be delivered. In January 1966, it became evident to both parties that Douglas would be unable to complete its DC-9-14 jets in time to meet the contract delivery dates. In an early exchange of letters on the subject, Douglas attributed the delivery delays to "our nation's rapidly increasing commitments in Southeast Asia," and Eastern replied by expressing concern and noting that "[i]t appears to us that some of this slippage really should have been avoidable."

Subsequently it appeared that the delays could not be confined to the DC-9-14 deliveries. During 1966 and 1967, Douglas repeatedly revised its scheduled delivery of DC-8's and DC-9-31's. These further delays were viewed with "great concern" by Eastern executives who informed Douglas that the late deliveries were imposing a "substantial burden" on the airline.

Throughout this period, Douglas was confronted with a mounting financial crisis which, to some extent, was the result of the DC-8 and DC-9 delivery delays. In the summer of 1966, Douglas forecast a loss of almost $30 million in its operations for the year. By November, Douglas' cash shortage reached such catastrophic proportions that the company's creditors insisted that a solvent merger partner be found. The natural choice was the McDonnell Aircraft Company whose military and space activities effectively complemented Douglas' strength in the commercial aircraft field. After McDonnell infused into Douglas over $68 million in new funds, a merger was consummated on April 28, 1967. The new McDonnell Douglas Corporation assumed all the obligations and liabilities of the former Douglas Aircraft Company.

Delivery delays continued after the merger until the last of the planes was delivered in January 1969. On the average, each of the 90 late planes was delivered 80 days after the month specified in the contract date. Several months after performance had been completed under the last of the eight contracts, Eastern wrote McDonnell on May 29, 1969 presenting a claim for damages resulting from the late deliveries over the previous three years. The airline alleged that these delays could not be deemed excusable under the applicable clause in the agreements. McDonnell rejected the claim and suit was filed in the District Court for the Southern District of Florida.

On the order of the District Judge, the trial was bifurcated with the liability phase to be tried first; to be followed, if necessary, by a trial on damages before the same jury. The greater part of the three-month liability trial was devoted to McDonnell's efforts to prove that the delivery delays were the product of events covered by the excusable delay clause in each contract. [The court's discussion of the excusable delay issue will be discussed in the final chapter of this book.]

McDonnell Douglas also contended that Eastern had failed to give timely and reasonable notice of the breaches, that one of the contracts was no longer enforceable, and that Eastern should be estopped from pursuing any of its claims. The District Court, however, ruled against McDonnell on all these issues.

At the close of the liability trial, the jury was instructed that McDonnell bore the burden of proving that the delays were caused by events which were excused under the contracts. Furthermore, according to the court's instructions, no event could be an excuse unless it was not reasonably foreseeable at the time the particular contract was entered into. On May 16, 1973, the jury's verdict, in the form of answers to special interrogatories, found that none of the 7,426 days of delay was excusable....

In its appeal, McDonnell Douglas' most fundamental contentions concern the District Court's rulings on excusable delay, Eastern's obligation to give reasonable and timely notice of breach, and the enforceability of one of the contracts....

III. *Notice of Breach Under the Uniform Commercial Code*

During the trial and in final instructions to the jury, the District Court held that Eastern need not prove, as a predicate for recovery in this suit, that it had given McDonnell Douglas reasonable and timely notice of the delivery delays. McDonnell strongly contests the trial judge's rulings for Eastern on this issue and argues either that the airline should, as a matter of law, be barred from any recovery or, alternatively, that the issue of timely notice should have been submitted to the jury.

The statute governing this question is § 2-607(3)(a) of the Uniform Commercial Code which provides in part as follows:

(3) Where a tender has been accepted

    (a) the buyer must within a reasonable time after he discovers or should have discovered any breach notify the seller of breach or be barred from any remedy;

... McDonnell contends that the trial judge denied it the benefits of this provision, both by ruling that § 2-607 does not apply to late deliveries and by holding in the alternative that Eastern gave adequate notice. Because we are unable to agree with the District Court's ruling on either ground, we hold that the question of timely notice under § 2-607 should have been submitted to the jury.

A. *Applicability of U.C.C. § 2-607(3)(a)*

Even though § 2-607, by its very terms, governs "any breach," the trial court found the notice requirement to be inapplicable to delivery delays because a seller necessarily has knowledge of this sort of contract violation. Relying on the case of *Jay V. Zimmerman Company v. General Mills, Inc.*, E.D.Mo., 1971, 327 F.Supp. 1198, 1204, the District Judge concluded that notice is useless where a breach is apparent to both parties.[20] The trial court apparently was of the view

---

[20] In relevant part, the Zimmerman opinion reads as follows:

    In the present, as in any case involving late delivery, both the seller and the buyer are necessarily fully aware *prior* to tender that the seller's contract obligation to timely deliver has not been complied with. It would be an unreasonable, if not absurd, construction of the statute to require a renewed notice of breach *after* acceptance of the goods under the facts

that the sole function of § 2-607 is to inform the seller of hidden defects in his performance. Under this approach, the only purpose of notice is to provide the seller with an opportunity to remedy an otherwise unknown nonconforming tender....

Section 2-607's origins, however, reveal that it has a much broader function. The Code's notice requirement was derived from decisional law in California and several other states which sought to ameliorate the harsh common law rule that acceptance of goods by the buyer waived any and all of his remedies.... This approach was codified under § 49 of the Uniform Sales Act which was adopted in California as Civ.Code § 1769.

... Pre-U.C.C. decisions in California and elsewhere, therefore, recognized that the primary purpose of notice is to inform the seller that, even though his tender has been accepted by the buyer, his performance is nonetheless considered a breach of contract.

Under § 49 it was irrelevant whether a seller had actual knowledge of a non-conforming tender. Instead, the critical question was whether the seller had been informed that the buyer considered him to be in breach. Consequently, in Professor Williston's words, "the section is applicable not only to defects in quality but to breach of any promise or warranty, as, for instance, *delay in time*." 5 S. Williston, Contracts § 714 at 409 (3d ed. 1961) (emphasis supplied).
...

As the drafters of Article 2 acknowledge, § 2-607 continues the basic policies underlying § 49 of the Uniform Sales Act. Indeed, the notice requirement developed in pre-U.C.C. cases is entirely consistent with the Article 2 goals of encouraging compromise and promoting good faith in commercial relations. As Comment 4 to § 2-607 indicates, the purpose of notice is not merely to inform the seller that his tender is nonconforming, but to open the way for settlement through negotiation between the parties. In the words of the California Supreme Court, "the sound commercial rule" codified in § 2-607 also requires that a seller be reasonably protected against stale claims arising out of transactions which a buyer has led him to believe were closed. *Pollard v. Saxe & Yolles Development Company*, 1974, 12 Cal.3d 374, 115 Cal.Rptr. 648, 525 P.2d 88.... Early

---

here involved. A party has notice of a fact when he has actual knowledge of it. Section ... 1-201(25) of the Uniform Commercial Code. The purpose of a notice in the context of this section ... is to *inform* the seller of matters which would not normally come to the buyer's attention until *after* the goods came into his possession. The legislative intent was to make provision with respect to the effect of acceptance of allegedly defective or inferior goods or those allegedly not meeting warranted standards of quality. In that situation it is reasonable to require the buyer to inform the seller of the existence of a possible factual dispute relating to matters of which the buyer presumably was not aware prior to his acceptance of a tender of the goods.

Jay V. Zimmerman Company v. General Mills, Inc., E.D.Mo., 1971, 327 F.Supp. 1198, 1204 (emphasis in original).

warning permits the seller to investigate the claim while the facts are fresh, avoid the defect in the future, minimize his damages, or perhaps assert a timely claim of his own against third parties....

Given these undeniable purposes, it is not enough under § 2-607 that a seller has knowledge of the facts constituting a non-conforming tender; he must also be informed that the buyer considers him to be in breach of the contract. The Code's notice requirement, then, is applicable to delivery delays as well as other breaches.... Accordingly, we decline to follow the reasoning of the *Zimmerman* decision, and we find that the trial court erred in not applying § 2-607 to the delivery delays at issue in this case.

B. *Adequate Notice Under § 2-607(3)(a)*

Turning next to the lower court's alternative rationale for ruling against McDonnell on the issue, we must determine whether the notice given by Eastern was both sufficient and timely as a matter of law. Finding the facts "essentially uncontradicted," the trial court concluded that Eastern adequately informed McDonnell that it considered the delivery delays to be an actionable breach:

> Eastern's management repeatedly protested the delays and requested negotiation of the dispute, but they were always put off by McDonnell Douglas with the assurance that the matter would be taken up once the assembly line was back on schedule. When production was again on-line many months later it became obvious to Eastern that no good-faith settlement negotiations would take place.

Because the court's ruling was, in effect, a directed verdict, it can be sustained only if there is no conflict in substantial evidence and the inferences from these facts "point so strongly and overwhelmingly" in favor of Eastern that reasonable men could not have arrived at a contrary verdict.... As will be demonstrated below, the adequacy and timeliness of notice under § 2-607 typically depend upon the reasonableness of the buyer's efforts to communicate his dissatisfaction.... Therefore, whether the notice requirement has been complied with is a question which is particularly within the province of the jury.... Applying this standard of review to the facts, we find that there was at least one substantial factual dispute before the court and that the trial judge's interpretation of the facts in the case was not the only reasonable inference that could be drawn from them. We, therefore, reverse on this issue as well. We do not agree, however, with McDonnell's contention that, as a matter of law, Eastern's notice was inadequate and untimely.

As we have seen, the contractual relationship between Douglas and Eastern stretched over a number of years and was governed by a series of separate agreements, several of which were amended a number of times. The complexity of these agreements and the large number of planes involved required the parties to be in constant communication with each other. Indeed, throughout this period, Eastern was informed of all significant developments by one of its own engineers who was in residence at the Douglas plant. Eastern, therefore, often knew of anticipated delivery delays before being formally informed of them by Douglas.

Eastern's first formal response to [four notifications of additional delays, sent to Eastern between October 1966 and September 1967] came on October 6, 1967. This letter informed McDonnell that "the delays in aircraft delivery have been very expensive to Eastern Airlines and we must view continuing slippage with great concern." Eastern went on to state that

> the delivery delays have cost Eastern so heavily that it would now appear that we made a mistake in going the DC-9 and DC-8-61 routes. Terms that were offered to us by another manufacturer would have been far less costly and although all aircraft manufacturers have suffered to some degree from common problems, it is apparent that the delivery schedule offered to us by your competitors have been more realistic than those attained by Douglas.... The delivery record of your current series of aircraft must necessarily be taken into account as we evaluate the purchase of the next series of airplanes. Unless there is concrete evidence that we can expect the DC-10 to be delivered in accordance with schedules offered by Douglas, it will be very difficult for us to decide in favor of your product as compared with that of another manufacturer.

On November 7, 1968, Eastern's Chief Financial Officer, Mr. Simons, wrote McDonnell Douglas asking that every effort be made to deliver several planes on schedule because a delay during the peak holiday season would place "a substantial burden on Eastern which is more severe than that imposed on your other customers."

There were no further significant written communications from Eastern until May 29, 1969 when McDonnell was formally presented with a claim for damages....

In addition to this undisputed documentary evidence, the District Court had before it testimony concerning Eastern's attitude toward the delivery delays. Eastern's Chairman, Floyd Hall, testified that he "talked with almost every one of the top officials [of Douglas and then of McDonnell Douglas] at one time or another.... [E]very time I met them I reminded them of the late delivery of their aircraft." W. Glenn Harlan, Eastern's Senior Vice President of Legal Affairs, also testified that he refused Douglas' request to waive the airline's claims concerning the late deliveries.

The record, however, also contains testimony that Eastern informed McDonnell executives that it did not intend to make a claim for the late deliveries. James S. McDonnell, Chairman of McDonnell Douglas, testified that, as late as October 1968, Eastern's President, Arthur Lewis, assured him that no damages would be sought. Another McDonnell executive, Jackson R. McGowan, also testified that Eastern's Chairman, Floyd Hall, told him that no legal action was contemplated. These allegations were denied by Eastern's witnesses.

Eastern contends that these facts are more than sufficient to constitute adequate notice as a matter of law. The Code, in Eastern's view, does not require the buyer to inform the seller that he is presenting a claim under the contract. This contention is based on Comment No. 4 to § 2-607 which states, in part, that "[t]he content of the notification need merely be sufficient to let the seller know that the transaction is still troublesome and must be watched." Eighth Circuit decisions and at least one commentary have relied on this sentence from Comment No. 4 for the proposition that almost any indication of dissatisfaction on the buyer's part meets the requirements of § 2-607. Under this standard, there would be little doubt that Eastern's letters concerning the delays constituted sufficient notice under the U.C.C.

It appears that Comment No. 4 was aimed at remedying a rule adopted under § 49 of the Uniform Sales Act by some courts that a mere complaint of a breach was not adequate notice....

These technical requirements were dispensed with because they frequently served to deny an uninformed consumer of what was otherwise a valid claim. As is noted in the draftsmen's comments, "the rule of requiring notification is designed to defeat commercial bad faith, not to deprive a good faith consumer of his remedy."[21] Eastern is therefore correct in asserting that notice under § 2-607 need not be a specific claim for damages or an assertion of legal rights....

However, the fact that the Code has eliminated the technical rigors of the notice requirement under the Uniform Sales Act does not require the conclusion that any expression of discontent by a buyer always satisfies § 2-607. As Comment 4 indicates, a buyer's conduct under § 2-607 must satisfy the Code's standard of commercial good faith. Thus, while the buyer must inform the seller that the transaction is "still troublesome," Comment 4 also requires that the notification "be such as informs the seller that the transaction is claimed to involve a breach, and thus opens the way for normal settlement through negotiation."

In arguing that these requirements have been complied with, Eastern cannot rely on the same minimal standards of notice developed for ordinary consumers. The measure of good faith required under the Code varies with a buyer's commercial status. Unlike an ordinary purchaser, a merchant's good faith is measured by "reasonable commercial standards of fair dealing in the trade." Therefore, as the comments to § 2-607 indicate, what constitutes adequate notice from an inexperienced consumer may not be sufficient in a transaction between professionals...

We note, moreover, that the trial judge's rationale for ruling against McDonnell on the notice issue appears to have been based on a single letter

---

[21]Uniform Commercial Code § 2-607, Comment 4.

written by Douglas in response to Eastern's March 15, 1966 request for aid in reducing its "pre-inauguration activities." In his post-trial memorandum, the District Judge appeared to infer a waiver of Douglas' right to notification concerning any future breaches from its request that this aid be postponed. In our view, though, the March 15 letter from Eastern does not constitute adequate notice as a matter of law. Indeed, a close reading of the communication reveals that Eastern's primary concern was the lack of early notification of impending delivery delays rather than the validity of Douglas' contention that these delays were the product of the Vietnam War. Although Eastern expressed the view that some of the delays should have been avoided, it requested merely that Douglas help to mitigate the delays' impact upon Eastern's operations. A jury, therefore, might reasonably infer from this correspondence that Eastern was not claiming a breach of the particular contract involved.

More importantly, the District Court's reliance on these two particular letters evidences a failure to recognize that the buyer's good faith is the governing criterion under § 2-607. As we have seen, the Code's draftsmen disposed of rigid technical requirements which would frustrate the notice requirement's design of defeating commercial bad faith. Therefore, the fact that dissatisfaction may once have been communicated to the seller should not preclude an inquiry into the buyer's good faith as evidenced by his entire course of conduct.... Even though adequate notice may have been given at one point in the transaction, subsequent actions by the buyer may have dissipated its effect. The buyer's conduct, then, taken as a whole, must constitute timely notification that the transaction is claimed to involve a breach.

It is particularly important in continuing contractual relationships — such as the one which bound Eastern and McDonnell Douglas together for almost four years — that all of a buyer's dealings with a seller be evaluated under the good faith standard. An overly mechanical application of the notice requirement to complex or ongoing agreements would frequently frustrate the § 2-607 design of defeating commercial bad faith.

Reviewing Eastern's entire course of conduct during the years 1965-1969, and recognizing that Eastern must be held to a higher standard of good faith than an ordinary consumer, we conclude that a jury could reasonably find, as one of its options, that adequate notice was not given. In analyzing the record before us ... we give McDonnell the benefit of every reasonable inference.

We note first that even Eastern's most strongly worded communications can reasonably be construed as an effort to prod McDonnell Douglas into minimizing the Vietnam War's impact upon production rather than as a claim for breach. As we have seen, Eastern's March 15, 1966 letter to Douglas — perhaps its single most forceful expression of dissatisfaction — can be viewed as a request for aid in minimizing the impact of the delays rather than an assertion that Douglas had violated the contract.

Eastern, moreover, did not dispute McDonnell Douglas' contention that the delays were caused by the Vietnam War until the airline presented its formal claim for damages in 1969. Indeed, throughout the life of all the contracts, Eastern was advising its shareholders, the public, and, in sworn testimony, the Federal Government, that war-related defense priorities were causing the delivery delays. Inasmuch as the "excusable delay" clause found in all the contracts provides that the "[s]eller shall not be ... deemed to be in default" on account of delays caused by "governmental priorities," Eastern may well have led McDonnell to believe that it was not in breach of the agreements.

We disagree with Eastern's contention that it "had no choice but to accept what Douglas was saying as the truth." Eastern was in constant communication with its own engineer who was in residence at the Douglas plant throughout this period. Furthermore, Eastern and, indeed, the entire aviation industry were aware that Douglas' catastrophic financial crisis was, to some degree, precipitated by internal management difficulties. As early as the summer of 1966, therefore, Eastern had ample opportunity to assert then, as it does now, that the delivery delays were caused by internal problems rather than the Vietnam War. It failed to do so.

Eastern's commercial good faith is subject to further challenge because it continued to negotiate new contracts and amend old ones throughout the period in which the delays occurred. Two of the agreements, in fact, were executed in October of 1967 after 44 of the planes were already late. At no time during the negotiation and execution of any of these contracts did Eastern seek a settlement of its claims or even dispute McDonnell's Vietnam excuse. This may very well have led McDonnell to believe that, even though Eastern was unhappy about the delays, it did not consider them to be a breach of the contract

In addition to supporting the inference that adequate notice was not given, the record reveals a conflict in the evidence which ... is sufficiently substantial to preclude a directed verdict for Eastern. As we have seen, both Mr. McDonnell and Mr. McGowan testified that Eastern's management had assured them that no damages would be sought because of the delivery delays. Eastern's witnesses disputed this contention. If such assurances were in fact given, Eastern's conduct may well have violated the requirements of commercial good faith. This conflict alone, then, is sufficient to render the question of notice an issue for the jury.

The evidence reflected in the record, however, is also insufficient to support a directed verdict in favor of McDonnell Douglas on the issue of notice. There was no evidence at trial concerning the "reasonable standards of fair dealing" in the commercial aviation industry. We, therefore, cannot determine whether Eastern's conduct failed to satisfy contemporary standards of commercial good faith. Additionally, the conflict in evidence described above, the testimony that Eastern in several instances refused to waive its legal rights and the dissatisfaction with the delays evident in several of the airline's communications with McDonnell, are sufficient to create a jury question. In conclusion, therefore, the issue of notice under U.C.C. § 2-607 should have been submitted to the jury with instructions that it determine whether Eastern's conduct throughout the life of the contracts constituted adequate and timely notice to McDonnell that it was considered to be in breach of the contracts.... [to be continued ...]

NOTES AND QUESTIONS

1. *The Fifth Circuit elaborates on Eastern Airlines:* The United States Court of Appeals for the Fifth Circuit explained its *Eastern Airlines* decision in *T.J. Stevenson & Co. v. 81,193 Bags of Flour*. In a dispute concerning whether or not the nation of Bolivia had given an adequate 2-607(3)(a) notice of its objection to insect infested wheat flour it was buying, the Fifth Circuit re-affirmed and explained its decision in Eastern. Applying Illinois law, the court observed:

> ... Courts have disagreed in their interpretations of § 2-607(3)(a)'s notification requirement. A few decisions, largely from the Eighth Circuit and from Oregon, have held that the seller need only be informed that "the transaction is still troublesome and must be watched." And if the troublesome nature of the transaction is moreover apparent or already known to the seller, no notice at all is required. In *Eastern Air Lines, Inc. v. McDonnell Douglas Corp., supra,* however, this Court decided that for merchant buyers § 2-607(3)(a) requires something more than the minimal notification endorsed by those Courts. 532 F.2d at 970-80. We held that the dual policies of "encouraging compromise" and "promoting good faith in commercial relations," *id.* at 972, underlay the notice requirement of § 2-607(3)(a). Notice consequently must fulfill those policies; merely indicating that the transaction is troublesome is not enough. One way in which the policies are fulfilled is by notice informing the seller that the buyer regards the contract as breached by the seller, though specific legal rights need not be invoked. *Id.* at 973, 976.
>
> The *Eastern Air Lines* interpretation of § 2-607(3)(a) has been adopted by the vast majority of Courts which subsequently have considered the issue....
>
> *Eastern Air Lines* therefore teaches two concepts. First, the factfinder's determination of the mixed law-fact issue of notice, if based on a correct understanding of the law, is to be given great weight. Second, § 2-607(3)(a) notice must be evaluated from the perspective of the policies which it seeks to encourage: compromise by the parties; and conduct within the bounds of commercial good faith....

The court then proceeded to consider a number of communications between Bolivia and ADM Milling Co., the seller. The wheat flour itself had been shipped from Mobile, Alabama to Arica, Chile. Bolivia initially refused to allow the flour to be unloaded in Chile, but eventually allowed the unloading of the flour; it was eventually sold in Chile at reduced prices. The court concluded its discussion of the notice issue:

We find four aspects of the record which indicate that Bolivia gave proper notice *after* accepting the flour in Arica: (i) the fact that, as stated above, communications concerning the flour problems were ongoing; (ii) prior communications, including the September 25 telex, indicated Bolivia's staunch position with respect to live infestation; (iii) Bolivia's action in refusing to allow the flour to be discharged in Arica, an action consistent with a position that the contract had been breached; and (iv) Bolivia's October 24, 1974, telex stopping further letter of credit payments and asserting that the flour was contaminated when it left ADM's hands. From these facts and inferences, the District Judge was entitled to conclude that *Eastern Air Lines'* first policy of encouraging compromise was fulfilled, since ADM had full knowledge that the flour was infested and that Bolivia regarded live infestation as a breach of contract.

Similarly, the second policy of encouraging commercial good faith is fulfilled under the facts and permissible inferences of this case. Bolivia acted in good faith.... ADM acted less reasonably. For example, the speed with which ADM declared that it had delivered uninfested flour suggests a lack of actual investigation into the condition of its deliveries. That ADM made its declaration recklessly and possibly with knowledge different from that it represented is moreover suggested by its immediate fumigation of the warehouse flour (although ADM now claims that it took that step solely to promote good customer relations).

We therefore have a situation converse to that in *Eastern Air Lines*. In the instant case, there is a factfinding, not a directed verdict, of adequate notice based on all the evidence. The notice encouraged compromise, notwithstanding ADM's adamant refusal to even consider doing so. And the buyer acted in commercial good faith in contrast to the seller's questionable conduct — as compared to the reverse situation in *Eastern Air Lines*. We cannot say that the District Judge was wrong in finding that Bolivia gave adequate notice of breach to ADM under § 2-607(3)(a). Bolivia's claim for damages for the *Arizona* and *Southwall* flour is therefore not barred under the U.C.C.'s notice requirement.

The court went on to find that ADM was not entitled to raise Bolivia's failure to comply with a notice procedure outlined in the ADM contract, since ADM had effectively waived that condition in the course of dealing with Bolivia after the infestation was discovered.

2. *Section 2-607(3)(a) and "good faith"*: The Fifth Circuit stated in its *Eastern Airlines* opinion that:

The evidence reflected in the record ... is also insufficient to support a directed verdict in favor of McDonnell Douglas on the issue of notice. There was no evidence at trial concerning the "reasonable standards of fair dealing" in the commercial aviation industry. We, therefore, cannot determine whether Eastern's conduct failed to satisfy contemporary standards of commercial good faith. Additionally, the conflict in evidence described above, the testimony that Eastern in several instances refused to waive its legal rights, and the dissatisfaction with delays evident in several of the airline's communications with McDonnell are sufficient to create a jury question.

Section 2-607(3)(a) itself says nothing about good faith. Section 1-203, however, tells us that "[e]very contract or duty within this Act imposes an obligation of good faith in its performance or enforcement." Section 2-103(1)(b) defines "good faith" in Article II "in the case of a merchant" as "honest in fact and the observance of reasonable commercial standards of fair dealing in the trade."

Burton[22] says:

> Good faith limits the exercise of discretion in performance conferred on one party by the contract. When a discretion-exercising party may determine aspects of the contract such as quantity, price, or time, it controls the other's anticipated benefits. Such a party may deprive the other of these anticipated benefits for a legitimate (or good faith) reason. The same act will be a breach of the contract if undertaken for an illegitimate (or bad faith) reason. Therefore, the traditional focus on the benefits due the promisee is inadequate.
>
> Bad faith performance occurs precisely when discretion is used to recapture opportunities foregone upon contracting — when the discretion-exercising party refuses to pay the expected cost of performance. Good faith performance, in turn, occurs when a party's discretion is exercised for any purpose within the reasonable contemplation of the parties at the time of formation — to capture opportunities that were preserved upon entering the contract, interpreted objectively. The good faith performance doctrine therefore directs attention to the opportunities foregone by a discretion-exercising party at formation, and to that party's reasons for exercising discretion during performance.

Does Burton's suggestion aid in resolving the *Eastern Airlines* case? Does the Fifth Circuit's opinion help Eastern gain the benefit of its bargain? Does it protect McDonnell Douglas from liability for risks it did not assume?

3. *Proof of good or bad faith*: As the Fifth Circuit notes, the question of good faith never was submitted to the jury in the *Eastern Airlines* case. For teaching purposes, we can sketch the situation based on reports in business publications

---

[22]Burton, Breach of Contract and the Common Law Duty to Perform in Good Faith, 94 Harvard Law Review 369, 372-373 (1980).

as well as opinions in the case, but, of course, a jury might find some of our "facts" not to have been proved. Given this qualification, let's first look at Eastern Airlines. It was not a healthy corporation. Despite government regulation of competition, it lost money in seven of the ten years from 1960 to 1970. It competed with Delta on many of its routes, and Delta was well managed and, unlike Eastern, many of its employees were not unionized. As the court notes, "Ever since the advent of the commercial jet age in 1959, Eastern had lagged behind its competitors in the purchase of jet-powered planes." It was the "last major trunk carrier to purchase a large number of jet aircraft." On many of its routes it flew the Lockheed Electra, a prop-jet that was both slower than a pure jet and unpopular with passengers because of a number of serious crashes when the plane was introduced. In the early 1960s, Eastern had alienated business passengers and had a reputation for trying to save money by providing poor service. Employee morale was very low. There was an organization of those who had to fly Eastern regularly which had a newsletter called "WHEALs" — the letters stood for "We Hate Eastern Airlines."

A new management tried to remedy the situation. It ordered 60 Boeing 727s, and it had received about half of them by 1965. It was heavily in debt for these purchases, but the 727 was not well suited for many of Eastern's routes. Thus, it entered eight contracts for Douglas DC 8 and DC 9 jets between July of 1965 and October of 1967. A major factor in selecting Douglas rather than Boeing planes was Douglas' willingness to lend Eastern the money to buy the DC-8s and DC-9s at favorable rates. When Douglas fell behind on deliveries in mid 1966, it disappointed all of the airlines that had bought planes from it. However, airlines such as TWA, United, Delta and Continental did not have to cancel flights on existing schedules. Eastern had to cancel about 5% of its June service because it had no pilots to fly additional piston aircraft since it had been concentrating on jet pilot training.

Eastern had a profit of $24.1 million in 1967, but it reported a loss of $11.9 million in 1968, and it had a sharp drop in earnings in the first half of 1969. In May of 1969, Eastern's Board of Directors instructed management to bring suit against McDonnell Douglas for the losses caused by the delays in performing the contracts to deliver the DC-8 and DC-9 aircraft. During the course of the litigation in the 1970s, Eastern's fortunes continued up and down. It had unsuccessful merger discussions with Pan American; it ordered the Lockheed L-1011, but it experienced great delays when Rolls Royce defaulted on the contract to produce the engines for that plane; and one of its L-1011s crashed in the Everglades under circumstances that generated negative publicity for both the plane and Eastern's pilots.

The Douglas Aircraft Corporation was the most successful producer of passenger aircraft in the world from the 1930s to the 1950s. However, it lost its position when it decided to produce the DC-7, the last piston engine transport sold in great numbers, rather than manufacture a jet aircraft. The Boeing Corporation developed a plane that could refuel jet bombers in flight so they could continue on patrol for longer periods, and when the United States Air Force bought the tanker, it paid to create the necessary manufacturing facilities. The tanker was converted by Boeing into the 707, the first successful passenger jet aircraft. Douglas found itself two to three years behind Boeing before it could offer the DC-8, and it lost its position as the major producer of commercial aircraft. Douglas saw a market for a smaller plane than either the 707 or the DC-8, and it developed the twin-engined DC-9. Technically, it was a fine aircraft. Douglas worked hard to sell it to the airlines, battling Boeing's 737. In order to make sales, Douglas was willing to tailor the DC-9 to the wishes of its customers, and so production could not be completely standardized.

The Wall Street Journal, Business Week, and Fortune all reported that Douglas was a victim of its own success because it sold more DC-9 aircraft than it could deliver on time. This point was the subject of great controversy in the *Eastern Airlines* trial. The business journals all reported that Douglas had underestimated the market and accepted orders exceeding its production capacity. It had to hire many new workers whose lack of experience delayed production. Douglas managers were reported to be better aircraft engineers and salespeople than experts in production. Douglas, however, pointed to the expansion of the Vietnam war as the major cause of its problems. It, and Boeing as well, experienced delays caused by Pratt and Whitney's inability to supply all the ordered engines; Douglas also was delayed by its suppliers of landing gear and galleys. Commercial jet aviation was in competition with military production, and war production came first. There was a debate about what part of the problem was caused by Douglas mismanagement and what part by the unexpected demands of the escalation of the war.

Douglas was in great financial trouble, and its major lenders pushed a merger with a profitable corporation to salvage the situation. The McDonnell Aircraft Corporation was primarily a producer of military aircraft, and it had the cash needed to keep Douglas in production. The two firms merged on April 28, 1967. It was clear that McDonnell was the dominant partner in the new firm; its people took over operation of Douglas. They set revised production schedules, and deliveries of DC-8 and DC-9s caught up to the new schedules in late 1967.

Suppose during 1966 to 1969, Eastern had been advised by lawyers who interpreted § 2-607(3)(a) exactly as the Fifth Circuit read it in the *Eastern Airlines* and *T.J. Stevenson* decisions. What would they have told Eastern's management to do? If Eastern had given a 2-607(3)(a) notice that would have passed the court's test, what would have been the likely result? Would Eastern have received more planes sooner or fewer planes later? Suppose Eastern had given proper 2-607(3)(a) notices. Douglas, in response, said that Eastern would have to give up its claims to damages or receive no special favors in the delivery of DC-9 aircraft. Would this be the exercise of economic duress or just the negotiations that the court says § 2-607(3)(a) is designed to bring about? Given Eastern's great need for the planes and Douglas' great difficulties which business publications attributed in part to bad management, what, if anything, was wrong with trying to get Douglas to perform and then suing for the damages caused by the delays?

4. *McDonnell Douglas' case for bad faith*: McDonnell Douglas' brief is not a cool and dispassionate document. A few excerpts will show its response to the idea that Eastern could "string along" Douglas:

> The acquisition of Douglas by McDonnell ... occurred only after McDonnell had been assured by Douglas that no claims had been asserted against it as the result of late deliveries of aircraft. True, letters from Eastern and other airlines had expressed concern over the status of future deliveries ... Eastern, like most of the other airlines, was vitally interested in witnessing the marriage of Douglas to a solvent bridegroom, so as to insure the delivery of the many planes still on order. Hence, Eastern refrained from asserting any claims which might have frightened the groom and cancelled the wedding....
>
> As late as 1968, Floyd Hall, Eastern's Chairman, and Arthur Lewis, Eastern's President, were assuring McDonnell's top officials that Eastern had no intention of asserting a claim.... Mr. James S. McDonnell, defendant's founder and Chairman, testified that ... he attended a luncheon ... held during the recess of an Eastern board meeting, at which Arthur Lewis reaffirmed the agreement reached the preceding evening [that Eastern would not pursue its claim for late delivery] but conditioned it upon a satisfactory resolution of the problems resulting from late deliveries of aircraft simulators by Conductron Corporation [a subsidiary of McDonnell Douglas] to Eastern. In accordance with this understanding, Mr. McDonnell instructed David Lewis, defendant's president, to resolve the Conductron dispute....
>
> Eastern had a change of heart as its financial picture deteriorated. When Charles Simon arrived on the scene [as Eastern's vice president in charge of financial affairs], he reversed the decisions previously made and persuaded Eastern to pursue the "fat-cat" McDonnell in order to brighten its financial outlook....
>
> Besides being morally suspect and inherently prejudicial, Eastern's conduct is precisely the type prohibited by § 2-607 of the U.C.C.... Eastern's string-along tactics deprived defendant of an opportunity to enter into meaningful settlement negotiations during the critical period when its entire production program was being disrupted and delayed; to take what steps it could to minimize its own potential damages, by preserving claims against subcontractors or suppliers or otherwise; or to prepare a proper defense to this action. Additionally, defendant's willingness to enter into further contractual arrangements with plaintiff would doubtless have been influenced had it been aware of Eastern's litigious designs....
>
> Although ... Eastern stoutly professes that it gave a series of notifications to McDonnell throughout the 1966-69 period, Eastern's true attitude and the

philosophy underlying the "string-along" theory is strikingly conceded ... [in] its brief, where it acknowledges that by making claims against defendant while some of the planes were still undelivered, it would be "in the awkward position of having to sue the seller to whom [it] must continue to look for further deliveries." Eastern therefore admits, in effect, that it gambled under § 2-607 ... and did not alert defendant to its designs for fear of jeopardizing the future deliveries which first Douglas and then McDonnell were working so hard to expedite. It is now time for Eastern to pay the price for that gamble....

5. *The settlement*: Macaulay reports what happened after the Fifth Circuit's reversal and remand for a new trial:

> The delays ... were an important factor in Eastern's decision to buy Lockheed L-1011 wide-body jets rather than the McDonnell Douglas DC-10. This was a serious loss to McDonnell Douglas.... The suit was filed in 1970, and the Fifth Circuit's opinion reversing the district court judgment was handed down almost six years later. Rather than retry the case, McDonnell Douglas and Eastern reached a complicated settlement. Eastern returned nine older model DC-9 jets and leased nine newer model DC-9s at a price lower than usual....
>
> The settlement reached gave Eastern much needed newer planes that were larger, quieter, and burned less fuel; importantly, it did not require Eastern to try to borrow money in order to do this. McDonnell Douglas apparently sought the resumption of close business relations after the earlier divorce.

The Fifth Circuit stressed that promoting compromise was an important objective of § 2-607(3)(a). All in all, the entire process did promote a compromise. However, it took two years of pre-trial proceedings, about 5 months of trial, and almost two years while the case was on appeal. Given that over $30 million was involved, was this a sensible investment of the time of lawyers, paralegal workers, secretaries, officials of the two corporations and judges? Suppose Eastern had given a proper § 2-607(3)(a) notice when Douglas fell behind on the delivery schedule for the DC-8s and DC-9s. What kind of a settlement could have been reached then?

6. *A contrasting example.* In *Paulson v. Olson Implement Company, Inc.*[23] two neighbors, doing business as the Breezy Prairie Farm, purchased a grain drying bin. They were given assurances by the dealer concerning the drying capacity of the bin. When the bin was delivered, it failed to live up to the representations. The seller, Olson Implement Company, made repeated efforts, over a two year period, to modify the bin so that it would perform better. In the meantime,

---

[23] 107 Wis.2d 510, 319 N.W.2d 855 (1982).

plaintiffs continued to use it. Finally, the plaintiffs brought suit alleging a breach of warranty. The trial court dismissed the suit on the ground that the pleadings did not allege a notice which would comply with the requirements of § 2-607(3)(a), and that a two year delay in giving notice would be unreasonable as a matter of law, so the failure could no longer be cured. The Wisconsin Supreme Court reversed, citing with approval the comments to § 2-607 which suggest that

> The content of the notification need merely be sufficient to let the seller know that the transaction *is still troublesome and must be watched.* There is no reason to require that the notification which saves the buyer's rights under this section must include a clear statement of all the objections that will be relied on by the buyer.... *Nor is there reason for requiring the notification to be a claim for damages or of any threatened litigation or other resort to a remedy....* It appears to us that the purpose of the notice provision, enabling the seller to cure the defect, has been effected. Only after the seller proved unable to remedy the situation did the plaintiffs commence the instant action. There is nothing in the record to indicate that the plaintiffs were not the good faith purchasers which the Uniform Commercial Code seeks to protect through liberal notice requirements. As we view the record, the defendants acknowledged the warranty and their responsibilities under it by attempting to repair the defects of which Paulson and Wachholz complained.... Thus we hold that Paulson and Wachholz provided the requisite notice to the defendants in this action....

7. *Distinctions*: Could the *Paulson* and the *Eastern Air Lines* decisions both exist in the same jurisdiction, assuming its courts were concerned about consistency? Suppose one were to argue that in the *Eastern* opinion the court distinguished consumers from merchant buyers, holding the latter to a much higher burden of giving notice in order to comply with § 2-607(3)(a). However, *Paulson* could be taken to suggest that more refined categories are needed. Consumers may constitute one group and large bureaucratically organized corporations well served by legal staff such as Eastern Air Lines may constitute another. However, Breezy Prairie Farms, Inc. is still a different kind of entity. Much as a consumer, such smaller businesses do not get day-to-day legal advice and are likely to deal less formally. Unlike an Eastern Air Lines, the Breezy Prairie Farms of the world cannot be expected to comply with unknown and hard to discover procedures. Do you see any problems with such an analysis? For example, what does the consumer/business distinction have to do with the Fifth Circuit's position on promoting settlements? Do you see any statutory basis for a distinction based on the type of buyer seeking to assert rights?

8. *Section 2-607(3) notices, and § 2-608(2) notices distinguished:* Most of us know very little about Gertrude Stein other than the fact that she authored that immortal line "A rose is a rose is a rose is a rose." Is it true that "A notice is

a notice is a notice?" It seems not. Different words may, for some purposes and in some situations, mean the same thing. It is equally true, though sometimes confusing and a bit inconvenient, that the same word may mean different things. U.C.C. § 2-607(3) requires that the buyer notify the seller of the breach "or be barred from any remedy." The very next section of the Code deals with revocation of acceptances, and provides, in § 2-608(2) that "[revocation] ... is not effective until the buyer notifies the seller of it." We have just seen that what constitutes a notice can prove to be a subject of great (and critical) controversy. Can we carry over to § 2-608 notices the jurisprudence of the meaning of notice under § 2-607? It *is* the same statute, the same Article, the same Part, and the words are inches apart in the statutes. But, asking the question as we have should suggest that the answer may be no.

The court in *Solar Kinetics Corp. v. Joseph T. Ryerson & Son, Inc.*[24] discussed the requirements for a notice of revocation. Solar Kinetics had been awarded damages for breach, but to sustain the award the plaintiff was required to prove that it had revoked its acceptance.

> Since revocation "is not effective until the buyer notifies the seller of it," Conn.Gen.Stat.Ann. § 42a-2-608(2), the third condition is met only if the buyer gives the seller effective notice of revocation within a reasonable time after the buyer knew or should have known of the seller's breach. Plaintiff insists that the jury has already decided this question and seeks to support this claim by reference to the following interrogatory:

>> Do you find the plaintiff has shown by a fair preponderance of the evidence that it gave Ryerson notice of any of its claims within a reasonable time after it knew or should have known of any breach of the contract by Ryerson?

> While the jury did answer this question in the affirmative, its findings does not, contrary to plaintiff's assertion, amount to a finding of notice of revocation. In order to have found that Ryerson was liable to Solar Kinetics for breach of warranty, the jury was only required to find that a notice of breach was given to the seller pursuant to § 42a-2-607(3). The content of the limited notice necessary to preserve a claim for damages need only "be sufficient to let the seller know that the transaction is troublesome and must be watched." U.C.C. § 2-607, Comment 4. The Official Comments to the section on revocation, however, make it clear that the *content* of notice required under § 2-608 is generally more than "the mere notification of breach" required under § 2-607....

---

[24]488 F. Supp. 1237 (D. Conn. 1980).

Consequently, when the jury concluded that adequate § 2-607 notice had been given, it had no occasion to consider and rule on the question of whether or not Solar Kinetics had given the more extensive § 2-608 notice necessary for revocation....

When the question is considered in light of the oral instructions given to the jury, it is clear that the jury was asked only to find whether Ryerson was given the limited notice required by § 42a-2-607. Thus, it is clear that the jury's affirmative answer to the question concerning adequate notice of breach of contract does not estop this court from reaching a different conclusion with respect to the notice required for revocation....

While the various authorities who have considered the question have uniformly insisted that a notice of revocation must contain more than a mere notice of breach, they differ widely over how much more. Some have suggested that as little as conduct manifesting a buyer's desire to get his money back will suffice.... An intermediate position requires the buyer to notify the seller that he considers the seller to be in breach and that he desires to revoke his acceptance as to particular goods. The strictest test was recently set forth in the case of *Lynx, Inc. v. Ordnance Products*, 273 Md. 1, 327 A.2d 502 (1974), where the court held that notice of revocation "should inform the seller that the buyer has revoked, identify the particular goods as to which he has revoked and set forth the nature of the nonconformity...." 273 Md. at 16, 327 A.2d at 513.... However, consideration of the cases reveals two significant trends. First, those cases which have found an effective notice of revocation based on minimal communications with the seller are generally cases where the dissatisfied buyer is the ultimate consumer. The notice required for revocation is generally more content-specific in a transaction between merchants....

Second, courts have been reluctant to allow a buyer in litigation to justify his earlier attempted revocation by reference to defects in the goods which he only discovered after the supposed revocation.... Both of these trends are in accord with the policy expressed in the U.C.C. Official Comment 5 to § 2-608, which provides:

> The content of the notice under subsection (2) is to be determined in this case as in others by considerations of good faith, prevention of surprise, and reasonable adjustment. More will generally be necessary than the mere notification of breach required under the preceding section. On the other hand the requirements of the section on waiver of buyer's objections do not apply here. The fact that quick notification of trouble is desirable affords good ground for being slow to bind a buyer by his first statement. Following the general policy of this Article, the requirements of the content of notification are less stringent in the case of a non-merchant buyer.

The first line of cases is in accord with the code's stricter treatment of interactions between merchants. The second line of cases adopts a rule designed to prevent surprise and to allow the seller to have an opportunity to make a reasonable adjustment with the buyer. Where the seller does not know the grounds for revocation it may be substantially prejudiced in its efforts to respond reasonably and in good faith to a supposed revocation. Thus, both of the rules adopted by other courts serve to highlight aspects of the Official Comment.... [The court discussed the communications between Solar Kinetics and the seller, finding in each instance that though there was a notice of a defect, there was no notice of revocation.]

Effective notice is an absolute prerequisite to the revocation of acceptance. Since Soklar Kinetics failed to set forth the particular nonconformity on which it was relying to revoke, its attempted revocation was ineffective.

Consider §§ 2-608, Comment 5, and 2-607, Comment 4, second paragraph. What functions should the notices required under these sections serve? That is, if a seller has delivered defective goods, why is it entitled to more notice than that given by the filing of a complaint in a court within the period of the statute of limitations (§ 2-725)? Why should more notice be given in a case where buyer wants to return the goods than where buyer wants to sue for breach of warranty after accepting the goods? What does the interplay between the two notice provisions as explained in the comments suggest about the decision in the *Eastern Air Lines* case?

9. *Written notices*: In *Prompt Electrical Supply Co., Inc. v. Allen-Bradley Co.*,[25] a former distributor sued Allen-Bradley. Allen-Bradley counterclaimed for payment for electrical equipment shipped to plaintiff. Plaintiff said that the goods were defective, Allen-Bradley would not accept their return, and they were destroyed in a fire in a warehouse. In granting summary judgment for Allen-Bradley, the court noted that while plaintiff gave Allen-Bradley *oral notice* of the alleged defects, Allen-Bradley's terms and conditions of sale required that notice of an alleged defect must be given Allen-Bradley *in writing* promptly upon discovery. The court cited §§ 2-607(3)(a) and 1-102(3) of the U.C.C. to justify the requirement of written notice. Should the court have cited § 2-607(3)(a) or § 2-608(2)?

Do you see a problem with upholding a written notice requirement which appears in the terms and conditions of a seller's printed form? See §§ 1-102(3) and 1-201(3), referring to varying provisions of the Code by "agreement" and defining that term as "the bargain of the parties in fact."

10. *Section 2-605 demands for specification of defects*: Suppose a seller has supplied goods that are defective in several respects. Buyer and seller negotiate about the problem. Seller demands in writing "a full and final written statement

---

[25]492 F. Supp. 344 (E.D.N.Y. 1980).

of all defects on which the buyer proposes to rely." Buyer makes such a statement. Later buyer discovers still another serious defect. Suppose seller could not prove that it had changed its position materially in reliance on the statement of defects. Why should buyer lose the right to seek a remedy for the unlisted serious defect in the goods? Wouldn't a contrary rule deter breaches by sellers and increase the level of quality generally?

e. Section 2-508: The Seller's Right to Cure

T.W. OIL, INC. v. CONSOLIDATED EDISON CO. OF NEW YORK, INC.

57 N.Y.2d 574, 443 N.E.2d 932 (1982)

FUCHSBERG, J. In the first case to wend its way through our appellate courts on this question, we are asked, in the main, to decide whether a seller who, acting in good faith and without knowledge of any defect, tenders nonconforming goods to a buyer who properly rejects them, may avail itself of the cure provision of subdivision (2) of § 2-508 of the Uniform Commercial Code. We hold that, if seasonable notice be given, such a seller may offer to cure the defect within a reasonable period beyond the time when the contract was to be performed so long as it has acted in good faith and with a reasonable expectation that the original goods would be acceptable to the buyer.

The factual background against which we decide this appeal is based on either undisputed proof or express findings at Trial Term. In January, 1974, midst the fuel shortage produced by the oil embargo, the plaintiff (then known as Joc Oil USA, Inc.) purchased a cargo of fuel oil whose sulfur content was represented to it as no greater than 1%. While the oil was still at sea en route to the United States in the tanker *M T Khamsin*, plaintiff received a certificate from the foreign refinery at which it had been processed informing it that the sulfur content in fact was .52%. Thereafter, on January 24, the plaintiff entered into a written contract with the defendant (Con Ed) for the sale of this oil. The agreement was for delivery to take place between January 24 and January 30, payment being subject to a named independent testing agency's confirmation of quality and quantity. The contract, following a trade custom to round off specifications of sulfur content at, for instance, 1%, .5%, or .3%, described that of the *Khamsin* oil as .5%. In the course of the negotiations, the plaintiff learned that Con Ed was then authorized to buy and burn oil with a sulfur content of up to 1% and would even mix oils containing more and less to maintain that figure.

When the vessel arrived, on January 25, its cargo was discharged into Con Ed storage tanks in Bayonne, New Jersey. In due course, the independent testing people reported a sulfur content of .92%. On this basis, acting within a time frame whose reasonableness is not in question, on February 14 Con Ed rejected the shipment. Prompt negotiations to adjust the price failed; by February 20, plaintiff had offered a price reduction roughly responsive to the difference in sulfur reading, but Con Ed, though it could use the oil, rejected this proposition out of hand. It was insistent on paying no more than the latest prevailing price, which, in the volatile market that then existed, was some 25% below the level which prevailed when it agreed to buy the oil.

The very next day, February 21, plaintiff offered to cure the defect with a substitute shipment of conforming oil scheduled to arrive on the *S.S. Appollonian Victory* on February 28. Nevertheless, on February 22, the very day after the cure was proffered, Con Ed, adamant in its intention to avail itself of the intervening drop in prices, summarily rejected this proposal too. The two cargos were subsequently sold to third parties at the best price obtainable, first that of the *Appollonian* and, sometime later, after extraction from the tanks had been accomplished, that of the *Khamsin*.

There ensued this action for breach of contract, which, after a somewhat unconventional trial course, resulted in a nonjury decision for the plaintiff in the sum of $1,385,512.83, essentially the difference between the original contract price of $3,360,667.14 and the amount received by the plaintiff by way of resale of the *Khamsin* oil at what the court found as a matter of fact was a negotiated price which, under all the circumstances, was reasonably procured in the open market. To arrive at this result, the Trial Judge, while ruling against other liability theories advanced by the plaintiff, which, in particular, included one charging the defendant with having failed to act in good faith in the negotiations for a price adjustment on the *Khamsin* oil (Uniform Commercial Code, § 1-203), decided as a matter of law that subdivision (2) of § 2-508 of the Uniform Commercial Code was available to the plaintiff even if it had no prior knowledge of the nonconformity. Finding that in fact plaintiff had no such belief at the time of the delivery, that what turned out to be a .92% sulfur content was "within the range of contemplation of reasonable acceptability" to Con Ed, and that seasonable notice of an intention to cure was given, the court went on to hold that plaintiff's "reasonable and timely offer to cure" was improperly rejected (*sub nom. Joc Oil USA v. Consolidated Edison Co. of N.Y.*, 107 Misc.2d 376, 390, 434 N.Y.S.2d 623 [Shanley N. Egeth, J.])....

II.   We turn then to the central issue on this appeal: Fairly interpreted, did subdivision (2) of § 2-508 of the Uniform Commercial Code require Con Ed to accept the substitute shipment plaintiff tendered? In approaching this question, we, of course, must remember that a seller's right to cure a defective tender, as allowed by both subdivisions of § 2-508, was intended to act as a meaningful limitation on the absolutism of the old perfect tender rule, under which, no leeway being allowed for any imperfections, there was, as one court put it, just "no room ... for the doctrine of substantial performance" of commercial obligations (*Mitsubishi Goshi Kaisha v. Aron & Co.*, 16 F.2d 185, 186 [Learned Hand, J.] ....

In contrast, to meet the realities of the more impersonal business world of our day, the code, to avoid sharp dealing, expressly provides for the liberal construction of its remedial provisions (§ 1-102) so that "good faith" and the "observance of reasonable commercial standards of fair dealing" be the rule rather than the exception in trade (see § 2-103, subd. [1], par. [b]), "good faith" being defined as "honesty in fact in the conduct or transaction concerned" (Uniform Commercial Code, § 1-201, subd. [19]). As to § 2-508 in particular, the Code's Official Comment advises that its mission is to safeguard the seller "against surprise as a result of sudden technicality on the buyer's part" (Uniform Commercial Code, § 2-106, Comment 2) …

[There are two parts to § 2-508. The first, which had its counterpart before the enactment of the Code, provides for a cure when the time for performance has not yet expired. The second part, new with the Code, provides an opportunity for cure in some cases even though the time for performance has passed.]

Since we here confront circumstances in which the conforming tender came after the time of performance, we focus on subdivision (2). On its face, taking its conditions in the order in which they appear, for the statute to apply (1) a buyer must have rejected a nonconforming tender, (2) the seller must have had reasonable grounds to believe this tender would be acceptable (with or without money allowance), and (3) the seller must have "seasonably" notified the buyer of the intention to substitute a conforming tender within a reasonable time.

In the present case, none of these presented a problem. The first one was easily met for it is unquestioned that, at .92%, the sulfur content of the *Khamsin* oil did not conform to the .5% specified in the contract and that it was rejected by Con Ed. The second, the reasonableness of the seller's belief that the original tender would be acceptable, was supported not only by unimpeached proof that the contract's .5% and the refinery certificate's .52% were trade equivalents, but by testimony that, by the time the contract was made, the plaintiff knew Con Ed burned fuel with a content of up to 1%, so that, with appropriate price adjustment, the *Khamsin* oil would have suited its needs even if, at delivery, it was, to the plaintiff's surprise, to test out at .92%. Further, the matter seems to have been put beyond dispute by the defendant's readiness to take the oil at the reduced market price on February 20. Surely, on such a record, the trial court cannot be faulted for having found as a fact that the second condition too had been established.

As to the third, the conforming state of the *Appollonian* oil is undisputed, the offer to tender it took place on February 21, only a day after Con Ed finally had rejected the *Khamsin* delivery and the *Appollonian* substitute then already was en route to the United States, where it was expected in a week and did arrive on March 4, only four days later than expected. Especially since Con Ed pleaded no prejudice (unless the drop in prices could be so regarded), it is almost impossible, given the flexibility of the Uniform Commercial Code definitions of "seasonable" and "reasonable," to quarrel with the finding that the remaining requirements of the statute also had been met.

Thus lacking the support of the statute's literal language, the defendant nonetheless would have us limit its application to cases in which a seller *knowingly* makes a nonconforming tender which it has reason to believe the buyer will accept. For this proposition, it relies almost entirely on a critique in Nordstrom, Law of Sales (§ 105), which rationalizes that, since a seller who believes its tender is conforming would have no reason to think in terms of a reduction in the price of the goods, to allow such a seller to cure after the time for performance had passed would make the statutory reference to a money allowance redundant. Nordstrom, interestingly enough, finds it useful to buttress this position by the somewhat dire prediction, though backed by no empirical or other confirmation, that, unless the right to cure is confined to those whose nonconforming tenders are knowing ones, the incentive of sellers to timely deliver will be undermined. To this it also adds the somewhat moralistic note that a seller who is mistaken as to the quality of its goods does not merit additional time (Nordstrom, *loc. cit.*). Curiously, recognizing that the few decisions extant on this subject have adopted a position opposed to the one for which it contends, Con Ed seeks to treat these as exceptions rather than exemplars of the rule ...

That the principle for which these cases stand goes far beyond their particular facts cannot be gainsaid. These holdings demonstrate that, in dealing with the application of subdivision (2) of § 2-508, courts have been concerned with the reasonableness of the seller's belief that the goods would be acceptable rather than with the seller's pretender knowledge or lack of knowledge of the defect....

It also is no surprise then that the aforementioned decisional history is a reflection of the mainstream of scholarly commentary on the subject....

White and Summers, for instance, put it well, and bluntly. Stressing that the code intended cure to be "a remedy which should be carefully cultivated and developed by the courts" because it "offers the possibility of conforming the law to reasonable expectations and of thwarting the chiseler who seeks to escape from a bad bargain" (*op. cit.*, at pp. 322-324), the authors conclude, as do we, that a seller should have recourse to the relief afforded by subdivision (2) of § 2-508 of the Uniform Commercial Code as long as it can establish that it had reasonable grounds, tested objectively, for its belief that the goods would be accepted (*ibid.*, at p. 321). It goes without saying that the test of reasonableness, in this context, must encompass the concepts of "good faith" and "commercial standards of fair dealing" which permeate the code.

As to the damages issue raised by the defendant, we affirm without reaching the merits. At no stage of the proceedings before the trial court did the defendant object to the plaintiff's proposed method for their calculation, and this though the plaintiff gave ample notice of that proposal by means of a preliminary statement and pretrial memorandum filed with the court.... And, even after the decision at nisi prius revealed that the Judge had acted on such an assumption, so far as the record shows, no motion was ever made to correct it....

For all these reasons, the order of the Appellate Division should be affirmed, with costs.

NOTES AND QUESTIONS

1. *Arguments by plaintiff and defendant:* Not surprisingly, Con Edison and Joc Oil emphasized different aspects of the dispute in their arguments to the jury. Mr. Goldstein, lawyer for Con Edison, attempted to describe as unreasonable Joc Oil's conduct upon discovering that the oil had a higher sulphur content than the contract provided. After noting that oil prices had fallen $4.50 per barrel since the contract was formed, Goldstein urged:

> What did Joc Oil offer to give us off on the oil that was defective? They offered to give us off at most 80 cents a barrel....
>
> Well, 80 cents a barrel as a reduction is nowhere near the prevailing market price for that oil, 1 percent oil, on February 14th or February 15th or February 20th or February 21st, any of those dates, because on those dates the oil was selling for $13 a barrel, so they wanted to take a price of $17.875 a barrel, which we had agreed to pay for .5 percent maximum sulfur oil and reduce that to not more than $17.075 a barrel, and ask us to pay that price for oil that was selling for $13 a barrel at the time they asked us to accept it....
>
> They wanted us to swallow a huge chunk of money because of their error....
>
> ... when you talk about a substitute shipment, you have to consider what is doing with this substitute shipment. It is very nice to say, o.k., we learned that the oil is defective that we delivered to you; we've got another barge and here it is, that is a reasonable way, perhaps, of offering a substitute shipment, because there is no delay there. But Joc Oil didn't do that, it said, we got a ship coming in, this is on February 21st, we have a ship coming in, it is due to arrive February 28th, we will give you that shipment at the old contract price.
>
> And we said we don't want that ship, we ordered a shipload of oil that was supposed to arrive between January 24 and January 30, and although it arrived it didn't meet specifications. Don't tell us you are going to give us a shipload of something that will meet specifications five weeks or six weeks later. We are not going to buy it at the old contract price because the market price is way down....

The argument of Mr. Maloof, counsel for plaintiff, emphasized the cure.

> ... [W]e were in the position to make Con Ed one hundred percent whole according to the contract. They should not have the advantage of a drop in the market that occurred from extraordinary military pressures in the Middle East, why should Con Ed get the benefit of that drop in the market and Joc Oil suffer so badly.... Mr. Elias ... offered 80 cents and Mr. Doyle

responded with an arbitrary offer of market value.... The market value, according to the papers and the guides was $13 a barrel. This meant that Joc would have taken a bath of 188,000 barrels times more than $4 a barrel, which is over $700,000, and this is what Con Ed wanted them to do because they were innocently surprised when the oil arrived at .92, and Mr. Goldstein admitted, admitted that we didn't know that it was .92, so we are innocent parties....

Now did we offer the conforming shipment on the APPOLLONIAN VICTORY seasonably? Well, on February 20th we had this meeting with Mr. Doyle, it broke up. On the next day we offered the conforming shipment. Seasonably means reasonably. I think that is pretty close. Nobody is going to talk about doing these things in a couple of hours. We were quite fortunate to find it, find that we owned it, and offered it on February 21st to be delivered on February 28th. I don't think there is a big question [about] that and I do hope that you will agree.

2. *Cure in a falling market*: When Joc Oil made its tender, the market price was falling. Section 2-508(2) calls for "seasonable" notice of an intention to cure and a "reasonable time to substitute a conforming tender." The trial court found that there was no showing of prejudice to Con Edison by "the relatively short delay arising from the substitute delivery...." What would Con Edison have to establish to show prejudice?

3. *Revocation of acceptance and cure*: Suppose a buyer accepts a defective performance. Then the buyer revokes acceptance under U.C.C. § 2-608. May the seller then cure under § 2-508?

The Supreme Court of Texas considered this problem in *Gappelberg v. Landrum*,[26] where the buyer purchased a large screen Advent television set from seller for about $3,700. Buyer had problems with the set and demanded his money back. Seller offered another Advent set as a replacement. Buyer refused this attempted cure and sued Seller.

The Texas court decided that a seller does not have a right to cure under § 2-508 when a buyer revokes acceptance under § 2-608. Seller argued unsuccessfully that under § 2-608(2)(c) a "buyer who so revokes has the same rights and duties with regard to the goods involved as if he had rejected them." One of the duties of a buyer who rejects is to accept a cure that meets the requirements of § 2-508.

The Supreme Court of Texas disagreed. "We do not consider paragraph (c) in U.C.C. § 2-608 as having any reference to U.C.C. § 2-508. It is more logically related to U.C.C. § 2-603 and 2-604, as U.C.C. § 2-608(c) makes absolutely no mention of seller's rights." Buyer "had seen one Advent television perform, or fail to perform as the case may be, and there certainly is justification for his not

---

[26]666 S.W.2d 88 (1984).

wanting to go through experiences with another Advent." Once a buyer's faith in a product is shaken, the buyer does not have to keep the product after repairs or take another of the same model. The court pointed out that the seller ordinarily is in a better position to maximize the return on the resale of repaired goods.

Often buyers will not have rights to revoke acceptances of goods that prove defective. Sellers usually disclaim warranties and limit remedies successfully. Frequently, buyers must be satisfied with replacement or repair at the seller's option. The Supreme Court of Texas does not explain why Advent large screen television sets are sold without effective remedy limitations.

f. CISG and Imperfect Performance

We have offered, in the preceding chapters, notes which offer a glimpse of the manner in which the Convention on Contracts for the International Sale of Goods deals with the topics of the course. In most cases, the CISG either adopts a rule which tracks the U.C.C., or chooses a variation which reflects the common law approach, or perhaps an approach which is widespread in other parts of the world. When it comes to the issue of the treatment of breach, notice, cure, and remedy, we have concluded that it is appropriate only to call your attention, in the broadest terms possible to the CISG approach. To do more would require more time and space than we believe appropriate here. Not that the differences are not significant, but rather the opposite. Professor Reitz suggests that, "The most important ... [differences between CISG and the U.C.C.] deal with the performance stage of sales contracts, particularly when a performance is late or is qualitatively or quantitatively deficient." The CISG creates, to some extent, a different structure than the Code; it rejects the perfect tender rule as a starting point for defining a buyer's rights, makes distinctions between late performance and the tender of non-conforming goods, provides for a remedy in which a buyer can insist on repair, adopts a concept which it calls "fundamental breach" as the critical point in establishing a right to "avoid" a contract, and generally "seeks to keep troubled contracts going forward despite failings to a greater extent than the rules of the Commercial Code." If you have a transaction governed by the CISG, you should realize that the CISG provides a different structure of rights and remedies. Our brief warning should also stand as more evidence that the rules which we have been discussing represent one set of choices from among competing possibilities, and not the inevitable result of the application of "legal science" to the problem.

4. TWO CLASSIC, BUT TROUBLESOME, PROBLEMS

a. Installment Contracts and the Failure to Perform Part of the Deal

Installment contracts often present several problems to lawyers and courts. Suppose supplier is to perform steps A, B, C and D while buyer is to pay $100,000. U.C.C. § 2-307 states the common law rule: "Unless otherwise agreed all goods called for by a contract for sale must be tendered in a single delivery and payment is due only on such tender...." The same idea is contained in the rule that when one performance takes time while the other can be done all at once, then the performance which takes time must be performed first. In other words, unless they agree otherwise, sellers of goods and services must complete the job before the buyer must pay for it.

Suppose, however, that supplier and buyer's contract looks like this:

Supplier does:	Buyer pays:
Step A	$25,000
Step B	$15,000
Step C	$35,000
Step D	$25,000
Total:	$100,000

Then assume that supplier completes step A, but supplier has not yet begun the other steps. Must buyer pay supplier $25,000 then? U.C.C. § 2-307 continues, providing: "but where circumstances give either party the right to make or demand delivery in lots the price if it can be apportioned may be demanded for each lot." If what we've called steps are orders for goods which are in no way interrelated, supplier may deliver item A without delivering the other three items. Buyer then should pay supplier $25,000. However, if A, B, C and D are interrelated steps necessary to produce the final product for which buyer has promised to pay $100,000, the result may differ. Buyer may have no use for step A without the other three steps. If this is true, then "circumstances [do not] give either party the right to make or demand delivery in lots."

Building contracts often provoke even more difficult problems. For example, suppose a builder has promised to do steps A, B, C and D. The owner has promised in turn to make the four payments indicated as each step is completed. Often the owner is not buying step A for $25,000. Step A may be worth much more or much less than $25,000. Rather, the parties have agreed on a payment schedule which serves several purposes. With such a payment schedule, the builder does not have to finance the entire job until completion. Rather than borrowing money to pay for needed materials, wages and subcontracts, the builder can settle its debts with the money the seller pays at designated times. Furthermore, the builder lessens its credit risk. It does not want to take the chance that it will build an entire structure and then discover that the owner cannot raise enough money to pay for it. In a pay-as-you-go contract, the builder only risks losing its investment of time and materials made between payments. Owners may benefit too from installment contracts. They can appraise the quality of performance at each step before they pay rather than waiting to the end when at least some defects will be harder to cure.

However, what happens when this nice system doesn't work to produce harmony? First, at the negotiation stage, builders often try to "front load" the contract. They seek to have owners pay far more than the builders have invested in the job at the early stages of performance and relatively little as performance is completed. This minimizes their risks as owners are paying in advance of the builders' performance. Moreover, builders can use owners' payments both to finance the particular job as well as pay bills due from past projects. Or builders can finance other projects until they have earned money under them. Owners, however, try to "back load" contracts. In this way, they limit the time during which they must borrow money and pay interest.

Second, what happens when one party fails to perform as called for by the contract? Suppose that builder completes step A and owner pays $25,000. Builder then completes step B, but owner fails to pay the $15,000 which is due. Must builder continue and finish steps C and D? Can it exercise *self-help remedies*? May builder suspend performance until owner pays the $15,000 which is due? May builder call off the entire contract and move its workers to another job? Suppose owner is eager to have builder complete the job and says that it will pay builder just as soon as it can. Should this matter?

Suppose builder sues for its *damages* caused by owner's breach of contract when the $15,000 was not paid when it came due. Should builder recover $15,000? If builder recovers $15,000 in addition to the $25,000 which builder paid when step A was completed, in some cases builder will be far better off than had the contract been performed. Can you imagine such a situation? Suppose that builder's costs to do steps A and B would have been $30,000. However, builder's costs to complete the entire job would have been $95,000. Or should builder recover the contract price less (a) the cost of completing the job and (b) the $25,000 which owner already has paid?

First, we'll look at installment contract problems in the setting of building contracts, and then we'll turn to transactions in goods and one of the Uniform Commercial Codes' less satisfactory sections.

ERVIN F. PALMER v. WATSON CONSTRUCTION COMPANY

265 Minn. 195, 121 N.W.2d 62 (1963)

SHERAN, J. The appeal is from an order of the district court denying defendants' motion for judgment notwithstanding the verdict or, in the alternative, a new trial.

The action was instituted by plaintiff to recover progress payments, retained percentages, and damages for breach of contracts for excavation and backfilling, one being dated August 26, and the other September 20, 1960. In response defendant Watson Construction Company asserted default by plaintiff and counterclaimed for damages occasioned by his failure to perform.

The subject matter of the contracts was excavation, backfilling, sodding, and seeding to be performed in connection with the construction of four buildings and connecting tunnels being built at the state hospital at Brainerd pursuant to a prime contract between defendant and the State of Minnesota.

Relevant contract provisions fixing the obligations of these parties included the following:

> The Contractor agrees ...
> h) To pay the Subcontractor on demand for his work or materials as far as executed and fixed in place, less the retained percentage, ...

The subcontractor's obligations are described as follows:

> Section 3. The Subcontractor agrees to complete the several portions and the whole of the work herein sublet by the time or times following: As required by the progress of the job. Sub-Contractor agrees to provide sufficient equipment to complete the excavation of the four buildings this fall and, further agrees that if he does not provide proper equipment to complete his contract, the contractor has the right to bring in additional equipment and charge the cost of same against his contract.

The contracts involved do not contain provisions governing resolution of disputes between the parties as to quantities of work performed for purpose of progress payments where, as here, there was no certification by the architect.[27]

On October 6, 1960, plaintiff submitted to defendant a statement for work completed as of September 20, 1960, which included a claim for $7,760 for excavation of 19,400 cubic yards of earth at 40¢/per cubic yard. Upon receipt defendant disputed the quantity of excavation for which it had been billed and sent plaintiff a check which included the sum of $5,400, less retained percentage, representing payment for excavation of 13,500 cubic yards of material. Protracted negotiations then ensued during the course of which plaintiff insisted that he was entitled to payment based upon his figures, which represented the quantity of material which he claimed he had in fact removed. Defendant persisted in its refusal to accept these figures on the theory that if the quantity of

---

[27]Neither party to the contracts insisted upon architect's certificates as to excavation done and hence the provisions of the contracts pertaining to payment upon the architect's certificate were waived and neither could insist on strict compliance or payment thereunder. Standard Const. Co. Inc. v. National Tea Co., 240 Minn. 422, 62 N.W.(2d) 201.

material claimed by plaintiff had in fact been removed, plaintiff had "overexca-vated," i.e., excavated from the foundation grade to the level of the ground at an angle in excess of that prescribed by defendant and by proper and customary standards of workmanship....

Although plaintiff submitted statements for and received payment on account of additional excavation performed during the month of November, the disagreement with respect to the quantity for which he was entitled to payment in connection with the digging done by him and included in the October 6 billing was never resolved. Apparently construction work on the project was resumed in February 1961, but plaintiff declined to perform further under his subcontracts unless he was paid in conformity with his calculations....

Correspondence between defendant and plaintiff and plaintiff's attorney during February, March, and April reveals that the parties had reached an impasse. By letter dated March 2, 1961, which reviews the February correspondence and reflects the persistence of the disagreement, defendant wrote, "Further, we are requesting at this time a definite statement from Mr. Palmer as to whether he intends to complete his contract." By letter dated March 6, 1961, defendant advised plaintiff that it was correcting the grade level in one of the basements and completing the backfilling on this building and would backcharge the expense to plaintiff. On March 16, 1961, defendant wrote to plaintiff, "If we do not hear from you by return mail that you intend to complete your contract on this project, it will be necessary for us to hire another contractor to complete your contract on a time and material basis. Any costs over and above your total contract price will necessarily have to be assumed by your firm." On March 20, 1961, plaintiff's attorney wrote to defendant as follows: "Mr. Palmer has always been willing to complete his contract but he is not going to complete the contract unless you fulfill your obligation to make payment as set forth above." In addition this letter contains a statement that plaintiff was unable to pay another subcontractor and that defendant was placing plaintiff "in a position where he cannot proceed with the contract by reason of this inability to pay."

The jury was instructed that if refusal by plaintiff to continue performance under the contract was justified, he was entitled to recover not only for the excavation and other contract services actually performed, but also for such profits as he would have realized had performance been completed and payment made according to the agreement. The jury was informed that if plaintiff's refusal to proceed was not justified, defendant was entitled to recover damages on its counterclaim. No instructions were given or requested that plaintiff would be entitled to recover in quantum meruit for the services in fact performed by him up to the point when the disagreement brought work to a halt....

... [I]t is our opinion that evidence does not sustain the verdict in so far as it includes damages for loss of the profit anticipated in the event of full perfor-mance. A party to a contract who is entitled to progress payments may treat the failure to make such payments when due as a breach of the contract which will justify him in refusing to perform further and which will give legal basis for a claim for the reasonable value of the services performed or material supplied pursuant to the contract.... His alternative course is to continue with performance and recover the contract price in full upon completion.... It is true that a party ready, willing, and able to perform may recover damages for breach of contract, as distinguished from the reasonable value of the services rendered or material supplied, if he is *prevented* from performance by an act or omission of the other contracting party.... We are committed in this state, however, to the rule that nonpayment of installment obligations is not in and of itself such prevention of performance as will make possible suit for loss of profits even though the party entitled to payment may lack working capital....

Although the letter written by plaintiff's attorney on March 20 stated that nonpayment was interfering with the discharge of Palmer's obligation to his subcontractor and thus preventing completion, there is nothing in the testimony of the subcontractor, who was called as a witness in behalf of plaintiff, to support this argument adequately. While the parties to a construction contract could make nonpayment of progress payments such an event as would empower the party entitled to the money to discontinue performance and sue for that which he would have earned had the contract been completed, we find no such provision in the agreements here involved. It is conceivable that refusal to make progress payments without justification and under circumstances where the refusal is intended to make performance by the contractor impossible could be considered such prevention of performance as would justify recovery of profits for breach of an indivisible contract. For the present, it is sufficient to say that this is not such a case.

Reversed and remanded for a new trial.

NOTES AND QUESTIONS

1. *An exercise in alternatives:* As an exercise, craft a list of possible rules to apply in cases like the *Palmer* case. Then critique them, both in terms of the quality of outcomes they would yield (using whatever criteria for evaluating quality you believe appropriate) and then in terms of their administrability. As a second exercise, describe the facts of the *Palmer* case as they might have appeared first, to Palmer, and then to Watson Construction. How could a court, or even the parties themselves, determine which version of the facts was "true?" Is it the case that one of the difficulties of making such an assessment arises because either party may have legitimate, but different, fears of what may happen next? For those familiar with game theory, is there something like a Prisoner's Dilemma here?[28]

---

[28]A "prisoner's dilemma" arises in a situation in which two persons must decide whether to cooperate or not. If both cooperate, both are slightly better off. If both choose not to cooperate, both are significantly worse off. However, both are tempted not to cooperate because if one chooses to cooperate, and the other chooses NOT to cooperate, the non-cooperating person receives

2. *The resources of the parties as affecting the outcome:* The General Contractor in the *Palmer* case thought that far too much dirt and rock had been taken away. It paid only a portion of the amount claimed by the Grading Contractor, the Grading Contractor then refused to continue until it was paid in full, and ultimately the parties found themselves before the Supreme Court of Minnesota. The General Contractor argued that if the Grading Contractor had performed properly, there was only a breach of the progress payment provisions and not the whole contract. It quoted *New York Life Ins. Co. v. Viglas*[29] as stating that to justify treating a contract as completely broken, a repudiation "must at least amount to an unqualified refusal or declaration of inability substantially to perform according to the terms of its obligation." The brief continued, saying that "[t]he trial judge in his memorandum attempts to distinguish ... case law ... on the basis that [the Grading Contractor's] financial resources were insufficient to let him finish the job.... [T]his contention has been repeatedly raised, examined on the merits in trial and has been held as a matter of law inapplicable." The General Contractor quoted a passage from *Beatty v. Howe Lumber Co.*:[30]

> It could make no difference with the legal liability of the defendant whether the plaintiffs were rich or poor. If they had been rich, or had ample means, it is evident, from the record, that they would or could have continued to perform the services ... [One may recover when another prevents performance] ... , but ... this right does not rest in the mere default in payment of an installment when it becomes due, especially when ... there was not denial of the legal right of the plaintiffs to proceed in the performance of the contract unaffected by the conduct or default of the defendant.

On March 20, 1961, the Grading Contractor's lawyer wrote the General Contractor, "Mr. Palmer has always been willing to complete his contract but he is not going to complete the contract unless you fulfill your obligation to make payment as set forth above." He then said that the General Contractor was placing Palmer in a position where he could not proceed with the contract because he required payments from the General in order to be able to pay the subcontractors. Suppose this were clearly the case. Would the result have been different? Suppose, instead, the *General Contractor* was short of working capital and could not make the progress payments required under the contract. Its managers looked for some item to question in order to delay paying the Grading Contractor. Would the result have been different?

---

a very significant gain.

[29] 297 U.S. 672 (1936).

[30] 77 Minn. 272, 79 N.W. 1013, 1015 (1899).

Like many legal questions, there is another view of the question of whether late payments constitute cause for a contractor's refusal to proceed. In *Cork Plumbing Co., Inc. v. Martin Bloom Associates, Inc.*,[31] the court stated:

> Because of the nature of construction contracts and the contractor's need for funds to meet expenses and proceed with construction, courts have distinguished construction contracts from other installment contracts with respect to the subcontractors's right to terminate for non-payment of installments. This judicial sentiment is expressed in *Brady Brick & Supply Co. v. Lotito*, 43 Ill.App.3d 69, 1 Ill.Dec. 844, 848, 356 N.E.2d 1126, 1130 (1976):
>
> The failure to pay an installment of the contract price as provided in a building or construction contract is a substantial breach of contract and gives the contractor the right to consider the contract at an end, to cease work, and to recover the value of the work already performed....[32]
>
> We recognize that the facts in every construction contract might not warrant a termination upon failure to pay an installment, but the present facts, particularly the repeated failure to keep payments current coupled with M.B.A.'s statements about future payments, permit such a resolution. We must consider the effect of delays on the builder's finances, and "[s]ince the builder's risks depend largely upon the financial resources of the debtor, ... a non-payment by an obligor who is of doubtful solvency ... *or who accompanies his non-payment by words of near repudiation is almost certain to be held a vital breach.*" (Emphasis added.) 3A Corbin on Contracts, § 692.

3. *Legislation by a private government — the American Institute of Architects forms*: The American Institute of Architects (AIA) has drafted form contracts covering most of the building process. These forms, or provisions modeled on them, are widely used in the construction industry. To what extent, if at all, do these provisions affect the resolution of disputes such as those in *Palmer v. Watson?*

---

[31]573 S.W.2d 947 (Mo.App. 1978).

[32]Does the court mean that the contractor can only recover restitution? Why shouldn't it be able to recover damages based on protection of its expectation interest? Corbin on Contracts § 693 (1952) says that if "the nonpayment is held to be a vital breach," the builder has four choices: He may stop performance and bring no suit. He may continue performance while either seeking no remedy or suing for the installment due. He may sue for restitution as an alternative remedy for breach. Or he may sue for damages for total breach. Under this last option, the builder would recover the contract price less the cost of completion and less any payments he has received from the owner.

AIA Document A401, Contractor-Subcontractor Agreement (12th ed. 1987)[33] provides:

> 4.7.1 If the Contractor does not pay the Subcontractor through no fault of the Subcontractor, within seven days from the time payment should be made as provided in this Agreement, the Subcontractor may, without prejudice to other available remedies, upon seven additional days' written notice to the Contractor, stop the Work of this Subcontract until payment of the amount owing has been received. The Subcontract Sum shall, by appropriate adjustment, be increased by the amount of the Subcontractor's reasonable costs of shutdown, delay and start-up.

> 7.1.1 The Subcontractor may terminate the Subcontract ... for nonpayment of amounts due under this Subcontract for 60 days or longer. In the event of such termination by the Subcontractor for any reason which is not the fault of the Subcontractor, Sub-subcontractors or their agents or employees or other persons performing portions of the Work under contract with the Subcontractor, the Subcontractor shall be entitled to recover from the Contractor payment for Work executed and for proven loss with respect to materials, equipment, tools, and construction equipment and machinery, including reasonable overhead, profit and damages.

While this might seem to clarify the situation, the subcontractor must establish that an amount is due or owing to trigger these sections. Section 6.1 provides that "any controversy or claim between the Contractor and the Subcontractor" shall be settled by arbitration. Arbitration is to be conducted as provided in the contract between Owner and Contractor.[34]

The result of the delay built into the agreement, plus the additional delays which accompany the arbitration process, is that a subcontractor may have to wait two months or even much longer before it can invoke the remedies described in the AIA Contractor-Subcontractor Agreement. An undercapitalized subcontractor might find it difficult to pay suppliers and workers while awaiting

---

[33]The American Institute of Architects.

[34]Arbitration is governed by a number of provisions in the General Conditions of the Contract for Construction. (AIA Document A201 (14th ed. 1987). © The American Institute of Architects.) Claims are submitted to the architect who must act within ten days. He or she may reject the claim, recommend approval, suggest a compromise or ask for additional supporting evidence. After the architect's initial response, if the claim has not been resolved, the party making the claim has ten days to respond. Then the architect has another seven days in which to decide the claim. The architect's decision is subject to arbitration under the Construction Industry Arbitration Rules of the American Arbitration Association. A demand for arbitration must be submitted within 30 days after the architect's decision. Pending final resolution of a claim, § 4.3.4 provides "the Contractor shall proceed diligently with performance of the Contract and the Owner shall continue to make payments in accordance with the Contract Documents."

a decision in situations such as involved in *Palmer v. Watson*. It might have to accept an offer such as the general contractor made in that case. Why do the AIA standard contract forms leave subcontractors in such a weak position?

4. *The measure of damages*: Suppose an owner or general contractor fails to make a progress payment. A court decides that the subcontractor is entitled to stop work on the job and sue for damages as well. What is the measure of recovery? Can the subcontractor recover the installments due or should damages be calculated in some other manner? Courts often distinguish between "partial" and "total" breaches of contract in discussing such questions. Under a *partial breach*, the contract continues despite the default. Nonetheless, the aggrieved party can recover a judgment for the payment that has been missed. Under a *total breach*, the contract is at an end. Now damages are not measured by the installment payments in the contract but are to be calculated in terms of the expectation, reliance or restitution interests. How do we know whether a breach is "partial" or "total?" Courts often ask whether the breach was substantial or material. To a great extent, the question is whether the aggrieved party should be required to continue to perform in the face of the other's breach.

The problem is reflected in *Fuller v. United Electric Co.*[35] The owner was constructing a new home in Las Vegas. She hired United Electric to do the electrical wiring. The total price was $1,410, and the contract provided that "80% of contract price payable on completion of rough-in and inspection thereof; balance payable on final completion and inspection." Rough-in was completed, and a municipal building inspector approved the work. The owner paid $500 on account but refused to pay more or to allow United Electric to complete the job, asserting that United Electric had breached. The trial court found that United had not breached but that the owner had.

The trial court awarded United Electric $1,048.60. It arrived at that sum by calculating that 80% of $1,410 contract price was $1,128. It then added 20% of $1,128 as a reasonable profit. United Electric was also entitled to $195 for extras. This totaled $1,548.60, and the court subtracted the $500 that had been paid to arrive at the award of $1,048.60. The Supreme Court of Nevada reversed. It explained:

> [T]he breach by defendant was not a partial breach with the contract continuing in effect notwithstanding, in which event an installment or progress payment due under the contract might be claimed in full. The breach was a total breach and was so treated by plaintiff. The contract was thereby terminated....
>
> In our view the contract in this case was clearly an entire one. The specified payment of 80% upon completion of rough-in was but a scheduled part payment upon the specified contract price and was not a full and fixed

---

[35] 70 Nev. 136, 273 P.2d 136 (1954).

payment allocated absolutely to that portion of the work done up to complete of rough-in. Upon a total breach, then, damages must be ascertained upon the entire contract without regard to those provisions having to do with the times at which portions of the contract price were to become payable.

The case was remanded for a determination of contract damages. "What is allowed is the profit, if any, which would have been realized had the contract proceeded to completion." United Electric, then, would have to show the difference between the contract price and its total cost of performance had the contract been completed. It would be entitled to this sum plus its reasonable expenditures in part performance. Of course, alternatively, United Electric might also bring a restitution action to recover the reasonable value of the work it had done in part performance.

Courts often discuss this problem in terms of "entire" and "divisible" contracts. Corbin objects to these words as terms of confusion.[36] We can imagine a divisible contract. For example, suppose a lawyer is to draft the documents necessary to incorporate client's business and also draft a will for that client. Both tasks are mentioned in the written contract between lawyer and client. The document states that the incorporation is to be done for a fee of $X payable when the articles of incorporation are filed. It also says that the will is to be drafted for $Y payable when it is presented to the client for execution. The contract then states the total fee to be $X + $Y. Unless a court were to find some relationship between the incorporation and the will, these seem to be distinct tasks and the fees would likely have been set independently for each one. If this were the case, one contract document expresses two "divisible" tasks, and the two sums mentioned are allocated to each one. If the lawyer completes the will, he is entitled to $Y although he has not begun the articles of incorporation. Furthermore, failure to pay $Y when the will was completed would not necessarily give the lawyer the right to abandon his or her work on the articles of incorporation under the contract.

However, suppose the entire purpose of the will was to deal with questions of control of the new corporation if one of its founders died. Furthermore, assume it was clear that the sum named for preparing the articles of incorporation was less than the usual charge for this service while the sum named for the will was a corresponding amount greater. It seems likely that the sums named were a payment schedule. That is, the writing meant that the lawyer was to get $X WHEN he produced the articles of incorporation and $Y WHEN he drafted the will. The parties named the amounts so that the new corporation could delay its need for cash until matters were settled but so that the lawyer would get something during the time he was performing.

---

[36]See 3 Corbin on Contracts §§ 694, 695, 955.

Now a court might find that the will and the articles of incorporation were not separate tasks purchased at the named prices. Rather, the payments of $X and $Y were partial payments of the total sum.

Suppose the client repudiates the arrangement and tells the lawyer to stop work. In this event, completion of the will before the repudiation would not entitle the lawyer to $Y. The lawyer would be entitled to expectation damages based on doing the entire job. If there had been no clear repudiation other than the failure to pay, it would be an open question whether the lawyer could stop work on the transaction.

Modern practice and the American Institute of Architects form contracts minimize the entire and divisible problem in building contracts. Contractors are required to allocate the entire contract price to designated portions of the work in a "schedule of values." This document is submitted to the architect for his or her approval before the contractor makes its first application for payment. Then payments are made in terms of the approved schedule. This means that payments are more closely related than in the past to the actual cost of the construction performed during the payment period. The specificity of the schedule of values and the degree to which the contractor can front load it are a matter of negotiation. The contractor makes a proposal and must get the architect to accept it. When a detailed and cost specific schedule of values is established, this practice creates something close to a divisible contract. Each installment payment will be a fair approximation of the contract rate for the work actually done.

b. Installment Contracts and the U.C.C.

Suppose instead of houses, a contract involves the delivery of 19 automobiles for use in Buyer's car rental business. Automobiles are movable at the time of identification to the transaction, and so Article II of the Uniform Commercial Code applies. Under the contract, one car is to be delivered when the contract is signed, ten are to be delivered four weeks later; and the final eight are to be delivered four weeks after that. The contract price is stated as $133,000, and it is payable in installments of $25,000 upon the signing of the contract; $60,000 when the ten cars are delivered; and $48,000 when the last eight cars are delivered. (Although it is not expressed this way in the written contract, $133,000 divided by 19 equals $7,000, which could be taken as the price per car. However, the buyer needed 19 cars, and there are reasons in the car rental business to have a number of the same make and model. Furthermore, a buyer who orders 19 similarly equipped cars of the same make and model will pay less per car than a buyer who orders only one or two).

Suppose: (1) the car delivered when the contract was signed was slightly defective — the engine needed tuning. Suppose, instead, that the first car is seriously defective — its brakes are improperly installed and will have to be rebuilt before the car is safe to drive. In either case, can the buyer call off the entire transaction and back out? If it were still possible to do it, would it have the right to stop payment on its check for $25,000 until the car was repaired satisfactorily? Can it successfully sue Seller for damages? For how much?

(2) buyer needs cars to rent to its customers. The first eleven cars are delivered with bad brakes. Buyer repairs them itself and puts the cars into service. When the next eight cars are delivered, two have bad brakes. Can the buyer call off the contract and return all of the cars to the seller?

(3) there are no defects in the cars. Seller delivers the first car and is paid $25,000. It delivers the ten cars four weeks later, but Buyer fails to pay the $60,000 called for by the contract. May Seller stop its preparations to deliver the remaining eight cars? May Seller sue for $60,000? For 10 x $7,000 or $70,000? For some other amount? See §§ 2-307 and 2-612 of the Uniform Commercial Code.

(4) all 19 cars are to be delivered at once, and the entire $133,000 is to be paid then. 17 of the cars are in merchantable condition while two are so seriously defective as to be unmerchantable. Must Buyer accept the 17 good cars or may it call off the entire deal and buy from another supplier? Is this an installment contract within the meaning of § 2-612? Would § 2-307 affect the result? If it is not an installment contract, the buyer's rights would be governed by § 2-601. Is there any reason that the analysis should differ depending on whether the 19 cars are all to be delivered at once or in three installments? Whether or not there is a good reason, the Code does structure the analysis differently depending upon whether an installment contract is or is not involved. Given modern business practices, it is not always easy to tell whether we are dealing with what the U.C.C. deems to be an installment contract.

BURROUGHS CORPORATION v. UNITED STATES

634 F.2d 516 (U.S. Court of Claims 1980)

BENNETT, J. This case comes before the court for review of a decision of the Postal Service Board of Contract Appeals (PSBCA) under the provisions of the Wunderlich Act, 41 U.S.C. §§ 321, 322 (1976). The parties have filed cross-motions for summary judgment. We have concluded that the PSBCA's decision against plaintiff was based on an erroneous interpretation of the contract and is therefore without finality. We reverse the decision and remand the case.

Under the contract in dispute, plaintiff was required to produce, deliver, and install 113 hardware systems combining a Multi-Position Letter Sorting Machine (MPLSM), a Zip Mail Translator (ZMT), and an Electronic Sort Processor (ESP). Prior to the contract, only experimental models of the ESP had ever been produced. Earlier systems then in use by the Postal Service had included MPLSM and ZMT units, but these units required modifications in order to function in combination with an ESP.

The negotiated contract price was subject to incentive price increases and penalty price decreases based on whether a system was completed early or late. The original contract schedule called for deliveries as follows:

Line Item	Identification	Time of Delivery
IV	Drawings and specifications (also called the technical data package or TDP)	
	Interim baseline drawings	Nov. 1975
	Final drawings	Mar. 1976
V	Operation and maintenance (O&M) manuals	
	Preliminary ESP	Nov. 1975
	Preliminary LSM	Mar. 1976
	Revised ZMT	Mar. 1976
VI	Maintenance training	Jan. 1976
I	Hardware	
	First articles	Mar. 1976
	Initial shipment	May 1976

The contracting officer later determined that no training would be needed on the MPLSM or ZMT units. On October 24, 1975, Modification 18 to the contract was executed to delete such training and to reduce the contract price. It was originally intended that the O & M manuals for the ESP would be a part of the materials provided to the Postal Service personnel to be trained by plaintiff. When it became apparent that the ESP O & M manuals would not be available in time, the contracting officer decided to purchase "interim" materials consisting of schematic drawings of the ESP cabinet. The training classes were conducted in January 1976, as scheduled, and the Postal Service made no contemporaneous objections to the quality of the instruction or materials provided.

During early 1976 it became apparent that plaintiff would not be able to meet the original delivery schedule in other respects, and new schedules were proposed by plaintiff which provided for the delivery of the TDP and the O & M manuals after the delivery and installation of the hardware but before its acceptance. By letter dated April 29, 1976, plaintiff was advised for the first time that any revised schedules "should reflect the contractually required delivery sequence," which in the opinion of the contracting officer was "(1) Delivery of an acceptable First Article; (2) Delivery of Drawings and Specifications which are authenticated with that acceptable First Article; (3) Delivery of Preliminary 'O & M' manuals;

and (4) Delivery of Production Hardware after the delivery of the foregoing first three deliverables."

In the Postal Service's view this delivery sequence was necessary to assure that hardware delivered to and installed in the field could be properly maintained. As one internal memorandum stated:

> If Burroughs was [sic] allowed to ship the hardware on the contract date of May 10, 1976, and not achieve their scheduled dates for the completion of the maintenance documentation, the Postal Service would be in a position of having equipment in the field and not being able to maintain it, due to the lack of maintenance documentation. The Postal Service cannot allow this situation to exist or even be put into a position where it may happen.

Plaintiff requested permission by a letter dated May 26, 1976, to begin hardware deliveries on June 7, 1976. Plaintiff proposed to deliver the O & M manuals on July 12, 1976, and the TDP in parts on June 21 and July 20, 1976. Plaintiff added:

> Burroughs assures the USPS that the preliminary manuals will be on site prior to final acceptance of the first systems. As further assurance, if for some unknown reason, the manuals are not available, Burroughs will entertain leaving an experienced field engineer at the site location to assist USPS in maintenance until the manuals arrive. Or, the USPS may elect not to accept the system until manuals are available. The choice would be up to the Postal Service.

By a letter dated June 9, 1976, the contracting officer denied the proposed schedule because of the "altered sequence of delivery."...

Plaintiff had to suffer penalties under the contract because of the Postal Service's refusal to permit plaintiff to begin hardware deliveries for a period of 49 days. Plaintiff argues that this refusal was improper because the contract did not require the delivery sequence demanded by the Postal Service, or, alternatively, that any contractually required delivery sequence was waived or changed by the Postal Service.

The PSBCA, with one administrative judge dissenting, concluded that the contract prescribed a delivery sequence which required O & M manuals and training materials to be delivered prior to the delivery of the hardware. The PSBCA did find that the delivery sequence of some software, such as certain training materials and the O & M manual for the ZMT, was rearranged by contract modifications to permit their delivery after the date of delivery for the hardware. However, the PSBCA apparently believed that the software not covered by the contract modifications was essential to the Postal Service for maintenance purposes and that, therefore, the Postal Service could insist on its delivery prior to the delivery of the hardware and did not waive its rights to so insist.

Uniform Commercial Code § 2-612(3) reflects the general rule of contract law with respect to installment contracts which require or authorize the delivery of goods in separate lots. It provides:

> (3) Whenever non-conformity or default with respect to one or more installments substantially impairs the value of the whole contract there is a breach of the whole....

The Uniform Commercial Code does not define what constitutes substantial impairment, but the prior Uniform Sales Act § 45(2) is somewhat more specific in this regard, providing that:

> (2) Where there is a contract to sell goods to be delivered by stated installments, which are to be separately paid for, and the seller makes defective deliveries in respect of one or more installments, ... it depends in each case on the terms of the contract and the circumstances of the case, whether the breach of contract is so material as to justify the injured party in refusing to proceed further and suing for damages for breach of the entire contract, or whether the breach is severable, giving rise to a claim for compensation, but not a right to treat the whole contract as broken.

Thus, the question in the present case is whether a failure to deliver the TDP and the O & M manuals before the hardware was delivered and installed would have constituted a substantial impairment or material breach of the whole contract. If so, the Postal Service was justified in suspending its obligation under the contract to receive delivery of the hardware and in insisting that any revised delivery schedule provide for the delivery of software before hardware. If not, the Postal Service could not treat the whole contract as broken and should have continued to perform its obligations under the contract, reserving any claims for actual damages for later settlement.

Defendant relies on several clauses in the RFP and the contract to establish that the breach was material. The RFP clause concerning time of delivery provides:

> ... If the offeror proposes his own schedule, it *must sequentially [sic] offer the same delivery pattern* as that contained in this RFP. (Hardware cannot be accepted before drawings, manuals, and trained maintenance people are available.) [Emphasis in original.]

The contract provision relating to early shipments[37] states:

> If a system is to be shipped, installed and accepted more than 30 days in advance of the contracted completion schedule, notification of early shipment, stating the time of delivery must be sent to the Contracting Officer in writing 120 days prior to factory shipping date. If units are to be shipped in advance of the contracted schedule, all other deliverable items (trainers, drawings, manuals, etc.) must be shipped in the same advanced rate.

Finally, Work Statement 102 which was incorporated into the contract provided with respect to O & M manuals: "In order to support early training requirements as well as to provide maintenance documentation with initial hardware shipments, the Contractor shall develop and deliver preliminary manuals in lieu of a review manuscript...."

Taken together, these clauses establish that the sequence of deliveries was *in general* a material consideration to the contract. Thus, plaintiff was not free to make major changes in the delivery sequence. The *particular* changes that would be considered to be major were left largely unspecified by the contract. Fortunately, one clause, the RFP clause quoted above, does address the problem of a particular variation in sequence by providing that manuals and drawings must be available before hardware can be accepted. Both acceptance and delivery are defined terms with specific meanings, and it must be assumed that the Postal Service was aware of the difference when it drafted this language. By establishing that the acceptance of hardware before the delivery of drawings and manuals would be an intolerable change in sequence, the Postal Service in drafting the contract implicitly excused, as a minor variation in sequence, the delivery of hardware before the delivery of drawings and manuals. Additionally, under the actual circumstances of the case, as discussed below, the inconvenience to the Postal Service through plaintiff's proposed change in sequence would have been in fact minor....

In judging the materiality of the delivery sequence, both parties lay almost exclusive stress on the terms of the contract and neglect the actual circumstances of the case. There was some dispute before the PSBCA as to the adequacy of the training conducted by plaintiff without benefit of the O & M manuals. The PSBCA cited testimony that some of the Postal Service personnel attending this training had to undergo retraining after the ESP O & M manuals were received in July 1976. This testimony was hearsay and so vague and uncertain as to lack sufficient assurance of its truthfulness. As such it does not constitute substantial evidence....

---

[37]The contract clause concerning late shipments contains no mention of any sequential requirement. The PSBCA, having erroneously decided that there was a delivery sequence established elsewhere in the contract, concluded that the "late shipments" clause did not modify this sequence.

Plaintiff was paid in full for the training at the time with no exceptions taken. The alleged deficiency in the training appears to have been an afterthought since litigation arose. Moreover, even if the training was in fact deficient, this can provide no logical justification for delaying delivery of the hardware since the training was already completed.

The Postal Service's contemporaneous justification for its insistence on the delivery sequence was that it could not risk having hardware installed in field post offices which could not be maintained after acceptance. Defendant argues that the only way to be certain of avoiding this risk was to insist on delivery of the manuals before delivery and installation of the hardware. Based on the evidence in the record, we cannot disturb the board's factual finding that the manuals were necessary for the proper maintenance of the hardware by Postal Service personnel. However, plaintiff assured the Postal Service that the manuals would be delivered before acceptance when the Postal Service assumed the responsibility for maintenance, and plaintiff in fact delivered the manuals before its proposed date of acceptance. Moreover, in the event that the manuals were delayed, plaintiff promised to leave an experienced field engineer at each site location to assist the Postal Service in maintenance. The Postal Service did not then and does not now provide any explanation as to why this proposal was not adequate protection against any risks.

Defendant, alternatively, argues that the contracting officer could properly have terminated plaintiff for default after it failed to meet the original schedule for the delivery of the manuals and the TDP. Even if this were true, it does not provide any basis for the contracting officer's actions here. It is well established that if the contracting officer does not decide to terminate a contractor for default within a reasonable time, any new delivery schedule unilaterally set by the contracting officer must be reasonable....

Just as the contracting officer cannot set an unreasonably short delivery date to insure a further default, he cannot set an unreasonable delivery sequence to increase the penalties incurred by the contractor. Having stressed the importance of time by putting incentive and penalty price adjustments in the contract, the Postal Service had a duty to cooperate and take all reasonable actions to permit completion on time or with as little delay as possible. As indicated above, defendant has failed to show that the Postal Service's actions were reasonable in view of plaintiff's assurances and promise to provide engineers for maintenance, if necessary....

Accordingly, upon consideration of the pleadings, motions, briefs, pertinent parts of the administrative record, and the board's opinion, without oral argument, plaintiff's motion for summary judgment is granted, and defendant's cross-motion for summary judgment is denied. The case is remanded to the Postal Service Board of Contract Appeals for further proceedings to determine the amount of the contract price adjustment, consistent with this opinion.

NOTES AND QUESTIONS

1. *The gaps in the drafting of § 2-612*: Peters, Remedies for Breach of Contracts Relating to the Sale of Goods Under the Uniform Commercial Code: A Roadmap for Article Two,[38] is still an often quoted important analysis of this part of the Code. Professor, and now Justice, Peters says of § 2-612:

[It] is reasonably clear at the extremes.

[A] If the breach is trivial and curable, the buyer must accept the installment and cannot categorically refuse further installments. He may, however, be able to reduce or postpone payments otherwise due upon delivery.... [She cites §§ 2-609 and 2-717 for this idea.]

[B] On the other hand, incurable breaches so substantial as to impair the value of the contract as a whole will privilege total rejection of installment and contract....

[C] It's the middle ground which remains unnecessarily uncertain. Consider the following cases:

   (1) the defect is trivial and uncurable;

   (2) the defect is trivial, curable, but not cured;

   (3) the defect is substantial as to the installment only and not curable;

   (4) the defect is substantial as to the installment only, curable, but not cured;

   (5) the defect is substantial as to the installment, and as to the contract, and seller actually tenders adequate cure....

The present language of 2-612 is a law professors' delight. Introduced at the proper moment, when the class in commercial law needs to be shaken up, it guarantees at least two class hours of wandering through a maze of inconsistent statutory standards and elliptical cross references....

Would the *Burroughs* case be an example of the second, the fourth or another of Peters' categories?

2. *The costs of contesting the importance of a default*: The Court of Claims raised § 2-612 on its own; neither Burroughs' nor the United States' brief discussed the section. The parties viewed the matter as one of interpretation of the contract as did the United States Postal Service Board of Contract Appeals. The Board found a delivery sequence requirement in the Request for Proposal accepted by Burroughs, and it was not concerned with the importance of this provision — it was enough that Burroughs had not complied.

---

[38]Reprinted by permission of The Yale Law Journal Company and Fred B. Rothman & Company from The Yale Law Journal, Vol. 73, pp. 225-227 (1963).

There is great concern about waste in government. Government procurement should be as efficient as possible. To what extent do cases such as the *Burroughs* decision excuse sloppy practice on the part of large corporations which supply the government and support the cynical folk-saying "close enough for government work?" Why isn't it enough to show a failure to comply with the contract? What would be the consequences of a more demanding standard?

c. The Long Wait: Delay and Calling Off the Deal After One Has Given Extensions

FAIRCHILD STRATOS CORP. v. LEAR SIEGLER, INC.

337 F.2d 785 (4th Cir. 1964)

BELL, J. [The Hufford Corporation Division of Lear Siegler, Inc. [hereafter Hufford], appealed from a judgment awarding Fairchild Stratos Corporation [hereafter Fairchild], damages upon a finding that Hufford breached a special warranties contract. The court affirms the finding of a breach but not the amount of damages.]

The background facts of this case are rather complex; the legal issues are reasonably simple. Generated by Fairchild's invitation to bid, Hufford on January 4, 1960, submitted proposals to design, fabricate, and install a stretch wrap forming press in Fairchild's Hagerstown, Maryland, plant. The press, according to the district court, was to be "a sophisticated piece of machinery, the purpose of which was, with a high degree of automation, to pull and stretch a sheet of aluminum to conform to dies for half sections of boat hulls so as to cause the formation of aluminum half-boat hulls which could be thereafter welded together to make a complete hull for certain aluminum pleasure boats that [Fairchild] desired to manufacture and sell." In its proposals, Hufford made certain affirmations of fact which are germane to the present controversy.

Hufford stated that "the equipment will be designed and built so that *no hand work* will be required in the formation of parts." (Emphasis in original.) Hufford further stated that "the stretch forming equipment will be capable of producing formed boat hull halves at a rate of ten (10) parts per hour or six (6) minutes per part on existing dies constructed by Fairchild...." This statement was qualified in two respects: first, by the statement that it could not be expected that the press would, immediately after installation, be capable of producing parts at the guaranteed rate until operators had been trained and the machine's functions refined, and second, as a consequence, Hufford was "to provide a qualified operating crew for a period of three (3) months to bring this facility to a full scale production capacity, simultaneously training [Fairchild's] personnel in operational procedures, maintenance, tooling, etc." The cost of providing the crew was to be borne by Fairchild.

Hufford agreed to manufacture and ship components in the order required for installation, so that installation could proceed concurrently with the latter stages of machine manufacture. Shipments were to start approximately four months from the date of receipt of the proposals and were to be completed two months thereafter. The purchase price was to be paid in six installments, five during the time that Hufford was shipping parts to Fairchild and installing them at Fairchild's plant and the sixth upon the completion of shipment, installation, and acceptance of the parts by Fairchild.

Fairchild issued a purchase order on January 21, 1960, accepting Hufford's proposals. Fairchild, in the purchase order, suggested that the cost of the operating crew be prorated, so that if less than three months was required, Fairchild's obligation would be accordingly reduced. Fairchild also suggested that shipments begin within four months from January 15, 1960, (the date of Fairchild's acceptance of the proposals by telephone) and be completed two months thereafter. Hufford agreed to these suggestions on February 2, 1960, and as of that date the terms and conditions of the contract were made explicit.

By the terms of the contract, Hufford was obligated to begin shipment of the components of the press on May 15, 1960, and to complete deliveries by July 15, 1960. This schedule was not met. Hufford's first shipment, that of rails for the press, was not made until July 12, 1960; the final shipment was not made until September 8, 1960; and not until November 21, 1960, did the press become operable. Thus, Hufford from the beginning was late in deliveries and acknowledged this fact in inter-company correspondence. For instance, a July 1, 1960, memorandum from Hufford's president stated:

> We are badly behind schedule on this machine. Our customer is in serious need for production from the machine to introduce their new line of boats in time to meet the marketing season.

The operating crew which was to be provided for a three month period arrived at Fairchild's plant and began work on the press on October 31, 1960. Initial attempts to stretch matching half hulls failed. Some measure of success was achieved on December 22, 1960, when a matching pair of half hulls was stretched; but it was found that when the half hulls were trimmed and put on the assembly jig, the tumble home area[39] lacked any formation at all. It was this area that was to present the major difficulties in the press' operation right up until Hufford's breach. After the December experience, Hufford undertook to redesign the machine assembly used in forming the tumble home area.[40] Discussions were

---

[39]Described by the district court as the area in the stern of the boat "where the sides bend inward to join. It may be likened to the base of an isosceles triangle."

[40]Formation of the tumble home area was to be achieved by imposing localized pressure on the aluminum sheets by the use of heavy pressure rubber rollers.

held within the period between January 6, 1961, and February 10, 1961, between representatives of the two companies to discuss problems in connection with the press and to try to work out an agreement as to what would constitute an acceptable half hull. Fairchild requested a completion date for the press' qualification, and Hufford's representative stated that Hufford expected the press to be ready for acceptance by April 7, 1961. Fairchild, waiving any claim it may have had to hold Hufford in breach at a prior date, orally advised Hufford that June 1, 1961, was the deadline for qualification.

Hufford, purporting to confirm the oral agreements between the parties, submitted a written memorandum in which it agreed to redesign and modify the machine element to provide configuration in the tumble home area and proposed a set of standards to determine whether the half hulls were in conformity with the die and with each other. Fairchild replied in writing, suggesting specific tolerances of stand off from the die in both the tumble home and forward areas of the boat and gave formal notice of the June 1, 1961, deadline. Hufford wrote and declined to accept specific tolerances as dimensional limitations, but it reiterated its memorandum position that the stand off in the tumble home area would be no more than that which could be pushed into position against the die by hand pressure. Hufford again acknowledged, without guaranteeing, its target date of April 7, 1961. On April 5, 1961, Hufford stretched two half hulls on the press. Although there was marked improvement in conformation on the second half hull, the stern area stood approximately two feet from the die, and it was impossible to force it into position by hand. Under these circumstances, Fairchild refused to give written confirmation that the machine was functioning properly.

Additional corrective work was done on the press by Hufford representatives and on April 15, 1961, they began stretching half hulls with Fairchild personnel as onlookers or helpers in loading and unloading the press. On April 24, 1961, Hufford representatives stretched three half hulls, and the third, as the most satisfactory, was left on the die for Fairchild's inspection. The following day, April 15, 1961, Hufford's representative advised Fairchild that he was ready for the qualification test. That same day, upon Fairchild's inquiry, Hufford's representatives prepared a test procedure and delivered it to Fairchild. It was agreed by the parties that the qualification run would consist of six half hulls of each hand rather than the ten upon which they had previously agreed.

The qualification run was never undertaken. Instead, Fairchild and Hufford reached an impasse. Hufford insisted that Fairchild accept the standards for forming sequence and procedures as set forth in Hufford's memorandum of April 25, 1961, and further insisted that if these standards were met by the qualification test, Fairchild must accept the press without regard to whether or not it could produce acceptable boat hulls. Fairchild adamantly refused, advising Hufford that it might undertake the qualifying test at any time but that Fairchild would accept or reject the press only on the basis of its operating characteristics and that there was no substitute for actual demonstration. This impasse came to a head on May 26, 1961, when Fairchild sent a telegram to Hufford stating that:

as parts and service. In addition, the utility industry had a general interest in the survival of competition in the reactor and power-generation industry; Westinghouse was an important player in that market. At one point, after three months of trial hearings had been held, a Pittsburgh judge was asked about his efforts to convince the parties to settle:

> The fiscal well-being, possibly the survival, of one of the world's corporate giants is in jeopardy. Likewise, the future of thousands of jobs.
>
> Any decision I hand down will hurt somebody and because of that potential damage, I want to make it clear that it will happen only because certain captains of industry could not together work out their problems so that the hurt might have been held to a minimum....
>
> Solomon-like as I want to be, I can't cut this baby in half...

There are also, of course, some pressures to proceed with the litigation. There is a chance that both parties overestimate their chances for winning the lawsuit, and so see the other side's position as unreasonable. One or both of the parties may in fact *be* unreasonable, making it more difficult to get agreement. And some reasons are more subtle. Professor Macaulay[48] has pointed out:

> [L]itigation may legitimate concessions in the eyes of outsiders who audit decisions. For example, the customers of Westinghouse are utilities whose rates are regulated. Without some strong justification, they could not negotiate a settlement with Westinghouse and then ask for approval of a rate increase to cover the balance of the loss. The chance that Westinghouse might win may serve to rationalize settlement, and the act of bringing suit might show the regulators that the utilities are not just giving money away. Consumer and antinuclear power organizations filed petitions in eleven states asking state utility regulators to scrutinize any out-of-court settlements that utilities may reach with Westinghouse. These groups assert that if utilities do not hold Westinghouse to its contracts, consumers will have to pay the extra fuel costs....
>
> The Wall Street Journal ... points to ... [an] assertion of norms that are not coterminous with the law of contract, in the Westinghouse cases:
>
> > [T]he electric utilities have canceled and stretched out contracts for atomic power plants, putting a financial squeeze on such companies as Westinghouse.

---

[48]Macaulay, Elegant Models, Empirical Pictures, and the Complexities of Contract, 11 Law & Society Review 507 (1977).

"You and I know that in the real world of business there's going to be some horse-trading," an industry person says. "You can bet that Westinghouse is reminding companies like Con Edison that it has gone along with them in stretching contracts."

Conduct in prior transactions generally is legally irrelevant in contract law, which focuses on the particular contract under litigation. However, the claim of prior accommodation to the needs of the utilities was highly relevant if any settlement was to be reached.

Although it would be hard to prove, the contract litigation process may also exert an indirect influence on the behavior of the managers of industrial enterprises even where they devote little thought to it. Those making bargains may tacitly rely on the law to fill gaps and provide sanctions, in order to avoid the costs of negotiating about unlikely contingencies or of constructing elaborate systems of security to insure performance. Contract law may crystallize business customs and provide a normative vocabulary, affecting expectations about what is fair. Westinghouse, for example, did not repudiate its uranium oxide contracts in the name of pure self-interest, but sought to cloak its actions in the language of the Uniform Commercial Code. Its positions, in that guise, may have been more palatable to some of its customers. It may be easier to negotiate with someone asserting a plausible claim of right than with an outlaw openly scorning those who had relied on its promise. (Perhaps the U.C.C. served as a means of self-justification so that executives at Westinghouse felt better about not honoring the commitment their firm had made.) We can only speculate about the situation had the drafters of the Uniform Commercial Code adopted a more rigorous standard that rarely excused nonperformance based on the occurrence of an unforeseen contingency. Suppose the rule had been that one who makes a promise must perform come hell or high water. Would Westinghouse have marched into bankruptcy trying to perform or would it have begged for mercy? Would the impact have been only on the amount of any settlement, since the likelihood of victory by Westinghouse would have been insignificant and thus worth little?

Ultimately, the cases brought by the utilities were settled. Judge Merhige, the federal judge presiding over most of the cases, pressed the parties to settle; the day the trial opened he told the assembled lawyers that "I don't ever expect to finish these cases.... I expect (them) to get settled."[49] There had been relatively little in the way of settlement negotiations up to that time. Lawyers for the utilities expressed surprise about this, but some who were following the case suggested that Westinghouse was digging up information about the international

---

[49]Pappas, Westinghouse, Utilities Under Pressure to Settle Uranium Suit Before Court Does, Wall Street Journal, June 2, 1978 at 32, cols. 1-3.

breach resulted in only two lost working days — by no reasonable standard a material breach.

Hufford's argument carries some force. Generally "in the contracts of merchants, time is of the essence," *Norrington v. Wright*, 115 U.S. 188, 203, 6 S.Ct. 12, 29 L.Ed. 366 (1885), and the failure of the seller to meet a promised day of performance permits the buyer to rescind. We think, however, that the present contract may not be viewed as an ordinary mercantile contract. It is more akin to the contract discussed in *Beck & Pauli Lithographing Co. v. Colorado Milling & Elevator Co.*, 52 F. 700 (8 Cir. 1892). There, in considering a seller's action for the purchase price of custom-made stationery, the Eighth Circuit reversed a directed verdict for the buyer. The court declined to accept the buyer's contention that the seller's delay of one day in delivery constituted a material breach of the contract, for as the court stated:

> "[I]n contracts for work or skill, and the materials upon which it is to be bestowed, a statement fixing the time of performance of the contract is not ordinarily of its essence, and a failure to perform within the time stipulated, followed by substantial performance after a short delay, will not justify the aggrieved party in repudiating the entire contract, but will simply give him his action for damages for the breach of the stipulation. *Tayloe v. Sandiford*, 7 Wheat. 13, 17 [5 L.Ed. 384]; *Hambly v. [Delaware, M. & V.] Railroad Co.*, 21 Feb.Rep. 541, 544, 554, 557." 52 F. at 703.

We think that this was, as in the Beck case, a contract for "work or skill" and "time [was] not ... of its essence." Thus, Hufford's delay of two working days in demonstrating that the press performed in accordance with its warranted capabilities, nothing else appearing, would not have justified Fairchild's rescission. But ours is a different case. It will be recalled that the contract contemplated that shipment of component parts of the press was to begin May 15, 1960, and was to be completed by July 15, 1960, at which time Hufford was given three months to bring the press up to its warranted capabilities. By October 15, 1960, Hufford was to have completed its contractual obligations and was to receive the final installment payment, and Fairchild was to begin mass production and distribution of aluminum pleasure boats. This schedule was not met, and in view of the sophistication of the press, the first of its kind, it seems improbable that the parties expected the schedule to be met to the day. Significantly, Fairchild waived a demonstration of the press' warranted capabilities until June 1, 1961. This date seemed an eminently reasonable deadline in view of Hufford's assurance, repeated in correspondence, that it would have the press ready by April 7, 1961. Thus, we are not faced here with the situation where a seller in a contract for "work or skill" fails to meet a specified day for performance. Rather we are faced with a seller who failed to meet a contract performance date, failed to meet a subsequent date set by himself, and then failed to meet an even later date set by the buyer. Even in out-of-the-ordinary mercantile contracts, there must come a day when a long suffering buyer may demand performance or opt rescission. In our case that day came on June 1, 1961....

We conclude that the district court correctly held that Hufford's failure to demonstrate the warranted capabilities of the press by June 1, 1961, constituted a material breach of the contract and entitled Fairchild to rescind....

NOTES AND QUESTIONS

1. *The reasons for Fairchild's actions*: Why did Fairchild let matters drag on for so long? Why did it then insist on calling off the deal? Lear Siegler contended that in July 1960 Fairchild was under pressure from its bankers to eliminate money losing projects. Its brief tells the story this way:

> In January, 1960, plaintiff was negotiating to become the sole source of supply for aluminum boats for Sears, Roebuck & Company and was interested in launching a program of boats of its own design. Plaintiff was also building F27 airplanes and radar antennas. For use in these projects, plaintiff requested and received from defendant a quotation on the desired stretch press, and on January 25, 1960, issued to defendant a purchase order for it. On February 3, 1960, the plaintiff's Directors voted ... to approve the purchase of the press. The basis of this approval was that a contract to assemble 1,300 boats for the 1960 Sears season had been received; and although the press was not involved in the Sears program for 1960, it would be required for the production for 1961 and subsequent years, as well as for plaintiff's own line of boats, its airplane and radar programs. The Sears program for 1961 contemplated a minimum of 10,800 and a maximum of 13,800 boats.
>
> On February 23, 1960, the plaintiff entered into a contract with Miracle Marine, Inc., Theodore Cromp, President, under which Miracle Marine, Inc. was to participate in design, development, advertising, sales promotion, and the establishing of dealerships for a line of marine products to be manufactured by plaintiff....
>
> Commencing in February, 1960, while the stretch press was being manufactured, plaintiff undertook the manufacturing of boats for Sears and Miracle Marine using boat hull halves from a Sears inventory and those purchased from Allied Products Incorporated. This effort was pursued vigorously until a Sears request for stop work was received on June 17, 1960, because of structural failure of plaintiff's boats in tests at the Sears Test Center, Fort Meyers, Florida. Manufacturing for inventory was allowed to continue until July 19, 1960, on the assumption that structural fixes would resolve the problem. Subsequent testing of the structural fixes showed that the problem was not resolved, therefore, a management decision was made on July 19, 1960, to stop work on the boat program....

On September 14, 1960, the Directors were told that the cooperative attitude of Sears would reduce by approximately one-half the indicated loss on the boat program and that expenses on the boat program had been written off as incurred. An attempt was then made to sell the boat program, including the press but the prospective purchaser, Miracle Marine, could not finance the purchase. Finally, on November 28, 1960, Fairchild advised all distributors that a decision had been reached not to renew their agreements at their expiration and immediate termination was invited....

[Thus, when Fairchild canceled the contract on June 1, 1961, its] boat program had terminated much earlier.... No practical or production use was to be made of the parts [produced at the demonstration of the machine] and they were nothing more than test pieces to be run for demonstration purposes.

As we might expect, Fairchild's brief sees the story differently:

The 1960 Sears boat program had absolutely no connection with or relevance to the pending lawsuit.

Difficulties with the Sears boats did not mean abandonment by Fairchild of its own boat program, based on mass production from the Hufford press. Fairchild's own program was only abandoned after June 1, 1961, when the Hufford press failed to prove out. The Hufford [Lear Siegler] brief fails to differentiate between the Sears boat program and the Fairchild boat program which was geared to the boat press.

The trial judge responded to Lear Siegler's argument by saying that "Fairchild's activities can only be characterized as those of prudence and caution, because it was obvious to Fairchild throughout the period that it was communicating with its distributors and seeking to sell the stretch press that Hufford was badly in default under the contract. That Fairchild sought to minimize its damages does not mean that it caused a breach of the contract. At most, Fairchild had a motive in failing to waive all of Hufford's defaults under the contract, but if, as is hereafter concluded, Hufford breached the contract, Fairchild's motive in asserting the breach is immaterial."

2. *Waiver and notice*: Is this decision consistent in reasoning and result with *Eastern Air Lines v. McDonnell Douglas*, *supra*? If Fairchild had given notice of its intention before it canceled the contract, would that have set the stage for the kind of negotiation so valued in the *Eastern Air Lines* case?

3. *The Fairchild case under the U.C.C.*: How would the *Fairchild* case be decided under the Uniform Commercial Code? Under § 2-601, Fairchild would have had a right to reject the defective delivery. Under § 2-606(1)(b), Fairchild may have accepted the goods by failing to make an effective rejection. However, it is questionable whether Hufford ever made a delivery or tender to start the reasonable time for inspection running. See § 2-602(1). Under § 2-503(1),

"[t]ender of delivery requires that the seller put and hold conforming goods at the buyer's disposition...." This was not done.

Perhaps under § 2-208(3), the course of performance showed a waiver of the original delivery date. Section 2-209(5) allows a retraction of a waiver "by reasonable notification ... that strict performance will be required of any term waived...." Yet Fairchild probably cannot demand that Lear Siegler meet the original contract date after Fairchild waived it. Section 2-209(5) blocks retractions of waivers when they would be "unjust in view of a material change of position in reliance on the waiver."

Could Fairchild, after such a waiver and reliance, then set a reasonable deadline for completion of the machine and declare the contract at an end if Lear Siegler failed to meet it? Section 2-309(1) provides that the "time for shipment or delivery or any other action under a contract if not provided in this Article or agreed upon shall be a reasonable time." We might think that after a waiver which has been relied upon, the time has not been "agreed upon." Then Lear Siegler would have a reasonable time in which to perform. Official Comment 1 tells us "[i]t thus depends upon what constitutes acceptable commercial conduct in view of the nature, purpose and circumstances of the action to be taken." However, this comment continues, saying "[a]greement as to a definite time ... may be found in a term implied from the contractual circumstances, usage of trade or course of dealing or performance as well as in an express term. Such cases fall outside of this subsection since in them the time for action is 'agreed' by usage." Fairchild's action in setting a new time and Lear Siegler's acceptance of it could be viewed as an agreement by course of dealing or performance.

The Code seems written to deal with contracts for delivery of "shelf goods." It does not seem too helpful when a seller and buyer enter a "quasi-partnership" to assemble a large custom-made machine in the buyer's plant and to work out difficulties as part of an ongoing process. We can always fall back on notions of agreement and the reasonable expectations of the parties. However, once the buyer allows the seller to miss deadlines for completion and gives the seller second and third chances in this kind of relationship, it is often hard to determine the reasonable expectations of the parties.

4. *"Time is of the essence" clauses*: Lawyers often draft clauses that attempt to give their client the right to cancel a contract if there is any delay in performance. Consider a few examples used by major corporations:

A. Buyers' Clauses

(1) The purchase order of Trane, a manufacturer of heating and air conditioning equipment provides:

> DELIVERY DATE. Time is of the essence and if delivery of items or rendering of service is not completed by the time promised, the Buyer reserves the right without liability, in addition to its other rights and remedies to terminate this contract by notice effective when received by

Seller, as to stated items not yet shipped or services not yet rendered, and to purchase substitute items or services elsewhere and charge the Seller with any loss incurred. Any provisions herein for delivery of articles or the rendering of services by installments shall not be construed as making the obligations of the Seller severable.

(2) The purchase order of Allis-Chalmers, a manufacturer of heavy machinery provides:

DELIVERY DATE. Shipment must be made to meet the required date specified. Time is of the essence. Production schedules established or commitments made to satisfy the required date must not contemplate production or procurement in advance of the current lead or procurement time required to meet such date, without the specific written approval of Buyer. On premature shipments, Buyer may return the goods at Seller's expense, and in any event payment will be withheld and any discount period will begin to run from the required date specified. Buyer, without waiving any other legal rights, reserves the right to cancel without charge or to postpone deliveries of any of the goods or services covered by this order which are not shipped in time to meet the required delivery date....

B. Sellers' Clauses

The following clauses are used by the Xerox Corporation on their standard forms:

1. DELIVERY — Customer shall accept delivery of ... equipment at the installation address(es) indicated herein in accordance with the delivery schedule quoted by Xerox and in no event later than fifteen (15) days after notification by the appropriate Xerox branch that the Equipment is available for delivery. In case of multiple unit purchases, Xerox shall have the right to make separate deliveries. Xerox shall deliver the Equipment within 120 days of acceptance of this Agreement, provided that if Xerox fails to make timely delivery of any individual installation of Equipment, the Customer may treat this Agreement as breached as to such individual installation only. If at the time of execution of this Agreement, Customer requests delivery more than thirty (30) days later than the delivery date quoted by Xerox, the Equipment Purchase Price shall be Xerox' Equipment price in effect at the time of actual delivery.

2. DEFAULT — Time is of the essence hereof and if Customer shall fail to pay when due any installment, or otherwise fail to observe, keep or perform any provisions of this Agreement required to be observed, kept or performed, or if Customer ceases doing business as a going concern, or if a petition is filed by or against Customer under any of the provisions or chapters of the Bankruptcy Act or any amendment thereto, or if Customer

shall make an assignment for the benefit of creditors or call a general meeting of creditors, or attempts an informal arrangement or composition with creditors or if a receiver or any officer of a court be appointed to have control of any of the property or assets of Customer or if Customer makes or has made any misstatement or false statement of fact in connection with this transaction, or if any of the foregoing occurs with regards to any guarantor, the unpaid time balance hereunder shall become immediately due and payable at Xerox' option and without notice.

If any of the foregoing occurs, Xerox shall have all of the rights and remedies of a secured party upon default under the Uniform Commercial Code or any similar law as enacted in the state where the equipment is located.

To the extent permitted by law, Xerox may recover the balance of all amounts due hereunder, enter upon the premises where the Equipment may be and render the Equipment unusable and/or take possession thereof and hereunder. In addition, Customer agrees at Xerox' request to assemble the Equipment and make it available to Xerox at a place designated by Xerox.

All rights and remedies of Xerox shall be cumulative and may be exercised successively or concurrently without impairing Xerox' security interest in the Equipment. Customer agrees to pay to Xerox reasonable attorneys' fees and legal expenses in exercising any of its rights and remedies upon default up to 15% of the unpaid balance and if such percentage is not so permitted, such other percentage or amount as is permissible under law. All the foregoing is without limitation or waiver or any other rights or remedies available to Xerox according to law.

One might ask, to what extent do Trane, Allis-Chalmers and Xerox Corporations gain greater rights by using these clauses than they would have if they said nothing about timely delivery or payment? To answer, one would begin by consulting U.C.C. §§ 2-507; 2-503; 2-601; 2-602(1); 2-612; 2-508; 1-201(3); 2-309(1); 1-204(1); 1-208. Xerox' rights as a secured creditor, and its rights in a bankruptcy or other insolvency proceeding are, of course, beyond the scope of this course.

The Restatement (Second) of Contracts deals with delayed performance in § 242. Two of the comments to that section suggest the Restatement's approach to common problems concerning delay that are found in the cases.

> *Substitute arrangements.* It is often said that in commercial transactions, notably those for the sale of goods, prompt performance by a party is essential if he is to be allowed to require the other to perform or, as it is sometimes put, "time is of the essence." The importance of prompt delivery by a seller of goods generally derives from the circumstance that goods, as contrasted for example with land, are particularly likely to be subject to rapid fluctuations in market price. Therefore, even a relatively short delay

in a rising market may adversely affect the buyer by causing a sharp increase in the cost of "cover." See Uniform Commercial Code §§ 2-712, 2-713. A less rigid standard applies to contracts for the sale of goods to be delivered in installments or to be specially manufactured for the buyer. On the other hand, considerable delay does not preclude enforcement of a contract for the sale of land if damages are adequate to compensate for the delay and there are no special circumstances indicating that prompt performance was essential and no express provisions requiring such performance....

Effect of agreement. The agreement of the parties often contains a provision for the time of performance or tender. It may simply provide for performance on a stated date. In that event, a material breach on that date entitles the injured party to withhold his performance and gives him a claim for damages for delay, but it does not of itself discharge the other party's remaining duties. Only if the circumstances, viewed as of the time of the breach, indicate that performance or tender on that day is of genuine importance are the injured party's remaining duties discharged immediately, with no period of time during which they are merely suspended. It is, of course, open to the parties to make performance or tender by a stated date a condition by their agreement, in which event, absent excuse ... delay beyond that date results in discharge ... Such stock phrases as "time is of the essence" do not necessarily have this effect, although ... they are to be considered along with other circumstances in determining the effect of delay....

M & I MARSHALL & ILSLEY BANK v. PUMP

88 Wis. 2d 323, 276 N.W.2d 295 (1977)

CONNOR HANSEN, J. The third party action is based upon long-term financing commitments the appellants obtained from Crown Life Insurance Company  (hereinafter Crown) for a 92-unit, four building apartment project to be constructed by the appellant at Menasha, Wisconsin. Construction financing for the project was provided by Richter-Schroeder Company (hereinafter Richter), a mortgage banking firm and a loan correspondent of Crown. Richter was acquired by M & I Marshall & Ilsley Bank (hereinafter Bank) while the construction was in progress.

In two financing commitments dated January 21 and 22, 1974, Crown agreed to lend appellants $1.16 million secured by two first mortgages for $440,000 and $720,000. These commitments provided that they would be null and void if the transaction was not completed within 253 days, unless extended in writing, at Crown's option. The commitments required, among other things, as conditions precedent, a title insurance policy without exceptions, payment of outstanding taxes and completion in strict compliance with the plans and specifications, including landscaping.

The appellants were unable to complete the project by the time the commitments expired in October, 1974, and requested an extension. At the request of the appellants, Crown ultimately agreed to four successive extensions of the commitments, first to December 15, 1974, then to April 15, 1975, then to July 15, 1975, and finally to a one-month extension to August 15, 1975.

During the period of the extensions, the appellants needed funds in addition to the original construction financing for the project. As a result, in June, 1975, the Bank agreed to advance appellants an additional $100,000, secured by a $250,000 second mortgage. This mortgage also covered a $116,000 rental holdback.

Appellants and Richter began preparations for closing in August, 1975, even though work continued on the project. The architect's certificate of completion was signed August 7th, but the project engineer indicated that this referred to the building itself and not to "odds and ends," such as hardware, carpeting, appliances or cleanup. He further indicated that some of the incomplete items, landscaping among them, were not included in the building plans. He admitted that building code violations existed the day he signed the completion certificate.

The closing did not occur because a title policy had not been obtained and the project was not completed. An inspection of the project on August 18th by Tom Richter showed that although the buildings were structurally finished the following work remained to be done:

1. Installation of appliances, including 28 refrigerators, three stoves and two dishwasher front panels;

2. installation of carpet padding in 35 apartments, and carpeting in 53 apartments;

3. installation of numerous electric fixtures, including those in 31 bathrooms and 21 hallways;

4. installation of numerous doors and door hardware;

5. removal of construction materials from underground garages and installation of garage doors and electric door openers;

6. fifty percent of the exterior painting and installation of some roof flashing;

7. the landscaping; and

8. correction of a number of building code violations, including the addition of fire-resistant materials and doors to the furnace rooms and on the basement stairs in each of the four buildings and the installation of a new ventilating system in the underground parking area in each building.

The building had 20 tenants on August 15th and approximately five more were due to move in.

A title insurance policy was not obtained because construction lien claims had been filed and potential unfiled claims existed. The appellants were also delinquent in real estate taxes.

The first two construction loans had been completely disbursed by June 15, 1975. Advances and draw requests being processed on August 15, 1975, depleted the $100,000 loan from the Bank. Crown's last extension of the commitments expired August 15, 1975. Richter attempted to get a further extension from Crown. However, on September 4, 1975, Crown advised Richter that the commitments would not be reinstated. The Bank then brought this foreclosure action in which the appellants counterclaimed against Crown seeking specific performance of the long-term financing commitments.... [The court summarized evidence tending to show the project was financially shaky.]

The trial court concluded that time was not of the essence in this transaction and in so doing recognized the general rule that when time is not of the essence, the appellants would be entitled to notice of default and a reasonable time in which to perform.

However, in this case, where the appellants had been granted four extensions and no showing had been made that performance within a reasonable time was practically possible, the trial court concluded notice was not required because it would be a mere formality. To support this conclusion the trial court found that the real estate taxes were in arrears, the cost to complete the project was in excess of $10,000 and acceptable title insurance could not be provided and therefore that Crown was relieved of the commitments after they expired on August 15, 1975. The trial court also found that these breaches were substantial and were of the very essence of the financing commitment agreements.

Although, as previously stated, this appeal is from the judgment of foreclosure, the issue presented relates solely to the judgment of dismissal of the appellants' counterclaim against Crown.

The issue is whether the appellants were entitled to notice fixing a reasonable time for performance after August 15, 1975, before Crown could be relieved of the obligation of the prior commitments. We are of the opinion the trial court correctly decided the issue when it entered judgment dismissing the appellants' counterclaim against Crown.

... When Crown granted the extensions requested by the appellants, none of them stated that time was of the essence. The respondents do not seriously challenge the finding of the trial court that time was not of the essence. Instead, they direct their attention to the exception relied upon by the trial court in its determination that under the facts of this case no notice was necessary.

The greater weight of the evidence in this case supports the finding that the appellants were in substantial default. Certainly it cannot be said that such finding is against the great weight and clear preponderance of the evidence. The original completion date requirement in Crown's commitments was October, 1974. At the request of the appellants, Crown gave them until August 15, 1975, to perform. They did not so perform....

... At 17A, C.J.S., *Contracts*, § 478(b), it is stated:

> A demand for a performance is unnecessary where it is apparent that it would be unavailing or constitute a useless formality, ... Thus a demand for performance is unnecessary where there has been a prior absolute refusal or repudiation, or where the party from whom performance is due has placed it out of his power to perform, or has demonstrated his inability to perform, or where demand has been waived.

Time and additional funding were necessary for the appellants to complete this building project. There is nothing in the record from which an inference could be drawn that the appellants had refused to complete the building or that it was physically impossible to complete it. The difficulty is that after the appellants had been accommodated by having the original commitments extended four times, they had been unable to complete the project or provide acceptable title insurance.

... The appellants were well aware of the fact that the last extension of the commitment would expire on August 15, 1975, and that their last extension had been limited to one month.

The appellants contend that they had substantially performed the construction project. But this is not the issue. The issue is whether they had substantially breached the terms of the financing commitment contract and Crown was thereby relieved of giving them notice that it would not extend the agreement a fifth time and afford appellants a reasonable time to complete the project....

This is a financing contract, where the closing actually begins a long-term relationship between the parties rather than ending one. Circumstances such as those presented here do not require the giving of a notice that the commitment will not be further extended or that the appellants be given additional time to comply with the contract provisions. This is not a situation in which a short additional extension of time would result in the transfer of a building with no further financial involvement of the parties. In that situation, where the court need only compute the completion costs and award damages, the delay in completion might not be considered a material breach. Here, when the project was finally completed and evidence of acceptable title available, Crown would be obligated to pay $1.16 million and receive repayment over an extended period of time. The long delay and inability to perform clearly present a material breach....

By the Court. — Judgment affirmed.

NOTES AND QUESTIONS

1. *Litigation rules and counseling rules*: Suppose you represent a bank which finds itself in a situation much like that in the *Marshall & Ilsley Bank* case.

Would you tell your client that it need not give notice that it is not going to renew financing or might you be more cautious?

2. *Notices and settlements once again*: Is this decision consistent in reasoning and result with *Eastern Air Lines v. McDonnell Douglas Corp., supra*? If the Bank had given notice, would that have set the stage for the kind of negotiation so valued in the *Eastern Air Lines* case?

3. *Delays in building contracts*: Delays in building construction contracts raise special problems. The *Marshall & Ilsley Bank* case points out that building construction often involves lenders. It also reminds us that completion dates often are waived.

On one hand, a builder or subcontractor's delay can be a material breach of contract. The owner or the general can terminate the contract and get someone else to complete the job. If the aggrieved party must pay more to complete construction, it can recover its increased costs as damages. On the other hand, an owner's failure to make payments may give the builder a right to suspend performance and in some situations to cancel and sue for damages. However, owners can delay performance in other ways as well. Often, they cannot get the necessary financing when they expected to have it, and they postpone the starting date until all the lenders have agreed to finance the project.

Professor Halper notes that builders can be hurt by such delays:

> A contractor bids for work in the expectation that he will not be prevented from organizing it efficiently. He expects to have the freedom to determine the methods by which the project will be constructed and the sequence of thousands of tasks that comprise the construction of a building. Within the framework of his bargain with the owner, he plans to perform the work during advantageous times of the year. If the starting date is postponed or the progress of the work is delayed unexpectedly, the delay may affect the seasons during which the work is scheduled, the construction methods, the construction sequences, or any combination of them.
>
> For example, a contractor may have assumed that the construction period would start in the spring of one year and end in the summer of the following year. Thus, he would be building during two spring seasons, one winter, and two summers. A six-month delay in the starting date might change that work period to two winters, two springs, and one summer. Pouring concrete in the winter is more expensive than doing it in the spring or summer. In fact, severe cold and snow will make almost any kind of outdoor operation go more slowly. The cost differences may be substantial....
>
> Notwithstanding the potential damage to the general contractor arising from excusable delays, relatively few construction contracts provide for an increase in the contract price when such delays occur. Most contractors are content to take the risk of short interruptions of the work schedule caused by an excusable delay. That is, they are willing to settle for an extension of the time period in which they are required to perform. On the other hand,

if the interruption lasts for a significant period of time, contractors usually seek much more drastic relief — the right to cancel the contract altogether....[41]

However, suppose *both parties* are responsible for the delay. In *United States v. Klingensmith, Inc.*[42] a subcontractor sued a general contractor for damages caused by the general's failure to coordinate the work of its subcontractors. The subcontractor contended that this caused delays which injured it. The trial court found that the subcontractor's own actions also contributed to the delays. The court concluded that neither party could collect delay damages from the other. The Court of Appeals reversed this decision. It said that each party should be able to recover to the extent of the injury caused by the other's delay. The subcontractor could recover whatever damages it proves that the general caused minus the amount of damages the general proves the subcontractor to have caused.

> Such a rule protects each party from losses due to the delay of the other throughout the period of performance. It also induces each party to avoid imposing losses on the other at any time during the period of performance.... Therefore, when both parties to a contract breach their contractual obligations by delaying performance, a court must assess the losses attributable to each party's delay and apportion damages accordingly.

Courts that follow this view still insist that the evidence must enable them to allocate the losses caused by each party's delay. Often this cannot be done, and the court will reject any claim for damages.[43] Other courts, however, say that when each party proximately contributed to the delay, "the law does not provide for the recovery or apportionment of damages occasioned thereby to either party."[44]

Some construction contracts contain "no-damage-for-delay" clauses. Often such clauses are found in standard form construction contracts entered as the result of competitive bidding on government contracts. Such a clause might provide: "The Contractor agrees to make no claim for damages for delay in the performance of this contract occasioned by any act or omission of the City or any of its representatives, and agrees that any such claim shall be fully compensated for by an extension of time to complete performance of the work as provided herein."

---

[41]Halper, Negotiating Construction Contracts III, 18 Real Estate Review 45, 48 (Summer 1988). Published by Warren, Gorham & Lamont, Inc., Boston.

[42]670 F.2d 1227 (D.C. Cir. 1982).

[43]See Lichter v. Mellon-Stuart Co., 305 F.2d 216 (3d Cir. 1962).

[44]See, *e.g.*, J.A. Jones Const. Co. v. Greenbriar Shopping Center, 332 F. Supp. 1336 (N.D. Ga. 1971).

Professor Halper comments,

> Contractors who agree to such a clause carry a heavy burden. They are already vulnerable to the risk of cataclysmic events that neither they nor the owners can control. The no-damages-for-delay clause adds the risk of delays caused by the owner's behavior (subject to possible relief from a court or arbitration panel). This risk would be best left to an insurance company or a Mississippi riverboat gambler.
>
> Nevertheless, contractors routinely agree to execute contracts that include a no-damages-for-delay clause. The nature of the competitive bidding process and the need of contractors to provide work to cover overhead and keep their supervisory staffs employed causes contractors to take such risks.[45]

Courts have upheld these clauses, but they have intervened to regulate them. In New York such a clause will not "excuse or prevent the recovery of damages resulting from the contractee's grossly negligent or willful conduct, i.e., conduct which 'smacks of intentional wrongdoing.' "[46] Morever, the New York courts allow a contractor to recover damages despite such a clause when the damages resulted from "uncontemplated delays caused by the contractee [the building owner]." They also will allow recovery when the contractee "is responsible for delays which are so unreasonable that they connote a relinquishment of the contract by the contractee with the intention of never resuming it."[47] Why have the courts created these exceptions to no-damages-for-delay clauses?

5. "ANTICIPATORY BREACH" AND "REASONABLE GROUNDS FOR INSECURITY"

a. Repudiation and the Power to Walk Away From the Deal

It is not uncommon that, before the time for performance arrives, one of the parties to a contract develops doubts about the other party's intention, or ability, to perform as required. Suppose that on January 2, Businessperson hires Linguist to accompany her as an interpreter on an extended trip to the Soviet Union and various Eastern European countries. The trip is to begin on August 1st. On January 25th, Businessperson is promoted to a new position and the trip is

---

[45]Halper, Negotiating Construction Contracts III, 18 Real Estate Review 45, 49 (Summer 1988). Published by Warren, Gorham & Lamont, Inc., Boston.

[46]Kalish-Jarcho, Inc. v. City of New York, 58 N.Y.2d 377, 461 N.Y.S. 746, 448 N.E.2d 413 (1983).

[47]See Corinno Civetta Const. Corp. v. City of New York, 67 N.Y.2d 297, 502 N.Y.S.2d 681, 493 N.E.2d 905 (1986). Compare Wes-Julian Const. Corp. v. Commonwealth, 223 N.E.2d 72 (S.J.Ct. Mass. 1967).

canceled. She immediately notifies Linguist that their contract is canceled. Linguist files suit on February 10th, alleging a breach of contract. Can he sue in February or must he wait until August 1st when the contract was to begin? After all, Businessperson has only said that she will not perform in the future, and she might change her mind between February and the end of July. Reading the contract literally, Businessperson has promised to perform in August, and she cannot fail to perform in August until it is August. However, in *Hochster v. De La Tour*,[48] the English court allowed an immediate suit to be brought, and this rule is followed by almost all American jurisdictions. The Queen's Bench said that this rule would encourage employees to get other employment as soon as they could. However, the employee did not have to sue but could await the day of the employer's performance.

The Queen's Bench could have dealt with the problem without allowing a suit for "anticipatory breach" to be brought before performance was due. All the employee really needs in most instances is to be sure that he or she can take another job between January and August in our example without breaching the obligation to perform under the original contract. If Businessperson repudiates the contract before her performance is due, Linguist is free to walk away from their contract at that point. In the language of the Restatement (Second) of Contracts, 253(2): "Where performances are to be exchanged under an exchange of promises, one party's repudiation of a duty to render performance discharges the other party's remaining duties to render performance." Clearly, this kind of self-help to avoid or mitigate damages is important, and in all but a few instances it is more important than the right to bring a lawsuit before the time for performance arises.

Suppose seller agrees to deliver one car on April 1st, ten on May 1st, and ten more on June 1st, and buyer promises to pay in specified installments for them. First, assume on March 20th, seller tells buyer that the deal is off and that no cars will be delivered. This would be an anticipatory breach since the repudiation came before the time specified for seller's performance. Second, assume there was no repudiation on March 20th, and seller delivered the first car on April 1st. However, seller fails to deliver the ten cars on May 1st and it is clear that seller will not deliver the ten cars due on June 1st. This would be a present breach of contract. (Anticipatory breaches are dealt with in Uniform Commercial Code §§ 2-610 and 2-611 while present breaches of installment contracts are governed by § 2-612.)

Does the distinction between anticipatory and present breaches make a difference? For many purposes a breach is a breach. The aggrieved party may sue or walk away free of obligation. However, there are a few distinctions. Suppose that seller changes his or her mind and decides to perform the contract after repudiating it. Under § 2-611(1), the seller can reinstate the contract by

---

[48]2 El. & B. 678, 118 Eng.Rep. 922 (Q.B. 1853).

retracting the anticipatory repudiation "unless the aggrieved party has since the repudiation canceled or materially changed his position or otherwise indicated that he considers the repudiation final."[49] After a present breach of contract, however, seller can reinstate the deal only with buyer's agreement. Seller, acting alone, cannot withdraw the repudiation even in the absence of reliance. Furthermore, § 2-725(1) provides that "[a]n action for breach of any contract of sale must be commenced within four years after the cause of action has accrued." A repudiation that is a present breach of contract starts the four year period running. However, § 2-610(a) says that after an anticipatory repudiation the aggrieved party may "for a commercially reasonable time await performance by the repudiating party." Would the cause of action accrue to trigger the statute of limitations before "a commercially reasonable time?"

What is a repudiation? Suppose seller, before the time for delivery arrives, writes buyer and says, "I doubt whether I shall be able to perform, and indeed, the way prices are going I doubt whether if I am able I shall care to do so." Restatement (Second) of Contracts § 250, Comment b., says that "mere expression of doubt as to his willingness or ability to perform is not enough to constitute a repudiation...."[50]

A more difficult issue is posed when one party insists on her rights under a contract as she sees them. Can a person repudiate a contract by insisting on an erroneous interpretation of a contract? Suppose that she honestly believes that her interpretation is the correct one, but a court later finds that she is wrong. Suppose most lawyers would say that the party's interpretation was plausible. To the extent that you can breach by insisting on a mistaken understanding of a contract, how can you maintain your position and avoid repudiating the deal? Consider the following:

BILL'S COAL CO., INC. v. BOARD OF PUBLIC UTILITIES OF SPRINGFIELD, MISSOURI

682 F.2d 883 (10th Cir.), *cert. denied* 459 U.S. 1171 (1982)

LOGAN, J. ... [Bill's Coal Company, Inc. had entered into a long-term contract in 1970 to supply all of the requirements of coal of the Board of Utilities of Springfield, Missouri ("Utility"). The contract provided for minimum and maximum amounts. The contract provided that before the end of each calendar year, Bill's Coal was to notify Utility as to the price for the next year, the price

---

[49]Restatement (Second) of Contracts § 256, states a similar rule for contracts other than those involving transactions in goods.

[50]However, the Second Restatement suggests that courts should expand Uniform Commercial Code § 2-609 to all contracts and allow a party who has "reasonable grounds for insecurity ... with respect to the performance of ... [the other party]" to demand adequate assurance of performance and to suspend performance until it is received. We will turn to this section of the Code later in these materials.

to take effect on April 1. The contract also contained an interesting termination clause. Utility was entitled to solicit bids from other coal companies. If Utility received a bid at least 25% under Bill's Coal's price, then Utility could terminate the contract effective March 31. If the bid was at least 15% less, then Utility could terminate, but not until the following March 31. The contract required Bill's Coal to quote its price F.O.B. its Garland, Kansas mine. Utility paid the cost of transportation from the mine to Springfield.

In March 1980, Utility notified Bill's Coal it was invoking the termination clause. Bill's Coal responded by bringing suit for breach of contract, and requesting both damages and injunctive relief. The trial court held that Bill's Coal had committed a bad faith breach by repeatedly urging an interpretation of the termination clause which it knew was contrary to the intentions of the parties. During discovery Bill's Coal had inadvertently given Utility a document which outlined an attorney's plan to assert that the contract required a comparison of the Bill's Coal price at its mine-head with the competitor's bid for coal delivered to Springfield. This interpretation would have given Bill's Coal a huge cost advantage with respect to other suppliers. The trial court had held that Bill's Coal had adopted this position in bad faith, and that such a position amounted to a repudiation of the contract because it manifested an intention not to be bound by the terms of the agreement. Bill's Coal argued (1) that Missouri would not recognize a claim grounded in a failure to abide by the U.C.C.'s good faith provision, (2) that Bill's Coal's interpretation was plausible and therefore could not be made in bad faith and, finally, (3) that even if the interpretation was made in bad faith, this did not interfere with any act of performance and so did not constitute a repudiation.]

... We do not address the first two arguments Bill's Coal makes since we agree that this type of bad faith behavior is not to be regarded as a contract breach or repudiation. In urging an interpretation of the termination clause it knew did not reflect the parties' intent, Bill's Coal did not affect either party's performance under the contract. A breach of a contract is a failure to provide the other party with the goods or services as the contract requires. See 20A *Mo. Ann. Stat.* §§ 400.2-601 to 608, 400.2-612; *Restatement (Second) of Contracts* §§ 235, 241, 243, 245 (1981). A repudiation is a party's manifestation that it is not going to provide those goods or services when they will be due at some future date. See 20A *Mo.Ann.Stat.* § 400.2-610; *Restatement (Second) of Contracts* § 250 (1981). The bad faith urging of a particular interpretation of a termination clause is neither a failure to perform contract obligations (breach) nor an indication those obligations will not be performed in the future (repudiation).

We can envision situations in which bad faith conduct might be actionable: for instance, if the Utility solicited bids from competing coal companies and Bill's Coal in some way coerced competitors into not submitting bids. That might constitute such a breach of Bill's Coal's good faith obligation as to allow the

Utility to cancel the contract.[51] But the mere urging of a particular interpretation is quite different. If a seller's interpretation of a termination clause is ludicrous, the buyer should ignore it; if the interpretation might prevail in a court of law, the seller has the right to urge it. If the party that wishes to invoke the termination clause is unsure of the merits of the other party's interpretation, it can either accept that interpretation, rely on its own interpretation, or obtain a declaratory judgment as to the meaning of the contract language.

Since we have found the trial court erred in its application of the law on the only issue it found against Bill's Coal in Phase II of the trial, the injunction we ordered reinstated should be continued in effect....

Our review of the trial court's rulings has been restricted to the one issue treated in this opinion. We express no view on its other rulings in Phase I or II of the trial. The Utility raises questions in its motion for clarification and instructions concerning price to be paid and whether additional bond should be required. These should be addressed by the trial court after remand, in light of the conclusions in this opinion and the trial court's other rulings interpreting the contract.

The case is hereby remanded for further proceedings consistent with this opinion.

[BARRETT, J.'s dissenting opinion, published at 685 F.2d 360 (1982)]

It is my view that the District Court correctly concluded that Bill's Coal's demand for more than it was entitled under the contract with Utility constitutes a repudiation under § 2-610 of the Missouri Uniform Commercial Code (20A U.A.M.S. § 2-610), fully justifying the Court's January 29, 1982, order dissolving the injunction. Thus, I would affirm the District Court.

The main issue generating this litigation involves the "take-out" provision of the 1979 amendment to the coal contract. That provision states, *inter alia*, that if Utility can secure a bid ... "at a delivered price of at least 25% less than the price quoted by [Bill's Coal] (adjusted to eliminate the depreciation credit referred to in paragraph 6) ... [Utility] may by written notice cancel this agreement as of the end of the then current fiscal year."

Utility had until March of the year to exercise the take-out provision. At a meeting later in the same day that the 1979 amendment was drafted, an attorney representing Bill's Coal noted that the contract language could be viewed to require a comparison of Bill's Coal quoted f.o.b. mine price to any competitor's delivered price. However, this attorney stated then that such was not the intention

---

[51]The only case the Utility cites that recognizes a cause of action for bad faith in connection with a termination clause, Baker v. Ratzlaff, 1 Kan.App.2d 285, 564 P.2d 153 (1977), is distinguishable. *Baker* holds that a party invoking a clause permitting termination in the event of nonpayment committed a breach of the good faith obligation if the party did not first request payment. A party's taking such affirmative acts is quite different from a party's urging a particular interpretation of the termination clause.

of the parties; rather, the parties agreed and intended that a comparison under the take-out clause would be delivery price versus delivery price.

In December, 1979, Bill's Coal became aware that Utility was going to solicit bids and attempt to utilize the "take-out" provision. Bill's Coal then formulated a "plan" to block a take-out by insisting that Utility make a comparison of Bill's Coal's f.o.b. mine price to competitors' delivered price. When Bill's Coal supplied Utility with its f.o.b. mine price for 1980, it also "demanded" that Utility make the bid comparison in accordance with Bill's Coal's "plan." An agent of Utility vehemently rejected Bill's Coal's proposed comparison formula and informed Bill's Coal if it insisted on the formula that Utility would see Bill's Coal in court.

Inasmuch as Bill's Coal's mine is located substantially closer to Springfield's power plant than any of its competitors, a comparison between Bill's Coal's f.o.b. mine price to competitor's delivery price could hardly, if ever, result in a bid sufficient to trigger the take-out provision. Bill's Coal's f.o.b. mine price was substantially higher than any competitor's f.o.b. mine price.

Utility proceeded to solicit bids and to compare Bill's Coal's f.o.b. mine price to competitors' f.o.b. mine price. On March 27, 1980, Utility gave Bill's Coal notice of termination under the take-out clause. Utility thereafter filed a declaratory judgment action against Bill's Coal seeking a declaration of the relative rights and liabilities of the parties under the 1979 amendment. Bill's Coal filed a separate action against Utility for breach of contract. Bill's Coal's action was subsequently consolidated with Utility's action. In all of its pleadings, Bill's Coal held fast to its interpretation of the comparison language of the take-out clause.

The parties agreed that the litigation should be divided into three phases. Phase I involved the interpretation of the take-out clause. The Court concluded that the take-out provision called for a delivery price versus delivery price comparison. It was only after this court finding that Bill's Coal finally abandoned its interpretation of the take-out clause. *It amended its pleadings to assert that the contract language was ambiguous and that the parties had always intended a delivery versus delivery price comparison. In response, Utility amended its complaint to allege anticipatory repudiation and bad faith on Seller's part.*

Phase II was conducted to determine liability. The Court found anticipatory repudiation by virtue of Bill's Coal's demand that Utility use a different price comparison than that which the parties had agreed to. The District Court recognized that although this is an unusual case on its facts, for anticipatory repudiation, the law appears clear that if a party, in bad faith, demands performance of the other party beyond the terms of the contract, and the demanding party conditions his own performance on the injured parties' performance of the additional terms, then there is an anticipatory repudiation by the demanding party. The District Court thus found anticipatory repudiation. It specifically found that Bill's Coal's interpretation of the take-out provision was the result of bad faith in that it was not an honestly held interpretation because

Bill's Coal had agreed to a different interpretation. The Court also found a separate cause of action for bad faith.

Based upon these conclusions, the District Court dissolved the injunction, and rendered detailed findings of fact and conclusions of law with which I agree. Specifically, the Court found that because Bill's Coal admitted that it knew at all times that the parties had in fact agreed to the delivery price versus delivery price interpretation of the "take-out" provision of the 1979 amendment, Bill's Coal did not entertain an honest mistake of contract interpretation when it insisted on its f.o.b. versus delivery price position. This, the Court concluded, was a bad faith contention. I agree.

When a party practices fraud, *i.e.*, assertion of a position it knows to be absolutely contrary to the agreement, it repudiates the contract if this false assertion, as here, impairs the value of the contract. This principle applies here inasmuch as the practical effect of Bill's Coal's false interpretation was to block any "take-out" and thus lock Utility into Bill's Coal's price. It follows that by forcing Utility to pay what may well be exorbitant prices under the contract, Bill's Coal impaired the value of the contract to Utility.

The majority opinion anchors its holding, it seems to me, on the proposition that Bill's Coal has "performed" under the contract because it has, at all times, delivered coal to Utility. This holding does not meet the issues addressed by the District Court relating to performance. What was the full performance promised? In terms of money values, it had to be Bill's Coal's promise to permit Utility to exercise the "take-out" provision in good faith by obtaining bona fide competitive bids based on delivery price versus delivery price. This plain intent was absolutely frustrated by the bad faith practiced by Bill's Coal. This bad faith could not be corrected. Accordingly, we are not here dealing with mere "deviations" from full performance which are inadvertent or unintentional. The "deviation" here is all pervasive and due to Bill's Coal's bad faith. It impaired the structure of the contract as a whole. It cannot be "repaired" and thus the contract must be terminated.

We have here an admitted, acknowledged manifestation on the part of Bill's Coal to frustrate the "termination" clause of the contract. The intention is unequivocal. *Restatement of Contracts* (First), §§ 314, 315 and 318 (1932), as supplemented, states that in a bilateral contract, one who has failed, without justification, to perform all or any part of what is promised in a contract has breached it (here, Bill's Coal's refusal to recognize the right of Utility to receive proper competitive bids) and, further, that one who, like Bill's Coal, has prevented or hindered Utility from determining whether it is bound to the condition of further purchases of coal from Bill's Coal (performance of a return promise to purchase) is guilty of an anticipatory breach which constitutes a total breach of contract. Under § 318(a) it is stated that "... a positive statement to the promisee or other person having a right under the contract, indicating that the promisor will not or cannot substantially perform his contractual duties" constitutes an anticipatory breach.

U.C.C. § 2-610, Comment 1 states that "anticipatory repudiation centers upon an overt communication of intention or an action which renders performance impossible or demonstrates a clear determination not to continue with performance." In *Neal-Cooper Grain Co. v. Texas Gulf Sulphur Co.*, 508 F.2d 283 (7th Cir. 1974), relied upon by the trial court, it was held that although a demand by a party to a contract for more than the contract calls for in the way of counter-performance is not in itself a repudiation, when a fair reading leads to the conclusion that it amounts to a statement of intention not to perform except on conditions which *go beyond the contract, it becomes a repudiation.* "In order to constitute an anticipatory breach of contract, there must be a definite and unequivocal manifestation of intention on the part of the repudiator that he will not render the promised performance *when the time fixed for it in the contract arrives.*" 4 Corbin on Contracts, § 973, p. 905. [Emphasis supplied]. And, "Where the two contracting parties differ as to the interpretation of a contract ... an offer to perform in accordance with his own interpretation ... [will] constitute such a breach, [if] the offer ... be accompanied by a clear manifestation of intention not to perform in accordance with any other interpretation." 4 Corbin on Contracts, § 973 at p. 911.

I would ... affirm the District Court.

NOTES AND QUESTIONS

1. *A duty to negotiate in good faith about modifying a contract?* In *Missouri Public Service Co. v. Peabody Coal Co.*,[52] Peabody and Missouri Public Service entered a contract in 1967, under which Peabody agreed to supply the requirements of coal at certain power plants for ten years. Even though the contract contained an escalator clause, it became very unprofitable for Peabody Coal. Peabody Coal asked to renegotiate, but was not satisfied with the price adjustment which Missouri Public Service offered. Missouri Public Service brought an action to require that Peabody Coal honor its contract. Peabody Coal showed its losses to be in excess of $3.4 million dollars (though the same inflationary events had caused a threefold increase in the value of its coal reserves).

Peabody asserted that Missouri Public Service had acted in bad faith in refusing to agree to a reasonable modification of the price under the contract. In rejecting this argument, the appellate court said,

[t]he fact that foreseeable economic trends or developments resulted in loss of anticipated profits or, as here claimed, actual financial loss, does not prevent Public Service from refusal of modification of price and to take advantage of a good bargain. Such is particularly true here, for the reason

---

[52] 583 S.W.2d 721 (Mo.Ct.Ap. 1979), cert. denied 444 U.S. 865 (1980).

that Public Service is a utility impressed with public interest and any increase in its cost in producing electricity would reflect in its rates to its public and private consumers. For this reason, its good faith, if it had agreed to a gratuitous modification upward of its costs, might properly be called into question.

The court also rejected Peabody's claim that it was excused under U.C.C. § 2-615. It provides for an excuse "if performance as agreed has been made impracticable by the occurrence of a contingency the nonoccurrence of which was a basic assumption on which the contract was made." Peabody was an experienced bargainer in long-term coal contracts. It had agreed to the escalator clause based on a particular price index, and thus it had assumed the risk of the index's adequacy. We will consider § 2-615 in more detail later. Of course, if Peabody had been excused by this section, then it would have had no duty to supply coal under the original contract. Its demands then would be just bargaining about a new contract rather than the repudiation of an old one.

2. *A demand for a modification as an anticipatory breach*: In *Unique Systems, Inc. v. Zotos International, Inc.*,[53] Duane Lilja was the chief officer of Unique Systems, Inc. which held a patent on a multi-station hair spray system intended for use in beauty salons. However, Unique lacked the resources needed to manufacture and market the systems. Zotos International, Inc. is a major manufacturer and distributor of shampoos, permanents and setting lotions for the professional hair dressing field.

Unique and Zotos entered a contract. Lilja was to develop, manufacture, and place in inventory hair spray systems. Zotos was to buy 15,000 systems over a two year period, and it had an option to buy 7,500 systems a year for the following two years. The actual stocking and distribution of the systems would begin with what the contract called "month one," a "mutually agreed date in the year 1974."

During 1974, several unanticipated delays occurred, some of which were the fault of Lilja, some the fault of Zotos, and some the fault of third parties. By January of 1975, "month one" still had not been set. In early 1975, Lilja told Zotos that he was ready to receive an order. However, other firms had introduced similar systems, and Zotos feared that the market had softened. Zotos demanded that Lilja demonstrate that its system would work. In July of 1975, a test was held, and Zotos' officials agreed that the system complied with the warranties in the contract. However, they refused to put their approval in writing or set "month one" unless Lilja would agree to a test marketing of the systems. There were proposals and counter-proposals, but Zotos insisted on test marketing before it would place orders.

---

[53]622 F.2d 373 (8th Cir. 1980).

Lilja notified Zotos that the contract had been repudiated and sued. The trial court entered a judgment in favor of Lilja and Unique Systems for $398,760, and Zotos appealed. The judgment was affirmed. The court found there was a repudiation under U.C.C. § 2-610. "If a party to a contract demands of the other party a performance to which he has no right under the contract and states definitely that, unless his demand is complied with, he will not render his promised performance, an anticipatory repudiation has been committed.... When Zotos told Lilja ... that it would not proceed until market tests were performed with results subject to Zotos's approval, Zotos repudiated the contract and was in total breach. No market tests were required by the contract, a fact that Zotos admits that it knew."

b. Anticipatory Repudiation and the Calculation of Damages

Suppose Buyer and Seller make a contract on November 1st for the sale of goods which are to be delivered several years later in installments. On December 1st, Buyer tells Seller that it will not perform the contract because the project for which the goods are to be purchased has been cancelled. Seller's officials are angry because they have invested engineering and selling effort in negotiating the deal and turned down other business opportunities. They seek to persuade Buyer's officials to reconsider and to reinstate the contract. On March 1st of the next year, Buyer's representatives tell Seller that the deal is off and there is no chance to going forward with it. How would damages be calculated under the Uniform Commercial Code?

The Code's drafters could have adopted a principle providing that, though a party may choose to treat an anticipatory repudiation as a breach and cancel the contract, or (in an appropriate case) bring an action for specific performance, they must wait until after the time for performance to actually bring a suit for damages. The rationale for such a rule would be that it would be too speculative to calculate damages in advance of the time for performance. The Code's drafters, however, did not choose such a rule. Instead, as U.C.C. 2-610 tells us, the party aggrieved by an anticipatory repudiation can choose to treat it as a breach and bring an action for damages immediately. Courts are often faced with the prospect of making awards of damages which entail predictions about the future, and the case of the anticipatory breach, while difficult, is no *more* difficult than other cases involving awards of damages for future injuries.

Seller's may choose the remedies identified in § 2-703. Buyers find their remedies identified in § 2-711. One need only consult these sections briefly to appreciate the difficulties of applying them in the case of the anticipatory breach. The remedy provisions were obviously drafted, generally, with an eye to measuring damages as of the time for performance. Turn to § 2-703 and ask yourself how the seller's choices identified in that section apply in cases of anticipatory repudiation. Could a seller choose 2-708(1) as a remedy, for example? The measure of damages in that case is the difference between the market price *at the time and place for tender*, and the contract price. The time for tender has not arrived, and so one can only speculate about what the market price would be. Is such speculation permitted? How often will this problem arise? Would the Code have been "better" if it had included a comprehensive set of rules to be used in cases of anticipatory repudiation?

The same kind of problems arise when the breach is a seller's breach and it is the buyer who is seeking a remedy. In such a case the language of the Code confronts us with a slightly different problem. Section 2-713 provides that the damages are "the difference between the market price *at the time when the buyer learned of the breach* and the contract price...." The time for performance is not the time identified as the time for calculating damages. The section was likely written in this way in order to protect buyers who first learned of the breach at some time after performance was due; measuring damages at this time protects buyers from the risk associated with a rising market, and more thoroughly protects a buyer's right to cover. How does the section apply, however, in the case of anticipatory repudiation?

The question was addressed in *Cosden Oil & Chemical Company v. Earl O. Helm Aktiengesellschaft.*[54] The court noted that there were three possible interpretations of the phrase "learned of the breach." The buyer learns of the breach: (1) when he learns of the repudiation; (2) when he learns of the repudiation plus a commercially reasonable time; or (3) when performance is due under the contract. After canvassing the advantages and disadvantages of each of these plausible interpretations, and acknowledging that "... the interplay among the relevant Code sections does not permit, in this context, an interpretation that harmonizes all and leaves no loose ends," the court opted for the second of the three choices it had identified. This tended to preserve a buyer's interest in investigating cover as a course of action, preserves the buyer's right to await performance for a commercially reasonable time, and reinforces the Code's preference for cover and cover-based damages.

c.   Uncertainty about the Other Side's Performance — The Code's Framework

AMF, INC. v. MCDONALD'S CORP.

536 F.2d 1167 (7th Cir. 1976)

CUMMINGS, J. ... AMF seeks damages for the alleged wrongful cancellation and repudiation of McDonald's Corporation's ("McDonald's") orders for sixteen computerized cash registers for installation in restaurants owned by wholly-owned subsidiaries of McDonald's and for seven such registers ordered by licensees of McDonald's for their restaurants. In July 1972, McDonald's of Elk Grove, Inc.

---

[54] 736 F.2d 1064 (5th Cir. 1984).

sued AMF to recover the $20,385.28 purchase price paid for a prototype computerized cash register and losses sustained as a result of failure of the equipment to function satisfactorily.... [T]he district court rendered a memorandum opinion and order in both cases in favor of each defendant. The only appeal is from the eight judgment orders dismissing AMF's complaints against McDonald's and the seven licensees. We affirm....

In 1966, AMF began to market individual components of a completely automated restaurant system, including its model 72C computerized cash register involved here. The 72C cash register then consisted of a central computer, one to four input stations, each with a keyboard and cathode ray tube display, plus the necessary cables and controls.

In 1967 McDonald's representatives visited AMF's plant in Springdale, Connecticut, to view a working "breadboard" model 72C to decide whether to use it in McDonald's restaurant system. Later that year, it was agreed that a 72C should be placed in a McDonald's restaurant for evaluation purposes.

In April 1968, a 72C unit accommodating six input stations was installed in McDonald's restaurant in Elk Grove, Illinois. This restaurant was a wholly-owned subsidiary of McDonald's and was its busiest restaurant. Besides functioning as a cash register, the 72C was intended to enable counter personnel to work faster and to assist in providing data for accounting reports and bookkeeping. McDonald's of Elk Grove, Inc. paid some $20,000 for this prototype register on January 3, 1969. AMF never gave McDonald's warranties governing reliability or performance standards for the prototype.

At a meeting in Chicago on August 29, 1968, McDonald's concluded to order sixteen 72C's for its company-owned restaurants and to cooperate with AMF to obtain additional orders from its licensees. In December 1968, AMF accepted McDonald's purchase orders for those sixteen 72C's. In late January 1969, AMF accepted seven additional orders for 72C's from McDonald's licensees for their restaurants. Under the contract for the sale of all the units, there was a warranty for parts and service. AMF proposed to deliver the first unit in February 1969, with installation of the remaining twenty-two units in the first half of 1969. However, AMF established a new delivery schedule in February 1969, providing for deliveries to commence at the end of July 1969 and to be completed in January 1970, assuming that the first test unit being built at AMF's Vandalia, Ohio, plant was built and satisfactorily tested by the end of July 1969. This was never accomplished.

During the operation of the prototype 72C at McDonald's Elk Grove restaurant, many problems resulted, requiring frequent service calls by AMF and others. Because of its poor performance, McDonald's had AMF remove the prototype unit from its Elk Grove restaurant in late April 1969.

At a March 18, 1969, meeting, McDonald's and AMF personnel met to discuss the performance of the Elk Grove prototype. AMF agreed to formulate a set of performance and reliability standards for the future 72C's, including "the number of failures permitted at various degrees of seriousness, total permitted downtime, maximum service hours and cost." Pending mutual agreement on such standards, McDonald's personnel asked that production of the twenty-three units be held up and AMF agreed.

On May 1, 1969, AMF met with McDonald's personnel to provide them with performance and reliability standards. However, the parties never agreed upon such standards. At that time, AMF did not have a working machine and could not produce one within a reasonable time because its Vandalia, Ohio, personnel were too inexperienced. After the May 1st meeting, AMF concluded that McDonald's had cancelled all 72C orders. The reasons for the cancellation were the poor performance of the prototype, the lack of assurances that a workable machine was available and the unsatisfactory conditions at AMF's Vandalia, Ohio, plant where the twenty-three 72C's were to be built.

On July 29, 1969, McDonald's and AMF representatives met in New York. At this meeting it was mutually understood that the 72C orders were cancelled and that none would be delivered.

In its conclusions of law, the district court held that McDonald's and its licensees had entered into contracts for twenty-three 72C cash registers but that AMF was not able to perform its obligations under the contracts (see note 1, *supra*). Citing § 2-610 of the Uniform Commercial Code (Ill.Rev.Stats. (1975) ch. 26, § 2-610) and Comment 1 thereunder, the court concluded that on July 29, McDonald's justifiably repudiated the contracts to purchase all twenty-three 72C's.

Relying on § 2-609 and 2-610 of the Uniform Commercial Code (Ill.Rev.Stat. (1975) ch. 26, §§ 2-609 and 2-610), the court decided that McDonald's was warranted in repudiating the contracts and therefore had a right to cancel the orders by virtue of § 2-711 of the Uniform Commercial Code (Ill.Rev.Stats. (1975) ch. 26, § 2-711). Accordingly, judgment was entered for McDonald's....

Whether in a specific case a buyer has reasonable grounds for insecurity is a question of fact. Comment 3 to U.C.C. § 2-609; Anderson, Uniform Commercial Code, § 2-609 (2d Ed. 1971). On this record, McDonald's clearly had "reasonable grounds for insecurity" with respect to AMF's performance. At the time of the March 18, 1969, meeting, the prototype unit had performed unsatisfactorily ever since its April 1968 installation. Although AMF had projected delivery of all twenty-three units by the first half of 1969, AMF later scheduled delivery from the end of July 1969 until January 1970. When McDonald's personnel visited AMF's Vandalia, Ohio, plant on March 4, 1969, they saw that none of the 72C systems was being assembled and learned that a pilot unit would not be ready until the end of July of that year. They were informed that the engineer assigned to the project was not to commence work until March 17th. AMF's own personnel were also troubled about the design of the 72C, causing them to attempt to reduce McDonald's order to five units. Therefore, under § 2-609 McDonald's was entitled to demand adequate assurance of performance by AMF.

However, AMF urges that § 2-609 of the U.C.C. is inapplicable because McDonald's did not make a written demand of adequate assurance of due performance. In *Pittsburgh-Des Moines Steel Co. v. Brookhaven Manor Water Co.*, 532 F.2d 572, 581 (7th Cir. 1976), we noted that the Code should be liberally construed and therefore rejected such "a formalistic approach" to § 2-609. McDonald's failure to make a written demand was excusable because AMF's Mr. Dubosque's testimony and his April 2 and 18, 1969, memoranda about the March 18th meeting showed AMF's clear understanding that McDonald's had suspended performance until it should receive adequate assurance of due performance from AMF....

After the March 18th demand, AMF never repaired the Elk Grove unit satisfactorily nor replaced it. Similarly, it was unable to satisfy McDonald's that the twenty-three machines on order would work. At the May 1st meeting, AMF offered unsatisfactory assurances for only five units instead of twenty-three. The performance standards AMF tendered to McDonald's were unacceptable because they would have permitted the 72C's not to function properly for 90 hours per year, permitting as much as one failure in every fifteen days in a busy McDonald's restaurant. Also, as the district court found, AMF's Vandalia, Ohio, personnel were too inexperienced to produce a proper machine. Since AMF did not provide adequate assurance of performance after McDonald's March 18th demand, U.C.C. § 2-609(1) permitted McDonald's to suspend performance. When AMF did not furnish adequate assurance of due performance at the May 1st meeting, it thereby repudiated the contract under § 2-609(4). At that point, § 2-610(b) (note 3, *supra*) permitted McDonald's to cancel the orders pursuant to § 2-711 (note 6, *supra*), as it finally did on July 29, 1969....

... McDonald's could cancel the orders under §§ 2-610 and 2-711 because of AMF's failure to give adequate assurance of due performance under § 2-609....

Judgment Affirmed.

NOTES AND QUESTIONS

1. *Materials from the briefs of the parties*: AMF argued that McDonald's Corporation had no grounds for insecurity since the machine with the defects was a prototype model, McDonald's knew of all the defects when it placed its order for the machines, and then McDonald's decided it could buy more advanced technology for less money and so it looked for a way out. If it had made a written demand for assurances, AMF could have responded by giving appropriate assurances.

McDonald's cited an internal AMF memo that stated:

On Tuesday, March 18, we had a meeting with McDonald's at which time they expressed their unhappiness with the last 2 months performance of the equipment and stated that they intended to cancel the order unless we could give them a warranty or assurance on the reliability of the production units, which reliability would have to be "considerably" better than the recent experience with the prototype.

What, if anything, would a formal written demand for assurances have added? Compare the approach of the court in *Eastern Air Lines v. McDonnell Douglas Corp.*, *supra*.

2. *Section 2-609 as the all-purpose tool*: Professor White[55] points out that the court used 2-609 to avoid considering whether the failure to perform the installment contract met the tests for breach in § 2-612. "In effect, the court applied § 2-609 to one party's routine negotiating behavior and gave it significant legal consequence — namely, repudiation by the other."

In another case in which the court declined to require a written demand for assurance, White says that the court used § 2-609 to magnify the importance of particular immaterial breaches and change them into material ones. "The analysis short-circuits the agonizing found in many common-law cases in which a court attempts to determine whether a breach in one installment so affects the expectations or behavior for other installments as to constitute a material breach."

In a third case, a buyer of specialized industrial burners for a plant in Yugoslavia discovered that similar burners in use in Syria and Sri Lanka had developed problems in operation. The buyer, before installation of the burners, asked that the seller take the burners back, or failing that guarantee they would operate properly, with the guarantee secured by a letter of credit. Seller refused, and buyer was awarded a full refund of the purchase price. The court held that seller had failed to provide meaningful assurances. Notice that by using U.C.C. § 2-609, buyer never had to prove that the burners would not meet the agreed specifications when they were installed in the Yugoslavian ammonia plant which had yet to be completed and put into operation at the time of the hearing on the motion for summary judgment. Of course, it looks as if neither buyer nor seller thought the burners would meet specifications if they had been installed. Buyer did not have to deal with questions of whether it had accepted the burners and whether seller still could cure or whether buyer was entitled to revoke its acceptance because of a defect that substantially impaired the value of the burners to the buyer.

3. *The relation among §§ 2-609, 2-610, and 2-611*: In the *AMF* case the court said "[w]hen AMF did not furnish adequate assurance of due performance at the May 1st meeting, it thereby repudiated the contract under § 2-609(4). At that point, § 2-610(b) ... permitted McDonald's to cancel the orders pursuant to § 2-711...." If § 2-609(4) is applicable, must one also meet the requirements of and be subject to the qualifications in §§ 2-610 and 2-611? For example, could AMF have withdrawn its repudiation under 2-611?

---

[55]Eight Cases and Section 251, 67 Cornell Law Review 841 (1982).

CHERWELL-RALLI, INC. v. RYTMAN GRAIN CO., INC.

180 Conn. 714, 433 A.2d 984 (1980)

PETERS, J. This case involves a dispute about which of the parties to an oral instalment contract was the first to be in breach. The plaintiff, Cherwell-Ralli, Inc., sued the defendant, Rytman Grain Co., Inc., for the nonpayment of moneys due and owing for accepted deliveries of products known as Cherco Meal and C-R-T Meal. The defendant, conceding its indebtedness, counterclaimed for damages arising out of the plaintiff's refusal to deliver remaining instalments under the contract. The trial court, *Bordon, J.*, trial referee, having found all issues for the plaintiff, rendered judgment accordingly, and the defendant appealed.

The trial court's unchallenged finding of fact establishes the following: The parties, on July 26, 1974, entered into an instalment contract for the sale of Cherco Meal and C-R-T Meal on the basis of a memorandum executed by the Getkin Brokerage House. As modified, the contract called for shipments according to weekly instructions from the buyer, with payments to be made within ten days after delivery. Almost immediately the buyer was behind in its payments, and these arrearages were often quite substantial. The seller repeatedly called these arrearages to the buyer's attention but continued to make all shipments as requested by the buyer from July 29, 1974 to April 23, 1975.

By April 15, 1975, the buyer had become concerned that the seller might not complete performance of the contract, because the seller's plant might close and because the market price of the goods had come significantly to exceed the contract price. [Do you see why this latter fact might cause plaintiff to worry about future deliveries?] In a telephonic conversation between the buyer's president and the seller's president on that day, the buyer was assured by the seller that deliveries would continue if the buyer would make the payments for which it was obligated. Thereupon, the buyer sent the seller a check in the amount of $9825.60 to cover shipments through March 31, 1975.

Several days later, on April 23, 1975, the buyer stopped payment on this check because he was told by a truck driver, not employed by the seller, that this shipment would be his last load. The trial court found that this was not a valid reason for stoppage of payment. Upon inquiry by the seller, the buyer restated his earlier concerns about future deliveries. Two letters, both dated April 28, 1975, describe the impasse between the parties: the seller again demanded payment, and the buyer, for the first time in writing, demanded adequate assurance of further deliveries. The buyer's demand for assurance was reiterated in its direct reply to the seller's demand for payment. The buyer, however, made no further payments, either to replace the stopped check or otherwise to pay for the nineteen accepted shipments for which balances were outstanding. The seller made no further deliveries after April 23, 1975, when it heard about the stopped check; the buyer never made specific requests for shipments after that date.

Inability to deliver the goods forced the seller to close its plant, on May 2, 1975, because of stockpiling of excess material.

The trial court concluded, on the basis of these facts, that the party in breach was the buyer and not the seller. The court concluded that the seller was entitled to recover the final balance of $21,013.60, which both parties agreed to be due and owing. It concluded that the buyer could not prevail on its counterclaim because it had no reasonable grounds to doubt performance from the seller and had in fact received reasonable assurances. Further, the buyer had presented no reasonably accurate evidence to establish the damages it might have sustained because of the seller's failure to deliver.

The buyer on this appeal challenges first the conclusion that the buyer's failure to pay "substantially impaired the value of the whole contract," so as to constitute "a breach of the whole contract," as is required by the applicable law governing instalment contracts. General Statutes § 42a-2-612(3). What constitutes impairment of the value of the whole contract is a question of fact....

The record below amply sustains the trial court's conclusion in this regard, particularly in light of the undenied and uncured stoppage of a check given to comply with the buyer's promise to reduce significantly the amount of its outstanding arrearages....

The buyer argues that the seller in an instalment contract may never terminate a contract, despite repeated default in payment by the buyer, without first invoking the insecurity methodology of General Statutes § 42a-2-609. That is not the law. If there is reasonable doubt about whether the buyer's default is substantial, the seller may be well advised to temporize by suspending further performance until it can ascertain whether the buyer is able to offer adequate assurance of future payments.

... But if the buyer's conduct is sufficiently egregious, such conduct will, in and of itself, constitute substantial impairment of the value of the whole contract and a present breach of the contract as a whole. An aggrieved seller is expressly permitted, by General Statutes § 42a-2-703(f), upon breach of a contract as a whole, to cancel the remainder of the contract "with respect to the whole undelivered balance." ... Nor is the seller's remedy to cancel waived, as the buyer argues, by a law suit seeking recovery for payments due. While § 42a-2-612(3) states that a contract is reinstated if the seller "brings an action with respect *only* to past instalments" (emphasis added), it is clear in this case that the seller intended, as the buyer well knew, to bring this contract to an end because of the buyer's breach.

The buyer's attack on the court's conclusions with respect to its counterclaim is equally unavailing. The buyer's principal argument is that the seller was obligated, on pain of default, to provide assurance of its further performance. The right to such assurance is premised on reasonable grounds for insecurity. Whether a buyer has reasonable grounds to be insecure is a question of fact. *AMF, Inc. v. McDonald's Corporation*, 536 F.2d 1167, 1170 (7th Cir. 1976). The trial court concluded that in this case the buyer's insecurity was not reasonable and we agree. A party to a sales contract may not suspend performance of its own for which it has "already received the agreed return." At all times, the buyer had received all of the goods which it had ordered. The buyer could not rely on its own nonpayments as a basis for its own insecurity. The presidents of the parties had exchanged adequate verbal assurances only eight days before the buyer itself again delayed its own performance on the basis of information that was facially unreliable. Contrary to the buyer's argument, subsequent events proved the buyer's fears to be incorrect, since the seller's plant closed due to a surplus rather than due to a shortage of materials. Finally, it is fatal to the buyer's appeal that neither its oral argument nor its brief addressed its failure to substantiate, with probative evidence, the damages it alleged to be attributable to the seller's nondeliveries.

There is no error.

NOTES AND QUESTIONS

1. *Material from the briefs and record*: Rytman, in its brief, asserts that in addition to the truck driver's statements about his "last load," Rytman had heard that Cherwell-Ralli was selling to others at the higher market price. Rytman had heard rumors that Cherwell-Ralli was going to close the plant because "they were held to a fast contract price with him and had problems with fuel and environmental protection." Rytman's lawyer wrote Cherwell-Ralli on April 28th, as follows:

> As I understand it, deliveries on this contract are quite late and there is some question in our client's mind as to whether your company is willing and able to comply with the terms of the contract. Our client requests delivery of this material and I hereby make formal demand for same. I can advise you that if we receive either delivery of the material or adequate assurance that the material will be delivered in accordance with the contract we will make satisfactory arrangements for payment of all present and future sums which may be due under the terms of the contract. In the meantime, our client will be damaged if you do not deliver the balance of the contract in accordance with its terms and this letter will give you notice that our client will seek compensation from your company for any and all damages which may result from your violation of the contract and will withhold all payments until this matter is resolved.

Cherwell-Ralli stockpiled the meal produced to supply Rytman, and on May 2d, the New Jersey plant stopped production.

2. *"Reasonable grounds for insecurity"*: Do you agree that Rytman's concern did not give it reasonable grounds for insecurity? Suppose Rytman had come to you for advice in late April of 1975. What would you have told him to do? Suppose, instead, Rytman's lawyer had showed you a draft of the letter of April 28th. Would you have advised him to change anything?

Justice Peters says that "subsequent events proved the buyer's fears to be incorrect...." Can one's fears be incorrect but reasonable within the meaning of § 2-609(1)?

d. Uncertainty About Performance — At Common Law

Suppose a case does not involve a transaction in goods and so Article II is inapplicable. Can a party who has "reasonable grounds for insecurity" suspend performance and demand assurances? There is relatively little authority on this point, but it was generally agreed that mere doubts about the other party's ability to perform did not justify a suspension of performance. In *Louis Koppelon v. W.M. Ritter Flooring Corp.*[56] a defendant had refused to proceed with a construction contract, asserting first, that the plaintiff's credit had become impaired, and so plaintiff was no longer a good risk and second, that the plaintiff was in fact insolvent. The court held that neither bad credit, nor the failure to perform other contracts, nor in fact insolvency would justify the defendant's refusal to proceed.

> The fact that the credit of a party to a building contract (to whom by the terms of the contract labor and material are to be furnished) has become impaired, so that he is no longer a good credit risk, and that he has failed to meet other independent obligations, does not relieve the other party from performance, and is no defense to an action for the breach of such contract, for it does not appear therefrom that he cannot and will not perform his part when his time for performance comes.
>
> It has been held that mere doubts of the solvency of a party to a contract, or mere belief that he will be unable to perform when the time for his performance comes, will not excuse performance by the other party.... If contracts could be repudiated upon the mere allegation that the credit of the other party had become impaired, there would indeed be much consternation in the business world, for contracts are made in view of the fact that credit fluctuates, and it is common knowledge that contracts are frequently fully performed by those whose credit has become impaired....
>
> [W]e think that the mere insolvency of a party to a building contract (to whom by the terms of the contract labor and materials are to be furnished) does not terminate the contract, in the absence of provisions to that effect therein, nor does it justify the other party in refusing altogether to perform, for it does not follow therefrom that the insolvent party could not and would not perform his part even though insolvent....
>
> It might well be that the insolvent party might find it advantageous and possible to carry out his part of the contract, since insolvency does not

---

[56] 97 N.J.L. 200, 116 A. 491 (1922).

necessarily mean a total lack of assets. To hold that mere insolvency of a party puts an end to a contract, and excuses the solvent party from the obligation altogether, would be intolerable. If the mere fact of insolvency terminates a contract every insolvent contractor would automatically be shorn of all property rights and beneficial interests in contracts. Of course, this cannot be....

The *Koppelon* case may represent an unusually strict view on the matter, but it is clear that Restatement (Second) § 251 represents an effort to expand the right of a party to refuse to perform in the face of well founded risks that it will not receive a counter-performance.

While the language of § 251 does not exactly track that of U.C.C. 2-609, it is clear that the Restatement is an effort to move courts in that direction. One can easily imagine that parties to contracts may wish to expand or modify the privileges afforded by § 2-609, or the probably more limited privilege arising under common law rules.

For example, a large manufacturing corporation uses the following clause on its purchase order:

> Buyer shall have the right to cancel and terminate this contract forthwith upon the happening of any one or more of the following events: (1) Seller's insolvency or commission of an act of bankruptcy; (2) filing of a voluntary or involuntary petition in bankruptcy by or against the Seller; (3) the execution by the Seller of an assignment for the benefit of creditors; (4) appointment of a receiver or trustee for the Seller by any court of competent jurisdiction, or (5) if at any time, in the judgment of the Buyer, the Seller's financial condition shall be such as to endanger its performance hereunder. The acceptance of goods or performances after the occurrences of any of the above events shall not waive the right of the Buyer to cancel and terminate this contract, nor shall cancellation, hereunder waive the Buyer's right to any damages to which the Buyer is otherwise entitled.

To what extent does Buyer gain greater rights under this clause than under U.C.C. § 2-609? Are there limits to the extent to which one can use a contract term to alter the result reached by 2-607? See 1-102(3) and 1-208.

What if, in a situation in which the preceding clause is contained in the agreement, Buyer makes an honest unreasonable judgment about seller's financial condition.

C. SELF-HELP IN THE FACE OF DEFAULT

1. DEDUCTING DAMAGES FROM WHAT IS DUE

PUROFIED DOWN PRODUCTS CORP. v. ROYAL DOWN PRODUCTS, INC.

87 FRD 685 (W.D. Mich. 1980)

HILLMAN, J. Plaintiff, a New York supplier of processed goose down and feathers, brings suit against defendant, a Michigan manufacturer of down-filled products, for recovery of the contract price of goose down and feathers shipped by plaintiff to defendant in 1976 and 1977. Defendant has counterclaimed for damages alleged to have resulted from defects in the material shipped by plaintiff....

I. FACTS

Plaintiff and defendant commenced business in early 1976, resulting in defendant's initial order for duck and goose down in June. Deliveries of down were thereafter accepted and paid for throughout that year. Additional orders were also placed by defendant in November, 1976, and January, 1977, with delivery to be completed by mid-1977.

In February, 1977, defendant concluded that, in its opinion, shipments of feather materials delivered by plaintiff failed to meet contract specifications. As a result, representatives of the parties met throughout March and early April in an attempt to resolve the dispute. On April 5, 1977, defendant's president formally notified plaintiff that the down shipped by plaintiff was defective and unmerchantable. In writing, defendant advised that it would hold plaintiff responsible for all damages flowing from the alleged breach. Defendant further advised that it was withholding payment due under the contract as a set-off, pending cure.

Plaintiff responded by proposing that defendant return the allegedly defective merchandise for reworking. The reprocessed goods were to be invoiced on a net 60 day basis at the original contract price. Defendant agreed.

Plaintiff shipped defendant an initial 5,000 pounds of replacement goods on April 6, 1977. Defendant thereafter shipped plaintiff 10,000 pounds of feather material, and received in return 5,000 pounds of reprocessed down on April 28, 1977. Defendant shipped back to plaintiff another 5,000 pounds of purportedly substandard down on April 28, 1977.

Upon receipt of the replacement, reprocessed feather material, defendant determined, upon inspection, that this down allegedly also failed to conform to contract specifications. Defendant notified plaintiff in writing, on April 11, and by telephone in April and early May, that the replacement material was unacceptable. At this point, plaintiff refused to return 5,000 pounds of down material awaiting reprocessing, and apparently repudiated its obligation to deliver 10,000 pounds remaining due under the agreement. On May 9, 1977, defendant's president again wrote to plaintiff advising that defendant would hold plaintiff liable for damages resulting from plaintiff's alleged breach. Plaintiff's attorney answered by telegram on May 19, 1977, threatening litigation.

The parties attempted to resolve the conflict, but negotiations failed. Meanwhile, time for payment passed with defendant refusing to pay for any of the material previously shipped. In the interim, defendant removed the allegedly defective down from the original packing containers, placed some of this material in a bonded warehouse, pledging it as collateral for business loans, and utilized the remainder in manufacturing down-filled products. Based upon defendant's refusal to pay for or return the down, plaintiff thereafter initiated suit in this court on June 24, 1977. Jurisdiction is based upon diversity of citizenship, with the matter in controversy exceeding $10,000. 28 U.S.C. § 1332. A jury trial has been demanded.

Plaintiff moved for summary judgment on November 4, 1977, arguing that defendant's acceptance of the goods, and its failure to pay, entitled plaintiff to judgment of the contract price as a matter of law. Plaintiff maintains that summary judgment in its favor will not act to prejudice defendant's counterclaim, but will simplify trial of the case.

Defendant opposes summary judgment, asserting that it has not breached the contract. While defendant admits having accepted the feather material in question, defendant nevertheless maintains that under M.C.L.A. § 400.2717 (U.C.C. § 2-717), it was permitted to offset its damages incurred as a result of plaintiff's alleged breach from the amounts due to plaintiff under the contract. For the reasons that follow, I hold that utilization of M.C.L.A. § 400.2717 bars granting summary judgment in the present case. Accordingly, I deny plaintiff's motion.

II. MOTION FOR SUMMARY JUDGMENT

In support of its motion, plaintiff relies on M.C.L.A. § 440.2607, M.S.A. § 19.2607 (U.C.C. § 2-607), which reads in part:

§ 2607. (1) The buyer must pay at the contract rate for any goods accepted....

Plaintiff argues that because defendant has accepted the goods, it is now liable for the remaining contract price.

However, plaintiff overlooks M.C.L.A. § 440.2717 (U.C.C. § 2-717), which reads:

§ 2717. The buyer on notifying the seller of his intention to do so may deduct all or any part of the damages resulting from any breach of the contract from any part of the price still due under the same contract.

That section authorizes the buyer to deduct damages from the purchase price, so long as the buyer notifies the seller of its intent to deduct damages, and provided that the buyer only deducts from the purchase price due on a contract such damages as arise under the same contract....

... [In an earlier case] the court held that § 2-717 of the U.C.C. operated to extinguish a purchaser's liability for goods sold and delivered where the purchaser offsets damages it has incurred by virtue of the seller's breach. Consequently, the court held, summary judgment may not be granted on a seller's counterclaim for goods sold where there are unresolved factual issues in the buyer's action for damages concerning whether the seller breached the underlying contract of sale....

The Michigan Court of Appeals similarly has ruled that setoff pursuant to M.C.L.A. § 440.2717 precludes summary judgment on the seller's behalf for the purchase price due under a commercial contract....

This interpretation of M.C.L.A. § 440.2717, as well as other courts' interpretations of U.C.C. § 2-717 generally, convince me that plaintiff's summary judgment motion should be denied. Whether plaintiff breached, and therefore, whether defendant has a right to set-off under M.C.L.A. § 440.2717, is a factual question which cannot be decided at this point in the litigation. Clearly, if defendant properly employed set-off available under M.C.L.A. § 440.2717, then defendant cannot be said to have breached the contract, and plaintiff cannot recover the purchase price allegedly due. Acceptance of seller's product, and refusal to pay, alone do not necessarily constitute breach.

Consequently, for the reasons set out above, plaintiff's motion for summary judgment is denied.

NOTES AND QUESTIONS

1. *What happened next?* The case was filed originally in June of 1977. Plaintiff's motion for summary judgment was denied on August 21, 1980. Pre-trial proceedings continued to April of 1982. There were many sets of interrogatories and depositions. Depositions were taken in states far from the Western District of Michigan, including New York, Washington, New Hampshire, and California. The case was dismissed with prejudice and without costs to any party on April 23, 1982, suggesting that a settlement had been reached.

2. *Deducting damages under one contract from payments due on another*: Section 2-717, Official Comment 1 says "[t]o bring this provision into application the breach involved must be of the same contract under which the price in question is claimed to have been earned." Suppose S and B have 5 separate contracts for goods which were made at different times. Seller breaches contract number 2, but Buyer discovers this only after paying for those goods in full. Why doesn't § 2-717 allow Buyer to withhold the damages on contract number 2 from payments due on contract number 4? Buyer can claim that the breach on contract number 2 gives "reasonable grounds for insecurity ... with respect to the

performance ..." of contract number 4, and demand adequate assurance of due performance under § 2-609 before making the payments on contract number 4. See § 2-609, Official Comment 3, which says that "a buyer who falls behind in 'his account' with the seller, even though the items involved have to do with separate and legally distinct contracts, impairs the seller's expectation of due performance." Is this inconsistent or are there reasons to limit the self-help remedy of § 2-717 and channel the problem to § 2-609?

3. *A check in full settlement of all claims*: When buyer and seller dispute the quality of goods supplied or the amounts due, often the buyer will send seller a check for an amount the buyer asserts is due. The check is restrictively endorsed and states that cashing it will constitute a full settlement of all claims. The common-law rule was that a creditor could not cash the check and disown the condition upon which it was tendered. See Restatement (Second) of Contracts § 281. U.C.C. § 1-207 may change the common-law rule and allow a creditor to cash the check if the creditor explicitly reserves her rights. The courts have divided on this issue. See, *e.g.*, *Flambeau Products Corp. v. Honeywell Information Systems, Inc.*,[57] where the Supreme Court of Wisconsin split 4 to 3 on the proper interpretation of U.C.C. § 1-207. The majority found that a creditor cannot cash the check without accepting the debtor's offer of an accord and satisfaction. However, there must be consideration for the settlement of the claim. See also Rosenthal, Discord and Dissatisfaction: Section 1-207 of the Uniform Commercial Code, 78 Columbia Law Review 48 (1978). In *Kelly v. Kowalsky*,[58] the court held that merely retaining the checks did not settle the claim when the debtors failed to ask that the checks be returned.

4. *Seller's self-help*: Sellers have a number of self-help remedies under Article II of the U.C.C. See §§ 2-718(2) & (3) which apply when a buyer has made payments. See § 2-702 which deals with "Seller's remedies on discovery of buyer's insolvency." See also §§ 2-703(a) and 2-705 on seller's right to withhold delivery or stop delivery in transit.

---

[57]116 Wis.2d 95, 341 N.W.2d 655 (1984).
[58]186 Conn. 618, 442 A.2d 1355 (1982).

Chapter 9
ADJUSTING TO CHANGED CIRCUMSTANCES: RISKS ASSUMED AND IMPOSED

A. MISTAKE, IMPOSSIBILITY, AND FRUSTRATION: CONTRACT DOCTRINE, RESTITUTION, AND COPING WITH THE PROBLEMS

People making contracts can be mistaken about the present situation, and can make wrong predictions of the future. Some mistakes are just the risks of the deal. For example, Seller, a used book dealer, sells an old book to Buyer for $5.00, and Buyer makes no misrepresentations. The book is a rare first edition, worth $25,000. Or Buyer thinks the value of land or corporate securities will increase after their purchase, but their value falls sharply. The risk of some mistakes, however, is not implicit in the deal, and our sense of fairness may require intervention and adjustment. While situations at the extremes may not present too much difficulty, often arguments can be made both that a risk was assumed and that it was not.

Legal culture at times distinguishes mistakes concerning existing facts from assumptions and predictions about the future. Typically, the law of mistake focuses on errors about facts at or before the contract was made. However, things may happen in the future that make it very difficult, impracticable, or virtually impossible to perform contractual duties. Lawyers often speak of this situation as one involving "impossibility." However, I may be able to perform my duties under a contract without difficulty, but events may rob my performance of any value to you. In the classic situation, I rent to you a place from which you plan to watch an elaborate parade. The parade later is canceled. You can still stand or sit there and watch whatever passes by, but this right is far less valuable to you than what you assumed you were buying. Lawyers label this as a problem of "frustration of purpose."[1] While these distinctions can be drawn,

---

[1] There is much discussion of frustration of purpose. However, Professor Wladis surveyed the cases and concluded: "The Krell case [which established the frustration doctrine and involved the rental of space overlooking the planned parade to celebrate the coronation of King Edward VII] can be deleted or reduced to the status of a footnote. For all the trouble it has caused generations of law students, and law professors, Krell has had virtually no influence upon the law." Wladis, Common Law and Uncommon Events: The Development of the Doctrine of Impossibility of Performance in English Common Law, 75 Georgetown Law Journal 1575, 1630-1631 (1988).

Uniform Commercial Code § 2-615 excuses sellers whose performance "has been made impracticable by the occurrence of a contingency the non-occurrence of which was a basic

as always we must ask whether the distinctions make any difference that matters. Many modern writers see mistake, impossibility and frustration as involving essentially similar problems, although the doctrinal tests may be stated in different terms.

Suppose, for example, Seller contracts with Buyer to deliver a machine built according to plans and specifications. Buyer is to pay on the date specified for delivery. The contract, however, says nothing about the effect of strikes, floods, fires and the like that delay production. Assume:

(a) Seller needs a special type of steel to build the machine. Seller's supplier's employees strike, and this kind of steel cannot be obtained elsewhere in time so that Seller can perform. Or

(b) Seller's own employees strike. Or

(c) There is a flood in Seller's plant, stopping production.

Seller fails to deliver on time. Buyer sues Seller for breach of contract. Does Seller have a defense in any, all or none of these situations?

Suppose, instead, Seller completes the machine a month after the delivery date. Seller's delay was caused by the strike or flood we've assumed. Seller then tenders the machine to Buyer. Buyer refuses to accept it. May Seller successfully sue Buyer for breach of contract or does Buyer have a defense? (These problems, of course, all raise issues of *impracticability* or *impossibility* since the seller cannot get the machine there on time.)

Suppose, finally, Seller could deliver on time, but Buyer is prevented from using the machine because of environmental protection regulations issued after the contract was made. The issue now is whether there is an excuse because of *frustration of purpose*.

1. CONTRASTING LEGAL APPROACHES

Consider the approaches taken by the common law in the 17th and 19th centuries and by the Uniform Commercial Code today. We can ask whether the legal system has gained any ground in 300 years. Whatever the reasons offered,

---

assumption on which the contract was made." However, the text of the section says nothing about buyers whose purposes have been frustrated. Official Comment 9 suggests that when a seller knows that a buyer's order is based on a definite and specific venture "the reason of the present section may well apply and entitled the buyer to the exemption." Following Wladis' suggestion we will leave frustration of purpose largely to this footnote.

For a recent case in which the court applied the frustration of purpose doctrine, see Chase Precast Corporation v. Paonessa Company Inc., 566 N.E.2d 603 (Mass. 1991). A subcontractor which had contracted to supply concrete median barriers to a highway construction contractor was denied a claim for lost profits when the state, acting in response to strong community protests, eliminated the use of median barriers on the project. The court characterized the frustration doctrine as a "companion rule" to the doctrine of impossibility.

we can see the spirit of *Paradine v. Jane* in some decisions interpreting the Uniform Commercial Code or applying contract doctrine to other than transactions in goods.

PARADINE v. JANE

Mich. 23 Car. Banco Regis.[2] Hil. 22 Car. Rot. 1178, & 1179

In debt the plaintiff declares upon a lease for years rendring rent at the four usual feasts; and for rent behind for three years, ending at the Feast of the Annunciation, 21 Car. brings his action; the defendant pleads, that a certain German prince, by name Prince Rupert, an alien born, enemy to the King and kingdom, had invaded the realm with an hostile army of men; and with the same force did enter upon the defendant's possession, and him expelled, and held out of possession from the 19 of July 18 Car. till the Feast of the Annunciation, 21 Car. whereby he could not take the profits; whereupon the plaintiff demurred, and the plea was resolved insufficient....

3. It was resolved, that the matter of the plea was insufficient; for though the whole army had been alien enemies, yet he ought to pay his rent. And this difference was taken, that where the law creates a duty or charge, and the party is disabled to perform it without any default in him, and hath no remedy over, there the law will excuse him. As in the case of waste, if a house be destroyed by tempest, or by enemies, the lessee is excused. [S]o of an escape. So in 9 E. 3. 16. a supersedeas was awarded to the justices, that they should not proceed in a cessavit upon a cesser during the war, but when the party by his own contract creates a duty or charge upon himself, he is bound to make it good, if he may, notwithstanding any accident by inevitable necessity, because he might have provided against it by his contract. And therefore if the lessee covenant to repair a house, though it be burnt by lightning, or thrown down by enemies, yet he ought to repair it. Now the rent is a duty created by the parties upon the reservation, and had there been a covenant to pay it, there had been no question but the lessee must have made it good, notwithstanding the interruption by enemies, for the law would not protect him beyond his own agreement, no more then in the case of reparations; this reservation then being a covenant in law, and whereupon an action of covenant hath been maintained (as Roll said) it is all one as if there had been an actual covenant. Another reason was added, that as the lessee is to have the advantage of casual profits, so he must run the hazard of casual losses, and not lay the whole burthen of them upon his lessor; and Dyer 56. 6. was cited for this purpose, that though the land be surrounded, or gained by the sea, or made barren by wildfire, yet the lessor shall have his whole rent: and judgment was given for the plaintiff.

---

[2]23 Car. refers to 1647, the 23d year of the reign of King Charles I.

NOTES AND QUESTIONS

1. *Historical context*: Some very simplified history may help make the case more understandable. Who was Prince Rupert who invaded the land with an army and prompted this case? The phrase "an alien, and an enemy of the King" is misleading. King James I had several children. One was Charles I, the King at the time of the *Paradine* case. Charles' sister, Elizabeth, married Frederick, the Elector of the Palatine (then a state in central Europe). In 1619, Prince Rupert was born to Frederick and Elizabeth in Prague. Thus, Rupert was Charles' nephew.

In 1618, a revolt in Bohemia began the Thirty Years' War. In 1619, Frederick became King of Bohemia. The Bohemians were defeated in 1620, and Frederick, Elizabeth and Rupert fled to Holland. James I attempted to aid his son-in-law by sending an army of 12,000 men to march to the Palatine, and it was landed in Holland. However, the army disintegrated because of sickness and lack of supplies. Frederick continued to fight in the Thirty Years' War, and Rupert joined him in battle when he was fourteen.

Paradine v. Jane is a product of the English Civil War which overthrew Charles I and brought Oliver Cromwell and the Parliamentarians to power. Several events produced this conflict. In 1603, James I asserted the absolute power to tax in order to finance his role in international affairs. Parliament resisted, asserting that only it could tax. Charles I became king in 1625. Soon he was involved in wars with Spain and France and needed money. In 1628, Parliament responded to Charles' actions with the Petition of Right which asserted that the King's power to tax, imprison and quarter soldiers was limited legally. Charles responded by dismissing Parliament in 1629.

Charles I also was involved in the religious battles of the time. Actions taken in his name drove the Puritans out of the Church of England to North America. In 1638, Charles tried to impose the Church of England on Scotland and prompted a revolt. The tensions between Catholics and Protestants were involved in the Thirty Years' War on the continent and in the conflicts in England as well.

Parliament met in 1640. It attacked the King's policies, and it seized some of his ministers. The King came to Parliament and tried to arrest its leaders, but he failed. The Civil War began in August of 1642. The King held the territory from Oxford to the North; the Parliament held London.

At the outbreak of the Civil War, Rupert came to England to join his cousin Charles at Nottingham in 1642. Although he offended various courtiers by "his rough manner and arrogance," he commanded the King's forces to a number of victories and proved himself one of the King's few able military leaders. He was named Earl of Holderness and Duke of Cumberland in 1644. In 1645, he became Governor of Bristol, but he surrendered it to Parliamentary forces. The King was angered by the surrender and banished Rupert, but Rupert brought about a reconciliation during that same year.

During most of the Civil War, neither side could win. Troops on both sides looted the estates of the nobility. This is the way armies of the time were paid and gained needed supplies. *Paradine v. Jane* involves one of the many minor actions in the war. Rupert's forces held the land from 1642 to 1645. Finally, in 1645, Cromwell organized what, for the time, was a professional army. It defeated the King's forces in a number of battles. In 1646, the King surrendered. The Parliamentary forces captured Rupert when Oxford surrendered. He was ordered to leave the country. Charles I was beheaded in 1649. Cromwell took power and ruled until his death in 1657. Charles II gained power in 1660. Rupert returned with him. He fought in the wars against the Dutch, and he was First Lord of the Admiralty from 1673 to 1679. He died in 1682.[3]

2. *Grant Gilmore on Paradine v. Jane*: Professor Gilmore comments on the significance of the case:[4]

No legal system has ever carried into practice a theory of absolute contractual liability. Our own system, during the nineteenth century, may be the only one which has ever proclaimed such a theory. The proclamation was made in this country long before Holmes came on the scene and, at least in this country, was steadfastly adhered to, mostly as a matter of ritual incantation, throughout the century. The source of the absolute liability idea in English law was always confidently stated to be the seventeenth century case of *Paradine v. Jane*. In that case, a landlord's action to recover rent, the tenant had pleaded that he should be excused from payment because, during the term of the lease, he had been evicted from the land by a royalist army under the command of Prince Rupert. The plea was held bad: "Though the whole army had been alien enemies, yet he ought to pay his rent." Two hundred years later we find Morton, J., for the Massachusetts court, explaining the "general rule" on excuse by reason of impossibility in this fashion:

... [W]here the party by his agreement voluntarily assumes or creates a duty or charge upon himself, he shall be bound by his contract, and the nonperformance of it will not be excused by accident or inevitable necessity; for if he desired any such exception, he should have provided for it in his contract.

---

[3]See Cook and Wroughton, English Historical Facts 1603-1688 (Rowman & Littlefield 1980).

[4]Grant Gilmore, The Death of Contract 44-7, copyright 1974 by the Ohio State University Press. Reprinted by permission.

This language was copied, almost word for word, from one of the seventeenth century reports of *Paradine v. Jane* — a case which, in all probability, Judge Morton had never read and which he did not cite.

The story of the transmission of the *Paradine v. Jane* language from mid-seventeenth century England to mid-nineteenth century America is one of the curiosities of the legal literature. In its own day *Paradine* does not seem to have been a particularly celebrated case, nor does its seventeenth century meaning, so far as we can determine it, necessarily have much or anything to do with what came to be its nineteenth century meaning. One possibility is that the seventeenth century court meant merely that the tenant could not interpose his plea in the landlord's action for the rent but could bring an independent action against the landlord to recover whatever damages he had suffered as the result of his eviction by Prince Rupert; indeed, *Paradine* is cited to that proposition in a case decided in 1723. Another possibility is that the court looked on the leasehold as a fully executed transaction, with the tenant bearing the risk of eviction in the same way that a buyer of chattels would bear the risk of their loss or destruction after receiving delivery of them from the seller. The modern vogue of *Paradine* dates from Serjeant Williams's edition, first published in 1802, of Saunders, which was a collection of late seventeenth century cases. One of the cases in Saunders, *Walton v. Waterhouse*, involved a covenant by a tenant to rebuild after a fire. In a lengthy note to *Walton v. Waterhouse*, Williams paraphrased the language used in the Aleyn report of *Paradine* and it was Williams' note which Judge Morton, in the Massachusetts case just referred to, cited and copied out. Indeed, there are several early nineteenth century references to *Paradine v. Jane* which assume that the case, given the context in which Williams had put it, involved a tenant's covenant to rebuild.

However, all this is mere bibliographical amusement. The importance of the story lies in the facts that the Williams edition of Saunders was highly successful — having been many times reprinted both in England and in the United States — and that the Note to *Walton v. Waterhouse* became celebrated — the apparent meaning of the Note being that English law for two hundred years past had steadfastly adhered to a theory of absolute contractual liability. Such a theory evidently made sense to the judges — particularly the American judges — of a hundred years and more ago. It would take us too far afield to inquire into the reasons for the success of such a theory; we might perhaps speculate that the Puritan ethic was somehow involved.... Let me repeat a point I have already made: the absolute liability idea was often preached but rarely practiced.... This comment makes the ideas themselves no less significant; it is always a matter of the highest interest when courts — like people generally — say one thing while doing its opposite....

Professor Gilmore invites us to speculate about the appeal of an absolute liability rule. In that spirit, we can ask whether the impact of such a rule would be random or would systematically benefit one group and disadvantage another? Recall Professor Horwitz' views, *supra*.

Professor Wladis reviews the history of the English law of impossibility. He says that law and history "are often incorrectly taught to law students. *Paradine*, for example, is usually cited for a proposition for which the case does not stand and which the judge had no intention of establishing." Wladis points to Aleyn's report which says: "when the party by his own contract creates a duty or charge upon himself, he is bound to make it good, *if he may*, notwithstanding any accident by inevitable necessity, because he might have provided against it by his contract." The key phrase is "if he may." And "*Paradine* was not a case in which the defendant's dispossession made payment of the rent impossible."[5] Wladis continues, noting "[f]ar from reflecting a general rule of the common law at the time, both the result and the reasoning in *Paradine* struggled for acceptance for some 150 years." He finds the first explicit recognition of the *Paradine* reasoning as a general principle in 1858, although he finds the decision used often in lease cases.

3. *The Diamond case:* We move next to a nineteenth century classic statement of individualistic ideology, reflecting some of the spirit of *Paradine v. Jane*. Although the case is 100 years old, the ideas are alive and well today. In *Wood v. Boynton*,[6] Mrs. Wood sued to recover an uncut diamond alleged to be worth $1,000 from Samuel B. Boynton, who operated a jewelry store in Milwaukee. She had sold the stone, which was "about the size of a canary bird's egg" and straw colored, to Boynton for $1.00. The trial court directed a verdict for Boynton, and the Supreme Court affirmed. "When this sale was made the value of the thing sold was open to investigation of both parties, neither knew its intrinsic value, and, so far as the evidence in this case shows, both supposed that the price paid was adequate."

Mrs. Wood made five trips to Boynton's store: (1) In September or October of 1883, she went to get a pin mended. While in the store, she showed Boynton the stone and asked what it was. "He took it in his hand and seemed some time looking at it. I told him I had been told it was a topaz and he said it might be." Boynton offered then to buy it "as a specimen" for $1.00, but she refused to sell. He asked where she found it, and she told him she found it in Eagle, Wisconsin. (2) About December 28th, "I needed money pretty badly, and thought every dollar would help, and I took it back to Mr. Boynton and told him I had brought back the topaz, and he says, 'Well, yes; what did I offer you for it?' and I says,

---

[5]Wladis, Common Law and Uncommon Events: The Development of the Doctrine of Impossibility of Performance in English Contract Law, 75 Georgetown Law Journal 1575, 1576, 1583-4 (1987).

[6]64 Wis. 265, 25 N.W. 42 (1885).

'One dollar;' and he stepped to the change drawer and gave me the dollar, and I went out." (3) She went into the store to get a clock repaired. Boynton questioned her about where she had found the stone. It came out of gravel thrown up when a well had been dug in Eagle, Wisconsin. Boynton then purchased the land where the stone was found.

(4) Boynton testified that "he sent word to her by her husband, that he wished to see her. She came to the store, and he told her, the stone he had purchased from her, proved to be of a good deal more value than he paid for it, and he intended to make her a nice present, not in jewelry, but in cash, when he got around to it. She said, 'Mr. Boynton, you do not owe me anything, ... you gave me more for the stone than I could get anywhere else'...." He replied that he did not propose to be a hog, supposed that he did not owe her anything according to law, but was going to make it all right with her, because the stone proved to be worth more than he paid for it. Mrs. Wood denied that such an offer had been made and denied that she said he did not owe her anything. (5) After an account of the diamond recovery appeared in the newspapers, she demanded return of the stone, tendering $1.10, which Boynton refused.

The day Boynton purchased the stone, he took a file and tried to cut it but could make no impression on it. He said to his son and partner, "Charlie, this is a diamond!" His son responded, "Pshaw!" His son then took it to several dealers who set diamonds, but they thought it was a sapphire. Boynton took it to Chicago and had it tested on a diamond wheel. Afterward he showed it to an expert from New York who said it was a diamond.

Mrs. Wood's lawyer's brief to the Supreme Court of Wisconsin concludes:

> Clearly there was in the minds of the defendants no such uncertainty or speculation as will justify them in claiming that they bought a diamond or anything which might turn out to be a diamond. The uncertainty in their minds was limited to a narrow range of species of inferior crystals of values ranging from fifty cents to forty dollars. Their uncertainty or speculation did not in any event include a diamond of any value, and it is just as clear that this stone was bought and sold under a material misapprehension of an existing fact going to the very substance of the sale, as it would be if they had bought it supposing it to be a diamond and it had turned out to be a topaz, and the plaintiff's right to rescind is just as clear as their's would have been in that case.

Boynton's counsel struck a very different note:

> The effort of counsel [for Mrs. Wood] to get this case before a jury is appreciated. Some of the phrases evidently conned for use before that body, are deftly fired at this court, on many pages of counsel's brief. Such as "the poor woman became pressed for money, so that even a dollar came to be regarded by her as an essential addition to her funds." "he felt too poor to

purchase jewelry at any price;" "a woman in desperate want of money;" etc., etc. Is Mrs. Wood, by reason of these conditions, entitled to any more remedies against the defendants, than Vanderbilt would have been, if he had sold us the stone? "A woman in desperate want of money," on one side, and two full-grown men on the other, with the disparity in value and price shown by this case, without a scintilla of proof of fraud, and without any mistake recognizable in the law, are the circumstances under which, counsel claims, that the case should have been submitted to the jury. The jury room has become the only legal refuge of the Commune in this country. Its jurisdiction ought not to be extended. Balancing the scales of justice with an eye to a "desperate want of money" by one party, is no better practice than a verdict based on color, sex or religion.

The "deal is a deal" principle is a powerful one. Judge Jerome Frank, a famous liberal judge, invoked it in 1951 in *Guttman v. Illinois Central R.R. Co.*[7] The dispute concerned the rights of preferred stockholders in the railroad to dividends. Between 1937 between 47 the railroad had chosen not to declare any dividends, though it would have been possible for them to do so. In 1950, the company declared dividends for both the preferred and common stockholders. The applicable rules required that preferred stockholders receive their dividend before common stockholders can be paid a dividend. Guttman, the holder of a stock designated as "non-cumulative preferred" sued to require that the preferred stockholders be paid all of the dividends which could have been paid to them from 1937 to 1947 before the common stockholders be paid any. The trial court dismissed the complaint, and Judge Frank, writing for the Second Circuit, affirmed.

Here we are interpreting a contract into which uncoerced men entered. Nothing in the wording of the contract would suggest to an ordinary wayfaring person the existence of a contingent or inchoate right to arrears of dividends. The notion that such a right was promised is, rather, the invention of lawyers or other experts, a notion stemming from considerations of fairness, from a policy of protecting investors in those securities. But the preferred stockholders are not — like sailors or idiots or infants — wards of the judiciary. As courts on occasions have quoted or paraphrased ancient poets, it may not be inappropriate to paraphrase a modern poet, and to say that "a contract is a contract is a contract."[8] To be sure, it is an overstatement that the courts never do more than carry out the intentions of

---

[7]189 F.2d 927, 930 (2nd Cir, 1951).

[8]Eds Note: The reference is to a line from Gertrude Stein's poem Sacred Emily: "Rose is a rose is a rose is a rose." Note that there are 4 roses, and not just 3, and no indefinite article to begin the line.

the parties: In the interest of fairness and justice, many a judge-made legal rule does impose, on one of the parties to a contract, obligations which neither party actually contemplated and to which the language of the contract is silent. But there are limits to the extent to which a court may go in so interpolating rights and obligations which were never in the parties' contemplation. In this case, we consider those limits clear.

4. *Rule and counter-rule:* Whatever the force of the ideas associated with *Paradine v. Jane,* it was possible to fashion a counter-rule well within the traditions of the common law. A court could find that what appeared to be an absolute unqualified promise was in fact a promise subject to an implied condition. Again, in the spirit of speculation, recall Professor Horwitz' views. Consider the text of what in the late-20th century is a better known case than *Paradine v. Jane.*

TAYLOR AND ANOTHER AGAINST CALDWELL AND ANOTHER

3 B. & S. 826, 122 Eng.Rep. 309 (1863)

The declaration alleged that by an agreement ... the defendants agreed to let ... The Surrey Gardens and Music Hall, Newington, Surrey, for ... Monday the 17th June 1861, Monday the 15th July, 1861, Monday the 5th August, 1861, and Monday the 19th August, 1861, for the purpose of giving a series of four grand concerts and day and night fetes, at the Gardens and Hall on those days respectively, at the rent or sum of 100£. for each of those days. It then averred the fulfilment of conditions &c., on the part of the plaintiffs; and breach by the defendants, that they did not nor would allow the plaintiffs to have the use of The Surrey Music Hall and Gardens according to the agreement, but wholly made default therein, &c.; whereby the plaintiffs lost divers moneys paid by them for printing advertisements of and in advertising the concerts, and also lost divers sums expended and expenses incurred by them in preparing  for the concerts and otherwise in relation thereto, and on the faith of the performance by the defendants of the agreement on their part, and had been otherwise injured, &c....

[The defendants answered:] That at the time of the agreement there was a general custom of the trade and business of the plaintiffs and the defendants, with respect to which the agreement was made, known to the plaintiffs and the defendants, and with reference to which they agreed, and which was part of the agreement, that in the event of the Gardens and Music Hall being destroyed or so far damaged by accidental fire as to prevent the entertainments being given according to the intent of the agreement, between the time of making the agreement and the time appointed for the performance of the same, the agreement should be rescinded and at an end; and that the Gardens ánd Music Hall were destroyed and so far damaged by accidental fire as to prevent the entertainments, or any of them, being given, according to the intent of the agreement, between the time of making the agreement and the first of the times appointed for the performance of the same, and continued so destroyed and damaged until after the times appointed for the performance of the agreement had elapsed, without the default of the defendants or either of them....

On the trial, before Blackburn, J., at the London Sittings after Michaelmas Term, 1861, it appeared that the action was brought on the following agreement:

Royal Surrey Gardens,

27th May, 1861.

Agreement between Messrs. Caldwell & Bishop, of the one part, and Messrs. Taylor & Lewis of the other part, whereby the said Caldwell & Bishop agree to let, and the said Taylor & Lewis agree to take, on the terms hereinafter stated, The Surrey Gardens and Music Hall, Newington, Surrey, for the following days, viz.: —

Monday, the 17th June, 1861,
" 15th July, 1861,
" 5th August, 1861,
" 19th August, 1861,

for the purpose of giving a series of four grand concerts and day and night fetes at the said Gardens and Hall on those days respectively at the rent or sum of 100£. for each of the said days. The said Caldwell & Bishop agree to find and provide at their own sole expense, on each of the aforesaid days, for the amusement of the public and persons then in the said Gardens and Hall, an efficient and organised military and quadrille band, the united bands to consist of from thirty-five to forty members; al fresco entertainments of various descriptions; coloured minstrels, fireworks and full illuminations; a ballet or divertissement, if permitted, a wizard and Grecian statues; tight rope performances; rifle galleries; air gun shooting; Chinese and Parisian games; boats on the lake, and (weather permitting) aquatic sports, and all and every other entertainment as given nightly during the months and times above mentioned. And the said Caldwell & Bishop also agree that the before mentioned united bands shall be present and assist at each of the said concerts, from its commencement until 9 o'clock at night; that they will, one week at least previous to the above mentioned dates, underline in bold type in all their bills and advertisements that Mr. Sims Reeves and other artistes will sing at the said gardens on those dates respectively, and that the said Taylor & Lewis shall have the right of placing their boards, bills and placards in such number and manner (but subject to the approval of the said Caldwell & Bishop) in and about the entrance to the said gardens, and in the said grounds, one week at least previous to each of the above mentioned days respectively, all bills so displayed being affixed on boards. And the said Caldwell & Bishop also agree to allow dancing on the new circular platform after 9

*o'clock at night, but not before. And the said Caldwell & Bishop also agree not
to allow the firework display to take place till a 1/4 past 11 o'clock at night.
And, lastly, the said Caldwell & Bishop agree that the said Taylor & Lewis shall
be entitled to and shall be at liberty to take and receive, as and for the sole use
and property of them the said Taylor & Lewis, all moneys paid for entrance to
the Gardens, Galleries and Music Hall and firework galleries, and that the said
Taylor & Lewis may in their own discretion secure the patronage of any
charitable institution in connection with the said concerts. And the said Taylor
& Lewis agree to pay the aforesaid respective sum of 100£. in the evening of the
said respective days by a crossed cheque, and also to find and provide, at their
own sole cost, all the necessary artistes for the said concerts, including Mr. Sims
Reeves, God's will permitting.*

(Signed) J. Caldwell.

Witness   Chas. Bishop.
(Signed) S. Denis.

On the 11th June the Music Hall was destroyed by an accidental fire, so that
it became impossible to give the concerts. Under these circumstances a verdict
was returned for the plaintiff, with leave reserved to enter a verdict for the
defendants on the second and third issues....

H. Tindl Atkinson shewed cause [to enter a verdict for the plaintiffs]. — First.
The agreement sued on does not shew a "letting" by the defendants to the
plaintiffs of the Hall and Gardens, although it uses the word "let," and contains
a stipulation that the plaintiffs are to be empowered to receive the money at the
doors, and to have the use of the Hall, for which they are to pay 100£, and
pocket the surplus; for the possession is to remain in the defendants, and the
whole tenor of the instrument is against the notion of a letting....

Secondly. The destruction of the premises by fire will not exonerate the
defendants from performing their part of the agreement. In *Paradine v. Jane* (Al.
26) it is laid down that, where the law creates a duty or charge, and the party is
disabled to perform it without any default in him, and hath no remedy over, there
the law will excuse him; but when the party, by his own contract, creates a duty
or charge upon himself, he is bound to make it good, if he may, notwithstanding
any accident by inevitable necessity, because he might have provided against it
by his contract. And there accordingly it was held no plea to an action for rent
reserved by lease that the defendant was kept out of possession by an alien enemy
whereby he could not take the profits.

Pearce, in support of the [defendant theater owner:]. — First. This instrument
amounts to a demise. It uses the legal words for that purpose, and is treated in
the declaration as a demise.

Secondly. The words "God's will permitting" override the whole agreement.

The judgment of the Court was now delivered by BLACKBURN, J. In this case the
plaintiffs and defendants had, on the 27th May, 1861, entered into a contract by
which the defendants agreed to let the plaintiffs have the use of The Surrey

Gardens and Music Hall on four days then to come, viz., the 17th June, 15th July, 5th August and 19th August, for the purpose of giving a series of four grand concerts, and day and night fetes at the Gardens and Hall on those days respectively; and the plaintiffs agreed to take the Gardens and Hall on those days, and pay 100£. for each day.

The parties inaccurately call this a "letting," and the money to be paid a "rent;" but the whole agreement is such as to shew that the defendants were to retain the possession of the Hall and Gardens so that there was to be no demise of them, and that the contract was merely to give the plaintiffs the use of them on those days. Nothing however, in our opinion, depends on this. The agreement then proceeds to set out various stipulations between the parties as to what each was to supply for these concerts and entertainments, and as to the manner in which they should be carried on. The effect of the whole is to show that the existence of the Music Hall in the Surrey Gardens in a state fit for a concert was essential for the fulfilment of the contract, — such entertainments as the parties contemplated in their agreement could not be given without it.

After the making of the agreement, and before the first day on which a concert was to be given, the Hall was destroyed by fire. This destruction, we must take it on the evidence, was without the fault of either party, and was so complete that in consequence the concerts could not be given as intended. And the question we have to decide is whether, under these circumstances, the loss which the plaintiffs have sustained is to fall upon the defendants. The parties when framing their agreement evidently had not present to their minds the possibility of such a disaster, and have made no express stipulation with reference to it, so that the answer to the question must depend upon the general rules of law applicable to such a contract.

There seems no doubt that where there is a positive contract to do a thing, not in itself unlawful, the contractor must perform it or pay damages for not doing it, although in consequence of unforeseen accidents, the performance of his contract has become unexpectedly burdensome or even impossible. The law is so laid down in 1 Roll. Abr. 450, Condition (G), and in the note (2) to *Walton v. Waterhouse* (2 Wms. Saund. 421 a. 6th ed.), and is recognised as the general rule by all the Judges in the much discussed case of *Hall v. Wright* (E. B. & E. 746). But this rule is only applicable when the contract is positive and absolute, and not subject to any condition either express or implied: and there are authorities which, as we think, establish the principle that where, from the nature of the contract, it appears that the parties must from the beginning have known that it could not be fulfilled unless when the time for the fulfilment of the contract arrived some particular specified thing continued to exist, so that, when entering into the contract, they must have contemplated such continuing existence as the foundation of what was to be done; there, in the absence of any express or implied warranty that the thing shall exist, the contract is not to be construed as a positive contract, but as subject to an implied condition that the parties shall be excused in case, before breach, performance becomes impossible from the perishing of the thing without default of the contractor.

There seems little doubt that this implication tends to further the great object of making the legal construction such as to fulfil the intention of those who entered into the contract. For in the course of affairs men in making such contracts in general would, if it were brought to their minds, say that there should be such a condition.

Accordingly, in the Civil law, such an exception is implied in every obligation of the class which they call obligatio de certo corpore. The rule is laid down in the Digest, lib. XLV., tit. 1, de verborum obligationibus, l. 33. "Si Stichus certo die dari promissus, ante diem moriatur: non tenetur promissor." The principle is more fully developed in l. 23. "Si ex legati causa, aut ex stipulatu hominem certum mihi debeas: non aliter post mortem ejus tenearis mihi, quam si per te steterit, quominus vivo eo eum mihi dares: quod ita fit, si aut interpellatus non dedisti, aut occidisti eum." The examples are of contracts respecting a slave, which was the common illustration of a certain subject used by the Roman lawyers, just as we are apt to take a horse; and no doubt the propriety, one might almost say necessity, of the implied condition is more obvious when the contract relates to a living animal, whether man or brute, than when it relates to some inanimate thing (such as in the present case a theatre) the existence of which is not so obviously precarious as that of the live animal, but the principle is adopted in the Civil law as applicable to every obligation of which the subject is a certain thing. The general subject is treated of by Pothier, who in his Traité des Obligations, partie 3, chap. 6, art. 3, § 668 states the result to be that the debtor corporis certi is freed from his obligation when the thing has perished, neither by his act, nor his neglect, and before he is in default, unless by some stipulation he has taken on himself the risk of the particular misfortune which has occurred.

Although the Civil law is not of itself authority in an English Court, it affords great assistance in investigating the principles on which the law is grounded. And it seems to us that the common law authorities establish that in such a contract the same condition of the continued existence of the thing is implied by English law.

There is a class of contracts in which a person binds himself to do something which requires to be performed by him in person; and such promises, *e.g.* promises to marry, or promises to serve for a certain time, are never in practice qualified by an express exception of the death of the party; and therefore in such cases the contract is in terms broken if the promisor dies before fulfilment. Yet it was very early determined that, if the performance is personal, the executors are not liable; *Hyde v. The Dean of Windsor* (Cro. Eliz. 552, 553). See 2 Wms. Exors. 1560, 5th ed., where a very apt illustration is given. "Thus," says the learned author, "if an author undertakes to compose a work, and dies before completing it, his executors are discharged from this contract: for the undertaking is merely personal in its nature, and, by the intervention of the contractor's death, has become impossible to be performed."... In *Hall v. Wright* (E. B. &

E. 746, 749), Crompton J., in his judgment, puts another case. "Where a contract depends upon personal skill, and the act of God renders it impossible, as, for instance, in the case of a painter employed to paint a picture who is struck blind, it may be that the performance might be excused."

It seems that in those cases the only ground on which the parties or their executors, can be excused from the consequences of the breach of the contract is, that from the nature of the contract there is an implied condition of the continued existence of the life of the contractor, and, perhaps in the case of the painter of his eyesight. In the instances just given, the person, the continued existence of whose life is necessary to the fulfilment of the contract, is himself the contractor, but that does not seem in itself to be necessary to the application of the principle, as is illustrated by the following example. In the ordinary form of an apprentice deed the apprentice binds himself in unqualified terms to "serve until the full end and term of seven years to be fully complete and ended," during which term it is covenanted that the apprentice his master "faithfully shall serve," and the father of the apprentice in equally unqualified terms binds himself for the performance by the apprentice of all and every covenant on his part. (See the form, 2 Chitty on Pleading, 370, 7th ed. by Greening.) It is undeniable that if the apprentice dies within the seven years, the covenant of the father that he shall perform his covenant to serve for seven years is not fulfilled, yet surely it cannot be that an action would lie against the father? Yet the only reason why it would not is that he is excused because of the apprentice's death.

These are instances where the implied condition is of the life of a human being, but there are others in which the same implication is made as to the continued existence of a thing. For example, where a contract of sale is made amounting to a bargain and sale, transferring presently the property in specific chattels, which are to be delivered by the vendor at a future day; there, if the chattels, without the fault of the vendor, perish in the interval, the purchaser must pay the price and the vendor is excused from performing his contract to deliver, which has thus become impossible.

That this is the rule of the English law is established by the case of *Rugg v. Minett* (11 East, 210), where the article that perished before delivery was turpentine, and it was decided that the vendor was bound to refund the price of all those lots in which the property had not passed; but was entitled to retain without deduction the price of those lots in which the property had passed, though they were not delivered, and though in the conditions of sale, which are set out in the report, there was no express qualification of the promise to deliver on payment. It seems in that case rather to have been taken for granted than decided that the destruction of the thing sold before delivery excused the vendor from fulfilling his contract to deliver on payment.

This also is the rule in the Civil law, and it is worth noticing that Pothier, in his celebrated Traité du Contrat de Vente (see Part. 4, § 307, &c.; and Part. 2, ch. 1, sect. 1, art. 4, § 1), treats this as merely an example of the more general rule that every obligation *de certo corpore* is extinguished when the thing ceases to exist. See Blackburn on the Contract of Sale, p. 173....

It may, we think, be safely asserted to be now English law, that in all contracts of loan of chattels or bailments if the performance of the promise of the borrower or bailee to return the things lent or bailed, becomes impossible because it has perished, this impossibility (if not arising from the fault of the borrower or bailee from some risk which he has taken upon himself) excuses the borrower or bailee from the performance of his promise to redeliver the chattel....

In none of these cases is the promise in words other than positive, nor is there any express stipulation that the destruction of the person or thing shall excuse the performance; but that excuse is by law implied, because from the nature of the contract it is apparent that the parties contracted on the basis of the continued existence of the particular person or chattel. In the present case, looking at the whole contract, we find that the parties contracted on the basis of the continued existence of the Music Hall at the time when the concerts were to be given; that being essential to their performance.

We think, therefore, that the Music Hall having ceased to exist, without fault of either party, both parties are excused, the plaintiffs from taking the gardens and paying the money, the defendants from performing their promise to give the use of the Hall and Gardens and other things. Consequently the rule must be absolute to enter the verdict for the defendants. *Rule absolute.*

NOTES AND QUESTIONS

1. *Application to production delayed by a strike*: Would *Taylor v. Caldwell* excuse late delivery or nondelivery of goods caused by a strike? The early cases which considered this question drew distinctions based on whether the strike was of the promisor's own employees, or involved a strike by the employees of a third party. If the strike involved the promisor's own employees, there were many cases which held that the promisor was expected to yield to the demands, at least if they were reasonable and if the strike was a peaceful one; failure to yield to a reasonable and peaceful strike destroyed any defense of impossibility. These cases, however, though reasonably numerous are of doubtful authority and pre-date modern labor law and labor practices. In light of the uncertainty associated with the early cases, it is usual for the parties to expressly address the question of strikes in their agreements.

Again, recall Professor Horwitz' views. Do these early cases on the impact of strikes reflect the domination of a capitalist ideology or do they reflect some counterview?

2. *The U.C.C. and strikes*: Apply Uniform Commercial Code §§ 2-615; 2-616 to the simple case of a delivery delayed by a strike by the employees of a manufacturer. Be sure to consider the Official Comments as well as the text of the statute. It is unlikely that you will find certain answers in the text or comments of the Code, but the exercise should make you sensitive to the

questions which must be answered in order to use the Code's provisions. Does the U.C.C. reflect *Paradine v. Jane*, *Taylor v. Caldwell*, or both cases?

3. *The mistake parallel*: Compare the famous "cow" case, *Sherwood v. Walker*,[9] with *Paradine v. Jane*, and *Taylor v. Caldwell*, and especially *Wood v. Boynton*. Generations of law students have struggled with the reconciliation of "the cow case" and "the diamond case" Can it be done? The cases were decided within two years of one another, on opposite sides of Lake Michigan. Sherwood, the buyer, sued for replevin of a cow and won in a Justice's Court. Walker, the seller, appealed. He argued that he was entitled to rescind because of a mutual mistake of fact. The judgment was reversed, with one judge dissenting. The majority opinion said that Sherwood, a banker, had called on Walker, a businessman,[10] seeking to buy some blooded cattle. "He was asked to go out and look at ... [some on Walker's Greenfield farm] ... with the statement at the time that they were probably barren, and would not breed." A few days later Sherwood called on Walker to buy a cow known as Rose 2d of Aberlone. The price was set at $80. Walker told Graham, his employee, to deliver the cow at King's cattle yard. Graham then discovered that the cow was with calf, and Walker refused to deliver her. The cow had cost Walker $850, and if it were not barren, it would be worth between $750 and $1,000. The majority of the Michigan Supreme Court said that there had been a "mutual mistake of a material fact as to the substance of the thing bargained for." "[T]he mistake was not of the mere quality of the cow but went to the very nature of the thing. A barren cow is a substantially different creature than a breeding one." The cow was "evidently sold and purchased on the relation of her value for beef, unless the plaintiff had learned of her true condition, and concealed such knowledge from defendants." A new trial was ordered to consider whether the cow was sold upon the understanding of both parties that she was barren.

The dissenting judge said that there was nothing in the record indicating that the cow was sold as beef. The buyer was told by the seller that the cow was barren, but the buyer thought she could be made to breed. The mistake went only to the quality of the animal rather than to the substance of the contract. "As to the quality of the animal, and as to this each party took his chances. If this were not the law, there would be no safety in purchasing this kind of stock."

How, if at all, does the right to rescind for mutual mistake about a material fact differ from the defense of an implied condition excusing performance when there has been the destruction of a specific thing essential for that performance? One could say that the theater owner promised to have a theater available on certain dates and that Walker had promised to sell Rose 2d of Aberlone; neither

---

[9]66 Mich. 568, 33 N.W. 919 (1887).

[10]We are told that this was Hiram Walker, a man whose business may be known to some readers.

qualified his promise expressly. Yet both courts were willing to look to what they saw as the real deal behind the formal one.

Nonetheless, are there differences as to when which doctrine would apply? Presumably, Rose 2d of Aberlone was with calf when Walker sold her to Sherwood. However, the theater was standing and available for performances when Caldwell agreed to let it to Taylor. The fire came about fifteen days later. Do we need different rules of law to cover these two situations or is the problem essentially the same? (Whatever your view on whether the difference as to when an event occurs makes a difference, you must recognize that, at least in form, mistake and impossibility are distinct doctrines.)[11]

Does the following decision indicate that the "a deal is a deal" ideology was still alive and well in 1983? Restatement (Second) of Contracts § 262 provides that "[i]f the existence of a particular person is necessary for the performance of a duty, his death or such incapacity as makes performance impracticable is an event the non-occurrence of which was a basic assumption on which the contract was made." Such events excuse performance. However, what should courts interpret "incapacity" to mean?

HANDICAPPED CHILDREN'S ED. BD. OF SHEBOYGAN CO. v. LUKASZEWSKI

112 Wis.2d 197, 332 N.W.2d 774 (1983)

CALLOW, J. This review arises out of an unpublished decision of the court of appeals which affirmed in part and reversed in part a judgment of the Ozaukee County Circuit Court, Judge Warren A. Grady.

In January of 1978 the Handicapped Children's Education Board (the Board) hired Elaine Lukaszewski to serve as a speech and language therapist for the spring term. Lukaszewski was assigned to the Lightfoot School in Sheboygan Falls, which was approximately 45 miles from her home in Mequon. Rather than move, she commuted to work each day. During the 1978 spring term, the Board offered Lukaszewski a contract to continue in her present position at Lightfoot School for the 1978-79 school year. The contract called for an annual salary of $10,760. Lukaszewski accepted.

---

[11]Sherwood v. Walker may no longer be the law of Michigan. In Lenawee Co. Bd. of Health v. Messerly, 417 Mich. 17, 331 N.W.2d 203 (1982), the court said "[w]e find that the inexact and confusing distinction between contractual mistakes running to the value and those touching the substance of the consideration only serves as an impediment to a clear and helpful analysis for the equitable resolution of cases in which mistake is alleged and proven. Accordingly, the holding ... of Sherwood with respect to the material or collateral nature of a mistake [is] limited to the facts of [that] case." The court called for a case by case analysis. Rescission is not available "to relieve a party who has assumed the risk of loss in connection with the mistake." The court said that had a risk of loss analysis been undertaken in Sherwood, "we believe that the result might have been different." Compare Florida v. Treasure Salvors, Inc., 621 F.2d 1340 (5th Cir. 1980).

In August of 1978, prior to the beginning of the school year, Lukaszewski was offered a position by the Wee Care Day Care Center which was located not far from her home in Mequon. The job paid an annual salary of $13,000. After deciding to accept this offer, Lukaszewski notified Thomas Morrelle, the Board's director of special education, that she intended to resign from her position at the Lightfoot School. Morrelle told her to submit a letter of resignation for consideration by the Board. She did so, and the matter was discussed at a meeting of the Board on August 21, 1978. The Board refused to release Lukaszewski from her contract. On August 24, 1978, the Board's attorney sent a letter to Lukaszewski directing her to return to work. The attorney sent a second letter to the Wee Care Day Center stating that the Board would take legal action if the Center interfered with Lukaszewski's performance of her contractual obligations at the Lightfoot School. A copy of this letter was sent to the Department of Public Instruction.

Lukaszewski left the Wee Care Day Care Center and returned to Lightfoot School for the 1978 fall term. She resented the actions of the Board, however, and retained misgivings about her job. On September 8, 1978, she discussed her feelings with Morrelle. After this meeting Lukaszewski felt quite upset about the situation. She called her doctor to make an appointment for that afternoon and subsequently left the school.

Dr. Ashok Chatterjee examined Lukaszewski and found her blood pressure to be high. Lukaszewski asked Dr. Chatterjee to write a letter explaining his medical findings and the advice he had given her. In a letter dated September 11, 1978, Dr. Chatterjee indicated that Lukaszewski had a hypertension problem dating back to 1976. He reported that on the day he examined Lukaszewski she appeared agitated, nervous, and had blood pressure readings up to 180/100. It was his opinion that, although she took hypotensive drugs, her medical condition would not improve unless the situation which caused the problem was removed. He further opined that it would be dangerous for her to drive long distances in her agitated state.

Lukaszewski did not return to work after leaving on September 8, 1978. She submitted a letter of resignation dated September 13, 1978, in which she wrote:

> I enclose a copy of the doctor's statement concerning my health. On the basis of it, I must resign. I am unwilling to jeopardize my health and I am also unwilling to become involved in an accident. For these reasons, I tender my resignation.

A short time later Lukaszewski reapplied for and obtained employment at the Wee Care Day Care Center.

After Lukaszewski left, the Board immediately began looking for a replacement. Only one qualified person applied for the position. Although this applicant has less an educational background than Lukaszewski, she had more teaching experience. Under the salary schedule agreed upon by the Board and the teachers' union, this applicant would have to be paid $1,026.64 more per year than Lukaszewski. Having no alternative, the Board hired the applicant at the higher salary.

In December of 1978 the Board initiated an action against Lukaszewski for breach of contract. The Board alleged that, as a result of the breach, it suffered damage in the amount of the additional compensation it was required to pay Lukaszewski's replacement for the 1978-79 school year ($1,026.64). A trial was held before the Court. The trial court ruled that Lukaszewski had breached her contract and awarded the Board $1,249.14 in damages ($1,026.64 for breach of contract and $222.50 for costs).

Lukaszewski appealed. The court of appeals affirmed the circuit court's determination that Lukaszewski breached her contract. However, the appellate court reversed the circuit court's damage award, reasoning that, although the Board had to pay more for Lukaszewski's replacement, by its own standards it obtained a proportionately more valuable teacher. Therefore, the court of appeals held that the Board suffered no damage from the breach. We granted the Board's petition for review.

There are two issues presented on this review: (1) whether Lukaszewski breached her employment contract with the Board; and (2) if she did breach her contract, whether the Board suffered recoverable damages therefrom.

I. It is undisputed that Lukaszewski resigned before her contract with the Board expired. The only question is whether her resignation was somehow justified. Lukaszewski argues that, because she resigned for health reasons, the trial court erred in finding a breach of contract. According to Lukaszewski, the uncontroverted evidence at trial established that her employment with the Board endangered her health. Therefore, her failure to fulfill her obligation under the employment contract was excused.

We recognize that under certain conditions illness or health dangers may excuse nonperformance of a contract. This court held long ago that "where the act to be performed is one which the promisor alone is competent to do, the obligation is discharged if he is prevented by sickness or death from performing it." *Jennings v. Lyons*, 39 Wis. 553, 557 (1876). See also Restatement (Second) of Contracts § 262 (1981); 18 S. Williston, *A Treatise on the Law of Contracts* § 1940 (3d ed. 1978). Even assuming this rule applies to Lukaszewski's failure to perform, we are not convinced that the trial court erred in finding a breach of contract.

A health danger will not excuse nonperformance of a contractual obligation when the danger is caused by the nonperforming party. See *Jennings v. Lyons*, 39 Wis. at 557-58. Nor will a health condition or danger which was foreseeable when the contract was entered into justify its breach. *Id.* It would be fundamentally unfair to allow a breaching party to escape liability because of a health danger which by his or her own fault has precluded performance.

In the instant case the trial court expressly found that the danger to Lukaszewski's health was self-induced. Lukaszewski testified that it was stressful for her to return to the Lightfoot School in the fall of 1978 because she did not want to work there and because she resented the Board's actions to compel her to do so. Citing this testimony, the court concluded: "The Court finds that the defendant's medical excuse was a result of the stress condition she had created by an attempted repudiation of her contract, and was not the product of any unsubstantiated, so-called, harrassment [sic] by the plaintiff's board." Lukaszewski further complained about the hazard of driving 45 miles to and from Sheboygan Falls each day. She alone, however, caused this commute by choosing to live in Mequon. The trial court pointed out in its decision from the bench that she could have eliminated this problem by simply moving to Sheboygan Falls. Thus the court clearly found that any health danger associated with performance of the employment contract was the fault of Lukaszewski, not the Board. This factual finding alone is enough to invalidate the medical excuse for Lukaszewski's breach.

The medical excuse is defective for a second reason. In order to excuse Lukaszewski's nonperformance, the trial court would had to have made a factual finding that she resigned for health reasons. The oral decision and supplemental written decision of the trial court indicate that it found otherwise. In its written decision the court stated:

"[Lukaszewski's] reasons for resignation were succinctly stated in her testimony, upon cross-examination ... as follows: '... I had found a job that was closer in proximity to my home and it offered a different type of challenge, ... also that the pay was, was more, and I asked them if I could be released from my contract.'" The trial court did not include the health danger. Indeed, the court appeared to doubt that Lukaszewski resigned for health reasons. The trial judge observed that Lukaszewski had a history of hypertension dating back at least five or six years. Her blood pressure would fluctuate at the slightest provocation. He further noted that she was able to commute between Sheboygan Falls and Mequon from January, 1978, through the middle of the following summer. In short, the decisions indicate that the court believed Lukaszewski resigned for reasons other than her health.

These factual findings by the trial court invalidate Lukaszewski's medical excuse and thereby establish a breach.... We conclude that the trial court's findings of fact are not against the great weight and clear preponderance of the evidence and, therefore, must be upheld. Accordingly, we affirm that portion of the court of appeals' decision which affirmed the circuit court's determination that Lukaszewski breached her employment contract....

By the Court. — The decision of the court of appeals is affirmed in part and reversed in part.

DAY, J. *(dissenting)*. I dissent. The majority opinion correctly states, "The only question is whether her resignation is somehow justified." I would hold that it was.

Elaine Lukaszewski left her employment with the school board. She suffered from high blood pressure and had been treated for several years by her physician for the condition. She claimed her hypertension increased due to stress caused when the Board refused to cancel her teaching contract. Stress can cause a precipitous rise in blood pressure. High blood pressure can bring on damage to other organs of the body.

She was upset over what she perceived was the unreasonable attitude of her employer in refusing to cancel her contract. Following an unpleasant exchange with the Board's Director of Special Education, Mr. Morrelle, she went to her physician. He found her blood pressure to be 180 over 100, which he testified was very high. He advised her to rest and to get out of the situation that was causing her symptoms, which she properly interpreted to mean "quit the job." He also told her that her elevated blood pressure made it dangerous for her to drive the ninety miles round-trip each day, that commuting from her home in Mequon to Sheboygan Falls entailed.

The trial court and the majority of this court conclude she could have obviated the danger of driving by moving to Sheboygan Falls. But the fact is that would not have eliminated her illness nor the hazards to her health that her condition posed. There is not a shred of medical evidence that her blood pressure problems would be cured or appreciably alleviated if she moved from her home to Sheboygan Falls.

Once the dangerous hypertension is established, and here the only medical testimony did just that, it should follow that one should be relieved of a contractual obligation for services unless malingering is shown. In this case no one denies she has the condition. But, the trial court says, the condition was one "she had created," which the majority on this court refer to as "self-induced." The majority here seized on the rationale that illness that is "self-induced" is somehow less worthy of judicial consideration than illness caused by others, or by outside forces over which the patient has no control.

It seems clear from the trial judge's comments that if he had found her physical condition had been caused by the Board's "harassment," he would have let her out of the contract. This is the only logical conclusion from the statement by the trial judge that, "The Court finds that the defendant's medical excuse was a result of the stress condition she had created by an attempted repudiation of her contract, and was not the product of any unsubstantiated, so-called, harrassment [sic] by the plaintiff's board."

In either instance, whether "caused" by the Board or "self-induced" because of her gnawing feeling of being unfairly treated, the objective symptoms would be the same.

Either, in my opinion, should justify termination of the contract where the physical symptoms are medically certifiable as they admittedly are here.

The majority makes the following assertion:

> It would be fundamentally unfair to allow a breaching party to escape liability because of a health danger which by his or her own fault has precluded performance.

Happily no authority is cited for this sweeping statement which means that it will be easier to ignore it, gloss over it, "distinguish" it, or overrule it in the future. Under this new found axiom, could a concert violinist under contract be sued to cover any added costs of his replacement if he lost an arm in an accident where he was found 100 percent negligent? Or could another party to a personal service contract be held liable if he was unable to perform because of a debilitating illness clearly caused by negligent health habits?

The majority cites a hundred-year-old case, *Jennings v. Lyons*, 39 Wis. 553 (1876), for two propositions:

> A health danger will not excuse non-performance of a contractual obligation when the danger is caused by the nonperforming party. See *Jennings v. Lyons*, 39 Wis. at 557-58. Nor will a health condition or danger which was foreseeable when the contract was entered into justify its breach.

Jennings is cited by the majority to bolster its position. The case is not really in point. In that case a husband and wife contracted to work on a farm for one year for the sum of $300. He was to do outside work and she to do housework. After four and one-half months she had to leave to have a baby and the husband had to go with her. The employer refused to pay either of them anything and they brought suit to recover for the time they had worked. The trial court instructed the jury that if at the time the plaintiff and his wife quit working for defendant, the wife was sick and unable to do her part of the work, plaintiff was not bound to a further performance of the contract and was entitled to recover the value of his and his wife's services for the time they actually worked. The trial court found for the plaintiff.

This court reversed and held that the defendant did not have to pay them anything. The court held that the rule is that performance is excused:

> ... as where performance has been rendered impossible by an act of God, by the act of the law, or by the act of the other party ... the obligation is discharged if he is prevented by sickness or death from performing it ... sickness or death is generally recognized as an act of God in such a sense that it excuses the nonperformance, and a recovery is allowed upon a quantum merit.... 39 Wis. at 557.

This court said that since the husband must have known his wife was four months pregnant when they took the job and that she would be unable to complete the year of work, therefore no recovery was allowed. This court said, "For when performance becomes impossible by reason of contingencies which should have been foreseen and provided against in the contract, the promisor is held answerable." 39 Wis. at 558. Nowhere did the *Jennings* court say "a health danger will not excuse nonperformance of a contractual obligation when the danger is caused by the nonperforming party."

The precedential value of *Jennings* is doubtful but to the extent the rules stated may still be valid it provides no support for the majority. Here, there is an illness, "an act of God," there is nothing in the record to show that the severe increase in Elaine Lukaszewski's hypertension was foreseeable when she signed the contract. Thus, even under *Jennings*, the teacher should be excused from performance.

Hypertension is a health problem that when caused by stress, however induced, may require a job change. That is what occurred here.

But the majority has discovered what it apparently regards as a "fall-back" position, that Elaine Lukaszewski really did not resign her teaching job for health reasons after all.

The majority says: "In short, the decisions [of the trial court] *indicate* that the court believed Lukaszewski resigned for reasons other than her health." (Emphasis added.) (*Supra*, p. 205.)

The word "indicate" has picked up increasing popularity in the jargon of the legal profession in the past few years mostly, I believe, because it does not say anything one can pin down precisely. *Webster's Third New International Dictionary* (1961) gives a wide range of possible meanings to the word "indicate," among them are: "SUGGEST, INTIMATE, HINT ... INDICATE signifies to serve as a sign or symptom pointing to (the inference or action), stressing only a general, unspecified connection between subject and object...."

"Indicate" seems to fall short on the definiteness required for a "finding of fact" by a trial court.

The first time the case came to the court of appeals they sent it back for further "findings" and it is the "original" remarks from the bench plus additional written comments by the judge on remand that form the bases for the appeal and this review.

What the trial court said was that the desire to take the better job brought on the physical symptoms when release from her contract by the Board was refused.

If the trial court had found that she quit merely for the better job and *not* because of her health problems brought on by the high blood pressure, this would be an entirely different case. However, that is *not* what the trial court found in my opinion. The trial court found her medical problems were self-induced and concluded they were therefore unworthy of consideration.

I would reverse the court of appeals decision that held she breached her contract....

NOTES AND QUESTIONS

1. *Brief of the Wisconsin Education Association Council as Amicus Curiae*:

The Wisconsin Educational Association Council (WEAC) is an unincorporated labor organization which serves, through its approximately 475 local affiliates, as the collective bargaining representative for over 45,000 teachers and other educational personnel in the State of Wisconsin. The WEAC is also a professional organization which seeks to advance and protect the educational profession and the individual rights of the members of the educational profession....

Both teachers and school districts encounter situations where the modification or termination of a teacher's individual employment contract during its term becomes desirable to one of the parties to that contract. For example, as a result of the statutory requirement that a teacher accept or reject by April 15 of each year an offer of continued employment with a particular district for the subsequent school year, a teacher is frequently in possession of a valid, binding contract of employment with one school district when that same teacher is under active consideration for employment in a different district. In order to enter into an employment contract with the latter district, the affected teacher must seek release from the former district....

The situation also arises where a school district can obtain economic and other advantages through the unilateral modification or termination of a teacher's employment contract during the term of that contract. An example of this situation, which is occurring with increasing frequency in this state, is where a school district finds it economically advantageous or programmatically feasible to reduce its complement of teachers. It is becoming increasingly common for school districts to attempt to implement such staff reductions by laying off teachers after those teachers have been issued individual employment contracts for the ensuing school year. In such situations, some school boards have claimed that their managerial authority to determine staffing levels and make layoff decisions entitles them to suspend or terminate a teacher's individual employment contract without incurring liability to the teacher for the teacher's lost employment and earnings, on the grounds that the economic savings to the school district sufficiently justifies the breach.

It is the position of the WEAC that the rules developed by the Wisconsin courts with respect to the breach of individual teacher contracts, and the principles for determining and awarding damages in breach-of-contract cases, should be reciprocal in nature and consistent with traditional contract law. The WEAC urges this Court to use the opportunity presented by its acceptance of this case to reaffirm the basic principle that neither party's unilateral interest in breaching an employment contract can excuse its obligation to compensate the non-breaching party for the damages incurred as a result of the breach.... In addition, the WEAC urges this Court to hold that either party's unilateral alteration, suspension, or termination of the individual employment contract constitutes an actionable breach of that contract.

Ms. Lukaszewski was not a member of WEAC. Would its argument help or hurt her case? What was WEAC's interest in this decision?

2. *Contrasts and distinctions*: Suppose a Wisconsin promoter contracted with the representative of Count Basie[12] on March 20, 1984. The contract called for Basie and his orchestra to appear in Milwaukee on June 1, 1984. Basie was born in 1904. Although Basie had suffered a serious heart attack and had been ill for about five years, he continued to perform with the band. Basie and the orchestra appeared in a concert in Hollywood on March 17, 1984. However, this was Basie's last appearance. Basie died of cancer on April 26, 1984. Assume that the contract with the Wisconsin promoter was silent about the risk of Basie's death. For purposes of this question, assume that the promoter would not have to accept an appearance of the Count Basie orchestra without Count Basie. Does the *Lukaszewski* case suggest that the promoter could sue Basie's estate successfully for the profits the promoter could prove it would have made from Basie's Milwaukee appearance? If not, how does the *Lukaszewski* case differ from our Count Basie hypothetical case as we have described it?[13]

---

[12]Some may know little about Count Basie. Along with Duke Ellington, he is one of the important sources of the small amount of serious American music. We prescribe listening to a recording as you contemplate this hypothetical. You might also want to follow this up with a biography like Murray, Good Morning Blues: The Autobiography of Count Basie (Random House 1985), which may change the way in which we hear the music — given its portrait of Basie's struggle, as a black musician, with the burdens of segregation [Is the foregoing side remark an irrelevancy? Construct an argument that it is not.]

[13]Of course, our hypothetical case is an unlikely one. The written contracts used in the music business typically deal with situations where a performer cannot appear because of illness or death. You must remember this problem whenever you draft a contract that calls for personal services to be performed by a specific person.

Indeed, you should also consider whether the services can be performed by anyone else and satisfy the contract. For example, the Count Basie Orchestra continued to perform after Basie's death. While many think the band is very good, most recognize that it is not the same as when Basie appeared with it. Should the contract negotiated with promoters during Basie's life give Basie's representative the right to tender a performance by the orchestra alone if Basie were unable to appear? Should the promoter have the option to accept or refuse such a performance? Should Basie's illness or death discharge the contract?

2. COPING WITH FLOODS, STRIKES, AND THE LIKE

a. Business Practices

Businesspeople often cope with unanticipated events that make performance of a contract very difficult or rob performance of its value. There is a great deal of negotiation and concession, but sometimes one party insists that the other assumed the risk:

— Interview with the Purchasing Agent of a manufacturer of heavy industrial items:

> It does not seem that a clause in a contract excusing delivery because of impossibility is really necessary. Any reasonable customer should not expect that material would be supplied if a supplier's plant is struck or under six feet of water.

— Interview with the Secretary-General Counsel of a maker of heating and cooling equipment:

> When we are purchasing, we often help a supplier in difficulty. We will not penalize him in monetary terms. We think a strike or fire is a justifiable impossibility excuse whether or not the courts would think so. Our suppliers work with us when we need to delay deliveries or cancel, and we work with them. You don't worry about legal niceties.

— Interview with the Purchasing Agent of a large manufacturer of agricultural machinery:

> We have gone to great lengths to help our suppliers when they face situations beyond their control. A number of years ago there was a flood in the Connecticut Valley that put many electrical manufacturers out of business ... Our Boston works sent in men and equipment to help clean up the mess so our suppliers could get back in operation.... You don't kick a man when he is down. Someday you may need help yourself.

— Interview with the Purchasing Agent of a manufacturer of automobile parts:

> On important raw material items we keep a careful record of the vendor's labor contracts. We know when they expire and we try to keep up on the labor problems faced by all our vendors. When the contract approaches the expiration date, we may ask for a monthly, or even weekly, report on negotiations with the union, and we may ask for an appraisal of the likelihood of a strike.... We may buy from nonunionized plants.... We may

buy from two vendors who deal with two different unions.... We like vendors who have several plants so that production can be transferred to the one still in operation.

b. Allocations: Solutions With a High Potential for Dispute

A fire, strike, or flood may destroy part but not all of a supplier's productive capacity. It is able to make some of its product but not enough to fill all of the claims on its supply. What can or must it do with what it has? Suppose, for example, a fire destroys part of a manufacturer's plant under circumstances that justify an impossibility excuse. It will be two months before the plant is back in full production. However, the manufacturer can still operate at exactly one-half of its former capacity — that is, before the fire it could produce 1,000 units a week but after the fire it can produce only 500 units. What can or must it do with the 500 units?

Before the fire, for example, the manufacturer had five contracts with five customers each calling for 100 units a week.

(1) One of these five contracts is legally unenforceable because of uncertainty as to price and quantity, but the parties have performed under it for six months before the fire.

(2) In addition to these five contract customers, the manufacturer had two regular customers who had purchased 100 units a week for five years but had no contract with the manufacturer at the time of the fire.

(3) Moreover, a division of the manufacturer's own company regularly took 100 units a week for use in its own operations.

(4) Shortly after the fire, the manufacturer received an order for 100 units a week from a large firm, but it has not yet accepted this order. The manufacturer had been trying to sell to this firm for years, and its business is more important to the manufacturer's continued success than that of any of its older customers.

(5) The manufacturer also received an order after the fire from a hospital that needs 100 units a week for purposes directly related to the treatment of seriously ill patients.

(6) One of the five customers that has a legally enforceable contract with manufacturer for 100 units a week is a race track. Another customer with a contract has an inventory of these units large enough to supply its needs for at least three months. The units are not readily available on the market at the present time.

You are the manufacturer's general counsel. Which actual and potential customers get how many units per week? See U.C.C. §§ 2-615(b)(c) and 2-616, and Official Comment 11 to § 2-615.

Some of the answers are fairly easy; many are not. Suppose that a manufacturer allocates its available goods in a manner that does not comply with § 2-615(b). A buyer who did not get enough sues. What is the consequence of the improper allocation? Does the manufacturer lose its entire impossibility excuse or will the buyer be limited to damages based on the difference between its allocation and what it would have received had an improper allocation not been made? See § 2-615(a) granting an excuse in certain cases to a seller "who complies with paragraphs (b) and (c)." May we assume that a seller who does not comply does not get the excuse granted by paragraph (a)?

Professor James J. White, of the University of Michigan Law School, studied contract administration in the chemical industry during a time of shortage.[14] There were widespread shortages and allocations in 1974 and 1975. White interviewed about 30 people at 10 chemical and pharmaceutical companies.

He found that no company had a written allocation plan or a fixed plan concerning all products. The predominate method of allocating production was on a pro rata basis in accordance with actual purchases over a historic period. This allowed allocations to both contract and spot purchase customers. Some contracts had clever clauses, but businesspeople did not refer to them, and often seemed not to know about them.

There were some deviations from pro rata allocations that seem justifiable. Some firms gave more product to military orders, to buyers who would otherwise have suffered extraordinary losses if all they received was their pro rata share, and to customers of a product not thought part of the pool such as a customer who had built a plant next door to the supplier's production facility.

There also were some deviations from pro rata allocations that seem unjustifiable. There were upstream diversions. The basic chemicals could be combined to produce a variety of products, but some firms found a product mix that produced the greatest yield for themselves. Often allocations were made only after all the internal needs were filled. One business person explained that he might be working next year for the president of the division that he had shorted this year, and he did not want to take this risk. Sales were made to new customers. "One should have a right to 'salt the market' because times of shortage were when one 'added to his market share.' We might serve new customers where in prior times we 'never got beyond the lobby.'" Extra allocations also were given to particularly good customers.

White concludes that "a large part of the behavior a lawyer might conceive as in response to the dictates of the law is in fact taken in ignorance or disregard of it." Lay agents of the seller ration subject to the sanctions within the corporations. Their decisions are largely based on immediate profitability and long-term relationships with buying companies. Furthermore, buyers are unlikely to discover or be able to prove that suppliers have not complied with the U.C.C. allocation rules. Other buyers who got more than they should have often are competitors and are unwilling to share information. Even if a misallocation were

---

[14]White, Contract Law in Modern Commercial Transaction, An Artifact of Twentieth Century Business Life? 22 Washburn Law Journal 1 (1982).

discovered, fighting could be costly; buyers might hesitate to lose what relationship they do have with a seller.

c. Restitution After an Excuse

Impossibility or frustration may excuse performance, but a contract that has been stopped in mid-course will likely cause many reliance losses. Who should take these losses? How far can doctrines such as restitution be used to shift some or all of them? If one party to a contract confers a clear tangible benefit on the other before the contract is discharged for impossibility, most courts will allow its recovery in a restitution action. The one receiving the benefit has been unjustly enriched — something has been handed over on the assumption that it would be paid for when the contract was fully performed and now the contract will not go forward to completion. However, many writers find the case more difficult when the alleged benefit was itself destroyed by the event that provoked the impossible excuse. At best, the unjust enrichment was temporary.

Suppose, for example, a court decides that one who is to construct a machine or make repairs or alterations on another's building is excused because of, say, a fire that has destroyed the partially built machine or the structure on which the builder was to make alterations or repairs.[15] This means that the buyer cannot sue the seller for failure to perform. However, usually the seller's performance also will be a condition to the buyer's promise to pay, and so the seller will be unable to recover on the contract. Suppose, however, the person trying to build the machine or make repairs has done a great deal of work trying to perform the contract before the fire. Can this seller of services or goods recover the value of that lost effort from the buyer? The answer is uncertain.

A seller whose duties were discharged by impossibility can recover for any benefits conferred in a restitution action. See Restatement (Second) of Contracts § 391. As always, the difficult question is what courts will call a benefit and how they will value it. Comment b to the Restatement section states:

> Usually the measure of reasonable value is appropriate. A benefit may be found if it was conferred before the occurrence of the event even though the event later resulted in its destruction, and in that case recovery may be limited to the measure of increase in wealth prior to the event, if this is less than reasonable value.... A party cannot, however, recover his reliance interest under the rule stated in this Section, and his expenditures in reliance

---

[15]Typically, a builder will not be excused if a partially constructed structure is destroyed by fire. The structure is under the builder's control, and placing the burden on builders gives them an incentive to insure or to insist that the owner buy insurance. Those repairing buildings, however, usually are excused if a building is destroyed making it impracticable for them to do their job. Of course, builders can contract for excuses in case of fire and place the burden on owners to obtain insurance; indeed, this is commonly done.

are not subtracted from what he has received in calculating benefit for which he is liable.... Furthermore, to the extent that the contract price can be roughly apportioned to the work done, recovery will not be allowed in excess of the appropriate amount of the price.

To what extent does this comment reflect the cases? More particularly, suppose Owner and Painter contract to have Painter paint three rooms in Owner's house. The house is destroyed by fire. Before the fire, the Painter has completed painting one room. He has also masked woodwork in another room with plastic sheets and tape so that painting the walls would not damage the woodwork. He has purchased the paint needed for the third room, and he has tinted it so that it is the proper color for the job. Paint so tinted cannot be sold to others. All of this paint remains in cans at Painter's place of business. Painter sues Owner for restitution of benefits conferred trying to perform the contract. For what items, if any, can he recover from the Owner? How will these items be valued?

The English common law view: In contracts discharged by impossibility, the English courts left all losses where they found them. Painter could recover nothing in restitution against Owner. A few early American cases also refused to allow either owner or contractor to recover for essential reliance expenditures which, arguably, had produced a benefit to the owner. Whether or not these old cases would be followed today in these states is uncertain.

The American view: While many states have no cases dealing with the problem, a number have allowed restitutionary recovery after a contract is discharged by impossibility. Owners have been allowed to recover advance payments made to builders. However, courts have used the "entire" and "severable" concepts to divide the losses. If the contract is entire, the contractor is entitled to the contract price only when the job is done, and the installment payments do not reflect equivalents for the work to date. However, the contract might be severable — that is, several contracts in a single document. Then the contractor would earn an amount specified in the contract as each step was completed. Suppose, for example, a painting contract is to paint a house. However, the owner is to pay specified sums as each room is completed. The court might construe the contract so that, for example, Painter would be entitled to keep any installments paid as the price of painting each room he had completed before the fire.

Does Painter have a restitutionary claim for work done before the fire? Many are troubled by the idea that Owner has been benefited by an attempt to perform the contract. Any benefit would seem to have gone up in smoke. Nonetheless, property concepts produce what some are willing to see as benefits. Suppose Painter finished the last room, doing the job perfectly. However, 5 minutes after Painter leaves with the money, the house burns to the ground. Painter is in no way responsible for the fire. The risk that the value of a coat of paint will be destroyed by fire, a leaking roof or a falling tree that crashes into the house are just part of the risk of owning property. Indeed, Painter handed over a tangible "thing." He left a thin layer of paint in the right places in the house, and this "thing" belongs to Owner. Thus, we can call it a benefit although it is destroyed immediately after the job is completed.

If we accept this property analysis, we can use it to tell us when a benefit has been conferred. When the paint is applied to the wall it becomes Owner's property, and thus he is benefited in a tangible way. Before the paint is applied, however, it still "belongs" to Painter, and thus the risk that it will be destroyed or rendered valueless is his. Painter could, for example, take paint purchased for Owner and sell it to a third party. On the other hand, Painter might take it to another job, add additional tinting pigments to modify the color, and apply it to the walls of another house. Thus, all these reliance expenditures by Painter will not become Owner's property until the paint is applied to the walls, and we could say that Owner will be benefited only at that point. A number of courts have taken just this approach.[16]

Massachusetts and reliance: In *Young v. Chicopee*[17] a contractor agreed to repair a wooden covered bridge by replacing timber wherever it had decayed. The contractor was to be paid compensation based on a sum per 1,000 feet of lumber actually used. However, so that public travel would not be stopped, the contract required that no work be begun until material for at least half the repairs was on the job site. The contractor stacked lumber on the bridge and on the river bank. It was possible that some or much of this lumber never would have become part of the bridge. The bridge and all the lumber was destroyed by fire. The court held that the contractor could not recover for the timber which had not been "actually wrought into the bridge" at the time of the fire.

The law of Massachusetts seemed to follow the property notions we have described — as each board was nailed into the bridge, it became the bridge owner's property and at that point the risk of loss changed from the contractor to the bridge owner. However, the Supreme Judicial Court of Massachusetts reconsidered the matter in the 1950s. That court overturned a contract between John Bowen Co. and the Commonwealth of Massachusetts to build the Chronic Disease Hospital and Nurses Home in Boston. John Bowen Co., although in

---

[16]Carroll v. Bowersock, 100 Kan. 270, 164 Pac. 143 (1917) draws distinctions based on this theory. A builder sued to recover for part performance of a contract to tear out an old reinforced concrete floor in owner's warehouse and construct a new one. The warehouse was destroyed before the job was completed. The court allowed the builder to recover for tearing out the old floor and for new concrete footings which had been completed when the building was destroyed. However, the court refused recovery for wooden forms into which concrete was to have been poured which were nailed in place and for steel reinforcing rods which were wired in place and would have become a part of the structure when the concrete was poured. Both could have been removed by the builder. The court said that "the liability of the owner ... should be measured by the amount of the contract work done which, at the time of the destruction of the structure, had become so far identified with it as that but for the destruction it would have enured to him as contemplated by the contract."

[17]186 Mass. 518, 72 N.E. 63 (1904).

good faith, had failed to comply with the statutory procedure for bidding on public work.[18] However, the court's decision came after subcontracts had been awarded by John Bowen Co. and work had begun. All of these subcontractors were discharged since it became impossible to continue the work. The court said that John Bowen Co. was discharged since, although it caused the impossibility by its method of bidding, "it must appear ... that, except for the defendant's conduct, there would have been in existence valid and enforceable contracts" in order for the subcontractors to hold John Bowen Co. in breach. Had John Bowen Co. complied with the correct procedure, it would not have been the low bidder and could not have been awarded the general contract. Hence, Bowen's obligations under the subcontracts were excused by impossibility.[19] Are you impressed with this argument? Why do the subcontractors have to take the risk of John Bowen Co.'s command of bidding procedures?

Though relieved of liability for expectation damages suffered by subcontractors, John Bowen Co. soon found itself defendant in a series of suits seeking to recover for the work that had been done before the general contract was overturned in the *Gifford* case.

In *M. Ahearn Co. v. John Bowen Co.*,[20] the plumbing subcontractor sued for labor and materials furnished before it was ordered to stop work. The court allowed recovery. The opinion, however, does not indicate whether the labor and materials had been "incorporated" into the structure, but the court did not seem to regard this as important. Bowen argued that it had received no "benefit" since it no longer held the general contract and would not be paid for this work by the Commonwealth. The court rejected this argument, saying that recovery in cases of excusable impossibility is *not* based "in the ultimate analysis on the principle of unjust enrichment ... wherein recovery is limited to benefits received."

The court allowed recovery, explaining:

[i]t is no longer necessary to find implications of a contract to support recovery. The implications are undoubtedly found in each case in accordance with what the court holds to be fair and just in the unanticipated circumstances and it is in order to proceed at once to that issue.

This is not a case where the defendant stands fully apart, as the plaintiff does, from the circumstances which caused the unexpected destruction of the subject matter of the contract. The defendant did those things with respect to the subbids discussed in *Gifford v. Commissioner* ... which caused its bid to appear the lowest, although in fact it was not. The Gifford decision has held that what the defendant did was not properly done. Even though we

---

[18]See Gifford v. Commissioner of Public Health, 328 Mass. 608, 105 N.E.2d 476 (1952).

[19]Boston Plate & Window Glass Co. v. John Bowen Co., 335 Mass. 697, 141 N.E.2d 715 (1957).

[20]334 Mass. 36, 133 N.E.2d 484 (1956).

assume, as the defendant urges here, that it acted in good faith, and in respects as to which the prescribed course was not clear, the fact is that its actions, in a field where it had a choice, had a significant part in bringing about the subsequent critical events — the awarding to it of an apparent contract which turned out to be void and the ensuing decision of this court. In the circumstances it is plain that this is not a case of fully excusable impossibility. The defendant's part in the train of events is amply sufficient to offset the consideration that it has suffered uncompensated loss. Whatever might be said against the application of our established rule (and we do not intend any suggestion) to a case where the contract subject matter is destroyed by an event completely unconnected with either party and where both parties were equally interested in making the contract for mutual profit, and neither, by insurance or otherwise, could have provided against the risk of the unexpected loss and there is no final benefit, it is clearly fair and just to say in the instant case that "it is enough that the defendant has actually received in part performance of the contract something for which when completed he had agreed to pay a price." Williston, Contracts (Rev. Ed.) § 1976, page 5551.

The Massachusetts court squarely faced the question of recovery for reliance losses in preparation for performance in *Albre Marble and Tile Co. v. John Bowen Co.*[21] Here the subcontractor was allowed to recover for "preparation of samples, shop drawings, tests and affidavits" which were required by the contract's provisions. John Bowen Co. relied on *Young v. Chicopee* and its requirement that work be "wrought into" the structure before recovery would be given. The court said that the "wrought into" test was merely a "variant" of the "enured to the benefit of the owner" requirement, and the term "benefit" could not be taken literally as was pointed out in the *M. Ahearn* decision. The court considered Fuller and Perdue, The Reliance Interest in Contract Damages.[22] It pointed out that John Bowen Co.'s responsibility for the impossibility was greater than the subcontractor's, although John Bowen Co.'s conduct was not so culpable as to render it liable for breach of contract. Later in its opinion, the court speaks of John Bowen Co.'s "fault."

The court noted that the efforts in preparation for performance involved in the case were not solely within the discretion and control of the subcontractor as they were to be approved by John Bowen Co. These samples, shop drawings and tests, by their very nature, could not be "wrought into" the structure. Under all these circumstances, the court was not disposed to "extend" the rule of *Young v. Chicopee* and deny recovery. The court concluded:

---

[21]343 Mass. 777, 179 N.E.2d 321 (1962).
[22]46 Yale Law Journal 52, 373 (1936-7).

The combination of factors peculiar to this case justifies this holding without laying down the broader principle that in every case recovery may be had for payments made or obligations reasonably incurred in preparation for performance where further performance is rendered impossible without fault by either party.... The damages to be assessed are limited solely to the fair value of those acts done in conformity with the specific request of the defendant as contained in the contract. Expenses incurred prior to the execution of the contract, such as those arising out of preparation of the plaintiff's bid, are not to be considered.

The Supreme Judicial Court of Massachusetts returned to the problem of restitution and reliance in impossibility cases in *R. Zoppo Co., Inc. v. Commonwealth*.[23] Here a construction company agreed to build a sewer for a sewage treatment plant in Boston. The contract called for a deep marine trench excavation, and the installation of "forty linear feet of sixty-inch precast reinforced concrete subaqueous pressure diffuser pipe between designed stations on the outfall sewer line." The work involving this pipe was subcontracted to the Perini Corporation. The pipe was specially designed and required fabrication of special forms for its manufacture. It had no salvage value since the only possible use for it was in performance of this contract. Perini, following the requirements of the prime contract, submitted to the Metropolitan District Commission's engineer detailed drawings for the sixty-inch pipe, and they were approved.

After the pipe was manufactured and delivered to the job site, tidal actions were discovered which in the opinion of the engineer required the final twenty-four linear feet of pipe to be deleted from the job. The Commission stored the deleted pipe.

The Massachusetts court found that performance in full was excused by impossibility. It then said,

We hold that this case is governed by *Albre Marble & Tile Co., Inc. v. John Bowen Co., Inc.*, ... There, as here, preliminary samples, shop drawings, and so forth, were prepared under a clause similar to that appearing in the contract we discuss. There, as here, the labor and materials for which action was brought were not actually wrought into the structure but the preparatory efforts of the contractor were under the supervision of the defendant.... [I]t appears just, having regard to all the circumstances of the case ... that the petitioner here may recover for those expenditures which it made pursuant to the specific request of the Commission.

---

[23]353 Mass. 401, 232 N.W.2d 346 (1967).

Is the *Zoppo* case just an application of the doctrine of *Albre Marble* or is it a major extension? Does it overrule whatever *Albre Marble* left of *Young v. Chicopee*?

Valuing the recovery under contracts discharged by impossibility: Suppose a court decides that impossibility excuses performance under a contract. It also decides that a party can recover for preparation or part performance under a reliance or benefit theory. How should it value the work? The Restatement (Second) of Contracts § 385 says that "as justice requires" a court may measure "benefit" either by what it would have cost to buy the performance elsewhere or by "the extent to which the other party's property has been increased in value or his other interests advanced."

Few cases deal with this issue. In a New Hampshire case[24] the court awarded a portion of the contract price measured by a fraction comprised of the ratio of the costs of completing the work to the anticipated total cost. Is this formula either of those suggested by the Restatement (Second)? By contrast, in *R. Zoppo Co., Inc. v. Commonwealth*,[25] mentioned earlier, the court found that plaintiff, who had performed work in good faith that was rendered valueless by tidal action, to be entitled to the costs incurred in doing the work, including a reasonable profit.

Loss splitting as the solution: A number of writers have suggested that "benefit" and "reliance loss" are inappropriate concepts when a contract has been excused by impossibility. Losses should be shared in such cases.[26] The writer of a Comment in the University of Chicago Law Review gives the following example:

> Plaintiff has agreed to install an elevator in defendant's building. The contract price is $2,500. Nothing has been said about time or terms of payment. When the plaintiff has expended $800 in preparing to install the elevator, but before any part of the installation has been made, the building is destroyed by accidental fire. The preparations have consisted primarily of procuring and readying specialized materials which were to be used in the installation and which because of their specialized nature and adaptation have a present market value of only $100. While it is clear that further performance on the contract would be excused, under present loss distribution schemes ... the plaintiff would probably bear the complete loss for the materials purchased and work done. Under a principle of equal sharing of

---

[24]Anderson v. Shattuck, 76 N.H. 240, 81 Atl. 781 (1911).

[25]353 Mass. 401, 232 N.W.2d 346 (1967).

[26]See Comment, Loss Splitting in Contract Litigation, 18 University of Chicago Law Review 153, 157 (1951); Sharp, Promissory Liability II, 7 University of Chicago Law Review 250, 269 (1940); Corbin, Frustration of Contract in the United States of America, 29 Journal of Comparative Legislation & International Law (3d Series, Part III-IV) 1, 8 (1947); Note, 59 Yale Law Journal 1511; Comment, 46 Michigan Law Review 401, 421 (1948).

essential reliance losses, since the net loss is $700 [$800 expenditures less the $100 salvage], the plaintiff could recover $350 from the defendant.

To what extent does this note on restitution actually offer a variety of loss sharing schemes when a contract's value is destroyed by an unanticipated event? On the facts of the example in the Chicago Comment, why shouldn't the elevator contractor share some of the owner's loss from the fire that destroyed the building? Why should the elevator contractor be entitled to add to the loss suffered by the owner? From this perspective can we view the "wrought into" test as a kind of rough loss sharing scheme that also has the virtue of some degree of certainty as compared to the Massachusetts recovery of some essential reliance loss in some cases?

A British solution to the problems: In *Fibrosa Spolka Akcyjna v. Fairbairn Lawson Combe Barbour, Ltd.*,[27] the House of Lords considered the impact of World War II on a commercial contract. In July of 1939, Fairbairn, an English manufacturer of textile machinery, contracted to supply machinery to Fibrosa, a Polish textile manufacturer. Fairbairn was to build specially designed flax-hackling machines in England and install them in Gdynia in Poland. Fibrosa paid 1,000 pounds as a down payment and was to pay 3,800 pounds on delivery.

In August of 1939, Germany invaded Poland, and Great Britain declared war against Germany. On September 7, 1939, Fibrosa's English representative asked for return of the 1,000-pound down payment since delivery of the hackling machines could not take place in Poland because of the German occupation and the English statutes prohibiting trading with the enemy. Fairbairn refused to return the down payment because considerable work had been done on the machines.

Fibrosa sued for the down payment. Fairbairn defended, asserting that performance of the contract was excused because it was frustrated by the German occupation of Gdynia. It said that Fibrosa had no right to the downpayment because of several 1900 British decisions that said that an excuse did not wipe out the contract retroactively, but only relieved the parties from further obligations. The Court of Appeal said that it hoped that the House of Lords would overrule these earlier decisions and adopt "the more civilized rule of Roman and Scottish law." The Court of Appeal assumed that it would have to determine how much of the 1,000 pounds Fairbairn should be allowed to retain to compensate it for its reliance losses and how much of the sum was "a pure windfall" and should be returned to Fibrosa.

The House of Lords did overrule the earlier cases, but it awarded Fibrosa the entire 1,000 pounds. It said that the consideration had failed totally, and, as a matter of quasi-contract, Fairbairn had no claim to the money since its expenditures had not benefited Fibrosa at the time performance was excused. The House

---

[27][1943] A.C. 32.

of Lords conceded that its position might work an injustice where there had been great reliance expenses which had not produced a benefit, but the common law did not furnish the court with a yardstick with which to apportion losses. "It must be for the legislature to decide whether provision should be made for an equitable apportionment of prepaid moneys...." However, we should note that Lord Roche mentioned that according to Fairbairn, the machines as far as completed were "realizable without loss."

Parliament reacted to the *Fibrosa* by enacting The Reform [Frustrated Contracts] Act of 1943 (6 & 7 Geo. 6, c. 40).[28] We can summarize a complicated statute as follows:

(1) The Act provides for recovery measured by benefits conferred (restitution) where there have been such benefits.

(2) The Act has no provision for equitably apportioning reliance losses if the seller has not received a down payment or if the buyer has not yet become liable to make payments.

(3) If there has been a downpayment, the Act provides that a court "may, if it considers it just to do so having regard to all the circumstances of the case," apportion the losses following frustration or impossibility although these losses produce no increase in the assets (tangible benefit) to the other party.

(a) Little direction is given for the exercise of this discretion.

(b) The court is directed not to give weight to whether either party has secured insurance.

The only reported case involving the Frustrated Contracts Act is *B.P. Exploration Co. v. Hunt*.[29] Nelson Bunker Hunt owned a concession giving him the right to drill for oil in Libya. He was required to start drilling by December of 1960, but he lacked the resources and experience needed to explore and develop the concession. He entered an agreement under which B.P. Exploration Co., a wholly owned subsidiary of British Petroleum, would explore and develop the concession. The Court described the arrangement:

Obviously the expenditure incurred in the exploration and development of an oilfield can be enormous. Under the agreement, however, up to the time when the field came on stream, all funds had to be advanced by B.P. Half such expenditure would be incurred for Mr. Hunt's account; but under the

---

[28]Swan and Reiter, Contracts 470-471 (3d ed. 1985) tell us that the Frustrated Contracts Act "was adopted by the Uniform Law Conference of Canada, and formed the basis for the legislation of all common-law provinces except Nova Scotia, Saskatchewan, and British Columbia. The latter province has legislation that is special to it; the others have retained the common law. The model act was largely adopted in the other Canadian provinces." Swan and Reiter also note that the British Columbia Act differs principally in the definition of the term "benefit." The British Columbia statute defines it as something done under a contract whether or not a benefit is received by the other party.

[29][1979] 1 W.L.R. 783, aff'd [1982] 1 All ER 925.

contract B.P. had no right of recoupment in respect of Mr. Hunt's share of
the expenditure until the oil came on stream. All oil produced from the field
belonged to both B.P. and Mr. Hunt, and was to be shared equally between
them, subject to the provision that B.P. was entitled to take and receive a
portion of Mr. Hunt's share of the oil, such proportion being called
reimbursement oil, in order to recoup both the expenditure incurred by them
for Mr. Hunt's account before the field came on stream ... plus 25 per cent.
Once the field came on stream, Mr. Hunt had to bear half the cost of
production, and of further development of the field.

A large and very valuable oil field was discovered and developed at great
expense. A large amount of oil was taken from the field, but Mr. Hunt's
obligation to B.P. for exploration and development had not been covered. In
1969, a revolution overthrew the Government of King Idris of Libya and
substituted the Government of the Revolutionary Command Council led by
Colonel Gaddafi. In 1971, the Libyan Government expropriated B.P.'s assets,
and in 1973, it expropriated Mr. Hunt's.

The court found that the work in exploration and development was a benefit
to Mr. Hunt. It then awarded B.P. an amount which was "just." It considered
Mr. Hunt's offsetting claims against B.P. B.P. was awarded a balance of
$15,575,823 and 8,922,060 pounds.

Justice Goff wrote a 67-page opinion. He noted:

> ... in addition to difficult and novel questions of law, the case involves
> substantial questions of fact and of accounting procedure. The sums involved
> are enormous; B.P.'s claim was advanced in a number of alternative ways,
> the sum claimed varying from nearly $45,000,000 to nearly $230,000,000.
> Furthermore, allegations made by Mr. Hunt relating to the manner in which
> B.P. developed the oil field led to an investigation of almost the entire
> history of the exploration, appraisal, and development of the field, and the
> production of oil from the field. This investigation required a substantial
> body of evidence, much of it technical; and the documents before the court,
> which were very largely concerned with these allegations by Mr. Hunt, were
> very numerous — I was told that there were over 15,000 documents in
> court. Many of these were of a technical nature; and in any event they
> represented only the tip of the iceberg of documents disclosed on discovery.
> Only by reason of the good sense and restraint shown by counsel on both
> sides, and the efficiency of their instructing solicitors, was it possible for a
> so substantial piece of litigation to be kept under control and for the hearing
> to take no longer than 57 days.

In dealing with whether the statute authorized the court to take into account the
time value of money, Justice Goff noted that the lawyers described the
consequences as involving "only $10 million."

Justice Goff was very critical of the Act itself, saying:

> ... all these difficulties would have been avoided if the legislature had
> thought it right to treat the services themselves as the benefit. [That is, to
> allow compensation for essential reliance whether or not defendant
> ultimately gained from it.] In the opinion of many commentators, it would
> be more just to do so; after all, the services in question have been requested
> by the defendant, who normally takes the risk that they may prove
> worthless, from whatever cause. In the example I have given of the building
> destroyed by fire, there is much to be said for the view that the builder
> should be paid for the work he has done, unless he has (for example by
> agreeing to insure the works) taken upon himself the risk of destruction by
> fire. But my task is to construe the Act as it stands. On the true construction
> of the Act, it is in my judgment clear that the defendant's benefit must, in
> an appropriate case, be identified as the end product of the plaintiff's
> services, despite the difficulties which this construction creates, difficulties
> which are met again when one comes to value the benefit.

How should losses caused by expropriation of a joint venture of this sort be
allocated among the parties? Does the Frustrated Contracts Act give a court
adequate guidance in solving the problem? Recall that one may look to essential
reliance losses only when there has been a down payment or the buyer has
become liable to pay a sum of money. In other cases, a court must find a benefit,
value it, and then determine a "just" allocation of this amount among the parties.
Beale, Bishop and Furmston[30] note,

> As [Justice] Robert Goff points out, the Act does not enable the court to put
> the parties into the position they would have been in if the contract had been
> performed (*e.g.*, no recovery of lost profit), nor to restore them to their pre-
> contractual position. Thus the licensees in *Taylor v. Caldwell* would still get
> nothing for the wasted advertising.... Perhaps this is right: the court has
> already determined that neither party was better able to prevent the
> frustrating event, and maybe each is the best insurer of his own expenses,
> since he alone knows the amount of them.

Furthermore, we can ask whether courts have the capability to carry out the
task given them by the statute. Even concluding that Justice Goff did a splendid
job, we must consider spending 57 days of court time plus all the lawyering that
went into this process. We may wonder about the impact of the case on contracts
to develop oil concessions in the future. Should we expect parties to provide in
their contracts ways to deal with the consequences of expropriation or are

---

[30]Beale, Bishop and Furmston, Contract: Cases and Materials 311 (London: 1985).

answers to this possibility so complex that parties will tend to avoid them by using vague and general phrases about equitable adjustments?

How would cases such as *Fibrosa* and *B.P. Exploration* be decided in the United States? There is no clear answer. Indeed, Nelson Bunker Hunt argued that the contract in the *B.P. Exploration* case was governed by the law of Texas rather than the British statute.[31]

Generally, American courts have looked for a tangible benefit conferred by performance before it was excused. However, outside of the area of building repair contracts, there is little authority. Nonetheless, in *Angus v. Scully*,[32] plaintiffs were to move a house from where it stood to another lot several blocks away. The house was moved about halfway and then left at the end of the work day. That night the house burned and was destroyed. The services rendered in moving the house part of the way to its new location were held to be a benefit to the owner, and plaintiffs recovered their fair market value.

Official Comment 6 to § 2-615 of the Uniform Commercial Code says, "[i]n situations in which neither sense nor justice is served by either answer when the issue is posed in flat terms of 'excuse' or 'no excuse,' adjustment under the various provisions of this Article is necessary, especially the sections on good faith, on insecurity and assurance and on the reading of all provisions in light of their purposes, and the general policy of this Act to use equitable principles in furtherance of commercial standards and good faith." Could a court reach results similar to the British Frustrated Contracts Act under U.C.C. § 2-615 and its Official Comments?

Notice that § 2-615 as such does not cover the typical frustration situation where delivery can be made on time but, because of changed circumstances, it has lost its value to the buyer. The text of § 2-615 speaks only of a seller's excuse. Official Comment 9, however, says:

> Even where notice is given by the buyer that the supplies are needed to fill a specific contract of a normal commercial kind, commercial understanding does not see such a supply contract as conditioned on the continuance of the buyer's further contract for outlet. On the other hand, where the buyer's contract is in reasonable commercial understanding conditioned on a definite and specific venture or assumption as, for instance, a war procurement subcontract known to be based on a prime contract which is subject to termination, or a supply contract for a particular construction venture, the reason of the present section may well apply and entitle the buyer to the exemption.

---

[31]See [1976] 1 W.L.R. 788.
[32]176 Mass. 357, 57 N.E. 674 (1900).

Practical solutions to the problems: Typically businesses use some type of "impossibility clause" on their contract forms if they use any legal provisions at all. However, the common clause is very brief. By far the most usual wording is no more than that the contract or order is "subject to" or "contingent on" certain specified events (such as "fire, strike or other circumstances beyond our control"). This simple phrase is found on the business documents of both large and small firms. One businessperson told us that only a simple clause was needed. "If you tried to cover every possible contingency in a contract, you wouldn't have time to get any other work done."

Larger firms with legal staffs often attempt to spell out matters in much more detail. A major producer of metal uses a form providing,

> Seller will not be liable for any delay or failure in performance of this order or in the delivery or shipment of products hereunder, or for any damages suffered by Buyer by reason of such delay or failure, when such delay or failure is, directly or indirectly, caused by or in any manner arises from acts of God, or of public enemies, fires, floods, explosions, accidents, epidemics, quarantine restrictions, riots, mobilizations, war, rebellion, revolutions, blockades, hostilities, governmental regulations, requirements, restrictions, interference or embargoes, strikes, lockouts, differences with workmen, inadequate transportation facilities, delays or interruptions in transportation, shortages of labor, fuel, raw materials, supplies or power, accidents to, breakdowns to, or mechanical failure of plant machinery or equipment arising from any cause whatsoever, or any other cause or causes (whether or not similar in nature to any of those hereinbefore specified) beyond Seller's control. In no event will Seller be liable for any consequential damages for delay in or failure of performance, whether or not excused by the foregoing.

There are a number of questions to be raised in drafting and considering an elaborate excuse clause. Some of the many can be suggested by an outline:

    (1) Who gets what excuse?
       (a) Who is excused, the buyer, the seller or both?
       (b) What excuse is given?
          (i) If a party is "not liable" for delay or failure to perform, must the other accept a partial or delayed performance?
         (ii) If a party is given an extension of time, is there any limit on how long the other must await performance?
        (iii) If one party has an option to cancel, what happens to the other's reliance losses?
    (2) How is the excusing event defined?
       (a) Are they defined generally or in detail?
       (b) Does the contract attempt to expand the "other causes" to include "similar or dissimilar" ones?

(3) What must the consequences of the event be in order to trigger an excuse? How serious an impact on the ability to perform? What about problems of multiple causation?

Realize also that courts may use their interpretive authority to avoid construing contracts that seem to undercut the spirit of the bargains the parties have made. That is, a court may strain to avoid literal application of a provision which allows a buyer to avoid risks which seemed inherent in the overall bargain the parties had made.[33] While we sometimes joke that, "The large print giveth, and the small print taketh away," the courts, like all the rest of us, seek to avoid such consequences if it seems inconsistent with what the parties expected and bargained for.

B. CONTRACTS INVOLVING LARGE ORGANIZATIONS AND GREAT EVENTS OF OUR TIME

Typically contracts are performed. Most problems can be anticipated and in long-term relationships other-than-legal sanctions serve to hold parties together. However, disaster can strike, and good faith may not be enough when millions or the very life of a multinational corporation are at stake. In the last thirty years or so, there have been many important events which have upset assumptions held by those in business — the Suez Canal was closed; the Vietnam War escalated; OPEC changed the price of energy suddenly; Japanese competition changed the way Americans had to do business. Cases arising out of these events prompt lawyers to bring forth many of the doctrines we have considered to this point, but these atypical cases tend to put the whole structure of contract law to the test.

We can offer quaint examples from the past, but both the person on the street and the commercial lawyer in an expensively appointed office accept the idea that a deal is a deal and those who lose bets have to pay up. Nonetheless, when losses get too big, other ideas are asserted. Perhaps, as has been said, the idea of capitalism without bankruptcy is like Christianity without Hell. Yet when Penn-Central, Lockheed and Chrysler are threatened, some begin to think of the impact of their failure on jobs and the economy as a whole. As we will see, the legal system and contract doctrine — the spirit of *Taylor v. Caldwell* — can be turned to salvage operations. There are lessons in these materials about doctrine, the legal system and lawyering, as well as questions of politics in the face of crisis cases.

---

[33]See, *e.g.*, Monolith Portland Cement Co. v. Douglas Oil co., 303 F.2d 176 (9th cir. 1962).

TRANSATLANTIC FINANCING CORPORATION v. UNITED STATES

363 F.2d 312 (D.C. Cir. 1966)

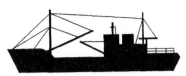

J. SKELLY WRIGHT, [On July 26, 1956, Egypt had taken over operation of the Suez Canal. On October 2, 1956 the U.S. contracted with Transatlantic Financing Corporation for the shipment of a full cargo of wheat aboard the SS Christos, a ship operated by Transatlantic, to a port in Iran. On October 27th, the SS Christos sailed from Galveston headed for Iran on a course which would have taken it through Gibraltar and the Suez Canal. On October 29 Israel invaded Egypt. On October 31, Great Britain and France invaded the Suez Canal Zone. On November 2, Egypt obstructed the Canal with sunken vessels and closed it to traffic. On November 7 a representative of Transatlantic contacted the U.S. and sought a promise that if the shipment of grain were shipped around the Cape of Good Hope that additional compensation would be paid to Transatlantic. The U.S. representative advised Transatlantic that they were expected to complete the charter, but that they should expect no additional compensation. Transatlantic made a claim against the U.S. for the additional costs it incurred when it proceeded to Iran via the Cape of Good Hope. The District Court dismissed the claim, and the D.C. Cir. affirmed.]

... Transatlantic's claim is based on the following train of argument. The charter was a contract for a voyage from the Gulf Port to Iran. Admiralty principles and practices, especially stemming from the doctrine of deviation, require us to imply into the contract the term that the voyage was to be performed by the "usual and customary" route. The usual and customary route from Texas to Iran was, at the time of contract, via Suez, so the contract was for a voyage from Texas to Iran via Suez. When Suez was closed this contract became impossible to perform. Consequently, appellant's argument continues, when Transatlantic delivered the cargo by going around the Cape of Good Hope, in compliance with the Government's demand under claim of right, it conferred a benefit upon the United States for which it should be paid in *quantum meruit*.

The doctrine of impossibility of performance has gradually been freed from the earlier fictional and unrealistic strictures of such tests as the "implied term" and the parties' "contemplation." Page, The Development of the Doctrine of Impossibility of Performance, 18 Michigan Law Review 589, 596 (1920). See generally 6 Corbin, Contracts §§ 1320-1372 (rev. ed. 1962); 6 Williston, Contracts §§ 1931-1979 (rev. ed. 1938). It is now recognized that " 'A thing is impossible in legal contemplation when it is not practicable; and a thing is impracticable when it can only be done at an excessive and unreasonable cost.' " Mineral Park Land Co. v. Howard, 172 Cal. 289, 293, 156 P. 458, L.R.A. 1916F, 1 (1916).... Uniform Commercial Code (U.L.A.) § 2-615, Comment 3.

The doctrine ultimately represents the ever-shifting line, drawn by courts hopefully responsive to commercial practices and mores, at which the community's interest in having contracts enforced according to their terms is outweighed by the commercial senselessness of requiring performance.[34] When the issue is raised, the court is asked to construct a condition of performance based on the changed circumstances, a process which involves at least three reasonably definable steps. First, a contingency — something unexpected — must have occurred. Second, the risk of the unexpected occurrence must not have been allocated either by agreement or by custom. Finally, occurrence of the contingency must have rendered performance commercially impracticable.[35] Unless the court finds these three requirements satisfied, the plea of impossibility must fail.

The first requirement was met here. It seems reasonable, where no route is mentioned in a contract, to assume the parties expected performance by the usual and customary route at the time of contract. Since the usual and customary route from Texas to Iran at the time of contract was through Suez, closure of the Canal made impossible the expected method of performance. But this unexpected development raises rather than resolves the impossibility issue, which turns additionally on whether the risk of the contingency's occurrence had been allocated and, if not, whether performance by alternative routes was rendered impracticable.

Proof that the risk of a contingency's occurrence has been allocated may be expressed in or implied from the agreement. Such proof may also be found in the surrounding circumstances, including custom and usages of the trade. See 6 Corbin, *supra*, § 1339, at 394-397; 6 Williston, *supra*, § 1948, at 5457-5458. The contract in this case does not expressly condition performance upon availability of the Suez route. Nor does it specify "via Suez" or, on the other

---

[34]While the impossibility issue rarely arises, as it has here, in a suit to recover the cost of an alternative method of performance, compare Annot., 84 A.L.R.2d 12, 19 (1962), there is nothing necessarily inconsistent in claiming commercial impracticability for the method of performance actually adopted; the concept of impracticability assumes performance was physically possible. Moreover, a rule making nonperformance a condition precedent to recovery would unjustifiably encourage disappointment of expectations.

[35]Compare Uniform Commercial Code § 2-615(a), which provides that, in the absence of an assumption of greater liability, delay or non-delivery by a seller is not a breach if performance as agreed is made "impracticable" by the occurrence of a "contingency" the nonoccurrence of which was a "basic assumption on which the contract was made." To the extent this limits relief to "unforeseen" circumstances, Comment 1, see the discussion below, and compare Uniform Commercial Code § 2-614(1). There may be a point beyond which agreement cannot go, Uniform Commercial Code § 2-615, Comment 8, presumably the point at which the obligation would be "manifestly unreasonable," § 1-102(3), in bad faith, § 1-203, or unconscionable, § 2-302. For an application of these provisions see Judge Friendly's opinion in United States v. Wegematic Corporation, 2 Cir., 360 F.2d 674 (1966).

hand, "via Suez or Cape of Good Hope."[36] Nor are there provisions in the contract from which we may properly imply that the continued availability of Suez was a condition of performance. Nor is there anything in custom or trade usage, or in the surrounding circumstances generally, which would support our constructing a condition of performance. The numerous cases requiring performance around the Cape when Suez was closed, see *e.g.*, Ocean Tramp Tankers Corp. v. V/O Sovfracht (The Eugenia), [1964] 2 Q.B. 226, and cases cited therein, indicate that the Cape route is generally regarded as an alternative means of performance. So the implied expectation that the route would be via Suez is hardly adequate proof of an allocation to the promisee of the risk of closure. In some cases, even an express expectation may not amount to a condition of performance.[37] The doctrine of deviation supports our assumption that parties normally expect performance by the usual and customary route, but it adds nothing beyond this that is probative of an allocation of the risk.

If anything, the circumstances surrounding this contract indicate that the risk of the Canal's closure may be deemed to have been allocated to Transatlantic. We know or may safely assume that the parties were aware, as were most commercial men with interests affected by the Suez situation ... that the Canal might become a dangerous area. No doubt the tension affected freight rates, and it is arguable that the risk of closure became part of the dickered terms. Uniform Commercial Code § 2-615, Comment 8. We do not deem the risk of closure so allocated, however. Foreseeability or even recognition of a risk does not

---

[36]In Glidden Company v. Hellenic Lines, Limited, 2 Cir. 275 F.2d 253 (1960), the charter was for transportation of materials from India to America "via Suez Canal or Cape of Good Hope, or Panama Canal," and the court held performance was not "frustrated." In his discussion of this case, Professor Corbin states: "Except for the provision for an alternative route, the defendant would have been discharged, for the reason that the parties contemplated an open Suez Canal as a specific condition or means of performance." 6 Corbin, *supra*, § 1339, at 399 n. 57. Appellant claims this supports its argument, since the Suez route was contemplated as usual and customary. But there is obviously a difference, in deciding whether a contract allocates the risk of a contingency's occurrence, between a contract specifying no route and a contract specifying Suez. We think that when Professor Corbin said, "Except for the provision for an alternative route," he was referring, not to the entire *provision* — "via Suez Canal or Cape of Good Hope" etc. — but to the fact that *an alternative route* had been provided for. Moreover, in determining what Corbin meant when he said "the parties contemplated an open Suez Canal as a specific condition or means of performance," consideration must be given to the fact, recited by Corbin, that in *Glidden* the parties were specifically aware when the contract was made the Canal might be closed, and the promisee had refused to include a clause excusing performance in the event of closure. Corbin's statement, therefore, is most accurately read as referring to cases in which a route is specified after negotiations reflecting the parties' awareness that the usual and customary route might become unavailable. Compare Held v. Goldsmith, 153 La. 598, 96 So. 272 (1919).

[37]Uniform Commercial Code § 2-614(1) provides: "Where without fault of either party ... the *agreed* manner of delivery ... becomes commercially impracticable but a commercially reasonable substitute is available, such substitute performance must be tendered and accepted." (Emphasis added.)

necessarily prove its allocation. Compare Uniform Commercial Code § 2-615, Comment 1; Restatement, Contracts § 457 (1932). Parties to a contract are not always able to provide for all the possibilities of which they are aware, sometimes because they cannot agree, often simply because they are too busy. Moreover, that some abnormal risk was contemplated is probative but does not necessarily establish an allocation of the risk of the contingency which actually occurs. In this case, for example, nationalization by Egypt of the Canal Corporation and formation of the Suez Users Group did not necessarily indicate that the Canal would be blocked even if a confrontation resulted.[38] The surrounding circumstances do indicate, however, a willingness by Transatlantic to assume abnormal risks, and this fact should legitimately cause us to judge the impracticability of performance by an alternative route in stricter terms than we would were the contingency unforeseen.

We turn then to the question whether occurrence of the contingency rendered performance commercially impracticable under the circumstances of this case. The goods shipped were not subject to harm from the longer, less temperate Southern route. The vessel and crew were fit to proceed around the Cape.[39] Transatlantic was no less able than the United States to purchase insurance to cover the contingency's occurrence. If anything, it is more reasonable to expect owner-operators of vessels to insure against the hazards of war. They are in the best position to calculate the cost of performance by alternative routes (and therefore to estimate the amount of insurance required), and are undoubtedly sensitive to international troubles which uniquely affect the demand for and cost of their services. The only factor operating here in appellant's favor is the added expense, allegedly $43,972.00 above and beyond the contract price of $305,842.92, of extending a 10,000-mile voyage by approximately 3,000 miles. While it may be an overstatement to say that increased cost and difficulty of performance never constitute impracticability, to justify relief there must be more of a variation between expected cost and the cost of performing by an available alternative than is present in this case, where the promisor can legitimately be

---

[38]Sources cited in the briefs indicate formation of the Suez Canal Users' Association on October 1, 1956, was viewed in some quarters as an implied threat of force. See N.Y. Times, Oct. 2, 1956, p. 1, col. 1, noting, on the day the charter in this case was executed, that "Britain has declared her freedom to use force as a last resort if peaceful methods fail to achieve a satisfactory settlement." Secretary of State Dulles was able, however, to view the statement as evidence of the canal users' "dedication to a just and peaceful solution." The Suez Problem 369-370 (Department of State Pub. 1956).

[39]The issue of impracticability should no doubt be "an objective determination of whether the promise can reasonably be performed rather than a subjective inquiry into the promisor's capability of performing as agreed." Symposium, The Uniform Commercial Code and Contract Law: Some Selected Problems, 105 University of Pennsylvania Law Review 836, 880, 887 (1957). Dealers should not be excused because of less than normal capabilities. But if both parties are aware of a dealer's limited capabilities, no objective determination would be complete without taking into account this fact.

presumed to have accepted some degree of abnormal risk, and where impracticability is urged on the basis of added expense alone.[40]

We conclude, therefore, as have most other courts considering related issues arising out of the Suez closure, that performance of this contract was not rendered legally impossible. Even if we agreed with appellant, its theory of relief seems untenable. When performance of a contract is deemed impossible it is a nullity.... If the performance rendered has value, recovery in *quantum meruit* for the entire performance is proper. But here Transatlantic has collected its contract price, and now seeks *quantum meruit* relief for the additional expense of the trip around the Cape. If the contract is a nullity, Transatlantic's theory of relief should have been *quantum meruit* for the entire trip, rather than only for the extra expense. Transatlantic attempts to take its profit on the contract, and then force the Government to absorb the cost of the additional voyage.[41] When impracticability without fault occurs, the law seeks an equitable solution, see 6 Corbin, *supra*, § 1321, and *quantum meruit* is one of its potent devices to achieve this end. There is no interest in casting the entire burden of commercial disaster on one party in order to preserve the other's profit. Apparently the contract price in this case was advantageous enough to deter appellant from taking a stance on damages consistent with its theory of liability. In any event, there is no basis for relief. Affirmed.

NOTES AND QUESTIONS

1. *Comparing Transatlantic Finance and Lukaszewski*: In what ways are the cases of *Transatlantic Finance Corporation v. United States*, and *Handicapped Children's Ed. Bd. of Sheboygan Co. v. Lukaszewski* alike? In what ways are they different? What about the opinions themselves — how do they compare? How do you account for the differences, whether stylistic or analytic, which you identify?

2. *The likely impact of U.C.C. § 2-615*: If the *Transatlantic Financing Corp.* case reflects the way most courts will use § 2-615, is that statute likely to excuse performance very often? Does the statute as applied reflect *Paradine v. Jane*, *Taylor v. Caldwell*, or something else?

---

[40]See Uniform Commercial Code § 2-615, Comment 4: "Increased cost alone does not excuse performance unless the rise in cost is due to some unforeseen contingency which alters the essential nature of the performance."...

[41]The argument that the Uniform Commercial Code requires the buyer to pay the additional cost of performance by a commercially reasonable substitute was advanced and rejected in Symposium, *supra*, Note 13, 105 University of Pennsylvania Law Review at 884 n. 205. In Dillon v. United States, 156 F.Supp. 719, 140 Ct.Cl. 508 (1957), relief was afforded for some of the cost of delivering hay from a commercially unreasonable distance, but the suit was one in which the plaintiff had suffered losses far in excess of the relief given.

3. *The virtues of uniform and relatively certain law*: Is it important that the *Transatlantic* case followed the British decisions denying relief based on the closing of the Suez Canal? Are there reasons in the international shipping area to have relatively certain uniform rules about such things as excuses?

4. *Industry response*: Goldberg[42] asserts: "Perusal of current shipping contracts indicates that the basic shipping form contracts were not altered after the *Suez* decisions. Closing of the canal is not an enumerated excuse in *force majeure* clauses. Hence, it would appear that the courts got it right." Why does Goldberg say that this failure to change standard form contract clauses means that the "courts got it right?" What does he assume that courts should do when one party seeks an excuse because of an event such as the closing of the Suez Canal?

EASTERN AIR LINES, INC. v. MCDONNELL DOUGLAS CORP.

532 F.2d 957 (5th Cir. 1976)

[See the statement of facts, *supra*. This portion of the opinion begins on p. 980 in the reporter.]

IV. *The Vietnam War as an Excuse for Delayed Deliveries*

Much of the trial below was devoted to McDonnell's defense that the delivery delays were the result of the escalation of the war in Vietnam and were therefore excusable under the contracts, the Defense Production Act, and the Uniform Commercial Code. To prove this contention, McDonnell introduced evidence of government pressure on its suppliers and subcontractors to accord military orders priority over civilian projects. McDonnell asserts that its efforts to raise the defense of government "jawboning" was frustrated by the trial judge's ruling and subsequent instructions to the jury which held that the only excusable delays were those resulting from formal ratings and directives issued in strict compliance with the Defense Production Act. Issue is also taken by McDonnell with the lower court's rulings that it had the burden of proof in establishing its defenses, that the U.C.C. is not applicable to this question and that any excusing event must have been unforeseeable.

Because we find that the Government's "jawboning" policy in effect during the years 1966-1969 comes within the terms of the contracts' excusable delay clause and the exculpatory provision of the Defense Production Act, we hold that the District Judge committed reversible error on this issue. The jury should have been instructed that McDonnell was not liable for any delays proximately caused by this government policy. The trial judge also erred in instructing the jury both

---

[42]Goldberg, Impossibility and Related Excuses, 144 Journal of Institutional and Theoretical Economics 100-116 (1988).

that these particular delays had to have been unforeseeable and that the Code's impracticability defense was not available to McDonnell.

A. The Government's "Jawboning" Policy

Although the origins of American involvement in Vietnam can be traced back to World War II, direct military intervention did not begin on a significant scale until after the overthrow of the Diem Regime in November of 1963. During the ensuing year, the United States increased the number of its troops stationed in that country from 1,000 to 23,000. This American commitment, however, constituted a relatively insignificant part of our total military budget and had no substantial effect on the national economy. Even after the Gulf of Tonkin Resolution of August 2, 1964, our troop commitment in Vietnam remained stable with the total size of the army, in fact, declining. The massive American buildup did not begin in earnest until January of 1965,[43] and it was not until mid-1966 that the United States assumed the bulk of the combat role in Vietnam.

Thus, in February 1965, when Eastern and Douglas signed the letter of intent concerning all the agreements ultimately executed between them, the Vietnam conflict was having no significant effect on the American economy. There was, moreover, little indication at that time of the proportions which the war was quickly to assume.[44]

It was not until 1966 that the war first began to have a substantial impact on the American economy. During that year, for example, the armed forces absorbed over two-fifths of the nation's available manpower. A substantial share of the remaining available work force was taken by firms confronted with a rising backlog of defense-related orders. As one expert testified at trial, this

---

[43]The bombing of North Vietnam did not officially begin until February 1966. As is indicated below, the number of American troops in Vietnam increased by 800 percent during 1965:

Date	Number of troops
December 31, 1964	23,000
June 30, 1965	103,000
December 31, 1965	184,000
June 30, 1966	322,000
December 31, 1966	455,000

[44]For example, Secretary of Defense McNamara announced in 1965 that "We have stopped losing the war." At the time, President Johnson estimated that the military budget for the fiscal year ending in 1965 would be lower than that of the previous year. As late as 1966, American fiscal policy was being formulated on the assumption that the war would be over by June 1967. In March of that year, therefore, Secretary of the Treasury Fowler publicly expressed the hope that "no one will base his economic decisions on the purely speculative assumption that our Vietnam needs will exceed current expectations." The cost of the war in the fiscal year ending in 1967, however, exceeded the Government's estimates by almost 100 percent.

military buildup was superimposed on an economy which was rapidly approaching full employment....

> Hence there wasn't the available capacity in the American economy to absorb the Vietnam requirements on top of existing civilian requirements.

This, of course, led to conflicts between already scheduled commercial production and sudden, unexpectedly large military needs. Rather than abandoning entirely the "guns and butter" policy upon which the war had been predicated, the Government sought instead to have military suppliers accord first priority to war production.

The vehicle by which military orders gained precedence over civilian production was the Defense Production Act of 1950 ("D.P.A."). 50 App. U.S.C. § 2061 *et seq.* Section 101 of the D.P.A. grants the President broad authority to require that priority be given to "contracts or orders ... which he deems necessary or appropriate to promote the national defense." Under § 704, the President is authorized further to "make such rules, regulations, and orders as he deems necessary or appropriate to carry out the provisions of this Act."

As provided under the D.P.A., the President in 1953 delegated his priority powers to the Director of what was then the Office of Emergency Planning ("O.E.P."), a part of the Executive Office of the President. Pursuant to this delegation, the O.E.P., in turn, delegated priority authority over the air transport and other industries to the Secretary of Commerce. Within the Commerce Department, the Business and Defense Services Administration ("B.D.S.A.") was charged with administering the Defense Production Act.

Pursuant to these delegations, the B.D.S.A. adopted rules and regulations governing the precedence to be given certain civilian and military orders. The highest priority under these regulations was achieved by "directives" issued by the B.D.S.A. or the Office of Emergency Preparedness to schedule production at a particular plant. "DX" ratings were intended to be used "to obtain products and materials in cases of extreme urgency," and were accorded precedence over "DO"-rated orders which, in turn, had priority over all unrated goods in a particular area of production.

Because of its importance both to the economy and to national defense, production for civil air carriers, ever since the Korean War, had been accorded the same general "DO" priority rating given military aircraft. By having equal preferential status with military production, the manufacturers of commercial planes were guaranteed prior access to the hardware and vital raw materials also being sought by less essential industries.

Occasionally, "DO"-rated civilian orders would delay military requirements with the same priority rating. Prior to 1966, these conflicts were usually resolved by a Defense Department application to the B.D.S.A. for a "bottleneck-breaking DX rating." After a number of weeks, the B.D.S.A. would issue the requested rating if it determined that civilian orders were in fact delaying military production.

By the end of 1965, however, the enormous increase in urgent military orders had made this process so unwieldy that the Defense Department sought to have the "DO" rating removed from commercial aircraft production. This request alarmed the entire aviation industry because it would have severely impeded its access to scarce raw materials and the heavy industry which was then processing these materials at full capacity. The airlines themselves were concerned that the loss of "DO" priority would further slow the production of planes already being delayed by a war-caused shortage of jet engines, and that non-urgent military orders would be filled at the expense of pressing commercial needs.

In the face of this widespread opposition, the military withdrew its request that the "DO" rating be removed from commercial aircraft production. As a *quid pro quo*, however, the Defense Department insisted that particular military orders be given preference on an individual and informal basis. It appears that the aviation industry agreed to the proposed arrangement....

[The court summarized evidence showing that jawboning of aircraft manufacturers was government policy.] ... Individual firms, moreover, were told that any resistance to informal requests by representatives of the military would result in a formal directive being issued against them. For example, Pratt & Whitney, the sole supplier of engines to Douglas, was "overwhelmed" in 1966 by government demands that its production of military engines be accelerated. These requests were being acceded to, in the words of one Pratt & Whitney executive, "to prevent the removal of the priority rating from the commercial [orders]."

Similar pressures were being applied to the manufacturers of Douglas' landing gear. Gerald Lynch, President and Chairman of Menasco, Inc., testified that the underlying reason for his firm's delay in delivering landing gear to Douglas was "the extraordinary unanticipated requirements for ... military spares." ... [Menasco felt obliged to give priority to military requirements.]

Cleveland Pneumatic Tool Company, the other supplier of landing gear to Douglas also gave military orders priority despite the "DO" rating given its civilian contracts....

Taking the view that the jawboning policy described above was voluntarily acquiesced in by the aviation industry, the District Court ruled and subsequently instructed the jury during the liability phase of the trial that only delays resulting from the actual issuance of formal ratings or directives could be deemed excusable. Consistent with this approach, the trial judge either excluded or struck evidence concerning government jawboning of Douglas' suppliers.

In an effort to blunt McDonnell's attack on the trial judge's rulings and instructions, Eastern devoted a great deal of its briefs and oral argument to a recitation of purported management difficulties at Douglas during the years 1965-1966. Eastern implied that even if the District Court erred in its approach to the Government's jawboning policy, there are no grounds for reversal because the delivery delays were in fact the product of Douglas mismanagement rather than the Vietnam conflict....

... However, there is ample evidence in the record to make this issue one for the jury. Not only does it appear that there was a substantial war-caused labor shortage in Douglas' recruiting area, but Douglas' suppliers testified that their own delays were the product of similar labor shortages. There is also direct evidence indicating that the delivery schedules of the manufacturers of Douglas landing gear and engines were delayed by the war. In short, the proof indicating that there were at least some war-caused delivery delays is not so inadequate as to eliminate the prejudicial effect of the trial court's rulings on military jawboning. We turn, therefore, to an examination of the legal basis for those of the court's rulings and instructions to the jury which related to McDonnell's Vietnam War defense.

B. The "Excusable Delay" Clause

McDonnell Douglas contends that the trial judge's instructions to the jury undercut the defense available to it under the excusable delay clause found in all of the contracts at issue in this appeal. In relevant part, the provision reads as follows:

> Seller shall not be responsible nor deemed to be in default on account of delays in performance ... due to causes beyond Seller's control and not occasioned by its fault or negligence, including but not being limited to ... any act of government, governmental priorities, allocation regulations or orders affecting materials, equipment, facilities or completed aircraft, ... failure of vendors (due to causes similar to those within the scope of this clause) to perform their contracts ..., provided such cause is beyond Seller's control.

1. Ejusdem Generis and the Applicability of U.C.C. § 2-615

McDonnell's first contention in this regard is that the District Court unduly narrowed the scope of this clause by instructing the jury that an excusable delay must be the result of "one or more of the listed events in the excusable delay clause of the contracts, or ... a similar cause beyond the defendant's control...." This instruction, in McDonnell's view, effectively construes the specifically listed excusable causes of delay as restricting the application of the more general phrase which exempts Douglas from liability for delays beyond its control and not due to its negligence. McDonnell feels, therefore, that its affirmative defense was unjustifiably limited to delays caused by events similar to those specifically listed when, in fact, the contracts excused all delays which were not its fault.

The trial judge's construction of the clause, moreover, affords McDonnell Douglas a narrower range of excuses than is available under the modern view of impossibility as it is codified in U.C.C. § 2-615. Simply stated, § 2-615 excuses delay or nondelivery when the agreed upon performance has been rendered "commercially impracticable" by an unforeseen supervening event not within the contemplation of the parties at the time the contract was entered into. Uniform Commercial Code § 2-615 [Cal.Comm.Code § 2615] Comments 1 & 8; see Restatement, Contracts §§ 454, 457 (1932); 6 A. Corbin, Contracts §§ 1321, 1339 (1962).

Under § 2-615, the impossibility defense is available to the seller only if he has not "assumed a greater obligation" than that imposed upon him by this provision. During the trial, the court below ruled that § 2-615 was not applicable for this reason. Although the trial judge failed to explain his holding, it must have been based upon his restrictive construction of the excusable delay clause. Presumably, then, the protections of § 2-615 were deemed to have been waived because the contracts were interpreted as limiting McDonnell's impossibility defense to delays caused by events similar to those specifically provided for in the excusable delay clause.

In support of this approach, Eastern argues that the District Court correctly applied *ejusdem generis*, a canon of judicial construction limiting the application of general terms which follow specific ones to matters similar in kind or classification to those specified....

This maxim, however, "is only an instrumentality for ascertaining the correct meaning of the words when there is uncertainty." ... Obviously, the application of the doctrine in this case would make superfluous the unambiguous words "including but not being limited to" which precede the specifically listed excuses for delay.[45] It is clear, then, that by excusing delays not within McDonnell's control nor due to its negligence, "including but not being limited to" governmental acts, priorities, or orders, the parties intended to excuse all delays coming within the general description regardless of their similarity to the listed excuses. Consequently, there is no basis for the trial judge's conclusion that McDonnell waived the protections of § 2-615 and that its contract excuses are narrower than those available under the doctrine of commercial impracticability.

2. *The Foreseeability Issue*

McDonnell also challenges the trial judge's jury instruction which limited excusable delivery delays to those resulting from events which were not "reasonably foreseeable" at the time a contract was executed. By writing a foreseeability requirement into the excusable delay clause, the District Court appeared to construe the contracts as constituting nothing more than an

---

[45]*Ejusdem generis*, by its very terms, applies only where the general terms of an exculpatory clause follow a more specific listing of excused events. Here, of course, the general terms of the excusable delay clause precede the more specific provisions....

application of the Code's commercial impracticability rule to those particular events specified in the contracts.

Although there has been some doubt expressed as to whether the Code permits parties to bargain for exemptions broader than those available under § 2-615, this concern is ill-founded.

... Comment 8 to this provision plainly indicates that parties may "enlarge upon or supplant" § 2-615. See *United States v. Wegematic Corp.*, 2 Cir., 1966, 360 F.2d 674, 677 (Friendly, J.).

There appear to be, however, certain strictures imposed upon judicial interpretation of such agreements. Comment 8 provides:

> Generally, express agreements as to exemptions designed to enlarge upon or supplant the provisions of this section are to be read in light of mercantile sense and reason, for this section itself sets up the commercial standard for normal and reasonable interpretation and provides a minimum beyond which agreement may not go.

While this provision could have been drafted in less vague terms, we presume that Comment 8 establishes "mercantile sense and reason" as a general standard governing our construction of agreements enlarging upon the protections of § 2-615. As we understand Comment 8, where there is doubt concerning the parties' intention, exemption clauses should not be construed as broadening the excuses available under the Code's impracticability rule. Applying this standard to the excusable delay clause, we cannot, in the absence of evidence to the contrary, hold that McDonnell is exempt from liability for any delay, regardless of its foreseeability, that is due to causes beyond its control. Exculpatory provisions which are phrased merely in general terms have long been construed as excusing only unforeseen events which make performance impracticable.... Courts have often held, therefore, that if a promisor desires to broaden the protections available under the excuse doctrine he should provide for the excusing contingencies with particularity and not in general language....

We realize, of course, that this rule of construction developed in the pre-U.C.C. era when the scope of the impossibility and frustration doctrines was unclear and varied from jurisdiction to jurisdiction. Because of the uncertainty surrounding the law of excuse, parties had good reason to resort to general contract provisions relieving the promisor of liability for breaches caused by events "beyond his control." Although the Uniform Commercial Code has ostensibly eliminated the need for such clauses, lawyers, either through an abundance of caution or by force of habit, continue to write them into contract....

Thus, even though our interpretation would render the general terms of the excusable delay clause merely duplicative of § 2-615, we will adhere to the established rule of construction because it continues to reflect prevailing commercial practices.

We reiterate, however, that we are applying only a canon of contract interpretation which generally reflects commercial standards of reasonableness. We disagree with the suggestion of one commentator that § 2-615 imposes a fixed standard governing the interpretation of exemption clauses. The Code establishes no absolute requirement that any agreement purporting to enlarge upon § 2-615 must do so in plain and specific language. Even in the absence of detailed wording, trade usage and the circumstances surrounding a particular agreement may indicate that the parties intended to accord the seller an exemption broader than is available under the U.C.C.

While we hold that the provision of the excusable delay clause exempting McDonnell from liability for delays beyond its control should be interpreted as incorporating the Code's commercial impracticability doctrine, we disagree with the trial judge's jury instruction on foreseeability insofar as it implies that the events specifically listed in the excusable delay clause in each contract must have been unforeseeable at the time the agreement was executed. The rationale for the doctrine of impracticability is that the circumstance causing the breach has made performance so vitally different from what was anticipated that the contract cannot reasonably be thought to govern.... However, because the purpose of a contract is to place the reasonable risk of performance on the promisor, he is presumed, in the absence of evidence to the contrary, to have agreed to bear any loss occasioned by an event which was foreseeable at the time of contracting. *Lloyd v. Murphy*, 1944, 25 Cal.2d 48, 54, 153 P.2d 47, 50 (Traynor, J.)....

Underlying this presumption is the view that a promisor can protect himself against foreseeable events by means of an express provision in the agreement.

Therefore, when the promisor has anticipated a particular event by specifically providing for it in a contract, he should be relieved of liability for the occurrence of such event regardless of whether it was foreseeable....

As Justice Traynor noted for the California Supreme Court under different but nonetheless analogous circumstances,

> the question whether a risk was foreseeable is quite distinct from the question whether it was contemplated by the parties.... When a risk has been contemplated and voluntarily assumed ... foreseeability is not an issue and the parties will be held to the bargain they made.

Glenn R. Sewell Sheet Metal, Inc. v. Loverde, 1969, 70 Cal.2d 666, 451 P.2d 721, 728 n. 13; see *Lloyd v. Murphy, supra*, 153 P.2d at 50. In this case, it is clear that Eastern specifically "contemplated and voluntarily assumed" the risk that deliveries would be delayed by governmental acts, priorities, regulations or orders. Moreover, unlike the only case cited to us by Eastern which construes a similar provision, *United States v. Brooks-Callaway Co.*, 318 U.S. 120, 63 S.Ct. 474, 87 L.Ed. 653 (1943), there is no indication from the wording of the excusable delay clause that McDonnell's defenses are to be limited to breaches caused by unforeseeable events. Therefore, we must conclude that the trial judge erred in instructing the jury that the events specifically listed in the excusable delay clause must have been unforeseeable at the time the contracts were entered into for McDonnell to claim exemption from liability.

3. *Informal Demands for Priority as an "Act of Government"*

Turning next to the question of whether the Government's informal priorities policy came within the ambit of the excusable delay clause, we have seen in Part IV-A of this opinion that McDonnell and its suppliers, in granting priority to the military, were cooperating with the established, publicly announced procurement policy of the Federal Government. Eastern contends, however, that this informal program did not come within the scope of the contract clause specifically excusing "any act of government, governmental priorities, allocations, or orders affecting materials." Asserting that the Defense Production Act authorizes the Government to obtain precedence for certain orders only by means of formal, published regulations, Eastern concludes that any other method is illegal, if not unconstitutional, and therefore cannot be deemed an act of Government. We disagree for the following reasons.

The Defense Production Act, in "a sweeping delegation of power," grants the President broad authority to require that defense-related contracts be given precedence over less essential orders. D.P.A. § 101(a), 50 App.U.S.C. § 2071(a). Congress created no detailed scheme by which this power was to be exercised, providing only that "[t]he President may make such rules, regulations, and orders as he deems necessary or appropriate." D.P.A. § 704, 50 App.U.S.C. § 2154. There is, moreover, nothing in either the legislative history of the D.P.A. or in the wording of the Act itself which gives any indication that the Government may not seek compliance with its priorities policies by informal means. It is reasonable to conclude, therefore, that Congress intended to accord the Executive Branch great flexibility in molding its priorities policies to the frequently unanticipated exigencies of national defense....

We note, moreover, that this case precisely fits an established pattern of decisions rejecting the contention that breaches of contract are excused only by formal or technical acts of Government. Whether predicated on a contractual provision or simply on the common law defense of impossibility these decisions indicate in the clearest terms that fundamentally coercive acts of Government, whatever their form, constitute an excuse for breach. Thus, a promisor is not liable merely because the government order causing a breach is technically deficient....

Consequently, we will not permit the form of the military priorities policy to disguise what was in substance a governmental act beyond the control of McDonnell Douglas. The excusable delay clause cannot be made to turn on a distinction which for so long has been held to be entirely artificial and unrealistic....

This approach, moreover, is consistent with that required under the Uniform Commercial Code. In Comment 10 to § 615, the draftsmen of Article 2 stated:

> Following its basic policy of using commercial practicability as a test for excuse, this section ... disregards any technical distinctions between "law," "regulation," "order" and the like. Nor does it make the present action of the seller depend upon the eventual judicial determination of the legality of the particular governmental action. The seller's good faith belief in the validity of the regulation is the test under this Article and the best evidence of this good faith is the general commercial acceptance of the regulation.

Given McDonnell's unquestioned good faith in complying with the Government's demands for priority and the uncontroverted evidence of the entire aviation industry's acceptance of the policy, we must hold as a matter of law that McDonnell is not liable for any delivery delay proximately resulting from the informal procurement program....

NOTES AND QUESTIONS

1. *The impact of a contract clause*: While the courts generally have interpreted U.C.C. § 2-615 very narrowly and offered few excuses, the *Eastern Air Lines* case reflects the very different approach that is common when a clause in a contract deals with the problem. In many instances, of course, this is just a matter of free contract. If a seller or buyer wants to condition its obligation so that it is not liable for strikes, national emergency priority schemes, or anything else, and if the other party agrees, we might expect courts to honor their wishes. In the *Eastern Air Lines* case, the court deals with the view that the introductory clause to § 2-615 and § 2-616(3) regulates impracticability excuses greater than those that would be provided by the statute absent such a provision. Instead of regulation, the court reads the language as a principle of interpretation.

While the Court's interpretation may simply implement free contract in a bargained-for deal between a sophisticated seller and buyer, should courts uphold clauses in standard forms that go beyond § 2-615 so that a seller no longer is assuming the normal risks in business? Could courts make such decisions without extensive and expensive evidence about trade custom?

2. *Judicial control of force majeure clauses*: In *Nissho-Iwai Co., Ltd. v. Occidental Crude Sales, Inc.*,[46] Occidental agreed to supply a Japanese oil distributor with crude oil produced from Concession 102 in Libya. The contract excused performances that could not be rendered because of "executive or administrative orders of acts [of the Libyan Government] ... or by any other event, whether or not similar to the causes specified above ... which shall not

---

[46] 729 F.2d 1530 (5th Cir. 1984).

reasonably be within the control of" Occidental. The Libyan government issued orders cutting back production of oil from this field.

The trial court charged that the jury had to find "the excusing event or events were not reasonably within the control of Occidental or its supplier." Occidental challenged this instruction on appeal. It argued that the "control" limitation only applied to "other events" and not actions of the Libyan government. The Court of Appeals, applying California law as specified in the contract, affirmed. It said,

> [T]he California law of force majeure requires us to apply a reasonable control limitation to each specified event, regardless of what generalized contract interpretation would suggest....
>
> The term "reasonable control" has come to include two related notions. First, a party may not affirmatively cause the event that prevents performance. The rationale behind this requirement is obvious. If a contractor were able to escape his responsibilities merely by causing an excusing event to occur, he would have no effective "obligation to perform...."
>
> The second aspect of reasonable control is more subtle. Some courts will not allow a party to rely on an excusing event if he could have taken reasonable steps to prevent it.... The rationale behind this requirement is that the force majeure did not actually prevent performance if a party could reasonably have prevented the event from occurring. The party has prevented performance and, again, breached his good faith obligation to perform by failing to exercise reasonable diligence....
>
> [Occidental's proposed jury] instruction would permit Occidental to rest on its legal rights and to refuse any demands by the Libyan Government that violated the contract between Libya and Occidental. When Libya imposed restrictions on Occidental's oil production in 1975, Occidental, acting on advice of counsel, withheld $117 million in payments that were due. The Government retaliated by imposing an embargo. Under Occidental's proposed instruction, the embargo would not have been within Occidental's reasonable control even if Occidental knew in advance that it could prevent the embargo by paying the $117 Million....
>
> It is clear Occidental was aware of the threatened embargo and could have prevented it by paying $117 million. This sum in [it]self was not unreasonable, since the entire figure represented back taxes, royalties, and oil costs that Occidental already owed the Libyan Government. Of course, even if Occidental had paid this sum and averted the embargo, it would still have faced production restrictions. A reasonable jury could have found, though, that Occidental would be able to recoup through arbitration or settlement any losses that might result from the restrictions. The company had already commenced arbitration proceedings against the Libyan Government; and, in December, it was able to reach a settlement. To be sure, the withheld payments and the resulting embargo were factors in producing that settlement. That is not to say, however, that a settlement would not have

been reached in the absence of an embargo. In the past, Occidental had been able to convince the Government to back down from production restrictions. A reasonable jury might have found that Occidental would again have been able to negotiate a reasonable settlement, particularly given the threat of arbitration proceedings.

How could Occidental show that the actions of the Libyan government were not within Occidental's reasonable control? Can it engage in aggressive negotiations without losing a defense under the court's construction? Can it seek to establish a reputation with the Libyan government as a hard bargainer willing to risk an embargo? Could Occidental contract around this problem so that it would be free of this heavy burden of proof in the future?[47]

Is *Nissho-Iwai* consistent with the *Eastern Air Lines* opinion?

1. DO THE RULES CHANGE WHEN THE GAME GETS BIGGER?

Westinghouse Electric Corporation sold nuclear reactors to twenty-seven power companies in the '60s and early '70s. In order to persuade the utilities to buy the reactors, Westinghouse agreed to supply the uranium oxide which the reactors used as fuel. The contract price averaged $9.50 per  pound. Westinghouse committed itself to supply 80 million pounds of fuel, though it owned at the time only about 15 million pounds; it was confident that it could buy fuel on the market as the need arose. Much to the dismay of Westinghouse, the price of uranium oxide rose from about $6 per pound in 1972 to $44 per pound in 1978.

---

[47]Compare International Minerals & Chem. Corp. v. Llano, Inc. 770 F.2d 879 (10th cir. 1985) where a buyer sought a declaratory judgment that it was excused from taking natural gas under the terms of a contract. It provided: "In the event ... Buyer is unable to receive gas as provided in this contract for any reason beyond the reasonable control of the parties ... an appropriate adjustments in the minimum purchase requirements ... shall be made."

The New Mexico Environmental Improvement Board later issued a regulation requiring emissions from industrial plants to be reduced "as expeditiously as practicable." The buyer converted its plant to a chemical precipitation process that used about 50-60% less natural gas.

The trial court found that the buyer voluntarily complied with the regulation and had come into compliance earlier than required. Thus, there was no excuse. The Court of Appeals reversed and found the buyer excused. The regulation was an event beyond the reasonable control of the buyer that rendered it "unable" to received its minimum amount of gas under the contract. The court said that "unable" was synonymous with "impracticable" as that term is used in U.C.C. § 2-615. It concluded that as a matter of policy those who cooperate with regulatory agencies and comply with the letter and spirit of legally proper regulations are to be encouraged. The court noted that the buyer's power was limited by the requirement of good faith. A buyer may not collude or induce a governmental agency to act so that the buyer can avoid a contract. However, cooperation to eliminate pollution "can hardly be termed improper collusion."

It doesn't take a nuclear physicist to see that the financial implications of this to Westinghouse were significant, if not dire.

On September 8, 1975 Westinghouse shocked its utility customers, and others in the business community, by announcing that it would not honor its contracts to supply the nuclear fuel. It argued that it was excused from performance by § 2-615(a) of the Uniform Commercial Code. That section provides a defense to an action for breach if the nonperformance is "the occurrence of a contingency the non-occurrence of which was a basic assumption on which the contract was made." Westinghouse argued that the extreme and unforeseen change in the market for uranium oxide amounted to just such a contingency. The power companies responded by bringing suits which charged that Westinghouse was simply seeking to avoid responsibility for the risk it took when it promised to deliver fuel it didn't own, electing to rely on an inherently risky market. Their theory was that Westinghouse had made a business misjudgment by gambling on the market and was trying to avoid taking the consequences. The claims of the utilities aggregated approximately $2.6 billion. The net worth of Westinghouse was $2.3 billion at the end of 1977. Many of the utility suits were joined in a single suit in the federal court in Richmond, Virginia, presided over by Robert Merhige, Jr.

Question: How would you assess the strength of Westinghouse's § 2-615 claim, acknowledging of course that you have only the sketchiest description of a very complicated story?

In 1976, documents surfaced in Australia which revealed an international uranium cartel which had been organized in 1972 to control sales by producing governments, and so to raise prices. The United States apparently knew about the cartel, but had chosen not to participate. It was not clear whether or not such a cartel was legal under international law. Westinghouse argued that the cartel was the reason for the price run-up. A Canadian subsidiary of Gulf Oil was a participant in the cartel. Westinghouse brought suit in October of 1976 against Gulf Oil and 29 uranium producers for price-fixing. It alleged that Gulf Oil's Canadian subsidiary provide the link between American uranium producers and the international cartel. Gulf Oil admitted the participation of its Canadian subsidiary, but said that the cartels plans had carefully excluded the American market from its plans. In May of 1978 Gulf filed a countersuit, alleging that Westinghouse itself had been seeking to monopolize markets for nuclear reactors, fabricated fuel, and uranium.

Question: What is the relevance, to the § 615 dispute, of the discovery of the international cartel?

From the very beginning, Federal Judge Merhige urged the parties to the suits between the utilities and Westinghouse to settle. Although the potential liability of Westinghouse exceeded $2 billion, most observers expected settlements in most, if not all, of the disputes. In addition to the risks associated with litigating and losing, the utilities had an interest in the survival of Westinghouse. Someone would have to continue to provide engineering for the reactor projects, as well as parts and service. In addition, the utility industry had a general interest in the survival of competition in the reactor and power-generation industry; Westinghouse was an important player in that market. At one point, after three months of trial hearings had been held, a Pittsburgh judge was asked about his efforts to convince the parties to settle:

> The fiscal well-being, possibly the survival, of one of the world's corporate giants is in jeopardy. Likewise, the future of thousands of jobs.
>
> Any decision I hand down will hurt somebody and because of that potential damage, I want to make it clear that it will happen only because certain captains of industry could not together work out their problems so that the hurt might have been held to a minimum....
>
> Solomon-like as I want to be, I can't cut this baby in half...

There are also, of course, some pressures to proceed with the litigation. There is a chance that both parties overestimate their chances for winning the lawsuit, and so see the other side's position as unreasonable. One or both of the parties may in fact *be* unreasonable, making it more difficult to get agreement. And some reasons are more subtle. Professor Macaulay[48] has pointed out:

> [L]itigation may legitimate concessions in the eyes of outsiders who audit decisions. For example, the customers of Westinghouse are utilities whose rates are regulated. Without some strong justification, they could not negotiate a settlement with Westinghouse and then ask for approval of a rate increase to cover the balance of the loss. The chance that Westinghouse might win may serve to rationalize settlement, and the act of bringing suit might show the regulators that the utilities are not just giving money away. Consumer and antinuclear power organizations filed petitions in eleven states asking state utility regulators to scrutinize any out-of-court settlements that utilities may reach with Westinghouse. These groups assert that if utilities do not hold Westinghouse to its contracts, consumers will have to pay the extra fuel costs....
>
> The Wall Street Journal ... points to ... [an] assertion of norms that are not coterminous with the law of contract, in the Westinghouse cases:
>
> > [T]he electric utilities have canceled and stretched out contracts for atomic power plants, putting a financial squeeze on such companies as Westinghouse.

---

[48]Macaulay, Elegant Models, Empirical Pictures, and the Complexities of Contract, 11 Law & Society Review 507 (1977).

"You and I know that in the real world of business there's going to be some horse-trading," an industry person says. "You can bet that Westinghouse is reminding companies like Con Edison that it has gone along with them in stretching contracts."

Conduct in prior transactions generally is legally irrelevant in contract law, which focuses on the particular contract under litigation. However, the claim of prior accommodation to the needs of the utilities was highly relevant if any settlement was to be reached.

Although it would be hard to prove, the contract litigation process may also exert an indirect influence on the behavior of the managers of industrial enterprises even where they devote little thought to it. Those making bargains may tacitly rely on the law to fill gaps and provide sanctions, in order to avoid the costs of negotiating about unlikely contingencies or of constructing elaborate systems of security to insure performance. Contract law may crystallize business customs and provide a normative vocabulary, affecting expectations about what is fair. Westinghouse, for example, did not repudiate its uranium oxide contracts in the name of pure self-interest, but sought to cloak its actions in the language of the Uniform Commercial Code. Its positions, in that guise, may have been more palatable to some of its customers. It may be easier to negotiate with someone asserting a plausible claim of right than with an outlaw openly scorning those who had relied on its promise. (Perhaps the U.C.C. served as a means of self-justification so that executives at Westinghouse felt better about not honoring the commitment their firm had made.) We can only speculate about the situation had the drafters of the Uniform Commercial Code adopted a more rigorous standard that rarely excused nonperformance based on the occurrence of an unforeseen contingency. Suppose the rule had been that one who makes a promise must perform come hell or high water. Would Westinghouse have marched into bankruptcy trying to perform or would it have begged for mercy? Would the impact have been only on the amount of any settlement, since the likelihood of victory by Westinghouse would have been insignificant and thus worth little?

Ultimately, the cases brought by the utilities were settled. Judge Merhige, the federal judge presiding over most of the cases, pressed the parties to settle; the day the trial opened he told the assembled lawyers that "I don't ever expect to finish these cases.... I expect (them) to get settled."[49] There had been relatively little in the way of settlement negotiations up to that time. Lawyers for the utilities expressed surprise about this, but some who were following the case suggested that Westinghouse was digging up information about the international

---

[49]Pappas, Westinghouse, Utilities Under Pressure to Settle Uranium Suit Before Court Does, Wall Street Journal, June 2, 1978 at 32, cols. 1-3.

cartel, and didn't want to discuss settlement until it had compiled that information. It was also noted that the utilities themselves had to be careful in reaching a settlement. If a rate-setting regulatory agency concluded that the utility had been too accommodating in reaching a settlement, they might refuse to allow the utility to pass along the extra fuel costs associated with settlement to customers. A Westinghouse representative said "If these were industrial customers, we could have arrived at settlements months ago."[50]

As a way of increasing the likelihood of settlement, Merhige appointed a law school dean to serve as a special master to "be utilized for purposes of encouraging and assisting the parties in reaching an amicable adjustment of the respective claims in these cases...." He also required the parties to file proposals for settlement. Something worked; the cases settled. In most cases, the settlements were not cash settlements, but instead involved a combination of cash and services. In one case involving Texas Utilities Services, Inc., the settlement (embodied in a 350-page settlement agreement!) was estimated to be worth $65 to $80 million to the utility, whereas Westinghouse estimated the settlement had cost it only $27 million. While it may be that the magnitude of the gap between the estimates reflects both sides' need to feel good about the settlement, it is quite plausible for a bargain to generate a substantial surplus of value. In fact, of course, every truly free bargain leaves both parties better off than they would have been with no bargain.

The antitrust suits which were brought against the 29 uranium producers, including perhaps most prominently Gulf Oil, were settled in the summer of 1981.

NOTES AND QUESTIONS

1. *The law firm's role*: James B. Stewart wrote a book about prominent American law firms.[51] Chapter Four is devoted to the Chicago firm of Kirkland & Ellis, whose partner, William Jentes, was principal outside counsel for Westinghouse. Stewart's book contains an interesting account of some aspects of the litigation between Westinghouse and the utilities:[52]

> One of the Uniform Commercial Code's most controversial provisions is one which provides an escape for sellers who would otherwise be locked into their contracts under common-law principles, and Jentes had mentioned it as a possibility at the first meeting with the Westinghouse lawyers.... [T]he provision had almost never been invoked or upheld in a court decision

---

[50]Wall Street Journal, op. cit.

[51]Stewart, The Partners: Inside America's Most Powerful Law Firms (Simon and Schuster 1983).

[52]Stewart, *id.*, p. 152 ff.

excusing nonperformance. Undaunted, Jentes assigned some associates to scour the case law for some support should Westinghouse assert the commercial impracticability clause.

Legal research, and the related preparation of a memorandum of law, are among the relatively few tasks mastered during the course of law school, and part of that assignment at Kirkland & Ellis fell to James Goold, a law student at the University of Chicago who was working as a summer associate for the firm....

Eventually [Goold's] task of researching the question of impracticability would take a full year — he barely attended class at the University of Chicago in order to complete the research — and resulted in a 200-page memorandum....

There was considerable debate inside Kirkland & Ellis about whether the facts surrounding the Westinghouse uranium contracts satisfied [the] conditions [for relief under § 2-615]....

As one general counsel for a major utility recalls, he found the Westinghouse default "almost unbelievable," given its scope; the legal opinion [of Kirkland & Ellis] he dismissed as "flimsy — obviously grasping at legal straws." The legal opinion may even have been a tactical error. Expected by Westinghouse to be interpreted by the utilities as an indication of how serious Westinghouse's plight had become, it was instead greeted as an audacious attempt by Westinghouse to wriggle out of the contracts rather than admit its own errors and ask the utilities to help restructure the deal. Jentes, however, doubts that the utilities would ever have expressed a conciliatory attitude. "They were not the least bit statesmanlike. They acted like we were repudiating the Bible." One by one, the utilities marched into courts across the country, all filing lawsuits against Westinghouse....

Meanwhile, another contingent of Kirkland & Ellis lawyers was assigned to shore up the legal positions. When he had been a student at the University of Chicago, Goold, who had now come to work full-time, had taken a class in contracts with Professor Soia Mentschikoff. Mentschikoff was the widow of Karl Llewellyn, the man who had actually drafted the Uniform Commercial Code which formed the basis for Westinghouse's defense, and Mentschikoff had worked closely with him on the project. Goold hired her as a consultant on the case, and together they began to sift through Llewellyn's files for more clues about the meaning of the impracticability provision.

Eventually they found a bundle of handwritten notes, some of them nearly tattered beyond legibility, and after piecing them together, they derived some small encouragement for the position that a price increase, if it was the result of some unforeseeable event directly related to performance of the contract, might excuse performance....

As Judge Merhige had urged, by 1980 all of the utilities had reached out-of-court settlements with Westinghouse which eliminated the need for the planned trial on the damages issue.... [The settlements] were handled internally by Westinghouse executives and the company's legal staff — and though nonmonetary aspects of the agreements make them difficult to value, it is estimated that they cost Westinghouse approximately $900 million, or about half of what the utilities had claimed. If Westinghouse and the utilities had simply split their differences in 1975, before resorting to litigation, the result would have been about the same.

In a review of Stewart's book, Peter W. Bernstein quotes this last paragraph about the final result in the Westinghouse cases.[53] He continues by saying,

> [y]ou'd think that such details would spur some serious rethinking about the possibly excessive use of corporate lawyers. Ironically, the Westinghouse case seems to have had almost the opposite effect. Stewart reports that despite Kirkland & Ellis's setbacks, "it is the widespread perception among members of the corporate bar — and in the firm itself — that it was Kirkland & Ellis that saved Westinghouse." It would seem that lawyers can convince themselves of anything.

Does the final result of these cases show "excessive use of corporate lawyers?" Had the utilities and Westinghouse split their differences in 1975, the result would have been roughly the same as reached in 1980 after a large amount was paid in legal fees. But had Kirkland & Ellis not been called in and played the § 2-615 card, would the utilities and Westinghouse have split their differences?

2. *Anticipating unforeseen risks at the drafting stage:* We sometimes forget that there are different ways to proceed in the face of similar problems. Often the participants in different business cultures, or subcultures, react differently to problems. In the *Westinghouse* cases we have just read about, the parties were reluctant to give up the gains they believed they had won by their bargain, and which they believed were embodied in their agreement; they chose to litigate the question of the contract's enforceability. Leon Trakman has written about the way that the multinational oil sellers respond, at the drafting stage, to the risks of unforeseen changes in oil supply and prices.[54]

> ... We analyzed the contract practices of multinational oil sellers and their international oil buyers, as described by their inside legal counsel....
>
> [C]ivil lawyers differed from common lawyers in their construction of the laws of nonperformance. Civil lawyers were generally much more willing to permit excuses from performance in the face of circumstances occurring beyond control than were their common-law counterparts. For instance, of

---

[53]Fortune, April 4, 1983, at 189, 191 (vol. 107, #7).

[54]Trakman, Nonperformance in Oil Contracts, 29 Oil and Gas Quarterly 716 (1981).

the civil lawyers who replied to the questionnaire, 100 percent favored an excuse from performance if the performance obligation had become "radically different" since the date of contracting; whereas only 63 percent of the common lawyers agreed. This difference in attitude is attributable partly to the jurisprudential differences between civil and common law systems, and partly to the political-economic havoc that was experienced in European civil law jurisdictions during the post-World War eras....

Crude oil contracts of sale provided for an array of performance risks and burdens in succinct language within their terms. The counsel structured their business obligations along predetermined lines. They established the contractual consequences that should ensue as a result of market and political unrest in the international crude oil market.

Nonperformance clauses in international crude oil contracts of sale were therefore the product of deliberate planning and compromise. As carefully formulated provisions, they constituted a means of avoiding deadlock and dissatisfaction over performance among oil companies. They summarized oil relations; and they embodied industry usages in their written terms. Most importantly, they ensured that crude oil transactors would not be left in doubt as to the nature and extent of their performance duties and as to their respective responsibilities in the event of nonperformance....

[A]fter each severe disruption in oil supply, international contracts for the sale of crude oil were revised to take specific account of fluctuating oil prices and severely impeded oil supplies. After each Middle Eastern War, inside legal counsel gave particular attention to the expanding role of governments in relation to crude oil contracts. They evaluated the effects upon performance of "royalty taxes," "new and changed government directions," and "increased government take...."

[A] majority of inside legal counsel who responded to the question indicated that, in their opinion, international oil contractors were not capable of foreseeing *all* categories of nonperformance risks. Nor were they capable of incorporating *all* such categories of nonperformance risks into their crude oil contracts of sale. They were even less likely to incorporate all categories of nonperformance risks into their agreements in an unambiguous manner....

3. *Dealing with the problem by renegotiating the contract*: Another way in which the parties might respond to an unforeseen development, and again this may depend on the business culture in which the event occurs, is to renegotiate the agreement. Can such a response be successful? Doesn't renegotiation constitute a repudiation of the rationale for the contract itself? Jeswald Salacuse

suggests that renegotiation is a common practice, at least in some international contexts:[55]

> ... In recent years we have seen many examples of the phenomenon of renegotiations. Since the outbreak of the international debt crisis in 1982, Western commercial banks and their Third World borrowers have been engaged in a constant process of renegotiating loans that developing countries have been unable to repay, an exercise commonly known as "debt rescheduling." The dramatic fall in the price of oil and gas from the heights of the early 1980s has forced purchasers to seek renegotiation of long-term supply agreements that once seemed profitable but have now become ruinous. And the rapid decline in the value of the dollar, particularly against the Japanese yen, has since 1986 prompted attempts to renegotiate other long-term contractual relationships.
>
> Renegotiation in international business is by no means peculiar to the 1980s. For decades, host country governments, often with the threat of nationalization in the background, have periodically sought to revise investment arrangements which they had previously made with foreign corporations but later judged no longer advantageous.... These examples illustrate a traditional theme in international business circles: the lament over the "unstable contract," the profitable agreement that the other party refuses to respect. One common response to contractual instability is renegotiation....
>
> Discussions of "renegotiation" apply the term to three fundamentally different situations, and it is important to distinguish each of them at the outset....
>
> (1) Post-Deal Renegotiations
> In this context, negotiations may take place at the expiration of a contract, when the parties, though legally free to go their own ways, nonetheless seek to renew their previous relationship....
>
> (2) Intra-Deal Renegotiations
> A second type of renegotiation occurs when the agreement itself provides that, during its life at specified times, the parties may renegotiate or at least review certain of its provisions. Here, renegotiation is anticipated as a legitimate activity in which both parties are to engage in good faith....

---

[55]Jeswald W. Salacuse, Renegotiations in International Business, 4 Negotiation Journal 347 (1988). © Negotiation Journal, 1988.

(3) Extra-Deal Renegotiations

The most difficult and emotional renegotiations are those undertaken in apparent violation of the agreement, or at least in the absence of a specific clause for redoing the deal. These renegotiations take place "extra-deal," for they occur outside the framework of the existing agreement. The renegotiations of the 1980s over Third World loans, petroleum prices, and currencies all fit within the category of extra-deal renegotiations, because in each case one of the participants was seeking relief from a legally binding obligation without any basis in the agreement itself for renegotiation....

Beyond mere disappointed expectations, extra-deal renegotiations, by their very nature, can create bad feeling and mistrust. One side sees itself as being asked to give up something to which it has a legal and moral right, and it views the other side as having gone back on its word, as having acted in bad faith by reneging on the deal. Indeed, the reluctant party may even feel it is being coerced into participating in extra-deal renegotiations, since a refusal to do so would result in losing the investment already made in the transaction or joint venture. Thus, it is very difficult for the parties to see renegotiations as anything more than a "zero-sum game," where one side wins and the other side loses.

The extra-deal renegotiation of an established arrangement may also have significant implications beyond the transaction in question. The party being asked to give up a contractual right may feel obliged to show various political constituencies, both inside and outside its own organization, that it is not "weak," and cannot be taken advantage of. Moreover, a party will usually fear that yielding to a demand for the renegotiation of one contract may encourage other parties to seek renegotiation of their agreements as well. This concern for the potential "ripple" effect from renegotiations clearly contributed to the reluctance of the international commercial banks to yield to demands by individual developing countries for a revision of loan terms. Concessions to Mexico would inevitably lead Argentina to demand equal treatment in its own renegotiation...."

While a request for extra-deal renegotiations may provoke bad feeling in one party, an outright refusal to renegotiate may also create ill will on the other side since it will be seen as an attempt to force adherence to a bargain that has become unreasonable.

Ultimately, the basic conflict between the parties in an extra-deal renegotiation will be over the type of changed circumstances justifying the negotiations. Such circumstances may cover a broad spectrum, ranging from sudden changes in objective conditions over which neither of the parties has control, such as rising exchange rates or closed trade routes, to conditions determined subjectively by one side alone. With regard to the latter, for example, host country governments often reassess their relations with foreign investors based on the country's current need for the investor's capital and technology....

Today, most contracts explicitly or implicitly deny the possibility of change and therefore make no provision whatsoever for adjustments to meet changing circumstances. This assumption of contractual stability has proven false time and time again. For example, most mineral development agreements assume they will continue unchanged for periods of from 15 to 99 years, yet they rarely remain unmodified for more than a few years.... As Raymond Vernon ... has argued, with reference to mineral investment agreements, a bargain, once struck, will inevitably become obsolete and issues once agreed upon will be reopened at a later time as circumstances change. Indeed, to borrow Vernon's phrase, international business negotiations should probably assume that most long-term deals are "obsolescing bargains."

4. *Arbitration as an alternative.* We have seen that the parties might deal with the unforeseeable by attempting to anticipate it in their drafting of the agreement, or by permitting renegotiation, or by resorting to judicial litigation. We must not forget private arbitration as another option. We offer an example which seems particularly apt, since it deals with the continued volatility of the uranium market, after the changes which prompted Westinghouse to repudiate its duty to deliver fuel to the utilities.

According to a 1985 story in the New York Times,[56] "once again, uranium is making lawyers glow." In 1976, with uranium selling for $40 a pound, a Switzerland-based utility, Kernkraftwerk Graben A.G., contracted to purchase uranium oxide for a twelve-year period from a New York Company, Freeport-McMoran, Inc. Over the next several years, the uranium contract price jumped up to $60 a pound. During the same time period, the market price plummeted to $17 a pound. To make matters worse, the Swiss government denied Kernkraftwerk a permit to build the nuclear power plant, thereby evaporating the utility's need for the uranium oxide.

Kernkraftwerk contended that the contract was no longer binding because of unforeseen circumstances. In 1982, the matter went to arbitration. Under a choice of laws agreement, the arbitrators applied New York contract law. Apparently, Kernkraftwerk had contractually agreed that it would not be excused from performing 'on account of force majeure or any other reasons whatsoever.' Yet, in August of 1984 the arbitrators agreed with Kernkraftwerk's argument that the purpose of the contract had been frustrated. In a decision which saved the utility $100 million, the arbitrators found that the dramatic price change and the Swiss Government's refusal to allow the nuclear power plant to be built, were events which the parties did not foresee and therefore the contract could not have been intended to cover these eventualities.

---

[56]N.Y. Times, Jan. 8, 1985, at 2, col. 1.

The New York Times reporter states that "the award illustrates the decline of the sanctity accorded to contracts since the heyday of laissez-faire in the last century." The reporter goes on to suggest that courts in Britain and the United States modify contracts, construe terms contrary to the parties' intention and help parties to evade duties and the like. Can you argue that the reporter does not understand what the arbitrators did? Would the arbitrators have to concede that they rewrote the contract in question here?

5. *Bankruptcy — another option:* Suppose that the parties to a contract failed to deal with the unforeseen in their drafting, they chose not to renegotiate, arbitration was not an option, and the law of contracts offered no excuses. What next? What are the consequences to letting the chips fall where they may? If a company cannot perform its contracts, we could award judgments for damages and leave salvage operations to the law of bankruptcy. This was the response followed when Braniff Airlines got into trouble. Braniff expanded its route structure after the airlines were deregulated. It ordered additional aircraft, hired pilots, flight attendants, maintenance workers, opened offices, rented space at airports and borrowed money. The officers who ran the company guessed wrong, and Braniff ran out of money needed to continue operations. After efforts to keep the airline flying failed, it ceased operations and attempted to reorganize under the federal bankruptcy laws. Undoubtedly, the experience will contribute some deterrence to officials of other airlines when they think about the risks they are willing to take. Undoubtedly, a case could be made that Braniff's failure will contribute to efficient allocation of resources. Braniff's creditors negotiated a limited resumption of service, but it was a far different, and smaller, airline.

While major surgery may prove beneficial in the long run, usually it is painful to many. What are the consequences to which groups of people are the victims of a collapse of a major corporation? Many people are likely to get hurt, and the injury often falls hardest on those free of fault and who had little choice in the matter. The following article from the Wall Street Journal[57] suggests the consequences likely to follow the collapse of any large business organization.

> Braniff officials won't comment on potential losses under current market conditions, but one lender says a confidential study by creditors confirms the general range of loss under such conditions. A source close to the carrier says the assumption of a one-third "haircut" is "in the ballpark."
>
> Losers in that case are legion. First and foremost, Braniff's 33,657 shareholders will lose their entire stake ...
>
> Next in line for a beating are Braniff's unsecured creditors.... As of Dec. 31, trade suppliers were owed an estimated $92.3 million. In a separate category, Boeing Co. is listed as an unsecured creditor to the tune of $84 million, partly because of the aborted sale of three 747s to Braniff....

---

[57]Copyright Wall Street Journal, May 17, 1982, at 4, cols. 2-4.

The unsecured creditors also include Braniff's 9,500 employees, plus retirees.... The employees and current retirees probably will see their pension benefits reduced because Braniff's unfunded liability for five different pension plans amounts to $148.7 million. Federal insurance may make up close to half of that amount, but the employees and retirees will be out the rest unless they succeed in realizing special claims on Braniff's assets ahead of secured creditors. [Research by Wisconsin Law School Professors Whitford and LoPucki indicates that unsecured creditors ultimately received only about 5% of their claims in the bankruptcy. Secured creditors did much better.]

One notable victim is likely to be Harding Lawrence, Braniff's former chairman who is widely blamed for engineering a rapid expansion that partly led to Braniff's downfall. His pension of $306,000 a year is apt to be slashed by $180,000, a source close to the company estimates....

While the collapse of Braniff had major negative consequences, the failure of even larger corporations might have even more serious impacts. In the Westinghouse litigation, all of the federal judges involved seemed well aware of the costs of destroying Westinghouse. Rather than using traditional contract doctrine in an orthodox manner, they pushed for a settlement and achieved it. The United States Congress, rather than the courts, dealt with the Lockheed and Chrysler "failures" by guaranteeing loans to keep them alive while they performed their obligations to many, if not all, concerned. However, there was a gap between American free enterprise rhetoric and the reality of what many saw the federal government doing. We can ask whether the federal courts did a better job in the Westinghouse situation than the Congress managed in the Lockheed and Chrysler cases. To what extent, if at all, does contract doctrine just get in the way of understanding what is involved? To what extent, if at all, does contract doctrine reflect an underlying world view that affects judgments in openly political settings?

The situations in the Westinghouse case, the "bailout" incidents involving Lockheed and Chrysler, and the Alcoa case which you are about to read seem structurally similar. In all these situations a company has voluntarily assumed burdens that turn out to be potentially capable of destroying a major business enterprise. A government institution is asked to intervene. In some cases the courts, and in others the legislature. What are the criteria which are used in such cases? Should the criteria for intervention be the same for each governmental organ, or can they legitimately differ?

We can ask who must bear the price of rapid unexpected economic change or unanticipated costs of technological change. Does it make a difference which institutions confront these problems?

NOTES AND QUESTIONS

1. *The rest of the story:* Well, what happened to Lockheed after it was bailed out? Did everyone live happily ever after? The Wall Street Journal wrote a follow-up story in 1983.[58] After briefly recapitulating the Congressional debate, the story notes that although Lockheed has reported record earnings, it is no longer among the top five U.S. defense contractors. David Packard, the deputy secretary of defense who ramrodded the Nixon administration effort to get the loan guarantees, indicated that, "Looking back on it, I don't think it would have been a disaster if Lockheed had gone under." Others note that the L-1011 project cost Lockheed $2.5 billion, and wasn't cancelled until 1981; it might have been better to have killed the jumbo jet project "in its cradle." Some company insiders suggested that Lockheed's competitive edge was dulled because executives became preoccupied with the task of just keeping the company alive. One former executive reports that Lockheed began "playing not to lose." Senator Proxmire noted that the loan guarantee didn't fulfill its promise of making Lockheed more diversified and stronger. Instead it simply hurt Boeing Co. and McDonnell Douglas because both would have benefitted from the early demise of the L-1011.

On the other hand, the fears that failing companies would descend on Washington looking for help just didn't materialize. The only other major bailout effort was the 1980 Chrysler loan guarantee. The official Lockheed position is that the bailout was a great success. The program didn't cost the taxpayers any money, and there was no interruption in production of the firms military programs. In fact, some have speculated that the real, though never acknowledged, reason for the loan guarantee was to satisfy the military's need for giant C-5A transport planes for use in Vietnam.

2. *Options:* Suppose a major corporation faced an economic disaster that threatens its survival. What could our society do? Our legal and political institutions *could* treat the situation as a matter of contract. The firm would have to perform its contracts, settle the claims of its creditors or seek some form of bankruptcy. In some instances this would mean that the firm would go out of business as its assets were liquidated to satisfy creditors. However, in other cases the firm would continue to exist. Creditors and shareholders would take some or all of the loss. Management might or might not continue in power. Labor would feel the pressure on management to cut wages and benefits or the number of jobs.

There are other possibilities as well. Courts might seek to save the corporation by finding excuses for performance or by refashioning terms of contracts to

---

[58]Roy Harris Jr., Survival Tactics: Back from the Brink, Lockheed Shows Signs of Prospering Again, Wall Street Journal May 12, p. 1, col. 1.

reflect changed conditions.[59] Legislatures could make loans to the sick corporation to give it time to deal with its problems. Of course, the threat of possible judicial or legislative relief could affect settlement negotiations. We also might nationalize the corporation and have it run by an agency of a state or the national government. Less drastically, we might condition any aid so the troubled corporation pursued certain goals rather than others. We could also subsidize a major corporation or a whole industry in our typically American way — that is, by such more or less hidden devices such as favorable tax treatment, formal or informal tariffs, or placing government procurement contracts with firms in economic difficulty.

Does it matter whether and how we offset large shocks to the economy? What should courts do when they face contracts cases involving major events that upset assumptions and expectations about the future? Is there any reason to think that legislatures will handle these problems better?

3. *Other examples*: Lockheed was not the only example of Congress protecting a large corporation in the face of major economic challenges. When the Chrysler Corporation approached bankruptcy in 1979, Congress passed the Chrysler Loan Guarantee Act. Various interests made concessions. A Loan Guarantee Board subjected Chrysler management to some oversight. Chrysler survived and was very successful during the early 1980s. Turkel and Costello[60] studied the arguments offered for the Chrysler arrangement and the acceptance of these ideas by laid-off Chrysler workers. The workers "overwhelmingly take basic features of capitalist market ideology, including competition, for granted." They felt that sacrifices made by workers had not produced satisfactory results. They felt that Chrysler management and various financial interests had been the beneficiaries of the loan guarantee. Reich and Donahue[61] analyzed the arguments for and against the results of the Chrysler Loan Guarantee Act. They say,

> The guaranteed loans were only a bargaining chip. What ultimately saved Chrysler was the sacrifice from labor, creditors, suppliers, and other constituents. The government's presence at the bargaining table radically changed the terms of the negotiations among claimants. It spurred greater sacrifice from these groups than they otherwise would have rendered. The government was able to broaden the terms of the bargain by threatening certain recalcitrant players, by verifying Chrysler's own threat to declare

---

[59]See, for a more extended treatment of these alternatives than we can possibly offer here, Robert Hillman, Contract Excuse and Bankruptcy Discharge, 43 Stanford Law Review 99-136 (N. 1990).

[60]Laid-Off Workers, the Chrysler Loan Guarantee and Corporatist Legitimacy: A Thematic Analysis, 9 Contemporary Crisis 229 (1985).

[61]New Deals: The Chrysler Revival and the American System (Times Books 1985). See also Reich and Donahue, Lessons from the Chrysler Bailout, 27 California Management Review 157 (1985).

bankruptcy unless sacrifice was forthcoming, and by orchestrating a single grand bargain incorporating all major parties.[62]

However, Reich and Donahue conclude "[i]f we opt to replicate the Chrysler bailout, we will need to develop a clearer consensus on the proper limits of the government's power to coerce concessions."[63] Consider the judge's role in major contracts cases. How is it similar to the role played by all agencies of the federal government in the Chrysler situation? How do the situations differ?

Finally, Stewart describes the role of Debevoise, Plimpton, Lyons & Gates in the Chrysler rescue.[64] His story describes great efforts to get the statute passed and to comply with its terms. However, he concludes, "[u]ltimately, it was politics, not the law, that saved Chrysler." To what extent, if at all, is this conclusion also true of the cases that follow?

4. *An anecdote:* A successful real estate developer was asked if he could summarize the secret of his success. He is reported to have said, "Well, some of it I attribute to the recognition that if you owe the bank $10,000 and can't pay, you're in trouble. But if you owe the bank $10 million and can't pay, the bank's in trouble."

ALUMINUM COMPANY OF AMERICA v. ESSEX GROUP, INC.

499 F. Supp. 53 (W.D. Pa. 1980)

TEITELBAUM, J. Plaintiff, Aluminum Company of America (ALCOA), brought the instant action against defendant, Essex Group, Inc. (Essex), in three counts. The first count requests the Court to reform or equitably adjust an agreement entitled the Molten Metal Agreement entered into between ALCOA and Essex. The second count alleges that the Molten Metal Agreement was modified by oral amendment and that Essex has breached the amended agreement. The second count seeks a declaratory judgment that the alleged breach by Essex excuses ALCOA's further performance and seeks as well an award of damages caused by the alleged breach of Essex. The third count asks for a declaratory judgment that ALCOA's prior notice of termination of the Molten Metal Agreement was proper or, in the alternative, that ALCOA may terminate the Molten Metal Agreement if it be determined by this Court to be a contract for the sale of goods. Essex denies all of ALCOA's material allegations. Essex further counterclaims that ALCOA is liable to it for damages based on ALCOA's failure to deliver to Essex the amounts of molten metal ALCOA is contractually obligated to deliver under the Molten Metal Agreement and seeks entry of an

---

[62]*Id.* at 174.

[63]*Id.* at 175.

[64]The Partners 201-244 (Warner Books 1984).

order specifically enforcing its right to receive molten aluminum from ALCOA in the amounts requested.

Jurisdiction is based upon diversity of citizenship and amount in controversy and is one of the few issues in the case *sub judice* not in dispute.

In 1966 Essex made a policy decision to expand its participation in the manufacture of aluminum wire products. Thus, beginning in the spring of 1967, ALCOA and Essex negotiated with each other for the purpose of reaching an agreement whereby ALCOA would supply Essex with its long-term needs for aluminum that Essex could use in its manufacturing operations.

By December 26, 1967 the parties had entered into what they designated as a toll conversion service contract known as the Molten Metal Agreement under which Essex would supply ALCOA with alumina which ALCOA would convert by a smelting process into molten aluminum. Under the terms of the Molten Metal Agreement, Essex delivers alumina to ALCOA which ALCOA smelts (or toll converts) into molten aluminum at its Warrick, Indiana, smelting facility. Essex then picks up the molten aluminum for further processing.

The price provisions of the contract contained an escalation formula which indicates that $.03 per pound of the original price escalates in accordance with changes in the Wholesale Price Index-Industrial Commodities (WPI) and $.03 per pound escalates in accordance with an index based on the average hourly labor rates paid to ALCOA employees at the Warrick plant. The portion of the pricing formula which is in issue in this case under counts one and two is the production charge which is escalated by the WPI. ALCOA contends that this charge was intended by the parties to reflect actual changes in the cost of the non-labor items utilized by ALCOA in the production of aluminum from alumina at its Warrick, Indiana smelting plant. In count one of this suit ALCOA asserts that the WPI used in the Molten Metal Agreement was in fact incapable of reasonably reflecting changes in the non-labor costs at ALCOA's Warrick, Indiana smelting plant and has in fact failed to so reflect such changes.

It is ALCOA's contention in count one of its complaint that the shared objectives of the parties with respect to the use of the WPI have been completely and totally frustrated, that both ALCOA and Essex made a mutual mistake of fact in agreeing to use the WPI to escalate non-labor costs at Warrick. ALCOA is seeking reformation or equitable adjustment of the Molten Metal Agreement so that pursuant to count one of its complaint, the pricing formula with respect to the non-labor portion of the production charge will be changed to eliminate the WPI and substitute the actual costs incurred by ALCOA for the non-labor items used at its Warrick, Indiana smelting plant. Essex opposes relief under count one contending that: 1) ALCOA cannot obtain reformation of the Molten Metal Agreement on the grounds of mutual mistake since ALCOA has failed to establish any antecedent agreement on pricing not expressed in the Molten Metal Agreement; 2) ALCOA assumed the risk that its prediction as to future costs would be incorrect; 3) ALCOA has failed to prove that enforcement of the Molten Metal Agreement would be unconscionable....

COUNT ONE

ALCOA's first count seeks an equitable modification of the contract price for its services. The pleadings, arguments and briefs frame the issue in several forms. ALCOA seeks reformation or modification of the price on the basis of mutual mistake of fact, unilateral mistake of fact, unconscionability, frustration of purpose, and commercial impracticability.

A.   The facts pertinent to count one are few and simple. In 1967 ALCOA and Essex entered into a written contract in which ALCOA promised to convert specified amounts of alumina supplied by Essex into aluminum for Essex. The service is to be performed at the ALCOA works at Warrick, Indiana. The contract is to run until the end of 1983. Essex has the option to extend it until the end of 1988. The price for each pound of aluminum converted is calculated by a complex formula which includes three variable components based on specific indices. The initial contract price was set at fifteen cents per pound, computed as follows:

A. Demand Charge	$0.05/lb.
B. Production Charge	
(i) Fixed component	.04/lb.
(ii) Non-labor production cost component	.03/lb.
(iii) Labor production cost component	.03/lb.
Total initial charge	$0.15/lb.

The demand charge is to vary from its initial base in direct proportion to periodic changes in the Engineering News Record Construction Cost — 20 Cities Average Index published in the Engineering News Record. The Non-labor Production Cost Component is to vary from its initial base in direct proportion to periodic changes in the Wholesale Price Index-Industrial Commodities (WPI-IC) published by the Bureau of Labor Statistics of the United States Department of Labor. The Labor Production Cost Component is to vary from its initial base in direct proportion to periodic changes in ALCOA's average hourly labor cost at the Warrick, Indiana works. The adjusted price is subject to an over-all "cap" price of 65% of the price of a specified type of aluminum sold on specified terms, as published in a trade journal, American Metal Market.

The indexing system was evolved by ALCOA.... ALCOA examined the non-labor production cost component to assure that the WPI-IC had not tended to deviate markedly from their non-labor cost experience in the years before the contract was executed. Essex agreed to the contract including the index provisions after an examination of the past record of the indices revealed an acceptable pattern of stability.

ALCOA sought, by the indexed price agreement, to achieve a stable net income of about 4 ovp(c)/per pound of aluminum converted. This net income represented ALCOA's return (i) on its substantial capital investment devoted to the performance of the contracted services, (ii) on its management, and (iii) on the risks of short-falls or losses it undertook over an extended period. The fact that the non-labor production cost component of ALCOA's costs was priced according to a surrogate, objective index opened the door to a foreseeable fluctuation of ALCOA's return due to deviations between ALCOA's costs and the performance of the WPI-IC. The range of foreseeable deviation was roughly three cents per pound. That is to say that in some years ALCOA's return might foreseeably (and did, in fact) rise to seven cents per pound, while in other years it might foreseeably (and did, in fact) fall to about one cent per pound. See Table I.

Essex sought to assure itself of a long term supply of aluminum at a favorable price. Essex intended to and did manufacture a new line of aluminum wire products. The long term supply of aluminum was important to assure Essex of the steady use of its expensive machinery. A steady production stream was vital to preserve the market position it sought to establish. The favorable price was important to allow Essex to compete with firms like ALCOA which produced the aluminum and manufactured aluminum wire products in an efficient, integrated operation.

TABLE I

YEAR	BASE WPI-IC[1]	WARRICK NON-LABOR PRODUCTION COSTS PER POUND[2]		PROFIT/LOSS PER LB.	POUNDS DELIVERED	PROFIT/LOSS
		¢	%			
1968	102.5	4.371	110.5	5.799	25,300,000	$ 1,467,147
1969	106.0	4.010	101.4	7.097	54,694,317	3,881,656
1970	110.0	4.397	111.1	6.517	84,370,265	5,498,410
1971	114.1	5.215	131.8	5.267	65,522,280	3,516,581
1972	117.9	5.309	134.2	5.721	83,128,209	4,755,765
1973	125.9	5.819	147.1	4.535	82,201,940	3,727,857
1974	153.9	9.009	227.1	2.070	86,234,310	1,785,050
1975	171.5	11.450	289.4	.189	76,688,530	144,941
1976	182.4	13.949	352.6	(.301)[3]	83,363,502	250,924
1977	195.1	17.806	450.1	(4.725)[3]	72,289,722	(3,415,689)
1978	209.4	22.717	574.2	(10.484)[3]	82,235,337	(8,620,504)

[1]The contract calls for a recomputation of the WPI-IC, so that the "Base Wholesale Price Index" = 100 in 1967.

[2]Warrick Non-Labor Production Costs 1967 - 100%.

[3]The profit (loss) shown in years 1976 through 1978 was affected by a temporary surcharge agreement. Without the temporary surcharge the loss in cents per pound would have been as follows: 1967 (1.699); 1977 (6.725); 1978 (10.984). The loss each year would have been as follows: 1976 ($1,416,346); 1977 ($4,861,484); 1978 ($9,031,631).

In the early years of the contract, the price formula yielded prices related, within the foreseeable range of deviation, to ALCOA's cost figures. Beginning in 1973, OPEC actions to increase oil prices and unanticipated pollution control costs greatly increased ALCOA's electricity costs. Electric power is the principal non-labor cost factor in aluminum conversion, and the electric power rates rose much more rapidly than did the WPI-IC. As a result, ALCOA's production costs rose greatly and unforeseeably beyond the indexed increase in the contract price. Table I illustrates the relation between the WPI-IC and ALCOA's costs over the years of the contract, and the resulting consequences of ALCOA.

During the most recent years, the market price of aluminum has increased even faster than the production costs. At the trial ALCOA introduced the deposition of Mr. Wilfred Jones, an Essex employee whose duties included the sale of surplus metal. Mr. Jones stated that Essex had resold some millions of pounds of aluminum which ALCOA had refined. The cost of the aluminum to Essex (including the purchase price of the alumina and its transportation) was 36.35 cents per pound around June of 1979. Mr. Jones further stated that the resale price in June 1979 at one cent per pound under the market, was 73.313 cents per pound, yielding Essex a gross profit of 37.043 cents per pound. This margin of profit shows the tremendous advantage Essex enjoys under the contract as it is written and as both parties have performed it. A significant fraction of Essex's advantage is directly attributable to the corresponding out of pocket losses ALCOA suffers. ALCOA has sufficiently shown that without judicial relief or economic changes which are not presently foreseeable, it stands to lose in excess of $75,000,000 out of pocket, during the remaining term of the contract.

B. ALCOA's Warrick Works, located in Indiana, are the designated source of supply. The Essex plant, where the bulk of the aluminum is used, is also located in Indiana. Essex takes delivery at the Warrick Works.

The contract declares "This Agreement shall be governed and interpreted in accordance with the laws of the State of Indiana." The parties surely have sufficient contacts with the State of Indiana and Pennsylvania so that the courts would enforce their agreement respecting the application of Indiana law. Restatement 2d Conflict of Laws § 187; *cf.* 13 Pa.C.S.A. § 1105(1) (U.C.C.). This Court must enforce it as well....

This case presents many issues which are governed by common law principles. Most fall within the interstices of the reported decisions of Indiana courts. Some touch principles announced in hoary Indiana decisions. Where the Indiana law remains undeclared, or where the declaration is far from current, the obligation of this Court is to discern the most probable state of current Indiana law for "the outcome of the litigation in the federal court should be substantially the same, so far as legal rules determine the outcome of a litigation, as it would be if tried in a State court." *Guaranty Trust Co. v. York*, 326 U.S. 99, 65 S.Ct. 1464, 89 L.Ed. 2079 (1945)....

In connection with these observations, the Court notes that the appellate courts of Indiana appear to join in the habits of thought and in the assessments of policy which have lately prevailed in most of the fine courts in this nation. The Indiana courts have joined the throng of state courts in (i) declaring that residential landlords are bound by an implied warranty of habitability. *Old Town Development v. Langford*, 349 N.E.2d 744 (Ind.App.1976); (ii) adopting the rule of strict products liability from the Restatement 2d of Torts § 402A, *Perfection Paint & Color Co. v. Konduris*, 258 N.E.2d 681 (Ind.App.1970); (iii) adopting the increasing prevalent view that harsh or unconscionable provisions in contracts of adhesion may be refused enforcement, *Weaver v. American Oil Co.*, 276 N.E.2d 144 (Ind.1971).

C. ALCOA initially argues that it is entitled to relief on the theory of mutual mistake. ALCOA contends that both parties were mistaken in their estimate of the suitability of the WPI-IC as an objective index of ALCOA's non-labor production costs, and that their mistake is legally sufficient to warrant modification or avoidance of ALCOA's promise. Essex appropriately raised several defenses to these claims. Essex first argues that the asserted mistake is legally insufficient because it is essentially a mistake as to future economic events rather than a mistake of fact. Essex next argues that ALCOA assumed or bore the risk of the mistake. Essex finally argues that the requested remedy of reformation is not available under Indiana law.

The late Professor Corbin wrote the best modern analysis of the doctrine of mutual mistake. Corbin took pains to show the great number and variety of factors which must be considered in resolving claims for relief founded on the doctrine of mistake, and to show the inappropriateness of any single verbal rule to govern the decision of mistake cases. Corbin on Contracts § 597 at 582-83 (1960).

The present case involves a claimed mistake in the price indexing formula. This is clearly a mistake concerning a factor affecting the value of the agreed exchange. Of such mistakes Corbin concluded that the law must consider the character of the risks assumed by the parties. *Id.* at § 605. He further concluded:

> In these cases, the decision involves a judgment as to the materiality of the alleged factor, and as to whether the parties made a definite assumption that it existed and made their agreement in the belief that there was *no risk* with respect to it. Opinions are almost sure to differ on both of these matters, so that decisions must be, or appear to be, conflicting. The court's judgment on each of them is a judgment on a matter of fact, not a judgment as to law. No rule of thumb should be constructed for cases of this kind. 3 Corbin on Contracts § 605 at p. 643 (1960).

The new Restatement 2d of Contracts follows a similar approach. After defining "mistake" as "a belief not in accord with the facts," § 293, the Restatement declares:

§ 294. WHEN MISTAKE OF BOTH PARTIES MAKES A CONTRACT VOIDABLE.

(1) Where a mistake of both parties at the time a contract was made as to a basic assumption on which the contract was made has a material effect on the agreed exchange of performances the contract is voidable by the adversely affected party unless he bears the risk of the mistake under the rule stated in § 296.

(2) In determining whether this mistake has a material affect on the agreed exchange of performances, account is taken of any relief by way of reformation, restitution, or otherwise.[65]

Both Professor Corbin and the Restatement emphasize the limited place of the doctrine of mistake in the law of contracts. They, along with most modern commentators, emphasize the importance of contracts as devices to allocate the risks of life's uncertainties, particularly economic uncertainties. Where parties to a contract deliberately and expressly undertake to allocate the risk of loss attendant on those uncertainties between themselves or where they enter a contract of a customary kind which by common understanding, sense, and legal doctrine has the affect of allocating such risks, the commentators and the opinions are agreed that there is little room for judicial relief from resulting losses. Corbin on Contracts § 598 and authorities there cited. The new Restatement agrees, § 296. This is, in part, the function of the doctrine of assumption of the risk as a limitation of the doctrine of mistake. Whether ALCOA assumed the risk it seeks relief from is at issue in this case. The doctrine of assumption of the risk is therefore considered below. The important point to note here is that the doctrine of assumption of the risk is not the only risk allocating limitation on the doctrine of mistake. Other important risk allocating limitations are inherent in the doctrine of mistake itself. They find expression in the cases and treatises in declarations that there has been no mistake, or no legally cognizable mistake, or a mistake of the wrong part.

ALCOA claims that there was a mutual mistake about the suitability of the WPI-IC as an index to accomplish the purposes of the parties. Essex replies that the mistake, if any, was not a mistake of *fact*, but it was rather a mistake in predicting future economic conditions. Essex asserts that such a mistake does not justify legal relief for ALCOA. The conflicting claims require the Court to resolve three questions: (1) Was the mistake one of "fact" as the cases and commentators use that word? (2) If so, was it of the sort of fact for which relief could be granted? (3) If the mistake was not one of "fact," is relief necessarily foreclosed?

---

[65]The quoted language in subsection (2), and in some of the comments which will be quoted contains variations from the published language. See n. 6. Those variations are not material to the decision of this case.

The initial question requires the characterization, as a matter of fact rather than of law, of the claimed mistake. The cases and commentaries contain useful thoughts and analogous problems which aid in this characterization. But the characterization is itself a question of fact. That it may have ultimate legal significance, and that it requires the exercise of judgment does not distinguish this determination from other determinations of fact. The distinction between questions of law and questions of fact is old. Its resolution is often doubtful. No simple and mechanical verbal formula can capture the distinction and resolve the hard cases. Factors affecting the characterization of a question include its suitability for jury or other fact-finder determination and its analytical separability from the final determination of legal consequences. The separation of fact from things which are not fact — opinion, prediction, desire, and the like — is principally a question of common sense or epistemology rather than of law, even when the separation must be done by courts. So it is here. ALCOA calls the mistaken assumption that the index was suitable a factual assumption. Essex calls it a prediction. This is a dispute of facts, not law. Its resolution will affect the decision of this case as factual determinations usually do. The law must be applied to it to yield a result. Neither is this question beyond the usual function and capacity of a jury or other fact-finder.

The first Restatement of Contracts notes, and the published Tentative Draft No. 10 of the Restatement Second stresses, the distinction between "existing fact" and prediction. See Restatement of Contracts § 502, Comment a; Restatement 2d of Contracts § 293. The approved final form of § 293 modifies the emphasis by deleting the word "existing." The Reporter, Professor Farnsworth of the Columbia University School of Law, related the circumstances of that change to the Court when he appeared on behalf of ALCOA.

> ... My clear recollection is that following the discussion of misrepresentation, a number of people came up to me and later saw me in the hallway and said that they agreed with the speaker that 'existing' should be dropped.
>
> It would be fair to say that there were probably as many reasons for dropping it given to me as there were people who had advanced the opinion.
>
> I would suppose at the end at least a dozen people had said they didn't like 'existing,' and nobody had defended it. *The reporter has the authority to change even the black letter when it is a matter of style, and since I did not bring it back to the Institute for a vote as a matter of substance, I think one would have to say that any change made was considered by the reporter to be a matter of style.*
>
> In any event, in response to the small but unanimous body of opinion that didn't like 'existing,' it was deleted in the draft that I finally sent off to the editor and it now reads 'Belief that is not in accord with the facts.'
>
> *I think that there is in the comment still a statement with respect to 'existing,' but the deletion from the black letter is at least a change that perhaps permits more flexibility with respect to the line between what is an*

existing fact or what is a fact and what is a pure presumption which is an extremely difficult line to draw in both cases.
Testimony of E. Allan Farnsworth 20-22 (Emphasis added).

The Comment Professor Farnsworth mentioned declares:

[T]he erroneous belief must relate to the facts as they exist at the time of the making of the contract. A party's prediction or judgment as to events to occur in the future, even if erroneous, is not a 'mistake' as that word is defined here....

The Court finds the parties' mistake in this case to be one of fact rather than one of simple prediction of future events. Plainly the mistake is not wholly isolated from predictions of the future or from the searching illuminations of painful hindsight. But this is not the legal test. At the time the contract was made both parties were aware that the future was unknown, and their agreed contract was intended to bind them for many years to come. Both knew that Essex sought an objective pricing formula and that ALCOA sought a formula which would cover its out of pocket costs over the years and which would yield it a return of around four cents a pound. Both parties to the contract carefully examined the past performance of the WPI-IC before agreeing to its use. The testimony was clear that each assumed the Index was adequate to fulfill its purpose. This mistaken assumption was essentially a present actuarial error.

The parties took pains to avoid the full risk of future economic changes when they embarked on a twenty-one year contract involving services worth hundreds of millions of dollars. To this end they employed a customary business risk limiting device — price indexing — with more than customary sophistication and care. They chose not a single index formula but a complex one with three separate indices.

... Here the practical necessities of the very long term service contract demanded an agreed risk limiting device. Both parties understood this and adopted one. The capacity of their selected device to achieve the known purposes of the parties was not simply a matter of acknowledged uncertainty like the ... prediction. It was more in the nature of an actuarial prediction of the outside limits of variation in the relation between two variable figures — the WPI-IC and the non-labor production costs of ALCOA. Its capacity to work as the parties expected it to work was a matter of fact, existing at the time they made the contract.

This crucial fact was not known, and was scarcely knowable when the contract was made.[66] But this does not alter its status as an existing fact. The law of mistake has not distinguished between facts which are unknown but presently knowable, *e.g.*, *Raffles v. Wichelhaus*, 2 H. & C. 906 (1864), and facts which presently exist but are unknowable, *e.g.*, *Sherwood v. Walker*, 66 Mich. 568, 33 N.W. 919 (1887). Relief has been granted for mistakes of both kinds.

To conclude that the parties contracted upon a mistake of fact does not, by itself, justify an award of judicial relief to ALCOA. Relief can only follow if the mistake was mutual, if it related to a basic assumption underlying the contract, and if it caused a severe imbalance in the agreed exchange.

The doctrine of mistake has long distinguished claims of mutual mistake from claims of unilateral mistake. Corbin on Contracts § 608. The standards for judicial relief are higher where the proven mistake is unilateral than where it is mutual. Compare, *e.g.* Restatement 2d of Contracts § 294 with § 295.

Essex asserts that ALCOA's mistake was unilateral. Mr. O'Malley, Chairman of the board of Essex Corporation, testified at trial that he had no particular concern for ALCOA's well-being and that in the negotiations of the contract he sought only Essex's best interests. Essex claims this testimony tends to rebut any possible mutual mistake of fact between the parties. The Court disagrees....

The law of mutual mistake is not addressed primarily to motivation or to desire to have a good bargain, such as that credibly testified to by Mr. O'Malley. As Mr. O'Malley struck the bargain for Essex, he understood the function of the Wholesale Price Index, as part of the pricing formula, to be the protection of ALCOA from foreseeable economic fluctuations. He further had every reason to believe that the formula was selected on the factual prediction that it would, within tolerable limits, serve its purpose. While he did not share the motive to protect ALCOA, he understood the functional purposes of the agreement. He therefore shared this mistake of fact. And his mistake was Essex's. The Court recognizes that Mr. O'Malley and Essex would cheerfully live with the benefit of their mistake, but the law provides otherwise. As a matter of law Mr. O'Malley's testimony of Essex's indifference concerning ALCOA's motivation for the use of the Wholesale Price Index as a gauge for tracking non-labor costs is immaterial.

Is it enough that one party is indifferent to avoid a mutual mistake? The Court thinks not. This situation resembles that in *Sherwood v. Walker, supra*, the celebrated case of Rose of Aberlone. There the owner of a prize breeding cow sold her for slaughter at the going rate for good slaughter cattle. The owner had unsuccessfully tried to breed her and had erroneously concluded she was sterile.

---

[66]Clear hindsight suggests the flaw might have been anticipated and cured by a "floor" resembling the 65% "cap" that Essex wrote into the price formula. To the extent this possibility might be thought material to the case, the Court specifically finds that when the contract was made, even people of exceptional prudence and foresight would not have anticipated a need for this additional limitation to achieve the purpose of the parties.

In fact she was pregnant at the time of the sale and she was much more valuable for breeding than for slaughter. There as here, the buyer was indifferent to the unknown fact; he would have been pleased to keep the unexpected profit. But he understood the bargain rested on a presumed state of facts. The court let the seller avoid the contract because of mutual mistake of fact.

In *Sherwood*, the buyer didn't know the highly pedigreed Rose was with calf. He probably could not have discovered it at the time of the sale with due diligence. Here the parties could not possibly have known of the sudden inability of the Wholesale Price Index to reflect ALCOA's non-labor costs. If, over the previous twenty years, the Wholesale Price Index had tracked, within a 5% variation, pertinent costs to ALCOA, a 500% variation of costs to Index must be deemed to be unforeseeable, within any meaningful sense of the word.

Essex has not seriously argued that the mistake does not relate to an assumption which is basic to the contract. The relation is clear. The assumed capacity of the price formula in a long term service contract to protect against vast windfall profits to one party and vast windfall losses to the other is so clearly basic to the agreement as to repel dispute. While the cases often assert that a mistake as to price or as to future market conditions will not justify relief, this is not because price assumptions are not basic to the contracts. Instead, relief is denied because the parties allocated the risk of present price uncertainties or of uncertain future market values by their contract. Where a "price mistake" derives from a mistake about the nature or quantity of an object sold, the courts have allowed a remedy; they have found no contractual allocation of that sort of risk of price error. Indiana cases hold that where land is sold as a tract for a set price, and it later appears that there was a material error in the parties' estimate of the quantity of land conveyed, the court will correct the error by adjusting the price, *McMahan v. Terkhorn*, 67 Ind.App. 501, 116 N.E. 327 (1917), or by allowing rescission, *Earl v. VaNatta*, 29 Ind.App. 532, 64 N.E. 901 (1902). See Corbin on Contracts §§ 604-05. Similarly many cases allow relief from unilateral price errors by construction contractors. An Indiana decision reached this result. *Board of School Comm'rs v. Bender*, 36 Ind.App. 164, 72 N.E. 154 (1904). See Corbin on Contracts § 609. Restatement 2d of Contracts § 295, Comment a. These cases demonstrate that price assumptions may be basic to the contract.

Essex concedes that the result of the mistake has a material effect on the contract and that it has produced a severe imbalance in the bargain. See Restatement 2d of Contracts § 294, Comment c. The most that Essex argues is this: ALCOA has not proved that enforcement of the contract would be *unconscionable*. Essex correctly points out that at the time of the trial ALCOA had shown a net profit of $9 million on the contract. Essex further argues that ALCOA has failed to prove that it ever will lose money on the contract, and that such proof would require expert testimony concerning future economic values and costs. These arguments are insufficient.

The evidence shows that during the last three years ALCOA has suffered increasingly large out-of-pocket losses.[67] If the contract were to expire today that net profit of $9 million would raise doubts concerning the materiality of the parties' mistake. But even on that supposition, the court would find the mistake to be material because it would leave ALCOA dramatically short of the minimum return of one cent per pound which the parties had contemplated.

But the contract will not expire today. Essex has the power to keep it in force until 1988. The Court rejects Essex's objection to the absence of expert testimony concerning future costs and prices. The objection is essentially based on the traditional refusal of courts to award speculative damages. But Essex presses the argument too far. The law often requires courts to make awards to redress anticipated losses. The reports are filled with tort and contract cases where such a awards are made without the benefit of expert testimony concerning future economic trends. Awards are commonly denied because they are too speculative where there is a claim for lost future profits and there is insufficient evidence of present profits to form a basis for protecting future profits.

Similarly the courts often decline to speculate concerning future economic trends in calculating awards for lost future earnings. Many states refuse to consider any possibility of future inflation in calculating such awards despite the presence of expert testimony and the teachings of common experience....

This demonstrates the law's healthy skepticism concerning the reliability of expert predictions of economic trends. Where future predictions are necessary, the law commonly accepts and applies a prediction that the future economy will be much like the present (except that inflation will cease). Since some prediction of the future is inescapable in this case, that commonly accepted one will necessarily apply. On that prediction, ALCOA has proved that over the entire life of the contract it will lose, out of pocket, in excess of $60 million, and the whole of this loss will be matched by an equal windfall profit to Essex.[68] This proof clearly establishes that the mistake had the required material effect on the agreed exchange. Indeed, if this case required a determination of the conscionability of

---

[67]The Court recognizes that ALCOA has suffered even larger losses of potential profits which it might have earned, but for the contract, in the strong aluminum market in recent years. Essex, rather than ALCOA, has enjoyed those profits. But their existence is immaterial to the questions raised in this case.

[68]The equivalence of ALCOA's loss and Essex's gain may distinguish this case from the concededly more difficult "Suez cases." Transatlantic Financing Corp. v. United States, 363 F.2d 312 (D.C. Cir. 1966); American Trading and Production Corp. v. Shell International Marine, 453 F.2d 939 (2d Cir. 1972); Glidden Co. v. Hellenic Lines, 275 F.2d 253 (2d Cir. 1960); Ocean Tramp Tankers Corp. v. V/U Sorracht (The Eugenia), [1964] 1 All E.R. 161 (C.A. 1963). In those cases an unexpected closing of the canal materially increased the cost of performing the contract leaving the courts to determine the allocation of a loss not balanced by an equal profit. Those cases might also be distinguished in that they involved the doctrine of frustration of purpose rather than the doctrine of mistake. However, the similarity of these doctrines renders this distinction doubtful.

enforcing this contract in the current circumstances, the Court would not hesitate to hold it unconscionable.

Essex next argues that ALCOA may not be relieved of the consequences of the mistake because it assumed or bore the risk of the market....

The Restatements and these cases reveal four facets of risk assumption and risk allocation under the law of mistake. First, a party to a contract may expressly assume a risk....

Customary dealing in a trade or common understanding may lead a court to impose a risk on a party where the contract is silent. Often the result corresponds to the expectation of both parties, but this will not always be true. See Berman, Excuse for Nonperformance in the Light of Contract Practices in International Trade, 63 Columbia Law Review 1413, 1420-24 (1963). At times legal rules may form the basis for the inferred common understanding. Equity traditionally put the risk of casualty losses on the purchaser of land while the purchase contract remained executory. This allocation was derived from the doctrine of equitable conversion. "Equity regards as done that which ought to be done." The rule could always be modified by express agreement. It survives today — where it does survive — largely by reason of its acceptance as part of the common expectations of real estate traders and their advisors.

Third, where neither express words nor some particular common understanding or trade usage dictate a result, the court must allocate the risk in some reasoned way....

Fourth, where parties enter a contract in a state of conscious ignorance of the facts, they are deemed to risk the burden of having the facts turn out to be adverse, within very broad limits. Each party takes a calculated gamble in such a contract. Because information is often troublesome or costly to obtain, the law does not seek to discourage such contracts. Thus if parties agree to sell and purchase a stone which both know may be glass or diamond at a price which in some way reflects their uncertainty, the contract is enforceable whether the stone is in fact glass or diamond. If, by contrast, the parties both mistakenly believe it to be glass, the case is said not to be one of conscious ignorance but one of mutual mistake. Consequently, the vendor may avoid the contract.

In this case Essex raises two arguments. First, it asserts that ALCOA expressly or by fair implication assumed the risk that the WPI-IC would not keep up with ALCOA's non-labor production costs. Second, it asserts that the parties made a calculated gamble with full awareness that the future was uncertain, so the contract should be enforced despite the mutual mistake. Both arguments are correct within limits, and within those limits they affect the relief ALCOA may receive. Both arguments fail as complete defenses to ALCOA's claim.

Essex first asserts that ALCOA expressly or implicitly assumed the risk that the WPI-IC would not track ALCOA's non-labor production costs. Essex asserts that ALCOA drafted the index provision; that it did so on the basis of its superior knowledge of its cost experience at the Warrick Works; and that ALCOA's officials knew of the inherent risk that the index would not reflect cost changes. Essex emphasized that, during the negotiation of the contract, it insisted on the inclusion of a protective "ceiling" on the indexed price of ALCOA's services at 65% of a specified published market price. Essex implies that ALCOA could have sought a corresponding "floor" provision to limit its risks.

Essex's arguments rely on two ancient and powerful principles of interpretation. The first is reflected in the maxim "expressio unius est exclusio alterius." The second is the principle that a contract is to be construed against its drafter. To agree to an indexed price term subject to a ceiling but without a floor is to make a deliberate choice, Essex argues. It is to choose one principle and to reject another. The argument is plausible but not sufficient. The maxim rules no farther than its reason, and its reason is simply this: often an expression of a rule couched in one form reflects with high probability the rejection of a contradictory rule. Less often it reflects a probable rejection of a supplementary rule. To know if this is true of a particular case requires a scrupulous examination of the thing expressed, the thing not expressed, and the context of the expression. The question here is precisely this: By omitting a floor provision did ALCOA accept the risk of any and every deviation of the selected index from its costs, no matter how great or how highly improbable? The course of dealing between the parties repels the idea. Essex and ALCOA are huge industrial enterprises. The management of each is highly trained and highly responsible. The corporate officers have access to and use professional personnel including lawyers, accountants, economists and engineers. The contract was drafted by sophisticated, responsible businessmen who were intensely conscious of the risks inherent in long term contracts and who plainly sought to limit the risks of their undertaking. The parties' laudable attention to risk limitation appears in many ways: in the complex price formula, in the 65% ceiling, in the "most favored customer" clause which Essex wrote into the contract, and in the elaborate "force majeur" clause favoring ALCOA. It appears as well in the care and in the expense of the negotiations and drafting process. Essex negotiated with several aluminum producers, seeking a long term assured supply, before agreeing to the ALCOA contract. Its search for an assured long term supply for its aluminum product plants itself bespeaks a motive of limiting risks. Essex settled on ALCOA's offer rather than a proffered joint venture on the basis of many considerations including the required capital, engineering and management demands of the joint venture, the cost, and the comparative risks and burdens of the two arrangements. When ALCOA proposed the price formula which appears in the contract, Essex's management examined the past behavior of the indices for stability to assure they would not cause their final aluminum cost to deviate unacceptably from the going market rate. ALCOA's management was equally attentive to risk limitation.... They selected the WPI-IC as a pricing element for this long term contract only after they assured themselves that it had closely tracked ALCOA's non-labor production costs for many years in the past and was highly likely to continue to do so in the future. In the context of the formation of the contract, it is untenable to argue that ALCOA implicitly or expressly assumed a limitless, if highly improbable, risk. On this record, the absence of an express floor limitation can only be understood to imply that the parties deemed the risk too remote and their meaning too clear to trifle with additional negotiation and drafting.

The principle that a writing is to be construed against its maker will not aid Essex here. That principle once sounded as a clarion call to retrograde courts to pervert agreements if they could. Today it is happily domesticated as a rule with diverse uses. In cases involving issues of conscience or of strong policy, such as forfeiture cases, the principle complements the familiar doctrine of strict construction to favor lenient results. In other cases it serves as an aid in resolving otherwise intractable ambiguities. This case presents neither of these problems. The question of defining the risks ALCOA assumed is one of interpretation. It implicates no strong public policy. Neither does it present an intractable ambiguity.

Neither is this a case of "conscious ignorance" as Essex argues. Essex cites many cases which establish the general rule that mistaken assumptions about the future are not the sort of mistaken assumptions which lead to relief from contractual duties.... The general rule is in fact as Essex states it. but that rule has limited application. The new Restatement notes that the rule does not apply where both parties are unconscious of their ignorance — that is, where both mistakenly believe they know the vital facts. See § 296 Comment C....

This distinction is sufficient to settle many cases but it is framed too crudely for sensible application to cases like the present one. The distinction posits two polar positions: certain belief that a vital fact is true and certain recognition that a vital fact is unknown. Such certainties are seldom encountered in human affairs. They are particularly rare in the understanding of sophisticated businessmen....

The ... notion of a range of uncertainty is not unknown to Indiana law. In *McMahan v. Terkhorn, supra,* the parties contracted to purchase and to sell a tract of land which they thought to contain 133 acres for $15,000. Before the date for performance the purchaser had the land surveyed. The surveyor reported the tract contained 104.52 acres. The parties then adjusted the purchase price to $12,000 and completed the conveyance on that basis. Later the vendor learned the survey was wrong; the tract contained 129 acres. He then sued for and won the value of the "excess" land conveyed. The court distinguished between the normal range of survey error which parties are deemed to expect and to risk, and gross errors for which a remedy is available....

Once courts recognize that supposed specific values lie, and are commonly understood to lie, within a penumbra of uncertainty, and that the range of probability is subject to estimation, the principle of conscious uncertainty requires reformulation. The proper question is not simply whether the parties to a contract were conscious of uncertainty with respect to a vital fact, but whether they believed that uncertainty was effectively limited within a designated range so that they would deem outcomes beyond that range to be highly unlikely. In this case the answer is clear. Both parties knew that the use of an objective price index injected a limited range of uncertainty into their projected return on the contract. Both had every reason to predict that the likely range of variation would not exceed three cents per pound. That is to say both would have deemed deviations yielding ALCOA less of a return on its investment, work and risk of less than one cent a pound or of more than seven cents a pound to be highly unlikely. Both consciously undertook a closely calculated risk rather than a limitless one. Their mistake concerning its calculation is thus fundamentally unlike the limitless conscious undertaking of an unknown risk which Essex now posits.

What has been said to this point suffices to establish that ALCOA is entitled to some form of relief due to mutual mistake of fact. But the stakes in this case are large, and the chances of review by higher courts are high. Therefore the Court thinks it appropriate to rule on two other theories which ALCOA presented in support of its first count.

D.   ALCOA argues that it is entitled to relief on the grounds of impracticability and frustration of purpose. The Court agrees.

In broad outline the doctrines of impracticability and of frustration of purpose resemble the doctrine of mistake. All three doctrines discharge an obligor from his duty to perform a contract where a failure of a basic assumption of the parties produces a grave failure of the equivalence of value of the exchange to the parties. And all three are qualified by the same notions of risk assumption and allocation. The doctrine of mistake of fact requires that the mistake relate to a basic assumption on which the contract was made. The doctrine of impracticability requires that the non-occurrence of the "event," Restatement Second of Contracts § 281, or the non-existence of the "fact," *Id.* § 286, causing the impracticability be a basic assumption on which the contract is made. The doctrine of frustration of purpose similarly rests on the same "non-occurrence" or "non-existence," "basic assumption" equation. *Id.* §§ 285, 286.

The three doctrines further overlap in time. There may be some residual notion that the doctrine of frustration and impracticability relate to occurrences after the execution of the contract while the doctrine of mistake relates to facts as they stand at the time of execution. But that view has never won general acceptance. The first Restatement does not specifically limit the mistakes of fact for which relief may be granted to facts existing at the time of the contract. §§ 500, 502. Corbin and Williston do not suggest such a limitation. And the new Restatement equivocates on the point. Section 293 defines "mistake" as "a belief that is not in accord with the facts." The word "existing" modified the word "facts" in Tentative Draft Number 10 but was deleted by the Reporter. Comment a to the section does declare:

> [T]he erroneous belief must relate to the facts as they exist at the time of the making of the contract. A party's prediction or judgment as to events to occur in the future, even if erroneous, is not a 'mistake' as the word is defined here.

This declaration is anomalous and unexplained. The Court believes the definition rather than the comment expresses the better rule. The denial of relief for mistakes of future facts is better understood to rest on policies of risk allocation discussed above than to rest on the definition of "mistake."

National Presto Industries, Inc. v. United States, 338 F.2d 99 (Ct.Cl.1964), is a prime example of the application of the doctrine of mistake to developments after the execution of the contract. There the corporation contracted to produce artillery shells for the Army at a fixed price, using a new and only partially proven production method. The method was contrived to reduce wasted steel by eliminating the need for shaving excess metal from the shells. After the contract was signed, the corporation spent large sums of money in unsuccessful attempts to make the method work. Eventually it became clear that some shaving would be required. The corporation purchased the necessary equipment and paid for the materials and labor. Then it sought and obtained relief in the Court of Claims for its added expense. The court held that there had been an actionable mutual mistake of fact. The assumed capacity of the new method to produce shells without a shaving step proved to be mistaken.[69] The court based its decision solely on mistake of fact. It does not appear that frustration or impracticability were considered.

Conversely the notion that the doctrines of frustration and impracticability apply only to events occurring after the execution of a contract appear to be drawn more from common experience with their application than from any inherent limitation of those doctrines. Nothing in the language of the first Restatement limits the doctrine to events occurring after the execution of the contract, though all three illustrations involve such supervening events. § 288. The new Restatement recognizes that circumstances existing at the execution of a contract may render performance impracticable or they may frustrate the purpose of one of the parties so as to excuse his performance. § 286.

Thus there is a substantial area of similarity between the three doctrines. Within that area, the findings and holdings with respect to the claim of mistake also apply to the claims of impracticability and frustration. It requires no further discussion to establish that the non-occurrence of an extreme deviation of the WPI-IC and ALCOA's non-labor production costs was a basic assumption on which the contract was made. And it is clear that ALCOA neither assumed nor bore the risk of the deviation beyond the foreseeable limits of risk.

The court must still consider those aspects of doctrines of frustration and impracticability which differ from the doctrine of mistake....

---

[69]The court further held that the corporation had not assumed the risk of the experiment by entering into an unconditional fixed-price contract. The court found that the parties did not contemplate the hazard and did not assign its risk. 338 F.2d at 109-110. The court further found that the actual cost of testing and development in attempting to perfect the new method exceeded the testing expense implicitly risked by the corporation. 338 F.2d at 109.

The focus of the doctrines of impracticability and of frustration is distinctly on hardship. Section 281 declares a party is discharged from performing a contract where a supervening event renders his performance impracticable. Comment d discusses the meaning of "impracticability." The comment states the word is taken from Uniform Commercial Code § 2-615(a). It declares that the word denotes an impediment to performance lying between "impossibility" and "impracticality."

Performance may be impracticable because *extreme and unreasonable difficulty, expense, injury, or loss to one of the parties will be involved....*

A mere change in the degree of difficulty or expense due to such causes as increased wages, prices of raw materials, or costs of construction, unless well beyond the normal range, does not amount to impracticability since it is this sort of risk that a fixed-price contract is intended to cover. Restatement 2nd Contracts § 281 com. (d).

Similarly, § 285 declares a party is discharged from performing his contract where his principal purpose is *substantially* frustrated by the occurrence of a supervening event. The extent of the necessary frustration is further described in Comment a: "[T]he frustration must be substantial. It is not enough that the transaction has become less profitable for the affected party or even that he will sustain a loss. The frustration must be so severe that it is not fairly to be regarded as within the risks that he assumed under the contract."

Professor Corbin explained this requirement of a severe disappointment by relating this doctrine to the broad public policies that parties should generally be required to perform their contracts.

> Variations in the value of a promised performance, caused by the constantly varying factors that affect the bargaining appetites of men, are the rule rather than the exception. Bargainers know this and swallow their losses and disappointments, meantime keeping their promises. Such being the business mores, court decisions that are not in harmony with them will not make for satisfaction or prosperity. Relief from duty, outside of the bankruptcy court, can safely be granted on the ground of frustration of purpose by the rise or fall of values, only when the variation in value is very great and is caused by a supervening event that was not in fact contemplated by the parties and the risk of which was not allocated by them. Corbin on Contracts § 1355.

This strict standard of severe disappointment is clearly met in the present case. ALCOA has sufficiently proved that it will lose well over $60 million dollars out of pocket over the life of the contract due to the extreme deviation of the WPI-IC from ALCOA's actual costs.[70]

Is this, then, a case of impracticability, of frustration, or both? The doctrine of impracticability and of frustration focus on different kinds of disappointment of a contracting party. Impracticability focuses on occurrences which greatly increase the costs, difficulty, or risk of the party's performance. Restatement 2d of Contracts § 281.

The doctrine of frustration, on the other hand, focuses on a party's severe disappointment which is caused by circumstances which frustrate his principal purpose for entering the contract.[71] Restatement 2d of Contracts § 285. The doctrine of frustration often applies to relieve a party of a contract which could be performed without impediment; relief is allowed because the performance would be of little value to the frustrated party. Illustration 1 of the new Restatement — abstracted from the Coronation Cases — typifies this aspect of the doctrine of frustration.

> A and B make a contract under which B is to pay A $1,000 and is to have the use of A's window on January 10 to view a parade that has been scheduled for that day. Because of the illness of an important official, the parade is cancelled. B refuses to use the window or pay the $1,000. B's duty to pay $1,000 is discharged, and B is not liable to A for breach of contract.

Nothing impedes the full performance of this contract. B is able to pay $1,000 and to use the window despite the cancellation of the parade. But B's purpose — to observe the spectacle — has been frustrated.

In the present case ALCOA has satisfied the requirements of both doctrines. The impracticability of its performance is clear. The increase in its cost of performance is severe enough to warrant relief, and the other elements necessary for the granting of relief have been proven. Essex argues that the causes of ALCOA's losses are due to market price increases to which the doctrine of impracticability does not apply. The doctrine of impracticability of the new Restatement is one of recent evolution in the law. The first Restatement used the term as part of the definition of "impossibility." The interesting legal evolution

---

[70]The Court recognizes the additional requirement that the frustration or impracticability must not be the fault of the party who seeks relief. Restatement 2d of Contracts §§ 281, 285. Essex has not claimed or shown that ALCOA's dealings during the contract caused or contributed to ALCOA's losses. The record sufficiently proves that the great cost increases of some of the non-labor cost components (power, electrolytes, carbon) were beyond ALCOA's control....

[71]Professor Corbin primely observed, "A 'contract' never has a purpose or object. Only the contracting persons have purposes; and the purpose of any one of these persons is different from the purpose of any other. The hopes and purposes and objects of one of the parties may be frustrated by supervening events, although the purposes of the other party may not be at all affected by those events." Corbin on Contracts § 1353.

from the strict standards of impossibility, evident at least by dictum in *Parradine v. Jane*, Aleyn, 26 (1647, K.B.), to modern standards of impracticability is traced in Professor Gilmore's The Death of Contract 35-90 (1974). The drafters of the Uniform Commercial Code adopted this line of development, particularly in § 2-615. The new Restatement expressly draws upon § 2-615 in defining the scope of the doctrine. Section 281 comments reporter's notes. The Official Comment to § 2-615 lends strength to Essex's claim.

> 1. This section excuses a seller from timely delivery of goods contracted for, where his performance has become commercially impracticable because of unforeseen supervening circumstances not within the contemplation of the parties at the time of contracting....
>
> However, ...
>
> 4. Increased cost alone does not excuse performance unless the rise in cost is due to some unforeseen contingency which alters the essential nature of the performance. Neither is a rise or a collapse in the market in itself a justification, for that is exactly the type of business risk which business contracts made at fixed prices are intended to cover. But a severe shortage of raw materials or supplies due to a contingency such as war, embargo, local crop failure, unforeseen shutdown of major sources of supply or the like, which either causes a marked increase in cost or altogether prevents the seller from securing supplies necessary to his performance is within the contemplation of this section.

Several of the cases cited by Essex rely on Comment 4 in denying claims for relief. [citations omitted] ... Each is distinguishable from the present case in the absolute extent of the loss and in the proportion of loss involved.

In *Publicker Industries*, the defendant Union Carbide had contracted in 1972 to sell ethanol in specified quantities over a three year period to the plaintiff. The price was set by a formula, adjusted annually to reflect the seller's cost for raw materials, and subject to a ceiling on adjustment increases. The raw materials were derivatives of natural gas; their price soared beginning in 1973 as did ALCOA's energy costs. The seller's costs for ethanol rose from 21.2 cents a gallon in 1973 to 37.2 cents per gallon in mid-1974. The ceiling contract sales price was then 26.5 cents per gallon. The seller's loss of 10.7 cents per gallon led to a projected aggregate loss of $5.8 million. The court refused to relieve the seller. It found that the ceiling provision constituted an intentional allocation of the "risk of a substantial and unforeseen rise in cost" to the seller. It based this finding in part on the twenty-five percent rise in prices by OPEC in 1971 which made future cost increases highly foreseeable. The court addressed the degree of loss issue, declaring:

> We are not aware of any cases where something less than a 100% cost increase has been held to make a seller's performance 'impracticable.'

... '[T]here must be more of a variation between expected cost and the cost of performing by an available alternative than is present in this case, where the promisor can legitimately be presumed to have accepted some degree of abnormal risk, and where impracticability is urged on the basis of added expense alone.'[72]

Publicker Industries is clearly distinguishable from the present case respecting the degree of loss which the seller suffered in comparison to what it foresaw at the time of contracting. The fact that the Publicker contract was made after the substantial price increase of 1971 may justify the court's finding that the seller had assumed the risk of further large price increases. The contract in the present case antedated the 1971 price increase. There is no similar factual basis for finding that ALCOA assumed the risk of the full loss which it is experiencing.

Transatlantic Financing Corp. v. United States, supra, was one of the "Suez" cases. The carrier had contracted to transport a cargo from the United States to Iran for a specified price. The contract did not specify the route, but both parties knew the most direct route was by way of Suez. When the Canal was closed the carrier had to divert its ships around Cape Horn, adding three thousand miles to the expected ten thousand mile voyage, and adding an expense of about $44,000 to the contract price of about $306,000. Judge J. Skelly Wright, for a unanimous panel, found that "circumstances surrounding the contract indicate that the risk of the Canal's closure may be deemed to have been allocated to Transatlantic." But he found this conclusion doubtful enough to cause him to reject a direct application of the risk allocation rule. He went on:

> The surrounding circumstances do indicate, however, a willingness by Transatlantic to assume abnormal risks, and this fact should legitimately cause us to judge the impracticability of performance by an alternate route in stricter terms than we would were the contingency unforeseen. *Id.* at 318-19.

Judge Wright then held, in the passage quoted in *Publicker Industries, supra*, that there must be more than a twelve percent cost increase to constitute impracticability.

Here ALCOA's loss is more than a thousand times greater than the carrier's loss. And the circumstances surrounding the contract show a deliberate avoidance of abnormal risks....

Eastern Air Lines Inc. v. Gulf Oil Corp., supra, follows the pattern of these cases except in one detail. Gulf had contracted to furnish jet fuel to Eastern in designated cities from June 1972 until January 31, 1977. The price was tied to a specific trade journal report of posted prices for a specified type of domestic

---

[72]Quoting Transatlantic Financing Corp. v. United States, *supra*.

oil. During the contract the price of imported oil soared. Domestic oil was subjected to a complex and shifting body of regulations including a "two-tier" price control scheme regulating the price of "old oil" but not the price of "new oil." The specified trade journal reacted to the new system by publishing prices only for the regulated "old oil." Gulf sought to escape the burden of its contract and Eastern sued to compel Gulf to perform it.

The court required Gulf to perform the contract. It found that Gulf had failed to prove its defense. The "cost" figures in evidence included built in intra-company profits such that the court could not "determine how much it costs Gulf to produce a gallon of jet fuel for sale to Eastern, whether Gulf loses money or makes a profit on its sale of jet fuel to Eastern, either now or at the inception of the contract, or at any time in between." *Id.* at 440. Thus Gulf failed to prove it had suffered losses on the contract.

In the course of the decision the court declared that relief was available under § 2-615 for an *unforeseeable* failure of a pre-supposed condition. It inferred this requirement from Comment 8 to § 2-615[73] and from the Suez cases. If it were generally adopted, this requirement would reduce the occasions for excusing performance under § 2-615. Judge Wright rejected such a requirement in *Transatlantic Financing*, declaring:

> Foreseeability or even recognition of a risk does not necessarily prove its allocation.... Parties to a contract are not always able to provide for all the possibilities of which they are aware, sometimes because they cannot agree, often simply because they are too busy. Moreover, that some abnormal risk was contemplated is probative but does not necessarily establish an allocation of the risk of the contingency which actually occurs. 363 F.2d at 318.

The question is important in developing doctrine of impracticability. The Indiana cases are silent on it. The Court believes that Indiana courts would find Judge Wright's approach is more in keeping with the spirit and purpose of the Uniform Commercial Code than is the strict approach of Judge King in *Eastern Air Lines*. The Code, embodied in Title 26, Burns Ind.Stat.Ann. (1974) seeks to accommodate the law to sound commercial sense and practice. Courts must decide the point at which the community's interest in predictable contract enforcement shall yield to the fact that enforcement of a particular contract would be commercially senseless and unjust. The spirit of the Code is that such decisions cannot justly

---

[73]8. The provisions of this section are made subject to assumption of greater liability by agreement and such agreement is to be found not only in the expressed terms of the contract but in the circumstances surrounding the contracting, in trade usage and the like. Thus the exemptions of this section do not apply when the contingency in question is sufficiently foreshadowed at the time of contracting to be included among the business risks which are fairly to be regarded as part of the dickered terms, either consciously or as a matter of reasonable, commercial interpretation from the circumstances....

derive from legal abstractions. They must derive from courts sensitive to the mores, practices and habits of thought in the respectable commercial world.

If it were important to the decision of this case, the Court would hold that the foreseeability of a variation between the WPI-IC and ALCOA's costs would not preclude relief under the doctrine of impracticability. But the need for such a holding is not clear, for the Court has found that the risk of a wide variation between these values was unforeseeable in a commercial sense and was not allocated to ALCOA in the contract.

The Court holds that ALCOA is entitled to relief under the doctrine of impracticability. The cases Essex relies on and the other cases discovered by the Court are all distinguishable with respect to the gravity of harm which the aggrieved contracting party was liable to suffer. Except for *Transatlantic Financing*, they are also distinguishable with respect to the question of allocation of the risk, inferred from the circumstances known to the parties at the time of the contract and from the contract terms.

ALCOA's claim of frustration requires more discussion. ALCOA's "principal purpose" in making the contract was to earn money. This purpose has plainly been severely disappointed. The gravity of ALCOA's loss is undisputably sufficient to meet the stern standard for relief. But the question remains whether the law will grant relief for the serious frustration of this kind of purpose, *i.e.*, for the conversion of an expected profit into a serious loss. All of the new Restatement illustrations center on purposes other than making a profit. However most of them bear on some stage of a profit oriented activity....

In § 1360 Professor Corbin demonstrates that at times courts should treat loss avoidance as a principal purpose of a party. That section deals with frustration of purpose caused by inflationary depreciation of money. Corbin demonstrates that the decisions are not uniform on this subject, but he rejects as reprehensible the nominalist rule that a dollar's a dollar no matter how small. The injustice of the nominalist position was clearly recognized in the case of *Anderson v. Equitable Life Assurance Society*, 134 L.T. 557, 42 T.L.R. 302 (1926). The facts in *Anderson* were these: In 1887 an Englishman in Russia took out a twenty-premium life insurance policy with premiums and benefits payable in German marks. The policy benefit was 60,000 marks. The premiums were paid from 1887 to 1907 and were converted, as both parties understood they would be, into pounds. Their value came to £2,377. The insured died in 1922 at the height of the German hyperinflation. At that time the value of 60,000 marks was less than an English penny. The insurer argued that it owed nothing on the contract, for it could not be required to pay a fraction of a cent. Astonishingly, the court agreed. Under English law the obligation to pay in foreign currency was absolute and unqualified by variations in exchange rates. The judges noted the harshness of the result and pressed upon the company its moral obligation to make some payment which they held the law would not compel.

Happily some American cases and the law of many foreign countries take a different view of the problem. The problem of serious, sustained inflation is not unique to modern America. During the Revolution and the Civil War, America witnessed serious inflation. And several other nations have recently experienced more severe inflation than America has. When the problem has arisen, here and abroad, courts and legislatures have repeatedly acted to relieve parties from great and unexpected losses. See Mann, The Legal Aspect of Money (1938); Corbin on Contracts § 1360 and cases there cited. The exact character of the relief granted is not important here. Neither is the exact explanation of the decisions found in the cases, because even the Civil War cases antedate the evolution of the distinct doctrine of frustration. What is important is this: first, the results of those decisions would be readily explained today in terms of frustration of purpose. Corbin discusses them in his chapter on Frustration of Purpose. And second, the frustration which they involved was a frustration of the purpose to earn money or to avoid losses. Thus it appears that there is no legitimate doctrinal problem which prevents relief for frustration of this sort. There remain the customary strictures concerning risk allocation and gravity of injury. Those have been addressed above and need not be considered again here. The Court holds ALCOA is entitled to relief on its claim of frustration of purpose.

E.   This leaves the question of framing a remedy for ALCOA. Essex argues that reformation is not available. It cites many Indiana cases declaring that reformation is only available to correct writings which, through mistake, do not reflect the agreement of the parties. The declarations to that effect are clear....

But the point is immaterial here. This case does not fall within reformation as a traditional head of equity jurisprudence. It does fall within the more general rules of equitable restitution. Courts have traditionally applied three remedial rules in cases of mistake, frustration and impracticability. In some cases courts declare that no contract ever arose because there was no true agreement between the parties, *Raffles v. Wichelhaus, supra*, or because the parties were ignorant of existing facts which frustrated the purpose of one party or made performance impracticable. Restatement 2d of Contracts § 286. In some other cases the courts hold that a contract is voidable on one of the three theories. In these cases the customary remedy is rescission. In both classes of cases where one or both parties have performed under the supposed contract, the courts award appropriate restitution in the light of the benefits the parties have conferred on each other. The aim is to prevent unjust enrichment. The courts in such cases often call this remedy "reformation" in the loose sense of "modification." See III Palmer, Law of Restitution § 13.9 (1978). In *Schwaderer v. Huron-Clinton Metropolitan Authority*, 329 Mich. 258, 45 N.W.2d 279 (1951), the plaintiff contracted to clear a tract of land of trees and brush. The parties mistakenly believed the tract contained 239 acres, and on that belief the plaintiff bid $59,000 for the job. In fact the land contained 545 acres. The court "reformed" the contract to award the plaintiff the value of the extra work it had performed. Professor Palmer says this of *Schwaderer* and similar cases:

> [T]he judgment is aimed at carving out and leaving intact an exchange that approximates or is in substance the one the parties had in mind, and at the same time readjusting the contract or its consequences so as to prevent unjust enrichment.
>
> The cases ... demonstrate that many situations do not fit neatly into a general scheme of classification. There are many typical cases for which a standard remedy is appropriate; there are also cases for which the relief given should be responsible to the particular facts. III Palmer, Law of Restitution § 13.9 at 61-62.

Indiana has accepted this remedial theory. In *McMahan v. Terkhorn, supra,* the parties had purchased and sold a tract of land at a price less than their contract price in reliance on a survey which erroneously showed there was less land in the tract than the parties had believed. After the sale and before the survey error was discovered the purchaser resold part of the land, making rescission inappropriate. The court "reformed" or modified the contract to require the purchaser to pay for the extra land which had been conveyed. There, in a fully executed contract, a price adjustment was necessary to protect the fair expectation of the parties and to prevent unjust enrichment.

The same ends can be achieved under a long term executory contract by a similar remedy. To decree rescission in this case would be to grant ALCOA a windfall gain in the current aluminum market. It would at the same time deprive Essex of the assured long term aluminum supply which it obtained under the contract and of the gains it legitimately may enforce within the scope of the risk ALCOA bears under the contract. A remedy which merely shifts the windfall gains and losses is neither required nor permitted by Indiana law.

To frame an equitable remedy where frustration, impracticability or mistake prevent strict enforcement of a long term executory contract requires a careful examination of the circumstances of the contract, the purposes of the parties, and the circumstances which upset the contract. For some long-term executory contracts rescission with or without restitution will be the only sensible remedy. Where developments make performance of the contract economically senseless or purposeless, to modify the contract and to enforce it as modified would be highly inappropriate. But in cases like the present one modification and enforcement may be the only proper remedy.[74] See *Parev Products Co. v. I. Rokeach and Sons, Inc.,* 124 F.2d 147 (2nd Cir. 1941). In this case Essex sought an assured long term supply of aluminum at a price which would let it earn a profit on its finished products. ALCOA, facing ordinary market risks in 1967, sought a long term, limited risk use for its Warrick Works. A remedy modifying

---

[74]The remedial provisions of the new Restatement agree. Section 296(2) declares that a court may frame a remedy by supplying a term which is reasonable in the circumstances to avoid injustice. The same provision appears in § 300(2).

the price term of the contract in light of the circumstances which upset the price formula will better preserve the purposes and expectations of the parties than any other remedy. Such a remedy is essential to avoid injustice in this case.

During the trial the parties agreed that a modification of the price term to require Essex to pay ALCOA the ceiling price specified in the contract would be an appropriate remedy if the Court held for ALCOA. The Court understands from the parties that ALCOA will continue to suffer a substantial but smaller out-of-pocket loss at this price level. But ALCOA has not argued that the ceiling price term is subject to the same basic assumptions about risk limitation as the indexed price term. Accordingly the Court adopts the ceiling price term as part of the remedy it grants to ALCOA.

The Court must recognize, though, that before the contract expires economic changes may make this remedy excessively favorable to ALCOA. To deal with that possibility, the Court must frame a remedy which is suitable to the expectation and to the original agreement of the parties. A price fixed at the contract ceiling could redound to ALCOA's great profit and to Essex's great loss in changed circumstances. Therefore the Court adopts the following remedial scheme. For the duration of the contract the price for each pound of aluminum converted by ALCOA shall be the lesser of the current Price A or Price B indicated below.

Price A shall be the contract ceiling price computed periodically as specified in the contract.

Price B shall be the greater of the current Price B1 or Price B2. *Price B1* shall be the price specified in the contract, computed according to the terms of the contract. *Price B2* shall be that price which yields ALCOA a profit of one cent per pound of aluminum converted. This will generally yield Essex the benefit of its favorable bargain, and it will reduce ALCOA's disappointment to the limit of risk the parties expected in making the contract. The profit shall be computed using the same accounting methods used for the production of plaintiff's exhibit 431. The profit and the resulting price shall be computed once each calendar quarter, as soon after the close of the quarter as the necessary information may be assembled. When Price B2 applies, ALCOA shall bill Essex periodically, as specified in the contract at the price specified at the last quarterly price computation. Essex shall pay those bills according to the payment terms previously observed by the parties. When the next quarterly price computation is completed, that price shall be applied retroactively to the aluminum converted during the previous quarter. ALCOA shall refund any surplus payment by Essex upon the computation of the price or shall bill Essex for any additional money due.

ALCOA shall keep detailed records of the pertinent costs, indices, and computations used to calculate Prices A, B1 and B2 and shall preserve them for two years beyond the termination of the contract. ALCOA shall send Essex, in the manner and at the times specified in the contract, the price information called for in the contract, as well as a quarterly statement of Price B2 whether or not that price then applies. The statement of Price B2 need not specify the elements from which it was calculated....

CONCLUSION

This case is novel. The sums of money involved are huge. The Court has been considerably aided by the thorough and commendable work of all of the counsel who have participated in the case. There remains a need for a few concluding remarks concerning the theory of Count One of this case and its limitations.

One of the principal themes in the development of commercial contract doctrines since the 1920's has been the need for a body of law compatible with responsible commercial practices and understandings. The old spirit of the law manifest in *Paradine v. Jane, supra,* is gone. The new spirit of commercial law in Indiana and elsewhere appears in the Uniform Commercial Code, in new developments of implied covenants, and in the new Restatement.[75]

At stake in this suit is the future of a commercially important device — the long term contract. Such contracts are common in many fields of commerce. Mineral leases, building and ground leases, and long term coal sales agreements are just three examples of such contracts. If the law refused an appropriate remedy when a prudently drafted long term contract goes badly awry, the risks attending such contracts would increase. Prudent business people would avoid using this sensible business tool. Or they would needlessly suffer the delay and expense of ever more detailed and sophisticated drafting in an attempt to approximate by agreement what the law could readily furnish by general rule....

Corporate managers are fiduciaries. Law, founded on good sense, requires them to act with care in the management of businesses owned by other people. Attention to risk limitation is essential to the fiduciary duty of corporate managers. Courts must consider the fiduciary duty of management and the established practice of risk limitation in interpreting contracts and in the application of contract doctrines such as mistake, frustration and impracticability. Corporate managers should not gamble with corporate funds. Generally they do not. Courts should not presume that they do, nor should they frame rules founded on such a presumption. Instead, courts should be alert to indications that the parties to a commercial contract sought to limit their risks, and should interpret the contracts and frame remedies to protect that purpose.

---

[75]The essential unity of the new spirit of commercial contract law appears in the recurring adoption of new statutory principles from the Code into the body of the common law by the Restatement and by the courts. See J. Murray, Intention Over Terms: An Exploration of U.C.C. 2-207 and New Section 60, Restatement of Contracts, 37 Fordham Law Review 317 (1969); J. Murray, Behaviorism Under the Uniform Commercial Code, 51 Oregon Law Review 269, 272 (1972); J. Murray, Under the Spreading Analogy of Article 2 of the Uniform Commercial Code, 39 Fordham Law Review 447 (1971).

Parev Products Co. v. I. Rokeach & Sons, Inc., supra, decided by Judges Clark, Frank and Learned Hand, illustrated an aspect of this point. There Parev, the plaintiff, by contract gave the defendant the exclusive right to produce and to market its product, Nyafat, a cooking oil, for fifty years for a specified royalty. The defendant had the option to cancel the contract at any time for a fee. The plaintiff agreed not to market the product or any similar product during the contract, and the defendant agreed not to market the product or any similar product after the end of the contract. In 1939 competitors began to sell Crisco and Spry, white semi-solid cooking oils which reduced the sales of the plaintiff's oil. The defendant responded to the falling sales by introducing a new product of its own, Kea, similar to Crisco and Spry. The plaintiff sued to enjoin this further competition with its product. Since the express negative covenants did not forbid this competition, the plaintiff argued that the court should imply a negative covenant to forbid it.

The court rejected the defendant's argument that only covenants intended by the parties may be implied. The court noted the then traditional "reluctance of courts to admit that they were to a considerable extent 'remaking' a contract in situations where it seemed necessary and appropriate to do so." 124 F.2d at 149. The court acknowledged that a discernible intent of the parties should control the case, but it found no sufficient indication of intent respecting this problem:

> Of course, where intent though obscure, is nevertheless discernible, it must be followed; but a certain sophistication must be recognized — if we are to approach the matter frankly — where we are dealing with changed circumstances, fifteen years later, with respect to a contract which does not touch this exact point and which has at most only points of departure for more or less pressing analogies. *Id.*

Thus the question of whether to imply some sort of covenant to protect the plaintiff did not rest on the parties' intent. It rested on the status, expectations and needs of the parties to preserve the mutual benefit of the long term contract under changed circumstances....

The court protected the "status" of both parties by implying a term requiring the defendant to compensate the plaintiff for royalties lost due to competition with the defendant's new product.

The court gave close attention to the legitimate business aims of the parties, to their purpose of avoiding the risks of great losses, and to the need to frame a remedy to preserve the essence of the agreement. To that extent the decision exemplifies the new spirit of contract law.

This attitude toward contract law and toward the work of the courts will disturb some people even at this late date. It strains against half-remembered truths and remembered half-truths from the venerated first year course in Contract Law. The core of the trouble lies in the hoary maxim that the courts will not make a contract for the parties. The maxim requires three replies. First, courts today can indeed make contracts for the parties. Given certain minimal indicators of an intent to contract, the courts are today directed to impose on the parties the necessary specific provisions to complete the process. See U.C.C. §§ 2-204, 2-207, 2-208; U.L.T.A. §§ 2-202-2-204. Second, a distinction has long been noted between judicial imposition of initial terms and judicial interpretations and implications of terms to resolve disputes concerning contracts the parties have made for themselves. The maxim bears less weight when it is applied to dispute resolution than it does when it is applied to questions of contract formation. This case is plainly one of dispute resolution. Third, the maxim rests on two sensible notions: (1) Liability under the law of contract rests on assent, not imposition. (2) Judges are seldom able business men; they seldom have the information, ability, or time to do a good job of contracting for the parties. Neither of these notions applies here. The parties have made their own contract. The Court's role here is limited to framing a remedy for a problem they did not foresee and provide for. And while the Court willingly concedes that the managements of ALCOA and Essex are better able to conduct their business than is the Court, in this dispute the court has information from hindsight far superior to that which the parties had when they made their contract. The parties may both be better served by an informed judicial decision based on the known circumstances than by a decision wrenched from words of the contract which were not chosen with a prevision of today's circumstances. The Court gladly concedes that the parties might today evolve a better working arrangement by negotiation than the Court can impose. But they have not done so, and a rule that the Court may not act would have the perverse effect of discouraging the parties from resolving this dispute or future disputes on their own. Only a rule which permits judicial action of the kind the Court has taken in this case will provide a desirable practical incentive for businessmen to negotiate their own resolution to problems which arise in the life of long term contracts.[76]

Finally, the Court notes that this case presents a problem of the appropriate legal response to problems of inflation. There are many long term contracts extant where inflation has upset the basic equivalence of the agreement. Courts will increasingly have to attend to problems like the present one....

The limitation of judicial relief to cases where the parties evidence a desire to limit their risks, where one party suffers severe out of pocket losses not adequately foreseen and provided for by the parties seems adequate to prevent a general disruption of commercial life by inflation. This limitation also seems generally compatible with the fair needs and understanding of responsible businessmen. Little more can be asked of the courts in the development of the law.

---

[76]The Court is aware of the practical incentive to negotiation which lies in the delay, expense and uncertainty of litigation. This case shows that at times these burdens are insufficient to prompt settlements.

The foregoing shall constitute findings of fact and conclusions of law as required by Federal Rule of Civil Procedure 52(a). An appropriate Order will issue.

NOTES AND QUESTIONS

1. *Judge Teitelbaum's background*: Judge Teitelbaum graduated from the University of Pittsburgh Law School in 1940. He was an FBI Special Agent and United States Attorney for the Western District of Pennsylvania. When he wrote his opinion in the *ALCOA* case, he was an Adjunct Professor at the Duquesne University Law School in Pittsburgh and a member of the American Law Institute. Perhaps he was more ready than many federal judges to consider the innovations of the Restatement (Second) of Contracts.

2. *Essex brief on appeal to the Third Circuit*: The case was appealed to the United States Court of Appeals for the Third Circuit. Lawyers for Essex Group argued,

> ... the decision endangers the future of long term contracts. It does this by replacing the escalated fixed price formula in a long term contract involving in excess of $300,000,000 with a new formula drafted by the court and never discussed or intended by the parties, essentially converting the contract into a cost plus agreement....
>
> ... [Essex] contends that the trial court's decision is without precedent in American jurisprudence. It has charted a course which, unless reversed, will henceforth inextricably embroil courts in the constant supervision and administration of commercial contracts. For reasons hereinafter set forth, both the applicable law and the largely undisputed facts in this case require that the trial court's judgment be reversed and that judgment be entered for ... Essex Group, Inc.

Essex charged that the escalated fixed price formula used in the contract had been developed by Alcoa's Department of Economic Analysis and Planning. According to Essex, Alcoa used the formula because it believed that its costs at the Warrick, Indiana plant were under control and the wholesale price index would increase faster than Alcoa's actual costs of aluminum production. Thus, the formula selected provided an opportunity to increase profits in a way a cost plus contract could not. During the period from 1960 when the plant opened to 1967 when the contract with the Essex Group was signed, while the wholesale price index was increasing, the actual cost of producing aluminum at the Warrick facility had declined dramatically. Moreover, Alcoa did not want to use an escalator clause based on actual costs because then it would have to reveal its costs to Essex (both a customer and a competitor) and questions of cost accounting could lead to disputes.

First, consider the assertions Essex Group's lawyers made about the trial court's opinion. Do they describe fairly Judge Teitelbaum's opinion? Second, consider the brief as an exercise in rhetoric. Note the use of the term "rewrite" and the phrase "without precedent." The Restatement (Second) of Contracts provisions are ignored here. Why? How many strands of classic contract ideology can you identify? Notice, too, the phrase "embroil courts in the constant supervision and administration of commercial contracts" with its image of burdening the judiciary.

3. *Alcoa's brief on appeal to the Third Circuit*: Alcoa's lawyers, supporting Judge Teitelbaum's opinion, responded as follows:

> First, Alcoa proved a sufficient underlying agreement for reformation under Indiana law....
>
> Second, the fact situation here fits exactly with the Restatement 2d of Contracts definition of mutual mistake of fact (§ 294) for which the remedy of reformation (§§ 297 & 300) is provided. Professor Farnsworth, the Reporter of the Restatement 2d of Contracts, presented an oral brief at the trial, which brief is included in the transcript ... Professor Farnsworth testified:
>
>> In my opinion, it is entirely possible that Alcoa could show at the trial that both parties at the time of contracting made a mistake as to the fact that the wholesale price index was then suitable for an escalation clause in an energy-intensive contract. An analogy by way of example would be to a mistake of two parties to a contract using specified equipment that the equipment was suitable to the task.
>
> Alcoa proved, and the trial court found, the facts to be as Professor Farnsworth suggested the evidence might show.
>
> If there is any difference between the provisions in the Restatement 2d of Contracts on mutual mistake of fact and the Indiana cases cited (Essex relies on the 1896 *Citizens National Bank* case), then certainly one would expect the Supreme Court of Indiana now to follow the Restatement as it has repeatedly done.
>
> Third, the trial court cited Restatement 2d of Contracts, § 300(2)[77] which allows a court to equitably adjust or supply a term that is reasonable in the circumstances to avoid injustice. As Professor Farnsworth stated in his oral brief, the Restatement has been liberalized to permit the formulation of a remedy to do justice and prevent an unconscionable result....

---

[77]This is now § 158 in the final version of the Restatement, and it is reprinted on page 118 of these materials.

Restatement 2d of Contracts § 300(2) which is entitled "RELIEF INCLUDING RESTITUTION; SUPPLYING A TERM" states at page 306 of Tentative Draft No. 14:

> In any case governed by the rules stated in this Chapter, if those rules together with the rules stated in prospective Chapter 16 will not avoid injustice, *the court may grant relief on such terms as justice requires* including protection of the parties' reliance interests. (Emphasis added).

Thus, Restatement 2d of Contracts § 300(2) constitutes an alternative theory of law for the trial court's remedy, even if reformation were somehow ruled inappropriate.

Alcoa's lawyers also responded to Essex Group's charge concerning the reasons the formula was used by saying: "the WPI was selected to meet Essex's desire for an objective and easily administered index to reflect Alcoa's Warrick non-labor costs, not to increase Alcoa's profits, and the trial court observing the testimony found it to be the fact."

Presumably, the *Alcoa* case was being tried under the law of Indiana as applied by federal courts. Whatever the merits of Judge Teitelbaum's opinion, did the Alcoa lawyers convince you that Indiana would adopt the new Restatement (Second) of Contracts approach? How would you argue this point for Alcoa or for Essex Group? As we have said several times in these materials, federal judges often develop state law dealing with contracts and statutes related to contracts problems. Federal judges must divine what a state court would do if it faced the problem. Yet diversity of citizenship jurisdiction keeps state courts from getting an opportunity to offer many modern clues.

4. *The outcome of the case*: The parties settled the case after oral argument to the United States Court of Appeals for the Third Circuit. Judge Arlin M. Adams, a member of the Third Circuit Court of Appeals, requested the parties to attend a conciliation session between the time briefs were filed and oral argument was scheduled, a relatively unusual procedure.

Following oral argument Alcoa indicated an interest in settling the case. The parties conferred at length, with Alcoa giving ground in its demands. It appears that the case was settled on the basis that the original contract would continue in effect until December 31, 1981; that during the balance of the original time of the contract, Alcoa would sell at a more favorable price; and that Alcoa would extend the time of the contract for a period of five years on a favorable price basis, albeit not as favorable as during the contract period.

Judge Adams settlement conference might not have promoted a settlement. Something might have happened during oral argument to cause Alcoa to re-evaluate its position, or it might have been waiting for what it thought was the right moment to strike a deal. There had been settlement discussions from time to time over a period of several years.

Why didn't the parties settle earlier and save all the investment in lawyering and judicial time? Did Judge Teitelbaum's opinion, work on the briefs, and the process before the Third Circuit serve some purpose?

5. *Scholarly criticism of the case*: The case provoked contracts scholars into print. The late *Professor John Dawson* was highly critical of the ALCOA decision. He said that the *Alcoa* approach "is the treatment that is now normally given frustrated contracts [in West Germany], a treatment described with the hope that our own courts can be dissuaded from a course so disastrous for the coherence and rationality of our law of contract."[78]

Professor Sheldon Halpern[79] notes that courts have not followed the ALCOA decision. He argues that Judge Teitelbaum's decision did not rest on an accepted theory of contract law. While the court rejected the often fictional search for the parties' intentions, all it could point to was the need to relieve hardship. Judge Teitelbaum went too far, too soon and with too little.

Judge, and formerly Professor, Richard Posner offered the following comments in *Northern Indiana Public Service Co. v. Carbon County Coal Co.*:[80]

> Since impossibility and related doctrines are devices for shifting risk in accordance with the parties' presumed intentions, which are to minimize the costs of contract performance, one of which is the disutility created by risk, they have no place when the contract explicitly assigns a particular risk to one party or the other.... *[A] fixed-price contract is an explicit assignment of the risk of market price increases to the seller and the risk of market price decreases to the buyer*, and the assignment of the latter risk to the buyer is even clearer where, as in this case, the contract places a floor under price but allows for escalation. If, as is also the case here, the buyer forecasts the market incorrectly and therefore finds himself locked into a disadvantageous contract, he has only himself to blame and so cannot shift the risk back to the seller by invoking impossibility or related doctrines. [Emphasis added].

6. *Scholarly defense of adjustment*: Several other scholars have defended judicial adjustment of contracts. For example, *Professor Leon Trakman* argues "[t]he need for a functional category of remedial adjustments, however, becomes more pressing when an all-or-nothing principle of law governs nonperformance and produces neither fairness nor economic efficiency."[81]

---

[78]See Dawson, Judicial Revision of Frustrated Contracts: Germany, 63 Boston University Law Review 1039 (1983); Dawson, Judicial Revision of Frustrated Contracts: The United States, 64 Boston University Law Review 1 (1984).

[79]Applicability of the Doctrine of Commercial Impracticability: Searching for "The Wisdom of Solomon," 135 University of Pennsylvania Law Review 1123 (1987).

[80]799 F.2d 265, 278 (7th Cir. 1986).

[81]Trakman, Winner Take Some: Loss Sharing and Commercial Impracticability, 69 Minnesota Law Review 471 (1985).

Professor Robert A. Hillman argues that a supplier is entitled to adjustment of a contractual obligation in at least some situations.[82] Hillman says the objective theory and interpretation seeking the reasonable expectations of the parties tell us whether there is a duty to adjust.[83] He points out that some contracts expressly provide for adjustment when the cost of performance is grossly inequitable. Such express provisions are common in some industries. Moreover, even if a supply contract contains no express agreement to adjust, the situation when the parties made the deal may show that they intended adjustments in light of changed circumstances. That they say nothing about adjustments in their written contract does not necessarily establish anything. Drafting a clause for what they see as unclear risks isn't worth the effort. Trade custom or the course of dealing or performance may establish a duty to adjust. Indeed, a party's duty of good faith may create an obligation to adjust a contract in light of changed circumstances.

Still, Professor Hillman recognizes that not every contract raises a duty to adjust if something goes awry. Large one-time deals involving standardized commodities usually involve assumption of the risk of market shifts. The parties may see adjustment as a matter of comity rather than legal obligation. Buyer may adjust seller's obligation as a favor which seller will return in the future. The parties may bargain about rising prices and shortages, and this suggests that the written contract reflects their risk assumption. However, even when this is true, they may not intend their written provision to govern an extreme shift in the market. Hillman recognizes that one of the most difficult questions is how much disruption triggers the duty to adjust.

Hillman also argues that parties may leave a gap in their agreement despite the appearance of settling their obligations in a formal writing. The evidence may not establish a duty to make adjustments, but a court may conclude that reasonable parties would not have expected the supplier to act as insurer. Courts could fill this gap in their agreement by finding a duty to adjust.

Are there any standards or must courts fly blind if they find a duty to adjust? Hillman argues there are standards. Courts may find that parties did not intend to allow a supplier to raise prices without a corresponding increase in its actual costs. They may find that parties did not intend buyers to be able to take advantage of a drastic market shift. Often they do not intend to allow buyers to raise their prices to third parties while insisting on seller's performance at a preinflationary price. Furthermore, courts can look to similar supply contracts made or adjusted under the changed conditions that provoked the problem. They can consider settlement offers. They can find large windfalls to be unjust enrichment. They can hold the supplier responsible to deliver at the old price

---

[82]Hillman, Court Adjustment of Long-Term Contracts: An Analysis Under Modern Contract Law, 1987 Duke Law Journal 1.

[83]Contrast Professor Hillman's view with that of Judge Posner quoted above. Recall, too, the debates about the parol evidence rule. Do we read the words on paper or do we look at these words in full context seeking the parties' real deal?

only long enough to allow a buyer to cover its reliance losses based on this old price.

Professor Richard Speidel attempts to rationalize the approach, if not the result, of the court in the ALCOA case.

> [C]an a case be made for imposing a duty on the advantaged party to accept a "fair and equitable" adjustment proposal made by the disadvantaged party? If so, what remedies are appropriate? Keeping the *ALCOA* facts in mind, a tentative case can be made that does not convert the law of contracts into a pervasive duty to be altruistic.
>
> First, the disadvantaged party must propose a modification that would be enforceable if accepted by the advantaged party. Under the Restatement (Second), [§ 89] this occurs if the disrupted contract is not "fully performed on either side" and if the modification is "fair and equitable in view of circumstances not anticipated by the parties when the contract was made." The changed circumstances are similar to but less than those required to discharge a contract for impracticability. This first requirement both neutralizes any opportunism by the disadvantaged party, *e.g.*, duress, and affirms that agreed adjustments are preferred — that contract is available to resolve the dilemma and has been employed by the disadvantaged party.
>
> Second, it must be clear that the disadvantaged party did not assume the risk of the unanticipated event by agreement, or under the test stated in the U.C.C. in § 2-615(a), or otherwise. If the disadvantaged party did assume the risk, then the advantaged party has no duty to accept any proposed modification. The risk assumption question is complicated, and the answer will probably not be clear at the time that the adjustment is proposed. Why should the advantaged party be held to reject at his peril? Because it is in this precise situation — where there are substantial unbargained-for gains and losses caused by unanticipated events — that a case for the duty to rescue can be made. In this setting where the risk of changed circumstances has not been allocated to either party, a refusal to adjust by the advantaged party leaves all of the loss on the disadvantaged party and permits the advantaged party to salt away all of the gains. Short of discharging the contract and leaving the parties to restitution, a duty to adjust is necessary to avoid opportunism.
>
> Thus, imposing the duty here is consistent with emerging notions of good faith performance and *ALCOA's* second peg in the "new" spirit, loss avoidance. More importantly, it is an imposition with little damage to the requirement of consent in contract law....
>
> Last, this conclusion is bolstered by what might be the imperatives of an emerging theory of relational contract law. In *ALCOA*, the parties, at the time of contracting, were unable adequately to deal with certain changed circumstances over the duration of a seventeen-year contract. Yet preserving the contract was important to the parties and to third parties dependent upon

its performance but not represented in the litigation. Ian Macneil has argued that in situations such as this there are relational norms that the contract should be preserved and conflict harmonized by adjustment. These norms put a high premium upon developing mechanisms for adjustment over time and good faith efforts to adjust in the light of change. Thus, if in an ALCOA-type case, the court concludes that the disadvantaged party is entitled to "some relief" but not discharge, and the advantaged party has refused to accept a reasonable adjustment in light of risks that the disadvantaged party did not assume, relational theory also supports a court imposed adjustment to preserve the contract, to adjust the price and to avoid the twin devils of un-bargained for hardship and unjust enrichment.[84]

7. *The relational exchange approach to contracts*: The economist *Victor Goldberg* has written about price adjustment in long-term contracts.[85] He notes that businesspeople often use "gross inequity" clauses in some long-term contracts. Under these clauses, parties leave to an arbitrator or judge the decision to adjust the contract or discharge the parties when performance would cause a gross inequity. Absent such clauses, courts will have to decide whether ever to grant any relief, what changes are sufficient to justify judicial action, and what relief they should grant.

Goldberg considers when parties might want a third party to make adjustments or award discharges. He says that the case for intervention is stronger "when the costs of a price dispute are high and the costs of settlement would be reduced by giving the disadvantaged party the right to call upon the court to revise the contract." There might be few such cases.

Goldberg points out that businesses have reason to use some form of price adjustment mechanism in their contracts. "Firms do not generally enter into multi-year contracts because of their concern for the future course of prices. Rather, they enter into the agreements to achieve the benefits of cooperation." Price adjustment clauses often are used when the contract calls for a complex product constantly redefined over the life of the contract. Adjustment also discourages the parties from wasting assets. Without adjustment, the below-market price of an input might cause a buyer to use too much of it. In addition, an adjustment clause reduces the likelihood that a party who had been a big loser on a contractual "bet" will try to recapture losses by minimal performance, retaliate by failing to cooperate, make threats to breach, or search for arguments to minimize the nature of the obligation.

---

[84]Speidel, The New Spirit of Contract, 2 Journal of Law and Commerce 193, 206-208 (1982); Speidel, Court-Imposed Price Adjustments Under Long-Term Supply Contracts, originally published at 76 Northwestern University Law Review 369 (1981).

[85]Goldberg, Price Adjustment in Long-Term Contracts, 1985 Wisconsin Law Review 527. Copyright © The University of Wisconsin.

Those who drafted the contract in *Alcoa v. Essex* used a price adjustment mechanism, but it didn't work. What kind of mistake was this, and should it warrant relief? Lawyers often find it hard to fashion an effective acceptable price adjustment mechanism. Price indices are the easiest to use, but often in a long-term contract there is no unique external market price to use.

Goldberg notes that in the *Alcoa* case the failure of the price index to measure the change in fuel prices accounted for only about ten to twelve cents of the difference between the contract price and the market price for aluminum in 1979. The balance of the difference may have reflected demand induced, rather than cost driven, market price increases. The contract did not track changing demand conditions and the demand for aluminum was soaring in the late 1970s. Moreover, the contract was not designed to adjust to large changes in the overall price level. "Sixty percent of the initial contract price (the demand charge plus the fixed 'profit') was unadjusted for the life of the contract." Nonetheless, Goldberg says it is a close question whether Alcoa should have bargained to index the remaining 60% of costs. He says that parties do not necessarily confront the same external price, and this makes it hard to use a price index based on aluminum prices. It is as if they are dealing in two different, imperfectly connected, markets.

> Alcoa's opportunity cost is the net price it could receive by using the Warrick capacity to produce ingot for export to other customers. Essex's opportunity cost is the price of delivered aluminum ingot. There is no a priori reason to believe that these will be close to each other. However, for an index to work it is not necessary that the prices be close, only that they move together over time. Whether these two opportunity costs (and the market price for aluminum ingot) move together over time is an empirical question which I intend to explore in a later paper.[86]

If we assume that the parties would have had difficulty finding an acceptable price adjustment mechanism, was the burden on Alcoa great enough to makes its performance impracticable? Goldberg argues, that in the *Alcoa* case, the court assumed something about future costs and prices and concluded that Alcoa stood to lose about $75 million.

> What does Alcoa lose if it must fulfill the contract? It loses the chance to sell aluminum to someone else. That is the true measure of the loss, and in this case it is considerably greater than the figure cited by the judge. In the year the suit was brought the loss was over thirty cents per pound, over $20 million.

---

[86]*Id.* at 540.

However, Goldberg says that we cannot define a magic number or percentage to allow us to judge whether relief should be granted. Even a very large difference between the market and contract prices for a standardized commodity might have little adverse effect on the expected value of the contract. On the other hand, at times a small difference might generate considerable joint costs and make revision valuable. However, if courts make relief too easy to get, this will generate additional joint costs as it will affect performance and demands for renegotiations. Part of the problem is that when the opportunity costs of buyer and seller differ, it is not clear how an arbitrator should set a new price.

Professor Thomas Palay commented on Goldberg's article.[87] Palay praised Goldberg's approach to the problem, but Palay cautioned that we cannot focus on the written document to tell us whether the parties in a long-term contract could benefit from or expect price adjustments. "Parties who have, or anticipate, strong relational ties with their contracting opposites are not particularly worried about initial terms of agreement."

Palay then discusses Oliver Williamson's approach to transactional governance structures. Williamson argues that three variables determine structural characteristics: (1) the degree to which uncertainty is present; (2) the frequency of exchange, and (3) the extent to which exchanges are supported by idiosyncratic capital that cannot be devoted elsewhere easily.

Williamson's third variable is particularly important. Those in idiosyncratic exchanges can protect themselves by demanding a price that compensates them for marginal costs and includes an insurance component covering opportunistic behavior. They also can gain credible commitments not to act opportunistically. This is done by the mutual exchange of hostages — investments of capital assets that will be destroyed if the contract falls apart.

Palay looks at the problems in *Alcoa v. Essex*:

> Alcoa's "hostage" was that portion of the Warwick capacity that was added for, or dedicated to, Essex. Alcoa might have believed that Essex had posted a similar hostage when it placed its fabricating facility near the Warwick smelter. The value of the fabricating facility, built specifically to receive aluminum from the Warwick plant, would diminish if the contractual relation failed. Alternatively, if Essex helped finance Alcoa's dedicated capacity, the arrangement could have led Alcoa to believe that Essex became tied to the aluminum manufacturer. After all, Essex could have lost its investment in Warwick if the contract failed.
>
> If these were the hostages Essex posted, imagining why they proved inadequate to force renegotiation of the contract is easy. Essex could receive aluminum from plenty of other sources if Alcoa were to breach, but any

---

[87]Palay, A Contract Does Not a Contract Make, 1985 Wisconsin Law Review 561. Copyright © The University of Wisconsin.

other source would entail additional transportation costs. This meant that as a hostage the plant was only worth the difference between its use in fabricating Warwick Aluminum and its use in fabricating aluminum that had to be transported from elsewhere. That is, as a hostage Essex's plant ranked right up there with giving the wicked king your lazy, shiftless third cousin. Using any of the financing aspects of the arrangement as a hostage would be similarly inadequate. Alcoa's pockets were simply too deep. Essex would know that Alcoa was never really in danger of defaulting on the "loan."

Thus, under this scenario, Alcoa's problem was not so much a "mistake" concerning the price term, but rather a mistake about the importance that Essex would place on the preservation of the relationship. Admittedly, many of my observations are little more than speculation — but they are reasonable hypotheses that require the researcher to look beyond the formal documents for confirmation.[88]

Assume Palay's speculation proved to be right. What significance would it have for our appraisal of Judge Teitelbaum's opinion? Would such a mistake fit into traditional notions of mistake or impossibility? Does it suggest what we should do?

8. *One economist offers a presumption as to the real deal*: Victor Goldberg[89] argues:

> Regardless of how the doctrine is labelled, courts, when considering a plea to excuse performance, should be constrained by the fundamental question: what would the parties have chosen? I will argue that, as a general rule, parties would not agree to excuse performance because of changed market conditions (neither supply nor demand shocks). The fact that market prices have doubled or tripled would be irrelevant. Parties are more likely to excuse performance if the supervening events adversely effect the costs of performing this particular contract for reasons that are essentially unrelated to overall market conditions....
>
> The crucial point is this. If the occurrence of a *force majeure* condition is not correlated with market conditions, the expected change in market price is zero, and therefore, the benefits anticipated at the contract formation stage from holding the promisor liable are likely to be low. However, if the seller refuses to perform because events subsequent to the formation of the contract have shown that the contract price is too low, the buyer does suffer. If the seller could perform, but would prefer not to, we can reasonably infer that the reason is that the contract price is too low; the seller could do better

---

[88]*Id.* at 564.

[89]Goldberg, Impossibility and Related Excuses, 144 Journal of Institutional and Theoretical Economics 100-116 (1988).

selling elsewhere. The changed conditions affect the market for the good or service involved. There is a widespread drought, the Suez Canal closes, etc. Discharging the contract in this instance carries a greater cost. If a seller could be excused simply because the contract price was below the market price, the substantial benefits from entering into a contract in a timely manner are sacrificed. While this sacrifice might be acceptable in some cases, it is clear that the costs of excusing a seller's performance when the contract price is too low are greater than excusing its performance in the event of a fire or other act of God.

Goldberg does note: "This is not to say that parties would never adjust the contract price. Price concessions in the face of changed market conditions are commonplace. But the grantor of the concession often expects a quid pro quo, either express (*e.g.*, an increase in the term of the contract) or implied (*e.g.*, enhanced good will). The grantor, that is, maintains the right to make (or not make) price concessions."[90]

9. *A Note on law and economics notes:* The two previous notes both rely on the commentary of an economist, and draw to some extent on the vocabulary of economics. This can be frustrating for those with little or no training in economics. A great deal of legal scholarship in the last 15 or 20 years has drawn on economic analysis. It is often controversial. Many reject the analysis and assert that it is not to be trusted because it contains concealed substantive or ideological biases. Others reject it by suggesting that it is not to be trusted because it is incomplete, but is presented as if it were not. Either or both of these critiques may be right (or wrong). But it is *not*, it seems to the authors, appropriate to reject the analysis because we are unable to understand it — though that is a very human tendency. Such a rejection would be akin to an English speaker asserting that a poem, or novel, is no good because it wasn't written in English. We offer this note to acknowledge the discomfort which the law and economics notes might cause some. As non-economists ourselves, we often share your discomfort. But we do need to be aware of, and take seriously, the accounts of our subject matter which are presented to us, and which often seem to illuminate the issue, even if they are difficult and make us uncomfortable. To the extent that there are those among this book's readers who would offer suggestions about improving its clarity, we welcome such comments.

10. *The role of jurists in the American system*: Professor Farnsworth, the Reporter for Restatement (Second) of Contracts, gave Judge Teitelbaum an oral brief that favored ALCOA. Interestingly, Professor Dawson tells us in his article on the United States' approach to judicial revision of frustrated contracts, "counsel for Essex ... had requested me to comment on the briefs that were being prepared for the appeal by Essex. I had thus had considerably earlier an

---

[90]*Id.* at n.3.

opportunity to form a highly adverse opinion of the trial court's decision." (note 71). Dawson calls the *Alcoa* opinion a "bizarre solution." Had the appeal gone forward, the Third Circuit might have had to choose between the views of Farnsworth and the Restatement (Second) and Dawson. The late Professor Dawson was a professor emeritus at the Harvard Law School, and a recognized expert in contracts, comparative law and legal history. Thus, each side could have pointed to a distinguished academic in its corner.

In what sense, if at all, are Professors Farnsworth, Dawson, Hillman, Halpern, Speidel, Trakman or the authors of the *Contracts: Law in Action* "experts" on what contract law ought to be? Should we fashion some mechanism so courts could call on contracts professors for assistance in major cases? Do you see any problem with Professor Farnsworth giving an "oral brief" to the court but being sponsored by ALCOA or Professor Dawson consulting with the Essex Group lawyers on their briefs in the case?

11. *Another judge, another case, another approach:* In 1981 Federal District Court Judge Merhige wrote an opinion on the question of liability in the case of *Florida Power and Light Company v. Westinghouse Electric.*[91] The dispute had arisen as a result of a contract entered into in 1966 in which Florida Power and Light had purchased two nuclear power plants from Westinghouse. As part of the agreement, Westinghouse had promised to remove and dispose of the spent nuclear fuel. The disposal of the fuel, which it appears Westinghouse had initially assumed would be dealt with as the nuclear power industry flourished, and as part of a comprehensive federal plan to reprocess, and/or dispose of spent fuel, became a major problem. There was no viable reprocessing option, and storage of spent fuel was a major problem. Westinghouse sought relief from its promises, on grounds substantially like those asserted in the *Alcoa* case. In an opinion which rejected many of Westinghouse's claims, and which represented a more cautious and traditional approach to the mistake/impossibility issue, Judge Merhige closed by leaving open the question of what remedy would be granted.

The closing paragraphs of the opinion suggest another judicial approach to litigating cases like Westinghouse (and Alcoa).

> Therefore, the parties will be granted ninety (90) days within which to attempt to reach agreement as to the form of the decree to be entered in this matter. Should they wish additional time, the Court may be willing to grant it, upon a showing that additional time would be productive. In the interim, the Court will meet and confer with counsel, in an effort to assist them in reaching agreement, and for the purpose of more fully apprising the parties as to the further information which the Court deems necessary to draft an appropriate decree in the event that the parties fail to reach an agreement. At such a meeting the parties should be prepared to render assistance in the

---

[91] 517 F. Supp. 440 (E.D. Va. 1981)

selection of an expert for the purpose of assisting the Court, should the court conclude that such assistance is necessary, in ascertaining the various alternatives, if any, leading to the removal and storage of the spent fuel.

In view of the fact that the interests of both parties and the public would best be served by an expeditious and final resolution of this matter, both parties are urged to use the initial time period in an intensive attempt to reach agreement, rather than in preparing to further litigate the issue of remedy.

This effort to persuade the parties to negotiate a settlement, and to use the power of the bench to do so, was typical of Judge Merhige's approach to major litigation, and raises important questions with respect to contracts-disputing which, though important, have little to do with judicial doctrine.

In the early 1970s, Judge Merhige ordered the Richmond, Virginia schools integrated. In the mid-1980s, he heard about 350 of the Dalkon Shield contraceptive device claims against A. H. Robins Co. He helped about 140 of these cases settle out of court. He also was in charge of most of the Westinghouse uranium litigation.

Emily Couric tells us more about Judge Merhige in the National Law Journal:[92]

U.S. District Judge Robert R. Merhige, Jr. of the Eastern District of Virginia tells a story: He privately brought together the two parties in a case before him. The case involved millions of dollars, and the trial, he predicted, would last at least six to eight weeks.

"I sat the two of them down on a Sunday night in my [home's] sun-room," the judge recounts. "I pointed out to them the expense of the trial and the fact that it was a business decision they could make better than six people who know nothing about business."

Then Judge Merhige left the room, and closed the door.

"In 45 minutes they came out," he continues. "I was in my library. They thanked me for the effort. One said, 'We've tried, judge, but it's impossible.'

"For you to tell me it's impossible really frightens me," Judge Merhige recalls answering, "because I didn't think anything was impossible for American businessmen. I didn't think people got to be executive vice presidents by having 'impossible' in their vocabulary."

One of the executives responded, "I guess that's not the right word. It's not impossible."

"Why then, why don't you try again?" suggested Judge Merhige.

The two men looked at each other, and retreated to the sun-room a second time.

---

[92]Copyright 1986. The National Law Journal, August 4, 1986, at 1. Reprinted with Permission.

Fifteen minutes later they had reached a settlement....

"Not infrequently, I will insist that the lawyers [in a case] bring their principals here because I want to satisfy myself that both principals recognize what [strong arguments] the other has," says the judge. "Even a pancake has two sides."...

Not everyone agrees that such an activist role in settling cases is appropriate for a judge....

"Judges can't settle cases," says Judge Merhige. "I'm not worried about someone saying, 'He forced us to settle.' Good lawyers can't be forced to do anything."

Despite Judge Merhige's efforts, the parties were unable to settle the case. The docket discloses that the parties filed joint reports of their efforts to resolve the dispute throughout 1981 and 1982. On October 10, 1983, there was a trial on the issue of damages that lasted almost six hours.

In *Florida Power and Light Co. v. Westinghouse Electric Co.*,[93] Judge Merhige reported "[t]he parties made a good faith effort to negotiate the remedy but failed." However, several things happened while the negotiations took place. The parties discovered that it was possible to "re-rack" the Turkey Point spent fuel storage pits a second time. This would provide sufficient on-site storage for all the spent fuel that the reactors will discharge over their useful life. As a result, the reactors will not have to shut down. FP & L will not have to spend a half-million dollars a day on substitute power. Westinghouse agreed to do the second re-racking at Turkey Point at no cost to FP & L.

Furthermore, the United States Government passed the Nuclear Waste Policy Act of 1982. The statute provides that the Department of Energy and the owners and generators of spent fuel are to enter into contracts. DOE takes title to the spent fuel and assumes full responsibility for it. The statute sets a time-table for the government to build a permanent storage facility. However, the site to receive spent fuel will not open until 1998 at the earliest. The Act encourages interim storage at the reactor sites through the use of techniques such as re-racking. FP & L entered a contract with the DOE and agreed to pay a fee of $70 million.

FP & L argued that Westinghouse should pay the $70 million fee, roughly $13 million for the first re-racking, and roughly $12 million for the second re-racking. Judge Merhige found that the United States Government had not acted in a timely fashion in honoring its implied commitment regarding spent fuel. This was a contingency, the non-occurrence of which was a basic assumption of the contract. It made performance of Westinghouse's implicit obligation to perform within a reasonable time impracticable under U.C.C. § 2-615. "Both Florida and Westinghouse were aware that reprocessing might not be available, but neither

---

[93]597 F.Supp. 1456 (E.D.Va. 1984).

of them anticipated that no alternative means of removal would be available until 1998 or after."

Judge Merhige said that an equitable allocation of the interim storage costs was in order. "In making the allocation, the Court must of necessity utilize its own sense of fairness." He said that there was "no reason to suspect that the costs of the permanent federal repository have been increased by the delays." As a result, he concluded that the $70 million DOE disposal fee should be borne entirely by Westinghouse. He then turned to the other costs caused by the delays. Florida Power & Light rate payers had benefited enormously from the use of nuclear power during the era of high oil prices. However, Westinghouse should not be rewarded for its lack of diligence during the early 1970s. Thus, Judge Merhige ordered the costs divided. "Without attempting mathematical precision, the allocation will divide the costs roughly as if Westinghouse were absorbing the costs of the first re-racking and Florida absorbing the costs of the second." He refused to award FP & L compensation for increased property taxes and insurance premiums. He concluded,

> The sums aforementioned are not intended to be precise. The Court is satisfied that the parties, who have worked so diligently toward settling their differences, will not be unable to draft an appropriate decree in accord with the Court's view as expressed herein.

The parties appealed Judge Merhige's decisions. The United States Court of Appeals for the Fourth Circuit rejected much of Judge Merhige's reasoning and reached a result more favorable to Westinghouse than his.

First, the Fourth Circuit found that the situation was a classic case of impossibility. Both parties had assumed that the spent fuel would be reprocessed, and both had assumed that either commercial reprocessing would be available or the government would provide this service. Westinghouse had not assumed the risk that neither reprocessing nor storage would be available. Moreover, there was no evidence that Westinghouse could have mitigated any of the losses under the contract as no reprocessing facilities ever were available after Florida Power & Light exercised its option to have Westinghouse remove the spent fuel.

Second, the court said that it must consider the equities of the parties after Westinghouse established that performance was impracticable. The parties had not challenged on appeal the District Court's allocation of the costs of reracking the storage facilities (though the Fourth circuit suggested it would have freed Westinghouse from its share, if Westinghouse had appealed this issue). The Court of Appeals concluded that the ratepayers had enjoyed tremendous benefits (about $10 billion) because of the much lower costs of nuclear power. Thus, it would be fair to charge them with the entire cost of storing the spent fuel until the federal storage facility went into operation. Since the Florida Public Service Commission had given Florida Power & Light the right to pass along these costs for the life of the Turkey Point facility, there was no reason to charge any of the DOE disposal fees to Westinghouse.

To what extent, if at all, does the Fourth Circuit's decision differ from Judge Teitelbaum's approach in the *ALCOA* case? Is the Fourth Circuit writing the contract it thinks the parties should have written if they had known that nuclear power would produce great savings compared to oil but that reprocessing would not be available and storage would not be available until far into the future? Is the Fourth Circuit acting as an administrative agency seeking to balance the interests of power users, utilities and equipment manufacturers? Were the interests of the ratepayers adequately represented before the Fourth Circuit by FP & L's and Westinghouse's lawyers?

The judge as mediator rather than as vindicator of rights: Judge Merhige's solution to this Westinghouse problem was to (1) press the parties to settle; (2) find Westinghouse bound by the contract and not excused by changed circumstances; (3) ask the parties to agree on a settlement; and (4) limit the remedy so there was some sharing of the losses. In the *ALCOA* case, Judge Teitelbaum considered the purposes of the parties and drafted a new pricing clause in light of changed circumstances. However, Essex appealed, and the Court of Appeals pressed the parties to settle. Finally, Essex and ALCOA reworked their arrangement.

In both cases the parties gained a compromise settlement after one or more federal judges played the role of "coercive mediator." Judge Merhige made "suggestions" in a judicial opinion, and Judge Teitelbaum wrote an opinion which would stand if not overturned on appeal. The parties were pushed to work out matters rather than stand on their rights. While ultimately Judge Merhige's effort was unsuccessful, the parties spent almost two years attempting to resolve the issue. Does this pressure to settle produce better solutions than the application of law school contract law producing a decision about breach and an amount of damages?

Judge Teitelbaum adjusted ALCOA's obligations and offered several options. Judge Merhige refused to excuse Westinghouse but then used notions of foreseeability and fault to limit the remedy. The Court of Appeals found commercial impracticability, but then used its equitable powers to fashion a remedy it saw as fair. To what extent do these approaches differ in substance?

One important function of a mediator is to make a concrete proposal. The parties may accept it as a fair compromise. However, even when they do not accept it, often it moves along the process. Parties can offer variations on the mediator's solution. It serves as a new starting point. If the parties cannot find a better solution, they always can fall back on the mediator's compromise. How does a federal District Judge's decision differ from that of a mediator? Remember that in both cases the trial judges' solutions were not final. The parties could and did appeal, and appellate courts could reverse these decisions. Moreover, at any time before the appellate courts acted, the parties could reach their own settlement.

Table of Cases

References are to pages. Principal cases and the pages
where they appear are in italics.

Index

A